DISCARDED

A Companion to the American Revolution

Blackwell Companions to American History

This new series provides essential and authoritative overviews of the scholarship that has shaped our present understanding of the American past. Edited by eminent historians, each volume tackles one of the major periods or themes of American history, with individual topics authored by key scholars who have spent considerable time in research on the questions and controversies that have sparked debate in their field of interest. The volumes are accessible for the non-specialist, while also engaging scholars seeking a reference to the historiography or future concerns.

Already published:

A Companion to the American Revolution edited by Jack P. Greene and J. R. Pole
A Companion to 19th-Century America edited by William L. Barney

In preparation:

A Companion to Colonial America edited by Daniel Vickers
A Companion to the Civil War and Reconstruction edited by Lacy K. Ford, Jr
A Companion to 20th-Century America edited by Stephen J. Whitfield
A Companion to the Vietnam War edited by Marilyn Young and Robert Buzzanco
A Companion to Native American History edited by Neal Salisbury and Philip J. Deloria
A Companion to the American South edited by John Boles
A Companion to the American West edited by William Deverell
A Companion to Women's History edited by Nancy Hewitt

A COMPANION
TO THE
AMERICAN REVOLUTION

Edited by

Jack P. Greene and J. R. Pole

BLACKWELL
Publishers

Copyright © Blackwell Publishers Ltd 2000
Editorial introduction and organization copyright © Jack P. Greene and J. R. Pole 2000

Some of the material in this book first appeared in *The Blackwell Encyclopedia of the American Revolution* 1991

First published 2000

2 4 6 8 10 9 7 5 3 1

Blackwell Publishers Inc.
350 Main Street
Malden, Massachusetts 02148
USA

Blackwell Publishers Ltd
108 Cowley Road
Oxford OX4 1JF
UK

Library of Congress Cataloging-in-Publication Data

A companion to the American Revolution / edited by Jack P. Greene and J. R. Pole.
    p.   cm.—(Blackwell companions to American history)
    Includes bibliographical references and index.
    ISBN 0-631-21058-X (alk. paper)
    1. United States—History—Revolution, 1775–1783.   I. Greene, Jack P. II. Pole,
J. R. (Jack Richon)   III. Series.
    E208. C67   2000
    973.3—dc21
                                                        99-36554
                                                         CIP

British Library Cataloguing-in-Publication Data
A CIP catalogue record for this book is available from the British Library.

Typeset in 9.6 on 11 pt Galliard BT
by Newgen Imaging Systems (P) Ltd, Chennai, India
Printed in Great Britain by MPG Books, Bodmin, Cornwall

This book is printed on acid-free paper.

Contents

Maps and Map Acknowledgements

The editors are grateful to the contributors for their help in preparing the maps. In addition, they would like to acknowledge the following sources for permission to adapt copyright material, as follows:

Map 1: Redrawn from page 41 of Lester J. Cappon (ed.) *Atlas of Early American History: The Revolutionary Era 1760–1790* (Copyright © Princeton University Press, 1976); Maps 3–6: Redrawn from Don Higginbotham *The War of American Independence* (copyright © Macmillan Publishing Company, New York, 1971), with additions and modifications; Map 7: Modified from Peter S. Onuf *Origins of the Federal Republic* (Philadelphia, 1983), based upon pages 16, 17 and 62 of *Atlas of American History: The Revolutionary Era 1760–1790*; Map 8: Reproduced courtesy of the Bodleian Library, Oxford, U.K., Copyright © Bodleian Library.

List of Contributors

John Algeo
University of Georgia

David L. Ammerman
Florida State University (ret.)

Robert A. Becker
Louisiana State University

Ruth H. Bloch
University of California at Los Angeles

Colin Bonwick
University of Keele

James C. Bradford
Texas A&M University

Maurice J. Bric
University College Dublin

Robert M. Calhoon
University of North Carolina at Greensboro

E. Wayne Carp
Pacific Lutheran University

Selwyn H. H. Carrington
Howard University

Robert J. Chaffin
University of Wisconsin at Oshkosh

Ian R. Christie
University College London

David W. Conroy
Alliance of Independent Scholars

Edward Countryman
Southern Methodist University

Peter D. G. Thomas
University College of Wales

Christine Daniels
Michigan State University

Horst Dippel
Universität Gesamthochschule

Murray Dry
Middlebury College

Jonathan R. Dull
The Papers of Benjamin Franklin

Mary E. Fissell
Johns Hopkins University

Alan Freeman
State University of New York at Buffalo

Sylvia R. Frey
Tulane University

Jack Fruchtman, Jr.
Towson University

Edwin S. Gaustad
University of California at Riverside

David P. Geggus
University of Florida

Norman S. Grabo
University of Tulsa

Jack P. Greene
Johns Hopkins University

Ronald Hamowy
University of Alberta

Don Higginbotham
University of North Carolina at Chapel Hill

Eric Hinderaker
University of Utah

Richard R. Johnson
University of Washington

Mark D. Kaplanoff
Pembroke College, University of Cambridge

Michael V. Kennedy
Michigan State University

Wim Klooster
University of Southern Maine

James T. Kloppenberg
Brandeis University

Isaac Kramnick
Cornell University

Mark Kwasny
Westerville, Ohio

Douglas Edward Leach
Vanderbilt University

Jan Lewis
Rutgers University at Newark

Donald S. Lutz
University of Houston

Elizabeth Mancke
University of Akron

Elise Marienstras
University College London

Peter Marshall
University of Manchester

Cathy Matson
University of Delaware

Kenneth Maxwell
Columbia University

Holly Mayer
Duquesne University

Michael A. McDonnell
University of Wales, Swansea

Elizabeth Mensch
State University of New York at Buffalo

James H. Merrell
Northwestern University

Frederick V. Mills, Sr.
LaGrange College

Alison G. Olson
*University of Maryland at
College Park*

Peter S. Onuf
University of Virginia

Edwin J. Perkins
*University of Southern
California*

J. R. Pole
St. Catherine's College, Oxford

Thomas L. Purvis
National American Biography

Jack N. Rakove
Stanford University

John P. Reid
*New York University School of
Law*

Clark G. Reynolds
College of Charlestown

Hans Rogger
*University of California of
Los Angeles*

Michal J. Rozbicki
Saint Louis University

Robert A. Rutland
University of Tulsa

Jan Willem Schulte Nordholt
University of Leiden (dec.)

Mary Schweitzer
Villanova University

Steven J. Sarson
University of Wales, Swansea

Robert E. Shalhope
University of Oklahoma

David S. Shields
The Citadel

James Sidbury
University of Texas

R. C. Simmons
University of Birmingham

W. A. Speck
University of Leeds

Rebecca Starr
*Cheltenham and Gloucester
College of Higher Education*

Ian K. Steele
University of Western Ontario

Peter D. G. Thomas
University College of Wales

Alan Tully
University of British Columbia

Maurice J. C. Vile
*University of Kent at
Canterbury*

Robert V. Wells
Union College

Betty Wood
University of Cambridge

Melvin Yazawa
University of New Mexico

Rosemarie Zagarri
George Mason University

Michael Zuckert
University of Notre Dame

Introduction

JACK P. GREENE AND J. R. POLE

The American Revolution marked an epoch in world history and a reversal of power between the few and the many, the center or imperial power and its scattered margins. In overall population, the North American colonies were heavily outnumbered by their British opponents; they had no tradition of inter-colonial government, had never maintained a regular army, were less well prepared for war and were frequently outgunned on land and sea. Moreover, their communications with each other, even their information about each other, were in many cases more tenuous and limited than their traditional connections with Britain. Several colonies had more friction and rivalry with their neighbours than with their common mother country. Yet, through more than seven years of conflict (and with the indispensable military and naval help of France, and financial aid from Britain's other European rivals), America's revolutionary generation ultimately achieved by force the overthrow of their ancient government while maintaining their dedication to the rule of law. This achievement was more extraordinary in the eighteenth-century context of power and resources than it may look to us in the light of what we know about subsequent history. This book has been designed to recreate these events in their historical context and in historical perspective.

Although the first British Empire emerged badly shaken from the years of turmoil, which began long before the fighting broke out, and ended with British recognition of American Independence, Britain survived as a world power. Offsetting the loss of the North American colonies, Britain retained Canada, the British West Indies, and India, forming the elements of the even vaster second British Empire. The newly created, self-declared United States (often written merely as "the united States" or even as "the u. States") failed to carry with them either the Canadians or the West Indians, and soon found that they had inherited many of the problems of their former British sovereigns. But the Americans nevertheless laid the foundations of a lasting (if imperfect) experiment in federal government founded on a written Constitution, adopted by popular votes in each of the states, and embodying the principles of government by representation and the rule of law; under the Constitution, as amended by addition of the Bill of Rights, the new republic's citizens gained legally protected rights to basic civil liberties. Although chattel slavery remained at the base of large swathes of American society, and grievous problems remained for an uncertain future, the American achievement had given new meaning to the old idea of republican government, and new hope to many peoples throughout the world who took inspiration from the American example (Thomas Paine dedicated *The Rights of Man* (1792) to George Washington). Meanwhile both nations continued to grow in wealth and population almost as though the separation had never happened.

Only a few people create revolutions, far more are caught in their train. Both these dimensions are reflected in this book, which has three aims. First, and above all, to present the American Revolution as a whole: as an event or series of events in the lives both of the militant actors and of their more passive contemporaries, while viewing it as an upheaval with lasting consequences in the wider world.

To do justice to this overarching aim, the book is organized in sections, each composed of chapters representing a group of related themes. We begin with a section on *Context*, whose chapters establish the structure of the British politics, domestic and imperial, within which the colonies lived and grew – and which eventually they shook off; these also deal with colonial administration; and with the strategic, political, demographic, and economic developments which made the Empire of ever-increasing importance but of ever-increasing complexity. This section encompasses religion, which, to many of the populations of both Britain and America, was of defining importance but of multiplying sectarian diversity; and the section also tracks the development of a civic culture, of medicine and language, and of an American version of Whig ideology. The next section deals with historical interpretation of the main events and trends which, directly or indirectly, fed into the themes of revolution, from the origins of Britain's "new" colonial policy in 1763 down to America's Declaration of Independence 13 years later. This thematic structure now becomes more chronologically oriented, and occupies the third section through the War of Independence, the Articles of Confederation and the debate on the Constitution; also dealing with loyalism and other domestic issues, changes in the role and status of women, developments in education, changing relations between church and state, and an interpretation of the problems of reform and continuity in the law. Some of the articles are new, others have been carefully revised from the *Encyclopedia*; we have improved on this volume's predecessor by commissioning new contributions on the Amerindians, on military operations, on the first American navy and aspects of internal dissent from the leadership of the American struggle.

The next two sections pass to *External Effects* and the *Internal Developments* which make the Revolution of lasting importance for America and for the world. We conclude with a section on the principal *Concepts* which defined the issues for participants and which they have passed down to their heirs. No reader can go far into the literature without noticing how often the political language which moved men and women in this period concerned itself with rights, property, liberty, equality, virtue and other powerful abstractions. We believe our contributors have presented new formulations on all these principal themes.

The second aim, in commissioning the chapters that follow, has been to draw on the expertise of historians who know their subject from original research in archival sources. Each of these essays, several of which are newly written for this edition, represents an expert's synthesis and interpretation of a specific theme. But these specialists are not addressing themselves only to other professionals: our third aim has been to make all the manifold aspects of the Revolution accessible to every class of reader, and all age groups. The information and the interpretations in these pages, though often in the public domain, derive from knowledge based on each writer's own research, and we hope that professional historians and teachers of history from the university professor to the high school teacher will find this book useful in preparing for classes just as will students in shaping their ideas for term papers and essays. The essays also discuss important issues of western settlement, which affected the intersection of British policies, Amerindian territorial interests, and colonial aspirations; the question of who was to control these vast tracts of land was vitally important to them all, and thence to the future of America. We hope also that the volume's unavoidable physical bulk will not deter general readers of history from propping it up on their desks or in their armchairs.

What we know of history does not consist of all the recorded events of the past. Before the records can be understood, before we can even think coherently about them, they must be captured, intellectually organized and presented in some ordered form. It is these forms that we call interpretations: and interpretations are inevitably products of the minds which think them up. For these reasons, certain philosophers have maintained that all history is the history of thought – an expression which can be too easily misunderstood to mean that history is nothing more than a projection of any historian's personal or political preferences. But points of view differ with differing routes from past to present. The first form of order, however, is the least controversial or subject to private opinion, and that is chronology. It makes a difference that the American Revolution preceded the French Revolution, because the upheaval within America, as well as the revolt against the British crown, affected all subsequent events, including the course of French history. Without a revolution in America, some disturbance would no doubt have taken place in France, but it would certainly not have been precisely the Revolution we know. Taking a long view, the events that were significant for the themes of this book are numerous, are often confusing, and begin a long way back. We have therefore come to the reader's help by including a long and detailed chronological table (by Steven Sarson) which records and dates events with occasional notes on their significance.

During the editors' professional lifetimes, the range and depth of historical knowledge have enormously increased, due both to the numbers of historians involved in research and to the more advanced techniques at their disposal. But it is more than the information that has changed; there have also been shifts in some important assumptions, and opinions about the content of history have been both enlightened and enlarged. We have both, in many of our own writings, tended to eschew nationalistic viewpoints of right and wrong; historians have become less interested in that sort of question and have tried to understand what those engaged on either side really wanted, how they themselves interpreted the crisis of their time, and why each side felt the other to be either ungrateful or threatening or both.

There is a strong sense in which the onset of the Revolution can be explained as a self-fulfilling prophecy. The British felt that after the war known in Europe as the Seven Years' War (which Americans from their own perspective called the French and Indian War), the colonies ought to make a more substantial contribution to their own defences, for which it would be fair to impose a moderate level of taxation. (The British landowner was paying a substantial land tax; Americans were lightly taxed and incurred few public expenses.) Although the colonies were not represented in Parliament, they had agents in London who were consulted about these plans. Americans, however, regarded taxation without direct representation as a gross violation of their rights, which portended even more oppressive impositions in the future. The British, who through Parliament had made a large subvention to Massachusetts to compensate for its heavy wartime losses, were outraged by what they conceived to be the ingratitude of the violent popular reaction against the Stamp Act. The repeal of the Stamp Act followed, but had to be accompanied by the assertion of absolute parliamentary sovereignty in the Declaratory Act, which meant that Parliament claimed the power to begin again whenever it chose; and when, just over a year later, Parliament agreed to Charles Townshend's new round of taxes, many colonial spokesmen perceived the unfolding of a deep-laid plot: "a settled design" to reduce the colonies to slavery. Both sides were affected in their pride and self-esteem as well as in their material interests. Habits of authority die hard. Whether or not British policies were intentionally repressive, as colonists believed, their attitudes were certainly paternalistic; the British sometimes referred to the colonists as their children, who ought to obey their parents, but they failed to observe that children have a habit of growing up. Meanwhile New England anxieties were aroused by a perpetual undercurrent of fear that Britain intended to impose the Church of England, with its panoply of bishops, in the Congregationalist colonies.

Mobilization of the colonial population incorporated women as never before into the activities generated by man-made policies. Gender relations were not transformed, but at least people became aware of issues, perhaps long suppressed, that involved potential tension as well as new possibilities, both public and private. The new state republics needed republican citizens, and political thinkers turned their attention to schooling for girls as well as schools for the people. The passionate rhetoric of colonial resistance to slavery aroused other sensations, already stirrred by English and American Quakers: what did it all mean for African slavery in a land of liberty? The question raised the issue of conflict between republican consciences and material self-interest; answers were neither swift nor simple. But many slaves took matters into their own hands, deserting to British lines or escaping to Canada. Others fought in their states' military forces, thereby gaining their freedom. By the end of the century, all the northern states had abolished slavery or provided for its eventual elimination. The Continental Congress, although it lacked the essential power to raise taxes, was not entirely inert; after appointing committees to make plans for the West, it adopted ordinances which provided for settlement and eventual representative government in the Northwest and, separately, in the Southwest. The Northwest Ordinance provided for eventual and very gradual elimination of slavery.

The whole period was charged with controversy and conflict, internal and external, on both sides. No honest record of these events could be a matter of bland agreement or neutral report, impoverished by demands for palatable but artificial consensus. While we have sought from each essayist a fully informed synthesis, we have also sought essays in which differences of opinion and ideology were fairly represented, with an appreciation of what was at stake for those who were involved in making (or resisting) the Revolution. The literature continues to proliferate; each essay is followed by an up-to-date list of recommendations for further reading. But readers should bear in mind that older books often contain wisdom which later generations keep rediscovering.

We have incurred many more debts than we can repay, but would particularly like to express our appreciation of the help of the (now) late Ian R. Christie, who checked for us all the British titles of aristocracy; and Don Higginbotham, who was most generous with his incomparable knowledge of the military history of the period. We also owe thanks to our publisher at Blackwells, Susan Rabinowitz, our desk editor Helen Rappaport, and to Fiona Barr, who compiled the index, an extremely laborious and taxing task.

Most of the changes from the *Encyclopedia* have been new additions on subjects previously omitted, and revisions to the original articles based on new evidence or altered perspectives. These changes, which make this *Companion* in many ways a substantially new book, represent our carefully considered response to the replies we received to our requests for comments addressed to a wide variety of readers who had used the book for teaching. But in the interest of making space for new contributions, while making this book cheaper, lighter, and more usable, we have dropped the illustrations, and have also removed the section of biographies. This loss is compensated for by the biographical information which occurs frequently in its proper place in the essays.

We hope to have recaptured and brought to life the multitudinous facets and contingencies of the era of the American Revolution, while doing justice to its vital spirit.

Jack P. Greene, Baltimore
J. R. Pole, Oxford
June 2, 1999

PART I

Context

Part I

Context

CHAPTER ONE

The structure of British politics in the mid-eighteenth century

W. A. SPECK

THE American Revolutionaries found it hard to put their fingers on the causes of their discontents. Where was the responsibility to be placed for the policies which sought to make them pay taxes without representation in the British Parliament? At first they blamed factions, cliques of ministers from George Grenville's ministry to Lord North's, whom they accused of taking a leaf out of Lord Bute's book by seeking to impose their allegedly unconstitutional views on Parliament and the Crown. Appeals to the legislature and to the King were consequently made to open their eyes to the machinations of these ministers. When these failed then Parliament itself was held to be the culprit. A body composed of a decadent aristocracy and a corrupt and unrepresentative Commons had arrogated unwarranted powers to itself. Addresses were therefore sent to the King to act as honest broker between the Houses and the colonies. Finally, when these too were unavailing, the Declaration of Independence laid the blame squarely on the shoulders of George III himself. The ultimate appeal was to British public opinion, to the majority of George III's subjects who should have been sympathetic to a just cause. Since they refused to be convinced, then a virtuous republic was fully justified in breaking away from a vicious monarchy.

Such contemporary confusion about the location of power in mid-eighteenth-century Britain demonstrates the complexity of its political structure. For the bodies held accountable for American woes – the Crown, factions, Parliament, and public opinion – all played a role in the functioning of the system. The problem now, as then, is to ascertain their relative significance.

1 The Monarchy

Constitutionally, Britain was a monarchy. Moreover, its monarchs were required to rule as well as to reign. It was not until the nineteenth century that the Crown made the transition from being an efficient part to becoming merely a dignified element of the constitution. In theory the monarchs directed all the affairs of the state. The Hanoverians still enjoyed the most essential prerogatives of their Stuart predecessors. Thus they appointed and dismissed ministers, summoned and dissolved Parliament, and declared war and made peace. Even in theory, however, they did not enjoy these prerogatives unreservedly. They were not absolute monarchs. Rather, limited monarchy was held to have been established in the Revolution Settlement of 1689. Where absolute monarchs were responsible to God alone, limited monarchs were accountable to Parliament.

Mixed monarchy was theoretically a balanced constitution wherein the three estates of Crown, Lords, and Commons were held in perfect equilibrium. Together they offset the tendency of each estate to arrogate more power to itself when it ruled singly. Thus the Lords and the Commons countered the Crown's aspirations towards tyranny; the Crown and the Commons countered the Lords' inclinations towards oligarchy; and the Crown and the Lords offset the Commons' tendency towards anarchy.

2   The Houses of Parliament

While the notion that the House of Lords represented the hereditary peerage was qualified by the presence there of 26 spiritual lords, the bishops of the Church of England, and, after the union with Scotland of 1707, the 16 Scottish peers elected by the noblemen of the northern kingdom, the regular summoning of about 160 titular peers of the realm – barons, viscounts, earls, marquises, and dukes – meant that the Upper House was largely a hereditary body. But the concept that the Lower House represented 'the Commons' strikes twentieth-century students as odd. The electoral system fell far short of enfranchising every adult male, let alone female. The highest estimate is that, about 1700, one in four men had the right to vote. Subsequently the growth of population and the actual erosion of the franchise in some constituencies reduced the proportion of enfranchised adults quite significantly, particularly by contrast with the American colonies, where between a half and four-fifths of white adult males could vote. Another development occurring during the first half of the eighteenth century which further qualified the claims of the Lower House to represent the Commons in general was the growth of oligarchy. The process whereby many small boroughs became progressively subject to the influence of patrons led to an increase in the number of members who were nominated by magnates rather than chosen by electors. As early as the general election of 1734 it became clear that the electorate as such enjoyed a genuine choice only in the minority of constituencies – counties and cities – with more than 500 voters, where the extension of influence could be resisted.

3   Relations between Parliament and the Crown

In practice, parliamentary limitations on the Crown were not usually irksome. There were statutory restrictions on the powers of appointment and the dissolution of Parliament. For example, judges could only be appointed on good behavior and not at the pleasure of the Crown, so that they could not be dismissed arbitrarily. Again, the

maximum interval between general elections was limited in 1694 to three years, which restricted the prerogative of dissolution. However, in 1716 the interval was lengthened to seven years, which greatly eased the restriction. Besides Acts of Parliament, conventions developed after the Revolution which made the monarchy more dependent upon Parliament. Thus the practice of laying treaties before the Houses for their approval was established. Annual sessions also date from 1689. No legislation necessitated these practices. It was the absolute necessity to have Parliament meet in order to vote supplies to sustain the unprecedented burden of war finance incurred in the conflict with Louis XIV which led to their adoption. It also became a convention, after the last use of the power by Queen Anne in 1708, that the monarch should not veto bills passed by both Houses.

Yet the Hanoverians did not allow the veto to lapse out of constitutional necessity. It atrophied because they found they did not need to use it. Their ability to influence the outcome of proceedings in Parliament was considerable, making resort to the vetoing of legislation unnecessary.

The Lords

Over the Lords, the Crown had virtual control throughout the early Hanoverian era. Although the first two Georges had in reserve the power to create peers for political purposes, unlike Queen Anne they did not exercise it, largely because they wished to preserve the elite status of the peerage, but partly because they were under no pressure to do so. The 16 elected Scottish peers were almost always those whom the government backed in the elections. The appeal of court patronage was a strong inducement to the impoverished nobility of Scotland to vote for the side which buttered their bread. Again, the 26 bishops who sat in the Upper House had all, by 1750, been preferred by George II or his father. These 42 spiritual and Scottish peers gave the Crown a sizable bloc vote in a House which numbered little more than 200 all told. Moreover most of the key ministerial posts went to peers, creating more dependents in the Upper House. Any nobleman ambitious to progress up the ladder of the aristocracy from baron to duke would think twice about risking his family's future by opposing the wishes of the Crown.

Not that the Upper House was puppet theater, with the strings manipulated by the kings. The Scottish contingent could refuse to cooperate if they thought that the interests of Scotland were threatened. Likewise the bishops could prove difficult if they felt the Church to be in danger. Individual lords could be the most independent of politicians. The journals of the House of Lords bear frequent testimony to the occasions when a minority in a division used their right to enter a protest in the official record. Moreover, the practice of proxy voting meant that it did not require a large attendance to mobilize opposition to the court. The Crown had therefore to tread carefully to avoid ruffling the prejudices of the peers. It could not treat the Upper Chamber as a rubber stamp. Nevertheless its influence over the House of Lords was sufficient to make problems of parliamentary management less formidable there than in the Commons. Often measures were allowed to pass the Lower House so that they could be stifled in the Upper, to avoid an embarrassing defeat in the elected Chamber.

The Commons

Even over the Lower House the Crown had formidable influence. Many Members of Parliament were offered, and accepted, posts in the administration. Some were major offices of state, such as the chancellorship of the exchequer or the attorney generalship, while others were sinecures. The numbers of MPs who were "placemen," as the occupants of such posts were called, varied, growing from about a quarter to over a third of the House during the early eighteenth century. To these might be added those members chosen with the help of the government in their boroughs. The court had considerable influence over the 45 tiny constituencies in Scotland, most of whose members supported the ministry in Parliament. Several small English boroughs also returned members with the assistance of the government, for example Harwich, where the Post Office employed many voters in its packet boat service to the Continent, or Queensborough and Rochester in Kent, where nearby military and naval installations gave the Admiralty and the War Office major interests.

Contemporary critics claimed that the systematic exploitation of its patronage, amounting to corruption, created for the court a built-in majority in the Commons. The promotion of MPs to places procured a well-drilled army of members ready to obey orders from the ministers, while the exploitation of the government's interest in elections reduced many boroughs with under 500 voters, which comprised over half the constituencies, to returning representatives of the court rather than of the Commons. Thus although opposition candidates trounced government supporters in the counties and cities, where electors numbered thousands, they were offset by those returned for the corrupt boroughs.

Such critics overstated their case. Not all MPs who accepted places became automatic lobby fodder, nor did their numbers ever amount to an overall majority. As for bribing voters, the government's direct electoral interest was restricted to a handful of boroughs. It was the court's cultivation of borough patrons which procured it a majority of seats in the smaller constituencies. Many noblemen and country gentlemen maintained electoral interests in local boroughs. The relationship between these patrons and the burgesses was sustained by a variety of means. In some it was merely a crude use of power, whereby landlords would turn out tenants who polled against candidates whom they had recommended, or refuse to deal with tradesmen who did likewise. But this was exceptional. The normal pattern was one of deference to the wishes of a social superior, provided he solicited the favor and did not demand it. Such deference sprang from a deeply hierarchical view of society. It was not just a duty owed by social inferiors to their superiors but required reciprocal duties too, being upheld by a subtle interdependence. The country house on the outskirts of a parliamentary borough engendered myriad social and economic links between the two communities. One was that the owner of the house would procure advantages for his neighbors as well as requiring obligations. Employment in the large households of peers or country gentlemen for the sons and daughters of neighboring burgesses was one way in which the relationship could be cemented. And Crown patronage was another. Local positions of all kinds were in the gift of the Crown, from deputy lieutenancies in the county militias and places on the commissions of the peace, which usually were bestowed on gentlemen, to posts in the revenue administration, such as gaugers in the excise. The judicious disposal of such places of status or of profit to the clients of noblemen and gentry in the localities could clinch their interests in parliamentary boroughs on the side of the government. In order to retain control of the Commons, therefore, ministers had to appeal to members other than the placemen or representatives of government boroughs. Traditionally they had done so since the accession of George I by forging a link with the Whig Party. The Whigs had upheld the Protestant succession in the House of Hanover against Tories, whom they accused of supporting the exiled House of Stuart. However much truth there might have been in the charge that the Tories were Jacobites, by 1750 there was really very little if any substance left in it. After the suppression of the Jacobite rebellion of 1745 it could be assumed that almost all active politicians were pro-Hanoverian. Although the terms Whig and Tory were still in use, neither side concerted their activities any more in a united party. The religious issues which had polarized them under Queen Anne were no longer as divisive. Under Queen Anne the Tories were known as the Church party because of their championing of the Church of England against Protestant dissenting sects such as the Presbyterians and the Independents. The Whigs, by contrast, upheld the claims of dissent against the Established Church. While most dissenters continued to support the Whigs under the early Hanoverians, time and time-serving caused many Anglicans to transfer their allegiance from the Tories to their rivals. Certainly by 1760 the Tory Party was not the Church party of the closing years of Anne's reign. Where on her death the incoming monarch had been in a position to choose between two parties, on the demise of George II his grandson

George III cannot be said to have been in a comparable situation.

4 Political Factions around 1750

At one level the state of affairs in the 1750s and 1760s can be seen as a choice between a number of connections. These were groups of politicians held together by kinship ties and electoral interests. For example, the Bedford connection, led by the fourth Duke of Bedford, included Lord Gower, to whom he was related, and MPs returned from constituencies such as Bedford, Lichfield, and Tavistock, where the two lords had family interests. Those associated with such interests tended to dominate debates in both Houses of Parliament. All told, they composed a small coterie of peers and politicians well known to each other. Their world was a small one, dominated by an aristocratic oligarchy. Politics at this level was a game between a small number of players; the kings, who were participants and not referees, much less spectators; the heads of connections which were in office; and the leaders of those who were struggling to get in.

Yet to see the political system as one confined to the "outs" against the "ins" is to take too narrow a view of politics. This was the mistake which the American colonists made when they brought themselves to believe that factions were at the root of their troubles. They soon learned that the parameters of the problem extended beyond the interplay of factions to Parliament itself. Alongside the placemen and the political connections was an amorphous mass of members who were independent in the sense that they owed neither a post to the government nor their seats to patrons. These included knights of the shires and the members for cities and large boroughs. Usually they were prepared to uphold the government of the day, since opposition was still regarded as disloyal. Opposition politicians had their work cut out to convince them to oppose the court. Conventional ploys were to try to persuade them that the ministry was intent on subverting fundamental liberties, either through corruption or the growth of a standing army. Occasionally they were presented with issues which could be turned to the government's disadvantage. The excise crisis of 1733, wherein Walpole miscalculated that he could persuade the Commons to replace the customs duties on tobacco and wine by inland duties, was the most celebrated of such episodes before the Stamp Act crisis of 1765–6. Since many independents represented large constituencies, pressure could be brought to bear upon them from their constituents. Thus addresses against the Excise Bill and the Stamp Act were organized to persuade these members to oppose these measures. In each case outside pressure was instrumental in obtaining the withdrawal of parliamentary support for them. By the middle of the eighteenth century the techniques of organizing constituency campaigns to pressurize the independent Members of Parliament were quite advanced. Since the final lapsing of the state censorship in 1695 the press had developed a nationwide network of communications which politicians were able to exploit. London boasted a number of newspapers – daily, tri-weekly, and weekly. Provincial towns also printed their own papers, some carrying two or even three. The main centers for these organs were precisely the kind of large parliamentary constituency whose representatives were sensitive to electoral pressure, such as Bristol, Newcastle-upon-Tyne, Norwich, and York. The first politician effectively to mobilize this network on behalf of a political campaign was John Wilkes.

By the accession of George III, therefore, there were two political structures in Britain. One was the restricted society of aristocratic connections, based for the most part on electoral interests in small boroughs, which made eighteenth-century politics appear so oligarchic. The other was the community of counties and large cities opened up by the development of the press and of turnpike roads, which was responsive to political campaigns such as that orchestrated by the Wilkites. The American colonists were to appeal first to the traditional political structure, then to the alternative to it which had emerged by the reign of George III. Apart from the successful campaign to repeal the Stamp Act, their appeals to both were to be in vain until after the battle of Yorktown.

FURTHER READING

Brewer, J.: *Party Ideology and Popular Politics at the Accession of George III* (Cambridge: Cambridge University Press, 1976).

Clark, J. C. D.: *The Dynamics of Change: the Crisis of the 1750s and English Party Systems* (Cambridge: Cambridge University Press, 1982).

Colley, L.: *In Defiance of Oligarchy: the Tory Party, 1714–1760* (Cambridge: Cambridge University Press, 1982).

——: *Britons: Forging the Nation 1707–1837* (New Haven: Yale University Press, 1992).

Cruickshanks, E.: *Political Untouchables: the Tories and the 'Forty-five* (London: Duckworth, 1979).

Namier, L. B.: *The Structure of Politics at the Accession of George III* (London: Macmillan, 1957).

O'Gorman, F.: *Voters, Patrons and Parties: the Unreformed Electorate of Hanoverian England, 1734–1832* (Oxford: Clarendon Press, 1989).

Rogers, N.: *Whigs and Cities: Popular Politics in the Age of Walpole and Pitt* (Oxford: Clarendon Press, 1989).

Speck, W. A.: *The Butcher: the Duke of Cumberland and the Suppression of the 'Forty-five* (Oxford: Blackwell, 1981).

Wilson, K.: *The Sense of the People: Politics, Culture and Imperialism in England 1715–1785* (Cambridge: Cambridge University Press, 1995).

CHAPTER TWO

Metropolitan administration of the colonies, 1696–1775

IAN K. STEELE

THE structure of British imperial administration altered little during the 80 years between 1696 and 1775, but political developments changed policies as well as officeholders and altered the relative importance of the various offices involved in colonial affairs. Basic assumptions, to protect metropolitan power in the colonies and to encourage colonial trades through England, were established long before 1700 and remained intact, but specific controls and their enforcement varied considerably. The Board of Trade brought thoroughness and creativity to colonial administration for a brief period after its foundation in 1696, but initiative subsequently passed to the Secretaries of State, who had many other responsibilities. The Duke of Newcastle held this post for 25 years, focusing on patronage rather than policy, and establishing colonial expectations of delegated power that would later be challenged. The change to a more vigorous British governance of the empire began before the Seven Years' War. The increasing role of the British Treasury and Parliament in governing the colonies after 1760, presaged in the Molasses Act, affected policy in ways that were central to the coming of the American Revolution.

Government of the colonies remained formally the King's business during these 80 years, though his executive power was delegated to royal officials and compromised by the increasing role of Parliament and colonial assemblies. The metropolitan administration of the empire included several departments, headed by major officers of state, who also had power in the Privy Council and the Cabinet. These departments had some direct colonial responsibilities, and developed a growing number of patronage positions in England and the colonies that became networks of influence. Routines, traditions, and precedents developed within the departments, enhancing the power of departmental secretaries, under-secretaries, and clerks, while masking the ignorance or inattention of some political appointees whom they served.

1 The Privy Council

The monarch appointed and replaced governors of royal colonies, issued royal proclamations, assented to legislation of Parliament affecting the empire, and heard petitions from myriad groups and individuals. These functions were performed by the King's Privy Council, after receiving political, administrative, legal, or strategic advice from within the government. Although it had lost executive power to the great officers of state, the royal Privy Council remained the official registry of decisions, called Orders-in-Council, on many imperial questions. Revival of a standing Privy Council committee on colonial affairs in 1714 was an initiative which added another stage of deliberation in many disputes. The Privy Council remained the final court of legal appeal for substantial colonial cases throughout the colonial period.

2 The Board of Trade

The Lords Commissioners of Trade and Plantations, usually called the Board of Trade, was the center of routine colonial administration from its founding in 1696. This office inherited the functions, but not the power, of a standing Privy Council committee of similar name, and reported to the Privy Council through the Secretary of State.

The Board of Trade prepared the commissions and instructions for royal governors, which evolved quickly and then ossified as formal and increasingly outdated assertions of royal prerogative. It corresponded with governors regularly and received additional information from royal officials, colonial councils, and assemblies, as well as petitioners and lobbyists. It encouraged colonial governments to appoint official agents to expedite their affairs in Whitehall, and it became a forum for agents and conflicting interests seeking government support or protection. While much of its work became reactive and routine, the Board did initiate policies, such as its early wars on piracy and proprietary government, and the later control of appointments under the Earl of Halifax.

3 The Secretary of State

The Secretaries of State were a decisive influence on the personnel and policies of colonial administration in the first half of the eighteenth century. In addition to wide-ranging diplomatic and military responsibilities, the Secretary of State for the Southern Department was the senior royal executive officer who reported to the Cabinet and the Privy Council concerning the colonies and issued resulting orders in the monarch's name. The Duke of Newcastle's long term of office (1724–48) demonstrated a preoccupation with patronage rather than policy in colonial administration. William Pitt the elder used that same office between 1756 and 1761 to dominate the government and direct the military conduct of the Seven Years' War.

A separate Secretary of State for the Colonies was established in 1768, giving cabinet rank to the Earl of Hillsborough, who also continued as President of the Board of Trade. In both capacities he advocated rigorous enforcement of legal controls over the colonies. His successor, the Earl of Dartmouth (1772–5), was more flexible but less diligent, leaving many of the details of policy preparation and enforcement

to his under-secretaries, John Pownall and William Knox.

4 The Admiralty

The Admiralty Board, chaired by its "First Lord," provided convoys for the colonial trades and royal navy "guardships" on colonial station to protect the colonies against enemies and pirates and to enforce the Acts of Trade. The permanent squadron at Jamaica (1695) and the naval bases at Antigua (1731) and Halifax (1749) expanded the regular naval strength available in America. The institution of vice-admiralty courts in the colonies created expeditious but arbitrary courts which decided whether ships captured from enemies were legal prize. These courts, without juries, also settled disputes between ship masters and crewmen and tried violations of the Acts of Trade. The Admiralty issued letters of marque to legalize privateers and Mediterranean passes to protect colonial merchant ships from Barbary corsairs, and provided the final court of appeal in maritime cases – the High Court of Admiralty. The Admiralty and its subsidiary Navy Board also encouraged subsidies for colonial pitch, tar, and turpentine, as well as more contentious measures to reserve colonial trees suitable as masts for the Royal Navy, and to force British and colonial merchant seamen to serve in naval vessels.

5 The Treasury

The Treasury collected English and colonial customs duties, postal revenues, and royal dues. Its Board of Customs Commissioners supervised collectors and comptrollers of customs in English and colonial ports, as well as overseeing the oddly titled "naval officers" who became bonded recorders of ship movements in colonial ports. Customs officers in America were supervised directly by two traveling Surveyors General of Colonial Customs. The General Post Office was also under the Treasury, though significant revenues were never received from the colonial Postmasters-General. However, the Post Office built a self-funding service in British America that improved communications within the empire. Royal revenues collected from the colonies were examined by another agent of the Treasury, the Surveyor and Auditor General of Plantations Revenues.

The greatest power of the Treasury was control over government payments, including salaries and contract purchases. This often equalled an effective veto of projects already apparently approved; the minister who controlled the Treasury was usually the Prime Minister. The Seven Years' War (1756–63) brought massive British expenditures in the colonies and increasing Treasury scrutiny of colonial currency laws and wartime expenses of colonial governments, a portion of which the British Government agreed to repay. The Treasury's role in colonial policy increased markedly thereafter, focusing on colonial taxation.

6 Parliament

Parliament's vital role in colonial administration was exemplified in the last of the Navigation Acts, passed in 1696. These acts, initially passed between 1651 and 1673, had evolved to exclude foreign shipping from the colonial trades and to ensure that major colonial products, led by sugar and tobacco, would be initially exported to England, where these had a monopoly but were subject to revenue-generating import duties. These duties, ultimately paid by English consumers of colonial luxuries, were by far the largest "colonial revenues." Parliament protected this imperial trade system, but was usually resistant to other administrative efforts to tighten imperial control before 1763. Parliament's own rise to power at the expense of the Crown in the seventeenth century became a model for the rise of colonial assemblies against their governors in the eighteenth century. The Seven Years' War transformed the role of Parliament, which thereafter legitimized Treasury initiatives to raise revenues in the colonies.

7 Officers in the Colonies

The Governor was the civil and military head of a colonial government throughout this period, though his freedom of action was gradually eroded both by the colonial assemblies and by London administrators. The Governor was both the royal representative and the civil and military head of local government. Other royal officers appointed from London included the Lieutenant-Governor, Secretary, Attorney-General, Deputy Auditor, Naval Officer, and Customs Collector. The appointed Council in royal colonies, usually manned by a dozen prominent colonists, served as a legislative upper house, the highest court in the colony, and executive advisory group to the Governor. Appointments to the Council rested with the British Privy Council, with the Governor usually nominating and the Board of Trade scrutinizing.

8 Development, 1696–1720

The Board of Trade was established by the Crown in 1696 to ward off a similar initiative by Parliament and to help execute the last of the Navigation Acts. During a generation of war and trade disruptions (1689–97, 1702–13) the defense of a self-sufficient empire was an administrative preoccupation. During an interlude of peace (1697–1701) the Board of Trade completed the vice-admiralty court system, inspired an effective campaign against piracy, and attempted to gain control over proprietary and chartered colonies. Regular scrutiny of colonial legislation, from all colonies except Connecticut, Maryland, and Rhode Island, required the regular assistance of the Attorney-General and the Solicitor-General until the Board acquired a legal officer in 1718. To tighten control of colonial legislation, after 1706 the Board began requiring suspending clauses which postponed implementation of specified types of colonial laws until these were confirmed by the Crown. The categories of law subject to this restriction expanded to create a significant colonial grievance. Intensifying British political partisanship in the decade after 1706 weakened the Board's expertise, thus expanding the imperial responsibilities of the Secretary of State.

9 Accommodation, 1721–48

Colonial policies gave way to pragmatic politics in the generation named for Robert Walpole and the style of imperial administration associated with the Duke of Newcastle as Secretary of State and Martin Bladen at the Board of Trade (1717–46). The triumph of patronage politics meant that administrative appointments, colonial and otherwise, were used to control a majority in Parliament. Peace and the complete victory of Whig politicians allowed the decentralization of political initiative. When there were military threats to the empire, in 1721 and 1739, the inclination was to encourage inter-colonial cooperation rather than British expense, even at the risk of fostering colonial independence. Colonial elites were able to consolidate their local positions by using British connections. This accommodative generation was marked by the continuing rise of the colonial assemblies and by fewer policy initiatives from the Board of Trade, the Secretary of State, or the colonial governors. Royal governors were not particularly inept, but their management of colonial councils and assemblies was further weakened by loss of control over minor local appointments to London.

The most explosive political battle of a comparatively stable period was linked to the excise crisis, which shook Walpole's administration between 1727 and the Molasses Act of 1733 (*see also* chapter 1, §4, and chapter 20, §2). Powerful interest groups raised public opinion against his plan to convert the import duties on wine and tobacco into excise taxes. In mustering the political support of interest groups, Walpole made numerous concessions that affected the empire. The powerful Irish lobby gained direct import of some colonial products in 1731. English hatters won the Hat Act of 1732, prohibiting the colonial export of hats. A well-organized philanthropic lobby gained a charter and government grants to establish Georgia. More significant was the lobbying of the West Indian sugar interest to restrict trade between the French islands and British North America. Inexpensive French colonial molasses had become central to the burgeoning American rum industry, as well as being widely used as a sweetener. The West Indians won a clear political victory with the passing of the Molasses Act, which allowed the legal importation of French West Indian sugar and molasses into

British colonies, but levied a higher duty on these than on products of the British islands. This differential duty was a new approach to channeling imperial trade; complete prohibitions had previously been customary. Although the Molasses Act was not primarily a revenue measure, it levied a substantial tax on imports into the colonies. Imperial centralists would later cite this Act as a precedent for taxing the colonies without their consent. American patriots would look back on the resulting smuggling as the beginning of the protest which undermined the legitimacy of imperial control in America.

Colonial administration in the Walpole era made another contribution to the coming of the American Revolution. Many colonials came to regard the accommodation of interests achieved in this period as the working of the true imperial constitution. "Salutary neglect" of a Whig-dominated British administration allowed colonial legislators and colonial agents considerable power. British imperial reformers and centralists looked back on the Walpole era as one of negligence and patronage-driven decisions which sacrificed the well-established prerogative powers of the Crown and undermined the right of Parliament to legislate for the empire.

Walpole was driven from office in 1742, early in a decade of renewed war against Spain (1739–42) and France (1744–8), but the Duke of Newcastle continued the same policies and practices as Secretary of State for the Southern Department for another six years in a government now headed by his brother, Henry Pelham. British commitment of resources to war in America was limited, avoiding serious challenge to the duke's style of colonial administration.

10 Transition, 1748–60

British political expediency, rather than a reappraisal of colonial administration, provoked change. To bolster its parliamentary support, the Pelham ministry was forced to accept a new approach when the Duke of Bedford was brought into the Cabinet as Secretary of State for the Southern Department in 1748, soon followed by the able and ambitious Earl of Halifax as President of the strengthened Board of Trade. The Board gained unprecedented control of all significant colonial appointments for a decade (1751–61) and oversaw the government-sponsored settlement of Halifax, Nova Scotia, It also became involved in schemes to control the upper Ohio valley and supported measures that led to Anglo-French confrontation there. Parliamentary grants for the colonies of Georgia and Nova Scotia and agreement of the British Government to pay the salary of the governor of North Carolina were new fiscal investments in empire made before the Seven Years' War, and these new costs brought new levels of parliamentary scrutiny.

A significant contest over colonial policy was emerging. Newcastle and his supporters favored continuing delegation of power and responsibility to the colonial assemblies. Halifax and the Dukes of Bedford and Cumberland led those favoring stronger measures against France in America, more commitment of British resources to the colonies, and assertion of imperial control. Some thought of the royal prerogative as the vehicle for this, but others, including Charles Townshend of the Board of Trade, saw constitutional as well as practical reasons why initiatives should be through Parliament. The unprecedented commitment of British men and money to the successful Seven Years' War in America greatly strengthened the argument of those holding these views.

11 Resurgence, 1760–75

The accession of George III and the victory over France in North America altered the contest over British colonial policy. George III pursued government by "King-in-Parliament," and this closer identification of the prerogative with Parliament made lobbying more expensive and complicated for colonial agents. The King's determination to manage his own ministries brought political instability, the unrestrained clash of interest groups, and more initiative for senior departmental bureaucrats committed to imperial control.

The costs of victory had been high, and the concern about revenues came to dominate colonial administration after the Peace of Paris (1763). The Treasury's search for American revenues was not to help repay Britain's war costs, but to offset the peacetime costs of administering and defending the enlarged North American empire (*see* chapters 15–17). The fiscal preoccupation of senior colonial administrators was also evident from the increased use of the Royal Navy for customs enforcement, from the establishment of an American Board of Customs Commissioners based in Boston (1767), and from the revitalization of the vice-admiralty courts (1768). These measures provoked continuing friction with the colonial mercantile community, highlighted by the Boston Massacre (1770) and the *Gaspée* incident (1772).

Although customs confrontations continued in America, Lord North's administration of the Treasury (1770–82) refrained from new initiatives. Nonetheless, colonial agents and their London supporters were becoming more isolated from British policy makers and more distracted by constitutional issues. The Tea Act of 1773 was not a revenue measure, but the sharp colonial reaction indicated that the contest had developed beyond a dispute about parliamentary right to tax the colonies. Administrative initiative shifted to the American Department, where Lord Dartmouth was Secretary of State, but the real authority rested with his undersecretaries, John Pownall and William Knox. Pownall, Secretary of the Board of Trade under Halifax and Under-Secretary in the American Department from its inception until 1776, was instrumental in the strong administrative and legislative response to the Boston Tea Party.

Before 1763 colonial assemblies had found that Parliament's Whiggish principles protected their expanding power against reassertions of royal prerogative. Growing fiscal initiatives of the ministry and Parliament encountered American resistance thereafter. By 1775 intercolonial congresses were urging the King to use his prerogative to save them from Parliament, and the King refused. Although the resulting struggle was political, constitutional, and eventually military, the administrative shift of imperial power had affected and reflected contentious revivals and innovations in colonial policy.

FURTHER READING

Clarke, D. M.: *The Rise of the British Treasury* (Hamden, Conn.: Archon Press, 1960).

Henretta, James A.: *"Salutary Neglect": Colonial Administration under the Duke of Newcastle* (Princeton, NJ: Princeton University Press, 1972).

Kammen, M. J.: *Empire and Interest* (New York: Lippincott, 1970).

Steele, I. K.: *Politics of Colonial Policy* (Oxford: Clarendon Press, 1968).

Wickwire, F. B.: *British Subministers and Colonial America, 1763–1783* (Princeton, NJ: Princeton University Press, 1966).

CHAPTER THREE

Intra-imperial communications, 1689–1775

RICHARD R. JOHNSON

THE European seaborne empires that burst upon, and fundamentally reconfigured, world history in the early modern period relied, to an unprecedented degree, upon communication as the lifeblood of their political, economic, and social systems. In each, communication was textured by the dictates of geography, currents, winds, and weather. But it also responded – and, in turn, gave shape – to the man-made processes of conquest, migration, commerce, and production, along with the bitter national rivalries each engendered. Between 1689 and 1775, as Britain's comparatively late-forming empire grew with dramatic speed, the increasing density and efficiency of its communications network both linked and helped to differentiate the functions of the network's component parts. Its refining of traditional methods of travel and trade, when combined with significant innovations in the deployment of print media, helped define the era of political revolution that followed.

Perhaps the best way to understand the obstacles and opportunities of eighteenth-century communication is to envision a world of oceans separated by land rather than one of lands separated by ocean. Britain's island Caribbean colonies were wholly dependent upon seaborne contact, and well into the nineteenth century all communication on the North American mainland that required the movement of any significant mass of people or goods necessitated coastal or riverine transport. It cost less to ship a ton of freight across the Atlantic than 20 miles inland on either side, a reality further illustrated by the postal rates set in 1697 that charged 12 pence to carry a letter by land from Boston to New York but only 2 pence to send it all the way to London.

Waterborne communication, however, had its own imperatives in an age of sail. The giant clockwise circulation of winds and currents within the North Atlantic encouraged ships leaving England to keep close to Europe as far south as the Azores or Madeira before seeking the aid of the trade winds en route to the Caribbean or the Chesapeake. Returning ships held to North American waters to take advantage of the Gulf Stream and the westerly winds that made the crossing from the Chesapeake several weeks faster than the eight to ten weeks required, on average, to get there. Bostoners seeking the fastest passage for Barbados would sail far out into the eastern Atlantic on a six-week voyage that covered double the direct distance to the island. As important as accurate navigation was the timing of voyages: vessels eager to share in the great cod fisheries off Newfoundland had to wait for winter storms and ice to clear, while ships loading the two other great staple products of British America, Chesapeake tobacco maturing in the fall and West Indian sugar in the early spring, had to balance market conditions against the perils of the late-summer hurricane season. Shipwrecks were uncommon, but epidemic disease was an ever-present menace to those who travelled packed together as emigrants or slaves: 10–15 percent of those brought as slaves to British America usually died in passage, and one contemporary estimated that 2,000 German migrants had died at sea in

1749. Finally, there were man-made dangers in this first age of literally overlapping empires: the state of war with France or Spain in effect during more than half the eighty years after 1689 exposed trade to enemy privateers, and the opening decades of the century were a golden age for pirates based in North Africa and the Caribbean.

To combat these dangers, mariners and merchants depended on maritime technology that had remained essentially unchanged for several centuries save for the refinement of sailing rigs and techniques of navigation. The vessels employed – sloops and schooners averaging 20–70 registered tons in the coastal trade and the larger (100–200 ton) ships and brigantines preferred for oceanic passages – altered little in size during the century. Traffic on rivers such as the Hudson, Delaware, and Savannah continued to rely on craft ranging from canoes and dugouts to rafts, scows, and flatboats, propelled by paddles, poles, and oars as well as sails. Rather, the evidence suggests, the British merchant fleet grew in number – some 4,000 vessels a year were recorded as entering British-American mainland ports alone by the 1760s – and in cost efficiency. Turnaround times spent in port diminished, and the threat of piracy and privateering was checked by convoy systems and naval escorts, permitting larger cargoes to be carried in ships with smaller crews and armaments, with lower insurance costs. Save for the development of a shorter and more secure northerly route to the Chesapeake (aiding the rise of Glasgow as a major tobacco-trading port), voyage times would remain much the same right up until the age of steam and iron. But the increased volume of trade, as the value of Britain and British America's trade with each other rose fivefold between 1700 and 1775, ensured more frequent and effective communication, sustaining the economic and societal specialization inherent in a system centered upon the exchange of Britain's manufactured goods for colonial agricultural products.

Transportation and communication by land responded much more slowly to the forces of imperial and commercial expansion. From the days of the first English settlements in America, the minority of colonists living out of reach of navigable waterways had developed a network of trackways, based on Amerindian paths, that could accommodate foot and horse traffic, along with animals and wagons being driven to market. Rivers might, for the most part, be crossed by bridges or ferries maintained by local government, although one traveller through Connecticut in 1704, Sarah Kemble Knight, complained bitterly about the state of both. Conditions had improved by mid-century when a horseback rider could travel with relative ease along the post road from New Hampshire as far as Philadelphia. South of Virginia, the lowland roads remained notoriously bad, choked with mud or dust according to season. Instead, thousands of incoming migrants took to what became known as "the Great Wagon Road," a network of inland piedmont trails that led from Pennsylvania down the Shenandoah Valley into the Carolina Country and as far as Georgia.

Migration embodied communication in its most complex form – moving people, cultures, and possessions, forming new ties and communities – and the Old World's exports to British America in these years included some 430,000 Europeans along with almost 2,000,000 Africans destined to labor as slaves, four-fifths of them in the plantations of the British West Indies. They contributed to the astonishing demographic growth that multiplied British America's white and black population eightfold between 1689 and 1775, to over 3 million people. Almost equally dramatic was the geographical expansion (and increasingly land-based character) of the arena for intraimperial communication, especially on the North American mainland. By mid-century, what had been a dotted line of coastal settlement from Maine to Carolina had grown and solidified to include Nova Scotia, Newfoundland, and Hudson's Bay to the north and Georgia to the south, with Spanish Florida and French Canada added after the victorious peace of 1763. Inland, to the west, internal migration was moving up to and, by the 1770s, beyond the Appalachian mountains.

However far-flung, settlers (and surviving Amerindian communities) continued to look to the Atlantic seaboard for many of the necessities of life. Merchants ordered

supplies – one estimate suggests that
Americans by 1775 spent over a quarter of
their incomes on imports from outside their
individual colonies – and political and social
leaders solicited for office and news from the
mother country. A stream of travellers
crossed the ocean to seek schooling, conduct
business, or serve as representatives of their
colonies at court. Religious denominations
such as the Quakers were especially active in
establishing a transatlantic network through
travel and correspondence. Congregational
minister Cotton Mather proudly listed in his
diary in 1706 the names of 50 correspondents scattered through Europe and America.

To convey correspondence, a regular mail
service took shape. To counter the disruption of intelligence in time of war, the
London government financed a special
packet boat service limited to letters and
light freight to the West Indies between
1700 and 1715, that was resumed in 1745.
A similar service to New York, based on a
round trip of 100 days, began in 1755 and
was later joined by others linking England,
the Caribbean, and South Carolina. Within
the North American mainland, a more reliable service than that provided by occasional travellers or coastal shipping grew
out of the granting of a royal patent to
English courtier Thomas Neale in 1692.
Neale appointed as his deputy in America
the energetic Andrew Hamilton, who persuaded several northern colonial legislatures
to endorse a mail service taken over by the
Crown in 1706. Through the next several
decades, this service, staffed by appointed
local postmasters and a schedule of (usually
weekly) horseback riders between the major
cities, was gradually extended to Annapolis,
Williamsburg, and then, in 1738, Charles
Town. Benjamin Franklin served as Philadelphia's postmaster after 1737, and in 1753
he received an appointment as deputy postmaster general of the colonies which he
shared with William Hunter and then John
Foxcroft until his dismissal in 1774. Franklin
greatly improved the uniformity and efficiency of the colonial mail service through
the inspection of branch offices, a more frequent schedule of riders (thrice weekly
between New York and Philadelphia), and
the appointment of reliable subordinates

(often his relatives and friends). Mail service
was extended as far as Canada after its
conquest from France.

Franklin had sought his appointments with
a clear-eyed appreciation of their advantage
for his career as printer and newspaper publisher, and a better postal service developed
in close conjunction with the spread of newspapers in the American colonies. When an
attempt in 1689 by a refugee printer from
London to found a Boston journal failed
after a single issue, the first successful newspaper, the *Boston News-letter* was established
by the town's postmaster, John Campbell,
in 1704. Others followed before 1730 in
Jamaica, Boston again, Philadelphia, New
York, and Annapolis, to number 17 by
1760 and more than 40, including those in
Quebec, Nova Scotia, and the Caribbean,
by 1775. Few had more than 300 or 400
subscribers per issue but their circulation, to
readers – and to others being read to – in
the taverns and coffeehouses springing up
in port cities and along highways opened
the way to a much larger readership. By
1762, the *New York Mercury* could claim
that it circulated throughout the neighboring provinces of New Jersey, Connecticut,
and Rhode Island.

The content of these papers revealed both
the circumstances of their composition and
their influence as forms of communication.
Overwhelmingly, despite their claims to
provide "the freshest Advices, Foreign and
Domestic," they printed news from Europe,
of wars, diplomacy, social and court hap-
penings, and the patterns of trade. Most
local news was already known by word of
mouth, and, besides, printing too much of
it might alienate local elites sensitive to any
hint of criticism and likely to retaliate by
curtailing the advertising and the government printing business on which profitable
publishing depended. The focus on foreign
events also followed from the manner in
which news arrived in the form of English
journals and letters from abroad, brought in
the commercial shipping that was still the
main source of contact with the outside
world. Yet there was a steady rise in the
printing of imported items, ranging from
political argument and theological disputes
to essays on the battle of the sexes, that

were plainly chosen for their relevance to local circumstances. Even before the opposition to Crown policies expressed in the 1760s, colonial newspapers had become a significant weapon in domestic political debate and in linking critical attitudes to government on both sides of the Atlantic.

By mid-century, moreover, the coverage given to what was coming to be termed "American" events was rising. Greater space was given to shipping news and to advertising the local availability of goods and services. As the European contest for North American empire intensified and moved from sea to land, colonists read more of frontier conflicts with the French and Amerindians and of such victories in America as the captures of Porto Bello and Louisbourg. A striking instance of the blending of transatlantic influences with an increasing sense of a shared American colonial experience came with the widespread religious revival that accompanied the travels within the colonies, beginning in 1739, of the renowned English evangelist, George Whitefield. The enormous publicity that Whitefield and such allies as Benjamin Franklin quite deliberately generated for this "great awakening" was built upon the evangelist's English fame. But it also forged, through such local publications as Thomas Prince's *Christian History* that hronicled by instalments the pace of revival, a sense of participation in what may in retrospect be termed British America's first collective experience. If the shape of intraimperial communication at the beginning of the eighteenth century had resembled a wheel with only the semblance of a rim connecting the spokes radiating from the hub of Britain, then by the later years of the century, that rim of intercolonial communication was now far more clearly marked.

The shifting balance between the continuities of transatlantic communication and the greater effectiveness of its intercolonial counterpart had implications for the colonies' political development. The minimum of several months that separated Britain from America had long hampered attempts to impose a closer supervision of colonial affairs. London's directives, and sometimes its representatives, might be captured or cast away, and colonial politicians had learned how to take advantage of the time and space that isolated Crown-appointed executives from their superiors in London. Laws could be locally passed and kept in operation for several years before Crown officials got around to disallowing them, a process that might be further delayed by the representations of the agents that each colony hired to represent their interests at court.

By the 1760s, as British officials strove to tighten up the imperial system, the colonists were better placed than ever before to unite in opposition. Their spectacular growth as a market for British manufactures gave compelling weight to the campaign of noncommunication – a refusal to buy goods from, or pay debts owed to, British merchants – that forced the London government to rethink such measures as the Stamp Act. This success in turn depended upon the capacity of colonial protesters to coordinate their arguments and tactics by means of such intercolonially established bodies as the Sons of Liberty and then, in the 1770s, the committees of correspondence established throughout the colonies. The print media joined in spreading the literature of protest: John Dickinson's *Farmer's Letters*, for example, appeared in twenty-one colonial newspapers and seven separate editions during 1768–9.

As resistance became rebellion, colonial patriots saw a need for autonomy in communication: during 1774, a group led by printer William Goddard set up a "constitutional post" separate from the mail service run by Crown-appointed officials. Patriot accounts of the clash at Lexington the following April reached Philadelphia in five days, Williamsburg in nine, and London in 40, the last arriving, to the dismay and anger of British ministers, almost two weeks before the official British version of events. The disparity foretold the difficulties that the London government would encounter in suppressing a revolt with armies sent and supplied from 3,000 miles away, and in countering sympathies for the colonial cause within Britain itself. As a Continental Congress met in America, and raised a truly Continental Army to mount a siege of Boston, the arteries of water that had nourished Britain's North American empire were giving way to the more complex and contiguous bonds of a nation united by land.

FURTHER READING

Bailyn, Bernard, and Morgan, Philip, eds.: *Strangers Within The Realm; Cultural Margins Of The First British Empire* (Chapel Hill: University of North Carolina Press, 1991).

Brown, Richard D.: *Knowledge Is Power: The Diffusion of Information In Early America,* *1700–1865* (New York: Oxford University Press, 1989).

Olson, Alison Gilbert: *Making The Empire Work. London And American Interest Groups, 1690–1790* (Cambridge, Mass.: Harvard University Press, 1992).

Shepherd, James F., and Walton, Gary M.: *Shipping, Maritime Trade, And The Economic Development Of Colonial North America* (Cambridge: Cambridge University Press, 1972).

Steele, Ian K.: *The English Atlantic, 1675–1740: An Exploration Of Communication And Community* (New York: Oxford University Press, 1986).

CHAPTER FOUR

The changing socio-economic and strategic importance of the colonies to the empire

ALISON G. OLSON

1 The Wars for Supremacy in Europe

FROM 1689 to 1713, with a five-year break after the Treaty of Ryswick in 1697, England and France were at war to determine the balance of power in Europe. In the first of the two wars William III of England, who was also Stadtholder of Holland, allied the English with Holland, Sweden, Spain, and the Holy Roman Empire against France. In the second the same countries were at war again, only this time the French king claimed the throne of Spain for his grandson and the Spanish were allied with the French. The war ended in 1713 with a British/Dutch triumph recognized in the Treaty of Utrecht.

In neither war were the tiny English colonies on the continent of mainland America important. They were small, isolated, economically insignificant except for tobacco, and lacked political clout in the councils of Europe. In the last decade of the seventeenth century English colonists, estimated to be 220,000 to 250,000 in number (compared with more than five million in the mother country), were settled thinly along the east coast of North America in a band stretching from eastern Maine to the northern border of the Carolinas, then again farther south in a ring around Charles Town. Farthest south of all were the English Caribbean islands, most notably Barbados, the Leeward Islands, and Jamaica. Rarely did the continental population extend more than 50 miles inland, and since the colonists

were constantly moving west their frontiers were marked by small civilian settlements rather than forts.

At no point did the English colonists run up immediately against settlements of Spanish or French. The 25,000 Frenchmen in North America were located in 15 or 20 fur trading centers along the Mississippi, the Ohio, the Great Lakes and the St. Lawrence River, and in Acadia, and the 2,000 Spaniards in Florida were mainly at St. Augustine. A far greater danger came from the Amerindian tribes that existed in between the English settlements and the French and Spanish. Many of the Amerindians had been seriously weakened in a related series of tribal wars with the English in the late 1670s, but the French and Spanish urged others to make periodic raids on the exposed English settlements: the French were particularly effective in provoking the Abenaki in Northern Maine and the Spanish encouraged the Creeks, Yamasees, and Tuscaroras against the Carolinas. It was with these, rather than with other European settlers, that the colonists were most concerned.

2 Trade in 1700

In 1700 the mainland colonies were still one of the least significant parts of the British Empire, and far less important to the British economy than continental Europe. They were required by a series of regulatory Navigation Acts passed between 1651 and 1673 to export most of their produce directly to England in English or colonial vessels and to pay duties in colonial ports for a few enumerated items allowed to be exported elsewhere. European products could be sent to the colonies only in English ships or those of the country where they originated, and they had to be brought to England for re-export. Nevertheless, the colonies' commerce was less than 6 percent of the value of total English commerce, and less than one-sixth that of Northern Europe; it was not quite two-thirds that of the West Indies and was less even than that of the East Indian trading stations. Only tobacco, at times taxed at more than 100 percent its worth, proved very profitable to the mother country. Tobacco from the Chesapeake averaged in value £200,000 per annum, and total Chesapeake trade with England (imports as well as exports, £490,000 per annum) accounted for two-thirds the value of all the mainland trade taken together. The other colonies were still of little economic consequence. The total value of New England's trade was only £133,000 (18 percent) per annum, of the middle colonies (wheat mainly from New York and Pennsylvania only £66,000 (12 percent) per annum, and the Carolinas (rice) only £25,000 (3 percent) per annum. Only New England and Pennsylvania fitted the mercantilist ideal of importing more from the mother country than they exported to her.

3 Military Considerations

Finally, the seaboard mainland colonies at the end of the seventeenth century had little effective way of appealing for military support from the home government, since they had weaker political organization in London than had any other part of the empire. The colonial trade was best handled by mercantile firms of two or three partners at the most, and the firms, with the exception of tobacco merchants, still found it hard to exert coordinated pressure on the government. The Atlantic seaboard trade did not lend itself to direction by a large and potentially powerful company (as did Hudson's Bay or India) and it was not in the hands of a combination of wealthy merchants and well-connected absentee landowners (as were the West Indies). Land in the

colonies was not yet particularly valuable – and hence not worth defending – and neither, in English thinking, were the settlers, who had a reputation for instability and lack of cooperation.

Not surprisingly the English put their military priorities elsewhere. The colonies were mentioned only as afterthoughts in the declarations of war, and for most of the fighting the inhabitants were left to carry on for themselves with the limited help of the British regiments that were there before the combat started. The colonists received no imperial help in defending themselves against French-inspired Amerindian raids on frontier villages in the Carolinas, New York, and Massachusetts. On three notable occasions they took the initiative themselves, once in each war when Massachusetts men captured Fort Royal in Acadia, and on another occasion, at the beginning of war in 1702, when Carolinians destroyed the town (though not the Fort) of St. Augustine. The English government generally confined its efforts to dispatching convoys to protect the tobacco fleets and appointing governors of New York with instructions to rally intercolonial support against the French in Canada. Only in 1710 did the British send any appreciable forces – 70 ships and 10,000 men to take Quebec – and that expedition, having sailed up the St. Lawrence, backed off without firing a shot. At the war's end, very little territory had changed hands.

The lack of American importance was further made clear by the provisions of the Treaty of Utrecht which ended the War of the Spanish Succession in 1713. In it Great Britain obtained, in addition to the asienta (the exclusive monopoly of supplying slaves to the Spanish colonies), Newfoundland, Nova Scotia, Hudson's Bay, Nevis, and the island of St. Kitt's. But all the mainland boundaries – the bounds of anything, in fact, that was not an island – were either left vague or entrusted to commissions to settle; the fate of the French who already lived in Newfoundland or Nova Scotia was undetermined; and the question of the French strengthening their trade routes along the. Mississippi and the Great Lakes was not addressed. France renounced special trading privileges in Spanish and Portuguese America; Spain promised never to give any of her

American territories to France, but for the time the European balance of power was more important than the American: the thrones of France and Spain were eternally to remain separate.

4 European Immigration

After the war the British Government aggressively encouraged immigration to the colonies, hoping particularly that settlers of non-English stock would take up residence in the areas left undefined by the treaty. Such settlement was in line with current mercantilist thinking. Non-English immigrants (or English convicts, 17,000 of whom were shipped directly to the colonies) would not subtract from England's supply of labor at home, while they would produce raw materials that could be processed in England for domestic use or re-export; they also created new markets for English manufacturers, and, when settled on the frontier, they constituted something of a buffer against the French and Spanish. "For every thousand who will be transported thither," it was argued, "[England] will raise the means for employing four thousand more at home."

After several batches of continental refugees arrived in England the British began actively assisting non-English to leave their homelands, not always an easy job when foreign princes were reluctant to lose manpower from their own territories or to lose money from fines levied on emigrants from other territories passing through. British agents were located in every major city of Holland and the empire to negotiate permission for would-be emigrants to leave home and pass toll-free through various principalities, to arrange transportation, food, and housing at local stopovers, to give security that emigrants passing through towns would depart by an agreed-upon time, and to leave the emigrants money. The Board of Trade often negotiated directly with ship captains to transport the settlers. With their encouragement, nearly 100,000 Germans and nearly a quarter of a million Scots Irish went to the colonies, in addition to thousands of Scots, Irish, Huguenots, and Swiss.

Once the settlers arrived in the colonies the Board of Trade worked with governors to get them land and then exemptions from paying taxes on it for seven to ten years. In 1740 Parliament passed a Naturalization Act authorizing governors by themselves to naturalize foreign Protestants who had lived in the colonies for seven years, and in 1747 Moravians in the colonies were allowed to become naturalized without having to take oaths. In 1732 Parliament voted the first of a series of annual grants to the newly chartered province of Georgia, created as a haven for continental emigrants as well as English debtors and as a buffer for the Carolina rice growers against Spanish Florida.

Such British encouragement of non-English immigration was regarded as a mixed blessing by the established colonists, though the merchants generally supported it. It gave promise of buffer areas against the French, Spanish, and Amerindians, provided field labor for farmers of particular crops and domestic labor that gave non-English families a satisfying chance to keep ties with the old country, and produced wheat for export markets and purchasers for local goods. But it also drained seaboard resources by requiring colonial governments to provide institutions and defense for the new settlers at the very time many of the immigrants were not yet paying taxes. In the eyes of many colonists it also diluted the very Englishness of colonial culture, and there was a good deal of resentment of the British Government for encouraging it all.

5 Expansion of Trade

With nearly a fivefold expansion in population over half a century, resulting from a combination of immigration and native increase, the mainland colonies became the fastest-growing part of the British Empire before 1750. (Britain itself had only a 25 percent population increase in the same period.) The value to Britain of mainland and West Indian trade (imports and exports combined with re-exports) increased more than 225 percent, from £1,855,000 per annum at the beginning of the century to £4,105,000 per annum at mid-century, making these colonies second only to Northern Europe in the total value of their trade. British trade with Northern Europe was growing much more slowly; in the same period it had increased from £4,500,000 per annum to £5,300,000 per annum, less than 20 percent. Trade with India was more than doubling, from £800,000 per annum in 1700 to £1,700,000 per annum in 1750, but even this growth was not as rapid as that of the American colonies. The increase in American trade value was accounted for by the mainland colonies: they contributed 10 percent of the value of British trade at mid-century compared with less than 6 percent a half century before. The value of West Indian trade grew from £1,121,000 per annum in 1700 to £2,073,000 per annum 50 years later, but while in 1700 it had been half as great again as the mainland colonies, in the later period it was only slightly greater.

As British trade with the mainland colonies grew, the number of Englishmen interested in the colonies increased accordingly. Englishmen smoked American tobacco, ate American sugar, grain, and fish, dressed in clothes colored with American dye, and sailed in ships with American masts. The number of occupations associated with American trade expanded, from the processing of American raw materials such as tobacco and sugar, to the textile manufacturing using American dyes, to the insuring of American ships and the warehousemen who supplied American merchandize to the merchants themselves.

Ever-growing numbers of merchants were trading with the mainland colonies. Unlike the East Indian nabobs, many of whom levied in the East for several years before returning home with substantial fortunes, or the absentee West Indian planters living handsomely in England off the profits of their Caribbean estates, the English merchants trading with Americans were active men of business, generally among the middling ranks of the mercantile community.

6   The Influence of English Merchants on Colonial Government

Increasingly over the first half of the century, the merchants trading to mainland America, so weakly organized at the beginning of the century, came to influence imperial decisions about the colonies. Gathered in coffeehouses and clubs, they organized effective lobbies to influence the Board of Trade, ministers, and Parliament. Individual mercantile leaders became important consultants to ministers on colonial policy. They testified before Parliament and the Board of Trade, addressed prime ministers almost at will, and several of them as a group called on William Pitt, prime minister during the Seven Years' War; one of them was actually a leading candidate for head of the Board of Trade. Possessing firsthand information about American trade that the government needed, the merchants were instrumental in shaping the government's decisions about America.

In general the English merchants supported the demands of their American correspondents – planters and merchants wealthy enough to be interested in colonial politics and/or interested in developing political connections in England – and most of these wanted the British Government to back colonial expansion and protect colonial trade. So in local American encounters with the French or Spanish or their Amerindian allies, the Board of Trade tended to support the aggressive activities of individual colonial governors even though the Prime Minister from 1721 to 1742, Sir Robert Walpole, was working to prevent a recurrence of war. Since the Treaty of Utrecht had left a number of boundaries undetermined and trade arrangements unexplored, governors had a good deal of opportunity to encourage activities of the settlers that might lead to conflict. Indeed, the most capable governors at the time of the treaty, men such as Robert Hunter of New York, anticipated that conflicts would soon enough escalate into a struggle for control of the entire North American continent. They urged that more soldiers and settlers be sent to the colonies, more forts be built, and more efforts made to cultivate the friendship of the Amerindians, and as a general rule the British Government followed their recommendations.

7   Defense of Colonial Frontiers

The Board of Trade stressed anew making frontier areas safe for certain settlement, and to this end they sent out governors with instructions to get the colonial assemblies to provide adequate defense and carefully reviewed the assemblies' legislation on defense. They backed the New Englanders in driving the French-inspired Abenakis out of Maine and in 1729 made a treaty with them in which the Abenakis recognized English authority. They took the government of the Carolinas away from proprietors who had provided no help in the colonists' war against the Yamassee Indians in 1715 and they appointed as governor Francis Nicholson, a military commander with extensive experience.

The British continued to rely on forts far less than the French, who concentrated on strengthening strategic defensible positions, building additional forts from the mouth of the Mississippi to the St. Louis area, then to the Great Lakes area and the enormous fort at Louisburg on Cape Breton Island at the mouth of the St. Lawrence, the only large island left to them after Utrecht. The British were aware of the French objective of encircling them with a string of forts, but they themselves centered into fort-building almost half-heartedly. The government supported New York's Governor William Burnet in building Fort Oswego on the south of Lake Erie to protect the fur trade, even though the Great Lakes were assumed to be under French, not English, occupation. They also backed Governor James Oglethorpe in his attempt to erect fortifications at the mouth of the St. John's River against the Spanish, even though the Savannah River, considerably to the north, was assumed by the Spanish to be their natural border. Much later George Washington was sent out to build British forts along the Ohio River, but backed down when the French arrived there first.

8 Relations between the Colonies and the West Indies

The Board of Trade also encouraged colonists from the middle and northern mainland provinces to expand their trade with the French West Indies, though this was not strictly in accord with mercantilist doctrine. As early as the 1720s northern colonies were already seeking to export wheat to the French West Indies in return for sugar which the New Englanders would distill into rum. Governors of British West Indian colonies protested against such attempts, but in 1724 the Board, having begun an investigation into the trade a year before, recommended that the government give the French trade open support. In 1733 the West India interest in England, having obtained very little from the Board of Trade, pushed through Parliament the Molasses Act, placing prohibitive duties on French sugars, but the Act was never enforced and there was scarcely a New England merchant by mid-century who did not engage in some French West Indian trade in violation of the law. The Molasses Act was the result of jockeying for influence between mainland and West India interests, with the West India interests able to do better with Parliament and the mainland interests better able to influence the Board of Trade, in good measure because they knew what laws could and could not be enforced among the colonists with whom they dealt. In the three and a half decades after Utrecht the British Government, urged on by the merchants trading with America, was thus encouraging the growth of New World settlement and trade.

The only relatively declining areas in North America were the West Indian islands: they were losing more of their lead with every year. Their amount of trade was going down because of a decline both in their own productivity and in the European market. By early in the eighteenth century, land in the smaller islands was losing fertility because of long use and lax management. It took increasing numbers of slaves to produce the same amount of sugar. The French islands, by contrast, more recently cultivated and better managed because their owners were not absentee, were increasingly productive, and over the first half of the eighteenth century French sugar captured the European market. The British consumption of sugar per capita doubled in the period, but whereas 40 percent of West Indian sugar in 1700 was re-exported from Britain, only 4 percent was re-exported by the 1730s. The British ended up paying considerably more for the domestic consumption of sugar. Nor were the islands improving as a market for British exports, since the non-slave populations of the islands remained stationary.

9 Results of Population Growth

Among the mainland colonies, the wealthiest were the middle colonies and the Chesapeake, which had large population increases in the generation after Utrecht. The Chesapeake colonies simply expanded the amount of their tobacco production as the population moved west: by 1751 their share of the total value of mainland trade with Britain had fallen to 39 percent, but their absolute trade had continued to expand from £490,000 per annum to £803,000 per annum, almost £300,000 per annum more than even the middle colonies. So rapidly was Chesapeake population growing that, by the 1740s, speculators, admittedly thinking of wheat rather than tobacco, were already looking to lands in the Ohio Valley. By the late 1740s agents of Virginia land companies, such as Christopher Gist and Dr. Thomas Walker, were sent to reconnoiter grants to the Ohio Company and the Loyal Company respectively. (They represented companies formed in 1747 and 1748 with large land grants from the King in the case of the Ohio Company and the Virginia Council in the case of the Loyal Company.)

The growth of the middle colonies was both faster (from 12 percent of mainland trade with Britain in 1700 to 25 percent in 1751, with an absolute increase from £88,000 to £506,000) and more complex. It was based on a combination of wheat, furs, and the carrying trade, and population growth was reflected not only in agriculture but also in the expansion of the largest ports, New York and Philadelphia. Indian tribes had begun moving into the Ohio area from both the east and the west to pursue the fur trade, the easterners because, with the overkill of the beavers in New England and eastern Canada, the remaining animals were moving west, and the westerners from Illinois in order to capitalize on the extension of European, and particularly

British, trade connections. In the late 1740s fur traders such as William Johnson of New York and George Croghan and Conrad Weiser of Pennsylvania joined land speculators from Virginia in the Ohio Valley; Weiser represented the colony of Pennsylvania in negotiating at Logstown, on the Ohio, a treaty in which the Amerindians agreed to do business with Pennsylvania traders.

10 Military Action, 1740–58

Despite the rapid growth of the mainland colonies (and the wealth of the middle and Chesapeake colonies in particular), and despite the Board of Trade's positive response to colonial pressure for expansion, transmitted by the merchants, the British Government was slow to recognize their military importance when war broke out with the French again in 1740. The War of the Austrian Succession (1740–8) was, as its title suggests, prompted by European politics. The only important fighting on the American mainland occurred in 1745, when an exclusively American effort took the French fort of Louisburg. Massachusetts supplied the manpower and New York, New Jersey, and Pennsylvania the equipment. And, much to the colonists' disgust, all conquered territories including Louisburg were returned to their prewar status by the treaty of Aix-la-Chapelle in 1748.

After the war the French, with some Amerindian allies, defeated the British and their Amerindian supporters at Pickawillany and began to erect a series of forts between the Ohio River and Lake Erie. The Governor of Virginia sent out troops but they proved powerless to stop the French. Even now, however, the British ministry still saw British interests as being primarily on the European continent, and when it was clear by 1754 that fighting was going to resume on the North American continent they simply planned a series of piecemeal attacks on the French, all of which came to failure. The first phase, in which troops starting from Virginia were to attack Fort Duquesne on the Ohio, and troops from New York and New England were to take forts on Lake George and Fort Niagara between Lakes Ontario and Erie, was headed for failure almost before it started, when General Braddock with a combination of British and American troops was defeated on his way to Fort Duquesne in 1755. From then until William Pitt became Prime Minister of Great Britain, three years later, the British suffered one defeat after another.

11 Pitt's Ministry

With Pitt's accession to power in 1758, the fortunes of the British on the North American continent turned around. Pitt's strategy and abilities have both been questioned, and it is recognized that American conquest was only part of his plan, which also included subsidizing the King of Prussia to fight the French on the European continent, blockading French continental ports so their navy could not get out, and sending troops to India.

Nevertheless his administration was important for the American empire in several indisputable ways. For one thing, his administration brought stability to a government that had endured one cabinet reshuffle after another from 1754 to 1757; for another, Pitt had close political ties with the very groups of middling merchants in London who had long urged an aggressive imperial policy, and his appointment showed clearly a shift in the balance of power in the ministry away from supporters of a continental and towards supporters of an imperial emphasis in the war. Pitt also favored extensive use of Americans in the war (many of his cabinet colleagues had doubts) and, though his initial overall plan was simply the traditional one of attacking the French up the Hudson River on the west and down the St. Lawrence from the east, he now added another prong up the Ohio and Allegheny, and he entrusted the campaigns to able generals such as James Wolfe.

Whatever the influence of Pitt, it is clear that four decades of colonial growth had greatly increased the number of British people with occupations related to America, the amount of coverage of American events in the British newspapers, the number of pamphlets devoted to American issues, the number of American books reviewed in British journals, the number of American products consumed, even (well before Pitt came to power) popular interests in the relationship between colonial and metropolitan society. British authors were contrasting the ruggedness of Americans with the effeminacy of Continentals – a far cry from their emphasis on the instability of the colonists in the seventeenth century – and some were even suggesting that America might sooner or later provide a model for social change in Britain. The debate over whether America or Europe should constitute Britain's first military priority was by no means confined to factions within the government.

12 Military Action, 1759–62

The campaign of 1759, the "annus mirabilis" of British military action in North America, was an extension of the plans begun the year before, combining attacks on Montreal and Quebec from the Great Lakes in the west, Lake George to the South, and the St. Lawrence entrance to the east. With larger armies than they had fielded in America before, better generals, and the support of Americans delighted with Pitt's promise of postwar reimbursement, and convinced by the press and the evangelists that the war was to determine for all time whether the North American continent was to be Protestant or Catholic, the Anglo-American forces succeeded in all their major campaigns, and in September 1759 took Quebec. Montreal was not captured until the following year, but in American thinking the war wound down with the fall of Quebec.

In the Caribbean and southern Europe the fighting did not end until 1762, mainly because the belated Spanish entrance into the war delayed its conclusion for ten months. In the Treaty of Paris signed the next year the British were clearly the heavy gainers, getting from the French all of Canada except Miquelon and St. Pierre (two tiny fishing islands), all the land east of the

Mississippi River except New Orleans, and former French possessions in Africa and India. From Spain the British received Florida. The various Caribbean islands retained their prewar allegiances.

13   Economic Results of War

For the mainland colonies the immediately visible result of the settlement was that they were no longer surrounded by a chain of Spanish and French forts. The long-run results of the war were less clear.

On the one hand, the colonies continued, after a brief postwar collapse, a spurt of economic growth that actually accompanied the mid-century conflicts. By 1772 the mainland colonial trade comprised 17 percent of the value of total British trade (though the mainland now included Canada), an increase of 7 percent in 20 years. Even the value of West Indian trade had increased an astonishing 5 percent, to 15 percent of the value of all British trade. The standard of colonial living climbed after 1740. Chesapeake exports expanded in value from £165,000 to £476,000 per annum, but the shift in the Chesapeake economy was revealed by the fact that per capita income from tobacco increased by only 17 percent while that from grain exports went up by 300 percent. Chesapeake exports continued to be the most valuable among those of the mainland colonies, but per capita income and the accumulation of portable wealth were growing far faster in the North, where shipping and shipbuilding were expanding rapidly in the third quarter of the eighteenth century. By the 1760s all American coastal trade and three-quarters of all direct trade between the northern colonies and Great Britain was in colonial hands; one-third of the British merchant marine was built in the middle or northern colonies.

The productivity of the colonies and their value to the empire, therefore, continued to increase, along with the colonial standard of living, during and after the mid-century wars. But as the value of their trade with Great Britain went up, their influence on the economic decisions of the mother country went down. After winning a "territorial"

empire in North America the British Government seemed to decide it had wanted a mercantile one all along. The Board of Trade, which had encouraged the expansion of colonial settlement as well as trade, abruptly lost power in successive shifts of the British Government.

With the British domination of Canada, the older mainland colonies found themselves competing for influence with a formidable new lobby of British merchants, whose interests were often competitive. The shifting influence was revealed in part through the Quebec Act of 1774, among other things assigning lands to Canada between the Ohio River and the Great Lakes, from which the New Englanders had been exporting furs. Even though the British now had undisputed title to lands east of the Mississippi, they immediately attempted to restrict colonial expansion into lands between the Appalachians and the Mississippi (by the Proclamation Line of 1763), and they withdrew support from the very land companies that had been awarded tracts of land in the late 1740s. Though the declining importance of the West Indian islands was shown by British disinterest in claiming more of them, Parliament passed, and this time seriously attempted to enforce, the Sugar Act, levying prohibitive duties on sugar from the French islands. Finally, the very importance of the North American lands, new and old, prompted Parliament to consider regulatory laws for the continent as a whole, leaving the colonies, used to lobbying on a regional basis, without influence.

The immediate results of the wars were thus mixed, more so for the Americans than the British, and so also were the long-term results of the American membership in the British Empire. The results for the mainland colonies have long been debated, partly on the basis of a counterfactual question – what would the American per capita income have been if they had not been required to handle the bulk of their trade through the British Isles? Historians stressing restrictions on commodities the colonists could manufacture, the overseas markets with which they could exchange goods, and the added charges when colonial produce was re-exported to other markets through Britain conclude that British economic policy was harmful to the colonists, enough so even to be a grievance promoting the American Revolution. Historians impressed with the bounties the British offered on certain American products such as indigo, with British knowledge of world markets the colonists lacked, with British provision for colonial defense, and overlooking the colonial smuggling of the important French West Indian sugar, point out that the colonists did not seem to think the economic restrictions a hardship and never complained of them until their effect was compounded by new laws in the decade before the Revolution. With counterfactual arguments now virtually exhausted, historians are concluding that the Navigation Acts cost the colonists approximately 1.8 percent of their income from exports and added 0.25 to 1 percent to the cost of imports, not a particularly onerous burden.

14 Advantages and Disadvantages of the Colonies to Britain

The arguments about British benefits from the American Empire, however, have not yet stabilized, some historians assuming that the British profited "handsomely" from their American trade and others going back to Adam Smith in calling the colonies "mere loss instead of profit." Contemporaries assumed that the colonies profited Britain because they provided a market for her manufacturers and with it jobs and profits for those in industry. Colonial consumption increased from 10 percent of England's exports in 1701 to 37 percent in 1772. Contemporaries also thought that raw materials imported from the colonies provided inexpensive consumer goods for the British public, or jobs and profits for people who processed them for re-export, and colonial trade stimulated the growth of British shipping. Recent historians have been doubtful of all these assumptions, suggesting mainly that the patterns of trade would have been essentially the same whether the colonies were in or out of the empire. They also argue that while the average British per capita income was

rising in the first part of the eighteenth century, while food prices were falling, the change could be explained in good part simply by the growth of English manufacturing.

Some economic historians further argue that the British might have been better off without American ties: they could have consumed more of their own manufactures more cheaply if they had not exported them to the Americans. Re-export profits were deceptive because once the per capita consumption of tobacco peaked and the consumption of sugar began profiting the French West Indian islands at the expense of the British, the continent began declining as a re-export market for colonial produce. The British would have done better to use their own manufacturers to cultivate trade with the more developed nations of continental Europe. Finally, the British emerged from the Seven Years' War financially exhausted, in part because of the heavy burden of defending the American colonies. Questions about the value of the first British Empire remained long after its demise with the American Revolution.

FURTHER READING

Deane, Phyllis, and Cole, W. A.: *British Economic Growth, 1688 to 1959* (Cambridge: Cambridge University Press, 1962).

Floud, Roderick, and McClosky, Donald: *The Economic History of Britain Since 1700*, vol. I: *1700 to 1860* (Cambridge: Cambridge University Press, 1981).

Greene, Jack P., and Pole, J. R. (eds.): *Colonial British America* (Baltimore: Johns Hopkins Press, 1984).

Henretta, James: *The Evolution of American Society, 1700 to 1815* (London: D. C. Heath, 1973).

McCusker, John J., and Menard, Russell: *The Economy of British North America, 1607–1789* (Chapel Hill: University of North Carolina Press, 1985).

Mitchell, B. R., and Deane, Phyllis: *Abstract of British Historical Statistics* (Cambridge: Cambridge University Press, 1962).

Savelle, Max: *The Origins of American Diplomacy: the International History of Anglo-America, 1492 to 1763* (New York: Macmillan, 1967).

Schumpter, Elizabeth Boody: *English Overseas Trade Statistics, 1697 to 1808* (Oxford: Oxford University Press, 1960).

Shepherd, James F., and Walton, Gary M.: *Shipping, Maritime Trade, and the Economic Development of Colonial North America* (Cambridge and New York: Cambridge University Press, 1972).

United States Bureau of the Census: *Historical Statistics of the United States, Colonial Times to 1957* (Washington, DC: Government Printing Office, 1960).

CHAPTER FIVE

The political development of the colonies after the Glorious Revolution

ALAN TULLY

DURING the last decade of the seventeenth century and the first three-quarters of the eighteenth, Britain's North American colonies went through a remarkable political evolution. At the time of the Glorious Revolution in 1689, they were a variegated collection of small, faction-ridden societies with little in common: by 1775 the colonies were capable of joining together to seek political independence by challenging the most powerful country in Europe. What gave them the political confidence to strike out on their own was their evolution into competent societies in their own right. The main political elements of that metamorphosis were the rise to power of the colonial assemblies, the appearance of politically able colonial elites, and the development of widespread public support for provincial political leaders. These developments took place in a political environment distinguished by strong institutions of local government, a comparatively broad colonial franchise, a largely unrestricted press, and freedom for most white males to associate for political purposes. All of these were important underpinnings of the kind of stable and deferential politics necessary to produce a coherent resistance to British authority, yet they were also shaded with enough ambiguity to foreshadow some of the political fragmentation that occurred under the stress of revolution.

1 The Colonies at the Time of the Glorious Revolution

Just as it was in Great Britain, the Glorious Revolution was an important turning point in the political development of the British American colonies. The early to mid-seventeenth century had seen the establishment of various institutions of representative government at the local and provincial levels in the Chesapeake and New England colonies. But the restoration of the Stuart monarchy in 1660 brought ambivalent policies to the English colonies. On one hand, the Crown granted colonizing rights to proprietors who, in the case of Pennsylvania, New Jersey, and the Carolinas, promised varying degrees of representative government as an inducement to immigration. On the other, the Stuart monarchs were determined to reduce the autonomy that the New England colonies frequently claimed as their right. The Crown accomplished that end in 1686 by establishing the Dominion of New England, a governmental unit running from New Jersey to Maine, which abolished the colonial assemblies and centralized colonial power in the hands of one governor and council. When the Glorious Revolution in Great Britain handed the North American colonists the opportunity to rid themselves of regimes associated with Stuart tyranny, they quickly did so. In Massachusetts, New York, and Maryland, popular uprisings overthrew colonial officials, who were tainted with the Stuart brush of autocracy and Catholicism. The new *ad hoc* governments attracted the support of colonists by claiming that they championed traditional English rights, rights that included a considerable measure of representative government.

Faced with the collapse of the Stuart experiment in colonial reorganization, the pragmatic William of Orange and his successors in England opted for new policies. They made no effort to consolidate the various colonies, and they accepted the claims that English colonies had a right to assemblies and local representative institutions. But they attempted to make the colonies more amenable to British direction by establishing the Board of Trade as a supervisory body, and by reorganizing some of the charter and proprietary colonies as royal governments. By the early 1720s only five colonies had escaped royalization (Connecticut and Rhode Island remained charter colonies, Pennsylvania, Delaware, and Maryland proprietary ones), and the governors of both charter and proprietary colonies were subject to many of the same laws and regulations that guided royal governors. The governors were intended to be the locus of power. As a representative of the monarch, the governor possessed vice-regal status and power. He symbolized the sovereignty of the Crown, exercised such prerogative powers as a veto over colonial legislation, and was responsible for the administration of both British regulations and provincial laws. His chief source of political support in each colony was the legislative and executive council, a body composed of approximately a dozen eminent appointees who were to take the lead in generating political support for Crown policies. Acting in concert, the governor and council were expected to dominate colonial politics, keeping the elected assemblies in a subordinate role.

2   The Rise of Colonial Assemblies

In the decades following the Glorious Revolution, the most important strand of political development was the emergence of the lower houses of assembly as the dominant force in provincial politics rather than the governor and his council. British hopes that the governor and council would be the focal point of governmental power were unrealistic, if not naive. The assemblies of various colonies had haphazardly and unevenly extended their powers in the seventeenth century, despite the autocratic forces arrayed against them. The Glorious Revolution, with its emphasis on the protection of English rights, encouraged the elected politicians in

the lower houses of assembly to push for powers consistent with the great importance they assigned to representative institutions as the chief protector of traditional liberties. The early eighteenth century saw the assemblies of four major colonies (Massachusetts, New York, Pennsylvania, and South Carolina) consolidate their power to the point where at worst they could battle the governor, council, and British Government to a stand, and at best they could control much of the provincial political agenda. In Massachusetts the constraints of a new royal charter, imposed in 1691, did little to curb the assertion of popular powers grounded in a half century of Puritan corporate autonomy. In New York, where James II's personal control had prevented the establishment of an assembly, the Glorious Revolution inaugurated a short period of speedy change. Once in existence, the New York Assembly moved quickly against a handful of corrupt governors to strip them of a number of their prerogatives and thus enhance popular powers. In the proprietary colonies of Pennsylvania and South Carolina the assemblies preyed on proprietary weakness. In 1701 Pennsylvania pried from William Penn a Charter of Privileges that quickly established its assembly as the most powerful in all the colonies; South Carolinians' continuous battles with their proprietors provided the assembly with incremental gains that they consolidated and expanded in the 1720s during the colony's conversion to royal government. The assemblies of other colonies, even of such long-established ones as Virginia and Maryland, did not stake out their ground with the same rapidity as the aforementioned quartet, but, as the eighteenth century wore on, all the lower houses of assembly were successful in expanding their areas of activity and influence.

The assemblies achieved their prominence by consolidating their power in a number of areas. Of first importance was their determination to control as much of the raising and distribution of tax money as they could. Initially they claimed the sole right to frame and amend money bills, and then they pushed for additional powers: the right to audit accounts, to control expenditures by specific appropriations, to appoint commissioners to oversee expenditures, to name local officers responsible for collecting provincial taxes, to keep royal officials on the short rein of annual salary grants, and to regulate administrative fees. Simultaneously, the assemblies tried to insulate themselves from executive influence. They claimed the right to control the ordering of their business and procedures, to oversee the conditions under which elections were held and resolve election disputes, to appoint their own officers, to regulate the release of governmental news to the press, and to direct agents responsible for conducting colonial business in London. Cumulatively, it was a formidable list.

The most common rationale leading assemblymen offered for their quest for power was an analogy to the British House of Commons. The structure of colonial government was close enough to the British model that apologists could liken the assemblies to the House of Commons and urge comparable powers for comparable bodies. This type of thinking was most explicit in the late seventeenth and early eighteenth centuries, when even royal governors occasionally accepted the analogy in order to help clarify the confusing relationship that often soured executive–legislative dealings. But that tendency fell out of favor as time wore on. Increasingly, governors tried to deflate assembly pretensions by reminding them that they were subordinate corporate bodies unlike those that composed Parliament. Assemblymen, meanwhile, recognized that as the lower houses gained powers beyond those of the British House of Commons, the analogy could be turned back on them.

What prompted the assembly politicians to assert their institutional power with such vigor was a number of circumstances, including an intense colonial awareness of English constitutional rights. Like many of their counterparts who remained at home in the British Isles, immigrants to North America were frequently well versed in the conflicts over constitutional rights that wracked Stuart England. In the seventeenth century and for the first quarter of the eighteenth century, this consciousness was reflected in various attempts by colonial assemblies to secure explicit statutory guarantees of the colonists'

rights to the laws of England, an effort that subsequently lost force with the customary, if selective, application of the common law by colonial judges throughout the late colonial period. The Glorious Revolution enhanced this rights consciousness, as did the writings of English radical Whigs who, throughout the eighteenth century, urged Englishmen to be ever vigilant of their liberties and freedoms. The belief that valued rights could be safeguarded only by an alert and powerful representative body accompanied that awareness. Moreover, many colonists believed that the corporate rights of the assemblies were synonymous with the rights of the people, and thus assembly rights were to be defended, clarified, and asserted without qualification.

Moreover, the exaggerated prerogative powers of the colonial governors underlined the apparent need for assembly vigilance. In theory, at least, colonial governors retained many prerogative powers that the Crown had lost in the wake of the Glorious Revolution in England. Not only did royal and proprietary governors have the authority to veto legislation, but, should the Crown's representative prove lax in his use of this power, the Privy Council had the right to disallow colonial acts upon their review in London (*see* chapter 2, §1). In addition, executive authority included the appointment of all judicial officers at pleasure, the right to set up chancery courts, and, in the case of most royal colonies, an unfettered power to prorogue, dissolve, and indefinitely extend the life of any assembly. The sweep of these powers seemed so extensive that colonial politicians felt popular liberties were constantly under siege. Responding to the perceived threat, they augmented the institutional power of the assemblies at every opportunity, much as they perceived Parliament had done in the face of Stuart tyranny in seventeenth-century England.

The assemblies' growing strength was, by and large, the result of a spontaneous political opportunism that developed unevenly among the various colonies. Yet popular politicians in all of the colonies shared common approaches and convictions: a consciousness of the importance of English rights and of the principal role the assembly should play

in protecting them; a determination to dupli-
cate, consolidate, and in some instances
extend traditional English rights in the
colonies; a conviction that the royal prerogative was a constant danger to colonial liberty;
and a historical perspective that encouraged
them to confine such power. Shared assumptions, along with the attention the assembly
leaders paid to the experiences of neighboring colonies, meant that by the Seven
Years' War many of the lower houses of
assembly had reached a stage of maturity that
inspired colonial self-confidence. They had
become formidable political institutions
strong enough to confront Parliament.

Powerful as the provincial assemblies
became, it is important to keep in mind that
gubernatorial influence was not completely
emasculated. Where they had them, the governors retained their powers of prorogation
and dissolution. They retained strong control over the judiciary, and they continued
to wield the veto power. More importantly,
a few governors were able to use what limited patronage they had to build court
parties within the assemblies. In New
Hampshire, Massachusetts, and Maryland,
court factions, supportive of the prerogative, took some of the initiative away from
the most outspoken advocates of assembly
power. In other colonies, such as New York
and Pennsylvania, political compromises
were reached which forced the assemblies to
back away from their most extreme claims.
In colonies such as Virginia and New York,
where the governors' councils retained prestige and maintained a voice on such issues
as land policy, the influence of the governor
and the Crown could softly seep into the
political groundwater of public opinion.
In other areas, where proprietary property
rights were growing more valuable as they
grew older, a political conservatism appeared
that expressed some partiality for royal
power and prerogative rights. All of these
developments were important qualifications
on popular power.

3 The Appearance of Colonial Elites

The second important feature of eighteenth-
century colonial political development (a
feature intimately connected with the growth

of assembly powers) was the appearance of
colonial elites who sought political power
commensurate with their emerging socio-
economic prominence. By the late seventeenth century the older provinces had
begun to produce a wealthy precocious
group of men who closely identified their
own and their families' fortunes with the
success of their colony. Among the new
colonies, such as New Jersey, Pennsylvania,
and the Carolinas, rapid growth and atten-
dant prosperity tended to enhance the process of elite development, so that they, too,
produced a recognizable group of social and
economic leaders by the early eighteenth
century. As time progressed, these elites
tended to strengthen themselves by involving new men who rose to prominence
in their midst, at the same time as they
stressed the importance of inherited wealth
and social position and the reputation of
their forbears as requirements for colonial
leadership. Whether immigrant or creole,
elites were concerned about entrenching
themselves behind upper-class barriers and
passing on their status to their children.
As a result, many turned to politics, hoping
through political activity to perpetuate
a socio-political climate protective of the
advantages they associated with colonial
residence.

Too numerous to be absorbed into the
governors' councils, and without the political leverage necessary to procure imperial
appointments, many prominent colonials
gravitated towards the assembly. Analogous
in a general way to the British House of
Commons, the assembly was the ideal vehicle for giving expression to their desire for
the consolidation of local political power
and for expanding areas of colonial autonomy. Although many of those who became
involved in assembly politics remained back-
benchers for all of their political life, there
appeared within all of the colonies a succession of politicians who dominated assembly
committees, mastered assembly procedures,
and led attacks against gubernatorial preten-
sion. These pre-modern versions of the professional politician, along with a sprinkling
of others who were more polemicists than
strategists, were instrumental in crystallizing
public opinion behind efforts to restructure

the royal prerogative and consolidate assembly powers.

As the early immigrant elites were replaced by creole sons, and as initial political gains were followed up by further successes, colonial political leaders became convinced of their own competence and of the soundness of their political judgment. Ironically, this development was prompted by a sense of inferiority that provincials often felt towards metropolitan centers. Aware of their rustic surroundings, prominent people in all of the colonies paid an obeisance to London by imitating the English in everything from style of dress to standards of professionalization. As the eighteenth century wore on, transatlantic shipping ties grew stronger and facilitated the Anglicization of colonial elites. That process strengthened political leadership in two ways. As the colonists selectively adapted a variety of English cultural norms, they became adept at turning standards of English political conduct back on the British – that is, in defending local autonomy on the grounds of British liberty. It also created a common cultural language among the various provincial elites, which helped to create a larger sense of colonial community. Inspired by the self-confidence that Anglicization and a primitivist sense of provincial rectitude bred, politically active provincials pushed their interests to the point where they could see the British imperial connection only from their blatantly colonial perspective. The power of the assemblies and their vigorous assertion of popular liberties during the mid-eighteenth century simply reflected the self-confidence of the colonial elites who manned the provincial legislatures.

Of course, there was no simple correlation between the longevity of the elites and the power of the colonial assemblies. Virginia had one of the oldest creole elites, but the Virginia assembly was relatively slow in its movement towards governmental dominance. Pennsylvania's case was very different. There, first-generation Quaker immigrants drove the assembly to a level of power never eclipsed by any other colony. But despite the variations that occurred from colony to colony, the overall tendency was the same: self-conscious colonial elites used the

assemblies to legitimize their search for political power, and, whatever their degree of political autonomy, they felt their position consistent with their loyalty to the British Empire.

It is important to recognize, however, that, no matter how closely colonial political elites were bound by social and economic interests, they were frequently fractured by factional disputes. In most colonies, the late seventeenth and early eighteenth centuries were distinguished by intra-elite conflicts that accompanied efforts to augment assembly power. Rarely were governor and council bereft of all support, and colonials warred among themselves over which faction should be the leading champion of assembly rights. As the eighteenth century wore on, the character of factional behavior varied from colony to colony. In Massachusetts a pro-governor court faction appeared in opposition to an assembly-based country faction. In the proprietary colonies of Maryland and Pennsylvania popular and proprietary parties imparted structure to intra-elite conflict. Virginia and New York were opposites: faction virtually disappeared in Virginia, while it split New York's elite at various junctures. While provincial elites shared a general interest in augmenting this sphere of colonial autonomy, that did not prevent periodic disagreements about who should take the lead, or at what point reconciliation with imperial demands should take place.

4 Local Government Institutions

One of the major reasons why the colonial assemblies and the political elites who directed them were able to consolidate their power so effectively in eighteenth-century America was that political activity was so broadly based. Levels of local government underlay the assemblies, a broad franchise included many citizens as voters, a comparatively open press provided opportunities for politicization and mobilization, and there were few impediments to open public expression of popular discontent. Local representative institutions were ubiquitous in the colonies, and they frequently served both as a proving ground for potential provincial leaders and as a vehicle for politicizing the population.

Of course, most local governmental institutions originated in the seventeenth century during the first years of each colony's life; but, no matter how the nature of local government changed over the decades, most maintained their vitality during the eighteenth century. Moreover, as most colonies expanded, they replicated and frequently elaborated their older institutions of local government. In New England town government marched with new settlers into vacant lands and bred in each settlement a sense of political competence. In the Mid-Atlantic, county government intersected with provincial government at numerous junctures. In the Chesapeake country, small planters participated in a great variety of local offices. Such widespread experience with local government built up feelings of self-reliance that in turn enhanced the confidence of politicians who would go on to become provincial leaders.

5   Political Awareness and the Franchise

One of the most distinctive features of the American colonies in the eighteenth century was the broad franchise that brought to many the opportunity to vote in provincial elections. Franchise requirements varied from colony to colony, but the level of property ownership, the rental value of real estate, or the amount of personalty they required in all cases was relatively low. While voting eligibility depended on the economic structure of different towns or townships, in most cases the majority of adult males had sufficient resources to qualify for the vote. The growing stratification of wealth in colonial cities may have decreased the percentage of eligible voters in such urban centers as Boston or New York City, but it is not clear that such trends were sufficiently widespread to reduce the percentage of voters who turned out for closely contested elections in the later colonial decades. Although provincial politicians occasionally voiced ambiguous feelings about the desirability of a broad and active electorate, frequent victories at the polls confirmed their right to govern and convinced them that in doing so they were speaking on their neighbors' behalf. Because colonists put considerable emphasis on the

existence of tangible ties between community and representative, widespread electoral support legitimized political leadership. But so, too, did electoral apathy. When voter participation dropped to very low levels, as it frequently did in the absence of contending personalities or contentious issues, political leaders argued that a *pro forma* ratification of their incumbency demonstrated the community's trust. In either case, the fact of a broad electorate encouraged confidence among members of the political elite.

As colonial populations increased during the eighteenth century, one of the most important means of politicizing and mobilizing the electorate was through the press. Newspapers began to appear in the colonies in the early eighteenth century, and their numbers gradually multiplied. Printers were generally prepared to publish any pamphlet that brought them a profit. Politicians quickly recognized that polemics could be used to persuade voters to support assembly battles against prerogative claims, or to strengthen their factional position over such issues as currency management, defense appropriations, or the conflicts of personality and advantage that from time to time divided them. There is no question that the informational infrastructure which the press represented did produce some notable instances of politicization and mobilization during the late colonial decades. In absolute terms, the numbers of colonial residents who occasionally responded to political appeals by voting in elections increased during the eighteenth century. In some areas, they increased in relative terms as well. In Boston, for example, the percentage of adult males who voted in provincial elections rose by approximately 10 percent between the 1720s and the early 1760s. But the trends were not always so clear. Despite the growing number of voters who turned out to support Philadelphia's politicians, in relative terms the percentage of voters was greater before 1750 than it was during the 25 years before the Revolution. While an active press could convince popular politicians that the community stood behind them, such signs of politicization did not always presage the willingness of voters to go to the polls in great numbers. Apparent politicization did not signify a predictable electoral mobilization.

A political environment in which the franchise was broad and the habits of local government weighted towards inclusion, and where an open press encouraged politicization, would seem to invite a robust articulation of community opinion anytime neighbors felt so inclined. In fact, colonial mobs did appear from time to time – to enforce community standards which elected or appointed officials ignored: to disrupt traditional electoral proceedings; to exert pressure on behalf of a particular governmental policy; or to express some social- or economic-based outrage at current conditions. Given the speed with which citizens could transform themselves into mobs, and the absence of a coercive force capable of containing the crowd (militia men were frequently mob participants), members of the colonial political elites were at times uneasy with what they perceived as their precarious perch atop the existing social order. Mitigating this sense of unease were the many instances in which established political leaders emerged unscathed from local crises. On some occasions they faced down mobs; on others, they either tacitly encouraged or passively accepted crowd activities in order to consolidate their claims to popular support. Such successes, and the absence of any major socio-political upheaval in any of the colonies in the eighteenth century, built up confidence among colonial leaders that they had the ability to withstand challenges and to control local affairs.

6   Stability and Deference

The political strength that the various colonial societies had developed by the mid-eighteenth century is best described by reference to the ways in which stability and deference characterized colonial politics. Two of the three most striking features of eighteenth-century politics were the rise to power of the assembly and the consolidation of colonial elites. Both tended to bring stability to colonial affairs. Institutionally, most assemblies quickly became strong enough to control a considerable portion of the provincial political agenda, and thus

they were able to prevent sudden changes in the relationship between colonists and imperial authorities – provided, of course, the British did not bring Parliament or the military into the equation. At the same time, tenacious colonial elites, distinguished by wealth, education, close kinship connections with other provincial politicians, and a gentry style of life, tightened their grasp on assembly seats. As they did so, the turnover rate of politicians dropped, suggesting fewer contested elections and growing electoral advantages for incumbents. Factional splits lost the quick-changing, life-threatening intensity that had distinguished them in the late seventeenth century, and evolved into what became familiar structural or ideological differences. Of course, there were occasional realignment crises in most colonies, but rarely did these upheavals produce much of a departure in the substance of politics, and never did they alter the status of those who occupied assembly seats.

When we add to these observations the third salient characteristic of eighteenth-century colonial political development – that colonists enjoyed an open political environment with a strong tradition of participatory government – it is clear how the notion of deference has come to play such an important part in explaining the stability of colonial politics. Time after time in the colonies, voters of middling and lower social rank elected the rich and the well-connected to represent them. Ordinary citizens deferred to gentlemen whose upper-class friends touted them as men of capacity, well fit to defend liberty on behalf of their fellow citizens. By voting as they did, and refusing to challenge the leadership of the provincial elites, the bulk of the politically active colonial population lent legitimacy and stability to regimes that in socio-economic terms were relatively narrow and exclusive. At the same time, the deference that middling and lower-class colonists ostensibly paid to their political leaders was of considerable importance in putting those leaders at ease. Without serious electoral challenges from the lower classes, members of the colonial elite frequently felt free to compete openly among themselves, and in the process to encourage political mobilization among members of the larger community. Encouraged by their long and tight control of elected offices, and confident of their abilities to continue leading the electorate, many members of the colonial elite were prepared to challenge British plans for reorganizing the empire during the late colonial years.

7 The Challenge to British Rule

Looking at the eighteenth-century political development of the British North American colonies from the perspective of the American Revolution, we must recognize the double-edged nature of that development. As the assemblies rose to power, the colonists focused their loyalty for British imperial government increasingly on the lower houses. The assemblies gained a *de facto* legitimacy that allowed them to challenge Great Britain on behalf of their respective communities during the late 1760s and early 1770s. At the same time, however, the assemblies remained integral to the imperial structure of government, and led the way to various accommodations with the Crown and with Parliament. During the crisis of Independence, for example, the Pennsylvania Assembly simply refused to repudiate British authority, and ultimately was swept away by the upheaval of revolution.

The elites who peopled the colonial assemblies were subject to the same problem of competing loyalties. Throughout the early and mid-eighteenth century, colonial elites consolidated their power, and were near unanimity in pushing for enlarged spheres of colonial autonomy. The confidence they gained in achieving that end, along with the experience they acquired in government, encouraged them to oppose British authority when imperial policy changed during the third quarter of the century. Yet, as in the case of the assemblies, there were members of the colonial elite who took the lead in accommodation with the British, and who saw themselves as quintessential Anglo-Americans. Many of these individuals were unwilling to jump into the void of independence. In some colonies, too, rivalries were so strong among the leaders of competing factions that the espousal of political radicalism by one group meant that others backed away from political risks they might otherwise have taken. Factionalism among the colonial elites fostered division in the revolutionary years.

A similar mixed legacy flowed from the colonial experience with vital institutions of local government, a broad electorate, an open press, and a tradition of legitimate community activism. The prevalence of widespread participation in local government reinforced the view that representative provincial institutions with a wide area of competency were essential for political legitimacy. However, just as a vital localism could contribute immensely to provincial strength, so could it undermine that power. In the contest over independence, and during the war that accompanied it, communities could withdraw into local non-involvement, or inter-act with provincial authorities in the most pragmatic and selective fashion. The broad franchise, of course, generated confidence among colonial leaders that they had the backing of the people. But either a sizable electoral vote or a low voter turnout did not always signify the kind of community support that provincial politicians chose to infer. A large turnout frequently meant a divided electorate, and a low voter count could mean apathy, quiet antipathy, or passive compliance rather than endorsement. As for the press and its power to politicize and mobilize, the record is mixed. Frequently provincial spokesmen were successful in mobilizing public opinion in support of their demands for colonial liberties, but the press could alienate as well as attract, and popular perspectives viewed from various social vantage points could extend beyond the horizons of political leaders. Politicization did not always mean mobilization in the way that established politicians intended. That was most evident in the case of community mobilization in public meetings, or in mobs. Although pre-revolutionary public demonstrations throughout most of the eighteenth century were tame affairs with limited objectives which rarely threatened popular political leaders, the potential was always there for more radical political action. As the points of tension between Great Britain and the colonies multiplied, existing popular leaders frequently found themselves unwilling and unable to speak for various social and economic elements in the community who demanded that public policy respond to their concerns.

In considering the deference and stability that permeated eighteenth-century colonial politics, we must also bear in mind some caveats. Both deference and the stability which accompanied it may have been increasing in some of the southern colonies; deferential attitudes may also have been growing stronger among some social groups in the Mid-Atlantic and New England colonies. But towards the end of the colonial period, there were indications that the old regimes had ossified and were showing signs of structural weakness. The Mid-Atlantic colonies and South Carolina were slow to extend representation to their burgeoning back-country, and a number of political demands were thus excluded from the assembly forums. Periodic tensions, born of economic and occupational stratification in the major colonial cities, may have fostered lower- and middle-class discontent with their political leaders. The consent of the governed may have come to rest less on deference than on performance in New England, on the tangible benefits of Quaker government in Pennsylvania, and on the interplay between power and clientage in New York. The competitive bidding for electoral support by competing political factions may have had a cumulative politicizing effect that encouraged lower social groups to speak out on their own behalf during the pre-revolutionary crises of authority. Finally, the professionalization of colonial politics may have brought some weakness as well as strength. Preoccupation with the processes of politics could lead to important political gains, but it could also blind provincial leaders to the larger concerns of those who composed colonial communities.

Unquestionably, the colonies did develop stable political regimes that were supported by deferential attitudes. But the kind of dynamic economic social and political adjustments that the colonies were undergoing in the third quarter of the eighteenth century meant that future periods of relative political stability would have to rest on a variety of new and different social bases. The political characteristics that distinguished the eighteenth-century colonies and made independence a possibility would not go through an era of revolution without some profound alterations.

FURTHER READING

Bailyn, Bernard: *The Origins of American Politics* (New York: Alfred A. Knopf, 1968).

Beeman, Richard: "Deference, Republicanism, and the Emergence of Popular Politics in Eighteenth-Century America," *William and Mary Quarterly, 3rd. ser.,* 49 (1992), 401–30.

Dinkin, Robert J.: *Voting in Provincial America: a Study of Elections in the Thirteen Colonies, 1689–1776* (Westport, Conn.: Greenwood Press, 1977).

Greene, Jack P.: *The Quest for Power: the Lower Houses of Assembly in the Southern Royal Colonies, 1689–1776* (Chapel Hill: University of North Carolina Press, 1963).

——: "Political mimesis: a consideration of the historical and cultural roots of legislative behavior in the British Colonies in the eighteenth century," *American Historical Review,* 75 (1969), 337–60.

——: *Peripheries and Center: Constitutional Development in the Extended Politics of the British Empire and the United States, 1607–1788* (Athens and London: University of Georgia Press, 1986).

Jordan, David W.: *Foundations of Representative Government in Maryland. 1632–1715* (New York: Cambridge University Press, 1987).

Kolp, John G.: *Gentlemen and Freeholders: Electoral Politics in Colonial Virginia* (Baltimore: Johns Hopkins University Press, 1998).

Labaree, Leonard W.: *Royal Government in America: a Study of the British Colonial System before 1783* (New Haven, Conn.: Yale University Press, 1930).

Murrin, John M.: "Political development," *Colonial British America: Essays in the New History of the Early Modern Era,* ed. Jack P. Greene and J. R. Pole (Baltimore: Johns Hopkins University Press, 1984), 408–56.

Nash, Gary B.: *The Urban Crucible: Social Change, Political Consciousness, and the Origins of the American Revolution* (Cambridge, Mass.: Harvard University Press, 1979).

Newcomb, Benjamin H.: *Political Partisanship in the American Middle Colonies, 1700–1776* (Baton Rouge: Louisiana State University Press, 1995).

Pole, J. R.: "Historians and the problem of early American democracy," *American Historical Review,* 67 (1962), 626–46.

——: *Political Representation in England and the Origins of the American Republic* (New York and London, 1966); repr. (Berkeley and Los Angeles: University of California Press, 1971).

Tully, Alan: *Forming American Politics: Ideals, Interests, and Institutions in Colonial New York and Pennsylvania* (Baltimore: Johns Hopkins University Press, 1994).

CHAPTER SIX

Population and family in early America

ROBERT V. WELLS

THE American Revolution was clearly a political and constitutional event. Nonetheless, in order to comprehend the social and economic context within which the Revolution occurred, it is necessary to understand the nature of the American population. The rapid growth of the population by 1775 made it possible for Americans to consider physical resistance to British rule, an option that would not have been possible a generation earlier. Because growth had occurred not only through natural increase (the excess of births over deaths), but also through immigration, only half the American people could claim English ancestry by 1775, and many of them had distant ties at best. Other characteristics of the population, such as age distribution, sex ratio, racial mix, and the presence of unfree people, gave life in the colonies a tone quite different from that in Britain, and even the various parts of America were sufficiently distinct from each other so that union was not an inevitable outcome. The importance of demography in the era of the Revolution becomes clearer when patterns on the continent are compared with those of Britain's island colonies.

Demographic structures are of interest not only for broad social and economic reasons, but also because they shape and are shaped by families. Families in early America were more important in the affairs of every individual than they are today, so we will examine how they were organized and what they did to and for their members. Finally, demographic patterns limited the choices that were available to American leaders during and after the Revolution. If nothing else,

political structures had to be found that could govern a heterogenous people, spread thinly over a vast territory, with a history of rapid expansion and independent action.

Before discussing the actual patterns of the population, some mention of the sources for our information is necessary. Nothing in the colonial period compares with the censuses of the twentieth century. The British Government did manage to get censuses taken in some of the colonies, especially after 1700. Their success was limited, however, for colonies such as New York and Rhode Island have a long series of counts, but Virginia has nothing resembling a census after 1703, and Pennsylvania, the second largest colony by 1775, never counted its people. The first comprehensive survey of all the American people occurred only with the first federal census in 1790. In spite of the gaps in the censuses, estimates of the population have been made, making use of tax and militia lists to fill the holes. These estimates outline the basic trends in the decades before the Revolution. In addition, scholars have painstakingly pieced together significant details of life in a number of communities from New England to the Chesapeake. From these studies, patterns of birth, death, and marriage have become clearer, and their effects on family life have been described. Such details can be used to reinforce and elaborate on the information from the early censuses.

1 Size, Growth, and Distribution

From tentative beginnings in Jamestown, Virginia, in 1607, the population of the colonies grew to about two and a half million in 1775. The early years of settlement, however, were anything but impressive. For example, the population of Jamestown was about 500 in October 1609, but by the time winter was over only 60 people were left alive. Between 1618 and 1624 the Virginia Company, which owned the colony, sent approximately 6,000 settlers to America to join those already there. The mortality of these people was so high that a census taken in 1624, after an Amerindian attack and years of mismanagement, showed fewer than 1,300 residents. The first winter for the pilgrims in Plymouth colony on Cape Cod was almost as bad, as about half the initial 100 settlers died and often no more than six or seven colonists were healthy at any one time. Later immigrants also went through a period of high mortality, known as seasoning, but by 1700 the colonies were clearly going to succeed.

Several features of Britain's colonies on the North American continent set them apart demographically from European colonies elsewhere in America or the rest of the world. When Europeans assumed control over new territory, their intent was to rule the conquered people for purposes of trade and extracting wealth. To these ends, the Portuguese and Spanish, for example, sent small garrisons of soldiers to rule the more numerous natives who did the work. By the time the English began to seek territories of their own, all the heavily populated parts of America were already claimed. They had to be satisfied with a few thinly settled islands in the Caribbean, which the Spanish no longer wanted, and the coast of North America, where there were few people and less gold to attract Britain's rivals. Within the first ten years of settlement, the companies and proprietors, who sponsored colonies for profit, realized that in order to make money they would have to recruit English men and women to work in the fields and provide markets for English goods. In 1618 the Virginia Company offered to potential settlers incentives that gave special shape to the future of American society. Anyone who moved to the new world received 50 acres of land for every passage paid. Thus, a man who brought his wife and two children to Virginia was granted 200 acres. The company also recognized that control over the colony from Britain was difficult, given uncertain transportation, and so provided for an assembly of local citizens to aid in government. Other colonies offered similar inducements, and added religious freedom. Thus, Americans quickly came to expect land, self-government, and religious toleration as part of living in the colonies.

Although the numbers were small at first, population began to grow rapidly by the middle of the seventeenth century, and continued to do so, through the era of the Revolution, down to the Civil War. This was one of the world's first great population explosions, with growth rates equaling or exceeding those in rapidly growing areas in the twentieth century. Table 1 provides details on this phenomenon, and shows figures for the population of the colonies that eventually became the United States. Two estimates of the population are given. The first, in column A, was made in 1909; the second was done in 1957. Although the numbers in column B are given to the last digit, they remain estimates and no more. Starting in 1790, the figures were derived from the census required by the Constitution of 1787. The two estimates, while in general agreement about the rapid growth of the population, differ over details. As is evident from the third column, which shows the ratio of the first estimate to the second, the figures produced in 1909 are almost always higher than the later estimates. Even more interesting are the differences in the growth rates for the various decades, as the first estimate shows a much more stable pattern of growth after 1670. Until the decade of the 1780s, growth according to the first study, ranged between 28.8 percent and 38.1 percent. In the second set of estimates, the range was from 19.3 percent in the 1690s to 43.9 percent in the 1750s, as growth exceeded 40 percent four times in the eighteenth century and was under 30 percent twice. Neither study provides a sufficient explanation of how the estimates were made to explain the difference, but the second set of figures appears to allow for more variation in the flow of

Table 1 Size and growth of the population in the colonies, 1610–1820

Year	A	B	Ratio A/B	Growth in decade ending in year given		% Black B
				A	B	
1610	210	350	0.60			
1620	2,499	2,302	1.09	1090.0	557.7	
1630	5,700	4,646	1.23	128.1	101.8	1.3
1640	24,947	26,634	0.94	390.3	473.3	2.2
1650	51,700	50,368	1.03	85.0	89.1	3.2
1660	84,800	75,058	1.13	64.0	49.0	3.9
1670	114,500	111,935	1.02	35.0	49.1	4.1
1680	155,600	151,507	1.03	35.9	35.4	4.6
1690	213,500	210,372	1.02	37.2	38.9	8.0
1700	275,000	250,888	1.10	28.8	19.3	11.1
1710	357,500	331,711	1.08	30.0	32.2	13.5
1720	474,388	466,185	1.02	32.7	40.5	14.8
1730	654,950	629,445	1.04	38.1	35.0	14.5
1740	889,000	905,563	0.98	35.7	43.9	16.6
1750	1,207,000	1,107,676	1.09	35.8	22.3	20.2
1760	1,610,000	1,593,625	1.01	33.4	43.9	20.4
1770	2,205,000	2,148,076	1.03	37.0	34.8	21.4
1780	2,781,000	2,780,368	1.00	26.1	29.4	20.7
1790	3,929,625	3,929,625	1.00	41.3	41.3	19.3
1800	5,308,483	5,308,483	1.00	35.1	35.1	18.9
1820	9,638,453	9,638,453	1.00			18.4

Sources: US Bureau of the Census: *A Century of Population Growth* (Washington, DC, 1909). 9–10 [A]; and US Bureau of the Census: *Historical Statistics of the United States* (Washington, DC, 1960), Z 1–19 [B].

immigrants in peace and war. It also may reflect the fact that the slave trade was uneven over the decades. Because the set of figures in column B tried to estimate the number of black Americans, they have been used to calculate the proportion of the population that was black.

The important aspects about the population are the same, whichever set of figures is used. From about 50,000 in 1650, the number of people reached 250,000 or more in 1700. This meant that the early fears about the colonies' survival no longer concerned either the English or the Americans. This fivefold increase was not matched in the next half century, but growth was still impressive, as the totals exceeded a million by a comfortable margin in 1750. By the outbreak of hostilities in 1775 the colonies counted about two and a half million inhabitants. Almost four million people were noted in the first census under the new government, and by 1820, when the revolutionary generation had given way to a new set of leaders, the country had almost ten million inhabitants. Between 1700 and 1800 the population increased almost 20 times. Both the English and Americans were aware of this growth and drew lessons from it that influenced their attitudes during the Revolution.

Ironically, the year in which representative government first made its appearance in Virginia (1619) was also the year in which the first black colonists were sold into bondage. The last column in table 1 traces the increase of the black part of the population, a change that has had lasting effects.

The legal definition of slavery had evolved out of a system of unfree labor, affecting many different colonists, to focus almost exclusively on Blacks by 1660, when they comprised only a small part of the population. Following upheavals among white servants in Virginia in 1676, the opening up of the slave trade to free market operation after 1690, and a decline in the number of immigrants from England, white landowners increasingly sought to purchase slaves to work for them. By 1700 one of every ten colonists was black. Heavy importations of slaves between 1730 and 1750 doubled the percentage of Blacks, so that at the time of the Revolution just over one of every five Americans was a slave. The end of major slave purchases lowered that proportion slightly by 1820, just before major influxes of Europeans reduced the percentage of Blacks in 1900 to the level of 1700.

Important sectional differences underlie the overall totals. New England, the middle colonies, and the South were distinguished by their demographic characteristics as much as by agriculture, culture, and climate. Table 2 illustrates several important points. In 1650 New England and the South were about equal in numbers, with just a scattering of Dutch and Swedes in the Hudson and Delaware valleys. By 1700 the South was slightly larger than New England, while New York, New Jersey, and Pennsylvania had started the growth that would take them past New England at the end of the century. By the time of the Revolution almost half of all Americans lived in the South, with the remainder divided equally between the other two sections.

One of the most pronounced differences among the sections was the presence or absence of slaves. In New England the proportion of Blacks never exceeded 3.1 percent. The corresponding figure for the middle colonies was 7 percent. In the South, Blacks accounted for 21.5 percent of the people in 1700 and 40.5 percent in 1770. Even these figures cover up more local differences. For example, in 1750 the proportion of Blacks in Rhode Island was 10.1 percent, about five times that of New Hampshire. In New York, 14.4 percent of the people in 1750 were black, compared with only 2.4 percent in Pennsylvania. South Carolina may have been the only mainland colony to have a black majority,

Table 2 Regional differences in population, 1700–90

	1700	1750	1770	1790
New England				
Local population	92,763	360,011	581,038	1,009,206
% of all	37.0	30.8	27.0	25.7
% white	98.2	96.9	97.3	98.3
% black	1.8	3.1	2.7	1.7
Middle colonies				
Local population	54,464	296,459	555,904	1,017,087
% of all	21.7	25.3	25.9	25.9
% white	93.3	93.0	93.7	93.8
% black	6.7	7.0	6.3	6.2
South				
Local population	104,588	514,290	1,011,134	1,903,332
% all	41.7	43.9	47.1	48.4
% white	78.5	60.2	59.5	64.4
% black	21.5	39.8	40.5	35.6
Total population	250,888	1,170,760	2,148,076	3,929,625

Source: US Bureau of the Census: *Historical Statistics of the United States* (Washington, DC, 1960), Z 1–19.

but Virginia was not far behind. North Carolina, however, had a population that was only 27.1 percent black. A look at Britain's island colonies places these figures in an interesting perspective. By 1774 Blacks accounted for 93.9 percent of Jamaica's population and 78.2 percent of Barbados's. Only Bermuda, with 45.1 percent black in 1774, was like even the most heavily slave-oriented continental colonies. Other demographic patterns also varied by region, but none so pronounced as race.

2 Demographic Composition

The composition of a population is as interesting as its size, and is often more important in determining the number of people available to work, run the government, or support social institutions such as churches or schools. As already mentioned, race was an important element in the population of the colonies, but so too were age, sex, ethnicity, and rural/urban residence.

In the early seventeenth century, colonies often had very unusual populations because of selective migration. Lists of passengers for Virginia in 1634 and 1635 record six men for every one woman going to the colony; only 5 percent of the migrants were under the age of 16. In contrast, New England received four women for every six men and many children in the years between 1620 and 1638. By the time of the Revolution, however, patterns had become more settled and similar among the mainland colonies.

Patterns for a select group of colonies are presented in table 3. Maryland is the only southern colony for which there is information after about 1700. Barbados, in 1773, and Bermuda, in 1774, provide interesting contrasts. The six colonies included in the table differed noticeably in size. Bermuda, with just over 11,000 inhabitants in 1774, was one of Britain's smaller colonies. Connecticut, New York, and Maryland were 15 to 20 times larger, and they in turn were eclipsed by Massachusetts, Pennsylvania, and Virginia. Of the latter, only Massachusetts counted her people after 1700, and that census was in 1764. One of the most obvious points of difference is in the proportion of Whites. Connecticut, with 97.6 percent white, was much like the rest of New England, with the exception of Rhode Island, where 91.5 percent were white. In New York, black slaves were more common, accounting for 14.8 percent of the population in 1737 and 11.8 percent in 1771. By 1755, the last year for which there is a census in the colonial period, Maryland's Whites made up only 70.5 percent of the people. In the islands the proportion of Whites was lower still. Bermuda, with 55 percent white in 1774, may have been a lot like South Carolina at the time. Barbados, on the other hand, was overwhelmingly committed to slavery, as fully 78.2 percent of her people were black, and that island

Table 3 Age and sex composition (Whites, selected colonies)

Colony and year	Total population	% white	under 10	% age under 16	60 up	Number of men per 100 women
Connecticut(1774)	197,842	97.6	32.0	–	2.2[a]	98
Rhode Island(1774)	59,607	91.5	–	46.0	–	91
New York(1737)	60,437	85.2	32.6	–	–	99
New York(1771)	168,007	88.2	–	46.2	5.6[b]	109
Maryland(1755)	153,505	70.5	–	49.3	–	113
Bermuda(1774)	11,155	55.0	–	37.1	–	93
Barbados(1773)	88,164	21.8	–	38.0	–	72

[a] Over 70
[b] Males only
Source: Wells Robert V.: *The Population of the British Colonies before 1776: a Survey of Census Data* (Princeton, NJ, 1975).

had more Whites than most of the Caribbean colonies.

The age composition of a population is important to study because the proportion of children affects the ratio of workers to consumers, the numbers in need of schooling, and the number of people old enough to assume political responsibility and military duty. In colonial America, 16 was the age at which young men were considered old enough to be taxed and serve in the militia. Attaining the age of 60 exempted one from these duties. Thus, many early censuses used 16 and sometimes 60 as ages for grouping the population. Women were also grouped in the same way, even though they did not pay taxes or serve in the militia. In general just under half of the population in the continental colonies was under 16 by the end of the eighteenth century, as is evident from the figures for Rhode Island, New York, and Maryland. Both Bermuda and Barbados had significantly fewer children. For some reason the Connecticut census of 1774 and the New York count of 1737 divided the population differently. In both cases, about one-third of the people were less than ten years old. This is normal in a population with about half under 16. The Connecticut census also recorded 2.2 percent over 70, while 5.6 percent of the males in New York in 1771 were 60 or older.

Since women were limited in their economic and political options in the eighteenth century, the ratio of men to women could also affect economic and political affairs. The main point illustrated by table 3 in this regard is that there were distinct regional differences among the colonies. By the outbreak of the Revolution, much of New England had a slight majority of females, at least among adults. As recently as 1755 Rhode Island's sex ratio had been 103 men for every 100 women. In Connecticut the ratio of men to women among those aged 20 to 70 was 98 to 100. There was a male surplus in the younger ages but an even more pronounced female majority over 70. South of New England, males generally predominated. The New York sex ratio for 1771 of 109 is much more in keeping with the full set of figures for that colony than is the ratio for 1737. New Jersey also had about 110 men for every 100 women from 1726 to 1772. The Maryland sex ratio reflects the presence of a number of white indentured servants, who were more likely to be male. In 1704, when servants had not yet given way to slaves in that colony, the sex ratio was 154 men to 100 women. The sex ratio in both Bermuda and Barbados shows a definite female majority. This was not always the case in the islands, for males were in the majority in most of the Leeward Islands in 1756. The island of Tobago, which had recently been acquired from the French, had a most unusual population in 1775. All the Whites listed were adult males; among the Blacks, who accounted for 95.7 percent of the total, 89.1 percent were adult, and there were 151 men for every 100 women. This last figure was down from 212 men to 100 women in 1771. The 1775 sex ratio for Tobago is similar to those of slave populations on the mainland in the eighteenth century. There were more black children on the continent, but they were not as prevalent as the white young.

By 1775 the population of Britain's colonies was increasingly not English. One out of every five Americans traced his or her roots to Africa, not Europe. But even among the Whites, English ties were growing rarer. In the late seventeenth century the population in England ceased to grow and may even have declined briefly. As a result the colonies, which had once been seen as an outlet for excess people, were now viewed as a threat to the English population. Although a few non-English had come to the colonies before 1700, after that year Germans, Irish, Scots, and Welsh all began to move to America. The traditional estimate was that about 30 percent of the total population were Whites from other than England. In the eighteenth century, Scots and Welsh, as well as Germans, were quite different from the English, and were proudly conscious of that fact. Recently, a new estimate of the ethnic composition of the United States in 1790 (which should reflect the situation in 1775) has suggested that there were more non-English than previously thought. In addition the unequal distribution of these people enhanced sectional differences. For example, Scots may have accounted for only 8.7 percent of Connecticut's population, compared with the 81 percent who were of English ancestry. In contrast, 32.9 percent of South Carolinians may have been Scots, and only 36.7 percent of the Whites were English. The estimates for Pennsylvania include 19.5 percent English, 33.3 percent German, and 42.8 percent Celtic (Welsh, Scots, and Irish). Overall, the white population of New England was about 75 percent English, but, from New York on south, non-English were in the majority. Of course this was also where the vast majority of Blacks lived.

Although the vast majority of Americans were farmers, a significant number lived in towns. Urban residents were significant beyond their numbers because they were most directly linked to the British Empire and were most immediately affected by changes in colonial policy. Because colonial governments were located in the colonial towns, the residents there were generally better informed about and more active in politics. Table 4 indicates the size of the most prominent colonial towns in the eighteenth century. Boston, which was the largest town in 1700, grew until about 1740, but then war and environmental problems brought on by too many people in too little space brought a half-century halt to its growth. In contrast, both Philadelphia and New York prospered during the century, with Philadelphia gaining a temporary edge after 1750. Newport experienced moderate growth until 1770, but was damaged severely during the Revolution and was eventually overtaken by its rival, Providence. Charles Town, South Carolina, was the single major town in the South until the rapid emergence of Baltimore after 1750. The most important southern city in the nineteenth century, New Orleans, was under French and Spanish control until 1804. Although these towns grew rapidly from 1700 to 1790, they did not keep pace with the rest of the colonies, with the result that their proportion of the colonial total fell from 6.1 percent to 3.7 percent.

3 Causes of Growth and Change

Three factors determine the size and composition of all populations: fertility (births), mortality (deaths), and migration. The exact balance of these forces has not yet been determined, but it is possible to indicate the general relationship among these factors within each of the major divisions of the colonies. In New England the major determinant of the population quickly became the balance of births and deaths. After 1650 immigration was minimal. Although New England was eventually outstripped by the other sections, growth was still rapid because

Table 4 Major centers of urban population, 1700–90 (estimates and counts)

City	1700	1750	1770	1790
Boston	13,000	15,731	15,520	18,038
Newport	4,640	6,600	9,200	6,716
New York	8,600	13,300	21,800	33,131
Philadelphia	8,500	13,400	28,000	42,444
Charles Town	n.a.	<8,000	10,863	16,359
Baltimore	n.a.	n.a.	n.a.	13,503
Salem, Mass.	n.a.	n.a.	4,500	7,921
Providence	3,916	3,400	4,320	6,371
Total	38,656	60,431	94,203	144,483
% of total population	6.1	5.5	4.4	3.7

Source: US Bureau of the Census: *A Century of Population Growth* (Washington, DC, 1909), 11, 163.

of high fertility and mortality levels that were probably as favorable as any in the world before 1800. The middle colonies shared in the rapid natural increase caused by high birth rates and low death rates. There, however, migration had a more significant impact. After 1700, Germans, Scots, Irish, and Welsh moved in to help swell the population. This immigration was uneven both in its impact on the individual colonies and over the course of the century. Some slaves were also imported, but not to the same extent as in the South.

Patterns in the South contrast sharply with those farther north. It is also necessary to distinguish the seventeenth from the eighteenth century. Migration to the South was higher throughout the entire colonial period. It did, however, undergo some marked changes, when English immigrants of the seventeenth century gave way to Blacks in the eighteenth along the coastal regions. In the middle of the eighteenth century, Scots and Germans moved into the western hill country. Mortality in the South was much higher in the seventeenth century than in the other sections, and although life expectancy improved after 1700 the climate continued to be favourable for diseases such as malaria. The birth rate was low in the early years because of the scarcity of women and high death rates. As the sex ratio came into better balance and mortality improved, family sizes in the South compared favorably with those elsewhere. The most distinct region in America was the Caribbean islands. They were almost the exact opposite of New England. Life was short for both Blacks and Whites, childbearing was low, and a steady stream of black slaves meant society was more New Africa than New England.

Migration

Migration deserves first detailed comment, if only because it was so influential in differentiating the sections. Estimates of the total number of immigrants to the mainland vary because records are scattered and uneven in quality. Recent work has, however, made it clear that immigrants were a major force in colonial life. Equally important, many of

them came involuntarily. About 350,000 slaves were imported in the eighteenth century alone. No less than 65,000 Germans arrived in Philadelphia between 1727 and 1776. Perhaps as many as 100,000 Scots and Irish came to America in the decade before Independence, joining the 17,500 convicts who were shipped to the colonies between 1718 and 1772. In the period between the Boston Tea Party and the end of the first year of actual fighting, 5,196 English and 3,872 Scots came to the increasingly rebellious colonies. In all, a million people may have moved to the colonies between 1607 and 1776.

Who were these people? The answer depends on the time and place. The differences in the early migrants to New England and Virginia have already been noted. Perhaps half to two-thirds of the Whites came as indentured servants. A study of 20,657 servants recorded in English registers at various years from 1655 to 1775 shows 81.6 percent were male and 75 percent were aged 16 to 25. The tendency for servants to be young males was more pronounced after 1700 than before. Interestingly, servants claimed skilled occupations 85 percent of the time in the 1770s, compared with 30 to 35 percent in the 1680s. Of the total, 55 percent of the women and 52 percent of the men went to the Chesapeake. Pennsylvania received 6 percent of the men and fewer women. Only 2 percent of both men and women went to the other mainland colonies. Barbados was the primary destination of servants in the 1650s, and Jamaica dominated from 1730 to 1749. Together, however, they attracted only 28 percent of the men and 26 percent of the women over the entire period. After 1750 almost all servants went to the Chesapeake, with a few heading to Pennsylvania.

The 9,364 migrants who arrived just as the imperial conflict was escalating can be described in detail. In general, two different groups moved to America. Single laborers from London and the immediate vicinity went to Maryland, Pennsylvania, and Virginia. Families left economic hardships in Scotland and the north of England for new farms in New York and North Carolina. As might be expected, children were more common among the Scots than the English. Only 3.4 percent of the latter were under ten, compared with 15.1 percent of the former (see table 3). Almost no older people went. Of the English, 83.8 percent were male, compared with 59.9 percent among the Scots. About two-thirds of the migrants went alone, as the proportion moving with their families was 18.2 percent for the English and 41.7 percent for the Scots. Artisans were the most common occupational group in both streams. The English, however, were much more likely to be indentured. About a quarter of the migrants indicated why they were moving. Most of the English saw the move as a new opportunity, while the majority of the Scots were fleeing a harsh life. Poverty was mentioned by 307 Scots as a reason to move; no English made this claim.

Fertility and mortality

Fertility and mortality also shaped the colonial population. Of these, fertility was the most important because it contributed to the high proportion under the age of 16. In general, families in the colonies averaged six to eight children during the eighteenth century. The corresponding figure for England was nearer four. One reason for the large family size was early marriage on the part of women, brought on by the number of men seeking wives. Once married, couples lived together for 25 to 30 years and so were able to have numerous children. Children arrived once every two years, much as in England, but they arrived over a longer period. The South did not achieve this level of child-bearing until the death rates declined after 1700. But by 1750 most colonists had large families.

Death rates were subject to greater variation. The terrible mortality of the early years lasted well into the seventeenth century in the South. In contrast, New Englanders quickly achieved remarkably long lives. Precise figures are rare because adequate records are missing. When illness and death were common, however, life expectancy may not have exceeded 25 years at birth. At best, life expectancy reached 45 or even a little higher. (At the end of the twentieth century it is over 70.) A life expectancy of 25 means that more than 300 out of every 1,000 babies will not see their first birthday. Under half will reach marriageable age, and only 170 will attain 60. With life expectancy at 45, 850 of the 1,000 infants will live to the age of one, 716 will survive to marry, and 430 will celebrate 60. Today, however, a higher proportion live to 60 than made it to one even under the best of colonial conditions. Smallpox, malaria, and tuberculosis were some of the more important killers the colonists faced. On the other hand, Americans may have been as well fed, housed, and clothed as any people in the world once the hardships of the early years passed.

4 Family and Population

The demographic patterns examined so far were both shaped by and in turn influenced families. Birth, death, and marriage were obviously closely linked to families. Single migrants sought to establish families as soon as possible when they were free to do so. The term "family" can be defined in a number of different ways. Perhaps the most common use of the word in the eighteenth century was to refer to a domestic unit of parents, children, and servants, all of whom were engaged in common economic activity under the control of a single head. Kin were also part of the family and could be called on to help in time of trouble, or to assist in family business.

Demography had a greater impact on three other aspects of the family: children born, households, and the life course. Once a man and woman married, they could expect to have between six and eight children if their marriage was not broken by an early death. This was the result of early marriages for women and good health for all. Because both fertility and mortality were unpredictable, individual experience varied considerably from the average. For example, both large and small families were common among one group of women, who averaged 7.4 children. Women who had ten or more children accounted for 24.3 percent of all wives. Another 10.9 percent had no more than three children. From the children's perspective, large families were relatively common, if only because one family with ten children had as many offspring as five couples with two each. Thus, 50.7 percent of the children lived in families with nine or more children. Where mortality remained high, or immigration created an imbalanced sex ratio, family life was more uncertain and children scarcer.

The household is another way to look at families. In this case, the perspective is on how many people lived together at any given moment, as births added new members, and marriages, deaths, and migration subtracted old. In the eighteenth century, white households on the continent contained an average of 5.5 to 7 persons. Once again, averages are deceiving. In Rhode Island in 1774, the average for all households was 6.3. Only 1.4 percent of the households were people living alone; 15.8 percent had at least ten members; 51.2 percent of the households had five to nine members. Since colonial houses were relatively small, crowding was common and the ability to get along was critical.

Several factors account for the variations in household size. As the age of the head of the family increased, so too did the number of people under his or her control. The longer a couple was married, the more children would be living at home until the head reached the age of 45 or 50. In addition, older householders often had enough money to be able to buy servants or slaves. When the family head was a woman, the household was generally smaller both because of the absence of a husband and because women were not as wealthy. Wealth also affected the size of households among men, with rich families being larger than poor. Generally, racial or ethnic minorities had households that were smaller than their neighbors'. Some of these factors are related, but at present the ties among age, race, and wealth cannot be separated. Perhaps a major source of variation among households was the presence or absence of servants or slaves. In 1790, for example, the average household size for Whites was 5.7. In South Carolina, households averaged 9.5 members when slaves are included. The average modern American household has under three people. As might be expected, households in the Caribbean colonies were quite different from those on the mainland. They were much larger, had many more slaves, and fewer children.

When a young man and woman married, prevailing demographic patterns provided some expectations about what course their lives might follow. The following, based on the experience of some Quakers in the middle colonies, is representative of the northern colonies in the latter half of the eighteenth century. The family was formed when marriage occurred, at about 25 for men and 20.5 for women. Children arrived quickly, and kept arriving every two and a half years for most of the next two decades. Once a woman reached 40 she was not likely to have more children, but the youngest would probably not marry for another 20 years. By this time, either the husband or wife would have been dead almost ten years. In contrast, childbearing at the end of the twentieth century seldom lasts even ten years, and couples can anticipate a long life together after their children have left home.

Probably no institution in colonial America was as important to the well-being of both individuals and society as the family. Families were the center of economic activity in an agricultural society. Both production and consumption occurred at home as parents, children, and servants worked at various tasks around the farm. In the absence of any welfare system, families took care of the sick, elderly, and orphaned. Even single people were placed in a family when they needed help. Government depended on families for taxes, voters (the head of the family only), militia, and control of subordinates. At a time when police were unheard of outside the towns, parents, and especially fathers, were expected to control their families. Although there were a few schools in the colonies, families provided much of the education, both to their own children and to apprentices. Churches taught obedience to women, children, and servants, and in exchange won members from the next generations. Paternal authority was the norm, and was enforced by custom, teaching, civil authority, and economics. In a world where age, sex, and race automatically disqualified a person from power both at home and in public, democracy was not yet widespread.

As the eighteenth century brought better life chances and a more even sex ratio to slaves, family life became a stabilizing force on plantations with numerous slaves. In the end, however, slave marriages were never recognized as legally binding by the masters, who felt free to separate families by sale or transfer to a new plantation.

The Revolution brought modest changes to family life by 1800. Divorce, which had been almost impossible in the colonial period, was made somewhat easier. Women experienced moderate gains in economic opportunities. Many reformers urged that the future mothers of the republic's citizens needed to be educated in order to raise their children properly. Children gave some evidence of resisting parental authority, both by insisting on more say in whom they would marry, and by starting their families before they were married. Although the connection is not clear, at least one group of Americans began consciously to limit the size of their families as the Revolution broke out. At the time few noticed these changes, but they became an increasingly important part of American society after 1800.

5 Population and the Revolution

Direct connections between demography and the resistance to Britain are hard to demonstrate. But population patterns did influence the course of events from 1760 to 1820. The most obvious link is between the growth of the colonies and their ability to fight. In 1700 military resistance to Britain would have been unthinkable; it was a possibility by 1775. Here, the contrast with the Caribbean is instructive. The island colonies agreed with many of the objections their northern counterparts raised about continued British control. In the end, however, they remained loyal, partly because they were small and isolated, and partly because the Whites who ruled were unwilling to give up British protection against the vast majority of slaves. Only Jamaica, with 209,000 people in 1774, rivaled the mainland colonies in size, but the critical point

was that almost 197,000 of the inhabitants were slaves.

The growth of the colonial population had a psychological effect in both America and Britain. By 1763, the English were well aware of the rapid growth that the censuses were recording. As the Seven Years' War came to a close and the royal officials began to consider how to restructure the empire, they debated what to do with the colonial population. One suggestion was to encourage the colonists to spread out so they would be unable to aid each other. The counter-proposal was to restrict the settlers east of the Alleghenies, where they would be accessible to British merchants and soldiers. In spite of efforts to enforce the latter policy, British governors were complaining in the 1770s about their inability to control the restless and independent pioneers.

Americans, too, were aware of growth, but they drew quite different conclusions. In one way or another, prominent Americans such as Benjamin Franklin; Ezra Stiles, President of Yale; and Edward Wigglesworth, a Harvard professor, all pointed with pride to the rapid increase. They saw this as a sign of American virtue (an important idea in republican thought), and told readers on both sides of the Atlantic that Americans would soon outnumber the English. This was an important conclusion in an age that believed that population meant wealth and wealth meant power.

After the war the creation of a union was rendered difficult by population patterns. The preferred form of government was a republic, but, according to theory, republics should be small and homogeneous. The new states were anything but that. A population of three and a half million was thinly scattered over the seacoast from what is now Maine to Georgia. In addition, immigration in the eighteenth century had produced a complex array of cultures, which had already led to political clashes before 1775. Slavery was another point that divided many Americans who were beginning to take seriously their rhetoric of freedom and equality. Thus, the debate in the Constitutional Convention over representation was serious not only in an abstract sense, but also because of the realities of population. The establishment of a regular census and the 3/5ths Compromise (which determined that five slaves would be counted as three free persons for purposes of taxation and representation) are two of the more obvious effects population had on the formation of the government. James Madison made an important contribution to overcoming the fears over an over-large republic when he suggested, in *Federalist*, No. 10, that republics might be safer with a large, complex population that could not agree on anything than in a small country where a tyrannizing majority might easily grab power.

The nineteenth century saw demographic revolutions that rivaled the political one of the previous century. Between 1800 and 1920, Americans swept over the continent to the Pacific, became an urban people, received 30 million immigrants, cut the size of their families in half, and improved their health and life expectancy. The world of Woodrow Wilson was no longer that of Washington or Jefferson. Just as Americans determined their political fate in 1776, they began to assert control over matters of life and death, and so transformed their existence in ways never before seen.

FURTHER READING

Bailyn, Bernard: *Voyagers to the West: a Passage in the Peopling of America on the Eve of the Revolution* (New York: Alfred A. Knopf, 1986).

Buel, Joy Day, and Buel, Richard: *The Way of Duty: a Woman and Her Family in Revolutionary America* (New York: W. W. Norton, 1984).

Dowd, Gregory E.: *A Spirited Resistance: the North American Indian Struggle for Unity, 1745–1815* (Baltimore: Johns Hopkins University Press, 1992).

Frey, Silvia R.: *Water from the Rock: Black Resistance in a Revolutionary Age* (Princeton: Princeton University Press, 1991).

McDonald, Forrest, and McDonald, Ellen Shapiro: "The ethnic origins of the American people, 1790," *William and Mary Quarterly*, 37 (1980), 179–99.

Potter, James: "The growth of population in America, 1700–1860," in *Population in History*, ed. D. V. Glass and D. E. C. Eversley (London: Edward Arnold, 1965), 631–88.

Taylor, Alan: *William Cooper's Town: Power and Persuasion on the Frontier of the Early American Republic* (New York: Alfred A. Knopf, 1995).

Ulrich, Laural T.: *A Midwife's Tale: The Life of Martha Ballard, Based on her Diary, 1785–1812* (New York: Alfred A. Knopf, 1990).

United States Bureau of the Census: *A Century of Population Growth: From the First Census of the United States to the Twelfth, 1790–1900* (Washington, D.C.: Government Printing Office, 1909).

Wells, Robert V.: *The Population of the British Colonies in America Before 1776: A Survey of Census Data* (Princeton: Princeton University Press, 1975).

——: *Revolutions in Americans' Lives: A Demographic Perspective on the History of Americans, Their Families, and Their Society* (Westport, Conn.: Greenwood Press, 1982).

——: "The population of England's colonies in America: old English or new Americans?" *Population Studies*, 46 (1992), 85–102.

CHAPTER SEVEN

Socio-economic development of the colonies

EDWIN J. PERKINS

THE economy of the North American colonies developed in very independent fashion in the seventeenth and eighteenth centuries. The economic events precipitating the independence movement began in the mid-1760s when Parliament tried to readjust the overall character of its political and economic relationship with the colonies by bringing them more within the administrative and fiscal sway of the home government. A large standing army was permanently stationed in North America to protect these highly valued overseas colonies from uncertain, ill-defined threats, and the British Exchequer sought tax revenues from the prime beneficiaries of this military protection to offset at least a small portion of defense costs. But the Americans resisted, claiming the new taxes violated their rights and liberties. Parliament insisted on demonstrating the superiority of its position, and the irreconcilable debate over the issue of sovereignty led to an armed rebellion and total independence. For an entire half century, from 1765 until 1815, economic interaction between Great Britain and the 13 political units in North America, which in tandem possessed the highest living standards around the globe, were periodically and often drastically interrupted, with the result that neither party in this prolonged conflict fully enjoyed all the mutual advantages accruing from the transatlantic exchange of goods and services.

The aggregate output of goods and services in the 13 colonies grew at a very rapid pace over the course of the seventeenth and eighteenth centuries. Fueled by burgeoning population growth and gradual but nonetheless steady increases in the productivity of workers, the size of the colonial economy expanded at a rate three or four times faster than that of Great Britain over the three-quarters of a century before American Independence. Starting from a very low base, colonial production in 1650 was minuscule on a comparative basis; by 1700 output was rising, but it remained less than 5 percent of the mother country's. By 1775, however, the future United States had developed a robust economy nearly two-fifths the size of Great Britain's. It was no longer a mere colonial outpost on a distant continent. Moreover, per capita incomes, or median living standards, for members of free, white households in British North America were higher than those in England and probably the very highest that the world had ever witnessed for a region with a population of over two million.

On the eve of their declaration of political independence, the rebellious colonies possessed a strong and vibrant economy, and they bitterly resented the persistent efforts of parliamentary leaders to consider them in an unequal, subservient light. Benjamin Franklin had projected, on the basis of prevailing rates of economic expansion, that North America would likely surpass Great Britain within two more generations – and his estimates were not far off the mark. Indeed, the most thriving economy under British rule was situated along the eastern shore of the North Atlantic. But British leaders in the 1770s insisted on taking a static rather than a dynamic view of political and economic developments within the empire. Their outlook was shortsighted and unrealistic since, by the third quarter of the eighteenth century, the underlying value of a close connection with North America was not within the realm of political control but linked instead to the steadily increasing opportunities for mutually advantageous trade in raw materials, manufactured goods, and shipping services.

1 Population Growth and the Economy

Demographics and economics were closely linked in colonial America. Population growth, stemming from immigration and natural increase, drove the economy forward at expansion rates as high as 40 percent or more per decade (*see also* chapter 6, §1). Birth rates were high as a result of early marriage, while death rates for both infants and adults were relatively low in comparison with those in Europe. American women married in their early twenties, several years sooner than in Europe. Most wives who survived to age 40 typically gave birth to six or seven children, of which four or five survived to adulthood. Because of the mild climate, hearty diets, and inexpensive wood for household heating, persons who survived childhood diseases generally lived into their late fifties and sixties.

The voluntary immigration of young people from Britain and northern Europe, who were responding to reports of unprecedented opportunities for upward mobility in North America, also contributed to the rapid climb in population. After 1670 the forced immigration of enslaved Africans had a demographic impact as well: by Independence, Blacks accounted for over 20 percent of the total population. In the southern colonies, where slavery reigned, Blacks comprised more than two-fifths of the work force. In 1775 the size of colonial population, at 2.6 million – including 2.1 million Whites, 540,000 Blacks, plus perhaps 50,000 Native Americans – was ten times greater than at the start of the century. Taking into account improvements in productivity as well, the aggregate economy was about 14 times larger when Thomas Jefferson penned the Declaration of Independence than in 1700.

2 Supply of Land

Three vital economic factors had a profound effect on population growth and the structure of the economy: the colonies had a surplus of fertile land and other natural resources but shortages of the labor and capital required for development. The ownership of land was the main goal of most pre-industrial peoples, and in North America that goal was within the reach of almost every free citizen. The availability of thousands of acres of undeveloped land stimulated immigration and likewise encouraged the formation of large family units because parents were confident that their many children would be adequately fed in youth and that, upon marriage, a couple could always earn an adequate living by farming. Except in certain areas of New England, population pressure did not hold down the median size of farms for succeeding generations. Farmers, who comprised about three-quarters of the colonial workforce, typically lived on properties containing 60 to 100 acres, a huge farm by European standards.

Only about one-third of farm property was planted in crops. The additional land was a combination of pasture and forest. The main food crops were maize (Indian corn), wheat, rye, and rice. Maize was an indigenous food source raised by Native American tribes from Maine to Georgia. The European settlers quickly adopted this food staple, for it complemented other agricultural crops ranging from grains to tobacco. Rye was planted extensively in New England, while wheat was important in the middle colonies and, after 1730, in the Chesapeake region. Rice was eaten in South Carolina and Georgia. Farmers also raised barley for brewing beer, apples for cider, and oats and hay for livestock. Vegetable gardens were planted in season. Ample forests provided wood for cooking and household heating.

The high incomes of farmers by contemporary world standards was revealed most clearly in their heavy consumption of meat and dairy products. Total meat consumption was around 200 pounds annually for adult males, with lesser amounts for women and children; the high protein content of diets translated into the achievement of near modern heights for the general population. Americans were on average about two inches taller than their English counterparts. Colonial farms kept a varied livestock. The typical farmer in Connecticut in the mid-eighteenth century, for example, owned ten cattle, 16 sheep, six pigs, two horses, and a team of oxen. Cows produced milk, cheese, and butter, chickens laid eggs, while sheep provided the wool for warm clothing. Virtually every farm household was self-sufficient in terms of food production. Except for the first few decades after the settlement of Virginia in 1607, starvation was not a serious threat in British North America.

In addition to producing enough food to provide a hearty diet for every member of the household, the family farm also generated surpluses available for sale in markets at home and abroad. Depending on the climate and fertility of the soil, households had the opportunity to divert up to two-fifths of total output to the market-place. Some families chose to divert extra grain into building their livestock herds, while others sold surpluses for cash or credit and purchased a variety of products and services from either neighbors, local towns, or overseas suppliers. By the mid-eighteenth century, roughly one-quarter of all goods exchanged in local markets had been transported across provincial borders. A substantial share of the discretionary income of colonial farmers was spent on imported English goods.

British credit to colonial merchants

The American market loomed ever greater in British foreign trade over the course of the century, and London merchants extended huge amounts of credit to colonial merchants and southern planters to finance that trade. The debts accumulated by colonial buyers were incurred because of the optimism of both English creditors and colonial debtors about the future prospects of the economy. The offering of credit was an inducement to increase sales, and colonial households with rising incomes responded accordingly. The old argument, sometimes advanced by earlier generations of historians, that linked American rebelliousness to the burden of indebtedness has been grossly

exaggerated. Large plantation owners in the Chesapeake were prone to complain in private about mounting debts and even expressed resentment about the tone of business relations with English merchants, but they kept buying and adding to their outstanding balances because of their over-riding desire to maintain the material component of their high life-styles. At no point in colonial history were Americans dependent upon the good will of English creditors for their well-being and prosperity. Credit was voluntarily extended and voluntarily accepted, with all parties, or the vast majority, obtaining the benefits bargained for and anticipated.

Land prices

Land prices were very low in the colonies compared with those in Europe. Indeed, the very existence of substantial tracts of land for sale in an impersonal market made the New World vastly different from the old. Even youths who failed to inherit substantial property were usually able to earn enough money from various labors to raise the down-payment to acquire a small farm. Unlike the situation in Great Britain, most tenant farmers did not remain landless over the course of their lives. Eventually the tenant household purchased the farm it occupied from the landlord, or the family pulled up stakes and moved into unsettled areas where land prices were very low.

The majority of farm households were independent units. Owners made their own decisions about crop selection and farm management, and they reaped the profits from the steady rise of land prices as local population increased. Since most married white males held title to sufficient property to meet requirements for voting, they were eligible to vote for all elected officials. The continuous availability of inexpensive, affordable land in every province was the major factor which led to the creation of a relatively highly participatory society in North America.

Distribution of wealth

In addition to its political impact, the large supply of salable land led to a surprisingly wide distribution of property. The majority of households had at least a modest stake in society, and they favored laws protecting property rights in land and in other bonded human beings, namely servants and slaves. The extremes of wealth and poverty so common in Europe were not as evident in the 13 colonies. Few Americans remained members of indigent households throughout their lives. Although up to one-third of all adult males held title to little tangible property, a careful analysis of the age distribution of wealth-holders reveals that most of the propertyless were unmarried persons under 30 years old. Over the course of the normal life-cycle, a person who survived to the age of 40 could anticipate living in a household of middling wealth and income. Only 3 to 5 percent of middle-aged white males were genuinely poor and dependent on charity; a higher percentage of older widows fell into poverty, however. Slaves and indentured servants held no property, yet the living conditions provided by owners were generally adequate to maintain good health. No occupational group in the colonies had reason to fear the possibility of starvation or long-term deprivation.

A few privileged colonial households did control a disproportionate share of the aggregate wealth. Families which arrived in a given locale when it was undergoing initial settlement and then proceeded to save and expand their land holdings over several generations formed the core of an American counterpart to the English gentry. Since primogeniture and entail were legal principles less vigorously applied in North America, and particularly in the northern colonies, the patterns of land-ownership rarely led to great extremes of wealth. Even the very richest Americans were persons of only modest wealth by English standards. The colonies had no inherited nobility, and no large land holdings controlled by religious orders. Large estates in the South relied upon slave labor rather than white tenant families.

By the 1770s, the top 10 percent of wealth-holders held somewhat over one-half of the region's net worth (assets minus liabilities) – a measurement that includes the ownership of indentured servants and slaves. The lower half of all wealth-holders laid claim to less than 5 percent of colonial net worth. The middle colonies – New York, New Jersey, Pennsylvania, and Delaware – had the least skewed distribution of property, with the wealthiest 10 percent holding only about two-fifths of net worth. The 13 colonies were certainly not a classless society. Differences in wealth and income were clearly evident in North America, but the rigid divisions so prevalent in European societies were modulated in the colonies. Equally important, movement upward from poor to middling status in one lifetime and then up to moderate wealth within several generations was a genuine possibility for white family units, given hard work and good fortune. Again, the primary economic factor promoting a relatively wide distribution of property among the upper half of wealth-holders was ready access to vast stretches of undeveloped land in the interior at prices which thousands of potential buyers could reasonably afford.

3 Supply of Labor

The shortage of labor in the colonies likewise had major consequences, some positive and others highly negative. On the plus side, artisans were in such demand that incomes typically exceeded the earnings of their counterparts across the Atlantic Ocean. As a result, artisans did not need to form guilds in an effort to hold up wages by placing restrictions on the entry of newcomers into labor markets. Few apprentices and journeymen remained dependent employees much beyond their mid-twenties; master artisans usually found substantial work at good wages in both urban and rural areas. The property qualifications for voting were applied in such a manner that most middle-aged artisans held the franchise, and some were elected to public office at the town and county levels.

The favorable market for labor also meant that unskilled youths seeking work opportunities prior to marriage were generally able to find at least part-time employment in the fields and shops of neighbors. In an agricultural economy based largely on the labor resources of the family unit, there were numerous times throughout the year when households sought to hire extra hands to plow fields, plant seeds, and harvest crops. In wheat-growing areas, the maturing crop had to be harvested quickly or left to rot in the fields. Households with numerous children but few males over the age of 12 invariably sought to employ unmarried youths living on neighboring farms to assist in the spring planting and fall harvesting. In households with many small children, parents often hired teenage girls from nearby farms to help with domestic work. Since employment opportunities came up regularly in any given locality, able-bodied children over the age of 12 were rarely an economic burden.

The shortage of labor had less fortunate consequences as well. In the southern colonies, where tobacco and later rice became plantation crops, land-owners could not recruit enough free labor to take full advantage of profit opportunities in exporting to European markets. Their solution was bonded labor. In the Chesapeake colonies of Virginia and Maryland, a market in white indentured servants quickly emerged in the seventeenth century. Adventuresome persons in England without the money to finance the ocean voyage essentially bartered a four to seven year claim on their labor services in return for transatlantic transportation, routine maintenance (food, shelter, clothing), plus modest freedom ducs upon the expiration of their legal contract. Between one-half and three-quarters of all Chesapeake arrivals in the seventeenth century came as indentured servants. In total, over the whole colonial period perhaps as many as 500,000 northern Europeans, some in complete family units, sailed to North America with an obligation to provide labor services under indenture contracts.

From the use of bonded white labor under contract for a fixed period of years, it was just another short step to the adoption of the pernicious system of black slavery. Slavery was a labor system based strictly on race in North America; only Africans and their children – and all future generations – were subject to permanent enslavement. Black slavery had been common in the Caribbean and South American colonies of European states since the sixteenth century, but it did not migrate to the Chesapeake tobacco colonies in full force until after 1670.

The shift from white indentured servants to black slaves occurred primarily because of movements in relative prices for bonded labor. Because of improving economic conditions in Great Britain, the number of servants willing to emigrate declined and the prices of indenture contracts rose. Meanwhile the number of slaves available for purchase along the coast of Africa rose steadily and the cost of transporting them across the Atlantic fell because of improvements in shipping services. Beginning in the 1670s the prices for slaves, after adjustment for the expected length of service, were competitive with servant contracts, and tobacco growers responded accordingly. The southern colonies embraced slavery because the system was compatible with the cultivation of their major exportable crops – tobacco, rice, and indigo – and it provided the most convenient and immediately profitable solution to the problem of short supplies of human labor for the development of abundant natural resources.

Occupations

The occupation profile of the colonial work force reveals that about 80 percent of all free males were involved primarily in agricultural pursuits. Artisans, both in rural and more urban areas, constituted from 10 to 15 percent of the male work force, depending on location and date. Merchants, professionals, and storekeepers comprised perhaps 5 percent of the population. Occupational overlapping was fairly common as well: most artisans kept some livestock and farmed a few acres for household consumption; few rural storekeepers could earn a livelihood on the profits of trade alone; and farmers were involved in some form of non-agricultural economic activity during the off-season. Male slaves were mainly field hands, but perhaps one-fifth did labor service as trained artisans or house servants.

White women performed domestic service – including child care, cooking, and cleaning – and they normally undertook related tasks such as tending livestock, churning butter, spinning thread, and sewing clothes. Except during the harvest season, free women did not routinely engage in field work. Many black women in the southern colonies, however, did perform double duty – working in the fields during the day for the owner and returning home at night to perform domestic services for their own family units.

4 Supply of Capital

The shortage of capital was likewise a handicap to economic development. Financial and credit markets were much less organized than those in England and Scotland. The colonies were unable to attract substantial amounts of capital from overseas to finance the direct development of natural resources. The largest volume of foreign capital entered the economy through the credit lines extended to American merchants and planters by numerous British firms involved in colonial trade. These sums climbed steadily throughout the eighteenth century, and by the mid-1760s the amount outstanding was on the order of £5 million annually.

The bulk of the capital for the conversion of raw land into productive farmland arose from the savings and investments of the colonists themselves. Most of the savings were not pecuniary, since no banks existed, but arose as a result of foregoing leisure and diverting the potential rewards of labor away from consumption and into clearing forests, constructing barns and fences, building livestock herds, and, in the South, enlarging the bonded work force. By Independence, the colonists had amassed total physical assets valued at approximately £110 million, or nearly $500 million, with just under one-fifth of the total accounted for by investments in bonded labor.

Monetary system

The monetary system of the colonies was based on the use of Spanish coins from mines in Latin America, since Parliament had refused to allow the export of English coins or the establishment of a colonial mint. The colonies supplemented the coinage with paper monies which the 13 assemblies issued independently at various times through two different mechanisms. In the first instance, they issued currency to pay pressing government debts. These sums were scheduled for retirement in future years through taxation. In a second instance, the assemblies created loan offices which advanced currency to borrowers who offered as collateral their equity in real-estate properties; the retirement of these currency issues was linked to the repayment of loans by private parties. In both instances, a given emission of paper money was scheduled to remain in general circulation for 10 to 20 years.

When assemblies failed to collect the scheduled taxes or private borrowers failed to repay their loans, colonial currencies depreciated heavily. Depreciation was a constant threat in New England in the first half of the eighteenth century, and Parliament forbade the issuance of any additional paper monies in those provinces after 1751. South Carolina was banned from increasing the volume of paper currency after 1731. The remaining colonies, however, collected the necessary taxes and insisted on the repayment of private loans, and their respective currencies retained their value relative to gold and silver.

Thus, it came as a profound shock when Parliament tried to suppress the remaining paper money in North America in 1764. The colonies which had acted responsibly for decades in managing their monetary affairs protested vehemently and unceasingly, and after much controversy Parliament finally agreed in 1773 to let them resume the issuance of currency under slightly revised legal tender terms. Thereafter, British creditors received ironclad protection from any losses associated with the depreciation of colonial currencies.

In their handling of financial affairs, the middle and southern colonies ranked among the most innovative societies in the early modern period for their persistent use of monies created from paper rather than metals. Because paper money was printed in a wide range of denominations, high and low, the ease and convenience of making routine exchange transactions was much greater in the 13 colonies than in most of Europe or elsewhere. The large infusions of paper money into some colonies at certain dates may have also served to stimulate their economies and pull them out of business and trade recessions.

Taxation

The level of taxation was very low in the colonies compared with the rates prevailing in the mother country. Local governments financed a large portion of their limited services through user fees – in particular, the court system. Farmers frequently accepted work assignments on roadways leading to local markets to meet their obligations to towns and counties. Since much of the population lived reasonably close to the Atlantic coastline or near the banks of navigable rivers, provincial governments invested little monies in developing an internal transportation system. Goods and persons destined for intermediate and longer distances usually traveled by water. Salaries for the governor and a small administrative staff were often the only major peacetime appropriations of the 13 assemblies. Several provincial governments collected sufficient interest revenues from the operations of their loan offices to cover all their normal annual expenditures. New Jersey and Pennsylvania collected no direct taxes at all from citizens for several decades.

Tax rates were minimal in large part because the governmental bureaucracy was small and defense costs were low. The British Navy patrolled the North Atlantic to protect ships engaged in trade within the empire, and, beginning with the Seven Years' War, Parliament reimbursed the colonies for a portion of the monies they had expended in that contest. Low taxes were among the factors which left the typical colonial household so much disposable income and allowed it to maintain the highest standard of living in the world by the mid-eighteenth century. Parliamentary efforts in the 1760s to raise imperial taxes and thereby shift at least a small portion of the tax burden for North American defense to the colonies themselves led instead to an

unanticipated rebellion (*see* chapter 16). The initial controversy over Parliament's attempt to impose a modest level of imperial taxation soon escalated in a full-blown debate over political rights and principles. During the trade boycotts organized to protest against imperial taxation, British merchants lost the opportunity to earn thousands of pounds in profits on foregone colonial sales. The lost private profits added up to a much greater sum than Parliament had ever hoped to raise in imperial taxes, which explains why representatives of the mercantile sector in London finally convinced the King's ministers to rescind all the controversial American taxes except the duty on tea. The tea tax remained as a symbol of the power and authority of Parliament, and its continued existence sparked an incident in Boston harbor in 1773 that put the two countries on the road to war (*see* chapter 24, §2).

5 Foreign Trade

Throughout the era, the economies of the 13 colonies received stimulation from both external and internal forces, with the impact varying by time and geography. The export sector was critical in the settlement and development of the three wealthiest southern colonies. The European demand for tobacco led to the expansion of Virginia and Maryland, while rice, and later indigo, produced the bulk of the wealth in South Carolina. By the mid-eighteenth century, the export of wheat and other foodstuffs from the middle colonies contributed greatly to the vitality of that region's economy. Indeed, foodstuffs combined, including all grain and livestock products, were more important to colonial foreign trade than tobacco. By the third quarter of the eighteenth century, the foreign trade sector was linked to the generation of roughly one-fifth of aggregate colonial income.

In typical mercantilist fashion, Parliament applied trade restrictions, a series of so-called Navigation Acts, on colonial trade beginning in the 1650s. The goal was to make certain that all trade reverberated to the benefit of the mother country and fostered its economic strength *vis-à-vis* competitive European powers. A few specific products were enumerated, meaning that they had to be shipped directly to British ports. Foremost in the enumerated category was tobacco. The negative effect of this policy was that colonial shippers were prohibited from seeking out buyers in other nations who might be willing to pay higher prices than British merchants. Another regulation required all trade within the empire to travel across the oceans in British vessels. This second rule became a boon to American interests. Because of the lower cost of raw materials, primarily wood, colonial shipbuilders received numerous construction contracts. Meanwhile, merchants in the New England and middle colonies garnered substantial earnings from the provision of shipping services. On balance, the Navigation Acts had a mildly negative effect on the American economy. Trade restrictions were once cited as one of the main grievances promoting the rebellion, but economic historians have reassessed the evidence and downgraded their importance in fomenting discontent.

Although foreign trade was crucial to the development of certain colonies, the volume of production destined for local consumption and internal markets was vastly greater. Some economic historians believe the expansion of domestic markets was by far the most dynamic factor in propelling the economy forward so rapidly. American producers specialized in growing certain crops for export because of comparative advantages linked to soil and climate, yet if foreign demand for those products had dwindled, the colonists possessed the flexibility and capacity to shift into other productive activities. The colonies imported increasingly large quantities of finished and manufactured goods from English suppliers by choice; if necessary, however, the colonists were fully capable of producing reasonably close substitutes, as they proved in convincing fashion during the organized boycotts of English goods in the 1760s and 1770s.

In addition to fertile land, the colonies had in abundance the natural resources necessary for the production of iron. The most advanced technology of the era still relied on wood as the primary fuel in smelting. England had undergone much deforestation by the eighteenth century and most of its

iron ore was far removed from large stands of trees. In North America, however, wood was plentiful everywhere. The colonies were smelting more iron ore than Great Britain by 1750. Pig iron became the fourth most valuable export in the bilateral trade with Great Britain, trailing only tobacco, rice, and indigo. Although American iron production lapsed after the War for Independence, the economy had demonstrated its capacity for manufacturing and the promotion of industrial ventures.

6　Patterns of Settlement

In terms of the mix of the rural versus urban population, the colonies revealed differing patterns over the decades. Because so many settlers initially hovered along the Atlantic Coast, the residents of towns and villages constituted a larger percentage of the total population in the seventeenth than in the eighteenth century. Although the size of port cities continued to expand, the number of settlers in outlying areas and along the frontier climbed at an even faster pace. Except for the port of Charles Town in South Carolina, the southern provinces had few large towns throughout most of the colonial era, although Baltimore and Norfolk were on the upswing after 1750. In the northern colonies the five largest cities by 1775 were Philadelphia, New York, Boston, Newport, and Providence – all thriving ports. With roughly 30,000 residents, Philadelphia was the largest colonial city by the 1770s, and indeed after London it ranked, along with Manchester, among the most populous and economically developed urban areas in all of Great Britain and North America.

The merchants in the larger ports were not only successful in accumulating wealth, but, unlike their counterparts in the mother country, many were also very active in political affairs. In the northern colonies, merchants often aligned themselves with provincial governors and thereby received numerous appointments to the upper chambers of their respective legislatures. Because of their direct involvement in government, they were able to sponsor laws that created a favorable environment for the promotion of trade and private initiatives of all varieties. The business orientation of American society – so prominent and so obvious to foreign critics and admirers in later centuries – had its roots deep in the nation's colonial heritage. When Adam Smith published *The Wealth of Nations* in 1776, he cited the British colonies in North America as the prime example of an economy which had profited from the application of his universal principles – namely the absence of monopolies and the existence of free markets in every sector from land to labor.

FURTHER READING

Brock, Leslie: *The Currency System of the American Colonies, 1704–1784* (New York: Arno Press, 1975).

Clemens, Paul: *The Atlantic Economy and Maryland's Eastern Shore: From Tobacco to Grain* (Ithaca, NY: Cornell University Press, 1980).

Doerflinger, Thomas: *A Vigorous Spirit of Enterprise: Merchants and Economic Development in Revolutionary Philadelphia* (Chapel Hill: University of North Carolina Press, 1986).

Galenson, David: *White Servitude in Colonial America: an Economic Analysis* (Cambridge and New York: Cambridge University Press, 1981).

Jones, Alice Hanson: *The Wealth of a Nation to Be: the American Colonies on the Eve of the Revolution* (New York: Columbia University Press, 1980).

Innes, Stephen: *Labor in a New Land: Economy and Society in Seventeenth-Century Springfield* (Princeton, NJ: Princeton University Press, 1983).

Lemon, James: *The Best Poor Man's Country: a Geographical Study of Early Southeastern Pennsylvania* (Baltimore: Johns Hopkins University Press, 1972).

McCusker, John J., and Menard, Russell: *The Economy of British North America, 1607–1789* (Chapel Hill: University of North Carolina Press, 1985).

Main, Jackson Turner: *Society and Economy in Colonial Connecticut* (Princeton, NJ: Princeton University Press, 1985).

Perkins, Edwin J.: *The Economy of Colonial America*, 2nd rev. edn. (New York: Columbia University Press, 1988).

Schweitzer, Mary M.: *Custom and Contract: Household, Government and the Economy in Colonial Pennsylvania* (New York: Columbia University Press, 1987).

Shepherd, James F., and Walton, Gary M.: *Shipping, Maritime Trade, and the Economic Development of Colonial North America* (Cambridge and New York: Cambridge University Press, 1972).

Walton, Gary M., and Shepherd, James: *The Economic Rise of Early America* (Cambridge and New York: Cambridge University Press, 1979).

CHAPTER EIGHT

Religion before the Revolution

EDWIN S. GAUSTAD

1   Colonial Religion, 1700

BY the beginning of the eighteenth century, religion in Britain's 12 mainland
colonies had assumed the following shape.
The two largest denominations, without
any genuinely close competitors, were first,
Congregationalism (a phenomenon almost
exclusively of New England), and second,
Anglicanism (strongest in the South but
with significant presence elsewhere). Followers of other denominations also visible
by this date included the Baptists, Quakers,
Dutch Reformed, Presbyterians, Roman
Catholics, and Lutherans. But the number
of churches in all these latter groups, even
added together, scarcely matched the Congregationalists in number of meeting-houses.

Congregationalism represented the one
truly effective establishment of religion in
colonial America, though such establishment
was limited to three colonies: Massachusetts,
Connecticut, and New Hampshire. Here the
close cooperation between ecclesiastical and
civil authority resulted in a homogeneity
that was as impressive as it was jealously
preserved. Dissenters were discouraged by
a variety of means: fining, jailing, exiling,
hanging. As a consequence, it was possible
to mold a "New England way" or "Puritan
mind" that had influence far beyond the
revolutionary era and far beyond the borders of these three colonies. The New
England town was dominated by the meeting-house in more than a merely architectural sense, as politics, education, family
life, and social organization all took on a
Puritan hue. When later in the eighteenth
century an Anglican missionary organization

began to send its agents into New England,
the Congregationalists could properly protest that no part of all America was as well-
churched, as thoroughly "gospelized," as
this corner of the country.

Rhode Island, however, was an irritating
exception to the unchallenged dominance
of Congregationalism in New England.
Founded by a Massachusetts exile in 1636,
this colony early became a haven for religious dissenters of all types: first Baptists,
then Quakers, then sectaries of many sorts
and dispositions. Its bubbling religious variety led the Puritan Cotton Mather early
in the eighteenth century to observe with
scorn that Rhode Island seemed to have
just about everything within its tiny con-
fines: "Antinomians, Familists, Anabaptists,
Antisabbatarians, Arminians, Socinians,
Quakers, Ranters – everything in the world
but Roman Catholics and real Christians"
(Mather, 1702, vol. 2, pp. 495–6).

The Church of England had an even earlier start as the official and established
church of Virginia, but by 1700 it was clear
that Virginia would have great difficulty
re-creating the national Church of England
on New World soil. Virginia had no towns,
the clergy had no bishops, the government
had little force or wealth or will with which
to bring about a full-fledged establishment.
Dissent had made no meaningful penetration by 1700, but the implacable forces of
economy and geography had certainly made
themselves felt. Nonetheless, Anglicanism
was stronger in Virginia than anywhere
else in the colonies, with dozens of parishes
duly laid out and even with its own
Anglican college, William & Mary, second

only to the Congregationalists' Harvard in point of time.

The neighbor with whom Virginia shared the closest economic ties, Maryland, followed a strikingly different path of religious development. Founded by English Roman Catholics in 1634, Maryland served as haven for those who experienced the heavy hand of government often raised against them. Nevertheless, by the end of that first century of its history, Maryland began to resemble its near neighbor religiously no less than economically. When in 1692 the proprietary colony became yet another royal colony, the Church of England lost little time in moving legislators at home and patrons abroad to support its position as the official church. Catholicism did not disappear and Quakers on the scene did not vanish, but Anglicanism in Maryland soon moved into a position of strength second only to that in Virginia.

South Carolina, a half-century or more behind Virginia and Maryland in origin, was likewise receptive to the Church of England, especially in and around the South's one real city, Charles Town. North Carolina (not a wholly separate entity until 1729) proved more hospitable to dissenters than to churchmen, with Quakers in particular making their presence felt. Later to be settled than either Virginia or South Carolina, North Carolina enjoyed no flattering reputation; in fact, scorn and ridicule were heaped upon what was regarded as an inhospitable wilderness, known (in the words of one early missionary) for its "damp Colds in Winter, and muschatoes in Summer" (Gaustad, 1976, p. 3).

Recognizing that the Church of England was not nearly as strong in England's own colonies as it ought to be, some churchmen (notably Thomas Bray) decided that private philanthropy promised more than governmental initiative for rectifying the situation. Founding both the Society for Promoting Christian Knowledge (1699) and the Society for the Propagation of the Gospel (1701), Bray did help Anglicanism to have a voice if not a commanding presence in all the colonies. Particularly in New York, New Jersey, and Pennsylvania, the strength of Anglicanism in the eighteenth century owed much to the efforts of these private societies that worked closely with sympathic bishops back in England. Even with such help, however, Anglicanism never attained the kind of effective, pervasive, enduring establishment that Congregationalism enjoyed in New England.

Apart from these two "power churches," the other denominational entities were either regional in scope or minimal in number. The Dutch early claimed as their own much of the area around the mouth of the Hudson River. Despite the English conquest in 1664, Dutch religion and culture continued to have significant presence in New York and East Jersey. William Penn's Quaker connection had great implications for the ecclesiastical history of Pennsylvania from the 1680s on, as did his dedication to the principle and (more importantly) practice of religious liberty. Penn's colony quickly became a haven for dissenters of many stripes: Mennonites, Moravians, Brethren (Dunkers), Scottish Presbyterians of varying loyalties, Welsh Baptists, German Catholics, and more beside. Presbyterians grew to major strength in the middle colonies, that strength augmented by a close cooperation with New England's Congregationalism. Lutheranism first appeared in Swedish garb along the Delaware River, but in the eighteenth century German Lutheranism, first in New York, then more vigorously in Pennsylvania, constituted Lutheranism's principal ethnic strain.

2 The Great Awakening

At the beginning of the century, then, national churches or colonial establishments dominated the American scene, a religious scene that was American only in a geographical sense, remaining European in virtually every other way. But this situation was soon to change radically, as by midcentury all the colonies experienced the tumult and tumble of waves of revivalism. Collectively known as the Great Awakening, these broadly based religious agitations permanently altered the religious landscape, creating a new and more characteristically American emphasis in denominational life: vigorously evangelical, slightly anticlerical, scornful of parish boundaries and liturgical niceties. Religion derived from and shaped by the Awakening would henceforth be the ally not so much of law and order as of individual experience and spiritual striving. The only message that counted was a biblical one: "Behold, I make all things new" (Revelation 21:5).

The Awakening traveled on the wings of Calvinism, the broadest theological tradition in the colonies at this time. Congregationalists, Presbyterians, Dutch and German Reformed stood solidly in the Calvinist tradition, as did Baptists after the Awakening and as did some Anglicans, notably George Whitefield, a regular visitor to America's shores. But like all revivalism, the Awakening tended to play down denominational differences and accentuate instead the necessity of conversion. "So many persons come to me under convictions," reported Whitefield, "that I have scarce time to eat bread. Wonderful things are doing here" (Whitefield, September 28, 1740, as quoted in Gaustad, 1957, p. 27). From Georgia to Maine, hundreds crowded to hear this mesmerizing orator as well as many other itinerants who moved freely, boldly wherever invited and even wherever not. Colonial boundaries counted for as little as denominational ones as a new and important inter-colonial community of like-minded evangelicals was created. The sweep of the movement was impressive: across lines of class, race, and gender. And the resulting realignments had long-lasting implications for politics and education, for theology and ecclesiastical order.

Of course, not all groups heartily joined in a movement that, to some, appeared little more than emotionalism run wild and obscurantism unleashed. The Church of England, Whitefield notwithstanding, held itself aloof from the raging storm, a quiet refuge for those seeking above all else decency and order. Quakers, Lutherans, and Catholics had little to do with this palpably Calvinist display. But members of the other denominations, even incipient Methodists, found themselves or made themselves part of this surge of religious passion. Both Congregationalists and Presbyterians were greatly affected and deeply divided by the Awakening, the former separating in the Old Lights (anti-Awakening) and New Lights (pro-Awakening), the latter in Old Side and New Side. While inevitably weakened by a bitter schism, both groups nonetheless acquired new blood and new energies that resulted in a revived theological and institutional life. Jonathan Edwards among others led in Congregationalism's intellectual rebirth, while Jonathan Dickinson was one of those who played a similar role among the Presbyterians.

Baptists, a relatively small denomination before the Awakening, took on a dramatically different character as a consequence of that movement. Now earnestly evangelical and possessing a gospel message preached in simplicity and accepted with gratitude, the Baptists (many of whom had separated from the Congregational establishment) moved from such early centers as Rhode Island and eastern Pennsylvania into all the colonies. Their proclamations seemed equally suitable for Blacks and Whites, for farmers and merchants, for rich or poor. Methodism, though not officially a separate denomination until 1784, had its chapels and lay preachers firmly in place long before the organizational structure caught up. For this Wesleyan pietistic movement within the Church of England, the Awakening was regarded as heavensent, drawing attention to the very kind of personal, experiential religion that Methodists in Britain no less than in America had been trying to promote. These two denominations, destined to become the largest in American Protestantism, did much to give colonial religion a distinctly American cast. Their imitators as well as their own unruly progeny (schisms abounding) made that new direction irreversible.

3 The Eve of Revolution

By 1775, therefore, the tone and direction of American religion differed sharply from that which had prevailed at the beginning of the century. National churches, having little appeal beyond their own ethnic enclaves, were engaged for the most part in a kind of holding action. The strongest national church of all, the Church of England, could not even do that, as revolutionary sentiment caused the populace to turn against all things English – its Church as well as its Parliament and its King. The campaign of some Anglican clergy to bring to America a bishop of their very own backfired badly (*see* chapter 22, §1). Lutheranism seemed mired in its Germanness, Dutch Reformed in its loyalty to Amsterdam, Catholicism in its obedience to Vatican direction. Those groups governed at home and, fired by revivalistic zeal, enjoyed enormous advantages which they played to the hilt.

The Congregational establishment, immune to the Anglophobia that so damaged the other establishment (the Church of England), did manage to hold its own, this despite the divisions provoked by the Awakening and despite the growing theological chasm that would later result in the Unitarian separation. Two factors helped Congregationalism to maintain its cultural force. First, Congregationalism was clearly a case of home rule (at times almost too much rule) – not subject to foreign control, not swayed by foreign influence. Second, Congregationalists (especially the New Lights) worked closely with the middle colony Presbyterians (especially New Side) to help break out of their New England confinement. Congregationalists and Presbyterians together had by far the largest number of churches and the largest degree of cultural dominance on the eve of the Revolution. The comment of King George III that the American Revolution was nothing more than a "Presbyterian rebellion" has more merit if one understands "Presbyterian" to include the Congregational forces as well. For the two groups were in fact theologically united, the thin line of separation being confined largely to their different notions of ecclesiastical governance and to their different areas of colonial settlement.

The Revolution, of course, was far more than a Presbyterian rebellion, however broadly that modifying term is understood. Persons of many other religions and of none joined in the revolt on the patriot side. Baptists and Methodists (the latter going against John Wesley's clear sentiments) enlisted heavily, with Dutch and Germans finding war against England no great crisis

of conscience. America's first Roman Catholic bishop, John Carroll of Baltimore, was part of an important diplomatic mission to Canada seeking help there, or failing that at least neutrality. Lutheranism's Henry Muhlenberg and his family form part of the mythology of the Revolution's clerical regiment. So the support for the American cause enjoyed a broad religious base.

Nor did loyalism follow clear religious lines. The closest thing to a regular pattern may be discerned in the missionaries sent out by the Society for the Propagation of the Gospel. With family and friends and employer back in England, it is no surprise that many sought an early opportunity to return to their homeland. Others were prompted to do so by a populace outraged by the prayers read for the King or by the mere failure to speak out in favor of this "most causeless, unprovoked and unnatural [rebellion] that ever disgraced any country," to quote the New York City Anglican Charles Inglis (Gaustad, 1982, p. 244). Yet, the patriotism of southern Anglicans, lay and clerical alike, was as evident as it was essential to the revolutionary cause. Anglicanism in the South had by 1775 become greatly Americanized, sufficiently distant from London's oversight as to see no need for a bishop in America, certainly not in Virginia. Middle colony and New England Anglicanism, on the other hand, dismayed by its minority status or even in some cases its extra-legal status, tied its cause much more closely to England's destiny.

In Pennsylvania many Quakers remembered that the King had been their benefactor and protector when so many others seemed determined to obliterate their struggling sect. Without Charles II, moreover, their colony might never have come into being. It was one thing to rail against Parliament, quite another to throw off or condemn the King. But Pennsylvania had a problem larger than pockets of Anglican or Quaker loyalism: namely, pacifism. Not only Quakers but Moravians and Mennonites and others made the revolutionary cause in that colony difficult, even problematic. Benjamin Franklin, the conciliator here as in so many other instances, persuaded many of the pacifists at least to serve as a kind of civil defense force, aiding the wounded and ill, assisting persons to find safety far from battle, acting as a fire brigade when necessary, and in general serving as a second line of defense behind the troops engaged in battle. In the Revolution as in every American war, however, pacifism aroused strong resentment outside those fellowships of faith, and sometimes even within the households themselves.

One final question about religion on the eve of the Revolution is frequently raised: how significant a factor was religion anyway? Was it a major cultural force or only a minor one? Here church membership data are often trotted out to make the point that only a minority of Americans were church members in 1775. While the data are far from solid (no census figures on religious membership are available for this period or for decades thereafter), it is almost certainly true that the majority of Americans were not members of any church or synagogue (only five synagogues are known to have existed at this time). But with equal certainty, one can indicate the vital role of the church as a social, cultural, and political force of unrivaled power. All pulpits tended to be "bully pulpits" in 1775

and all meeting-houses served as information centers and propaganda disseminators. Membership was selective and restrictive; congregational attendance and participation was neither. The church, standing virtually alone as a community and cultural gathering place, therefore reached (and often persuaded) an "auditory" of far greater breadth than scanty membership figures can possibly suggest.

FURTHER READING

Bonomi, Patricia U.: *Under the Cope of Heaven* (New York: Oxford University Press, 1986).

Gaustad, Edwin S.: *The Great Awakening in New England* (New York: Harper & Brothers, 1957).

——: *Historical Atlas of Religion in America*, rev. edn. (New York: Harper & Row, 1976).

——: *Documentary History of Religion in America* (Grand Rapids, Mich.: William B. Eerdmans Publishing Co., 1982).

Goen, C. C. (ed.): *The Works of Jonathan Edwards*, vol. 4: *The Great Awakening* (New Haven, Conn.: Yale University Press, 1972).

Henry, Stuart C.: *George Whitefield, Wayfaring Witness* (New York: Abingdon Press, 1957).

Mather, Cotton: *Ecclesiastical History of New England* (1702) (New York: Russell and Russell, 1967).

CHAPTER NINE

The cultural development of the colonies

MICHAL J. ROZBICKI

THE question whether British colonies in America developed a distinct culture of their own has for long been a staple of colonial historiography. Did colonial culture evolve new, original features or was it merely imitative of the distant metropolis? Was it homogeneous or a mosaic of several cultures? What main periods in its development can be distinguished? What sort of yardsticks should be used to judge it; those of the high culture of the cultivated elites, or those of the vernacular, popular culture of the common folk? These are some of the key questions that we must ask when attempting to gain a comprehensive overview of American colonial culture.

To explain colonial America with all its diversity and regionalism we need a rather broad understanding of the concept of culture, one that brings whole regions of experience into simultaneous focus. Such a perspective helps to correlate the local and particular facts and expressions of social life which together make up a culture and permit attempts at some generalizations. Culture may be defined as the framework of socially established and inherited practices, meanings, values, and norms shared by members of a society. These patterns can be formulated explicitly but usually they have to be abstracted from a society's behavior and from its symbolic products such as language, artifacts, and institutions. Culture gives meaning to social reality; one of its central functions is to create order and make sense of life – both vital needs of all people.

The cultural history of colonial America may be divided into several periods. The early stage, from the founding of Jamestown in 1607 to the 1680s, was characterized by a high degree of fluidity, fragmentation, and disorientation. The death rate, especially in the southern areas, was so high and the ratio of men to women so unbalanced that more permanent patterns of interaction, with the notable exception of the tiny New England settlements, were slow to evolve (see also chapter 6 §1). By the last decades of the seventeenth century the societies of the older colonies had become more stable, native-born elites began to form, and the economy was becoming more diversified. With the second decade of the eighteenth century we observe a crystallization of social hierarchies and the entrenchment of creole ruling groups which had concentrated substantial – at least in relation to colonial realities – wealth and power. At the upper levels of social hierarchy a certain standardization of genteel tastes was taking place, enhanced by similarities in political and legal patterns across the colonies as well as by the rapid growth of commerce. Finally, the years from 1763 to the Revolution brought a gradual increase in the awareness of America's differences from Britain, as well as the first explicit and specific articulations of separate cultural identity that had been objectively developing over the preceding decades. The Seven Years' War mobilized the colonists towards greater intercolonial cooperation and educated American military and political leaders who would play a central role in the Revolution. At the same time, the new and more aggressive imperial policy of London forced many colonists to reassess the status of

America against Britain not only politically, but also in cultural terms. While previously they strived to achieve the standards of metropolitan culture, the revolutionary confrontation enabled colonial leaders to claim that they now represented the liberties and virtues which Britain had forfeited through political corruption and decadent luxury. It must be noted, however, that the process of developing a new and mature American identity was gradual and continued long after Independence.

1 High and Vernacular Culture

Those who would identify culture only with its high version and assign it to the educated elite may come close to dismissing colonial culture as practically nonexistent. Such an approach would be as restrictive as that which assumes that American culture was an attribute only of the European population, or that which claims that it was merely a copy taken from the British matrix. As in any society, colonial American culture did not exist as one, homogeneous set of patterns shared by all. Even though there was less social stratification than in Britain, there was by the eighteenth century a substantial cultural distance between the narrow elite and the majority, many of whom could not read or write. Even in the late seventeenth century, a Maryland governor complained that too many colonists occupying such official positions as justices and sheriffs could not even sign their names. It is therefore useful to distinguish, especially with regard to the eighteenth century, two major traditions in early American culture: the high culture of the elites, and the vernacular culture of the common folk. These two traditions were by no means hermetic, separate worlds; there were many similarities and a constant interactive relationship between them. Common folk acquired certain tastes from the elites. In the mid-seventeenth century the Massachusetts magistrates felt obliged to pass a law in which they lashed out against men and women of "mean condition" who wore gold, silver, silk scarves, and other attributes deemed exclusive to those higher on the social scale. Similarly, the cultivated gentlemen of

Virginia were far from separated from the popular culture, as they had to deal personally on an everyday basis with the reality of business and the daily running of their plantations. Another example of the osmosis between the high and low traditions can be found in the witch trials of 1692 in Salem, Massachusetts, when 20 people were executed for being possessed by evil spirits and over 200 more were accused. The persecutions cannot simply be ascribed to folk superstition since distinguished theologians and learned men such as Cotton Mather elaborated formal theories of witchcraft grounded in old and widespread folk beliefs; through their agency, these ideas – now authoritatively sanctioned by church leaders – were recycled among the broad public. Similarly, forms of play and entertainment often provided common experiences that cut across social classes. For instance, in the plantation region, horse races and cockfighting were widely attended and enjoyed by the gentleman as well as by plain white folk and African slaves, thus becoming an enduring ingredient of popular culture in the South.

The American colonists were no different from other societies in that they had certain aesthetic needs, a receptivity to symbolic expressions of their desires and fears, a need for leisure time, and a need for information. Economic and educational opportunities differentiated the ways in which these needs were fulfilled: these varying opportunities can be observed in different cultural tastes reflecting the status of their publics. Notably, such stratification had political implications; cultural values when durably internalized in the process of education and socialization tended to reproduce behavior, including the social order. This was why the dominant groups in society insisted on control over certain cultural meanings. The genteel-style silk scarves worn by commoners and criticized by the Massachusetts magistrates belonged to a specific class of symbolic meanings which mediated status and power relations. One of the functions of the genteel life-style was to set the elite groups apart from the common folk. Consequently, its exclusiveness was closely guarded; an open questioning of this style was perceived as an attack on the status of the elite.

For instance, the simple life-styles of the Virginia Baptists in the eighteenth century contrasted sharply with the conspicuously "high" style of the wealthy gentry; the latter group asserted their style and persecuted the Baptists in part for ostentatiously questioning some of its elements such as pleasure, gaming, dancing, and physical aggression.

The culture of the common people was based on folk traditions and inherited patterns of behavior. It was much more diverse; there was no central, metropolitan authority such as the court in London which legitimized models of politeness and taste for the upper classes. Folk traditions were also more heterogeneous and tended to change less over time than the conventions of elite culture. Whether in Virginia or in Maine, a gentleman could immediately recognize his counterpart by style and manner, but carpenters and blacksmiths looked, spoke, and behaved differently depending on the local and individual circumstances, often influenced – at least in the early stages of colonization – by the particular characteristics of their region of origin in Britain. These various imported patterns usually disappeared in the second and later generations and were often homogenized and replaced by local ones, sanctioned by the community rather than by British tradition; such was the case of the common design of house construction in seventeenth-century New England. But when we view the entire cultural map of the colonies, what must strike us is the great diversity of American experience, an outcome arising out of a combination of the enormous extent of the land, with its varieties of terrain and climate, the divergent economic practices, ethnic makeup, and religious identities. The world experienced by common folk was primarily local; it was observed from the perspective of their villages and farms, and it was not until the Revolution that greater numbers of people experienced the world outside of their localities and encountered ideas that were to become part of a common identity. And even then, although the new political system was a major unifying factor, cultural identity was to remain strongly local for a long time to come.

2 The Bourgeois and the Genteel Values

In Europe one of the defining divisions between the bourgeois and the genteel culture was marked by the first putting value on the practical and the utilitarian and the latter on disinterested virtue and dilettante demeanor. In colonial America this division was much less significant. In the eighteenth century, the first group of values was perhaps best exemplified by the works of Benjamin Franklin, and the latter by the life-styles and worldviews of the great planters of the South, modeled on the English landed class. Franklin, pragmatically oriented and free of ambition to achieve classical elegance, saw the written word mainly as an effective tool for educating society. His *Poor Richard's Almanack* (1733–58) had the popular form of a calendar supplemented by a compilation of various kinds of useful information, humor, maxims, proverbs, and illustrations, all with the secular purpose of instilling the virtue of frugality and promoting self-education. Franklin, like Daniel Defoe whom he admired, believed that trade was a way of life as noble as the landed life-style. "Franklinian" thinking typically distrusted purely theoretical learning and emphasized practical results. The American Philosophical Society which he founded in 1743 had the words "useful knowledge" in its full title. It was this intellectual stance that animated such American scientific undertakings as those of the naturalists John Bartram, Cadwallader Colden, Alexander Garden, or the instrument maker and astronomer David Rittenhouse. The bourgeois nature of values espoused by people like Franklin may be seen in their praise for hard, honest work and in the sharp criticism of idleness. It is no wonder that they often ridiculed the gentleman as worthless to the community since well-born status prevented him from doing any work with his hands.

In contrast, the genteel current in colonial culture, limited to a small but politically and economically powerful elite, put prime emphasis on the ideals of cultivation, accomplishment, and elegance. It was often accompanied by conspicuous consumption, something that was particularly abhorrent to those who, like Franklin, were influenced by Puritan traditions. By the mid-eighteenth century – with growing prosperity and increased leisure time – this subculture was playing a major role in integrating the elites. It looked for its norms and tastes to London; news about the fashions, manners, and style of the court supplied by the colonial press would be closely followed and their manifestations displayed at public gatherings such as church, court, elections, fairs, or horse races. But it is important to note that the American gentleman was mostly self-made and his wealth was usually a result of economic entrepreneurship rather than inheritance. Unlike the old English gentry, he did not fully share the belief that commercial activities were "beneath his quality." On the contrary, materialist ambitions and commercial occupations were not seen as inherently antagonistic to polite status and were keenly pursued by colonial gentry, a distinctively American development with consequences for the future cultural identity of the new nation.

3   Regional Differences

In the past, the "exceptionalist" approach, emphasizing new and homogeneous features of colonial America, not only minimized the British cultural inheritance but also, in order to recover the origins of a uniform American culture, downplayed local and regional differences among the colonists. Today, we are better aware of the strength of these regional cultures. Until Independence, the colonists identified themselves mainly with their localities – they considered themselves Virginians or Pennsylvanians rather than Americans. The very difficulty in organizing collective public action during and after the Revolution is evidence of such regional orientations.

New England was conspicuous as a region in that it was relatively stable from its beginning, its organization based on the family unit and town covenants and its ideals made cohesive by the domination of Puritanism. In the second half of the seventeenth century the orthodox Puritan ethos was challenged by the growing secularism and individualism of wealthy merchants and entrepreneurs, creating spiritual and political tensions. It has for long been a popular assumption that colonial New England, with its literate and stable communities, represented the prototypical American society, and that its cultural patterns radiated as norms across the rest of British America. More recently, it has been pointed out that the New England society, except for the earliest decades, was not monolithic but often mobile and differentiated, and after the 1660s significantly more commercialized, urbanized, and individualistic. As Jack P. Greene has shown, the model of colonial New England "declining" from the original integrity and coherence is not particularly useful for analyzing cultural change in the region, and even less so in the colonies to the south. New York and Pennsylvania were from their beginnings much more pluralistic, multi-ethnic, cosmopolitan, and tolerant than New England. The early plantation society that developed in the Chesapeake region was distinct in a very different way: it was highly mobile, demographically unbalanced, more atomized and secular, with initially weaker social ties and authority, settlements widely dispersed, and an exploitative agrarian capitalism producing for export markets. New England attempted – successfully – to remain traditionally English as long as possible, while the tobacco colonies were giving rise to a more original, dynamic, and individualistic society. Individualism and attitudes oriented towards economic achievement were destined to become the dominant values of American culture, and in this sense early New England was an exception rather than the rule, until later in the colonial period a noticeable cultural convergence between the regions began to take place.

4   A Multi-ethnic Society

A common element of the American scene that profoundly contributed to the originality of colonial culture was the prominent presence of two ethnic groups other than the British: the Amerindians and the Africans. Unlike earlier, narrow portrayals of colonial life in which the Amerindians only supplied the British with certain technical skills, traded goods, and fought against common enemies, while the Africans primarily labored on the plantations, we now have a vastly better and deeper understanding of how close interactions among these three groups constituted a major formative influence on the shaping of early American culture. The Amerindians had been prominent players in this process. The arrival of Europeans created a New World, a new order, both for the Amerindians and for the colonists. They found ways to adjust to the presence of one another by extensively pursuing mutual trade and economic relations. Despite intensive competition to define cultural space, there was much interplay and mutual influence. A good example of such osmosis is the history of place names so many of which, even along the east coast, in the oldest areas of settlement, have remained Amerindian to this day. For the colonists arriving from Britain the consequences of these confrontations were profound. They did not possess culturally established patterns of reacting to such alien cultures, so inter-ethnic confrontations were among the first aspects of colonial reality which forced them to modify cultural assumptions transplanted from Europe. They had to incorporate the Amerindian, and later the African, into their notions of world order. After a brief period of initial Anglo-Amerindian cooperation, the colonists gradually developed separatist and exclusionist attitudes towards non-Europeans. The English, unlike the Spaniards, never incorporated the Amerindians into their society and culture but they did use the new situation to reassert their own identity – disrupted by emigration from the mother country – in terms of "civilization" as opposed to the "savagery" of non-Europeans. The emergence of the class of black slaves further facilitated white solidarity and muted class tensions by creating the assumption of common interest and by fostering self-definition in terms of opposition to the two other ethnic groups. In this sense, the presence of Amerindians and Africans also contributed to a faster assimilation of non-British immigrants such as Germans, Scots, Irish, Swedes, and Dutch into English culture.

By the early eighteenth century slavery became one of the central realities of life in British America and Africans living in the colonies were fast becoming an integral part of the emerging American culture. In the first eight decades of the century the number of arriving slaves was twice as large as the number of European colonists. As a result, the map of the American labor market not only included a huge sector of unfree workers but this sector of society produced an equally massive portion of the country's wealth. A distinct ethnic subculture may be said to have emerged among slaves in the plantation region. The institution of slavery, however inhumane and oppressive, had created an inseparable, organic relationship between Whites and Blacks generated by close and complex encounters which forced them to engage one another in many ways which mutually defined both sides. Even in the old tobacco region around the Chesapeake Bay many plantations remained small and white folk often worked alongside slaves. These everyday contacts involved various economic exchanges, violence, sex, religion, and recreation. The European patriarchal ideal was revitalized in the plantation region as a useful means of legitimizing the system of slavery and sanctioning the "obligations" of the slave towards the master, as well as reinforcing the authority of the latter by stressing his duty to supervise and protect his dependents. It was an ethos well-grounded in British history and based on a widely believed premise that the upper class had the title to rule over those considered socially inferior but also had the obligation to protect them. The latter, in turn, owed loyalty and subservience to the powerful. It was within this world order that the great planter Landon Carter of Virginia could consider himself a benevolent gentleman and, as he noted in his diary, "a very kind Master" who took pains to administer medical help to his slaves but who also felt fully justified in whipping them for any infringement of his rule. What is striking is that many slaves participated in this cultural worldview. Although it may on the surface seem that it was entirely contradictory to their objective interests to buy into an ideology of their oppressors, it is not at all surprising; people tend to crave making sense of their situation and this was an attempt to make existential sense by participating in the system, something that historians who have studied totalitarian systems are quite familiar with.

As Philip D. Morgan has shown, a new, black American culture developed under colonial slavery, one that combined African and European elements. African religion was not extensively practiced but elements of magical practices remained a part of their culture long after Christianization. As always when people use culturally familiar ways to interpret and make sense of the unfamiliar, the slaves participated in Christian services and sang hymns but also used amulets, invoked or placated evil spirits, and presented offerings at burial ceremonies. One of the characteristic examples of cultural fusion was the slaves' religious music, influenced both by Christian and African elements. The songs and lyrics were European but African-style rhythm and percussion were added which together with syncopation and antiphonal singing made for new and highly original forms. Slaves, for whom music carried great value in everyday life, absorbed European influences but transformed them according to their own needs and styles. Their gift for music was widely recognized and admired by Whites. Slaves often played music at dances and they were especially renowned for being excellent with that European instrument, the fiddle, which was often accompanied by the African-descended banjo and – mostly during all-African ceremonies – the drums. White colonists were also influenced by African dancing styles; for instance, the jig was immensely popular in Virginia despite complaints by genteel visitors from Britain that the dance, unlike the properly refined European minuet, lacked politeness and order.

5 Colonial Architecture

The development of colonial architecture illustrates well the process of cultural evolution taking place in British America. The first phase involved simple continuity of transplanted designs. The early English colonists in Massachusetts reproduced typical English wooden-frame cottages with mud and plaster walls and thatched roofs. Since they soon found that these constructions required change in order to resist a climate that was much harsher than in England, this traditional pattern was modified in the second half of the seventeenth century; the frames as well as the roofs were covered with shingles or clapboards. A characteristic version of such a New England house was the so-called salt-box, where the roof was continued down on the rear side to cover an additional storey and a half. The plans of New England towns also usually reflected English traditions; each had a town common where a rather large meeting house was placed centrally, evidence of the role of religion in the life of these Puritan communities. Since the meeting-house served for political and other gatherings as well, it may also be regarded as a symbol of the close social cohesion within the settlements of this area. Further south, the first Dutch colonists in New Amsterdam also reconstructed the familiar as they built Flemish-style urban brick houses with crowstepped gables and – in the countryside – Walloon-style farmhouses with low roofs and two chimneys on both sides. Similarly, the Swedes who settled around Fort Christina transplanted their ethnic styles, building stone houses with high gambrel roofs. The Chesapeake area was different; in contrast to New England, the plantation system and easy individual access to the numerous waterways created a dispersed settlement system which gave a distinct character to the culture of the region. Although English architecture was also reconstructed – in the early period often with a lack of adaptation to the hot and humid climate – there were more attempts here to transplant European high style than in the North. The wealthier owners of plantation residences often aspired to imitate the English country houses of the gentry. Many were colonists who originally came to America as humble indentured servants, made their fortunes on tobacco, and aspired – as most immigrants – to higher social status and respectability. Such was the case of Adam Thoroughgood, whose house in Norfolk, Virginia (1636–40), displays brick masonry and traces of Elizabethan and Jacobean styles in its proportions, all surmounted by a large, medieval chimney. The proportions of another Virginia residence, the 1655 Arthur Allen house (known as Bacon's Castle) with its projected towers in front and rear, massive chimney stacks and Flemish gables, may have lacked harmony but displayed a typical early southern example of amateur design combined with an ambition to express current European taste.

Urbanization

A separate chapter in the history of colonial architecture was related to the progress of urbanization, begun in the second half of the seventeenth century and much accelerated in the eighteenth. It brought about the founding of new cities as well as a rapid development of the older ones on the Atlantic seacoast which became prominent centers of trade and culture. Plans for newly established cities often reflected Enlightenment, rationalist ideas of harmony and a strong desire to create a well-ordered society. Symmetrical squares and rectangles as well as the regularity of space division were common to diverse urban projects in different regions. New Haven is said to have been planned by John Davenport according to the layout of the New Jerusalem in the Revelation of St. John. Philadelphia, founded in 1682 and designed by William Penn on a grid pattern, was divided into four quadrants by Broad and Market Streets, with a large square for public buildings at their intersection, a central square in each of the quadrants as a public center, and individual buildings within each block spaced by gardens. The only major city founded in eighteenth-century colonial British America, Savannah in Georgia, was established in 1733 on a pattern designed by Robert Castell, with broad straight streets, divided at regular intervals by squares and parks. In Williamsburg, which was laid out in 1699 as the new capital of Virginia, the central axis of the town was formed by a 99-feet broad boulevard closed at one end by a square with a capitol and at the other

by the building of the College of William and Mary. The boulevard was intersected by a perpendicular street leading to the Governor's Palace surrounded by formal gardens. The plan was so meticulous that it even defined the size of the houses and their distance from the axis of the street.

The colonial Georgian style

The eighteenth century which brought an increase in wealth, better education of the well-to-do classes, and more frequent contacts with the metropolis also generated ambitions to model styles more closely on England's currently legitimate fashions. More impressive residences were sought to establish a more refined environment for an emergent upper class and to emphasize social authority. In architecture, this period witnessed the rise of the colonial Georgian style. Because it was based on a set of abstract, normative principles, and because information about it was mostly obtained from a few standard British books and manuals, it displayed much more uniformity across the colonies than had been the case with any style in the preceding century. It was clearly distinguishable in buildings constructed from Maine, through New Hampshire, Massachusetts, and Pennsylvania, to the Chesapeake colonies. Its distinctive elements consisted of Ionic or Corinthian pilasters, richly decorated entrances, quoins at the corners, high ceilings allowing for more space, and indoor ornamentation. In the first half of the eighteenth century colonial style was influenced mostly by the concepts of Inigo Jones and Christopher Wren, and in the second half by the ideas of James Gibbs, whose *Book of Architecture* (1728) was at that time the most popular of its kind in America.

A good early example of the colonial Georgian style, typical of the buildings designed by Christopher Wren and constructed in England, is the Governor's Palace in Williamsburg. Its shape is rectangular, it is symmetrical in plan and facade, harmoniously divided into horizontal ranges by means of balustrades, roofs, cornices, and string courses, while the articulation of details such as windows and edges is enhanced by classical ornaments. The neighboring College of William and Mary (1695–1702), built in similar style on an axial plan with a rear court, a forward central pavilion covered with a steep gable, and a prominent cupola on a hipped roof, provided a model for other college halls, such as Harvard and Yale. Many churches were built in the style of Wren in the first decades of the eighteenth century, but after 1730 chiefly Gibbs's concepts were followed. The most often reproduced model was his St. Martin-in-the-Fields in London; its emulations include the red brick Christ Church (1727–54) in Philadelphia and the woodframe First Baptist Meetinghouse (1774–5) in Providence, both designed by amateurs using Gibbs's plates.

The southern mansions, usually standing alone on large tracts of land and often set in landscaped gardens, are well exemplified by Westover, the residence of William Byrd II in Charles City County, Virginia. Designed by the owner himself and built in red brick, it was externally symmetrical, with a steep roof, string courses between floors, an ornamented main door, and extensions on both sides of the main building. Since such residences were usually centers of large plantations, the various dependent buildings housing kitchens and other service facilities were often connected by covered passageways with the main building. Some residences also boasted sophisticated interior design with grand staircases and paneled walls with pilasters and entablatures. Mansions comparable in size and style, ornamented with classical pilasters and pedimented doorways, were built for wealthy New England merchants in Salem, Newport, and Marblehead as well as in New York and Philadelphia, but they more often resembled English town houses than country seats.

Most of the great colonial Georgian houses were not designed by professional architects, who were rarely available, but by gentlemen-amateurs who took their models from books. A prominent case was Peter Harrison (1716–75) of Newport, Rhode Island, who designed several sophisticated Georgian buildings, including the Touro synagogue, the first of its kind in America, and the Palladian-style Redwood Library,

both in Newport. The lack of architects meant that a significant role in the final outcome of these projects was played by trained carpenters and builders, who often had to solve practically, with the help of handbooks, many problems concerning details and ornamentations. A high degree of competence was also achieved by other artisans, especially those producing furniture to equip the newly spacious residences and public buildings. This was especially so in Philadelphia, which in the second half of the eighteenth century grew into the most urbane of American cities, and became known for its artisans turning out elegant furniture in the style of Thomas Chippendale. Locally made high chests with rococo ornamentation could easily compete with their imported British counterparts. Furniture of equally high quality was also made in Newport by John Goddard and John and Edmund Townsend.

6   Fine Art

While applied art made rapid advances as wealth increased in the colonies, fine art was scarce and aesthetic theory almost nonexistent. Painting, in the sense of creating ideal forms, had not reached a point where it would be classified by colonial culture as a virtuous activity. While the eighteenth-century English gentry is known to have greatly increased its demand for painting, colonial elites, although they increased spending on luxury goods during the same period, showed little interest in fine art. This was mainly the result of a combination of the old Protestant distrust for symbolic or sensual painting, manifest since the Reformation, with a utilitarian frame of mind which was so prominent in the colonies. Unlike in Europe, paintings had low resale value in British America, a fact reflecting a very circumscribed demand. Relatively rapid social ascent of new elites bred a pragmatic attitude to artistic products, often treated as means of asserting status. Portraits were bought less for beauty than for their cultural value as symbols of family social prominence and as suggestions of lineage. Not infrequently they were produced by journeyman painters whose skills were not outstanding. Two accomplished early painters – both born in England – must be mentioned here: John Smibert and Peter Pelham, John Singleton Copley's stepfather. Also, a number of Dutch artists in New Amsterdam where traditions of painting were stronger, produced portraits of a quality higher than the colonial average. The wealthiest colonists commissioned portraits in England. Much other painting was based on imitating or copying from engravings imported from Europe; in this process form was typically made simpler and plainer. As with architecture and furniture, much depended on the availability of imported books with appropriate models. The utilitarian inclination of the market did much to prevent artists from venturing into the area of pure art. Two well-known examples were Benjamin West and John Singleton Copley, both outstanding painters, who decided – despite or perhaps because of their early successes – to leave America for Europe, the former in 1760 and the latter in 1774. As can be seen from Copley's letters, they aspired to an audience different from the colonial one which treated painting "as no more than any other useful trade... like that of a carpenter, tailor, or shew maker, not as one of the most noble arts in the world."

7 The Theater

Reactions to cultural imports from England, which varied with the regions, reflected a significant diversity of the colonial scene. Such was the case with the theater which met with opposition from some circles and enthusiastic support from others. It was welcome in the polite company of Annapolis and Charles Town but ardently opposed in Philadelphia and Boston. The prolonged debate on whether theater performances should be allowed at all revealed the various cultural forces at work in America, especially the contrast between the tastes of the leisured elite and those of the urban middle class. In the 1760s the American Company, a dynamic group of professional English actors which toured the colonies producing the latest drama and encouraging the construction of theaters,

attracted much publicity by stirring a deep controversy between the supporters and opponents of theater. Attempts to erect a playhouse in Philadelphia brought angry petitions of citizens to the government, demanding an end to such practices. Theater was perceived by many, especially Puritans and Quakers, as a form of extravagance equivalent to such excesses as drinking and gambling and, consequently, deserving equal condemnation. Religious arguments that plays demoralized and corrupted were widely invoked. Merchants and tradesmen opposed plays on economic grounds – that they not only drew people away from industry and spoiled a healthy business mentality by making leisure a virtue but also took scarce money out of circulation.

It was the emergence of a wealthy leisured class in the South, with its markedly more secular worldview, that allowed for the development of theater in the early eighteenth century. The first stage was built in 1716–18 in Williamsburg, followed by another in 1752. Plays were also staged in Charles Town, first in the Court House and after 1736 in a permanent theater. By the mid-eighteenth century drama by English playwrights such as William Shakespeare, John Dryden, Joseph Addison, and William Congreve was performed in the colonies by students or professional, itinerant actors. Among the best known of these groups was the troupe led by Thomas Kean and Walter Murray who produced several plays in Philadelphia and New York, and the company headed by Lewis Hallam which performed in Charles Town, Annapolis, Williamsburg, New York, and Philadelphia. Almost all plays performed were English. The earliest play written by a native-born American was *The Prince of Parthia*, written by the Philadelphia poet Thomas Godfrey and produced in 1767. It was a romantic, blank-verse tragedy set in the early Christian era and, like much of Godfrey's poetry, highly imitative of the styles of English authors, both contemporary and Elizabethan.

8 Music

The beginnings of American musical history are associated with the New England music of worship, particularly psalmody, practiced both at religious gatherings and at home. The so-called *Bay Psalm Book* (1640), which unlike many Anglican compositions was not very complicated and so made it easy for the common folk to sing its pieces, gained such popularity that it went through at least nine editions in the seventeenth century. The concern of ministers to improve church music led to the publication of instruction books ("tunebooks") and then to the establishment of the singing-school movement, a unique system of musical education that paved the way for American composers. The singing-school became an important musical and social institution in British America. Its students, who usually assembled in taverns and schoolhouses, came from all strata of society, giving an early egalitarian cast to this cultural institution. Native-born itinerant singing-masters offered instruction not only in New England but also in the middle and southern colonies. In the early eighteenth century one encounters advertisements in Boston newspapers by teachers of music, who not infrequently were also music dealers and dancing masters. We do know the program of what was probably the first public concert given in Boston in 1729. Music was more often performed privately than publicly, and was typically produced by ensembles of gentlemen-amateurs such as, for instance, those gathered at the Tuesday Club in Annapolis in Maryland. The second half of the eighteenth century which saw a rise in the demand for cultivation also witnessed a rising number of immigrant musicians who found positions, mostly as teachers but also as performers and dealers in musical articles. This was followed by an increased local production of instruments. The most distinctive and stylistically homogeneous group of early American composers was the New England school which emerged in the 1770s and included such popular authors of music as William Billings, Daniel Read, Jacob French, Jacob Kimball, Samuel Holyoke, and Oliver Holden. Characteristic of their Yankee musical style was the "fuging tune." It typically began with a choral hymn with the principal air in the tenor voice, which then gave way to entrances by each of the voice parts as it was led to a full close, followed by the repetition of the "fuge."

9 Culture and the Public Sphere

Influenced by the theories of Jürgen Habermas, historians interested in the formation of colonial American cultural identity have recently devoted much attention to the construction and nature of the public sphere in the eighteenth century – a development by which private individuals came together to become a public. This approach is grounded in Habermas's concept of culture as a set of subjective meanings held by individuals about themselves and their world. Culture is thus seen as being legitimated by interactions of social classes as well as by institutions that articulate and translate these norms into collective behavior; society is therefore literally created by language and communication. Colonial historians have been using these productive concepts to take a broader look at the public sphere as a theater where a constant struggle to define its boundaries as well as to seek agreement takes place. In this approach the public sphere is viewed as an entity larger than just the state and the ruling class. Such a communicative perspective allows for an effective inclusion of plebeian culture and women's roles. It also facilitates a more integrated interpretation of the various forms of social life which participated in the construction of the public, one that reveals how culture, print, and political action all interacted and influenced one another. This prompted a new interest in institutions which were part of this process such as newspapers, magazines, coffeehouses, salons, clubs, and taverns. For instance, Michael Warner (*The Letters of the Republic*) fruitfully applied Habermasian theory to show the interrelationship between republicanism and literature, and David S. Shields (*Civil Tongues and Polite Letters*) to analyze literature as part of the discourse of civility, as a set of performances that served to create and culturally define group identities in a society. Shields's study uncovers the prominent role of oral communication in colonial culture; a focus on discursive practices rather than on rigid norms of manners and politeness not only brings culture closer to real life and away from grand theory but also reveals interactions between the oral, non-print culture of the common folk and the printed one of the elites. Various private associations such as coffee-houses, clubs, and tavern groups are shown functioning as a social territory outside of government control, and engaged in propagating civility viewed as an ingredient of an ordered society. At the same time, these pursuits of pleasure were also forms of associating and as such helped constitute the public sphere, a zone where public opinion formed independently of the state. It was this emphasis on private action that, in contrast to Europe, was to become a major ingredient of American political culture.

10 Newspapers

The role of the printed word, especially newspapers, in the political energization of Americans during the revolutionary era is rather well known, but the press, long before it became politicized in the 1760s, also played a significant role in the cultural consolidation of colonial society. It is important to bear in mind that in the first century of the British American colonies printed text was treated mainly as a tool to expand religious knowledge and to inform the elites of matters of local political significance. Secondly, when the printed word was directed to the general public it was within the framework of a hierarchical society; persons of authority addressing deferential readers. A violation of this concept would be seen as a potential threat to authority and hierarchy, which explains why a number of early American newspapers were suppressed by local governments. The idea of print as a means of openly communicating information to a wide public found its way into culture only much later, in the second half of the eighteenth century. Even then the literary patterns used – for instance the traditional form of a genteel letter so common in colonial newspapers – as well as topics covered in them make it quite plain that they were primarily addressed to the educated elite. Before 1750, it was the essay that dominated colonial papers, but in the second half of the century news rapidly gained prominence.

The appearance of the historically first colonial newspaper was marked by an episode of censorship. The short-lived, three-page *Publick Occurrences both Forreign and Domestick*, was published in Boston on September 25, 1690 by printer and bookseller Benjamin Harris who intended to produce it monthly and cover news of general interest. It was suppressed days later by the Massachusetts government amid complaints that it was unlicensed and contained information both politically unacceptable and immoral. The first regular newspaper, the Boston *News-Letter*, began appearing only in 1704, produced by printer Bartholomew Green and postmaster John Campbell. Two other newspapers, Andrew Bradford's *American Weekly Mercury* in Philadelphia and William Brooker's *Boston Gazette*, appeared in 1719. Characteristically, postmasters – who had the advantage of good access to news sources and who also controlled distribution systems – were involved in publishing all three. The next decade brought the founding of five more colonial newspapers. Boston, with its high literacy and education rates was clearly becoming the leader in the field; in 1721 Benjamin Franklin's elder brother James launched another newspaper, the *New England Courant*. All these papers published an often eclectic mélange of rumors, gossip, news brought by ships, items reprinted from British sources, and political information; the distance meant that news was often old, sometimes up to six months. Political news was especially prominent in Franklin's *Courant* which ventured into critical commentary, a quality that did not please the authorities; he paid for it with time in jail and ultimately removed himself to Rhode Island. His brother Benjamin had much more success with the *Pennsylvania Gazette* which he took over in 1729. New Yorkers had the *New York Gazette* to read from 1725, but it was John Peter Zenger's *New York Weekly Journal*, established in 1733, that forcefully took up what was going to become an American tradition – political criticism of local authorities. As in earlier cases, Zenger paid the price; he was accused and tried for libelling New York Governor William Cosby and jailed. His ultimate victory in this celebrated and widely publicized trial, in which Andrew Hamilton argued that the truth of the printed information precluded accusations of libel, contributed not only to the establishment of political freedoms but also to making the right to free expression one of the future ingredients of American cultural identity. Another pioneer of colonial journalism was William Parks who had two print shops (in Annapolis and Williamsburg) and who founded two major newspapers, the *Maryland Gazette* in 1727 and the *Virginia Gazette* in 1736. Like other publishers, he looked towards England for news and cultural styles but he also appealed to the practical needs of colonists; he advertised his paper as a useful tool for publicizing the sale of houses, land, goods, cattle, and giving public notice of runaway servants and slaves. Newspapers were as a rule printed on a single sheet folded into four pages. The type was set by hand, each letter separately, placed in a frame, inked, and then put in a press; the paper made from rags, then dried, and the reverse side printed on. On the eve of Independence there were 37 regular newspapers in colonial America.

During the first half of the eighteenth century newspapers did not have a large reading public; they reached mostly, though not only, the elites and the educated intelligentsia, groups they were addressed to in the first place. By 1750 the average circulation of papers was about 600 annually. Newsprint was given a major impetus by the French and Indian Wars and the growing conflict with Britain, events which electrified the public and provided a catalyst for the growth of the press. They also fostered interest in the news among the more common folk. Such interest was reflected in the fact that many owners of taverns kept newspapers for their clients to read and even advertised their availability. Public houses provided an important forum, where not only informal political discussions took place but also where the elite and the common folk mingled over drink and exchanged

views. After 1765, current news from papers – especially related to local affairs – was eagerly consumed and debated there. Tavern keepers also held occasional book sales for their customers; for instance, in 1726 the Royal Exchange Tavern in Boston sold over 700 books ranging from law and science to poetry and drama.

11 Books

Book reading began to emerge on a wider scale as a cultural phenomenon by the mid-eighteenth century. They were clearly in demand in Boston; local newspapers published numerous notices asking for a return of books. Massachusetts with its widespread personal use of the Bible boasted a high percentage of literate public; even in the seventeenth century many households owned books, but up to the second decade of the eighteenth century the overwhelming majority of them were of a religious nature. In all colonies relatively high prices still limited purchases on a wider scale but the rising demand was reflected in the institution of public libraries. Perhaps the best known was the Library Company of Philadelphia, founded in 1731 by Benjamin Franklin. It was a subscription library; members contributed a certain sum of money annually towards the purchase of books for the collection. Among the first titles selected by Franklin and Thomas Godfrey were the *Spectator,* the *Tatler,* the *Guardian*, Algernon Sidney's *Discourses Concerning Government*, Richard Bardley's *A Complete Body of Husbandry*, as well as Plutarch's *Lives* and Homer's *Iliad* and *Odyssey*. Notably, the overall character of the collection was practical, dominated by handbooks, atlases, and histories.

By the last decades of the century, books took on a greater role as a consumer commodity. As reading for pleasure became more widespread, the book public expanded and was no longer limited to narrow elites or utilitarian-oriented readers. Permanent as well as circulating libraries made books available to a wider public, the majority of which owned very few or no books. Booksellers often played the role of printers and publishers. These changes were signaled by the slow rise in the popularity of fiction, especially the novel, read mainly for entertainment. As in other areas of early American culture, two distinct currents were discernible among the book-buying and reading public: the elite and the popular, the first influenced by high, European tastes, and the second by local, vernacular, strongly Protestant traditions. By the end of the colonial period two reading publics could be distinguished; the first consisting of professional and wealthy classes, with preferences for more sophisticated, learned, often classical texts, and the second, made up of those non-elite groups who, like the urban middle classes or farmers, especially sought almanacs, Bibles, and schoolbooks. But it must be noted that even collections in colonial gentlemen's libraries tended to be heavily dominated by works of a utilitarian nature, useful for self-improvement and practical affairs. A separate group were academic libraries which in the eighteenth century grew considerably in number and scope of collections. For instance, in 1723 Harvard College library held 2,961 titles (of which 58 percent were in theology, 9 percent literature, 8 percent science, 7 percent philosophy, 7 percent history, and 2 percent law).

12 Literature

Just as in other spheres of culture, for most writers in colonial America the spiritual home was Britain; in belles lettres, America – conscious of its provincial status – was, through most of the colonial period, trying to replicate legitimate metropolitan styles. As a result, its literature did not draw much on the realities of local life. In this sense we cannot speak of a distinctly American literature before the Revolution. Britain was not only a source of form and style for American writers but in many cases also of a reading public, since the circles of cultivated readers of polite letters in the colonies were very narrow. Even long after the Revolution literary ambitions were often expressed in efforts to meet the standards of European belles lettres. Such were, for instance, the products of the Connecticut Wits, a literary group based in Hartford who celebrated American society and history

by writing poetry entirely modeled upon current English styles; the results were peculiarly overloaded with hyperboles and grandiose sentimentality and spiced with orthodox Calvinism and Federalist social conservatism. But a broader understanding of culture as a style of life and the meaning that a society gives to its common experience does not restrict it to the sophisticated, intellectual rendering of this experience by small elites. Literature in a wider sense of the term always reflects the realities of life in the society which creates it and colonial America was no exception. Its literature was already taking on a number of native, local qualities, even if at times somewhat in spite of itself.

Most of seventeenth-century writing originated in New England, a fact of profound importance to the future development of American culture. The society of this region was significantly more literate than elsewhere in America; this was where the first colonial printing presses were established. Furthermore, the Puritan mission as well as the relative success of early Massachusetts attracted several prominent and erudite ministers and theologians such as, for instance, Thomas Hooker and John Cotton. Messianic and millennial sentiments provided a powerful stimulus for publications in which New England affairs were inseparably linked with those of the Church, and local history was presented as a series of God's interventions. It is worth noting that the writings of Puritan intellectuals were not only often printed in London but also aimed at the English public. Even in these mostly theologically oriented texts one can observe certain American peculiarities. A lack of opposition made the colonial writings noticeably more dogmatic in content and the pietist fervor imposed a heavy emphasis on didacticism in style. For instance, *Day of Doom*, the poem by Michael Wigglesworth published in Cambridge in 1662, had a very practical aim: to popularize Puritan theology in an easy ballad meter. The morbid verse seldom approached the poetic but, because of its simple and appealing style, it became immensely popular and was reprinted many times. Another case in point is the wilderness baroque of Cotton

Mather whose attempts to give a heroic and epic dimension to New England Puritanism in his huge compendium *Magnalia Christi Americana* (1702) resulted in a didactic, grandiloquent style, full of digressions, anecdotes, puns, and anagrams, all saturated with erudition. Even if not quite compatible with European belletristic standards, Mather's writings revealed a characteristically American amalgam (later discernible in Walt Whitman's works) of an enthusiastic vision of a new man, rendered in an exaggerated style. In marked contrast to such writing was Robert Beverley's *The History and Present State of Virginia*, published in London in 1705. The author, who in a typically Virginian fashion had little interest in ecclesiastical problems or providential history, wrote in simple language and demonstrated strong local patriotism towards his native colony. New England had to wait until 1764 for a history more secular than Mather's: it was only then that Thomas Hutchinson's *History of the Colony of Massachusetts Bay* appeared in London. Notable for its objectivity, and its solid foundation in manuscript sources, it was the most sophisticated and thorough work of colonial historical writing, exemplifying a keen Enlightenment mind as well as considerable literary talent.

Puritan anti-aestheticism and didactic orientation both steered literature away from the belles lettres models. Only a few New England writings, such as, for instance, the fine verse of the pastor of Westfield, Massachusetts, Edward Taylor (*c*.1644–1729), a follower of the English metaphysical poets, carried truly outstanding aesthetic value. Nevertheless, the influence of colonial Puritanism on American literature has been profound, complex, and enduring. The sense of mission echoed in American writing for a long time, just as did the inclination to analyze the soul, to see the world in symbolic and allegorical terms, and to refer to Biblical motifs. The tendency to explain the world rationally while holding feelings suspect has also been attributed to the Puritan worldview and to its belief that purely aesthetic experience was superfluous and vain; the conspicuous lack of love scenes in American literature until the first

decades of the twentieth century may be partly explainable by that heritage. The Puritan culture of New England expressed itself particularly well in the prosaic and polemic form of the pamphlet, widely used to explain and justify church government. The years preceding the Revolution witnessed the greatest boom in this genre, with such famous examples as Thomas Paine's *Common Sense* and *The Federalist*.

Colonial writing as a whole was dominated by what may be categorized as literature of fact: diaries, histories, relations, pamphlets, travel, and promotional tracts. Colonial authors rarely endeavored to create belles lettres. They wrote mostly for practical purposes: to record events, describe the country and its people, promote religion, or educate. Captain John Smith, member of the Jamestown expedition, wrote his *General History of Virginia* (1624) after he had returned to England to refute his enemies and to promote colonization. William Bradford, governor of the Plymouth colony for three decades, wrote *Of Plymouth Plantation* (1620–48) not so much for publication but as a testimonial to the achievements of the founders of New England society. John Winthrop, leader and several times governor of Massachusetts, kept a detailed journal of events from 1630 to 1649, mostly understood as a record of God's providential acts; it was published in full only in the mid-nineteenth century. Smith's style was typically Elizabethan: colorful, dramatic, and at times consciously introducing episodes that have all the marks of legends. Bradford's was plain, simple, and direct, while Winthrop's was rather dry; both have the unmistakable stamp of Puritan solemnity. A diametrically different approach to life was seen in the writings of the great Virginian planter William Byrd II. His *History of the Dividing Line Run in the Year 1728*, a journal of his journey to the frontier between Virginia and North Carolina, is a witty, observant narrative, full of lively comment and biting humor, conspicuously secular and often pragmatic. A similarly worldly style is present in his extensive diary. Not intended for publication, it was deciphered and published only in the twentieth century and remains one of the major sources on the culture of the great planters. The contrast between the diaries of Bradford and Byrd exposes not only a basic dividing line between the cultures of New England and the South but also between the more egalitarian approach of the former, earlier author and the elitist perspective of the latter, reflecting a growth in social polarization as well as the maturing of the identity of the American gentry by the third decade of the eighteenth century. But this gentry – however much it modeled itself on the British landed class – was also peculiarly American in that it combined European polite style with businesslike and utilitarian attitudes. In his description of the North Carolina frontiersman's life Byrd took such a position when, deploring the primitive subsistence economy of the squatters, he proclaimed them to be useless to society because they were unable to cultivate the land efficiently.

Only in the last decades of the eighteenth century do we witness a significant and deliberate concern – spurred by Independence – with the creation of an original, distinctly American literature, an effort accompanied by conscious attempts to disconnect it from English models and styles so as to reflect American experience. This period brought literary works idealizing the American frontiersman and explicitly rejecting an aristocratic view of society, a view that was now seen as tinged with European cultural decay as opposed to the simplicity of American virtue. Such was John Filson's *Kentucke* (1784), with its famous fragment on the exploits of the legendary pioneer Daniel Boone, who was presented as a person free from the corruption and artificiality of civilization, living a simple but noble life based on the inherently good rules of Nature. This motif was to reappear later in American literature in the works of James Fenimore Cooper, Mark Twain, and Walt Whitman. Perhaps the best known arguments for such a concept were given by Michel Guillaume St. Jean de Crèvecoeur in his *Letters from an American Farmer*, published in London in 1782, where he used it to define the newly emergent American culture. Aware that the multi-ethnic, immigrant society of America had one basic, common element of identity – the fact that almost all of its members came from Europe in search of economic opportunity – he turned this quality into a central value and made it the distinctive feature of the new society. Opportunities for economic advancement implied, in his view, a freeing from the old, European society with its hierarchic dependencies; the new American man had new opportunities for education, self-reliance, and independence from the system inherited from the Old World. Crèvecoeur juxtaposed European high culture, which he saw as inseparable from wars, poverty, and disease, with the harmonious and dignified life of an American farmer. His image may have been a Rousseauistic idealization but it was also an early and forceful articulation of the concept that American culture grew out of new and egalitarian principles.

13 From British to American Cultural Identity

From the 1760s America underwent an acceleration of cultural change. It is this period that saw the first native epic poetry, novels and musical compositions, the establishment of the first permanent theater, the first professional staging of an American play (in Providence in 1761), and the major paintings of West and Copley. More importantly, the Revolution stimulated an outburst of nationalism and, consequently, more frequent articulations of a new concept of American cultural identity, emphasizing education and common sense in place of inheritance and other traditional English patterns. Noah Webster, a fervent Federalist, designed his famous *Spelling Book* (1782) to meet American needs and help standardize American orthography that differed from the English; in his essays he argued against foreign education for Americans, and advised them instead to obtain a better knowledge of their own country.

J. P. Greene has pointed out (*Pursuits of Happiness*) that despite deep regional differences a social and cultural convergence between the various colonies was gradually taking place during the century after 1660 and especially in the decades preceding the Revolution. It was reflected in a growing coherence and propelled by the common experiences of provincialism, economic opportunity, increasing economic diversity and ties with the metropolis. Especially important in this process was a certain frame of mind that characterized the colonists from the earliest times and therefore may be viewed as a formative element of a distinct, American culture – individual expansiveness associated with favorable conditions for the pursuit of individual ambitions. These included the acquisition of land, especially in newly colonized areas, rapid demographic growth in the eighteenth century, abundant food, average standard of living better than in Europe, and the existence of a large – relative to other countries – social sector of independent individuals. American society was – despite much exploitation and dependency – less hierarchically structured than Europe and had less poverty. Although the extent of available opportunities varied widely, there can be little doubt that their very existence combined with the immigrants' powerful dreams and ambitions of attaining a better life in the New World to provide by the late colonial period an increased homogeneity to American cultural identity. One need only look to the novels of Daniel Defoe (son of a London butcher) in which this immensely popular author successfully promoted emigration to America. Many of his heroes, such as Moll Flanders or Colonel Jacque, were simple folk who by resettling in America acquired wealth, independence, and social respectability that they could never hope for in Britain. According to Greene, an exceptionalism of sorts was inherent in such beliefs, since colonists as well as many foreign visitors to British America were convinced that the new society being created there was significantly different from the societies of contemporary Europe.

Having achieved Independence, Americans used this concept of distinctiveness as a means of constructing a new identity. Dreams of a new and better life in the New World were powerfully enhanced by the success of the Revolution which triggered a major cultural shift; whereas formerly the colonists looked keenly towards Britain for legitimate models of culture, often only to be rejected as provincials, after the Revolution they could claim that virtue was preserved in America while Britain was becoming corrupt and dissolute through excessive luxury. This in turn enabled national leaders such as John Adams and Thomas Jefferson to assert that America was exceptional in that it represented the future of mankind where its best achievements would be upheld and opportunity for everyone would be ensured. Looking for a usable past, Americans could root this newfound sense of respectability and legitimacy intellectually and culturally in their own, by now venerable, history of the founders, harking back to the belief of early Puritan colonists that creating a new society in America represented God's peculiar design – a millennial New Jerusalem.

At a more general level, two major factors underlying the early shaping of American cultural identity may be identified: first, that the colonists were exiles, and second, that their lives were played out in the situation of the frontier. All who crossed the Atlantic were compelled to come to terms with these two facts of life. America was not and could not be a simple extension of England or a microcosm of English society and culture. Not only were the immigrants by definition a socially selective group but the colonies lacked many institutions which profoundly influenced culture and society in Britain, to mention only the King, the court, bishops, and the aristocracy. Furthermore, frontier life brought confrontations with new and unfamiliar cultures. On the other hand, anthropology has taught us that when the inhabitants of a country abandon their old cultural space and are transferred to a new and substantially different environment they are usually very slow to abandon their historically internalized worldviews and assumptions. At the same time the new environment together with the mere physical distance from the mother country forced them to function on the cultural periphery of the old country. Even by 1700 most of America was still very rural and life-styles remained simple; it was a wilderness environment that not a few Europeans viewed with apprehension. It was only in the period that followed that the colonies underwent accelerated growth which brought with it ambitions to replicate European cultural patterns and rebut their provincialism. Such reassertions of metropolitan identity may be seen as a reaction to the culturally disrupting experience of life in the New World, a means of seeking stability and making sense of the new environment. In particular, the emergent, early eighteenth-century elites had a stake in seeking a metropolitan recognition of their Englishness. It was quite typical of Virginia minister and educator Hugh Jones to argue in his 1726 description of the colony – addressed to the British reading public – that the life-styles of Virginians were "much the same as about London," that "they talk good English without idiom," and that "they wear the best of Cloaths." Such emphasis betrayed a characteristic sensitivity to provincialism and to the disdain often shown by metropolitan elites towards the colonials as a lesser sort of people and second-rate citizens.

It would be accurate neither to label colonial culture as primarily imitative nor to claim, as has so often happened in the past, that America was, from the beginning, born new and different. Continuity rather than imitation is a term that more appropriately describes the selectively replicated elements of European culture in the colonial period, both high and vernacular. Many patterns were reproduced not so much by deliberate mimesis as by an unconscious application of historically inherited taken-for-granted knowledge. This process was enhanced by the fact that Americans were relatively isolated from the deep changes taking place in contemporary Britain and by the original intent of many immigrants to escape from some of these developments. Most colonists, however, felt they were an integral part of British culture and society; after all, the Revolution undertaken to win the same rights as those enjoyed by Englishmen in Britain was itself an indicator of such attitudes. But it was also an indication that the society was ripe for change and was becoming conscious that there were many forces at work that made America different. Independence greatly stimulated the awareness of this separateness. The new country was never a blank space to be merely filled by imported cultural forms, for these forms operated in a new context and in new configurations which gave them new meanings. Native populations, climate, landscape, decentralization, pioneer individualism, Protestant appeals to individual conscience, denominational system, relative prosperity, personal independence, and economic organization were all becoming ingredients of this new American mix. Their various combinations brought to the forefront such values as individualism, ambition, localism, optimism, practicality, and orientation towards economic achievement, all of which were emerging by the end of the colonial era as distinctive components of an original American culture.

FURTHER READING

Bushman, R. L.: *The Refinement of America: Persons, Houses, Cities* (New York: Alfred A. Knopf, 1992).

Carson, C., Hoffman, R., and Albert, P. J. (eds.): *Of Consuming Interests: The Style of Life in the Eighteenth Century* (Charlottesville: University Press of Virginia, 1994).

Fischer, D. H.: *Albion's Seed: Four British Folkways in America* (New York: Oxford University Press, 1989).

Greene, J. P.: *Pursuits of Happiness: the Social Development of Early Modern British Colonies and the Formation of American Culture* (Chapel Hill and London: University of North Carolina Press, 1988).

——: *Imperatives, Behaviors, and Identities: Essays in Early American Cultural History* (Charlottesville: University Press of Virginia, 1992).

Greene, J. P., and Pole, J. R. (eds.): *Colonial British America: Essays in the New History of the Early Modern Era* (Baltimore and London: Johns Hopkins University Press, 1984).

Morgan, P. D.: *Slave Counterpoint: Black Culture in the Eighteenth-Century Chesapeake and Lowcountry* (Chapel Hill: University of North Carolina Press, 1998).

Rozbicki, M. J.: *The Complete Colonial Gentleman: Cultural Legitimacy in Plantation America* (Charlottesville: University Press of Virginia, 1998).

Shields, D. S.: *Civil Tongues and Polite Letters in British America* (Chapel Hill: University of North Carolina Press, 1997).

Warner, M.: *The Letters of the Republic: Publication and the Public Sphere in Eighteenth-Century America* (Cambridge, Mass.: Harvard University Press, 1990).

CHAPTER TEN

The emergence of civic culture in the colonies to about 1770

DAVID SHIELDS

THE term "civil society" has been embraced by various schools of political theory to describe developments in the body politic, particularly the emergence of an organized zone of communal life beyond the management of governments in Western nations. Attempts to apply the term globally – for instance, by policy makers of the "Civil Society Organizations and Participation Programme" of the United Nations Development Programme – have proved difficult, but historiographically useful, since the engagement of ideals of civil order and voluntary association with values of non-Western cultures reveals several historically specific elements of the concept. First, civil society in Europe and North America is invariably understood as a concomitant of the state. Civil society is where the citizenry enjoys the benefits of civil order, exercises its right of association, forms public opinion, projects communal interest, and elaborates ideas of the good life. Civil society is not so much a creation of the state as an organic communal culture that permits states to function peacefully. Civil society tends not to operate under state superintendence, though certain of its institutions – royal courts, levees, state balls – have served as informal organs of government.

Civil society operates in tension with the state. Political theorists also see it existing in tension with the market. Corporations, stock companies, bourses, exchanges, and commercial coffeehouses, while possessing the sociability, lack the civility that animates civil society. There is an aesthetic dimension to the civil society not found in bodies created to serve commercial imperatives. In Western literature civil society is viewed as the place where one refreshes oneself after turning aside from work and trade.

When we consider the role of civil society in British America, the theoretical abstract takes on several peculiarities. In colonies where a strong government was often lacking, civil society often supplied the regularity and social integrity needed for commerce and public life to occur. This was particularly the case when a welter of different ethnic populations competed for power and resources. In New York City, or Charleston, or Newport, or Bridgetown young men belonged to societies of their countrymen (Charleston in the eighteenth century had its St. George's Society, St. David Society, St. Patrick Society, German Friendly Society, St. Andrew's Society, and French Coffeehouse). Yet there was invariably a space – a city tavern, a dancing assembly, or in the case of Charleston, "the court room," a tavern long room on Union Street – in which men and women of every European group could mix and constitute a local "beau monde." In this space a common, cosmopolitan image of life – civility – was projected. Civility was an international code of manners and a style of presentation that enabled persons of different countries, sexes, classes, and ranks to interact agreeably. Civility was a broader code than gentility, pertaining to the manners of the broad imperial public engaged in commerce. Artisans, tradesmen, and merchants were expected to master the civil attributes – conversational ease, a friendliness, good humor, honesty, tastefulness, moderation, and politeness – if they were to be successful.

In the metropolis civility served as an antidote to the vulgarity and profanity of the lower orders. When the Reformation of Manners movement blossomed in London during the 1690s, civility became the Whig ascendancy's vehicle for disciplining the urban mob. In British America the use of civility as an ethical hammer to anneal sailors and artisans into proper form also took place, but a more fundamental opposition to civility was embodied in the "savagery" of Native Americans. From the time of the initial settlement, English adventurers presumed the culture of Native Americans to be primitive – equivalent to that of the ancient Picts or early Britons – lacking the refinement of manners and institutions that mark civil culture. For John Locke and other political theorists Native American males virtually manifested that radical liberty of the state of nature prior to the social contract and so comprised the ground against which politics and civil society became visible. The question whether such "natural," "savage," "primitive," "free" persons could be incorporated into the British Empire was open. While there was little doubt that the grace of Christianity's all-sovereign God could work the spiritual transformation needed to make a Native American a Christian, there was intense debate whether a cultural conversion could be performed. Optimists linked the Christian conversion and the European acculturation, putting particular hope in academies that would train Native American evangelist/leaders. Every colonial college from Harvard to Dartmouth announced as its mission the task of transforming Native Americans into civil Christian citizens; every college suffered the frustrations of scant success. Indeed, there were astute commentators who feared that the colonists assimilated more easily to native ways than vice versa. William Byrd's caricature of North Carolina as a lubberland of colonial dropouts going native in his *History of the Dividing Line* conveyed a sense of the fragility of civil society on the margins of settlement; how it is a mental construct that is easily surrendered by those who fear the labor of improvement.

Libertarians among the colonists who bridled at the repeated attempts by Whitehall during the eighteenth century to reform the imperial scheme, embraced the Amerindian as an emblem of the self-sufficiency of the free citizen. Chief Tamanny of the Delawares became the focus of a political cult and his motto – "Kawania Che Kee-teru" – "I am master wherever I am" – the watchword of American radicals, as resonant as the 1680s motto of the original Whigs, "Every man a king." Yet there is a sense in which this symbolic identification with the personal sovereignty of the state of nature was a masquerade. While colonial radicals may have resisted the imposition of state power, they did not reject the contractual obligations of civil society. Indeed, the devotees of Tamanny invariably formed themselves into parties and clubs. These private societies – from the Schuykill Fishing Company of the 1730s to the network of Tamanny Clubs of the 1780s – instituted laws and practiced sociable rites. Radical individualism was entertained as a symbolic possibility in British America. In practice, however, British Americans were an inveterately social people.

"Love of society" was understood to be an innate disposition of humanity by thinkers of all persuasions. (Indeed, the eighteenth century's fascination with hermits and feral persons can be viewed as a dialectic outgrowth of Western culture's consciousness of its own prejudice favoring society.) Family, community, church, and nation gave formal expression to this love. Yet each of these forms of social love served a necessary end: the reproduction of the species, the protection of the neighborhood, the working of God's will on earth, the survival of a race or culture. Civil society expressed the love of society in terms other than necessity. It elevated the aesthetic dimension of communal being, making visible its pleasurable, permissive, supplementary, and voluntary features. Utility, not necessity, impelled it. Friendship, not love, bound it. Shared appetites, interests, and affections grounded its institutions, not perpetual custom or divine mandate. Boston merchant Matthew Adams (he whose library supplied the youthful Franklin with reading matter) wrote: "Society is to unloose and unbend the Mind, and ought to have something of Gaiety and Sprightliness in it. If it should be serious, it ought also to be Chearful, and should never be affected; but above all, it must be Useful." The Club, the Coffeehouse, the Salon, the Tea Table, the social Library, the Drawing Room, the Rout, the Dancing Assembly, the Fraternity, the Conventicle, the private society all were organized upon these premises. All had come into being in the European metropolises during the seventeenth century, and all had become established in North America early in the eighteenth century.

The importance of these institutions for the well-being of the citizenry was such that Whig theorists viewed the creation of the arts and institutions of peace as the purpose of Britain's commercial empire. Since the vast emigrant population could not participate directly in the exercise of the state's political power, its sense of belonging to the imperial enterprise depended on the impression that it partook of the blessings of an extended imperial civil society – that the manners, fashions, entertainments, conveniences, news, commodities, and improvements of London were available in the hinterlands. The printing press was important in promoting this sense of connectedness. But the colonial executives played an important role too, if they chose. Those who attempted to create a provincial imitation of the royal court gave a focus to society in the colony. The sponsorship of state balls, levees, and royal birthday illuminations served both the ends of state and the ends of social pleasure. These civic occasions, in particular, supplied women with a place in public. Certain executives gained broad favor by the largesse of their public diversions and their cultivation of private society: Governor Robert Hunter in New York, Governor Gooch in Virginia, Lt. Governor Keith in Pennsylvania, Governor Burnet in Massachusetts. Conversely, certain executives too narrowly set on personal gain, earned contempt, as did Governor Dinwiddie of Virginia.

Two rhetorics grew up around the attempts by colonial executives to create provincial courts and thereby assert governmental dominion over civil society. Recent historiography has emphasized the oppositional rhetoric – the critique of governors' efforts

to organize politics by class, creating a gentry party centered in the court. This critique borrowed the republican attack on aristocratic luxury and the rapacity of an established governing class. American adaptations of this critique stressed the speciousness of attempts to establish an aristocracy in the colonies. One jaundiced politician, commenting on the history of the court party in New York, observed how,

> a Governour
> Was vested with an ample pow'r
> To punnish and reward.
> Out of this mob was chose some few,
> That something more than others knew,
> To be his aid and guard;
> To Set him right if he went wrong,
> And help him with their heads and tongue,
> In giving of advise.
> They were Yclep'd the councill board:
> Each man a leather apron Lord:
> For there was not much choice.
> The Chieftain, brought a patch work train
> Of Such as ne'r return'd again;
> But made our Gentry here.

The second rhetoric identified the goals of government with the wishes of civil society. This rhetoric posited the "public spirit" as a congruence of the desires of the government and citizenry for the welfare of the community. There were simple-minded and sophisticated constructions of public spirit. Whig partisans could assert the unity of public spirit, imagining that the interests of the governors and the governed coincided in the aims of ameliorating social conditions, refining manners, and increasing the wealth of a citizenry. Often these Whig visions (the poem "The Publick Spirit" (1718) by the sometime Virginian, John Fox, is an example) were so rarified that class and ethnicity made no appearance. More circumspect and politically astute were the descriptions of the public sphere provided by Shaftesbury and the Scottish "Common Sense" theorists who followed him. For Shaftesbury a *sensus communis* sufficiently broad to manifest the public spirit had to emerge from the institutions of civil society. Only in clubs and circles where persons had permission to test the opinion of their fellows by raillery and debate could an opinion be formed with sufficient sturdiness and incisiveness to stand as public opinion. Such a public opinion truly manifested the wish and will of the people, since it emerged from the conversation of civil society, and did not parrot the propaganda of a government.

Shaftesbury's account of the creation of public opinion allows us to understand one of the subtlest of political distinctions in eighteenth-century Anglo-America – the difference between the public and civil society. The public was the sphere of political action that encompassed the government and the citizenry, defined by a common sense of issues, expressed as opinion, and enacted in the name of the people for the welfare of the commonality. Civil society was that zone of communal exchange where the privacy of contractual obligation and the liberty of self-regulated conversation gave rise to authentic opinion and enabled "happiness in society." For the public to operate authentically, it had to be perpetually renovated by an injection of opinion formed and tested in civil society. In light of this theory, court parties were invariably suspect, for they lacked sufficient distance from the interest of the government to claim to be the opinion of the people.

When judging the accuracy for the British American scene of Shaftesbury's account of the origins of public opinion on the initiatives of civil society, one finds both substantiations and counter-cases. There is no doubting the proliferation of projecting bodies in civil society – clubs, agricultural societies, conventicles, societies for the reformation of manners – that had public influence. The projects growing out of Franklin's junto are perhaps the most conspicuous examples. Charitable societies and groups enabling the education of likely youths proliferated over the course of the eighteenth century. Freemasonry flourished. Yet for every benevolent initiative, one could cite a group formed to promote a private interest. Furthermore, elements of the imperial scheme militated against a confluence of governmental and popular opinion except on the broadest sentiments (anti-popery, promotion of trade, increase of territory). When executives appointed by the Crown or by proprietors appeared in the colonies

bearing instructions intent on preserving Crown prerogatives, public opinion in governmental actions was ideally (for the governors) reduced to the mechanical assent of the local assembly. What in fact happened was the creation of popular parties in local legislatures intent upon containing or hindering the exercise of prerogative. To a great degree popular opinion was oppositional, and political clubs and bodies formed to increase the power of local legislatures in the conduct of affairs. Electioneering occupied much of the activity of these bodies until the Stamp Act crisis, when the organization of resistance became the chief end. While the mechanisms of popular opposition remained much the same from the time of the antiproprietary Old Charter men of 1720s Massachusetts to Boston's Long Room Club and the Sons of Liberty in the 1770s, the boldness with which these groups claimed to speak and act for the entire people increased; so did their willingness to abandon the code of civility to convey the seriousness of their political convictions. The symbolism of the masquerade of the Boston Tea Party was lost on no contemporary commentator.

One must be wary of the political teleology that lurks behind most accounts of the working of opinion in British America. Civil society, whence opinion came, did not wholly absorb itself (or even largely occupy itself) with the creation, reformation, or development of the empire, nation, colony, or state. The judgments rendered in society were just as often about individual character, taste, fashion, manners, and accomplishments as they were about the *res publica*. Women played a large part in rendering these judgments and forming the "talk of the town." Feminine opinion was formed at the tea table, in the salon, and in the drawing room. In many locales groups of "town madams" exercised social discipline. Those who defied their judgment regarding conversation, appearance, or action risked exclusion from the hospitality of the elite, or could be denied access to the marriage market and recognition in social spaces. Gossip and scandal constituted an alternative news, shaping reputations with reports validated by the personal convictions of the speaker. Against this report printed news had little power. While a man could remain politically effective without a gentlemanly reputation – one thinks of Andrew Hamilton in Pennsylvania – such a character proved a liability outside the Assembly chamber. One's reputation influenced the reception of one's ideas in public. The stories of scores of the excommunicated survive, predominantly tales of men whose crudity, political zeal, sexual impropriety, or free-thinking landed them in social limbo. Their fates are well captured in the comic Scots elegy that Archibald Home, secretary of New Jersey, penned about the rebuffs endured by his hard-drinking, hard-swearing, bachelor friend from Elizabethtown, George Fraser:

To ithers too he had made Proffers,
To Share wi' them his weel pang'd Coffers,
Shame fa them! They refus'd his offers.
    In troth Miss_____
When you and_____play'd the Scoffers
    Ye shaw'd your Folly.

Not even wealth – Fraser's "weel pang'd Coffers" – could purchase reprieve from the feminine judgment.

While the opinions of the tea table policed society, enforcing manners, they also carried great weight concerning matters of consumption. Fashion – particularly the reception of metropolitan modes of dress and household furnishing – was a matter largely under the jurisdiction of the tea tables. Given the place that the sale of luxury and manufactured goods had for Britain's commercial empire, the good opinion of women at the places of vendue mattered greatly. Consequently, when the patriots campaigned against duties, groups of women played a key part in organizing non-importation. Certain circles, the Ladies' Association of Mecklenberg, N.C. in particular, won continental renown for their stalwartness in turning away luxury imports. Yet women and fashionable consumption were so closely linked in the imaginations of elite men, that confirmed patriots doubted the ability of American women to make do with homespun and yappon tea. Robert Bolling's "The Association" satirically warned southside Virginian women of the costs

of wavering in their resolves. The presumption also underlies the empire's selection of tea, the feminine beverage, as the one commodity with which to assert the parliamentary right to tax the colonies.

A fear of patriot radicals was that republican virtue was too austere, too devoid of pleasure, to appeal to women. A sense of the seductiveness of the world led many to consign women wholly into the domestic sphere, distanced from such enticements and absorbed in private duties to household and family. Elite women did not wholeheartedly embrace the idea that they should evacuate civil society and keep to home. The 1770s and 1780s would see an ongoing crisis in manners in which elite women were principal actors. Contentions over Meschianza, the culture clash over the Sans Souci social club, culminated in the paper war over the republican court, Martha Washington's national drawing room. Republicans perceived in her gatherings, and her campaign for a hybrid republican-courtly style of manners, echoes of the French salons and specters of aristocracy, dynastic marriage, and the rule of women in public life. Jefferson's dismantling of the republican court did not quash the demand by women of parts for a place in public life and a civic social space in which to project their values and desires.

Apart from a modest number of radical republican ideologues, there were few in the colonies or the United States to overthrow the rule of manners or the institutions of civil society. The American Revolution was political, not cultural. Indeed, the hunger for civil order, social custom, peace, and a regular commerce is revealed in that other eighteenth-century American revolt – the Regulator Rebellions of the 1750s and 1760s. In these agitations, frontier communities organized and armed themselves to coerce the extension of the mechanisms of state (courts, chartered markets, militias) that were being monopolized by ruling coastal oligarchies. Charles Woodmason's petitions on behalf of the South Carolina Regulators poignantly expressed the passion of backcountry settlers to partake in the benefits of ordered society. In these petitions the dependence of civil society on a functioning state is laid out unambiguously. Unless life and property were secured, there could be no commerce and no improvement of society. Government enabled civil society. Civil society made governments worth enduring and sometimes enabled them to work to a public good.

FURTHER READING

Conroy, David: *In Public Houses: Drink and the Revolution of Authority in Colonial Massachusetts* (Chapel Hill: University of North Carolina Press, IEAHC, 1995).

Elias, Norbert: *The Civilizing Process,* vol. I, *The History of Manners,* trans. Edmund Jephcott (New York, 1982).

Ferguson, Adam: *An Essay on the History of Civil Society* (London: T. Caddel, 1773).

Goldgar, Anne: *Impolite Learning: Conduct and Community in the Republic of Letters 1680–1750* (New Haven: Yale University Press, 1995).

Griswold, Rufus Wilmot: *The Republican Court; or, American Society in the Days of Washington* (New York, 1855).

Hearn, Frank: *Moral Order and Social Disorder: The American Search for Civil Society* (New York: Aldine de Gruyter, 1997).

Norwood, Joseph White: *The Tammany Legend* (Boston, 1938).

Seligman, A.: *The Idea of Civil Society* (New York: Free Press, 1992).

Shaftesbury, Earl of: *Sensus Communis: An Essay on the Freedom of Wit and Humour in Characteristics of Men, Manners, Opinions, Times, Etc.,* ed. John M. Robertson, 2 vols. (London, 1900).

Shields, David: *Civil Tongues and Polite Letters in British America* (Chapel Hill: University of North Carolina Press, IEAHC, 1997).

CHAPTER ELEVEN

Ideological background

ISAAC KRAMNICK

THE political, economic, and social confrontation between the colonies and Great Britain was filtered through the lens of political ideas. Available to the parties on both sides of the Atlantic was a varied set of intellectual perspectives that served both to explain events and to inform positions. In their pamphlets, sermons, broadsides, and editorials, colonial polemicists could call upon a large number of available political and intellectual traditions. Present-day scholars may disagree about which of these traditions played the larger or more seminal role, but most agree that at least six ideological perspectives were available to the revolutionary mind: liberalism, Protestantism, juridical rights, republicanism, the Enlightenment, and the Scottish school.

1 Lockean Liberalism

Especially evident in the rhetoric of the revolutionary period was the language of Lockean liberalism. James Otis's *Rights of the British Colonies Asserted and Proved* (1764), Richard Bland's *An Inquiry into the Rights of the British Colonies* (1766), Samuel Adams's *A State of the Rights of the Colonists* (1772), and, of course, Thomas Jefferson's *Declaration of Independence* (1776) are all grounded in the writings of the Englishman John Locke, whose *Second Treatise of Government*, written in the early 1680s, proved extremely useful to opponents of Britain's new colonial policy. Government for the liberal was a voluntary creation of self-interested individuals who consent to be governed in order to protect their personal rights to life, liberty, and property.

Originally equals in a natural society without government, men entered into a contractual relationship of trust with a government which serves at their will as a common umpire protecting individuals from other individuals who would interfere with their natural rights. Should the agent-government not protect the rights of the individuals who have consented to its creation, or should that government itself invade individual rights, then Locke allows for the dissolution of that government and its replacement with another.

At the heart of Lockean liberalism is individualism. Neither God, tradition, divine right, nor conquest is the source of political obligation. Self-regarding individuals intent on protecting their individual private rights provide legitimacy to government by their individual acts of consenting to be governed. That government is then a servant granted only the very limited task of safeguarding individual rights to life, liberty, and property. In so privileging individualism and individual freedom, liberalism symbolized the new social ideals challenging the older vision of a static hierarchical politics which had individuals subordinate to larger corporate entities, as well as assigned or ascribed to specific social ranks.

A particularly important source of Lockean liberal ideas on individual freedom in politics, religion, and the economy for revolutionary America was its articulation by a group of English Protestant dissenters in the 1760s and 1770s, whose writings were well known to fellow non-Anglicans in the colonies. Writers such as Richard Price, Joseph Priestley, James Burgh, and Thomas

Paine gave Locke's political ideals a social as well as political relevance for the highly individualistic culture emerging in colonial America.

Locke's suggestion in chapter V of his *Second Treatise of Government* that unlimited acquisition of money and wealth was neither unjust nor morally wrong was a move absolutely essential for a liberal agenda of competitive individualism and equal opportunity. Locke's very Protestant God commands men to work the earth, and in turn the hard-working and industrious have the right to possess what they work. Since God had given "different degrees of industry" to men, some have more talent and work harder than others. It is just and ethical, then, for them to have as many possessions as they want. This is crucial to the emerging ideology. If individuals are to define themselves in terms of what they achieve in the race of life, and if this sense of achievement is seen increasingly in terms of work and victory in a market society where talent and industry have their play, then the traditional Christian and moral economy barriers to unlimited accumulation have to fall. How else can achievement and sense of self be known if not by economic success?

An utterly new understanding of the individual and society emerges in the liberal world-view. Ascription, the assignment to some preordained rank in life, came more and more to be replaced by achievement as the major definer of personal identity. Individuals increasingly came to define themselves as active subjects. They no longer tended to see their place in life as part of some natural, inevitable, and eternal plan. Their own enterprise and ability mattered; they possessed the opportunity (a key word) to determine their place through their own voluntary actions in this life and in this world.

The political implications of these liberal social ideals are clear. Governments could tax property, the fruit of virtuous labor, only with the individual's consent, and more profoundly even, ruling classes of idle nobility and useless monarchy would be challenged everywhere by the assertive hard-working men and women of real ability and individual talent.

2 Protestantism

Closely allied to Lockean liberalism is another intellectual tradition available to colonial Americans, Protestantism and the Protestant ethic. Many Americans knew work-ethic Protestantism derived from Richard Baxter, John Bunyan, and the literature of the calling and of "industry." In the later decades of the eighteenth century it was this discourse that monopolized the texts of the English dissenters whose writings were so influential in the founding generation.

Central in work-ethic Protestantism was the vision of a cosmic struggle between the forces of industry and idleness. Its texts vibrate with the dialectic of productive hard-working energy, on the one hand, and idle unproductive sloth, on the other. Work was a test of self-sufficiency and self-reliance, a battleground for personal salvation. All men were "called" to serve God by busying themselves in useful productive work that served both society and the individual. Daily labor was sanctified and thus was both a specific obligation and a positive moral value. The doctrine of the calling gave each man a sense of his unique self; work appropriate to each individual was imposed by God. After being called to a particular occupation, it was a man's duty to labor diligently and to avoid idleness and sloth. Virtuous man is a solitary and private man on his own, realizing himself and his talents through labor and achievement; corrupt man is unproductive, indolent, and in the devil's camp. He fails the test of individual responsibility.

The American response to English taxation centered on a dual policy of self-denial and commitment to industry. Richard Henry Lee, as early as 1764, when hearing of the Sugar Act, assumed it would "introduce a virtuous industry." The subsequent non-consumption and non-importation policy of colonial protestors led many a moralist to applaud parliamentary taxation as a blessing in disguise, recalling America to simplicity and frugality. As Edmund Morgan notes (1967), the boycott movements were seen by many as not simply negative and reactive. "They were also a positive end in themselves, a way of reaffirming and rehabilitating the virtues of the Puritan Ethic."

Early Puritan settlers had seen themselves as a chosen people who with God's help were building a city on a hill for all the world to imitate. Although this conception of the New England experiment rarely penetrated south of the Hudson River and lost force even in New England during the eighteenth century, a secular variant that saw the colonies as the home of liberty everywhere was apparent. The Quaker Thomas Paine could tap that tradition in his plea in *Common Sense* that Americans, like Old Testament prophets, reject monarchy. Their calling was to provide an asylum for freedom so recently evicted from Europe by its useless kings.

3 Juridical Rights

Paradoxically, one of the secular signs of their special covenant with God was the colonists' unshakable commitment to the rights of Englishmen. If their pamphlets and sermons spoke often of universal, transcendent, and abstract natural rights and natural law, they just as often were grounded in discussions of historical and contingent rights, the positive rights of Englishmen. Sam Adams, for example, used the conventional formula familiar to all colonial pamphleteers which depicted the English common law and statutory Acts of the British Parliament as sources of "the absolute rights of Englishmen," or "the Rights, Liberties and Privileges of Subjects born in Great Britain." In their political formulation these legal rights focused on the supremacy of the legislature, the rule of law as opposed to arbitrary decree, and the illegality of government seizure of property without the subject's consent "in person, or by his representative."

This tradition of juridical rights was of profound importance to the colonists and the ideal of law as a restraint on the Crown informed much of the rhetoric of colonial protest. Statutory as well as common law, the intricate set of legal precedents and customs, which had evolved over time, guaranteed the sanctity of an Englishman's life,

liberty, and property, as well as the rights of trial by jury, representative government, and habeas corpus. In the hands of seventeenth-century jurists such as Sir Edward Coke (1552–1634) the juridical rights tradition emerged as a major constraint on Stuart monarchical pretensions as well as the principal defender of an "Ancient Constitution" which protected the liberty and property of Englishmen against the claims of royal prerogative. Older even than the common law, this "Ancient Constitution" was assumed to have roots in Saxon England and to have been reaffirmed, in the wake of Norman assaults, through great charters such as the Magna Carta.

According to the juristic notion of the "Ancient Constitution," Parliament was an age-old institution, by no means created by or dependent on the will of monarchs. English liberties and freedom of the subject were born in the forests of the tribal past and survived the attack of the "Norman Yoke" only through the assiduous care of lawyers and parliamentary statesmen. No matter that many historians faulted the historical assumptions of the "Ancient Constitution," its political success in the constitutional struggles of seventeenth-century England ensured its appeal to colonial Americans.

For many in the colonies the particular figure in the juridical school cited over and over again in the late eighteenth century was Sir William Blackstone, whose *Commentaries on the Law of England* (1765–9) was regarded as the definitive statement on the British Constitution. Blackstone, it was assumed, codified the ideal of the "Ancient Constitution" as the source of the unique British tradition of parliamentary government and the common law as constitutional alternatives to arbitrary rule.

4 Republicanism

To this point we have looked at the ideological background of the Revolution very much in British terms: Lockean liberalism, Puritanism, and the British Constitution. The set of traditions available to the colonists was by no means so provincial. Indeed, in recent decades a good deal of attention has been given to an intellectual influence on the revolutionary era that has roots far broader than merely Britain. Chroniclers of this republican or civic-humanist tradition see it, in fact, as much more influential than Lockean liberalism.

Part Aristotle, part Cicero, part Machiavelli, civic humanism conceives of man as a political being whose realization of self occurs only through participation in public life, through active citizenship in a republic. The virtuous man is concerned primarily with the public good, *res publica*, or commonweal, not with private or selfish ends. Seventeenth-century writers such as James Harrington and Algernon Sidney adapted this tradition, especially under the influence of Machiavelli (according to J. G. A. Pocock), to a specifically English context. This significantly English variant of civic humanism, "neo-Machiavellianism" or "neo-Harringtonianism," became, through the writings of early eighteenth-century English Augustans such as Davenant, Trenchard, Gordon, and especially Henry St. John, Viscount Bolingbroke, the ideological core of the "country" ideology that confronted Walpole and his "court" faction. Bolingbroke provided a crucial link in this intellectual chain by associating corruption with social and political themes, a critical concept in the language of eighteenth-century politics. Much richer than simple venality or fraud, the concept is enveloped by the Machiavellian image of historical change: corruption is the absence of civic virtue. Corrupt man is preoccupied with self and oblivious to the public good. Such failures of moral personality, such degeneration from the fundamental commitment to public life, fuel the decline of states and can be remedied only through periodic revitalization by returning to the original and pristine commitment to civic virtue. Calls for such renewals, for *ridurre ai principii* (Machiavelli's phrase), form the response to corruption.

Bolingbroke's achievement was to appropriate this republican and Machiavellian language for the social and economic tensions developing in Augustan England over the rise of government credit, public debt, and central banking as well as for political issues, such as Walpole's control of Parliament through patronage or concern over standing armies. Themes of independence and dependence, so critical to the republican tradition (the former essential to any commitment to the public good), were deployed by Bolingbroke into a social map of independent country proprietors opposing placemen and stock jobbers and a political map of a free Parliament opposing a despotic court. In addition, Bolingbroke stamped this eighteenth-century republican-country tradition with its socially conservative and nostalgic quality, in terms of not only its anti-commercialism but also its anti-egalitarianism.

To a great extent, the innovative scholarship of J. G. A. Pocock has shaped this new way of looking at English political thought. His writings on Harrington and his magisterial *The Machiavellian Moment* (1975) have made the concept of civic humanism and republicanism a strikingly useful tool with which to understand the political mind of late seventeenth- and early eighteenth-century England. However, in the hands of Pocock and others, this insightful reading of early eighteenth-century politics through Bolingbroke's dichotomy of virtuous country and corrupt court does not stop with Augustan England. It becomes the organizing paradigm for the language of political thought in England as well as America throughout the entire century.

Locke and possessive individualism in this scheme have had to go. A chorus of distinguished scholars has joined in de-emphasizing the importance of Locke throughout eighteenth-century Anglo-American thought. "Eighteenth century English political thought," according to Gordon Wood (1972), "perhaps owed more to Machiavelli and Montesquieu than it did to Locke." Indeed, Bernard Bailyn has persuasively argued (1967) that "the effective triggering convictions that lay behind the [American] Revolution were derived not from common Lockean generalities but from the specific fears and formulations of the radical publicists and opposition politicians of early eighteenth century England."

Pocock has applied this revisionist verdict about Locke to an alternative reading of

America and its founding. American political culture, according to Pocock, has been haunted by myths, the most mistaken of which is the role of Locke as "the patron saint of American values." The proper interpretation "stresses Machiavelli at the expense of Locke." The Revolution was, in Pocock's reading, "the last great act of the Renaissance ... emerging from a line of thought which staked everything on a positive and civic concept of the individual's virtue." The Revolution was a Machiavellian *rinnovazione* in a new world, "a republican commitment to the renovation of virtue." America was born in a "dread of modernity," according to Pocock.

Americans could come to republican ideas directly, as well as through the mediation of Renaissance Italy or English Commonwealth or Country Ideology. Greek and Roman authors were well known to the colonial mind. From Cicero, Aristotle, and Polybius, all widely read in America, notions of a higher law as well as constitutional arguments for mixed and separate powers in a stable government could be found. Perhaps the most influential text from antiquity in eighteenth-century America was Plutarch's *Lives of the Noble Greeks and Romans*. In it the greatest historical glory is reserved for the "law giver" as "the founder of commonwealths." This classical celebration of those who serve the common good is found in Hamilton's republican aspirations. In a pamphlet written in 1777 attacking congressmen for not better realizing the potential of their position, Hamilton had written of true greatness and fame. He signed the pamphlet with the pseudonym "Publius," a fabled figure in Plutarch's *Lives* and the name later used by him and his fellow authors of *The Federalist*. Hamilton's vision transcended the walls of Congress in the infant nation and spoke to the historic discourse of republicanism.

The station of a member of C ... ss, is the most illustrious and important of any I am able to conceive. He is to be regarded not only as a legislator, but as the founder of an empire. A man of virtue and ability, dignified with so precious a trust, would rejoice that fortune had given him birth at a time, and placed him in circumstances so favorable for promoting human happiness.

He would esteem it not more the duty, than the privilege and ornament of his office, to do good to mankind.

5 The Enlightenment

Another primarily non-British source of political ideas and ideals for the colonists was the Enlightenment, which, to a great extent, took the secular wisdom of classical antiquity as a source for its crusade against both Christianity and the *ancien régime*. The writings of Jefferson, Franklin, and John Adams reveal deep understanding and familiarity with the ideas of the French *philosophes*, and their European connections as well as correspondents were often leading figures in the Enlightenment. From them they acquired a rational skepticism about supernatural religion as well as a passionate commitment to ameliorative and practical science and technology as engines of progress and reform. The French Enlightenment with its rejection of original sin and pessimism directed energy to this world and spoke to the ease of reforming outdated social institutions. Jefferson's transformation of Locke's sacred triad of life, liberty, and property to life, liberty, and happiness bears the stamp of the this-worldly, more hedonistic orientation of the French Enlightenment.

The generally secular and liberalizing tone of the Enlightenment pervaded the educated revolutionary mind. In addition to Jefferson, Franklin, and Adams, America's own *philosophes*, ordinary pamphleteers were familiar with and cited Montesquieu on the influence of climate, or the intricacies of the separation of powers. The Italian legal reformer Beccaria was a frequent source, as were other Enlightenment luminaries such as Rousseau, Pufendorf, Grotius, Vattel, and Burlamaqui.

6 The Scottish School

The final component of the ideological background of revolutionary America requires a return to Great Britain, but not to England, for a powerful influence on the eighteenth-century colonial mind was the Scottish Enlightenment. Much the most interesting group of writers and thinkers in Britain during the eighteenth century were the Scottish intellectuals from Glasgow, Edinburgh, and St. Andrews. They offered a conception of human nature and a reading of history quite different from those offered by Lockean liberalism or neo-classical republicanism. Francis Hutcheson as well as David Hume and Adam Smith depicted men as neither asocial nor autonomous, as liberalism did. Men, they wrote, were moved to community by a common "moral sense" which produced sociability and benevolence. Nor was the quest for a moral life the product of a disinterested and rational perception of the common good; it was informed by sentiment and affection. A "moral sense" was innate in all mankind, giving them an intuitive knowledge of what is right and wrong. In a fundamental sense, then, all people were seen as equal by the moral sense school, since all people had the moral capacity for sociability and benevolence.

If the thrust of the Scottish school's views on human nature runs counter to liberal views, then its attitude to history runs directly contrary to much of the republican tradition. Scottish writers such as Hume, Smith, Adam Ferguson, and Lord Kames did not see history as a repetitive cycle of corruption and virtuous revitalization. Nor did they see economic modernity as a morally inferior era of luxury and selfishness. They depicted history as evolving in terms of developmental stages characterized principally by the mode of production. Societies moved through four such stages, the ages of hunting, herding, agriculture, and commerce. Commerce produced economic abundance and a freer, more civilized social order. For David Hume and for Adam Smith, modern market society not the classical or Saxon past produced freedom and happiness.

The Scots differed among themselves, to be sure. Thomas Reid, for example, shared few of his countrymen's historical concerns. His "Common Sense" philosophy, however,

had a great deal of influence on American thought in the revolutionary generation.

Americans, in turn, differed in their evaluations of Scottish thinkers. David Hume, a particularly influential member of the Scottish school, is a case in point. His writings on politics with their emphasis on factionalism, his conviction that politics could be reduced to a science, and his widely read historical judgments made him an often cited writer in the revolutionary generation. Yet Jefferson disapproved of Hume because of the allegedly Tory sentiments of his *History*. Madison, on the other hand, was very much influenced by Hume in crafting his social and political worldviews. Whether he turned to Hume more often than to Locke or republicanism is, alas, another, perhaps unanswerable, question.

FURTHER READING

Bailyn, B.: *The Ideological Origins of the American Revolution* (Cambridge, Mass.: Harvard University Press, 1967).

Greene, J. P.: *The Intellectual Heritage of the Constitutional Era* (Philadelphia: Library Company of Philadelphia, 1986).

Kramnick, I.: *Republicanism and Bourgeois Radicalism: Political Ideology in Late Eighteenth-Century England and America* (Ithaca, NY: Cornell University Press, 1990).

McDonald, F.: *Novus Ordo Seculorum: the Intellectual Origins of the Constitution* (Lawrence: University Press of Kansas, 1985).

Morgan, E.: "The Puritan ethic and the American Revolution," *William and Mary Quarterly*, 24 (1967), 3–43.

Pocock, J. G. A.: *The Machiavellian Moment: Florentine Political Thought and the Atlantic Republican Tradition* (Princeton, NJ.: Princeton University Press, 1975).

Pole, J. R.: "Enlightenment and the Politics of American Nature," *The Enlightenment in National Context*, ed. Roy Porter and Niklaus Teich (Cambridge: Cambridge University Press, 1982).

Wills, G.: *Inventing America* (New York: Vintage Books, 1979).

Wood, G.: *The Creation of the American Republic* (New York: W. W. Norton, 1972).

CHAPTER TWELVE

The Amerindian population in 1763

ERIC HINDERAKER

THE end of the Seven Years' War in 1763 brought dramatic changes to the balance of power in North America and set the context for the American Revolution in Amerindian country. For more than half a century, Amerindian peoples of eastern North America had cultivated economies and political identities in relation to the French and British empires. In the treaty of Paris that ended the Seven Years' War, France ceded to Britain all of its claims to North America east of the Mississippi, while Spain handed over East Florida. Britain's American empire, which had consisted primarily of a string of coastal settlements until that point, suddenly stretched from the Mississippi delta to the rocky outcroppings of Newfoundland and embraced half a continent. For eastern Amerindians this was a decisive change: their ability to navigate between European powers suddenly disappeared, and they faced instead British officers and Anglo-American colonists who were determined to cast Amerindian relations and western policy in a new mold. These changes led Amerindian communities throughout eastern North America to reconsider their relations to the British colonies and Crown.

1 Accommodation

By 1763, the Amerindian societies of North America had been adjusting to the wrenching effects of European colonization for more than a century and a half. Dozens of distinct peoples, often sharing some broad cultural patterns but speaking many languages and pursuing a variety of social, economic, and political strategies, faced unprecedented

challenges to their survival. European diseases devastated Amerindian communities, destroying some altogether and reducing the populations of others by as much as 90 percent. English settlers fought desparate wars for control of Amerindian lands, while new patterns of trade and alliance led some Amerindian groups to make all-out war on others. Communities and polities disintegrated and collapsed, and new, multi-ethnic villages and composite political groupings emerged from the ruins. Gradually a kind of equilibrium returned to Amerindian country, based on increasingly stable patterns of trade, alliance, mediation, and accommodation. Perhaps 150,000 Amerindian people still inhabited the eastern woodlands in 1763.

They faced an uncertain future. For two generations, Amerindians and Europeans had cultivated political, economic, social, and cultural ties that knitted together backcountry communities and improved intercultural relations. The Iroquois confederacy cultivated alliances with the British colonies of New York and Pennsylvania through its easternmost tribe, the Mohawks, and another alliance with New France through the Senecas in the west, while the confederacy council at Onondaga maintained an official policy of neutrality toward both empires. This allowed the Iroquois to trade both in Canada and New York while they steered a middle course in diplomacy. The Shawnees in the Ohio Valley sought alliances with Pennsylvania and New France at the same time, and many Ohio Amerindian communities had regular contacts with traders from both empires. In the Gulf South, the Choctaws played French and British interests off one another as well.

These play-off strategies gave some Amerindian groups latitude and leverage in their relations with the European powers.

The fur trade in the north and the deerskin trade in the south brought both prosperity and dependency to Amerindian communities and gradually transformed the material conditions of their residents' lives. Amerindians hunted with guns and wore European clothing; in many Amerindian towns traditional wigwams and longhouses stood alongside single-family cabins in the European style. Cash economies often prevailed in trading communities, and Amerindian women began to raise chickens, pigs, and cattle to supplement traditional diets. As alcohol devastated some Amerindian towns, Christian missionaries who preached abstinence and individual moral responsibility occasionally gained headway. At the same time, colonists grew maize, adopted useful Amerindian technologies like the canoe, and learned new methods of hunting and warfare. By the mid-eighteenth century, diplomatic protocols between colonies and Amerindians were sufficiently well-established that conflicts could often be settled peacefully. All these developments reflected growing contact and interdependence between Amerindian and European communities.

The Seven Years' War disrupted these patterns and unleashed unprecedented levels of violence throughout the British backcountry. The worst fighting between colonists and Amerindians came in western Pennsylvania, Maryland, and Virginia, where the Ohio Amerindians raided mercilessly for several years, and in Cherokee country, which was invaded by the South Carolina militia in 1760. New levels of mistrust reigned among Amerindians and colonists alike in many of the regions touched by war. When France withdrew from North America in 1763, Amerindian leaders throughout the eastern woodlands feared that British commanders might scorn their interests and Anglo-American colonists might trample their claims to land.

Their fears were well-founded. In 1761 General Jeffery Amherst, Commander-in-Chief of British forces in North America, imposed stringent regulations on the Amerindian trade and diplomatic gifts at the many western posts that had just been captured from the French. These regulations struck especially hard in the Ohio Valley and Great Lakes region, where the fighting had devastated local crops; now, because Amherst – who, like most British officers, deeply mistrusted the western Amerindians – wanted to keep their hunters "scarce of Ammunition," it was difficult for many Amerindian towns to support themselves (Hinderaker, 1997, p. 148). The last years of the war brought privation, famine, and disease to many parts of Amerindian country. At the same time, land-hungry colonists were drawn to the vicinity of new western posts like Fort Pitt, where they began to occupy Amerindian territory at an alarming rate. Almost immediately, Britain's victory in the Seven Years' War appeared to have disastrous implications for Amerindians in the West.

2 Resistance

Many Amerindian communities with long-standing ties to the French, especially the Great Lakes groups around Detroit, hoped to revive French power in North America when they discovered British intentions. Western nations – including Delawares, Shawnees, Senecas, Ottawas, Chippewas, Potawatomis, Huron-Petuns, Wyandots, Kickapoos, and Miamis – met in various combinations between 1760 and 1762 to consider an alliance of western Amerindians that might resist British expansion in the West and facilitate the return of French soldiers and administrators, with whom many of them had maintained ties of diplomacy and trade for a century or more. In the end, it was impossible to reconcile the conflicting interests and concerns of all the communities and peoples represented in these meetings to forge a single, coordinated confederacy, but their discussions reflect the widespread anti-British sentiment that quickly took root following the Seven Years' War.

At the same time, many Ohio and Great Lakes Amerindians turned to the teachings of several prophets to explain their declining fortunes. The most notable of them was a Delaware man named Neolin who came from a village on the Tuscarawas River in the Ohio Valley. Inspired by a vision in which he was instructed by the Master of Life, Neolin preached a gospel of cultural purification to restore the spiritual power that he believed Amerindians had lost as a result of their contact with Europeans. Neolin, like other Amerindian prophets of the day, believed that Amerindians and Europeans were created as different peoples and must remain separate and distinct from one another. To punish Amerindians for their reliance on European guns and their love of alcohol and other alien goods, the Master of Life had made game increasingly scarce. Neolin emphasized the need to resist English expansion and reform Amerindian societies to restore the world's balance. "If you suffer the English among you," he warned "you are dead men. Sickness, smallpox, and their poison will destroy you entirely" (Dowd, 1992, p. 34). His program of reformation required that Amerindians purge themselves of European impurities and embrace new rituals to restore their power.

These two movements – one to create a pro-French, pan-Amerindian alliance, the other to restore spiritual power to western Amerindian communities – were distinct but mutually reinforcing. Both helped to inspire a young Ottawa war leader named Pontiac when he convinced a group of villagers living near Detroit to take up arms against the British garrison there in the spring of 1763. Word of their attack spread quickly throughout the region and prompted uprisings elsewhere, until by summer's end every British post in the West had been attacked: Forts Edward, Augustus, and Michilimackinac on Lake Michigan, St. Joseph, Miami, Ouiatanon, and Sandusky between Detroit and the Ohio River, and Presque Isle, Le Boeuf, and Venango along the Allegheny River all fell to the attackers, while the garrisons at Detroit and Fort Pitt held out against prolonged sieges. These attacks, which have come to be known collectively as Pontiac's Rebellion, were not part of a coordinated offensive effort, but they illustrate the depth of hostility to British power that prevailed among western Amerindians in the wake of the Seven Years' War.

3 Division

British administrators and army officers learned an indelible lesson from Pontiac's Rebellion: they could not hope to control the West through force and intimidation. It took two years for the British army to reassert its control over the western posts; in the meantime, British administrators had ample opportunity to rethink their western policy. The Proclamation of 1763, issued in October, represented the ministry's first attempt to articulate its new approach. The Proclamation created a boundary between the colonies and Amerindian lands. Beyond the line, settlement was forbidden, land purchases were to be made only by the Crown, and licenses were required for Amerindian traders. The ministry hoped to reduce its expenses in the West to a minimum while it considered the possibility of slow colonial expansion at some future date.

The Amerindians of the trans-Appalachian West were divided and uncertain how to respond to British power in the wake of the western rebellions. From the country of the Creeks and Cherokees in the South to the Great Lakes, Iroquoia, and beyond, the end of the Seven Years' War brought crises, new choices, and sharp disagreements. Disease and famine challenged the survival of Cherokee and Ohio Amerindian communities; the loss of French ties seriously disrupted the economies of many groups in the Mississippi and Great Lakes basins; the return of British traders flooded Amerindian towns with unprecedented quantities of liquor; along the margins of colonial settlement, squatters were taking up Amerindian lands at an alarming rate. The deerskin trade among the southeastern Amerindians, especially the Creeks and Choctaws, fell into the hands of a few traders who were especially adept and ruthless in their commercial activities. Carrying large quantities of rum to Amerindian towns, they sold it at great profit to hunters returning home with a season's take of deerskins. Hunters might trade the product of three or four months' work for a drinking binge, only to find that they had nothing left with which to provide for their families. Drinking was an especially destructive force in Amerindian communities.

It led to fights, murder, and discord; it set community leaders against hunters and wives against husbands; it sapped a town's economic resources and encouraged overhunting of animal populations. The rum trade drove many men, and even entire communities, into debt; when this happened, traders gained leverage to acquire grants of Amerindian land.

While some Amerindian leaders continued to counsel resistance to British power and cultural purification of Amerindian communities, others argued that it was necessary to cooperate with imperial officials in order to regulate trade, restrain settlement, and mediate conflict. John Stuart, the superintendent for Amerindian affairs for the southern colonies, advised the king's ministers in London of the need to restrain unscrupulous traders and keep squatters off Amerindian lands if the empire hoped to avoid another expensive and bloody Amerindian War. William Johnson, Stuart's counterpart in the northern colonies, argued that Britain needed to adjudicate the proliferating boundary disputes between the colonies and western Amerindians and carefully control any future westward expansion. Stuart maintained especially close ties with the leaders of the Creek confederacy, while Johnson identified primarily with the concerns of the Six Nations of the Iroquois confederacy. The Iroquois claimed to speak for Amerindian groups throughout the northeast, including those of the Ohio country, by right of conquest. Johnson hoped to capitalize on this claim to centralize and streamline Indian policy by conducting all of his Amerindian diplomacy through Iroquois spokesmen who would act as intermediaries with other groups. Thus the Iroquois confederacy became increasingly pro-British in its official policy, but the Amerindians of the Ohio Valley and Great Lakes chafed under the yoke of Iroquois domination.

In many Amerindian communities, an older generation of leaders had had its fill of war and advised cooperation with British officers. But their authority was challenged with increasing frequency by younger, militant men, some of whom continued to be influenced by nativist prophets. One observer noted that younger men among the Ohio Delawares "began to despise the counsel of the aged, and only endeavored to get into favor with these preachers, whose followers multiplied very fast" (Dowd, 1992, p. 37). In the Ohio Valley, these Amerindian prophets were often competing directly for adherents with Moravian missionaries who were also gaining followers, especially among the Delawares. The Moravians planted a series of mission towns, first in Pennsylvania and later in the Ohio Valley, where they imparted Christian beliefs to their converts and at the same time encouraged them to adopt European-style farms, houses, and crafts. Travelers were struck by the "regularity, order, and decorum" of the Moravian Amerindian towns (Calloway, 1995, p. 1). Some Delaware leaders who were not attracted to Christianity nevertheless welcomed the Moravian influence for other reasons. They hoped the missionaries might teach their people craft skills that would make Amerindians less dependent on Europeans. Following the Moravian example, a number of Amerindian towns banned alcohol to control its devastating effects. Though they were not Christian converts, the Delaware counsellors White Eyes and Killbuck hoped to convince the King to appoint a schoolmaster and an Anglican minister to teach their children English language and customs.

The struggles and divisions that emerged after 1763 in Amerindian country grew, ironically, from the pursuit of a common goal: the preservation of Amerindian autonomy and independence in the face of rising British power. The future was uncertain; no one knew whether that goal would best be secured through cooperation with British officials and a partial adoption of European ways, or whether the only viable option was to reject British influence and resist the empire with force. Time would show that the British Empire, though its power was unmatched anywhere on the globe at the end of the Seven Years' War, was incapable of controlling events in the American backcountry. But in 1763 that realization lay still in the future.

FURTHER READING

Anderson, Fred: *Death and Taxes: The Seven Years' War and the Fate of the British Empire* (New York: Knopf, forthcoming).

Calloway, Colin: *The American Revolution in Indian Country: Crisis and Diversity in Native American Communities* (New York: Cambridge University Press, 1995).

Dowd, Gregory: *A Spirited Resistance: The North American Indian Struggle for Unity, 1745–1815* (Baltimore: Johns Hopkins University Press, 1992).

Hatley, Tom: *The Dividing Paths: Cherokees and South Carolinians through the Revolutionary Era* (New York: Oxford University Press, 1995).

Hinderaker, Eric: *Elusive Empires: Constructing Colonialism in the Ohio Valley, 1673–1800* (New York: Cambridge University Press, 1997).

Mancall, Peter: *Deadly Medicine: Indians and Alcohol in Early America* (Ithaca: Cornell University Press, 1995).

Martin, Joel: *Sacred Revolt: The Muskogees' Struggle for a New World* (Boston: Beacon Press, 1991).

Merrell, James: *The Indians' New World: Catawbas and Their Neighbors from European Contact Through the Era of Removal* (Chapel Hill: University of North Carolina Press, 1989).

Snapp, J. Russell: *John Stuart and the Struggle for Empire on the Southern Frontier* (Baton Rouge: Louisiana State University Press, 1996).

White, Richard: *The Middle Ground: Indians, Empires, and Republics in the Great Lakes Region, 1650–1815* (New York: Cambridge University Press, 1991).

PART II

Themes and Events, to 1776

CHAPTER THIRTEEN

The origins of the new colonial policy, 1748–1763

JACK P. GREENE

IN the decades following World War II, most historians have come to agree that, by the mid-eighteenth century, Britain's North American colonies were well socialized to the British imperial system and that they were driven to resistance and rebellion primarily by changes in metropolitan colonial policy that occurred after the conclusion of the Seven Years' War in 1763, changes that gradually over the next dozen years led to the alienation of colonial affections from Britain and eventually in 1775–6 to the emergence of broad support for Independence. More recently, however, it has been shown that British officials developed this "new" British colonial policy not during the early 1760s but more than a decade earlier, during the late 1740s. As early as 1748, the metropolitan government began to abandon its long-standing posture of accommodation and conciliation towards the colonies for a policy of strict supervision and control, a policy that in both tone and content strongly resembled that usually associated primarily with the post-1763 era.

1 Reasons for the Change

The explanation for this change is to be found in four separate conditions. Far and away the most important was the phenomenal growth of the colonies in the decades following the Peace of Utrecht in 1713. Between 1710 and 1750, the extent of settled territory, the size of the population, the volume of immigrants. the number of African slaves, the volume of commodity production, the amount of foreign trade, and the size of

major urban centers all increased at an extraordinarily rapid rate (*see* chapters 6 and 7). Demographic growth was unparalleled. The free population rose by 160 percent between 1710 and 1740 and by 125 percent between 1740 and 1770, while the slave population grew by 235 percent during the former period and 200 percent during the latter.

Territorial and demographic growth in turn made it possible for the colonists both to send to Britain increasing quantities of raw materials, many of which were subsequently profitably re-exported by British middlemen, and to purchase ever larger quantities of British manufactures, thereby providing an important stimulus to the development of British industry. During the eighteenth century, in fact, the colonial trade became the most rapidly growing section and accounted for a significant proportion of the total volume of British overseas trade. Imports from the colonies (both continental and West Indian) accounted for 20 percent of the total volume of English imports in 1700–1 and 36 percent in 1772–3, while exports to the colonies rose from 10 percent of the total volume of English exports during the former year to 37 percent during the latter. The colonial trade was thus a critical segment of the British economy and was becoming more important with every decade.

For the British political nation, the extraordinary growth of the colonies was, however, a source not only of celebration for the vast power and profits it brought but also of acute anxiety, which manifested itself through the middle decades of the eighteenth century in the frequent expression of two related ideas. The first was that the colonies were of crucial importance to the economic and strategic welfare of Britain. The second was that the colonists secretly lusted after and might possibly be on the verge of trying to achieve their independence from Britain.

At least since the closing decades of the seventeenth century, metropolitan officials and traders had intermittently voiced the fear that the colonies might eventually seek independence, set up their own manufactures, and become economic rivals rather than subordinate and complementary partners with Britain. By lending increasing plausibility to this fear, the extraordinary growth of the colonies, along with the concomitant increase in their economic and strategic worth to Britain, contributed to a significant rise during the late 1740s and the 1750s in the frequency and urgency of explicit expressions of anxieties within metropolitan circles over the possible loss of the colonies. Such expressions were everywhere manifest in Britain: in official reports prepared by the Board of Trade, in correspondence between metropolitan officials and royal governors, in parliamentary debates, and in a proliferating number of tracts, both published and unpublished, on the state of the colonies and the need for reforms in their administration. So consequential had the burgeoning colonies become to Britain that, as Horace Walpole put it, any "Apprehension of their being lost" could "easily … create a consternation."[1]

If the long-term rapid and substantial growth of the colonies, along with the corresponding increase in their importance to Britain, was the single most important precondition behind the shift in British policy beginning during the late 1740s, a second, closely related, medium-term precondition was the threat of French or perhaps even Spanish conquest of such valuable possessions. The Treaty of Aix-la-Chapelle, signed in October 1748 at the conclusion of the third inter-colonial war, was widely understood as offering only a temporary respite from the decade of conflict between Britain and the Latin powers that had begun in 1739 with the War of Jenkins's Ear. The stakes in the prospective conflict were widely recognized to be no less than supremacy over the entire western, and even some of the eastern, world.

With so much at risk, there could be no question of allowing the colonies to be lost, and British officials were particularly concerned following the peace of 1748 to strengthen colonial defenses in preparation for a renewal of hostilities. The areas of greatest vulnerability seemed to be the two ends of the chain of colonies stretching along the east coast of North America from the Altamaha River in the South to the Strait of Canso in the North. At the northern end, Nova Scotia relied for its defense almost entirely upon a small British military establishment that lived in perpetual fear of rebellion by the numerically dominant "neutral" French in the Annapolis Valley or of attack from the superior French military force at Louisburg on nearby Cape Breton Island. Despite more than 15 years of government support, including major expenditures from parliamentary revenues, Georgia, at the southern end, was in an obvious state of decay, perhaps even an easy prey for the small Spanish garrison at nearby St. Augustine. Fear of colonial independence and French or Spanish conquest combined to stimulate still a third fear: that strong and rebellious colonies might sell their favors to the highest bidder among Britain's European rivals.

The actual timing of the change in British colonial policy can be accounted for by the temporary cessation of hostilities in 1748 and two additional short-run circumstances. First was the end of the domestic political turmoil that had begun with the outbreak of war in 1739 and was intensified by the vigorous competition for power through the mid-1740s following the fall of Sir Robert Walpole in 1742. Having already won the confidence of George II and wooed many opposition leaders to the side of government, Henry Pelham finally managed to establish his administration on a sound basis as a result of the government's overwhelming victory in the elections of 1747. For the next seven years, until Pelham's death in 1754, the government enjoyed a new freedom from domestic distractions that enabled its leaders to devote significant attention to the colonies for the first time since the mid-1730s.

A second, and even more important, short-run condition that determined the timing of the shift in colonial policy was the apparent breakdown of metropolitan authority in many colonies during the late 1740s. For the previous 30 years, metropolitan officials had held the colonial reins loosely. Preoccupied with domestic concerns and relations with continental European powers, they rarely gave close attention to colonial problems unless they were perceived as threatening to powerful economic interests within the home island. There were two important results of what Edmund Burke later called this "wise and salutary neglect." One was the relaxation of tensions that had characterized relations between metropolis and colonies for much of the period between 1660 and 1720. The second was the emergence of a functional balance between metropolitan authority and local power based upon the existence of undefined and unacknowledged ambiguities in the nature of the metropolitan–colonial relationship. These ambiguities permitted local leaders to achieve a large measure of *de facto* control over the internal governance of the colonies without calling into question long-standing assumptions within Britain about the supremacy of the metropolis over all aspects of colonial life.

But a number of corollary developments between 1720 and 1750 rendered this balance extremely precarious by making it increasingly difficult for metropolitan authorities to retain even an illusion that they had the colonies under any kind of firm control. With the administration showing so little interest in the details of colonial matters, metropolitan institutions charged with overseeing the colonies atrophied. The Board of Trade, the only body for which the colonies were a primary concern, gradually became little more than a housekeeping organization, and a very sloppy one at that. Moreover, the colonial bureaucracy became increasingly politicized during these years, as the ministry expropriated administrative resources for political purposes, and patronage, not expertise or competence, became the main criterion for appointments. These developments helped to break the spirit of governors and other royal officials in the colonies. In all but a few settlements, governors found themselves with insufficient resources to resist strident demands

for power from the colonial lower houses and in many instances simply capitulated to local interests. By 1750, more and more of the governors had become thus creolized.

By the late 1740s, these several developments seemed from the perspective of London to have produced a much more ominous one: the breakdown of metropolitan political control in many of the colonies. From the dispatches and papers that had accumulated in the colonial office, especially after 1745, the situation in America appeared to be truly alarming. Metropolitan merchants complained that the legislatures of several colonies, in direct violation of metropolitan prohibitions, had issued large sums of paper money during the war and were subsequently refusing to enact measures to protect British debts against its rapid depreciation. At the same time, West Indian sugar planters and metropolitan customs officials in the colonies charged that merchants from the continental colonies were violating the Molasses Act of 1733 at will, to the severe economic detriment of the sugar producers. In both instances, colonial behavior showed a blatant disregard for metropolitan authority.

A review of conditions in individual colonies seemed to reveal even greater cause for concern. The situation was most serious in New Jersey, where the inability of the royal administration to restrain widespread rioting against the East Jersey proprietors after 1745 had produced what Lord Chancellor Hardwicke described as "disorders and confusions" that had been "carried almost to the height of revolution."[2] In New Hampshire and North Carolina, legislative activity had been brought to a halt and civil government rendered tenuous as a result of the desperate efforts of the governors to enhance royal power by altering the apportionment of representatives to the lower houses. The same result had been produced in Bermuda by Governor William Popple's vituperative altercation with the assembly over a number of issues. In New York, where Governor George Clinton had engaged in violent quarrels with the lower house over the extensive financial powers it had wrested from him and his predecessor during the early years of the Spanish and French war, the situation was marginally better but only because opposition leaders had not yet, in contrast to their coun-terparts in New Hampshire, North Carolina, and Bermuda, become so enraged with the governor as to cut off all further business with him. In Jamaica, a powerful faction was challenging Governor Edward Trelawny's right to remove judges, while Barbados had only just been rescued from a distracted political state by the prudent behavior of its new governor, Henry Grenville.

From all these colonies and others – from all of the royal colonies except Virginia, Massachusetts, and the Leeward Islands – governors complained frequently, and in ago-nized tones, that they were powerless to carry out metropolitan directives against the opposition of local interests. They charged that the elected assemblies had far too much power and called for the remodeling of the constitutions of the colonies. A growing number of governors thought that the situa-tion could only be corrected through the intervention of Parliament.

In the face of so many such complaints, no wonder that to authorities at a distance in London the whole American empire from Barbados to Nova Scotia seemed to be on the verge of disintegration. At the precise moment at which the economic and strate-gic worth of the colonies was becoming apparent to all and the French seemed to be preparing themselves to challenge British hegemony over them, there thus seemed to be a grave – and general – crisis of metro-politan control over the American Empire. This crisis of control in turn helped to gen-erate a serious crisis of confidence. Colonial officials in Britain responded to the peace of 1748 not with exultation but with strong feelings of unease and anxious fears about the impending loss of the colonies and the consequent decline of Britain itself. Such fears underlay and provided the primary impetus for the shift in colonial policy that would eventually lead to the rebellion of the colonies a little more than a quarter of a century later.

2   Beginnings of the New Policy, 1748–1756

As early as 1745, the Board of Trade responded to the apparent breakdown of

metropolitan authority in the colonies by showing signs of a vigor it had not demon-strated since the early decades of the cen-tury. But it received little support from the administration during the war. Not until November 1748, when the ambitious and energetic George Montagu Dunk, Earl of Halifax, was appointed as the new president of the Board, did the systematic and sus-tained attention called for by the situation begin to be accorded to colonial affairs. For the next eight years, from 1748 until the revival of hostilities with France in 1756, metropolitan officials engaged in a vigorous effort to deal effectively with the many out-standing problems relating to the colonies. This effort fell into two distinct periods.

The first lasted from the fall of 1748 through the winter of 1751–2 and was a period of activity and frustration. Inspired and driven by Halifax, the members of the Board worked with diligence in an effort to define the problems facing it and to work out a system of priorities for dealing with them. The Board gave top priority to the problem of strengthening the defenses of the northern colonies against French Canada by making Nova Scotia into a fully-fledged British colony. In a series of detailed memo-randa and reports emphasizing the colony's strategic importance for the security of the North American Empire, the Board provided the justification that enabled the administra-tion to secure an annual parliamentary grant for Nova Scotia similar to one extended to Georgia for the previous 15 years and suffi-cient to support the subsidized settlement of the colony with British and New England colonists which began in earnest in 1749. At the same time, the Board was less suc-cessful in its efforts to respond to the clam-ors of British merchants against colonial paper currencies. Its bill, introduced into Parlia-ment in March 1749, to restrain the further issuance of paper money in the colonies and to prevent those already in existence from being legal tender, was not enacted.

If Halifax and his colleagues gave highest priority to the settlement of Nova Scotia and the restraint of colonial paper money, they were by no means neglectful of the many problems relating to the internal gov-ernance of the colonies. Initially, the Board's approach to these problems was almost entirely piecemeal and *ad hoc*, as it sought to find an appropriate solution for the particular difficulties of each colony. But its actions all tended in the same general direction: towards much closer supervision over and more intimate involvement with colonial affairs. Demonstrating an impressive attention to detail, the Board read the dispatches and papers transmitted from the colonies with far greater alacrity and care than it had in the past and made increased use of its legal counsel, Matthew Lamb, and the Attorney-General and Solicitor-General to scrutinize colonial laws to determine if they were suitable for confirmation.

In the colonies themselves, the Board insisted that royal governors adhere as strictly as possible to their instructions from the Crown and was quick to censure those who assented to laws in violation of those instructions. Indeed, the Board tried to give those instructions legal standing by including in its 1749 Currency Bill a clause declaring any colonial legislative enactments contrary to those instructions null and void. But this clause provoked such an outburst of opposition from several colonial agents that the administration agreed to reserve it for future consideration.

In the meantime, the almost invariable refusal of all colonial assemblies to comply with the instructions meant that the only effects of the Board's careful scrutiny of colonial legislation and gubernatorial conduct was to deepen discord in the colonies by intimidating governors into taking unyielding stands that were unacceptable to local interests. After 1748, governors had to contend not only with recalcitrant legislatures and other powerful leaders in the colonies but also with a group of metropolitan officials who, given the conditions that had developed over the previous 30 years, were demanding a standard of conduct that was wholly unrealistic. Henceforth, governors had to keep one eye on their adversaries in the colonies and the other closely on their superiors in London.

The positions of the governors in each of the major trouble spots – Bermuda, New Hampshire, North Carolina, New York, and New Jersey – were rendered even more difficult by the Board's inability to secure prompt action upon their several problems. Overwhelmed by a tremendous volume of business, the Board either put the governors of those provinces off or altogether ignored their plaintive letters. During these early years, the Board managed to produce long reports on the two colonies with the most serious problems, New Jersey and New York, recommending sending troops to quiet the riots in the former and the passage by Parliament of a declaratory bill to restrain the extensive authority of the legislature in the latter. But the Board had no authority to enforce its recommendations. Although the Privy Council followed its suggestions for the disallowance of many colonial laws and the ministry in 1751 guided through Parliament a bill to prohibit further issuance of legal tender paper money in the four New England colonies, neither of the reports on New Jersey and New York received ministerial support sufficient to secure its implementation.

Rumors circulated on both sides of the Atlantic that the delays in dealing with the problems of these and other colonies were the result of the ministry's determination "to settle a general plan for establishing the King[']s Authority in all the plantations" before dealing with any of them in particular.[3] In anticipation of such an event, several favor seekers and aspiring imperial statesmen, including James Abercromby, Henry McCulloh, Robert Hunter Morris, and Thomas Pownall, submitted elaborate plans for the overhaul of both metropolitan administration and the colonial constitutions. But no such plan ever received serious ministerial attention. However desperate the colonial situation might appear to Halifax and others who were well informed about it, the ministry exhibited no inclination to undertake comprehensive reform.

Except for the Nova Scotia settlement, the Currency Act of 1751, and a desk full of unheeded reports, Halifax and his colleagues at the Board had little to show for three years of diligent application. Not a single one of the convulsed situations Halifax had inherited when he assumed office had been resolved. To make matters worse, the Board's aggressive behavior towards the governors was even then in the process of escalating relatively minor problems in South Carolina, Jamaica, and the Leeward Islands into major ones. If anything, metropolitan control over the colonies must have seemed to be even more tenuous at the beginning of 1752 than it had four years earlier.

The result was wholesale frustration in both the colonies and the Colonial Office. Clolonial governors still had no more than vague promises from a body that, it was becoming increasingly clear, was unable to deliver on them. The endless delays, punctuated only at infrequent intervals by perfunctory and evasive letters from the Board, drove governors to distraction and despair. That matters of such importance had been so long delayed in resolution was equally dispiriting to Halifax, who pushed hard, beginning in the summer of 1750, to have himself appointed as a separate Secretary of State with broad jurisdiction over and full responsibility for the colonies. Although he failed in this effort because of opposition from George II and the two existing Secretaries of State, he finally succeeded in early 1752 in securing enlarged powers for the Board of Trade. An order in council of March 11 gave the Board exclusive authority over the appointment of all governors, councilors, attorneys-general, and secretaries in the colonies and made those officers directly responsible to the Board.

The enlargement of the Board's powers marked the beginning of a second phase in the metropolitan effort to come to grips with the apparently declining authority of the parent state in the colonies. This period, lasting until the outbreak of the Seven Years' War in 1756, was one of renewed activity – and failure. Armed with its new powers and building upon its experiences over the previous four years, the Board embarked upon an even more vigorous campaign to bring the colonies under closer metropolitan control. It immediately moved to secure more up-to-date information on the colonies by insisting that governors provide new answers to the formal queries hitherto required only irregularly and send home all public papers promptly, and in 1755 it sought to establish more regular communications with the colonies by setting up a packet boat system. The Board also moved to strengthen the defenses of the continental colonies, continuing to promote the settlement of Nova Scotia and converting Georgia into a royal colony in 1754.

Halifax also seems to have sought more effective personnel for appointments both to the Board and to colonial offices. At least in part because he was unable to resist the patronage of his superiors, the caliber of his initial appointees to colonial governorships was not very high. Sir Danvers Osborne of New York committed suicide shortly after his arrival, while Charles Knowles of Jamaica, John Reynolds of Georgia, and William Denny of Pennsylvania proved to be such maladroit politicians that each was either encouraged to resign or cashiered after a stormy tenure in office. Robert Dinwiddie of Virginia, Charles Lawrence of Nova Scotia, Robert Hunter Morris of Pennsylvania, and Arthur Dobbs of North Carolina all performed significantly less well than Sir William Gooch of Virginia and William Shirley of Massachusetts, the most successful of the previous generation of governors. Following these initial mistakes, however, Halifax and his colleagues do seem to have done consistently better during the last half of the 1750s. Most of their appointees served capably, managing to walk the narrow line between the competing demands of their metropolitan superiors and the local political establishment without giving major offense to either.

The standards to which the governors were expected to adhere had been mostly worked out over the previous four years and revolved around the Board's dictum that only in the most extreme circumstances should they ever deviate from their instructions. The Board's insistence upon this point was only a general policy designed to achieve several more specific goals the Board had come to regard as essential for the retention of the colonies as viable parts of the empire. One of the most important of those goals was to check the power of the lower houses of assembly. The Board never seems to have entertained any thought of governing the colonies without assemblies. In both of the new royal colonies of Nova Scotia and Georgia, it insisted upon the establishment of representative government, in the former case even against the opposition of the governor on the spot. But the Board did hope to reduce the power of the assemblies in the older colonies by depriving them of many powers they had long enjoyed, including the right to establish new constituencies, apportion representatives, determine their own tenures, settle accounts, appoint local officers, and exercise a wide variety of other privileges and powers.

To that end, the Board continued to review colonial legislation carefully, to secure disallowance of objectionable statutes, and to insist strenuously, and with few exceptions, upon the inclusion of a clause suspending operation until metropolitan approval had been accorded in an ever-wider variety of colonial laws. It also recommended, though unsuccessfully, that the legislatures of all the colonies follow the example of the Virginia Assembly in reducing all earlier statutes into a clear and well-digested body of laws that (as had happened in the Virginia case) could carefully be pruned of improper statutes by metropolitan authorities. To decrease the extraordinary financial powers of the lower houses, the Board urged the governors to secure laws creating a permanent revenue that would support the entire civil list independent of further legislative appropriations.

In addition to striking at the power of the colonial assemblies, the Board pursued several other policies aimed at securing the same general objectives. After 1752 it sought, whenever the opportunity arose, to rationalize the court systems of individual colonies and to alter the ordinary terms of judicial tenure from good behavior to royal pleasure. It also endeavored to prevent the emission of any further legal-tender paper currency by adamantly insisting that the colonies south of New England comply with the terms of the Currency Act of 1751, even though it did not actually apply to them, and made preliminary investigations aimed at checking the further engrossment of land by large owners, especially in Virginia, New York, and Jamaica. It also sought to extend its jurisdiction over the private colonies, demanding that the corporate colonies of Rhode Island and Connecticut transmit their laws to the Board for information, and seeking

to force the proprietors of Pennsylvania and Maryland to follow the example of the Board in attempting to curtail the authority of the lower houses in those colonies. In the case of Pennsylvania, the Board actually managed to gain a major voice in the selection of governors. Finally, in response to continued complaints from West Indian interests about violations of the Molasses Act by traders from the northern colonies, the Board toyed with the idea of recommending that Parliament revise that act in such a way as to produce a revenue.

The outbreak of hostilities between the Virginians and the French Canadians along the Ohio River in 1754–5 provided an opportunity for Halifax to try to achieve still another of his ideas for augmenting metropolitan colonial authority. The Board had proposed to send troops to quell the riots in New Jersey as early as January 1749. Immediately upon securing enlarged powers for the Board in 1752, Halifax pressed for the appointment of a governor-general for North America who, also acting as governor of New York and New Jersey, would preside over a military force to restore some semblance of metropolitan control in those two colonies. Halifax conceived of this proposal as a major step in the creation of a continental military union that might help the colonies to put forth a concerted effort in the event of a war with French Canada.

This plan got nowhere in 1752 for want of ministerial backing. But the proposal for a unified military command gained steady support in 1754–5 following Braddock's defeat and the Albany Congress. As part of the decision to send more metropolitan troops to the colonies to fight the French, the government appointed a Commander-in-Chief with full military authority over all the colonies. The appointment of two royal commissioners of Indian affairs in 1754 was a slightly earlier and similar move to shift responsibility for Amerindian diplomacy from individual colonial governments to officials directly responsible to Whitehall. The main purpose of this concentration of authority over military and Amerindian affairs was to produce a more effective military effort against the French. But several writers pointed out that the large contingent of British troops being sent to America might also be used to force the colonists to comply with metropolitan measures.

Few people in Britain in 1756 were yet persuaded of the necessity for such draconian measures, but the results of the accelerated effort to tighten metropolitan control over the colonies after 1752 had done little to allay the fears that lay behind such proposals – fears, as one writer put it, that without the "Colonys in America" Britain would lose the "greatest part of" its "Riches and Glory" and become, once again, "a small state not more respectable than Danemark, Sweden, [or] Switzerland."[4] Almost everywhere, in fact, metropolitan initiatives ran into stiff opposition, as the lower houses and other powerful local interests in the colonies refused to accede to them. In one colony after another, the assembly denounced every effort to diminish its authority or enhance metropolitan power as an attack upon their established constitutions and a violation of the traditional and long-standing relationship as it had been gradually worked out over the previous century. Even with its increased power and its new assertiveness, the Board of Trade could not effectively cope with such opposition. It could intimidate its governors into a faithful observance of their instructions. But that only reduced their room for maneuver when, in the absence of effective support from London, they needed all the latitude possible to accomplish the difficult assignments demanded of them.

Not that the metropolitan campaign did not achieve some limited successes. By taking extraordinary pains, the Board of Trade managed in the new civil polities of Georgia and Nova Scotia to make them the models of colony government that, it hoped, would eventually be emulated by the older colonies. In addition, by 1756 political conditions in North Carolina, New Hampshire, New Jersey, and Bermuda were much improved from the chaotic circumstances of the late 1740s. With the possible exception of North Carolina, however, these results owed more to local developments than to metropolitan initiatives. Indeed, the Board's jealous defense of the prerogative and its zealous attacks on the powers of the assemblies had

contributed significantly to the development of new problems in the Leeward Islands, Virginia, South Carolina, Pennsylvania, Georgia, and Massachusetts and had been in major part responsible for throwing Jamaica into total civil chaos. No less than their predecessors a decade earlier, new governors who went to the colonies in the mid-1750s still, despite vigorous metropolitan efforts after 1748, complained that their powers were reduced within narrow limits.

By the beginning of the Seven Years' War in 1756, Halifax and his colleagues were painfully aware that their campaign to amplify metropolitan authority in the colonies was a failure. Especially in the older colonies, both on the continent and on the islands, metropolitan control was not significantly greater in 1756 than it had been eight years earlier when the whole campaign had begun. Unable to accomplish its objectives with the prerogative powers at its command, the Board of Trade from the late 1740s on had been increasingly driven to threaten the intervention of Parliament. Except in the case of the Currency Act of 1751, however, the ministry had proven reluctant to involve Parliament in its reform efforts. But in 1757, the House of Commons, acting with the full approval of the Colonial Office, actually did intervene in the purely domestic affairs of a colony for the first time since 1733. It thereby created an important precedent when it censured the Jamaican Assembly for making extravagant constitutional claims while resisting instructions from London. That metropolitan authorities were quite willing to take similar actions against other colonies was clearly indicated by the pains they took to inform all the colonies of the Commons' action in the Jamaica case.

The metropolitan program of reform between 1748 and 1756 engendered among the colonists considerable, if mostly only temporary, individual, group, and local dissatisfaction with specific metropolitan actions. But it did not produce either the sort of generalized discontent that might have brought the colonists to rebellion or a significant predisposition towards revolution among them. The impact of most of its components was too local to invite collective opposition, and the program as a whole was sufficiently diffuse and contingent as to conceal from those not at or near the center of metropolitan administration its general thrust and implications. Not until the Stamp Act had brought representatives from several colonies together and put earlier metropolitan actions in a new perspective did colonial leaders begin to perceive that, as Christopher Gadsden wrote from South Carolina in December 1765 following his return from the Stamp Act Congress, the "late attacks on different parts of the Constitution in different places" carried "the appearance of design" and were "very alarming."[5]

The result was that the whole program could be interpreted by the colonists as nothing more than some additional episodes in the ongoing efforts of metropolitan administrators to enhance the prerogative in the colonies. By the 1750s such efforts may even have come to seem less threatening than they had been 50 or 100 years earlier when the colonists had had less experience in coping with them. Yet, despite the fact that colonial leaders in most instances had effectively frustrated metropolitan designs between 1748 and 1756, the new aggressiveness in metropolitan behavior clearly exacerbated traditional colonial fears that metropolitan officials were intent upon establishing some extraordinary power over the colonies. By the mid-1750s, some were beginning to worry that the conclusion of the war would bring renewed efforts to strengthen prerogative power in the colonies, while others, disturbed by the rising volume of threats of parliamentary intervention into colonial affairs, were anxious lest Parliament might lend its support to such efforts. Still others predicted that the troops sent to the colonies might eventually be used to keep them in subjection.

However exaggerated such rumors might have been, the efforts of Halifax and his colleagues between 1748 and 1756 clearly constituted a major transformation in metropolitan behavior towards the colonies, the general thrust of which involved a dramatic shift from an essentially permissive to a fundamentally restrictive philosophy of colonial administration. The deep fear that Britain might lose the colonies resulted in the widespread conviction that the colonies had too

many privileges and that those privileges ought to be reduced. In pursuit of such goals, metropolitan authorities between 1748 and 1756 attempted to implement a wide range of measures, many of them the very ones colonials found so objectionable between 1764 and 1776, which seemed to threaten or actually to violate fundamental aspects of the traditional relationship between Britain and the colonies as the colonists had come to perceive that relationship over the previous century.

Yet, the causal significance of this shift in metropolitan posture and policy for the American Revolution lies much less in the relatively localized and transitory pockets of discontent it created in the colonies than in its almost total failure to achieve any of the objectives for which it had been undertaken. For this failure served both to intensify metropolitan fears that the colonies would sooner or later get completely out of hand and to increase metropolitan determination to secure tighter control over the colonies.

3   The Seven Years' War and the New Colonial Policy, 1756–63

The need for a concerted effort against the French during the Seven Years' War forced the suspension of the metropolitan reform effort starting in 1756. But experience during the war exposed the weakness of British colonial authority more fully than ever before and thereby intensified the reform impulses in London. Throughout the war, aggressive lower houses openly used the government's need for defense funds to pry still more authority away from the governors; many colonial traders flagrantly violated the Navigation Acts, in many cases with the implicit connivance of the colonial governments and even of imperial customs officials; and many colonial legislatures failed to comply with metropolitan requisitions for men and money for the war effort – even with the promise of reimbursement. By the concluding years of the war, the question was no longer whether imperial administration would be reformed but how.

Not surprisingly, as soon as the British and colonial armies had defeated the French in Canada in 1759 and 1760 and colonial support for the war was no longer so essential, metropolitan officials undertook a variety of new restrictive measures calculated to restrict the colonists' scope for economic and political activity. Between 1759 and 1764, they both revived most of the measures they had pursued unsuccessfully between 1748 and 1756 and inaugurated several new ones in an attempt to diminish the inflated privileges of the colonial assemblies and to resolve problems that had come to the fore during the war, including especially the lax enforcement of the Navigation Acts.

In these new efforts, metropolitan authorities had the benefit of two important lessons they had learned from their earlier failures. The first was that only a sweeping reformation of the government and trade of all the colonies would be effective. The kinds of *ad hoc* and local solutions attempted between 1748 and 1756 obviously had not worked. The second was that any such comprehensive reconstruction would have to be undertaken by Parliament. Whether even the authority of Parliament would be accepted in the colonies seems not to have been doubted in London. The issue had never been put to the test, and, in the absence of colonial resistance to parliamentary authority, metropolitan officials could comfortably assume that Parliament had jurisdiction over colonial affairs and that its regulations would effectively be obeyed.

4 Lessons and Significance

The conclusions drawn from the experience by the metropolitan political nation, not the many specific and local and largely unconnected grievances they generated among the colonists, are thus the primary reason why the reforms of 1748–56 must be assigned a central place in the causal pattern of the American Revolution. It need not be argued that revolution was logically inevitable thereafter or that, in response to different empirical conditions, metropolitan officials might not have reverted to their earlier policy of salutary neglect. But, by contributing to building sentiment for still more restrictive and, the officials hoped, more effective measures when a favorable opportunity presented itself, metropolitan experiences between 1748 and 1756 helped to stiffen the determination to put colonial affairs on

a more rational – and more controllable – footing. That determination would continue powerfully to inform metropolitan behavior between 1759 and 1776 and would ultimately constitute the primary animating force in driving large and strategic segments of the colonial population to resistance, rebellion, and independence.

REFERENCES

1 Walpole to Duke of Newcastle, June 18, 1754, Newcastle Papers, British Library, London.
2 Hardwicke to Jonathan Belcher, August 31, 1751, in *The Life and Correspondence of Philip Yorke, Earl of Hardwicke*, ed. Philip C. Yorke (Cambridge: Cambridge University Press, 1913), II, 27–9.
3 Cadwallader Colden to George Clinton, February 12, 1750, Clinton Papers, Box 10, William L. Clements Library, Ann Arbor, Michigan.
4 W. M. to William Pitt, November 16, 1756, Chatham Papers, PRO 30/8/95, Pt. I, ff. 194–5, Public Record Office, London.
5 Gadsden to Charles Garth, December 2, 1765, in *The Writings of Christopher Gadsden, 1746–1805*, ed. Richard Walsh (Columbia: University of South Carolina Press, 1966), 67.

FURTHER READING

Basye, Arthur H.: *The Lords Commissioners of Trade and Plantations* (New Haven, Conn.: Yale University Press, 1925).
Bumsted, John: "'Things in the womb of time': ideas of American independence, 1633 to 1763." *William and Mary Quarterly,* 31 (1974), 533–64.
Dean, Phyllis, and Cole, W. A.: *British Economic Growth, 1688–1959: Trends and Structure* (Cambridge, Mass.: Harvard University Press, 1962).
Ernst, Joseph A.: *Money and Politics in America, 1755–1775* (Chapel Hill: University of North Carolina Press, 1973).
Greene, Jack P.: "An uneasy connection: an analysis of the preconditions of the American Revolution," in *Essays on the American Revolution*, ed. Stephen G. Kurtz and James H. Hutson (Chapel Hill: University of North Carolina Press, 1973), 65–80.
——: *The Quest for Power: the Lower Houses of Assembly in the Southern Royal Colonies, 1689–1776* (Chapel Hill: University of North Carolina Press, 1963).

Greene, Jack P., and McLoughlin, William G.: *Preachers & Politicians: Two Essays on the Origins of the American Revolution* (Worcester, Mass.: American Antiquarian Society, 1977).

Henretta, James A.: *"Salutary Neglect": Colonial Administration under the Duke of Newcastle* (Princeton, NJ: Princeton University Press, 1972).

Knollenberg, Bernhard: *Origin of the American Revolution: 1759–1766* (New York: Macmillan, 1960).

Rogers, Alan, *Empire and Liberty: American Resistance to British Authority, 1755–1763* (Berkeley: University of California Press, 1974).

CHAPTER FOURTEEN

The Seven Years' War and its political legacy

THOMAS L. PURVIS

1 Territorial Rivalries Precipitate War

GREAT Britain and France sparred for dominance in North America during three inconclusive conflicts fought between 1689 and 1748 (*see* chapter 4). In response to a French policy of encircling the mainland Anglo-American colonies with military posts at strategic points in disputed regions, Britain authorized armed expeditions to oust French troops from the forks of the Ohio, Lake Champlain, and the Isthmus of Chignecto during 1754 and 1755. The Newcastle ministry hoped to avoid outright war through victories so decisive that the Bourbon court would consider retaking those areas by force to be either futile or prohibitively expensive.

The French held their frontiers everywhere except Acadia, however, and delivered a rude awakening to British illusions of a quick and easy triumph by their stunning upset of General Edward Braddock's army near the forks of the Ohio (July 9, 1755). At the battle of Braddock's Defeat, French and Amerindians not only routed a British force three times their own number, but furthermore inflicted 30 percent casualties while sustaining only minor losses themselves. Braddock's regulars had been destroyed as an effective fighting force; as they limped into Philadelphia, cynics sneered that the king's soldiers had taken up winter quarters in August. Two consequences ensued from this catastrophe: first, it disabused Anglo-Americans of their impulse to idealize the British military as invulnerable – a sentiment that would have

formed a considerable deterrent to risking a war for independence if not dispelled well before 1776; second, it left the Newcastle ministry no alternative but to issue a formal declaration of war against France, which George II proclaimed on May 17, 1756.

2 Wartime Frictions Emerge

The Seven Year's War became the first intercolonial conflict in which large numbers of British regulars fought alongside provincial soldiers in North America. Both forces initially found it awkward to work amicably together. The dismal record of British generalship furthermore encouraged skepticism among Anglo-Americans about both royal troops and the king's ministers through 1757.

Britain's commanders-in-chief for North America at first experienced repeated frustration in getting colonial legislatures to raise the number of soldiers they needed. No assemblies complied fully with requisitions from Whitehall, and a few (Maryland, North Carolina, and Georgia) provided virtually no men or supplies. All the assemblies, to greater or lesser degrees, used the home government's desperate need for colonial aid to coerce governors into signing appropriation bills that either sacrificed their prerogative powers or violated specific instructions from the Board of Trade. The legislatures won their most notable victories by forcing every chief executive to accede to large emissions of legal-tender paper money, which British policy strenuously opposed, as the price of raising provincial troops.

Royal officers generally criticized the quality of provincial units, which rarely came to the field with adequate equipment, sufficient training, or experienced officers. Colonial troops furthermore received their discharges in late fall, sometimes before the British commander-in-chief declared that year's campaign over, and the cycle would have to be repeated the following spring when fresh levies took their place. "And for my part," wrote an exasperated British colonel in 1757, "I wou[l]d rather have no Troops than to be at the Trouble & expense to form them, & when the[y] could begin to be able to perform their Duty, be oblig'd to disband them."[1]

Royal officers likewise encountered many local leaders and ordinary citizens who acted more like adversaries than allies when regular forces sought recruits, logistical supplies, or winter billets. Magistrates issued writs of habeas corpus to release servants from British recruiting parties that had unlawfully inveigled them to join the service without their masters' consent; they also intervened to void enlistments by free men if evidence surfaced that they had been enrolled through fraud, deception, or alcohol. Sheriffs and justices of the peace often sympathized with farmers who refused to comply with royal impress orders obliging them to surrender horses or wagons needed by the military, and neglected to fine them. Despite the urgent need to find winter housing for royal troops once the campaign season ended, dozens of town councils and several assemblies vigorously fought army efforts to quarter soldiers in private homes, even though no barracks or other practical alternative existed to furnish the necessary shelter. Lord Loudoun, British commander-in-chief, summarized the view of most royal officers in 1756 when he alleged that "[t]here is resistance against everything that is military in this country."[2]

Royal officers expressed additional disappointment that many American officers seemed unwilling to give them any more than grudging cooperation. Bad blood had been left simmering, between the two corps of officers by a War Office directive of November 12, 1754, which defined rank between them. This order gave British

officers precedence over all colonials with identical rank through major (grades in which few provincials outranked any British counterparts), but then severely discriminated against colonial commanders of battalions, regiments, and brigades (colonels and generals) by subordinating them to any major of regulars. That policy generated enormous ill-will between British and American field-grade officers, besides sowing indignation among both junior officers and colonial elites, who interpreted it as a gratuitous insult belittling their own colony's contribution to the war effort.

Ordinary colonial soldiers also took strong exception to the frequent failure of British commanders to honor the term of service for which they joined. Entire provincial units were kept on duty weeks past their expected discharge dates, while colonists in the regular army might wait for their discharges many months, or more than a year, after their enlistment had ended. Thousands of Americans reacted to this predicament with deep disaffection and sullen insubordination that sometimes ended in mutinous disorders.

These tensions between the British military and Anglo-Americans resembled, on a smaller scale, conflict sparked by the Royal Army's expansion in Great Britain. English magistrates and other officials vigorously resisted efforts to quarter troops in their communities, invalidated the enlistment of apprentices by recruiting parties, and sometimes confined army or navy officers to jail on trumped-up charges. Crowds frequently assaulted army recruiters or navy press gangs and rescued persons thought to have been tricked into enlisting. Innumerable communities harbored deserters and protected them from arrest. Extensive rioting convulsed ten English shires in 1757, when rumors circulated that men would be drafted from the militia into the regulars; the government only restored order after deploying 5,200 infantry and cavalry against mobs who swore "that they had rather be hanged in England, than Scalped in America."[3]

From 1754 to 1757, the Newcastle ministry had much difficulty building support for the war effort, because it appeared to have blundered into an expensive struggle that was enormously disruptive of its citizens' lives, without offering much hope of a decisive outcome. A sizeable minority of Englishmen acted as if a large-scale military mobilization threatened their personal liberty and property rights, and even many colonists behaved as if they were ambivalent toward a war raging on their own frontiers. Beginning in mid-1757, however, support for the government's war policy swelled dramatically in both the British Isles and America.

3 The Mainland Colonies Mobilize for Victory, 1757–1763

The year 1757 brought new military setbacks for the British, but it also marked a critical turning point, in which the empire began to summon the political will to defeat France once William Pitt became prime minister. Pitt's oratory electrified the House of Commons, and he soon captured the empire's imagination with his fighting spirit and grim determination; under his leadership, the war inexorably evolved from a desultory stalemate in the wilderness to a crusade aimed at forcing France to sue for peace from a position of military weakness and then cede valuable possessions. Pitt recognized that the colonies' manpower resources had barely been tapped and could prove decisive, so he gave priority to mobilizing the largest possible number of provincials for ensuing campaigns.

Pitt stimulated a groundswell of military support from American legislatures by promising to reimburse the bulk of costs incurred by them in raising soldiers. In both 1758 and 1759, the colonies sent 21,000 provincials into battle, fully half the troops under the British Commander-in-Chief for North America, and enabled Britain – for the first time in the war – to attempt the conquest of Canada. Since the Seven Years' War was a global struggle, in which Britain's limited population resources strained its ability to field armed forces equal to its enemies, the colonial mobilization had strategic ramifications far beyond Canada: by eliminating the need for the ministry to send any significant reinforcements of regulars to

North America after 1757, the provincial levies freed many thousands of redcoats raised in Britain to fight in Germany, the Caribbean, and India, where they were desperately wanted.

Pitt and his generals devised practical solutions to problems that had bedeviled relations between regulars and provincials. The prime minister ended the rank controversy that had aroused so much animosity between senior officers of both corps by decreeing that colonial field-grade officers would no longer have to take orders from any regulars of a lesser grade (modified only by a special warrant promoting all British lieutenant colonels in America to brevet colonels). The British government also took steps to improve the quality of provincial units by supplying them with stands of new arms, camp equipage, and other necessary items whose former shortages had seriously hobbled the colonials' effectiveness.

Friction between Anglo-American civilians and the British army also subsided substantially after 1757. The controversy over quartering redcoats in private homes had largely abated by 1759, since most royal troops spent their winters garrisoned at frontier outposts, while those few behind the lines occupied barracks built for them at provincial expense. The British army likewise had developed a satisfactory logistics system by the late 1750s, and no longer made extensive use of the hated impress orders to seize wagons and draught animals from reluctant farmers. Regular soldiers moreover seem to have conducted the enlistment service more reputably than earlier in the war, so that magistrates were called on less often to investigate complaints that servants were wrongfully recruited or freemen were deceived – if not shanghaied – into joining the army.

The war years of 1758 through 1763 marked the pinnacle of British and Anglo-American cooperation. By the conflict's end, at least 60,000 Anglo-Americans had served in provincial units against the French and another 12,000 enlisted in British regular units, whereas only about 21,000 redcoats had been sent from Britain to fight in the Canadian theatre of operations. If the number of men who performed duty on privateers, as rangers, or in the *bateaux* corps were also included, perhaps two-fifths of all adult males completed some military service during the war, a higher ratio of the population than entered the army or navy from Great Britain.

4   The Political Legacy of the Seven Years' War

Victory invariably heals most wounds between fractious allies, and so, for Anglo-Americans in 1763, the British Empire's triumph over France far outweighed fading memories of wartime frictions with redcoats in the war's early years. The conflict enshrined British statesmen and soldiers at the forefront of the colonists' pantheon of heroes. William Pitt had innumerable communities named after him. Almost every college consistently lauded James Wolfe, the daring victor at Quebec, in its annual commencement poem well into the 1770s, while Israel Putnam, a future rebel general, named his Connecticut tavern the "Genl Wolfe." The Massachusetts Assembly commemorated just one fallen hero from the war with a monument, and that was to honor George Augustus Howe, a general in the Royal Army enormously popular among provincials, who died leading Americans at Ticonderoga. The Seven Years' War imbued the colonists with pride in the British Empire and a visceral sense of English identity.

The war left Britain's upper class grousing that the colonists had not made contributions in the struggle equal to their abilities, however. This perception stemmed in part from lack of information about colonial participation in military campaigns, a point that Benjamin Franklin noted as early as 1756. "They say," wrote Franklin, "that last Year, at Nova Scotia, 2000 New England Men, and not more than 200 Regulars, were join'd in the Taking [of Fort] Beau Sejour; yet it could not be discover'd by the Account sent by Govr. Lawrence, and publish'd in the London Gazette, that there was a single New England-Man concern'd in the Affair."[4]

Britain's political elite also tended to discount the colonial military contribution because, from their perspective, the most important measure of support for a war effort was not the number of soldiers mustered, but the amount of taxes paid and debt incurred. The aristocracy and landed gentry, who owed most taxes, endured increasing levies on their rent rolls that peaked at 25 percent of annual income. Britain's national debt moreover nearly doubled from £72,289,673 in 1755 to £129,586,789 by 1764, with annual interest charges exceeding £5,000,000, while the accumulated colonial debt was about £1,000,000 in 1764. England's landed elite, whose members dominated Parliament, felt enormous resentment that Parliament had voted over £1,000,000 in subsidies for the 13 colonies, about 40 percent of their total military expenditures, for raising troops in a war initiated to defend the Anglo-Americans' very own frontiers. When it was learned that garrisoning and governing the conquered territories of Canada and Florida would entail annual costs of nearly £250,000, irresistible pressure began building for the colonies to bear part of that expense through a parliamentary tax.

As British public opinion turned increasingly antagonistic toward Anglo-Americans, political support materialized for measures that would reform imperial administration through stricter supervision and control over the colonies. The Board of Trade had unsuccessfully tried to strengthen metropolitan authority from 1748 to 1755; it abandoned those efforts during the Seven Years' War to avoid offending American legislators, whose help was needed against the French (*see* chapter 13). The war confronted Whitehall's bureaucrats with several problems that reinforced their predisposition for tighter control over the colonies: allegations of widespread American smuggling indicated that enforcement of the Navigation Acts had grown too slack; as the amount of paper money circulating expanded by 355 percent in North America from 1754 to 1764, British merchants lobbied the Board of Trade to resume its former antagonism against fiat currencies; Pontiac's uprising of 1763 stirred concern that Anglo-American expansion, if left unchecked, could trigger future Amerindian conflicts that would drain the Treasury; and most importantly, Whitehall concluded from the recalcitrance shown by a handful of colonies (Maryland, Pennsylvania, and North Carolina) that to comply with royal requisitions for wartime assistance, Parliament should establish a tax in America to help offset the cost of occupying the former enemy territories of Canada and Florida. It was consequently issues arising out of the Seven Years' War that furnished the very rationale underlying those British policies most objectionable to Anglo-Americans in the early 1760s, namely the customs service's crackdown on colonial smuggling that spawned the writs of assistance controversy, the Proclamation of 1763, the Sugar Act, the Currency Act of 1764, the Quartering Act of 1765, and the Stamp Act (*see* chapters 15 and 20).

The impact of these measures, as James Otis observed in 1764, was to "set people a thinking, in six months, more than they had done in their whole lives before."[5] The Grenville ministry's program struck the colonies like a thunderbolt precisely because the Seven Years' War had absorbed their population's energies to an unprecedented degree. Like other Americans, Otis took immense pride in the provincial contribution to victory over the French. "In the late war the *northern colonies* not only raised their full quota of men but they went even beyond their ability," he affirmed, "the flower of *our* youth were annually pressed by ten thousands into the service."[6] Despite what Otis and other Americans saw as incontrovertible evidence that "the Colonies had been so remarkable for loyalty," they discovered themselves facing a sudden barrage of new restrictions, unprecedented taxes, and an unmistakable posture of hostility directed against them from Britain.

An especially spirited boldness marked the protests of colonies that had been most energetic in prosecuting the Seven Years' War. Virginia, Massachusetts, and New York had exerted themselves to an extraordinary degree against the French in the number of troops raised, money expended, and indebtedness incurred. These three colonies took the lead in protesting the Grenville program, and this forwardness sprung in large part from an intensely felt sense of betrayal

upon realizing that their wartime sacrifices had not brought the esteem to which they thought themselves entitled, but rather rank ingratitude, punitive laws, and unconstitutional taxes.

It was the crowning irony of the Seven Years' War to create conditions that would precipitate a constitutional crisis at the very moment when the 13 colonies had made significant contributions to Great Britain's emergence as Europe's foremost imperial power. The colonial military mobilization had been essential in enabling Britain to conquer Canada, but the assemblies attracted frequent criticism at Whitehall because – like most democratic institutions (including Parliament) – they not only tended to wage war inefficiently, but also constrained royal officials to accept help on their own terms, often in violation of British policy. By the war's end, a consensus had emerged among British leaders that the colonies needed to be brought under closer supervision; mounting pressure came simultaneously from the aristocracy and landed gentry to relieve their crushing tax burden by finding new sources of revenue in the provinces. Once the Grenville program came in response to these impulses, Anglo-Americans opposed it vigorously, in large part because they had taken fresh stock of themselves and grown in self-confidence after making unprecedented sacrifices to help defeat western Europe's largest kingdom. Having left in its wake a never-ending financial crisis that would drive British leaders repeatedly to seek a colonial revenue, while stiffening American readiness to oppose parliamentary taxes, the Seven Years' War created the political circumstances chiefly responsible for producing the Stamp Act crisis and the Townshend Acts crisis (*see* chapters 16 and 17).

REFERENCES

1 Henry Bouquet to Arthur Dobbs, Sep. 29, 1757, in J. L. Tottenham and L. M. Waddell, eds., *The Papers of Henry Bouquet*, 5 vols. to date (Harrisburg, Pa.: Pennsylvania Historical and Museum Commission, 1951–), I, 201.

2 Loudoun to Commodore Holmes, Sep. 30, 1756. Loudoun Papers, Henry E. Huntington Library, San Marino, California.

3 J[ob] S[tanton] Charlton to Duke of Newcastle, Aug. 27, 1757. Newcastle Papers, British Library, London.
4 Benjamin Franklin to Sir Everard Fawkener, July 27, 1756, in Leonard W. Labaree, et al., eds., *The Papers of Benjamin Franklin*, 33 vols. to date (New Haven: Yale University Press, 1960–) VI, 473.
5 *The Rights of the British Colonies Asserted and Proved* (Boston, 1764), 54.
6 Ibid., 72.

FURTHER READING

Anderson, Fred: *A People's Army: Massachusetts Soldiers and Society in the Seven Years' War* (Chapel Hill: University of North Carolina Press, 1984).

Greene, Jack P.: "Social Context and the Causal Pattern of the American Revolution: A Preliminary Consideration of New-York, Virginia and Massachusetts," *La Revolution Americaine et L'Europe*, Colloques Internationaux du Centre National de la Recherche Scientifique (No. 577, 1979), 25–63.

Knollenberg, Bernhard: *Origin of the American Revolution: 1759–1766* (New York: Macmillan Press, 1961).

Leach, Douglas E.: Roots of Conflict: British Armed Forces and Colonial Americans (Chapel Hill: University of North Carolina Press, 1986), see chapters 5, 6, 7.

Middleton, Richard, *The Bells of Victory: The Pitt–Newcastle Ministry and the Conduct of the Seven Years' War, 1757–1762* (Cambridge: Cambridge University Press, 1985).

Purvis, Thomas L., "The Seven Years' War (1754–1763)," in Alan Gallay, ed., *Colonial Wars of North America, 1512–1763: An Encyclopedia* (New York: Garland Publishing, 1996), 686–93.

Rogers, Alan, *Empire and Liberty: American Resistance to British Authority, 1755–1763* (Berkeley: University of California Press, 1974).

CHAPTER FIFTEEN

The Grenville program, 1763–1765

PETER D. G. THOMAS

THE Stamp Act of 1765 is conventionally taken as the commencement of the sequence of events immediately comprising the American Revolution. But it was only the most famous of the series of policy decisions concerning the colonies enacted by George Grenville's ministry of 1763–5. For by 1763, after a generation of war and a century of neglect, the British Government had turned its attention to America. The measures enacted during the next two years forced the colonies to face up to the implications of imperial rule.

The key decisions for new colonial expenditure and for consequential taxation of America had already been made when Grenville became Prime Minister in April 1763. There always had been an army in America. The change in 1763 was that this would be much larger than before in peacetime. The reason given to Parliament on March 4, 1763 by the Bute ministry was France's decision to maintain 20,000 soldiers in its West Indian colonies. This potential menace from Britain's traditional enemy, and the need to control the new subjects of Canada, then estimated at 90,000, meant that the army would be garrisoned for the most part outside the 13 old colonies – in Canada, the Floridas, and the wilderness of the Mississippi and Ohio valleys. It is a long-exploded myth that the British Army was in America to maintain military control over the settlement colonies. Nor was it to be the size of 10,000 men customarily stated. That was the establishment only for the transitional year of 1764. Thereafter it was 7,500 until further reductions took place from 1770.

The Bute ministry assumed that the cost burden of this army would be unacceptable to Parliament. Estimated in 1763 at only £225,000, the average annual cost between 1763 and 1775 was to be £384,000. The announcement of the decision about a large American army was therefore coupled with a promise that after the first year the colonies themselves would pay for the American army.

These were not the only policies inherited by the Grenville ministry. Lord Egremont, the minister responsible for the colonies as Southern Secretary, already had a scheme ready to fix a western boundary for the existing colonies. New settlements in Amerindian territory had been discouraged since 1761. There was to be military occupation only of the western lands, and regulation of trade with the Amerindian tribes. The policy was recommended by Egremont to the Board of Trade on May 5, 1763 and, after news of the Pontiac Rising, enacted by the Proclamation of October 7. New colonies were created in Quebec, East Florida, and West Florida, with the area west of the mountain watershed left as an Amerindian reservation (*see* chapter 19).

More central to Grenville's colonial policy, and certainly closer to his heart, was the detailed investigation during 1763 into American evasion of the trade laws: the Customs Board estimated the average annual revenue from the American customs to be a mere £1,800. This state of affairs was found intolerable by a Prime Minister whose guiding principles were strict adherence to legality and financial solvency. Attempts to enforce the existing trade regulations, as by incentives to naval officers and customs officials, preceded their alteration by Parliament in the American Duties Act of 1764. That comprised numerous alterations in the trade laws and new methods of enforcement. The most controversial was the creation of a new vice-admiralty court for the trial of smuggling cases at Halifax, Nova Scotia, a location remote from local pressures, and a mode of procedure where judges sat without juries (*see* chapter 20, §2).

1 The Molasses Act

But the most famous provision of this measure, which has often given it the name of the Sugar Act, was the alteration of the molasses duty so as to convert it into a source of revenue as well as a trade regulation. This was the first deliberate attempt to tax the colonies and to fulfil the promise of 1763: for the money was to be used towards the cost of the army in America. The Molasses Act of 1733 had imposed what was intended as a prohibitive 100 percent duty of 6d a gallon on the import of foreign molasses, used to make rum. This was evaded by smuggling and by collusion with the customs officers, who charged about 10 percent of the duty. The revenue had been around £700 a year, instead of the £200,000 to be expected from a trade estimated at eight million gallons. Grenville's Treasury Board dropped the idea of prohibition, accepting that the trade was vital to the economy of New England, which bought the molasses with its fish and lumber. The rate of duty that would produce the highest revenue became the Treasury's sole concern. At the end of 1763 this was calculated to be 3d a gallon, which would reduce molasses imports by two-ninths but yield £78,000. On February 27, 1764 the Treasury Board confirmed this decision by rejecting a memorial from colonial agents asking for a duty of only 2d.

The proposal was introduced to Parliament as part of Grenville's Budget on March 9. He justified the decision by reminding MPs of Britain's vast expenditure on behalf of America during the recent war; and explained that the molasses duty had the twofold aim of producing a revenue and maintaining imperial preference, since there would still

be no duty on molasses from the British West Indies. There was little criticism, for the idea of a colonial tax was popular with independent opinion in the Commons. The right of Parliament to raise such taxation was generally assumed, and no MP publicly challenged it. The Duke of Newcastle, head of the main opposition party, was under pressure from the West Indies interest not to delay the Bill. The only important debate arose over the rate of duty, when an amendment at the Committee stage on March 22 for a reduction to 2d was defeated by 147 votes to 55.

2 The Currency Act

There was also parliamentary legislation in 1764 on the status of colonial paper money as legal tender. The assemblies issued paper bills of credit for a specified number of years, and they served as legal local currency. The Currency Act of 1764 applied only to the nine colonies south of New England, which had had a similar act since 1751. Only two colonies, Virginia and North Carolina, had a suspect currency, but the British Government thought a general regulation preferable to a discriminatory measure. The problem centered on the use of depreciated Virginia currency for the payment of debts due from that colony to British creditors. Early in 1763 the Board of Trade, during the Bute ministry, had warned the Virginia Assembly to mend its ways, but without effect. The Board thereupon took up the matter at the end of the year, and on February 9, 1764 its President Lord Hillsborough sent to the Privy Council a report condemning the practice of legal-tender paper money as fraudulent and unjust. It recommended a ban both on all future issues and on extending the time-limit of current paper money when it expired. The Grenville ministry, however, showed no inclination to enact the proposal that session, and it might have lapsed but for the initiative of Anthony Bacon, an MP concerned in trade to North Carolina. On April 4, he moved for a bill to prohibit immediately all colonial paper money as legal tender, and met a favorable reception for this idea. Colonial agents and parliamentary friends of America thereupon at once agreed to accept the Board of Trade report, since that would not cancel existing monetary issues. That was the basis of the Currency Act, which therefore had little immediate effect and did not incur sustained colonial criticism until after the Stamp Act crisis.

3 The Stamp Act

That the American colonies should, like Britain, pay stamp duties was an idea often proposed before 1763, when such a suggestion from the London merchant Henry McCulloh found favor with Grenville, then seeking a colonial revenue. On September 8 the Treasury instructed McCulloh to consult with Thomas Cruwys, Solicitor to the Stamp Office, about drafting appropriate legislation. Preparation of the Bill continued until March 9, 1764 in the expectation that it would form part of Grenville's financial plans. In his Budget speech that day Grenville spoke of the stamp duty as a measure intended for that year, and moved a resolution accordingly. He then changed his mind during the debate, accepting the argument of John Huske, a native American, that due notice of such an important step ought to be sent to the colonies, and it was postponed until 1765.

Since various colonial agents formed conflicting impressions of Grenville's intention, they had a meeting with the Prime Minister on May 17 to clarify the point. Grenville explained his determination to introduce a Stamp Duties Bill in 1765, but he would listen to any colonial suggestions on the subject: one agent, Charles Garth, even thought he was willing to accept an alternative parliamentary tax. What Grenville made clear was that he would not agree to the 26 colonies in North America and the West Indies each taxing themselves instead. There is no substance in the contemporary and historical allegation that Grenville on March 9 said that he would allow this, and then later withdrew the offer. Grenville agreed to meet the agents again early in 1765 before any legislation was enacted, in order to learn the view of the colonists. He apparently envisaged the colonial role as combining general consent to the proposed taxation, which might establish a valuable precedent for prior

consultation, with the opportunity to suggest detailed modifications.

Grenville, however, failed to send his proposal through the proper channel of an official letter to colonial governors. It is not known whether every colony was even informed by its agent. Certainly no suggestions about either the stamp duties or alternative parliamentary taxes were received by the British Government. Instead colonial agents were instructed to oppose the Stamp Bill, and a delegation met Grenville on February 2, 1765 to suggest the adoption of the traditional method of requisitions, whereby the Crown asked each individual colony for money. Grenville believed that this procedure had not worked satisfactorily even in wartime, and rejected the idea.

The postponement of the Stamp Bill was for political reasons, and there is little evidence to substantiate the idea that lack of detailed information was a motive; for during the summer of 1764 the ministry did little more than obtain precise details of legal documents used in the colonies. Thomas Whately, Treasury Secretary, was the politician in charge of the Bill, and on December 6 he explained the principles to the Treasury Board. The duties were to be lower than the equivalent ones in Britain, but they would be widespread for fairness, more than 50 altogether. Only nine, all non-recurrent, were over £1, and those likely to be paid often were nearly all 1/- or less. The final draft of the Bill stipulated that stamped paper would have to be used for newspapers, many legal documents, and ships' clearance documents, so the tax would be paid regularly by printers, lawyers or their clients, and merchants. A whole range of other items would also be taxed, such as liquor licenses, land grants, press advertisements, pamphlets, playing cards, dice, and calendars. Very few colonists would escape altogether.

By the time the Stamp Bill was introduced into Parliament the chief motive of the Grenville ministry had changed from the collection of revenue to the assertion of sovereignty. News of colonial protests during 1764 against Parliament's intention to tax America (*see* chapter 16, §1) caused Whately to write to an American correspondent on February 9, 1765 of "the important point it establishes, the right of Parliament to lay an internal tax on the colonies. We wonder here that it was ever doubted. There is not a single member of Parliament that will dispute it" (Thomas, 1975, p. 86). The Grenville ministry did not proceed with the Stamp Act in ignorance of colonial opinion, but thought the measure would be accepted under protest.

The main parliamentary debate took place on February 6, when Grenville introduced the stamp tax resolutions. He used the argument of virtual representation as the basis of Parliament's right to tax America, and said that in Britain fewer than 5 percent were directly represented. Nor had any colony been granted exemption, by charter or otherwise. The defense of America was expensive, and the burden of the colonists' own internal taxation very light. The revenue from stamp duties would increase as the colonies prospered, and the tax would be largely self-enforcing through the nullity of unstamped documents. Colonial objections were to all taxation, not to this particular method. If Parliament backed down now, he said, America would never be taxed. Although a dozen MPs during the subsequent debate opposed imposition of the tax, none challenged Parliament's right to do so, not even Isaac Barré, who on this occasion made his famous reference to Americans as "Sons of Liberty," whose ancestors had fled from tyranny in Britain. The West Indies planter and City radical William Beckford, a follower of the absent William Pitt, put a procedural motion to postpone a decision, but it was defeated by 245 to 49. That was the only parliamentary vote on the stamp tax in 1765. This test of opinion deterred critics of the Bill subsequently from more than desultory sniping. During its passage, however, the ministry shifted its ground from Grenville's initial contention of virtual representation to the claim of the right of Parliament to tax and pass laws for the colonies as the supreme legislature of the British Empire. On February 21 a clause was added to enforce the measure by vice-admiralty courts; but to meet complaints about the remoteness of Halifax, three more would be created at Boston, Philadelphia, and Charles Town. There was no debate in the House of Lords on the Stamp Bill, which received the royal assent on March 22.

Great care had been taken to make the Stamp Act acceptable to the colonies. The total tax envisaged was small. The wide range of duties, which averaged only about 70 percent of their equivalent in Britain, had been devised to provide an equitable distribution of the burden. All money raised by both this tax and the 1764 molasses duty would be handed over to army paymasters in the colonies. There was never any foundation for the contemporary and historical myth that Britain would drain money from America. The two revenue measures would cover only one-third of the annual army cost in the colonies, now being estimated at £350,000, and Britain would have to cover the balance. The Stamp Act, moreover, was to be administered by leading resident colonists, not by officials sent out from Britain. This decision was implemented as soon as the legislation had passed. The key post was that of Stamp Distributor, one for each colony. It would provide income, power, and prestige, and was bestowed as patronage; for colonial resistance was not anticipated in London at the time, even by men, such as Benjamin Franklin, recently arrived from America.

4 The Quartering Act

Before the Stamp Act was passed the Grenville ministry unexpectedly found itself called upon to initiate what would be another controversial colonial measure, the Mutiny Act, also known as the Quartering Act. On March 1 there arrived a letter from General Thomas Gage, army Commander-in-Chief in America, complaining of difficulties over the quartering of soldiers and other problems caused by colonial obstruction. The Secretary at War Welbore Ellis informed Lord Halifax, now Southern Secretary, that Britain's Mutiny Act did not apply to the colonies, and was directed to prepare one. His first draft authorized the billeting of soldiers in private houses when necessary, and was altered by Grenville to a vague phrase endorsing previous practice. This was still liable to the same political objection, billeting being an infringement of personal liberty, and was fiercely attacked in the Commons on April 1 for that reason. The ministry faced a parliamentary storm over the Bill, and used the Easter recess to consult colonial agents and other experts. The solution was a clause authorizing the billeting of soldiers on uninhabited buildings if no barracks or ale-houses were available. A further new clause stipulated that in such cases the colony concerned should provide the soldiers, free of charge, with heat and light, bedding and cooking utensils, and beer or cider. This provisions clause was to be the controversial part of the Mutiny Bill, but in 1765 no complaint was anticipated about a measure deliberately altered to meet colonial objections as understood in London.

5 Grenville's Influence

The notion of a "Grenville program" for America is too modern a concept. That Grenville's ministry gave so much attention to the colonies was due not to any positive ideological approach, but to the need to solve problems, old and new. The phrase also implies a coherence that did not exist, for the colonial measures sprang from diverse antecedents. The Proclamation of 1763 was for the most part based on earlier wartime decisions. The policy of maintaining a large army in America, and the crucial public commitment to finance it by a colonial tax, were both legacies of the Bute ministry. The initiative for the Currency Act came from an independent MP. The Mutiny Act was prompted by a request of General Gage. Yet there are two circumstances that

do give the phrase "Grenville program" some validity. Grenville's American measures can be seen as part of a wider British attempt in the 1760s and 1770s at a reconstruction of the empire that involved tighter control over not only America but also India and Ireland, while there can be no doubt that the conscientious and industrious Grenville left his personal mark on American policy. A great deal was done in a short time. Grenville, a financier with a legal background, was shocked at the disorder and defiance of authority revealed in the American scene. Hence the comment of an anonymous contemporary, "Mr. Grenville lost America because he read the American despatches, which his predecessors had never done" (Thomas, 1975, p. 113). The Stamp Act was introduced to restore Britain's authority as much as to raise money.

FURTHER READING

Bullion, J. L.: *A Great and Necessary Measure: George Grenville and the Genesis of the Stamp Act, 1763–1765* (Princeton, NJ: Princeton University Press, 1982).

Ernst, J. A.: "Genesis of the Currency Act of 1764: Virginia paper money and protection of British investments," *William and Mary Quarterly*, 22 (1965), 33–74.

Lawson, P.: *George Grenville: a Political Life* (Oxford: Clarendon Press, 1984).

Morgan, E. S.: "The postponement of the Stamp Act," *William and Mary Quarterly*, 7 (1950), 353–92.

Thomas, P. D. G.: *British Politics and the Stamp Act Crisis: the First Phase of the American Revolution, 1763–1767* (Oxford: Clarendon Press, 1975).

CHAPTER SIXTEEN

The Stamp Act crisis and its repercussions, including the Quartering Act controversy

PETER D. G. THOMAS

THE Stamp Act crisis was the first phase of the American Revolution. It raised the basic issue of Britain's sovereignty over her settlement colonies. The measures of Grenville's ministry, and especially the passage of the Stamp Act, were based on British assumptions that Parliament had complete legislative authority over the empire. It was a sovereignty that had never hitherto been exercised in this positive manner. While British opinion could see no distinction between taxation and other modes of legislation, the American colonists certainly did. Although the first colonial challenge concerned only taxation, the implications embraced the whole of Parliament's sovereignty, as Grenville pointed out when on February 6, 1765 he introduced the Stamp Act resolutions. "The objection of the colonies is from the general right of mankind not to be taxed but by their representatives. This goes to all laws in general" (Thomas, 1975, p. 89). He was referring then to the protests of 1764. After the passage of the Stamp Act in 1765 the colonists did more than complain. They nullified the operation of that measure, and adopted retaliatory devices to compel a change of British policy. This was achieved in 1766, but not as the Americans either believed or would have wished.

1 The Colonies Complain in 1764

In 1764 the American colonies were confronted with the news of the Sugar Act and of the prospective stamp duties. They were already suffering from a postwar economic depression. News of the actual and intended taxes, on top of what seemed a bleak future, prompted alarm. It was natural for the colonists to question the constitutional right of Parliament so to alter their lives. But while there could be no doubt over the ominous significance of the proposed stamp duties, the Sugar Act was the adaptation of trade regulations to an additional purpose of revenue. The wording of the act showed the molasses duty was intended as a tax (*see* chapter 15, §1), but the traditional method employed led to a confused response. It was also one limited geographically, since that duty would directly affect only a few colonies. The Massachusetts politician James Otis did challenge the Sugar Act as a tax in his pamphlet *Rights of the British Colonies Asserted and Proved*. But his stand was not a typical response.

Massachusetts, Rhode Island, and New York had already protested about the Sugar Act before its passage, though their complaints had arrived too late. They were the colonies most likely to suffer from it. Of the 127 rum distilleries listed for North America in 1763 which used molasses as their raw material, 64 were in Massachusetts and 40 in Rhode Island and Connecticut; none were south of Pennsylvania. Aware of the potential damage to their trade and industry, Massachusetts and Rhode Island complained about the Sugar Act only on economic grounds, but the New York

Assembly protested about this exploitation of a trade duty to extract revenue. "All impositions, whether they be internal taxes, or duties paid for what we consume, equally diminish the estates upon which they are charged: what avails it to any people, by which of them they are impoverished" (Morgan and Morgan, 1963, p. 56). But North Carolina was the only other colony to complain about the Sugar Act as a tax.

The prospect of a universal stamp tax provoked a wider response. Massachusetts sent a petition to the Commons asking for a continuation of the "privilege" of internal taxation, evidently with the proposed stamp duties in mind. Altogether the assemblies of at least eight colonies protested against the proposed Stamp Act, the others being Rhode Island, Connecticut, New York, Pennsylvania, Virginia, North Carolina, and South Carolina. The evidence may be incomplete, for South Carolina's agent told his colony that all the agents had been instructed to oppose the measure. No colony took up Grenville's offer to consider modifications of the stamp duties or suggested alternative parliamentary taxation. To do so would have been an acknowledgment of Parliament's right. It was this invariable and possibly unanimous response of the colonies that Grenville perceived as a challenge to parliamentary sovereignty over America, and made him determined to proceed with the Stamp Act.

2   The Colonies Protest in 1765

News of the passage of the Stamp Act reached the American colonies during April 1765. The initial response was not indignation, but resignation. William Smith, an author of the 1764 New York protest, commented that "this single stroke has lost Great Britain the affection of all her colonies" (Morgan and Morgan, 1963, p. 121), but he did not envisage any riposte. Still less did Lieutenant-Governor Thomas Hutchinson of Massachusetts, who on June 4 wrote from Boston that "the Stamp Act is received among us with as much decency as could be expected. We shall execute it" (Gipson, 1961, p. 291). None of the assemblies still in session made any response until May 29.

The Virginia House of Burgesses was only one-third full when the young lawyer Patrick Henry, a nine-day member, rose to win instant fame. The legend that he defied shouts of treason has long been exploded. But he did carry five resolutions asserting the doctrine of no taxation without representation. The evidence as to precisely what happened is unsatisfactory, but it would appear that his boldest resolution, claiming for the assembly the exclusive right of taxation, was carried by only one vote and expunged the next day. The opposition to Henry came from men who had put forward similar doctrines in the 1764 petition, and merely reflected personal animosity. The significance of the Virginia Resolves was the publicity afforded them in the colonial press, and the more so in that it was misleading. Henry had drafted seven resolutions, and one of the others was a declaration to disobey parliamentary taxation. The Virginia Assembly had discussed the question of resisting the Stamp Act, but had decided not to endorse such a stand. But the American newspapers conveyed the opposite impression by printing all of Henry's resolutions as if they had been voted by the assembly.

The Virginia Resolves changed the mood of America. This was demonstrated when assemblies met again later in the year. In September that of Rhode Island, which had made no complaint in May, voted all that Virginia was thought to have done. Other assemblies, perhaps better informed on that point, did not go so far; but Pennsylvania and Maryland also voted declaratory resolutions that month, and by the end of the year Connecticut, Massachusetts, South Carolina, New Jersey, and New York had also done so. In June even Massachusetts had merely decided to send respectful petitions to King and Parliament; but it had also proposed, on the suggestion of James Otis, a meeting in New York of delegates from the various colonies to frame a joint petition. That proved the crucial step. Nine colonies were to send a total of 27 delegates to what has since become known as the Stamp Act Congress when it met in October. New Hampshire declined, but later approved what was decided. Virginia, North Carolina, and Georgia were prevented from attending by the refusal of their governors to summon assemblies; but Delaware and New Jersey overcame the same obstacle by unofficial choice of delegates.

The issue that concerned the Congress was not the financial burden of the Stamp Act but the belief that it was unconstitutional. The delegates were agreed on that point, but it took about a fortnight's discussion before 14 resolutions were devised. These set out the colonial view of the imperial relationship. Allegiance to the Crown and subordination to Parliament were acknowledged. But the colonists, who claimed the rights of British subjects, were not and could not be represented in Parliament, only in their assemblies, which therefore alone had the power to tax them. The Stamp Act and other revenue measures were condemned for "a manifest tendency to subvert the rights and liberties of the colonists." This was a distinction between taxation and legislation, which would not be acceptable at Westminster. The additional argument was then put that since the colonies were obliged to purchase Britain's manufactures they indirectly contributed to the taxation levied there. The final resolution was a decision to petition King, Lords, and Commons for repeal of the taxes, and these petitions were drafted before the Congress broke up on October 25.

The chief argument within the Congress had been whether to balance the denial of Parliament's right to tax the colonies with an acknowledgment of its right to regulate trade. Those who argued for this statement believed that it was necessary to make such an offer to persuade Britain to give up the right of internal taxation, but they failed to get their way. Since the Sugar Act had shown how trade duties could be used to raise revenue, the majority of delegates would not risk any admission. The declaration merely made a vague statement of the "due" subordination of the colonies to Parliament, without mention of any specific legislation such as the trade laws.

Historians have differed in opinion as to the precise nature of the colonial objection to Parliament's right of taxation. The traditional interpretation, as championed by Gipson (Gipson, 1961), is that the Americans objected only to "internal taxes," such as the Stamp Act, and not to "external taxes," revenues deliberately raised from customs duties. This was generally understood to be so in Britain, and that is why Charles Townshend chose such duties as his mode of taxation in 1767. When the Americans thereupon denied altogether any parliamentary right of taxation, they were then and have often subsequently been held to have changed their ground. Morgan argues that this was not the case, and that they had objected from the first to all taxation (Morgan, 1948; Morgan and Morgan, 1963). Both interpretations can be supported by selective evidence, but it would seem that the colonists had the Stamp Act in mind, whether they spoke of "taxes" or "internal taxes." Americans may not have specifically denied Parliament all powers of taxation; but neither did they make any positive acknowledgment of Parliament's right to raise money from the colonies – hence the cautious refusal of the Stamp Act Congress to admit even a right to regulate colonial trade, since that might be used to produce revenue.

3 Colonial Resistance to the Stamp Act

Words of protest were accompanied by deeds of resistance. This took three forms. Firstly, the Stamp Act was prevented from coming into operation on its due date, November 1. Secondly, the colonists then continued most of the relevant activities, for to refrain from doing so would have been a tacit admission of that Act's validity. Thirdly, methods of retaliation were devised to bring pressure on Britain for its repeal. This resistance was often characterized by caution and initial hesitation. The colonists were aware of the enormity of the challenge they were making to Britain, but they also knew there was no constitutional way to change parliamentary decisions, and MPs had seemed deaf to their earlier pleas. Physical resistance appeared to be the only method to alter Parliament's attitude. The Achilles' heel of the Stamp Act was the appointment of local men as the Stamp Distributors who were to supervise its operation in each colony. If they could be prevented from doing so the whole taxation measure would be nullified.

Boston was to show the way. The initiative there did not come from the Massachusetts political leaders such as James Otis and Samuel Adams. But they may well have directed the artisans and shopkeepers who comprised the small ginger group called the Loyal Nine, later expanded into the Sons of Liberty, who instructed the mob that first erupted on August 14 (*see* chapter 23, §2). Andrew Oliver, rumored to be the Massachusetts Stamp Distributor, was then hanged in effigy and had his house wrecked after he had fled for his life; next day he promised to resign. The ostensible object had been achieved. Yet on August 26 the Boston mob again went on the rampage, attacking the homes of several officials, notably that of Lieutenant-Governor Thomas Hutchinson. Although Hutchinson had attempted to stop the attack on Oliver and was deemed a supporter of the Stamp Act, such other motives as personal enmities and the destruction of customs and legal records better explain this second riot.

News of the first Boston riot led to a similar disturbance in Newport, Rhode Island, from August 27 to 29, which caused the resignation of the Stamp Distributor Augustus Johnston. After these events the mere threat of violence usually sufficed to secure the resignation of Stamp Distributors elsewhere. In New York James McEvers resigned as early as August 22, stating that he had a warehouse containing £20,000 worth of goods at risk. The notorious New York City mob was not, however, deprived of its riot, for a clash with the military and civil authorities occurred on November 1, when that port, like many others in America, went into public mourning to mark the formal commencement of the Stamp Act. By that date the Act had been effectively nullified by the resignation of all the other Stamp Distributors. On September 2 William Coxe in New Jersey resigned before any threat, and the same day Zachariah Hood in Maryland fled after having his house wrecked. Two others who had, like Hood, obtained the appointment for themselves in Britain, resigned

immediately on arrival back in America, George Meserve for New Hampshire on September 11 and George Mercer in Virginia on October 31. A fourth who had done so, Jared Ingersoll in Connecticut, resisted mob pressure for some weeks before resigning on September 19. John Hughes, appointed at Benjamin Franklin's request for Pennsylvania and Delaware, also resisted pressure until October 7, when he promised not to act. Caleb Lloyd of South Carolina gave the same undertaking on October 28. No news of the appointment of Stamp Distributors for North Carolina and Georgia had even arrived by November 1, when there was not one willing to act in the 13 colonies. In any case the stamped paper was unobtainable: some had been destroyed, some had not arrived, and most had been stored for safe-keeping in forts or on navy ships. North Carolina's Stamp Distributor was to resign when his appointment was notified on November 16; but in Georgia the only non-American, George Angus, did officiate for a fortnight after his arrival on January 4, 1766, before discretion prevailed.

Governors outside Massachusetts blamed Boston for this sequence of events. But the resolutions of Virginia and other colonies, and of the Stamp Act Congress, logically implied some action; and the speed and unanimity of the colonial response shows that Boston was merely a convenient scapegoat. The Sons of Liberty became a general phenomenon as resistance crystallized in each colony.

Boston took the lead only in violence. Other colonies opened the ports first. Everywhere in America as many ships as possible had sailed before November 1, but this apparent reluctance to break the law was soon overcome by commercial pressures, as customs officials were coerced into acting without stamped papers. Philadelphia never really closed, by the device of issuing clearance papers before November 1 to ships not yet loaded. Virginia reopened after one day, on November 2, Rhode Island on November 25, and Pennsylvania, New York, and New Jersey early in December, but Boston not until December 17. Connecticut and New Hampshire opened by the end of December, Maryland in January 1766, and the two

Carolinas and Georgia in February. Ports in all 13 colonies were open before news of the prospective repeal of the Stamp Act.

Opening the law courts was another matter. Lawyers faced the problem that decisions on unstamped papers would be invalid. Delays of several months were customary in legal proceedings, and many people, such as debtors, were happy to see the courts closed. Judges and lawyers sometimes changed their minds, and often found it easier to resort to adjournments until news came from Britain; the impending repeal relieved the pressure for awkward decisions. There is therefore no consistent pattern, nor even any clear picture of the colonial response, for the evidence is incomplete. It would seem that only in Rhode Island did the courts never close, and that they might not have opened in such colonies as New York or Virginia, but that in most there was a gradual trend towards resuming normal legal business.

The printers, together with the merchants and lawyers, formed the third main occupational group whose livelihood was directly affected by the Stamp Act. The colonial press in 1765 played a key role in American resistance both by deliberate propaganda and by simply reporting words and deeds of defiance. The newspaper printers had no intention of paying the stamp duties, but most adopted the cautious response of suspending publication from November 1. Of the 23 colonial newspapers then in existence, it would seem that only eight continued publication without a break, and some then by altering titles or appearing anonymously. During the ensuing weeks, though it was sometimes months, there was a gradual resumption of publication by the others, either under local pressure or from fear of losing their customers, for four new papers were founded to exploit market gaps that had arisen. Most newspapers were defying the law long before news of repeal arrived.

Refusal to pay the stamp duties, and ignoring the Stamp Act by the resumption of taxable activities, produced only a stalemate. What America wanted was repeal of the Stamp Act, and, while this was requested in petitions, direct pressure on Britain was deemed necessary. There was talk both of refusal to pay debts to British creditors and of armed resistance, but these ideas were not seriously canvassed, although awareness of them in Britain helped to swing opinion there in 1766. The method that was adopted was the economic pressure of a refusal to purchase British goods. This was instigated by individual ports, for the Stamp Act Congress had confined itself to verbal remonstrances. New York City took the initiative on October 31, when two hundred merchants there signed an agreement to stop ordering British goods until the Stamp Act was repealed. Four hundred Philadelphia merchants did the same on November 14 and two hundred Boston merchants on December 9. Elsewhere, as in Rhode Island, merchants usually suspended British orders without formal agreements. The propaganda impact of this boycott was enhanced by a publicized campaign for the colonial manufacture of clothing and other goods customarily bought from Britain. It was the threat implied by the boycott that was to be of significance in resolving the Stamp Act crisis, rather than its actual effect. For this must necessarily have been limited in the time-scale involved: and in any case Britain's trade to America amounted only to about one-eighth of her total exports. But the confusion of the boycott threat with the commercial and industrial recession already in existence was to produce an exaggerated effect on British opinion.

4   The British Decision on Policy

In July 1765 Grenville's ministry was replaced by one headed by the 35-year-old Marquis of Rockingham, who earlier in that year had succeeded Newcastle as head of the political group that liked to regard itself as the Whig Party. Young and inexperienced, the new administration was faced by the hostility of Grenville, while Pitt and his followers acted as a neutral third party who might support or oppose the ministry. The reasons for this change were unconnected with America: Grenville had given personal offence to George III. But it was important that at the time of the Stamp Act crisis there should have come to office an administration not responsible for the measures that had aroused discontent in the colonies. A change of policy was not inevitable, for the men of the new ministry had made little resistance to Grenville's legislation, but they would be more likely to consider conciliation of some kind.

News of the colonial resistance to the Stamp Act gradually reached Britain during the second half of 1765. In August the new ministry thought the Virginia Resolves did not truly represent American opinion, and did not anticipate much difficulty in enforcing the Stamp Act. But by October America was on the political agenda. News had come of the Boston and Newport riots, and of various protests and resistance elsewhere. The ministry played for time by sending formal orders, through Southern Secretary Conway on October 24, that the law should be upheld, but the governors had no military force or other means to obey this instruction. The ministry tacitly postponed any policy decision on whether or not to enforce the Stamp Act until the end of the year, awaiting more information. There was still hope that opposition was not widespread, that the crisis would resolve itself. The administration meanwhile came under pressure for suspension or repeal of the Stamp Act, from Benjamin Franklin and other agents, and from British merchants concerned about the threat to trade; one of them, Barlow Trecothick, instigated a national campaign to petition Parliament by circulating 30 towns on December 6. Rockingham himself approved this letter. He foresaw that British complaints about the American trade slump would assist any move to persuade Parliament to make concessions over the Stamp Act. This was the first sign the Prime Minister had decided on conciliation.

The decline in colonial trade and the economic depression in Britain had begun before the Stamp Act crisis. The evidence that was to be presented to Parliament in February 1766 depicted an industrial recession in Britain that had already lasted for some time. But the colonial boycotts of imports did not begin until October 31, 1765, and news of them did not reach Britain until mid-December. The Rockingham ministry, in assuming that the economic recession in Britain was caused by the colonial trade embargo, misunderstood the situation.

By December 1765 the Rockingham ministry could no longer hope that the Stamp Act would come into operation after colonial disturbances had ceased. The apparent choice was between military coercion and some form of concession, which might be modification, suspension, or complete repeal of the Act. But ministers knew that it would be impossible to assemble the army needed to enforce the taxation in the face of such overwhelming colonial hostility: they had been told so by General Gage, Commander-in-Chief for North America. Conciliation was therefore the only possible short-term solution. But simple repeal would be unacceptable to British political opinion, as too obvious a surrender to mob violence. The administration faced up to reality, and, after numerous consultations and private discussions, on December 27 produced a preliminary policy decision. There would be a Declaratory Act to assert the supremacy of Parliament over the colonies, and a subsequent offer of "relief" to America, ostensibly on economic grounds. Members of the government held different opinions as to what this should be. The ministry had not only to agree on a policy but to devise one acceptable to King and Parliament. George III had no firm opinion, and would as usual accept his ministry's decision, albeit with reluctance. The key to Parliament was the attitude of William Pitt. While both public rumor and the behavior of his followers pointed to his support of conciliation, he rebuffed a ministerial enquiry about his opinion, stating that he would give it only to Parliament, which was to meet on January 14, 1766. No final policy decision was therefore taken before then, and the King's Speech to Parliament reflected this ministerial predicament. Ostensibly a statement of policy, its vague wording left open a wide choice of possible options.

The debate on the Speech resolved the situation. Pitt attended the Commons after a two-year absence, and spoke in favor of complete repeal. Adopting what was generally thought in Britain to be the colonial view, he denied that Parliament had any right to levy internal taxation on America, since the colonies were not represented there. His speech made it possible for Rockingham to convince his colleagues that repeal was both the inevitable course of action and one that Parliament would accept, with Pitt's advocacy, if there was the palliative of a Declaratory Act to allay uneasiness about the implications of such a turnabout. For Pitt's denial of the right of taxation had offended many independent MPs, who would not want repeal to be seen as an endorsement of this view.

On January 19 the Rockingham ministry came to a final decision on American policy. This would comprise a Declaratory Act that would avoid mention of taxation so as not to offend Pitt; it would be followed by the complete repeal of the Stamp Act, on the alleged grounds of its inherent faults and the detrimental effect it had had on the British economy. The Declaratory Act would assert the right of Parliament to legislate for the American colonies "in all cases whatsoever." This formal statement was an expression of political faith, and was to be an integral part of future Rockinghamite attitudes to America. But there was also the motive of tactical expediency, based on the realization that King, Lords, and Commons would all be unwilling to accept any surrender to colonial defiance.

5 The Repeal of the Stamp Act

The ministry faced opposition to their policy on two flanks. Grenville would obviously resist repeal, while Pitt's denial of the right of taxation would cause him to challenge the Declaratory Bill. The campaign was therefore carefully planned. Parliament was kept fully informed about the gravity of the colonial crisis; but this tactic may have been counter-productive, for there is evidence of parliamentary resentment against America. A less subtle attempt to influence parliamentary opinion was the battery of petitions organized by Trecothick with ministerial blessing. In January 1766, 24 petitions from British ports and manufacturing towns were submitted to the House of Commons.

The case for the Declaratory Act was established first. The Lords and Commons both read through the American papers, and examined witnesses on the colonial resistance. On February 3 both Houses debated the declaratory resolution. Pitt's followers, led by Camden, forced a vote in the Lords, losing 125 to 5, but there was none in the Commons, even though Pitt spoke against the right of internal taxation. Government lawyers in both Houses deployed a wealth of precedents and arguments to deny that representation was necessary for taxation, or that there was any distinction between internal and external taxation or between taxation and legislation. The most important result of the debates was to clarify the point that the phrase "in all cases whatsoever" did include taxation.

The ministry took a buffeting in Parliament during the next few days. There were defeats in the Lords over opposition amendments to government motions, while in the Commons Grenville seized the initiative with resolutions of his own about compensation for riot victims and an indemnity for any offenders now willing to pay the taxes. He then announced that on February 7 he would move to enforce the Stamp Act. That would be the crucial test of parliamentary opinion. Rockingham therefore obtained permission from George III to make public the King's support of repeal. This news, a warning by Pitt that bloodshed would be the consequence, and another by Conway that Britain's European enemies might intervene in any conflict, combined to produce a majority of 274 to 134 against Grenville.

Even yet the success of the ministerial policy was not assured. George III let it be known that his personal preference would have been for modification rather than complete repeal, had that been a viable option, and customary government supporters then felt free to vote against repeal without offending their sovereign. Opinion in the Commons was still volatile over what was to many the unpalatable choice of complete repeal, and there was also the hurdle of the House of Lords.

Emphasis on Britain's economic distress was the chief ministerial tactic in securing the consent of the House of Commons to repeal. All the government witnesses examined in February, bar two, were merchants and manufacturers concerned with British trade to America. They had been carefully selected, and some were rehearsed beforehand. All, even under cross-examination, gave repeal as the only satisfactory solution. Trecothick, on behalf of the London merchants, was the most important witness, on February 11: his evidence included the calculation that colonial debts to British merchants amounted to £4,450,000, with the obvious implication that much of this was at risk. The tale of economic woe throughout Britain by the procession of witnesses succeeded in alarming independent MPs. They were already aware of hunger riots in Britain, and feared more general disorder. While ministers sought to arouse such fears of disturbances is Britain, they played down the deliberate violence and constitutional claims of the colonists. They were portrayed respectively as spontaneous mob riots and as a challenge to Parliament only over internal taxation; the most famous witness, Benjamin Franklin, told MPs so on February 13.

The great debate on repeal took place on February 21. It was significant for the public formulation of British attitudes on America. Conway explained ministerial policy when he affirmed Parliament's right of taxation but said it was a right that ought not to be exercised. A tax revenue of £60,000 was not worth the sacrifice of British trade to America. Those who favored amendment were told that modification gave up the substance while keeping the shadow, a shadow that would frighten the Americans. Pitt put what was to be his characteristic view of the colonial relationship: that it was unfair both to tax America and to control its economy. Grenville argued vainly that the colonies were well able to pay all his taxes. The resolution for repeal was carried by 275 votes to 167. The key to this ministerial success had been the effort to win over independent opinion, for many customary government supporters had deserted.

On March 4 Pitt challenged the passage of the Declaratory Bill by moving to omit the words "in all cases whatsoever," but did not force a vote; the Commons passed the repeal the same day by 250 to 122. The ministry was nevertheless apprehensive about the House of Lords. Independent peers were few in number, and Rockingham did not deploy witnesses on the economic situation. He relied instead on royal pressure on important peers. This strategy proved successful in the only Lords vote over repeal, on March 11. The ministerial majority was 73 to 61, increased by proxies to 105 to 71. Both bills received the royal assent on March 18.

Repeal required practical implementation. The scanty revenue was secured, surviving stamped paper returned to Britain, and the accounts of officials settled. The gross revenue was £3,292, but with costs incurred of £6,863. An Indemnity Act was passed in May, to wipe the slate clean. Compensation for riot victims was recommended to the relevant assemblies, but Rhode Island proved evasive, New York did not vote enough, and Massachusetts refused to comply. This recalcitrance aroused indignation in Britain, and in December the Massachusetts Assembly, warned by its agent that the new Chatham ministry was adamant on the subject, voted to pay compensation to Thomas Hutchinson and other victims. But the same measure also pardoned all offenders in the Boston riots, the British indemnity having covered disobedience and not violence. This usurpation of the royal power of pardon infuriated both administration and opposition in Parliament. In 1767 they argued only as to the best method of nullifying it, before on May 13 the Privy Council declared the whole measure void.

6   The American Trade Act of 1766

The Stamp Act was not the only American legislation of the Grenville ministry with whose consequences the Rockingham administration had to grapple. The other revenue measure, the alteration of the duty on foreign molasses to 3d a gallon in 1764, had also been a failure. The ministerial argument then had been that the planters in the French West Indies would reduce their price to keep the market, and the stability of the molasses price in North America seemed initial confirmation of this view. But that the continuance of widespread smuggling was the true reason was revealed by the failure of the 3d duty to produce the anticipated revenue of £78,000; it yielded only £5,200 in 1764 and £4,090 in 1765.

Consideration of that question formed part of the general review of the trade laws in 1766. While the ministry was concerned with the parliamentary contest over the Stamp Act, the North America and West Indies merchants agreed on March 10 that the duty on foreign molasses imported into America should be reduced to a realistic 1d a gallon. Rockingham accepted this idea, and witnesses told the Commons on March 27 how desirable such a change would be. America needed profits from the West Indies trade to purchase British goods. Repeal of the Stamp Act might restore the will of the colonists to trade with Britain, but such changes were needed to enable them to do so. West Indies planters, however, refused to endorse the 1d duty agreed by the merchants; as the planter William Beckford had the support of his mentor William Pitt, and Grenville also criticized the change, political opposition threatened to wreck the plan.

The Chancellor of the Exchequer William Dowdeswell nevertheless proposed the 1d duty to the Commons on April 30. It was criticized by Beckford as harmful to the British West Indies and by Grenville as a surrender to colonial smugglers. The ministry resolved the problem by direct negotiations with the West Indies lobby, offering concessions concerning inter-island trade in return for the remarkable new concession that molasses from the British, as well as foreign, islands would pay the 1d duty. The advantage would be the elimination of fraud: hitherto foreign molasses had often been passed off as British. But the change meant that the molasses duty was now simply a tax, and it was to be the only effective one devised by British politicians in the revolutionary period. This agreement, made on May 8, was confirmed by the Commons the same day and enacted without debate as part of another American Duties Act by June 6.

The Rockingham ministry, sympathetic to growing colonial complaints about the scarcity of legal-tender money, also considered alteration or repeal of the 1764 Currency Act, but the dismissal of the administration in July prevented enactment of any measure on that subject. This came about because George III had ascertained that Pitt was willing to form a ministry in disregard of what the King detested as "faction"; such an administration had been George III's aim since his accession. Royal disapproval of the Rockingham ministry's American policy was not the reason for its removal: it was only afterwards that the King came to see repeal of the Stamp Act as the measure fatal to Anglo-American union.

7 The Significance of the Stamp Act Crisis

Although the Stamp Act crisis was concerned ostensibly with the issue of taxation, it had raised the wider question of Britain's sovereignty over the colonies, and had consequences on both sides of the Atlantic. British opinion would not be satisfied with the formal claim of the Declaratory Act after such a rebuff, and would especially seek a colonial revenue. Within Britain politicians were now categorized according to their attitudes on America, even though these had largely been shaped by the chance of who was in administration or opposition when decisions were being made. Henceforth Grenville and his friends were hardliners or "Stamp men"; the Rockinghamite party would be pragmatic in approach, championing sovereignty in theory but not its exercise in practice. Those sympathetic to America were few in number – Pitt and his followers, a handful of radicals, and some Rockinghamites and independents. In America the colonists would now be suspicious of any British government policy, while in some individual colonies the Stamp Act crisis had considerable impact on local power structures. Those politicians identified with support of Britain, such as the Hutchinson–Oliver party in Massachusetts and Jared Ingersoll in Connecticut, had their influence weakened or destroyed. Conversely, championship of America had brought new men to power, notably Patrick Henry, or given established politicians victory over their rivals. Neither in general nor in detail would the Anglo-American relationship return to what it had been before the Stamp Act crisis.

8 The Quartering Act Controversy

The American Mutiny Act of 1765, known to colonists as the Quartering Act (*see* chapter 15, §4), was soon found to be defective by both the army and the colonies. The army had to accept that billeting on private houses, which had occasionally been the practice in the past, was now implicitly illegal, while the new dependence on assemblies for barrack supplies made the vote of army provisions a political weapon by which displeasure with the British Government or local governors could be manifested. The colonists had a double grievance. The provisions clause was regarded as a new tax; and it was one whose incidence was accidental and uneven, and therefore unfair. Postings were irregular and rarely permanent, and some colonies, such as Virginia, escaped a military presence almost altogether.

New York, containing the main port for the arrival and departure of soldiers, was the colony likely to bear the heaviest burden. At the end of 1765 its assembly refused to comply with the request of General Gage, army Commander-in-Chief in North America, for provisions under the Quartering Act. Gage tried again, in May 1766, and in June the assembly did agree to supply firewood and candles, bedding, and utensils, but not the alcohol stipulated. The assembly also passed resolutions stating that the total number of soldiers for whom provision might have to be made was unknown, implying that the colony faced an unlimited demand on its resources, but that New York was willing to pay a proportionate share of the total American expense. New York had a real grievance, but such defiance of an Act of Parliament could not be allowed to pass without reprimand by any British government. The Chatham Cabinet on August 5 therefore decided that Southern Secretary Shelburne should write to the Governor stating that it was expected there should be "all due obedience" to parliamentary statutes; he did so on August 9. The response of the assembly in December was a unanimous decision not to vote any supplies at all, and a complaint that the burden on New York would be greater than that on any other colony. The New Jersey Assembly in December voted only what New York had done in June, and declared that the Quartering Act was as much a tax as the Stamp Act, and more unfair, as soldiers were stationed in few colonies. Resistance to the Quartering Act was not universal. Pennsylvania fully complied with the Act up to 1774, the only colony to do so. Connecticut and even Massachusetts at this time supplied casual detachments of soldiers. That Georgia was defying the act in 1767 remained as yet unknown in Britain. It seemed that only New York was being obstructive.

The British ministry was determined to enforce the Quartering Act on that colony. The absent Chatham ruled that the matter should be referred to Parliament, and on March 12, 1767 the Cabinet met to decide what proposal to put to the House of Commons. Southern Secretary Shelburne's solution was the coercive billeting of soldiers on private houses. Northern Secretary Conway suggested a direct levy on New York by additional trade duties. Both proposals were rejected in favor of an idea of the Chancellor of the Exchequer Charles Townshend, that the New York Assembly should be prohibited from exercising its legislative function until it fully obeyed the Quartering Act. Not until May 13 did Townshend put this proposal to the Commons. It was more moderate than the alternatives preferred by the opposition parties. The Rockinghamite solution was to quarter soldiers on private houses, the same as Shelburne's idea in cabinet. Grenville suggested a direct order to the colony's treasury. The debate reflected almost universal agreement about the policy of coercing New York into submission. In that sense the majority for Townshend's motion, of 180 against 98, was a victory for moderation; and there is evidence that many MPs did not think New York would risk further defiance.

That proved to be the outcome. Early in June, before Parliament had passed the New York Restraining Act, the colony's assembly voted a sum sufficient to pay for all items stipulated in the Quartering Act, but without formal reference to that measure. The Governor reported this as compliance with it, and Shelburne agreed that the Restraining Act, due to go into operation on October 1, had been rendered unnecessary. The matter was ended as far as the ministry was concerned, but the Quartering Act continued to be an intermittent colonial grievance during the next few years. The Massachusetts Circular Letter of February 1768 complained of the financial burden, and later that year Gage met obstruction in Boston that caused him to request a revision of the Act. This was accomplished in 1769, after both the Grafton Cabinet and the Commons had rejected the idea of billeting on private houses; it was proposed respectively by the American Secretary Lord Hillsborough and the Secretary at War Lord Barrington, and killed by Lord North. During a routine renewal of the Quartering Act the former Massachusetts governor Thomas Pownall carried an amendment giving army officers and civil magistrates discretion to make mutually satisfactory arrangements. Another amendment even allowed colonies to opt out of the Quartering Act if they passed their own legislation for the same purpose. The Cabinet rejected this suggestion from Hillsborough, but the Commons adopted the Pownall amendment to that end. No colony took advantage of this choice, but Hillsborough devised a pragmatic solution to the problem in 1771. Since 1767, colonies with army detachments had made provision for them with little protest except in the heated atmosphere of 1769 during the Townshend Duties crisis, but New Jersey refused to pay in 1771. Hillsborough's answer to the problem was the withdrawal of army units from disobedient colonies, rather than coerce New Jersey, as had been the case with New York in 1767. This would prompt realization that the economic and military benefits of an army presence outweighed the financial burden. A regiment might spend £6,000 a year in pay, quite apart from its maintenance costs, while soldiers could sometimes be useful to maintain order. The removal of New Jersey's regiment in 1771 aroused alarm that all the middle colonies were going to be evacuated. New York and Philadelphia voted their contributions promptly, and so did New Jersey when regiments later returned. Apart from the special case of Massachusetts, the problem of the Quartering Act had virtually been resolved.

FURTHER READING

Gipson, L. H.: *The British Empire before the American Revolution*, Vol. X: *The Triumphant Empire: Thunder-Clouds Gather in the West, 1763–1766* (New York: Alfred A. Knopf, 1961).

Knollenberg, B.: *Origin of the American Revolution, 1759–1766* (1960), 2nd edn. (New York: Collier Books, 1961).

Langford, P.: *The First Rockingham Administration, 1765–1766* (Oxford: Oxford University Press, 1973).

Morgan, E. S.: "Colonial ideas of parliamentary power, 1764–1766," *William and Mary Quarterly*, 5 (1948), 311–41.

——: *Prologue to Revolution: Sources and Documents on the Stamp Act Crisis, 1764–1766* (Chapel Hill: University of North Carolina Press, 1959).

Morgan, E. S. and Morgan, H. M.: *The Stamp Act Crisis: Prologue to Revolution* (1953), 2nd edn. (New York: Collier Books, 1963).

Schlesinger, A. M.: *Prelude to Independence: the Newspaper War on Britain, 1764–1776* (1957), 2nd edn. (New York: Vintage Books, 1965).

Shy, J.: *Towards Lexington: the Role of the British Army in the Coming of the American Revolution* (Princeton, NJ: Princeton University Press, 1965).

Thomas, P. D. G.: *British Politics and the Stamp Act Crisis: the First Phase of the American Revolution, 1763–1767* (Oxford: Clarendon Press, 1975).

CHAPTER SEVENTEEN

The Townshend Acts crisis, 1767–1770

ROBERT J. CHAFFIN

THE Townshend Acts of 1767 consisted of a series of taxes on goods imported into the American colonies, a reorganized Board of Customs Commissioners stationed in Boston to collect the taxes and enforce other revenue measures, and the New York Restraining Act. Reasons for passing these measures included a symbolic gesture to show the colonies that the mother country had the right to tax the colonies, raise a revenue to support some governors and justices, and punish New York for refusing to abide by the Mutiny Act (also known as the Quartering Act). As a consequence of these measures, relations between Britain and its provinces deteriorated. The crisis did momentarily pass with minor alterations of the tax measures in 1770, but not before the Boston Massacre had taken place. Additional changes in the tea tax three years later, however, led to the Boston Tea Party, setting the two sides on the road to war.

1 Britain's Need for Revenue from the Colonies

Shortly after assuming office in 1766, the Chatham ministry concluded that the colonies should contribute additional revenue to the Treasury. Augustus Henry Fitzroy, third Duke of Grafton, led the Treasury Board. With the assistance of Charles Townshend, Chancellor of the Exchequer, Grafton directed his staff to transmit a report on colonial quitrents.[1] He wanted to know how quitrents were collected, how much was received, and the provincial legislation relative to it. He also sought each colony's sources of income, expenditures, and taxes. The inference was that once the Board obtained a complete report of colonial accounts, it could devise new tax measures.

The Chancellor of the Exchequer simultaneously gathered data for his system of colonial revenue. Ambitious and opportunistic, the 41-year-old Townshend was the most experienced member of the Chatham Cabinet. Not even Pitt, the once "Great Commoner," could boast of such a varied background. During his two decades in Parliament, Townshend had served under George Montagu Dunk, Earl of Halifax, at the Board of Trade, where he had received a thorough education in colonial affairs. Later he held such posts as Secretary at War, President of the Board of Trade, First Lord of the Admiralty, and Paymaster of the Army, all of which dealt directly or indirectly with the colonies.[2]

In October 1766 William Dowdeswell, Townshend's predecessor at the Exchequer, wrote that "a rebate of part of the customs on teas imported to America" would be "a very good thing" if the English market could be effectively supplied and American smuggling controlled.[3] The heart of Dowdeswell's suggestions – an amply supplied English market and the control of smuggling – offers a clue to one aspect of Townshend's schemes. In negotiations with the East India Company in the spring of 1767, the government agreed to lower the inland duty on teas going to Ireland and America. In return for these concessions, the company agreed to pay the government £400,000 annually. The settlement caused the price of tea to drop, increased exports to the colonies, and placed the company in a stronger position against smugglers and its continental competitors.[4] Townshend also considered placing a 6d per pound duty upon tea imported into the colonies, but finally reduced it to 3d in the Committee of Ways and Means, presumably because the higher rate would have increased the price of tea.[5]

Aware that the previous administration had considered permitting colonies to import wines and assorted fruits directly from Spain and Portugal without first stopping in England, Townshend incorporated that scheme into his tax program.[6] Besides tea, wines, and fruits, other items attracted Townshend's attention. From the London Customs House he learned that the value of china exported annually amounted to more than £51,000. Because the china carried a tax rebate when exported to the provinces, it provided an attractive taxable item. He dropped the rebate in his revenue acts. Salt also held enticing tax possibilities. He considered placing upon it a duty of five to ten pence, depending upon quality, and granting a bounty upon salted fish exported from the colonies. He never introduced the salt tax, however, because colonial agents persuaded him enforcement would prove difficult.[7]

In drawing up his tax plans, Townshend showed himself a skillful innovator rather than a creative genius. The idea of laying import duties upon unimportant items had its origins in 1710, when the government considered laying an import tax upon all goods imported into New York. As Townshend said in 1754, he thought it unwise to encumber with duties important British manufactured products going to America. For this reason, then, he chose articles of little consequence upon which to place his taxes: wine, fruits, white and green glass, red and white lead, painters' colors, and paper and pasteboards. Unfortunately, no evidence exists to suggest why Townshend chose those particular items. Several possibilities are apparent, however. The plan to lay duties upon fruits and wines was taken from the Rockingham administration, as already noted. Articles such as glass, paper products, lead, and painters'

colors were unimportant in the total amount of American trade, and taxes on those items would leave established patterns of trade undisturbed. Moreover, England monopolized trade in those articles, for colonies were prohibited from purchasing them elsewhere. While conceding that Britain had the right to lay duties upon colonial imports, Benjamin Franklin had admitted during his House of Commons interrogation in February that colonies might begin to produce their own manufactures if such an event occurred. Perhaps for this reason Townshend chose items difficult to manufacture. Glass, for instance, took a degree of technical sophistication almost unknown in the provinces. Quality paper, paper boards, and painters' colors likewise were not produced in America. And except for wine, none of the articles was suitable for smuggling. His calculations showed that he could obtain £43,420, exclusive of the tea duty – not a large amount, but new tax measures often are small and increase only after the taxpayer has grown accustomed to paying them. Moreover, the duties were sufficient for their immediate purpose, which was to provide independent salaries for some governors and magistrates.

In the House of Commons, on January 26, 1767, Townshend promised to lay a new set of duties upon America without first obtaining the Cabinet's permission. William Wildman, Lord Barrington, Secretary at War, moved for £405,607 for the army in the colonies. George Grenville, father of the Stamp Act, immediately proposed an amendment calling for the troops to be supported by the colonies.[8] Townshend quickly rose in opposition; nonetheless, he spoke "warmly for making America bear her share of the expense." In his pocket diary, Sir Roger Newdigate recorded in his minute scrawl that Townshend "pledgd. himself that something shd. be done this session … towards creating a revenue in the colonies."[9] When pressed to explain himself more fully, Townshend replied that he did not mean to create a revenue immediately adequate to meet all colonial expenses, but would do everything "to form a revenue in time to bear the whole," that he would "plan by degrees" and use "great delicacy."

Clearly Townshend intended to begin his program with small levies, gradually increasing them until the income was sufficient to relieve England of all colonial expenses. Impressed with Townshend's plans, the House voted down Grenville's motion.

2 Difficulties with the New York Assembly

Townshend's promise to lay fresh taxes on the colonies was only one of the problems the ministry faced. A second was a petition from New York merchants. With remarkably poor timing they had petitioned Parliament, complaining that their trade was severely restricted by certain Navigation Acts passed in 1764 and 1766.[10] William Petty, second Earl of Shelburne, Secretary of State for the Southern Department, thought the petition ill-advised, especially since the New York Assembly had refused to abide by the Mutiny Act and provide fully for the troops stationed in the colony.[11]

Already perturbed because of the petition, both the Cabinet and Parliament were prepared to deal harshly with New York because of its refusal to abide by the Mutiny Act. Fearful that unqualified support of the British Army would set a precedent for a new tax act, the New York Assembly had carefully restricted its grants. This action not only violated the Mutiny Act, but it also implicitly repudiated the Declaratory Act, which stated that Parliament had the right to legislate for the colonies. Britain's answer to this challenge to its authority was the New York Restraining Act, officially a part of the Townshend Acts.

In April Shelburne offered a plan to Chatham, one that would have strengthened the Declaratory Act. The general consensus in the Cabinet, he said, was to pass an act reiterating the Declaratory Act and "to recite the new effect of that law in the instance of the Mutiny Act."[12] Because colonists had failed to see the significance of the Declaratory Act, Shelburne believed the government should grant a general pardon for all past violations. But after three months he wanted it declared "*High Treason* to refuse to *obey* or *execute* any laws or statutes made by the King with the advice of Parliament under the pretence that the King and Parliament hath not sufficient authority to make laws and statutes to bind his American Colonies." Moreover, anyone who questioned the Declaratory Act by writing, preaching, or speaking against it should be tried for misprision of treason.

Spurred on by pressure from the opposition, the ministry finally reached a decision on April 26.[13] Shelburne probably did not offer his harsh corollary to the Declaratory Act. A second plan, offered by Henry Conway, Secretary of State for the Northern Department, was to place a "local extraordinary port duty" on New York. Townshend earnestly objected to Conway's tax proposal because it would have obstructed trade between the West Indies and England, increased smuggling, and failed to achieve the principle they were seeking – colonial recognition of Parliament's supremacy. Townshend suggested "addressing the Crown to assent to no law whatever, till the Mutiny Act was fully obeyed."[14] The attractive feature of this plan was its simplicity. Merely by refusing to sign any legislation, the governor could compel obedience to the Mutiny Act. Townshend recognized, of course, that the ministry might have to provide the governor's salary if the Assembly refused to bend. The Lord President of the Council, Robert Henley, Lord Northington, immediately disapproved, partly because the address applied only to one colony, and partly because an address carried little weight. Agreeing that an act was preferable to an address, the Cabinet ordered Townshend to write what later became a part of his Acts.

Townshend confronted the Cabinet with the question of army extraordinaries on March 12. He threatened to resign, Grafton reported to the ill and absent Chatham, unless "the reduction of them was not determined before the closing of the Committee of Supply, by drawing the troops nearer the great towns, laying the Indian charges upon the provinces, and by laying a tax on American ports,"[15] the same system, in short, that he and Grenville had earlier agreed upon in debate. He had committed himself to colonial taxes in the House, he continued, upon what had been discussed in the Cabinet, implying that cabinet discussions had led him to believe the ministry favored American taxation.[16]

Townshend, in the meantime, continued to work on the budget, drawing up duties, regulations, and savings. Shelburne and Grafton apparently had agreed with Townshend that a civil list free from colonial control was desirable. They wanted it funded with quitrents, however.[17] Townshend was not opposed to a colonial revenue fund based upon quitrents, a favorite scheme of Shelburne's. He asked Grafton for permission to introduce the plan, which would "be of infinite consequence tomorrow and of little use afterwards."[18] He also urged Grafton to obtain the King's permission to allow him to introduce his own tax schemes when he opened the budget. No evidence shows that Grafton answered Townshend or approached the King. The Chancellor of the Exchequer never mentioned quitrents when he introduced his budget.

After a two-day postponement because of illness, Townshend presented his budget to the House of Commons. Townshend noted that he had collected more than £469,000 out of the savings of office and cash dormant in the Exchequer. The House approved the budget without a division, and the next day it adjourned for the Easter holidays.[19]

3 Plans for a Customs Commission

During the adjournment, Townshend's plans to create a customs commission in America reached maturity. Who first suggested the commission is uncertain, though Charles Paxton, the Boston customs official who had also advised Townshend on his duties plans, might have been responsible. Shelburne informed Chatham on February 1 that the Chancellor of the Exchequer had a "plan for establishing a Board of Customs in America."[20]

In one of two reports to Townshend in January 1767, the British Board of Customs explained the problems it faced in America.[21] It noted that the great distance between the colonies and Britain, lack of supervision of colonial customs officers, and the hardships under which they worked posed onerous problems. Moreover, colonists started prosecutions against revenue men upon the slightest pretense, the report complained, the result of which was that

several officers had "lately been fined and imprisoned for obeying their instructions." To remedy the situation in America, the report proposed that "seven commissioners be appointed, three of whom to constitute a Board, and to reside at Philadelphia, for managing the said American duties." The Customs Board estimated the commissioners, their secretaries, and assistants would cost £5,540 in salaries; savings resulting from the dissolution of old offices would amount to £3,071. The new system would, consequently, incur about £2,469 in additional expenses. But because the new Board would result in a more efficient collection, it would soon compensate for the increased costs. Without such a system, the report warned, American duties would soon have to be abandoned because they would fail even to "yield sufficient income … to defray the salaries of the officers."

Attached to the first report was a list of customs officers the Customs Board wished to see provided for.[22] Henry Hulton, a plantation clerk, was named one of the seven commissioners, as were the four colonial Surveyors General – John Temple, Charles Steuart, Peter Randolph, and Thomas Gibbs. The report called for two more commissioners, but made no effort to name them. Only two on this list, Hulton and Temple, actually became members of the American Board of Customs. John Robinson, who suffered much in the Stamp Act riots, became a third; William Burch, about whom nothing is known, was named a fourth; and Charles Paxton, Townshend's tax advisor, was appointed to the fifth post.

Though the Treasury Board accepted the proposal, not until the following August, two months after the Bill became law, was the number of American commissioners finally agreed upon as five and their permanent residence fixed at Boston. Why the number was reduced from seven to five remains unexplained. Each commissioner was to receive £500 annually. Perhaps the prospect of saving £1,000 enticed the Treasury Board to name only five commissioners. Because Paxton, Robinson, and Temple were residents of New England, the shift from Philadelphia to Boston may have been made simply on grounds of convenience to the new commissioners.

4 Townshend's Program

Plans to punish New York and establish an American Board of Customs were agreed to by the end of April, and Shelburne and Grafton had accepted the idea of an independent civil list for America. But the First Lord of the Treasury still proved reluctant to grant Townshend authority to present his tax schemes to the House. On May 13, the New York Restraining Bill was considered by the Committee of the Whole House. Though some colonies had abided by the Mutiny Act, Townshend noted, New Jersey had complied evasively and New York had "boldly and insolently" defied it and the authority of Parliament. Because New York had been the most refractory, he thought it should receive "an adequate punishment to deter others."[23] Moving on to the subject of taxes, he cautioned that they should be moderate and prudent. With all the characteristics of a compromise between himself and Grafton, he next proposed to "mention some tax not as Chancellor of the Exchequer but as a private man for the future opinion of the House in the committee of Ways and Means."[24]

Speaking as a private man he thus dissociated himself from the ministry. Later, he said, he would recommend levies on fruit, oil, and wine from Spain and Portugal imported directly to the colonies and taking off all or part of the tax rebate on articles such as china, glass, red and white lead for painting, and colored papers for furniture.[25] The new duties would, in his estimation, amount to between £30,000 and £40,000 yearly, a sum sufficient to pay some colonial governors and magistrates their salaries. And to assure the collection of the duties, he called for the creation of an American Board of Customs. He realized, he concluded, that his plans might exacerbate relations between Britain and the colonies, but the "quarrel must soon come to an issue. The superiority of the mother country can at no time be better exerted than now."[26] With that, he moved his resolutions that "New York had been disobedient to the acts of the legislature of Great Britain," that the colony's act for providing for troops was "void and derogatory to the honor of the King and legislature," and that "instructions

be sent to the Governor to give no assent to any acts of assembly till a compleat and entire submission to an execution of the Billeting Act" was accomplished.[27]

In proposing his program, Townshend urged moderation and prudence, punishment for New York, an independent civil list, and a Board of Customs to ensure the collection of duties. He had shrewdly sidestepped Grafton's roadblock when introducing his tax plan for future consideration by declaring himself a private man. In spite of his bluster and threats, it is doubtful that he would have attempted even that maneuver without prior consultation with Grafton.

At one o'clock in the morning – after eight hours of debate – the vote was taken. The first two propositions, that New York had become disobedient and that its Provisioning Act was null and void, were passed unanimously. The House divided over the New York restraining resolution after Grenville proposed an amendment to enforce the Mutiny Act. The question whether Townshend's proposal should stand as first offered was carried by a comfortable majority, 188 to 98.[28] Upon the committee report on May 15, the opposition offered new propositions. But by majorities of three to one Townshend carried the day. It was his personal triumph.[29]

A fortnight later, on June 1, Townshend proposed his duties plan to the Committee of Ways and Means. He gave up his proposal for direct trade between Spain, Portugal, and the colonies because, as Franklin reported, the British merchants trading to those countries made such a clamor. By dropping the duties on fruit, he lost some £12,000 from his original estimates. But he compensated for this reduction with his proposal for a 3d per pound duty on tea payable in the colonies, which would bring an estimated £20,000. By dropping the rebate on china and placing small duties on glass, various kinds of paper, pasteboards, red and white lead, and painters' colors, the government could obtain an additional revenue. Townshend estimated that china earthenware would bring £8,000; glass, £5,000; paper and pasteboard products, £9,000; and lead and painters' colors, £3,000. The purpose of the duties was, as the preamble of the Acts showed, "for making a more certain and adequate provision for the charge of the administration of justice, and the support of the civil government, and defraying the expense of defending, protecting and securing the said colonies."[30]

The committee presented the Duties Bill, along with the measure for creating the American Board of Customs, on June 10. Several amendments were offered by the opposition, but the Bills survived substantially the same as Townshend had first presented them. Receiving the Bills on June 15, the House of Lords returned them unchanged at the end of the month.[31]

After signing the bills on July 2, 1767, the King prorogued Parliament. George III observed in his speech (written by his ministers) that it was not "expected that all the great commercial interests should be completely adjusted and regulated in the course of this session." Yet he was persuaded "that by the progress you have made, a solid foundation is laid for securing the most considerable and essential benefits to this nation."[32] Obviously the King and authors of the speech believed the Townshend Acts would provide gains that would strengthen Great Britain.

5   Reactions to the Townshend Acts

Both were wrong. The Acts aggravated an already tense situation in the colonies. The provinces responded to Townshend's measures in three ways: philosophically, politically, and economically. Each activity, often interwoven with the others, confirmed the colonists in the righteousness of their cause – resistance to perceived British encroachments on their rights.

John Dickinson's Letters

Many colonists reacted to the Townshend Acts in newspapers and pamphlets. None, however, was as influential as the 12 *Letters from a Farmer in Pennsylvania* by John Dickinson. The *Letters* were first published in the *Pennsylvania Chronicle and Universal Advertiser*, beginning with the

issue for December 2, 1767, and their popularity and circulation surpassed that of all other publications in the revolutionary war period save Thomas Paine's *Common Sense*. They were reproduced in 19 of the 23 English-language colonial newspapers; at least seven pamphlet editions were printed, as were two editions in Europe.

Joseph Harrison, a Boston customs collector, thought the *Letters* were "dangerous and alarming," and "the principal means of spreading … general disaffection among the people."[33] Georgia's Governor James Wright was convinced they had "sown the seeds of sedition," which had been "scattered in very fertile soil."[34] They received a mixed review in England. The conservative *Critical Review* considered them seditious and superficial, while the liberal *Monthly Review* thought they presented a full enquiry into the rights of Parliament that would be difficult to refute.[35]

Offering nothing new or profound, the *Letters* documented and dignified radical ideas already held by many colonists. The author utilized such popular Whig themes as the executive's threat to the liberties of assemblies, the loss of power to tax themselves, the proliferation of offices, the danger of standing armies, and worse tax measures to follow if colonists allowed the Acts to set precedents.[36] Dickinson admitted that Britain could regulate trade for the benefit of the empire. But he also argued that the mother country could levy no taxes on the colonies, because they had no representatives in Parliament. Fidelity to the monarch, mutually beneficial trade, traditional affection – these were the tenuous ties that bound the two together. Always the reluctant rebel, Dickinson suggested few methods of redress. Besides petitions to the King, he advised boycotting British goods until colonial grievances were rectified. In that way, he said, colonists could achieve their goals, disappoint their enemies, and elate their friends.

Adams's Circular Letter, Massachusetts Assembly

The Massachusetts Assembly followed Dickinson's advice. Called into session on December 30, 1767, it devoted the next

18 days to preparing remonstrances against the Acts. Among those remonstrances was the Circular Letter. Mainly the work of Samuel Adams, Clerk of the Lower House, the Letter urged other colonies to resist the Acts, and argued that no people could enjoy full freedom if the monarch had the right to pay salaries of, as well as appoint, colonial officials.[37] The Letter went on to note that Parliament had no legal right to tax the colonies for the *sole* purpose of raising a revenue, a position put forth most vigorously by the Pennsylvania farmer.

The British Government's response to the Assembly's activities heightened tensions even further. Wills Hill, first Earl of Hillsborough, had recently become Secretary of State for the new American Department. In a circular of April 21, he ordered all governors to prorogue or dissolve their assemblies rather than allow them to countenance Massachusetts' Circular Letter.[38] In addition, Hillsborough ordered the Massachusetts Governor Francis Bernard to require the Assembly to rescind the Letter and resolutions and declare its dissent from those measures.[39] Aware that his directive might lead to trouble, Hillsborough also alerted General Thomas Gage at New York to prepare his troops in case they were needed in Boston.[40]

Dissolving assemblies in wholesale fashion to oblige obedience to the British ministry was at the very least an extraordinary step for the Cabinet to take. It was a dangerous experiment that could only result in arousing a spirit of unity Britain wished to avoid. In contrast to the New York restraining measure, debated upon at length in the House of Commons and applying only to one colony, Hillsborough's actions were indicative of the ministry's determination to gain colonial recognition of Britain's sovereignty as spelled out in the Declaratory Act. Except for deepening the Townshend Acts crisis, the policy failed.

The conflict between Bernard and the Assembly grew even more acute in the spring session of 1769. Troops had arrived in Boston in October 1768 at the instigation of the Governor and customs commissioners. The town was torn by turmoil as the Governor attempted to find suitable housing for the soldiers. Actions by the

British Government added to these tensions. Meeting in December 1768, Parliament had confirmed the ministry's use of troops in Boston and proposed that Boston ringleaders be brought to trial under the 35th Henry VIII. This obsolete law, entitled "An Act for the Trial of Treason Committed out of the King's Dominion," would have enabled the ministry to bring to England any colonist accused of treason.

Bernard was chagrined but not surprised to find that, of the 17 members who had voted to follow Hillsborough's commands to rescind the Circular Letter in 1768, only five had been re-elected and only two of those were courageous enough to attend. Out of a House of 120 members, no more than ten could be counted on as firm supporters of the government.[41] With the radical character of the House so apparent, Bernard braced for battle. It was not long in coming. At the first meeting, the House sent the Governor a message filled with "insolent terms." After choosing their speaker, members of the House elected councilors for the Upper House, declaring openly that "they would clear the Council of tories." Accordingly, they turned out four of those who had in the past shown an inclination to support the government. Bernard retaliated by vetoing six radical choices before a council was agreed upon by both sides. For the first fortnight the House's attention was dominated by the question of troops in Boston. No other business was conducted until the Virginia Resolves arrived (*see* chapter 16, §2). Similar to resolutions already passed by Massachusetts, the House readily agreed with them. This was too much for Bernard; he prorogued the House and recalled it at Cambridge, hoping thereby to modify the legislature's high spirits. It was a futile gesture.

As impertinent as the House appeared, Bernard was unprepared for the resolves it passed in the first week of July. To Commodore Samuel Hood, rarely given to exaggeration, the resolves were "of a more extraordinary nature than any that have yet passed an American assembly." Governor Bernard – "whom fear acts upon very powerfully," Hood caustically observed – viewed the House's actions as the opening of a revolt. Aware that General Gage intended to reduce the number of troops at Boston, the Governor felt that the resolves' tendency "was such that it seemed rather to require a reinforcement" of troops, not a reduction.[42]

Largely the work of Samuel Adams, the resolves declared that "no man can be justly taxed by, or bound in conscience to obey, any law to which he has not given his consent in person, or by his representative." Formerly the House, like most colonial assemblies, had agreed it could not be taxed without representation. Now it went to the next logical step and maintained it need not abide by any legislation in which it had not participated. The resolves also accused Bernard of giving "a false and highly injurious representation of the conduct" of the Council, magistrates, and inhabitants of Boston so that he could "introduce a military government into the province; and to mislead both Houses of Parliament into such severe resolutions." Furthermore, establishment of a standing army in the province in peacetime without the Assembly's consent was an invasion of the people's natural rights, the Magna Carta, and the Bill of Rights, as well as the charter of the colony. Finally, the resolves declared that instituting the 35th Henry VIII was "highly derogatory of the rights of the British subjects," because it denied them the privilege of being "tried by a jury from the vicinage, as well as the liberty of summoning and producing witnesses on such trial."[43]

After 46 days of frustrating and acrimonious disputes between the Governor and Assembly, Bernard prorogued the House until the following January. Rarely had the House sat so long; never had it accomplished so little. With justification, Bernard complained that the Assembly had devoted most of its time "in denying the power of the Parliament, arraigning and condemning its acts, abusing the king's ministers at home and his principal officers in America." Members of the House had implied "in plain if not direct terms their right and intention to separate themselves from" the British Government.[44]

The Assembly thus displayed increasing – almost hysterical – hostility towards Governor Bernard and Great Britain. At first

according Parliament control over trade, the House had moved by 1769 to the point where it denied that legislature any power over Massachusetts. Few other assemblies were prepared to go as far in denying the mother country's control. Yet few others had endured as much as Massachusetts. The home government had arbitrarily dismissed the Assembly because it had refused to rescind the Circular Letter and had stationed troops in Boston. Customs commissioners, rigidly interpreting the Navigation Acts, were attempting to enforce all the revenue laws; the Governor had become almost paranoid, sending exaggerated reports to the ministry; Parliament had violently condemned the colony and threatened to have arrested and sent to England for trial anyone suspected of treason. No other colony had to contend with such factors. But this was the price the province had to pay for leading resistance to the Townshend Acts.

The effects of the New York Restraining Act

Citizens of New York understandably showed less immediate concern for the Townshend Duties Act than for the Restraining Act directed at their colony. In 1766 the Assembly had refused to fulfill all requirements of the Mutiny Act because it was considered an unconstitutional tax, and because the measure placed no limit upon the number of troops a colony could be required to support. Faced with the prospect of having none of its legislation become law as a result of the Restraining Act, the Assembly responded in 1767 with more generous support of the army. But even the threat of a restraining measure failed to force the legislators to recognize Parliament's right to impose such acts upon them. Ignoring the Mutiny Act by name, the Assembly passed a bill appropriating £3,000, a sum thought adequate to provide all items called for by the Act.[45]

At the end of the year a Committee of the Whole House drew up a set of constitutional resolves that asserted the rights of the colony's citizens – a bill of colonial rights. Besides a list of privileges, the resolution noted that the legislature in which both king and citizen were represented could not constitutionally be suspended by Parliament. Only the Crown had such authority, it argued. The resolution also declared firmly in answer to Hillsborough's instructions that the Assembly had the right to correspond with any of its neighboring assemblies or any part of the dominion.[46]

Disturbed at the Assembly's surprising behavior, Governor Moore attempted to explain and justify it to Hillsborough. The Restraining Act had never gone into effect, he observed, troop maintenance had been settled, and merchants and traders had paid the Townshend Duties for almost a year with little complaint. Why, then, the angry memorials and resolves? He believed that a small faction in the House supported by Sons of Liberty in the city had intimidated other members. An equally important reason for the Assembly's actions was that "a rash and intemperate measure approved" in one colony "will be adopted in others." To have done less would impugn the patriotism of the colony.[47]

Regardless of its reasons, New York made clear its attitude towards the Townshend Acts. Unlike their frequent complaints about the Navigation Acts, the legislators viewed the Townshend measures as violating fundamental constitutional principles. Repudiating the Declaratory Act, they held that a mere Act of Parliament could not abridge such venerable documents as the Magna Carta and Bill of Rights. The British Constitution, as Samuel Adams had already observed, was an unchanging instrument.

South Carolina's response to the Townshend Acts

Slow to respond to the Townshend Acts, South Carolina became by 1770 one of their most uncompromising opponents. In April 1768 the House directed its Committee of Correspondence to order the South Carolina agent in London, Charles Garth, to work for the repeal of the Acts and to prevent the clause for billeting troops in the colonies from being inserted in the next Mutiny Act. The Commons House had begun to look upon continued support of His Majesty's troops as an unnecessary burden. Before it received the

Massachusetts Letter, the House was prorogued. But the speaker, Peter Manigault, assured Speaker Thomas Cushing of the Massachusetts Assembly that he would lay the Circular before the House at the first opportunity.[48]

That opportunity was long in coming. With the triennial term approaching its end, the extreme heat, and the absence of the ill Governor Montagu, the opening of the new session was postponed until November 1768. Lieutenant-Governor William Bull hoped the delay would prevent "the forming of precipitate and disagreeable resolutions" which were "more easily prevented than rescinded." He was aware, however, that many remained "fixed in the opinions adopted and encouraged from the north."[49]

The new Commons House opened on schedule in November and closed less than a fortnight later. With the doors barred, the legislators considered the Massachusetts and Virginia Circular Letters, resolved they were founded on constitutional privileges, and agreed to petition the monarch for relief from the Townshend Acts. The Committee of Correspondence was directed to keep Garth informed of the House's resolutions and advise him to continue to work for the repeal of the Townshend Acts. Because of Hillsboroughs's directive, Governor Montagu was left with little choice. He dissolved the House.[50]

A new Commons House met in June 1769, but, from the Governor's point of view, it was no improvement over the legislature he had dismissed some seven months before. It affirmed the Virginia Resolutions on August 19 and declared it lawful and expedient to join with other colonies in circulars that supported the "violated rights of America." In answer to the threat of the 35th Henry VIII, the House believed that Parliament had misconstrued the Act in "an arbitrary and cruel" way. Since the colony had adequate laws to handle felonies, treason and misprision of treason, the House saw no need to transport suspects to England to stand trial. Aroused by what they perceived as a threat to keep colonies cowed, members of the House agreed to petition their sovereign "to quiet the minds of his loyal subjects … and to avert from them those dangers and miseries" which would "ensue from the seizing and carrying beyond [the] sea any person residing in America suspected of any crime whatsoever." As they interpreted the ministry's intentions, not only those suspected of treasonous activities, but those accused of any kind of crime, could be transported to the mother country to stand trial.[51]

Fear and hostility were similarly evident in the House's response to Governor Montagu's request of August 17 to provide supplies for British troops in transit through the colony. Destined for St. Augustine, the troops were ordered to wait in South Carolina until sufficient barracks could be built in Florida. Many members of the House had already declared publicly that they would grant no further supplies to the army. They confirmed that promise on August 19.[52] The legislators reasoned that South Carolina was not bound to support troops even if the colony had applied for them. After all, they argued, the Townshend Acts were passed expressly for "protecting, defending and securing his Majesty's dominions." Let the government use these "illegal" revenues to pay for the troops' expenses. Indeed, the Commons House firmly declared that "under the circumstances … we are constrained to refuse making the desired provision during the existence of those acts – acts which strike at the very root of our Constitution, by taking our property without our consent, and depriving us of the liberty of giving to our sovereign." Furthermore, the Governor had acted unjustly and improperly by requesting support for the troops while the Townshend Acts were in force. The House promised to maintain this stern posture until the acts were repealed.[53]

By using the Townshend Acts as an excuse to withhold supplies from the army, the House had presented a remarkable rebuttal which, if assumed by other colonies, could have had dangerous repercussions for Britain. Why other provinces never vigorously pursued a similar policy after South Carolina initiated it is difficult to understand. Hillsborough candidly admitted to Gage that the Commons House position had "a face of plausibility." He was convinced that Parliament would have to alter

the Mutiny Act to counter arguments that South Carolina offered against it. Bull made no effort to refute the House's contentions and, rather than dissolve the Assembly, he quietly prorogued it after signing ten bills.[54]

6　The Colonies Boycott British Goods

Besides their political reactions to the Townshend measures, colonies also responded with boycotts of British goods. Boston's radicals quickly developed boycott plans that found a welcome in other Massachusetts communities. By the middle of January 1768, at least 24 towns had voted to abide by an agreement. Encouraged by the response, a Boston town meeting in December 1767 unanimously decided to instruct its representatives in the General Court to recommend bounties on domestic manufactures and to petition Parliament to repeal the Townshend Acts.[55]

The Assembly responded by passing a resolution in February 1768 calling for economy. With the tacit approval of the Assembly, the boycott gained momentum. Ninety-eight merchants meeting on March 1 voted to give consideration to non-importation. As Bernard observed, "This may be said to be the first movement of the merchants against the acts of Parliament." Concerned over the growing unfavorable balance of trade, the merchants claimed that restricting British imports under certain conditions would help correct the deficiency. On March 4 they concluded that the Townshend Acts had increased the specie shortage, slowed trade, caused further indebtedness among the traders, and threatened the Constitution. Accordingly, they resolved not to import for one year any goods save necessities, such as fish hooks, wire, and lead, and would invite other trading towns in Massachusetts, New York, New Jersey, and Pennsylvania to cooperate with them. They also agreed to encourage manufacturing, inform British merchants why they were withholding orders, and appoint a committee to correspond with other colonial merchants.[56]

New York's merchants stirred themselves to action in April 1768. Already unhappy over the hostile reception their petition of

December 1766 had received, distressed over declining trade, and encouraged by Boston's example, the merchants of the city signed a non-importation agreement even more restrictive than that of their New England neighbors. Meeting on April 28, the traders agreed to rescind all orders sent to Britain after August 15 and stop further importation after November 1. Subscribers who violated the agreement would be considered "enemies of their country." By September the association of merchants widened its restrictions with the threat to withhold its patronage from those traders who refused to abide by the agreement. Other towns fell in line behind the city. Albany concurred with the merchants' plan, though some of its traders wanted to continue importation of Indian trade goods.

South Carolina also joined the boycott, but not without controversy. Some individuals had the "integrity and resolution to withstand" intimidation and "flattering arguments," Lieutenant Governor Bull wrote, because the agreement was "contrary to their opinion and conscience." To make an example of these recusants and simultaneously show how few their numbers were, the general committee of merchants ordered circulated throughout the colony handbills on which 31 names were listed. The handbills, the standard colonial weapon with which to beat those who refused to cooperate, sparked the controversy between those who opposed and supported non-importation.[57]

William Wragg, planter, trader, and leader in the Commons House for a decade before 1768, saw his name on the list as an "honourable certificate." It proved to him that he was one of those who refused to violate his judgment by "swimming with the stream." The Constitution and common law alike indicated to him that he had the right to withhold his assent to propositions he disapproved. Believing non-importation would be "destructive of the end proposed," he saw neither reason, justice, nor charity in forcing one to forego British goods. He would, he said, endure anything "rather than have the freedom of my will or understanding limited or directed by the humours or capricious proscriptions of men not having authority."[58]

The second response to the handbills came from William Henry Drayton, nephew of Lieutenant-Governor Bull. Born to wealth and educated at Oxford, the 26-year-old Drayton was firmly fixed in the ethereal regions of Charles Town society. Under the name "Freeman," he had attacked non-importation in August 1769. "That Harlequin Medley Committee," he wrote, in its efforts to stigmatize him, had only given public testimony of his "resolution and integrity to persist in acting agreeably to the dictates" of his reason. He abhorred "the laying illegal restraints upon the free wills of free men, who had an undoubted right to think and act for themselves." He was, he thought, at least as capable of thinking for himself as those "gentry" were for themselves.[59]

Their angry rhetoric aside, Wragg and Drayton touched upon a fundamental dilemma for all non-importation associations. In their haste to protect the traditional freedom of representation and taxation, subscribers to associations violated an equally important freedom – liberty of conscience. Though good tactics, printing names of those who refused to accept the agreement was more insidious than mere physical abuse which some suffered in some communities. For the handbills attacked the individual's reputation and character, two delicate elements that were quick to wound and slow to heal.

Boycotts began to fail by 1770. While complex, the causes for their ultimate breakdown began in New York, where many issues were at work. A keen distrust of Boston, an acute currency shortage, and growing unemployment were all factors that influenced the merchants to renew importation. Even in the face of New York's desertion, many colonists were determined to carry on the fight. They believed that the ministry offered them no great concessions, and that the critical question of parliamentary sovereignty remained unanswered. Yet their protests were muffled by merchants who thought they had sacrificed enough and who refused to cooperate further. As non-importation began slowly to break apart, trade was resumed, and normalcy returned to all colonies by the beginning of 1771.

Non-importation failed as an instrument of protest in 1770, but colonists learned their lessons well. All the associations "were drawn up in a hurry and formed upon erroneous principles," the Virginian George Mason wrote in December. Differences between the various schemes adopted in different provinces caused increasing frustration. To correct weaknesses in non-importation, he felt that all colonies had to agree to one general plan of non-importation "exactly the same for all the colonies." Only in that way could intercolonial suspicions and jealousies be removed. "Such a plan as this is now in contemplation," Mason concluded; "God grant we have no cause to carry it into practice." Of course, the first Continental Congress carried just such a plan into operation when its members formed the Continental Association in October 1774[60] (see chapter 24, §4, and chapter 26, §5).

7 Repeal of the Townshend Duties

The British ministry had thrown out hints that if the Americans would behave, would stop boycotting British products, the government would consider altering the Townshend Acts. "Upon the whole, it was not a very lively debate," William Samuel Johnson said of the debate to alter the Townshend Duties Act on March 5, 1770.[61] London merchants presented their petition to the House, setting off the debate. After the petition was read, Lord North suggested that the interruption of trade about which merchants complained was the result of non-importation associations in America. Many people had attempted to persuade him to support repeal of the whole Act, North continued. But tea was not an article of English manufacture; it was a luxury item. Of all taxable goods, it was the most proper to carry a tax. Furthermore, as a result of the agreement with the East India Company, the price of tea had actually fallen in the colonies, acting in effect as a bounty for Americans. In answer to those who claimed the tea duty produced only trifles, he made an observation that had generally been ignored. Without equivocation or

qualification, he observed that the tea tax

was one of the best of all port duties. When the revenue is well established, it will probably go a great way towards effecting the purpose for which it was laid, which was to give additional support to our government and judicatures in America.[62]

North and presumably others in the ministry thus looked upon the tea tax as the most effective way to make some colonial civil administrations independent of the people – the very purpose Charles Townshend had in mind when he first proposed his measures.

North pointed out that not only was the tea duty profitable, but colonial complaints towards it were really aimed at the preamble. Americans "had laid it down as a rule that England has no right to tax her for the purpose of raising a revenue; they therefore desire to have all these duties repealed." A total repeal would mean giving up the preamble, which stated that the duties were for the purpose of raising a revenue. England, North cautioned, should never give up its rights to raise levies in America. "If you are to draw a line, it is better to draw a line with this act." Yet he repeated the assurances given in a Hillsborough circular of the previous May that his ministry had no intention of further taxing Americans for revenue.

Other reasons convinced North that Parliament need repeal only part of the duties. Doubtless using information supplied by the Boston publisher John Mein and Robert Hallowell, a customs official, North noted that, by "the last letters from Boston," it appeared the people had already begun to feel the bad effects of non-importation. "Many of the chief promoters have indulged in little deviations from the line they struck out." Prices had risen as much as 100 percent; a new subscription had ended with few names; some traders who had consented to hold their goods had begun to sell. Most important, in North's view, "many ships are gone full freighted from England to America, and there is every reason to expect that these associations will not long continue."

North's carefully prepared arguments were clear: those duties on British goods should be repealed to relieve the plight of English merchants, not to meet American demands. Parliament should retain the tea duty because it was the most profitable way to carry out Charles Townshend's goals, and because its retention would protect the government's right to tax the colonies. And because of the unmistakable evidence that non-importation agreements were breaking apart, there was no need to go further. With that, North moved "to bring in a bill to repeal so much of the said act as lays duties upon glass, red lead, white lead, painters' colours, paper, pasteboards, mill boards, and scaleboards."

Although the opposition urged the repeal of all the taxes, neither North nor any of his colleagues attempted to refute their arguments. There was no need to do so, for when the vote for an amendment to include the tea duty in the repeal was put, it was defeated by 204 to 142. The main question, the repeal of the lesser items, was carried without a division. The fight to repeal all the Townshend Duties was nearly at an end.

The opposition made one last effort to include the tea duty in the repeal on April 9, when one of its members moved to bring in a bill for that purpose. He reminded the House of the value of American trade, the monopoly Britain held over it, and the absurdity of raising a revenue in the colonies. Members of the ministry quickly disputed the propriety of the motion, arguing that it violated a well-known House rule that any motion which had once received a negative could not be introduced again in the same session. Rejecting the motion, the House voted by 80 to 52 in the negative. This vote moved William Samuel Johnson to observe that "it is now absolutely and finally determined not to repeal the duty on tea in this session."[63]

It would be inaccurate to claim that a major part of the Townshend Acts had been repealed. The revenue-producing tea levy, the American Board of Customs and, most important, the principle of making governors and magistrates independent all remained. In fact, the modification of the Townshend Duties Act was scarcely any change at all. Charles Townshend had always been fearful lest the colonies become infected with the bacillus of independence; his antidote had been to buttress the executive and judicial branches of colonial administration.

The North ministry agreed with that position and put it into effect. In Massachusetts, the Governor and Lieutenant-Governor, along with the jurists on the Superior Court, received their salaries from revenue collected from the tea duty. By 1772 the tea duty supported almost every important civil office in Massachusetts. Similarly, New York's governors obtained their salaries from those funds, as did the Chief Justice of New Jersey.[64]

The major concession Britain made had nothing to do – at least directly – with the Townshend Acts. That concession was the pledge never to raise another tax for revenue in the colonies. The Grafton ministry first made it, and North repeated it in the repeal debates. Admittedly, the administration could not bind future ministries to that promise, but once given up it would be difficult to re-establish. It was manifest why the ministry felt it could be magnanimous on the question of future taxation: it planned to strengthen the power of colonial officials. Little wonder that Lord North fought vigorously to retain the duty on tea. But if the struggle to end the Townshend Acts was finished in England, the battle continued in the colonies, especially in Massachusetts.

8   The Boston Massacre

"The madness of mobs or the insolence of soldiers, or both, should, when too near each other occasion some mischief difficult to be prevented or repaired," Franklin observed upon learning that the government had ordered troops for Boston in 1768. Franklin's fears proved tragically reliable, for resentful citizens and hostile soldiers made a volatile brew. But the explosion did not occur until the spring of 1770. In the meantime, radical tactics exacerbated a situation already made serious by ministerial blunders.[65]

Like many March evenings in New England, it was clear but cold and crisp that night of the 5th. Snow and ice clung stubbornly to the shaded and protected cobblestones, the last evidence of a hard winter. With disquieting suddenness the meetinghouse bells began to ring, bringing the curious into the streets. Standing in King Street with their backs pressed against the customs house, Captain Thomas Preston and a small contingent of soldiers faced a milling, taunting crowd. "Fire, damn you! Fire!" someone shouted. Those in the rear pressed the front of the mob towards the pointed bayonets. A stick flew out of the darkness, striking the gun barrel of Private Hugh Montgomery. He stepped back, or slipped on the icy street, and fired his weapon. Knocked to the ground, he screamed to the other soldiers, "Fire! Fire!" Panicked by now, the troopers followed Montgomery's example and shot point-blank into the mass of bodies. The solid mass flew apart as the mob shoved and pushed and trampled to escape the line of fire. One soldier was seen to take careful aim at the back of a fleeing youngster, but his shot missed. Within seconds King Street was deserted except for the soldiers, the wounded, and the dead. Three were killed outright, two lay mortally wounded, and six others were less seriously wounded. The meeting-house bells continued to chime and were soon supported by the staccato drum beat of the call to arms. Originally rung by a member of the mob, the bells could now more properly be tolled for the dead.[66]

The streets quickly filled with angry, armed citizens. Expresses were sent to neighboring towns requesting support against the army. Only after receiving assurances from Acting Governor Thomas Hutchinson that those soldiers responsible would receive proper punishment did the crowds sullenly disperse. Before dawn the next morning Captain Preston and eight soldiers were remanded to jail and ordered to stand trial for the murder of one Crispus Attucks, a runaway slave from Framingham, Massachusetts.

The evidence seems to suggest that this affray was the tragic and final product of an accumulation of small, hostile acts between soldiers and citizens, with each event growing more serious, making the social fabric more flammable. Only a spark was needed to ignite it; that came in the form of an insult. On Friday March 2, Samuel Gray, a rope-maker at John Hancock's wharf, and later one of the massacre victims, asked a passing trooper of the 29th Regiment if he wanted a job. When the underpaid soldier nodded in the affirmative, the rope-maker laughingly told him to clean out his privy. The trooper took the remark as an insult and attacked Gray. Soon other dock workers and soldiers joined in the battle with clubs, sticks, and cutlasses. Both sides came away badly bloodied, though there were no deaths. Fighting continued the following day, but eased somewhat on the Sabbath.

On Monday March 5, fighting again broke out. At first isolated frays occurred. Corporal John Eustace and one Mr. Pierpoint met as Eustace walked from his post at the Neck guard house. Words were exchanged and a fight ensued. Other fights continued that evening, and intensified when several soldiers attacked and beat two boys, one 11 years old and the other 14. A crowd gathered and in a frenzy attempted to charge into the main barracks after the soldiers. Several officers held off the mob with their swords. Frustrated and hearing the noise of another group not far away, the mob departed. Shortly thereafter several of its members broke into the meeting-house and began to ring its bell, the signal for fire, bringing hundreds of people into the streets.[67]

Captain Preston, the 40-year-old officer of the day, was informed that the ringing bell signified that inhabitants were assembling to attack the troops. As he made his way to the main guard house, the gang which had assaulted the barracks passed by, heading towards the customs house. There it joined a group of youths who were already taunting the lone sentry. A townsman informed Preston, he later claimed, that the mob intended to kidnap and possibly murder the sentry. Preston immediately sent off a non-commissioned officer and six soldiers to protect both the guard and the King's revenue. He soon followed the troops because he feared the non-commissioned "officer and soldiers by insults and provocations of the rioters, should be thrown off their guard and commit some rash act." Why he sent only a handful of soldiers – fewer than a dozen – to face a howling mob, he left unexplained. This body of men was large enough to feed the mob's anger, but too small to do anything more than barely defend itself.[68]

The "rash act" – the massacre – resulted in the removal of all soldiers from Boston to Castle William in Boston harbor at the insistence of the inhabitants. This was a prudent decision, for, had the troops remained, it was a "moral certainty" – as Hutchinson put it – "that the people ... would have taken to their arms and that the neighbouring towns would have joined them."[69]

The key issue in Preston's long trial, which began on October 24, 1770, was whether he had actually ordered his men to fire upon the mob. As the evidence unfolded, it became apparent that Private Montgomery, not Preston, had yelled out the order. During the trial, Justice Peter Oliver observed that it "appears quite plain to me that he must be acquitted; that the person who gave the orders to fire was not the captain, and indeed if it had been he, it at present appears justifiable." Within three hours after retiring, the jury had decided upon an acquittal for the officer.

Begun on November 27, the trial of the eight soldiers lasted more than seven days. The basic facts were that, though there were eight defendants, only six or seven shots were fired. It was shown convincingly that Private Montgomery shot Crispus Attucks and that Private Matthew Kilroy shot Samuel Gray. But much doubt remained over which of the other troopers fired into the mob. At least one of them did not fire at all. Led by John Adams and Josiah Quincy, the defense pointed out that a reasonable doubt existed over who fired their weapons. Adams went on to say the soldiers were under an extraordinary provocation by a "motley rabble of saucy boys, negroes and mulattoes, Irish teagues, and outlandish jack tarrs" – that is, outside agitators. Placing the blame of the assault on the soldiers to outsiders was a shrewd tactic, for it offered the jurors a way to bring in an acquittal without impugning the town's reputation. Six of the eight soldiers were found innocent, but Montgomery and Kilroy were found guilty of manslaughter, a capital crime. Both later pleaded benefit of clergy, were branded on the thumb, and released.[70]

Undoubtedly the Townshend Acts accelerated the deterioration in relations between the mother country and her colonies. By sending troops to Boston to assist in enforcing those measures, the ministry implicitly admitted it could control Massachusetts only with an army. For a nation rightfully proud of its benign rule, this was a terrible confession. Unfortunately, the troops' presence exacerbated a situation already made volatile by radicals, Bernard, and the customs commissioners. Had the ministry declared martial law instead of carefully abiding by legal and constitutional restrictions, perhaps it could have brought a semblance of peace to the colony. As it was, the small army became the ugly symbol of an oppressive regime attempting to enslave a free people. With few restrictions on their behavior, skirting the law at will, radicals made life miserable for the soldiers. The troops responded with predictable pugnacity.

The British Government ignored the lesson of the massacre – that the madness of mobs and insolence of soldiers made an explosive setting. After the Tea Party in 1773, the North ministry again sent troops to Boston. Shortly thereafter the Revolution began. And it must surely rank as the supreme irony of the pre-revolutionary decade that the massacre occurred on March 5, the same day that Parliament moved to temper the measures which had occasioned it.

REFERENCES

1 Treasury Minutes, Sept. 23, 1766, Class 29, Pieces 38–41, Public Records Office, London.

2 Namier, Lewis, and Brooke, John: *Charles Townshend* (New York, 1964).

3 Dowdeswell Papers, post, Oct. 25, William L. Clements Library, Ann Arbor, Michigan.

4 Labaree, Benjamin W.: *The Boston Tea Party* (New York, 1964), 13–14.

5 Whately to Grenville, Oct. 20, 1766, in *The Grenville Papers*, ed. William J. Smith, 4 vols. (London: John Murray, 1852–3), III, 332–6.

6 "Proposals for Regulating the Plantation Trade," March 14, 1766, Rockingham Papers, Wentworth-Woodhouse Collection, Sheffield City Library, England.

7 Sosin, Jack: *Agents and Merchants* (Lincoln: University of Nebraska Press, 1965), 104–5.

8 Conway to George III, Jan. 26, 1767, in *Correspondence of King George III*, ed. Sir John Fortescue, 6 vols. (London: Macmillan, 1927–8), I, 451.

9 Newdegate Papers, Box B26, B2548/3, Warwick County Public Record Office,

Warwick, England [NB The spelling of Newdigate was changed by his descendants].

10 Dec. 9, 1766, Colonial Office Papers, Series 5/1137, 8–10.

11 Shelburne to Chatham, [Feb. 16, 1767], in *Correspondence of William Pitt, Earl of Chatham*, ed. W. S. Taylor and J. H. Pringle (London, 1838, 1840), III, 206–9.

12 Shelburne to Chatham, April 26, 1767, Chatham Papers, 30/8, LVI, 86–90, Public Record Office, London.

13 Ibid.

14 Townshend Papers, Buccleuch MSS, VIII/31, Dalkeith, Midlothian, Scotland.

15 Lord Charlemont to Henry Flood, March 13, 1767, *Correspondence of William Pitt*, III, 231–2.

16 Shelburne to Chatham, March 13, 1767, Ibid.

17 April? 12, 1767, Grafton Papers, Public Records Office, Bury St. Edmunds, England.

18 Ibid.

19 Sackville to Irwin, April 20, 1767, in Historical Manuscripts Commission: *Manuscripts of Mrs. Stopford-Sackville*, 2 vols. (London: Eyre and Spotiswoode, 1905), I, 123.

20 Shelburne to Chatham, Feb. 1, 1767, *Correspondence of William Pitt*, III, 105.

21 Jan. 6, 1767, Townshend Papers, Buccleuch MSS, VIII/31.

22 Ibid.

23 West to Newcastle, May 13, 1767, Newcastle Papers, Add. MSS 32891, 323, British Museum.

24 Ibid.; Ryder shorthand notes, May 13, 1767, Doc. 46, Hanrowby MSS, Sandon Hall, England.

25 Charles Garth to Committee of Correspondence, May 17, 1767, *South Carolina Historical and Genealogical Magazine*, XXIX (1928), 228–9.

26 Ryder shorthand notes, May 13, 1767, Doc. 46, Harrowby MSS.

27 Ibid.

28 Cobbett, William (ed.): *Parliamentary History of England* (London, 1806–20), XVI, 331.

29 Bradshaw to Grafton, May 16, 1767, in *Autobiography and Political Correspondence of Augustus Henry, Third Duke of Grafton* (London: John Murray, 1898), 179–81.

30 Garth to Committee of Correspondence, June 6, 1767, *South Carolina Historical and Genealogical Magazine*, XXIX (1928), 295–305; *London Magazine*, XXXVII (1767), 179.

31 *London Magazine*, XXXVII (1767), 177; Newcastle Papers, Add. MSS 33037, 65–173.

32 *Boston Gazette* (Sept. 14, 1767).

33 Rockingham Papers, RII, 63.

34 To Hillsborough, May 23, 1768, Colonial Office Papers, Series 5/678, 48.

35 *The Critical Review*, XXVI (London, 1768), 16; *The Monthly Review*, LIX (London, 1768), 18.

36 Halsey, R. T. H. (ed.): *Letters from a Farmer in Pennsylvania* (New York, 1903).

37 Commager, Henry Steele (ed.): *Documents of American History*, 6th edn. (New York: Appleton Century Crofts 1958), 66–7.

38 Shelburne Papers, LXXXV, 182–3, Clements Library, Ann Arbor, Michigan.

39 April 23, 1768, Colonial Office Papers, Series 5/757, pt. 1, 113–17.

40 Gage Papers, Colonial Office Papers, Series 5/86, 109.

41 Bernard to Hillsborough, Jan. 23, April 29, June 1–17, 1769, Colonial Office Papers, Series 5/758, 95–7, 227–8, 255–65.

42 Hood to Philip Stevens, July 11, 1769, and Bernard to Hillsborough, July 7, 1769, ibid., 334–42, 309–14.

43 *Boston Post-Boy and Advertiser* (July 3, 1769).

44 Bernard to Hillsborough, July 17, 1769, Colonial Office Papers, Series 5/758, 349/54.

45 Assembly address to Moore, June 3, 1767, Colonial Office Papers, Series 5/1098, 657.

46 Assembly Journal, Dec. 1–31, 1768, Colonial Office Papers, Series 5/1100, 5–54: Gerlach, Don R.: *Philip Schuyler and the American Revolution in New York, 1733–1777* (Lincoln: University of Nebraska Press, 1964), 149–70.

47 Moore to Hillsborough, Jan. 4, March 30, 1769, Colonial Office Papers, Series 5/1100, 37–43, 265–6.

48 *South Carolina Gazette* (Sept. 6, 1768); Montague to Hillsborough, Nov. 25, 1768, Colonial Office Papers, Series 5/409, 57.

49 Bull to Hillsborough, Oct. 23, 1768, Colonial Office Papers, Series 5/409, 55–6.

50 Resolutions of the Commons House, Nov. 19, 1768, Colonial Office Papers, Series 5/391, 155–8; Montagu to Hillsborough, Nov. 25, 1768, Series 5/409, 57.

51 Resolutions of the Commons House, Aug. 17–19, 1769, Colonial Office Papers, Series 5/379, 71–2.

52 Resolutions of the Commons House, Aug. 23, 1769, Colonial Office Papers, Series 5/392, 93–4; Montagu to Hillsborough, June 30, 1769, Series 5/409, 63.

53   Resolutions of the Commons House, Aug. 23, 1769, Colonial Office Papers, Series 5/392, 93–4.

54   Hillsborough to Gage, Dec. 9, 1769, Colonial Office Papers, Series 5/87, 367/8; Bull to Hillsborough, Aug. 28–9, 1769, Series 5/409, 67–70.

55   Bernard to Shelburne, Sept. 14, Nov. 14, 1767, Colonial Office Papers, Series 5/756, 243–5, 295–6; *Boston Post-Boy and Advertiser* (Dec. 28, 1767).

56   Bernard to Hillsborough, March 21, Aug. 9, 1768, Colonial Office Papers, Series 5/757, pt. 1, 151–7, pt. 3, 749–50; Diary, March 1, 4, 9, 1768, in *Letters and Diary of John Rowe, Boston Merchant*, ed. Anne Cunningham (Cambridge, Mass.: W.B. Clarke, 1912), 152–3.

57   Bull to Hillsborough, Sept. 25, 1769, Colonial Office Papers, Series 5/409, 72–3.

58   *South Carolina Gazette* (Sept. 25, 1769).

59   Dabney, William, and Dargan, Marion: *William Henry Drayton and the American Revolution* (Albuquerque: University of New Mexico Press, 1962), 25–39; *South Carolina Gazette* (Aug. 3–17, 1769).

60   Mason to unknown correspondent, Dec. 6, 1770, in Kate M. Rowland: *Life and Correspondence of George Mason*, 2 vols. (New York, 1892), I, 148–51.

61   Johnson to Trumbull, March 6, 1770, Massachusetts Historical Society Collections: *Trumbull Papers* (Boston, 1885), IX, 421–6; Cavendish shorthand notes, Egerton MSS, 221, foll. 4–53, British Museum, London.

62   Cavendish shorthand notes, Egerton MSS, 4–53.

63   Johnson to Trumbull, April 14, 1770, Massachusetts Historical Society Collections: *Trumbull Papers* (Boston, 1885), IX, 430–2.

64   Dickerson, Oliver M.: "Use Made of the Revenue from the Tax on Tea," *New England Quarterly*, XXXI (1958), 240.

65   Franklin to Cooper, Feb. 24, 1769, Franklin Papers, Clements Library, Ann Arbor, Michigan.

66   Wroth, L. Kinvin, and Zobel, Hiller B. (eds.): *Legal Papers of John Adams*, 3 vols. (Cambridge. Mass.: Harvard University Press, 1965), III, *passim*; Zobel, Hiller B.: *The Boston Massacre* (New York: W. W. Norton, 1970), *passim*.

67   Depositions of John Eustace, July 24, 1770, Alexander Mall, Aug. 12, 1770, Henry Malone, July 24, 1770, Jeremiah French, July 25, 1770, Hugh Broughton, July 24, 1770, Colonial Office Papers, Series 5/88, 521, 425–?, 431, 519, 451–?.

68   Deposition of Capt. Thomas Preston, no date, Colonial Office Papers, Series 5/759, 247–53.

69   Hutchinson to Hillsborough, March 12, 1770, ibid., 119–22.

70   Wroth, L. Kinvin, and Zobel, Hiller B. (eds.): *Legal Papers of John Adams*, 3 vols. (Cambridge, Mass., 1965), III, esp. 1–34, 67, 77, 115, 118–19, 314.

FURTHER READING

Barrow, Thomas: *Trade and Empire: the British Customs Service in Colonial America, 1660–1775* (Cambridge, Mass.: Harvard University Press, 1967).

Brooke, John: *The Chatham Administration, 1766–1768* (London: Macmillan, 1956).

Bullion, John L.: *A Great and Necessary Measure: George Grenville and the Genesis of the Stamp Act, 1763–1765* (Columbia: University of Missouri Press, 1982).

Christie, I. R.: *Crisis of Empire: Great Britain and the American Colonies, 1754–1783* (New York: W. W. Norton, 1966).

Donoughue, Bernard: *British Politics and the American Revolution, 1773–1775* (London: Macmillan, 1964).

Flower, Milton: *John Dickinson, Conservative Revolutionary* (Charlottesville: University of Virginia Press, 1983).

Greene, Jack: *The Quest for Power: the Lower Houses of Assembly in the Southern Royal Colonies, 1689–1776* (New York: W. W. Norton, 1972).

Labaree, Benjamin W.: *The Boston Tea Party* (New York: Oxford University Press, 1964).

Langford, Peter: *The First Rockingham Administration* (New York, 1973).

Namier, Sir Lewis, and Brooke, John: *Charles Townshend* (New York: St. Martin's Press, 1964).

Ritcheson, Charles R.: *British Politics and the American Revolution* (Norman: University of Oklahoma Press, 1954).

Thomas, P. D. G.: *British Politics and the Stamp Act Crisis: the First Phase of the American Revolution, 1763–1767* (Oxford: Clarendon Press, 1975).

CHAPTER EIGHTEEN

The British Army in America, before 1775

DOUGLAS EDWARD LEACH

DURING the latter part of the seventeenth century the need for regular troops in the North American colonies was only occasional, but in the eighteenth century, with the growth of international rivalries and civil challenges to British authority, the army's involvement and responsibilities increased significantly. Gradually the enlarged garrison force, owing allegiance directly to the monarch, became closely linked with British imperial administration, being based in particular colonies under the command of provincial governors, many of whom were themselves professional military officers. In its simplest form the army's assignment was twofold: to defend imperial territory against Amerindians or European foes, and to aid local authority in repressing any civil insurrection. From time to time, depending on circumstances, one or the other of these two missions was dominant. Given the well-known conditions of colonial development, with growing conflict between American and British interests as well as mutually antipathetic attitudes, it is not surprising to discover considerable and sometimes intense friction between regulars and colonists. Thus the military presence is properly recognized as a contributing factor in the coming of the American Revolution.

1 The Seventeenth Century: Action and Communications

The first large-scale use of regulars occurred in 1677, when more than 1,000 soldiers landed in Virginia to stamp out Bacon's Rebellion, only to find that the royal governor had already done the job for them. At Boston in 1689 and New York in 1691, during the colonial version of the Glorious Revolution, regular troops again played a repressive role (although in Boston it was the redcoats, not the citizenry, who were disarmed). These seventeenth-century episodes did much to plant in the American mind the idea that the regulars were essentially a police power.

The British Army in the colonies operated under heavy handicaps. Consider, for example, the great length of its line of communication from London in the era of sail. Royal governors and military commanders alike often had to choose between inaction while awaiting instructions and action that might later be censured. Even when specific orders did arrive they were not always helpful, for the ministry at home usually had a clouded view of American conditions, including geography. Officers posted to North America found themselves in an unfamiliar environment amidst a diverse and sometimes perverse people. Each colony had its peculiarities, including currency. There was a great variety of ethnic and religious groups. One heard foreign tongues as well as strange accents. There were thousands of Africans, nearly all held in slavery. And there were numerous Amerindians, to many officers an enigma and to many soldiers a terror. Towns were few and widely scattered, interconnected only by water routes or primitive roads that would have been scorned by Roman legions. Moving troops and supplies over such long distances across wilderness territory often proved extremely difficult.

The very attitude of many colonists was hampering. Farmers and merchants alike profiteered at the army's expense, while taxpayers in general made clear to their representatives in the assemblies that taxes should not be increased just to aid the army in its mission. Usually the colonists backed the army when it was furthering their own interests, but then might shift into stubborn opposition if the troops seemed troublesome. Commanders soon realized that they had to be diplomats as well as soldiers.

Service in America had an adverse effect on the army in many ways. Commanders and other officers were frequently frustrated by what they viewed as provincial hostility. Among the officers there was a fairly high level of absenteeism, some officers, especially colonels of regiments, lingering long in Britain before rejoining their units. The enlisted men were often accommodated in badly deteriorating barracks or makeshift quarters, subject to rampant disease, scorned by the local community as immoral or vicious. Soldiers who tried to supplement their meager pay by working for hire during off-duty hours were accused of competing with local labor. Many seized an opportunity to desert, sometimes aided by colonists, which in turn angered the officers who were struggling to fill vacancies in the ranks. Altogether it makes for a picture of a garrison force far from home, discouraged, unappreciated, neglected, deteriorating.

2 Action, 1702–48

These severe difficulties should be kept firmly in mind while examining the army's role in North America during the first three-quarters of the eighteenth century. Queen Anne's War (1702–13) brought additional troops into the colonies. This was especially true in 1711, when about 4,300 redcoats used Boston as a base in preparation for a joint army–provincial expedition against Quebec. By accident this large and expensive venture came to grief in the treacherous currents of the St. Lawrence River, adding little to the reputation of army or navy.

During the long interlude following the Peace of Utrecht (1713) the colonists saw little of the regular army excepting the few independent companies permanently stationed in South Carolina and New York. Such companies were unaffiliated with any regiment, being specially constituted and maintained for garrison duty in certain locations. These small units typically remained for many years where assigned, suffering greatly from imperial neglect, with the result that their aging members lost both military polish and pride, becoming objects of local contempt. At best they remained as visible symbols of imperial authority, weak props for royal government amidst a growing and expanding colonial populace.

Increasing friction between Britain and Spain culminated in the War of Jenkins's Ear (1739–48), again bringing the British Army to the fore. One regiment had already been sent to the defense of the recently founded colony of Georgia under the overall command of General James Oglethorpe, participating in both the futile expedition against St. Augustine in 1740 and the successful defense of Georgia two years later. Then France entered the war in 1744, thereby providing New England with an opportunity to strike at the menacing French fortress of Louisburg on Cape Breton Island. After a motley New England army aided by the Royal Navy had besieged and forced the surrender of Louisburg in 1745, the victorious provincials were relieved by a substantial garrison of redcoats, who remained there until the area reverted to France at the Peace of Aix-la-Chapelle (1748).

3 Character and Organization

Here we may pause briefly to examine the character and organization of the mid-eighteenth-century British Army. Most of the commissioned officers were career soldiers drawn from the lower ranks of the British aristocracy and the upper middle class. Their commissions had been purchased rather than earned by merit, although some officers were highly experienced and competent. The enlisted men, by contrast, had been enticed into the army from their places in the lower levels of British society, mostly by the lure of guaranteed maintenance and security plus the prospect of adventure. Some but not all had been at odds with the law.

Having clutched the King's shilling, the new recruit was outfitted with a uniform consisting of tricornered hat; shirt and stock; waistcoat; tight white breeches; gaiters; shoes; and (most distinctive of all) a red outer coat with brass buttons, facing, and tails. He was also issued a 0.75 caliber Brown Bess musket with attachable bayonet. This muzzle-loading flintlock gun was deadly at close range, but quite ineffective beyond about a hundred yards.

The army was a fully professional fighting organization equipped and trained in accordance with the prevalent military concepts of the day, featuring exacting parade-ground drill and harsh discipline. Approximately 80 percent of the personnel were infantry, most of the remainder being mounted troops not used in America before the Revolution. Engineers and artillerymen were specialists ordinarily outside the normal line of military command until temporarily attached for a particular mission.

In speaking of infantry organization there is danger in being too precise, for numbers changed with changing circumstances. A company of foot soldiers usually numbered about 40 men under the command of a captain or other superior officer, who was assisted by a lieutenant, an ensign, and several non-commissioned officers. Nine or more companies comprised a battalion or regiment (in America the two terms were virtually interchangeable, although some regiments in the army did include more than one battalion). Thus a typical regiment, identified by the name of its colonel or, more frequently, its assigned number, consisted of about 400 officers and men. Headed by a colonel who owed his office to royal favor, the regimental staff also included a lieutenant colonel, a major, a quartermaster, and a surgeon.

Tactics were traditionally and officially linear, the units of infantry confronting the enemy while standing erect in drill-perfect lines at short range. The troops were intensively trained to load, fire, and reload their muskets simultaneously by units at the words of command, the objective being to deliver one or more devastating volleys, followed, if necessary, by a bayonet charge to clear the field. It is incorrect, however, to assume that the British Army was totally ignorant of any other style of fighting, including guerrilla warfare; nevertheless, most officers were more thoroughly versed in the traditional tactics and felt most comfortable employing them.

4   The Great War for the Empire

In the opening phase of the Great War for the Empire (1754–63) the disastrous defeat of General Edward Braddock's 44th and 48th regiments shocked the British world, and planted in the American mind a notion that redcoats were vulnerable to irregulars. As the British suffered further defeats in 1756–7, American respect for the regulars was further eroded, while colonial self-interest worked to shift more and more of the burden of the war onto the imperial government. Determined to win despite the inadequacy of American support, the ministry dispatched many more regiments to North America, also shouldering more of the cost, a policy that produced major victories in 1758–60 and the eventual defeat of France. The British Army emerged from the war with considerable glory and increased contempt for the provincial troops with whom they had shared the field: many colonists who had experienced British arrogance and insensitivity reciprocated.

5   The Americans' Resistance to British Taxation

Conquered territory in the West needed careful guarding, so London decided to retain 15 regiments in North America, the bulk of these troops to be stationed in a string of frontier posts stretching from the St. Lawrence through the Great Lakes, down the Mississippi Valley, to the Gulf of Mexico and Florida. Their main mission was to keep the various Amerindian tribes pacified by preventing British colonists from abusing them in the fur trade and encroaching on tribal lands. The government intended to defray at least part of the heavy cost by colonial taxation, but neglected to clarify for the Americans the nature of the army's mission. Americans would resist the taxation while suspecting the army's motives. Pontiac's Uprising of 1763 revealed the army's unreadiness, and,

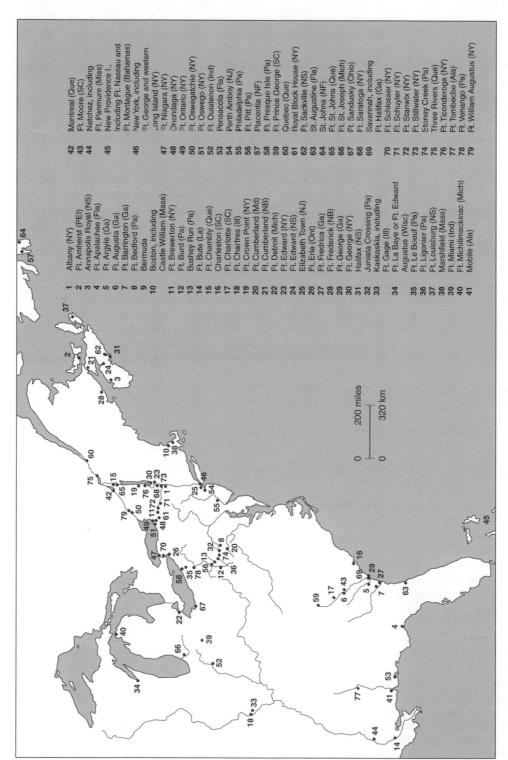

1	Albany (NY)
2	Ft. Amherst (PEI)
3	Annapolis Royal (NS)
4	Ft. Apalachee (Fla)
5	Ft. Argyle (Ga)
6	Ft. Augusta (Ga)
7	Ft. Barrington (Ga)
8	Ft. Bedford (Pa)
9	Bermuda
10	Boston, including
11	Castle William (Mass)
12	Ft. Brewerton (NY)
13	Ft. Burd (Pa)
14	Bushey Run (Pa)
15	Ft. Bute (La)
16	Ft. Chambly (Que)
17	Charleston (SC)
18	Ft. Charlotte (SC)
19	Ft. Chartres (Ill)
20	Ft. Crown Point (NY)
21	Ft. Cumberland (Md)
22	Ft. Cumberland (NB)
23	Ft. Detroit (Mich)
24	Ft. Edward (NY)
25	Ft. Edward (NS)
26	Elizabeth Town (NJ)
27	Ft. Erie (Ont)
28	Ft. Fredrica (Ga)
29	Ft. Frederick (NB)
30	Ft. George (Ga)
31	Ft. George (NY)
32	Halifax (NS)
33	Juniata Crossing (Pa)
34	Kaskaskia, including
	Ft. Gage (Ill)
	Ft. La Baye or Ft. Edward
35	Augustus (Wisc)
36	Ft. Le Boeuf (Pa)
37	Ft. Ligonier (Pa)
38	Ft. Louisburg (NS)
39	Marshfield (Mass)
40	Ft. Miami (Ind)
41	Ft. Michilimackinac (Mich)
	Mobile (Ala)

42	Montreal (Que)
43	Ft. Moore (SC)
44	Natchez, including
45	Ft. Panmure (Miss)
	New Providence I.,
	including Ft. Nassau and
	Ft. Montague (Bahamas)
46	New York, including
	Ft. George and western
	Long Island (NY)
47	Ft. Niagara (NY)
48	Onondaga (NY)
49	Ft. Ontario (NY)
50	Ft. Oswegatchie (NY)
51	Ft. Oswego (NY)
52	Ft. Ouiatenon (Ind)
53	Pensacola (Fla)
54	Perth Amboy (NJ)
55	Philadelphia (Pa)
56	Ft. Pitt (Pa)
57	Placentia (NF)
58	Ft. Presque Isle (Pa)
59	Ft. Prince George (SC)
60	Quebec (Que)
61	Royal Block House (NY)
62	Ft. Sackville (NS)
63	St. Augustine (Fla)
64	St. Johns (NF)
65	Ft. St. Johns (Que)
66	Ft. St. Joseph (Mich)
67	Ft. Sandusky (Ohio)
68	Ft. Saratoga (NY)
69	Savannah, including
	Ft. Halifax (Ga)
70	Ft. Schlosser (NY)
71	Ft. Schuyler (NY)
72	Ft. Stanwix (NY)
73	Ft. Stillwater (NY)
74	Stoney Creek (Pa)
75	Three Rivers (Que)
76	Ft. Ticonderoga (NY)
77	Ft. Tombecbe (Ala)
78	Ft. Venango (Pa)
79	Ft. William Augustus (NY)

0   200 miles

0   320 km

Map 1   Forts and posts occupied by the British Army up to 1775.

although the regulars did eventually prevail, they simply were not capable of fulfilling the ministry's expectations.

The Quartering Act of 1765

By 1768 the imperial government had recognized the failure, while feeling intensified concern over American insubordination, causing a shifting of major troop strength from the West to the populated coastal area, with concentrations at Halifax, New York, Philadelphia, and St. Augustine. The troops were housed in barracks where available, otherwise in taverns and other non-domestic buildings. There was doubt as to whether or not the British Constitution permitted forced quartering in occupied dwellings; nearly all Americans were certain it did not, and except under emergency conditions British commanders avoided forcing the issue. The Quartering Act of 1765, even though it did not authorize domestic quartering, had imposed a form of taxation and raised American ire (*see* chapter 15, §4, and chapter 16, §8). One should be aware that under the British Constitution the army had no free hand. Troops could not be employed against rioters until summoned by a civil magistrate. A governor would be foolish to make such a request without the support of his council whose members, in turn, were reluctant to offend their fellow colonists. Although the army was expected to act decisively, it often could not.

Further complicating the situation was the military office of Commander-in-Chief, the unfortunate Braddock having been first in a succession that included Governor William Shirley of Massachusetts, the Earl of Loudoun, General James Abercromby, General Jeffrey Amherst, and, from 1763, General Thomas Gage. Army headquarters were in the town of New York. The office tended to blur the authority of the provincial governors, who traditionally had control of all military forces within their respective jurisdictions. Most governors after 1754 tended to defer to a strong Commander-in-Chief.

The Boston Massacre

The seaport of Boston was in the forefront of American resistance to British taxes and the customs service, yet no garrison force had been sent there. In 1768 the ministry ordered Gage to remedy that deficiency. Before this could be accomplished the Liberty Riot occurred as a blatant affront to royal authority, causing London to dispatch a sizeable force. The first units began landing on October 1, 1768, covered by the menacing guns of several warships. By the end of the year the garrison consisted of the 14th, 29th, 64th, and 65th regiments plus part of the 59th. These were sufficient to prevent all but petty harassment by the sullen inhabitants, who viewed the soldiers as the arm of ministerial oppression. After the situation had stabilized, Gage eventually withdrew most of the troops, leaving only about 600 men to shiver through the winter of 1769–70 under the taunt of "lobsterback" and even less flattering epithets hurled by Boston's gamins.

That same winter saw violence in New York, where the Sons of Liberty had erected a liberty pole as a symbol of defiance. After redcoats of the town garrison cut down the pole, rioting patriots brawled with the troops on Golden Hill, fortunately without loss of life on either side. Elsewhere in the colonies, wherever redcoats and patriots were in proximity there was likely to be tension if not open violence, as tempers on both sides grew shorter. This was especially true in Boston, where the townsfolk made every effort to discomfort the soldiery.

The culmination was the Boston Massacre of March 5, 1770. On that tragic evening an ugly-spirited mob so harassed and frightened a small party of troops on guard duty that first one and then others of the soldiers discharged their muskets into the crowd, killing five. Later brought to trial and defended by John Adams, all but two of the soldiers were acquitted and none was hanged. Local radicals seized upon the "massacre" as proof of British bestiality, emitting whole volleys of skillful propaganda excoriating the garrison. To ease the situation, the troops were withdrawn to Castle Island in the harbor.

The Boston Tea Party and the Coercive Acts

Boston again showed its determination not be coerced when its Sons of Liberty organized and hosted the now-famous Tea Party of December 16, 1773, efficiently destroying 90,000 pounds of dutiable tea in less than three hours (*see* chapter 24, §2). It is noteworthy that, although both the navy and the army were within call, neither took preventive action. Outraged by the defiant destruction, Parliament passed the Coercive Acts, two of which in particular affected the army. A new Quartering Act required the colonies to provide quarters for troops *wherever needed*, but still failed to endorse forced billeting in private homes. The Administration of Justice Act (applying only to Massachusetts) was intended to secure a fair trial for any royal official or soldier accused of killing a colonist in the line of duty by permitting the case to be transferred to another colony or even to England. Radicals charged that the new law gave soldiers a license to murder. Also, in the spring of 1774 Massachusetts acquired a new royal governor – none other than General Gage – who now moved from New York to Boston, combining civil authority and military command in one person.

The authority of the new governor was supported by large numbers of additional troops. By the beginning of 1775 the offending town was garrisoned by nine regiments plus portions of two others, which meant one redcoat for every five inhabitants, surely enough to keep the lid firmly clamped down on the Boston teapot. It should have been clear to everyone, even the most radical patriot, that Parliament and the Crown meant business.

FURTHER READING

Dunn, W. S., Jr.: *Frontier Profit and Loss: the British Army and the Fur Traders, 1760–1764* (Westport, CT: Greenwood Press, 1998).

Frey, S. R.: *The British Soldier in America: a Social History of Military Life in the Revolutionary Period* (Austin: University of Texas Press, 1981).

Higginbotham, D.: *The War of American Independence: Military Attitudes, Policies, and Practice, 1763–1789* (New York: Macmillan, 1971).

Leach, D. E.: *Arms for Empire: a Military History of the British Colonies in North America, 1607–1763* (New York: Macmillan, 1973).

——: *Roots of Conflict: British Armed Forces and Colonial Americans, 1677–1763* (Chapel Hill: University of North Carolina Press, 1986).

Shy, J.: *Toward Lexington: the Role of the British Army in the Coming of the American Revolution* (Princeton, NJ: Princeton University Press, 1965).

CHAPTER NINETEEN

The West and the Amerindians, 1756–1776

PETER MARSHALL

IN the West, constant conflict and change marked the 20 years preceding Independence. Though the elimination of the French empire in North America and the acquisition of Spanish colonies had demonstrated beyond doubt a British ascendancy, the victor's inability to establish effective control over an immense expanse, where Amerindians, settlers, speculators, colonial governors and imperial officials were continually in conflict, was even more clearly evident. During these years expansion to the west made a significant contribution not to the profits but to the bankruptcy of an imperial policy so recently marked by military humiliation during the Seven Years' War and the Rebellion of Pontiac, followed by failure to organize the regulation of Amerindian affairs, and incapacity in Westminster and Whitehall to manage Western settlement and establish new colonies. Victory in war had therefore only magnified the problems of the ensuing peace.

Frontier traders, settlers, and speculators regarded the British declaration of war on France in May 1756 as an event of no great significance: Washington's surrender at Fort Necessity in July 1754, the expulsion of the Acadians from Nova Scotia, and Braddock's defeat and death on the Monongahela in the following year made a far greater impression. The converse did not hold good: the conflict in America drew the attention of Europeans to the particular prospects and distinguishing features of New World societies. Throughout the eighteenth century the Amerindian presence had attracted constant attention marked by a determination to incorporate mythical qualities within the imperial structure: the visit of the four Amerindian "Kings" to London in 1710 secured a popular response that owed far more to the imagination than to facts but which saw one of their number, Chief Hendrick, remain a figure of some prominence until his death, fighting with the British, at the battle of Lake George in 1755. Distant exoticism contrasted sharply with contiguous antipathies. Yet, if neither colonists nor Amerindians held each other in trust or esteem, by 1756 both needed to define relations. Self-sufficiency had long been abandoned. As John Stuart, Superintendent of Indian Affairs south of the Ohio, reported to London in 1764:

The original great tie between the Indians and Europeans was mutual conveniency. This alone could at first have induced the Indians to receive white people differing so much from themselves into their country.... A modern Indian cannot subsist without Europeans; and would handle a flint ax or any other rude utensil used by his ancestors very awkwardly: so what was only conveniency at first is now become necessity and the original tie strengthened. (De Vorsey, 1966, p. 12)

Despite its generation of continual conflict and dispute, trade bound Amerindians and colonists together. For the Amerindians it afforded essential recourse to arms, ammunition, tools, strouds and rum: the colonists might obtain furs, deerskins and, with increasing frequency, land grants of uncertain extent and validity.

1 The Need for a Coordinated Amerindian Policy

In the early 1750s the western districts of Virginia and the Carolinas proved centers of conflict between settlers and Amerindians. Movement from the north had brought, from the 1730s, Scots-Irish and Germans to settle close to Amerindian lands and had also encouraged Pennsylvanian and Virginian territorial claims. The organization in 1747 of the Ohio Company and in 1749 of the Loyal Company, Virginian enterprises whose immediate lack of success would not extinguish their land claims, marked the beginning of corporate ventures in a region where settlement was not inhibited by Amerindian numbers or geographical access. New York's proximity to New France and exaggerated estimates of Iroquois fighting strength focussed political and military attention on threats developing north of the Ohio. The Albany Congress of 1754 testified to colonial support for a coordinated Amerindian policy, the likelihood of which seemed to grow in the following year with the appointment of an Amerindian Superintendent for the Northern District. William Johnson, long resident among and linked with the Mohawks, his influence among the Iroquois unsurpassed, was the obvious candidate for the post. What powers were bestowed upon him remained uncertain: although, when Loudoun became Commander-in-Chief in 1756, Johnson's new commission was accompanied by a letter that declared "the whole management of this branch of the service will be left entirely to your discretion," the superintendents' finances depended totally on military funds. If Johnson's standing and activities were such as to permit a certain freedom of action, or at least room for financial argument after the event, no such advantages accrued to Edmond Atkin, appointed Superintendent for the Southern District in 1756. All Atkin had demonstrated before his death in 1761 was that a capacity to write at some length on Amerindian history and policy did not insure an ability to transact Amerindian affairs. His successor, John Stuart, would exercise, until the coming of the Revolution, altogether more effective control, even if he did not equal the status

and prominence of his colleague to the north.

2 The Amerindian Population and their Relations with the Colonists

The number of Amerindians in contact with colonial expansion can only be roughly calculated, particularly since estimates were provided by those whose interests seemed more personal than scientific. Figures were offered in terms of warriors, and needed to be multiplied four- or fivefold to calculate the total population. In 1763 Johnson declared that his district contained some 8,020 warriors: the Iroquois and their dependents accounted for 2,230; Canadian Amerindians allied to them, 630; the Amerindians of the Ohio Valley 1,100; while the remainder, for whom accurate figures could not be given, were to be found round the Great Lakes. Stuart's figures, provided in the following year, indicated a somewhat larger and even more widely dispersed body of Amerindians. The Cherokees, located at the southern end of the Appalachians, and the nation most in contact there with the colonists, were estimated to comprise 2,750 warriors; the Creeks, to their south and west, possessed 3,600; on lands located in the present State of Mississippi were to be found 5,000 Choctaw and 450 Chickasaw warriors. Taking these conservative totals, the Amerindian population in the South amounted at least to some 60,000, and the two superintendents were responsible for relations with more than 100,000 Amerindians.

During the Seven Years' War, and in its aftermath, colonists and Amerindian officials could never rely on the maintenance of peace and friendship. In the North only Johnson's adopted Mohawks, in the South only the Chickasaws, could be considered faithful. Proof of Amerindian duplicity and capacity to wipe out frontier posts remained only too recurrent: until the summer of 1758 French regiments and Amerindian raiders inflicted death and devastation, and the Cherokee war of 1759–61 brought much slaughter but little military glory to South Carolina. If the events of 1759 brought a dramatic and, as it proved, conclusive end to French power in North America, Pontiac's

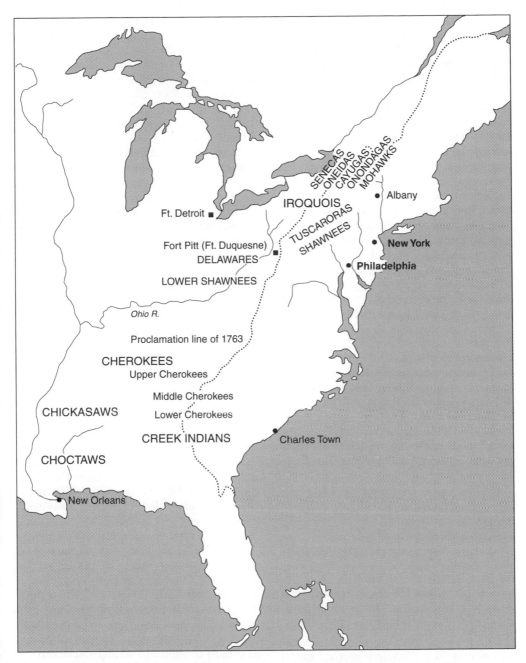

Map 2 The location of some major Amerindian nations in the years
leading up to the Revolution.

Rebellion in 1763 demonstrated a continued capacity to attack. French regiments might have departed but Amerindian warriors still commanded fear and respect.

The British conquest might have seemed to transform Amerindian relations but appearances proved deceptive. Two commanding features remained unchanged and unaffected: the cultural meeting of Americans and Amerindians in a complex set of circumstances denoted and entitled by Richard White "the middle ground," and the constant involuntary migration and splintering of Amerindian communities so as to render assertions of coherent "tribes" and "nations" as ventures into unreality. These processes, long under way, became significantly less subject to control as a consequence of the end of French power. British authority had lost its recognized antagonist but, far from governing unopposed, possessed totally inadequate resources to implement its rule. Traders, missionaries, officers and officials, settlers, both came into conflict and shared interests with Amerindians who were better identified in terms of villages than of nations. The basic distinction between French and British forms of territorial exploitation resided in the magnitude and extent of settlement. This alone served to eliminate any possibility of peaceful coexistence, especially in the absence of effective imperial direction. As Richard White has observed:

The irony of British policy in the years between the French and Indian War and the American Revolution was that although it aspired to control Indians, it foundered on the British government's inability to control its own subjects. And the more British officials failed to control their own people through law, the more events forced them to appeal to the customs of the middle ground. (White, 1991, p. 344)

Conquest was never as complete as the victors may have thought it would be.

3   Results of the Proclamation of 1763

The establishment of supremacy in North America had involved Britain in unprecedented costs and commitments. One North American consequence was the need to create three more colonial governments. The province of Quebec, as delimited in 1763, saw a reduction of the extent of New France,

both in the Gulf of the St. Lawrence and, much more significantly, west of the Ottawa river, so excluding from any form of civil rule the entire Great Lakes region; in the far south, Spanish Florida became the colonies of East and West Florida. The Proclamation of October 7, 1763, which detailed these arrangements, also sought to protect Amerindian lands. Governors of all the colonies were forbidden to acquire lands within their limits reserved for the tribes, or "beyond the heads or sources of any of the rivers which fall into the Atlantic Ocean from the west or north-west." The withdrawal was ordered of any colonists already settled further west. Within the colonies, only governors would purchase Amerindian lands, and trade, though "free and open," was to be conducted under licenses and regulations which, if breached, would lead to a cancellation of permit and forfeiture of security payment. The Proclamation had been issued before news reached London of the attacks on the western posts attributed to Pontiac. Intended as an interim, not a permanent, measure, it left undrawn the lines that divided settled from Amerindian lands. The task of repairing this omission would occupy much of the superintendents' attention until the Revolution.

Between 1763 and 1774 the problems of western expansion and of Amerindian relations appeared both incompatible and inseparable. Prominent figures, such as Sir William Johnson, saw no contradiction as existing in a dual commitment. Imperial authority had to be maintained, defined, and paid for; conflicting colonial claims demanded resolution; innumerable land schemes pursued by individuals, syndicates, and companies testified to ambitions of territorial gain extending seamlessly from Nova Scotia to Florida. The process of growth stimulated continual change, challenging and disturbing a variety of interests that ranged from imperial order to Amerindian custom. It must be said that in these years ambition, rather than achievement, had the upper hand.

4   Imperial Control of Trade with the Amerindians

Amherst's   refusal,   as   Commander-in-Chief, to accept that after the French had surrendered the Amerindians still posed a military threat and that notice needed to be taken of the procedures of the middle ground, had been totally invalidated by the events of 1763. The overwhelming of so many military posts seemed to have proved Johnson's assertions of the necessity to keep good Amerindian relations. Official recognition of this was provided by the Board of Trade in its circulation, on July 10, 1764, of an elaborate plan for the future management of Amerindian affairs. These proposals, 43 in number, seemed to incorporate Johnson's preferences. Amerindian trade would be placed under imperial control and be confined to posts in the North and to Amerindian towns in the South, each being provided with a commissary, an interpreter, and a smith. The superintendents would assume sole responsibility for Amerindian relations and diplomacy, be independent of military commanders, and negotiate all treaties and land grants on behalf of the colonies. The commissaries would fix the places and rates of trade for those licensed to conduct it. Liquor, swan shot, and rifled guns were not to be supplied, and a precise Amerindian boundary would be established. It was estimated that the plan would cost about £20,000 a year, the sum to be raised either by a duty on the trade or by traders' payments.

The raising of revenue required the listing of places where trade would be conducted, the tariffs which were to be imposed, and the passage of legislation. The Board of Trade circulated the plan and awaited comments from the colonies. Two years later to the day, the Board was writing to Johnson to explain that "it has been impossible for us, amidst the other pressing business that has occur'd, so to prepare our thoughts & opinion upon this important subject, as to be able as yet to lay them before His Majesty." Ministerial changes, diverse colonial responses, the Stamp Act crisis, had inhibited progress. Lacking formal authority, Thomas Gage, now Commander-in-Chief, reluctantly condoned an unofficial and partial implementation of the plan. He was particularly fearful of financial outlays likely never to be approved or recovered. The superintendents continued to perform their duties without legislative support: imperial control of Amerindian affairs accordingly remained dependent not on statute but on individuals.

The superintendents' uncertain standing encouraged their tendency to confuse personal and official activities. This was particularly the case with Johnson as he sought to reconcile the responsibilities of office, his attachment to the Mohawk, his standing with the Iroquois, his greed for land and his political ambitions. In the case of New York this presented particular problems since any acquisition of Amerindian territory had to be set against an affirmation of Iroquois preeminence. The outcome was an attempt to direct settlement and speculation towards the western extents of Pennsylvania and Virginia. There, the territory might seem more accessible, a greater demand might be satisfied, and Amerindian resistance prove less significant. The lands in this region of the Delawares and Shawnees might be surrendered by the Iroquois on behalf of their "nephews." Johnson concluded that this would lessen pressure on "his" Amerindians, allow him to continue to secure land profits, and maintain peace on the frontier. By relinquishing claims to lands they could no longer control, the Iroquois would not suffer. A similar solution was adopted by Stuart in respect of the Cherokee. Continual demand for land in conditions that lacked formal means of regulation or provision of title resulted inevitably in reliance on temporary expedients that guaranteed enduring problems.

Boundary negotiations

No matter how mixed their motives may have been, the superintendents had devoted much attention to the establishment of a boundary line. Building upon the Congress of Augusta, held in November 1763, Stuart concluded eight treaties between 1763 and 1768. Johnson completed 11 between 1764 and 1766. Boundary negotiations proved easier in the South, where they principally concerned the Cherokee. Stuart reached agreement with them in October 1768 at the Treaty of Hard Labor. This completed a line which, in the Carolinas, ran well to the east of that indicated in the 1763

Proclamation. In the North the boundary awaited the making by Johnson of the Treaty of Fort Stanwix in November 1768, and even then the line north of the Mohawk River remained undemarcated.

5   The Return of Amerindian Affairs to Colonial Control

By the end of 1768 the completion of the boundary line had been overtaken by events. The authority to finalize it, received by Johnson in February, had been undermined with the receipt in July of the Board of Trade's report of March on American affairs. The proposals of the plan of 1764 were now set aside. Imperial regulation of Amerindian trade was to be abandoned and, as far as possible, the army was to withdraw from western posts. Although the boundary line was still intended to be run, in future the superintendents would be restricted to diplomatic, not administrative duties. This return of Amerindian affairs to colonial control proved a signal for disorder: local arrangements were quite inadequate and attempts to initiate intercolonial cooperation were quashed by the ministry. With the steady removal of garrisons from the western posts – 24 had been abandoned by the beginning of 1773 – imperial management of the interior had been almost totally relinquished. This did not mean, however, any necessary improvement of prospects for the Amerindians.

It is almost certain that even wholehearted imperial intervention in Amerindian affairs would have failed to keep order, since the West was far too extensive an area to permit the control of trade, the provision of military protection, or the prevention of further settlement. The acquisition of land, whether by individuals or companies, exerted a particular attraction. So by 1766, much of the Monongahela Valley in western Pennsylvania had been peopled without official consent or even Amerindian purchase. The Ohio Company of Virginia, though lacking in vigor, still maintained an interest in the region of Pittsburgh, while the Mississippi Company, formed in June 1763, represented a further attempt to secure a tract of two and a half million acres further down the

Ohio. In the East, moreover, Pennsylvanians faced a challenge from the Susquehannah Company, organized in Connecticut in 1753 and, revived and redeveloped after the war, claiming land under its colony's sea-to-sea charter. If, in the new colonies, attempts to attract British migrants to Quebec had proved pitifully unsuccessful, applications for land grants in the Floridas were altogether more abundant. Although in a large majority of these cases receipt of grant was not a prelude to successful settlement, the disturbances engendered by land claims can hardly be overemphasized.

Extending the boundaries

The most serious attempt at communal land acquisition had its origins in a bid to secure traders compensation for losses suffered at the hands of the French and Amerindians, both in 1754 and in 1763. This had led to the emergence in 1765 of a group, including Johnson's assistant, George Croghan, backed by the Philadelphia trading enterprise of Baynton, Wharton, and Morgan, which had obtained the Superintendent's support for claims in respect of their 1763 losses. In May 1765 the Six Nations and the Delawares offered, at Johnson's insistence, these "suffering traders" a grant of land between the Ohio and the Alleghenies, to be called Indiana. In the following year Johnson, while continuing to urge approval of this grant, was pressing the Board of Trade to recognize the Illinois Company and consider its petition for the grant of 1,200,000 acres on the Mississippi near Fort Chartres. Half of this company's shares were owned by Baynton, Wharton, and Morgan, a quarter were divided unobtrusively between Johnson and William Franklin, the Governor of New Jersey. The London advocate of this project was, not surprisingly, the latter's father, Benjamin Franklin. By the summer of 1767 the ministry lacked leadership and was beset by conflict between the Chancellor of the Exchequer, Charles Townshend, who required a reduction in American expenses, and Lord Shelburne, responsible as Secretary of State for a policy submerged in detail and uncertainty. It had discussed but not confirmed a proposal that new colonies be established at Illinois and Detroit.

The Board of Trade report of March 1768 considered at length and rejected the case for inland colonies. This, however, did not deter the speculators, who soon derived great encouragement from the lands obtained in November by Johnson at the treaty of Fort Stanwix. That much of the territory ceded by the Iroquois was not theirs to surrender could be ignored. Although Hillsborough, the new, and specifically appointed Secretary of State for America, saw no merit in the Superintendent's achievement, others were anxious to profit from it. In return for meeting the costs of the Fort Stanwix treaty (calculated to amount to £10,460 7s. 3d.), a group of Philadelphia traders, headed by Samuel Wharton, their numbers expanded, after Wharton's arrival in England to secure a grant of 2,400,000 acres, by the addition of the politician and banker Thomas Walpole, Benjamin Franklin, other influential officials and Members of Parliament, aimed to establish a proprietary colony south of the Ohio. The proposal, under the name of the Grand Ohio Company, was quite unacceptable to Hillsborough, who resisted its acceptance until after a hearing of the case before the Privy Council committe. From this, Wharton emerged much the superior and secured a report that favoured the application: in August 1772 Hillsborough, unable to win support in the Cabinet, resigned from office. By 1773 the establishment of the first inland colony, to be named Vandalia as a supposed compliment to the Queen, appeared imminent.

6 Collapse of Imperial Authority

There was little time for Wharton to contemplate prospects of success. Conditions on the Ohio were out of control: the competing interests of Virginians, Pennsylvanians, and would-be Vandalians turned the region into a chaos that became even more evident in the summer of 1774 when Lord Dunmore, as Governor of Virginia, made war on the Shawnee. By that time the disintegration of imperial control rather than the creation of another colony was the significant issue. The only new development was the boundary revision included in the imperial legislation of July 1774: the Quebec Act not only extended the province to the Ohio but followed the river to the Mississippi and then turned north to meet the territories of the Hudson's Bay Company. The entire Great Lakes region now enjoyed, under British rule, a unity of government that France had continually sought to achieve. In terms of the northern district, imperial regulation and colonial government had completely parted company.

The opposition aroused by this despairing attempt to impose some measure of control upon the territories and peoples of the West contributed to the grounds on which, less than a year later, hostilities would begin. The number of settlers to have entered Amerindian country by the time of the Revolution can only be estimated: there may have been 50,000 west of the Appalachians, few of whom remained loyal to the Crown. The departure of the garrisons and the death of Johnson in 1774 confirmed the collapse of imperial authority. The situation to the south was no better. Stuart despaired at Whitehall's failure to create and impose imperial regulations. As one who found traders more likely than Amerindians to cause conflicts, he regarded the massive growth in commercial competition after 1763 as a permanent invitation to the spread of uncontrolled violence.

By 1776 there may have existed an overlap of economic, social, and cultural interests between Amerindians and settlers more than sufficient to constitute a "middle ground." This did not extend to political relations. It was not surprising that most Amerindians proved unwilling to opt for either side at the outbreak of war. In the South, where Stuart remained Superintendent, only the Cherokees moved, in the summer of 1776, against the Carolinas. Prompt and effective American counterattacks devastated their lands and villages and cowed other tribes. In the North the new Superintendent, Guy Johnson – Sir William's nephew – was unable to launch the Six Nations against the rebels. Twenty years' endeavor to link imperial and Amerindian interests could be seen to have made a minimal contribution to British efforts to maintain authority in

North America. Whatever the Declaration of Independence would claim, "the merciless Indian savages" were not to play a major part in the drama of the Revolution.

FURTHER READING

Abernethy, Thomas Perkins: *Western Lands and the American Revolution* (New York: Russell & Russell, 1959).

Alden, John Richard: *John Stuart and the Southern Colonial Frontier* (Ann Arbor: University of Michigan Press, 1944).

Calloway, Colin G.: *The American Revolution in Indian Country* (New York and Cambridge: Cambridge University Press, 1995).

De Vorsey, Jr., Louis: *The Indian Boundary in the Southern Colonies, 1763–1775* (Chapel Hill: University of North Carolina Press, 1966).

Jones, Dorothy V.: *License for Empire* (Chicago: University of Chicago Press, 1982).

Snapp, J. Russell: *John Stuart and the Struggle for Empire on the Southern Frontier* (Baton Rouge: Louisiana State University Press, 1996).

Sosin, Jack M.: *The Revolutionary Frontier, 1763–1783* (New York: Holt, Rinehart and Winston, 1967).

White, Richard: *The Middle Ground: Indians, Empires, and Republics in the Great Lakes Region, 1650–1815* (New York and Cambridge: Cambridge University Press, 1991).

CHAPTER TWENTY

Trade legislation and its enforcement, 1748–1776

R. C. SIMMONS

1 Trade and Power

SOME discussions of the Revolution have stressed British trade legislation and the measures taken to enforce it as fundamental colonial grievances. For important planting and merchant interests, especially after 1763, the disadvantages of the commercial (including currency and credit) system seemed increasingly to outweigh its advantages. Other discussions have accepted contemporary denials of any wish to end traditional commercial subordination. Discontent arose because of new legislation seeking less to regulate trade than to raise revenue. Most American evasions of duties and attacks on customs officials, even if fueled by resistance to the Stamp Act, were not part of any principled opposition to the Trade Acts. About Great Britain, however, there is general agreement. Fears that Americans might try "to get loose from the Acts of Navigation" led to substantial support for firm action, support fostered by the belief in the inter-dependence of the parts of the British commercial empire. George III shared these fears, prophesying the West Indies following the Americans "not [into] Independence but must for its own interest be dependent on North America: Ireland would soon follow the same plan...then this Island would be reduced to itself, and soon would be a poor Island indeed, for reduced in Her Trade Merchants would retire with their Wealth to Climates more to their Advantage, and Shoals of Manufacturers would leave this country for the New Empire" (Fortescue, 1927–8, IV: p. 351).

The essence of British commercial thought was that colonies had value only in so far as they benefited the mother country economically. Trade legislation and its enforcement had been laid down in the seventeenth century, as the importance of overseas commerce and colonies grew together. Governments had learned to enjoy revenues that could be obtained relatively easily from taxes on imports. They now began to appreciate that commerce could be aided by the possession of colonies producing valuable staples. These, if re-exported, particularly in manufactured form, contributed to a favorable balance of trade, to wealth and employment in the mother country, and to a satisfactory maritime sector. Colonies might also become large markets for metropolitan goods. Commerce more than agriculture was the foundation of national wealth, power, and happiness. It sometimes needed fostering and always needed regulating. All European economic thought in this period was strongly protectionist, emphasizing competition between states as the natural order of things. Despite literary and philosophical effusions about the civilizing effects and cultural benefits of commerce, war was seen as a proper extension of commercial rivalry. These ideas were not seriously challenged until after the publication in 1776 of Adam Smith's *Inquiry into the Nature and Causes of the Wealth of Nations* (which included an analysis of American commercial relations with Great Britain and a statement that, although the denial to Americans of complete economic freedom broached "the most sacred rights of mankind," it had not hurt them or prevented them from becoming wealthy). Edmund Burke, despite his pro-American sympathies, believed the old commercial system to have been a triumphant success needing little change. So did William Pitt, architect of British colonial supremacy over France. In his epitaph for Pitt (who died in 1778), Burke praised him for "raising his nation to a high pitch of prosperity and glory," for uniting commerce with and making it "flourish by war." Few persons of his generation would have seen any reason to question this judgment.

2 Laws and Institutions

The commercial system in 1748 and until 1776 rested on seventeenth-century legislation. Early laws had been aimed at the Dutch in an attempt to prevent them from engrossing colonial commodities and the carrying trade. Basic legislation (1651, 1660, 1661) prohibited non-English owned and manned ships from carrying goods to and from England's overseas possessions. But – and this was important – the colonies and colonial settlers were here counted as English. The law also prohibited the colonial export of enumerated commodities (indigo, sugar, tobacco, ginger, cotton, and some dyestuffs) unless these went directly to England, for use there or for re-export, or to other English colonies. Additions to these enumerated commodities continued: rice and molasses (1704; although rice was later allowed to be sent directly to European destinations south of Cape Finisterre), naval stores (1704, 1725), copper (1721), beaver and other furs (1721), and iron (1764). In 1663 a complementary Act forbade the colonial import (with some few exceptions) of European goods that had not passed through the mother country.

Enforcement of this legislation was parceled out to a variety of agencies. Colonial governors were charged with enforcing Acts of Trade and Navigation, including the taking of bonds and the keeping of records, and in theory were liable to financial penalties and dismissal for failure. Some governors appointed their own officials ("naval officers") to carry out these duties. By

an Act of 1673, ships' masters without appropriate English documentation had to pay a duty at the colonial port of clearance and to deposit a bond promising that any enumerated goods not carried to another English colony would be taken to England. The English Customs Commissioners were to "order and manage" the levying and collection of rates and duties within the colonies. A process of appointing colonial customs officers (begun in 1671) followed. By the 1680s this was complete for the Americas, and the customs officials were empowered to use the navy to seize offenders. Indeed, three sets of officials – gubernatorial, customs, and naval – were as often rivals as colleagues. An Act of Trade of 1696 also dealt with enforcement, placing further obligations on colonial governors, subordinating naval officers to customs officials (whose powers of search were also enlarged), and extending vice-admiralty courts to America. Unlike in the mother country, vice-admiralty courts could be used for dealing with trade offenses, though there was also provision for such offenses to be tried by ordinary courts with juries. In the same year (1696) the government created the Board of Trade, whose special responsibilities included oversight of the colonies and of commerce.

With some amendments, the legislative structure just outlined lasted to 1776. Other more or less significant developments also took place by the middle of the eighteenth century. Restrictions were placed on some forms of colonial manufacturing that might have competed with that of Britain, mainly by forbidding exports of any manufactured goods across colonial boundaries: woollens (1699), hats (1732), iron (1750). This policy complemented British prohibitions on the emigration of skilled workmen and on the export of certain machines and tools. However, shipbuilding, a major and profitable colonial industry, and certain types of iron manufacturing were never forbidden. Encouragement was also given to commodity production useful to the mother country, notably naval stores and indigo, by paying bounties on them as they entered Britain.

A striking piece of new legislation resulted in part from lobbying by sugar traders and illustrates the clash of interests within the system. British West Indian sugar had a virtual monopoly in the home market, although heavily taxed, since foreign sugar was taxed even more. A sugar lobby also sought a trade monopoly with the North American colonies, where distilleries used great quantities of non-British sugar products. The Molasses Act (1733) set a high duty on the import of foreign sugar, rum, and molasses into British North America. North Americans were also the main suppliers of provisions and timber products to the West Indian slave societies. If the French (and to a lesser extent the Dutch) could no longer sell the continentals sugar, they could also not pay for these vital goods, which might lead to a glut, forcing down their price to the British islands. The position was complex, since the imports and profits from the foreign West Indian trade and from the northern colonies' exports of rum helped pay for their British imports. This Act seemed to attempt to raise a revenue in North American ports, whereas most trade legislation did so at British ones. But another interpretation is that the high duties were meant to exclude or regulate rather than to raise revenue and, in fact, the British Government made little effort to enforce the Act. Widespread evasion continued even in times of war.

The operation of the commercial system has been viewed from several angles. One portrays it as working satisfactorily and to the advantage at least of Great Britain and the mainland colonies, whose commerce rapidly expanded. The most important North American commodity, tobacco, had a semi-protected market and found successful re-export destinations; by the 1750s the Chesapeake had begun to diversify, with wheat exports becoming important money-earners. The northern and middle colonies developed a considerable shipping sector, good export markets, and substantial craft and proto-manufacturing sectors in ship-building and iron; British restrictions on other forms of manufacturing had marginal impact, since capital was lacking and skilled labor expensive. Moreover, North Americans were able to import large and growing amounts of relatively cheap British manufactured goods, and their trade, shipping, and territory received the protection of the British military and the credit and insurance benefits of an expanding empire. Although enforcement was lax and smuggling occurred, the majority of officials were competent (in eighteenth-century terms) and the majority of transactions were legal. A differing interpretation emphasizes the prevalence of evasion (by collusion, fraud, and smuggling) and the looseness of enforcement. Therefore, ultimately market factors – supply and demand – not commercial legislation, formed the channels of trade.

One aspect of legislation which affected trade and which has received recent attention is the place of paper money and of credit. British and some colonial merchants certainly lobbied for restrictions on the issue in the colonies of paper money and bills, mainly to protect themselves against the depreciation of such instruments. Private banks were forbidden by law in 1741; in 1751 a Currency Act set certain restrictions on the issue of paper bills by the New England governments (*see* chapter 7, §4). Later this and new legislation, together with the growing feeling that American trade was too closely tied to British credit and its sometimes frightening fluctuations, as well as the growth of Chesapeake planter indebtedness, provided a context for growing disillusionment with the workings of the commercial system.

The year 1748 saw the appointment of George Montagu Dunk, Earl of Halifax, as a strong reforming President of the Board of Trade. It was apparent that the Peace of Aix-la-Chapelle was only a temporary measure and that North America and the West Indies would have a central place in the coming struggle between France and Britain. Halifax's main concerns were therefore strategic rather than commercial, although ways of tightening up the enforcement of legislation and of increasing state revenues were also under active consideration. During the war years (1754–63), cooperation with the colonies rather than reform was obviously a paramount consideration, but sustained complaints about colonial trade with the French and Spanish in the West Indies, often carried out under special licenses or flags of truce but seen as treasonable by many in the mother country, stimulated investigations and suggestions for action during the 1750s. After British victory these evasions, together with a huge budget deficit created by the war, provided conditions in which reform seemed crucial. Its main implementation was during George Grenville's premiership (*see* chapter 15).

The bedrock of reform as it affected trade legislation was a drive for adequate enforcement in order to improve revenue collection. Executive threats of dismissal for absentee customs officers and other measures aimed at efficiency were followed by an Act (April 1763) for "the improvement of His Majesty's revenue of customs," which provided for the inspection of ships below 50 tons burden in coastal waters and sought to ensure cooperation between naval ships and customs officials in the prevention of smuggling. The government over the next two years also moved in response to long-standing reports of deficiencies in the Customs Service to increase the numbers of customs officials and provide for staffing by persons from Britain rather than local men who, experience seemed to show, were unwilling or unable to act forcefully. A Customs Fees Act, which tried to guarantee payments to colonial customs officers, became law in 1765 but created problems of enforcement.

Major parliamentary legislation also sought strict enforcement of the Acts of Trade. A complex "Bill for granting certain Duties in the British colonies …" became law in April 1764 and is now generally (perhaps misleadingly) known as the Sugar Act. It incorporated the permanent continuation of the Molasses Act of 1733 but with the duty lowered from 6d to 3d per gallon; a total prohibition of the import of foreign rum and spirits into the colonies; a requirement for increased documentation to be held by ships' captains in a wide variety of cases, including intercolonial trading: the extension of the list of enumerated products to cover pimento, coffee, coconuts, whalefins, raw silk, hides, and skins; a requirement that all duties and fines be paid in sterling; a stipulation that the burden of proof in the event of seizures for non-payment of duties should rest with the defendant; and a

provision that the prosecutor or informant be allowed to choose the court, including vice-admiralty courts, in which he wished to have trade cases tried. The Act also made reference to a new vice-admiralty court, to which any case could be sent, and which was established in the autumn of 1764 at Halifax, Nova Scotia. In 1764 the government further legislated to extend the provisions of the Currency Act of 1751 to colonies from New York south, prohibiting

paper bills of credit, hereafter to be issued, in any of His Majesty's colonies or plantations in America, from being declared to be a legal tender in payments of money; and to prevent the legal tender of such bills as are now subsisting from being prolonged beyond the Periods limited for calling in and sinking the same.

This Act was in fact aimed at preventing English and Scottish merchants in the Chesapeake tobacco trade from being paid in depreciated colonial paper.

To what extent the Stamp Act of 1765 may be viewed as trade rather than fiscal legislation is arguable; it certainly sought to raise money by duties on many commercial transactions, but some of its provisions (i.e., that stamps to the value of 4d be applied to bills of lading) were, perhaps, aimed at preventing fraud rather than obtaining revenue. It also gave the Halifax vice-admiralty court appellate jurisdiction and allowed all the vice-admiralty courts to hear cases arising from offenses against its provisions. But some Americans, notably Franklin, and some Englishmen argued that there was a difference between legislation to raise "internal" and "external" (i.e., customs or port duties) "taxes," and that the latter aspect of the old commercial system had been acceptable while the Stamp Act was not. Others joined to this or advanced separately the argument that the "old" commercial system had not sought to raise revenue, except as a kind of incidental method of enforcement, but only to regulate trade and manufacturing. The new system (i.e., 1764 and after) – "our newly adopted system of colonial policy," Burke called it – with its fiscal objectives, therefore broke a kind of original compact with the colonies. If Americans "share your taxes," will they not "claim the right of manufactures, of free trade, of every other privilege of the mother country?" (Simmons and Thomas, 1982–7, II: p. 83). But Grenville, his followers, and successors vigorously maintained that "the distinction between internal taxes and commercial regulation was a distinction without a difference. Paying duties upon imports was paying internal taxes ..." (Simmons and Thomas, 1982–7, II: p. 610), and that the Acts of Trade and Navigation had always included a substantial revenue component as well as regulatory purposes.

Certainly the Stamp Act created an opposition which forced all these questions into the public arena. Other Acts of the Grenville administration in 1765 were conciliatory, exempting undecked boats of under 20 tons used in the American coastal trade from the need to carry detailed documentation and allowing the direct export of colonial iron and lumber to Ireland. While repealing the Stamp Act in 1766, however, the Rockingham ministry did not uphold any idea that the Acts of Trade in their American context should be used only to shape and regulate commerce and not to raise a revenue. It reduced the duty on foreign molasses imported into North America to 1d per gallon but established the same tax for imports from the British islands and allowed the importation of foreign sugar into North America on payment of a duty of 5s. per cwt. It also created two freeports in the Caribbean, a radical departure from precedent, but extended the requirements of earlier statutes that ships give bond not to land cargoes in Europe north of Cape Finisterre, except in Great Britain. The ministry's measures were conciliatory in that no further action was taken to tighten up customs or vice-admiralty jurisdiction, and it adopted a sympathetic attitude to the problems of American currency.

Rockingham's government had also contemplated but did not undertake a method of raising revenue by allowing the direct importation of certain specified European commodities into America on payment of duties at the port of entry – another break with the "old" system. Under the subsequent Pitt–Grafton administration the same idea formed the basis of the Townshend

Duties Act of 1767. Townshend claimed to base his policy "upon laying taxes upon America, but not internal taxes, because though he did not acknowledge the distinction it was accepted by many Americans and this was sufficient" (Simmons and Thomas, 1982–7, II: p. 464). He also believed in adequate enforcement, and the Townshend Act allowed the issue at will of writs of assistance by the supreme or superior court in each colony. This was accompanied by legislation placing the management of the customs service in America under a new American Board of Commissioners in Boston. In March 1768 another Act created three new superior vice-admiralty courts (Boston, Philadelphia, Charles Town) to add to that at Halifax. The creation of an American Civil List was also expected to improve enforcement by reducing the dependence of colonial officials on popular assemblies.

Lord North's government did not materially add to these measures and, of course, repealed all the Townshend Duties except that on tea (see chapter 17, §7). In fact North sought conciliation. He refused to contemplate further reforms in the Act of Trade, since it was obvious that the government was powerless properly to enforce them, and legislated in 1773 to allow some relief from the Currency Act. Colonies would be able to establish loan offices issuing legal-tender bills for public obligations. North's government in addition legislated on an annual basis to allow certain concessions to American exports; the famous Tea Act did not alter the duty levied on tea imports into America and was meant to lower the actual price of tea to Americans.

3 Commerce and Revolution

Much of the legislation discussed above represented responses to reports of the difficulties of enforcement and administration in the colonies. The Sugar Act sought to take account of years of complaints about deficiencies in the Acts of Trade and Navigation, the Townshend Acts in part to correct deficiencies arising from the operation of the Grenville legislation. However, there was no coherent or at least no successful overall administrative review, and the operation of the Acts of Trade remained subject to technical and administrative problems. Characteristic of the 1760s were continual bickerings among governors, customs officials, and naval commanders – the three main agents of enforcement – who were, in fact, rivals for the rewards of successful searches and seizures, since some payments based on the values of the cargoes were made to them. Enforcement came also to rely more and more on the navy, whose presence in North American waters was considerably increased. Admiral Lord Colvill, the naval Commander-in-Chief from 1763 to 1766, reputedly hoped to make his fortune from customs seizures and tended to treat colonial governors like midshipmen. His and other officers' brusque attitudes led contemporaries to ask "Are the gentlemen of the navy judges of the nature of commerce and the liberty of the subject?" Later, the patriotic historian George Bancroft wrote of "A curiously devised system, which bribed the whole navy of England to make war on colonial trade." When the British Government sent regiments to Boston in 1768, it also seemed that the army was being brought in to do on land what the navy did at sea, particularly to support the American Board of Customs Commissioners.

One famous early struggle, preceding Grenville's reforms, involved writs of assistance and a legal argument in Boston in 1760–1 over the rights of customs officials to search for suspected goods under their authority. The Superior Court, after a reference back to London, eventually found in favor of the officials, though even in the future these writs were used only with difficulty and were challenged in the colonial courts. Here the argument over the enforcement of trade laws, linked to the politics of the day, eventually led on to a general statement by James Otis that certain forms of parliamentary legislation attacking liberty and property were void. The Boston merchant community (perhaps jealous of the non-enforcement of customs legislation in neighboring Rhode Island) and the Boston press joined in the condemnations of the "rats" gnawing at the subject's property. On January 4, 1762 the *Boston Gazette* appealed

to the rights of Englishmen against "the great *patrons* of this writ." Governor Bernard believed that Thomas Hutchinson's connection with "the Admiralty and Customs House," through his granting writs of assistance, made his house the target of the Boston mob during the Stamp Act disturbances. Later the Townshend Act's amendments to writs of assistance were themselves poorly drafted, and it is not clear how often they were successfully used after 1767. What is clear is that, in the New England colonies, the writs entered popular and political rhetoric as despotic instruments that allowed brutal customs officers to raid the homes of innocent families, and were seen as similar to the general warrants used in London against John Wilkes, friend of America and another victim of oppression and corruption. General warrants were condemned as illegal in Britain both by the Court of Common Pleas and by parliamentary resolution. The use in America of writs of assistance, which so closely resembled them, added to colonial grievances, to the sense of unequal treatment.

The other instruments and agencies for operating the revitalized commercial system were also condemned with similar language and charges. The vice-admiralty courts, unlike the revenue courts which tried trade offenses in England, were juryless. Their judges were often Englishmen appointed in England. Their officials had an interest in the fees they could collect. Cases were often brought before them as a result of information laid by persons who would also gain financially from conviction. Similar charges were brought against active customs officials. In the political climate that prevailed in many colonies after 1765 these facts were used to bewail the inequality of American and British rights and the alleged cavalier disregard of British ministries for American liberty and property. The colonial courts became involved both in writs of assistance and in vice-admiralty cases, demonstrating the general problem of trade enforcement, since it was commonplace for them not only to find against customs officers but to admit counter-claims for false arrest and the like and award substantial damages against them, even to imprison them. Governors, even if well disposed, could not provide protection or redress. Sometimes customs agents could find no lawyers willing to act for them and were forced to appeal or return to England for assistance. It is also obvious that crowd or group action was another obstacle to enforcement and that the threat of violence shadowed customs and naval personnel.

In number the cases of mob or crowd action were in fact few (and, unlike such affrays in eighteenth-century Britain, involved no deaths), but they were widely reported and helped to shape public opinion in America and government actions in the mother country. In Charles Town, South Carolina, in May 1767 Captain James Hawker was attacked by a mob led by gentlemen, who (he claimed) insulted the King, Parliament, and the British flag. In Norfolk, Virginia, in September 1767 the people, headed by the mayor, attacked Captain Morgan and his men, who had come ashore looking for deserters. Considerable parliamentary attention was given to the seizure in June 1768 of the *Liberty*, owned by John Hancock of Boston, which led to threats to the American Customs Commissioners and their flight from the city. Two years later, a New Jersey collector was severely beaten and his son beaten, tarred, and feathered. In 1772 the burning of the royal navy schooner *Gaspée* and the wounding of her commanding officer caused outrage in British Government circles.

Such incidents, although sometimes involving attacks on ships' captains who were known or believed to be customs racketeers, were seen by the home authorities with other forms of colonial resistance as evidence of the need for severe responses. Among Americans (and they were widely reported in the press) they were incorporated into the prevailing political rhetoric and ideology. Novel and oppressive legislation enforced by brutal and corrupt agents was part of the attack on liberty. Such beliefs came to be held by otherwise conservative merchants such as Henry Laurens of South Carolina, whose experiences with the customs service led him to radical pamphleteering and ultimately to revolution.

Yet there is some debate as to how far colonial opinion was ready to deny the Acts of Trade and call for free trade. The most common patriot point of view from about 1765 onwards seems to have been to deny that the raising of revenue was a legitimate part of the Acts but to assert that the colonists accepted an obligation to

carry the chief of their produce there [Great Britain] and to take off her manufactures in return; and as they must conform to her price in both buying and selling, one would think the advantage she reaps by their trade sufficient.

There was a strength of feeling in the northern and middle colonies for freer intercourse with the West Indies, expressed, for example, in an outspoken New York merchants' petition presented to Parliament in 1767 and some (largely ineffectual) attempts at encouraging home manufactures in order to lessen dependence on British imports during and after the Stamp Act crisis. By the 1770s protests at British restrictions on manufacturing were appearing in petitions to the mother country. There was also disquiet about a British credit crisis in 1772–3, which had severe American effects, particularly in the Chesapeake, and may have further increased doubts about the real benefits of the colonies' place in the existing system. But if statements were made or positions taken that seemed to look beyond the Acts of Trade and Navigation to the rise of America as an independent economy with a developing manufacturing sector and a profitable export trade of great agricultural surpluses to the rest of the world, it is doubtful if these had much general circulation before 1776 or were important in the causes of the Revolution.

On the British side no politician failed to defend the Acts of Trade and Navigation. Indeed Chatham in January 1775

observed that if… the views of America were ultimately pointed to defeating the act of navigation, and the other regulatory acts, so wisely framed and calculated for that reciprocity of interests, so essentially necessary to the grandeur and prosperity of the whole empire… there was no person present, however zealous, would be readier than himself to resist and crush any attempt of that nature in the first instance. (Simmons and Thomas, 1982–7, V: p. 273)

Burke, Barré, and other friends of the American and the merchant community tended to take the line that the evident and increasing opposition to British rule, including British commercial legislation, was due to mistaken British policy after 1763 – not only the introduction of the Stamp Act but the attempt to collect substantial revenues by the Sugar Act and the Rockingham legislation of 1766. A return to the status quo before the Sugar Act was advisable, presumably including a return to the lax enforcement of legislation. Their argument rested on an almost religious belief in the importance of North America's commerce to Britain and other parts of the empire. Its loss would mean ruin. "You have not a loom nor an anvil but what is stamped with America," Barré told the House of Commons in March 1774, and Shelburne, in December 1775, reminded the House of Lords of "the great Palladium of our Commerce, that great source of all the advantages that we now happily enjoy."

Lord North and his ministers countered with the arguments that Americans indeed wished to destroy British commerce, since they were aiming at the dismantling of the Acts of Trade, and anyway, when the "clearest rights" of the legislative power of Britain were invaded and denied and when in consequence the people so denying were in "actual and open rebellion," that then there were points of greater importance to be settled than those of "commerce and manufacture ..."

Before 1776 the struggle between America and Britain was largely fought out in terms of attacks on each other's commerce, with trade boycotts on the American side after the Stamp Act and the Townshend Duties and with movements to greater American self-sufficiency. Some of the bitterness of the conflict was undoubtedly due to the economic recession following the Seven Years' War. Yet from about 1770 to 1774 British–American trade was possibly never greater and customs revenues never higher. In 1774 and 1775 British retaliation against colonial actions was directed first against Boston as a commercial center, then against the trade of all 13 colonies. On the American side independence meant throwing open American ports to all comers. During the war, trade questions were obscured. After it they once more became central, stimulating the move towards federal union, and causing many Americans to protest as vigorously against their exclusion from the British commercial system as they had before 1776 at its enforcement.

FURTHER READING

Andrews, C. M.: *The Colonial Period of American History*, vol. IV, *England's Colonial and Commercial Policy* (New Haven, Conn.: 1938; repr. New Haven and London: Yale University Press, 1964).

Barrow, T. C.: *Trade and Empire: the British Customs Service in Colonial America, 1660–1775* (Cambridge, Mass.: Harvard University Press, 1967).

Dickerson, O. M.: *The Navigation Acts and the American Revolution* (Philadelphia, 1951; repr. New York: A. S. Barnes and Co., 1963).

Engerman, Stanley L., and Gallman, Robert E., eds.: *The Cambridge Economic History of the United States*, vol. 1 *The Colonial Era* (Cambridge: Cambridge University Press, 1996).

Ernst, Joseph A.: *Money and Politics in America, 1755–1775* (Chapel Hill: University of North Carolina Press, 1973).

Koehn, Nancy F.: *The Power of Commerce: Economy and Governance in the First British Empire* (Ithaca: Cornell University Press, 1994).

McCusker, J. J., and Menard, R. M.: *The Economy of British America, 1607–1789* (Chapel Hill and London: University of North Carolina Press, 1985).

Owen, David R., and Tolley, Michael C.: *Courts of Admiralty in Colonial America: The Maryland Experience, 1634–1776* (Maryland Historical Society and Durham, North Carolina Academic Press, 1995).

Simmons, R. C., and Thomas, P. D. G.: *Proceedings and Debates of the British Parliaments Respecting North America, 1754–1783*, vols. I–VI (White Plains, NY: Kraus-Thomson, 1982–7).

Tucker, R. W., and Henderson, D. C.: *The Fall of the First British Empire: Origins of the War of American Independence* (Baltimore and London: Johns Hopkins University Press, 1982).

Ubbelohde, Carl: *The Vice-Admiralty Courts and the American Revolution* (Chapel Hill: University of North Carolina Press, 1960).

CHAPTER TWENTY-ONE

Ongoing disputes over the prerogative, 1763–1776

JACK P. GREENE

HISTORIANS have traditionally stressed the centrality of the issue of parliamentary authority in the constitutional debates that preceded the American Revolution, and they have been correct to do so. Beginning with the Stamp Act crisis in 1764–6, the long-standing conflicts over the relative balance between prerogative power and colonial rights, conflicts that had been an endemic feature of metropolitan–colonial relations ever since the middle of the seventeenth century, had been subordinated to the new and more pressing debate over the extent of Parliament's colonial authority, over the respective jurisdictions of Parliament and the several legislatures in the American colonies. Yet the older conflict over the boundaries of metropolitan executive authority in the colonies remained alive. Manifest in a variety of important incidents and controversies, it continued throughout the era from 1763 to 1776 to function as a major irritant in constitutional and political relations between metropolis and colonies.

1 1763–6

Indeed, not since the late 1740s had there been so many serious controversies between metropolitan authorities and local legislatures as there were in the years just before and during the Stamp Act crisis. During the early 1760s, there were several serious confrontations over the extent of the King's prerogative in the colonies. Though they were often intensely fought, most of these, such as the altercation that occurred in Massachusetts in the fall of 1762 over Governor

Francis Bernard's attempts to expend public funds without prior legislative authorization, elicited a sudden burst of protest but were soon resolved and rarely involved authorities in London.

In a few instances, however, these disputes lasted for years and seriously disrupted provincial political life. Such had been the case in Virginia, where the so-called Two Penny Act controversy persisted for the better part of six years between 1758 and 1764. Involving the Crown's insistence by royal instruction that, no matter what the apparent exigencies of the situation, the Virginia legislature could pass no law that modified a measure already confirmed by the Crown without a clause suspending its operation until it had been reviewed and approved in London, this dispute elicited widespread denunciation among Virginians of the Crown's attempt to use its prerogative powers to reduce the scope of legislative authority in the colonies.

At roughly the same time, New York was the scene of an even more debilitating battle between metropolitan prerogative and colonial privileges. Throughout the early 1760s, a running dispute raged between Lieutenant Governor Cadwallader Colden and local leaders over two related issues: the tenure of the colony's superior court judges and the authority of the Governor and the Council to overrule jury decisions on appeal from the defendant.

Since the Revolution Settlement in 1688–1701 the Crown's judges in Britain had held office during good behavior, which meant, in effect, for life. But metropolitan officials had always resisted the extension of this practice to the colonies, where, they argued, it would be "subversive of that Policy by which alone colonies can be kept in a just dependance upon the Government of the Mother Country."[1] Instead, they insisted that colonial judges, like English judges before the Glorious Revolution, should hold their commissions only during the Crown's pleasure. Such a tenure made colonial judges, also like English judges under the Stuarts, subject to removal whenever they decided a case contrary to metropolitan orthodoxy, thereby depriving them of that celebrated independence enjoyed by judges in Britain.

Notwithstanding metropolitan attitudes on this subject, however, New York judges had enjoyed tenure during good behavior since the mid-1740s, a privilege that had been wrested for them from a weak executive. When, upon the death of Chief Justice James De Lancey in 1760, metropolitan authorities refused to grant similar terms to his successor, New York leaders, unsurprisingly, regarded that ruling as an attack upon an established constitutional right. The ensuing fight over this question between the Assembly and Colden persisted for two years, during which the first Crown appointee resigned in frustration and the Board of Trade responded by issuing a categorical general instruction prohibiting governors of all colonies from appointing judges during good behavior and thereby setting the stage for similar altercations in New Jersey, South Carolina, and North Carolina during the following decade. In all these colonies, the local political establishments lost the battle for colonial judicial independence. Deeply resented, this defeat was attributed by colonial leaders to an aggressive prerogative that was bent upon depriving colonists of constitutional protections routinely enjoyed by Britons in the home islands.

The second issue in New York arose out of Colden's decision in 1764 to hear an appeal from Waddel Cunningham in a case in which a jury had convicted him of assaulting Thomas Forsey and awarded Forsey damages of £1,500. Local leaders regarded Colden's actions as a judicial innovation that struck at the sanctity of the jury system by enabling a governor to subvert the Englishman's traditional right to trial by jury. The decision of the British Privy Council in 1765, at the height of the Stamp Act crisis, to back Colden and order him to hear the appeal raised the specter of still another unwarranted exertion of prerogative by Crown officials in the colonies and called forth condemnation not just by New York leaders but by the Stamp Act Congress. When it met in New York in October 1765, that body pointedly endorsed trial by jury as the right of all British subjects, whether in the colonies or in England. Unlike the controversy over judicial tenure, however, this dispute was settled in favor of New York when the Board of Trade, in consultation with the Crown's chief law officers in London, ruled against Colden's hearing such appeals.

Similarly prolonged and even more intense disputes left both South Carolina and Jamaica without an operative legislature for long periods and were resolved only by the resignation or removal of the royal governors. In South Carolina, beginning in September 1762, legislative government came to a virtual halt when the Commons House of Assembly, despite some minor irregularities in a by-election held the previous March, voted to admit the Charles Town merchant Christopher Gadsden as representative from St. Paul's Parish. Endeavoring to force the Commons House to pass a new election law conformable to metropolitan stipulations, Governor Thomas Boone seized this occasion to illustrate the looseness of the existing law. Refusing to administer the oath of office to Gadsden, he charged the Commons House with acting contrary to the existing election law, precipitately dissolved that body, and called for new elections.

When the new legislature met in the fall, it denounced Boone's behavior as a blatant violation of its exclusive constitutional right to judge the legitimacy of the elections of its own members, a right that had been long enjoyed by the British House of Commons and had not been disputed in South Carolina for nearly 40 years. Accordingly, the Commons House voted to do no further business with Boone until he had apologized for his actions. Boone's refusal to apologize resulted in a complete stoppage of legislative business for the next 19 months. Despite the urgent need at one point for legislative action to defend the backcountry against attacks by Creek Indians, the Commons House stubbornly refused to resume legislative intercourse with the Crown's executive until May 1764, after Boone, in despair, had left for England to seek support from metropolitan authorities.

In Jamaica, Governor William Henry Lyttelton was reluctantly drawn into a controversy in which he took measures that also could be seen as an effort to restrict the customary parliamentary privileges of the local legislature. Members of the Jamaica House of Assembly had long enjoyed exemption from suits at law during legislative sessions, and when, in late 1764, court officials seized the coach and horses of representative John Olyphant in partial fulfillment of a judgment against Olyphant, the Jamaica House took into custody and charged with contempt both the two judicial officers who had carried out the seizure and the plaintiff in the suit.

These events set the stage for a long and bitter impasse between the Assembly and the Governor. Unable to resolve the matter by informal persuasion, Lyttelton, in response to a petition from the jailed men, issued a writ of habeas corpus to free them, whereupon the Assembly passed a series of resolutions denouncing this action as an unwarranted and unconstitutional violation of its privileges, and refused to do any further business with Lyttelton until he had made reparation. The London authorities took Lyttelton's side in this controversy, and over the following year Lyttelton thrice dissolved the Assembly and called new elections. But the Assembly remained adamant and did not again transact business with the royal Governor until after Lyttelton had been recalled in the summer of 1766, more than 18 months after the onset of the dispute.

With the exception of the Two Penny Act controversy and the quarrel over judicial tenure in New York, all of these incidents arose out of maladroit or unavoidable actions by Crown governors in the colonies and were not immediately provoked by directives from London. In both the South Carolina and Jamaica cases, metropolitan officials eventually found that effective government could

not be restored unless they catered to local opinion by removing the offending governors, and they actually condemned Boone for his rash behavior in stimulating and perpetuating discord in South Carolina. In every case, however, the actions of the governors had been to some considerable measure conditioned by the growing insistence by metropolitan authorities that governors strictly observe their instructions from the Crown and resist efforts by the assemblies to increase the scope of their authority. In the Jamaican case, moreover, metropolitan officials strongly backed Lyttelton until after it had become clear that he had lost all political credibility within the colony.

Underlining the persistence of the long-standing tensions between metropolitan authorities in London and local legislatures in the colonies, these battles all revolved around the familiar issues of the previous century: whether the royal prerogative in the colonies should be placed under the same restraints to which it had been subjected in Britain in the wake of the Glorious Revolution, whether royal instructions had constitutional standing, whether the rights of British people in the colonies were equal to the rights of those who continued to reside in the home islands, whether colonial legislatures were entitled to the same privileges and powers enjoyed by the metropolitan House of Commons, and whether custom had the same constitutional authority in the colonies as it had traditionally had in Britain itself. Underlying these battles, moreover, were the same old fears. While metropolitan authorities worried that the continual grasping after power by these distant colonial legislatures would eventually erode all control from the center, colonial leaders were anxious lest the Crown's continuing efforts to extend the "prerogative beyond all bounds"[2] should sooner or later cheat the colonists "out of their liberties" and thereby actually degrade them "from the rank of Englishmen" to "a condition of slavery."[3]

2 1767–76

Throughout the last half of the 1760s, during the crisis over the Townshend Acts, this ancient contest between prerogative and liberty was superseded or at least pushed into the background by the debate over Parliament's relationship to the colonies. Coincident with the repeal of most of the Townshend Duties, however, a new series of quarrels developed over the scope of the Crown's colonial authority, quarrels that punctuated the so-called period of quiet during the early 1770s and revealed that the debate over the limits of the Crown's prerogative was still a live and profoundly significant issue between metropolis and colonies.

Major controversies developed in several colonies. In Georgia during the spring of 1771, Governor James Wright, acting on directions from Lord Hillsborough, Secretary of State for the Colonies in London, rejected the Georgia Commons' nominee as speaker, and thereby initiated a dispute over the Governor's right to negative the legislature's choice of speaker that agitated Georgia politics for nearly 21 months. In proprietary Maryland in late 1770, following the failure of the two houses of the legislature to agree on a bill for that purpose, Governor Robert Eden's proclamation setting the scale of officers' fees instigated a three-year controversy over the Governor's authority by virtue of proprietary prerogative to set the fees of public officers without legislative consent. In North Carolina in late 1773, the Assembly devised a new superior court law that pointedly ignored a recent royal instruction forbidding colonial governors to assent to any laws providing for the attachment of the property of non-residents in suits for debts. The ensuing dispute seriously disrupted legislative affairs in the colony and left it without superior courts for the last three years before the Declaration of Independence.

Even more serious were conflicts in two other colonies, Massachusetts and South Carolina. In the former, Crown officials led by Hillsborough sought by instruction in the summer of 1768 to punish Boston for its leading role in opposing the Townshend Acts by encouraging Governor Francis Bernard to call the Massachusetts General Court to meet in Cambridge or Salem instead of in Boston, the capital and customary meeting-place of the legislature. When Bernard in June 1769 and his successor Thomas Hutchinson in March 1770 acted on this instruction by removing the sessions to Cambridge, they set off a constitutional crisis of major proportions.

At issue was the question of whether the Crown by virtue of its prerogative powers could legally employ the royal instructions to alter or violate established customary constitutional practices in the colony. With metropolitan authorities standing firmly behind him, Hutchinson argued that he was bound to obey his instructions, while a series of General Courts insisted that instructions could not supersede the colony's basic rights as manifest in provincial laws and customs, railed against the use of ministerial mandates to overturn the settled constitution of the colony, and charged the Crown officials with trying to incapacitate the legislature so that it would be less able to resist efforts by both Parliament and prerogative to subvert colonial liberty. Only after a protracted struggle of more than two years was this controversy ended, in June 1772, with an inconclusive compromise.

The more prolonged Wilkes fund controversy in South Carolina was never resolved. For several decades, the South Carolina Commons House had assumed authority to issue money from the public treasury without the consent of the Governor and Council, a practice the British House of Commons had never been bold enough to attempt. The existence of this peculiar constitutional tradition first came to the attention of London officials following the Commons House vote in December 1769 of a gift of £1,500 sterling to the Society of the Gentlemen Supporters of the Bill of Rights, a London organization formed to pay the debts of John Wilkes, who over the previous few years had successfully set himself up as the chief symbol of resistance to arbitrary ministerial authority in the metropolis. London officials responded to this audacious act by issuing an instruction on April 14, 1770 that threatened both the royal Governor and the Treasurer with severe penalties if they permitted any money, including the sum voted to Wilkes, to be issued from the South Carolina treasury without executive approval.

Regarding this instruction as an attack upon a constitutional custom it had long enjoyed, the South Carolina Commons House refused to act in accordance with its stipulations. For the next five years, the instruction was the central issue in South Carolina politics. The normal processes of legislative government were entirely suspended. No annual tax bill was passed in the colony after 1769 and no legislation at all after February 1771, and local leaders became increasingly resentful of what they regarded as an unconstitutional effort by metropolitan authorities to deprive the Commons House of its customary legal rights through the use of what they denounced as ministerial mandates. Only the outbreak of the War for Independence and the assumption of legislative authority by a provincial congress in 1775 brought this bitter altercation to an end.

3 Significance

With the exception of the Maryland controversy, all of these disputes revolved around metropolitan efforts to use royal instructions to curb the power of local assemblies. In one sense, they were merely the latest rounds in the ongoing contest in the extended polity of the British Empire between central prerogative power and local colonial rights as championed by the several provincial assemblies. From the 1670s on, and more systematically since the late 1740s, the "Governing of colonies by Instructions," as Franklin observed in January 1772, had "long been a favourite Point with Ministers" in London.[4] Ministers, they believed, had made so many "daring and injurious attempt[s] to raise and establish a despotic power over them"[5] that, as the Maryland lawyer Charles Carroll of Carrollton remarked during the fee controversy in Maryland in May 1773, it had long since become "a common observation confirmed by general experience" that any "claim in the colony-governments of an extraordinary power as … part of the prerogative" was "sure to meet with the encouragement and support of the ministry in Great-Britain."[6]

From the perspective of the crisis over the Stamp and Townshend Acts and the debate over Parliament's new pretensions to authority over the internal affairs of the colonies, however, these old questions about the Crown's relationship to the colonies acquired a new and heightened urgency. If, as an impressive number of colonial spokesmen had begun to argue during the late 1760s, sovereignty within the empire rested not in the Crown-in-Parliament but in the Crown alone, then it became especially important for the colonists to establish the boundaries not just of parliamentary but also of royal authority in the colonies. For that reason, colonial defenders in all of the battles of the early 1770s revealed a pronounced tendency to build upon their own particular local constitutional heritages to argue, as their predecessors in earlier generations had often done, that, no less than in Britain itself, the Crown's authority – the freedom of its "will" – in the colonies had been effectively limited over the previous century by specific idiosyncratic constitutional developments in each of the colonies. Again just as in Britain, these developments had led, colonial leaders believed, irreversibly in the direction of increasing authority in the hands of the local legislatures and greater restrictions on the prerogatives of the Crown. By this process, they argued, the rights of the inhabitants in the colonies had gradually been secured against the power of the metropolis.

As refined and elaborated during the contests of the early 1770s, this view of colonial constitutional history powerfully helped to reinforce traditional views of the colonial legislatures as both the primary guardians of the local rights of the corporate entities over which they presided and, like Parliament itself in Britain, the dynamic forces in shaping the colonial constitutions. Insofar as the constitution of the empire was concerned, this emphasis upon the peculiarity and integrity of the several colonial constitutions comprised a vigorous assertion of what one recent scholar has referred to as constitutional multiplicity that had profound implications for the new, post-1764 debate over the nature and location of sovereignty within the empire.

For, together with the emerging conviction that Parliament had no authority over the colonies, the renewed contention that the Crown's colonial authority was also limited by local constitutions as they had emerged out of not just the colonists' inherited rights as Englishmen and their charters but also local usage and custom pushed the colonists towards a wholly new conception of sovereignty in an extended polity like that of the early modern British Empire. That conception implied that ultimate constitutional authority – sovereignty – lay not in any institution or collection of institutions at the center of the empire but in the separate constitutions of each of the many separate political entities of which the empire was composed.

That by no means all of the constitutional grievances that drove the 13 colonies to revolt could be laid at the door of Parliament was dramatically revealed in the Declaration of Independence (*see* chapter 32). Although Parliament was certainly responsible for those grievances the colonists found most objectionable, especially the effort to tax them without their consent, 17 of the 18 counts of unconstitutional behavior by the metropolitan government listed in that document referred to actions or policies undertaken not by the Crown-in-Parliament but by the Crown and its officers acting in their executive capacities. The content of this list made clear that the Crown's ancient claim for more extensive prerogative powers in the colonies than it enjoyed in Britain continued to be an important source of unease throughout the constitutional struggles that preceded the American Revolution. Indeed, the many continuing contests between prerogative and liberty during the years between 1763 and 1776 only gave added force to the conviction, explicitly articulated in the Declaration, that a connection with Britain of the kind advocated by many colonial leaders from the late 1760s through mid-1776 – that is, one through the Crown independent of Parliament – would not provide a safe foundation for the security of colonial rights.

REFERENCES

1   Board of Trade Report, November 11, 1761, in *Documents Relative to the Colonial History of the State of New York,* ed. E. B. O'Callaghan (Albany: Weed, Parsons, 1853–87), vol. 7, 473–5.

2   James Otis: *A Vindication of the Conduct of the House of Representatives of the Province of Massachusetts-Bay* (Boston: Edes & Gill, 1762), 51.

3   [Nicholas Bourke]: *The Privileges of the Island of Jamaica Vindicated* (London: J. Williams, 1766), 47, 64.

4   Benjamin Franklin to James Bowdoin, January 13, 1772, in *The Papers of Benjamin Franklin,* ed. Leonard W. Labaree et al., 26 vols. to date (New Haven, Conn.: Yale University Press, 1959–), vol. 19, 11.

5   William Bollan: *The Free Britons Memorial* (London: J. Williams, 1769), 15.

6   First Citizen's Third Letter, May 6, 1773, in *Maryland and the Empire, 1773: The Antillon-First Citizen Letters,* ed. Peter S. Onuf (Baltimore: Johns Hopkins University Press, 1974), 149.

FURTHER READING

Greene, Jack P.: *The Nature of Colony Constitutions: Two Pamphlets on the Wilkes Fund Controversy by Sir Egerton Leigh and Arthur Lee* (Columbia: University of South Carolina Press, 1970).

——: *Peripheries and Center: Constitutional Development in the Extended Polities of the British Empire and the United States, 1607–1788* (Athens: University of Georgia Press, 1986).

——: *The Quest for Power: the Lower Houses of Assembly in the Southern Royal Colonies, 1689–1776* (Chapel Hill: University of North Carolina Press, 1963).

Klein, Milton M.: "Prelude to Revolution in New York: Jury Trials and Judicial Tenure," *William and Mary Quarterly,* 17 (1960), 439–62.

Knollenberg, Bernhard, *Origin of the American Revolution, 1759–1766* (New York: Macmillan 1960).

Lord, Donald C., and Calhoon, Robert M.: "The Removal of the Massachusetts General Court from Boston, 1769–1772," *Journal of American History,* 55(1969), 735–55.

Metcalf, George: *Royal Government and Political Conflict in Jamaica, 1729–1783* (London: University of London Press, 1965).

Peter S. Onuf (ed.): *Maryland and the Empire, 1773: the Antillon-First Citizen Letters* (Baltimore: Johns Hopkins University Press, 1974).

CHAPTER TWENTY-TWO

Bishops and other ecclesiastical issues, to 1776

FREDERICK V. MILLS, SR.

THE Treaty of Paris ended the Seven Years' War in Europe and the French and Indian War in America. By this treaty Great Britain gained French Canada, the Spanish Floridas, all North America to the Mississippi, much of the West Indies, and India. The military success of the British meant that the freshly acquired territory in the New World would be organized according to the directions of King and Parliament. Then, too, colonial policy as it related to the previously developed colonies was subject to review. Between 1763 and 1776 the development, revision, and implementation of policy for British America was the focal point of activity within the empire. The governance of Canada by royal proclamation until the enactment of the Quebec Act in 1774 and the announcement of the Proclamation Line in 1763 foreshadowed the coming of a new era. This shift in policy from "salutary neglect" in the pre-1750s to one of imperial direction was a change of major importance.

1 Archbishop Secker's Initiative

The structuring of imperial policy provided an opportunity for advocates of the Church of England to press their case to King George III and his ministers for support in extending the Church as a Christianizing and culturalizing agent in British America. To churchmen the advancement of the Anglican Communion spread the Christian gospel but had the added benefit of promoting loyalty to the British Constitution and hence stabilizing society. The Archbishop of Canterbury, Thomas Secker, took charge of the effort to extend the Church into the newly acquired territories and to strengthen it where it already existed in America. He confided to a long-time promoter of the colonial church, Dr. Samuel Johnson, President of King's College, New York City, "Probably our ministry will be concerting schemes this summer, against the next session of Parliament, for the settlement of His Majesty's dominions; and then we must try our utmost for bishops" (Mills, 1978, p. 29).

It was the office of bishop, of all the features of the Anglican Communion, that provoked controversy between churchmen and dissenters on both sides of the Atlantic. To churchmen a bishop was a third order of the clergy, consecrated and essential to the existence of the Church in addition to his royal appointment. Dissenters, those who opposed the Church of England and rejected communion with it, viewed bishops as royal officials subsidized by Parliament and ecclesiastically unnecessary for a church. The possibility that such a royal ecclesiastical person might be sent to a colony or region where dissenters were dominant, e.g., Massachusetts or New England, was regarded as a threat to the internal colonial constitution. Indeed, it was primarily the constitutional-political implications of Anglican episcopacy that caused the issue of a colonial episcopate to become intertwined with the mounting tensions between Whitehall and the colonies between 1763 and 1776.

The Church of England in British America in 1763 was the established church in the five colonies from Maryland to Georgia and in the counties surrounding New York

City. In the dozen years before the outbreak of the War for Independence, Anglicanism experienced remarkable growth from New England to Georgia. The Society for the Promotion of Christian Knowledge and the Society for the Propagation of the Gospel in Foreign Parts were major contributors to this advance. But a persistent problem was the absence of a bishop to perform ordination, confirmation, and the consecration of churches. Royal governors acted as ordinaries of the Bishop of London, in whose diocese the colonies were located, but they were hardly a substitute for a bishop. Nor were commissaries, licensed by the Bishop of London, although they could convene, examine, and reprove the clergy; but they could not ordain, and their decisions were subject to appeal to the Bishop of London.

Archbishop Thomas Secker, assisted by the Archbishop of York, Robert Hay Drummond, petitioned King and ministry in 1764 to procure bishops for British America, including the British West Indies. Their approach was low-keyed and highly confidential. Secker, as a member of the Privy Council, naturally would be consulted on ecclesiastical matters. But, unexpectedly, the Reverend East Apthorp, SPG missionary in Cambridge, Massachusetts, published in 1763 *Considerations on the Institution and Conduct of the SPG*. Apthorp intended to vindicate the SPG, but the inclusion of the subject of episcopacy in his treatise ignited a controversy. Jonathan Mayhew, a Congregational minister from Boston, challenged Apthorp's assessment of the SPG and charged that a plot, including an episcopate, was afoot "to root out all New England churches" (Bridenbaugh, 1972, pp. 224–9). Mayhew's counter-blast in his *Observations on the Charter* was so severe that Archbishop Secker, writing anonymously, supplied the rebuttal in *An Answer to Dr. Mayhew's Observations on the Character and Conduct of the SPG*. On the matter of an episcopate, Secker stated that the bishop would not reside in New England but only visit there and instead reside in a colony that invited him. No tax support would be sought, no political influence exerted. In past clashes between dissenters and churchmen, their disagreements ranged over many issues, but after the Apthorp–Mayhew encounter the

other issues became secondary to the subject of a colonial episcopate.

In correspondence with Dr. Samuel Johnson in May 1764, Archbishop Secker expressed guarded optimism about the episcopal plan but cautioned that it might depend on "various circumstances." What had happened was that two ministries in four years had fallen and a third was likely to be changed. After a dispute over war policy, William Pitt resigned in October 1761. Lord Bute, his successor, did not last two years in office. The Duke of Newcastle, after a disagreement with George Grenville over the conduct of the Treasury, left office. At the time Secker wrote he could not know that in 1765, Grenville, whose ministry gave the episcopal plan "a hearing," would fall from power even before the repeal of the Stamp Act. Understandably the Archbishop advised his American friend, "I beg you attempt nothing without the advice of the Society, or of the bishops" (Mills, 1978, pp. 28–34). The problem of ministerial instability continued until Lord North came to power in 1770, but his ministry, like those of his predecessors, was reluctant to introduce intentionally measures that would generate controversy as the episcopal issue had.

2 The Campaign of Drs. Johnson and Chandler

In spite of these conditions Thomas B. Chandler, supported by Dr. Johnson, called a voluntary convention of Anglican clergy to meet in Elizabeth Town, New Jersey, in October 1766. The convention's sole purpose was "to use their joint influence and endeavors *to obtain the happiness of bishops*" (Mills, 1978, p. 48). Nineteen clergy were present, from Connecticut, New York, New Jersey, and Pennsylvania. Dr. Johnson, Dr. Chandler, Samuel Seabury, Charles Inglis, Myles Cooper, Jeremiah Leaming, Abraham Jarves, and Bela Hubbard were there. Richard Peters (rector of Christ and St. Peter's churches in Philadelphia) and his assistant, William Sturgeon, attended. Two prominent clergy, Provost William Smith of the College of Philadelphia and Henry Caner from Boston, were absent. Zeal for their church, which in most cases was their adopted faith, was the moving force behind their High Church view on episcopacy. The completion of their historic and apostolic tradition was at stake, and no substitute for bishops was acceptable. To this end petitions were sent to the Archbishop of Canterbury, the Bishop of London, and the Bishop of Oxford. Agents were authorized and sent to the governors of Maryland and Virginia in the hope of securing support from the major colonies where Anglicanism was established.

The idea of an American episcopate had been raised earlier, during the tenure of Henry Compton as Bishop of London (1675–1713), and it came close to realization before the death of Queen Anne in 1714 ended it. The Bishop of London in 1748, Thomas Sherlock, revived the idea of suffragan bishops for America, but he too failed. At the conclusion of the French and Indian War, a pamphlet written by the Dean of Gloucester, Josiah Tucker, again promoted the idea of a suffragan bishop, but this time for Canada. Richard Peters presented to the Archbishops of Canterbury and York a treatise entitled *Thoughts on the Present State of the Church of England in America*, in 1764, which favored the appointment of four suffragan bishops by the King, without recourse to Parliament, within the archdiocese of Canterbury for service in America. When this same Peters in the Elizabeth Town convention in 1766 offered an alternative plan, prepared by Provost Smith, which called for the appointment of commissaries, the other delegates were shocked. The only difference between previous commissaries and the new ones was an enlargement of their respective jurisdictions from one to two colonies.

This Smith–Peters plan met defeat at the Elizabeth Town convention. Hostility to the idea of commissaries was expressed in letters to the Bishop of London and the SPG. Commissaries simply could not ordain, confirm, and consecrate. This counter-proposal, which might have won acceptance in England and avoided controversy in the colonies, was rejected. But the paradoxical conduct of Richard Peters from 1764 to 1766 actually reflected the changed reality in Pennsylvania. At the end of the war Great Britain was hugely admired, but the new imperial policy expressed especially in the Stamp Act of 1765 generated hostility towards the British Government. Moreover, Peters and Smith were aware that the Pennsylvania proprietors, Sir Thomas and Richard Penn, were opposed to any possible extension of royal authority in America and particularly in Pennsylvania. In this colony a considerable political faction was seeking to have the home government convert Pennsylvania into a royal colony. The creation of a colonial bishop, no matter how defined or wherever located, would have the appearance of extending royal authority. Smith and Peters were prepared to put the local interest of the Church ahead of a particular ecclesiastical issue, even episcopacy, to preserve what the Church had already achieved and to avoid involving it in unnecessary controversy.

In the fall of 1767, New Jersey Anglicans hosted another inter-colonial convention under Chandler's leadership, and this time the delegates urged him to prepare a pamphlet setting forth the episcopal cause. *An Appeal to the Public on Behalf of the Church of England* was the result. It was believed that a rational approach to the subject of bishops would allay dissenter fears and rally indifferent and passively resistant Anglicans to the cause. The *Appeal* stressed that only "a purely spiritual episcopate" was sought for America: one with no temporal power, no special relations with the state, no state functions, and no exclusive civil privileges as the bishops had in England. The fury of independent opposition to the *Appeal* found expression in Charles Chauncy's response. Chauncy, the most influential clergyman in New England, was minister of First Church, Boston. His tract, *An Appeal to the Public Answered*, was the initial blast in pamphlet and newspaper intended to refute totally the position stated in Chandler's *Appeal*. In time, the pamphlet contest included *The Appeal Defended* by Chandler; this was answered by Chauncy, *A Reply to Dr. Chandler's "Appeal Defended." The Appeal Farther Defended* was answered by *A Compleat View of Episcopacy*.

The second phase of the controversy exploded with a series of newspaper articles entitled "The American Whig," which appeared in Parker's *New York Gazette* in March of 1768 and ran for 57 issues. Behind the series were three Presbyterian laymen: William Livingston, William Smith, Jr., and John Morin Scott. Their objective was to explode the idea that Anglicans wanted a primitive bishop. The episcopal plan was described as a veiled attempt to secure a benign episcopate and later endow it with full prelatical powers. Although Samuel Seabury, Charles Inglis, and Myles Cooper contributed a series of articles entitled "Whip for the American Whig," which appeared in Gaine's *New York Mercury*, they had a difficult time handling their opponents' arguments. "The American Whig" series also appeared in the *Boston Gazette* and the *Pennsylvania Journal*. In Philadelphia, Francis Alison, John Dickinson, and George Bryan, all Presbyterians, articulated their opposition to the *Appeal* in a series entitled "Centinel," which was countered by Provost Smith in a series labelled "Anatomist."

The rancorous rhetoric used by both sides in the episcopal controversy served to emphasize the essential constitutional problem and caused many churchmen, especially in the colonies where the Church of England was established, to downgrade the importance of episcopacy and resist the Johnson–Chandler plan. When three clergy in Maryland tried to advance the scheme, Hugh Hamersley, secretary to Lord Baltimore, wrote, "His Lordship by no means wishes to see an episcopal palace rise in America," and this virtually foreclosed the subject. On June 4, 1771, when 12 clergy out of more than 90 in Virginia met in convention, the subject was raised. Four of the clergy present openly opposed the scheme. Press coverage of the event extended from May 30, 1771 to March 5, 1772 and included some 23 letters for and against episcopacy, with the opposing side making the most forceful and effective case. William Nelson, President of the Virginia Council, stated succinctly, "We do not want bishops" (Mills, 1978, p. 85). No record exists of an attempt in North and South Carolina or Georgia to raise the issue. But the harsh treatment the Johnson–Chandler plan received in the two colonies where the Church of England was strongest was a major setback. In Maryland, the scheme

was viewed as an encroachment upon the proprietor's prerogative; in Virginia it was perceived as a threat to their local ecclesiastical arrangements.

3 Other Ecclesiastical Issues

In the period 1763–76 the Church of England in America was in a paradoxical position. At the very time when colonial resentment over the Proclamation Line, Revenue Act, Stamp Act, and Townshend Duties reached fever pitch, the Anglican Communion was experiencing remarkable growth. It was not until zealous churchmen cooperated with and then initiated an episcopal plan that grave difficulties were encountered. As long as the Church itself was perceived to be under local control it did not become an object of abuse, as did stamp agents, revenue commissioners, and admiralty judges. The suspicion, however, that the zealous advocates of episcopacy were also desirous of an extension of British authority proved correct. In the 1775–6 period, Thomas B. Chandler wrote at least three pamphlets supportive of Great Britain's policies and critical of America's actions. Myles Cooper and Charles Inglis did likewise, but Samuel Seabury, in his *Letters of a Westchester Farmer*, became the most noted loyalist of the group.

Tensions between Anglicans and Congregationalist-Presbyterians flared up over related ecclesiastical matters in at least three northern colonies. In 1763, the Privy Council disallowed a Massachusetts law creating an Indian Mission under Congregational auspices, and Archbishop Secker was suspected of playing a role in the defeat. Then, too, Anglicans in Massachusetts were unable to win Assembly approval for a proposed college to be located in the Berkshires. Churchmen in both Massachusetts and Connecticut frequently complained to British authorities that they were denied tax money whenever their parishes were without a minister. But it was in New York that the episcopal controversy became so deeply involved in local issues that the labels "Anglican" and "Presbyterian" were used to identify political factions. Livingston, Smith, and Scott, with other Presbyterians, fought against Anglican domination of King's College and endeavored to have the Ministry Act of 1693, which provided tax support for Anglicans, repealed. The acrimony and emotion expressed over these issues in local contexts simply added another dimension to the larger episcopal controversy.

It is worthy of note that in spite of repeated assurances from dissenters and churchmen alike, similar to what Thomas Hollis wrote in 1763, "You are in no real danger at present, in respect to the creation of Bishops in America if I am rightly informed," the episcopal controversy continued throughout the decade (Mills, 1978, p. 149). Why was this so? The need for resident ecclesiastical oversight of the American part of the Anglican Communion was real, and the sincerity of the proponents was compelling. On the other hand, dissenter fears of episcopacy, though based largely on accounts of seventeenth-century prelacy, were real. The interrelatedness of Church and State under the British Constitution clearly made bishops officials of the State as well as of the Church. This meant that a bishop, even a suffragan one, resident in the colonies would represent, at the very least symbolically, an extension of British authority over the internal affairs of the colonies. This idea posed a potential threat to the evolving colonial constitution to which dissenters and large numbers of churchmen subscribed. To have acquiesced in the settlement of a resident bishop between 1763 and 1776 would have been a contradiction to the argument used by the colonists to oppose the emerging imperial policy.

FURTHER READING

Bridenbaugh, Carl: *Mitre and Sceptre: Transatlantic Faiths, Ideas, Personalities, and Politics, 1689–1775* (New York: Oxford, 1962).

Clark, J. C. D.: *The Language of Liberty 1660–1832: Political discourse and social dynamics in the Anglo-American world* (Cambridge: Cambridge University Press, 1994).

Cross, Arthur L.: *The Anglican Episcopate and the American Colonies* (New York: Longmans, Green and Co., 1902).

Mills, Frederick V., Sr.: *Bishops by Ballot: an Eighteenth Century Ecclesiastical Revolution* (New York: Oxford, 1978).

Overton, J. H., and Relton, F.: *The English Church from the Accession of George I to the End of the Eighteenth Century* (London: Macmillan, 1906).

Sykes, Norman: *Church and State in England in the Eighteenth Century* (Cambridge: Cambridge University Press, 1934).

CHAPTER TWENTY-THREE

Social protest and the revolutionary movement, 1765–1776

EDWARD COUNTRYMAN

"MOBS, a sort of them at least, are constitutional" (Maier, 1982, p. 24). The year of the statement was 1768. Its author was Thomas Hutchinson, the Lieutenant-Governor of Massachusetts. Three years earlier Hutchinson had seen his own house virtually demolished by one of the most destructive mobs of the era. Thanks to Pauline Maier we know that even after that ordeal he still believed that popular uprisings could be legitimate. Thanks to her and to many others we now have a well-developed understanding of how ordinary people took part in the American Revolution, including its riots, of the difference they made to the Revolution's course, and of the difference that taking part made to them.

The phrase "social protest" is too simple to describe what took place. The "progressive" historians of the early twentieth century, who first posited the idea that there was an internal American Revolution, put their arguments in terms of flat, hard confrontation. In Carl Becker's words, the Revolution was a struggle for "the democratization of American politics and society" as well as for "home-rule." To him the history of pre-Independence political parties fed directly into "the history of the Federalist and Anti-Federalist parties under the confederation" (Becker, 1909, pp. 5, 276). Three-quarters of a century later the questions that Becker and his contemporaries raised remain valid, but we reject most of their precise formulations. Instead of flat confrontation, historians of the Revolution's internal dimensions and conflicts now see process, change, and development. This is so at every level from individual consciousness to the grand coalitions of resistance, of revolution, and of national construction.

Popular upheaval was central to the revolutionary process. Among the major events were the Stamp Act risings of 1765 and 1766 (Boston, New York, Newport, and Albany, among other places), the *Liberty* riot (Boston, 1768), the Battle of Golden Hill (New York, 1770), the King Street Riot (or "Boston Massacre," 1770), the destruction of the British revenue vessel *Gaspée* (Providence, 1772), the Boston Tea Party (1773), the popular response to the Coercive Acts (especially in rural Massachusetts, 1774) and to the news of war (1775), and the destruction of the Pennsylvania provincial government (1776).

In addition there were movements in many parts of the countryside. In the crisis decade itself came the Regulator uprisings in the two Carolinas, the Hudson Valley tenant insurrection of 1766, and the guerrilla warfare against New York authority that resulted in the birth of Vermont in 1777. Reaching backwards, we might also cite the New Jersey land riots of the late 1740s, Hudson Valley tenant unrest throughout the 1750s, and the Paxton Boys' march on Philadelphia in 1763. Reaching forwards, the list includes militant popular loyalism during the war in the Deep South, in Maryland, and in New York, Shays's Rebellion in Massachusetts in 1786, and the Whiskey Rebellion in Pennsylvania in 1792.

Nor were these outright uprisings the only form of protest. Virginia was the only province/state that did not experience explicitly political internal upheaval. But the emergence within it of militant evangelical churches – Baptists and Methodists – came close to the same thing (*see* Isaac, 1982). In large part (though not entirely) the direct risings were the work of white males. However disadvantaged some of these may have been, all of them were members of both the ruling race and the ruling gender. But during the Revolution both Blacks and women began to find voices of their own and to act together to change their situations.

1 The Nature of Popular Upheaval in the Colonies

The upheavals of the Revolution emerged from the social fabric and the culture of colonial America and, by extension, of the European world of their time. Thomas Hutchinson's observation that crowd risings could be "constitutional" reflects their ubiquity in the world he knew. In part, as Maier notes, risings were so frequent because colonial society had no other way to defend itself. The posse, the volunteer fire company, the militia unit: these were simply crowds that had received official sanction and leadership. A crowd that drove away smallpox victims to prevent contagion or that closed down a house of prostitution was doing much the same work as they. Rioters of this sort might cover the entire social spectrum from wealthy merchants, often clad in working men's costume, to journeymen and apprentices. Women did join some of these "constitutional" mobs, and there were occasions when men rioted in female disguise. "A rabble of negroes and boys" was the standard phrase to describe a mob that did not have official approval. But the phrase appears so often in the sources that we may be sure Blacks and youths rioted as well.

"Mixed" crowds acted to defend a community when there was no other way; these were the sort of which a man like Hutchinson might approve. But even these had a distinctly plebeian flavor, and there were other times when uprisings grew out of the experience of class rather than of community. In Boston and New York, and perhaps elsewhere, lower-class crowds celebrated

"Pope's Day" each November 5, with parades, bonfires, and sometimes a brawl. This popular ritual commemorated the discovery of the "Popish Plot" to blow up the House of Commons early in the seventeenth century; the day is still celebrated in England. Pope's Day created a brief moment of "misrule," when the social order could be inverted. It also kept alive the most radical traditions of English Protestantism. Among those traditions were the memories of Oliver Cromwell, of Cornet George Joyce, the reputed captor of Charles I during the English Civil War, and of the regicides who found shelter in New England after the Stuart restoration in 1660. All of those memories came forcefully to the surface during the American Revolution.

Lower-class crowds had more mundane concerns as well. Among the most important was the long-standing tradition that society's rulers bore the duty to control the market place so that poor and middling people could get basic necessities at affordable prices. If they failed, direct action became legitimate, either to remedy the problem itself or to convey its seriousness to society's rulers. The French called this *taxation populaire*; Edward Thompson has described its English variant as the "moral economy of the crowd" (Thompson, 1971); students of early America have referred to it as "corporatism." We know that this tradition of social responsibility crossed the Atlantic; it figures prominently in the social thought of New England Puritanism. We know as well that in eighteenth-century America its salience increased as urban development created wealth, poverty, and greater dependence on the complexities of the market place. This tradition, too, fed into popular revolutionary militance.

If Hutchinson had been pressed, he would probably have agreed that urban crowds were more likely to be "constitutional" than rural ones. Both in Britain and in America the same authorities who tolerated risings by townsfolk over bread or smallpox used all the force they could muster to put down risings by country people. Parliament showed the way with its response to the Scottish insurrections of 1715 and 1745 and with the "Black Act" of 1723 against illicit hunting. The colonial and state legislatures of South and North Carolina, Maryland, New York, and Massachusetts and the United States Congress all found reason to follow its example. The reason may have been that an urban riot was an event, growing from a specific issue, but a rural rising was a movement, directed against the larger pattern of authority and social relations.

Popular upheaval may be central to the process of the great revolutions, but by itself it is not necessarily revolutionary. The very fact that Hutchinson and men like him could regard rioting with equanimity suggests that far from posing a danger to the world they controlled it was a functioning part of that world. The deep *ancien régime* background that historians have uncovered on both sides of the Atlantic explains why and how popular upheaval appeared in revolutionary America. But by itself it does not explain why American crowds became revolutionary.

2   The Sons of Liberty

For that, we must turn to the Sons of Liberty, who made themselves into the Revolution's popular leadership. The term was coined not in America but by a sympathetic Member of Parliament, Colonel Isaac Barré, during the debates on the Stamp Act. The Americans adopted it quickly, both as a general description for people committed to resistance and as a name for the organized radical leadership.

The first group to emerge was the "Loyal Nine," who planned the Stamp Act resistance in Boston. Other groups took shape from Charles Town, South Carolina, to Portsmouth, New Hampshire. As a formally constituted network the Sons existed only for the duration of the Stamp Act crisis in 1765 and 1766. But for practical purposes they never disbanded at all. Their members remained active in local, provincial, and eventually continental radical politics (*see* chapter 26, §1, and chapter 27, §1).

The social makeup of the Sons varied widely. According to John Adams, the members of the Loyal Nine in January 1766 were "John Avery Distiller or Merchant, ... John Smith the Brazier, Thomas Crafts the Painter, [Benjamin] Edes the Printer, Stephen Cleverly the Brazier, [Thomas] Chase the

Distiller, Joseph Field Master of a Vessell, Henry Bass [merchant]" and "George Trott Jeweller" (Maier, 1972, p. 307). Charles Town's Sons were mostly master artisans. In New York the Sons were led by small merchants such as Isaac Sears and Alexander McDougall, but they had a strong artisan following. There were gentlemen of the first order among the Sons in Maryland and in Virginia.

To these must be added the Revolution's radical intellectuals. The most important, perhaps, was Samuel Adams, a Harvard graduate who was driven by a vision of turning Boston into a Christian Sparta where pious, virtuous men would put the public good ahead of their own. But Adams found he could work closely with a man as unlike himself as Dr. Thomas Young. Young was a self-taught physician and a man of startlingly unorthodox belief about the nature of God and the universe. He loathed the landlord-ridden society of his native province of New York as much as he scorned conventional religion. A wanderer, he helped found the Sons of Liberty in Albany – his name comes first on a list of their members made in 1766 – before moving to Boston and eventually to Newport and Philadelphia. He also involved himself at a distance with the Green Mountain insurrection that created Vermont.

What the groups of Sons shared was not specific social characteristics but rather commitment to determined action in the face of the British crisis. They were as much a coalition of different sorts and groups as the revolutionary movement they created and led. Their tactics varied as well, as the contrast between their revolutionary journalism in Boston and in New York City shows. In the former town, Benjamin Edes's *Boston Gazette* confined its politics solely to the British issue. In the latter, John Holt's *New York Journal* published article after article on New Yorkers' own "distressed situation."

Whether or not their press gave prominence to local issues, however, the Sons understood two cardinal rules of revolutionary politics. One was to establish discipline among the people they led; inchoate rage and uncontrolled violence had no place in their movement. Perhaps the best example was provided in February 1770 by the Boston radical William Molyneux. An angry crowd had attempted to confront a known customs informer named Ebenezer Richardson, and anger turned to outrage when a panic-stricken Richardson opened fire, killing an 11-year-old boy, Christopher Sneider. But though Molyneux had been active in organizing the confrontation, he personally saved Richardson from the crowd's vengeance for the boy's murder.

But for all their insistence on discipline, their other great principle was militance, and they understood that militance required making the British issue come alive in terms of people's lives. The Loyal Nine provided a fine example in the way they generated the first American resistance to the Stamp Act.

Boston's resistance to the Stamp Act

The action happened on August 14, 1765. By then the Virginia House of Burgesses had given a stirring lead, condemning the Act itself and (depending on the published version of their resolves) seeming to call for outright resistance. The Loyal Nine set out to dramatize the effect of the Act on everyday life, and they set up a mock stamp office on Boston Neck, the narrow spit that connected Boston to the mainland. They carried out their business beneath America's first Liberty Tree, in which they had placed effigies of Stamp Distributor Andrew Oliver and the Devil peeping out of an old boot. The boot's sole was green and vile with corruption. The effigy represented a double pun, on both the name of the Earl of Bute, the hated Scot who had been George III's first Prime Minister, and that of George Grenville, Bute's successor and the prime mover of the Stamp Act. But the two effigies were also strongly reminiscent of the effigies of the Pope, the Devil, and Guy Fawkes with which lower-class Bostonians paraded each November 5. The Loyal Nine may have shunned any appeal to outright class resentment. But they appealed directly to lower-class culture.

When night began to fall, a crowd gathered, as the Loyal Nine had anticipated. The Nine had already recruited Ebenezer Macintosh, a shoemaker who was leader of one of the two traditional Pope's Day crowds, and he led a parade with the Liberty Tree effigies. When the crowd reached the waterfront it leveled a brick building that Andrew Oliver had under construction. Then it advanced on Oliver's house, where it did minor damage before dispersing. Oliver immediately resigned his office, which meant that there was no one in Boston legally capable of distributing the stamps. Crowds elsewhere followed Boston's widely reported example, and by November 1, when the Act was due to take effect, it was virtually unenforceable.

To the Loyal Nine, and to others like them, that was all that was necessary. But their "followers" went further. On August 26, 12 days after the Liberty Tree demonstration, another crowd gathered in Boston and marched on another great man's house. The intended victim was Thomas Hutchinson, who was Oliver's brother-in-law and who was simultaneously Lieutenant-Governor, Chief Justice, and holder of several other high offices. He opposed the Stamp Act as unwise, but he believed in British authority. A native Bostonian, Hutchinson had long been unpopular; when his house caught fire in 1749 bystanders had cried, "Let it burn." By 1765 that house was also an island of opulence in a Boston that was suffering from long-term economic stagnation and from the general trading depression that followed the end of the Seven Years' War. Oliver had escaped with minor damage; Hutchinson saw his property utterly devastated.

Other cities follow Boston's example

Nor was Hutchinson's house the only victim of such destruction. On October 31 it happened to carriages and sleighs in New York that belonged to Lieutenant-Governor Cadwallader Colden and to a house in the same city that had been rented by Major Thomas James of the British Army. In Newport it happened to the houses of Martin Howard and Dr. Thomas Moffatt. The following May a New York City crowd poured into a newly opened theater, disrupting the performance and then destroying the building. There was discipline in the American movement, but there was also genuine anger.

In some of these instances the crowd's motivation seems obvious. Major James had been directly responsible for putting Fort

George, at the foot of Manhattan Island, in a state of preparedness, which included training its guns on New York City itself. Hutchinson, Colden, Howard, and Moffatt were all outspoken supporters of British authority. The Loyal Nine repudiated the sacking of Hutchinson's house and together with the town fathers they took strong steps to bring Boston under control. But the New York radical leadership made no objection to what happened to Colden's property and to James's rented house. They actually led the crowd that sacked the Chapel Street theater, and the crowd's members shouted "Liberty! Liberty!" as they paraded with the wreckage. It would seem that more was involved than the British issue by itself.

3   Imperial Issues Versus Domestic Distress

Underlying this urban rioting was a combination of sharp distress, stemming from the mid-1760s depression, and the "corporatist" tradition of political economy. Hutchinson's house and Colden's carriages and sleighs were symbols of opulence and privilege, and they were resented for their own sake as well as for the politics of their owners. In the case of the New York theater the imperial issue did not count directly at all. The events that took place early in 1770 in New York and in Boston help to show how imperial issues and domestic distress meshed and balanced.

In both places, British soldiers and American working men came to blows. New York City saw a week of civilian–soldier rioting in January. In Boston five Americans died when troops who were guarding the Customs House opened fire on a crowd on the evening of March 5. One reason for the violence lay in the Whig political language of the era, which taught that any standing military force betokened imminent tyranny. Benjamin Edes never stopped making that point to his Boston readers and the troops who were stationed in his town seemed determined to drive it home. Their mission was to protect the American Board of Customs Commissioners from the townspeople's hostility, while the commissioners presided over an outright despoliation of the American maritime

economy by their minions. The soldiers took over Boston Common for a camp ground and a number of public buildings for barracks. They paraded on Sunday mornings, disrupting church services with their racket. To stop desertion, they established guardposts, including one at Boston Neck. Bostonians who remembered the mock stamp office of August 14, 1765 must have remembered the Loyal Nine's predictions each time they had to stop for a sentry's challenge. In New York Alexander McDougall pressed the same point, that troops portended tyranny, in his impassioned address "to the betrayed inhabitants." The "betrayal" was by politicians who had given in to British demands that the city's garrison be supplied from provincial funds.

But other themes appeared as well. While McDougall was writing of betrayal, "Brutus" was telling New Yorkers that off-duty soldiers were taking employment away from people who needed it: themselves. Seeking part-time work was the soldiers' customary right, and it made the difference between lives of misery and lives with any comfort or enjoyment. Heretofore it had caused little distress, for New York's garrison had always been small and Boston had had none at all. But now each city contained several regiments, and the times were hard. In these maritime towns, with economies that were suffering both from British "customs racketeering" and from a severe trading slump, the soldiers' customary right turned into explosive provocation.

The Boston Massacre

The Boston events are particularly revealing. Only a few days before the riot, an off-duty soldier from the 29th Regiment approached a ropewalk seeking work. One of the ropeworkers offered the soldier a job cleaning his "necessary house," and the soldier took the offence that the rope-worker intended. He gathered comrades from his barracks and a brawl broke out. Boston leaders and British officers joined to break up the brawl. But the town was already seething because of the death of Christopher Sneider, and feelings remained high. Soldiers from the same regiment were guarding the Customs

House on the night of March 5, and a crowd began pelting them with snowballs. Thinking they had received an order, the soldiers fired, killing five members of the crowd. What the Boston crowd did in those late weeks of winter makes sense only against the background of its whole situation. In 1770, as in 1765, the town's Sons of Liberty strove hard to maintain control, and by and large they succeeded. But the sustained revolutionary militance that people like those rope-workers were developing grew from the problems they faced in their daily lives as well as from the great dispute with Britain. Had there been no British crisis, the domestic problems would not have led to revolution. But had there been no domestic problems, the response to the British issue would have been muted rather than militant.

4 The Involvement of Country People

Though the great port towns were the Revolution's "urban crucible" (Nash, 1979), their people comprised less than a twentieth of the whole American population. The movement could not have become a genuine revolution without the massive involvement of the countryside. The land riots in New Jersey and New York, the Regulator movements in the Carolinas, and the Paxton Boys' march in Pennsylvania show that the backcountry was as ridden with turmoil as the port towns. But these were parallel to the direct movement against Britain rather than part of it. When the New York City radical John Morin Scott joined in suppressing the Hudson Valley rising of 1766, one British army officer quipped that the Sons of Liberty were "of opinion that no one is entitled to Riot but themselves" (Countryman, 1981, p. 67). How, then, and why did country people become involved in the main movement?

Massachusetts provides the clearest picture. In 1772 the Boston Town Meeting established a committee of correspondence and gave it the job of rousing the interior. From then until the aftermath of the Boston Tea Party the committee strove to raise rural consciousness. Its extensive papers show that towns all over the province agreed with its analysis of the situation America faced. This analysis held that a major plot against

American liberty had been hatched in London and that it had to be resisted. But as in the case of townsfolk, it took more than political language to generate a movement of resistance and then to turn it into a movement of revolution.

At first the farmers confined their commitment to words. Even in 1773 and early 1774, some were so removed from the great political issues that they feared the whole movement stemmed from a plot among Boston merchants to sell off their excess goods. Fears and doubts dropped away, however, when the news arrived of Britain's response to the Boston Tea Party. Boston's port was closed; the royal charter of Massachusetts was altered; Crown officials accused of misdeeds in Massachusetts could now be tried far away; troops could be billeted on the people. The response was strong: all across the interior town meetings decided not simply to protest against Parliament's new laws but to nullify them.

The result was that when the judges of the county courts assembled for their new session late in the summer of 1774 they found themselves unable to open for business. The court houses were surrounded by armed men, drawn up in their militia units and insisting that the judges resign. The judges were the immediate representatives of British authority, for they held their commissions under the reformed Massachusetts charter. Through them the farmers were confronting the whole structure of British power, because closing the courts meant closing down the government. The farmers knew it: they would not accept the judges' private resignations. Instead they insisted that they humble themselves by doffing their ceremonial wigs and robes and walking through the ranks of the crowds as they read their resignations aloud. Resistance was becoming revolution, and by the autumn of 1774 the royal governor, General Thomas Gage, found that his authority extended only where his troops could march.

On the surface it would seem that the issues were purely constitutional, and that social protest had nothing to do with the farmers' rising. The leaders of Massachusetts certainly insisted that was the case. According to their official explanation, what was happening was not a revolution against British authority. It was a restoration of legitimate authority in place of illegitimate. The Massachusetts Government Act was a nullity; the old charter was still in effect; the provincial assembly, meeting in Salem, was administering it. The governorship and the judiciary were vacant, but the province would do without them until the Act was formally repealed and they could be restored.

But, as in the port towns, more was at stake than simple constitutionality. As Richard Bushman has shown, the farmers' uprising sprang from problems that were rooted deep in their society and their historical memory as well as from the immediate issue of relations with Britain (Bushman, 1976). From the beginning, rural New England had been trying to maintain a precarious balance between the medieval world and the modern. On the one hand, it completely repudiated feudal forms of landholding and its people loathed the whole idea of lordship and vassalage. On the other, its village way of life was in many ways pre-commercial and even communal (*see* Berthoff and Murrin, 1973). By the time of the Revolution, demographic change and economic development were bringing the New England way under ever-greater pressure. But the vision of living together, in harmony and without overlords, retained its power.

The land question

The key issue was land. By 1774 the experiments with open-field farming of the early years were a distant memory. Freehold farmers took pride that each of them could sit "under his own vine and fig-tree." But they also understood that their tenure could be precarious. They knew that late in the seventeenth century their ancestors had faced down another British attempt to change the terms of their government and to challenge their hold on their property. Perhaps the worst of it had been that Sir Edmund Andros, whom James II had named to rule them, had regarded their land as open to seizure for the benefit of his henchmen and himself. They had been quick to clap Andros in jail when the news arrived that his royal master had been overthrown in England's Glorious Revolution of 1688.

Now it seemed the nightmare had returned. Governor Thomas Gage was no Edmund Andros, but he was still a British general on active duty, commanding all the troops in North America as well as governing the province. His task was to enforce Parliament's will. Parliament had shown clearly enough that its will was to impose taxes the farmers could not pay. Failure to pay could lead to court proceedings that would end in the seizure of a person's land. Land that was so condemned could easily be bought up by someone with money to spend, and such a person might readily make himself lord of a new estate, worked by tenants who had once been the land's owners. The logical candidates for the new role of landlord were men of the sort that had risen to positions on the bench of the county courts. They were Massachusetts men, not Englishmen, but they held their commissions by the Governor's favor, and they had attracted his favor because they were already possessed of prominence and wealth.

By closing the courts the farmers were not just confronting Britain's latest assertion of its claim to rule them; they were also confronting their strongest memories and fears, and asserting their sense of what their world should be like. As they reached into the past they found models to emulate as well as bogeys to fear. Alfred Young has noted the importance to them of the memory of revolutionary England (Young, 1984). New Englanders took pride that after the Stuart Restoration in 1660 the surviving regicides, who had executed Charles I, found refuge among them. Oliver Cromwell, who had led the Puritan Revolution, was a figure of evil to the orthodox English Whig tradition, but to these people he remained a hero. A Massachusetts farmer named Asa Douglass addressed Washington himself as "Great Cromwell" in 1776, and new-born boys all over the region were being christened Oliver in Cromwell's honor. As Young puts it, a New Englander then would have spoken Cromwell's name with the same respect that an African-American would speak of "Malcolm" or "Martin" now.

Was this social protest? Perhaps not, if we are looking for outraged peasants attacking the castle. But the rising of the New England farmers drew on their whole social experience. It opened the possibility of remaking their political world so that it would suit their sense of what society should be like. By 1776, when it had become clear that Parliament would not back down and the old charter would never be restored, the farmers were looking to the future they would make themselves rather than to the past their ancestors had bequeathed to them (*see* chapter 45, §4).

Moreover, their rising had much in common with rural protest elsewhere in the colonies. The Hudson Valley had been in turmoil since mid-century as New England migrants crossed the Berkshires and joined New York tenants in confronting New York's manorial land system. The Green Mountains were claimed by New York, which intended to create a society of landlords and tenants there as well. But they were being settled by New Englanders who wanted to re-create the village world they knew. The landlord–tenant issue underlay the mid-century rioting in New Jersey as well, and it figured in the North Carolina Regulator movement. Not all of these issues fed directly into the movement against Britain. In some places, including the Hudson Valley, Maryland's eastern shore, and the Carolina interior, protest led to loyalism rather than to revolutionary patriotism, as discontented farmers found that their own opponents were among the Revolution's leaders. But whatever the precise course politics took, social discontent and social protest ran through rural experience during the era.

5 Revolution and Radicalism in Philadelphia

As the independence movement gained strength, social protest and political experience began combining to create new public identities. The case of Philadelphia shows the process particularly well. Pennsylvania's capital took little part in the great uprisings of the Stamp Act period; its stamp distributor resigned with little ado and there was virtually no rioting. But by the end of the 1760s relations within the city were growing tense. The issue was the non-importation movement with which the colonies had responded to Parliament's Townshend Duties of 1767. These were an attempt to meet the supposed colonial objection to "internal" taxes, such as the Stamp Tax, by imposing "external" duties on colonial imports. The colonials had long accepted Parliament's right to impose duties in order to control their behavior, such as the Molasses Act of 1733. By and large they were even paying the duties imposed by the Sugar Act of 1764. It seemed to the British that they had made the external–internal distinction themselves. On all counts, it looked as if Parliament had found a way of taxing the colonials that the colonials would accept.

They did not accept it. Instead, they agreed to boycott British commerce until the taxes were repealed. To the merchants of the great ports it was a disagreeable necessity: they would not accept Parliament's right to tax them, but transatlantic commerce was their life. But to Philadelphia's artisans it was another matter. Like New Yorkers and Bostonians, Philadelphians were enduring the depression that had settled on the colonies at the end of the Seven Years' War. It seemed to the artisans that non-importation offered a chance to bring prosperity back. Without British imports there would be more of a market for their own goods. But when Parliament repealed four of the five Townshend Duties in 1770, leaving only the duty on tea in place, non-importation began to collapse.

To the merchants the issue was simple: they were the traders and they had the right to decide whether to import or not. But to one Philadelphia "tradesman" the "consent of the majority of the tradesmen, farmers and other freemen ... should have been obtained." A "lover of liberty and a mechanic's friend" wrote that a "good mechanic" was "one of the most serviceable, one of the most valuable members of society" but that merchants were only "weak and babbling boys – clerks of yesterday." "Brother Chip" asked Philadelphia artisans whether they did not have "an equal right of electing or being elected ... Are there no ... men well acquainted with the constitution and laws of their country among the tradesmen and mechanics?" (Countryman, 1990).

The issue was one of social and political consciousness more than it was one of overt social conflict. The Philadelphia artisans wanted an equal voice in the making of their community's major decisions. But in their self-assertion they were also redefining the terms of their membership in the community. In the colonial period they may have accepted that their political position and their social rank were inferior. Now they were casting such beliefs aside and developing instead the ideology of equal rights which would become dominant in American political culture.

The involvement of artisans

From its slow start in 1765, Philadelphia went on to become the most radical urban center in revolutionary America. Politically the culmination came in June 1776, when the old provincial government was forcibly overthrown. One element in the coalition that overthrew it was the militant members of the Continental Congress, who were determined to have independence and who recognized that the Pennsylvania Assembly formed the last major obstacle to it. But they were joined by Pennsylvanians whose vision of America demanded transformation as well as independence. Many of them were master artisans, the people who had asserted their right to an equal political voice in 1770. But now they were joined by lesser men, most notably the journeymen and laborers who formed the bulk of the city's revolutionary militia. The artisans had found the means to express themselves in the city's committee of safety. Like similar committees elsewhere this had begun to take shape in the aftermath of the Boston Tea Party, and by 1776 its voice was dominant in the city's popular politics. The emergence and triumph of such committees was the surest possible sign that a full political revolution was underway. The spread of their membership to include men who would never have had such a voice in running the old order was as sure a sign that the Revolution had a profound social dimension (*see* Ryerson, 1978; Countryman, 1981).

But Philadelphians took it further. They met the final crisis as a bitterly divided people. For reasons of both religion and self-interest the city's old elite of Quaker and Anglican merchants were rejecting the Revolution. The non-Quaker patriot elite,

typified by the lawyer and pamphleteer John Dickinson, proved unwilling to accept the consequences of what they had helped to begin. In 1768 Dickinson's own *Letters from a Farmer in Pennsylvania* had been enormously influential in rousing opposition to the Townshend Duties and his "Liberty Song" had been sung from New Hampshire to Georgia. In it he had urged, "Come join hand in hand, brave Americans all, and rouse your bold hearts at fair Liberty's call," but now his own heart was timid and he held back from joining his own hand to the cause of independence. It was Dickinson and his like, not open loyalists, who were using the old provincial assembly to put the moment of independence off, and it was their power that dissolved when the popular committee and the Continental Congress joined their own hands to bring the assembly down.

The militia

Meanwhile another group had also taken on shape and consciousness: the privates of the city's militia. Philadelphia's Quaker pacifist heritage meant that it had no military tradition, which meant that there were no established lines of military authority. When a militia became necessary its officers were drawn from the better and middling sorts, and the privates came from the city's journeymen, apprentices, laborers, and servants. But the terms of the militia law were lenient, and a man who had conscientious objections could easily avoid service. To the city's Quakers it was a matter of religious belief. But to the militiamen liability to military service became a matter of political principle.

The consequence was that the militiamen established their own committee and formulated their own program for the Revolution. Equal liability to service was only one of the points they put forward. They scorned the paternalistic willingness of some of their officers to equip the troops they commanded; instead they wanted officers and men alike to be uniformed in simple hunting shirts. They wanted to elect their officers themselves, rather than serve under men appointed by higher authority (*see* Rosswurm, 1987). Their demands found echoes elsewhere. Hunting shirts became the costume of revolutionary commitment in Virginia. A committee of artisans took shape in New York City, and in May 1776 it issued a strident set of demands to the "elected delegates" in the province's provincial congress. One of those demands was that under the new order the system of popular committees that had taken power during the final crisis be able to reconstitute itself whenever the people might choose.

Thomas Paine's "Common Sense"

The need for governmental simplicity and responsiveness became one of the dominant themes in popular political discourse. No one put the point more clearly than the pamphleteer Thomas Paine. His first great piece in a long career of radical political writing was *Common Sense*, published in Philadelphia in January 1776 (*see* chapter 31). Paine was a former corset-maker and British customs official, and he had migrated from England only in 1774. He had known Benjamin Franklin there, and through the famous former printer he found an entrée to the artisan community just at the point when it was awakening to political consciousness.

Paine set himself three distinct projects in *Common Sense*. One, after nine inconclusive months of war, was to convince Americans that reconciliation was impossible. Full independence was the only course worth following: "the weeping voice of nature cries 'tis time to part." The second was to argue the case for simple republicanism: "let the assemblies be annual, with a president only." The third was to put his case in a political language that would be sophisticated but also simple. Paine's predecessors in the Revolution's pamphlet literature had been gentlemen and they had written for other gentlemen. Paine's own roots were plebeian, and he wrote for people like himself (*see* Foner, 1976).

His impact was enormous. *Common Sense* sold some 150,000 copies and was read and discussed from one end of the 13 provinces to the other. People had been waiting for an unequivocal call for independence. Artisans and farmers were ready for a major piece of political writing that was neither beyond

them nor condescending to them. Paine had made himself the voice of these people. The power with which he spoke for them was a measure of their own importance to the revolutionary movement. It was also a measure of how much their consciousness and situation had changed over the decade since the crisis first began. His call for republican institutions of the simplest sort, directly responsive, open to anyone's participation, devoid of the complications and balances of the old order, expressed the conclusions that the people who devoured *Common Sense* were drawing from their experience in the revolutionary movement.

6 Later Developments

The fullest measure of social protest in revolutionary America came after 1776, and it is beyond the main scope of this article. Independence brought the collapse of existing political institutions, and the collapse provided opportunity for many sorts of Americans to try to change their situations. Paine's people – white working men – pressed for institutional settlements of the sort he sketched in *Common Sense*. Their fullest opportunity came in Pennsylvania itself, where the patriot wing of the old elite gave way to panic and lost control. The result was the state's radical constitution of 1776, and its provisions found echoes elsewhere. It was copied directly in the Green Mountains, where the New England settlers seized the moment and cut themselves free of New York. Their choice of the Pennsylvania model suggests the political mentality of revolutionary rural America. So does the equally simple New England proposal called *The People the Best Governors*. Following Paine, the Pennsylvanians repudiated the whole idea of a governorship, appointing a "president only" to see to public business. The title bore none of the quasi-regal meaning it would later take on in American political culture, and others proposed it as well: South Carolina, Delaware, and New Hampshire in their first constitutions and New York in a constitutional proposal of 1776.

All of these changes took place among white men. Mary Beth Norton, Linda Kerber, and Ira Berlin have pointed the way for understanding the terms on which women and African-Americans confronted the Revolution, entered it, and tried to take advantage of the possibilities it presented (Norton, 1980; Kerber, 1980; Berlin and Hoffman, 1983). (Both groups receive full treatment elsewhere in this volume.) Enough here to make four points. The first is that they started from situations far less privileged than those of any white males. The second, springing from the first, is that neither women nor Blacks found themselves in a position to claim full political equality or direct political power. The third is that members of each group were to at least some extent actors in the main events between 1765 and 1776. The most notable case is that of Crispus Attucks, who was black and who was one of the five Bostonians slain in the King Street Riot in 1770. The fourth is that some members of both groups did make the most they could of the political and the ideological opportunities that the Revolution presented.

The American Revolution does not, perhaps, fit a mechanistic model of a social revolution. But that is not to say that the Revolution did not have a profound social dimension, both in its origins, to which this article has referred, and in its short-term and long-term consequences. One starting point for the people who made the Revolution was their common membership in a dependent, colonial yet British society. The other was their many different situations within that society and their relations with one another. During the political crisis with Britain they found themselves confronting their own social situations and relationships as well as the large imperial issues. The process and the great transformations of the Revolution grew from its domestic and social aspects as well as from its imperial and political ones.

FURTHER READING

Becker, Carl Lotus: *The History of Political Parties in the Province of New York, 1765–1776* (Madison: University of Wisconsin Press, 1909).

Berlin, Ira, and Hoffman, Ronald (eds.): *Slavery and Freedom in the Age of the American Revolution* (Charlottesville: University Press of Virginia, 1983).

Berthoff, Rowland, and Murrin, John M.: "Feudalism, communalism and the yeoman freeholder: the American Revolution considered as a social accident," in *Essays on the American Revolution,* ed. Stephen G. Kurtz and James H. Hutson (New York: W. W. Norton, 1973).

Bushman, Richard L.: "Massachusetts farmers and the Revolution," in *Society, Freedom and Conscience: the American Revolution in Virginia, Massachusetts and New York,* ed. Richard M. Jellison (New York: W. W. Norton, 1976).

Countryman, Edward: *A People in Revolution: the American Revolution and Political Society in New York, 1760–1790* (Baltimore: Johns Hopkins University Press, 1981).

——: "'To Secure the Blessings of Liberty': Language, the Revolution and American Capitalism," in *Beyond the American Revolution: Further Explorations in the History of American Radicalism,* ed. Alfred F. Young (Dekalb: Northern Illinois University Press, 1990).

Foner, Eric: *Tom Paine and Revolutionary America* (New York: Oxford University Press, 1976).

Isaac, Rhys: *The Transformation of Virginia, 1740–1790* (Chapel Hill: University of North Carolina Press, 1982).

Kerber, Linda K.: *Women of the Republic: Intellect and Ideology in Revolutionary America* (Chapel Rill: University of North Carolina Press, 1980).

Maier, Pauline: *From Resistance to Revolution: Colonial Radicals and the Development of American Opposition to Britain, 1765–1776* (New York: Alfred A. Knopf, 1972).

Nash, Gary B.: *The Urban Crucible: Social Change, Political Consciousness and the Origins of the American Revolution* (Cambridge, Mass.: Harvard University Press, 1979).

Norton, Mary Beth: *Liberty's Daughters: the Revolutionary Experience of American Women, 1750–1800* (Boston: Little, Brown, 1980).

Rosswurm, Steven: *Arms, Country and Class: the Philadelphia Militia and the "Lower Sort" During the American Revolution* (New Brunswick. NJ: Rutgers University Press, 1987).

Ryerson, Richard A.: The *Revolution Is Now Begun: the Radical Committees of Philadelphia, 1765–1776* (Philadelphia: University of Pennsylvania Press, 1978).

Thompson, E. P.: "The moral economy of the English crowd in the eighteenth century," *Past & Present,* 50 (February 1971), 76–136.

Young, Alfred F.: "English plebeian culture and eighteenth-century American radicalism." in *The Origins of Anglo-American Radicalism,* ed. Margaret Jacob and James Jacob (London: Allen & Unwin, 1984).

CHAPTER TWENTY-FOUR

The tea crisis and its consequences, through 1775

DAVID L. AMMERMAN

THE Boston Tea Party initiated a series of events which led directly to the American Revolution. On December 16, 1773, a group of Bostonians, disguised as Amerindians, boarded three vessels and threw the cargo of tea into the harbor. The party ended three weeks of negotiation between the town and Governor Thomas Hutchinson. The citizens did not want the tea landed because they feared that paying taxes on it would establish a precedent. The Governor was determined to land the tea, in part because of his conviction that any failure to enforce the law would encourage disregard for British authority.

In response to the destruction of the tea, the British Government adopted four Acts. These Acts, known in the colonies as the Coercive or Intolerable Acts, closed the port of Boston, redesigned the government of Massachusetts Bay to increase British authority, provided for moving trials of British officials to another colony or to England when local opinion was inflamed, and permitted the housing of British troops in unused buildings. The British considered the Acts essential for the effective governing of the colonies; the Americans viewed them as an unwarranted exercise of arbitrary power.

A fifth Act, the Quebec Act, was not adopted in response to the Boston Tea Party, but was unpopular in the colonies and was included – by the Americans – with the Coercive Acts because it seemed to favor the Catholic church in Canada, provided for a government without an elected assembly, and – perhaps most importantly – transferred large areas of western lands to the Canadian colony, thus threatening land speculators.

News of the Coercive Acts aroused widespread dissatisfaction in the colonies and led to the calling of the First Continental Congress. This body adopted an embargo of British goods and called for the repeal of the Coercive Acts as well as all legislation levying taxes or altering traditional rights of trial by jury. Congress authorized the election of Committees of Inspection in local communities throughout the colonies as a means of enforcing the embargo. It also provided for non-exportation to begin in the fall of 1775 if Great Britain did not agree to its demands.

The British ministry, faced with the demands of Congress as well as the impossibility of enforcing its will in Massachusetts, decided on an armed response. The Colonial Secretary, Lord Dartmouth, acting on instructions from the Cabinet, ordered General Thomas Gage (the recently appointed Governor of Massachusetts Bay) to march into the countryside either to arrest leaders of the resistance or to confiscate arms being stored at Concord. The resulting skirmishes at Lexington and Concord touched off the American Revolution.

1 The Tea Act of 1773

It is unusual, perhaps unprecedented, for a revolution to begin over lowered commodity prices. Yet that was the case with the American Revolution. It has been a continuing source of puzzlement to historians that the Boston Tea Party – and subsequent events leading to the American Revolution – occurred in response to a British measure which reduced the price of tea throughout the colonies.

By 1773 the East India Company was on the verge of bankruptcy and the government undertook to save the company – and the nation – from such a fate. One aspect of this effort involved helping the company to sell the large quantities of tea stored in its warehouses. The company had had difficulty selling tea since 1767 when the American colonies had adopted a boycott of all products, including tea, taxed by the Townshend Duties. When the other duties were repealed in 1770, the government had maintained the tax on tea and the colonies had continued their boycott. By 1773 it seemed that one way to help the East India Company increase its profits would be to lower the price of tea in America and thus increase sales.

The simplest way to reduce the price of tea would have been to repeal the 3d tax levied in the colonies. That was unacceptable to the ministry. When the government repealed the Townshend Duties, it had kept the tax on tea as a means of demonstrating to the colonists that Parliament had the right to levy taxes. The same considerations proved determinative in 1773. England kept the colonial tax, but still managed to lower the price of the commodity in America. The means adopted to achieve this goal were to prove lethal to the empire, but the method was simple. Since all tea had to be imported to England before being sent on to the colonies, and since a tax was charged when the cargo arrived in the mother country, a rebate was arranged. Merchants who exported tea from England to the colonies were refunded the original tax. Thus the price was lowered and the colonial tax was maintained.

One other provision of the Tea Act would arouse the ire of colonial merchants. It gave the East India Company the right to select certain merchants in America and consign shipments of tea to each. Thus, in effect, the company decided who could sell tea in the colonies, and the resulting monopoly naturally irritated those to whom consignments were not made.

Colonial objections came from three different groups. Professional patriots charged that lowering the price of tea while maintaining the colonial tax constituted another attempt by the British Government to trick them into accepting taxation. Merchants, as noted above, were upset over the implications of permitting the East India Company to select its own factors. This constituted a monopoly of tea sales, they said, and might well lay the groundwork for similar measures in the future. Finally, smugglers were irritated over the prospect of lowered prices on legal tea. It seemed not unlikely that the prospect of buying legal tea at prices lower than smuggled tea would lure away their customers. This combination (professional patriots, merchants, and smugglers) provided formidable opposition.

2 The Boston Tea Party

In the summer of 1773 the East India Company dispatched shipments of tea to the four major ports in the colonies: Charles Town, Philadelphia, New York, and Boston. The effort proved unsuccessful. In New York and Philadelphia the colonists refused to allow the cargo to be unloaded and the vessels simply left the harbor. In Charles Town the situation was more complicated, but in the end the tea was unloaded and stored without paying the tax. Only in Boston did the situation lead to violence.

To say that Thomas Hutchinson, acting Governor of Massachusetts Bay, was a man of conviction, would not be an overstatement. And one of his convictions held that the common people of Massachusetts Bay – if not all America – had gotten out of hand. If government is to govern, Hutchinson believed, it must do precisely that. Compromise and submission only encouraged mob rule, and the time had come to put an end to such encouragement which had already caused problems in Massachusetts Bay. Hutchinson believed that the shipment of tea to Boston provided a unique opportunity to restore order and authority. Once the ships had entered the harbor, British law forbade their leaving until all taxes had been paid. Fortuitously, from the acting Governor's point of view, the guns of Castle William controlled egress from the harbor and permitted Hutchinson to stop the ships from leaving Boston.

Captain Rotch, the commander of the three vessels which brought the tea to Boston, is one of those historical figures caught in the flow of events. Hoping only to extricate himself from a difficult situation, he traveled back and forth between the town meeting – which repeatedly refused to allow his ships to unload – and the acting Governor – who repeatedly insisted that the ships remain in port.

Hutchinson apparently believed that he had the citizens of Boston in a bind. Authorized by law to unload a cargo which waited in port for three weeks without paying the required taxes, the acting Governor apparently intended to do just that. He would then presumably be able to use military force to unload the cargo and see that it was disposed of according to the provisions of the law. A commercial transaction would, in effect, become a governmental transaction. Thomas Hutchinson's thoughtful preparations failed. As the ships bobbed in Boston harbor and the frantic captain ran between the town meeting and the Governor trying to avert disaster, colonial leaders planned a fateful step. Samuel Adams, serving as moderator of a massive town meeting in Old South Meeting Hall, listened to Rotch explain Hutchinson's final refusal to permit the ships to leave. Then, according to tradition, he banged his gavel three times and declared that since "*this* meeting" could do no more to protect the rights of America it stood adjourned. Subsequently, a group disguised as Amerindians swooped down on the harbor and tossed the tea into the salty water. Boston must have been deceptively quiet that night as the colonists celebrated their apparent victory behind closed doors and shuttered windows.

3   The Reaction of the British Government

What makes the Boston Tea Party so significant was not the event itself but the response of the British Government. Crowd action, as historians have repeatedly demonstrated, was not unusual in the eighteenth century

and the Boston Tea Party was a classic example of this phenomenon. The decision of the North ministry, however, to use the event as a justification for closing the port of Boston, restructuring the government of Massachusetts Bay, and ordering changes in the system of justice was unprecedented.

It seems clear, in retrospect, that the British Government saw the Boston Tea Party as an opportunity to restore its authority in the American colonies. Ever since the repeal of the Stamp Act, there had been a growing belief in England that – as General Gage would later put it – the colonists would be lions "whilst we are Lambs." The clear implication of such an attitude was that at some point the British Government must take a stand and maintain it at all costs. The Tea Party appeared to present a perfect opportunity for decisive action.

In the first place the actions of the Boston mob were almost universally condemned in England. Few, even among the supporters of the colonists, could justify the destruction of private property and the flouting of established law, especially when that law had resulted in reducing the price of tea. Even many colonists believed that the Bostonians had taken events to the extreme. George Washington and Benjamin Franklin were among those prominent Americans who expressed reservations about the events of December 16. Moreover, Massachusetts Bay seemed to stand alone. Although New York, Philadelphia, and Charles Town had refused the tea, none of these cities had gone to the extreme of destroying it. Consequently it was possible to single out Boston and Massachusetts Bay for punishment and, since this city and province were thought to be the center of colonial resistance, bringing them to order would presumably entail a lesson for all America. No one seems to have considered the inherent contradictions in a policy which sought to isolate a group as a means of teaching a lesson to other groups.

The Coercive Acts

Parliament adopted four specific Acts in direct response to the Boston Tea Party: the Boston Port Act, the Massachusetts

Government Act, the Justice Act, and the Quartering Act. A fifth Act, usually lumped together with these four, termed the Coercive or Intolerable Acts in the colonies, was the Quebec Act, which was not attributable to the events in Boston Harbor.

The Boston Port Act closed the port of Boston. Declaring shipping to be unsafe in that area, Parliament forbade ships to enter or leave the port until compensation had been made for the tea. Even then, commerce would not be restored until the King determined that it was safe.

The Massachusetts Government Act altered by parliamentary fiat, as the colonists saw it, the basic structure of colonial government. It provided that the upper house, or Council, should henceforth be appointed by the King rather than selected by the governor from a list nominated by the lower house. It also brought local administration more directly under the control of the governor. Towns were allowed to hold their cherished meetings only once a year and were forbidden to concern themselves with other than local matters. The thrust and intent of the law was to limit the "democratic" features of New England government.

The Justice Act was intended to protect British officials in their efforts to enforce the law. It provided that in capital cases government officials, or those working under their direction, be protected from vindictive local juries. If the governor determined that a fair trial could not be had, he might order a change of venue either to another colony or even to Great Britain itself.

The Quartering Act altered existing legislation in an effort to provide more effectively for British troops. It stipulated that when the colony offered quarters which were unacceptable, the governor could take over unoccupied public buildings for the use of the troops. It did not, as generations of American school children were taught, permit the housing of troops in private homes.

Because of its timing and provisions, the Quebec Act was also considered by the colonists to be a part of this punitive legislation. In fact the Act was an enlightened effort on the part of the British Government

to organize the recently acquired colony of Quebec. It allowed the Catholic Church to continue at least a quasi-established position in the colony and also continued French civil law – a system which did not guarantee trial by jury. It set up a government without an elected assembly and, perhaps most galling to the English colonists, it added the Old Northwest Territory – where many of the original 13 colonies had land claims – to Quebec. To the colonists the Act favored Catholics, established a government without representation, interfered with their land claims, and limited trial by jury.

4 The First Continental Congress

Perhaps the major miscalculation of the North ministry in adopting these measures was the assumed isolation of Massachusetts Bay. Although many of the other colonies were reluctant to rush precipitously into a trade boycott – as Boston asked – they clearly rejected the Coercive Acts as an unwarranted intrusion into colonial affairs. During the late spring and early summer of 1774, leaders in every colony except Georgia had arranged for the election of delegates to attend a "Grand Congress" in Philadelphia. Moreover, virtually all of those colonies had committed themselves to some sort of trade boycott and some – such as Virginia – had already adopted measures directed at that objective.

The First Continental Congress met in Philadelphia in September 1774 and immediately set itself three objectives. The delegates proposed to draw up a clear statement of colonial rights, list the Acts of Parliament which violated those rights, and propose measures to secure the repeal of that legislation. It is notable that the first of these objectives proved impossible, the second was accomplished with some clever sleight of hand, and only the last – the decision which led to revolution – was achieved with little debate and adopted by acclamation.

In drawing up a statement of rights, Congress rejected outright Parliament's right to tax, to interfere with traditional rights of trial by jury, or to adopt the Coercive Acts. All of these were beyond the authority of the British Government in the American colonies. The divisive issue concerned Parliament's right to regulate trade. Five colonies wanted to approve that right, five wanted to deny it, and two – including Massachusetts Bay – found themselves split on the question. In the end the delegates adopted an ambiguous document wrapped around such statements as "the necessity of the case" which said little and guaranteed nothing.

Turning to its list of grievances, Congress once again stumbled on the issue of trade regulation. Should the delegates complain of the Acts of Trade and Navigation? What about the Hat Act or the Woolens Act? In the end they adopted a clever, if devious, solution. Deciding that a conspiracy to deprive Americans of their rights had been hatched about the year 1763, they concluded that legislation passed before that year could be passed over for the time being. It is significant that Congress did not legitimatize such legislation but simply decided to limit its debates to Acts passed after the agreed-upon date.

It must have been with some relief that the delegates turned to that issue upon which they were virtually unanimous – the means by which the colonists should secure repeal of grievances. Without apparent dissent, the delegates invoked non-importation to begin in December 1774 and followed that with a resolution to begin non-exportation the following fall if Parliament had not rescinded the objectionable legislation. A number of delegates wanted to begin non-exportation immediately but apparently submitted to the representatives of Virginia, who adamantly refused a measure which would prevent them from marketing tobacco that was already in the ground.

The Continental Association

In pursuing these objectives Congress endorsed a document known as the Continental Association. That document listed the Acts that Parliament was to repeal and endorsed non-importation and delayed non-exportation as a means of securing that repeal. It also called upon towns and counties throughout the colonies to establish Committees of Inspection, each of which would take responsibility for enforcing the trade boycott. In establishing local committees for the purpose of enforcing what might easily be viewed as a piece of legislation, Congress took an enormously important step in the development of a quasi-legal governmental structure. One of the problems facing a revolutionary movement is the maintenance of order. These committees, in effect, would become the means by which both the Provincial and the Continental Congresses would provide local government as the Revolution progressed.

Another aspect of the Association merits mention. In an effort to encourage the colonists to develop an economic independence from Great Britain – and, perhaps, not incidentally, to demonstrate their determination to the government – the delegates approved a number of resolutions designed to promote self-sufficiency. Americans were asked to protect sheep in order to encourage the production of woolen cloth. They were warned to avoid the exchange of expensive (and imported) gifts at funerals and to develop domestic manufacturing in order to lessen their dependence on Great Britain. In brief, Congress asked all Americans to adopt a frugal and independent life-style which would not only promote economic self-sufficiency, but would also demonstrate to the mother country their determination and willingness to sacrifice.

Galloway's Plan of Union

Despite the unanimity with which Congress adopted its trade embargo with England, a number of delegates remained dissatisfied with the ambiguous Statement of Rights. They argued that Congress had been instructed not just to secure repeal of colonial grievances, but also to establish a firm basis on which the connection with England could be maintained. Individuals such as James Duane and Joseph Galloway believed that the failure of Congress to recognize Parliament's right to regulate colonial trade was unacceptable. The matter, in the opinion of such delegates, remained unsettled.

It was in this context that Galloway introduced his now famous Plan of Union. Although often touted as a conservative alternative to the trade embargo, it was nothing of the sort. Galloway's proposal came after Congress had endorsed non-importation and non-exportation and it was, in fact, an attempt to deal with the question of the imperial relationship rather than immediate problems. The Galloway Plan of Union was one of the most radical proposals put forth in Congress. It envisioned a reorganization of the empire, with an American Congress sharing power with the British Parliament. Had it been endorsed by the Congress it would almost certainly have been rejected by the British Government.

The plan was rejected by Congress. When first proposed by Galloway the delegates voted, by the margin of a single colony, to lay it on the table. Historians have occasionally suggested that the plan was rejected by a single vote, but that was not the case. Those colonies which voted to table it simply indicated a willingness to consider it at a later time. When it was brought up for resolution, near the end of the meetings, it was rejected, but by what margin was not recorded. New York voted for the plan, but there is no evidence that any other colony did, and it is even possible that Pennsylvania, whose delegation had been altered by the addition of John Dickinson, did not support the proposal in the final vote.

Resolutions adopted by Congress

Before adjourning, Congress adopted two resolutions which had far-reaching effect. Fearing that Massachusetts Bay – which was widely regarded as more radical than other colonies – might initiate conflict with the troops stationed in Boston, Congress sought to avoid that possibility. The delegates asked Massachusetts to avoid taking aggressive measures and promised that if the Bay Colony was attacked it would be supported by the other colonies acting in concert.

The delegates further agreed to call a second meeting of Congress in the spring, allowing enough time for Great Britain to respond to their measures. Their timing, as it turned out, would be propitious, since news of the conflict at Lexington and Concord reached many of the delegates as they set out for the May meeting of the Second Continental Congress.

5 Support for Congress in the Colonies

As the delegates left Philadelphia they were almost certainly divided in their expectations. More militant members such as Sam Adams and Richard Henry Lee were certain that the efforts of Congress would not change British policy. They had argued, unsuccessfully, that Congress should instruct the colonists to prepare for war. Others – James Duane and John Dickinson are notable examples – hoped that the decisions of Congress would persuade the British that the colonists were united and determined and thus lead to a modification of government policy.

The work of Congress was widely acclaimed and supported throughout the colonies. From the point of view of most Americans, the delegates had adopted a moderate but determined stand. They had rejected all proposals for military preparation, had petitioned the government in respectful terms, and had invoked an embargo policy which had, apparently, proved ineffective in previous crises provoked by the Stamp Act and the Townshend Duties. Consequently a substantial majority of colonists determined to show their support for Congress by adopting and enforcing its resolutions. In town, county, and provincial meetings throughout the continent they approved the program adopted by the Congress, appointed committees to see to its enforcement, and took steps to ensure their economic independence from the mother country.

Committees of Inspection

One of the most important gauges of support for the Continental Association was the swift appointment of committees. In New England the response was almost unanimous. Hundreds of committees were appointed, even in the smallest and most remote of communities. The sincerity of these community efforts is perhaps best demonstrated by the town of Sutton, Massachusetts. Noting that the punishment for violating the resolutions of Congress was social ostracization, citizens discussed the exact meaning of that term. They concluded that those who spoke to offenders might be forgiven if they had done so inadvertently, to convince the offender of his or her error in ignoring the resolutions of Congress in a situation which involved a threat to their lives or the lives of their domestic animals, or for purposes involving religion and the state of the offender's soul.

It is somewhat more difficult to assess support for Congress in the middle colonies. Certainly the embargo was effective in the major port cities of New York and Philadelphia, and committees actively enforced the dictates of Congress in both. Records in smaller towns and counties are fragmented, but where they exist they show general approval. New York was the only colony – excepting Georgia, which sent no delegation to Congress – in which the Assembly failed to ratify the Continental Association.

In the southern colonies there was generally enthusiastic support for Congress and the appointment of committees seems to have been the rule. Virginia, of course, led the way. The Virginia *Gazette* reported the formation of nearly 50 county committees to enforce the Association. In South Carolina the Provincial Congress appointed committees, and while it is difficult to assess local support the committees apparently operated effectively. Counties in Maryland appointed quite large committees, each of which seems to have divided into smaller groups to provide effective local surveillance.

It would be difficult to overemphasize the significance of these committees in the development of revolutionary government in the colonies. Literally thousands of citizens were brought into the movement through their activities as committeemen. This included not only the pre-crisis leaders (Governor Dunmore reported from Virginia that local Justices of the Peace were active *only* as committee members) but others who had not previously been active in government. In Maryland, for example, members were constantly added to the committees, which suggests a conscious effort to broaden the basis of support for the patriot program.

The activities of these Committees of Inspection were nearly as varied as the localities in which they were appointed. In major port cities a large proportion of time was spent enforcing the embargo through the inspection of incoming vessels, merchant inventories, etc. In other communities the committees went from house to house collecting signatures on copies of the Continental Association or calling citizens before them to explain reports that they had drunk a cup of tea. Newspapers reported a number of incidents in which individuals were forced to recant before local committees for having cast aspersions on various members or on the committee itself. As the crisis deepened, the Committees of Inspection gradually evolved into Committees of Safety and took upon themselves responsibility for such governmental policies as collecting taxes for the revolutionary governments and recruiting soldiers.

Significantly, these committees acted not under the authority of the Provincial Assemblies or even the Provincial Congresses, but considered themselves enforcement agencies of the Continental Congress. In New York, for example, where the Provincial Assembly did not specifically endorse the work of Congress or call on local communities to enforce its resolutions, many communities appointed committees anyway. In nearly every colony Committees of Inspection were appointed before any provincial body had met or acted on the decisions of Congress. Even many conservative colonists supported local committees because they were rapidly becoming the only bulwark between order and chaos. As provincial and local government ceased to function under the authority of King and Parliament, it was essential that some form of authority step into the void. That authority was most often the local Committee of Inspection.

6 Reaction in Britain to the Congress

In Great Britain the response to the resolutions of the Continental Congress was, at first, confused. By the time word of the events in Philadelphia arrived in England the government was, for the most part, dispersed and already engaged in the general inactivity which characterized the Christmas holidays. Rumors circulated in the colonies that the ministry had been favorably impressed with the work of the Congress and that the King and Parliament would respond in a conciliatory fashion. Nothing could have been further from the truth, but the state of communications in the eighteenth century and the inactivity of government during the holidays prevented the contradiction of those reports for several months.

The British Government faced a situation which virtually demanded vigorous action. Massachusetts Bay was clearly in rebellion and the regular government had ceased to function outside the city of Boston. Governor (General) Thomas Gage had dissolved the General Court of the colony in June 1774 when he learned that the delegates were appointing representatives to the Continental Congress. When he ordered new elections under the provisions of the Massachusetts Government Act, which had established an appointive Council, the deputies simply refused to meet with the so-called mandamus councilors. Instead, they gathered in Concord and invited the previous Council – organized under the provisions of the Charter granted by William and Mary – to meet with them. They also invited Governor Gage to participate but he, not surprisingly, refused.

Even in Boston Gage found it hard to govern. The Massachusetts Government Act had decreed that town meetings should be held only once a year, a provision that the Boston Town Meeting had rendered ineffective by simply adjourning from week to week. So difficult had Gage's position become that he wrote to the Cabinet proposing that the Coercive Acts be "suspended" until Great Britain was in a position to see them enforced. Before leaving England the Governor had believed that the colonists could be brought to heel by a show of force and determination. On the spot in Boston he discovered that opposition in Massachusetts Bay was not confined to the "rabble" and a few radical

leaders, but, rather, had infected the entire province.

The government could not avoid taking action. According to the Declaratory Act of 1766 the King and Parliament had the right to legislate for the colonies "in all cases whatsoever," and in adopting the Massachusetts Government Act they had done so. Massachusetts had simply refused to abide by the terms of that legislation, and the duly appointed governor of the Bay Colony now sat impotently in Boston while the province proceeded to flout British law. The only possible means of avoiding a confrontation with the colonists would have been for the government to adopt a conciliatory position towards the resolutions of Congress and begin negotiations based on the assumption that the Coercive Acts would be repealed. That was not possible. Even Gage's suggestion that the acts be "suspended" was scoffed at by the Cabinet and by Dartmouth, who wrote that he was not aware of any provision in British law for "suspending" Acts of Parliament.

Ignoring the resolutions of Congress, the evidence from a number of British officials in the colonies that the Americans were united in their determination to resist the Coercive Acts, and the insistence of Gage that his forces were inadequate to enforce the law, the government continued to believe that the crisis could be ended through a show of force. Perhaps the fatal flaw in British policy at this time was the failure of the government to acknowledge the extent of colonial resistance. It was conventional knowledge among the ministry that opposition in the colonies was the work of a few radical leaders who had inflamed the rabble. If only the government would take a stand, show that they were determined to enforce it, and send the royal standard out into the countryside, the vast majority of the colonists would rally to the cause. Cabinet members even suggested, privately, that Gage's about-face since his arrival in Massachusetts Bay was evidence of cowardice on his part.

As events stood in January 1775, conflict was virtually inevitable. Both sides had made up their minds that a show of determination and force was needed. Many colonists were convinced that British policy reflected a failure on the part of the King and Parliament to recognize colonial unity. If the government could be persuaded, they believed, that the American colonies stood united, then concessions would follow. Similarly with the members of the British government: failure in the past, they concluded, had resulted from a perception in the colonies that the government did not have the will to enforce its legislation. Failure to enforce the Stamp Act and then the Townshend Duties had, the British leadership believed, contributed to a lack of respect for order in the colonies. Now was their chance to correct that perception. The laws would be enforced and, when the colonists realized that the mother country meant business, resistance would fall apart.

Military action

In the early part of 1775 the Cabinet began to consider measures to deal with the crisis in America. After considering and rejecting a number of possibilities the ministers decided to follow through on their assumptions about the weakness of the opposition and take action in Massachusetts Bay. Lord Dartmouth was instructed to draft a letter to Governor Gage instructing him to use the forces he had at hand to make a show of force in the countryside outside Boston

The Cabinet's instructions to Gage left little room for interpretation. Gage was informed that his observations about the extent of resistance in the province had been considered and rejected. He was ordered to take action. The Cabinet would have preferred that he march into the countryside and arrest certain presumed leaders of the resistance movement, but admitted that since he was on the scene he would have to be the judge of that. Nevertheless, he was to do something. If he decided that it was impossible to make such arrests he was to confiscate military stores or in some manner indicate that the time for concession was past.

Dartmouth reported the Cabinet's overwhelming belief that, despite Gage's assertions to the contrary, the resistance would collapse once British troops showed a determination to enforce British law. He

acknowledged Gage's conclusions that military action would precipitate civil war but informed the General that the Cabinet disagreed. Even if Gage were correct, the Cabinet had determined that if war were inevitable it would be better to begin the conflict immediately rather than allow the colonists to become better prepared for military conflict. These lengthy instructions reflect the contempt of the British Government, not only for colonial unity but for colonial military prowess. It was apparently inconceivable to the Cabinet that the Americans had either the will or the ability to resist the British military.

Meanwhile in Massachusetts Bay, Samuel Adams, among others, awaited the conflict which he knew was coming. The Provincial Congress, meeting in Concord without the mandamus councilors or the Governor, proceeded to conduct business, collect taxes, and govern the province outside Boston. Although the delegates avoided precipitating armed conflict with the British – perhaps because they remembered the promise of Congress to come to their assistance provided that they were the aggrieved party – they were preparing for an expected attack. If men like James Duane in New York and John Dickinson in Pennsylvania still held out hope for overtures of peace, most of the Massachusetts leadership knew better. They even provided for patrols on the roads leading out of Boston in order to alert the countryside when the British finally decided to march. Paul Revere, William Wadsworth Longfellow aside, did not just happen to be in place on the "18th of April in seventy-five." Similar patrols had been active for some time.

The British march on Lexington and Concord is too well known to be detailed here. Gage, following specific orders, determined that his best chance was to send a force to Concord to destroy or confiscate military stores collected there. In the early hours of the morning of April 18, 1775 British regulars approached Lexington Green, where they were confronted by a small force of militiamen who had been alerted of their approach. As the Americans began to disperse, having made a show of resistance, a shot rang out, and before the British officers could stop the firing a number of colonists had been injured or killed.

Continuing on to Concord the British did, indeed, seize and destroy some of the military stores collected there. Even as they marched, however, militia from throughout Massachusetts and Connecticut were marching towards the temporary colonial capital. By the time the regulars began their retreat to Boston they found themselves harassed by increasing numbers of colonials who fired from behind barns, hedges, and stone walls. The remnants of the expedition straggled back into Boston demoralized and defeated. It appeared, as a minor British governmental official would later comment, that the colonists had been more determined than anticipated.

News of Lexington and Concord was electric throughout the colonies. In New York thousands signed the Association and turned out in support of the upcoming Congress. Reports of the battle reached Patrick Henry in Virginia, who responded with his now famous "Give me Liberty or Give me Death" speech. Perhaps more important, reports of the conflict reached many of the delegates to the Second Continental Congress as they approached Philadelphia, and the news set the tone for the meeting. George Washington appeared on the scene in the uniform of his native Virginia and would soon accept the command of the American army offered by Congress. Meanwhile, thousands of militiamen headed towards Boston, where they surrounded the city and effectively bottled up the British troops, ultimately forcing them to withdraw.

7 Summary

In retrospect it appears that the British Government did virtually everything wrong. In adopting the Coercive Acts they had seriously miscalculated the possibilities of isolating and punishing Boston as an example to the rest of the colonies. The Acts themselves touched on almost every sensitive point in the colonial mind, almost as if calculated to provoke resistance. The Massachusetts Government Act had altered a colonial charter by fiat, a move which

threatened many colonists regardless of the alterations made. The Justice Act interfered with traditional British concepts of trial by jury, prompting even so conservative a colonist as George Washington to refer to it as the "Murder Act." The Boston Port Act appeared to many as a virtual declaration of war, with British naval vessels sent to blockade an American port. The Quebec Act managed to incite colonial Protestants by protecting the Catholic Church in Canada, and threatened land speculators through its transfer of territory to a distant – and "foreign" – jurisdiction. Nearly every colonial interest felt threatened by these Acts. Moreover, the Massachusetts Government Act, unlike the Port Act, the Quebec Act, or even the Justice Act, could be enforced only with provincial cooperation or through force. It was inconceivable that the British Government could permit its army to sit idle in Boston while the rest of the province ignored an Act of Parliament. By adopting this Act the ministry put itself in a position of either acknowledging its weakness or taking forceful action.

Having aroused almost universal opposition and having put its prestige on the line, the British Government proceeded to initiate conflict in such a manner as to allow Massachusetts to proclaim its innocence and its suffering "in the common cause." Since the First Continental Congress had promised to come to the assistance of Massachusetts in case of attack, the delegates had little choice but to follow through on that assurance. And, propitiously for the men from the Bay Colony, the attack was undertaken on the eve of the second meeting of the Congress.

Finally the British suffered a disastrous defeat, both in actuality and in the propaganda war. The vaunted reputation of the redcoats was in tatters and their casualties were far greater than those of the colonists. They had retreated in disarray. It appeared that regular troops were no match for the virtuous wrath of an aroused citizenry. The colonists stood aggrieved, attacked, and victorious, and the British Government was totally unprepared to subdue a continent. Before further activities could be undertaken by the ministry, troops would have to be raised, taxes collected, and plans for conquest formulated. And while the British undertook these preparations, the colonists had time to raise an army, organize an intercolonial government, embark on measures of wartime finance, and win the initial military successes of the war in New England.

FURTHER READING

Ammerman, David: *In the Common Cause: American Response to the Coercive Acts of 1774* (Charlottesville: University Press of Virginia, 1974).

Brown, Richard D.: *Revolutionary Politics in Massachusetts: the Boston Committee of Correspondence and the Towns, 1772–1774* (Cambridge, Mass.: Harvard University Press, 1970).

Countryman, Edward: *The American Revolution* (New York: Hill and Wang, 1985).

Donoughue, Bernard: *British Politics and the American Revolution: the Path to War, 1773–1775* (New York: St. Martin's Press, 1964).

Gross, Robert A.: *The Minutemen and their World* (New York: Hill and Wang, 1976).

Labaree, Benjamin Woods: *The Boston Tea Party* (New York: Oxford University Press, 1964).

Maier, Pauline: *The Old Revolutionaries: Political Lives in the Age of Samuel Adams* (New York: Knopf, 1980).

Marston, Jerrilyn Greene: *King and Congress: the Transfer of Political Legitimacy, 1774–1776* (Princeton, NJ: Princeton University Press, 1987).

Middlekauff, Robert: *The Glorious Cause: the American Revolution, 1763–1789* (New York: Oxford University Press, 1982).

Nash, Gary B.: *The Urban Crucible: Social Change, Political Consciousness, and the Origins of the American Revolution* (Cambridge, Mass.: Harvard University Press, 1979).

CHAPTER TWENTY-FIVE

The crisis of Independence

DAVID L. AMMERMAN

FROM the Battle of Lexington and Concord in April 1775 until the Declaration of Independence in early July 1776, the American colonists engaged actively in warfare with Great Britain but did not declare independence. It is unusual in history for colonies to take up arms against the mother country while proclaiming that their only objective is reunification, and the refusal of the colonists to declare their independence hindered the war effort, thus making their situation even more remarkable. Delegates to the Second Continental Congress refused to open their ports to foreign nations because it violated British law, they held back on entering into negotiations for foreign military assistance because their objective was to return to the empire, they inventoried captured equipment and arms so that they could be returned to England after the conflict was over, and they toasted the health of the King and carried on business in his name until well into 1776.

A majority of Americans expected that their demands would ultimately be met by the British, which explains their behavior. They held on to the hope that George III and the opposition in Parliament would reverse the course of the ministry once it became clear that the colonists sought only to restore their rights as Englishmen and remain within the empire. These expectations proved unrealistic, yet they prevented a declaration of separation from Great Britain for over a year.

The actions of the British ministers and their colonial governors ultimately persuaded a majority of Americans that their only choice was between independence and submission.

During the latter half of 1775 England declared them in rebellion, closed their ports, hired foreign mercenaries to carry on warfare against them, and made it clear that the government was determined to force them to accept the authority of Parliament. It became increasingly clear that the King himself supported these measures, and that the opposition in Parliament was ineffective. These events, and others like them, brought the colonists to accept the necessity for separation.

By February 1776 a majority in the Second Continental Congress supported independence. But even at that late date their majority was small. A number of colonies, including New Jersey, Delaware, New York, Pennsylvania, and Maryland, still opposed it. Indeed, Congress had to encourage a revolution in the government of Pennsylvania to win the support of that colony, and the New York delegates did not have instructions on how to vote when the issue came to the floor on July 2. Not until February 1776 was independence even debated on the floor of Congress.

North Carolina, on April 12, 1776, became the first colony to instruct its delegates to agree, in concert with others, to independence. Two months later Richard Henry Lee, acting on the instruction of the Virginia Convention, proposed that the colonies "are, and of right ought to be, free and independent States." Several delegates threatened to leave Congress unless the vote was postponed, but their endeavors were only a delaying tactic. The vote was put off until early July, but the fact that a date had been set gave evidence of the approaching victory of those gathering support for independence. On July 2, 1776 Congress voted for independence, and two days later the document was embossed and signed. The decision to declare independence had been made. The effort necessary to win it remained.

1 Divided Opinion in Congress

Armed conflict between the British and their American colonists broke out at Lexington and Concord on April 18, 1775, and news of that battle swept rapidly through the colonies. War had begun. And yet the delegates who assembled for the Second Continental Congress in May of that year were far from convinced that the empire was irrevocably shattered. It would, indeed, be more than a year before the Americans declared themselves independent, and during the intervening months many, if not most, of them continued to hope for reconciliation.

Certainly the colonists in North America did not look upon themselves as revolutionaries. In their determined insistence that they had been forced to arms in order to protect the traditional rights of Englishmen, they maintained the fiction that they were fighting not the King but only the machinations of wicked counselors. Until early 1776 Washington and his officers continued to toast the health of George III and to refer to their armed opponents as the "Ministerial Troops."

For many these protestations were propaganda and window-dressing. Leaders such as Samuel Adams not only expected independence but actively pursued it, and it seems unlikely that George Washington would have accepted command of the Continental Army had he expected the colonies to return to the British fold. For others, however – John Dickinson of Pennsylvania and James Duane of New York come immediately to mind – independence was virtually unthinkable. Such men were clearly "reluctant Revolutionaries" who accepted each step towards separation in the hope that it would be the last.

It did not take long for the divisions which separated the American colonists to make themselves felt in the Second Continental Congress. Three distinct groups rapidly emerged. The radicals, which included John and Samuel Adams, Thomas Jefferson, George Washington, and Benjamin Franklin, had little hope for reconciliation and were prepared for independence. Dickinson and Duane, along with John Jay of New York, provided leadership to a group on the other end of the spectrum. These conservatives, although determined to protect American rights, adopted military measures with great reluctance and hoped that petition and moderation would produce a change in British attitudes. No doubt the largest group in Congress stood between these extremes. The moderates, including Robert Morris of Pennsylvania, John Hancock and Thomas Cushing of Massachusetts, and the Rutledges of South Carolina, hoped for a return to the empire but had little faith that this could be accomplished by petition and moderation. They supported military measures as the only means of persuading the British to grant colonial demands. One of the considerations that separated the three groups in Congress was their respective reading of political conditions in Great Britain. The radicals had no expectation that the British would moderate their demands. They were convinced that the ministry had the full support of George III and that neither petition nor armed resistance would result in reconciliation. The conservatives believed that there was strong opposition to British measures in Britain itself. They wanted, in so far as possible, to avoid armed conflict and relied on petition and remonstrance to convince the government, and particularly the King, that the Americans were loyal subjects whose grievances should be redressed. The moderates, like the conservatives, hoped for reconciliation but, like the radicals, had little hope that this could be achieved through peaceful means. They were not ready to endorse independence, but they were prepared to support military resistance as the only hope of forcing Great Britain to meet colonial demands.

The radicals were correct. George III not only supported the ministry but in many cases pushed for more determined measures. Moreover, opposition in Parliament was small, divided, and demoralized. Anticipating the possibility of an extended contest with the Americans, Lord North had called for parliamentary elections and had won a resounding victory. Not until after the Battle of Yorktown in 1781 would the ministry face an effective opposition in Parliament. Throughout the American Revolution the government could count on comfortable margins in support of its measures.

In a very real sense, then, the months between the Battle of Lexington and Concord and the Declaration of Independence were a period of educating the moderates and conservatives in Congress to the realities of British politics. One by one the measures of the British Government brought new recruits to the radical block and ultimately to the acceptance of independence. Prohibiting trade with the colonies and declaring them in rebellion, encouraging opposition among the slaves and the Amerindians, hiring Hessians as combat troops were among the measures that gradually convinced the most reluctant of revolutionaries that it was independence or submission.

2   The American Military Reaction to Lexington and Concord

There were a number of issues which Congress faced that influenced the question of independence. Perhaps the most immediate was what to do with the troops surrounding Boston. Incorporating the troops into a Continental Army and appointing officers were clearly the acts of a sovereign nation. Yet there seemed to be no alternative. The troops were there, and popular enthusiasm for fighting the British was at its height after Lexington and Concord. Moreover, Congress was more or less committed to such an action. Towards the end of the meeting of the First Continental Congress in October 1774 the delegates, in an effort to restrain the "radicalism" of Massachusetts, made a promise to the Bay Colony: if the Bostonians would avoid aggressive action and were attacked by British troops in spite of this moderation, all of America would come to their support. That was now the case.

The issue first arose when the New York Committee of 100 asked what to do if British troops arrived in New York City. Congress, determined to act on the defensive, told the committee to act only defensively. If the British committed hostile acts or attacked private property the New Yorkers could resist with force, but otherwise they should avoid conflict.

A few days later the delegates in Philadelphia learned that troops under the command of Ethan Allen and Benedict Arnold had captured Fort Ticonderoga on Lake Champlain and also Crown Point. While the Massachusetts Provincial Congress rejoiced, the Continental Congress worried about how to deal with this obvious act of colonial aggression against the mother country. In the end, the delegates ordered that a strict inventory of all arms and supplies be made so that they could be returned to England when the dispute was settled.

On May 26 Congress resolved that hostilities made it necessary to adopt a state of defense, and two weeks later the delegates committed themselves to raising troops and turned to the appointment of a Commander-in-Chief. George Washington, apparently the only member of Congress who appeared on the floor in military attire, was rumored to be available for the position. The Virginian was particularly acceptable because, as a member from one of the southern colonies, he would help solidify support for the New Englanders. His appointment on June 15 proved popular both in Congress and throughout the continent although, if John Adams is to be trusted on the issue, highly upsetting to John Hancock of Massachusetts, who had coveted the position himself. By instructing Washington "to command all the continental forces, raised, or to be raised, for the defence of American liberty," the Congress took a major step towards independence.

On June 22 the delegates made yet another advance. News of the Battle of Bunker (Breeds) Hill led to the election of eight brigadier generals and a vote to issue $2 million in paper money. Moreover it was decided to take command of the garrisons at Ticonderoga and Crown Point. These were clearly the acts of a sovereign power, although the letters and notes of the delegates indicate more concern with the politics of who would command the army than with the impact of the decision to create one.

Washington's acceptance of command is almost certainly indicative of his decision to pursue independence. It is almost inconceivable that he would have assumed this position had he expected reconciliation with the British Empire. Any outcome other than independence would have left the newly created general in a difficult position. Curtis Nettels, in his *George Washington and American Independence* (1951), has argued, persuasively if perhaps one-sidedly, that from the time of his appointment onwards the Virginian used every means within his power to advance the cause of independence. Certainly his push to create a navy, to define treason, and to insist that captured Americans be treated as prisoners of war and his numerous other activities helped commit the colonists to separation. The decision to invade Canada, coming some three weeks after Congress had resolved that no colonists should undertake or assist in such a venture, was further evidence of Washington's influence.

Was it not contradictory for the Congress to insist that it opposed independence and wanted to avoid conflict, even as it created an army, issued paper money, took command of the captured forts at Ticonderoga and Crown Point, and authorized an invasion of Canada. Certainly in many instances it was. John and Samuel Adams, Richard Henry Lee, and others clearly held neither a hope nor a desire of returning to the empire. For others, however, the position was not hypocritical. The Declaration of the Causes and Necessity of Taking up Arms, adopted on July 6, fairly clearly – and no doubt honestly – expounded their position. They did not want armed conflict nor independence, and yet the presence of British troops and engagements such as those at Lexington, Concord, and Bunker Hill forced them to adopt measures to provide for their own defense.

3 Britain's Retaliatory Measures

The apparently contradictory position of seeking reconciliation while adopting war measures is again a reflection of misinformation about the state of affairs in England. The Reconciliationists continued to hope that a change would be forthcoming in British policy. They clung to the belief that George III would heed their petitions and oust the evil ministers who had brought about this unwanted state of affairs. They continued to hope that the people of England – and the opposition in Parliament – would take control of the situation. None of those scenarios was even remotely possible. George III was, if anything, more committed to settling the issue with America than was his Cabinet. The opposition in Parliament was completely ineffective.

Slowly but purposefully the British Government adopted measures which dashed the hopes of the Reconciliationists and forced them to the reluctant conclusion that there was no alternative to independence except submission. On March 30, 1775 the North ministry obtained passage of an Act restraining trade with New England, and on April 13 the measure was extended to Pennsylvania, New Jersey, Maryland, Virginia, and South Carolina. New York, Delaware, North Carolina, and Georgia were not at first included because the government hoped to drive a wedge between the colonies by offering a more conciliatory policy towards those that seemed less aggressive. North accompanied these Acts with a motion on reconciliation which proposed, in essence, that the colonies would not be taxed if they agreed to tax themselves. This so-called Olive Branch Resolution was widely viewed in America as window-dressing, and so it was. North himself admitted in his correspondence with the King that he was more concerned with the opposition in England than with the possibilities of conciliation with America. Congress ultimately rejected the petition as having no substance.

4 Local Government

Almost daily the delegates in Philadelphia faced problems that forced them to make decisions leading to independence. A major problem concerned the establishment of governments in the several colonies. Only a few legal governments were functioning, and it was imperative, if only to maintain order in the various provinces, that some sort of government be in place.

The First Continental Congress had, indeed, taken an important step in the direction of creating local governments when it authorized the appointment of committees of inspection to enforce the Continental Association. That Association, which provided for non-importation of British goods, amounted to a national law adopted by a national Congress. This measure took on even more important implications because of its method of enforcement. Congress had authorized the establishment of town and county committees with power to inspect cargoes and punish those who failed to abide by the terms of the agreement. In doing so the delegates to the First Congress had bypassed provincial governments and thus established an embryonic national government with the committees acting as its agents. In time these committees raised taxes, enlisted soldiers, and took over most of the functions of local government. Although the First Continental Congress may have been unaware of the implications of this arrangement, the Association was a step in the direction of independence since it authorized the creation of local governments which in no way depended upon the support or the authority of the Crown or Parliament.

When Congress, during the second half of 1775, confronted the issue of entire provinces without government, the issue was more clearly tied to the question of independence. If Congress were to authorize the establishment of colonial governments acting in every way as sovereign powers but without the authority or approval of the British Government, would they not, in effect, be declaring independence colony by colony? Yet even the conservatives were forced to acknowledge that some such measure was necessary. John Adams recorded in his diary a conversation with a debtor who thanked him – and the Massachusetts Provincial Congress – for closing the courts since it was no longer necessary to pay debts. This had clearly not been one of Adams's objectives in leading the opposition to Great Britain, and it was certainly not an objective of more conservative colonists. If order was

to be maintained, government must function, and in the absence of an established British-based authority, the Congress had to take responsibility for the creation of new, and non-imperial, governments.

The situation in Massachusetts is illustrative. With the failure of the British successfully to enforce the Massachusetts Government Act, the legal government had ceased to function. There had, in fact, been no royal government in the Bay Colony since Gage had dissolved the Assembly as it was electing delegates to the First Continental Congress in June 1774. Council members appointed by the King had either been forced to resign or had fled to Boston. The Assembly, meeting in Concord, invited the council elected before passage of the Government Act to meet with them and also issued an invitation to Gage to work with them until the crisis had passed. Gage, of course, had no intention of accepting that offer, and so government – outside of Boston – passed effectively to the lower house.

Conflicts among the patriots themselves brought the issue to the attention of the Continental Congress. The eastern towns and counties were, by and large, content simply to resume government under the terms of the Charter granted them by William and Mary in 1691. The western portion of the colony, chafing under what it perceived to be under-representation in the government, agitated for a return to the original Charter of 1629. On June 9, 1775 the Continental Congress resolved that the Assembly of Massachusetts Bay should elect a council, essentially as had been done under the Charter of 1691, and that the legislature should then govern until such time as a royal governor would act according to the terms of the Charter. In doing so, of course, the Congress endorsed the refusal of Massachusetts Bay to abide by the terms of the Massachusetts Government Act, and also put its weight and authority behind the creation of an independent government, albeit a temporary one.

Authorizing Massachusetts to resume government under the terms of a charter voided by Parliament and the King was a bold step, but still stopped short of actually instructing a colony to assume government based on the will of the people. On October 18, 1775 the New Hampshire Assembly asked Congress for instructions as to the creation of a new government for that colony. In responding to this request the delegates faced a more difficult decision than that taken with regard to Massachusetts Bay. In the end Congress recommended that New Hampshire assemble a "full and free representation of the people," and that if the representatives so decided they should establish a government as would "best produce the happiness of the people." In adopting this measure the Congress officially put itself in the position of authorizing provincial governments based on the will of the people rather than on the authority of England.

5 Congress Moves from Reconciliation to Separation

Nonetheless the majority in Congress continued to oppose independence and hoped for reconciliation. Until early February 1776 those colonies favoring independence were in a minority even though the Reconciliationists were gradually forced to adopt measures characteristic of an independent nation. New York and Pennsylvania strongly opposed independence until at least June 1776, and even Maryland was not far behind. In November 1775 the New Jersey Assembly declared that reports of the colonies seeking separation from the British Empire were completely groundless, and on January 11, 1776 the Maryland Convention instructed its delegates not to consent to independence. Even the Massachusetts delegation, so long as it included Robert Treat Paine, Thomas Cushing, and John Hancock, was not committed to separation despite the fulminations of the two Adamses.

Events continued to strengthen the hands of the radicals. On July 8, Congress adopted its second petition to the King in which the delegates blamed the ministry for the present unrest in the empire, and explained the necessity of adopting "defensive" measures against those who sought to destroy the peace and harmony which had existed before their misdirected innovations. They begged the King to use his influence to end the armed conflict. Expectations of support

from George III received a shattering blow when, in November, the news arrived that the King had refused even to receive the petition. Indeed, on August 23, 1775 a royal proclamation declared parts of America in open rebellion and threatened those in England who assisted the colonists with "condign" punishment. The punishment for treason at that time called not just for death but for dismemberment and other similarly drastic measures. It is doubtful that the ministry envisioned such punishment for William Pitt and Edmund Burke, but they clearly hoped to curtail the opposition in Parliament.

On December 22, 1775 Parliament passed the Prohibitory Act, putting a complete stop to American commerce. In effect, all American vessels and cargoes were declared forfeit to the Crown and the British Navy was legally entitled to seize them on the seas and in port. These two measures had enormous impact on sentiment in Congress and seriously weakened the arguments of those who continued to push for reconciliation. By declaring the colonies in open rebellion and refusing to hear the petition of Congress, the King made clear his intention to force submission from America. Similarly, Parliament's Prohibitory Act, adopted by wide margins in both the Commons and the Lords, served as tangible evidence of the weakness of the opposition.

As if this were not enough the ministry proceeded to enlist foreign mercenaries to help fill the ranks of the army. Samuel Adams, who seems to have had an uncanny knack for predicting the actions of the British Government, had long argued that England would enlist German mercenaries to fight Englishmen in America. This step, which was objectionable to virtually every shade of opinion in America and to the opposition in England, had long been downplayed by those in Congress who sought reconciliation. In late January 1776 the ministry entered into treaties with several German states to provide nearly 20,000 mercenary troops. These troops were to be used not only for garrison duty in Europe but were to be sent to America to engage in combat with the colonists. That George III would permit the "slaughter" of his own subjects by mercenary troops unquestionably forced many opponents of independence to alter their stance.

But more than events in England served the cause of those seeking independence. British governors helped inflame colonial opinion. In July Governor Martin of North Carolina had called for a pardon for the Regulators and then fled to a British warship. Meanwhile in Virginia the efforts of the legislature to establish some sort of agreement with Governor Dunmore came to naught. In July and August 1775 the Virginia Convention – acting without the governor or any semblance of royal authority – levied taxes on the people, issued paper money for the purpose of conducting military resistance, and created two regiments. Governor Dunmore, also in residence on a British warship, probably ended all hope of a peaceful resolution of conflict in that colony when, in November, he offered freedom to all slaves who joined him in fighting their former masters. Few, if any, potential horrors loomed more menacing on the horizon in the southern colonies than the prospect of racial warfare, and the encouragement of such an event by a royal governor ended any influence he may have had. Less significant, but certainly objectionable to the Virginians, was the shelling of Norfolk, which destroyed much of the city on New Year's Day 1776. That much of the destruction was the result of actions by colonial troops had little impact on public opinion.

During the latter months of 1775 several other issues related to independence had come before Congress, but most of them had been left to lie on the table. On July 21 Benjamin Franklin had proposed a plan for union but, even though the union was to last only until the end of the conflict, such a step proved too much for those who feared separation from the empire. Clearly the establishment of an authorized continental government was not consistent with plans for reconciliation. The proposal was placed in a stack of unfinished business and left there. Similarly with proposals to open the ports of America to foreign trade and to negotiate with foreign nations. Both were advisable and both appeared increasingly

necessary, but like the proposal for a union of the colonies such steps seemed too drastic for the more conservative members of the Congress, and no real progress was made until 1776. For example, Franklin and Richard Henry Lee had proposed in July that if the Acts restraining American commerce were not repealed the Congress should throw open all colonial ports to the ships of foreign nations, but, like the plan of union, these suggestions were tabled and ignored.

Changes took place during the first two months of 1776 which would put the supporters of independence in control. One important event took place in Massachusetts, where the assembly replaced Thomas Cushing with Elbridge Gerry, thus giving the radicals firm control of that delegation. Another important development was the publication of Thomas Paine's *Common Sense*, a pamphlet which unquestionably had an enormous impact not only on the public at large but upon the members of Congress. Within weeks more than 100,000 copies of the writing had been published and letters from the delegates in Philadelphia reveal that most, if not all, of them, had been impressed with Paine's reasoning and style.

Two factors played a part in the importance of *Common Sense*. In the first place, Paine blamed the King directly for the misgovernment of America. He roundly condemned the entire system of monarchy and found the "royal brute" of England particularly culpable. The significance of this straightforward attack on George III assumes even greater significance when one notes that as late as mid-March the Continental Congress refused to adopt language blaming the King rather than the ministry for the war. Paine's persuasive prose was strong medicine for many who had been brought up to revere the monarchy.

Then, too, Washington began to speak more clearly in support of the need for independence. When he arrived in New York in April 1776 he found the citizens supplying the British with the apparent approval of the Provincial Congress. The General found this absolutely inexplicable given the fact that American ports had been closed, colonial trade destroyed, property seized, towns burnt, and citizens made prisoners. They must, Washington wrote, consider themselves "in a state of peace or war with Great Britain," and there was no doubt as to where his sympathies lay.

6 The Move to Independence

The first indication that the majority in Congress had been won over to independence came at the end of February 1776. The delegates, for the first time, considered the question of separation from Great Britain, and although no decision was reached the radicals apparently constituted a majority. The debate was ended because "five or six" delegations did not have the authority to agree to independence without consulting their respective provincial governments. Perhaps more significant was the decision, on April 6, to open the ports of America to all nations except Great Britain and its dominions. That determination was certainly a declaration of economic, if not political, independence. North Carolina was to be the first colony actually to mention independence – from a positive point of view – in its instructions to its delegates. On April 12, 1776 the convention empowered its representatives in Congress to combine with the other colonies in separating from the empire. In May of the same year Rhode Island virtually declared its separate independence by refusing to continue the administration of oaths in the name of the king who had violated the compact of government. The colony then joined North Carolina in giving its congressional delegation the authority to join in a declaration of independence.

Still, no colony had actually instructed its delegates to call for independence, and an effort to achieve that result in Massachusetts Bay failed because of internal divisions in the colony. It was left to Virginia to initiate the move for independence. On May 15, 1776 the Virginia legislature, by roll-call vote, instructed its delegation in Congress to move for separation from the empire. North Carolina soon followed suit, and on May 27 the resolutions of these two colonies were laid before Congress.

On June 7, 1776 Richard Henry Lee rose in Congress to present three resolutions. The most important of these was that "these United Colonies are, and of right ought to be, free and independent States." But the battle was far from over. By then the delegates generally agreed that independence was inevitable, but the debate concerned timing. A number of colonies wanted to delay as long as possible, and as late as early June several – including New York, New Jersey, Delaware, and Maryland – were unprepared to vote for independence. Threats to walk out of the Congress produced a compromise which, in the end, worked for those who favored independence. Congress agreed to delay a final vote on independence until July 1.

In the meantime, an important political revolution had been engineered in Pennsylvania. Elections there on May 1 had given the opponents of independence a dramatic victory. The leaders of the independence movement in Congress recognized that they must have the support of that pivotal province. Consequently they successfully connived with the radical factions in Pennsylvania to bring down the provincial government and replace it with a more democratic system. In a desperate effort to avoid its demise the Pennsylvania Assembly rescinded its instructions against independence, but it could not protect itself. The assembly lost its power and Pennsylvania was removed from the list of opponents of independence.

Events now moved rapidly. Shortly after Congress voted to delay a decision on independence until July 1, the new Pennsylvania Provincial Conference met and unanimously endorsed independence. On June 15 Connecticut called for separation from Great Britain, and Delaware followed suit on the same day. Maryland soon gave in, in part because of threats of internal disruption, and New York faced a similar situation. The New Yorkers moved so slowly that their delegates were not empowered to vote either yea or nay on July 2, 1776, but faced with a decision for independence by the other 12 colonies they also came around.

Resistance to independence did not dissolve in late June and early July. John

Dickinson refused to sign the Declaration of Independence and the conservative party in Pennsylvania had clearly yielded to coercion. Many feared that independence would lead to the dissolution of government or, what was almost as bad, to the implementation of democracy. One is reluctant to quote again John Adams's comment about the difficulties of making 13 clocks strike as one, but the simile is apt. It had been a difficult battle and friction in Congress had been great. Nevertheless 13 colonies declared their independence on the same day.

7   The Philosophy of Independence

The Declaration of Independence is a statement of political philosophy which tells us a great deal about the struggle for separation from Great Britain. Interestingly enough the delegates did not directly mention Parliament in their explanation of declaring independence. Having spent well over a decade in conflict with Parliament, the colonists moved to the position that their only tie with the empire had been through the monarch. The major part of the Declaration is a list of ways in which George III had violated his contract of government with the colonies. Only one oblique reference is made to Parliament, when the delegates accused the King of having combined "with others" to deprive them of their liberties.

This statement of philosophy raises questions about the objectives of the colonists throughout the years of controversy following the end of the Seven Years' War in 1763. Certainly the Stamp Act Congress, which met in 1765, believed that the colonists were to some extent under the governance of Parliament. As late as 1774, when the First Continental Congress met to consider the Coercive Acts, the delegates were not prepared to reject entirely the authority of Parliament, although they left vague the exact boundaries of that authority. Were the colonists, as many in England believed, simply testing the boundaries of British authority? Were they, indeed, demanding independence all along but hoping to be able to obtain it without making a formal declaration?

The strength of the British position was consistency. Upon repeal of the Stamp Act in 1766, Parliament clearly stated that the government in England could legislate for the colonies "in all cases whatsoever." Not until late in the war did Parliament offer to back off from that position, and after the war was over George III claimed that his only error had been in agreeing to the repeal of the Stamp Act. Perhaps, as Ralph Waldo Emerson once put it, "a petty consistency is the hobgoblin of little minds."

The Americans were confronted with an unprecedented situation in 1764 when the Revenue Act for the first time imposed taxes for the purpose of raising money for the empire. Their halting steps in resisting that measure have led to accusations of hypocrisy but are more likely the result of confusion. Perhaps they were not initially clear in understanding exactly what they wanted, but, as Edmund Morgan has pointed out, they generally objected to revenue taxes while trying to construct a policy which would permit Parliament to continue its regulation of trade. By 1774 it was becoming increasingly clear that this was a distinction without a difference, at least in the hands of those who proposed to raise a revenue by whatever means came to hand. So the colonies moved slowly but surely towards independence, although that was almost certainly not their original objective.

The debates, letters, and diaries of the period between the Battle of Lexington and the Declaration of Independence suggest that the majority of American leaders opposed independence. Early on they did not understand that their definition of dependence was not compatible with the expectations of the British Government. In retrospect it is now clear that, with the adoption of the Continental Association in 1774, war was inevitable. While the British Government was adopting legislation to reconstruct the government of Massachusetts Bay, the delegates to the First Continental Congress were arguing about whether or not Parliament had the right to establish a Post Office in the colonies. Historians have often condemned the so-called radicals in the First Congress for rejecting Joseph Galloway's Plan of Union, but the simple fact is that such a plan would not have had a hearing in England. When all is said and done, the

American colonists were determined to be governed a bit less, and the British were determined to govern a bit more.

The extent to which the "crisis of independence" was simply an issue of educating Americans to the reality of British politics is striking. Again and again the conservatives in Congress were encouraged by reports of commissioners being sent to negotiate a settlement, only to learn that the commissioners had no authority to make concessions. Again and again the conservatives persuaded Congress to make yet another "humble petition" to the King, only to be rebuffed by a monarch who believed that the time had come to settle the issue with the colonists. The correspondence of Samuel Adams is instructive on this issue. At least as early as 1774 he apparently understood that his independence – and he was certainly one American who had independence in mind at an early stage of the game – would be accomplished by the British. He repeatedly predicted that the British response to plea and petition would increase the ranks of those who supported independence. It was a knowledge of events in England that determined whether one was for or against independence after 1775, and the declaration of that independence took place when a majority in the Congress understood that their hopes for reconciliation, at least on the grounds they were willing to accept, were unrealistic.

FURTHER READING

Green, Jack P. (ed.): *The American Revolution: its Character and Limits* (New York: New York University Press, 1978).

Jensen, Merrill: *The Founding of a Nation: a History of the American Revolution, 1763–1776* (New York: Oxford University Press, 1968).

Maier, Pauline: *From Resistance to Revolution: Colonial Radicals and the Development of American Opposition to Britain, 1765–1776* (New York: Alfred A. Knopf, 1972).

Middlekauff, Robert: *The Glorious Cause: the American Revolution, 1763–1789* (New York: Oxford University Press, 1982). [Vol. II of the Oxford History of the United States].

Nash, Gary B.: *The Urban Crucible: Social Change, Political Consciousness, and the Origins of the American Revolution* (Cambridge, Mass.: Harvard University Press, 1979).

Nettels, Curtis: *George Washington and American Independence* (Boston: Little, Brown, 1951).

Rakove, Jack N.: *The Beginnings of National Politics: an Interpretative History of the Continental Congress* (New York: Alfred A. Knopf, 1979).

Ryerson, Richard Alan: *The Revolution is Now Begun: the Radical Committees of Philadelphia, 1765–1776* (Philadelphia: University of Pennsylvania Press, 1978).

Shy, John: *Toward Lexington: the Role of the British Army in the Coming of the American Revolution* (Princeton, NJ: Princeton University Press, 1965).

Young, Alfred F. (ed.): *The American Revolution: Explorations in the History of American Radicalism* (DeKalb: Northern Illinois University Press, 1976).

CHAPTER TWENTY-SIX

Development of a revolutionary organization, 1765–1775

DAVID W. CONROY

COLONISTS in North America initially organized in 1765 to protect what they conceived to be the traditional liberties of Englishmen in the British Empire, not to repudiate their connection with it. Indeed leaders of the Sons of Liberty all idealized the British Constitution as a model of political organization which staved off the twin evils of tyranny and anarchy. Thus when Parliament repealed the Stamp Act in 1766, the Sons dissolved their organizations amidst profuse professions of loyalty to a benevolent King. From the start, organization to resist new imperial policies possessed a dual purpose – to maintain order and discipline in resistance as much as to foment and execute it. The character and timing of activity received close attention. As late as 1774, leaders chose to organize non-importation associations – to demonstrate political virtue through collective sacrifice and austerity – as the primary means of resistance. Nevertheless Parliament's determination to reorganize colonial administration and extract new revenues gradually convinced colonial leaders of the existence of a conspiracy to abridge their liberties. By the 1770s, they even implicated the King. Extra-legal organization within the colonies became more extensive, communication between them more vital, and cooperation in a Continental Congress more imperative. Moreover the progressive experience of creating, leading, and following resistance organizations gradually transformed colonial political behavior by expanding the number of leaders, purging those reluctant from elected bodies, and making an informed and active citizenry the

sovereign source of all political authority. As organizations of limited resistance gradually cast off traditional restraints governing political behavior, they became revolutionary harbingers of a new political order in which a King and all inherited privilege could have no place.

1   The Sons of Liberty

Passage of the Stamp Act provoked groups in all of the mainland colonies to organize to resist its enforcement during the summer months of 1765 (see also chapter 23, §2). Leaders of the nascent Sons of Liberty sprang from the upper and middle ranks of colonial society. Several groups originated in urban voluntary associations such as the Loyal Nine, a social club in Boston, and the Charles Town Fire Company in South Carolina. In other colonies such as North Carolina, leaders of the Assembly took the initiative. The Sons of Liberty had ample precedents to draw upon in planning acts of resistance. Extra-legal crowd actions with specific, limited goals had long been an informal means of resolving public dilemmas, often with the tacit approval of constituted authorities. In this tradition, the Sons of Liberty organized street demonstrations in the major port towns and capitals, the hanging and parading of effigies, and acts of further intimidation to frighten Stamp Distributors to resign their commissions. This was accomplished in all of the colonies by November 1 except Georgia, where stamps were issued briefly.

To accomplish their goals, and justify their actions, steering committees recruited popular support and manpower. In Boston the Loyal Nine persuaded the North and South End gangs to put aside their traditional rivalry in order to unite in street protest. But when these aroused workmen later destroyed Lieutenant-Governor Hutchinson's house in an unplanned sacking of private property, leaders took steps to impress upon the rank and file of resistance the importance of restraint. The movement must not be discredited by the specter of anarchy and violence. A similar emphasis on discipline pervaded the organization of the Sons of Liberty in other colonies. In Maryland they formalized their organization in early November by the creation of the Society for the Maintenance of Order and Protection of American Liberty. These dual concerns also informed the rules that the Albany group wrote and published for itself in 1766, promising to discourage actions which slandered the character of individuals by disciplining its own membership. Local leaders insisted that they acted to uphold and defend established institutions, not overturn them. Thus the organization of the Sons of Liberty became as much an antidote to disorder as a weapon of resistance.

The strongest and most active groups organized in the major towns, but rural counties and towns emulated them to various degrees. As organizations multiplied within colonies to arouse the populace at large, prominent leaders of the Sons made efforts to establish ties between colonies to form an intra-colonial movement. In December 1765, representatives of the New York and Connecticut Sons met and subscribed to an agreement of mutual aid, the first of a series of pacts which linked groups from New Hampshire to Georgia. But organization receded or dissolved upon news of the repeal of the Stamp Act in 1766. The Sons were not revolutionaries. Nevertheless they had changed as well as defended the old order by creating organizations which mobilized ordinary colonists to participate in the resolution of issues of imperial import.

2 Non-Importation Organizations

Organization flowered anew in response to the Townshend Duties enacted in 1767. In some colonies such as New York and South Carolina, the Sons revived their organizations, but they now acted in assistance to a new layer of organized resistance: non-importation associations. Such agreements had emerged during the Stamp Act crisis, but now became the primary means of resistance to duties considered to be thinly disguised taxation. Boston merchants formed progressively more strict associations to boycott English products in 1767 and 1768 providing that New York and Philadelphia merchants followed suit. New Yorkers responded swiftly, but Philadelphia merchants delayed until 1769. Still, by the end of 1769 all colonies but New Hampshire had associations pledged to either non-importation or non-consumption. Such associations perpetuated the spirit of vigorous but orderly resistance by adopting tactics which prescribed sacrifice and discipline. Everyone was enjoined to subscribe to or support associations which organized colonists into a collective demonstration of superior social and political virtue. Non-importation fused protest and self-imposed austerity together.

Like the Sons of Liberty, the instigators of non-importation acted in close harmony with their respective colonial assemblies, and did not seek to usurp constituted authority. In Maryland, 22 of the 43 signers of the association were delegates to the Assembly, and the Connecticut, New York, and New Jersey Assemblies all passed resolutions commending the associations. But these organizations also moved beyond their predecessors by assuming the authority to police enforcement. Association committees examined suspected cargoes, adjudicated violations, and punished infractions with alacrity. The association in Maryland published the proceedings of a committee appointed to investigate one shipment as a separate pamphlet and distributed it in all the counties, thus providing a model for extra-judicial proceedings. The movement also witnessed the emergence of artisans as a distinct voice in resistance organizations agitating for stricter enforcement. Artisans in Charles Town made sure that they be given equal representation to merchants and planters on the committee of enforcement. In Philadelphia, artisans challenged the right of merchants to dissolve the association when all of the duties except that on tea were repealed. They would later form their own "Patriotic Society," and help to elevate John Dickinson to the leadership of resistance over the objections of more conservative merchants. As the conviction arose that the Stamp Act and the Townshend Duties represented a concerted plan to curtail colonial autonomy, all members of elite governing groups came under scrutiny as to their devotion to the cause.

3   Committees of Correspondence

The associations disbanded in one colony after another when Parliament repealed all of the duties in 1770 except that on tea, which continued to be boycotted. Resistance leaders received fresh provocation, however, to develop new organizations between 1770 and 1773. Belief in a conspiracy hatched in Whitehall made it seem imperative to sustain and extend the networks of communication established in past years. When the Crown decided to use customs revenues to salary superior court justices in Massachusetts, Samuel Adams decided that the time was ripe to create a Boston Committee of Correspondence to elicit more formal and systematic expressions of support from the towns. This committee of 21 men, one-third of whom possessed degrees from Harvard, was formally created by the Boston Town Meeting. It sent plainly written explanations of the past and current state of imperial controversy to all of the towns in the colony, inviting them to elect their own committees and respond to the Boston leaders' concerns. More than half did reply, and the committee succeeded in encouraging participation in the controversy by the people at large on an unprecedented level. Continuing correspondence provided proof of the broad base of support for extra-legal actions against "unconstitutional" acts. Communication between the colonies was also raised to a more systematic level when the Virginia House of Burgesses wrote to all of the colonies requesting them to establish provincial Committees of Correspondence. Appointed by their assemblies, but able to act out of session, these committees strengthened ties between radical colonies and those less active or divided.

They also reoriented communication away from England to intracolonial networks at a time when faith in the efficacy of petitions and protests to the Crown was waning.

The Tea Act of March 1773, granting a monopoly of the sale of the still-dutied commodity, immediately stirred leaders to act. In the major ports they once again sought to involve and organize the people, but cautiously and with every appearance of propriety. Mass meetings of the people became the vehicles to inform the populace, identify tea consignees, and pressure them to resign their commissions first in Philadelphia, then in New York, Boston, and Charles Town. Fall meetings in Philadelphia enlarged the committee of 12 to 24, as radicals pressured hesitant merchants to make a decisive response. In Charles Town, a mass meeting in December demanded and received the resignation of all the tea consignees and appointed a steering committee to prepare for future meetings. Carefully orchestrated "Meetings of the People" in Boston resolved to prevent the tea from being landed. When Governor Hutchinson refused to allow reshipment, a disguised delegation from a December meeting dumped it in Boston Harbor. These self-constituted mass meetings were beyond the reach of the law and therefore could act free of the restraints which bound town and province government. At the same time, leaders such as Adams delayed taking any radical steps until every means of removing the tea legally had been formally explored. Publicly, "the People" had acted in Boston only after all other avenues of redress had been exhausted. Discipline in resistance was still paramount, especially when "the People" moved to destroy property.

4   The First Continental Congress

Reactions to the Boston Tea Party in the other colonies were mixed. But when news of the Port Act reached the colonies, followed by the other "Intolerable Acts," they united behind Boston. They became convinced, as suggested to them by a Boston Committee of Correspondence Circular, that Parliament planned similar punitive measures for all the colonies if they remained defiant. The previous establishment of regular communication between the colonies bore fruit as leaders in Providence, Philadelphia, and New York issued calls for an intercolonial congress. Virginia Burgesses meeting unofficially in a Williamsburg tavern proposed going beyond the Stamp Act Congress of 1765 by making it the first of regular annual congresses. But royal governors attempted to prevent their colonies from electing delegates by dismissing their assemblies. This only stimulated the creation of a new layer of extra-legal organization. Seven colonies in the spring and summer of 1774 convened provincial conventions to choose delegates. South Carolina's convention elected a Committee of 99, which became virtually the temporary government of the colony. The still growing Committee of 43 in Philadelphia called a convention and developed a comprehensive committee system in the counties to coordinate resistance, all but overwhelming the voices of a conservative group of merchants. All of the colonies witnessed a new burst of extra-legal meetings and activities as the Intolerable Acts seemed to confirm beyond a doubt the sinister intentions of the British ministry. The Acts became the spark for the convening of the First Continental Congress on September 5, 1774 attended by representatives from all of the colonies except Georgia (*see also* chapter 24, §4).

This Congress represents a milestone in the development of a revolutionary organization in the colonies. Heretofore, organization had developed most extensively and effectively at the colony level, and particularly in major ports. Massachusetts' more radical posture had sometimes threatened to isolate it in the past. With the organization of the Congress, however, the colonies now possessed a vehicle with which to speak with a united voice, and a potential means of integrating and consolidating the resistance organizations and conventions which had sprung up with renewed vigor in 1774, bringing several colonies close to the establishment of revolutionary governments.

5 The Continental Association

In formulating a pan-colonial policy, the Congress continued to adhere to principles clarified in 1765 counseling order and restraint in resistance. It adopted and recommended to the colonies the Continental Association as the principal means of forcing England to redress colonial grievances. Modeled on an association already drawn up by Virginia, the Continental Association prescribed comprehensive non-importation and non-exportation within a scheduled framework. Once again colonists were enjoined to unite self-sacrifice and discipline with vigorous opposition. Choice of such a tactic served to restrain the popular violence which threatened to weaken and divide the movement amidst the passions unleashed by Parliament's punishment of Boston. But it also served to encourage and extend organization in a uniform way in every colony by recommending the election of committees of inspection and observation in every town and county by all those qualified to vote for representatives in their respective colonies. Congress authorized these committees to become its local agents by policing the observation of the Association and punishing violators with public censure and ostracism. This program for organizing resistance was more elaborate and comprehensive than any previously adopted by a town or colony. The Congress proposed mass participation in resistance, but through mass organization to boycott trade with England.

Congress fell short of its goal of stimulating the election of committees in every locality, particularly in New York, whose delegates had refused to endorse the Association. But by April 1775, committees were in operation and the Association in effect to some extent in all the colonies. In Virginia, 51 of 61 counties elected committees, in Maryland 11 of 16 counties, and in Massachusetts at least 160 towns responded. The membership of these committees tended to be larger than that of their predecessors, ranging from an average of ten in Massachusetts to 100 in Maryland. By the spring of 1775, at least 7,000 persons had publicly identified themselves as leaders of a movement which the Crown had already condemned as rebellion. Local and colony organizations had brought the Congress into existence, but they now multiplied at the behest of Congress. The linking of so substantial a number of local leaders to an intercolonial congress vertically integrated organized resistance to a new level of refinement, efficiency, and impact. Local committees often acted as engines of mobilization, as in Wilmington, North Carolina. Here the Committee pledged the entire town to sign the Association by sending a delegation to each household to secure signatures. The Committee proclaimed a boycott of those who refused, and within a few days they agreed to sign. In large sections of the colonies, organized resistance no longer existed apart from the political community, but became coterminous with it. Many committees did not limit themselves to enforcement of the Association, but also began to set prices, promote manufactures, and regulate morals. They did not supplant existing institutions of local government, but they did assume authority for acting on issues of "continental" importance.

6 Provincial Congresses

The erection of committees of inspection across the colonies during the winter of 1774 and 1775 not only invested resistance with new force and urgency, but also accelerated the transformation of traditional political values and behavior. Back in 1765, the Sons of Liberty had organized to preserve the rights of Englishmen in the colonies, professing their continuing reverence for King and British Constitution. By 1774, however, the proliferation of resistance organizations had multiplied the numbers of people holding positions of leadership, and encouraged the population at large to scrutinize carefully and regularly the beliefs and behavior of those leaders. In resistance organizations colonists had begun to act out what would only later be elevated to a revolutionary ideal: the sovereignty of the people over all branches of government, and the accountability of all elected officials to the people's will. The prestige of the hitherto idealized British Constitution with its much acclaimed balance between monarchy, aristocracy, and democracy faded as colonists began to construct alternative governments in 1774 entirely derived by direct or indirect vote of a politically aroused citizenry. Besides their local committees, voters elected provincial congresses and conventions far more democratic and representative than their assemblies had been at the outset of resistance. In both New Jersey and Maryland, the number of

delegates in their provincial congresses was more than twice that of their previous regular assemblies. The South Carolina Congress had 180 members, triple the size of its Assembly. Substantial, educated men continued to dominate, but were joined by new faces elevated to authority by the movement. Philadelphia's leadership increasingly departed from the traditional model by being younger and more diverse in occupation, ethnic composition, and religious affiliation. Similar changes occurred in parts of New York, where large landowners had dominated local government. Resistance organizations thus became the seedbeds not just for a revolt against England, but for a repudiation of traditional models of government and political behavior. Magistrates could no longer expect deference from the small farmers and artisans now engaged in stripping royal government of what authority it could still muster.

7 The Continental Army

The final layer of organization which propelled the colonies towards revolution was once again sparked by events in Massachusetts. Although controversial, military preparations had begun in the New England colonies and in Maryland and Virginia by early 1775. Maryland's Provincial Congress had recommended to each county that they tax their inhabitants in order to purchase military provisions. By February 1775, the Massachusetts Congress had taken steps to prepare the colony for war. Already local minutemen companies drilled throughout the colony in anticipation of a foray by General Gage from Boston into the countryside to destroy munitions. After the Battle of Lexington and Concord in April 19, the Massachusetts Congress ordered the mobilization of 13,600 soldiers. Thus when the Second Continental Congress convened on May 10, it confronted the problem of addressing a state of war in Massachusetts.

The decision to organize a Continental Army commanded by Washington did not come easily. Heretofore, organization to resist imperial policy had been consciously designed to avoid violence and preserve every chance of reconciliation and restoration to a revered King. The Sons of Liberty had organized only to render the "unconstitutional" Stamp Act unenforceable. Non-importation associations had been formed only to force repeal of the equally loathed Townshend Duties. Committees of Correspondence had been created to expose the dark designs of a "corrupt" British ministry. The Intolerable Acts had been answered by a more comprehensive employment of tactics used previously. Each layer of new organization had been created and refined to counteract policies deemed violations of the British Constitution. But the cumulative experience of organized resistance had gradually eroded colonists' confidence in this Constitution of balanced social orders. It now seemed an inadequate guarantor of traditional political liberties. Meanwhile the gradual, vertical integration of local committees, provincial congresses, and the Continental Congress had become an operating alternative in which the voting citizenry became the ultimate source of all layers of political authority. This refined state of organized resistance made the planning of military operations conceivable from a continental perspective. And now, after the Battles of Lexington, Concord, and Bunker Hill, it seemed necessary if the carefully constructed unity of the colonies

was to endure. Some members of the Second Continental Congress still hoped for reconciliation, as did numerous moderates and loyalists at the local level. But as Massachusetts had already demonstrated, the organization of an army was but a tiny step short of using it. Organization for resistance had become organization for revolution in 1775.

FURTHER READING

Ammerman, David: *In the Common Cause: American Response to the Coercive Acts of 1774* (New York: Norton, 1974).

Brown, Richard D.: *Revolutionary Politics in Massachusetts: the Boston Committee of Correspondence and the Towns, 1772–1774* (Cambridge, Mass.: Harvard University Press, 1970).

Maier, Pauline: *From Resistance to Revolution: Colonial Radicals and the Development of American Opposition to Britain, 1765–1776* (New York: Vintage Books, 1974).

Ryerson, Richard Alan: *The Revolution Is Now Begun: the Radical Committees of Philadelphia, 1765–1776* (Philadelphia: University of Pennsylvania Press, 1978).

Weir, Robert M.: *"A Most Important Epoch": The Coming of the Revolution in South Carolina* (Columbia: University of South Carolina Press, 1970).

CHAPTER TWENTY-SEVEN

Political mobilization, 1765–1776

REBECCA STARR

WHEN John Adams ventured the remark that one-third of all Americans were patriots, one-third were loyal to King George, and one-third were undecided, he was saying something about the success of radicals like himself in mobilizing public opinion for independence. Rhetorical claims to the contrary, political mobilization is an induced, not a spontaneous, process. It usually happens from the top down, led by a politically astute elite. But in a reasonably fluid society (such as was America in this period), it can also come from politically self-conscious minorities, such as artisans or women.

All mobilization, however, depends on some degree of organization. Because of its superior command of the channels of communication, the elite usually dominates the first step in the mobilization process – creation of organizations. But while a small leadership may supply the initiative required to formalize an association's structure, the organization's collective aims and ideals must encode ideas, values, attitudes, assumptions, and beliefs latent in the social practices and moral patterns already established in the society. At least in its early stages, political mobilization is the reification of values already present in the prevailing political culture. As mobilization progresses, however, not only is the way prepared for the reformulation of those values into new patterns of thought, but initiative for that change moves down through the hierarchy. Passing from the hands of a few official leaders, it spreads laterally into those of its constituency.

Political mobilization also requires an explicit message: hence an organization's first task is to provide a forum where generally shared ideas may be articulated, debated, refined, and agreed to in a consensus-making exercise. Its second purpose is to broadcast those ideas to the public. The broader the organization's basis, the wider the dissemination of its ideas.

But while a formal organizational structure supplies an umbrella for the already committed, mobilization of an unorganized and unconvinced public relies on tactics. Tactics then are the true focus of the mobilization task. A successful tactical program will spread and increasingly intensify a shared body of ideas until a critical mass is reached. Then only some triggering event is needed to transform ideas into action. The first organization to evolve a set of tactics aimed at politicizing the public was the Sons of Liberty (on the organizational history of the Revolution, *see* chapter 26). Although its purpose was specifically limited to achieving the repeal of the Stamp Act, the strategies and tactics developed by the Sons of Liberty set a pattern for subsequent public opinion mobilization right down to the Revolution.

One cannot talk about organizations and politics in this period without considering mobs and street action. Not truly organizations since they lacked formal structure, mobs still had an important, although unintended, impact on popular thought. Recent scholarship on crowd behavior has shown that mobs sometimes acted in the public welfare when civil authority failed, but most eighteenth-century men feared the anarchy of mob rule as much as they deplored a despotic monarch.

In political mobbing, if no law was broken or property destroyed, most leaders of the American opposition did not openly disapprove. A few individuals, such as Samuel Adams, might openly approve violence when all other legal means to secure redress had been exhausted, but most leaders simply refrained from commenting on actions like the Boston Tea Party.

Yet to say mob violence served no tactical purpose is to miss its most important, if unintended, consequence. Nameless, faceless, and without overt leadership, mob violence forced both the conservative public and established authority to look to a responsible opposition as an alternative to social instability. Mobs served to cast an aura of legitimacy on an opposition that insisted on practicing only constitutional tactics to secure redress.

1   The Stamp Act and the Sons of Liberty, 1765–6

The Stamp Act of 1765 levied a tax on a seemingly endless list of items including newspapers, wills, deeds, contracts, diplomas, almanacs, playing cards, even dice. Because it affected nearly everyone, the Stamp Act set off a wave of resistance that cut across all divisions of rank, class, and interest. By the summer or 1765, Sons of Liberty groups were springing up almost spontaneously in most of the colonies. As Pauline Maier has written (1974), the organizing effort was intended not to create the Sons of Liberty, but to assemble them into formal structures. Some local groups went under other names. "The Respectable Populace" of Newport, Rhode Island, and the "Loyal Nine" of Boston are examples. These groups soon changed their names or were subsumed into the Sons organizations. Others, such as the Charles Town [South Carolina] Fire Company, kept their name, but declared that they were the "brethren of the Sons of Liberty of America."

By late 1765, the idea of regularizing an intercolonial movement against the Stamp Act surfaced in several of the colonies, but New York's early and intense organizational effort made it the unofficial hub of the movement. Its clear leadership emerged by the following April when New York proposed a congress of the Sons of Liberty, but repeal rendered it unnecessary.

The central strategy of the Stamp Act resistance was unity. Hence the first priority of the Sons of Liberty, and of the later movements as well, consisted in winning a mass base by converting the populace at large into Sons of Liberty. Tactics included mass meetings, meant to draw in as many persons, and of as great an assortment in rank and condition, as possible. The mass meeting not only formed linkages across society, but imbued their proceedings and resolves with the authority of "The Body of the People."

Since mass appeal precludes secrecy, the Sons deliberately practiced openness, hoping to inform and engage the public politically as either activists or supporters. Newspapers (and their editors) were central to this strategy and became a forum for formulating an agreed-on public policy. In them, the Sons' leading committees published their sentiments and resolutions for public response and amendment.

At the same time, official committees of correspondence of local Sons organizations exchanged views among themselves at the township, county, and provincial levels, as in Maryland and New Jersey. The first to move across provincial lincs, Manhattan and Albany's organizations formed a correspondence circuit with Boston which soon enlarged to include several other Massachusetts towns, as well as centers in Portsmouth, New Hampshire, and Providence and Newport, Rhode Island. In the South, Charles Town's radicals established links with sympathetic Georgians in a pattern similar to New York's plan. Correspondence and circulars knit these networks together and helped to foster a uniform ideology at the top, which in turn encouraged a consistent, coordinated, and informed program for mobilization at the level of the public.

Potentially their most radical strategy lay in the military and police powers which the Sons assumed. There was always the possibility that the British might send soldiers to enforce the Stamp Act. If that happened, the Military Association of the Sons of Liberty declared that it could "assemble

50,000 fighting Men" in New Jersey and New York to resist.

At the same time the Sons took on a domestic peace-keeping role. The September Stamp Act riots in Boston and Newport which exploded before the Sons formally organized had proved politically counterproductive. Violence and property destruction alienated support and "hurt the good cause." Once they were organized, the Sons' brief was to uphold civil government in all its functions, only excepting the enforcement of the "unconstitutional" Stamp Act. That they must resist in order to save the constitution. To give credit to that claim, Sons of Liberty must strictly limit their resistance tactics to constitutional (lawful) means. (The Sons made a distinction between violence and coercion, such as was used to force Stamp Act distributors to resign.) This commitment to law and order also required that the Sons act to suppress popular anti-Stamp Act disorders. In Charles Town, it was the Sons of Liberty who dragged rioting sailors to jail in late 1765. And in New York, Providence, and Boston, Sons directly intervened in support of civil magistrates. In their readiness to repel invasion, and their commitment to curb domestic violence, the Sons of Liberty set themselves up as the defenders of the public welfare, a stated object of government. This strategic but decisive step was the first in the shift of American resistance from the role of an opposition to that of a civil government.

At this early stage, however, resistance not revolution was their purpose. The Sons made no claim to overturning established government. Upon news of the Stamp Act's repeal, they immediately dissolved their organizations in the belief that their task was done. But the business of learning tactical resistance had begun. Thus, when opposition resurfaced in 1767 upon the passage of the Townshend Acts, colonials had a body of methods to draw on that could mobilize the public behind a cause. With the Townshend legislation, Sons of Liberty across the colonies reorganized specifically to support non-importation, deemed the most effective of the tactics that had won the Stamp Act repeal. Building on previous methods of political mobilization not only lent an invaluable continuity, but partook of the lessons those methods embodied. To be legitimate, an opposition must involve the whole body of the people (an intimation of the doctrine of popular consent). It must rest on legal procedures, and it must have peaceful, not violent, enforcement measures.

2 Tactical Advances and the Townshend Acts, 1767–9

The Massachusetts circular letter

With the passage of the Townshend Acts, Massachusetts radicals reactivated the tactic of the circular letter. This time, however, the letter expressing colonial concern was drafted in the provincial legislature's Committee of Correspondence, and was not sent to the colony's agent in England as the committee's correspondence normally was. Instead, it was sent to the various colonial assemblies, and suggested a coordinated resistance. Generating the letter in the legislature, the people's elected representatives imbued it with an authority that popular protest could not have done. Circulating it to the other elected assemblies, where its reception had to be approved by a majority vote, affirmed the tactic's legitimacy while endorsing the letter's proposals. Royal government response in Massachusetts was to attempt to force the legislature to rescind the letter. Ninety-two of 109 members refused.

In South Carolina, the royal Governor warned the newly elected Commons House of Assembly not to receive the Massachusetts letter. The moment a quorum assembled, however, the 28 members present voted unanimously to do so. Overnight, the "Ninety-Two Anti-rescinders" and the "Unanimous Twenty-Eight" achieved a rhetorical and symbolic power equal to that of number 45 in the Wilkes controversy. Ninety-two toasts were drunk to the Anti-rescinders and 28 to the unanimous Carolina assembly. Candles of these numbers were solemnly lighted at meetings and 92 and 28 cheers were shouted in street demonstrations. The mobilizing and unifying force of such rallying cries cannot be overlooked.

Another strategic development from the circular letter controversy in Massachusetts was the idea of a convention of towns. It was conceived originally as a protest against the dissolution of the House of Representatives after the Anti-rescinder victory, and against the proposed introduction of troops at Boston. When Governor Hutchinson refused to call a new assembly to consider the crisis, Samuel Adams and Thomas Cushing, Speaker of the Massachusetts House, called (in September 1768) for the election of delegates to a convention of towns. More than 100 of 250 towns sent representatives. The convention elected Thomas Cushing as chairman, and went on to adopt a petition to the King and an address to the Governor. They ordered their proceedings published, then dissolved themselves without incident. Although the Governor scorned the whole episode, "the people," wrote Andrew Elliot, "have, at present, great confidence in them [the delegates to the convention]." Thus radical leaders found a method of mobilizing local activism which bypassed regular political channels.

Non-importation associations

With the enactment of the Townshend legislation, the tactics of petition and non-importation immediately revived. The former remained unchanged, since it was an ancient procedure whose form was prescribed by law. But non-importation, an extra-constitutional method, made significant strides, especially in the matter of broadening its base. As a strategy, non-importation reached its most mature form in the South.

Merchants remained at the core of northern associations. Success depended largely on an unexceptional compliance by the importers. To protect themselves, merchants could boycott entire communities, as when New York, Philadelphia, and Boston imposed an absolute boycott on Newport and Providence, Rhode Island, when merchants there tried to withdraw from the agreements. Despite merchant dominance of the movement in the North, the popularity of non-importation with the public

allowed political leaders to pull its base line of support within the constitutional framework. The Boston Town Meeting for example supported domestic manufacturing and violators. Provincial assemblies in New York, New Jersey, and Connecticut passed resolutions commending the movement to the people. These measures lent legitimacy to the *ad hoc* associations, even though the organizing impulse imposed non-importation from the top down.

In the South, however, the movement assembled at the level of the people. The Virginia Association took the form of a social compact among its subscribers, described as "his Majesty's most dutiful and loyal subjects." In Charles Town the association began with a "General Meeting of the INHABITANTS" which sought to be as inclusive as possible. In this way, its decisions might claim to represent the "Sense of the Whole Body [of the people]." After several plans foundered, the meeting adopted a compromise plan whose Enforcement Committee consisted of an exact balance between the colony's three main economic interests: planters, merchants, and artisans. Interest representation ensured concurrence among the three major economic and social subcommunities of Charles Town. The other southern agreements (in Maryland, Virginia, and North Carolina) also stipulated that membership of Enforcement Committees come from the community at large rather than merely from the trading community, but none attempted the internal balance of the South Carolina plan.

Less a policy of non-importation than of non-consumption, the southern plans shifted responsibility for success onto the willing cooperation of the entire population. Enforcement committees could only discover and publicize names of non-signers, but the economic boycotts, social ostracism, and shaming of offenders came from the consuming public. Moreover, non-consumption meant not only refraining from doing ordinary business with non-signers, but abstaining from the purchase of most luxuries from anyone. Emphasizing virtue and sacrifice, the non-importation leader Christopher Gadsden forbade the purchase of mourning for his wife's funeral.

Patriotic austerity knit the community and mobilized participation and support in a way that enforcement from the top never could have done.

The general meeting and the committee structure proved a major advance in the art of political mobilization. Committees became institutional bridges for the will of the people as expressed in public meetings, such as town meetings (as in New England) and the general meetings of the inhabitants (as in the South), reflecting that will back through its implementation of policy. Committee resolutions resembled rules and its enforcement procedures were judgments. What the non-importation association as a grass-roots movement erected, as William H. Drayton of South Carolina recognized, was a new legislature.

But the committee could also serve as a mobilizing agent of nascent political forces, a method that reached its highest development in the Massachusetts Committees of Correspondence organized between 1772 and 1774.

3 Committees of Correspondence, 1772–4

Upon repeal of the Townshend Acts (except for the tax on tea), the non-importation associations disbanded, expecting that Great Britain would eventually resume its policy of taxing the colonies, since she had not surrendered that right. Massachusetts opposition leaders used the relatively quiet period from 1772 to 1773 to arouse the radicalism latent in the assumptions and habits of mind of townsmen. In September 1771 Samuel Adams proposed a network of corresponding societies to instruct and arouse the public.

The first of these was the Boston Committee of Correspondence. Created by the Boston Town Meeting, it partook of the people's unspoken acceptance of its town meeting's authority to create whatever committee it saw fit. The tactic of overlapping memberships in both the new Committee and the General Assembly lent an additional official status to the group. Moreover, the Committee met regularly, sitting even when the Assembly was out of session.

In addition to the well-established methods of influencing the public through newspaper essays, pamphleteering, and publishing its proceedings, the Boston Committee of Correspondence carefully drafted individual replies to all correspondence sent from the 58 Corresponding Committees set up in other towns on the Boston model. These replies were read aloud in town meetings which all voters could attend. The Boston committee replies reinforced the beliefs and ideas expressed in the towns' letters, concentrating by reflecting them back to the writers. The Committee flattered and approved, generally pointing to some passage or sentiment in the town's own proceedings, quoting it back with assurances that Boston agreed and joined in the sentiment. Gradually initiative passed from Boston to the towns themselves, as individuals in previously apolitical communities become politically activated. By the collapse of royal government in the summer of 1774, it was the towns that supplied a replacement political structure by creating ad hoc county conventions composed of two elected deputies.

The famous Suffolk Resolves adopted by the first Continental Congress grew out of a joint meeting of four county conventions, whose views were generally re-enacted by all nine of the Massachusetts county conventions. By that time public opinion was so thoroughly mobilized that the role of the Boston Committee of Correspondence in provincial politics had become superfluous.

The call by the Virginia House of Burgesses in March 1773 to form committees of correspondence in all the provinces made the movement inter-colonial. Provincial Committees of Correspondence met regularly, whether the elected assemblies were sitting or not. Thus they formed an alternative structure for mobilizing public opinion in the face of increasing official efforts to thwart such activity by dissolving the legislatures.

4 The Association of 1774

The British response to the Boston Tea Party was a series of acts popularly known as the Coercive Acts or the Intolerable Acts.

Chief among these were the Boston Port Act, the Massachusetts Government Act, the Act for the Better Administration of Justice of Massachusetts Bay, and the Quebec Act. With a few pen strokes, Parliament altered the structure of Massachusetts's internal government, threatened its religious autonomy by establishing the Roman Catholic Church in nearby French Canada, interfered with jury trial procedures, and declared economic war on Boston by closing its port. These Acts were intended not merely to punish the Boston radicals, but to establish once and for all the principle of the British Parliament's supremacy over Massachusetts's internal affairs.

The Boston Committee of Correspondence countered with its only major tactical blunder. It tried to force the provincial towns to accept a plan for a commercial boycott of Great Britain before a general congress could meet to consider the crisis. As stated above, initiative for political decision-making in Massachusetts had already passed to the individual towns, most of which overwhelmingly rejected the Solemn League and Covenant (as the Boston plan was called) in favor of some concerted colonial action. Instead, a completely uniform, continental approach was to be the cure for all the tactical miscalculations of the earlier non-importations. Inconsistencies among the colonies in prohibited items, incongruities in timing, and the difference in scope between simple non-importation and non-exportation agreements and the broader-based non-consumption agreements were blamed for the incomplete success of the past.

In its emphasis on non-consumption, the Continental Association was a direct descendant of the southern pattern of non-importation agreements during the Townshend Acts. As a strategy for altering British policy, the association was a failure. But as a tactic for mobilizing those who were previously politically inert, either because they were geographically remote from the radical power centers in the seaports or major inland towns, or because of social or economic distance from the top in a hierarchical society, the association succeeded to an unexpected degree.

The association agreement that was hammered out by the delegates to the 1774 Continental Congress not only remedied all the mistakes of the past, it also supplied the final and crucial ingredient missing from previous agreements for a full political mobilization of ordinary Americans. It provided for committees of enforcement to be established not just in the major seaports, but in every township, county, and parish of every province. These committees recruited leaders for the American cause at the most parochial level.

David Ammerman (1974) has estimated that local committee elections brought some 7,000 Americans into local leadership positions. If the total colonial population stood at about three million, the Association conservatively created one new leader for every 430 citizens, in addition to the elected, appointed, and voluntary leaders already in place. Once a saturation of local leadership had been achieved, the habit of deference did much to weld residual local opinion to that of its leaders. But other methods were dusted off and improved. Leaders in South Carolina, for example, realized that occupational and religious interest-groups were two additional handles by which the public's opinion-forming machine might be turned.

After the Continental Association plan granted an exemption to the non-exportation of rice, low-country indigo growers and up-country provisions exporters felt slighted, and the whole province was bitterly divided along both sectional and interest lines over the partiality shown to the rice planters. In response to the crisis, South Carolina's proponents of the association devised an elaborate scheme whereby these smaller producers could swap a portion of their crop for rice at a fixed ratio of value. In this way the burden of non-exportation would be shared by all, at the same time preventing the general economic collapse that would have followed a complete embargo on rice, the colony's premier cash crop. The plan was to be administered by special committees in each parish. Although never implemented, as a consciousness-raising exercise it brought the smaller planters and outlying farmers into the opposition movement in a more direct way than ever before.

An appeal to the largely apolitical but deeply evangelical back country was made on the religious interest. When the General Committee in Charles Town sent three emissaries to obtain support for the association from the violently opposed population of back-country producers, it sent two dissenting ministers, but only one Whig politician, to obtain signatures. Philadelphia radicals also played the religious card in declaring a "solemn pause" on June 1, the date the Boston Port Act took effect. In its appeal to the Quaker disposition for silent worship, it strove to clothe a political cause in religious garb.

An additional tactic borrowed from America's dissenting religions was the powerful and informal language forms that emerged from religious revival movements, lending an evangelical strain to Whig ideology. It infused the egalitarian rhetoric of the classical Whiggery with ardor, and injected it with a meaning and imperatives it never originally possessed, thus empowering the dispossessed with a mobilizing impulse all their own. The rhetoric of Patrick Henry harks from this tradition. The power of Thomas Paine's *Common Sense*, on the other hand, sprang from another non-classical rhetorical tradition whose touchstone was its unembellished, direct, and "plain" speech. It is not hard to imagine that it shared stylistic links with the striving for plainness and pietism of Old Light Calvinist faiths.

Religion and religious organizations also served as the natural route for mobilizing the political opinions and activities of women. Especially in New England, but in other colonies as well, groups of women dressed in homespun met at the home of their local minister. Here they spent the day spinning the cloth they no longer purchased from importers and discussing the issues that their labor supported. For refreshment they ate local produce and drank herbal tea. Occasionally, they competed in a match format for the production of the greatest quantity and quality. These ladies, reported the *Boston Evening Post* on a Long Island spinning bee, "may vie with the men in

contributing to the preservation and prosperity of their country, and equally share in the honor of it."

At least some of these "Liberty's Daughters," as several newspapers referred to them, may have been among those who saw in the struggle with Great Britain the ingredients for social reform. Certainly the ladies of Phliadelphia had strong views on the political significance of their gender as well as their individual political identities. After canvassing for donations from house to house in a fund-raising effort organized and led entirely by women, the ladies objected to General Washington's suggestion that the money be spent on cloth for shirts for the soldiers. They felt the soldiers might consider this part of their normal entitlement from the public, and miss the point that women as women were promoting the war effort. When they were unable to dissuade the General from his views, the women complied, but pointedly signed the pocket of each shirt with their names, lest the wearer overlook their contribution as individuals as well as women.

Other groups belonged to the liberal wing of Whig ideology that fostered mobilization from the bottom up. We have already discussed the Sons of Liberty, whose rank-and-file members came from artisan classes. In some places it was the militia that became a school for political education, somewhat like Cromwell's New Model Army. In Philadelphia, the militia was by 1775 a center for intense debate. It organized its own Committee of Correspondence, and began putting pressure on conservative members of the legislature for a stronger stand on independence.

When in 1766 radical Whig politicians led by Samuel Adams moved the House of Representatives to build a public gallery, Thomas Young said it would turn the legislature into a "School for Political Learning," implying that enlightened elites would instruct the masses. But instruction worked both ways. Boston opinion was much more radical than that of the interior towns, and Adams's supporters from the city streets packed the galleries to exert pressure on the country members. The incident illustrates the complexity of the political mobilization movement, with its intermixed dynamics of inducement, argument, and coercion, all straining towards the goal of consent. It also re-emphasizes that mobilization flowed not only from the politically powerful at the top, but from the powerless at the bottom as well.

FURTHER READING

Ammerman, David: *In the Common Cause: American Response to the Coercive Acts of 1774* (Charlottesville: University of Virginia Press, 1974).

Brown, Richard D.: *Revolutionary Politics in Massachusetts: the Boston Committee of Correspondence and the Towns, 1772–1774* (Cambridge, Mass.: Harvard University Press, 1970).

Drayton, William Henry: *The Letters of Freeman, etc.: Essays on the Nonimportation Movement in South Carolina*, ed. with an Introduction and Notes by Robert M. Weir (Columbia: University of South Carolina Press, 1977).

Maier, Pauline: *From Resistance to Revolution: Colonial Radicals and the Development of American Opposition to Britain, 1765–1776* (New York: Vintage Books, 1974).

Marston, Jerrilyn Greene: *King and Congress: the Transfer of Political Legitimacy, 1774–1776* (Princeton, NJ: Princeton University Press, 1987).

Nash, Gary B.: *The Urban Crucible: Social Change, Political Consciousness, and the Origins of the American Revolution* (Cambridge, Mass.: Harvard University Press, 1979).

Norton, Mary Beth: *Liberty's Daughters: the Revolutionary Experience of American Women, 1750–1800* (Boston: Little, Brown, 1980).

Pole, J. R.: *The Gift of Government: Political Responsibility from the English Restoration to American Independence* (Athens: University of Georgia Press, 1983).

Rosswurm, Steven: *Arms, Country, and Class: the Philadelphia Militia and "Lower Sorts" During the American Revolution, 1775–1785* (New Brunswick, NJ: Rutgers University Press, 1987).

Ryerson, Richard Alan: *The Revolution is Now Begun: the Radical Committees of Philadelphia, 1765–1776* (Philadelphia: University of Pennsylvania Press, 1978).

Starr, Rebecca: *A School for Politics: Commercial Lobbying and Political Culture in Early South Carolina* (Baltimore and London: The Johns Hopkins University Press, 1998).

Stout, Harry S.: *The New England Soul: Preaching and Religious Culture in Colonial New England* (Oxford and New York: Oxford University Press, 1986).

CHAPTER TWENTY-EIGHT

Identity and Independence

JACK P. GREENE

BEGINNING in the early decades of the seventeenth century, immigrants, at first mostly from England but later and increasingly from elsewhere in the British Isles, began to establish settlement societies in North America and the West Indies. Like other European immigrants to America during the early modem era, they carried with them explicit and deeply held claims to the culture they left behind and to the identities implicit in that culture. The Protestantism and, increasingly during the eighteenth century, the slowly expanding commercial and maritime superiority of the English nation were significant components of the emerging identity of English people. Far more central, however, was the English system of law and liberty. Epitomized by the consensual institutions of juries and parliaments and by the tradition of the subordination of the monarch to the law, this system, contemporary English and many foreign observers agreed, constituted the principal distinction between English people and all others on the face of the globe. Together, England's status as the palladium of liberty and the English people's profound devotion to law and liberty were the principal badges of Englishness, the essential – the most deeply defining – hallmarks of English identity.

For English people migrating overseas to establish new communities of settlement, the capacity to enjoy – to possess – the English system of law and liberty was thus crucial to their ability to maintain their identity as English people and to continue to be so thought of by those who remained in England. For that reason, as well as because they regarded English legal arrangements as the very best way to preserve the properties they hoped to acquire in their new homes, it is scarcely surprising that, when establishing local enclaves of power and authority during the first years of colonization, English settlers overseas made every effort to construct them on English legal foundations.

Among the inherited liberties these distant colonies sought to incorporate in their new polities, none were more essential to the colonists' identities as English peoples than the rights, in the words of New York justice William Smith, "*to choose the Laws by which we will be Governed*" and "*to be Governed only by such Laws.*" Because the colonies were too far from Britain to permit them to send representatives to the British Parliament, they contended that colonial legislatures with full legislative authority over the colonies' internal affairs were necessary in order to secure to them these inherited rights. Colonial writers often quoted Sir William Jones, Attorney General under Charles II, that the King could not levy money on his subjects in the plantations without their consent through an assembly of their representatives. This position implied a conception of colonies as extensions of Britain overseas and of colonists as fellow-subjects who, though living in different parts of the world, together with those who resided in Britain formed, as the political economist Arthur Young remarked in 1772, "one nation, united under one sovereign, speaking the same language and enjoying the same liberty."

For those who viewed the empire in this *expansive* way, the transfer of English liberties to the colonies was precisely the characteristic that distinguished the British Empire from others. Just as Britain was the home of liberty in Europe, so also was the British Empire in America. "Without freedom," Edmund Burke remarked in 1766, the empire "would not be the British Empire." In America, said Young, "Spain, Portugal and France, have planted despotisms; only Britain liberty." "Look, Sir, into the history of the provinces of other states, of the Roman provinces in ancient time; of the French, Spanish, Dutch and Turkish provinces of more modern date," George Dempster advised the House of Commons in 1775, "and you will find every page stained with acts of oppressive violence, of cruelty, injustice and peculation."

If ideas of consent and liberty were central to one contemporary conceptualization of the empire, there was an alternative and, in Britain, more pervasive view of colonies and colonists. This competing view saw the colonies less as societies of Britons overseas than as outposts of British economic or strategic power. In this *restrictive* conception, explicit in the Navigation Acts and other Restoration colonial measures, the colonies were, principally, workshops "employed in raising certain specified and enumerated commodities, solely for the use of the trade and manufactures of the mother-country." Increasingly after 1740, and especially during and after the Seven Years' War, this view gave way to a complementary emphasis upon the colonies as instruments of British national or imperial power. Between 1745 and 1763, the intensifying rivalries with France and Spain, together with the growing populations and wealth of the colonies, produced, among metropolitan analysts, an unprecedented discussion about the nature and workings of the empire.

Most of the contributors to this discussion started from the assumption that the very "word 'colony,'" as Charles Townshend subsequently declared, implied, not equality, but "subordination." Contending that the colonies had been initiated, established, and succored by the metropolitan state for the purpose of furthering state policy, they argued that the colonies always had to be considered in terms of "power and dominion, as well as trade." In this view, the original purpose of colonization was to "add Strength to the State by extending its Dominions," and emigrants to the colonies had always been "subject to, and under the power and Dominion, of the Kingdom" whence they came. So far, then, from being in any sense equal to the parent state, colonies were nothing more than "Provincial Governments ... subordinate to the Chief State."

Such conceptions of the colonies suggested that colonists were something less than full Britons; not "fellow subjects," as Benjamin Franklin put it in 1768, "but subjects of subjects," people of "vulgar descent" and unfortunate histories, the miserable outcasts of Britain and Europe. During the Stamp Act crisis of 1765–6, Franklin, who throughout much of the period from the mid-1750s to the mid-1770s resided in London and acted as a self-appointed cultural broker for the colonies, was dismayed to see metropolitan newspaper writers dismiss the colonists with the "gentle terms of *republican race, mixed rabble of Scotch, Irish and foreign vagabonds, descendents of convicts, ungrateful rebels & c.*," language that, he objected, conveyed only the most violent "contempt, and abuse." By "lumping all the Americans under the general Character of 'House-breakers and Felons'" and by "raving" against them "as 'diggers of pits for this country,' 'lunaticks,' 'sworn enemies,' 'false,' and 'ungrateful'... 'cut-throats,'" Franklin protested during the decade after 1765, metropolitans repeatedly branded the colonists as a people who, though "descended from British Ancestors," had "degenerated to such a Degree" as to become the "lowest of Mankind, and almost of a different Species from the English of Britain," a people who were "unworthy the name of Englishmen, and fit only to be snubb'd, curb'd, shackled and plundered." Such language identified colonists as a category of others, "foreigners" who, however much they might aspire to be, could never actually become English, and who on the scale of civilization were only slightly above the Amerindian.

The expansion of British activities in India and the massive employment of enslaved Africans and their descendants throughout the British American colonies strongly reinforced this image in Britain. The more Britons learned about India, the more convinced they became that, as Dempster remarked in Parliament, the "eastern species of government" and society was replete with "rapines and cruelties." Beginning in the late 1750s, the transactions of Robert Clive and others persuaded many Britons that, in their rapacious efforts to line their own pockets, their countrymen in India had themselves often turned plunderers and been guilty of "Crimes scarce inferior to the Conquerors of *Mexico* and *Peru*." Already by the late 1760s, the term *nabob*, initially a title of rank for Indians, had become, as a contemporary complained, "a general term of reproach, indiscriminately applied to every individual who has served the East India Company in Asia" and "implying, that the persons to whom it is applied, have obtained their fortunes by grievously oppressing the natives of India."

Throughout the latter half of the eighteenth century, the rapidly growing antislavery movement more and more focused attention on the association of racial slavery with the colonies and fostered the conviction in Britain that "no People upon Earth" were such "Enemies to Liberty, such absolute Tyrants," as the American colonists. With "so little Dislike of Despotism and Tyranny, that they do not scruple to exercise them with unbounded Rigour over their miserable Slaves," colonists were obviously "unworthy" of claims to a British identity or to the liberty that was central to that identity. No less than the image of the nabob, that of the dissolute "creolean planter" – a despot schooled by slavery in "ferocity, cruelty, and brutal barbarity," whose "head-long Violence" was wholly unlike the "national" temperament of the "native genuine English" – shaped contemporary metropolitan conceptions of colonists.

The images presented in the anti-slavery literature suggested that no people who consorted with the corrupt and despotic regimes of the East or held slaves in the American colonies could be true-born Britons, lovers of liberty. To reassure themselves that Britain actually was the land of freedom, metropolitan Britons had to distance themselves from such people and Britain from such places.

The long debate that preceded the American Revolution provided colonists and their advocates in Britain with an opportunity to combat this negative image. In protesting that the extensive free colonial populations were mostly descendants of Englishmen or Britons, colonial protagonists penetrated to the essence of Englishness and Britishness as contemporaries understood it. What distinguished them from the colonists of other nations – and identified them with Britons at home – was not principally, they insisted, their Protestantism or their economic and social success, but their political and legal inheritance. "*Modern* colonists," in James Otis's view, were "*the noble discoverers and settlers of a new world*, from whence as from an endless source, *wealth* and *plenty*, the means of *power*, *grandeur*, and *glory*, in a degree unknown to the hungry chiefs of former ages, have been pouring in to *Europe* for 300 years past; in return for which those colonists have received from the several states of *Europe*, except from *Great Britain* only since the Revolution, nothing but ill-usage, slavery, and chains, as fast as the riches of *their own* earning could furnish the means of forging them." Not just the Catholic and despotic Spanish, Portuguese, and French had been so guilty, but even the Protestant and free Dutch, who shamelessly admitted that "the liberty of Dutchmen" was "confined to Holland" and was "never intended for provincials in America or anywhere else." If "British America" had thus long been "distinguished from the slavish colonies around about it as the fortunate Britons have been from most of their neighbours on the continent of Europe," colonial advocates argued powerfully, Britain's "colonies should be ever thus distinguished."

To colonial protagonists in the 1760s and 1770s, the colonists' claims to share in this central component of British identity seemed unassailable. "To the infinite advantage and emolument of the mother state," the colonists, as the Providence merchant Stephen Hopkins announced in 1764, echoing several earlier generations of colonial theorists, had "left the delights of their native country, parted from their homes and all their conveniences[, and] ... searched out ... and subdued a foreign country with the most amazing travail and fortitude." They had undertaken these herculean tasks on the assumption "that they and their successors forever should be free, should be partakers and sharers in all the privileges and advantages of the then English, now British Constitution," and should enjoy "all the rights and privileges of freeborn Englishmen." Exulting in their identity as Britons, colonists took pride in having come "out from a kingdom renowned for liberty[,] from a constitution founded on compact, from a people of all the sons of men the most tenacious of freedom." They expressed their happiness that, unlike the inhabitants of most other polities, they were not "governed at the will of another, or of others," and that they were not "in the miserable condition of slaves" whose property could "be taken from them by taxes or otherwise without their own consent and against their will." Rather, they militantly asserted, they lived, like Britons in the home islands, under a "beneficent compact" by which, as British subjects, they could "be governed only agreeable to laws to which themselves [they] have some way consented, and are not to be compelled to part with their property but as it is called for by the authority of such laws."

This assertion that the colonists enjoyed "the Liberty & Privileges of Englishmen, in the same Degree, as if we had still continued among our Brethren in Great Britain" was a reiteration of the colonists' long-standing demand for metropolitan recognition of their identities as Britons. Not just "Our Language, ... our Inter-marriages, & other Connections, our constant Intercourse, and above all our Interest[s]," they cried, but also, and infinitely more important, "Our Laws [and] ... our Principles of Government," those preeminent characteristics of true Britons, identified colonists as Britons who, "descended from the same Stock" as their "fellow-Subjects in Great Britain" and "nurtured in the same Principles of Freedom; which we have both suck'd in with our

Mother's Milk," were "the same People with them, in every Respect."

Vociferously, then, the colonists objected to being taxed or governed in their internal affairs without their consent because such actions subjected them to a form of governance that was at once contrary to the rights and legal protections traditionally enjoyed by Britons and, on the deepest level, denied their very identity as a British people. To be thus governed without consent was to be treated not like the freeborn Britons they had always claimed to be, but like a "conquered people"; not like the independent proprietors so many of them were, people who "possessed ... property" that could be "called" their "own" and were therefore not dependent "upon the will of another," but like "miserable ... slaves" who could "neither dispose of person or goods," but enjoyed "all at the will of" their "masters"; and certainly not like people of property in Britain, as *free agent[s]* in a *political* view" with full rights of civic participation, but like those many people in the home islands who had little or no property, people who were *"in so mean a situation*, that they" were "supposed to have no will of their own" and were therefore ineligible even to vote. "Unless every *free agent* in America be permitted to enjoy the same privilege[s]" as those exercised by similarly free agents in Britain, the young Alexander Hamilton declared in 1775, the colonists would be "entirely stripped of the benefits of the [British] constitution," deprived of their status as British peoples, "and precipitated into an abyss of slavery."

That such was the return made by metropolitan leaders to the colonists "for braving the danger of the deep – for planting a wilderness, inhabited only by savage man and savage beasts – for extending the dominions of the British Crown – for increasing the trade of British merchants – for augmenting the rents of the British landlords – [and] for heightening the wages of British artificers" seemed to colonists to be understandable only as an act of "Tyranny and Oppression" intended to deny colonial Britons an equality of status with metropolitan Britons by "destroy[ing] the very existence of law and liberty in the colonies." Only by exercising their inherited right, a right "secured to them both by the letter and the spirit of the British Constitution," to employ force to defend their "British liberties" against such "Violence & Injustice," only by actively "resist[ing] such force – force acting without authority – force employed contrary to law," they decided in 1775–6, could they manage to "transmit" their British heritage "unimpaired" to their "Posterity" and to make good their own claims to a British identity.

The various measures at issue between the colonies and Britain between 1764 and 1776 thus forcefully brought home to the colonists the problematic character of their pretensions to a British identity. Once the actions of the metropolitan government seemed aggressively to contest those pretensions, colonists made every effort to articulate and secure metropolitan acknowledgment of them, to make clear, as Burke said, that they were "not only devoted to liberty, but to liberty according to English ideas and on English principles." On a deep, perhaps the deepest, level, the American Revolution was thus the direct outgrowth of metropolitan measures that seemed to call into question colonial claims to a British identity. Colonial resistance to those measures needs to be understood, in the first instance, as a movement by colonial Britons to establish that they too were Britons.

FURTHER READING

Anderson, Benedict: *Imagined Communities: Reflections on the Origin and Spread of Nationalism* (New York: Verso, 1991).

Colley, Linda: *The Britons: The Forging of a Nation, 1707–1837* (New Haven, Conn.: Yale University Press, 1992).

Greene, Jack P.: "Empire and Identity from the Glorious Revolution to the American Revolution," in *The Eighteenth Century* ed. P. J. Marshall (Oxford: Oxford University Press, 1998), 208–30.

Greenfeld, Liah: *Nationalism: Five Roads to Modernity* (Cambridge, Mass.: Harvard University Press, 1992).

Helgerson, Richard: *Forms of Nationhood: The Elizabethan Writing of England* (Chicago: University of Chicago Press, 1992).

Wilson, Kathleen: *The Sense of the People: Politics, Culture, and Imperialism in England, 1715–1785* (Cambridge: 1995).

CHAPTER TWENTY-NINE

Loyalism and neutrality

ROBERT M. CALHOON

THE loyalists were colonists who by some overt action, such as signing addresses, bearing arms, doing business with the British Army, seeking military protection, or going into exile, supported the Crown during the American Revolution. Historians' best estimates put the proportion of adult white male loyalists somewhere between 15 and 20 percent. Approximately half the colonists of European ancestry tried to avoid involvement in the struggle – some of them deliberate pacifists, others recent emigrants, and many more simple apolitical folk. The patriots received active support from perhaps 40 to 45 percent of the white populace, and at most no more than a bare majority. Amerindians split into the same pro-British, pro-American, and neutralist alignments, with those tribes that British Indian Super-intendents had courted since the 1740s proving most likely to support British arms.

Because the loyalists were a military asset and a political liability for the British, their history throws light on why the British lost the War for Independence and why the Americans had to expend more than six years of fighting, and secure French assistance, to win the struggle. Likewise, the loyalists articulated views of liberty and order at variance with those of the patriots and thereby deepened ideological struggle within the Revolution; as the patriots learned how to identify, isolate, discredit, conciliate, and ultimately reintegrate loyalists, they gained political capacity and maturity.

1 The 1760s: Antecedents to Loyalism

While loyalism became a distinct phenomenon in late 1774 and 1775, there were important antecedents to loyalism during the pre-revolutionary decade. The Stamp Act crisis of 1765–6 exposed many Crown supporters to the rage of the populace. Lieutenant-Governor Thomas Hutchinson of Massachusetts and his kinsman, stamp distributor Andrew Oliver, had their homes pillaged by mobs (*see* chapter 23, §2). Lieutenant-Governor Cadwallader Colden of New York in vain tried to prevail on the British commander, Thomas Gage, to use military force against anti-stamp demonstrators in New York City demanding the surrender of tax stamps; Gage insisted that he could do so only on order from civil officials, placing the onus on Colden to issue such an order, which the Lieutenant-Governor declined to do. In South Carolina, Attorney-General Egerton Leigh and former Councillor William Wragg, both future loyalists, and Henry Laurens, who would become a leader of the Revolution, all opposed boycotts and remonstrances against the Stamp Act and became public pariahs as a result. In Georgia, where James Wright alone among royal governors had personal command of British troops, stamps were protected and legally sold – the only province where the Act was enforced. Several future loyalists sought during the late 1760s and early 1770s to devise solutions to the disputes between Britain and the colonies. William Smith, Jr., of New York, a member of the popular faction led by William Livingston, devised in 1767 a plan for imperial reorganization which he promoted so discreetly that almost no one knew its full terms until it was published in 1965. Also discreet and obscure was Hutchinson's contribution to reconciliation – an imagined dialogue between a knowledgeable British subject and a colonist about the merits of imperial policy and administration and colonial opposition. In contrast to Smith's and Hutchinson's penetrating private analyses, a group of high Anglican clergymen led by Thomas Bradbury Chandler, Samuel Seabury, and Myles Cooper constructed and published searing attacks on colonial individualism, opposition politics, and dissenting religious practices, which they astutely and accurately blamed for the pre-revolutionary assault on British authority.

Seeking appropriate labels for themselves and their adversaries in the pre-revolutionary controversy, the advocates of colonial resistance called themselves "Whigs" and their enemies "Tories" – appropriating partisan labels from the politics of the reign of Queen Anne and before that the contending sides in the struggle in 1679–83 to exclude the Duke of York from succession to the English throne. English Whigs favored toleration of religious dissent, parliamentary supremacy, and an anti-French foreign policy, while Tories resisted each of those tendencies. After 1720 the terms lost much of their meaning as Tories became politically marginal and Whig factions multiplied and dominated English politics. Nor did the terms describe divergent colonial ideologies very aptly. Whigs and most Tories in America had so internalized John Locke's teachings about consent as to be predisposed to resist arbitrary governmental action; however, Tories – even those with a Lockean outlook – reacted with visceral anxiety to the idea of concerted, organized opposition against British authority. Thus, while Whig and Tory polemics from 1765 to 1775 were volleys which went past their respective targets, this nomenclature indicated where the dispute was heading and the libertarian Whig and prescriptive Tory assumptions underlying the controversy. Indeed, a case before the 1754 Privy Council – the "Pistole Fee dispute" over the power of the Virginia Assembly to regulate Anglican

salaries – turned on the very question of whether colonial government depended in the final analysis on the "prescriptive" power of the parent state or on the "custom" of colonial autonomy built up by precedent. That distinction re-emerged on the eve of the Revolution as the crux of Whig–Tory disagreement (Greene, 1963, p. 163).

2   The Coercive Acts

When the British ministry decided in 1774 to impose the Coercive Acts and to use force to reimpose its authority in Massachusetts (*see* chapter 24, §3), the pre-revolutionary debate had already aroused the supporters of the mother country – "the King's friends," or persons "inimical to the liberties of America," or "friends of government," as the earliest "loyalists" were variously called.

The text of the Coercive Acts, General Thomas Gage's governorship of Massachusetts, and substantial reinforcement of the British garrison in Boston all occurred during July and August 1774. No one was more surprised by the abolition of the old elected Council and its replacement with a new appointed body than the 12 prominent Crown supporters named to the new Royal Council. After a short period of deceptive calm, crowds gathered in front of the homes of several of the new "mandamus" councilors and demanded their resignations and apologies. Those directly confronted complied, and all of the new appointees quietly slipped into Boston and repudiated resignations offered under duress. They soon discovered that Gage's authority did not extend beyond the Boston patrolled by British troops. By serving as a focus for outraged but largely non-violent demonstrations, the mandamus councilors unwittingly enabled popular leaders to seize control of the Massachusetts countryside by September 1774, the same month in which the last House of Representatives elected under royal rule converted itself into a Provincial Congress and began to oversee preparations for resistance.

Disastrously misreading the situation, the ministry in London dismissed Gage's request for 20,000 troops to restore order throughout Massachusetts and ordered him to march soldiers already under his command into the countryside to arrest the leaders of the insurrection. When Gage obeyed that order on April 19, 1775, he provoked a famous skirmish at Lexington Green, heavy fighting at Concord Bridge, and an outpouring of militiamen which forced the British troops to retreat ignominiously to Boston. Within days thousands of minutemen, volunteers from all parts of New England, surrounded Boston, effectively isolating Gage and British forces within the town. Gaining *de facto* control of the countryside by the fall of 1774 and compelled to organize armed insurgency by the late spring of 1775, revolutionary leaders in New England focused their attention at this early stage on their potential opponents – prominent British supporters who had taken refuge in Boston and who went into exile when Britain evacuated the city in March 1776, as well as smaller fry who were neighbors and kinsmen hostile to colonial resistance and fit subjects for interrogation and surveillance by local committees of safety, correspondence, and inspection. Committee dealings with "persons inimical to the liberties of America," as these early loyalists were labelled, sought to define the community as a holistic and virtuous entity and Tories as offenders against the public good who acted out of ignorance, cupidity, or moral obtuseness. Encouraged by the committees to apologize in these terms, Tories were typically restored to good standing by their own candor and humility or ordered to post bond equal to the value of their property assuring their continued good behavior.

3 Southern Backcountry Loyalists

North Carolina

In a much more rudimentary, recently settled, and conflict-ridden setting such as the southern backcountry, loyalists posed a more serious threat to the Whig movement. In North Carolina a widely scattered and diverse population of Highland Scots, Scots-Irish, German-speaking, and English settlers had never coalesced into a unified political community. Opposition to British policy was strong but limited to pockets in the coastal lowlands, the Neuse and Roanoke River valleys in the east, and the two western counties of Rowan and Mecklenberg. The great influx of recent settlement lay in a broad, politically neutral belt in the upper Cape Fear River valley and central Piedmont region. With the aid of a Scottish officer in the British Army and a handful of his own agents, Governor Josiah Martin succeeded in encouraging backcountry supporters – chiefly newly arrived Scottish settlers on whom he had lavished generous land grants – to prepare to fight against the rebels. Though forced to take refuge on a British warship, Martin received word on January 3, 1776 that a British expedition had been dispatched to the mouth of the Cape Fear River, the site of the town of Wilmington; and he called on the backcountry loyalists to rise, march to the coast, and occupy Wilmington in advance of the arrival of British regulars. By February 14, 1776, 1,400 volunteers – two-thirds of them Highland Scots – assembled in the upper Cape Fear. At first successful in eluding a force of rebel militia, the loyalists headed south for Wilmington, but other patriot troops positioned themselves on wooded slopes on the bank of a creek in the path of the loyalists' line of march. Rashly trying to cross a partially dismantled bridge, which crossed Moore's Creek, the loyalists were completely routed by cannon fire. When General Henry Clinton, commanding the British expedition to the Carolinas, learned of the disaster, he canceled his plans to land troops at the mouth of the Cape Fear.

South Carolina

In the South Carolina backcountry the loyalists had far better leadership than in North Carolina, and with almost no help from the royal governor they came very close to seizing control of the South Carolina–Georgia frontier in the summer and fall of 1775. The Whig leadership dominated the lowland aristocracy and the Charles Town merchant community; and in the first six months of 1775 the Whigs seized effective control of the lowlands, forcing the newly arrived governor, William Campbell, to seek refuge on a British warship in Charles Town harbor.

The device that the South Carolina Whigs employed was an "Association," or oath, which all inhabitants were required to sign. When they tried to secure signatures in the backcountry, however, the new Council of Safety encountered stubborn resistance. The most powerful figure in the region, militia Colonel Thomas Fletchall, enormously overweight and vain, was irked at not receiving a more important position in the revolutionary movement, and he successfully blocked efforts to require all militiamen in the backcountry to sign the Association. Playing on Fletchall's vanity and influence, a number of committed loyalist leaders sensed an opportunity to make their region a bastion of British strength at the very moment imperial authority was rapidly eroding everywhere else. Not a single militiaman under Fletchall's command signed the Association; instead they adopted a counter-Association denying that the King had forfeited their allegiance or violated the British Constitution.

At this critical juncture, the Sons of Liberty in the Georgia backcountry seized and tortured Thomas Brown, an obstinate landowner recently arrived from Great Britain, by jabbing burning splinters into the soles of his feet. The enraged Brown escaped, made his way to District Ninety-Six in the western portion of South Carolina, and became a fiery leader of the growing loyalist movement there. The Council of Safety sent one of its most politically adroit members, William Henry Drayton, to District Ninety-Six to counter the influence of the loyalist leadership. By skillful maneuver, Drayton managed to separate Fletchall from the loyalist leaders and negotiate in September 1775 a truce between Fletchall's militia and the Whig forces. The truce collapsed in late November, and more than 2,000 rallied to arms to fight for the Crown against a patriot force of 550. A blizzard occurred, which made marches and discipline extremely difficult, and after three days the fighting sputtered out and the loyalists dispersed. The loyalists had been waging a defensive campaign, most of them just wanting to be left alone. The Whigs had a more clearly defined aim: to discredit the leadership of the ambivalent Fletchall and the intransigent loyalists.

4 Northern Loyalists

New Jersey

In northern New Jersey, the British enjoyed both military supremacy and a large pool of loyalist volunteers in arms. After his successful occupation of New York City, William Howe's holding of New Jersey thrust into view both the state's revolutionary leadership and its large loyalist population and initiated bloody internecine combat. In line with Howe's aim of expanding the area under British control, British troops occupied Burlington, Bordentown, and Trenton, on the Delaware River, as well as Princeton and New Brunswick. Howe sent Cornwallis in chase of Washington, but the cold wet weather of November 1776 was an inauspicious season for grim pursuit. Howe was briefly tempted in early December to catch his prey at Trenton, but again Washington responded quickly to Howe's movements and whisked his force across the river into Pennsylvania. Howe paused and issued another proclamation promising pardon to defectors from the rebel cause. He sought to multiply the psychological impact of these defections by holding frequent public drills of occupying British forces and by paying generous prices to loyalist farmers who brought goods to a procurement center at Bordentown. By spring, some 2,700 New Jersey residents had signed Howe's oath and received pardon. But as his forces moved across New Jersey they seized livestock and produce without ceremony and looted fine homes of silver plate, jewelry, clothing, and other household finery. British officers vied with each other to equip field headquarters with the fine mahogany furniture of the region. Uncomfortable in the New Jersey winter, troops appropriated all available firewood and destroyed farm buildings for more fuel. Numerous reports of rape and killing by British and Hessian troops appear to have been grossly exaggerated, but the offenses that did occur further fanned abhorrence of the British occupiers during the winter of 1776–7, when patriot morale was at its lowest ebb and the machinery of revolutionary government in New Jersey in near ruin. The combined effect of Washington's stunning victories against exposed British outposts at Trenton and Princeton plus resentment over the depredations of armed loyalist forces was to bring Howe's offensive in New Jersey to a halt.

New York

A more controlled environment for loyalist policing of British military control occurred in the garrison towns of New York, occupied from 1776 to 1783, and Philadelphia, held from September 1777 until the following June. The British commandant in New York, General James Robertson, struggled to reconcile the needs of the army and the interests of loyalist exiles who flocked to the city from patriot-held territory to the north and loyalist and neutralist inhabitants. He ended vandalizing and looting by British soldiers and protected loyalists from unauthorized seizure of their homes by British troops. Robertson located cramped quarters for British and Hessian troops and wives and children of British officers who had joined them in New York City – some 2,500 dependents by 1779. Warehouses were converted to handle British war supplies; churches were used as hospitals; and prisons had to be improvised in empty buildings and ships in the harbor. Housing for returning loyalists and refugees remained the most pressing problem in occupied New York City. Most rented rooms cost four times their prewar amounts. Not until 1780 did the army develop machinery to regulate and prevent abuses in its occupancy of private homes. Moreover, the army was supposed to pay loyalists for the use of their homes but regularly neglected these obligations. Loyalists in turn were not above falsely claiming ownership of buildings used by the British. In spite of General Robertson's tireless efforts to be fair, the shortage of accommodation and the absence of a court system to settle disputes over housing created persistent friction between loyalist inhabitants and the British Army.

General Howe appointed Andrew Elliot Superintendent of Exports and Imports for the port of New York. Elliot, the son of a Scottish official, had grown up in Philadelphia, married into wealth, established himself as a New York merchant, and held, from 1764 to 1776, the post of Receiver General and Collector for the port of New York. He also served as head of the Board of Police in occupied New York City. Elliot was the most important loyalist during the first half of British occupation of New York City. A civilian, he was responsible for the enforcement of detailed regulations and procedures preventing the illegal re-export of goods to other parts of the rebelling colonies. With his cronies, the former mayor David Mathews and the police magistrate Peter Dubois, Elliot monopolized political influence and authority in New York during the first half of the war. As prominent members of the Board of Police, the trio were responsible for a wide range of governmental functions: "suppression of vice and licentiousness," support of the poor, direction of the night watch, regulation of ferries, and maintenance of the "economy, peace, and good order of the city."

Philadelphia

The British occupation of Philadelphia in 1777–8 offered even more promising opportunities for loyalist allies of the Crown to help restore imperial administration of an American colonial community. Joseph Galloway, an experienced Pennsylvania politician and advocate of compromise with Britain at the First Continental Congress in 1774, sought a position in occupied Philadelphia, analogous to Elliot's in New York, which he could expand into that of a powerful administrative overseer of British policy. He conceived of his role as Superintendent of Police more as that of a long-range constitutional theorist than that of a mere overseer of policy subordinate to the British commander. Galloway assumed the duties of political overlord of the Pennsylvania campaign as soon as the troops landed, on August 25, at Head of Elk, at the northern end of Chespeake Bay. He hired intelligence agents, organized efforts at supply operations, and ordered

Cornwallis to destroy a bridge the rebels had built across the Schuylkill River. Loyalists who helped prevent the burning of Philadelphia by retreating rebels received rewards for their courage from Galloway. He sought lucrative governmental positions for other conspicuous loyalists and forged his subordinates into an effective and adaptable administrative agency.

Galloway's personal corps of loyalist troops did conduct a wide range of irregular raids in Pennsylvania during the winter of 1777–8, seizing rebel provisions and supplies bound for Valley Forge, capturing many supporters of the Revolution within a 30-mile radius of Philadelphia, and collecting military intelligence. When Cornwallis had failed for six weeks to erect batteries on Mud Island in the Delaware River because tides kept washing over the foundations, Galloway organized and supervised a crew that built batteries there in less than a week, to the astonishment of the army's chief engineer. Galloway also conducted a census of the entire population of the city, designating the loyalty or disaffection of every inhabitant. He designed a campaign of newspaper proclamations urging voluntary restrictions on price increases, which prevented the kind of inflation rampant in occupied New York City. Events, however, frustrated Galloway's initially successful attempt to convert Philadelphia into a showplace of benevolent, vigorous, confident reimposition of royal authority. Howe, for example, vetoed his scheme to kidnap the revolutionary Governor and Council of New Jersey. When news came that Philadelphia was to be abruptly abandoned to the Americans, the loyalist community asked permission to negotiate directly with General Washington for their safety. Habitually prone to overreaching himself, Galloway seemed to British officials in America as vain and undependable as he was loyal and efficient. Rebuffed, he went to London, where his testimony before a parliamentary inquiry discredited the cautious tactics of General William Howe and encouraged British legislators to believe that a vigorous military effort would tap vast reservoirs of loyalist support and crush the rebellion.

5 Amerindians Serving the Loyalist Cause

The North

Through the work of Superintendents of Indian Affairs on the northern and southern frontiers from the late 1740s onwards, the British Government had built up a large reservoir of good will among Amerindian tribes which traded with the colonists and had fought with them against the French. Some Amerindians regarded themselves as allies of the British, acting from considerations of self-interest, while others concluded that British protection and support was a moral debt. The use of Amerindians as counter-revolutionaries was, however, fraught with difficulty. They made up about a third of an offensive strike force, commanded by Lieutenant Colonel Barry St. Leger, which marched from Oswego on Lake Ontario in late July 1777 in support of Burgoyne's offensive to rendezvous with Burgoyne near Albany, New York. Sir John Johnson, son and successor of Sir William Johnson – legendary Indian Superintendent from 1754 to 1774 – led a group of Amerindians and white loyalists as a part of the St. Leger offensive, which ambushed and destroyed a patriot force at the battle of Oriskany and in the aftermath burned a neutral village of Oneida Amerindians, another Iroquois tribe. That act destroyed the delicate web of Iroquois unity and provoked vengeful attacks by patriots and Oneidas upon Mohawk settlements. This mutual destruction of villages and crops in turn wiped out the food supply of Amerindians on both sides of the conflict; these tribes had so widely adopted the white man's agricultural techniques to the neglect of hunting that, from 1777 onwards, famine and hunger became weapons of war that took a terrible toll. Deep divisions developed among white loyalists about the proper use of Amerindian warriors. Guy and John Johnson and their allies – Joseph Brant, a brilliant Mohawk leader, and his sister Mary Brant – wanted the Amerindians to operate as a disciplined, elite, and independent military force. But Governor Guy Carleton in Quebec wanted the Amerindians to serve a defensive and subordinate role, and he placed them under the command of the Johnsons' rival, Colonel John Butler, a wealthy western New York loyalist. Butler preferred to recruit braves by getting them drunk, and therefore most of the Amerindians he enlisted for the St. Leger offensive were so hungry and ill-clad that they did little fighting; when St. Leger's forces failed to capture Fort Stanwix and dispersed, the Amerindians robbed and assaulted retreating British and loyalist soldiers. With the surrender of Burgoyne at Saratoga, frontier New York ceased to be a strategic theater of the war, but it was nevertheless the scene of successive Mohawk and white loyalist terrorist attacks on patriot settlements and equally savage retaliation by patriots against Mohawk villages and crops.

The South

Similar divided counsel in the British offensives in the South from 1778 to 1781 prevented effective use of pro-British Amerindian tribes such as the Creeks and Cherokees. The Indian Superintendent in the South, John Stuart, realized that Amerindian fighting capacity was a highly expendable commodity, while headstrong loyalists such as Thomas Brown and the East Florida Governor Patrick Tonyn wanted to use Amerindians to terrorize frontier patriots. Poorly supplied and with confusing lack of military direction, loyalist Amerindians in Georgia and the Carolina backcountry contributed little to the British conquest of the region in 1780. Amerindians sensed, with good reason, that a victorious independent American republic would be far less restrained than the British administration had been in dispossessing them of their land and extirpating their way of life.

6 African American Loyalists

African Americans, both free and enslaved, saw in the Revolution an opportunity to attain and enhance their own freedom. Just as 4,000–5,000 slaves in the Mid-Atlantic states extricated themselves from bondage during the War for Independence by working on American merchant vessels and supporting the revolutionary cause in other ways, probably 3,000–4,000 runaway slaves worked in the British garrison towns and followed the British into exile when General Guy Carleton evacuated New York in December 1783.

The first black loyalists were Virginia slaves who responded to Lord Dunmore's November 15, 1775 proclamation calling on indentured servants and slaves belonging to rebellious planters, and who were ready and willing to bear arms in the service of the Crown, to flee their masters and repair to the British standard at Norfolk. Dunmore's Ethiopian Regiment wore "Liberty to Slaves" badges on their chests mocking the white Virginians' motto of "Liberty or Death." More than 800 succeeded in reaching Norfolk, but probably ten times that number heard news of Dunmore's appeal, were ready to respond, but were prevented or dissuaded by patriot surveillance from responding to it. The Ethiopian Regiment fought valiantly alongside British Regulars and white loyalists, but the Virginia patriots overwhelmed them at the battle of Great Bridge on December 9, forcing Dunmore to evacuate by sea his base at Norfolk and taking his black volunteers with him.

The leadership core of the Ethiopian Regiment may have come, not from tidewater Virginia plantation slaves, but from members of a maroon community in the Great Dismal Swamp in southside Virginia where runaway Blacks had lived as free men and women since the 1720s and with whom Dunmore was in contact. Most of the African Americans who fought under Dunmore later died at sea from diseases to which they had no immunity.

Another key leader of African American loyalists in the Carolinas was Thomas Peters, a slave millwright in Wilmington, North Carolina. On the eve of General Sir Henry Clinton's impending occupation of Wilmington in March 1776, Peters threw off his enslavement and organized Blacks in the lower Cape Fear valley to support

British military operations until the defeat of loyalists, making from the upper Cape Fear in the battle of Moore's Creek, forced Clinton to suspend his landing of British troops in Wilmington. Peters made his way to Nova Scotia and in 1792 to Sierra Leone as a leader of the black Tory émigré community.

In South Carolina in 1775, a free black named Thomas Jeremiah – a Charleston boat pilot, fisherman, and fire fighter worth more than £1,000 – allegedly told his slave brother-in-law that "there is a great war coming" which would "help the poor Negroes" and that he "had powder enough ready," but not yet enough guns, to organize a black force to oppose the patriot rebels. Charging him with insurrection, the South Carolina Committee of Safety publicly hanged and burned Jeremiah on August 18, 1775 over the impotent but anguished protests of British royal governor, Lord William Campbell.

The most widespread instance of African American loyalism was the presence of Blacks in Methodist revivals on the Delmarva Peninsula from 1777 to 1782, where Methodist evangelists preached against the Revolution and inspired a lower-class and yeoman farmer Tory insurgency against the authority of the Whig elites in tidewater Virginia and Maryland and in the northern part of Delaware. When Delaware loyalists descended on the home of the Whig judge, Robert Appleton, in 1782 to destroy legal papers relating to the prosecution of area loyalists, they ordered the judge to read aloud the text of a Methodist sermon, and failing to secure that degree of ritual abasement, had him submit to being whipped with a rope by a black man – a symbolically rich tableau.

7 Religious Groups

Pietists

A number of ethnic, religious, and social groups, sometimes labeled "cultural minorities" by historians of loyalism, had the same misgivings about American independence and stood aloof from the struggle for self-determination. The most visible were religious pacifists in Pennsylvania, both Quakers and German pietists. Of the latter, the most vulnerable were the Mennonites, who refused to sign a Test Oath prescribed by the Pennsylvania revolutionary government in 1777. The Mennonites were willing to sell grain to the Continental Army, to supply teamsters and wagons to the government on request, and to pay commutation fees in lieu of military service. But they refused to take the compulsory oath of allegiance to the state imposed in June 1777, and they refused to pay special war taxes. They objected not only because it was an oath – a mere affirmation would have satisfied the law – but also because it required renunciation of their allegiance to the King and affirmative endorsement of authorities in Philadelphia whom they had no reason to respect or support. Moreover, the oath implied their approbation of the warfare necessary for the establishment of the new government.

The Brethren, Dunkers, and Schwenkfelders suffered similar pressures. In 1776 the Ephrata community of Brethren simply declared their neutrality on the ground that they were subject to a higher magistrate "and consequently emancipated from the civil government." Though opposed to both military service and oaths of allegiance, the Brethren were far less strict in enforcing these prohibitions and ruled that the payment of fines in lieu of military service "would not be deemed so sinful" as actually bearing arms if it was done under "compulsion" and not "voluntarily." The Schwenkfelders adapted themselves to the conditions of war still more adroitly. The Church established a charitable fund to pay fines for non-participation in the militia. It was not military service but oaths or affirmations of allegiance that caused the greatest friction between pietist sects and the revolutionary government. One member of the sect refused on the ground that he had taken an oath of allegiance to the King when he was naturalized, and, second, the outcome of the war was still in doubt and it was not yet clear "upon what side God almighty would bestow the victory." As opportunistic and equivocal as the reasons appear, they represented an important pietist belief and one that distinguished these pacifists from the Quakers: the assurance that divine providence ultimately controlled the military struggle and that men could not alter oaths of allegiance until God had granted victory and spiritual legitimacy to one side or the other.

Quakers

The most serious conflict between the government of Pennsylvania and pacifist citizens, of course, involved the Quakers. The Philadelphia Quakers were too wealthy and influential a group to be ignored by revolutionary leaders. Quaker aversion to any complicity with the war effort was both ingenious and scrupulous, but there were just enough wealthy Quakers who were outright British sympathizers to taint the neutrality of the whole sect. The Philadelphia Meeting for Sufferings called on Friends in the city "with Christian fortitude and firmness" to "withstand and refuse to submit to the arbitrary injunctions and ordinances of men who assume to themselves the power of compelling others … to join in carrying on war by imposing tests not warranted by the precepts of Christ … or the laws of the happy Constitution under which [the Friends had] long enjoyed tranquillity and peace" – language that came perilously close to being non-neutral. Congress asked Pennsylvania officials to arrest 11 prominent Quakers – including James, Israel, and John Pemberton, Henry Drinker, Samuel Thomas Fisher, and Thomas Wharton – and to add to the list other names of persons "inimically disposed toward the American states," and recommended that Pennsylvania officials deport the prisoners to confinement in Virginia. The Council first ordered the militia to transport 20 unrepentant prisoners to Reading. A judge then ordered their release on a writ of habeas corpus, but a special *ex post facto* law denied the group the protection of habeas corpus. After a few days they were taken to Winchester, Virginia, arriving there in September 1777, just three days after the British had occupied Philadelphia. There they lived under lenient confinement until sympathy for the exiles persuaded the Supreme Executive Council to return them to Lancaster, Pennsylvania, and release them.

Quakers in New England were more vulnerable to harassment and more willing to seek an accommodation with revolutionary leaders as a demonstration of their peaceableness. Led by Moses Brown, the New England Friends sought to achieve a practical compromise between the demands of conscience and the actual exigencies of the time, between church government that imposed discipline on its members and one that responded to the concerns of its constituents. The first step was thoroughly conventional: the establishment of the New England Meeting for Sufferings, in June 1775, modeled on the Philadelphia Meeting for Sufferings, which had dealt with the legal and financial needs of pacifists and brought relief to other victims of war since 1756. Between December 1775 and January 1777, using funds contributed largely by Philadelphia Quakers, Brown and his co-workers assisted more than 5,000 destitute Boston-area residents whose incomes had been cut off by the commencement of hostilities.

Throughout the early years of the War for Independence, the New England Friends continued to seek a moderate means of practicing pacifism without appearing to be openly hostile to the revolutionary cause, and to maintain the unity of the fellowship without becoming narrowly exclusive. The New England Quakers agreed that they should not accept paper money issued by the Continental Congress or by revolutionary state governments because the issuance of this money was a means of financing the war. But, under Moses Brown's guidance, monthly and yearly meetings imposed no arbitrary prohibitions on transactions payable in the new currency and left the matter, instead, to the conscience of each individual. Open dissension arose over payment of taxes. Some purists wanted to refuse any tax payments to new state governments on the ground that support of a revolutionary regime was as evil as complicity in warfare, while a strong minority argued that Quakers had a responsibility to contribute to the costs of government even if by so doing they inadvertently contributed to the support of military activity as well. Trying to mediate between the two camps, Brown believed that on the issue of paying taxes members should be answerable only to their consciences and should be disciplined only for unauthorized public statements on matters that weakened Quaker solidarity. The longer the war lasted, the stronger became the influence of doctrinaire Friends, and Brown only narrowly prevented the adoption in New England in 1780 of a rule making non-payment of taxes mandatory.

Methodists

Methodist preachers had just begun to arrive in the colonies in the early 1770s, preaching a message of assurance and grace which appealed to people living on the fringes of polite society in the middle colonies and the Chesapeake. Their founder and leader, John Wesley, vociferously condemned the American Revolution, and this factor added to their reputation as outsiders and troublemakers. Methodist revivals on the Eastern Shore of Maryland and in adjoining portions of Delaware and Virginia therefore helped foment a kind of lower-class Tory populist revolt against the authority of patriot governments. Some Methodists were outright British sympathizers, while a larger number relegated politics to the level of worldly concerns, insignificant compared with the work of salvation. Dutch Reformed settlers in the Hackensack Valley of northern New Jersey split between a Tory faction aligned with church authorities in Holland and a patriot one bent on further Americanization of the Church; Dutch families around Albany, New York, with the greatest internal solidarity and distrust of English neighbors, were more prone to be loyalist than the families which had more varied social and business dealings; those prominent Dunkers in North Carolina, who were deeply involved in land speculation and estranged from humbler church members, saw General Charles Cornwallis as their savior and became avowed loyalists, while the bulk of the Dunker community simply feared disintegration of their communities under the pressures of war and fled North Carolina as soon as the conflict ended.

8 War in the South

The inability of the Continental Congress and Army to defeat the British in the Mid-Atlantic states between 1776 and 1778 and British failure to smash Washington's forces and induce a majority of the inhabitants of the region to return to affirm their allegiance to the Crown made loyalism and neutrality possible and also precarious; in the southern states from 1778 to 1781, a bold but poorly planned and executed British offensive also summoned loyalists to arms and encouraged the uncommitted to withhold their support from the revolutionary cause. But the war in the South also spread warfare beyond the battlefield and into the lives of non-combatants.

The southern offensive began auspiciously when forces sailing from the British base at St. Augustine, Florida, recaptured Savannah, Georgia, in February 1779 – enabling the British to re-establish civilian government in coastal Georgia and inland Augusta, the only instance during the war that regular British administration supplanted martial law in North America. Then in May 1780 General Henry Clinton brought an invading force from New York, landed near Charles Town, South Carolina, cut off supply lines to the city, and compelled the American defenders to surrender. Over the next eight weeks, resistance throughout South Carolina collapsed, and Clinton returned to New York leaving a portion of his forces under the command of General Charles Cornwallis to complete the pacification of Georgia and South Carolina, to occupy and pacify North Carolina, and then to march north into the Chesapeake.

The strategic weaknesses of the southern campaign became apparent as soon as Cornwallis tried to invade North Carolina in the early autumn of 1780. Clinton had saddled Cornwallis with two ungovernable subordinates, Major Patrick Ferguson and Lieutenant Colonel Banastre Tarleton, both commanding loyalist troops and both brilliant, reckless officers. Ferguson allowed himself to be cut off from Cornwallis's army and trapped atop a spiny hogback ridge called Kings Mountain by a huge force of "over the mountain men" from what later became Tennessee. In savage hand-to-hand combat on October 7, 1780, the patriot frontiersmen annihilated the loyalists. Tarleton's defeat at Cowpens in January 1781 further eroded the offensive power of British arms. Most North Carolina loyalists abandoned any idea of rallying to the King's standard, and a few who did try to rendezvous with Cornwallis – when he occupied the state capital at Hillsborough – fell into an ambush set by Colonel Henry "Lighthorse Harry" Lee. Bereft of loyalist support and bogged down in a hostile wilderness, Cornwallis lost a quarter of his men to death and injury in an inconclusive battle at Guilford Courthouse in March 1781. He marched to the port of Wilmington to be resupplied and then decided to risk an invasion of the Chesapeake rather than fight on in North Carolina or return to Charles Town and adopt a defensive position in South Carolina. He was not convinced that the war could be won only if Britain transferred all of its available forces to the Chesapeake. And so he marched north into Virginia, where he occupied the town of Yorktown just before the French fleet entered Chesapeake Bay in force, severing British supply lines, communications, and means of reinforcement. Alerted of French naval plans, Washington and General Rochambeau moved their armies from New England, New York, and New Jersey to Virginia, besieged Yorktown, and forced Cornwallis to surrender.

When the British departed from North Carolina in June 1781, they left behind a state exhausted from the struggle against the invader. Loyalists filled the vacuum. Major James Craig occupied Wilmington in January 1781 and in July appointed David Fanning commander of loyalist militia, already operating under Fanning's leadership. Craig and Fanning had finally learned how to fight irregular war in America successfully. Fanning devised a new guerrilla strategy based on what one authority calls "quickness, mobility, deception, and improvisation" (Watterson, 1971, p. 98). Fanning's raids concentrated on freeing Tory prisoners, capturing the most notorious persecutors of the loyalists, operating widely in eastern North Carolina under cover of darkness, "plundering and destroying our stock of cattle and robbing our houses of everything they can get." Fanning's men were disciplined and violence was carefully targeted against key officials. Throughout Cumberland, Bladen, Anson, and Duplin counties, pockets of dispirited loyalists felt emboldened by Fanning's exploits. General Nathanael Greene and Governor Thomas Burke sensed almost immediately what was happening. The only safe remedy was to hunker down and wait for events outside North Carolina to shift advantage away from the British irregulars. The use of retaliatory terror against known or suspected loyalists only played into Craig's and Fanning's hands, enabling them to present themselves as agents of justice for the oppressed and targets of barbarity. The Fanning–Burke duel in North Carolina in the summer of 1781 therefore pitted against each other for the first time in the war adversaries who thoroughly understood the relationship between conventional and guerrilla warfare in the Revolution.

9   After Independence: Reintegration

Had the British kept sea lanes open between New York and the Chesapeake when Cornwallis encamped at Yorktown – or if the French fleet had not chosen to descend in force into the Bay in September 1781 – Cornwallis might well have savaged the Virginia tidewater during the winter and spring of 1782 and then marched back into North Carolina to capitalize on Fanning's successful demoralization of the Whig regime in that state.

Instead, the surrender at Yorktown destroyed the political credibility of the ministry and forced the creation of a new government committed to peace even at the cost of conceding independence to the rebellious colonies. The treatment of the loyalists was the most difficult issue for British and American negotiators to resolve in 1782. The Crown insisted on the restoration of all confiscated property and amnesty from prosecution for all crimes allegedly committed by the loyalists in the course of the war. American negotiators were instructed to refuse any concessions in favor of the loyalists. Britain broke the impasse by abandoning its rigid defense of the loyalists' interests, and the Americans responded by agreeing that Congress would "earnestly recommend" to the states that loyalists who had not borne arms for the British could reclaim their property, and that those who had fought for the Crown or gone into exile would have one year to purchase back their confiscated estates from the new owners. The American Secretary for Foreign Affairs rightly called the loyalist clause of the peace treaty "a very slender provision... inserted [by Britain more] to appease the clamors of these poor wretches than to satisfy their wants" (Norton, 1972, p. 180).

In 1783–4 most states ignored the provisions of the treaty protecting loyalists and British creditors. But in 1785 Alexander Hamilton in New York, Benjamin Rush in Pennsylvania, and Aedanus Burke in South Carolina each mounted public campaigns to restore property and political rights to most former loyalists. They argued that public vengeance was a self-inflicted wound on the American body politic, that a fragile republican polity would ill-afford the corrosive effects of such recriminations and retribution. By 1787 most states, needing the commercial skills of departed loyalist merchants, began repealing anti-Tory legislation.

Meanwhile 60,000 to 80,000 loyalists who departed with the British or fled to Canada or the West Indies after 1783 created new communities in the portions of British America which did not revolt. Half of the exiles settled in Quebec, New Brunswick, and Nova Scotia. Of these, about a thousand black loyalists were eventually resettled in Sierra Leone in West Africa. Seven thousand made their way to England. Disappointed by the ambiguous loyalist provisions in the peace treaty, the exiles in London redoubled their efforts to secure redress from the British Government. Parliament responded by creating a commission dealing with the losses and services of the American loyalists. Its investigation began in 1783 and lasted for six years. Hearings were held in London and also in Canada, at Halifax, St. Johns, and Montreal. The commission, which heard 3,225 claims for property and income lost on account of claimants' loyalty to the Crown during the Revolution, and which granted compensation to 2,291 claimants, did its work well. It eliminated fraudulent and inflated claims and required each claimant to produce witnesses from among other loyalist exiles and Crown officials who could testify to his character, devotion to the Crown during the Revolution, and the pre-revolutionary value of his estate or Crown office. The claimants did not recoup all of their losses, but the compensation of more than £3,000,000 amounted to 37 percent of the successful claimants' estimates of their losses.

During the 1780s and 1790s, an assortment of loyalists with experience in mobilizing and leading pro-British Amerindians along the southern, Ohio valley, northwest, New York, and Vermont frontiers – notably Thomas Dalton and William Augustus Bowles – promoted the idea of systematic loyalist and Amerindian military activities in North America; during the War of 1812 loyalists played a key role in repulsing American incursions into Canada.

FURTHER READING

Brock, Peter: *Pacifism in the United States from the Colonial Era to the First World War* (Princeton, NJ: Princeton University Press, 1968).

Calhoon, Robert M.: *The Loyalists in Revolutionary America, 1760–1781* (New York: Harcourt, Brace, Jovanovich, 1973).

——: *The Loyalist Perception and Other Essays* (Columbia: South Carolina University Press, 1989).

Frey, Sylvia R.: *Water from the Rock: Black Resistance in a Revolutionary Age* (Princeton: Princeton University Press, 1991).

Greene, Jack P.: *The Quest for Power* (Chapel Hill: University of North Carolina Press, 1963).

Hancock, Harold B.: *The Loyalists in Revolutionary Delaware* (Newark: University of Delaware Press, 1977).

Holton, Woody: "'Rebel against Rebel': Enslaved Virginians and the Coming of the American Revolution," *Virginia Magazine of History and Biography*, 105 (1997), 157–91.

Leaming, Hugo Prosper: *Hidden Americans: Maroon Communities of Virginia and the Carolinas* (New York Garland Publishing, 1995).

Nash, Gary: "Thomas Peters: Millwright and Deliverer," H-Net, November 24, 1997.

Nelson, William H.: *The American Tory* (Oxford: Oxford University Press, 1961).

Norton, Mary Beth: *The British-Americans: the Loyalist Exile in England, 1774–1789* (Boston: Little Brown and Co., 1972).

Watterson, John S. III: "The Ordeal of Governor Burke," *North Carolina Historical Review*, 48 (1971), 95–117.

Weir, Robert M.: *Colonial South Carolina: A History* (Millwood, NY: KTO Press, 1983).

CHAPTER THIRTY

Opposition in Britain

COLIN BONWICK

OPPOSITION in and out of Parliament to the American policy of successive British governments grew slowly during the 1760s, reached a climax during the critical years of 1774–6 and continued throughout the war. Until the final crisis following General Cornwallis's surrender at Yorktown in 1781 it was always the stance of a minority. Within Parliament the critics included major statesmen such as William Pitt, his supporter and successor the Earl of Shelburne and their small group, the Marquis of Rockingham, his adviser Edmund Burke and their somewhat larger group, and Charles James Fox, who collaborated with Rockingham but retained political autonomy. Their failure to develop effective opposition was partly a consequence of Lord North's control of the House of Commons after 1770, but they could agree on only one principle: that the Anglo-American dispute should be – and could be – resolved within the framework of a continuing imperial connection. Their ability to form tactical alliances was seriously hindered by the fragmented nature of British parliamentary politics during the revolutionary era. Coherent parties in the modern sense were non-existent; in their place were shifting associations which centered on particular individuals and made sustained cohesion impossible. The problem was especially acute during the 1760s, when ministries changed frequently, but continued until well after the American war. Development of concerted opposition was also complicated before 1775 by the demands of issues such as Ireland, India, and the Falkland Islands overseas, and the Wilkes affair and Middlesex Election of 1768–9 at home, which frequently commanded greater attention.

1 The Gathering Crisis, 1763–75

During the early years of the American dispute parliamentary opposition was limited in scope and largely pragmatic in character. All politicians applauded British success during the recently concluded Seven Years' or French and Indian War, and recognized that acquisition of Canada, Florida, and the lands east of the Mississippi River required systematic reorganization of the American empire, including provision for defence of the new territory and a revenue to finance it. George Grenville's Revenue or Sugar Act of 1764 was opposed only on matters of detail, and, apart from protests by General Conway, Isaac Barré, and a handful of others, the Stamp Act of 1765 passed with little opposition. Rockingham, Grenville's successor as Prime Minister, gained a reputation as sympathetic to America but repealed the Stamp Act in 1766 for political reasons rather than on grounds of principle. Moreover, his decision was influenced not by colonial resistance but by the complaints of British merchants about the damage to their trade. Simultaneously Rockingham clarified his constitutional position in a Declaratory Act which stated that Parliament possessed authority to legislate for America "in all cases whatsoever," and revised the Sugar Act to improve the profitability of the revenue on American trade. He carefully evaded the question of whether parliamentary authority extended to taxation, but his general principle was simple: "I shall always consider that this country, as the parent, ought to be tender and just; and that the colonies, as the children, ought to be dutiful." Balancing this belief in parliamentary supremacy, however, was an appreciation of the strength of the colonies and an acceptance that policies should be adjusted to particular circumstances rather than directed by rigid adherence to constitutional principle. Outside government William Pitt, who enjoyed a great reputation in America, had demanded immediate repeal of the Stamp Act but attempted to distinguish between legislation and taxation. He applauded the colonists for defending their liberty but declared: "Let the sovereign authority of this country over the colonies be asserted in as strong terms as can be desired, and be made to extend to every point of legislation whatever. That we may bind their trade, confine their manufactures, and exercise every power whatsoever, except that of taking their money out of their pockets without their consent." Revenue received from duties on trade was acceptable in his view, provided it was incidental to the regulation of commerce.

Even the Townshend Duties of 1767, which skirted American objections to the Stamp Act and would finance the salaries of colonial officials, failed to arouse opposition in England commensurate with protests in America. Ironically they had been imposed by a government nominally headed by Pitt (now Earl of Chatham). They were also compatible with Rockingham's previous policy and were not opposed by his group in the House of Commons. Nor was there any protest from British merchants, since improved trading conditions in Europe had made their American trade relatively less important. When Chatham collapsed the same year, an attempt was made to construct a coalition from his followers and the Rockingham group. Such a government might have been more conciliatory than the ministry formed by Lord North in 1770, but negotiations broke down for personal reasons. Thereafter the Rockinghamites remained out of office until 1782 and were joined by the Chathamite rump in 1770. While North consolidated his position, opponents of his American policy remained divided, partly because Chatham was fiercely

independent in his views and personally erratic. They mustered 142 votes against retention of the tea tax in 1770 but were easily beaten, and Burke made a shallow speech in a debate on the Boston Massacre, but it merely demonstrated opposition weakness. In any case America virtually left the political agenda for a time.

2 The Critical Years, 1774–5

The Coercive or Intolerable Acts of 1774, introduced in response to the Boston Tea Party of the previous December, stimulated the beginnings of sustained opposition. No one condoned the destruction of property, and opposition to the Boston Port Act was negligible; only John Sawbridge, a London radical, denied Parliament's claim to tax the colonies. The other legislation aroused considerable opposition. Edmund Burke, adviser to the Marquis of Rockingham, insisted that imperial relations should be based on the principles of English liberty and warned of the dangerous consequences of using the army. Charles James Fox argued that Americans would only consider themselves attached to Britain if the right to taxation was abandoned. But opposition was ineffectual. The government's program passed through Parliament with exceptionally high majorities in both Houses. Later the same year a general election in which America was seldom an issue confirmed North's control of the Commons. Nevertheless, one difference of great significance emerged very clearly. Ministers were convinced that colonial resistance was the work of a small and malign minority of radicals. Their opponents were impressed by the evident maturity of American society and the colonists' willingness to defend their rights; they believed that resistance represented widespread American opinion.

Yet if the opposition's arguments are more congenial than those of the government, their constructive proposals contained serious weaknesses. They shared a common view that the foundations of the imperial connection must rest on mutual affection and common interests but beyond this could agree only on the necessity of some form of legislative supremacy. Chatham particularly feared the destruction of his achievements during the Seven Years' War. On January 20, 1775 he introduced a Conciliatory Bill in response to North's recent proposals. He reiterated the principles that the colonies were dependent on the Crown and subordinate to Parliament and affirmed the Crown's right to deploy troops in America and Parliament's authority fo regulate trade. But his Bill also recognized Congress as a permanent imperial institution, renounced the use of force against American liberties, abandoned claims to taxing power, acknowledged the sanctity of colonial charters and repealed or suspended all parliamentary legislation since 1764 against which there was protest. However, although he recognized the colonial legislatures' sole right to raise revenue, he envisaged authorization of a permanent revenue that would be placed at Parliament's disposal. Benjamin Franklin was impressed by the proposals, but they left crucial questions unanswered and had no prospect of acceptance.

A few weeks later, on March 22, Edmund Burke spoke for the Rockingham group. He had been dismayed by the opposition's previous lack of energy, and presented a second alternative to North's coercive policy. As always his arguments were directed towards practicalities, but though he denied being a speculative philosopher they were grounded in philosophical ideas. He was convinced that the government ought to come to terms with circumstances and that since peace was the grand objective some form of reconciliation was necessary. Conciliation required concessions, and Britain could afford them. The real issue, he argued, was "not whether you have a right to render your people miserable; but whether it is not your interest to make them happy. It is not what a lawyer tells me I *may* do; but what humanity, reason and justice tell me I ought to do." Burke's proposals conceded almost everything demanded by the First Continental Congress. In particular they included repeal of all unacceptable legislation enacted since 1763 and the principle that financial contributions to imperial expenditure should be made voluntarily, as before that year. His speech was generous and even noble in spirit and his proposals were sufficiently

flexible to allow for growth. Yet quite apart from their certain unacceptability to the government and probable unacceptability to the Americans his plan was flawed: he could not escape from the Rockinghamite commitment to the central principle of the Declaratory Act. All he could propose in a second speech on conciliation in November was that parliamentary supremacy should remain but by self-denying ordinance its powers should not be exercised. His first motion was defeated by 270 votes to 78, and his second by 210 to 105.

3   The War Years

Efforts to construct a united opposition after the outbreak of war were unsuccessful. Chatham had annoyed the Rockingham group by failing to warn them of his proposals, and the summer of 1775 exposed their political weakness. An attempt to establish a chain of personal connections between the two groups failed during the following winter. Divisions were exacerbated by publication of Richard Price's *Observations on the Nature of Civil Liberty* early in 1776. As a close friend and protégé, he commended Shelburne's Chathamite proposals for reconciliation with America but damaged relations with the Rockinghamites by launching a ferocious attack on the Declaratory Act: "I defy anyone," he said, "to express slavery in stronger language." But it was more their inability to influence government policy that demoralized the opposition, and in November 1776 the Rockinghamites formally seceded from Parliament in a futile gesture of protest.

General Burgoyne's surrender at Saratoga in October 1777 marked the beginning of a change of fortune. Nevertheless its effects were not felt immediately and it did nothing to unite the two groups. Chatham refused to modify his position and continued to insist that the connection with America must remain the basis for any peace settlement. Shelburne supported him in this view. Such a principle was now completely impractical and led to a final breach with the Rockingham group. Lord North attempted to exploit the breach by bringing him into the government but negotiations were abruptly halted by

Chatham's death. Fox and some members of the Rockingham group naively hoped for some form of federal arrangement which they wishfully believed was compatible with independence. In contrast Rockingham drew the conclusion from Burgoyne's disaster that American independence would have to be conceded, and believed that it should be recognized immediately in the hope of averting war with France. Thereafter this new principle became the central plank in his policy, and in 1780 he refused to negotiate a coalition with North unless it was accepted as government policy.

News of the second British surrender, by General Cornwallis at Yorktown in October 1781, at last brought victory for the opposition. The attack on North's government began in earnest with a motion from Sir James Lowther, leader of a small independent group who had always opposed the war, which argued that operations against America should be terminated but implied that the war against France should continue. From January 1782 onwards the attack became relentless. Attendance in the House of Commons was extremely high, rising to about 500, and government support slowly drifted away. On February 27 General Conway's motion that offensive operations should be discontinued was passed by 19 votes. Privately North had already accepted that the war was lost, and on March 20 he resigned in order to avoid a motion of no confidence. The opposition had worked hard to achieve their victory, but the tide was turned by the disillusionment of independent members and the temporary defection of about 45 supporters of the government. Thereafter the two opposition groups formed an uneasy coalition government under Rockingham's leadership. Disagreement between the partners delayed negotiation of a peace treaty, for whereas Rockingham and Fox proposed immediate recognition of American independence, Shelburne still hankered after some form of connection. After Rockingham's death in July 1782 Shelburne became Prime Minister and concluded the treaty by recognizing American independence and offering generous terms as a means of encouraging reconciliation.

4 Radicals and Dissenters

Throughout the war Rockingham had stressed the importance of opposition outside Parliament. In general government policy was popular until the final crisis, but a small minority consistently supported the Americans and opposed coercion. The most prominent opponents were the "Commonwealthmen" or "Real Whigs" whose intellectual ancestry dated back to the radicalism of the seventeenth century, but whose numbers had fallen away in more recent years. Many were also religious dissenters or nonconformists, but some were members of the rationalist liberal wing of the Church of England. They included the dissenting ministers Richard Price and Joseph Priestley, both of whom were notorious radicals in orthodox eyes, Catharine Macaulay, author of the so-called republican *History of England*, and John Jebb, who had left the Church because he could no longer subscribe to its Articles of Religion. Other publicists included the parliamentary reformers John Cartwright and Granville Sharp, who campaigned for many reform causes but unusually was a devout Anglican. John Wilkes, who became the focus of radical activity in the 1760s and whose fate aroused much concern in the colonies, also supported the Americans after entering Parliament in 1774; whether he was entirely sincere remains open to question.

Radical opposition derived in part from a strong sense of the reality of transatlantic community. To a high degree Price and many others shared a common intellectual inheritance with the American revolutionaries. They corresponded extensively with their American counterparts on matters such as theology, the anti-slavery campaign, and later the Anglo-American dispute, and read extensively in the literature of colonial protest, much of which was reprinted in Britain. Above all they enjoyed friendships with Americans living in London, particularly Benjamin Franklin. These associations encouraged a highly favorable view of colonial society, except for its tolerance of slavery, and made them receptive to colonial arguments. Moreover some Americans participated in reform politics; Arthur Lee of Virginia in particular was an active member of the Wilkite Society of Supporters of the Bill of Rights and frequently introduced American issues into its propaganda.

Opposition gathered pace slowly outside as well as within Parliament. During the 1760s dissenters among the radicals campaigned against Archbishop Thomas Secker's efforts to establish an American bishopric (*see* chapter 22, §1); Thomas Hollis, who died in 1774, was especially active in distributing colonial tracts on the subject. Their objections lay in their fear that such an appointment would be accompanied by the apparatus of ecclesiastical authority and religious discrimination against which they had protested for decades in England. The coincidence of the bishopric campaign, the American legislation, and the Wilkes affair at home convinced the radicals that both parts of the empire faced a single crisis and that British ministers were attempting to suppress liberty on both sides of the Atlantic.

Attitudes crystallized as the crisis degenerated into war from 1774 on. Both London and Bristol were divided. Elsewhere the colonists' friends were widely scattered, though dissenters commonly were supportive. Sympathy for America was often a manifestation of long-running social divisions. Well-organized and vocal London supporters were mostly wholesale or retail shopkeepers and craftsmen, not great merchants. Outside the capital, sympathizers were usually men of middling social rank who were excluded from public authority and political patronage. After 1775 London critics were able to continue their orchestrated attacks on the government, but provincial opponents fell virtually silent since they lacked national organization and were largely unaware of each other's existence. Radical opposition to the government was directed towards finding a solution acceptable to both sides within the framework of a continuing empire. Dr. John Fothergill used his connections as a physician to act as an intermediary between Franklin and the American Secretary Lord Dartmouth during the winter of 1774–5, but without success. More prominent was the radical contribution to public debate. Over one thousand pamphlets were printed on various aspects of the American crisis between 1764 and 1783, including many written by radicals. Several focused on the critical problem of representation and all rejected parliamentary supremacy. In 1774 John Cartwright published *American Independence the Interest and Glory of Great Britain.* Its title was misleading, for he proposed only legislative separation, not total independence, and argued that in practice Britain would become the dominant partner. Granville Sharp also argued in favor of local legislative autonomy coupled with continued loyalty to the Crown in his *Declaration of the People's Natural Right to a Share in the Legislature*, but it was Price's *Observations on the Nature of Civil Liberty* which caused the greatest outcry. In his view Britain should welcome the development of free states within the empire and should seek to bind them only by ties of affection and interest; it was absurd that a small group of men on one side of the Atlantic should control a vast continent on the other. His solution to the problem of government was a federal community within which each state would be self-governing and a senate representative of the general confederacy would balance the interests of individual members against the needs of the empire as a whole.

Those who opposed the government at first refused to accept the thrust of the Declaration of Independence. Cartwright and Sharp both insisted that Americans would accept parliamentary reform as a token of British good faith and would then negotiate a reconciliation. Only after Saratoga did they reluctantly come to recognize that the real alternatives were coercion or separation. Having done so they enthusiastically supported independence, in good measure because they regarded the United States as a model for political reform, and (a matter of great importance for dissenters) as an example of the practicality of religious liberty. During the closing years of the war the radical program of parliamentary reform at home and an end to hostilities against America attracted wider support, but only because the war had become unpopular.

Other than the Real Whigs there were few notable critics of government policy. Quakers had very strong connections with America and deplored the war but advised their members to remain true to the principles of pacifism and submission to lawful authority. At the other extreme *The Crisis*, a scurrilous newspaper published in 1775–6, attacked the King and made veiled threats of domestic revolution. Thomas Paine, the most notorious eighteenth-century radical, spent the Revolution in America, though *Common Sense* was reprinted several times in Britain, initially in an expurgated edition. The exception was Josiah Tucker. Far from being sympathetic to America he deplored its political culture and argued that the colonies had become a liability. He rejected mercantilist arguments and insisted that British as well as American trade would flourish if both economies were permitted to develop in freedom. Separation was in the British interest and independence should be welcomed.

FURTHER READING

Bonwick, Colin: *English Radicals and the American Revolution* (Chapel Hill: University of North Carolina Press, 1977).

Bradley, James E.: *Popular Politics and the American Revolution in England: Petitions, the Crown, and Public Opinion* (Macon, Ga.: Mercer University Press, 1986).

——: *Religion, Revolution and English Radicalism: Nonconformity in Eighteenth-century Politics and Society* (Cambridge: Cambridge University Press, 1990).

Clark, J. C. D.: *The Language of Liberty, 1660–1832: Political Discourse and Social Dynamics in the Anglo-American World* (Cambridge: Cambridge University Press, 1994).

Derry, John: *English Politics and the American Revolution* (London: J. M. Dent, 1976).

Guttridge, G. H.: *English Whiggism and the American Revolution* (Berkeley and Los Angeles: University of California Press, 1942, repr. 1966).

O'Gorman, Frank: *The Rise of Party in England: The Rockingham Whigs, 1760–82* (London: George Allen & Unwin, 1975).

Peters, Marie: *The Elder Pitt* (London and New York: Longman, 1998).

Reich, Jerome R.: *British Friends of the American Revolution* (Armonk, NY: 1998).

Sainsbury, John: *Disaffected Patriots: London Supporters of Revolutionary America, 1769–1782* (Kingston and Montreal: McGill-Queen's University Press and Gloucester: Alan Sutton, 1987).

CHAPTER THIRTY-ONE

Common Sense

JACK FRUCHTMAN, JR.

THE appearance of Thomas Paine's *Common Sense* (January 10, 1776) was one of the most remarkable publishing events of the eighteenth century. Not only did it for the first time publicly present strong arguments for America's separation from England, but it also enjoyed phenomenal sales. Although exact figures are uncertain, scholars have estimated that well over 100,000 copies were sold in the first year of its publication. This does not consider sales after 1776 nor those of the French translation which appeared later. Paine turned all of his profits over to the American cause. More important than its sales history, the pamphlet became the conscience of the Revolution, providing "a summary of a large segment of the ideology of the American Revolution as well as a substantial contribution to that very ideology" (Aldridge, 1984, p. 17).

In early 1776, many Americans were still wavering about the idea of separation from Britain. Paine's pamphlet, first signed anonymously "By an Englishman," proved so popular that, in galvanizing opposition to the British Crown, it served as the final catalyst for those uncertain whether America should break with Great Britain. In so doing, it successfully shattered the residual American psychological resistance to independence, because Paine undertook a dual assault. First, he launched a frontal attack on the British monarchy in terms so graphically violent that only the most committed loyalist came away without a sense of hatred and loathing for Britain and its King. Second, he unequivocally showed, for the first time, how the relationship with Britain, should it continue, fatally threatened American republican virtue

and simplicity. His goal was to awaken Americans to British ignorance and prejudice and thus teach them to reverence themselves. "Every thing that is right or natural pleads for separation," he wrote. "The blood of the slain, the weeping voice of nature cries, 'TIS TIME TO PART" (Penguin edn., p. 87).

The pamphlet was accessible to many Americans for two reasons. First, because it cost but a shilling a copy, it was relatively cheap. Second, and perhaps more important, Paine's style attracted not only merchants and manufacturers, but also the artisans, tradesmen, and craftsmen (*see* §2 below).

1 An Outline of the Work

Paine divided *Common Sense* into four principal sections. For the second edition, he enlarged it and included an Appendix as well as a reply to the Quakers, who were distressed over the non-pacifist views Paine presented in the first edition. In the first part, Paine reviewed the history of man using Lockean themes of a state of nature and the social contract (*see* chapter 11, §1). He told how man, at one time unconnected to his fellows by any form of government, at long last decided principally for security reasons to join others to form civil government. In this section, using the quotable turn of phrase for which he was so well known, he formulated one of his most famous remarks about the natural good of society and the corresponding evil of government: "society in every state is a blessing, but government even in its best state is but a necessary evil; in its worst state an intolerable one ... Government, like dress, is the badge of lost innocence" (p. 65). The British Constitution, with its divisions into King, Lords, and Commons, was not a republican form of government as its supporters claimed it was (*see* chapter 84). For Paine, the House of Commons was the only republican element in British government.

This discussion led directly to the second part, which was a consideration of monarchy and hereditary succession. Here Paine inquired into the origins of kingship and the hereditary principle and gave long quotations from scripture. They described how the Bible condemned the ancient Hebrews, who were at one time free, as a sinful people because they wanted a monarchy when they had an opportunity to create a republic. For Paine, because human beings were created equal in the sight of God, it was an abomination for one family to set itself up in perpetuity over all others. England's problems grew out of its long history of monarchy and hereditary succession. These problems intensified because of William the Conqueror: "a French bastard landing with an armed banditti and establishing himself king of England against the consent of the natives is in plain terms a very paltry rascally original" (p. 78).

In his third section, Paine turned to the situation in America. His thoughts rested on nothing but the "simple facts, plain arguments, and common sense" (p. 81). Common sense told us that the relationship between America and Britain had become so bad that Americans had only one choice: they must stop negotiating a settlement with England and separate. "'TIS TIME TO PART" because America had entered "the seedtime of continental union, faith, and honor" (pp. 87, 82). America must become independent to ensure its protection and security from a Europe that was hopelessly corrupt. By separating from England, America would develop into a free port and enjoy a strong, lasting commerce. Its prosperity would be assured, its people happy, and the nation safe.

This would be realized when the Americans called a constitutional convention to draft a republican constitution with annual assemblies and a president who would be chosen each year from a different colony. Congress would be empowered to pass laws but only by a three-fifths majority. Unlike the rest of the world, America had the opportunity to be a free nation. All other countries had expelled freedom. It was time for America to "receive the fugitive, and prepare in time an asylum for mankind" (p. 100).

In the final part, Paine reviewed America's strengths, giving particular attention to her navy, and predicted that in a war with Britain America would be victorious. In the meantime, he recommended that America tell the world of her mistreatment by the British Government by means of a manifesto, somewhat like the Declaration of Independence of a few months later.

In the Appendix to the second edition, Paine briefly responded to some of the criticisms from those who wanted reconciliation, not independence. In his exploration of the consequences of separation, he made the remark most often quoted from this text:

we have every opportunity and every encouragement before us, to form the noblest, purest constitution on the face of the earth. We have it in our power to begin the world over again ... The birth-day of a new world is at hand. (p. 120)

Paine concluded the work with an explanation of why war with Britain was necessary despite the arguments of the pacifist Quakers.

2   The Language and Style of *Common Sense*

Paine's work has been acclaimed as masterfully capturing the essence of the argument for independence in a style accessible to his American audience. He wrote not in the learned style of an educated man but on a level that appealed to most Americans, no matter what their station or class. The use Paine made of this style is controversial. For Foner, "Paine was the conscious pioneer of a new style of political writing, a rhetoric aimed at extending political discussion beyond narrow bounds to the eighteenth century's 'political nation'" (Foner, 1976, p. 83). For Wilson, however, "Paine's style is better understood as part of a wider 'revolution in rhetoric' that was taking place during the late eighteenth century" (Wilson, 1988, pp. xi–xii, 20–5). They agree that Paine's plain style was accessible to all his readers.

Beyond lucid writing, Paine also used exciting imagery to enhance his work. Although his formal education consisted only of attendance in grammar school, Paine developed a colorful, imaginative manner of presentation, perhaps the result of his participation in the tavern debates in Lewes and Philadelphia. He used powerful phrases and strong images that were richly graphic and engaging. Some examples will demonstrate how he captivated his audience.

First and foremost was his image of King George III. He mocked the King by dehumanizing him, saying he has "sunk himself beneath the rank of animals, and contemptibly crawl[s] through the world like a worm" (p. 114). Even worse, he compared the King to Saturn devouring his children, a favorite eighteenth-century theme: the father-king relished his children, the Americans, as his main meal. "Even brutes do not devour their young," he exclaimed. Still, the lovers of liberty have fled England to America in hopes of escaping "the cruelty of the monster" (p. 84; *see* Jordan, 1973). Meantime, aristocrats fared no better than kings. He called them the King's "parasites," who hold their station only because of hereditary right. They produced nothing by their own skills because they had no skills, and they "fed off the work and sweat of their subjects" (p. 84).

Paine also employed images from science and medicine, in particular health, disease, and youth, to distinguish the corruptions of monarchy from the virtues of the republic. He referred to "a thirst for absolute power" as "the natural disease of monarchy" (p. 69). Later he asked, "why is the constitution of England so sickly, but because monarchy hath poisoned the republic, the crown hath engrossed the commons?" (p. 81). In contrast to rotten England, the virtues and vigor of the republic would be fruitful. With great fanfare, he drew an image of how in America the law, as founded on true constitutional principles, would reign supreme. In contrast to the arbitrary laws of England, based only on the whim of the King and his ministers, American law would be protected by divine ordinance. God himself had ordained American separation.

[L]et a day be solemnly set apart for proclaiming the charter [the new constitution]; let it be brought forth placed on the divine law, the word of God; let a crown be placed thereon, by which the world may know, that so far as we approve of monarchy, that in America THE LAW IS KING. For as in absolute government the King is law, so in free countries the law 'ought' to be King; and there ought to be no other. But lest any ill use should afterwards arise, let the crown at the conclusion of the ceremony be demolished, and scattered among the people whose right it is. (p. 98)

The smashing of the crown ended America's relationship with Britain for ever.

3 The Impact of *Common Sense*

The widespread distribution and huge readership of *Common Sense* had a multiple impact. First, responses, pro and con, in the form of pamphlets, broadsides, and penny numbers as well as newspaper articles, began to appear. All were devoted to the controversial issue of separation, but Paine himself was always the central focus, especially for the opposition. The most important of these were John Adams's *Thoughts on Government* and James Chalmers's *Plain Truth* (Aldridge, 1984, pp. 158–215). Moreover, *Common Sense* convinced many Americans that a separation was not only the inevitable but the only course for America. The pamphlet profoundly transformed the debate over America's relationship with Britain and the meaning of republican government (Foner, 1976, pp. 107–44).

Finally, *Common Sense* brought into the public arena many of the more radical Philadelphia writers, such as Benjamin Rush and Timothy Matlock, Charles Willson Peale and David Rittenhouse. Some of these men later assumed positions of leadership in Philadelphia after America's break with Britain. Their participation in politics was immediately made evident during the drafting of the Pennsylvania Constitution of 1776 shortly after the Declaration of Independence. With its unicameral legislature, it was one of the most radical of the state constitutions of the time (*see* chapter 34, §4).

These factors all made *Common Sense* one of the most successful political pamphlets ever written. It aroused public opinion in America in an unprecedented way and it led ineluctably to the promulgation of the Declaration of Independence. Thomas Paine's genius and style endowed the work with all that was necessary to stimulate Americans to think seriously about their future, especially the end of their ties to Britain.

FURTHER READING

Aldridge, A. O.: *Thomas Paine's American Ideology* (Newark: University of Delaware Press, 1984).

Foner, E.: *Tom Paine and Revolutionary America* (New York: Oxford University Press, 1976).

Fruchtman, Jack, Jr.: "Nature and Revolution in Paine's *Common Sense,*" *History of Political Thought*, 10 (Autumn, 1989): 421–38.

——: *Thomas Paine and the Religion of Nature* (Baltimore: Johns Hopkins University Press, 1993).

Greene, J. P.: "Paine, America, and the 'Modernization' of Political Consciousness," *Political Science Quarterly*, 93 (1978), 73–92.

Jordan, W. D.: "Familial politics: Thomas Paine and the killing of the king," *Journal of American History*, 60 (1973), 294–308.

Newman, S.: "A Note on *Common Sense* and Christian Eschatology," *Political Theory*, 6 (1978), 101–8.

Paine, T.: *Common Sense* (Philadelphia: 1776); 2nd edn., repr., ed. I. Kramnick (Harmondsworth: Penguin, 1976).

Wilson, D. A.: *Paine and Cobbett: the Transatlantic Connection* (Kingston and Montreal: McGill–Queen's University Press, 1988).

CHAPTER THIRTY-TWO

The Declaration of Independence

RONALD HAMOWY

WHEN the Second Continental Congress convened in May 1775 few delegates supported complete independence from Great Britain. The events of the following eight months, however, were to make a reconciliation between the colonies and the mother country close to impossible. On August 23 the King proclaimed the colonies in "open and avowed rebellion" and in December Parliament enacted legislation declaring the colonies beyond the protection of the Crown and proscribing all trade with them. These responses to the colonists' petitions for a redress of their grievances and to the outbreak of hostilities at Lexington and Concord in April 1775 could only serve to strengthen the forces for separation. By early spring of 1776 the delegations of the two most populous colonies, Massachusetts and Virginia, were united in supporting independence, while the advocates of compromise in Congress, although still representative of a substantial portion of public opinion, found their task increasingly difficult.

The proponents of some accommodation with the Crown were dealt a decisive blow in January 1776 with the publication of Thomas Paine's *Common Sense* (*see* chapter 31). In dramatic language, Paine argued the case for a complete break with Great Britain from whom, he concluded, the colonies derived no benefit or advantage. And in an electrifying passage, he called upon Americans to embrace their destiny to serve as an oasis of freedom and enlightenment in a world of oppression and darkness. Paine's pamphlet proved an astonishing success. Some estimates put the sales of *Common Sense* during the course of 1776 at approximately half a million, and newspapers throughout the colonies ran substantial excerpts from it. Its effect was almost immediate and the debate between the radicals and those supporting reconciliation which raged throughout the colonial press following its publication tipped decisively towards independence.

By May 1776 it was apparent to most that a complete separation between the colonies and Great Britain was inevitable. On May 10 the Continental Congress had enacted a resolution calling upon the various colonies to form their own governments, and five days later a far more radical preamble to this resolution, drafted by John Adams, was adopted. Not only did the preamble recommend that the colonies assume full powers of government but also that all exercise of authority under the Crown be suppressed. While the Congress was thus committing itself to this militant position in Philadelphia, the Virginia Convention, meeting in Williamsburg, instructed its delegates to the Congress to propose that that body declare the colonies "free and independent states, absolved from all allegiance to, or dependence on, the Crown or Parliament of Great Britain." In compliance with the instructions received from Virginia, Richard Henry Lee, the colony's senior delegate, moved on June 7 "that these United Colonies are, and of right ought to be, free and independent States, that they are absolved from all allegiance to the British Crown, and that all political connection between them and the State of Great Britain is, and ought to be, totally dissolved."

The pro-separatist forces, aware that so radical a measure would have far greater impact if supported by all the colonies, agreed to postpone consideration of Lee's resolution for three weeks, by which time, it was hoped, the Congress would be able to act unanimously. Inasmuch as the ultimate outcome of a vote was clear, however, the Congress on June 11 appointed a committee to draw up a preamble to the resolution, consisting of John Adams, Benjamin Franklin, Thomas Jefferson, Robert Livingston, and Roger Sherman. Jefferson, in turn, was selected by the committee to prepare a draft of the document which, as it was to turn out, was submitted to the Congress after only minor modifications.

In drafting the Declaration Jefferson set out not only to catalog the specific reasons which constrained the colonies to separate from Great Britain but also, and more importantly, to lay bear the ideological underpinnings upon which the Revolution rested. In doing so, he did not seek to offer an original theory of government, "not to find out new principles, or new arguments never before thought of," as he was later to put it, but to "place before mankind the common sense of the subject." The philosophical preamble of the Declaration attempts to set forth the ideological substance of American revolutionary thought, which was grounded in a theory of natural, inalienable rights and which reflected, Jefferson was later to write, "the harmonizing sentiments of the day, whether expressed in conversation or letters, printed essays, or in the elementary books of public right, as Aristotle, Cicero, Locke, Sidney, etc."

The principles of government expounded in the Declaration bear the unmistakable imprint of Whig revolutionary thought and particularly of its chief exponent, John Locke. The popularity of Locke's political views among the colonists, both directly through his works and through those writings heavily influenced by him, such as Trenchard and Gordon's *Cato's Letters*, was immense. Indeed, if any one work could be said to have captured "the harmonizing sentiments of the day" during the period immediately before the Revolution, it would be Locke's *Second Treatise of Government (see* chapter 11, §1).

The principal argument of the *Second Treatise,* echoed in the Declaration's preamble, is easily understood. All men enter the world possessed of certain rights, which are theirs by virtue of their nature as human beings. These rights exist in advance of the establishment, and independent, of any civil authority and not as a consequence of the actions of that authority. The powers of the civil magistrate are founded on the consent of those who are governed and may be exercised solely in their interests. When any government violates this trust, it is the right of the people to abolish it and to create a new government more likely to effect those ends for which governments are established. Locke and the Declaration thus link a theory of natural rights to the notion that the authority of government rests on individual consent. That the Declaration articulates the principle that popular consent is the only legitimate basis of political authority should not, however, be taken to mean that governments may act in any manner consonant with popular approval. The Declaration is eminently clear on this point. While the authority of the magistrate rests on the consent of the people, that authority is by its nature severely limited.

Governments may act only insofar as they respect the inalienable rights with which all men are endowed. These rights are not the creatures of government but are rooted in man's very nature and, as such, are unconditional. Nor are they transferable by virtue of man's having entered into civil society. The purpose of government is the more efficient protection of these rights. The Declaration clearly affirms this when it asserts that all men "are endowed by their creator with certain unalienable rights, that among these are Life, Liberty, and the pursuit of Happiness" and "That to secure these rights, Governments are instituted among Men."

An analysis of the logical structure of the Declaration reveals that the rights to which Jefferson refers – and here he clearly follows Locke – are to be understood not as mandating individual or collective action of any kind but rather as restraining men from acting in certain ways. Or, put more simply, my right to something, say my liberty, entails only prohibitions on others and not positive commands. To the extent that I am free, I am "let alone" or "unhindered" by others. The only boundaries limiting the actions of other men are those prohibitions which extend around my liberty. There are no circumstances under which they are required to act but only a narrow set of instances where they are prevented from acting. When rights are thus negatively conceived it is apparent that there exist no conditions under which the liberty of one person can conflict with the liberty of another, for it is perfectly consistent with the liberty of each person that they be constrained not to act in any manner invasive of the liberty of another. It further follows from this reading that, since the transcendant function of political authority is to secure to each of us our inalienable rights (and since these require that we be prevented from acting in certain ways but never that we be forced into certain positive actions), the Declaration gives voice to a political philosophy of extremely limited government.

Of equal importance, Jefferson's claim that all men are created equal must be understood within the framework of this notion of rights. Men are equal in that all possess the same absolute rights, which others may not transgress under pain of violating the fundamental laws by which all men are governed. The equality to which the Declaration refers is not one of social or economic condition, nor does the Declaration make as one of the tests of government whether men become, in some sense, equal in attainments. We are equal only in that we are all invested with certain indefeasible rights, including the rights to our lives and our liberties and the right to pursue our happiness as we individually see fit, free from the intrusions of others, whether acting individually or collectively.

It is a tribute to Jefferson's stylistic abilities and to his skill in distilling the common political sensibilities of the day that his draft of the Declaration received only minor revision at the hands of the other members of the drafting committee. On July 2 the Congress adopted Lee's resolution, with 12 delegations voting in favor of independence and New York abstaining. Having thus declared the united colonies free states, independent of the British Crown, the Congress immediately turned its attention to a consideration of the Declaration, which offered a justification for the decision just reached.

While a number of alterations and deletions to Jefferson's draft were made by the Congress, at that point meeting in Committee of the Whole, it is significant that no attempt was made to tamper with the document's philosophical preamble. Nor is this particularly surprising; the American revolutionaries had long embraced the legal and political principles expounded in the natural-law theories of Hugo Grotius and Samuel Pufendorf, through Locke and the other Whig radicals, and in the continental writers inspired by them, particularly Jean Jacques Burlamaqui. The central thrust of congressional revision was reserved for the main body of the Declaration, a list of specific charges against Great Britain. These charges were leveled not against the Parliament but against the Crown, in keeping with the colonists' conception of the constitutional status of the North American colonies. Americans regarded the colonies as linked to Great Britain only in that they acknowledged a common monarch. Parliament of Great Britain, it was argued, had no more legal authority over various colonies than the legislature of one of the colonies had over its sister colonies or, indeed, over Great Britain itself. While the colonists conceded fealty to the British Crown, they did not regard themselves as British subjects and they predicated the right to rebel against tyrannical government not on the privileges granted them as British subjects but on the natural rights which they shared with all men.

It has been noted, with some justification, that the deletions and amendments made to the Declaration by Congress in almost all cases contribute to both its force and its elegance. It is particularly remarkable, as one eminent critic has observed, that a public body chose to reduce rather than increase the number of words in a document so political. Indeed, it is a reflection on how widely accepted were Jefferson's philosophical views by the delegates meeting in Philadelphia that the Declaration, with all its eloquent subtleties, is as brief as it is. There was one important exception, however. Jefferson included in his draft a fierce denunciation of the slave trade – for which he blamed George III. This was correctly regarded by delegates from southern states as an oblique attack on slavery itself, and to Jefferson's chagrin they insisted on striking it out.

The Committee of the Whole, having completed its revisions, reported the Declaration to the Congress on the evening of July 4 where it was duly approved without dissent. The document was then ordered authenticated and printed, at which point John Hancock signed the authenticated copy "by order and in Behalf of the Congress." Five days later the New York provincial congress, meeting in White Plains, voted unanimously to ratify the Declaration, thus bringing New York into line with the other 12 colonies who had voted for independence on July 2. As a consequence of New York's action, the Congress directed on July 15 that the word "unanimous" be added to the document's title "Declaration of the Thirteen United States of America," and that it be engrossed on parchment. Finally, on August 2 the engrossed copy was signed by the members of the Continental Congress sitting in Philadelphia. Copies of the Declaration were dispatched throughout the colonics immediately upon its passage in early July, where it was reprinted in all the newspapers and read before solemn assemblies of soldier-citizens, now more acutely aware that the struggle in which they were then engaged was energized by the highest principle.

FURTHER READING

Becker, Carl L.: *The Declaration of Independence: a Study in the History of Ideas* (New York: Alfred A. Knopf, 1942).

Boyd, Julian P.: *The Declaration of Independence: the Evolution of the Text* (Princeton, NJ: Princeton University Press, 1945).

Dumbauld, Edward: *The Declaration of Independence and What it Means Today* (Norman: University of Oklahoma Press, 1950).

Fliegelman, Jay: *Declaring Independence: Jefferson, Natural Language and the Culture of Performance* (Stanford, Calif.: Stanford University Press, 1993).

Friedenwald, Herbert: *The Declaration of Independence: an Interpretation and Analysis* (New York: Macmillan, 1904).

Gerber, Scott Douglas: *To Secure These Rights: The Declaration of Independence and Constitutional Interpretation* (New York: New York University Press, 1996).

——: "Whatever Happened to the Declaration of Independence?" A Commentary on the Republican Revisionism in the Political Thought of the American Revolution," *Polity* 26 (Winter, 1993), 207–32.

Jayne, Allen: *Jefferson's Declaration of Independence* (Lexington: University Press of Kentucky, 1998).

Maier, Pauline: *American Scripture: Making the Declaration of Independence* (New York: Knopf, 1997).

White, Morton G.: *The Philosophy of the American Revolution* (New York: Oxford University Press, 1978).

PART III

Themes and Events, from 1776

CHAPTER THIRTY-THREE

Bills of rights and the first ten amendments to the Constitution

ROBERT A. RUTLAND

AMONG the many ironies created by the American Revolution was the colonists' insistence that they must fight the mother country in order to preserve their birthrights to English liberty under the law.

Five generations of American-born subjects had lived on the Atlantic seaboard (between Canada and Florida) and grown accustomed to exercising certain civil liberties when the break with Great Britain occurred. Proud emigrants from England spoke of their rights as Englishmen when they passed the Massachusetts Body of Liberties in 1641, giving solid form to their notions of a rule of law first embodied in the Magna Carta. Meanwhile, colonial charters in Maryland, Carolina, Pennsylvania, and New Jersey from 1639 onwards had encouraged English-American subjects to expect that the common law and certain personal rights were part of their heritage. These rights were sometimes called "natural," and in everyday practice they involved guarantees for jury trials, the rights of accused persons, and freedom of conscience, and provisions for peaceable assemblies, petitions to law-making bodies, and an exuberant (if often unbridled) press. The "not guilty" verdict that freed John Peter Zenger from a New York jail in 1735, after he was accused of printing sedition in his newspaper, was more than a legal landmark. Zenger's release indicated the unmistakable direction in which Americans were moving. Clearly there was more latitude for expressing ideas in America, but the colonists worshiped, assembled, and exercised other rights in the belief that their demonstrations were simply liberties conferred by the British Constitution. "We claim Nothing but the Liberty & Privileges of Englishmen, in the same Degree, as if we had still continued among our Brethren in Great Britain," the Virginian George Mason wrote during the Stamp Act aftermath of 1766 (Mason, 1970: 1, p. 71). Few American leaders would have disagreed.

1 The First Continental Congress

Parliamentary interference in domestic affairs ended the truce that followed the Stamp Act crisis. Punitive laws aimed at the citizens of Boston boomeranged to create unity in all the colonies. Amidst the tension exacerbated by the Boston Port Bill, delegates went to the First Continental Congress in Philadelphia to deliberate a course of action. Samuel Adams, the Boston firebrand who had labored overtime to bring on the crisis between Great Britain and her colonies, realized the importance of linking colonial grievances with time-honored British landmarks. "Should America hold up her own Importance to the Body of the Nation and at the same Time in one general Bill of Rights," Adams wrote to a Virginia delegate, "the Dispute might be settled on the Principles of Equity and Harmony restored between Britain and the Colonies" (Rutland, 1983, p. 26). When the delegates concentrated on propaganda weapons to use in prying concessions from Parliament, Adams's brainchild was a declaration of rights couched in terms any British MP would understand and ranging from assurance for jury trials to the old bug-bear of illegal "standing armies." The heart of the matter was the fifth resolution claiming that "the respective colonies are entitled to the common law of England," for had the mother country conceded this proposition there probably would have been no need for a Continental Congress, or a rebellion, or a bill of rights discussed beyond the pale of Westminster.

Before the Congress delegates adjourned they went a step further by sending a "Letter to the Inhabitants of Quebec," which may have been conceived as a propaganda ploy but still showed how the Americans were attached to the categorizing of rights. Congressmen admitted in the letter that French-speaking *Canadiens* might be ignorant of the "unspeakable worth" of an Englishman's rights, but since 1763 they had been George III's subjects and needed a lesson on their libertarian legacy. Rights similar to those in the Declaration passed two weeks earlier were listed and the delegates ordered this version of an Englishman's rights translated into French, published in pamphlet form, and dispersed where it would do the most good for their cause. The rights included jury trials and habeas corpus along with others that seemed to require a pedagogical tone. The importance of a free press, Congress insisted, involved "the advancement of truth." Did the Canadian subjects enjoy liberty of conscience? No, Congress answered, "God gave it to you," but Parliament denied the right by maintaining an established church in their midst (Rutland, 1983, p. 28).

If the American propaganda converted no Canadians, it reinforced local ideas on the right to resist perceived tyranny. Armed with the right of resistance, Washington took the time to write to English subjects in Bermuda for aid to his army besieging the British in Boston. "As Descendents of Freemen and Heirs with us of the same Glorious Inheritance," Washington told the Bermudians, "we flatter ourselves that tho' divided by our Situation, we are firmly united in Sentiment." Washington's plea was in vain, but the tone of his remarks was an echo of Jefferson's statement that he wanted Americans to move not forwards, but back-wards, to claim their hallowed rights as transplanted Englishmen. Once the American leaders shared this view, when the time came to break all bonds with England the next logical step was to rewrite the British Constitution in American terms. To that end, the Virginia Convention of 1776 met in Williamsburg in May, committed to preparing a declaration of rights and constitution to replace the British laws and traditions that lost all their force on American soil after July 4, 1776.

2 The Virginia Convention

Action by Virginia was expected, for her sons had been in the front ranks of the resistance movement from the start. Thus by mid-May 1776 the largest and most populous of the American colonies had (through her representatives) called on Congress "to declare the United Colonies free and independent states." A sister resolution from the Virginia Convention established a committee to prepare a declaration of rights and constitution for what would be the foremost of those free states. No time could be wasted. By late May a committee was busy with the details that independence required; and in this emergency George Mason, who had professed complete loyalty in 1766, showed he had undergone a change of heart and allegiance. "Things have gone such Lengths," Mason later recalled, "that it is a Matter of Moonshine to us, whether Independence was at first intended, or not" (Mason, 1970: 1, p. 435). What mattered was the business at hand, the drafting of an American bill of rights. "As Colo Mason seems to have the Ascendancy in the great work," a colleague noted, "I have Sanguine hopes it will be framed so as to Answer it's end, [which is] Prosperity for the Community and Security to Individuals" (Rutland, 1983, pp. 33–4).

Within days Mason's draft had been studied by the whole committee, slightly altered, and then sent to the full Convention. The opening resolution said that "all men are by nature equally free and independent," and they possessed immutable rights, "namely, the enjoyment of life and liberty, and the means of acquiring and possessing property, and pursuing and obtaining happiness and safety." Then came several general statements about the role of free government and the evils of hereditary office-holding, and praise for the separation-of-powers principle. Next came Mason's catalog of specific rights, enumerating the right of suffrage and a long list of limitations on governmental power. Free governments could not suspend laws, or deny accused persons their legal rights, or fine them excessively, or punish convicted criminals with "cruel and unusual" means; and general warrants for searches and seizures were condemned as "grievous and oppressive." Mason's draft went on to laud the use of juries in civil law suits as an ancient right that "ought to be held sacred," called freedom of the press "one of the great bulwarks of liberty," praised the use of militiamen and condemned standing armies "in time of peace ... as dangerous to liberty," and insisted that "the military should be under strict subordination to, and governed by, the civil power." Two resolutions concerned the jurisdiction of the gigantic state of Virginia and the need for a government based on "frequent recurrence to fundamental principles." The last resolve aimed a blow for religious liberty, perhaps broader than Mason had intended when he first wrote in support of "the fullest toleration" for religious sects. James Madison, serving his first term in an elective body, suggested that the clause be altered to an all-encompassing statement that "all men are equally entitled to the free exercise of religion, according to the dictates of conscience." Mason consented, the delegates approved, and for the first time in recorded history a public body had taken a stand in favor of freedom of religion for "all men" (Mason, 1970: 1, p. 289). (To complete the business, a decade later Jefferson's "Statute for Religious Freedom" was passed to erect in Virginia an impregnable "wall of separation" between church and state.)

The message that Virginians had given a priority to human rights as they fashioned a new government was soon broadcast to the other erstwhile colonies. On June 12, 1776 the Virginia Convention approved the 16 resolutions in its Declaration of Rights, and it was soon printed in the Williamsburg newspaper, then reprinted in other journals along the Atlantic seaboard week by week until, by harvest time, leaders in every corner of the new republic knew its contents. "We all look up to Virginia for examples,"

John Adams remarked to Patrick Henry (Rutland, 1983, p. 37). Adams's flattering statement proved to be prescient, for the Virginia model was to be copied (sometimes verbatim) in seven other constitution-drafting states. When the wave of constitution-writing ended in 1784, 11 states had some form of a bill of rights, while Connecticut and Rhode Island operated under provisions of their colonial charters that carried substantial guarantees for personal rights.

3 The First Ten Amendments

The idea that a free government must operate within the limits imposed by a bill of rights, to which Americans had given a new twist by taking traditions and writing them into their laws, impressed Europeans already influenced by Enlightenment precepts from Montesquieu, Beccaria, and other writers. Thus a similar approach was followed by the French National Assembly when it adopted a Declaration of Rights in 1789. Three months before the French acted, James Madison had already fulfilled a pledge he made during the ratification struggle over the Constitution drafted in 1787. Madison introduced in the House of Representatives of the First Federal Congress a series of amendments for the Constitution that was ratified only after promises concerning a bill of rights had been extracted from the leading proponents of ratification. Eschewing originality, Madison relied on the Virginia Declaration of Rights for most of his proposed amendments. Pared by a committee from the preliminary list of 16 to 12 amendments, ten were finally ratified in 1791, and these became the national Bill of Rights.

Fortuitously separated from the original Constitution, these ten amendments in time became the most admirable aspect of American law-making. The First Amendment, now considered the cornerstone of American civil liberty, prohibited congressional interference in religious matters and forbade federal curbs on freedom of speech, "or of the press; or the right of the people peaceably to assemble, and to petition ... for a redress of grievances." The Second Amendment reflected an American preference for a home-grown militia instead of a detested standing army, and hence proclaimed "the right of the people to keep and bear Arms." Other amendments (Three, Four, and Five) prohibited the peacetime quartering of troops with civilians, general search warrants, and "unreasonable searches and seizures" by federal officers, and gave accused persons safeguards against self-incriminating testimony or the threat of a double-jeopardy prosecution, while providing that nobody could "be deprived of life, liberty, or property, without due process of law." A speedy jury trial in the vicinity of the offense was guaranteed to the accused by the Sixth Amendment, along with other legal safeguards for criminal trials, and the Seventh Amendment reinforced the American partiality for jury trials "in Suits at common law." Excessive bails and fines were forbidden in the Eighth Amendment, as were "cruel and unusual punishments"; the wording was familiar since it was borrowed verbatim from the 1689 English Bill of Rights. The Ninth and Tenth Amendments broadened the concept of the people's liberties but provided nothing specific (and thus never became useful in practice). These guarantees applied only to the federal government, and left to the states the practical matter of enforcing promises of unfettered liberties.

To gain acceptance of his list of amendments, Madison had been forced to browbeat reluctant colleagues into their passage and transmittal to the state legislature for ratification. That process proved to be cumbersome but effective, and by December 1791 the first ten amendments to the Constitution were in place. To many Americans on both sides of the dominant issues of the day, and to Madison and Jefferson in particular, these amendments proved that the spirit of freedom aroused by the American Revolution had been rekindled. Although their full enforcement was delayed until the twentieth century, the first ten amendments – the American Bill of Rights – provided a symbol for the new nation's commitment to liberty under the law.

FURTHER READING

Brant, Irving: *The Bill of Rights: its Origin and Meaning* (Indianapolis: Bobbs-Merrill, 1965).

Conley, Patrick T. and Kaminski, John P. (eds.): *The Bill of Rights and the States* (Madison, WI: Madison House, 1992).

Dworkin, Ronald: *Freedom's Law: The Moral Reading of the Constitution* (Cambridge, MA: Harvard University Press, 1996).

Levy, Leonard W.: *Constitutional Opinions: Aspects of the Bill of Rights* (New York: Oxford University Press, 1986).

——: *Original Intent and the Framers' Constitution* (New York: Macmillan, 1988).

Mason, George: *The Papers of George Mason*, ed. R. A. Rutland, 3 vols. (Chapel Hill: University of North Carolina Press, 1970).

Rutland, Robert A.: *The Birth of the Bill of Rights, 1776–1791* (Boston: Northeastern University Press, 1983).

Schwartz, Bernard (ed.): *The Bill of Rights: a Documentary History*, 2 vols. (New York: Chelsea House, 1971).

CHAPTER THIRTY-FOUR

State constitution-making, through 1781

DONALD S. LUTZ

THE early state constitutions stand as the fulcrum in American constitutional history. On the one hand they were the culmination of colonial political forms, and thus embodied and summarized that rich experience. On the other hand, they formed the ground upon which first the Articles of Confederation and then the United States Constitution was erected. Even the Declaration of Independence owed most of its contents to the state constitutions. Although each state maintained a basic continuity with its colonial institutions, and despite considerable innovation in some instances, the state constitutions written between 1775 and 1781 converged towards a common model characterized by a dominant bicameral legislature, a weak executive, and annual elections using a broad electorate. The standard model gradually evolved towards a more balanced executive–legislative relationship, and moved the power for adopting constitutions from the legislature to the people. This evolution achieved full expression in the 1780 Massachusetts Constitution, which became a model for later state constitutions, and, some feel, for the United States Constitution as well. The 1776 Pennsylvania Constitution represented a more radical alternative, and for a while was widely copied. However, the struggle in state constitution-making between those seeking a more radical, direct form of democracy and those inclined towards a government based on direct popular consent but structured by balanced institutions to become indirect in its actual operation was eventually won by the latter persuasion.

1 Early Forms of Colonial Government

In order to lay out the essentials of this process, it is necessary to begin with a discussion of colonial political institutions. Every American colony had started as an aggregation of communities, with each community having its own local government. In New England these local communities were towns, in the South they were counties, and in the middle colonies they were a blend of towns and counties. Thus, although colony-wide governments had important duties, most government remained at the local level. Elected colonial legislatures served as umbrella organizations for local communities in their relationship with Britain, which was usually represented by a governor appointed by the Crown. Local and colony-wide government rested upon an electorate that was much broader than it was in England at the time, and a popularly elected legislature was the centerpiece of colonial politics at all levels. When colonists began to organize politically to contend with what they considered to be British tyranny, the wellspring of organization was the same electorate and set of local institutions that had been used to run colonial government, and from these sources were derived, not surprisingly, the same basic institutions that had been erected earlier.

The move from colony to statehood was not a sudden one arising from a single act, but the result of a political process that took several years. The process actually began during the middle 1760s when, in reaction to Acts of Parliament such as the Stamp

Act, the colonists in America developed experience in organizing for political resistance, an ideology to justify that resistance, and institutions for collective action independent of existing, legal ones. In many respects the Revolution began in 1765.

Events quickened in 1774, and the process that led explicitly to the writing of state constitutions began. Local committees of correspondence and safety began to spring up everywhere in early 1774 as a means of organizing for dealing with perceived threats from Britain. These committees were sometimes needed because royal governors failed to convene local or colony legislatures.

The committees of safety and correspondence successfully organized often took the lead in resisting Britain either by reconstituting their colonial legislature or replacing it with a parallel organization. The new or reconstructed legislature, now termed a convention or a provincial congress, constituted a political entity somewhere between a colony and an independent state. Typically, the congress appointed an executive committee to replace the recently departed governor, and these executive committees, frequently called committees of safety, ran provincial affairs when the congress was not sitting. The Continental Congress, composed of delegates from all the colonies, provided during these early years guidance to the several colonies.

The exceptions to this more or less spontaneous pattern that arose between 1774 and 1776 were Connecticut and Rhode Island, which had been virtually self-governing and had elected their own governors since the early 1660s. The Connecticut Charter of 1662 was essentially the same as the Fundamental Orders of Connecticut written and adopted by the colonists in 1639, while the Rhode Island Charter of 1663 preserved the government created by the colonists in the Acts and Orders of 1647. In both colonies, the governor was popularly elected, and the two charters functioned so effectively as constitutions that Connecticut and Rhode Island lived under them as fully constituted states well into the nineteenth century.

In the spring of 1776 John Adams introduced a resolution in the Continental Congress calling for all colonies that did not have a permanent constitution based upon the authority of the people to provide themselves with one. On May 10, 1776 the Continental Congress passed the resolution, and many considered this action equivalent to a declaration of independence. Still, it is difficult to point to one act as being decisive. Three of the 13 former colonies were already operating under state constitutions by the time Adams's proposal was approved, and most of the others were already at work on new documents. Every new state document adopted in 1776 and 1777 after approval of Adams's resolution, including the pre-Declaration constitutions of Virginia and New Jersey, was based upon a specific recommendation by the Continental Congress that a provincial congress write a constitution, and each individual recommendation by the Continental Congress was therefore, in effect, a declaration of independence. Indeed, the list of grievances that forms three-fourths of the official Declaration of Independence was essentially a compilation and summary of the lists of grievances found as preambles to the state constitutions adopted before July 4, 1776.

2   Massachusetts, New Hampshire, and South Carolina

The first state constitution put into effect was that of Massachusetts. On May 16, 1775 the Provincial Congress of Massachusetts suggested that the Continental Congress write a model constitution for it and the other colonies. Afraid of alarming those who still hoped for reconciliation with Britain, the Continental Congress did not oblige. But on June 2, 1775 it did suggest that Massachusetts consider its charter of 1691 as still in force and the offices of governor and lieutenant-governor as temporarily vacated. It also recommended that new elections held and a new governor's council be elected by the Provincial Congress. On June 19, 1775 the Massachusetts Congress elected a 28-member council that replaced the governor as executive. With this one alteration, the replacement of the governor with an executive council, the Massachusetts Charter of 1691 became the first state constitution. It was replaced in 1780 but in the meantime constituted, along with the Connecticut and Rhode Island charters, the most obvious link between colonial and statehood political institutions.

On October 18, 1775 New Hampshire put to the Continental Congress the same question that Massachusetts had asked the previous May. The intent of the request was to press the issue of independence, since a recommendation to frame a state constitution would be regarded by many as a declaration of independence. There was no functioning colonial charter which the Continental Congress could use to dodge the issue, so it advised the New Hampshire provincial congress to "establish such a government, as in their judgment will best produce the happiness of the people." The letter to the New Hampshire Provincial Congress added, however, that such reorganization should endure only until the conflict with Britain was over. In the face of this ambiguous recommendation, on December 21, 1775 the New Hampshire Provincial Congress met to draft a document. Prominent during these proceedings were Matthew Thornton, Meshech Weare, John Langdon, and John Sullivan. On January 5, 1776 New Hampshire became the first state to write a new constitution. As in Massachusetts, the major change from colonial practice was the election of a council by the House of Representatives. The council, the upper house in what was now a bicameral legislature, in turn elected a president who replaced the Crown-appointed governor.

South Carolina received the same recommendation from the Continental Congress on November 4, 1775. Prominent figures during the proceedings included John Rutledge, Christopher Gadsden, Henry Laurens, Charles Pinckney, and Rawlins Lowndes. As elsewhere, there was great hesitation to break openly with Britain, and the document approved on March 26, 1776 by the Provincial Congress of South Carolina amounted only minimally to a constitution. Designed to be in effect only until hostilities with Britain were over and passed as a normal piece of legislation by a legislature that underwent no special election to frame such a document, the "constitution" did not carry enormous authority

and would be replaced in 1778. The indeterminate nature of the constitution reflected the position of the South Carolina Congress that wrote and adopted it. When it wrote the document, this body was simultaneously the old revolutionary legislature, the constitutional convention, and the new legislature created by the old legislature. During the morning of March 25, 1776, the men in this group acted in the first two capacities; in the afternoon of the same day they acted as an Assembly under the new government and elected the Council, which became the new upper house in the new bicameral legislature.

These first three state constitutions had a half-hearted quality to them. Rather short and incomplete as foundation documents, written and adopted by a sitting legislature in a manner indistinguishable from normal legislation, and bearing the marks of compromise between proponents for independence and supporters of reconciliation, they could in truth be viewed either as temporary expedients implying no significant alteration in colonial status or as manifestations of the intent to break with Britain. If the American Revolution had not been successful, perhaps history would have recorded them as the former. However, since the Revolution did conclude successfully and no other constitutional action was necessary for Massachusetts, New Hampshire, and South Carolina to assert their independence, we can view these three documents as being the constitutions of states establishing their independence. Still, their transitional status is clearly reflected in the fact that, by the time the United States Constitution was written in 1787, only these three states of the original 13 felt the need to write and adopt a second state constitution – South Carolina in 1778, Massachusetts in 1780, and New Hampshire in 1784.

3 Virginia and New Jersey

There was no half-heartedness about the next constitution. The Virginia Provincial Congress had its share of reluctance about writing a state constitution, since such an action was viewed as equivalent to a declaration of independence. However, by

May 15, 1776 the Virginia Congress had instructed its delegates at the Continental Congress to vote for independence. Thus, when Virginia turned to writing a declaration of rights and a state constitution, there was no doubt in the minds of the delegates about what they were doing. Although a committee of the Provincial Congress was charged with the task, George Mason was largely responsible for both the Declaration of Rights adopted on May 27, 1776 and the new constitution adopted unanimously on June 29, 1776. The similarity in wording between Virginia's Declaration of Rights and that found in the first two paragraphs of the Declaration of Independence can probably be accounted for by the close juxtaposition in time between the two documents, and Mason's close connections with his fellow Virginian Thomas Jefferson. Many of Virginia's most visible leaders were not available. George Washington was leading the army, and Jefferson was away serving in the Continental Congress, as were Richard Henry Lee and George Wythe. However, Virginia was blessed with a host of good minds, and among these Edmund Pendleton, Richard Bland, James Madison, Patrick Henry, Edmund Randolph, and Mason were in attendance and prominent in debates.

The New Jersey Provincial Congress barely missed beating Virginia. Although it did not start drafting a document until June 21, 1776, it was able to adopt a new constitution on July 2, 1776, only nine days after starting. The Virginia Congress had put in very long hours to write its document in 45 days, so one might conclude that the New Jersey Congress either worked around the clock, or, as is likely, was not scrupulously concerned about its new document. It is doubtful that such speed would have been possible in either Virginia's or New Jersey's case if there had not been a long colonial experience upon which to draw and an existing form of government successful enough to warrant close approximation. That New Jersey's hastily framed and adopted constitution lasted 44 years before being replaced is testimony to the utility of having an existing political system upon which to model a new constitution. Prominent in New Jersey's deliberations were

the Reverend Jacob Greene, John Cleves Symmes, Lewis Ogden, Jonathan D. Sergeant, and Theophilus Elmer. Greene was the most influential and is reputed to have received considerable help from another cleric, the famous John Witherspoon.

4   Pennsylvania and Delaware

Thus, by the time the Declaration of Independence was adopted, seven fully constituted states were already in existence, counting Connecticut and Rhode Island. Almost three months elapsed before another group of state constitutions appeared, during late 1776. The brief hiatus allowed enough time for experience and evolving constitutional theory to support a number of innovations. The first of these was to use a specially elected rather than an already sitting legislature to write a constitution. Pennsylvania initiated the innovation, but Delaware, copying its neighbor, was the first to finish a constitution using the method.

Among proponents for independence there were two viewpoints concerning the method for writing new state constitutions. On the one hand were those who wished to emphasize the continuity between colonial and statehood institutions in service of the basic premise that Americans were breaking with Britain in order to preserve their constitutional tradition. The provincial congresses were the bearers of that continuity and thus were the bodies that should write constitutions. Also, during the colonial era constitution-like documents had occasionally been adopted by the legislature.

On the other hand, there were those who felt that the American commitment to popular sovereignty and the need to engage as many people as possible in support of the legitimacy of the new governments required both a distinction between constitutions and normal legislation and a more direct linkage with popular sentiment. Since masses of people could not directly write a constitution, the best alternative seemed to be a body elected specifically for the purpose. The second group gradually won its point as constitution-writing progressed. Americans would eventually move a step further and require that constitutions written by a special convention also be approved by the people at large in a referendum. As logical as this next step was, it was not taken until 1780, in the fifteenth state constitution adopted.

Delaware was slow in moving from a colonial assembly to a provincial congress, and did so only on June 15, 1776, when all public officials were requested to continue their power from that date forward in the name of the people of specific counties rather than in the name of the King. On July 27, 1776 elections were called for a legislature that was first to sit as a constitutional convention. This specially elected legislature convened on September 2, 1776 and adopted a declaration of rights nine days later. The process was speeded along by copying much of Pennsylvania's declaration. The convention adopted a constitution on September 20, 1776, with both George Read and Thomas McKean being mentioned as the document's primary authors. Despite the haste, the document would not be replaced for 39 years.

Pennsylvania's new state constitution was interesting for far more than its being written by a specially elected legislature sitting as a constitutional convention. More than any other state until that of Massachusetts in 1778–80, Pennsylvania worked at developing a constitution that would reflect the latest in constitutional theory. The result was the most radical document of the era, certainly the most innovative, and until the adoption of the 1780 Massachusetts document the primary contender as a model for future state constitutions. It was at least partially adopted by several states.

Like Delaware, Pennsylvania was slow to move to provincial status, and for the same reason – there were many who did not wish to replace the old government. The legal assembly proved unwilling to act, and the election of May 1, 1776 failed to alter significantly the make-up of the legislative assembly. The proponents for independence absented themselves from the legislature, thereby denying the assembly its quorum and rendering it impotent. Then a convention of county committees of inspection was called by the Philadelphia Committee of Inspection in an attempt to bypass the legal assembly. This convention met for a week in Philadelphia, and its 108 delegates in June scheduled an election for July 8, 1776. Ninety-six men were elected by an electorate that was potentially broader than usual, since the normal property requirements were waived, but was in fact narrower than usual, since it excluded from voting anyone who did not attest to their support for independence. These men became a legislature parallel to the legal one, but they first assembled as a constitutional convention and met across the street from the Continental Congress in Philadelphia.

The Pennsylvania Constitutional Convention was dominated by pro-independence men, and several of its more radically democratic members were prominent in writing the new constitution. Benjamin Franklin had a considerable impact on the document, but James Cannon, Timothy Matlack, and Cannon's good friend George Bryan (who was not a delegate but worked closely with Cannon nonetheless) were the primary authors.

Pennsylvania's Declaration of Rights owed much to Virginia's, although Pennsylvania's was both longer and more far-reaching. The resulting constitution, adopted along with the Declaration of Rights on September 28, 1776, was distinguished by creating a unicameral legislature, an extremely broad electorate, and a set of institutions designed to make the government as responsive to popular consent as possible. For example, in order to become a law a bill had to be passed in two consecutive sessions of the legislature. Since Pennsylvania had what became the standard American practice of annual elections, and bills approved the first time had to be published for public perusal, legislators were subject to explaining their past and future votes between elections. Also, the constitution established a statewide grand jury, called a Council of Censors, which was to be elected every seven years to review and evaluate all aspects of governmental action. Vermont would later copy most of this constitution, including its Council of Censors, and Georgia would emulate its unicameral legislature. Indeed, during the 1820s, 1830s, and 1840s the next generation of state constitutions would bring to widespread fruition many of the potentially highly democratic aspects of Pennsylvania's 1776 constitution.

5 Maryland, Connecticut, Rhode Island, North Carolina, and Georgia

On July 3, 1776 the Maryland Provincial Congress resolved that a new congress should be elected and that, in addition to acting as a legislature, it should write a new constitution. The electorate, defined by the same requirements as had chosen the current congress, was thus put on notice that they were selecting a constitutional convention as well as a legislature. Between August 14, 1776 and November 8, 1776 the body elected mixed constitutional matters with normal legislative concerns, although beginning in mid-October the congress focused on the constitution and deferred all but the most pressing legislative matters until a constitution had been approved. Charles Carroll of Carrollton and Samuel Chase were among the most energetic figures during the debates. A declaration of rights was approved on November 3, 1776, and the constitution itself was adopted and put into effect on November 8, 1776.

By this time state constitutions were taking on a standard pattern. Annual elections, a bicameral legislature (except in Pennsylvania and Georgia), and a weak executive were among the usual features of state constitutions. Maryland's was standard except for the striking innovation of using an electoral college to select the senate, an innovation that was used in the United States Constitution for electing the President. In one way or another, most of what is found in the national Constitution and its Bill of Rights can be traced back to one state constitution or another – usually several of the state documents.

Connecticut and Rhode Island had continued operating under their colonial charters as if they had been state constitutions all along. However, minor adjustments were made that amounted to recognition of complete independence. In October 1776, Connecticut's general assembly passed a law confirming that its 1662 charter was still in effect and functioning as its constitution. Rhode Island had passed a law in May of 1776 that the name of the King be stricken from all legal documents. These minor actions secured independence and ratified constitutional government under their respective colonial charters.

North Carolina followed a path that reflected its resolute commitment to independence and its participation in mainstream American constitutionalism. It had been among the earlier states to instruct its delegates to the Continental Congress to vote for independence (April 12, 1776). In the letter of instruction to its delegates, the Provincial Congress claimed competence to frame and adopt a state constitution, and on April 13, 1776 it established a committee to write a temporary constitution. It approved a number of resolutions on May 11, 1776 as being a "temporary civil Constitution," but these resolutions did little more than create a council of safety for the entire colony. The result was so obviously interim, and the institutional structure so minimal, that it is not usually considered a true state constitution.

In August 1776 the 13-member North Carolina Committee of Safety called an election for October 15, 1776 and announced that the elected representatives would also write a state constitution in addition to their regular legislative duties. The new congress first met on November 12, 1776, and by borrowing copiously from the constitutions of Virginia, Maryland, and Pennsylvania had their own constitution ready in about a month. Prominent in the debate were Richard Caswell, Willie Jones, Thomas Person, and Abner Nash. The resulting document was mainstream in content and contained no notable innovation. The Provincial Congress adopted the constitution on December 14, 1776 and the Declaration of Rights three days later.

Georgia followed a pattern almost identical to that of North Carolina. Georgia's Provincial Congress on April 15, 1776 adopted a set of eight "rules and regulations" that amounted to a transitional "constitution," although the document was not called a constitution in its title and is usually not considered one. The eight laws essentially ratified the position of the Provincial Congress as the legislature and reflected the loss of its Crown-appointed governor by establishing a president, executive council, and court system. On August 8, 1776 the Provincial Committee of Safety scheduled an election for a new congress that would write a constitution as well as pass legislation. The new congress began meeting in October 1776, and on January 24, 1777 it appointed a committee to prepare a final draft of a constitution. The new constitution was approved by the Congress on February 4, 1777.

Borrowing heavily from the constitutions of other states, as had North Carolina, Georgia opted for Pennsylvania's unicameral legislature. This departure from what was becoming the standard format for state constitutions led to immediate and continued agitation in Georgia for a new constitution, as it did in Pennsylvania. In 1789 Georgia replaced its 1777 document with one establishing a bicameral legislature. (Pennsylvania replaced its 1776 constitution with one creating a bicameral legislature in 1790.)

6 New York

Discussions about a new constitution began in New York early in the spring of 1776, but differences of opinion as to whether the current Provincial Congress had the power to write one or whether a new congress had to be explicitly elected for that purpose clouded the issue and delayed action. By late May the Provincial Congress had decided to call for an election, and the new congress assembled on July 9, 1776. Significant opposition arose concerning this method, an opposition that had until now been scattered and inconsequential in other states. Some argued that no legislature, however elected, had the power to approve a constitution. Rather, by right, only the people could approve a constitution and put it into effect. This opposition was not nearly strong enough to carry the day, but it gave explicit expression to some of the logical implications of popular sovereignty for constitution-making in the American mode.

Constantly distracted by the presence of British troops in New York, the new congress several times had to move in order to avoid capture. The delay that resulted had one important consequence in that it gave members of the Provincial Congress time to reflect on what other states had been doing, and, rather than merely borrow the institutions of others, New York began an historically important alteration in the developing pattern of state constitutions.

During the colonial era politics had revolved around a competition for power between a popularly elected legislature and a governor who was in most cases appointed by the Crown. Gradually the legislatures had gained the upper hand, and with the coming of Independence Americans were not eager to re-create strong executives which they associated with the abuse of power. Thus, except for the elected governors in Connecticut and Rhode Island, constitutions adopted before New York's generally had created an executive that was hardly worthy of the name. Appointed by the legislature, having few independent powers, carefully watched by a privy council drawn from the legislature, and sometimes simply replaced by a legislative committee, governors were no longer an important part of government in America.

New York began the process of defining an executive branch with sufficient independent powers to balance the legislature. Without such a balance the separation of powers as a constitutional strategy would have been impossible, and the United States Constitution might well have taken a radically different form. John Jay is generally credited with having actually written the document, with considerable help from Gouverneur Morris and Robert Livingston. Also prominent in the proceedings and influential on the outcome were James Duane, Robert Yates, and William Duer. The changes initiated in New York reached fruition in the 1780 Massachusetts Constitution, but one can see the New York document as a kind of half-way house. For example, the governor was made part of a council of revision which included the chancellor and supreme court judge as well. This council could veto acts of legislation, although the legislation could override the veto with a two-thirds vote. There was also a council of appointment composed of the governor and four senators which appointed the rest of the executive branch.

That such anemic powers can be considered a significant increase in executive strength is a measure of how debilitated the executive branch had become in the early state constitutions. In the 1780 Massachusetts Constitution, written largely by John Adams, the governor alone would have a veto, subject to two-thirds override, and the power of appointment with senate approval. The United States Constitution would follow the Massachusetts example, but New York began pointing the way in the constitution adopted by the Provincial Congress on April 20, 1777. Another notable feature of the New York Constitution was its use of reapportionment to produce equal representation by district in what amounted to a "one man, one vote" provision.

7   The Revisions of South Carolina and Massachusetts

South Carolina, not satisfied with its "provisional constitution" from two years earlier, adopted a new one on March 19, 1778. The general assembly that began its session in January 1777 had been elected with the understanding that it would write a new state constitution. The assembly followed a highly deliberative process that included hearings and on March 5, 1778 passed a new constitution as a piece of normal legislation. However, President John Rutledge (the chief executive in South Carolina was not at this time called governor) vetoed the bill on the technical grounds that since he had been sworn in to uphold the constitution of 1776 he could not legally approve its demise. Public sentiment was against him, he resigned, and on March 19, 1778 the new governor approved the legislation establishing the new state constitution.

On June 16, 1780 Massachusetts, after a lengthy process, adopted a constitution that replaced the 1691 charter. No constitution to this point had either been subjected to such a searching analysis or been the result of such careful process. The result was a state constitution that was to become the primary model for all later state constitutions as well as for the United States Constitution. Many believe that this document brought the design of state constitutions to its highest level during the eighteenth century.

The process began with an earlier constitutional proposal that was defeated. On May 2, 1776 the Massachusetts legislature, called the General Court, removed all references to the British Crown from the 1691 charter upon which it had based its legitimacy since June 19, 1775. It was clear that, despite claims to the contrary, Massachusetts government needed a more secure legal basis. There were desultory efforts during the summer of 1776 to draft a new constitution, but no document resulted. In September the General Court asked the towns to approve a method of adoption whereby the inhabitants would have an opportunity to examine the proposed constitution written by the General Court before the legislature also approved it. Seventy-four towns replied in the affirmative, which was a clear majority, but 23 towns said no with enough vigor to bring the process to a standstill.

There appeared to be strong sentiment, and cogent arguments, against the legislature writing and adopting a constitution that was supposed to limit the legislature. The minority opinion swayed the General Court to propose that the legislature write a constitution after voters had a chance to elect a new body and that the document be ratified by the electorate counted as individuals rather than as part of corporate units such as towns. Ratification would require two-thirds of all males free and over 21 years of age, which meant the property requirements were being waived in this constitutional referendum.

The House of Representatives (the lower house of the General Court), newly elected and authorized to write a constitution, met and began its work in June 1777. By February 1778 a new constitution had been drafted, and in March, for the first time in American history, a proposed constitution was submitted to a popular referendum. It was overwhelmingly defeated, 9,972 to 2,083. The arguments against the document were so diverse that some despaired of ever finding a majority in a referendum. However, many towns provided lengthy explanations for their opposition, and one in particular, the Essex Result written by Theophilus Parsons, clearly showed that more popular control rather than less would be required if the people were to be satisfied.

After mulling it over for a good while, the General Court asked the towns whether they would like to proceed with a new constitution if it were written by a constitutional convention instead of the legislature. By a margin of almost three to one the towns responded in the affirmative in April 1779. Elections were held for delegates to a constitutional convention, and the first such body in Western history, elected solely for the purpose of writing a constitution, convened on September 1, 1779. Samuel Adams, James Bowdoin, and especially John Adams were most prominent in the framing process. The final version was approved on March 2, 1780 and sent to the voters. The returns from the towns were very complex, and for a while no one could figure out how to count the votes. Finally, the convention simply declared that the draft had been accepted in its entirety by at least two-thirds of the voters, even when taking into account reservations about specific passages, and the constitution went into effect on October 25, 1780.

Massachusetts currently has the oldest functioning constitution in the world – in effect since 1780. The other early state constitutions, once Massachusetts, New Hampshire, and South Carolina adopted their second, permanent documents, would last, on average, more than half a century. The essential stability indicated by these figures resulted from the constitutions being built upon the secure base of a century and a half of colonial political experience.

8 Popular Sovereignty in the Colonies

The notion of popular sovereignty had never taken hold in Britain. The sovereignty of the King had been replaced by parliamentary sovereignty after the Glorious Revolution of 1688, a constitutional alteration signified by the convention of "king in Parliament." In America, however, political institutions were effectively based upon popular sovereignty, even though they still technically rested upon the legal authority of the British sovereign. By 1776 Americans

generally assumed that government in its formation and operation should rest upon popular consent, and this assumption was an important source of the controversy between Britain and America (see chapter 85, §§1 and 2). Americans did not elect Members of Parliament, were not represented there, and thus argued that Parliament could not pass laws directly affecting Americans without breaching the assumption of popular sovereignty. The British considered sovereignty to reside in Parliament and denied that popular consent was required either to create Parliament or to justify its acting. Parliament had not, after all, been created by an act of popular sovereignty. Americans, on the other hand, had for a century and a half been erecting their own legislatures on the basis of documents which they approved themselves.

Logic, therefore, would seem to dictate that new state constitutions should have a special status accorded them in keeping with the American practice of popular sovereignty. This did not at first occur. The initial constitutions were adopted by provincial and state legislatures rather than by constitutional conventions and were treated as pieces of legislation. Continuity between colonial political institutions was thereby assured, but the failure until 1780 to take the writing and approval of constitutions out of the hands of the legislature and thereby to distinguish between constitutions and normal legislation seemed implicitly to deny the basic American doctrine of popular sovereignty. The key to understanding this seemingly odd situation lay in how Americans viewed their legislatures.

During the colonial era the legislature was not generally viewed as distinct from the people. Rather, it was looked upon as a buffer between the people and the government (the Crown), with the majority of the legislature more or less automatically representing the interests of the community at large. The people could not all gather together to frame a constitution any more than they could gather to write legislation, so the body designed to embody the will of the people, the legislature, was the obvious instrument for both tasks. What made such a position plausible was the very close control maintained by the people over the legislature.

A much more broadly defined electorate than that found in England used relatively frequent elections as the primary instrument of control. Furthermore, since the community was viewed as being an entity in which everyone's long-term interests were the same, the strong link between an electoral majority and a legislative majority made them appear indistinguishable.

Events during the Revolution led to an altered view of the legislature. Factions within the population undercut the notion of a community with common interests. Divisions within the legislature furthered this perception, and the fact that legislative factional divisions frequently did not match those within the population led to many rethinking the assumed identity of the people with its legislature. Among the many important political matters that increasingly divided Americans was the animosity and suspicion between the wealthier, more cosmopolitan cities and towns along the coast, and the smaller, more locally oriented towns and counties further inland. The legislatures represented these splits with varying accuracy. The outcome of bitter legislative debate was more likely to reflect the balance of forces within the legislature than the pattern of sentiment in the general population.

The response to the new perceptions was a logical and straightforward one. If the legislatures could not be trusted any longer automatically to reflect the interests of the community, then the community had to become more directly involved with matters of government, especially when it came to the writing of constitutions. Put another way, whereas before popular sovereignty was seen as being transmitted from the people through the legislature in the writing of constitutions, increasing doubt concerning the reliability of the legislature led many to wish the legislature removed as a link in the chain of constitutional design.

Perceptions changed faster than the ability to design new institutions. Like everything else during the founding era, political processes tended to evolve rather than break out in revolutionary new directions. The assumption of popular sovereignty led to a gradual move towards popularly elected constitutional conventions

to write constitutions, coupled with popular approval of the document the convention produced. By 1780 the new institutional format for transmitting popular sovereignty was in place with the adoption of the Massachusetts Constitution.

9 The Common Political Culture of the Colonies

What is striking about the early state constitutions as a group is that, despite some institutional diversity, there were strong similarities among them that reflected a common political culture. That is, the political institutions developed in relative isolation by each colony converged over time, and during the revolutionary era the similarities became even stronger. To a certain extent this can be explained by the common practice of borrowing from other state constitutions, but it is doubtful that such borrowing would have been likely, or so successful, unless fundamental similarities had not already existed.

A general look at the 15 state constitutions adopted between 1775 and 1781 reveals the following patterns. All but two states used a bicameral legislature. Georgia went bicameral when it replaced its 1777 document in 1789, and Pennsylvania did so when it replaced its 1776 document in 1790. In all 15 constitutions the lower house was elected directly by the people. Although the percentage of white adult males enfranchised varied from state to state, on average the percentage was at least four times larger than it was in Britain.

Of the 13 constitutions creating bicameral legislatures, all but one had the upper house (senate) elected directly by the people, usually using the same electorate for both houses. Maryland, the one exception, used an electoral college to elect its senate. With only one exception, 1776 South Carolina, all constitutions provided for annual elections for the lower house. Of the 13 bicameral states, eight had annual elections for the senate, two had biennial elections, and three had staggered, multi-year elections.

In nine of the constitutions the executive was elected by the legislature, three used a popular election, and three used a popular election to identify the major candidates from among whom the legislature picked the governor. Eleven constitutions provided for annual elections of the governor, two for biennial elections, and two for triennial elections.

Twelve of the constitutions required voters to own property, usually about 50 acres or the equivalent, and three required voters to have paid taxes. Of the 13 bicameral legislatures, ten had the same property requirement to vote for the upper house as for the lower house. Of the nine states that involved the people in selecting the governor, eight used the same property requirement to vote for the governor as was required to vote for the lower house. All but one of the constitutions had property requirements to run for office, and nine for the 13 bicameral legislatures required more property to run for the upper house than for the lower house.

Ten of the early state constitutions included bills of rights. These bills of rights varied in length and detail, but generally had similar content. Virtually all rights later found in the United States Bill of Rights could be found in an earlier state constitution, usually in several.

Fourteen of the 15 constitutions were written and adopted by the respective state legislature, usually after an election where it was made clear that the new legislature would also write a new constitution.

Far from exhausting the similarities, the ones listed here indicate that, despite differences resulting from colonial experiences, regionalism, size, diversity, or degree of radicalism, there was a coherent shared political culture underlying the early state constitutions. Perhaps most obvious is the manner in which they produced political systems dominated by a bicameral legislature. The executive was invariably quite weak and a creature of the legislature. This was in keeping with both the colonial tendency to focus upon the legislature as the embodiment of the people, and the colonial distrust of executives and executive privilege.

Typical provisions in state constitutions towards this end, in addition to having the legislature elect the executive, included the requirement that the legislature approve

executive appointments, the creation of a small body drawn from the legislature to assist the governor in giving executive approval to legislation, granting pardons, or just generally telling him what to do. The extent to which separation of powers was actually found in state constitutions, aside from the 1780 Massachusetts document, was limited to a prohibition on anyone holding simultaneously a position in the legislative and executive branches.

In this regard, the United States Constitution built upon and evolved out of state constitutionalism. The national executive was stronger than state executives, although only somewhat more so than the Massachusetts governor. The movement away from the radical model of direct, popular consent was also only a matter of degree with respect to the Massachusetts Constitution. When taken together, some believe, the state constitutions and the political process that produced them show the extent to which the national Constitution was in most respects a logical development out of, or deflection from, what had come before rather than a radical departure or a conservative reaction. Regardless, the early state constitutions were the American laboratory for liberty, the base upon which the Continental Congress rested as it successfully prosecuted the War of Independence and the first true written constitutions in world history. Even those who prefer to minimize the impact of these documents upon the United States Constitution admit the importance of the early state constitutions in these other respects.

FURTHER READING

Adams, Willi Paul: *The First American Constitutions: Republican Ideology and the Making of the State Constitutions in the Revolutionary Era* (Chapel Hill: University of North Carolina Press, 1980).

Dargo, George: *Roots of the Republic: a New Perspective on Early American Constitutionalism* (New York: Praeger, 1974).

Green, Fletcher M.: *Constitutional Development in the South Atlantic States* (Chapel Hill: University of North Carolina Press, 1930).

Lutz, Donald S.: *Popular Consent and Popular Control: Whig Political Theory in the Early*

Constitutions (Baton Rouge: Louisiana State University Press, 1980).

——: *The Origins of American Constitutionalism* (Baton Rouge: Louisiana State University Press, 1988).

Main, Jackson Turner: *The Sovereign States, 1775–1783* (New York: New Viewpoints, 1973).

Nevins, Allan: *The American States During and After the Revolution, 1775–1789* (New York: Augustus M. Kelley, 1969).

Peters, Ronald M., Jr.: *The Massachusetts Constitution of 1780: a Social Compact* (Amherst: University of Massachusetts Press, 1978).

Selsam, J. Paul: *The Pennsylvania Constitution of 1776: a Study in Revolutionary Democracy* (New York: Octagon Books, 1971).

Thorpe, Francis N. (ed.): *The Federal and State Constitutions, Colonial Charters, and Other Organic Laws of the United States*, 7 vols. (Washington, DC: Government Printing Office, 1907).

Wood, Gordon S.: *The Creation of the American Republic, 1776–1787* (Chapel Hill: University of North Carolina Press, 1969).

CHAPTER THIRTY-FIVE

The Articles of Confederation, 1775–1783

JACK N. RAKOVE

THE Articles of Confederation established the first formal charter of national government for the 13 American states. Drafted by the Continental Congress in 1776 and 1777, the Articles were not formally ratified by all 13 states until February 1781. By then, many American leaders already sensed that Congress lacked effective authority to carry out even the tasks that the Articles had assigned to it. Efforts to amend the Articles began as early as 1781; ultimately they culminated in the Federal Convention of 1787, which proposed the new Constitution that replaced the Articles of Confederation in March 1789.

1 Resistance and Confederation

When resistance to the claims of parliamentary authority over America reached crisis proportions in the summer of 1774, 12 of the 13 colonies appointed delegates to the Continental Congress that met in Philadelphia in September and October (only distant Georgia went unrepresented). A Second Congress of all 13 colonies assembled in May 1775, after war had erupted in Massachusetts. Save for a short adjournment that summer, this unicameral body, which was formally known as the United States in Congress Assembled, served continuously as the effective national government of the new republic for the remainder of the war. The power Congress exercised ultimately rested on popular support and the success of the struggle against Britain. But by 1775 some delegates concluded that its authority should rest on a more solid foundation.

Drafting formal articles of union would help to clarify the relations between Congress and the individual colonies (later states). Equally important, such a step would give Congress a credible basis for negotiating with potential allies in Europe.

Those delegates who believed that the British Government was intent on crushing the rebellion hoped that independence would be declared only after the creation both of a formal union and of legal governments in the individual states. By contrast, a number of delegates still hoped for reconciliation with Britain. In their view the act of confederating was tantamount to independence, and they accordingly opposed allowing Congress even to discuss the topic at all. Several rough drafts of a confederation had in fact been prepared by the winter of 1776. Benjamin Franklin presented the best known of these to Congress in August 1775; members of the Connecticut delegation prepared at least two others. But, in practice, the pressing need to maintain consensus within Congress favored the position of the moderate delegates well into 1776.

By early June, however, even they sensed that independence was imminent. On June 7 Richard Henry Lee of Virginia offered a set of resolutions calling for independence, the negotiation of foreign alliances, and the drafting of a confederation. Five days later Congress appointed a 13-member committee (one from each colony) to draft Articles of Confederation. Its leading member was John Dickinson of Pennsylvania, the celebrated author of *Letters from a Farmer in Pennsylvania*, a pamphlet that had played a crucial role in rousing resistance to the Townshend Duties of 1767. The most influential opponent of independence still sitting in Congress, Dickinson had long feared that separation from Britain would lead to endless conflict among the American colonies. Other members of the committee, such as Samuel Adams of Massachusetts and Roger Sherman of Connecticut, were far more militant.

2 Drafting the Articles

Although the committee kept no records of its deliberations, Dickinson evidently prepared the original set of articles: a first draft in his hand came to light only in the middle of the twentieth century. Dickinson envisioned a confederation that would restrain the autonomy of the states in significant ways. One notable article would have protected the freedom of religious exercise within the states while prohibiting the latter from making any further alteration in the existing structure of church–state relations, a recurring source of controversy throughout America. More important, Congress was to be vested with exclusive authority over peace and war, the conduct of foreign relations, the direction of the war, the resolution of disputes between states, and the disposition of the vast and unsettled western lands whose ownership was already the source of bitter conflict and rivalry among the states.

The committee met frequently during the second fortnight of June. Most of Dickinson's original plan survived its scrutiny (though the article on religion was rejected). A revised set of articles was reported to Congress on July 12. By then Dickinson had left Congress, and, in his absence, none of the other members of the committee appears to have assumed the role he might have played as leading spokesman for their plan.

The draft articles were debated in a committee of the whole house from mid-July until August 20, 1776, when Congress ordered the printing of a revised report that would provide the basis for a final round of discussion. Some of the most important provisions the Dickinson committee had proposed were accepted with little if any

dissent. Indeed, it is striking how little controversy arose over the task of dividing the basic functions of government between the union and the states. There was nearly unanimous agreement that Congress should retain exclusive control over the great affairs of war and foreign relations, while the states preserved full legal authority to regulate their "internal police" – that is, all the ordinary business of daily life. The states would retain the right to levy their own taxes and to determine how they would mobilize the other resources of men and materiel that the war would require. But, in both instances, the delegates expected that the states would faithfully execute whatever measures Congress asked of them.

On the whole, the surviving records of the deliberations of July–August 1776 do not suggest that the delegates were deeply concerned with the perplexing theoretical issues that are inherent in any system of federal government. There was no discussion, for example, of the whole question of the location of sovereignty – though that issue had been at the heart of the previous decade of constitutional debate with Britain. Instead, the framers of the Articles sought to divide major powers of government in a pragmatic way, creating two broad and largely exclusive spheres of authority for the union and the states, and trusting to patriotism and the imperatives of war to persuade these two levels of government to cooperate for the common good.

But if abstract questions of sovereignty and federalism did not figure prominently in the debates of 1776, other concerns of a different nature threatened to prevent either Congress or the states from agreeing upon any draft of confederation. The true sources of controversy centered on three other issues in which certain groups of states feared that their particular interests would be jeopardized.

The first of these involved the question of representation and voting in Congress. The drafting committee had followed the precedent set by the First Congress of 1774 of giving each state one vote in Congress, regardless of disparities in population and wealth. While delegates from the populous states of Pennsylvania, Virginia, and Massachusetts vigorously opposed the injustice of this measure, their colleagues from such small states as Rhode Island, Maryland, and Delaware argued just as vehemently that they deserved an equal vote because they were as fully committed to the revolutionary cause as their larger neighbors.

The problems posed by the two other controversial issues reflected the delegates' awareness that winning independence would not come cheaply. Northern and southern delegates disagreed whether the common expenses of the war should be apportioned among the states on the basis of total population (including slaves) or free population only. Similarly, a coalition of five states whose western boundaries were fixed by their colonial charters (Rhode Island, New Jersey, Delaware, Pennsylvania, and Maryland) argued that the vast territorial claims of the so-called landed states (of which Virginia was the most important) should be transferred to Congress in order to create a common stock of lands whose later sale could provide a relatively painless way to discharge the national debt. Only the united effort of all the states would bring the interior under American control, they argued; what would have to be gained at common expense should be used for the common benefit. On this issue the landed states were adamant, and they succeeded in striking every proposal designed to vest Congress with authority over western lands.

Continuing disagreement over these three issues of voting, expenses, and western lands helps to explain why Congress largely abandoned discussion of confederation after August 20, 1776. The tentative decisions the Committee of the Whole had taken on these points reflected neither compromise nor consensus. The objections of the dissenting minorities remained so strong that many members doubted whether the state legislatures could ever be brought to ratify the Articles. Moreover, the repeated defeats the American Army suffered in the summer and fall of 1776 left Congress with little time to continue its debate over the confederation.

3 Completing the Confederation

Not until April 1777 was Congress able to return to the Articles. Almost immediately, the delegates approved one amendment of major importance. Thomas Burke, a new delegate from North Carolina, proposed an article affirming that each state would retain "its sovereignty, freedom, and independence, and every power, jurisdiction, and right, which is not by this Confederation expressly delegated" to Congress.[1] After brief debate, this formula was approved by 11 of the 13 delegations. While it made no substantive changes in the actual allocation of power between the union and the states – one would have to look elsewhere in the Articles for that – it strongly implied that the ultimate power of sovereignty resided in the states. Yet this provision (Article 2 of the completed Confederation) had its ambiguities; even Burke later acknowledged that "the United States ought to be as One Sovereign with respect to foreign Powers, in all things that relate to war or where the States have one Common Interest."[2]

Once Congress adopted Burke's amendment, it soon found itself mired in the impasse over representation, expenses, and western land. By the summer of 1777 the subject of Confederation was again tabled. It was not resumed until October, when Congress (resettled at York, Pennsylvania, following the British occupation of Philadelphia) finally mustered the determination to complete the Confederation.

Two expedient calculations probably led to this decision. First, Congress was anxious to respond to the growing problem of inflation and the accompanying depreciation of its paper currency by submitting a comprehensive set of financial resolutions to the states. Second, Congress hoped that the dramatic American victory at Saratoga would at last persuade the French Government to conclude a treaty of alliance. In both cases, the delegates appear to have concluded that the completion of the Articles of Confederation would strengthen the hand of Congress *vis-à-vis* the states and its potential ally.

There were, however, no magical solutions to the problems that had delayed the completion of the Articles for more than a year. The speed with which Congress now dispatched these issues indicates that the delegates had decided to accept imperfect solutions in the interest of completing the Confederation. The issues of voting and western lands took only one day each to resolve. On Octobr 7 Congress endorsed the one state, one vote precedent of 1774; on the 15th it rejected a final flurry of motions designed to give the union the power to set state boundaries and manage the land that would then lie beyond. The one issue that took time to resolve was the apportionment of expenses, which consumed five days of maneuvering before Congress narrowly accepted an unwieldy formula to base each state's share of the costs of national government on the value of its settled lands "and the buildings and improvements thereon."[3] By November 15, 1777 Congress had at last completed its work, and was prepared to submit the 13 Articles of Confederation to the states.[4]

The first three Articles gave the Confederation its title ("The United States of America"), recognized the principle of state sovereignty in the language of Thomas Burke's amendment, and declared the general purpose for which the states had united. Article 4 prohibited the states from discriminating against each others' citizens, provided for the extradition of fugitives, and obliged each state to give "full faith and credit" to the judicial determinations of other states. Article 5 defined the institutional character of Congress: it would meet annually; delegates could serve no more than three years out of every six, and were subject to recall by their states at any time; each state would have one vote.

The sixth Article demonstrated that the reserved sovereignty of the states was less than absolute by imposing a series of restrictions on their authority, especially in the general realm of external affairs. Article 7 dealt with the appointment of military officers, and Article 8 regulated the apportionment of common expenses among the states.

Article 9, enumerating the powers of Congress, was the most important. It gave Congress "the *sole* and exclusive right and power of determining on peace and war," conducting foreign relations, and "directing [the] operations" of military and naval forces. It established a detailed if cumbersome procedure for adjudicating disputes between states without allowing Congress itself to become a direct party to their resolution.

Article 9 also gave Congress the authority to determine the expenses of the union and to appropriate the necessary funds; to emit bills of credit and borrow money; to set the size of the army and to require the states to raise the necessary numbers of men. In exercising all of these major powers, the consent of nine states would be necessary.

The concluding four Articles tied up a few loose ends. Article 10 prohibited the committee of the states – a body made up of one member from each state, which was to sit in the recess of Congress – from exercising any of the major powers that required the approval of nine states. Article 11 invited Canada to join the Confederation, but no other state was to be admitted without the consent of nine states. Article 12 extended the "public faith" to all debts contracted by the union before the formal completion of the Confederation. Finally, Article 13 obliged the states to "abide by the determinations" of Congress "on all questions which, by this confederation, are submitted to them." It also stipulated that the Articles must be ratified by all the states, with later amendments to be first proposed by Congress and then similarly approved by all the states.

The conditions under which the Articles of Confederation were framed had not encouraged the delegates to give sustained thought to the long-term nature of the union they hoped to consolidate. By 1777 their major concern was simply to complete a document that the states could quickly and unanimously approve. Had they proposed vesting Congress with authority to levy its own taxes or to coerce delinquent states into fulfilling their federal obligations, the prospects for ratification would have diminished. Rather than consider whether Congress would be able to command the continued allegiance of the states, the framers simply presumed that the states would have to do their duty.

4   Ratification

The hope that the Confederation would be ratified quickly came to nought. By June 1778 it was known that ten of the state legislatures had either ratified or were preparing to ratify the Articles. With the first ambassador from France expected to arrive soon, Congress brushed aside the numerous amendments that had been proposed by the states, and proceeded with a partial but legally meaningless ceremony of ratification. Many delegates expected the three remaining states – Delaware, New Jersey, and Maryland – to fall into line. These states balked at signing the Confederation because it failed to provide for the creation of a national domain in the West. By 1779 Delaware and New Jersey had swallowed their objections – though only under protest. But Maryland held out until February 1781, and the Articles did not take effect until March 1, 1781. By then the landed states had initiated the process of ceding their western land claims, which eventually led to the creation of a national domain northwest of the Ohio River. But by then, too, the war itself was almost over: the climactic victory at Yorktown was only months away. The Articles of Confederation thus proved largely irrelevant to the victory they were meant to secure.

More than that, the nearly three and a half years that had elapsed between the submission of the Articles to the states and the final act of ratification had revealed that many of the assumptions that had guided the framers of 1776–7 were flawed. The failure of the states to meet congressional requisitions for men, supplies, and taxes seemed to demonstrate that the Articles had placed too much confidence in the willingness and ability of the states to serve as the administrative agents of the union. Indeed, Congress had begun considering the need to secure amendments even before the Confederation took effect.

Some delegates were attracted to the idea of giving Congress "coercive" powers over the states. But how could a recalcitrant state be coerced to do its duty? and how could the states ever be expected to approve so drastic an increase in federal power? Rather than pursue so impractical a measure, most members instead favored asking the states to grant Congress independent sources of revenue. On February 3, 1781 – several weeks before the Articles were to take effect – Congress asked the states to grant it the power to collect a duty

(or impost) on foreign goods imported in America.

This modestly drawn measure drew intense opposition in Rhode Island, which effectively blocked its adoption. But the problems the impost was meant to address did not disappear. Even with the war winding down in 1782, Congress needed revenues both to meet its current expenses and to service the enormous national debt incurred during a long and costly war. At the urging of Robert Morris, its newly appointed Superintendent of Finance, Congress spent the months between the summer of 1782 and the spring of 1783 struggling to frame a comprehensive revenue program. After a prolonged period of intense political maneuvering marked by rumors of an insurrection of unpaid soldiers and various threats from Superintendent Morris, Congress proposed (April 18, 1783) two new amendments to the Confederation. One was a revised version of the impost; the other proposed altering the method for calculating each state's share of the national expenses from the impractical formula based on the value of improved lands to a simple apportionment on the basis of population (with slaves counted at the three-fifths ratio that the Federal Convention of 1787 would later adapt to the issue of representation).

Like the impost of 1781 – as well as two further amendments that Congress proposed a year later – these two measures failed to secure the unanimous approval of the states. With the struggle for independence successfully concluded, it quickly became apparent that the states no longer shared the same overriding sense of a common national interest that had carried them, though with great difficulty, through the war. It would take only a few years for many Americans to conclude that the Articles of Confederation no longer provided an adequate framework either for mediating conflicting interests or for carrying out national policy on those rare occasions when Congress proved capable of decision.

REFERENCES

1 Ford, Worthington C.: *Journals of the Continental Congress, 1774–1789*, 34 vols.

(Washington, DC: US Government Printing Office, 1904–37): vol. 9, 908.

2   Smith, Paul H.: *Letters of Delegates to Congress, 1774–1789*, 13 vols. to date (Washington, DC: US Government Printing Office, 1976–): vol. 8, 435.

3   Ford, vol. 9, 800–1.

4   For the complete text, see Ford, vol. 9, 907–25.

FURTHER READING

Jensen, Merrill: *The Articles of Confederation: an Interpretation of the Social-Constitutional History of the American Revolution, 1774–1781* (Madison: University of Wisconsin Press, 1940).

——: *The New Nation: a History of the United States during the Confederation, 1781–1789* (New York: Alfred A. Knopf, 1950).

Onuf, Peter S.: *The Origins of the Federal Republic: Jurisdictional Controversies in the United States* (Philadelphia: University of Pennsylvania Press, 1983).

Rakove, Jack N.: *The Beginnings of National Politics: an Interpretive History of the Continental Congress* (New York: Alfred A. Knopf, 1979).

CHAPTER THIRTY-SIX

The War for Independence, to Saratoga

DON HIGGINBOTHAM

IN the winter of 1774–5, the British ministry, frustrated and angered by a decade of disturbance and controversy in the North American provinces, elected to respond with military force. To be sure, scarlet regiments had been sent to Boston in 1768 and again – in larger numbers – in 1774. But their presence in the Masssachusetts capital had scarcely intimidated the so-called Whigs or patriots there, nor had those steps had a sobering effect on popular leaders in the other English-speaking seaboard colonics. The landing of 3,500 troops in Massachusetts in 1774, the combining of civil and military authority in the appointment of General Thomas Gage as successor to the departing Governor Thomas Hutchinson, and the passing of the Coercive Acts had instead resulted in the First Continental Congress and in a groundswell of American sympathy for the beleaguered Bostonians.

1 Britain's Opening Military Gambit: Lexington and Concord

If the ministry did not want an all-out war, it did instruct General Gage to engage in a major display of muscle; the Massachusetts politicians would surely be sobered by such an act. So it was, then, that Gage, hesitant to move on his own in such a tense atmosphere, dispatched a troop column on the night of April 18 to destroy the Massachusetts Provincial Congress's military stores at Concord. Recently formed Massachusetts minutemen companies responded to the challenge. Although the next morning the locals were dispersed at Lexington Green,

Lieutenant Colonel Francis Smith's column found only a portion of the munitions that had been assembled at Concord. They also found, on their return journey to Boston, an aroused countryside as minuteman companies from surrounding communities subjected them to such a deadly rain of musketry that they were fortunate to reach the safety of the city, their casualties in all categories numbering approximately 275.

Rather than pulling back or giving pause, Britain sought a military solution to its decade-old political problem: the constitutional relationship between the metropolitan center and the colonial peripheries of empire. It did so without taking a long view of the implications. While the mailed fist approach never received a full airing in official quarters, it did trigger warnings of overwhelming costs, of French and Spanish intervention, and, as Lord Chatham put it, of the wreckage of both Britain and America. But instead of acknowledging concerns of the parliamentary opposition, the government only half-heartedly entertained ideas for halting the bloodshed before the American war became a full-scale international conflict.

These schemes need not long detain us. In 1776 Admiral Richard, Lord Howe, and his brother General William Howe were appointed joint Commanders-in-Chief in America and peace commissioners, but, as commissioners, they could merely listen to American grievances and inform the colonists that their views would receive a hearing in London *after* they put down their arms. The Howes' peace offer (such as it was) had no chance of success, and in fact it was only presented to America after the

Declaration of Independence. The second British peace initiative also amounted to too little, too late. Cobbled together after Burgoyne's disaster at Saratoga, it essentially proposed to turn the clock back to 1763 in terms of British–American relations and to renounce Parliament's right to tax the colonists. Reaching America after the signing of the Franco-American alliance of 1778, it was as ill-timed as the previous olive branch.

2   The Military Resources of the Colonists

Even so, the American cause did not rely solely on Britain's international difficulties. The colonists drew up military ideas and practices that had served them reasonably well in the century and a half before Lexington and Concord. The militia, seemingly a dying institution in Stuart England, became the colonists' mainstay of defense in the seventeenth century. Provincial publicists never tired of touting the virtues of the militia over professional or "standing armies." The sturdy yeomanry of Virginia or Massachusetts were infinitely superior to long-enlisted European soldiers who fought for pay and not for patriotism. John Adams averred that the militia was a cornerstone of New England society, along with the county court, the town meeting, and the Church. The Reverend Ebenezer Gay praised the universality of militia service. There were "no Exceptions ... for the High, nor the Low; for the Rich, nor the Poor; for the Strong, nor the Weak; for the Old, nor the Young." If the militia bore the burden of defense, it still fell short of its admirers' claims. Normally the militia served as a body from which volunteers and draftees were obtained for more extended duty in reconstituted militia companies and regiments. As the years passed, people on the upper end of the social scale received exemptions, and those at the very bottom – "loose, idle, dissolute persons" – fell outside the system.

While the eighteenth-century militia continued to be a valuable instrument of social control at home – it put down riots and disorders in the colonial period and disarmed and tyrannized the loyalists in the Revolution – its place in the more sophisticated post-1688 imperial wars was taken by semi-professional forces, which were a hybrid between the militia and a standing army. The term applies to men who received a bounty in return for a year's enlistment and agreed to fight outside their own colonies and be governed by a more rigorous military code than applied to the militia. Their officers also saw themselves as a cut above their militia counterparts, whom they criticized for their ignorance and lack of leadership. Semi-professional officers not infrequently devoured European military treatises and hoped to learn first-hand from observing British regulars during the French wars of the mid-century.

Massachusetts and Connecticut in particular felt heavy demands for manpower in these struggles. Massachusetts provided the bulk of the 1745 New England expeditionary force that employed European siege tactics in the capture of the fortress of Louisburg on Cape Breton Island. So many Connecticut officers and men shouldered arms in the Seven Years' War that the province's military organization became an American likeness of a mercenary European army.

Washington, Virginia, and the Continental Army

The case of Washington and Virginia is especially instructive because of the former's subsequent role in the War of Independence. Washington had not yet reached the age of 24 when he became colonel of the Virginia Regiment in 1755, but he had read several military books, talked extensively to older Virginians who had held British commissions, and kept notes on British Army procedures he observed while an unofficial aide to General Edward Braddock before the latter's death in the Battle of the Monongahela. Despite innumerable obstacles during his three-year command, Washington made impressive strides in the training and disciplining of his regiment. He and his officers thought of themselves as professionals and petitioned British authorities to take their unit into the royal service. If they were rebuffed in these efforts, they nonetheless drew praise from Generals John Forbes and Robert Monckton.

Seventeen years later when the Second Continental Congress, meeting in the aftermath of Lexington and Concord, adopted the New England forces besieging General Gage in Boston and appointed Washington their Commander-in-Chief, the legislators were taking a logical and predictable step in the history of early American military institutions: from seventeenth-century militia, to eighteenth-century semi-professional forces, to professional army in 1775. In some respects this new Continental Army, as it was called, appeared to be an extension of a semi-professional colonial force of the Seven Years' War, for many of its officers had held commissions in the last imperial war, and its soldiers were enlisted for a year or less.

Although a second and smaller American army under Richard Montgomery and Benedict Arnold was driven out of Canada after initial successes, Washington's main American Army was not tested by its British counterpart in Boston – except in the bloody but inconclusive Battle of Bunker Hill, which occurred before the Virginian's arrival in the Bay colony. Those months from July of 1775 to March of 1776 were crucial in two ways: one, Washington demonstrated that an American army need not be feared by its own citizens; and second, he had time to bring order and system to his command as he watched the enemy from his well-entrenched positions overlooking the city. Finally, William Howe, Gage's successor, sailed away on March 17, St. Patrick's Day, preferring to regroup, await reinforcements, and attack where the Americans seemed more vulnerable than in Massachusetts, the hotbed of American radicalism.

3   The British Campaign of 1776

The campaign of 1776 saw Britain take the offensive; but it is hardly accurate to say, as did earlier generations of historians, that she possessed the lion's share of the advantages. Problems of transportation, communication, and supply bulked large two hundred years ago. So did her lack of sufficient men

under arms. Her generals and admirals were competent enough, though little more than that – Generals Gage, Howe, and Clinton were too cautious; Burgoyne and Cornwallis were too aggressive. Admiral Howe was hesitant and perhaps more interested in winning over the colonists by the carrot than by the stick; Sir Henry Clinton called Howe's naval successors – Gambier, Graves, and Arbuthnot – "old women"; they fumed and strutted and got along poorly with their army counterparts. The generals in America, who were Members of Parliament with alliances to rival political factions, also distrusted each other.

The recruitment of Germans and loyalists

With human resources decidedly limited in an age when the productive elements of society were excluded from shouldering arms, Britain turned to her time-honored tradition of buying military manpower. That undertaking always included looking to the German states. This traffic in human flesh, so roundly condemned by Enlightenment philosphers, brought 30,000 German troops from six principalities into the American war. Valuable though they were, their presence deeply embittered Americans and doubtless converted many fence-sitters to the idea of independence. But even greater animosities stemmed from Britain's recruitment of the loyalists, from her urging royalist-oriented colonists to spy, obstruct, and fight their fellow Americans. British authorities, as well as loyalist leaders such as Joseph Galloway, persisted for years in the notion that opposition to the Crown was the work of a small minority that intimidated the larger populace. Acknowledging that for the time being British forces were inadequate to throttle the rebellion in New England, the ministry sent a small fleet in the spring of 1776 to the coast of the Carolinas to tap this reputed source of fidelity. The outcome should have demonstrated the myth of ubiquitous loyalism: the rebels' destruction of a 1,400-man Tory contingent at Moore's Creek Bridge near Wilmington, North Carolina, and the repulse of the royal naval squadron at Charles Town, South Carolina, in June of

1776. Although illusions persisted, Britain undertook no new significant southern ventures for several years.

The middle colonies were the focus of British operations in 1776 and for some time thereafter. Lord George Germain, the Colonial Secretary and director of the war effort (instead of the non-assertive First Minister, Lord North), was an eternal optimist, but even he acknowledged that it would take a massive show of force to crush the rebellion in a single campaign. Certainly he expended abundant energy that year as the creaky machinery of Hanoverian government assembled huge quantities of supplies, dozens of vessels, and a formidable fighting force. In fact, Germain and company made their greatest effort in that year: raising and sending to America the most imposing military expedition in English history, a feat never again equaled in the war and, in relative terms, never repeated until the twentieth century.

The battle for New York City

In August of 1776 the Howe brothers rode at anchor before New York City. Their armada, drawn mainly from England but also containing elements from the former garrison at Boston and from the abortive southern expedition, consisted of 73 warships carrying 13,000 seamen and several hundred transports bearing 32,000 troops. Their strategy was to take New York City, cut off New England from the other rebel colonies, and then crack the heart of the rebellion, which they were convinced was in the Puritan colonies. In the process, they hoped to draw Washington into a major battle that would bring a climactic triumph. In all of this Germain and the Howes were supposedly in agreement. But, as we have already indicated, the Howes were also peace commissioners, and the Admiral in particular seems to have hoped to persuade the rebels to lay down their arms before the above-mentioned scenario unwound. To what extent these desires influenced his conduct and carried over to his brother, the General, will probably never be known.

But we can say that the campaign opened on a high note for the British, a low note

for the Americans, although it concluded as something of a draw. Washington was eager to defend New York City, as was the Continental Congress, not only because of its strategic importance but also because New York had been a divided colony and loyalism was still potent there. Given the various islands, bays, and rivers in the area, Washington faced the danger of being isolated and cut off from retreat; but he became even bolder when he ferried the bulk of his militia-dominated army from Manhattan to Brooklyn on Long Island, where William Howe's army had assembled. Digging in on Brooklyn Heights, Washington hoped Howe would assault him frontally, with the kind of crimson carnage that had marked Bunker Hill. Instead, the British executed a skillful nocturnal flanking movement and hammered unsuspecting American units that had been posted in advance of the main line. American losses in all categories came to nearly 1,500 compared with Howe's fewer than 400. Howe, as was to be his custom, did not immediately press his advantage. With his back to the water, Washington subsequently under cover of darkness transported his remaining 9,000 men back to Manhattan.

Although Washington had reunited the two wings of his army on Manhattan, his situation remained extremely precarious. He risked the danger of a retreat northwards being cut off by a British landing at the far end of the island. General Howe's coming ashore at Kip's Bay on September 15 posed that very threat, but the Briton failed to drive swiftly across the island and Washington pulled back just in the nick of time. The next two months witnessed a series of minor battles and skirmishes at Harlem Heights, White Plains (on the mainland), and elsewhere as Howe continued his unsuccessful efforts to encircle Washington's army, which capitalized on a measure of luck and Howe's lethargic movements. But the Briton did overrun and capture the garrison of Fort Washington, which the American commander had unwisely left behind on Manhattan.

With the greater New York City area and its nearby islands securely in British hands, Washington fled across New Jersey and over the Delaware River, while Howe,

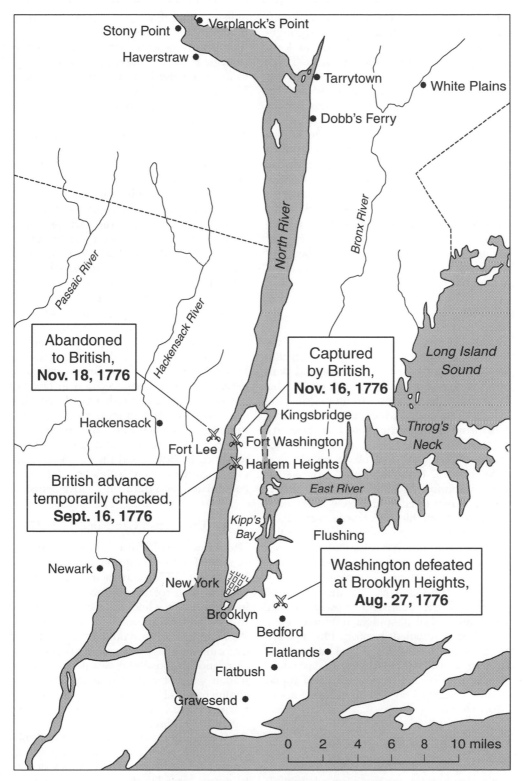

Stony Point •

Haverstraw •

Verplanck's Point

Tarrytown •

White Plains •

Dobb's Ferry •

North River

Bronx River

Passaic River

Hackensack River

**Abandoned
to British,
Nov. 18, 1776**

**Captured
by British,
Nov. 16, 1776**

*Long Island
Sound*

Hackensack •

Kingsbridge

*Throg's
Neck*

Fort Lee

Fort Washington

Harlem Heights

East River

**British advance
temporarily checked,
Sept. 16, 1776**

*Kipp's
Bay*

Flushing •

Newark •

**Washington defeated
at Brooklyn Heights,
Aug. 27, 1776**

New York

Brooklyn

Bedford •

Flatlands •

Flatbush •

Gravesend •

0   2   4   6   8   10 miles

Map 3 Campaigns around New York.

dividing his forces, seized Newport, Rhode Island, and established outposts throughout the Jersies. For the moment, at least, the Revolution had reached its nadir. Those were the times, as Thomas Paine wrote in *The Crisis*, that "tried men's souls." Yet the year had not been a total loss for the Americans. The British had given up Boston, suffered the loss of a large loyalist body in North Carolina, and been repulsed at Charles Town. Moreover, a second British offensive that year directed by General Guy Carleton, who pressed southwards from Canada, encountered Colonel Benedict Arnold's small-ship flotilla on Lake Champlain. The Battle of Valcour Island saw Arnold's outgunned vessels get the better of Carleton, who now, with the approach of winter, retired northwards.

The Trenton–Princeton campaign

General Howe, now Sir William, had hardly earned his knighthood in the campaign of 1776, which, in fact, did not end with the calendar. For Washington launched his brilliantly unorthodox Trenton–Princeton winter campaign, which continued from Christmas through the New Year. Sensitive to the psychological need to end the campaign on an upbeat note, he once again took risks, but this time with positive results for his now-minuscule 3,000-man force. Howe, settled down to enjoy the New York social scene, had left his widely separated New Jersey garrisons ripe for the picking. After crossing back into that colony on Christmas night, Washington surprised the celebrating Hessians at Trenton, capturing or killing 1,000 of the Germans. He then returned briefly to the Pennsylvania side of the Delaware, called up militia reinforcements, and then reoccupied Trenton. Out maneuvering Lord Cornwallis, who had hastened in pursuit of him, Washington dashed to Princeton, defeated its garrison, and found winter sanctuary in the mountains about Morristown.

Britain's lack of strategy

The campaign of 1776 revealed ambivalences and contradictions that plagued Britain's military effort throughout the War of Independence. Part of the problem lay in the fact that British generals were not trained in strategic thinking; indeed, the word strategy in its later sense had not come into being. Military men lacked a body of theoretical and historical doctrine from which to choose alternatives for practical application. That development came in the next century in the studies of Jomini and Clausewitz, who analyzed Napoleon's revolution in warfare. There were, however, as Ira Gruber has pointed out, implicit options in the military literature available to commanders of the time. There was the then prevailing philosophy of circumscribed war, associated with France's Marshall Saxe, with its stress on eschewing decisive engagements and exhausting the opponent by a variety of undertakings. At the same time, there was a tradition dating from antiquity, best exemplified by Caesar, stressing mobile, aggressive operations leading to the destruction of the enemy in combat. Beginning with the Howe brothers in 1776, British chieftains never made a clear-cut decision in favor of one or the other, but rather tried one, then the other, and sometimes both in the same campaign. Furthermore, the relationship between the land war and the naval war remained muddled, and the navy's blockading operations were sporadic and rarely coordinated with the army's movements.

4   The British Campaign of 1777

The Howes had grown increasingly pessimistic about cracking the American rebellion in late 1776, and their state of mind was less than totally optimistic the following year. For a while, at least, they seemed to look to new approaches. If annihilating Washington's army would be difficult and overrunning the continent even more so, then another possibility would be a naval war in which the fleet strangled American commerce and the army captured port towns for use as naval bases. After advancing and then discarding a number of plans, Sir William decided to move against Philadelphia, the rebel capital, a conquest that might well damage American morale but hardly prove fatal to the cause if Washington's

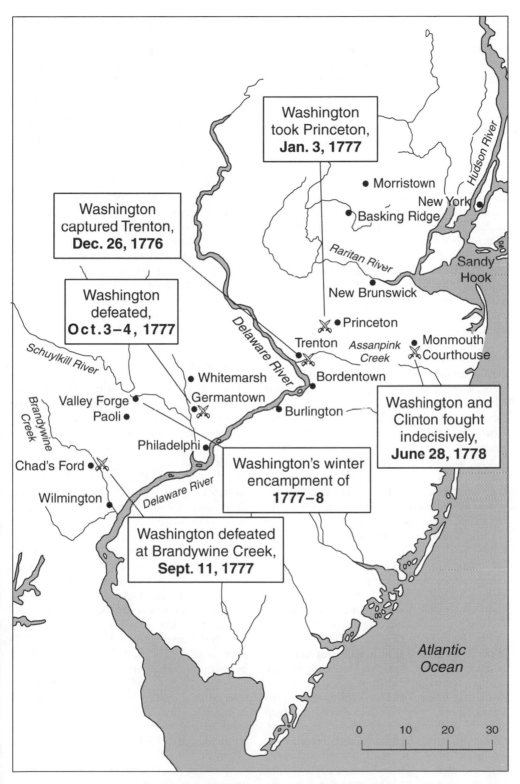

Washington
took Princeton,
Jan. 3, 1777

Washington
captured Trenton,
Dec. 26, 1776

Washington
defeated,
Oct. 3–4, 1777

Washington and
Clinton fought
indecisively,
June 28, 1778

Washington's winter
encampment of
1777–8

Washington defeated
at Brandywine Creek,
Sept. 11, 1777

● Morristown

● New York

● Basking Ridge

Hudson River

Raritan River

Sandy
Hook

● New Brunswick

✗ ● Princeton

Delaware River

Trenton   *Assanpink
Creek*   ✗ Monmouth
Courthouse

Schuylkill River

✗

● Whitemarsh   Bordentown

Germantown ✗

● Valley Forge

Paoli ●

● Burlington

Brandywine Creek

Philadelphia ●

Chad's Ford ● ✗

Wilmington ●

Delaware River

Atlantic
Ocean

0   10   20   30

Map 4   Operations in New Jersey and Pennsylvania.

army remained intact. Howe had little if any interest in the British force in Canada, previously commanded by Carleton but now headed by General John Burgoyne, who seemed to be all the things that Howe was not: confident, bold, and aggressive.

·

General Howe's victories at Brandywine Creek and Germantown

Amazingly, Colonial Secretary Germain sanctioned the campaign of 1777 without imposing a unifying concept. Scholarly opinion no longer holds that Howe had orders to advance up the Hudson for a union with Burgoyne. It may be that Burgoyne believed that Howe would at the very least clear the lower Hudson Valley before heading for Philadelphia. But Germain did not instruct Howe to do so, nor did Burgoyne later act as if he needed Howe's assistance in conducting his own operations. Few in the highest positions in England or America evidently worried about how the Canadian Army might cope in the northern wilderness. Germain, however, had assumed that Howe would advance on Philadelphia by land and that he would keep in touch with Burgoyne. But Howe, though leaving garrisons at New York City and Newport, Rhode Island, took the bulk of his army – 13,000 men – to Philadelphia by sea, which for weeks isolated him from the outside world and allowed Washington to maneuver between Burgoyne and himself. One can only speculate as to Howe's motives. Certainly he disliked interior campaigning, and his descent on the Quaker city by sea was consistent with his campaign of the year before and would extend the blockade down the coast, all of which must have found favor with his brother, the Admiral.

On July 23, 1777 the Howe brothers' expedition headed southwards, put in briefly at Delaware Bay, and then returned to sea, finally debarking its human cargo at the head of Chesapeake Bay, even farther from Philadelphia, now 57 miles away. Amazed at Sir William's desertion of Burgoyne, Washington endeavored to turn Howe back on September 11, at Brandywine Creek; but the British general executed a skillful flanking movement, similar to his successful tactics on Long Island, and defeated Washington in a hard-fought contest, Sir William's casualties in all categories amounting to 500, half the number of Washington's.

The Virginian was hardly intimidated; after Howe finally reached Philadelphia, Washington, stalking nearby, again offered battle, attacking Howe's 9,000-man force quartered at Germantown on the night of October 3. The American plan was probably too complicated, involving as it did four converging columns, and the outcome was indecisive. Each general's losses were approximately what they had been two weeks earlier at Brandywine. Yet Howe was paying a heavier price in manpower than Washington, who, after both Pennsylvania encounters, replenished his own depleted ranks. If Washington was game for another round, Sir William had no stomach for more costly bloodletting, convinced now that the war could not be won in 1777.

General Burgoyne's defeat at Saratoga

Meanwhile, Burgoyne's army from Canada got off to a good start, as was almost always true of British campaigns in the revolution. Moving down Lake Champlain in June of 1777, with 7,000 men – Amerindian scouts, loyalist parties, British regulars, and German Brunswickers – he forced the American evacuation of Fort Ticonderoga. From that time on Burgoyne did few things right. He halted at Skenesborough after skirmishing with the American rearguard, in no hurry to press his advantage while the rebels were back on their heels. He gave General Philip Schuyler, the commander of the American Northern Department, time to plant obstructions in the already arduous pathway to the Hudson, with the result that the Canadian-based army needed 24 days to travel the next 23 miles. Burdened by excessive paraphernalia in rough country, Burgoyne was already in trouble when he learned that one of his diversionary parties in the Mohawk Valley had been halted by rebel irregulars and that a second probing contingent had been routed at Bennington, Vermont.

Crossing the Hudson, Burgoyne encountered a well-entrenched and revitalized

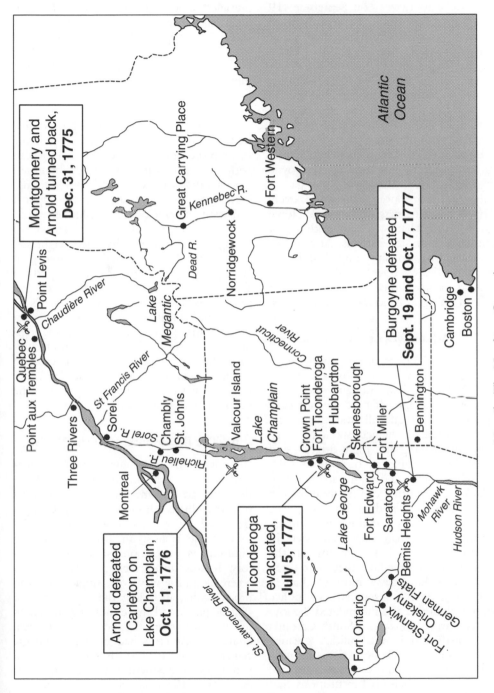

Montgomery and Arnold turned back, **Dec. 31, 1775**

Burgoyne defeated, **Sept. 19 and Oct. 7, 1777**

Arnold defeated Carleton on Lake Champlain, **Oct. 11, 1776**

Ticonderoga evacuated, **July 5, 1777**

Atlantic Ocean

Point Levis
Quebec
Point aux Trembles
Chaudière River
Three Rivers
Montreal
Sorel
Sorel R.
Chambly
St. Johns
Richelieu R.
St Francis River
Lake Megantic
Valcour Island
Lake Champlain
Crown Point
Fort Ticonderoga
Hubbardton
Skenesborough
Fort Miller
Bennington
Lake George
Fort Edward
Saratoga
Bemis Heights
Mohawk River
Hudson River
German Flats
Oriskany
Fort Stanwix
Fort Ontario
St. Lawrence River
Connecticut River
Dead R.
Kennebec R.
Norridgewock
Great Carrying Place
Fort Western
Cambridge
Boston

Map 5   The Northern Campaigns.

American Northern Army, now commanded by General Horatio Gates, ably assisted by General Benedict Arnold and Colonel Daniel Morgan. Twice – on September 19 and October 7 – Burgoyne sent forward substantial columns which thrashed about in search of Gates's lines. Both times Gates dispatched regiments to claw at his opponent from advantageous wooded locations. Burgoyne's casualties in the first and second battles of Bemis Heights exceeded Gates's by roughly 1,200 to 470. Soon surrounded, and aware that the small British garrison remaining in New York City could hardly break through to his rescue, Burgoyne capitulated at the village of Saratoga on October 17. A European army was scarcely equipped for wilderness warfare (the Howe brothers knew that), to say nothing of fighting a countryside in arms. And invariably, when the British plunged into the interior of the continent, that was what happened: people turned out in their militia units and bolstered American regular forces.

5   The Advantages of the Americans

It was no small advantage to Americans to be fighting on their own soil and to be more flexible in their military operations than their opponents. If they did not contemplate a massive guerrilla war, they nonetheless resorted advantageously at times to winter campaigning and night attacks, and they effectively employed backwoods riflemen, light infantry, and militia in harassing the flanks, interrupting communication and supply routes, and raiding isolated posts. Militia were no more useful in formal fixed-position warfare than they had been in the colonial period, but operating on the fringes and behind the lines they were often most effective; and never more so than in serving as a local constabulary or police force that disarmed and intimidated the loyalists. As James Simpson, a South Carolina loyalist, expressed it, the militia's greatest contribution to the rebel cause was in helping to erect and sustain civil governments, for it was "from their civil institutions that the rebels derive the whole of their strength."

The greatest burden, however, fell on Washington and his Continental Army, and

it steadily improved. No longer do serious historians dismiss the Continental Army as an assortment of "ragtag and bobtail" that prevailed almost in spite of itself. Even in defeat, as at Long Island and Brandywine, it could fight surprisingly well, and it learned from its mistakes. To be sure, it shrank in size each winter, as it did during the dark months at Valley Forge following the campaign of 1777. But the spring months saw its ranks swell, sometimes dramatically. Drawing on the American semi-professional tradition from the colonial era, it became more professional with each passing year, with longer enlistments, larger bounties, stricter articles of war, and better training. Washington and his staff, with the support and assistance of Congress, fashioned a military instrument that showed remarkable staying power in a war that lasted eight and a half years. No small credit was owing to certain European professionals. Friedrich Wilhelm von Steuben standardized drill procedures and served as Washington's *de facto* chief-of-staff; and French volunteer officers formed a first-rate corps of engineers and introduced a scientific and technical tradition that would lead to the creation of the United States Military Academy and to the army's nineteenth-century role in the development of the West.

6   The Disadvantages of the British

If the strengths of the militia and Continentals were less clear in the spring of 1778 than they are in retrospect, it is nonetheless true that British leaders were increasingly frustrated by waging a war 3,000 miles from home against an armed population diffused over enormous stretches of territory. It was disheartening to seize somewhere along the way every single American urban center, including the capital city of Philadelphia, and have nothing to show for it other than the possession of real estate, for America had no vital strategic center. Thus far, too, British efforts to win over all the Amerindian tribes and drive American settlers out of the West had met with limited success. If the frontier war raged back and forth, with neither side able to assert firm dominance, it produced such colorful figures as Daniel Boone and George Rogers Clark of Kentucky for the Americans and such controversial individuals as Colonel Henry Hamilton, British commandant at Detroit, the alleged "Hair-Buyer."

Moreover, France threatened to turn the conflict into an international war. Already she had made available to the patriots aid in the form of arms, munitions, and clothing, funneled through Caron de Beaumarchais' fake "Hortalez and Company" (*see* chapter 44, §1). She had also assisted the tiny Continental Navy and rebel privateers by clandestinely allowing them the use of her ports. Since under no circumstance could Americans contest the waves with mighty Britannia, French succor, then as well as in later years, made American sea raiders, and particularly the exploits of John Paul Jones, a nuisance and an embarrassment to England, causing insurance rates to skyrocket in London's mercantile circles. Emboldened further by British failures in 1777, the Bourbon kingdom concluded treaties of commerce and alliance with the United States on February 6, 1778, an action that soon led to France's entering the war on the side of the Americans in hopes of settling old scores with England. Consequently, Britain had to distribute her military and naval forces more thinly in the American theater in order to anticipate Gallic threats in Europe, the West Indies, India, and on the high seas.

7 The International Impact

When Sir Henry Clinton, who succeeded William Howe as military Commander-in-Chief, evacuated Philadelphia with orders to concentrate his forces in New York City and dispatch units to the defense of the West Indies, Washington broke camp at Valley Forge and gave chase across New Jersey. Clinton's long baggage train extending over a dozen miles was tempting to the Continental commander who had been dogged by reversals in 1777. On June 28 American advance regiments, under General Charles Lee, caught up with Clinton's rearguard at Monmouth Courthouse. Becoming disorganized, Lee's troops fell back and were met by Washington, who arrived with the main army. The Continentals stood firm, exchanging volley for volley with some of Clinton's veteran regiments, which had been hastened back to Monmouth. In military terms, the outcome was indecisive, but it was a moral victory for Washington's soldiers, proof of how far they had come under the tutelage of Steuben at Valley Forge. While Clinton continued to New York City, Washington followed more slowly and encamped at White Plains, New York, close enough to watch his adversary. As the American commented, the two armies were juxtaposed in almost the same location they had occupied two years before. The unproductive meanderings of Howe and Clinton elicited a bit of doggerel from the London *Evening Post:*

Here we go up, up, up
And here we go down, down, downy
There we go *backwards* and *forwards*
And here we go round, round, roundy.

FURTHER READING

Carp, Wayne E.: *To Starve the Army at Pleasure: Continental Army Administration and American Political Culture, 1775–1783* (Chapel Hill: University of North Carolina Press, 1984).

Ferling, John E. (ed.): *The World Turned Upside Down: The American Victory in the War of Independence* (Westport, Conn.: Greenwood Press, 1988).

Gruber, Ira D.: "British strategy: the theory and practice of eighteenth-century warfare," *Reconsiderations on the Revolutionary War: Selected Essays,* ed. Don Higginbotham (Westport, Conn.: Greenwood Press, 1978), 83–103.

Higginbotham, Don: *The War of American Independence: Military Attitudes, Policies, and Practice, 1763–1789* (New York: Macmillan, 1971).

Royster, Charles: *A Revolutionary People at War: the Continental Army and American Character, 1775–1783* (Chapel Hill: University of North Carolina Press, 1979).

Shy, John: *A People Numerous and Armed: Reflections on the Military Struggle for American Independence* (New York: Oxford University Press, 1976).

Wright, Robert K.: *The Continental Army* (Washington, DC: Government Printing Office, 1983).

CHAPTER THIRTY-SEVEN

The War for Independence, after Saratoga

DON HIGGINBOTHAM

THE year 1778 brought home to Britain the new international character of the war (*see* chapter 44, §3). The French Admiral the Comte d'Estaing appeared in American waters that summer and narrowly missed intercepting a convoy of British transports bound from Philadelphia to New York. The Frenchman suffered equally poor luck when a storm obliterated his favorable chances of defeating Admiral Howe off Narragansett Bay and sealing off the British garrison in Rhode Island. Even so, Britain had little to boast of after three years of campaigning. If she possessed Newport and New York City, she had evacuated Boston and Philadelphia, and later in 1778 she gave up Newport as well. For the next two and a half years Washington remained a short distance from New York City as the opposing sides watched each other and limited their activities to occasional raiding expeditions.

1 Britain's Southern Strategy

The war that began in New England and shifted in 1776 to the middle states now took on a southern complexion. Thus far unsuccessful in the North and short of manpower after France entered the fray, Britain adopted a southern strategy. The region below the Potomac had experienced little of the war since 1776, the year in which the British assault on Charles Town had been turned away and uprisings of loyalists in North Carolina and Cherokee in the backcountry had been crushed. Although the South had yet to be tested, Colonial Secretary Germain and his London colleagues believed reports that the region was overwhelmingly devoted to the Crown. That meant fewer troops would be needed than had been the case in the North. It also meant, to London planners, that royal regiments would not directly occupy every bit of territory gained from the rebels. Rather, they would "Americanize" the conflict: the loyalists would police and defend many areas, thus freeing the King's regulars for combat elsewhere.

In pushing the new strategy – pressed by loyalist exiles and royalist officials from the South – Germain ignored the advice of Sir William Howe, who, before returning to England, had warned the Colonial Secretary that it was hazardous to put great dependence on the King's friends anywhere in America. Nowhere were they so ubiquitous and dedicated that they could be counted on to hold districts previously overrun. Howe's concerns, of course, received scant attention at Whitehall, which likewise ignored the danger of dispersing Britain's military resources from New York to the Floridas, an arrangement that might well have encouraged the French Navy to return to American waters and cooperate with the rebels in picking off British bases.

But the southern plan seemed so simple and desirable that it was beguiling. Step by step the regulars–loyalists combination would roll up the lower South and then the upper South. Perhaps Britons believed so fervently in the southern strategy because they really had no alternative to winning the war after it had become an international conflict. Moreover, it was noted that the South was nearer the West Indies and therefore British forces in both theaters could coordinate their efforts. And certainly the South produced commodities of greater value to England's mercantile scheme of things than New England and the middle states. As one Briton put it, the war had "begun at the wrong end" of America.

2 The Conquest of Georgia and South Carolina

Although the initial undertaking in the South resulted in the reduction of Georgia in the winter of 1778–9, the French naval danger reappeared in 1779 when d'Estaing and American forces laid siege to Savannah. But the Admiral's concern over the approaching hurricane season led to a direct assault on the British positions, which resulted in heavy Franco-American losses, the sudden departure of d'Estaing, and an American withdrawal. Once again the British were lucky in their encounter with d'Estaing, and the French continued to be dogged by ill-fortune. The year 1779 had been curious in terms of implementing the new British strategy. Sir Henry Clinton, perhaps ambivalent about the southern approach and not entirely reconciled to giving up the idea of a climactic battle with Washington, had moved slowly to commit the preponderance of his resources to the South.

As Whitehall reiterated its wish to focus on the South, Clinton was at long last already moving. Soon after heavy reinforcements reached Georgia, Clinton, himself leading the advance, besieged Charles Town, South Carolina. The American commander, Benjamin Lincoln, a solid if unimaginative general, had initially bowed to the Carolinians' insistence that the city be defended; but later, fearing its destruction, they persuaded him to surrender his more than 5,500 men, presenting Clinton – on May 12, 1780 – with the biggest bag of American prisoners captured in the entire war. A second, hastily assembled American Southern Army under General Horatio Gates appeared in upper South Carolina in early August. Eschewing the prudence he had displayed against Burgoyne, Gates hastily advanced and stumbled upon a British column at Camden on August 16. Gates's militia, holding one side of his main

line, broke and fled, and Cornwallis soon swept the field.

With the stain of British conquest spread over Georgia and South Carolina, London officialdom predicted that North Carolina and Virginia would be back in the royal fold in short order. Yet late twentieth-century experience reminds us that pacification of the countryside is difficult. Guerrilla warfare often continues, and so it was in the American Revolution. Clinton, just after the fall of Charles Town and before his own return to New York, had issued a proclamation freeing prisoners of war from parole and restoring their full citizenship, *provided* they take an oath to the Crown and support British efforts to bring law and order to South Carolina. The proclamation was disastrous in two respects. First, it compelled former rebels, many of whom were now willing to sit out the war quietly, to take sides – to opt for outright loyalism or rebellion. Second, it was too tolerant for the hardline loyalists to accept. Bitter and hardened by their earlier misfortunes, furious with Clinton's leniency, loyalists so terrorized former Whigs that their behavior drove countless Carolinians and Georgians back into the field on the revolutionary side.

3 The Americans Regain Lost Ground

If Clinton had helped exacerbate the problem of pacification, he did recognize that Lord Cornwallis, now in command in the South, should not launch a northward thrust before South Carolina was completely subdued. Cautious and methodical, Clinton was very different from the bold, aggressive Cornwallis, who wasted little time in launching an invasion of North Carolina. At Charlotte he learned of the destruction of his 1,000-man loyalist left wing, at the hands of far western frontiersmen, at Kings Mountain, just below the Carolinas' border. Even when successful, Cornwallis had trouble in grasping that the defeat of American armies did not mean American capitulation. For that matter, in a people's war Continental armies had a way of reappearing.

Still another small southern army entered South Carolina, commanded by General Nathanael Greene, Washington's ablest

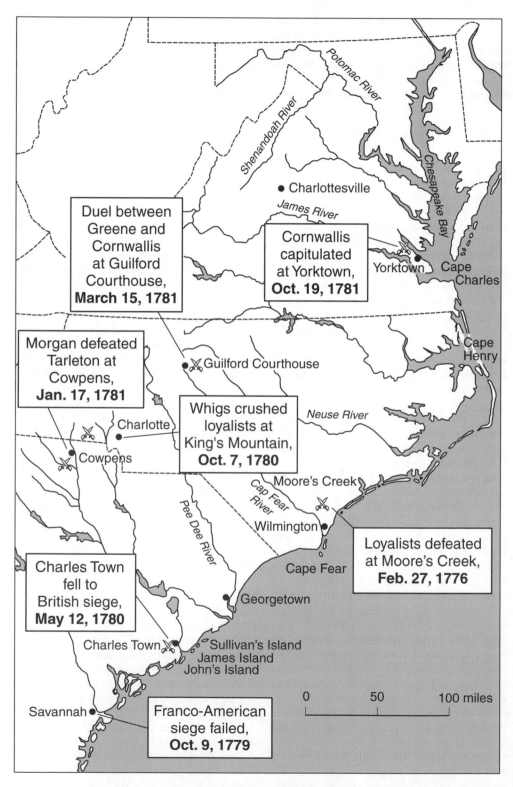

Map 6 The Southern Campaigns.

lieutenant and former quartermaster-general. The ex-Quaker from Rhode Island, a flexible, resourceful general, resolved to play the guerrilla role until he could augment his thin ranks. Dividing his army so that each division sat on the flanks of Cornwallis at Winnsboro, Greene took a position on the Pee Dee River, while General Daniel Morgan, with the other division, advanced southwestwards into the state, rallying guerrilla parties and checkmating the loyalists in his vicinity. When Cornwallis sent Banastre Tarleton's Tory Legion after Morgan, the Americans won a lopsided victory at the Cowpens on January 17, 1781. Tarleton lost more than 900 men as compared with Morgan's 72.

Now began a merry chase, with Cornwallis setting out after the retreating Morgan, and with Greene endeavoring to reunite with Morgan before Cornwallis overtook his subordinate. Linking up in central North Carolina, the Americans retired briefly into Virginia and then returned to challenge Cornwallis at Guilford Courthouse (near present-day Greensboro). Greene's reinforced army had a heavy numerical advantage; but Cornwallis had the veterans. The Briton also held the field, and Greene withdrew after inflicting heavy losses – more than 500 as against Greene's own 250. Cornwallis, his army no longer an effective fighting machine after King's Mountain, Cowpens, and Guilford Courthouse, limped to Wilmington on the coast before proceeding to Virginia.

With Cornwallis's posts in South Carolina vulnerable, Greene returned to the Palmetto State. One by one the interior stations fell – until Lord Rawdon, the British commander there, pulled back his remaining units to the coast. Greene never won an open-field battle against either Cornwallis or Rawdon, but he outmaneuvered them and wore them to a frazzle. The war wound down to occasional raids and skirmishes as Greene's army kept Savannah and Charles Town under observation until the British evacuated those cities in 1782. A masterful strategist, Greene had made the most of his slender resources. He made the British play his game, ever on the move and never letting up to allow his adversaries to regroup. If guerrilla warfare was scarcely understood by professional soldiers in his day, he employed methods that have been the stock-in-trade of revolutionists in recent times.

Cornwallis, meanwhile, continued his meanderings in tidewater Virginia, his southern campaign having failed. He had not pacified the lower South before moving into North Carolina, and his efforts to Americanize the war had proved unsuccessful. Cornwallis, however, did have a curious theory about how to smother the flames of sedition in the lower South. In possession of North Carolina, he would then have the South Carolina guerrillas isolated and cut off from supply lines to the north. Then, failing in the Tarheel State, he claimed that he must overrun Virginia to complete the subjugation of North Carolina. Undoubtedly, he and other British leaders had exaggerated the strength of loyalism, but they had hardly given Americanization a meaningful test. As he had moved northwards, allegedly pacified areas erupted in brutal civil war between loyalists and Whigs. Such was the "bizarre chain of ideas and circumstances" that brought Cornwallis to Virginia, where he lacked a plan of operations and stood exposed to encirclement from land and sea on the tip of the Virginia peninsula.

4 The British Surrender at Yorktown

In the Old Dominion, Cornwallis had taken under his command British raiding parties led by the turncoat Benedict Arnold (who had gone over to the royal side in September 1780) and William Phillips. Following two months of indecisive campaigning, he retired to Yorktown on the coast and began erecting fortifications, all of which displeased his superior in New York, Sir Henry Clinton, who had never intended to make that state the center of operations in the South. If Cornwallis's thinking was muddled, Clinton erred in not explicitly ordering Cornwallis to get out of Virginia and to consolidate British gains in the lower South before undertaking new initiatives.

Just as Clinton realized that the Chesapeake region was vulnerable to French sea power, so too did the Franco-American allies find his Yorktown base an inviting target. There had been no major allied campaigning since d'Estaing's earlier failures; but since 1780 5,500 French troops under the Comte de Rochambeau had been stationed in Rhode Island, along with the Comte de Barras's French naval detachment at Newport. Washington, who had thought of Rochambeau's joining him in an attack on New York, proved that he was flexible and opportunistic when he received word that the French Admiral de Grasse was in the West Indies and crowding sail for Chesapeake Bay with 20 ships of the line and 3,000 soldiers. Washington and Rochambeau, on August 17, 1781, wrote to the Admiral that they would hasten southwards to cooperate in snaring Cornwallis on the Virginia peninsula. As a small American force under La Fayette, operating in the Old Dominion, positioned itself to block Cornwallis's escape up the peninsula, de Grasse arrived in time to transport the regiments of Washington and La Fayette from Chesapeake Bay to the James River. With the appearance of de Barras's French squadron from Newport, the allies had completed a remarkable feat of coordination and synchronization, unprecedented in an era without modern, instantaneous means of communication.

Cornwallis's only hope now was the Royal Navy, which did not rise to the occasion, partly at least because the Cabinet in London had felt – after d'Estaing's setbacks – that any French naval push in support of the rebels could easily be scotched. Clinton in New York sent an outmanned naval expedition under Admiral Thomas Graves in a game effort to save Cornwallis. After a day of indecisive bombardments, Graves and de Grasse pulled apart, then jockeyed for position between September 6 and 9, after which Graves returned to New York.

Cornwallis's time of reckoning was not far away as he drew his 8,000 men back to his entrenchments immediately before Yorktown. Although the allied force numbered 17,000, it was the artillery – a military arm that had grown increasingly significant in the eighteenth century – that hastened the British defeat. Nothing was spared as French gunners and General Henry Knox's American artillerymen pinpointed gun batteries, ships in the harbor, and troop encampments. On October 17 a British drummer and officer sounded the parley and waved a white flag. Two days later the articles of surrender were signed and British soldiers in new scarlet uniforms stacked their arms while their musicians appropriately played an old tune called *The World Turned Upside Down*.

5 The Effects of War on American Life

The ultimate meaning of Yorktown for Britain was hardly transparent at the time to the Americans, who suffered from an acute case of war-weariness and internal discord after more than six years in arms. If the Crown's followers had their share of misery, so did the Revolutionists. There were massacres of civilians by loyalists and Amerindians in western New York, and there were destructive raids in Kentucky and other frontier areas, as well as along the coast. The fierce, partisan war in the southern backcountry took the lives of untold non-combatants on both sides. In the absence of men, in military service, women had to protect home and hearth; their letters displayed a growing knowledge of business and financial affairs, and men not infrequently responded by referring to "our farm" and no longer to "my farm." While the Revolution did not erase the differences between the work roles of men and women, these were certainly eroded.

The economy

The vicissitudes on the economic front seemed endless. Neither enlisted men nor officers turned a profit from their army duty. Both soldiers and civilians felt the pain of hardships stemming from mounting inflation and soaring prices. Such upward trends were probably inescapable in a country without a stable national currency and hardly any sizeable manufactures. There was no alternative for Congress and the states but to emit vast quantities of paper currency, which, lacking specie backing, declined sharply in value. People on fixed salaries were particularly hard hit; for although wages increased they hardly kept pace with inflation. Planters and merchants not infrequently accused each other of exacerbating inflation. Although merchants may well have profited more than any other single component of the population, those engaged in privateering and importing military stores combined private gain with public service. Despite their complaints, some farmers may have benefited from inflation, since their obligations, taxes and debts did not necessarily increase at the rate of their produce. Some were successful – if not patriotic – in selling only a part of their crops to meet obligations and then held back the remainder in anticipation of still higher prices later.

In any case, the war profoundly disrupted the American domestic economy. The decline of external commerce, which had been the linchpin of the prewar economy, cut off patterns of exchange and weakened incentives normally motivating farmers and others to generate the surpluses so desperately needed by the Continental Army. Particularly harmful was the curtailment of trade with the West Indies and southern Europe, which had brought to the colonies goods and occasionally cash. Some states appear to have suffered more than others. Connecticut, for example, bordered the early combat zones and for seven years felt the impact of Britain's occupation of New York City. Price inflation, currency devaluation, hoarding, and illicit commerce with the enemy in nearby New York all extracted their heavy toll on public morale, patriot loyalties, and governmental machinery. Despite the valiant efforts of state leaders, many citizens saw stringent taxation, price-fixing, and impressment as abridgments of privacy and personal liberty.

Civil–military relations

At the same time that home-front economic problems went from bad to worse, civil–military relations showed severe strains. That fact is hardly surprising given traditional Anglo-American reservations about standing armies and given the agonizingly protracted nature of the conflict. Throughout, Washington was expected to respect the home front, to be the servant of Congress, and to be sensitive to the concerns of state and local officialdom. These requirements placed on the army's conduct produced frustrations in the officer corps, as did the failures of Congress and the civilian sector to meet the Continentals' needs. Prominent generals such as Nathanael Greene and Charles Lee bluntly

voiced their unhappiness, Lee excoriating the federal lawmakers for "having no military men in their body" and therefore "continually confounding themselves and everybody else in military matters."

In this tense atmosphere, punctuated by more battlefield defeats than victories and by stressful winter army encampments at Valley Forge and Morristown, dire rumors seemed permanently to threaten civil–military relations. There were widely circulated, albeit erroneous, reports towards the end of 1777 that Congress, displeased by Washington's twin setbacks at Brandywine and Germantown, would replace the Commander-in-Chief with Horatio Gates, the victor over Burgoyne. Washington himself believed that Generals Gates and Thomas Conway and a faction of congressmen sought his ouster. The episode, known as the Conway Cabal, amounted to little if anything since Washington's detractors were few in number and unorganized. The truth was that Washington and his subordinates were overly sensitive owing to their military reverses, pitiable winter conditions, and unhappiness with Congress over pay and other benefits. Spring brought green foliage, new recruits, a healthier frame of mind at Valley Forge, and an end to the Conway Cabal.

Yet some Americans were uncomfortable with Washington, not because of either his successes or failures in battle but rather because he was praised excessively and sometimes in language reminiscent of kingship. John Adams fumed about the "stupid veneration" accorded the Virginian. The one attempt to encourage Washington to accept a crown took place some months after Yorktown when Colonel Lewis Nicola, an Irish-born Huguenot, wrote to the Commander-in-Chief to that effect. Washington, replying that Nicola's screed left him with "painful sensations," admitted that the army's legitimate needs had not always been met; but he sternly warned the colonel that he would work to obtain them only in what he called "a constitutional way."

The Newburgh Addresses and troop revolts

Small though the army was as the war wound down in 1782 and 1783, it nevertheless frightened some Americans as never before. The officers complained of their pay being in arrears, and they reminded Congress of its earlier promise in 1780 to award them half-pay for life as compensation for their extended services and sufferings. Rumors were rampant, including one that a segment of the army had lost faith in Washington for not having pressed harder for the military's demands. Discontent climaxed on March 10, 1783, at Washington's encampment at Newburgh, New York. There circulated that day the anonymous "Newburgh Addresses," penned by 24-year-old Major John Armstrong (*see also* chapter 47, §2). Calling for a gathering of officers, they urged Washington's subordinates not "to be tame and unprovoked when injuries press down hard upon you."

The meaning of the addresses, especially the possibility of taking violent action, is subject to differing interpretations, as is the question of whether the leaders wished to include or exclude Washington from their subsequent measures of seeking relief. One view holds that the affair was "the only known instance of an attempted coup in American history." If so, it appears to have been almost completely limited to the younger officers. And it may well be that the whole affair was more an effort on the part of disgruntled public creditors and advocates of a stronger central government to use the army than it was any movement initiated within the military ranks. In any event, Washington himself seized the initiative, calling the officers together and persuading them to work through him and other legitimate channels to secure their just rewards. Washington was keenly aware that military tensions are inherent in free and open societies – for the precise reason that the military does not have a blank check in such societies – and he labored successfully to keep those tensions under control. He demonstrated that a professional army was not incompatible with civil liberty and constitutional government.

At the time, however, the army's fidelity to its civilian masters was not as clear as it is in retrospect, a statement that holds true for enlisted men as well as officers. While the congressmen also sought relief in 1783 for officers, in June that body faced a mutiny – the last of several – on the part of several hundred troops, who surrounded the Pennsylvania State House where Congress and the executive council of the state were in session. Boisterous from liquor, the soldiers demanded that their complaints be addressed at once. As the civilians inside steeled themselves and passed through the cordon of milling soldiers, the latter heaped verbal abuse upon the congressmen. Word of the approach of loyal Continentals under General Robert Howe resulted in the mutineers' dispersing. Another crisis had been averted.

A professional army

Still, the overall record of the army, officers, and enlisted men is exceedingly impressive. In a war twice the length of the Civil War or World War II, it displayed staying power, the ability to survive. Its desertion rate, about 20 percent, may seem high by present standards, but it was remarkably low compared with that of European armies of the day. It was never numerically more than a shadow of the more than 60,000 men that Congress had agreed to raise for the duration in 1776. Consequently, it had to resort to militia drafts, short-term enlistments, and, in time, to the bottom of the barrel of human resources. British deserters and prisoners of war found their way into the Continental ranks, as did men in bondage, both white indentured servants and Blacks. By 1778 the army was heavily sprinkled with slaves and free Negroes. The ideals of the Revolution, combined with the service of Blacks in the cause of freedom, brought a profound change in the legal status of Negroes above the Mason–Dixon line. If the Revolution failed to produce any significant alteration in the status of women in America, females nonetheless played a role with the Continental Army, not only in gathering clothing and other necessities but also by their presence in the camps. They performed valuable domestic duties, and some of them shouldered arms. Without the distaff side, admitted Washington, some of the best soldiers would have deserted.

This was the heterogeneous army that became an object of concern for British commanders, a source of intimidation for the loyalists, a rallying point for the militia, and a living, day-to-day symbol of the Revolution and of emerging American nationality. A scavenger for soldiers and supplies, Washington faced the additional challenge of wiring it together, making it fight and occasionally win – all without unduly antagonizing civilians and public officials. Yet he prevailed over these internal obstacles and the British foe alike.

6 Britain's Decision to End the Offensive

Britain, to be sure, did not suffer total military defeat. Even after Yorktown, she held New York, Savannah, and Charles Town, and the King's Amerindian friends remained troublesome on the frontiers. Although George Rogers Clark had several years earlier launched a spectacular campaign in the Illinois country highlighted by the capture of Vincennes, and though General John Sullivan razed the homelands of the Iroquois in western New York, the tribesmen were sheltered and resupplied at Detroit and Niagara. Indeed, the international war seemed to be going in Britain's favor. In 1782 she struck back sharply at France and her ally Spain, which had entered the war in 1779. In April, Admiral George Rodney defeated Admiral de Grasse in the West Indies. Almost simultaneously in India, the French under the Balli de Suffren were repulsed by Admiral Sir William Hughes. Nor did the Bourbons fare better at Gibraltar, where Lord Howe's fleet and General George Eliot's determined resistance saved that rocky eminence for England.

British military resurgence, however, did not translate into a fresh burst of enthusiasm at home for continuing the conflict. The administration's majorities had steadily declined until a motion to renounce all attempts to regain America passed the House of Commons. North and Germain resigned their posts and the King formed a new government drawn largely from the opposition forces of the Marquis of Rockingham and the Earl of Shelburne, both of whom were committed to peace. To have continued the struggle against both the Bourbons and America could have meant imposing heavy taxes, regimenting the economy, and drawing productive citizens into the army and navy. Very few, least of all the King and his ministers, were willing to pay that price. They would not risk derailing their mercantile economy, nor would they chance arming citizens who might in turn demand a greater part in the political system in exchange for their service. No European monarchy in the period before the French Revolution would take that gamble.

Still, the failure to regain America was painful for both material and psychological reasons. Britain, like America in the 1960s, with its Vietnam involvement, suffered from a superpower mentality. For the leaders of a country that could boast of such a long winning tradition against its continental opponents, to accept military and naval failures and the possibility of anything short of total victory was extremely difficult. Moreover, there is another applicable Vietnam analogy: the North cabinet, as was true of the Lyndon Johnson administration nearly two centuries later, persisted in prosecuting a war as long as it did because of a foolish belief in the domino theory – for Britain this meant that the loss of the mainland colonies would lead to secessionist movements in Ireland, the West Indies, and elsewhere and to the collapse of its hegemony in international trade; for the Johnson team, it meant the fall to communism, one by one, of most Southeast Asian states.

7 The Consequences of American Independence

Britain

What were the consequences of the War of Independence for Europe and for the United States? Britain, notwithstanding the loss of America, remained supreme in the colonial and maritime field. Already she had begun to lay the basis for a "Second British Empire," whose vital center was the great subcontinent of India, and which led to new fields of commerce in the Pacific and the South China seas. And American trade soon fell back into its prewar channels with Britain, the most industrial nation of the time. Shelburne's generosity to the Crown's rebellious American subjects in the 1783 Treaty of Paris was owing in part to his desire to pry America away from France and to pull the colonies back into the imperial orbit. But for a variety of reasons, including the collapse of Shelburne's ministry and Britain's unwillingness to adopt American free trade ideas, Anglo-American relations did not show dramatic improvement for more than a century.

France

France in the long run gained little at Britain's expense. America was a restless satellite, scarcely willing to remain unequivocally in the diplomatic constellation of Versailles. Since the French alliance had been a marriage of convenience, America soon returned to a unilateral approach to foreign relations more in harmony with her world outlook.

In fact, the colonists might well have kept Britain from restoring royal control throughout America even without direct French military intervention. Once again America's late twentieth-century experience in Vietnam reminds us of the difficulties of waging distant wars against a mass insurgent movement. One view goes so far as to assert that France's entry into the conflict probably discredited moderates and appeasers in Parliament, saving the North ministry from collapse after Burgoyne's disaster and steeling the kingdom to fight with an infusion of new vigor.

What then was crucial about the French alliance? Simply put, it brought the war to an end before America unraveled; the country was showing signs of approaching such a condition with the collapse of the economy and the restlessness of the army. Without international pressures, Britain might have held on to several major cities and their environs, making American Independence hardly meaningful, and leaving unresolved the ownership of the trans-Appalachian West, which, to the amazement of European diplomats, Britain ceded to America in 1783. Finally, an endless struggle – neither side capable of winning outright – might have wrenched the Revolution to the left, generating the guerrilla war American leaders had thus far avoided (except in the lower South) in order to preserve the fabric of American political and cultural life.

While the Revolutionists never turned to bush fighting as their principal means of resistance, some European officers were fascinated by certain unorthodox features of the war, especially in the South but at times elsewhere too, such as in the Burgoyne campaign, where partisan forces cooperated with the Continental Army in cutting off Burgoyne's communications and in sealing off his retreat. But any tactical lessons were learned mostly from small-unit engagements and woodland fighting, not from the major battles of the Continental Army, which usually dueled its British counterparts in the European manner. Because European *chasseurs* and *Jägers* were not unlike American guerrillas in some respects, as were partisan fighters in the Low Countries and the Balkans, American practices lent weight to evolving trends instead of creating new ones. By employing productive citizens (along with the lower echelons of humanity, of course), Americans did reject the concept of the soldier as necessarily set apart from his own countrymen, a creature without his stake in society. This use of the citizen as soldier did fire the European imagination, especially since it conformed to Enlightenment principles on the "natural" way to wage war. Here then was a political ideal as well: confidence in the individual as a trustworthy citizen. And it was chiefly in the political arena – not that of military strategy or tactics – that the American Revolution influenced the French Revolution; but the War of Independence also helped to precipitate the upheaval in the Bourbon monarchy, beginning in 1789, because of the huge debt France incurred in aiding the United States a short time earlier.

America

As for America, it required an extended period of peace in which to recover and complete its unfinished business, which meant getting the nation solidly on its feet. It needed to disband the army, deal with the public debt, organize the western lands, and grapple with the Articles of Confederation. Many felt that this first Constitution of the nation, ratified in 1781, was inadequate without amendments or even more extensive alteration to meet the internal and external requirements of the United States.

Some of those needs would take years to resolve; but not the departure of the army, which melted back into civilian life from which it had come. There was real poignancy in Washington's farewells to the officers of the army and to Congress. The Commander-in-Chief met with his subordinates for a final time at Fraunces Tavern in New York City. After calling each man present to come forward – and "take my hand" – he was off to Annapolis, Maryland, where Congress was in session and where once again emotions surfaced. As he phrased it, he bade "an Affectionate farewell to this August body... and take my leave of all the employments of public life."

Washington and certain other military men, as well as numerous congressmen and diplomats, emerged from the war as nationalists, and they worked for a stronger union, their efforts bringing the culmination of the Revolution in the writing and ratification of the Federal Constitution in 1787–8. That document also embraced the twin military traditions of the Revolution: it provided for a professional army and navy – *in time of peace* as well as in time of war – without constitutional limits on the size and length of service of those forces; and it recognized the continued role of state militias; but the latter, now for the first time, would in certain instances be subject to federal control. The nationalists' military plan had been enunciated as early as 1783 in Washington's "Sentiments on a Peace Establishment," an essay drafted at the request of Congress. Much of it was implemented in the 1790s,

providing military institutions that survived with little change down to the beginning of the twentieth century. Such military power would never have been written into the new national parchment had Washington's Continental Army threatened the liberties of his countrymen. From the time that it took its modern form in late seventeenth-century England, the concept of civil control of the military had never been severely tested by the pressures of a divisive war that strained Britain to the breaking point. It was in America rather than in the mother country that such a test first took place, between 1775 and 1783.

FURTHER READING

Higginbotham, Don: *George Washington and the American Military Tradition* (Athens: University of Georgia Press, 1985).

Kohn, Richard H.: *Eagle and Sword: the Federalists and the Creation of the Military Establishment in America, 1783–1802* (New York: Free Press, 1975).

Kwasny, Mark V.: *Washington's Partisan War, 1775–1783* (Kent, Oh.: Kent State University Press, 1996).

Mackesy, Piers: *The War for America, 1775–1783* (Cambridge, Mass.: Harvard University Press, 1964).

Royster, Charles: *Light-Horse Harry Lee and the Legacy of the American Revolution* (New York: Alfred A. Knopf, 1981).

Wilcox, William B.: *Portrait of a General: Sir Henry Clinton in the War of Independence* (New York: Alfred A. Knopf, 1964).

CHAPTER THIRTY-EIGHT

The Continental Army

HOLLY A. MAYER

ON June 14, 1775 delegates to the Second Continental Congress voted "the American Continental Army" into existence. Thus it was that over a year before it declared the Independence of the united colonies, Congress shouldered the responsibility for existing and proposed forces that were to defend against any hostile actions taken by British forces in North America. Besides proposing to raise ten companies of riflemen to come from Pennsylvania, Maryland, and Virginia, the delegates adopted the New England troops encamped around Boston, the other New England provincial forces that had mustered for service elsewhere, and the New York units being formed to defend strategic positions in that province. They also appointed a committee to draft the rules and regulations that were to govern the army. When they met again the next day, they chose the Virginian George Washington to be the new army's Commander-in-Chief. Their decision was based on political as well as military concerns: they not only needed someone militarily qualified for the position but a person from outside New England, for they had to show that there would be continental participation and support in military as well as political endeavors. The decisions of the delegates to Congress on those two days and over the course of the eight long years following – until the war was won and the Confederation Congress dismissed some and incorporated other continental units within the United States Army in 1783 – along with those of officers, soldiers, and observers reveal that the Continental Army had two roles: the

primary one was to execute the war; the secondary one was to represent the Confederation and the American people.

1 Execution

The Continental Army's principal mission was to apply force to defend the people, property, and liberty of the united colonies. Once Independence was declared, the army's mission expanded. It had to exercise the will and power behind the words, for it had to execute the separation from Great Britain and thus ensure the success of the Revolution. Washington reminded both his troops and the civil authorities of this time and time again during the war. In a circular to some of the states in January 1782, as he urged them to continue their recruiting efforts, he wrote that it was a priority

to have a powerful Army early in the field; for we must suppose the Enemy are either disposed, "to prosecute the War" or to enter into "a negotiation for peace"; there is no other alternative; on the former supposition, a respectable Army becomes necessary to counteract the Enemy and to prevent the accumulating expences of a lingering War; on the latter, nothing but a decidedly superior force can enable us boldly to claim our rights, and dictate the law at the pacification. (Washington, 23: 478–9)

Some Americans preferred to think of the Continental Army as an enlarged militia or provincial force similar to earlier colonial semi-professional units (precedents which, along with British and European ones, did affect this army's practices; see "The Military Resources of the Colonists" in chapter 36), but Washington and his subordinate commanders, with the support of civil adherents, immediately began to shape it into a regular army. In taking such an offensive course, even for defensive reasons, they escalated the rebellion. The King, George III, responded to the news of fighting at Lexington and Concord, the formation of an army at Cambridge, and other revolutionary acts by declaring on August 23, 1775 that the colonies were in a state of rebellion. He followed that up by engaging German forces to support the additional British units he was sending to America. The increasing threat then confirmed to many, though still not all, Americans that a regular – properly organized and disciplined – army was needed.

Organization

In the fall of 1775, after reviewing the troops encamped outside of Boston, contemplating the dissolution of his army in December when most of the soldiers would go home upon the expiration of their enlistments, and consulting with his senior officers, Washington submitted proposals for a new, more effective organization of the army to the congressional committee investigating the issue. The committee passed the proposals to Congress, which then adopted them in November. Washington officially implemented the reorganization of the main army on January 1, 1776. Under the new organization, which made manifest that this was to be no militia force, the main army consisted of one artillery and 26 infantry regiments. Each infantry regiment was to have three field officers (major, lieutenant colonel, and colonel), a staff consisting of an adjutant, paymaster, quartermaster, quartermaster sergeant, sergeant major, chaplain, surgeon, surgeon's mate, drum major, and fife major, and eight companies. Each company was supposed to present 4 officers (a captain and subalterns), 2 musicians, 8 non-commissioned officers (sergeants and corporals), and 76 privates. When at full strength, a regiment would thus have 640 men (privates and corporals) in the ranks. The artillery regiment, commanded by Henry Knox, had a few more field officers, a staff similar to those of the infantry regiments,

and 12 companies which in theory each had 5 officers, 8 non-commissioned officers, 2 musicians, 8 bombardiers, 8 gunners, and 32 matrosses. Those were the planning figures; they were not the actual ones, for, as it turned out, not enough men volunteered for service and thus none of the regiments was at full strength for the 1776 campaign. That spring the army had approximately 828 officers, 694 sergeants, 365 drummers and fifers, and 12,510 rank and file (Wright, 1983, pp. 47, 53, 56).

The personnel problem continued throughout the war. A major contributing factor to that was the colonial legacy of short enlistments. Had such a practice continued unabated, it would have undermined continuity and efficiency. Therefore in 1776, in the course of planning for the next reorganization of the army, Congress came to agree with Washington that enlistments should be for the duration of the war. Some states, leery of a standing army, responded by raising units in which soldiers enlisted for three years, and then Congress, responding to the reluctance of men to enlist for an indefinite period, also allowed individuals to enlist for three years instead of the duration. It was not quite what Washington wanted, and it did cause problems as the war marched into the 1780s, but it did mean that he would not have to perform a major reorganization every winter. Furthermore, as such soldiers then endured more training and battle experience, it also meant that Washington would have more disciplined troops.

Congress and the military command still did reorganize the army a number of times throughout the war. They added more regiments, modelled upon those of 1776, in 1777. The next year, admitting that 110 regiments (Congress had added 16 to the 88 initially approved for 1777) could not be filled, they reduced the number of regiments and the personnel in each regiment. Washington, however, did create several new specialized units to serve in engineering, light dragoon, policing, and other roles. Washington managed to stave off major reorganizations for a time after that, but by 1780, with the main army's strength depleted by recruiting problems and the reassignment of some units to the Southern

Department, and in response to a series of military failures and considerations of combined operations with the French, Washington and Congress again contemplated changes. In the 1781 reorganization, the army could retain most of its specialty units, such as the Corps of Engineers, but it was to rearrange and consolidate other units into 49 infantry regiments, the Canadian regiment, 4 artillery regiments, 4 legionary corps, 2 partisan corps, and a regiment of artificers. Under this plan, an infantry regiment at full strength would not be as strong as the 1776 arrangement, but better than the 1778 one, for it would have 544 rank and file, 40 sergeants, 24 company officers, and 3 field officers (ibid., pp. 157–9). Again, as with all other plans, the army could not fully implement this one; even so it had developed into a more effective fighting force – as it proved in the Yorktown campaign.

Staff departments, such as the adjutant general, quartermaster, commissary, ordinance, clothing, and hospital departments, suported the line regiments. They faced a multitude of problems as they tried to supply, succor, quarter, and move the troops. The frequent reorganization of the combatant units was one problem, their own reorganizations another. Complicating the situation, as revealed in disputes over pay and subordination to civil and military authorities, was the fact that both military and civilian personnel served within these departments. Moreover, while many of their military members and civilian employees were dedicated public servants, the departments did have to deal with both corruption and noncompliance among their own personnel (wagoners, for example, because some embezzled and destroyed supplies, and were often damned as untrustworthy and unreliable) as well as within the American populace. The necessity of subordinating personal to state interests, and the problems that could crop up when that did not happen, were therefore particularly obvious in staff department affairs.

Structure and discipline

The United States had to learn how to wage war while it was in the midst of one. The lesson was made especially difficult due to that war being part of a Revolution. This affected the army's demand for and application of discipline as much as its strategy and tactics (for the latter points, see chapters 36 and 37). Washington emphasized the connection on January 1, 1776 when he expressed the hope that the troops understood the importance of their cause and acknowledged "that an Army without Order, Regularity & Discipline, is no better than a Commission'd Mob." He continued with a plea: "Let us therefore, when every thing dear and valuable to Freemen is at stake; when our unnatural Parent is threat'ning us with destruction from every quarter, endeavour by all the Skill and Discipline in our power to acquire that knowledge, and conduct, which is necessary in War" (Washington, 1931–44, 3, p. 1).

Americans had to create and serve in an authoritarian institution while engaging in the profoundly anti-authoritarian process of rebellion and while implementing a more democratic political system. Military requirements thus harshly challenged revolutionary beliefs, practices, and peoples; but needs dictated the means. Washington and his supporters insisted that the creation of a hierarchical organization and the imposition of discipline were necessary in order to turn citizens into soldiers, soldiers into effective fighters, and the fighters into a force that could beat the British Army. The Commander-in-Chief was willing to use militia and state regiments to supplement army operations when need be, but he wanted seasoned troops as the core of his forces.

To foster proper subordination, Congress and the army collaborated to create a military justice system by which officers, soldiers, and associated civilian personnel were controlled not only by civil laws but by the more stringent rules of war. The congressionally mandated Articles of War established the ordinances governing the army. They provided military commanders with a legislative as well as a strategic or tactical basis for issuing the orders that compelled actions conducive to military success. In addition, military and associated personnel were bound by the custom of war, which encompassed the established principles and practices peculiar to army life. The combination of laws, orders, and custom helped establish an institutional culture and professional ethos that emphasized deference to one's superiors in the chain of command and national interest above self-interest. Joseph Plumb Martin, a soldier of many years service, gave evidence of that when he wrote that the militia would not have endured the torments that the army did.

They would have considered themselves (as in reality they were and are) free citizens, not bound by any cords that were not of their own manufacturing, and when the hardships of fatigue, starvation, cold and nakedness... begun to seize upon them... they would have instantly quitted the service... they would not have answered the end so well as regular soldiers... The regulars were there and there obliged to be; we could not go away when we pleased without exposing ourselves to military punishment, and we had trouble enough to undergo without that. (Martin, 1963, p. 239)

Even so, mutinies did erupt on occasion, desertions were frequent, and insubordination was commonplace. The application of discipline could not fully control the social and political practices and expectations that were part of the Revolution.

2   Representation

The issue of discipline – and especially its corollary, subordination – both supported and interfered with the Continental Army's secondary role as America's marching band. In addition to its military mission, the army had the political one of ensuring separation without undermining or threatening the Revolution. The army was to represent, and not only demonstrate, the unified will of the revolutionary American states and people to both friends and foes, foreign and domestic. As Washington reminded his troops in August 1776, "the honor and success of the army and the safety of our bleeding country depends upon harmony and good agreement with each other. That the Provinces are all united to oppose the common enemy, and all distinctions sunk in the name of an American, to make this honorable and preserve the Liberty of our Country, ought

to be our only emulation" (Washington, 1931–44, 5, pp. 361–2). As it turned out, the army displayed both the ideals and the reality of the Revolution: it represented unity but reflected divisions – from the administrative level down to the soldiers in the ranks.

The Continental Army was also to be the image if not the embodiment of the American citizenry and their virtues. It was supposed to reflect what some leaders hoped was already inherent – if perhaps too deeply buried – in the people. Given that supposition it does not appear that the army had a prescribed social mission: Congress and the American people did not specifically charge the army to execute social change; it was just to exercise the American spirit. In the process of doing so, however, especially as it attempted to foster recruiting and retention while implanting discipline, the army became a manifestation of some of the young nation's social issues and concerns.

Administration

In accordance with its political mission, the Continental Army was supposed to exemplify civilian control of the military. Washington certainly promoted such civil power even as he dealt with the difficulties that ensued as a result of it. The biggest problem was not so much civilian authority as it was civilian authorities. Washington found that he had to apply to them constantly for support even as he trod carefully between congressional and state exertions of their respective powers over the army. To have had to comply with 13 sovereign heads instead of one would have made Washington's assignment impossible, so he made it clear that Congress, having created the army, had ultimate control of it even though the states were expected to support it.

Congress, unfortunately, was often ineffective as a command body and inefficient as an administrative one. Initially this was due to its attempts to oversee the army via committees. Congress moved to change that in 1777 when it made the Board of War a permanent body rather than a standing committee and expanded its duties to include the supervision of recruitment, prisoners, and weapons production. Problems developed, however, due to political and personal challenges – specifically by Major Generals Horatio Gates, who had been appointed president of the Board, and Thomas Conway – against Washington's leadership. After Congress dismissed the criticisms and confirmed Washington's command, the Board became, once again, simply an administrative rather than a command body. Congress looked to Washington to formulate military policy, and he returned the favor by always doing it in conjunction with and through Congress. This essentially continued even after Congress transformed the Board of War into an executive department, that of the Secretary at War, in October 1781.

Personnel

An inspection of the Continental Army's officers, soldiers, and camp followers provides a glimpse of America's social organization and reveals some discrepancies between that reality and the ideal image touted by some revolutionaries. While they could easily characterize officers as Cincinnatus, the citizen-soldier, it was more difficult to cast many of the soldiers, those from the disrespected and dispossesed ranks of society, in that role. The Continental Army, and its attending civilians, reflected a stratified eighteenth-century American society and culture. Yet American egalitarianism was also evident in the army's struggles to maintain deference and order in the face of democracy and individualism.

Both soldiers and officers, by their origins and ambitions, represented the equalitarian nature of American society in comparison to their European allies and foes. That egalitarianism was perhaps more evident in the composition of the officer corps than in the companies of men, for a good many, if not the majority of the soldiers, especially after 1776, came from the lower orders. Many had little or no property or marketable skill, some were quite young, and quite a number of them were foreign-born or black. Such social origins did not, however, translate into subordinate behavior. These soldiers – and many officers – struggled with army and

civilian officials to have their needs met and their rights recognized at the same time as they fought for the nation's independence.

The legions of civilians who travelled with and served the army also revealed much about America's social as well as military organization. These camp followers included the minor merchants called sutlers, the civilian employees of the staff departments, and the servants and family members of the officers and soldiers. They came from all the states and from all social ranks. The majority – the laborers, servants, and wives and children of soldiers – were of modest or lowly origins, but there were some – merchants, staff department administrators, and officers' wives – who represented the middling and upper orders. Most of these people mixed personal interest with public service, and many gave the former priority over the latter.

Servant and symbol

As Americans associated a standing army with tyranny, Congress and Washington endeavored to make the Continental Army a citizens' army, in image if not always in fact. They tried to make it a reality through the various measures that they adopted and by insisting that the army respect citizens' rights and property. They made it clear that the army was not to be used as a coercive force against the people. The militia in policing loyalists on the home front could and did do that. Furthermore, although the army was separate from the militias and state forces, it still had to work with them. In supporting them and being supplemented by them, the army's connection to the civilian populace was reinforced.

The Continental Army was supposed to symbolize and serve a virtuous people by exhibiting moral and military courage. The republicanism of the Revolution rested upon such assumptions of an actively engaged and virtuous citizenry both in and out of the military. In actuality, the army, in its composition, organization, and operations, stood and fought for a people and nation in search of independence and virtue, but not fully in possession of either.

REFERENCES

Martin, Joseph Plumb: *Private Yankee Doodle: Being a Narrative of Some of the Adventures, Dangers and Sufferings of a Revolutionary Soldier* (Hallowell, ME: 1830); repr., ed. George F. Scheer (New York: Popular Library, 1963).

Washington, George.: *The Writings of George Washington from the Original Manuscript Sources 1745–1799*, 39 vols, vols. 3, 5, and 23, ed. John C. Fitzpatrick (Washington, D.C.: Government Printing Office, 1931–44).

Wright Robert K., Jr.: *The Continental Army* (Washington, D.C.: Center of Military History, United States Army, 1983).

FURTHER READING

Higginbotham, Don: *The War for American Independence: Military Attitudes, Policies, and Practice, 1763–1789* (1971), repr. (Boston, MA: Northeastern University Press, 1983).

Martin, James Kirby, and Lender, Mark Edward: *A Respectable Army: The Military Origins of the Republic, 1763–1789* (Arlington Heights, IL: Harlan Davidson, 1982).

Mayer, Holly A.: *Belonging to the Army: Camp Followers and Community During the American Revolution* (Columbia: University of South Carolina Press, 1996).

Neimeyer, Charles Patrick: *America Goes to War: A Social History of the Continental Army* (New York: New York University Press, 1996).

CHAPTER THIRTY-NINE

Militia, guerrilla warfare, tactics, and weaponry

MARK V. KWASNY

GUERRILLA warfare, known as partisan warfare or *petite guerre* in the eighteenth century, was an important characteristic of the American Revolutionary War. Generals and statesmen deliberately used it in pursuit of their war aims, but even without this push from the top, local militia forces and Amerindians all engaged in guerrilla activities from the start. Forces ranging in size from a dozen to over 1,000 fought each other in a series of brutal encounters using mostly muskets, rifles, sabers, axes, and knives. These partisan fighters fought for their homes, their families, and their very survival, in a fashion that guerrilla warriors in the twentieth century would easily recognize.

The first clashes initiated this guerrilla warfare. The Massachusetts militia mobilized in April 1775 to resist the march of the hated British Army through the countryside, while in the South, local Whig militiamen rallied to suppress the Tories by defeating them at Moore's Creek on February 27, 1776. Lord Dunmore, royal governor of Virginia, launched raids in 1775 against Whig plantations, tried to get the Ohio Amerindians to attack the Virginia frontiers, and offered freedom to enslaved Blacks to enlist in his Loyal Ethiopians. British policy quickly incorporated the native warriors along the frontiers. In the South, the British encouraged the Cherokee to attack, while to the north, agents working from British bases in Niagara and Detroit urged the natives to strike.

General John Burgoyne used the threat of guerrilla warfare during his campaign in upstate New York in 1777. With several hundred Canadian and Iroquois Amerindians, Burgoyne threatened the rebels with the terrors of Amerindian attacks if they resisted. Burgoyne tried to control the Amerindians, but they grew disgusted with these restraints and most went home. The major effect of Burgoyne's threat was to strengthen the opposing American militia, as frightened and enraged inhabitants took up arms.

After the capture of Charleston, South Carolina in May 1780, Lord George Germain, Secretary of State, urged Sir Henry Clinton, the British commander, to use the Tory militia as the rebels used their own militia: to garrison forts and pacify areas by suppressing rebel activity. Ultimately, the British policy failed because they relied on the Tories too much. Tories could not handle the more numerous Whig forces without substantial support from the British Army.

American leaders relied heavily on the partisan qualities of their militia from the start. George Washington used the militia to fight a partisan war around the British in New York City. Washington and the state governments used the militia to suppress Tories, a job the militiamen did effectively, and to stand guard between the British and American armies as a forward defense. If the British advanced, militia and Continental detachments would swarm on the flanks and rear of the British columns. Philip Schuyler used small parties to slow Burgoyne's march southward from Ticonderoga in the summer of 1777, and his successor, Horatio Gates, had militia forces threaten and ultimately cut Burgoyne's communications with Canada.

Daniel Morgan's riflemen, armed with the long rifle and dressed in hunting shirts, joined Gates and helped neutralize the Amerindians. In the South, as Gates advanced toward the town of Camden in August 1780, he sent out detachments of Continentals to join with partisan leader Thomas Sumter, and ordered Francis Marion to take command of the militia operating in the lowlands of North and South Carolina. Gates's successor, Nathanael Greene, relied even more heavily on this guerrilla warfare. Thus, guerrilla warfare influenced the strategies employed by both sides.

Region by region, this partisan activity had many similarities and yet a few distinctive characteristics. After the evacuation of Brooklyn in 1776, Jonathan Trumbull, governor of Connecticut, and Washington urged the Connecticut militia to raid Long Island. Over the next seven years, Whig militia units, occasionally joined by Continental troops, crossed the sound in whaleboats and attacked Tory settlements and forts, and Tories raided Connecticut ports. For example, in May 1777, a detachment of Continentals and militia crossed to the island, attacked a Tory battalion, lost one man, killed six Tories and captured 90, destroyed a quantity of forage gathered for use by the British Army, and then returned to Connecticut, having traveled 90 miles in 25 hours. In August 1777, General Samuel Parsons led 200 Continentals and militia to Setauket, Long Island, besieged a fort held by 150 Tories, then withdrew to Connecticut. Swift raids, where success occurred immediately or not at all, were the usual tactics. To counter the threat of Tory attacks, Trumball ordered militia guards along the coast throughout the entire war, and by 1778 Washington stationed detachments of Continental soldiers near the coast. The British augmented their island defenses too. In the winter of 1778–9, 1,000 Tories, the Queen's Rangers, and a detachment of British grenadiers garrisoned Long Island, while in the summer of 1779, the British Light Infantry and the 17th Regiment, in addition to the Queen's Rangers, were all stationed there.

In southwestern Connecticut, William Tryon, former royal governor of New York, and other Tories burned towns and took the local inhabitants hostage. By 1781, the region was a virtual no-man's-land. The local militia, however, continued to patrol the area and intercept as many of the plundering raids as possible.

In Westchester County, New York, in what would be called the Neutral Ground, Whig and Tory militiamen, as well as parties loyal to no one, infested the countryside. The most notorious Tory unit was James DeLancey's "Cowboys." The destruction grew so bad that in 1778 Washington ordered the newly created Light Infantry Corps, consisting of infantry, militia, and dragoons, to guard the Neutral Ground. The corps skirmished with Hessian *Jägers* and Colonel John Simcoe's Queen's Rangers. Simcoe personally believed the constant fighting was bad for the British and good for the rebels, whom he considered experts at scouting and skirmishing. In an attempt to rid the area of the hated "Cowboys," Washington sent Continentals and militia to make a surprise winter attack on DeLancey's base at Morrisania in January 1781. The raiders burned the barracks, killed 30 and captured 45 Tories, while losing only 25 men. British soldiers from a nearby fort joined the surviving Tories to pursue the raiders, but after a brief skirmish the pursuers gave up the chase. The plundering continued through 1783 with neither side exerting much control over it.

The guerrilla activity began in New Jersey in December 1776, when the inhabitants reacted to the outrages and plundering done by the Germans, British, and Tories. Breaking their newly sworn oaths of allegiance to the King, men took up arms and began to harass the local British garrisons. They captured Tory leaders, killed lone British soldiers, and sniped at enemy garrisons. In the midst of these partisan attacks, Washington launched his winter offensive that culminated in the successes at Trenton and Princeton. Through the next six years, New Jersey militiamen and detachments of Continentals skirmished almost constantly. Washington encouraged, but did not always control, these activities. One prominent leader was New Jersey militia general, Philemon Dickinson. In January 1777 he led 400 militia in a surprise winter attack across a partially frozen river and forced an equal number of British foragers to retreat from Somerset Courthouse. In November 1777 Dickinson led 1,400 Jersey militia onto Staten Island but failed to trap the Tory and British garrisons. They skirmished throughout the day and then withdrew.

The war for forage was a bitter struggle that constantly escalated, forcing the British to use ever larger detachments. When they ran into rebel militia or Continentals, part of the foragers would delay the Americans while the rest tried to gather the supplies and return to New York. One trick used against British foragers was to drive a herd of cattle near the British lines and then hide foot and horse soldiers in the nearby woods. A few militiamen dressed as farmers would stay with the cattle. At first the British and Germans ignored the ruse, but by late winter 1777 meat was scarce and they took the bait more than once.

The British struck back, raiding coastal towns by boat, burning buildings, and dragging off militiamen or prominent civilians. Often the British targeted Continental detachments. In January 1780, about 300 British infantry crossed from Staten, surprised a Continental garrison in Newark, and inflicted 42 casualties. The British took no losses. At the same time, Simcoe raided into New Jersey with 200 dismounted Rangers in an attempt to capture Washington, but was met on the coast by the militia and forced to retreat. The British and Tories learned that they had to act swiftly because the local militia would muster quickly once the alarm spread.

The British watched as their casualties mounted and their soldiers became fatigued by this constant guerrilla activity, even during the winter months. Whenever British forces moved, they were surrounded by militia and Continentals. The best example of this occurred in New Jersey in June 1778. Washington ultimately sent over 5,000 militiamen and Continentals, including Morgan's riflemen, to harass the British flanks and rear as they tried to march from Philadelphia to New York City. At Monmouth Courthouse on June 28, the two armies met and fought a pitched battle, but the British took more casualties from the constant skirmishing than they did in the conventional battle.

In the South, the partisan units fought a guerrilla war characterized by mounted forces sweeping across long distances. This fierce struggle began with the brutality of one man in particular, Banastre Tarleton. On May 29, 1780, Tarleton launched a frontal charge against a detachment of Continental soldiers at the Waxhaws, and even after the Continentals surrendered, Tarleton's legion continued to cut them down with sabers. Around the same time, Tories burned down the home of Thomas Sumter, who then collected militiamen enraged by the massacre and the plundering. Sir Henry Clinton issued a proclamation on June 3 demanding that the people either help the British or be considered rebels. Many southerners feared they would be forced to serve in the British Army and instead resisted. Germain's policy to use Tories for pacification merely worsened the situation, as newly organized Tory units sought revenge against their hated Whig neighbors. Whig militia acted swiftly to suppress any Tory uprisings as the guerrilla war escalated.

On June 20, 1780 about 1300 Tories gathered at Ramsour's Mill. Whig militiamen launched a surprise attack and scattered the Tories. During the month of July Tory and Whig militia fought twelve engagements, intimidating the pro-British element. From July on, few groups rallied to the British Army. When Cornwallis issued a proclamation in North Carolina in February 1781 calling out the Tories, few responded.

Isaac Shelby and Elijah Clarke defeated Patrick Ferguson and 500 British regulars and Tories on August 17, the day after the battle of Camden. The Whigs lured Ferguson into an ambush, but the British charged, putting the rebel riflemen at a disadvantage. Shelby rallied his 40 reserves, let out a rousing Amerindian yell, and counter-charged. Ferguson's men were routed, losing over 220 men. The rebels lost 11. Ferguson ran into worse trouble in October after marching through the western counties. At King's Mountain, over 900 backcountry riflemen caught him, dismounted, and fought a typical forest battle, where individual movement and fire took precedence over unit actions. Ferguson's men could not emulate the riflemen's tactics or their rage, and in the end, Ferguson and about 200 Tories were killed, and 700 others captured.

Partisans Francis Marion and Thomas Sumter attracted a lot of attention. Marion operated in the low counties near Georgetown and the Santee River, harassing Tories and disrupting the movement of British reinforcements and supplies. In September 1780 a party of 250 Tories tried to catch Marion but he kept out constant patrols and was almost impossible to surprise. Instead, he attacked with 53 men and routed the Tory advance guard. The other 200 Tories pursued and Marion retreated, laying an ambush in nearby woods. The Tories followed carelessly, fell into the trap, and were routed. Sixty additional recruits joined Marion the next day. A little later 700 British and Tories hunted him. This time Marion simply dismissed the local members of his band and fled into North Carolina. He then returned on September 25 in a swift night march to Black Mingo Creek. After launching a diversionary attack to the front, Marion swept around the flank of a Tory unit and routed the already alerted Tories. Marion realized that the Tories had been warned by the sound of horses crossing a nearby bridge, so from then on he used blankets to cover bridges he had to cross. On October 26 Marion launched a dawn assault against another Tory force, sending out two flanking columns and personally leading the strongest party frontally. The surprise worked and the Tories fled, losing over 430 men. Marion had no casualties. Twice in October and November Marion unsuccessfully attacked fortified Georgetown. Cornwallis finally sent Tarleton to hunt Marion, but Marion avoided him and fled the area.

Sumter's security arrangements were not as good as Marion's, enabling the British 63rd Regiment to catch and rout Sumter at Fishing Creek. Then Tarleton returned from his pursuit of Marion and on November 20 struck Sumter on the Tyger River, scattering his men and wounding Sumter.

When Greene arrived in the South in December 1780, he sent Lieutenant Colonel Henry Lee with 150 infantry and 150 dragoons to join Marion, while Daniel Morgan led over 600 Continentals westward to coordinate with the local militia. Morgan launched cavalry raids under the command of Lieutenant Colonel William Washington, who captured 100 Tories at Rugeley's Mill by bluffing them with a fake cannon. Cornwallis sent Tarleton after Morgan, which resulted in the total defeat of Tarleton at the Cowpens. As Greene and Morgan fled through North Carolina, Greene left Marion, Sumter, and Andrew Pickens behind to harass the British garrisons and prevent reinforcements from getting to Cornwallis. Sumter unsuccessfully attacked a couple of forts, while Pickens followed into North Carolina. He joined Lee to eliminate 400 Tories commanded by Colonel John Pyle on February 25, 1781. By pretending to be Tarleton's men, they rode alongside the Tories, then suddenly turned and sabered or shot them. About 100 were killed and many wounded. There were no rebel casualties. This incident squelched most of the British recruiting in North Carolina.

After Cornwallis retreated to the coast following the battle of Guilford Courthouse, Greene re-entered South Carolina and urged Pickens, Sumter, and Marion to attack as many British posts as possible. Greene unsuccessfully besieged Fort Ninety-six, while Pickens attacked Augusta, Georgia. Marion, supported by Lee, captured Ft. Watson by building a tower and having his riflemen fire into the fort. They then captured Ft. Motte by setting fire to the nearby buildings. Meanwhile, Sumter's forces were cut up badly in June by Lord Rawdon, British commander in the South. Sumter, Marion, and Lee together attacked the 19th Regiment and a party of Tories at Quinby in July. The British formed a hollow square so Sumter attacked in a half-moon with Lee's cavalry in reserve. The forces engaged in a firefight until the Americans ran low on ammunition and retreated, having taken 35 casualties. The British lost 70 men, including 50 captured by Whig cavalrymen who circled around behind the British. In August, Marion slipped south of Charleston, joined the local militia, and with 400 men engaged 550 regulars and Tories. He then ambushed 100 of the Tories as they pursued him across a causeway but the infantry arrived and Marion's men, low on ammunition, melted into the swamps.

Pickens, Marion, and Lee rejoined Greene for the battle of Eutaw Springs in September 1781, and despite their defeat, they confined the British in Charleston and Savannah. Partisan and Continental forces fanned out and by the summer of 1782 had stamped out any remaining Tory resistance. In one of the last fights, 200 British and black dragoons encircled Marion's men, but the Whigs used muskets firing buckshot and dropped 20 dragoons and ten horses. Marion, however, had no mounted support, so he kept his troops in the woods until the British withdrew.

Along the frontiers, a 150-year war of extermination continued unabated. British agents convinced several nations of the Iroquois Confederation, and Mohawk Chief Joseph Brant, to join the British against the rebels. After the British failure at Ft. Stanwix in 1777, the Iroquois, supported by Tory and occasionally British regulars, began a series of devastating raids. Similar to the swift raids of the southern partisans, the attackers had no artillery and thus usually could not take forts, but individual families and unfortified buildings were in danger. Often the Amerindians used feigned withdrawals and ambushes. In the Wyoming Valley of Pennsylvania, 110 Rangers and over 460 Amerindians attacked in June 1778, trapping 800 militiamen in a nearby fort. When 400 emerged to attack the raiders, the Amerindians outflanked and routed the militia, killing about 300 men. The fort surrendered and the raiders burned the settlements. In the Mohawk Valley, Brant led a similar raid, but the local inhabitants remained safe in the forts. Brant's men burned the homes and killed the livestock.

Americans retaliated by burning Tioga and Unadilla in September and October 1778. Butler led 150 Tory rangers, 50 British regulars, and over 300 Amerindians in November against Cherry Valley, New York. Again the locals remained safe in the fort while the Amerindians burned the village. In 1779, Washington sent General John Sullivan to attack the Iroquois homeland with over 4,000 Continentals from the east, while Colonel Daniel Brodhead led over 600 from Fort Pitt. Only at Newtown

on August 29, did about 800 Tories and Amerindians resist. Sullivan's men spotted the ambush and outflanked the Amerindians. Casualties for both sides were light and the defenders retreated. Sullivan destroyed crops and numerous villages, and forced the Iroquois to winter at Niagara.

In 1780, Iroquois war parties terrorized the frontier of New York and Pennsylvania, eliminating several settlements. The Mohawks even attacked the Oneida, who were helping the United States. Meanwhile, Amerindian war parties raided from Canada, burning towns near Ft. George and Ft. Anne. At least 300 or more people were killed, six forts captured, and 700 buildings burned in 1780. The local militia often pursued but rarely did more than skirmish with the withdrawing Amerindians. The year 1781 saw similar raids, but finally in the summer of 1782, the British called a halt to Brant's attacks.

In Kentucky, Simon Kenton and Daniel Boone led the local settlers in their defense against the Shawnees and other Ohio Amerindians. By the end of 1776, some families had already fled to the east. Fortunately for the settlers, the Amerindians could not take forts. Harrodsburg's fortification repulsed three attacks in 1776–7, but at Boonesboro in April 1777, a party chased a few Amerindians and ran into an ambush. The men never returned. Throughout 1777, war parties made it deadly to leave a fort.

In 1778–9, General George Rogers Clark captured Cahokia, Kaskaskia, and Vincennes, thus threatening the Ohio Amerindians with encirclement from the east, south, and west. Then in 1779 Colonel John Bowman invaded Ohio with 250 men and burned Chillicothe. In response, the British sent 100 regulars and 70 Canadians from Detroit, with a couple of cannon, to join 300 Amerindians. They quickly captured a small fort but the British commander, Captain Henry Byrd, was disgusted at the massacre of the garrison. They next captured 500 Americans, and Byrd ended the campaign and escorted the prisoners to Detroit. The Amerindians went home, knowing they could do little against forts without the cannon.

In March 1780, Clark led 1,000 men into Ohio, destroyed Chillicothe, and then engaged a force of about 300 Amerindians. Both sides tried to outflank each other, but the superior numbers and American cannon forced the Amerindians to retreat. American casualties numbered about 30, but the Amerindians took triple that loss. Clark then destroyed Piqua and returned to Kentucky, having marched 480 miles in 31 days. The Amerindian wars were typified by these long, rapid marches culminating in brief clashes and destroyed settlements.

By 1781, the Ohio Amerindians realized they could not eliminate the Kentucky settlements. Still, they attacked, increasingly targeting white travelers along the Ohio River. In retaliation, Colonel David Williamson led an attack in 1782 against the Moravian mission of Gnadenhutten and killed 96 unresisting Amerindians. British captain, William Caldwell, and Brant led 1,000 Indians and 50 British against Wheeling, Virginia, but aborted the attack and turned against Kentucky. A nearby fort held out, and Kentucky militiamen came to the rescue. The first 176 men immediately pursued rather than wait for Simon Kenton and 470 reinforcements. The 176 men crossed the Ohio River and were wiped out in an ambush. Clark hit Ohio in November 1782, destroying Chillicothe and Piqua again while meeting no resistance. Finally, the fighting subsided in 1783, though the war along the Ohio River and into Ohio would continue for decades.

In the South, the Amerindian wars ended sooner. In 1776, Whig militiamen and Continentals mounted two separate campaigns into Cherokee territory, destroying villages and crops. The Cherokees sued for peace and the other southern Amerindians remained quiet. Fearing a renewal of Cherokee attacks in 1780, western riflemen swept through the Cherokee villages, burning them once again. When the Tories of Georgia called for the Creeks to help them in 1780–1, the Creeks refused to help.

Clearly, guerrilla warfare was an integral part of the Revolutionary War. The basic tactics of ambush, hit-and-run, surprise attacks, and trickery were similar throughout the regions, as were the muskets, sabers, and lack of cannon. Rifles and mounted parties gave the southern fighting a distinctive flavor, while the viciousness of the Amerindian wars typified the frontier war. Individual leaders, such as Brant, Marion, Sumter, Kenton, and Clark became experts at this guerrilla warfare.

The impact of this fighting was critical. British movement in the middle states was severely hampered, Burgoyne was surrounded, British control of the South was destroyed, and the western settlements of New York, Pennsylvania, and Kentucky were saved. British and German soldiers, Continentals, and most of all, militiamen and Amerindians participated in eight years of guerrilla war

FURTHER READING

Buchanan, John: *The Road to Guilford Courthouse: The American Revolution in the Carolinas* (New York: John Wiley & Sons, Inc., 1997).

Eckert, Allan W.: *That Dark and Bloody River: Chronicles of the Ohio River Valley* (New York: Bantam Books, 1995).

Ewald, Johann: *Treatise on Partisan Warfare*, trans. Robert A. Selig and David Curtis Skaggs (New York: Greenwood Press, 1991).

Graymont, Barbara: *The Iroquois in the American Revolution* (New York: Syracuse University Press, 1972).

Kwasny, Mark V.: *Washington's Partisan War, 1775–1783* (Kent, OH: Kent State University Press, 1996).

CHAPTER FORTY

Naval operations during the War for Independence

CLARK G. REYNOLDS

NAVIES played a major role in the war of the American Revolution before and after the conflict became global in 1778. Britain's Royal Navy, with undisputed control of North American coastal waters, sealifted and supported army units at will along the coast between Halifax, Nova Scotia and Jamaica in the West Indies until France and its navy allied with the United States in 1778. Thereafter, General George Washington based his strategic movements on exploiting the French fleet to neutralize Britain's fleet long enough for the Franco-American army to achieve a decisive victory on land. This was finally accomplished by the Battle of the Virginia Capes on September 5, 1781, resulting in the surrender of Major General Lord Charles Cornwallis's army at Yorktown, Virginia and American Independence. Naval operations included blockade, shore bombardments, commerce raiding, coastal defense, and battles on inland lakes as well as at sea.

During the summer of 1775 six American armed schooners began attacking British supply ships off Boston, advanced base of the British North American Squadron. Its commander, Vice Admiral Samuel Graves, responded by dispatching four small warships to destroy Falmouth (now Portland), Maine and 13 anchored merchant ships. This was accomplished by a naval bombardment and a landing party of sailors and marines on October 18. Instead of intimidating the patriots, the incident only heightened their resolve. First Lord of the Admiralty, the Earl of Sandwich, replaced an indecisive Graves with Vice Admiral Lord Richard Howe early in 1776, with orders to blockade and seize the major American ports and destroy colonial shipping. But Howe elected to seek a peaceful settlement to the revolt by calling in all but six of his 75 blockading warships, an unsuccessful ploy.

The Continental Congress issued letters of marque and reprisal to merchant captains to arm their vessels as privateers for attacking British commerce and created the Continental Navy to construct and convert ships as men-of-war. From Philadelphia, a flotilla of eight of them took several merchantmen as prizes and briefly occupied Nassau in the Bahama Islands in March 1776. The defenders of Fort Ticonderoga in upstate New York built a squadron of gunboats to augment their defenses on Lake Champlain. Washington's pressure against Boston forced the British navy to abandon the city and retire to Halifax in March, enabling Washington to shift his army to New York.

In June 1776 Howe sent an amphibious force to capture Charleston, South Carolina, only to have it repulsed by the defenders of Sullivan's Island at the harbor entrance. In July, Howe landed troops on Long Island and forced Washington out of the city of New York by December. On the shores of Lake Champlain a British Army force from Canada constructed a force of 20 makeshift gunboats that destroyed the American squadron of similar size commanded by General Benedict Arnold at the battle of Valcour Island on October 11. But winter weather forced the British to withdraw. The Royal Navy clamped a vigorous blockade on all American seaports which prevented major exports, especially farm products, as well as imports from reaching the rebelling states – a damaging economic blow that lasted the duration of the war.

The British ministry of Lord North and Sandwich planned to crush mercantile New England in a grand pincers movement executed by armies from Canada and New York. Lieutenant General Sir William Howe (the admiral's brother) would march north from New York along the Hudson River to meet up with General John Burgoyne coming south from Canada via Lake Champlain. But coordination was impossible. Burgoyne easily captured Fort Ticonderoga in July 1777, only to discover the Howe brothers had decided that instead of pushing up the Hudson they would move by sea against Philadelphia, which they captured in September. The same month Burgoyne's army was defeated and captured at the battle of Saratoga by an American army. Washington meanwhile controlled the countryside around Philadelphia, forcing Admiral Howe to supply his brother's army inside that city by sea via the Delaware River and Chesapeake Bay, hindered by American shore batteries and small naval vessels.

By the start of 1778 the British held only New York and Philadelphia. The seaward approaches to the latter were threatened by floating mines, the work of inventor David Bushnell, who had also devised the world's first submarine for use against Howe's ships off New York. Both devices had only nuisance value, but they displayed the same Yankee audacity as a small American squadron of two brigs and a cutter, which operated out of French ports against British shipping in European waters during the spring of 1777. The North ministry had proved so inept in directing the war that Admiral Howe retired from the navy in disgust.

The American successes convinced France to conclude an alliance with the United States in February 1778. The French Navy, undergoing a major expansion, aimed at humbling the British Empire and allowed an American sloop-of-war under the command of Captain John Paul Jones to operate successfully out of Brest against British merchantmen in home waters. The French Mediterranean fleet sailed for America, and in June France declared war on Britain.

The arrival of these 12 ships of the line under Vice Admiral Count J. B. d'Estaing caused the British Army to abandon Philadelphia late in June 1778 and march overland to New York. The deep-draft hulls of the French ships prevented them from passing over the Sandy Hook bar to attack New York, and in August a storm prevented them from dislodging a British garrison at Newport, Rhode Island. D'Estaing thereupon established his base of operations at Boston, and the British fleet remained at New York. General Washington now realized that the key to victory lay in the French Navy neutralizing the British fleet in American waters.

France, however, viewed the American campaign as only one theater of the war and honed its Atlantic fleet at Brest of 32 of the line and 13 frigates in order to deny Britain naval supremacy in European waters and ultimately to invade England. During training exercises off Ushant on July 27, 1778 this fleet encountered the British home fleet of 30 of the line and six frigates. For three hours the two fleets pounded each other before the French broke off the action. But Britain could not take advantage of the absence of the French Mediterranean fleet in America for vigorous operations in Europe because of the growing threat of Spain and its sizeable navy entering the war on the side of France. The French Navy's capture of Dominica in the British West Indies in September 1778 motivated the British to reinforce their North American fleet. It thereupon seized the island of St. Lucia in November and Savannah, Georgia in December. Major naval operations in America thereupon shifted from the northern colonies to the Caribbean.

Early in 1779 France and Spain developed plans to invade England, with Spain declaring war in June. Their combined fleets of 66 ships of the line so outnumbered Britain's naval forces in European waters that the latter could not maintain a close blockade of French and Spanish ports. Spain's fleet easily joined up with the French Atlantic fleet off Cape Finisterre to cover the invasion transports assembling at

France's English Channel ports. The two allies sluggishly coordinated their preparations, however, and both were easily intimidated by aggressive British counteractions.

British Home Fleet movements emanated from the actions of its chief of staff, Captain Richard Kempenfelt. With the Royal Navy outnumbered, Kempenfelt adopted a "fleet in being" strategy in August 1779: while active frigate cruiser squadrons patrolled each end of the English Channel to prevent the invasion transports from concentrating, the Home Fleet of 25 of the line stood ready in the Western Approaches of the Channel to respond to enemy fleet movements. The French and Spanish fleets sortied late in the month, seeking battle to clear the way for invasion. But the British fleet avoided contact, skillfully maneuvering until disease-ridden Franco-Spanish crews became too exhausted to keep up. France and Spain thereupon abandoned their invasion scheme, hoping to resurrect it later.

This was not to be, because Kempenfelt's policy remained in force until new warship construction began to restore British naval supremacy. "Flying squadrons" of British cruisers attacked enemy merchant shipping while protecting their own convoys, and the Home Fleet actively patrolled the Western Approaches. This open blockade of French and Spanish ports included the seizure of neutral merchantmen, a policy which, however, antagonized other European powers. Kempenfelt simultaneously introduced aggressive battle tactics into fleet doctrine.

With the active Home Fleet on the defensive in the Channel, Britain conducted offensive naval operations on a global scale. They cleared most of Indian Ocean waters of the French, kept Gibraltar supplied against a siege by the Spanish, continued the pressure against the American revolutionaries in New England, and attacked French and Spanish West Indian colonies and shipping. France improved its naval skills under a series of aggressive admirals in American waters, including operations out of Boston to support the patriots.

The American campaign of 1779 began with Admiral d'Estaing's capture of the British West Indian islands of St. Vincent and Grenada in the early summer. On July 6 his 25 ships of the line frustrated 21

British ships in the naval battle of Grenada. A British expeditionary force occupied the shores of Penobscot Bay in Maine in June for a new base. The Americans responded in July with their own expedition in 22 transports, escorted by a frigate, six smaller warships, and 12 privateers, which besieged the British garrison. In August, the British fleet at New York dispatched seven men-of-war thence, which drove the Americans upriver, forcing them to scuttle most of their vessels. During the autumn, d'Estaing used American troops in a fruitless attempt to dislodge the British garrison holding Savannah.

As 1780 began, Britain detached Home Fleet units for offensive operations in the West Indies and against the southern colonies, all coordinated with the defense of Gibraltar and the fleet maintaining its strategic position in the Channel. Britain's blockade of neutral shipping, however, caused Russia, Sweden, and Denmark to form the Armed Neutrality in February. They moved their fleets into the North Sea to protect their merchantmen from seizure by the British. Among several other powers which eventually joined this anti-British coalition was the Netherlands, already actively supporting the Americans.

Early in January 1780 Rear Admiral Sir George B. Rodney took 22 of the line to supply the garrison at Gibraltar at the entrance to the Mediterranean Sea before proceeding to the West Indies. He captured a Spanish convoy and its seven-ship escort and on the 16th attacked a Spanish squadron of 12 ships blockading Gibraltar off Portugal's Cape St. Vincent. Rodney captured half the Spanish vessels in the so-called "Moonlight Battle." He then resupplied Gibraltar before crossing the Atlantic. In February, 11 British warships departed New York and landed an expeditionary force near Charleston to besiege the city and three frigates of the fledgling Continental Navy anchored there. The city fell in May. Supplied through Charleston and Savannah, General Cornwallis then undertook a lengthy ground campaign in the southern states.

When Rodney arrived in the West Indies in March 1780 he immediately sought battle with the reinforced French fleet of 23 of the line under Rear Admiral Count de Guichen. They clashed off the French base of Martinique on April 17. When Rodney ordered the captains of his 20 ships of the line to mass individually on the rear of the French fleet, they instead clung to the antiquated formalist doctrine of a strict line ahead formation. This enabled de Guichen to fire into their riggings and break off the action. Rodney then drilled his subordinates in the new melee tactics of massing on a portion of the enemy line. He again closed on the French fleet near Martinique on May 15, with much the same indecisive result. De Guichen then returned to Europe, escorting a large convoy.

In July 1780 another French convoy, escorted by seven of the line, delivered a French army under Lieutenant General Count J. B. D. de Vimeur de Rochambeau to Newport, earlier evacuated by the British. Although British warships from New York blockaded the French ships at Newport, the combined Franco-American army under Washington controlled the countryside from the outskirts of New York to Boston. The arrival of Rodney in September with half his ships from the Caribbean, however, frustrated Washington's plans to attack New York. The Continental Army could do nothing until a French fleet could deal with its British counterpart. Rodney returned to the West Indies, only to find that the fleet contingent he had left behind had been decimated by a hurricane and an earthquake, thereby restricting his operations.

The growth and aggressive leadership of the Royal Navy gave Britain sufficient confidence to declare war on the Netherlands at the end of 1780 for supplying both the French and the Americans. Aside from one minor naval battle in 1781, however, the Dutch had to depend on the French Navy to protect their trade and colonies in the West and East Indies.

With the French Navy at peak strength, France organized naval expeditions to America and the Indian Ocean. The former was commanded by Vice Admiral Count F. J. P. de Grasse-Tilly, the latter by Rear Admiral Pierre-André de Suffren de Saint-Tropez. The two forces sortied together from Brest in late March 1781 while the British Channel fleet was absent escorting a supply convoy to the beleaguered defenders of Gibraltar. Suffren's squadron of five of the line separated from de Grasse's America-bound fleet near the Azores Islands. In April Suffren attacked a British squadron gathering at the Cape Verde Islands for a descent on the Dutch colony at the Cape of Good Hope in southern Africa. Though Suffren was repulsed, his audacity persuaded the British to abandon their designs on the Cape, to which place Suffren then proceeded and landed troops. He continued on to the Indian Ocean where he operated successfully against British merchant shipping and a naval flotilla for the next two years.

De Grasse with 26 of the line escorted a large transatlantic convoy to Martinique, the main French base in the Caribbean, arriving on April 29. Britain's Rear Admiral Sir Samuel Hood, standing offshore with 18 of the line, opened fire on de Grasse's larger force but could not prevent de Grasse from protecting his convoy and anchorage.

The arrival of de Grasse's fleet encouraged Generals Washington and Rochambeau to seek its employment against the British Army in North America. In March 1781 the French squadron of eight of the line at Newport had sailed toward the Chesapeake Bay to support a French army force under Major General the Marquis de Lafayette in Virginia. On the 16th it drove a British squadron of equal strength away from the entrance of the bay but could not prevent the latter from anchoring inside it, forcing the French ships to return to Newport. General Cornwallis then moved his British Army overland from the Carolinas to Yorktown, Virginia. This action convinced Washington and his French allies to shift their ground forces from watching New York to attack Cornwallis in Virginia. They dispatched a ship to de Grasse in the Caribbean urging him to actively participate in their campaign. De Grasse replied by the same vessel in the affirmative.

In mid-August 1781 de Grasse headed north with 28 of the line, taking a longer but elusive course for the Chesapeake Bay where he planned to make contact with Washington's army, at that time marching south from the New York countryside toward Virginia. In addition, the eight-ship French squadron at Newport sortied, escorting a convoy of transports laden with heavy siege guns for Washington's army. It took a wide circuitous route in order to avoid the British fleet which had reconcentrated at New York. In the Caribbean, Admiral Hood, learning of de Grasse's departure, sailed directly from the West Indies to the mouth of the Chesapeake, where his 14 of the line arrived on the 27th. Seeing no French ships inside the bay, he proceeded immediately to New York, where he reported to the new fleet commander there, Rear Admiral Thomas Graves, on the 30th.

The British had expected the Franco-American army attack to come at New York or Newport. But because de Grasse had not arrived at either place, and the French squadron at Newport had departed, Graves sailed from New York next day, August 31, hoping to intercept de Grasse off the Chesapeake Bay. Graves commanded 19 of the line and seven frigates; Hood led one of its squadrons. De Grasse's more indirect course to the Chesapeake did not bring his fleet into the bay until August 30. He dropped anchor just inside the capes and established contact with Lafayette, operating against Cornwallis at Yorktown. On the morning of September 5 Graves arrived off the bay and was surprised to see de Grasse's fleet anchored inside. The latter was no less surprised, expecting instead the French squadron from Newport. Both fleets nevertheless deployed for action in what came to be known as the Battle of the Virginia Capes.

Graves intended to attack the French fleet inside the bay, but de Grasse headed out to sea at noon in order to draw the British fleet away from Cornwallis and the anticipated French convoy en route from Newport.

As the 24 French ships of the line formed their line heading into the open sea, Graves signaled all of his ships – then heading west toward the bay – to come about and re-form their line to parallel the eastward track of the French line. After his captains made their turns, a murderous cannonade began about 4:00 p.m., with the firing spreading from the van squadrons to those in the center as they came within gun range of each other. Graves ordered Hood in the rear to close up with the enemy rear, but Hood delayed, enabling the larger French fleet to mass its withering fire on Graves's van. After two hours the British ceased firing, having suffered the heaviest damage, though no ships sank on either side.

Next day, both fleets continued their eastward courses, but Graves elected not to renew the fight and soon had to scuttle his most heavily damaged ship. De Grasse maneuvered offshore for four more days, thereby preventing Graves from relieving Cornwallis at Yorktown and enabling the French convoy from Newport to deliver its siege guns to Lafayette. De Grasse then anchored in the bay, where his ships helped transport Washington's army, arriving at the head of the bay from the north, to complete the isolation of Cornwallis at Yorktown.

Graves hastened back to New York, consumed several weeks effecting repairs to his battered ships, and sortied on October 19 with 23 of the line, embarking 6,000 troops to reinforce Cornwallis's 8,000 at Yorktown. But he was too late. De Grasse, now reinforced to 36 of the line by the arrival of the Newport squadron, had transported Washington's and Rochambeau's army down the bay – 16,500 troops, strengthened by the siege guns from Newport. Besieged and cut off from seaborne supplies, Cornwallis had no choice but to surrender on the same day as Graves's sortie, the 19th. With British forces hard-pressed throughout the world, King George III's government decided to grant the Americans their independence.

The loss of America brought down the North cabinet and led to a shakeup in British naval commands. Rodney, then in England, replaced Graves in order to save the West Indies, toward which the French mounted a naval offensive following Cornwallis's surrender. Admiral Hood followed de Grasse to the Caribbean, where the French admiral with his 25 of the line landed troops on St. Kitts in mid-January 1782. On the 25th Hood's 22 ships ran past de Grasse into the roadstead, then repelled his subsequent attack. Next day, de Grasse attacked Hood's ships anchored across the entrance of the harbor and suffered heavy damage. In mid-February Rodney arrived from Britain with 12 more of the line, joining up with Hood and assuming overall command.

On April 12 Rodney and Hood with 36 of the line broke up a French invasion force bound for Jamaica by defeating de Grasse's 30 in the Battle of the Saints, named for several islets near Dominica. The British line broke through two gaps in the French line, classic melee tactics, capturing five French ships, including the flagship with Admiral de Grasse on board. Admiral Howe, recalled to active duty in command of the Home Fleet, meanwhile attacked French convoys and protected Britain's trade in Atlantic waters during 1781–2. In September 1782 Howe with 34 of the line and 12 frigates relieved Gibraltar, besieged but not challenged by 49 Franco-Spanish ships of the line. Naval battles continued in the Indian Ocean until April 1783, four months after peace had been concluded.

The French fleet's victory at the Battle of the Virginia Capes proved decisive in the securing of American independence. Just how fortunate the Americans were to capitalize on this achievement lies in the fact that this battle was the only major French naval victory against a British fleet during their many wars between 1690 and 1815.

FURTHER READING

Buel, R., Jr.: *In Irons: Britain's Naval Supremacy and the American Revolutionary Economy* (New Haven: Yale University Press, 1998).

Dull, J.: *The French Navy and American Independence: A Study of Arms and Diplomacy, 1774–1787* (Princeton: Princeton University Press, 1976).

Fowler, W. M., Jr.: *Rebels Under Sail: The American Navy during the Revolution* (New York: Scribner's, 1976).

James, W. M.: *The British Navy in Adversity: A Study of the War of American Independence* (New York: Longmans, Green, 1926).

Jenkins, E. H.: *A History of the French Navy* (London: Macdonald and James, 1973).

Mahan, A. T.: *The Major Operations of the Navies in the War of American Independence* (London: 1913), repr. (Westport, Ct.: Greenwood, 1969).

Reynolds, C. G.: *Navies in History* (Annapolis: Naval Institute Press, 1998).

Yerxa, D. A.: "The burning of Falmouth, 1775: a case study in British imperial pacification," *Maine Historical Society Quarterly*, 14 (1975), 119–61.

CHAPTER FORTY-ONE

The First United States Navy

JAMES C. BRADFORD

GREAT Britain's North American colonies all bordered the Atlantic Ocean and their economies consequently depended to varying degrees on the sea. Americans often ignored legislation enacted by Parliament to regulate overseas commerce as they traded with the West Indies and even with Britain itself. After the Seven Year's War, Britain stepped up efforts to enforce imperial policies creating tensions that escalated toward revolution. Prior to the outbreak of war the British Government's main instrument of coercion was the Royal Navy and once an army was sent to the colonies it was dependent on seaborne logistical support. Indeed, British strategy for subduing the rebels often required ocean transport such as for the Southern Campaigns of 1776 and 1779–80 as well as the capture of New York in 1776 and Philadelphia in 1778.

Clashes between the colonials and British naval forces were inevitable. In 1772 residents of Rhode Island attacked and burned the armed revenue schooner *Gaspée* in retaliation for its enforcement of navigation acts and theft of local produce and livestock. Boston workers often fought with off-duty sailors who they believed were taking their jobs and driving down wages.

It was only natural that when war began, the Americans moved to counter British power at sea. Four types of naval forces served the American cause during the War for Independence: forces raised by army officers for operations in limited areas, most notably the cruisers commissioned by George Washington to prey on British shipping in 1775 and the flotilla assembled by Benedict Arnold to contest British passage of Lake Champlain in 1776; navies established by 11 of the 13 states; privateers commissioned by the Continental Congress and state governments; and the Continental Navy, operated between 1775 and 1785.

The first of these government-sanctioned forces was a by-product of the April 1775 clashes at Lexington and Concord. Two weeks after "The Shot Heard Round the World," the British schooner and two sloops put into Machias, Maine, to load wood for the British Army occupying Boston. A group of patriots led by Jeremiah O'Brien seized the vessels, killing Midshipman James Moore in the process. Fitted with guns from the schooner, one of the American sloops put to sea as the *Machias Liberty* and captured another British naval schooner. These two vessels became the first ships of the Massachusetts State Navy. Most of the 11 state navies were formed to assist in coastal and riverine defense, lasted for relatively short periods of time, and were disbanded without accomplishing very much. The exceptions were Pennsylvania's navy, whose men and vessels contributed significantly to the defense of the Delaware River before the British destroyed it in 1777, and Massachusetts', which suffered an inglorious demise in the ill-fated attempt to dislodge a British garrison from the Penobscot River in 1780.

In October of 1775 George Washington used his authority as Commander-in-Chief of the Continental Army to hire Captain Nicholas Broughton, lease the schooner *Hannah*, and order Broughton to intercept supplies en route to the British garrison in Boston. Over the next few months Washington expanded the force to seven vessels, mostly schooners, under the command of John Manley. By the time the British Army withdrew from Boston in March 1776, 35 of their ships with cargoes valued at over $600,000 had fallen prey to the Americans. Of most importance was the November 5, 1775 capture of the ordnance brig *Nancy* whose 2,000 muskets and supply of flints and shot were immediately issued to soldiers in Washington's army. Washington's navy lasted for another year, into early 1777, and took 55 prizes in all before its remaining vessels and all but one of its captains gradually shifted into the Continental Navy.

That force was created by the Continental Congress and had been established though a series of acts passed in late 1775, the first of which, passed on October 13, 1775, provided for the dispatch of two ships to intercept British supplies en route to Canada. A fortnight later Congress increased the number of vessels to four and provided that they "be employed ... for the protection and defense of the United colonies," thereby giving the new force an air of permanence. In December Congress appointed a Marine Committee, ordered construction of 13 frigates, and commissioned the navy's first officers.

In part to counter southern opposition to a navy, Congress ordered the squadron gathering at Philadelphia to sail to the Chesapeake and rid the bay of enemy, mostly loyalist, raiders that preyed on commerce and plantations along the many rivers that fed the bay. From there Esek Hopkins, commander of the squadron, was to proceed to Carolina and then to Rhode Island and clear those coasts of the British. Taking advantage of a loophole in his orders, and, perhaps fearing an encounter with ships of the Royal Navy, Hopkins sailed his eight vessels to the Bahama Islands where they captured the forts guarding New Providence and carried off 58 cannons, 15 mortars, and other ordnance. En route home, the American ships were so roughly handled by a single British frigate, the *Glasgow*, and her tender that Hopkins was ultimately relieved of his command.

Meanwhile, to the northward, General Benedict Arnold was forming a squadron of his own to contest British passage of Lake Champlain. An American army had invaded Canada in the fall and winter of 1775, but the arrival of the Royal Navy compelled the Americans to withdraw into upstate New York. There Arnold worked at a feverish pace to assemble a flotilla of 15 small vessels that could dominate Lake Champlain and the roads running along its shore. The British commander, Sir Guy Carleton, countered by constructing 29 vessels of his own.

In October 1776 Carleton overwhelmed Arnold at the battle of Valcour Island and forced the Americans to destroy the remainder of their ships and flee into the woods of Vermont. Arnold's delaying action led Carleton to withdraw to Canada for the winter. The Americans used this respite to prepare for the campaign of 1777 and at Saratoga inflicted a defeat on the next British Army that invaded from Canada. Victory at Saratoga paved the way for the Franco-American Alliance of 1778, an alliance vital to victory at Yorktown and the winning of independence three years later.

Unheralded, but nonetheless significant in the American war effort, was the assault by privateers on British commerce. Congress issued over 2,000 letters of marque licensing privately owned vessels to seize British ships in retaliation for British actions against Americans. The states commissioned as many privateers as Congress; and by the end of the war Lloyd's of London estimated that American maritime marauders had captured or destroyed 2,208 British merchantmen.

The operations of American naval forces were never well coordinated. Alongside the Marine Committee, Congress formed a Naval Committee composed of a congressman from each state. In 1779 Congress tried to streamline naval administration by replacing both committees with a single five-man Board of Admiralty, two of whose members were congressmen. This group proved unworkable and in 1781 Congress provided for a secretary of marine. No one was appointed to fill the post and Robert Morris soon added the responsibilities of

"Agent of Marine" to his burdens as "Super-intendent of Finance."

Congress expected its naval forces to assist in coastal defense, to transport diplomats abroad and return with money and supplies, to capture badly needed supplies, and, most importantly, to join privateers and state naval forces in waging a *guerre de course* upon Britain. Such expectations were unrealistic. Britain had 78 warships in American waters in 1775 (only 53 ships served in the Continental Navy at any time during the war), a number which trebled before the end of the war. During the entire war the Continental Navy had only 53 ships in all theaters of operation.

One officer, John Paul Jones, advocated a different strategy, one of raiding British outposts in Africa, Florida, and Canada, as well as attacking ports in the British Home Islands. American leaders never adopted Jones's ideas, but acting under discretionary orders Jones attacked British fishing villages in Nova Scotia in 1776, spiked the guns guarding Whitehaven, England, in 1778, and attempted to lay Leith, Scotland, under contribution in 1779.

Though never employed in pursuit of a coordinated plan, the Continental Navy made notable contributions to American victory by capturing supplies badly needed by Washington's army, destroying British commerce, and winning a few key battles that raised American morale and won the nation respect in Europe.

The most important captures of British supplies occurred in 1776 when American needs were greatest. Commodore Esek Hopkins's January raid on New Providence was followed in May by Captain Nicholas Biddle's capture, in the *Andrew Doria*, of ten prizes, including two British troop transports, and John Paul Jones taking 16 prizes in the *Providence* during the fall. In November Jones, promoted to command of the *Alfred*, captured the *Mellish*, an armed transport carrying 10,000 winter uniforms.

In 1777 and 1778 Captains Lambert Wickes, Gustavus Conyngham, and Jones carried the war to European waters. After transporting US commissioners Benjamin Franklin, Silas Deane, and Arthur Lee to France, Wickes and the brig *Reprisal* took five prizes off the French and Spanish coasts in January and February 1777; then sailing from Nantes with two other ships in May they captured 18 British ships in their home waters. Conyngham and the cutter *Revenge* sailed from Dunkirk to seize another 20 British vessels before British protests led France and Spain to bar Conyngham from their ports.

In April 1778 Jones singed British pride by leading the *Ranger* on a cruise in the Irish Sea. After setting fire to the coal fleet at Whitehaven, Jones and a landing party tried to kidnap a Member of Parliament from his home on St. Mary's Isle in Scotland. The next day Jones and the *Ranger* captured the Royal Navy sloop of war *Drake* and took it into Brest, France. A year later Jones led the *Bonhomme Richard* and several other vessels on a cruise counter-clockwise around the British Isles. On September 23, 1779, after a bitterly fought engagement, Jones and the *Bonhomme Richard* captured the newer, more powerful *Serapis* in the Battle of Flamborough Head and sailed his prize into Texel, thereby precipitating a crisis in Anglo-Dutch relations.

These successes were balanced by the Continental Navy's loss of the *Cabot*, *Hancock*, *Reprisal*, and *Lexington* in actions during 1777, and the *Randolph*, *Alfred*, *Columbus*, *Virginia*, *Independence*, and *Raleigh* in 1778.

British Army operations resulted in the destruction of several other American ships. During the summer of 1777 the Royal Navy transported Major General Sir William Howe's 18,500-man army from New York City to the head of Chesapeake Bay. From there they marched overland and captured Philadelphia in September. For almost two months Americans maintained control of the Delaware River, preventing Britain from supplying her army by sea. Finally overwhelmed by Admiral Richard Howe's fleet and the fall of Forts Mifflin and Mercer, the Americans destroyed five vessels belonging to the Continental Navy and the entire Pennsylvania State Navy on November 21. With the Delaware River under British control, Americans decided to burn the frigates *Effingham* and *Washington* to keep them out of British hands. The advance of British parties up the Hudson forced Americans to destroy the *Congress* and *Montgomery* for the same reason.

The one bright spot in American waters in 1778 was the arrival of a French fleet in July. With the signing of the Franco-American Alliance in February 1778 George Washington changed his strategy for winning American independence. He wanted France to send a fleet to American waters to operate jointly with his army. In July Vice Admiral Charles Henri Comte d'Estaing arrived off New York with 12 ships of the line, but much to Washington's disappointment he refused to attempt to enter the harbor and engage the inferior British fleet. Instead d'Estaing proposed an attack on the British garrison at Newport. Washington reluctantly agreed and began shifting part of his army to Rhode Island. D'Estaing took control of Narragansett Bay, but before an attack could be launched against the British outpost Admiral Richard Howe arrived with a relief expedition. D'Estaing put to sea to give battle, but a storm badly damaged and scattered both fleets. After repairing his ships at Boston, the French admiral departed for operations in the Caribbean, the center of French interests in the New World.

Naval operations were equally disappointing for France and America in 1779. A Franco-Spanish invasion of southern Britain collapsed in failure when operations were delayed so long that disease decimated the men of the fleet. In July Massachusetts dispatched Captain Dudley Saltonstall with a large force to evict a British force from the Penobscot River in Maine. The naval component included three ships of the Continental Navy, three from the state navies of Massachusetts and New Hampshire, and 13 privateers leased by the Massachusetts state government. The Americans laid siege to the British garrison for three weeks before Commodore Sir George Collier brought in a superior British naval squadron that spread fear among the Americans. Most fled upriver where they burned their vessels to keep the British from capturing them. The Penobscot fiasco of August 1779 achieved nothing for Massachusetts, but added significantly to the state's debt, thereby leading indirectly to the high taxation of the 1780s which precipitated Shays's Rebellion. In

another attempt to dislodge a British garrison, the French fleet joined an American army in an unsuccessful assault on Savannah, Georgia.

Against these defeats, the Americans could count only the July capture of 11 vessels from a British West Indies convoy, the taking of a few other scattered prizes, and the spectacular voyage of John Paul Jones in the *Bonhomme Richard* which resulted in the capture of the *Serapis* and the *Countess of Scarborough* off Yorkshire in September. There were not even such limited American victories in 1780 to balance against the loss of four Continental Navy vessels engaged in a fruitless attempt to protect Charleston, South Carolina, from capture by the British. Indeed, nothing done by state or Continental navies after 1779 approached in importance what they accomplished between 1776 and 1778. Cruising alone or in pairs, ships of the Continental Navy continued to harass British shipping. James Nicholson, captain of the *Trumbull*, fought the *Watt* to a bloody draw on June 1, 1780. John Barry, captain of the *Alliance* captured two British brigs a year later, and in the last naval engagement of the war, on March 10, 1783, repelled an attack by the *Sybille*. Continental Navy ships continued ferrying diplomats to Europe and transporting supplies, but such activities had little impact on the war.

In the end it was a naval engagement that made victory possible in America's struggle for independence, but the battle was not won by American forces. Since the start of the war George Washington had understood the need for sea power if America was to expel the British from its borders. Finally in 1781 the elements came together to execute his strategy of combined operations by an American army and a French navy. By late summer Americans encircled Lord Cornwallis's army at Yorktown, Virginia. In late August Vice Admiral François Comte de Grasse arrived in the Chesapeake with a French fleet to close the trap. On September 5 it drove off a British fleet commanded by Admiral Thomas Lord Graves that had been sent to extricate Cornwallis's army from the Franco-American trap at Yorktown. The Battle of the Virginia Capes sealed the fate of Cornwallis's army and its surrender resulted in the signing of the treaty of Paris, ending the war and granting Independence to the United States.

The war over, few Americans saw the need for a navy. By 1785 all of its ships had been sold, its officers and seamen returned to civilian life, and its administrative network of naval agents and prize courts disbanded. Looking back, John Adams, among the firmest proponents of a navy, told a friend that when reviewing the record of the navy he found it "very difficult to avoid tears." On the surface it is difficult not to agree with Adams. By the end of the war American naval forces virtually ceased to exist. But before their demise, those same forces had contributed significantly to American victory in what became a protracted war of attrition.

In the opening stages of the conflict, prizes taken by George Washington's schooners, the Continental Navy's raid on New Providence, and John Paul Jones's capture of the *Mellish* provided the Continental Army with much needed supplies. In 1776 Benedict Arnold's squadron on Lake Champlain suffered tactical defeat but delayed the enemy advance long enough to provide the Continental Army with vitally needed time to prepare the defenses in the Hudson River Valley that contributed immeasurably to American victory at Saratoga in 1777. The exploits of Conyngham, Wickes, Jones, and others in 1778 and 1779 raised foreign awareness of the American rebellion and embarrassed the Royal Navy when it proved unable to stop their depredations. Less tangible, but perhaps as important, were the symbolic contributions of the Continental Navy. Flying the American flag throughout the North Atlantic its warships were tangible representations of American independence and unity. In their "David vs. Goliath" contest with Britain's Royal Navy, ships such as the *Bonhomme Richard* won battles important to American morale at home and the image of the new nation abroad.

These American achievements at sea were made possible in part by the failure of Britain to use her sea power effectively. Rather than blockade the American coast and economically strangle the colonies, or seek out and destroy American commerce raiders, the Royal Navy was employed primarily as an adjunct to the British Army. In 1776 its ships evacuated army units from Boston and supported attacks on Charleston and New York. In 1777 they transported troops to the Chesapeake Bay for the campaign against Philadelphia. The next year warships were used to evacuate supplies and civilians from Philadelphia and to defend the garrison at Newport. In 1778 the Royal Navy transported army units to Savannah at the start of the Southern Campaign and the following year it carried other troops on raids in Chesapeake Bay. In 1780 it supported the army's capture of Charleston.

With so many ships tied to army operations in North America, the Royal Navy lost control of the Caribbean in 1779 and 1780. Ultimately, Britain lost her American colonies not because of actions by the Continental Navy or by privateers but because the French Navy defeated the Royal Navy at the Battle of the Virginia Capes, thereby forcing the surrender of Lord Cornwallis's army at Yorktown. The following year its fortunes changed when it reasserted British control of the Caribbean. Still, the War for American Independence was a humbling experience for the Royal Navy, a great fighting force which had racked up an unparalleled series of victories during the Seven Years' War and would do so again during the Wars of the French Revolution and Empire beginning a decade later.

Englishmen may assess their navy's performance in the American Revolution negatively, but Americans view the accomplishments of their naval forces with pride. For a century they debated the naval lessons of the war, but Americans never forgot the gallantry of leaders such as John Paul Jones, Gustavus Conyngham, and Lambert Wickes. Acts of bravery in the face of overwhelming odds – the courage of the men who fought on Lake Champlain and the Delaware River and the men of the *Randolph* who lost their lives engaging a far superior ship of the line inspired later generations and laid the basis for one of the greatest naval traditions in world history.

FURTHER READING

Allen, Gardner W.: *A Naval History of the American Revolution*, 2 vols. (Williamstown, Mass.: Corner House Publishers, 1970 [1913]).

Fowler, William M., Jr.: *Rebels Under Sail: The American Navy during the Revolution* (New York: Charles Scribner's Sons, 1976).

Miller, Nathan: *Sea of Glory: The Continental Navy Fights for Independence 1775–1783* (New York: David McKay Co., 1974).

Morison, Samuel Eliot: *John Paul Jones: A Sailor's Biography* (Boston: Little, Brown and Co., 1959).

Tilley, John A.: *The British Navy and the American Revolution* (Columbia: University of South Carolina Press, 1987).

CHAPTER FORTY-TWO

The home front during the War for Independence: the effect of labor shortages on commercial production in the Mid-Atlantic

Michael V. Kennedy

DURING the Revolution, the colonies confronted the problem of producing supplies needed for the war as well as filling the normal labor needs of colonial households. A labor shortage unusual even in colonial experience developed, however, and made the improbable task of conducting a revolution against the world's most powerful empire that much more difficult.

Labor shortages have been a recurring theme in the historiography of colonial British America, and they became an acute problem during the War for American Independence. Historians have blamed a lack of available labor for the retardation of commercial and industrial development in the British colonies, and have posited that a dearth of skilled labor precluded the need for guild systems, but nonetheless ensured satisfactory incomes to master craftsmen who owned shops and tools. They have also argued that, especially in rural and frontier areas, many farmers taught themselves to build and repair as needed. Easy access to land also resulted in a lack of sufficient unskilled labor willing to work for wages, goods, or food, and an independent spirit made British colonists, whether newly arrived from Europe or native-born creoles, unwilling to work for others. Those who did commanded wages higher than could be had in Europe, and made it difficult for most potential employers to afford workers they needed.

The generally accepted historical theory on bound labor states that, as a result of the unavailability of free labor, both agricultural and commercial interests in the British colonies turned to indentured servitude by the second decade of the seventeenth century. By 1660 or so, servitude was complemented by African slavery, first in the West Indies, then in mainland North America. By the early eighteenth century, slavery had superseded indentured servitude in the Chesapeake and the lower South and had equaled it in the Mid-Atlantic. Outside of New England, bound labor was vital, for in its absence, the exploitation of resources and economic development beneficial to the British colonies and Britain itself would have been impossible.

While servitude and slavery were both important in the Mid-Atlantic region – Maryland, Delaware, Pennsylvania, New Jersey, and New York – for more than a century before the American Revolution, bound workers never satisfied the area's labor needs. Large numbers of free workers complemented family labor on farms, particularly at harvest; worked in craft shops, stores, construction, and maintenance jobs, particularly in urban areas; and made viable commercial production possible in urban and rural industries, including saw, oil, fulling, and commercial grist mills, distilleries, breweries, tanneries, and ironworks.

The steady development of surplus production in agriculture and industry in the long-established areas of the Mid-Atlantic took place, in fact, because no labor shortage existed by the end of the seventeenth century. Free wage laborers, complemented by smaller percentages of bound labor, accomplished the region's work. The labor situation in the Mid-Atlantic was the result of managerial decisions to limit the *full-time* work force for most of the year, which caused frequent searches for sufficient labor to meet seasonal needs.

These problems of seasonal labor management were generated by several factors. The seasonality of agriculture and the concentration of landholders to acquire needed labor, particularly at harvest, has been examined historically for decades. Productive industries were also seasonal during the colonial period. All commercial milling operations in the Mid-Atlantic, including iron production, shut down from two to four months each year, as the shallow, fast-flowing creeks and streams that powered water wheels froze over. Grist and oil mills were often shut down for longer periods. While ancillary work could be done from winter's onset to spring thaw, including cutting wood and repairing mills, the size of the necessary work force dwindled dramatically.

As a result, owners and managers of commercial operations acquired a minimum number of bound workers (servants and slaves) and hired a skeleton crew of free laborers for year-round work, in order to reduce expenses during off-peak months. While entrepreneurs often complained about labor shortages, their own designs made an annual hunt for workers necessary.

Most available free workers in the region were also reluctant to contract for year-round work in industry, and preferred to work only for a few weeks or months at a time. They either moved from job to job or took periodic "vacations" from work. By mutual agreement, therefore, the majority of commercial industry's labor force worked part-time throughout the eighteenth century. The tables below list the number of commercial industries in the Mid-Atlantic, and the approximate number of people employed annually, designated as full- or part-time workers, free and bound, 1765–85.

Tables 1 and 2 show a steady expansion of Mid-Atlantic industrial operations from the end of the Seven Years' War until after the American Revolution. This rise in productive industries was accompanied by a rise in the industrial work force until 1775, when the War for Independence depleted

Table 1 Commercial industries in Mid-Atlantic 1765–85

Industry	Year				
	1765	1770	1775	1780	1785
Gristmill	314	348	397	432	493
Sawmill	1,136	1,272	1,434	1,581	1,769
Fulling	150	175	205	230	262
Oil mill	94	112	135	153	174
Distill	330	417	538	568	646
Tannery	244	278	319	344	392
Forge	88	98	111	121	132
Furnace	54	63	73	77	84
Other	51	58	66	72	79
Total[a]	2,461	2,822	3,278	3,578	4,031

[a] Approximately 30 percent of these businesses were located in complexes that combined between two and five different operations at the same site. The grist mills listed here account for commercial sites only, not small to moderately sized family-run operations.

Table 2 Annual work force in Mid-Atlantic commercial industry

Year	Industrial work force[b]	% Servants	% Slaves	% Free
1765	74,000	6.9	15.9	77.2
1767	77,000	6.9	15.9	77.2
1770	84,000	6.8	15.3	77.9
1772	88,000	6.2	15.1	78.8
1775	97,000	5.3	14.7	80.0
1777	82,000	5.7	18.1	76.2
1780	84,000	3.3	17.3	79.4
1782	89,000	3.4	16.5	80.1
1785	114,000	4.0	12.9	83.1

[b] Approximate number based on 157 sets of business records and extrapolated to cover all contemporary production sites.

the number of available laborers. Military service drew workers from their jobs, as former employees fought in local militia companies, or the Continental Army, or joined the ranks of loyalist units. Immigration dropped, and with it the supply of new indentured servants. The number of immigrant servants who entered the Mid-Atlantic during the Revolution fell by over 90 percent from the previous decade. As older servant indentures expired, the bound labor force declined. By 1780, only native-born apprentices, debt and convict servants remained. Such laborers collectively had never amounted to as much as 10 percent of the servant population in the British colonies. Although several hundred prisoners of war, hired out by Congress for regular assignment or special projects, also supplemented the bound labor force, they did not constitute a significant amount of the labor force. The importation of slaves was also curtailed, although natural increase kept the number of slaves available for industrial work relatively steady during the war. Bound laborers who ran away during the Revolution also contributed to the shortage of labor in commercial industries. The preceding factors affecting the labor shortage during the American Revolution will be examined in turn.

Nearly 15 percent of workers employed in industry between 1770 and 1780 appeared at some point on the muster rolls of state militias or the Continental Army.

Table 3 Bound workers in Mid-Atlantic commercial industries

Year	Avg. bound per company	Avg. # servants	Avg. # slaves
1765	6.75	2.04	4.71
1767	6.77	2.05	4.72
1770	6.54	2.01	4.53
1772	6.33	1.84	4.49
1775	5.91	1.57	4.34
1777	5.80	1.36	4.44
1780	4.91	0.78	4.13
1782	4.84	0.83	4.01
1785	4.77	1.13	3.64

Laborers who served in loyalist units, plus runaways who enlisted under assumed names, would certainly increase this total to over 20 percent.

Owners of businesses made significant efforts to forestall enlistment by servants, slaves, and free workers. The Continental Congress and state legislatures recognized the necessity of maintaining work forces in all industries producing military supplies, including commercial grist and saw mills, tanneries, and ironworks, yet their actions were varied and often vague. Initially the Continental Congress encouraged the recruitment of servants in an effort to fill the army's ranks. The legislatures of Maryland and New Jersey declared servants eligible for military service without their masters' consent, but provided masters with compensation for the lost workers. New York and Delaware, however, permitted servants to enlist only with their masters' consent and offered no compensation. In Pennsylvania, servants were exempted from the military at first, but not banned. In all states, an avalanche of complaints ensued, led by business owners who decried servant enlistment on the grounds that production would quickly halt.

Maryland and New Jersey responded to this outcry by exempting servants and free workers in industries vital to the war effort from military service. As a result, notices appeared, such as one from Mount Holly Ironworks in New Jersey, which advertised for nailers, woodcutters, colliers, and general laborers, and declared "the workmen at these works are, by a law of this state, exempt from military duty" (New Jersey Archives, Ser. 2 v. 1, Newspaper Abstracts), and encouraged workmen to avoid wartime service. The New York legislature continued to allow servants to enlist, but barred their active recruitment and allowed exemptions for specific numbers of men at various commercial sites. Iron companies, for example, could specify five workmen from each phase of operations, servant or free, to be exempted from the military. The Council of Safety in Pennsylvania, in response to industries' complaints of disappearing workers directed on July 7, 1776 that "all such workmen as are necessary to be employed at the Iron Works … be ordered not to leave their Respective Works, nor to March with the Militia" (Colonial Records of Pennsylvania v. 10, Minutes of the Council of Safety, p. 662). The Continental Congress, on the other hand, decided on exemptions for servants in key industries one company at a time, based on individual circumstances, and never revoked its call for servant enlistments.

Government decrees could, in theory, confirm that bound laborers should remain at work in important industries, but in fact governments could not control runaways who fled to join either side in the conflict, or who simply took advantage of wartime disruptions to seek their freedom. Lord

Dunmore's call for servants and slaves to run to the British lines, for example, spread quickly. His promise of freedom for those who joined his ranks also encouraged non-loyalist bound laborers to consider flight. Also, the wishes or needs of both government officials and business owners had no effect at all on the actions of free workers who, as noted in table 2, made up over 75 percent of the work force.

The number of free workers in commercial industry fell by 21 percent between 1775 and 1778 before slowly rebounding. This decline, however, had a greater effect than the number alone would indicate. The number of *full-time* wage laborers dropped by 23 percent (table 5) over the course of the war, while the slight rebound in the total number of free workers after 1779 was due to an increase in part-time or casual labor hired by companies desperate for employees of any kind. Skilled free workers were also at a premium; their numbers in industry declined by nearly 40 percent between 1775 and 1780. The full-time work force, including bound labor, dropped by over 32 percent during the war, and while most workers had always been employed only part-time, full-time skilled laborers were vital to most operations. Their absence affected both the ability of the Council of Safety to conduct the war and the capability of businesses to support ordinary commercial demand.

Before the outbreak of the Revolution, over 40 percent of full-time workers in commercial industry were bound laborers. Their numbers declined during the war by 44 percent due to several factors. Increasing numbers of slaveowners in the Mid-Atlantic region, particularly Pennsylvania, manumitted their slaves during the war. While few owners of commercial businesses took part in this movement, even a slight decline in the numbers of slaves available for hire from nearby families decreased the controllable work force, increased hiring costs, and limited production capabilities. In fact, the numbers of slaves *hired* in industry *increased* during the Revolution, as business owners sought to replace free workers and servants. Most newly hired slaves, however, did not work full-time. Slaves available for

Table 4 Average number of bound workers owned or hired by companies

| Year | Servants | | Slaves | |
	Bound	Hired	Owned	Hired
1765	1.01	1.03	2.63	2.08
1767	0.94	1.11	2.79	1.93
1770	0.93	1.08	2.82	1.71
1772	0.82	1.02	2.72	1.77
1775	0.77	0.80	2.59	1.75
1777	0.64	0.72	2.23	2.21
1780	0.33	0.45	1.80	2.33
1782	0.34	0.49	1.69	2.32
1785	0.54	0.59	1.59	2.05

Table 5 Average numbers full-time and part-time workers

| Year | Full-time employees | | | | Part-time employees | | | |
	Servants	Slave	Free	Total	Servants	Slave	Free	Total
1765	1.74	4.15	7.79	13.68	0.30	0.56	15.06	15.92
1767	1.72	4.11	7.78	13.61	0.33	0.61	15.15	16.09
1770	1.69	3.92	7.86	13.47	0.32	0.61	15.20	16.13
1772	1.57	4.02	7.93	13.52	0.27	0.47	15.48	16.22
1775	1.37	3.94	7.84	13.15	0.20	0.40	15.85	16.45
1777	0.75	3.12	6.89	10.76	0.61	1.32	11.21	13.14
1780	0.38	2.60	6.17	9.15	0.40	1.53	12.58	14.51
1782	0.36	2.92	7.12	10.40	0.47	1.09	11.84	13.40
1785	0.75	2.58	8.56	11.89	0.38	1.06	14.87	16.31

full-time work in industry declined by 34 percent, while slaves working part-time increased by 283 percent, and the real cost of slave hires rose by 15 percent during the Revolution. Their owners simply could not afford to keep slaves from other duties for very long.

In addition to the drop in full-time hires, slave imports virtually ceased during the war, and industries were unable to replace aged, injured, or deceased slaves. Natural increase among slaves owned by commercial industries was almost nonexistent, as males outnumbered females by approximately eight to one in industrial settings, and children constituted less than 3 percent of such slave populations. As a result, the average number of slaves owned by ironworks, mills, and other commercial industries in the region dropped by 35 percent between 1775 and 1782.

The shortage of servant labor became progressively more acute as the Revolution dragged on. Before 1775, over 90 percent of servants were recently arrived immigrants with four to five year indentures. Between 1775 and 1781, immigration to the Mid-Atlantic dropped by 91 percent. As a result, more than 80 percent of what had come to be the normal labor pool of servants was not replaced. If an "average" servant possessed a five-year indenture, the servant population in the Mid-Atlantic fell by an average of 16 percent per year. By the end of 1780, therefore, the servant population cannot have been more than 20 percent of what it had been five years earlier.

The effect on commercial industry was dramatic. The average number of servants working per company fell by over 50 percent. As with slaves, the number of servants available to work full-time in commercial industry dropped to only 26 percent of its prewar total. Between 1775 and 1777, servants who worked part-time for commercial operations rose by 205 percent, as their masters met some of the immediate needs of industry, and charged a per-day hire rate nearly 20 percent higher than the pre-Revolution norm. From 1778 to 1781, however, even servants available for day or limited task work disappeared as they completed their indentures and were not replaced by new arrivals.

Prisoners of war filled some of the depleted servant ranks, but their numbers were too small to have a sustained effect. The Continental Congress and state legislatures hired out several hundred prisoners during the war in the Mid-Atlantic region, mainly to iron companies and saw and grist mills. No individual company, however, acquired more than a handful of prisoners even temporarily. While Elizabeth Furnace in Pennsylvania, for example, hired a total of 22 Hessian prisoners, no more than eight worked at any one time. The company paid Congress for their services in cast ball and shot, perhaps made by the prisoners themselves. George Ege, the manager of Charming Forge, was assigned 34 prisoners to help build a slitting mill and race, and to cut a channel through a ridge to supply the mill with water. After they had completed this task, however, the prisoners were split up and sent elsewhere. Most companies spent more time *requesting* prisoners than such men actually served.

The average commercial operation in the Mid-Atlantic region, therefore, lost 19.9 percent of its labor force during the course of the Revolution. More importantly, prewar averages for full-time laborers declined by over 32 percent. This labor shortage was unmatched at any time prior to or succeeding the American Revolution, even during other wars. During the Seven Years' War, for example, the region's work force in commercial industry declined by only 4.9 percent, while full-time employees dropped by 8 percent. The complaints of labor shortage from 1775 to 1781 were certainly more justified than those voiced at any other time.

Owners and managers of productive industries had additional labor problems with the bound workers available to them during the Revolution. While fewer servants and slaves fled from bondage during the American Revolution than during the decade that preceded it, the rapidly shrinking labor force could not spare even a small number of runaways.

Table 6 demonstrates that the annual number of runaways advertised in the Mid-Atlantic region declined by more than 67 percent during the Revolution. The number of indentured servant runaways declined most precipitously because many fewer servants were under indenture by 1777. Also, most servants inclined to flee evidently ran, many to British lines, during 1775 and 1776.

At least 25 percent of all runaways in the Mid-Atlantic region left commercial production sites, a percentage roughly equivalent to prewar proportions and to the proportion of bound laborers in the region who worked in industry each year. Between 1765 and 1774, for example, approximately 23 percent of runaways had been employed in commercial industries. Despite the consistency of percentages, the smaller the pool of workers, the greater effect any percentage of lost workers would have on production.

In all, 1 percent of servants and slaves working in industry ran away during the American Revolution, and while most companies never experienced the problem of runaways, those that did lost a significant percentage of their labor force. For example, in 1777, six servants ran together from the Batsto Furnace at Little Egg Harbor, New Jersey. They had constituted nearly 4 percent of the ironworks' total labor force and 15 percent of its full-time workers. John Cox, owner of Batsto, had contracted in the spring to supply the Council of Safety in Philadelphia with shot and cannonballs. His servants' disappearance slowed production considerably.

Servants and slaves hired from other sources constituted 63.8 percent of the

Table 6   Mid-Atlantic runaway servants and slaves 1765–1783[c]

Pre-Revolution				Revolution			
Year	Servants	Slaves	Total	Year	Servants	Slaves	Total
1765	242	46	288	1775	296	33	329
1766	316	46	362	1776	232	39	271
1767	265	31	296	1777	72	27	99
1768	256	32	288	1778	38	31	69
1769	281	40	321	1779	20	28	48
1770	270	46	316	1780	14	21	35
1771	276	22	298	1781	11	22	33
1772	270	27	297	1782	12	20	32
1773	340	41	381	1783	20	23	43
1774	372	28	400				
Avg.	278.8	35.9	324.7		79.5	27.1	106.6

[c] Compiled from notices in the *Pennsylvania Gazette*, the *Pennsylvania Journal & Weekly Advertiser*, the *Pennsylvania Chronicle*, the *Pennsylvania Chronicle & Universal Advertiser*, the *Pennsylvania Packet & General Advertiser*, the *New York Mercury*, the *New York Gazette & Weekly Mercury*, the *New York Gazette or Weekly Post Boy*, *Rivington's New York Gazetteer*, and the *New York Journal and General Advertiser*, all for the years 1765–1783, and including ads for Pennsylvania, New York, New Jersey, Delaware, and Maryland.

runaways from commercial operations during the war. They ran, in other words, at twice the rate of workers bound directly to companies. The act of running could have been a protest against being hired out, intensified by the pressures of wartime work in commercial industrial settings where productive labor was at a premium. In any case, hired or owned runaways resulted in added anxiety for company managers, who were forced to advertise, offer rewards, and deal with masters whose servants had run from their supervision, all while they suffered from wartime labor shortages.

Insufficient labor caused a number of iron companies to close down operations for at least part of the war. This interruption, in turn, caused shortages in colonial supplies of ball and shot. The middle states had the greatest concentrations of iron ore on the Atlantic coast, and consequently most of the iron companies. While it quickly became apparent that these iron companies could not supply all the arms and ammunition necessary for the conduct of the Revolution, and that much would be purchased overseas, the Continental Congress and Councils of Safety nonetheless expected a significant

proportion to be produced domestically. Labor shortages, however, slowed production significantly, and the closure of as many as half of the colonies' iron companies for several weeks to more than a year made hopes for domestic supply ephemeral.

The difficulty of acquiring enough labor to operate became most acute when the war came to the home front itself. When British forces were situated in the Mid-Atlantic region between 1776 and 1780, local militias repeatedly called men to arms and depleted the work force. British soldiers also occupied and closed a number of works in lower New York State, the northern half of New Jersey, and southeastern Pennsylvania between 1776 and 1779. When such occupations ended, companies often had to gather entirely new labor forces in order to restart operations.

Another problem that slowed production in the face of increased labor shortages was caused by the number of loyalists counted among industrialists at the outset of the Revolution. When possible, the rebel Councils of Safety captured the property of loyalists, assessed its value, and offered it for sale at auction in order to raise revenue. This program often slowed or halted production beyond the damage caused by simple depletion of the work force. In 1776, for example, Joseph Galloway, the owner of the Durham Ironworks in Bucks County, Pennsylvania, approximately 40 miles from Philadelphia, and a member of the Continental Congress, worked vigorously on a compromise to fighting, sought a negotiated peace that would settle the conflict between Britain and her colonies, and keep the empire together. In the late spring and early summer of 1776, however, as the movement for independence gained majority sway in Philadelphia, Galloway balked. He refused to support the July declaration, and before he left Philadelphia for his rural estate, told rebel George Taylor, who had leased and operated the ironworks since 1773, to cease munition production on *his* property.

Taylor refused, and continued to manufacture ammunition until the British Army moved into the area, occupied Philadelphia, and effectively shut down Durham and several other nearby operations. The Continental Congress, reconvened in Lancaster from September 1776 to June 1778, when the British withdrew from Philadelphia. The Congress continued to make production arrangements with other ironworks after the exodus, but Durham was idle.

Galloway announced himself a loyalist and supported the British efforts during Philadelphia's occupation. As a result, the Continental Congress announced the forfeiture, in absentia, of Galloway's lands and property. When the British (and Galloway) left Philadelphia, the Continental Congress secured his property in and around Philadelphia, including Durham, to auction it off for revenue, despite Taylor's protest that as lessee, he should resume production. Not until the end of July did the Supreme Executive Council decide to "pay due respect to the written agreement between Mr. Joseph Galloway, Esq'r, & the Honble George Taylor," and not to "disturb Mr. Taylor" (Colonial Records of Pennsylvania, v. 11, Minutes of the Supreme Executive Council, p. 538) for the remainder of his lease, which Congress extended until April 1, 1780. By July 1778, the production facility

had lain idle for 21 months while colonial troops scrambled for munitions. Also, the time had passed for Taylor to assemble a new work force to begin a lucrative blast before agricultural harvest cycles occupied available workers, and he was forced to suspend operations until the following spring. Food production was, in many ways, more vital than local manufacture of shot, and finding sufficient workers to bring in crops during the war was an additional problem that had to be met.

The ability to continue production in commercial industry during the War for American Independence was hampered by unavailability of agricultural supplies to maintain work forces and keep many companies operating. All Mid-Atlantic industries depended on local farmers to supply 80 to 90 percent of the foodstuffs necessary to feed their full-time work forces, as well as some of their part-timers. Several types of mills, including grist, oil, fulling, and hemp mills acquired the majority of the resources they processed from farmers in market areas of approximately 300 miles surrounding their operation. As labor shortages, mobilization and movements of armies, foraging operations, battles, and destruction of the enemies' support lands by both rebels and loyalists disrupted normal agricultural production and distribution, commercial industries were less able to maintain even the smaller work forces left by the drain of military service, lower immigration figures, and runaways.

Two-thirds of the region's bound labor were occupied primarily in agriculture on the eve of the American Revolution, and these work forces were affected in the same ways as commercial industries. Servants and slaves were in short supply by 1777 as fewer new bound workers entered the region. Fifty-nine percent of runaway servants and slaves came from the area's farms. Families dependent on bound labor were less able to produce surpluses that were normally sold to local industries.

The free labor force in agriculture, landed, and tenant farmers, as well as hired farm workers were also affected. Several thousand adult males served in the Continental Army during the war, most from farm families. While militia companies were generally unreliable, tens of thousands of men from the Mid-Atlantic region's pool of over 200,000 between the ages of 16 and 60 saw some militia service. While women routinely took over male duties on farms across the eastern seaboard, disruptions of drill, mobilization of units, and battlefield action caused a decline in farm production between 1776 and 1780.

While the Mid-Atlantic remained the center of land-based military operations between the summer of 1776 and the fall of 1779, the movements of the Continental Army and British regulars, militia companies and loyalist units, civilian marauders and Hessian mercenaries all caused havoc with routine agricultural production. The quartermaster corps established by the Continental Congress continually confiscated livestock and foodstuffs in the region, paying farmers in chits and Continental dollars whose value depreciated veritably by the day. British units sent out foragers to gather up supplies from the farms of friend and foe alike, usually without any payment.

Eighty percent of the major battles fought in the region between 1776 and 1779 were fought during the height of the growing season through the end of the normal harvest cycle. Not only were people drawn from farm work at vital times, but engagements fought in fields, gardens, and grazing areas destroyed needed supplies.

Civilian raiders took the opportunity afforded by war to avenge themselves on neighbors with whom they had long-standing quarrels and feuds. Rebel and loyalist-oriented marauders burned fields, barns, and homes, and destroyed cattle of their enemies. Bands of runaways, like that led by "Colonel Tye," formerly Titus, a runaway Monmouth County, New Jersey slave raided throughout the region, encouraged by British officers. For example, Colonel Tye and more than 50 other runaway slaves were landed at Shrewsbury in southern New Jersey on July 15, 1779, where they fired the village and surrounding fields, plundered homes, and stole livestock before being picked up by a British ship. While actions like these were not daily occurrences, they added to the inability of Mid-Atlantic

farmers to reach normal production levels, support themselves and supply the area's commercial work forces. The difficulties in acquiring food supplies during the war certainly hastened the attempts by many commercial operations that had the means to provide a greater percentage of their own supplies on company lands after the war. While the conflict continued, however, food shortages added to both the inability of industries to operate normally, and the difficulty of the rebel government to keep the armies in the field fully supplied.

The disruptions of the American Revolution not only caused immediate shortages of labor and hampered the abilities of commercial industry to engage in normal production, but made owners and managers of businesses in the Mid-Atlantic region more acutely aware of the limitations of carrying on operations with a majority of part-time workers. More control over labor was necessary, and solutions that better balanced seasonality with industrial necessity had to be found.

Across the region, solutions varied. In Maryland, where the number of slaves had increased to more than a third of the population by 1790, many commercial industries increased both direct purchases of slaves and the hiring of slaves on an annual basis during the 20 years succeeding the American Revolution. This practice insured the availability of a much larger core of full-time employees. In order to maximize the profitable efforts of these larger full-time work forces, an increasing number of Maryland entrepreneurs added to their existing operations. Combinations of ironworks and several types of mills, and/or tanneries allowed owners of permanent labor forces to move workers around complexes as seasonality dictated, in attempts to extract the highest possible number of productive work days.

New York, New Jersey, and Delaware, despite increased numbers of manumissions between 1781 and 1800, contained a combined slave population of 8.5 percent. Most commercial businesses in these states saw their annual work forces decline after the Revolution, as the average company employed 9.6 percent fewer workers. This trend, however, reflected employment of more full-timers. During the 20 years after the Revolution, the number of full-time workers in industry increased by 15 percent as the number of full-time slaves employed rose by 36.7 percent over the pre-revolutionary figure, and full-time free labor increased by 8.7 percent. As in Maryland, the number of commercial complexes in New York, New Jersey and Delaware increased, and owners rotated more full-time employees among production facilities as seasons changed.

The situation in Pennsylvania differed significantly. The decline in the number of slaves in the state between 1775 and 1800 negated the possibility of industries increasing their full-time slave labor forces. Instead, slaves working in commercial businesses full-time in Pennsylvania *declined* by 31.8 percent. The overall number of full-time workers in Pennsylvania industry rose by 10.1 percent in the period, however, because of the significant rise (23.7 percent) of *free* full-time labor. This rise probably resulted because companies could no longer rely on slaves or large numbers of servants, and instead increased offers of full-time work to free people during the post-revolutionary decades. In other words, it was not so much a change in attitude by most people toward industrial work, as it was a change in opportunity to make a year-round living at it. Owners and managers of companies in Pennsylvania had reassessed the composition of their labor forces. As slavery was gradually eliminated and the number of available indentured servants declined steadily, full-time employees had to be drawn from a free labor market. When offers increased for full-time wage work, a significant number of laborers accepted. Full-time work contributed to increased geographic stability among a greater percentage of families, enabled households to build basic competencies more easily, and as a result allowed more families to acquire land in the early nineteenth century.

The unusual labor shortage during the American Revolution did not alone herald changes in management decisions with regard to labor, nor did all companies make major changes over the post-revolutionary generation. The enhanced awareness of the damage a labor shortage could cause to commercial industry, however, certainly caused many entrepreneurs in the Mid-Atlantic to rethink the demographics of their work forces.

FURTHER READING

Grubb, Farley: "Servant Auction Records and Immigration into the Delaware Valley, 1745–1831: The Proportion of Females Among Immigrant Servants," *Proceedings of the American Philosophical Society* 133 (1989), 154–69.

Morris, Richard B.: *Government and Labor in Early America* (New York: Columbia University Press, 1946), esp. chs. 6–8.

Papenfuse, Edward C.: *In Pursuit of Profit: The Annapolis Merchants in the Era of The American Revolution, 1763–1805* (Baltimore: Maryland Bi-Centennial Series, 1975).

Price, Jacob: "Economic function and the growth of American port towns in the eighteenth century," *Perspectives in American History* 8 (1974), 121–86.

Smith, Billy G.: *The 'Lower Sort': Philadelphia's Laboring People, 1750–1800* (New York: Cornell University Press, 1990).

Soderlund, Jean R.: "Black importation and migration into southern Pennsylvania, 1682–1810," *Proceedings of the American Philosophical Society* 133 (1989), 144–53.

Wax, Darold D.: "Black immigrants: the slave trade in colonial Maryland," *Maryland Historical Magazine* 73 (1978), 30–45.

Wokeck, Marianne S.: "German and Irish immigration to colonial Philadelphia," *Proceedings of the American Philosophical Society* 133 (1989), 128–43.

CHAPTER FORTY-THREE

Resistance to the American Revolution

MICHAEL A. MCDONNELL

RESISTANCE to the Revolution came in many forms, and from many quarters. The most obvious forms of resistance – initiated by outright and active loyalists, by thousands of Amerindians, and by enslaved Americans everywhere – was only the most direct and explicit of the resistance offered the revolutionary movement. What is often less acknowledged is the fact that there were also thousands of ordinary Americans throughout the new states who offered resistance to the means and ends of patriot leaders of the Revolution in more subtle, often passive, but no less debilitating ways than sustained, direct, and armed opposition: farmers who refused to sell supplies to the army, to pay their wartime taxes, or to take oaths of allegiance to the new states; laborers who refused to be conscripted into the army, who charged high bounties for that service, or deserted as soon as they could; whole counties or towns who ignored, evaded, or resisted new tax, conscription, or militia laws. All of these actions were seen as resistance by the patriot leadership – the actions of those who were often condemned as the "disaffected" – and all adversely affected the War for Independence and ultimately the course of the Revolution.

As many forms of resistance as there were, there were almost as many reasons for that resistance. And though resistance was not always offered for clear and coherent reasons – for the Crown, for individual freedom from bondage, or for native sovereignty, for example – there was often an underlying rationale that can be rediscovered, with some effort. But until recently, historians have been slow to acknowledge

and therefore understand "disaffection" as anything other than what patriot leaders at the time attributed it to – war weariness or as often, loyalist-leaning sentiment. The division of colonists into two categories – Tory and patriot – has too often and too easily muted the voices of those normally considered "inarticulate," or perhaps more appropriately, less "accessible" than the elite leadership, behind whom the middling and lower sorts are thought to have rallied, either for the Crown or Constitution. Such an approach masks the extent and nature of *alternative* popular political ideologies. For resistance to *the* Revolution was not always a function of loyalism, but was often a manifestation of adherence to a *different* kind of revolution – or at the very least to a different conception of social, economic, and political relations than that envisioned by the Revolution's leadership. During the Revolution, if not before, the populace or "mob" did indeed "think and reason" as much as Gouverneur Morris feared. Ultimately, the demands and turmoil of the war gave many an opportunity to express their dissatisfaction with the status quo.

1 Spectrum of Resistance

Active loyalism, or the bearing of arms against patriot forces, is what usually comes to mind when considering resistance to the Revolution, yet this hardly does justice to the full range – or subtlety – of resistance offered. Even "treasonous" activity, perhaps the easiest and most recognizable form of resistance, was defined differently by different states at different times of the war.

Though usually most governments included levying war against the states and some kind of adherence to the enemy under its rubric, the range of activity defined as treasonous varied. New York, New Jersey, and Delaware, for example, used more strict English common and statutory law in defining treason, whilst other states, including Pennsylvania, North Carolina, and Connecticut defined it widely, sometimes embracing any and all manner of cooperation with the enemy, including trade.

Yet it was the laws passed in the different states concerning activities that amounted to something less than treason that reveal that resistance to the revolution came in many more different forms than treasonous and overtly loyalist acts could account for. States officially condemned the recognition of the sovereignty of the King, for example, and encouraging others to forsake American allegiance, but they also outlawed the discouraging of enlistments in the patriot military service, advice against resisting armed invasion, expressions of hostility to the state governments, the dissemination of false information, and any communication with the enemy or their adherents. They also implemented emergency measures to deal with counterfeiters, those who refused to accept the new currencies, those who resisted tax collections, and of course, they passed laws dealing with desertion and mutiny within the army (see Higginbotham, 1981, pp. 268–9). The very range and nature of the laws passed by the states is testimony to the widespread existence of activities that could be and were labeled as "resistance," which might be defined as anything that tended to undermine the authority, power, and legitimacy of the new state governments.

Active loyalists, while generally beyond the scope of this essay, declared their open opposition to the new patriot regime by joining or running away to the British to serve in their armed forces or by recruiting for them. Thousands of Americans chose this option, and thousands more were tempted according to the fortunes of the war. Others offered random, but persistent and often devastating, violence against patriots. Outside of regular British military activity, loyalist-leaning Americans incited insurrections, kidnappings, attacks on stores and supplies, and individual acts of violence against patriot authorities. This kind of resistance was wide-ranging and affected most of the new states in varying degrees. Some areas, like the Georgia backcountry, Carolina Piedmont, Long Island and the Delmarva Peninsula, for example, were plagued by chronic and persistent internal violence and strife. Less overt but as damaging to the patriot cause were the acts of those "occasional" loyalists who traded with the enemy or assisted them when they were near. Everywhere the British went, they were aided in some degree by local residents. When William Howe made his move on Philadelphia, for example, Marylanders along the way offered aid and supplies and at least one militia officer opposed calling up his men to go against the British and refused to muster himself. Even in the most ardently patriot communities, the British experienced few problems in securing temporary supplies, particularly as specie grew scarce and the invading forces offered ready money.

Such activities point to the fact that there were many thousands who shifted allegiances as circumstances dictated on different occasions in the war. In Poughkeepsie, New York, for example, 21 men who had signed the Association of 1775 ended the war as outright loyalists, whilst four who refused to sign the Association ended up volunteering for the Continental line. One man signed the Association in 1775, joined the militia, and was elected second lieutenant. In 1777, however, he signed a petition asking for clemency for a Tory teenager sentenced to hang, and by 1783 he was indicted for "adhering" to the enemy, though he stayed in the county at least until 1790 (Clark, 1994, pp. 292–4). Many apparently patriot colonists were also quick to take paroles from advancing British forces which essentially absolved them from future participation in the patriot militia. The situation grew so severe in Virginia where farmers actively sought out the British to get "captured" and then gain a parole, that Governor Jefferson felt obliged to outlaw the practice and send a severe protest to the British commanders responsible for encouraging such behavior.

Yet probably the largest group of those offering resistance to the revolutionary movement were not those who were openly disloyal to the patriot regime, but those who were and are often classified as neutrals, or loyalist-neutrals: those who simply refused to help the patriots unless forced to do it, if then. Large numbers, if not majorities of these kinds of men could be found throughout the states, but particularly in the small-farming regions of North and South Carolina, Georgia, and Virginia, and up through the Delmarva Peninsula, New Jersey and southeastern Pennsylvania to southern New York and up into western Connecticut. But there were also substantial pockets of such people in towns like Philadelphia, New York, Portsmouth, Charleston and smaller places like Savannah, Norfolk, and Newport. In some places, like Queen's County, New York, it has been estimated that over 60 percent of the population were neutrals, while 12 percent were active patriots and 27 percent were actively loyalist (see Tiedemann, 1988, pp. 419–20). Where local studies have been conducted, the numbers of "neutrals" have always been high.

Defining neutrality is difficult as it is often blurred into more active loyalism *or* patriotism. Local farmers could offer free supplies and forage to troops one year, and illegally hide it from desperate soldiers the next; patriot Continental soldiers could serve for two or three years, then become anti-revolutionary draft-dodgers the next; a young member of the militia might turn out against British raids one week, and turn against his patriot betters the next for denying him a political voice. Wavering patriots, or neutrals, most often revealed themselves by refusing to sign oaths of allegiance to the new state governments that were required shortly after declaring independence. Most states, like Virginia in the summer of 1777, passed some kind of law requiring an oath of allegiance from all free white males over the age of 16. In many places, however, the laws met with resistance or were ignored.

Many men also expressed their (sometimes occasional) dissatisfaction with the Revolution by refusing to join the patriot armed forces. Many simply refused to volunteer for the armed services when there was a choice, such as in the early minutemen units or the state or national regular forces, or actively opposed being forced to join the patriot forces either in the compulsory militia, or when conscription was introduced for the Continental Army. In Virginia, for example, entire counties sometimes refused to respond to militia call outs by the state government. Moreover, resistance to compulsory drafts for the armed services resulted every time the state tried to force men into service. The repeated confrontations culminated in violent rioting in 1781 all across Virginia. In one county as many as 700 men assembled to stand in opposition to conscription, and in another, hundreds more gathered at the courthouse wielding clubs to prevent the draft from taking place. Baron von Steuben summed up mobilization problems in 1781 when he wrote with some disgust: "the opposition made to the law in some counties, the entire neglect of it in others, and an unhappy disposition to evade the fair execution of it in all afford a very melancholy prospect." Resistance to serving and draft protests crippled the war effort not just in Virginia – where less than a quarter of the men needed in 1781 were actually raised – but throughout the states. When Washington called for an additional 2,200 men from Connecticut in 1781 to guard the Highlands, for example, he got less than 800, or about 40 percent of the call. Even if drafts did take place, the results were the same. Again in Connecticut in 1780, of 158 men drafted or "detached" for six months' service, 130 refused to go or absconded (Buel, 1980, pp. 253–4).

Perhaps worse than the resistance itself, as von Steuben's comments indicate, such anti-revolutionary activity was aided and abetted by local inhabitants, local officials, and sometimes the very militia officers in charge of implementing the laws. When Connecticut towns were asked once again to draft men from their militia in 1780, there was widespread disobedience. One sergeant, after being ordered to draft a man, told his captain that his "orders are not worthy of my notice." Another captain refused to comply because he said the

Assembly had set an unfair quota for his town. Other officers were elected who were openly disaffected, while local officials' reluctance to "doom" delinquent divisions of militia when they failed to produce recruits showed a general and growing antipathy towards patriot service (Buel, 1980, pp. 231–2). Civilian officials in Braintree, Massachusetts went further when they voted to indemnify its militia officers if they were ever fined for failing to carry out state levies of men, particularly drafts (Gross, 1976, p. 150).

Within the military, too, many thousands of ordinary Americans who found themselves for one reason or another in the armed forces often showed their dissatisfaction with the patriot regime through acts of protest and defiance. The most common expression, of course, was desertion. In Virginia, a conservative estimate puts the number of those who fled from the militia at half, and from the Continental service at a third of those who served. And most of those deserters found hiding places among sympathetic family and friends, employers, or other friendly neighbors. Resistance in the army now and again blossomed into outright mutiny, such as the Connecticut brigade who mutinied in 1778 mainly because they were getting no relief for being paid in rapidly depreciating currency.

Thousands more Americans resisted patriot efforts when they refused to offer supplies or submit to impressments. When Connecticut's Assembly was forced to requisition grain from each town in 1779 for the supply of the militia supporting d'Estaing, not one bushel was ever collected, even though local officials were given summary power to collect from individuals as they saw fit. None wanted to risk popular opposition (Buel, 1980, p. 203). Perhaps worse, many people took it upon themselves during the war years to seize supplies intended for the army or hoarded by elites and merchants. The Chesapeake was plagued in the early years of the war with salt shortages that usually culminated in armed riots and seizures of the commodity. In both Virginia and Maryland in 1775 and 1776, large numbers of farmers banded together to raid and attack the plantations of prominent

and active patriots who were suspected of engrossing or hoarding salt supplies. Even George Washington's estate at Mount Vernon, managed by his cousin Lund Washington in his absence, narrowly avoided a public ransacking when neighbors came to ask for salt. Lund, torn between risking the wrath of his neighbors and unrest among his own white and black servants and slaves if supplies ran low, actually hid his extra salt and "told the people I had none."

Tax resistance also helped cripple the patriot war effort. Evidence indicates that tax resistance levels were high throughout the states, but in most cases, violence was avoided by the failure of local tax collectors to apply pressure on their neighbors. In Connecticut, for example, locally elected selectmen in each town had a discretionary power to abate taxes where they felt there was a need, or good cause. Though custom put the proportion of abated taxes at about 5 percent this rose to 20 percent in the first years of the war and up to 25 percent in the latter years. This had a direct effect on mobilization, as taxes were most often used to pay for recruiting. A tax of two shillings, six pence laid in Connecticut in 1781 to pay for new recruits and supplies was supposed to raise £288,223 in specie. Abatement of up to 20 percent reduced this to £231,017. The government actually received only £160,792, but of this, £120,260 came in as orders on the treasury of goods and services already supplied. Thus the government ultimately only received about £40,000, or just 14 percent of the original request (Buel, 1980, pp. 256–7).

As resistance grew increasingly collective, local authorities were forced to adapt, temporize, or even ignore laws that they were asked to implement and oversee. Those local officials who did not use any discretionary power to avert open confrontation, were often faced with even more uncontrollable violent resistance. In supposedly Tory Newtown, for example, the Whig tax collector was "menaced with personal abuse and injury" and "something else more dreadful than death" unless he stopped collecting. In nearby Norwich, a minor riot broke out in the face of new tax impositions and participants broke open the town jail to free those who had already been imprisoned for delinquency. Similarly, when officials in Hampshire County, Virginia tried to conscript farmers for the army shortly after a 2 percent tax was ordered raised in 1781, they precipitated a "dangerous insurrection." The region was in turmoil for months afterwards as local officials struggled to regain control over the situation. The situation, with local variations, was replayed throughout Virginia and most other states over the course of the war.

2 Reasons for Resistance

While patriot leaders attempted to come to terms with the outward manifestation of disaffection in the form of laws preventing the disruption of mobilization efforts, rarely did they stop to examine and consider the motives behind what they generally dismissed or condemned as "Treasonable and destructive" activities. Most believed that pro-British sentiment was behind much of the resistance, and that more often than not only a few active Tories were primarily responsible for stirring up trouble among a normally acquiescent population. More sympathetic leaders believed that apathy, war-weariness, and a general disposition to evade onerous or oppressive laws was at the root of resistance. Yet the reasons behind the myriad forms of resistance to the Revolution were rarely as simple or as clear-cut as elite leaders wanted to believe. And when the patterns of resistance are investigated closely, what were labeled as the actions of the disaffected, or even the war-weary, begin to appear as the actions of the dissatisfied – those who, in one way or another simply disagreed with the means and/or ends of the revolutionary agenda pursued by patriot elites, and sometimes pursued their own.

For example, *some* of the Maryland salt rioters were accused of being pro-British and it was reported that "by their declarations against the present measures of the country and in favour of the King shew themselves intirely disaffected to our cause." Yet another group, however, was defended as being more patriotic than the wealthy patriots they attacked and plundered for hoarding and engrossing salt. One man

attempted to defend them by noting they had neither "through any dastardly conduct or conversation endeavoured to disunite and weaken our cause; which too many of our first Gentlemen have done and in public acts, and speaks with such timid duplicity, which leaves the ignorant in doubt" (Mason, 1990, pp. 34–5). By attacking those who hoarded much needed supplies, they were only taking the law into their own hands and rectifying an injustice – an action which clearly had parallels with the larger struggle against Britain. Indeed, George Mason, worried about popular upheaval in his home state of Virginia, warned that "the same Principles which first induced us to draw the Sword will again dictate Resistance to Injustice & Oppression, in whatever Shape, or under whatever Pretence, it may be offered." In sum, resistance to the Revolution could reveal a range of beliefs and values that might represent pro-British sentiment, class conflict, dissatisfaction with the status quo, or *extra*-revolutionary behavior.

Undoubtedly, many who acted against the patriots did so because of strong and explicit pro-British feelings. One rare account of a New Yorker of at least middling rank relates that he confessed that he had taken an oath of allegiance to the Crown, "and that in point of Conscience he cannot take up arms against the Forces of the King." Others actively fought for a neutrality that was becoming increasingly difficult to protect. One Brookhaven, New York man who was charged with raising a loyalist volunteer group told his accusers that on the contrary, "all the Combinations & Inlistments were for the purpose of Neutrality & call'd them a Club of Sivility that intended to fight on nither side" (Kammen, 1976, pp. 152–3, 172). Others were more ambiguous. Edward Bacon, James Otis's political rival in Barnstable, Massachusetts, called himself a Tory and said he "was determined not to go to fight," but "if they [the British] landed and come to destroy his house he did not know what he should do." Still others, it was believed, fought on the side of the British or disrupted Whig mobilization for mercenary reasons, or the "Allurements of Gain" (Kammen, 1976, pp. 34–5).

More usually, though, farmers often fought against the patriots (or at least did not fight for the patriots) to protect what property they had rather than gain anything they did not. William Holland, a militia captain in the northern neck of Virginia told his neighbors that he would not oppose the British because "the people in Boston, New York & Phil: that stayed by their property rescued it, & those that flew into the Country & took up arms lost it totally." Holland had "swore by God if the enemy came upon the spott, he would not take up arms in defence of his country, but would stay by his property & would make the best terms he could." Similarly, many landless laborers refused to serve in the patriot armies because they saw better economic opportunities at home. An army recruiter in Cumberland County, Pennsylvania in 1777 found that there was no hope of procuring troops "while wages in the country were so high." Farmers were offering "five pounds per month for common ploughmen and men will not be so foolish ... when they earn double and stay at home" (Knouff, 1994, p. 52). But even wealthy Whigs were willing to sacrifice the cause for the preservation of their property; Samuel Tucker, a staunch Whig and first president of the New Jersey Provincial Congress turned himself over to the British in the fall of 1776 and took an oath of allegiance to the King in an attempt to save his property from confiscation.

Yet many others showed a general lack of belief in the principles of the Revolution and betrayed emerging class resentments. One Marylander declared in 1776, for example, that "it was better for the poor people to lay down their arms and pay the duties and taxes laid upon them by King and Parliament than to be brought into slavery and to be commanded and ordered about as they were." Another refused to sign a loyalty oath because he felt that American opposition to Britain was not designed "for the defence of American liberty of property, but for the purpose of enslaving the poor people thereof" (Hoffman, 1976, p. 285). Later in the war, militia from eastern Virginia refused to serve against the British any longer because

many of them felt that "the Rich wanted the Poor to fight for them, to defend their property, whilst they refused to fight for themselves."

Some of this wartime opposition, which was anti-authoritarian in character, was a result of prewar tensions and factionalism. Social conflict in North and South Carolina during the Regulator movement spilled over into the Revolution as some upland farmers refused to join the army because they believed the rice planters of the lowlands wanted the people of the Piedmont "to go down and assist them against the Negroes and the British." Where unpopular landlords were pro-British, tenants often became patriots; but if a landlord was pro-patriot, tenants could turn against the movement when the going got rough. Prewar ethnic and religious divisions also contributed to the determination of loyalties. Some of those who refused to join the patriot cause with any enthusiasm were recent arrivals who had not yet found their "place" – Scottish Highlanders, for example, along with Dutch farmers in New York and New Jersey, and Germans from Pennsylvania, Maryland, and North Carolina. Many of those who refused to support the Revolution were also from pacifist sects in places like West Jersey, Philadelphia, northern Maryland, northwestern Virginia and backcountry North Carolina (*see* chapter 29).

Yet as important as prewar conditions were in determining enthusiasm for the cause, most people made their choices in the midst of the protracted and costly war itself. As the war slowly ground onwards, more and more people offered resistance to new patriot measures simply out of a weary unwillingness and/or inability to comply. In one of the few studies done of wartime morale, the inhabitants of Westchester County, New York, were described by the end of the war as "almost desolate," "exhausted," "debilitated," and in a "truly deplorable" and "almost incredible" state. They were physically and economically exhausted, and the constant fear, anxiety, and uncertainty of the previous eight years had drained them of any political commitments and norms. Even in the midst of the war in 1778, one army officer wrote that the county and its inhabitants had been so ravaged that even "good Whigs" were "determined" to do nothing for the cause. A survivalist instinct replaced any positive adherence to the Whigs or loyalists vying for their attention and though they traded with anyone who offered profit, needed goods, or safety, they offered no overt allegiance to either side (*see* Kim, 1993, p. 887). Many others across the new states simply got tired of the war – of shortages, or worthless money, of high taxes, of constant calls for armed service.

When people resisted wartime laws and regulations, however, it was usually for particular and sound reasons, reasons which many lawmakers failed to acknowledge. Many militia, for example, refused to serve on particular call outs because it would have meant economic disaster for their farms. Backcountry Pennsylvanians refused to muster in September 1777 as they had "not yet finished their harvests" (Knouff, 1994, p. 50). Less wealthy Virginians refused to serve for too long, or at critical times in the growing season because they had large families who needed their support. They were worried that if they ever did return from fighting, it would be to find their "Wives & Children dispers'd up & down the Country abeging, or at home aslaving," while their wealthier neighbors were "aliving in ease & Affluence." Rather, they would fight when they could, for as long as they could, but no more.

Many of those who broke the law or resisted wartime legislation believed the laws were simply unjust, or arbitrary. Salt rioters seized stores "and paid what price they thought proper." A group of women from Poughkeepsie broke into the store of a merchant they felt was charging too much for tea, vandalized it, drank his liquor, and tried to stone him and his servants. Militia and Continental soldiers often refused to march until they got the bounty money and pay that was due to them, and many men across the states joined in collective, sometimes violent protests against what was seen as arbitrary conscription laws, even if they themselves were exempt from the particular law. And throughout the states, many "subscriptions" were circulated and new

"associations" formed to resist taxes, impressments, and mobilization laws which were seen to be far more onerous and unjust by ordinary people than any that the British had ever imposed.

A desire for just laws also translated into a concern that equal sacrifices be made. Militias in Philadelphia, composed of many from the "lower sort," refused to serve until a compulsory militia law was passed that forced all inhabitants to do their turn, or at least pay for it if they did not (*see* Rosswurm, 1989). This was a common refrain throughout the war. As early as 1776, complaints were raised in Connecticut that militia mobilization penalized the poor and left the rich alone. Protest against mobilization laws – which were usually tantamount to a heavy and essentially regressive tax and thus seemed to favor the wealthy – also plagued the war effort in the South. Militia from Orange County in Virginia, for example, refused to comply with mobilization laws after 1779 because they targeted the "poor militia" of the county who had already been "so liberal in their contributions" while allowing "many that possess great estates" to refuse "to contribute one farthing." And as much as poorer farmers wanted more wealthy ones to make appropriate sacrifices, they also insisted that neighbors and neighboring counties and states do their equal bit as well as it was believed that the "obligation is equal on all men, to defend their liberty and property." When prevaricating patriots refused to do their part, including even wealthy ones, the militias were almost quicker to act against them than they were the British, much to the chagrin and embarrassment of state officials who were unable to protect their lukewarm colleagues.

Farmers also insisted on local autonomy and put local concerns ahead of state or national needs. Virginia militias banded together and pledged not to march out of the state; others refused to march much beyond their county borders. Pennsylvania backcountry farmers who joined the army were incensed to find themselves attached to Washington's army in the east after they had been promised they would be only used to protect the frontier. Both officers and men "understood they were raised for the defense of the western frontiers" and the fact that "their families and substance [were] to be left in so defenseless a situation in their absence, seems to give sensible trouble" (Knouff, 1994, p. 52). Many of those who refused to sign patriotic loyalty oaths in Virginia in 1777 did so because they believed they could then be "compelled to go to the northward whenever the Governor pleased to order them." Militia in Delaware even went to the trouble of disrupting elections in 1777 because they had heard that if the Whigs got into the Assembly, they would be "drafted and obliged to go to camp." Backcountry farmers were particularly worried about Amerindian war parties who might threaten their homes in their absence while more eastern militias worried about the hostile enslaved in their midst and British plunderers on their coastal borders. Men were thus not so much anti-revolutionary, as many state leaders complained, as they were pro-localistic.

But personal and collective autonomy were also insisted upon. Pennsylvania riflemen who had voluntarily marched to Cambridge in 1775 mutinied when some of their men were court-martialed by officers in the Continental Army. After their uprising was put down, many of them were so disillusioned that they began deserting to the enemy (Knouff, 1994, pp. 53–4). Control over the conditions or terms of service was critical – when, where, and how they would obey rules or be punished was seen as negotiable by those making real sacrifices. Whether or not they were allowed to elect their own officers was often the particularly determinative element in a successful call to arms – as it was in Virginia as early as the summer of 1775.

When men were not allowed to elect their own officers, serve for as long as they thought necessary, or fight only for local defense, they more often than not simply refused to do what was seen as someone else's bidding. More democratic-minded militia were particularly resentful when they had to serve under high-minded, more authoritarian Continental officers. Captain Jesse Barefield joined the notorious Little Pedee Loyalists because of the supercilious treatment he received at the hands of

low-country gentry patriot officers (Hoffman, 1976, p. 296). Militia from Caroline County Virginia bonded together and with the "most rivited disgust" formed a pact never to serve again after they had been "wantonly" used by a "Brutal ... Major Mcgill, a Regular Officer."

3 Meanings and Consequences

Just as many enslaved Americans, Amerindians, and loyalists used and resisted the Revolution and patriot forces to struggle for liberty or at least a greater degree of freedom, for their own sovereignty, or to restore a traditional way of life under the Crown, so too did many thousands of ordinary white Americans within the new states also struggle against the new revolutionary regime. Some resisted it passively, some actively or even occasionally in order to be left alone or to challenge what were seen as unfair or unjust measures. In effect, the "disaffected" as they were so often called, were expressing their dissatisfaction with a particular kind of revolution that had only little, occasional, or no appeal to them at all.

By dividing colonists into Whigs and Tories as did the patriot leadership so often, we can too easily miss the point that for a huge number of ordinary Americans, perhaps even a majority, the Revolution was not, in some way, satisfactory. The degree of dissatisfaction might range from the ardent loyalist who took up arms to defend the King, to the family that wished to stay neutral, and to stay out of the way of the conflict, to the groups of normally patriotic militia who protested conscription, to those who wanted to foment or pursue something much more radical than that proposed. All of these people – a majority of the population – "resisted" *the* Revolution somehow – they all expressed their dissatisfaction in some way – by silent protest, withdrawal, individual and collective violence, and sometimes by petitions. For most of these people, the ideals, means, and ends of the Revolution as dictated by the majority of the patriotic leadership simply failed sufficiently to interest, entice, and rouse them to positive action on behalf of the patriot movement for any length of time, if at all.

In the end, a great deal of resistance to the Revolution resulted from this disillusionment with the limits of truly revolutionary activity. Thus it is that we now know, for example, that the Fort Wilson, Pennsylvania confrontation of October 1779 was not caused by loyalist insurgents nor by simple "war-weariness" as contemporaries sometimes assumed. Rather, it was the culmination of almost four years of internal conflict in Pennsylvania between the militia – whose grievances included the fact that the middling and poor had borne a disproportionate burden of the war, that there was too much leniency shown to Tories and neutrals, and that they suffered while serving their country by price gouging and hoarding merchants – and those merchants themselves and the political leaders of the new state who had failed to do anything to rectify the situation (Rosswurm, 1989). Similarly, internal conflict within Virginia throughout the war often stemmed from small farmers' desire to make sacrifices as free and equal men, under terms drawn up by themselves, and under officers and officials elected collectively, rather than as "mercenary" soldiers under rigid regulations enforced with corporal punishment and administered by officers appointed by their supposedly social betters. Such demands clashed with many patriot gentlemen's belief in a more rigid military hierarchy, which could and should enforce discipline and respect for authority above all else (see McDonnell, 1998). Under the strain of wartime conditions, the people "out of doors" were more willing, or sufficiently desperate, to make their views heard through individual and collective protest.

Patriot leaders preferred to dismiss or condemn such worrying subtleties as "treasonable" or the actions of the "disaffected." It was safer to do so, for in resisting the authority and legitimacy of the national and state governments and their revolutionary policies, ordinary people posed implicit and explicit challenges to the ruling patriot elite. In the end, resistance to the Revolution was often a more subtle manifestation of the struggle over who would rule at home – a struggle that represented not so much a direct political attack on the haves by the have-nots, but rather an indirect attack on different forms of authority – one which saw a steady erosion of political and social authority and legitimacy *because* of resistance to Britain and the war.

Yet because most direct or overt resistance to the Revolution – like the Fort Wilson uprising – was quelled or dismissed, the reasons behind, and therefore the consequences of, such resistance have largely been left unexplored or ignored. Indeed, too often historians, consciously or unconsciously, separate what is seen as the "constructive" political Revolution from the "destructive" military War for Independence, when they ought to be looking for the connections (Shy, 1990, p. 110). The Revolution was a mighty and destructive struggle involving in some way most of the population of the eastern half of North America, male and female, black, white, and red, rich and poor. Quite apart from the social, economic, and cultural changes that resulted from the upheaval, we have barely begun to uncover the political consequences. And until we understand and acknowledge the full extent and nature of popular dissatisfaction with the Revolution, we cannot possibly comprehend the process that culminated in the birth of the nation in the form of the Constitution.

Such consequences may have been incorporative or reactive. Certainly many ordinary Americans learned a lesson in oppositional politics as they began to understand how and when to voice their grievances. Collective wartime protests helped initiate a dramatic rise in petitioning throughout the states, for example, not just on those issues that were actively agitated against, but also on much broader political issues that might affect them. Local politics and political culture also appear to have undergone dramatic changes that we have only begun to discover. Paradoxically, the movement that created a new nation may have also reinforced and even strengthened localism amongst many, as the stresses of war increased mistrust of more centralized governments and allowed new, more local and more popular leaders to emerge. More explicitly, the active and collective tax resistance and popular politics of the 1780s were probably a consequence of wartime lessons; the formation of republican societies in the early 1790s might thus have been another legacy of the lesson in collective opposition.

Moreover, the bitter and divisive experience of the war and postwar period might help explain the change of mood, as John Shy has put it, "between the euphoria at Philadelphia in 1776…and the hardheadedness of many of the same men, when eleven years later, in the same city, they hammered out a federal constitution" (Shy, 1990, p. 132). Though the consequences of wartime resistance to the Revolution are difficult to measure in the long term – and certainly beyond the scope of this essay – the possibilities are suggestive. Clearly, state and national leaders were affected not just by the arguments and debates of their colleagues in the legislative chambers, but more fundamentally by the voices and actions of those they lived with, listened to, and often struggled against. Further recovery of the other half of that dialogue throughout the period would not just enrich but irrevocably alter our understanding of the early Republic.

FURTHER READING

Buel, Richard Jr.: *Dear Liberty: Connecticut's Mobilization for the Revolutionary War* (Middletown, Conn.: Wesleyan University Press, 1980).

Gross, Robert A.: *The Minutemen and Their World* (New York: Hill and Wang, 1976).

Hoffman, Ronald: "The 'Disaffected' in the Revolutionary South," in *The American Revolution*, ed. Alfred F. Young (Dekalb, Ill.: Northern Illinois University Press, 1976).

Kammen, Michael: "The American Revolution as a *Crise de Conscience*: The case of New York," in *Society, Freedom, and Conscience: The Coming of the Revolution in Virginia, Massachusetts, and New York*, ed. Richard M. Jellison (New York: W. W. Norton & Company, 1976), 125–89.

Kim, Sung Bok: "The limits of politicization in the American Revolution: The experience of Westchester County, New York," *Journal of American History* 80 (1993), 868–89.

Knouff, Gregory T.: "'An Arduous Service': The Pennsylvania Backcountry Soldiers' Revolution," *Pennsylvania History* 61 (1994), 45–74.

Mason, Keith: "Localism, evangelicalism, and loyalism: the sources of discontent in the Revolutionary Chesapeake," *Journal of Southern History* LVI (1990), 23–54.

McDonnell, Michael A.: "Popular mobilization and political culture in revolutionary Virginia: the failure of the Minutemen and the Revolution from below," *Journal of American History* 85 (1998), 946–81.

Rosswurm, Steven: *Arms, Country and Class: The Philadelphia Militia and the 'Lower sort' during the American Revolution* (New Brunswick, NJ: Rutgers University Press, 1989).

Shy, John: *A People Numerous and Armed: Reflections on the Military Struggle for American Independence* (Ann Arbor: The University of Michigan Press, 1990).

Tiedemann, Joseph S.: "A Revolution Foiled: Queens County, New York, 1775–1776," *Journal of American History* 75 (1988), 417–44.

CHAPTER FORTY-FOUR

Diplomacy of the Revolution, to 1783

Jonathan R. Dull

THE American Revolution was the first successful colonial war of independence. This unprecedented success was achieved against one of the greatest powers of Europe, a nation which indeed could claim to be the greatest naval and financial power in the world. It was not accomplished, however, by American efforts alone. The United States received the direct or indirect assistance of a number of European states which found it to their advantage to weaken Great Britain's position in the European balance of power or to procure territorial or commercial benefits at Britain's expense. The American Revolution thus had a diplomatic impact throughout Europe, an impact much more immediate than the gradual spread of its example to the other nations of the world.

The American Revolution posed in itself a question of diplomacy: were the American colonies an inseparable part of the British Empire or were they free to combine into an independent state with its own foreign policy? For Americans who came to believe the latter, the central diplomatic issue was that of procuring British recognition of their independence. This issue did not arise, however, until many months after the Battles of Lexington and Concord. The task of the Second Continental Congress, which convened only weeks after those battles, initially differed little from that of the First Continental Congress of 1774. That task was to secure from the British Crown redress of American grievances. Like its predecessor, this Congress followed the traditional method of petitioning the Crown, but it also coordinated the successful military

blockade of Boston. The British Government offered an uncompromising answer to the Olive Branch Petition and to the news of the Battle of Bunker Hill. It declared America to be in rebellion, warned the other states of Europe not to intervene, and began to assemble an army large enough to crush the insurrection.

1 The Period of Limited French Aid

In November 1775 Congress learned that the Olive Branch Petition had been ignored and that Britain was planning to expand its military efforts. Its reaction was cautious and measured. It rejected a proposal to send an ambassador to France, instead establishing a Committee of Secret Correspondence to communicate with America's friends "in Great Britain, Ireland, and other parts of the world." Other parts of the world, however, had already taken steps to communicate with America. A few weeks after its establishment the committee met secretly in Philadelphia with a foreign visitor, a young French nobleman named Julian-Alexandre Achard de Bonvouloir. He had been sent to America by the French ambassador to Great Britain. Speaking "unofficially" for the French Government, Bonvouloir told the five commiteemen that France had no designs on Canada, that she wished the Americans well, and that she would permit them to use her ports. In reply, the Americans asked for further assurances of French goodwill, in particular the use of two military engineers and the right to exchange in French ports American raw materials (such as tobacco) for war material.

It was thus the need for supplies of war, particularly gunpowder, which stimulated America's first contact with France. Already that need had produced an extensive private smuggling network reaching from France and the Netherlands to the American coast via the Dutch Caribbean island of St. Eustatius. This smuggling network was insufficient for the needs of the American Continental Army, however, and in March 1776 Congress decided to send a purchasing agent to France, a former congressional delegate from Connecticut named Silas Deane.

Bonvouloir's mission produced even more dramatic results in France. His report of the meetings with the Committee of Secret Correspondence provoked a major foreign policy debate within King Louis XVI's chief advisory body, the *conseil d'état*. The French Controller General (finance minister), Anne-Robert-Jacques Turgot, was reluctant to see France become involved in the American rebellion. He argued that the French monarchy's most urgent needs were those of reforming its budget and reducing its debts. He believed, moreover, that France would benefit from a British victory over the rebels, which would leave Britain to bear the expenses of a continued military occupation of America. The French foreign minister, Charles Gravier, Comte de Vergennes, argued, however, that the British economy and the British Navy were dependent on Britain's maintaining her monopoly of American trade and that hence the French Government should subsidize the American rebellion. Vergennes, whose central interest was not colonies but France's position in European affairs, believed that weakening Britain would improve France's own position in the European balance of power and increase her long-term security. In early May 1776 the King decided in favor of Vergennes and soon thereafter forced Turgot from the *conseil*. Providing a direct subsidy was too dangerous, so the French Government devised a stratagem to funnel military supplies to America. It loaned 1,000,000 *livres tournois* (about £40,000) to a trading company, which would purchase arms at reduced prices from government arsenals. The company would

then sell the arms to the Americans on credit and would eventually be repaid in American tobacco. To head the company Vergennes chose a former secret agent of King Louis XV, the playwright Pierre-Augustin Caron de Beaumarchais. Beaumarchais named the new company Roderigue Hortalez & Co. France furthermore persuaded Spain, which was anxious to see Britain's troubles prolonged, to provide matching funds.

France's commitment to the American cause was less than absolute. The astute Vergennes may have realized that providing arms to the Americans was likely to lead eventually to war with Britain, but he was too prudent to alarm the naive young King Louis XVI, who was still concerned with domestic reforms and far from ready to contemplate a war. At the moment the question of hostilities was still academic. The French Navy would need almost two years to refill its arsenals and repair its ships before it could think of going to war. Vergennes left the question of finding funds for naval rearmament to his ally in the *conseil d'état* Naval Minister Antoine-Raymond-Gualbert-Gabriel de Sartine. It was Sartine's success in maneuvering the King into giving these funds which, as much as the activities of Roderigue Hortalez & Co., began France on the way to war.

The French policy of limiting her aid had the further advantage that it would prolong the American rebellion without alarming American public opinion, which was still mistrustful of Catholic states in general and France in particular. News of King Louis XVI's decision reached Congress about September 15, 1776, the date the British captured the city of New York. The military situation was so threatening it is hardly surprising Congress reacted enthusiastically to the promise of French assistance. It decided to establish a diplomatic mission at the French court and then elected three commissioners to fill it: Silas Deane, the purchasing agent already in Paris, Arthur Lee, a former colonial agent who was presently the London agent of the Committee of Secret Correspondence, and Benjamin Franklin, who was, with the possible exception of George Washington, America's best-known public figure. Franklin, a congressional dele-gate from Pennsylvania and member of the Committee of Secret Correspondence, had already undertaken two futile diplomatic missions on behalf of Congress. The first had been to Montreal during the last weeks of the American occupation; he was thus a witness to the first failure of American foreign policy, that of winning Canadian support for the Revolution. Secondly, on September 11 he and two colleagues met unsuccessfully with Admiral Richard Howe, British naval commander and peace com-missioner, who had hoped to arrange a re-conciliation but lacked the power (and inclination) to recognize American indepen-dence. Franklin's election as commissioner to the French court proved vital to establish-ing the credibility of the American mission.

Franklin soon sailed to France, where in late December he joined his colleagues. Initially they were authorized to offer nothing more than American trade in exchange for France's signing a commercial treaty which would surely provoke Britain to war. As a result of the near collapse of Washington's army in December 1776 Congress amended the commissioners' instructions, permitting them to discuss with France joint military planning. It did not matter, however, since France was still unprepared for war and Vergennes dared not meet openly with the commissioners. He entrusted discussions with them to his under-secretary (*premier commis*) Conrad-Alexandre Gérard. Although Hortalez & Co. continued its vital shipments of war supplies, the commissioners were restricted to waiting for the French Government to recognize their existence. Their contacts with Gérard and Vergennes were often tense, particularly because of the use of French ports by American privateers, which threatened to provoke a premature war with Britain. Because the American mission was full of British spies (e.g., the commissioners' unofficial secretary Edward Bancroft), the French Government could not tell the com-missioners about the French Navy's con-tinued unreadiness for war. In the late summer of 1777 British threats forced the French to expel a squadron of American warships, leading to considerable bitterness.

The British threats were probably hollow; determined to end the American rebellion quickly, the British Government stopped short of treating the French provocations as a cause of war.

2   The Treaties of Alliance and of Amity and Commerce

In spite of their frustrations, the commis-sioners wisely refrained from issuing ultima-tums to the French Government. Their patience was rewarded on December 4, 1777 when a messenger from America brought news of Burgoyne's surrender at Saratoga. For Vergennes the timing of the news was opportune. French naval rearma-ment was finally almost complete and he had already begun to press the Spaniards about jointly intervening directly in the war. The news of Saratoga provided an argu-ment he could use with both Spain and King Louis XVI (who was still reluctant about hostilities): unless the Americans were promised military assistance they might make a compromise peace with Britain and attack the French and Spanish West Indies. It is impossible to know with any certainty how genuine were Vergennes's fears, but on their face they seem illogical; why should the Americans abandon their claims to independence after just winning a major victory? The British Government, however, unwittingly bolstered Vergennes's arguments by sending a secret agent to meet with the commissioners. Neverthe-less Vergennes's arguments failed to con-vince the astute Spanish Foreign Minister, José de Moñino y Redondo, conde de Floridablanca. Spain was happy to pro-long Britain's difficulties – the governor of Spanish Louisiana, Bernardo de Gálvez, was particularly helpful in providing gun-powder to the Americans – but Spain had no interest in American independence. Floridablanca postponed any decision, how-ever, until the treasure fleet from Mexico reached Spain. Vergennes was more success-ful in overcoming the scruples of King Louis XVI. News that the treasure fleet had been delayed at Havana meant there was lit-tle reason to postpone negotiations with the American commissioners. Vergennes feared that the Americans might balk at signing a treaty of military alliance as well as a commercial treaty, but the commissioners' only major objection was that the proposed treaty of alliance would not take effect until the start of hostilities. (The French wished this so they could choose when and where to commence war with Britain.) Once American suspicions on this point had been removed the negotiations went quickly. The treaties, both of them drafted by France, were signed on February 6, 1778. The Treaty of Amity and Commerce was exceptionally generous so as to win American support for the alliance. It gave the Americans most-favored-nation status and generally avoided extracting commercial advantages for France. The Treaty of Alliance was also highly beneficial to the United States. France rejected any claim to Canada (although not to the vitally important Newfoundland fishery), promised not to make peace until Britain recognized American independence, and guaranteed in perpetuity American "liberty, sovereignty and independence." Each party to the alliance guaranteed whatever territories might be conquered during the war by the other. A secret addendum to the treaty invited Spain to join the alliance. The terms of the treaties reflected the European-centered nature of France's war aims; Vergennes wished, above all, not for colonies or even trade, but rather to weaken Britain.

Copies of the treaties were sent to Philadelphia, where Congress immediately ratified them (May 4, 1778). Two clauses in the commercial treaty dealing with export duties, which had been left to Congress's discretion, were deleted. The chief questions now facing France were those of breaking relations with Britain and of beginning hostilities. A few weeks of further discussion with Spain convinced Vergennes there was little point in delay. The British Government knew from its secret service of the existence of the treaties, but chose to ignore them. The French Government forced its hand by announcing on March 13 the Treaty of Amity and Commerce (although not the Treaty of Alliance). Britain had no choice but to recall its ambassador to the French court. France reciprocated and then publicly recognized

the commissioners as diplomatic representatives of the United States and began openly preparing for war.

Britain now modified its campaign plans for the coming year by ordering the evacuation of Philadelphia, the concentration of British forces in New York, and the sending of a large detachment to attack the strategically important French Caribbean island of St. Lucia. All this, however, would require considerable time. France's plans called for seizing the initiative and exploiting the advantage of surprise. A dozen ships of the line (the large warships that were the primary basis of naval strength) would be sent from the Mediterranean naval base of Toulon directly to America in hopes of capturing New York and thereby ending the war in a single stroke. The French hoped that the British, fearing the squadron might be *en route* to the English Channel to support an invasion of Britain, would not be able to reinforce New York in time. The French squadron sailed from Toulon on April 13. Aboard Admiral d'Estaing's flagship *Languedoc* was Gérard, who had been selected as France's first minister plenipotentiary to the United States. He was accompanied by Deane, recalled by Congress for his excessive generosity in distributing in France commissions in the Continental Army.

3 The Beginning and Expansion of Hostilities

D'Estaing had been ordered to commence hostilities when he arrived in America. For diplomatic reasons, however, France hoped hostilities would begin in Europe. It was important to her for Britain to appear the aggressor. War was soon expected in Central Europe between France's nominal ally Austria and the other great German power, Prussia. Austria had provoked the confrontation by bribing the new ruler of Bavaria into ceding considerable territory to her. Vergennes did not wish France to become involved in the dispute, particularly in support of Austria. The Austro-French treaty of alliance was defensive in nature; if either nation was attacked she could call on the other for assistance. If France could claim she was attacked by Britain she could call for Austrian assistance; if, as expected, Austria refused, France would have an excuse to remain neutral in the Austro-Prussian dispute. (This strategy worked; the subsequent Austro-Prussian war lasted only a few months before Russian threats to intervene on Prussia's behalf forced Austria to return most of her newly acquired territory.) Britain on her part wished to appear the victim of French intervention so she could call for help on the Netherlands under terms of *their* defensive alliance. Hostilities commenced on June 17 in a manner sufficiently ambiguous for both combatants to claim to be victims (and for both Austria and the Netherlands to evade any obligations): a French frigate encountered the British home fleet, became involved in a dispute over protocol, and ended by fighting a British counterpart for a number of hours. Both countries reacted to the incident by authorizing reprisals against the other's shipping; neither issued a formal declaration of war. Six weeks later a major fleet battle off the French coast ended any doubts the two countries had gone to war.

At approximately the same time, d'Estaing was vainly attempting to break through Admiral Howe's defensive line off New York. D'Estaing's failure to win a decisive victory changed the diplomatic and military situation. During the 1778 campaign Britain, still awaiting sailors from incoming overseas convoys, had been unable fully to man her fleet. By the opening of the 1779 campaigning season, however, the French Navy could expect to be outnumbered by about 90 ships of the line to 65. Its only hope of survival, let alone victory, lay with the 50 ships of the line of the Spanish Navy. Britain could purchase Spanish neutrality by offering her Gibraltar, but refused to do so, believing she could defeat both navies combined. France did not have the luxury of bargaining and had to offer whatever price Spain demanded for her participation in the war. The price was high. France had to agree to a risky joint invasion attempt on England itself, which Spain wished in order to end the war quickly and protect the Spanish colonial empire. France also had to promise to continue the war until Spain

acquired Gibraltar and to help Spain achieve as many as possible of her other territorial objectives, such as the reconquest of Florida and the Mediterranean island of Minorca. Floridablanca delayed making an agreement until he was certain Britain would not meet his demand for Gibraltar, but it was finally signed at the Spanish palace of Aranjuez on April 12, 1779.

The entrance of Spain into the war (although not into a formal alliance with the United States) completed the transformation of the war into a European conflict; already the main theater of Western Hemisphere naval operations had shifted to the Caribbean. The agreement to continue the war until Spain acquired Gibraltar may not have been compatible with the Franco-American alliance's emphasis on American independence, but the disparity of naval resources left France no alternative. The issue of Gibraltar might bedevil any future peace negotiations, but France took immediate steps to forestall the United States further complicating matters. Through Gérard, Vergennes asked Congress to define its peace objectives. Vergennes had no interest in America beyond seeing her achieve her commercial and political independence, so he instructed Gérard to help moderate the congressional demands. His lobbying was partially successful; Congress insisted on the Mississippi as a western border (although Florida would be left to Spain to reconquer), but the delegates of New England were foiled from demanding a share of the Newfoundland fishery as a peace ultimatum.

Congress was also badly divided by news of dissension among its diplomatic representatives – charges by Arthur Lee against former commissioner Deane and a bitter dispute between Lee and Franklin, which the newly arrived commissioner John Adams (who replaced Deane) vainly attempted to mediate. Gérard's arrival in America caused the dissolution of the unwieldy American diplomatic arrangements in France. Protocol dictated that the United States accredit a minister plenipotentiary to the French court. Congress would also need to elect a peace commissioner for the time Britain was ready to begin negotiations. Furthermore Congress wished to send a diplomatic representative to Spain. The election of these representatives added to congressional bickering but a compromise was reached among the various political factions by which Franklin was elected as minister to France, Adams as peace commissioner, and President of Congress John Jay as minister to Spain.

Gérard's influence in Congress was less the product of his political skill than of America's growing dependence on France. (Gérard, who resigned his position for reasons of health at the end of the year, was actually less adept than was his successor, Anne-César, chevalier de la Luzerne.) This dependence was manifested by George Washington; in 1778 he had opposed asking French help in capturing Canada, but by late 1779, with the British having opened a new front in Georgia and South Carolina, he was willing to encourage the French to send an expeditionary force to the United States. Washington's message was conveyed to Vergennes by the general's former aide, the Marquis de La Fayette, who presently was serving with the French Army.

4 The Decisive British Defeat in North America

Washington's change of attitude was welcome at the French court. As Vergennes had feared, the attempted invasion of England proved to be a fiasco. At the end of 1779 France convinced Spain the allies should shift their strategy. By using their superiority in ships and troops against all the points held by the overextended British they might wear them down until there was the opportunity for a decisive victory. The idea of an expeditionary force in North America fitted well with this strategy and King Louis XVI quickly approved the plan. On May 2, 1780 a force of 6,500 men under command of Jean-Baptiste-Donatien de Vimeur, Comte de Rochambeau, sailed from France for Newport, Rhode Island. Rochambeau's army reached America safely. The British also failed to intercept critically important French and Spanish reinforcements for the West Indies. The British Navy had won a victory off Gibraltar in January 1779 which almost forced Spain out of the war, but it

was unable to follow up the victory. The troops which reached America and the West Indies in 1780 were those which would win the decisive victories of 1781.

The major diplomatic development of 1780 occurred in Northern Europe. Since the beginning of the Revolution Britain had attempted to deprive America of war supplies by intercepting neutral shipping carrying them. In 1778 she also began intercepting supplies bound for France. She thereby became embroiled with Dutch and other neutral shippers, who considered naval material such as timber and masts to be legitimate cargo. On February 28, 1780 Empress Catherine II of Russia announced the formation of a League of Armed Neutrality to protect the rights of such neutral shippers. Her action stunned the British, who considered themselves particular friends of Russia and who had hoped for Catherine's support. During 1780 other neutrals such as Denmark and Sweden joined the League while Britain watched helplessly. Britain was not prepared, however, to see the Netherlands, the most important neutral shipper, also join. To preclude this, on December 20, 1780 Britain opened hostilities on them (thereby negating their eligibility). In so doing they added another 15 ships of the line to their enemies and opened the North Sea as another theater of operations for the overcommitted British Navy.

By the beginning of 1781 even the few ships of the Dutch Navy were critical because all the other combatants were strained to their limits. Spain had already almost dropped out of the war; without the Spanish Navy to put pressure on Gibraltar and to help threaten another invasion attempt on England, the British could detach enough ships from Europe to gain an overwhelming superiority in the Western Hemisphere. The American Navy was negligible – its only ship of the line was still under construction – but the Continental Army was vital to pinning down the British in New York and newly captured South Carolina. By now the Americans, their currency virtually worthless, were completely dependent on French financial help. Congress consequently became totally acquiescent to

French wishes. John Adams, who had returned to France to await the summons to a peace conference, alienated Vergennes by his rudeness and ignorance of diplomatic protocol. At France's request Congress replaced him as peace negotiator by a five-member peace commission consisting of Adams, Franklin, Jay, the former President of Congress Henry Laurens, and Thomas Jefferson. It even instructed the peace commission to accept the advice of King Louis XVI when negotiations finally began. France was in as nearly desperate a condition. Money was available for the 1781 campaign, but should it fail Vergennes admitted he might have to reconsider his commitment to American independence, possibly through accepting Russian mediation.

Luckily for the United States it was the British who broke first. Britain failed to provide enough ships of the line for North America and the Comte de Grasse (commanding a French fleet which arrived from the West Indies), Rochambeau, and Washington trapped at Yorktown Britain's only remaining mobile striking force. Cornwallis's surrender on October 17, 1781 was only one in a string of British defeats from mid-1781 to early 1782 – the Spaniards captured West Florida and Minorca, de Grasse the Caribbean islands of Tobago, St. Christopher, and St. Eustatius – but it was the one which delivered a fatal blow to the government of Lord North and to Parliament's determination to suppress the American rebellion.

5 The Peace Negotiations

Parliament's February 27, 1782 decision to end offensive war against the Americans doomed the existing government and on March 20, North resigned. He was succeeded by Charles Watson-Wentworth, Marquis of Rockingham. Rockingham's Colonial Secretary, William Petty, Earl of Shelburne, moved immediately to open negotiations with his old acquaintance Franklin, using as his agent an elderly Scottish merchant, Richard Oswald. Negotiations with France, however, were the responsibility of Rockingham's Foreign Secretary, Charles James Fox. Fox selected his own agent to meet with Vergennes, a young nobleman, Thomas Grenville. By early May both Grenville and Oswald had begun their negotiations in Paris.

By then the military situation was shifting. Freed from defending exposed outposts such as Minorca and Yorktown, the British Navy began a resurgence. Now it was the French Navy and its allies that were overextended, as was shown by the defeat and capture of de Grasse on April 12, 1782, while beginning an operation against Jamaica. This defeat at the Battle of the Saintes and other failures undermined Vergennes's confidence in the French Navy. France, moreover, was approaching the limits of its ability to borrow money and a major diplomatic crisis was developing in Eastern Europe (where a dispute over the Crimean peninsula seemed likely to lead to a general war between the Russians and the Turks). These factors made Vergennes anxious to conclude peace.

The British Government, however, was ill-prepared to exploit France's difficulties. Because of the divisions within the Rockingham Cabinet, Britain herself was vulnerable to the United States. Fox wished to take control of all the peace negotiations, hoping by the offer of independence to detach the Americans from the French alliance. Then Britain could, if she chose, crush France, Spain, and the Netherlands, extracting from them compensation for her loss of America. Shelburne's approach was totally different. He was reluctant to offer the Americans independence and hoped for some form of federal union with the former colonists; he did not share Fox's Francophobia and wished a general peace with all Britain's opponents. These differences presented enormous leverage to Franklin, temporarily the sole American negotiator. (Jay joined him in Paris on June 22 but fell ill from influenza, Adams was at The Hague negotiating a Dutch–American commercial treaty, Laurens was a prisoner in London, and Jefferson was still in the United States.) He could have chosen to deal with Grenville, but instead wisely chose to continue discussions with Oswald. Fox had overreached himself and on June 30 was repudiated by the rest of the Cabinet.

By coincidence Rockingham died the next day and was succeeded as First Lord of the Treasury (and *de facto* Prime Minister) by Shelburne.

The peace negotiations now entered a new phase. Shelburne, like Vergennes, sincerely wished peace, but time was against him. The British military position was strengthening, Shelburne's support in Parliament was unreliable, and the King (and British public opinion) was wavering between wishing peace and wishing revenge on France and her European allies. Ironically Shelburne soon adapted Fox's negotiating strategy for his own purposes. He moved to divide his enemies by conceding the demands of the patient Franklin. The Americans could have not only British recognition of their independence, but also the territorial boundaries they wished (except for Canada). The threat of a separate American agreement could then be used to force a general peace, since such an agreement would free the garrisons of New York and Charles Town to attack the West Indies. First, however, the stalled negotiations with France must also be revived. Soon after the offer to Franklin, Shelburne sent word to Vergennes that he was ready to offer generous terms to all Britain's enemies. He used de Grasse, an honored prisoner of war, to carry the message.

Vergennes doubted Shelburne's sincerity, but decided to send a representative to England to sound him out. His undersecretary Joseph-Mathias Gérard de Rayneval (brother of Conrad-Alexandre Gérard) held a series of meetings in mid-September at Bowood, Shelburne's country estate. Shelburne repudiated the extravagant offers conveyed by de Grasse, but nevertheless managed to convince Rayneval that Britain was not only willing to make a reasonable peace with France, but would also help contain the Russian threat in Eastern Europe.

The mission to Bowood saved the Anglo-French negotiations; it also indirectly resolved a serious problem that had arisen in the American negotiations. John Jay, now recovered from his influenza, had joined Franklin and then, when his older colleague was stricken with a kidney stone, had taken over the negotiations. Jay distrusted Shelburne as much as did Vergennes, and hence demanded a confirmation of his intention to recognize American independence. For seven weeks the negotiations were stalled by a dispute over the wording of Oswald's commission to deal with the United States.

During these weeks the British crushed a Spanish attack on Gibraltar, thereby increasing the bellicosity of the British public and reducing Shelburne's freedom to make diplomatic concessions. Jay, however, was suspicious of Vergennes as well. When the American commissioner learned of Rayneval's mission to England he feared Britain and France were preparing their own settlement at the expense of the United States. He quickly accepted a compromise on the wording of Oswald's commission. In October detailed discussions began in Paris on the substantive issues still separating Britain and the United States: the boundary between the United States and Canada, compensation for American loyalists who had lost their property, and the extent of American rights off Newfoundland and the other fisheries. During the discussions Jay was gradually joined by Franklin, Adams, and finally Laurens.

European negotiations meanwhile were proceeding in Paris among Alleyne Fitzherbert (Grenville's replacement), Vergennes, and Pedro Pablo Abarca de Bolea, conde de Aranda, the Spanish ambassador to the court of France. France had agreed to surrender most of her conquests in order to speed the peace, but Spain refused to concede her demand for Gibraltar. Finally after another trip to England by Rayneval a complicated exchange of territories was arranged: Spain would receive Gibraltar but would return Minorca; in addition, Britain would receive the French Caribbean islands of Guadeloupe and Dominica, for which France would be compensated by the undeveloped Spanish colony of Santo Domingo (now the Dominican Republic).

6 The Agreements

A few days later the arrangement collapsed. On November 29 the American and British negotiators (acting separately) signed a provisional agreement conceding British acknowledgment of American independence, generous borders for the United States, and even American participation in the Newfoundland and St. Lawrence fisheries. (For further discussion of the treaty's negotiation and its long-term consequences *see* chapter 49.) In deference to the Franco-American alliance the agreement was made conditional upon a general peace being reached, but this was largely a sham. The war-weary American people were hardly likely to continue fighting in order to help France and Spain obtain their war objectives. The British hence would be free to use the New York and Charles Town garrisons against France and Spain; Jay, embittered by his treatment in Spain, even encouraged the British to attack the Spanish garrison of West Florida.

British public opinion was so shocked by the generous terms given the Americans that Shelburne claimed he could no longer count on parliamentary approval for the cession of Gibraltar. He withdrew his agreement to the exchange of territories and for several weeks peace was in doubt. A huge Franco-Spanish naval and military expedition was preparing to sail from Europe for another attempt on Jamaica (a potential exchange for Gibraltar). At Vergennes's request its commander, Admiral d'Estaing, explained to King Carlos III of Spain the obstacles to its success and was delaying its departure as long as possible, but once it sailed the chance of peace would disappear. At this desperate conjuncture the Spaniards finally relented; Aranda took the responsibility of conceding on Gibraltar in exchange for Spain's obtaining Minorca and all of Florida. Vergennes took upon himself the task of negotiating on behalf of the Netherlands, surrendering to Britain a small trading post in India in exchange for the vital Dutch port of Trincomalee in Ceylon. (The Dutch were not in a position to refuse the intervention since France was currently occupying the Dutch island of St. Eustatius and the Cape colony of southern Africa.) In a final compromise France agreed to a return to the *status quo ante bellum* in India and to return all its conquests in the West Indies except the small island of Tobago;

Britain returned St. Lucia and agreed to improved French fishing rights off Newfoundland, the abolition of British rights to maintain a commissioner at Dunkirk (to prevent fortification of that famous privateering port), and French retention of Senegal. A general armistice was signed at Versailles on January 20, 1783; the final treaty of September 3, 1783 merely confirmed the terms reached eight months earlier.

7 Results of the War

The results of the war proved the wisdom of Turgot, who had predicted American independence would bring France no real benefit. Within a few years American trade with Britain had revived, while her trade with the rest of Europe languished. British prosperity revived and Britain soon regained her position in the European balance of power; France, crippled by debt, saw her influence in Europe continue to decline. The Dutch, the war's most unwilling combatants, were humiliated by their failures; their subsequent attempts to reform their political institutions were foiled by foreign intervention. Spain permanently regained Minorca as a result of the war, but her recovery of Florida was only temporary; within half a century all her possessions on the American continent were gone. Ironically the most important territorial gains were made by Russia; with the powers of Western Europe distracted by the American war she was able to gain the Crimea from the Turks. Within a few years of the war's end the great powers of Europe had largely forgotten America and had turned their attention to the problems and opportunities presented by the declining strength of the Poles and Turks. It would take another great revolution, that of 1789, to return France and Britain to the center of events.

FURTHER READING

Dull, Jonathan R.: *A Diplomatic History of the American Revolution* (New Haven, Conn., and London: Yale University Press, 1985).
——: *The French Navy and American Independence: a Study of Arms and Diplomacy,*

1774–1787 (Princeton, NJ: Princeton University Press, 1975).

Harlow, Vincent T.: *The Founding of the Second British Empire, 1763–1793*, 2 vols. Vol. 1, *Discovery and Revolution* (London: Longmans, Green & Co., 1952).

Hoffman, Ronald, and Albert, Peter J. (eds.): *Peace and the Peacemakers: the Treaty of 1783* (Charlottesville: University Press of Virginia, 1986).

Hutson, James S.: *John Adams and the Diplomacy of the American Revolution* (Lexington: University Press of Kentucky, 1980).

Madariaga, Isabel de: *Britain, Russia, and the Armed Neutrality of 1780: Sir James Harris's Mission to St. Petersburg during the American Revolution* (New Haven, Conn.: Yale University Press, 1962).

Morris, Richard B.: *The Peacemakers: the Great Powers and American Independence* (New York, Evanston, Ill., and London: Harper & Row, 1965).

Scott, H. M.: *British Foreign Policy in the Age of the American Revolution* (Oxford: Clarendon Press, 1990).

Stinchcombe, William C.: *The American Revolution and the French Alliance* (Syracuse, NY: Syracuse University Press, 1969).

Stourzh, Gerald: *Benjamin Franklin and American Foreign Policy*, rev. ed. (Chicago and London: University of Chicago Press, 1969).

CHAPTER FORTY-FIVE

Confederation: state governments and their problems

EDWARD COUNTRYMAN

BETWEEN 1776 and 1787 the 14 newly independent states (including Vermont) were the scenes of exciting political innovation and of great political achievement. Yet those same states became the despair of the men whom most Americans regarded as the wisest and most experienced in the country. The states had good claim to call themselves genuinely sovereign, acknowledging no political superior. Yet they were part of a larger emerging nation, and there were points when their actions put the whole of American nationhood at risk. They made themselves the most democratic polities on earth. Yet by 1787 and 1788 enough Americans were unhappy with what they had achieved and what they stood for to accept the radically different vision of the future that the Federalists put forth. The states had won a revolutionary war but it seems that in the eyes of many of their own people they lost the peace that followed.

1   The New Political Men

The states were born in diversity, from passionate democratic experiment in Pennsylvania to sober institutional balance in Massachusetts. But beneath the differences among their constitutions lay a common set of developments and problems. In terms of political sociology one of the most important developments was the entry into the center of public life of men who might, at best, have watched from the periphery during the colonial era. People who had cut their political teeth in the Sons of Liberty during the years of resistance and in the committees

and conventions of the independence crisis were now becoming assemblymen and state senators. Jackson Turner Main (1966) has called this process the "democratization" of the legislatures, leading to "government by the people."

This democratization had two primary sources. One was a simple enlargement of the opportunity to take part. Before independence, assembly elections were held at intervals that varied widely: annually in New England; roughly triennially in Virginia; far less often in New York. After it, they took place annually in every state but one. Under the old order some of the assemblies had been remarkably small: New Hampshire's had 34 members in 1765, New York's 28 in 1769, and New Jersey's 20 in the same year. But by the mid-1780s New Hampshire's lower house had 88 members, New York's had 65, and New Jersey's had 39. Large or small, the colonial institutions had been dominated by men of wealth and standing: "gentlemen of long-tailed families" in Virginia's House of Burgesses; lowland planters and Charles Town merchants in the South Carolina Commons House of Assembly; port-town merchants, Harvard graduates, and the "river gods" of the Connecticut Valley in the Massachusetts General Court; the DeLanceys and Morrises and Livingstons and Van Rensselaers who ran public life in colonial New York; the Philadelphia merchant and Quaker elite in Pennsylvania.

The Revolution brought the withdrawal, whether voluntary or forced, of many of these men and groups. Some became neutrals or outright loyalists, such as Pennsylvania's Joseph Galloway and the New York political faction centered on the DeLancey family. The DeLanceys controlled their province from their victory in the assembly election of 1769 until the independence crisis. Then, effectively, they vanished. Others who chose the Revolution nonetheless lost their nerve and with it their ability to rule, most significantly the patriot wing of the old Pennsylvania elite. The panic with which such men as John Dickinson faced the moment of independence cost them their chance to shape their province's future, at least until they found their political footing again. Still others moved to a higher sphere, as generals, congressmen, and diplomats. Ultimately these included the Adams cousins of Massachusetts, New Yorkers as diverse as John Jay and Alexander McDougall, and George Washington himself. For these men the Revolution meant a leap from mere provincial prominence to national and even world fame.

In every province, both the newly created seats and the vacant places began to be filled by the new men of the Revolution. Abraham Yates, a shoemaker turned lawyer turned politician, of Albany, New York, had been denied a seat in the colonial assembly when he sought one in 1761, thanks to the hostility of Sir William Johnson. Now, deeply hostile not only to loyalists such as Johnson's heirs but to all "high flyers," he graduated from the chairmanship of his city's revolutionary committee to a position of power in the state senate. His story was repeated hundreds of times, as artisans, freehold and even tenant farmers, and small-time professionals and traders became makers of high public policy. Some stayed a session or two and then returned to obscurity. Others, such as Yates, William Findley of Pennsylvania, and Abraham Clark of New Jersey, became men of considerable political consequence.

Massachusetts

Numbers alone did not guarantee power, for in the upheaval of the mid-1770s the most basic and valuable political skill was the ability to organize. With it, a few might well take charge of many, as the case of Massachusetts shows. Based on the separate representation of each town, the state's assembly was huge, with a potential membership of more than 200. The farmers of the interior had the power to exercise absolute control in the lower house, but a number of factors kept them from doing so. One was simple inexperience. To these men parliamentary procedure and the correct mode of drafting bills were arcane mysteries, not skills to be taken for granted. A second was the inability, or unwillingness, of many of the interior towns to provide salaries and expenses. These were absolute necessities if a farmer or a village artisan or even a small-town lawyer was to go to Boston for an extended legislative session. A third was the reluctance of the men of the interior actually to act together politically: everything in their political culture told them that this was partisanship, and all of them knew that partisanship was fundamentally wrong.

The result was that the merchants and professionals of the seaboard counties, men such as Nathaniel Gorham of Boston and Jonathan Jackson of Newburyport, took effective control. They, too, were "new men," but they stepped into places vacated by the likes of Samuel Adams, not Joseph Galloway or James DeLancey. They did not share the political culture of the interior villagers, or even of the Boston crowd, and they had no scruples about organizing privately in order to take public power. Until the aftermath of Shays's Rebellion, these men would run the commonwealth according to their view of its best interests.

New York

Developments elsewhere were more complex. The young elite of New York's revolution – landholders such as Robert R. Livingston, Gouverneur Morris, and Philip Schuyler, and professionals such as John Jay and Egbert Benson – understood the importance of organization and coordination. In 1777, after they succeeded in writing and implementing a state constitution that was to their own taste, they reminisced to one another about the "well-planned delays, indefatigible industry and minute … attention to every favourable circumstance" that had enabled their "council of conspiracy" to achieve its institutional goals. They planned to dominate the new government as well and deployed themselves carefully: Schuyler (as they expected) to the governor's chair; Livingston and Jay to the high posts of Chancellor and Chief Justice; Benson, Morris, and a clutch of lesser Livingstons to the assembly. "They may chuse who they will," Schuyler smugly predicted during the first election. "I will command them all."

But the governorship in fact went to George Clinton, who would hold it until 1792. Like Schuyler he was a seasoned man of public affairs, having served with some prominence in the colonial assembly. But to the men who had so confidently expected to rule, "George the governor" (as one of their confidants dismissively described him) was a plebeian. His "family and circumstances" did "not entitle him to so distinguished a predominance." In the assembly Benson found himself not the *de facto* leader he had expected to be but rather obliged, thanks to his possession of the necessary technical skills, to draft bills for men whom he scorned and on behalf of causes that he loathed.

To repeat such accounts 14 times would be tedious. Each separate state had its own separate story. But from New Hampshire to Georgia the Revolution brought obscure men to prominence and responsibilities that none of them must ever have expected. Their presence was a gain, for it brought to the fore men of energy, commitment, and local sensitivity, if not of wide experience, deep learning, or "family and connections." But it also brought problems, as the many bungled pieces of legislation they passed and the partisanship they provoked would show.

2 Legitimizing the New State Governments

The new governments had to establish their own legitimacy, and the men in charge soon found that more was necessary to do it than simply proclaiming a constitution and calling an election. Anticipating trouble, the ever-astute John Adams wrote in 1776 of the need to "glide insensibly" from the old

order to the new. But his desire was not fulfilled. Instead, during their earliest years the governments had to prove their ability to rule both to their supporters and to their enemies. In some states they nearly broke under the effort.

New York

New York, Pennsylvania, Maryland, and South Carolina provide the clearest examples. New York entered independence as a mere fragment of the province that it had been. In August 1776 the British conquered the southern district, comprising Manhattan, Long Island, Staten Island, and the lower portion of Westchester County. They would remain until the end of 1783, and to large numbers of the district's people that was perfectly acceptable. A few months after the invasion, at the very beginning of 1777, what had been the New York counties of Cumberland and Gloucester, together with part of Charlotte (now Washington) County, broke free to establish Vermont. Geographically, the free New York that adopted a republican government in April 1777 was no more than a strip running along the Hudson and Mohawk valleys.

Had Continental troops and state militia not stopped the British Army under General John Burgoyne at Saratoga in October 1777 there would have been no state to be governed at all. Even after the major military threat was ended, profound instability remained. Although the state constitution was proclaimed in April, the legislature did not assemble until the fall. It was scattered almost immediately, when a minor British expedition took and burned Kingston, the temporary capital, during the Saratoga crisis. The legislature did not actually begin permanent operations until early in 1778.

Moreover, it faced immense difficulty from its own "subjects." Popular loyalism was intense in the landlord-ridden counties along the east bank of the Hudson and in the Mohawk Valley. Among the patriots, the revolutionary committees of the independence crisis persisted. Despite the denunciation by the state constitution itself of the "many and great inconveniences" that attended "government by Congresses and Committees," they continued meeting until well into 1778. New York's state constitution was never an issue of serious debate, despite its relatively conservative institutions and despite its never being submitted for the popular ratification that the artisans of New York City had demanded as early as May 1776. But during the first years, the survival of the state government was by no means a certainty.

Pennsylvania

For Pennsylvania the problem was just the reverse. There the difficulty was not loyalists, or separatism, or, for the most part, the course of the war. It was the state's radical constitution, adopted in 1776 (*see* chapter 34, §4). The document reflected the most democratic impulses of the Revolution, as its emulation by Vermont and the similar proposals that came forward in many other states show. But it also reflected the precise balance of Pennsylvania politics at the moment of independence. Pennsylvania's moderates acted swiftly to regain power, establishing their Republican Society and dedicating themselves to the abolition of a government that they believed to be the height of political folly. With leadership that included the jurist James Wilson, the merchant and financier Robert Morris, the physician Benjamin Rush, and the writer-politician John Dickinson, they were formidable, despite the abilities of Joseph Reed, Charles Willson Peale, and George Bryan on the other "Constitutionalist" side.

The Constitutionalists enjoyed real popular support. But the Republicans appreciated the importance of their state's social complexity and its fundamentally commercial economy in a way the Constitutionalists never did. The state constitution never became an object of general veneration and respect, providing a framework within which disputes might be worked out. Instead, it became and remained the primary object of dispute itself. In 1790 a constitutional convention finally got rid of it, establishing an upper legislative house and a governorship to bring Pennsylvania into live with the dominant American model.

Maryland

Maryland's problems were akin to New York's, and almost as severe. The state never had to endure massive invasion or protracted warfare. But it did have many militant loyalists, particularly on the eastern shore of Chesapeake Bay. Maryland loyalism drew on many roots. These included the economic difference between eastern-shore small farmers and the opulent tobacco planters who had written the state constitution and who dominated the new government, the dissent of Methodists and Baptists in a state dominated by Anglicans and newly enfranchised Catholics, and the possibility of an alliance between poor Whites and slaves. In Maryland, as in New York, the militia was unreliable, the courts could not be opened, and taxes were almost impossible to collect.

The situation was not helped by having a political system that was deliberately "closed." Maryland's planter elite lacked the social confidence of its Virginia counterpart. The Virginians boldly set up institutions that were almost as democratic in formal terms as Pennsylvania's, secure in the certainty that their own sort would continue to rule. But the Marylanders erected a "fortress of institutions" around themselves. They established high property qualifications for public office, the only assembly that was chosen for a term longer than a single year, and a system of electors that stood between the voters and the state senate. The document reflected the well-justified fear of the elite that it might lose control of the whole situation.

South Carolina

South Carolina's instability sprang from a combination of pre-independence tensions and the fortunes of war. Despite the homogeneity of lowcountry society – later referred to as the "harmony we were famous for" – the state's people entered independence with many conflicting interests and possibly with different ideas about its future. Like the great northern ports, Charles Town saw a rapid growth in political awareness among artisans during the independence crisis. As in Philadelphia or New York, these formed the core of the town's Sons of Liberty. Again as in the North, some of them found in the non-importation of the late 1760s a chance to advance their own prosperity, with no over-seas rivals in the local market for the goods they made. For the town's merchants, who lived by overseas trade, and for artisans who served the long-distance economy, non-importation had a different meaning. The interior was even more split, with deep hos-tility between the planter dominated low-lands and a backcountry where slavery and the plantation system had not yet taken full shape. It may or may not be the case that backcountry people wanted a different social model; it is certainly the case that they thoroughly mistrusted the lowcountry gentlemen who ruled their province. When the lowland planter and jurist Williams Henry Drayton set out to rally the back-country in 1775, he met indifference and resistance rather than support.

To this essential social instability was added a massive British invasion early in 1780. Sir Henry Clinton's forces quickly captured Charles Town and the lowcountry, and the people who did not flee took the oaths of submission that the conquerors required. In an address to Clinton, a large number of Charlestonians and planters repudiated independence and the "rank democracy" to which it had led, calling it a "tyrannical domination, only to be found among the uncivilised part of mankind." Among the men who sought British protec-tion were the former president Rawlins Lowndes, Colonel Charles Pinckney, and Henry Middleton, who had been president of the Continental Congress. In the interior, the invasion led to the most vicious warfare the Revolution saw, both between British and American and between patriot and loy-alist. What was left of the revolutionary government fled the state.

New laws of taxation

For three of these states, New York, Maryland, and South Carolina, the answer to the problem of legitimacy came in the form of dramatic demonstrations of responsiveness to public demands. In New York it happened in 1779, when the legisla-ture totally reversed its previous policies on loyalism and taxation. Instead of simply controlling the "disaffected," the state would punish them: the Confiscation Act passed that fall was only the first of a series of harsh laws that would eventually be long enough to fill a sizeable volume. Instead of taxing as lightly as possible, the state would strike at the rich, allowing assessors to rate them according to "circumstances and other abilities to pay taxes, collec-tively considered." This mode of taxation was never elegant and by 1782 Alexander Hamilton had concluded that it was "radically vicious." But in a state where the rich had never had to pay before, it proved popular.

Even earlier, Charles Carroll of Carrollton had begun to argue "the wisdom of sacri-fice" to his own kind in Maryland, insisting that they recognize the social need for tax-ing the rich and for issuing cheap paper cur-rency. To his father, Charles Carroll of Annapolis, it surpassed "in iniquity all the acts of the British Parliament." But to the son all "great revolutions" brought "partial injustice and suffering" and these had to be endured. Better for the planter elite to lose some of its property than all of its power. In South Carolina the change came somewhat later. But by the revolution's end "the inhabitants" had adopted the egalitarian "mode of respectful Representation" when they addressed their legislators, instead of the "humble petitions" of an earlier day. They began assuming that "people who were no better than they but who happened to sit in the legislature would act" to do what the people wanted. To its historian Jerome Nadelhaft, "that was the revolution" there.

A governor of no "family and connec-tions" in New York; an intensely democratic but deeply divisive institutional experiment in Pennsylvania; the elite's need to accept "the wisdom of sacrifice" in Maryland; the "snarls of invidious animals" in South Carolina: these were the political situa-tions that the early state governments faced. There was no real question of "gliding insensibly" from the old order to the new.

Instead, there was a pressing need for change.

3 The New Governments and the Economy

Beneath these questions of political sociology a deeper issue was also crystallizing, with equally long-range causes and consequences. This was the proper stance of the government in relation to the economy. Like the question of institutional responsiveness, it came to a head in the late 1770s, as the states tried to grapple with the runaway inflation that accompanied wartime shortage and the collapse of the Continental dollar. But in larger terms a major change in political economy was underway.

Throughout the colonial period the imperial, provincial, and local governments had operated on the principle that they had a duty as well as a right to intervene in the economy for "the public good." At the imperial level the whole crisis had been about establishing the nature and scope of the public good, and independence meant the definitive American rejection of Parliament's assertion that it could do so. At the provincial and local levels, intervention had usually been for the sake of controlling the market place, with the goal of establishing a balance among the good name of local wares in the larger world and the direct interests of producers, traders, and consumers. Assizes of bread, laws against such market offences as "forestalling," "regrating," and "engrossing," and the regular use of embargoes to counter shortages were normal and accepted parts of economic life.

At the end of the 1770s, popular pressure for such intervention became intense, due to the unprecedented demands of a large-scale wartime economy and to the worst and most widespread inflation Americans had ever known. All over the northern states, particularly, people responded to the crisis in ways that both long-established custom and revolutionary experience legitimated. They rioted, taking goods they needed, and paying according to "just" prices that they set themselves. They treated "monopolisers" and "hoarders" just as they had learned to treat loyalists, ostracizing

them, carting them about for public ridicule, and sometimes tarring and feathering them. They put pressure on the state governments for action, in the form of price-control legislation and embargoes. In 1779 they elected new popular committees and gave them the task of bringing the economy under control. As they did so, they were starting to repeat the steps that had brought down the old order, for these committees, like the revolutionary committees of 1774, 1775, and 1776, claimed a mandate to take direct action. A dual crisis faced the new governments. Both the working of the economy and their own fragile legitimacy were at stake.

For many Americans the long-standing belief in "corporatist" political economy was an article of faith, just as much as the newly founded belief in republicanism. Indeed, the two reinforced each other. In Gordon Wood's phrase (Wood, 1969), corporatism and classical republicanism were both "essentially anti-capitalistic" in their assertion of the primacy of the small community and of stasis over the individual and change. In Pennsylvania the Constitutionalist Society made acceptance of corporatist political economy a condition of membership during the 1779 crisis. But two new elements were now present, and both pointed towards a redefinition of the whole issue.

One was the sheer dimensions of the problem. The enormous economic disloca tions of the war years were part of the birth pangs of a national economy that would be much more powerful and much more tightly integrated than the old economy of the British Empire had ever been. There had been wars and depressions and inflation and shortages before, but never over so large a scale or for reasons that were so thoroughly interlinked. Beneath economic corporatism, as most Americans understood it, was a working assumption that the local economic unit could and sometimes should isolate itself. The larger economy of the Atlantic world had always impinged on colonial life, but it usually had been possible to shut it out, at least for a while. The demands of the war could not be shut out. If the army was not to collapse, if the French were not to take the aid they were supplying and go home, and if the British were not to triumph, there had to be cooperation across community and state lines. In the new situation locally focused embargoes and price controls would be ineffectual at best and pernicious at worst.

The second element was ideological. Throughout the western world advanced thinkers were developing the idea that a free market was superior to any form of controlled economy. The trend found its supreme expression in Adam Smith's *The Wealth of Nations*, published the same year that independence was declared, but it had been taking shape for over century. Now its American moment arrived, as men with an awareness of large-scale national need and of the new dimensions and possibilities of the market place contemplated the economic mess that surrounded them and rejected the old solutions. Let the price "limitation" be "limited to the City of Albany" urged Egbert Benson of New York, writing to John Jay. Jay agreed. So did Pennsylvanians such as James Wilson and Robert Morris; so did the hard-headed men who had taken control of the revolution in Massachusetts. Nor was the new sense restricted to the elite, for so did Thomas Paine and so did the organized leatherworkers of Philadelphia.

The consequence was that during the late 1770s and the early and middle 1780s the state governments became arenas in which two economic ideologies contended. There could not have been any Americans who doubted the fundamental importance and even sanctity of private property. But the social nature of private property became the subject of intense dispute. In Massachusetts, liberal market-place values won handily; even before the adoption of the Constitution of 1780 the commonwealth adopted policies of hard money and high taxation. There would be no attempts at all to use public power to cushion the state's citizens against the larger demands of the economic world. There would be no cheap paper money that debtors could use to pay what they owed, or legal procedures that they could use to stave off their creditors.

But elsewhere the older beliefs remained strong and men who held them were still able to shape policy. Not really paradoxically, these tended to be precisely the obscure men whom the Revolution had brought to prominence. Paper money, stay laws, compulsory debt arbitration, laws that disadvantaged British and loyalist creditors, tender laws, and continuing attempts at embargoes and price controls were the result. As often as not, the legislation was ill-drawn and poorly thought out. In larger terms and in the long run it was bound to be ineffectual, for no amount of locally focused effort could stave off the growing power of the national and Atlantic economic spheres. But in the short run the effect was to aid profoundly in stabilizing the new political institutions. People with real grievances and real fears – of bankruptcy, of losing their farms, of the debtors' prison – came to the conclusion that the new state governments could be theirs to control and to use.

4   The Emergence of Partisanship

By and large the new men of state politics did not enter public life as part of an organized attempt to seize power. Perhaps the only exceptions came in Pennsylvania and Vermont. In the first, the coalition of backcountry Scotch-Irish Presbyterian farmers and Philadelphia artisan-radicals that created the state's constitution of 1776 began quickly to consolidate itself as the Constitutionalist Party. In the second the former Green Mountain Boys who had waged a decade-long guerrilla struggle against New York now had to create and lead a state.

But the effect of such men's entry was division. The patriots of 1776 created a remarkable political coalition, held together by a common view on the issue of independence. The great desire that year was for unity: even men who had been openly loyalist were welcomed back to the fold if they would make the necessary gestures of commitment to the revolutionary cause. The political foe was Britain and its minions, not Americans of differing backgrounds or beliefs or interests or political opinions. Inherently fragile, however, the unity of 1776 could not last. Although partisanship was a dirty word in virtually everyone's political vocabulary, it was the necessary outcome both of American social reality and of people's revolutionary experience.

One reason was the fact that the Revolution was teaching people to regard themselves in specific social terms as well as in terms of a new national identity. Men of power and wealth had always known that for political purposes they were merchants, planters, and landlords as well as Pennsylvanians or Virginians. They had begun to show it in the late years of the old order by organizing groups such as New York's Chamber of Commerce. They had always known how to cooperate in their own interests, even when they were also thinking in terms larger than themselves. That was what had made them a ruling elite. But even they needed reminding about the facts of political life. In 1784 and 1785 Alexander Hamilton conducted a remarkable campaign aimed at convincing New York's aristocrats, who had fallen to squabbling among themselves, to forget their disputes and "endeavour to put men in the Legislature whose principles are not of the *levelling kind*."

The novelty was the emergence of such political consciousness, assertiveness, and mutual cooperation among the lesser men who traditionally had been the ruled rather than the rulers. The two clearest cases are urban artisans and small farmers. Artisan consciousness had grown steadily during the years of resistance, from hesitant offers to cooperate with "our neighbours the merchants" for the sake of the grand cause to strident assertions that in "Questions of … great Consequence, the Consent of the Majority of the Tradesmen, Farmers and other Freemen" was needed. By 1773 New York artisans were meeting "at Beer Houses" in order "to concert Measures"; the following year they purchased their own meeting place, naming it Liberty Hall. In Philadelphia even the privates in the militia developed their own consciousness, electing a committee to represent them, making their own political demands, and providing much of the driving force for the "corporatist" attempt to resolve the inflation crisis of 1779.

This did not lead immediately to partisanship in the modern sense. Except in Pennsylvania, where Constitutionalists and Republicans rapidly faced one another down, there were no recognized labels, no party organizations, no coordinated campaigns. But it did form the raw material from which partisanship could emerge. By and large the revolutionaries expected that in the republican political order people would put citizenship ahead of self-interest, the public above the private. But definitions of citizenship and of what was genuinely public differed, as the inflation crisis showed. For many, perhaps most, Americans the "public" meant the small cohesive community, held together by custom and mutuality. For a growing number it meant the nation, whose immediate interest was keeping the army supplied. And for at least some it meant a large-scale commercial society, in which the maintenance of stable, predictable conditions of contract and exchange would be regarded as more important than the prevention of local and personal suffering.

New York

Within this context partisanship emerged in fits and starts. From its first session in 1777 until 1781, voting patterns in New York's legislature were essentially chaotic, with little predictability about how a man would vote or who his associates would be from one issue to the next. There was ample conflict but there was not yet structure. But in the fifth session (1782), predictability from one issue to another did begin to emerge. By the eighth session (1784–5), the assembly was splitting the same way on fully half of its roll-call votes, whatever the ostensible issue. Land policy; treatment of loyalists; taxation; the future of old institutions such as New York City's Trinity Church; paper currency: issue after issue provoked the same split. The fundamental question at stake was what kind of society independent New York would be.

During the war years men did try to manage elections. But these first efforts were haphazard, ill-coordinated, and local in focus. At the war's end there was still no generally accepted label for either of the developing sides. Writing of New York City's first free election, at the end of 1783,

Robert R. Livingston described the efforts of "the tories... the violent Whigs... and those who wish to suppress all violences," but his reference was specific to the town, not general for the whole state. Historians have sometimes written of "Clintonians" and "Anti-Clintonians," but those terms are anachronistic. Only slowly did Governor George Clinton emerge as an openly partisan leader. As late as 1786 his name was at the head of an assembly ticket put forward by men who in fact wanted him out of office.

But the divisions of the mid-1780s did directly prefigure the split between Federalist and Anti-Federalist in the state in 1788. The only exception was the New York City's "late exiled Mechanics," who had been the "violent Whigs" of 1783, now joined the merchants and professionals – the former "tories" and their friends who had wished to "suppress all violences" – in favoring the Constitution. The frantic attempts at unity among all patriots of the independence period had given way to open expression of difference, open organization, and open political labels as well-recognized sides maneuvered in order to get power.

New York's experience of partisan development had much in common with that of its two major neighbors, Pennsylvania and Massachusetts. In all three, a coalition of farmers, artisans, and merchants came apart along its own internal lines of stress. In all three the fundamental issue was the shape of the republican future. In all three that issue lay behind debates on such seemingly diverse issues as debtor–creditor relations, loyalism, education, and land policy. In all three, as well, the issue of the government's stance *vis-à-vis* the demands of a mobilized citizenry had to be confronted. Finally, in all three the "radical" or "democratic" or "popular" position developed two poles. Artisans and farmers alike clung to a vision of a society of equal, productive men, which merchants and urban professionals did not share. Neither artisans nor farmers were enamored of the idea of a free market, at least as envisaged by a Robert Morris or an Alexander Hamilton. But in none of these states did they develop a strong alliance. In 1788 most artisans in New York City,

Philadelphia, and Boston found that they had good reason to support the Constitution. Most farmers in the three states found equally good reason to oppose it.

Pennsylvania

But in New York the course of partisan development worked to strengthen the state government. In Pennsylvania and Massachusetts, it did not. From the point of view of legitimating the new order, Pennsylvania's partisanship developed too quickly and cut too deep. It took almost half a decade for New York's independence coalition to split, another three years for genuinely coherent partisanship to solidify in the legislature, and two more for party labels and organization to appear. But in Pennsylvania the split came suddenly and was tied directly to the issue of independence. New York's conservatives – a Robert R. Livingston or John Jay – may have been reluctant to make the leap, but they made it. They may have wanted leniency for Tories during the war and they may have been willing to work with them after it. But no one could have accused them of being loyalists themselves. Pennsylvanians such as Dickinson, however, were tainted in exactly that way, at least to the eyes of their patriot foes, thanks to their fatal attempt in 1776 to keep hesitating past the moment when hesitation was still possible. To the Constitutionalists, the Pennsylvania Republicans would always be crypto-loyalists.

The second problem in Pennsylvania was the very clarity of focus and intensity of organization that partisanship took from the beginning. With the constitution of 1776 as the main issue there was no room for temporizing; as on independence, one was either for or against. The Constitutionalists recognized this by their policy of requiring an oath of loyalty on the part of voters and office-holders, not simply of Pennsylvania's independence but to the constitution itself. With so sharp a division on so fundamental a question it is not surprising that both sides were fully organized by 1779, the year that New York's independence coalition first came under serious strain. In one sense the emergency of the

Republican and Constitutionalist clubs so early was a measure of the vitality of Pennsylvania's political life. But in another it was a sign of forced hot-house growth, with the branches taking on weight and density before the stem had the strength to hold them up.

Massachusetts

In Massachusetts the problem was not the too-rapid development of partisanship but rather its stunting. The state's independence coalition was as tense in its internal relationships as it was passionate in its commitment against the British. When the countryside mobilized in response to the Coercive Acts, some villagers were fearful that the whole crisis stemmed from the desire of Boston merchants to secure a market for their surplus goods by cutting off external trade. Their fear sprang from a loyalist canard, spread by the Tory press of John Mein, but the charge struck a responsive chord in Puritan village culture. More than any other Americans, New England farmers clung to the ideal of a cooperative, communal society, and more than most they had always been able to live relatively free of the large commercial market place. Their collective life, with its town meetings and its gathered churches, reinforced their sense that they could run their own affairs to suit themselves. Ordinary Bostonians shared some of this ethos, as their passionate attachment to town-meeting government demonstrates. But of necessity Boston was much more immersed in the world of commerce than most of the towns of the interior. Within Boston the tension between commerce and community reached right back to the founding. But in the aftermath of independence its men of commerce took firm control not only of the town but of the whole state.

Meanwhile Boston's mechanics fell politically silent. They would remain so until 1788, when they emerged under the leadership of Paul Revere as a strong pro-Constitution force. The farmers' whole ethos, in turn, told them that the proper way to organize themselves was in consensual groups, not in partisan formations.

Throughout the Confederation years they gathered to voice their grievances, but their medium was the town meeting or the county convention. The delegates they sent to the legislature felt themselves bound by town-meeting instructions, but neither they nor their constitutents accepted the legitimacy of state-level cooperation in the manner that New Yorkers or Pennsylvanians did. In consequence, despite the state's adoption of policies that glaringly favored one social interest at the expense of another, the legislature did not become a focus of party development. Its members did not develop the kind of creative political dialogue with their constituents that the New Yorkers engendered or the Pennsylvania Constitutionalists had fondly expected. There was no state figure like New York's George Clinton, slowly taking on a partisan role on the "popular" side, or Pennsylvania's president Joseph Reed, known as a Constitutionalist and ably administering the state during the worst years of the war. Most people in Massachusetts accepted their state's constitution of 1780. But all over the interior there were men who found that, though it was easy enough to make their wishes known, there was no way to turn them into governmental action.

Shay's Rebellion

The result was Shay's Rebellion. This uprising of central and western Massachusetts farmers was not an isolated event, springing from causes peculiar to its own region. There were "combustibles in every state," and as David Szatmary (1980) shows, the rising itself was a New England-wide movement. Even in distant South Carolina, 1785 and 1786 saw debtors gathering to close courts and demand state laws to protect them from the effects of the postwar depression. But it was in Massachusetts that the issues and forces involved crystallized.

The problem was threefold. First, like most of America, Massachusetts found itself caught in a contracting network of debt that reached all the way to London. Second, in Massachusetts, unlike most other states, there was no structure of state laws to cushion debtors against creditors or, in an alternative reading, to protect virtuous patriots against the British and former loyalists. Third, there was no partisan structure able to channel popular demands to and through the institutions of the state government. The fundamental issue was the emerging power of an increasingly capitalist economy, with Boston looking towards the future and the towns trying to cling to the past. The new large situation required predictability and stability for the enforcement of contractual obligations, conditions that the Federal Constitution would in fact guarantee. But both long tradition and the history of the Revolution told the farmers they were correct to resist.

This is not the place to recount the story of either the uprising or its suppression (see chapter 47, §4). The important point is the transformation in political practice that ensued. Although the farmers' amateur militia proved no match for the state's troops, and though the insurgents found themselves obliged to crawl before the triumphant state authorities, the interior finally realized the power of its numbers and organized to win the next election. John Hancock replaced James Bowdoin as governor. More towns than ever before elected representatives, 228 in all, and 60 percent of the men they chose were new to the assembly. Even in the 40-member state senate, established specifically to protect property, 16 new faces appeared.

It might have heralded a genuinely radical alteration in the state's direction, but in fact it did not. The year was 1787, and both the rebellion in Massachusetts and the subsequent election served to convince the coalescing Federalist movement that radical change of another sort was in fact required. The real outcome of Shays's Rebellion came not in changes to the state's laws but in the ncar-victory of Massachusetts' Anti-Federalism in 1788. When the state's ratifying convention met, the two sides were almost evenly matched. This was a direct reflection of the political awakening of the interior, just as the strength of Anti-Federalism in the New York convention – which significantly met in Poughkeepsie rather than New York City – reflected that state's decade of partisan development.

As Gordon Wood has shown (1969), the major concern of the emerging Federalists was the states, not the Articles of Confederation. James Madison framed his "Vices of the Political System of the United States," the preparatory notes that he wrote before the Federal Convention, around the problem of controlling and limiting the state governments. Originally he wanted the central authority to have an absolute veto on state legislation. To the Federalists the state administrations were filled with "Characters too full of Local attachments and Views," men of "narrow souls" who pandered "to the vulgar and sordid notions of the populace." "The vile State governments are sources of pollution which will contaminate the American name for ages ... Smite them," wrote Henry Knox, who had commanded the expedition that smote the Shaysites, to Rufus King, sitting in the Philadelphia convention.

5   The Ratification of the Constitution

Enough ordinary white adult male Americans agreed, for one reason or another, to accept the Constitution and thus end the era of state autonomy. Some did it with reluctance and on the promise of the amendments that became the Bill of Rights. Others did it with enthusiasm, as the great ratification parades of the major towns showed. But even in 1788, at the Federalists' moment of triumph, the states and what they stood for still commanded wide support, so much that in the three key states of Virginia, Massachusetts, and New York ratification was a close-run thing. Had the Anti-Federalists won at the right moment in any of them, or even in strategically important New Hampshire, it might have been stopped completely and the states would have gone on as before.

Even in 1788, to many of their citizens – the term "subjects" had fallen out of use and the change is telling – the state governments were not "vile" but rather popular, responsive institutions, a vast improvement on what had gone before. This belief developed at an uneven pace, but the local story in each of the states grew from the large complexities of the Revolution. What took place in the states between 1776 and 1788 did not complete the Revolution; that was to be the Federalists' great achievement. But it did express in its complexity both the hopes and the experience of the many sorts of people who had joined in agreeing on independence but who thereafter found themselves disagreeing on where independence should lead and what it should mean.

FURTHER READING

Bogin, Ruth: *Abraham Clark and the Quest for Equality in the Revolutionary Era* (Rutherford, NJ: Fairleigh Dickinson University Press, 1982).

Brown, Richard D.: "Shays' rebellion and the ratification of the Federal Constitution in Massachusetts," *Beyond Confederation: Origins of the Constitution and American National Identity*, ed. Richard Beeman et al. (Chapel Hill: University of North Carolina Press, 1987), 113–127.

Countryman, Edward: *The American Revolution* (New York: Hill & Wang, 1985; Harmondsworth: Penguin, 1987).

——: *A People in Revolution: the American Revolution and Political Society in New York, 1760–1790* (Baltimore: Johns Hopkins University Press, 1981).

Main, Jackson Turner: "Government by the people: the American Revolution and the democratization of the legislatures," *William and Mary Quarterly*, 23 (1966), 391–406.

——: *Political Parties Before the Constitution* (Chapel Hill: University of North Carolina Press, 1973).

——: *The Sovereign States, 1775–1783* (New York: New Viewpoints, 1973).

Nadelhaft, Jerome J.: *The Disorders of War: the Revolution in South Carolina* (Orono: University of Maine Press, 1981).

——: "'The snarls of invidious animals': the democratization of revolutionary South Carolina," *Sovereign States in an Age of*

Uncertainty, ed. Ronald Hoffman and Peter J. Albert (Charlottesville: University Press of Virginia, 1981).

Patterson, Stephen E.: *Political Parties in Revolutionary Massachusetts* (Madison: University of Wisconsin Press, 1973).

——: "The roots of Massachusetts federalism: conservative politics and political culture before 1787," *Sovereign States in an Age of Uncertainty*, ed. Ronald Hoffman and Peter J. Albert (Charlottesville: University Press of Virginia), 31–61.

Pole, J. R.: *Political Representation in England and the Origins of the American Republic* (New York: St. Martin's Press, 1966; repr. Berkeley: University of California Press, 1971).

Ryerson, Richard Alan: "Republican theory and partisan reality in revolutionary Pennsylvania: toward a new view of the Constitutionalist Party," *Sovereign States in an Age of Uncertainty*, ed. Ronald Hoffman and Peter J. Albert (Charlottesville: University Press of Virginia, 1981), 95–133.

Szatmary, David: *Shays' Rebellion: the Making of an Agrarian Insurrection* (Amherst: University of Massachusetts Press, 1980).

Sydnor, Charles S.: *Gentlemen Freeholders: Political Practices in Washington's Virginia* (Chapel Hill: University of North Carolina Press, 1952).

Weir, Robert M.: "The harmony we were famous for: an interpretation of pre-revolutionary South Carolina Politics," *William and Mary Quarterly*, 26 (1969), 473–501.

Wood, Gordon S.: *The Creation of the American Republic 1776–1787* (Chapel Hill: University of North Carolina Press, 1969).

——: "Interests and disinterestedness in the making of the Constitution," *Beyond Confederation: Origins of the Constitution and American National Identity*, ed. Richard Beeman et al. (Chapel Hill: University of North Carolina Press, 1987), 69–109.

Zemsky, Robert M.: *Merchants, Farmers and River Gods: an Essay on Eighteenth-Century American Politics* (Boston: Gambit, 1971).

CHAPTER FORTY-SIX

The West: territory, states, and confederation

PETER S. ONUF

THE establishment of effective authority along the northern and western frontiers represented one of the leading challenges to the United States during and after the Revolution. Reports of fabulously fertile frontier lands inspired a rage for emigration, particularly in areas where land was overused and in short supply. But the rapid expansion of settlement kept the frontiers in an uproar, stretching the political capabilities of state and central governments to the limit and provoking chronic conflict with the Amerindians. Meanwhile, frontiersmen invoked revolutionary notions of popular sovereignty and self-determination as they sought increased representation in the state assemblies or recognition as new states. Separatist movements were, in turn, symptomatic of pervasive jurisdictional confusion, the leading legacy of British rule. State boundary claims in frontier areas were rarely clearly defined; the claims of large, "landed" states, generally based on vague and often mutually contradictory colonial charters, were particularly controversial. Not surprisingly, the small, "landless" states were reluctant to recognize large state claims. How, they asked, could a union of such unequal states survive? Beyond these political and constitutional issues was the question of land titles. Jurisdictional confusion led to conflict, sometimes violent, between rival groups of land speculators, settlers, and their political allies and sponsors.

The American Congress thus confronted a daunting array of challenges in the West. Before the Revolution, imperial officials focused their attention on the increasingly rebellious coastal cities. Chaotic conditions on the frontiers were bound to set Americans squabbling among themselves, British commentators believed, and so serve the counter-revolutionary cause. Congress, made up of delegations from states with conflicting claims, was singularly ill-equipped to resolve jurisdictional disputes. As a result, the western problem dominated congressional politics over the next few years, absorbing more energy – to less apparent effect – than anything other than the conduct of the war itself. Yet, paradoxically, congressional inaction helped keep jurisdictional issues at bay during the war years, when any decisive action was bound to be dangerously divisive.

With the coming of peace, the states moved with surprising rapidity to negotiate a broad settlement of the western lands controversy. Legendary for its impotence in other policy areas, Congress acted quickly and effectively to establish its authority over the new national domain in the region north and west of the Ohio River. In three short years (1784–7), Congress passed a series of ordinances for selling public lands and exercising federal jurisdiction that established a framework for the future development of the national frontier and the expansion of the union. In 1776, the West appeared to be a source of discord and conflict that jeopardized the common cause. But the image of the West was dramatically different in 1787. In a "critical period" of deepening inter-sectional tension, the development of the national domain represented one of the few clear, substantial interests shared by all the states. Congress's western policy was predicated on a commitment to the union and on the belief that the new nation's future prosperity and power depended on frontier development.

1   Congress and the West

Pressures from settlers and speculators for access to frontier lands mounted after Anglo-American victory over the French and their Amerindian allies in the American Seven Years' War. The Vandalia Company, a consortium of influential American and English investors, sought a Crown charter for a new colony in western Virginia. Other groups, such as Connecticut's Susquehannah Company, enjoyed the support of their colony governments. Claiming that Pennsylvania's Wyoming Valley fell within the limits of the Connecticut Charter of 1662, the Susquehanna Company sent hundreds of settlers into the contested region. New Hampshire's royal governor Benning Wentworth enriched himself and his associates by granting town charters in the northeastern counties of New York. Other speculators, including the Illinois and Wabash companies and a group headed by Judge Richard Henderson of North Carolina, sought royal confirmation for private purchases from Amerindian proprietors. Eager settlers, including large numbers of "squatters" as well as land company titleholders, pushed the frontiers of settlement into regions reserved to the Amerindians by the royal Proclamation of October 7, 1763. Americans generally saw the Proclamation as a temporary measure, designed to placate the Amerindians.

The result of all this frenetic activity was sporadic conflict between Whites and Amerindians, beginning with Pontiac's "rebellion" (1763), as well as jurisdictional controversy between colonies and chronic confusion about the imperial government's position on various title and boundary questions. Distracted by mounting resistance to British policy throughout the colonies, imperial authorities failed to articulate or implement a coherent western policy. The new American Congress inherited all of these unresolved problems: settlers continued to pour into contested areas; speculators turned

first to the new state governments and then to Congress for confirmation of their grants and purchases; and the states themselves sought to extend their claims at each other's expense. How, under such circumstances, could the Americans hope to mount a united effort on behalf of their rights?

Congress's liabilities as putative successor to the imperial government were obvious to contemporaries. As colonists, Americans had acknowledged the ultimate authority of Privy Council to adjudicate inter-colonial conflicts. The colonists also recognized that private titles ultimately depended on royal sanction. In theory, the King was the original titleholder to all of British America, and he retained his title in frontier regions, except in proprietary or charter colonies. Not only did the King "own" all ungranted, public lands in the West, but the authority of Crown officials to manage relations with the natives and regulate the activities of Whites in the region was unquestioned.

In all these respects, Congress found itself at a relative disadvantage. The new states were reluctant to accord extensive powers to Congress, particularly where those powers – for instance, in determining boundaries – jeopardized their vital interests. After independence, representatives of the "landed" states with extended western claims insisted that the states, not Congress, succeeded to the Crown lands. The Articles of Confederation (drafted in 1777; ratified in 1781) gave Congress general powers over Amerindian affairs, but with crippling qualifications: Congress was to have "the sole and exclusive right" of "regulating the trade and managing all affairs with the Indians, not members of any of the States, provided that the legislative right of any State within its own limits be not infringed or violated." In other words, the Articles upheld the authority of the states to govern frontier areas within their own limits. And because all American territory fell within the limits of one state or the other, Congress's "sole and exclusive right" was at best prospective: Congress could not have a western policy until it gained title, by cession from the states, to frontier territory.

The revolutionaries recognized that failure to resolve the western problem endangered the common cause. Under British rule, jurisdictional controversies were usually only of local significance, particularly to speculators and their client-settlers. Colony officials might have a personal stake in the outcome of these conflicts, but they generally did not engage the interest of the larger community. After independence, however, boundary and title questions took on a new importance to public-spirited citizens concerned with their states' prospects for future development as well as with the more immediate benefits of public land sales revenue. As a result, endemic local controversies merged into a larger, more fundamental debate over the organization of the union. Jurisdictional confusion on the frontiers thus constituted a double threat to the American cause. Title and boundary conflicts that had erupted into violence before independence – including the Green Mountain Boys' guerrilla war against New York in what would become Vermont, as well as violent conflict between Connecticut and Pennsylvania forces in the Wyoming Valley – fragmented the patriot coalition and offered obvious counter-revolutionary opportunities to the British. These controversies also raised basic questions about Congress's role in ascertaining and enforcing the states' respective territorial claims.

2   Landed and Landless States

The great division among the states was between the large, landed states with their extensive western claims – Massachusetts, Connecticut, New York, Virginia, North Carolina, and Georgia – and the small, landless states. Led by Maryland, the landless states sought to curb landed state claims and establish Congress's title to the western lands. Small state delegates warned that, if their large neighbors monopolized frontier development, the resulting inequalities in population and power would destroy the union. Sales of western lands would provide the landed states an inexhaustible source of revenue, enabling them to lower taxes and so attract settlers from overpopulated and overburdened landless states. Not coincidentally, many influential politicians in landless Maryland and Pennsylvania were

investors in the Indiana Company – successor to the Vandalia scheme – and other speculative ventures. Landed state leaders thus concluded that private interest, not legitimate political or constitutional concerns, explained the landless states' hostility to their claims. Virginians, whose extensive claims in the Kentucky District and in the vast region north and west of the Ohio River constituted the leading target of landless state machinations, vigorously defended the sanctity of charter boundaries. They insisted that Congress's role was to protect the rights of its members, from each other as well as against the common enemy.

The landless states first sought to set limits to large state western claims in the Articles of Confederation. Congress, they argued, was the logical successor to the Crown's jurisdictional and property rights in the West. The problem with this formulation was that it made Congress an interested party in the western lands controversy, thus compromising its position as an impartial, superintending authority. The landed states successfully rebuffed this direct challenge to their claims, and the final draft of the Articles sent out to the state legislatures in 1777 guaranteed the states' territorial pretensions. By withholding their approval of the document, however, Maryland and other landless estates hoped to force territorial cessions from the claiming states. The Articles would be acceptable once the landed states had relinquished their western claims to Congress. In effect, the landless states acknowledged that national title would have to be built on state titles. Maryland kept up the pressure by refusing to ratify the Articles until 1781. Thereafter, the landless majority in Congress continued to campaign for unconditional cessions.

The protracted impasse over the western lands revealed a general awareness of the importance of the West for the future of the union. Because Congress could not act decisively without jeopardizing its authority, some sort of accommodation among the states was prerequisite. On September 6, 1780, Congress first called on the landed states for territorial cessions, thus establishing a framework for compromise. Congress further pledged, in a resolution of October 10, that the western lands would be developed for the common benefit of the United States and that new states eventually would be formed in the national domain. Landed state leaders agreed, at least in principle, that Congress should exercise control over the western lands. As the central government's financial obligations mounted and successive efforts to establish a national impost failed, revenue from public land sales seemed increasingly critical to the survival of the union. Furthermore, jurisdictional confusion subverted congressional efforts to coordinate and direct military and diplomatic efforts on the frontiers. The radical defects of Congress's authority thus became conspicuous as general agreement on the broad outlines of western policy emerged.

The landed states responded to the call for cessions with a series of offers which were rejected by the landless majority in Congress. Most controversial was Virginia's cession of January 1781. Landless state delegates complained about the extensive region, including the Kentucky District, that Virginia withheld from its cession; furthermore, Virginia insisted on the invalidation of all private titles in the ceded territory that it had not sanctioned. But Congress could avoid these embarrassing conditions by accepting New York's unconditional cession (February 1780) of much of the same territory covered by the Virginia cession. New Yorkers sought to trade their western claims, based on its supposed "suzerainty" over the Iroquois, for congressional support of their claims in the New Hampshire Grants (Vermont). On October 29, 1782, after a delay of more than two and a half years, the small states finally mustered a majority in favor of accepting New York's offer.

Congress hoped to avoid considering the relative merits of overlapping state titles by gaining cession from all the states. But Congress's inability to establish a plausible title on the basis of New York's cession exposed the limitations of this policy. Whatever the merits of its charter claims, Virginia had been militarily and politically active in the region north and west of the Ohio River and therefore had concrete interests to protect. Suspicions of congressional motives had led the state's leaders to stipulate specific cession conditions, securing Virginia's interests and guaranteeing that the new national domain otherwise be dedicated to the common benefit of the entire union. To Virginians, rejection of their state's offer and acceptance of New York's revealed Congress's partiality for the interests of private "landmongers." Such machinations convinced the usually moderate James Madison that "the present Union will but little survive the present war."

Although completion of the New York cession proved a hollow victory for the landless states and their land company allies, it did set the stage for ultimate resolution of the western problem. Splitting the landed bloc and gaining control over Congress did not enable the small states to dictate policy to Virginia. To the contrary, small state delegates were increasingly hard pressed to explain why they found Virginia's conditions unacceptable. Meanwhile, American victory on the battlefield and rapid progress towards a definitive peace meant that western policy issues – treaty agreements with Amerindian nations, the distribution of military bounties, the sale of public lands, and the organization of new settlements – could not be evaded. Jurisdictional questions were no longer speculative or prospective. If the American states did not act quickly, the national government would never gain control over frontier development.

In the negotiations leading up to the completion of its cession in March 1784, Virginia enjoyed a decisive advantage: Congress could not organize or govern the Northwest Territory until Virginia relinquished its claims. At the same time, however, Virginians were more and more conscious of the difficulties and dangers of preserving their state's authority over such a vast region. With the onset of peace, traders, speculators, and squatters poured across the Ohio; meanwhile, Kentuckians complained of the inconveniences and inequities of Virginian rule. New state, separatist movements gained momentum in Kentucky and in southwestern Virginia as well as in frontier regions of other large states; rumors of secret negotiations between disaffected

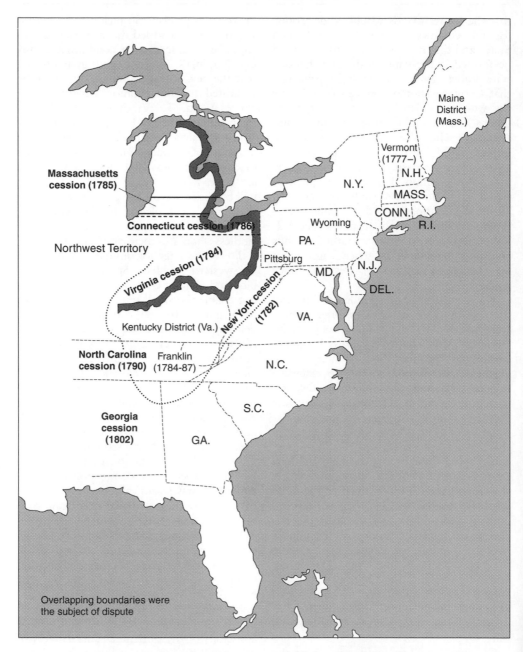

Map 7 Western land cessions and new state movements.

elements and the Spanish and English spread rapidly. Responding to these developments, many Virginians became convinced that their state would be best served by sanctioning a new state in Kentucky and relinquishing jurisdiction over the trans-Ohio region to Congress. It was crucial in both cases to draw the various interested parties into binding agreements that would protect Virginian land titles and other essential interests.

The most controversial provision of Virginia's offer was its invalidation of unauthorized purchases by private land companies. Small state delegates ultimately realized, however, that their refusal to accommodate Virginia on this point jeopardized Congress's future rule in the West. Clearly, completion of the western land cessions would serve the interests of the landless states. The cessions would strengthen the union by helping to equalize the states and by guaranteeing that all of the states would share equally in the benefits of frontier development. Meanwhile, the ceding states – Virginia, Massachusetts (1785), and Connecticut (1786) – could be assured that the national domain would be administered according to the conditions and within the limits set forth in their cession acts.

3 Western Policy and the Union

The furor over the western lands often obscured general agreement on the most desirable outcome: all parties agreed that Congress should develop and govern the new nation's vast hinterland. But could Congress be trusted to promote the national interest, or would it favor a particular group of states, or influential private interests? These, of course, were the same questions Americans asked about the proposed new national government in the ratification debates of 1787–8. The western lands controversy thus raised fundamental questions about the organization of the union under the Articles of Confederation. In effect, completion of the cessions amended the Articles, enlarging Congress's power by giving it direct jurisdiction over national territory while guaranteeing that that power would be exercised only for limited purposes.

Once the constitutional issues were resolved, congressmen had little trouble agreeing on the main lines of western policy. Congress had already committed itself to the eventual creation of new western states and to the development of the national domain for the "common benefit." Anticipating the rapid completion of the Virginia cession, Congress thus named a committee headed by Thomas Jefferson to prepare an ordinance for implementing those principles. The first territorial government ordinance, adopted on April 23, 1784, a few weeks after the completion of the Virginia cession, articulated the basic principles that subsequently governed American territorial policy. The ordinance set forth boundaries for future states in unceded areas of western Virginia, North Carolina, and Georgia, as well as for ten new states in the trans-Ohio region recently ceded by Virginia. Settlers in the national domain were promised that, once the free population of any one of these embryonic states had reached 20,000, they would be entitled to "establish a permanent constitution and government for themselves." Then, when the number of "free inhabitants" in a new state equalled that of the "least numerous of the thirteen Original states," it would be admitted to the union "on an equal footing."

Meanwhile, another committee, also including Jefferson, sought to secure the common benefit by establishing a system for the sale of public lands. But disagreement over the cost of land, the size of parcels, and the relation between surveys and sales led Congress to reject the first proposed land ordinance (on April 30, 1784). The major contribution of the rejected ordinance was the grid survey system that was later incorporated in the land ordinance adopted by Congress on May 20, 1785. Congressmen then agreed that surveys should precede sales, that federal lands should sell for a minimum of a dollar an acre, and that townships (of six miles square) should be sold alternately by individual lot (640 acres) and as a whole. Lands would be sold at auctions in each of the original states.

Jefferson and his fellow policy-makers anticipated that the territorial government and land ordinances would work together to govern the process of frontier settlement. They thought the key to political and social order was the regular distribution of property and the elimination of title conflicts that ordinarily produced so much conflict on other frontiers. But efforts to implement the new system soon showed the need for revisions. When the Seven Ranges, the first series of townships surveyed by United States Geographer Thomas Hutchins and his surveyors, were brought to auction late in 1787, only 72,934 acres were sold, producing a mere $117,108.22 in revenue. Impatient to gain a quicker, more substantial return from the national domain, congressmen began to look more favorably on large-scale speculative enterprises, such as the Ohio Company, which promised to settle the region beyond the Seven Ranges with industrious and orderly New Englanders. In exchange for a substantial reduction in price – the company paid a total of $1,000,000 (in depreciated Continental securities) for 1,500,000 acres – the Ohio Associates agreed to assume responsibility for extending the survey system.

Congress had to offer more attractive terms for its lands, and so modify the 1785 ordinance, because of the need to compete for settlers with states with extensive public land reserves, such as New York and Massachusetts, as well as with British Canada. Yet the demand for Ohio lands, already well known for their productivity, was potentially great. In order to exploit that demand, however, Congress would not only have to sell its lands at competitive prices but would have to establish effective temporary government for the region. The experiences of federal surveyors and military garrisons on the Ohio showed the inadequacy of Congress's original western policy, embodied in the territorial government and land ordinances of 1784 and 1785. Federal lands would be worthless unless the illegal settlers who swarmed into the region were driven off, and bona fide purchasers were able to develop their property in peace.

The Northwest Ordinance, adopted on July 13, 1787, represented the culmination of protracted efforts to elaborate provisions for the temporary government of the national domain. The authors of the new ordinance did not abandon the commitment to create new and equal states set forth in the 1784 ordinance. But because the statehood promise was grounded in the prior cession "compact" between Virginia and the United States, the new territorial government committee felt free to draft an entirely new ordinance. Major changes included a reduction in the number of prospective new states from ten to between three and five and a new population threshold – 60,000 "free inhabitants" (a fixed rather than variable standard that would probably accelerate the admission of new states). But most crucial was the institution of direct congressional rule, to be gradually relinquished in successive stages. While the 1784 ordinance stipulated that settlers would establish their own temporary government, the 1787 document gave legislative as well as executive and judicial authority to the governor and three territorial judges – all federal appointees. Only when there were 5,000 free male inhabitants in the territory would a popularly elected assembly exercise any authority. In the event, self-government was long-delayed: the first assembly in the Northwest Territory was not convened until 1799.

What is most remarkable about this new, avowedly "colonial" system of territorial government was that it aroused so little controversy in Congress. At a time when inter-sectional tensions were running high and disunionist sentiment was on the rise, northerners and southerners in Congress agreed that a "high-toned" administration of the Northwest Territory was essential. The explanations for this consensus are straightforward. First, continuing rumblings on the frontiers – threats of Amerindian wars, separatist movements, foreign adventurism, and widespread defiance of state and federal officials by illegal settlers – underscored the immediate threat to the common interests of the states in Congress. Before the resolution of the western lands controversy, Maryland and other landless states had encouraged new state movements and other assaults on large state jurisdictional pretensions. Now, of course, the small states would not countenance any challenge to federal jurisdiction or property interests in the new national domain. Regardless of their distinctive interests on other questions, notably on the regulation of commerce or on the navigation of the Mississippi, congressmen agreed on the importance of public land sales as a source of desperately needed revenue.

Congressmen recognized that the institution of effective temporary government on the northwestern frontier represented a crucial test for the durability of the union. Awareness that the national domain was jeopardized by separatist movements, diplomatic intrigues, and Amerindian wars dictated a united front. For many policy-makers and commentators these prudential concerns were reinforced by the belief that the development of the West was the key to the nation's future prosperity and power. "If we make a right use of our natural advantages," an Independence Day orator promised in 1785, "we soon must be a truly great and happy people." But this "right use" was not foreordained. If Congress failed to act expeditiously, all would be lost. The value of the western lands, as a source of revenue and of economic growth, depended on attracting orderly, industrious commercial farmers to the region. The land ordinance would assure that new settlements would extended gradually and systematically from the old, thus facilitating the extension of trade routes and the establishment of civil authority. Restrained within defensible limits, these settlements would coexist peacefully with their Amerindian neighbors, so eliminating expensive and debilitating wars. The national frontier would thus be a valuable source of revenue, not a drain on the treasury. Most important, carefully regulated settlement was the best guarantee of continuing "union" between the East and the frontiers, a union based on complementary and common interests.

Prospective settlers could only be attracted to the Ohio country if their lives and estates were protected against the depredations of the "white savages" and "banditti" who infested it. Mannasseh Cutler, lobbyist for the Ohio Associates, carried this message to New York, where Congress was sitting, and helped spur final passage of the Northwest Ordinance. By establishing a strong territorial government, the Ordinance guaranteed the continuing federal presence that potential purchasers of federal lands demanded. Yet the compact articles of the Ordinance promised that the federal hold gradually would be relaxed as the new states grew towards social and political maturity. The most famous article, the sixth, was supposed to prohibit the future importation of slaves into the region; introduced at the final stages of deliberations, the slavery ban was probably a concession to the Yankee sensibilities of the Ohio Associates.

Every state delegation then represented in Congress voted for the Ordinance. This remarkable unanimity stands in contrast to congressional divisions during the western lands controversy and to contemporaneous sectional splits on other questions. Challenges to national authority in the Ohio country helped clarify the common interests of the eastern states in regulating frontier development. The overarching conflict was between western farmers and speculators who sought unlimited access to western lands and eastern policy-makers who were determined to restrain settlement and thereby foster development and strengthen the union. Congress's hostility to westerners was apparent both in its military actions against illegal settlers and in its efforts to attract easterners to the national domain. Western policy-makers hoped to restrain the dangerous centrifugal tendencies of uncontrolled settlement; they were convinced that the survival of the union depended on easternizing the West.

Congressional western policy was most notably successful in establishing a durable federal presence and protecting national property interests in the Northwest Territory. And by asserting its control over new state formation, Congress effectively discouraged the separatist agitation that kept frontier settlements in a turmoil in the mid-1780s. The immediate effect of congressional rule was to depoliticize the frontier and so reassure eastern congressmen that they would not be overwhelmed by delegates from poor, lightly populated western states. The drafting and implementation of the land and government ordinances thus created a framework for economic development and the expansion of the union that successfully addressed easterners' fears about losing population, wealth, and political power to the frontiers. Limited expansion would be integrative, drawing old and new states closer together by fostering common interests. Congress would exercise direct rule while these bonds remained weak and undeveloped, thus holding localistic tendencies in check.

Although congressional western policy established a broad framework for territorial expansion, its original scope necessarily was limited. As long as vast stretches of the American hinterland remained under state jurisdiction, the political aspirations of frontiersmen jeopardized national security and competition from state land offices undercut the value of federal lands. The new national government therefore sought to normalize frontier politics and extend the national domain. In 1790, North Carolina ceded its western claims to the United States; although the Southwest Territory added little to the national domain – most lands had already been transferred to private hands – the federal government extended its authority over an area that had been a hotbed of separatism and chronic conflict with the Amerindians. Shortly thereafter, in 1791 and 1792 respectively, the independent republic of Vermont and the Kentucky District of Virginia were admitted to the union.

The great achievement of western policymakers was to secure the union of East and West during a period of political crisis and constitutional change. By resolving a divisive legacy of jurisdictional confusion on the frontiers, the American states were able to define their common interests more clearly.

FURTHER READING

Abernethy, Thomas Perkins: *Western Lands and the American Revolution* (New York, 1937; repr. New York: Russell & Russell, 1958).

Aron, S.: *How the West was Lost* (Baltimore: Johns Hopkins University Press, 1996).

Bellesiles, M. A.: *Revolutionary Outlaws: Ethan Allen and the Struggle for Independence on the Early American Frontier* (Charlottesville: University Press of Virginia, 1993).

Cayton, Andrew R. L.: *The Frontier Republic: Ideology and Politics in the Ohio Country, 1790–1825* (Kent, Ohio: Kent State University Press, 1986).

Jensen, Merrill: *The Articles of Confederation: an Interpretation of the Social-Constitutional History of the American Revolution, 1774–1781* (Madison: University of Wisconsin Press, 1940).

——: *The New Nation: a History of the United States During the Confederation, 1781–1789* (New York: Alfred A. Knopf, 1950).

Onuf, Peter S.: *The Origins of the Federal Republic: Jurisdictional Controversies in the United States, 1775–1787* (Philadelphia: University of Pennsylvania Press, 1983).

——: *Statehood and Union: a History of the Northwest Ordinance* (Bloomington: Indiana University Press, 1987).

Rakove, Jack N.: *The Beginnings of National Politics: an Interpretive History of the Continental Congress* (New York: Alfred A. Knopf, 1979).

Slaughter, Thomas P.: *The Whiskey Rebellion: Frontier Epilogue to the American Revolution* (New York: Oxford University Press, 1986).

CHAPTER FORTY-SEVEN

Demobilization and national defense

E. WAYNE CARP

AS a result of the Continental Congress's inability to pay its soldiers, the demobilization of the Continental Army, a process spanning nearly two years from the American victory at Yorktown (1781) to the signing of the Paris Peace Treaty (1783), was an inglorious affair. It was punctuated by a revolt of the Pennsylvania Line and a potential *coup d'état* by nationalist army officers at army headquarters in Newburgh, New York. For the majority of enlisted men, moreover, demobilization was particularly bitter: they simply left camp and drifted home, unpaid and unheralded. Revolts and rumored coups renewed America's distaste for standing armies in peacetime. These ideological fears, coupled with the Confederation Congress's political and economic weaknesses, made the postwar establishment of permanent military institutions a difficult, piecemeal process. In 1784, Congress rejected George Washington's proposals for a small peacetime army and a national militia. But soon thereafter, forced to defend the frontier against the Amerindians, Congress authorized the First American Regiment, a regular army of 700 men drawn from state militias, which would remain in service throughout the Confederation period. With little cooperation from the states, this small force proved unable to cope with foreign intrigue, Amerindian raids, and, most importantly, Shays's Rebellion. In 1787, the nation's leaders met in Philadelphia to remedy the weaknesses of the Articles of Confederation. Despite strong opposition from the Anti-Federalists, the Constitution significantly strengthened the nation's capacity to defend itself militarily. Nevertheless, it took several American defeats at the hands of the Northwest Amerindians (1790, 1791)

before Congress created the Legion of the United States and finally accepted in principle a permanent peacetime regular army and reorganized the state militias under the Militia Act of 1792.

1 Localism and Real Whig Ideology

The demobilization of the Continental Army and the establishment of permanent military institutions must be understood within the context of colonial American political culture and the experience of the American Revolutionary War. Two aspects of colonial American political culture, localism and Real Whig ideology, particularly influenced the colonists' military beliefs and practices. The colonists' localistic perspective resulted largely from more than a half century of "salutary neglect" by British officialdom and the emergence in the colonies of a *de facto* system of self-government. During the imperial crisis of the 1760s and 1770s, Americans viewed Parliament's taxation and its claims of undivided sovereignty as threats not only to their liberty and property, but also to their traditional way of life.

The militia symbolized and reinforced Americans' attachments to their local communities. Springing up with the first English settlements, the militia was composed of part-time soldiers, existing primarily for local defense, who rarely ventured beyond their provincial borders or engaged in offensive war. During the eighteenth century, as settlement grew and population increased, the militia's fighting skills atrophied. Colonists ceased to depend on the militia for defense and instead relied on volunteers and draftees commanded by British regulars or Americans. Thus, although by mid-eighteenth century the militia had long ceased to be an effective shield against foreign or Amerindian attack except on the frontier, the colonists continued to believe that it was invincible when defending the local community.

The colonists' beliefs in Real Whig ideology, which led them to distrust professional standing armies, reinforced their faith in the militia. Real Whig anti-military sentiment was primarily a legacy of the English Civil War and Oliver Cromwell's Protectorate, during which the civilian government was replaced with what amounted to a military dictatorship. Throughout the seventeenth and eighteenth centuries, Real Whig political writers repeatedly warned that a standing army endangered English liberties, that professional soldiers were a source of social oppression, and that the very existence of a professional army was evidence of a corrupted people. Real Whig arguments against standing armies became deeply embodied in most colonial Americans' ideological worldview.

One of the greatest ironies of the American Revolution is that those aspects of the colonists' political culture most responsible for propelling Americans into revolt – their fear of concentrated power, their tradition of self-government, and their abhorrence of standing armies – made waging war, mobilizing manpower, and supplying the army almost impossible. By 1780, as a result of military defeats, manpower and supply shortages, public apathy, and financial chaos, the Revolution had nearly collapsed. The experience of fighting a war under a weak central government, uncooperative state legislatures, and repeated military defeats convinced many revolutionaries, who considered themselves nationalists, of the necessity to strengthen Congress's powers. Although the Continental Army, now composed of seasoned regulars, eventually defeated the British at Yorktown with the aid of the French, most Americans congratulated themselves on their own and the militia's patriotic resistance against tyranny. The debate over America's national peacetime military establishment was shaped, but distorted, by the experience of fighting a war shackled by ideological fears of standing armies and a strong national government.

2 The Newburgh Addresses and the Revolt of the Pennsylvania Line

In the midst of celebrating military victory over the British, the demobilization of the Continental Army reignited the nation's anti-military prejudices. A series of alarming events revolving around the issue of pay for officers and enlisted men appeared to pose a serious threat to civilian government. In particular, officers' demands for pensions escalated into a threat of a *coup d'état*. Historians still disagree on the exact details of the "Newburgh conspiracy," but the broad outlines are clear. In late 1782, as the approximately 10,000-man Continental Army unofficially began to demobilize at its final cantonment at Newburgh, New York, an impoverished and bitter officer corps feared that the army would disband before Congress made good its promise to fund their half-pay for life pensions. Congress viewed the officers' pension proposal as a European military affectation that America should avoid; the officers believed the pensions were just recompense for their financial sacrifices during the war. In December 1782 a committee of three, representing the disgruntled officers, carried a petition to Congress offering to accept a commutation of half-pay for life to some equivalent lump-sum payment and warning of the "fatal effects" if denied. Extreme nationalists such as Alexander Hamilton, Robert Morris, and Gouverneur Morris, their plans for a strong central government thwarted, seized the opportunity presented by the potentially mutinous army to attempt to coerce reluctant congressmen to strengthen Congress's taxing power. Their effort failed, and amid a chorus of denunciation of officers' greed and fears that a half-pay settlement would corrupt America's republican society, Congress rejected a resolve to commute half-pay for life to six years' full payment, preferring that the state legislatures handle the problem of officers' pensions. When word reached camp of Congress's refusal to meet their demands, a second group of officers, encouraged by extreme nationalists and led by General Horatio Gates, issued the inflammatory Newburgh Addresses calling upon the army to refuse to disband if its grievances were not redressed. At an officers' meeting on March 15, 1783, Washington's dramatic appeal to the army's tradition of subordination to civil authority effectively dissipated the officers' enthusiasm for rebellion. A week later, tension was further defused when word arrived that Congress had voted the officers ful pay for five years and enlisted men full pay for four months, although the source of funding was left to the future. Yet, as Richard H. Kohn has written, "the Newburgh conspiracy was the closest an American army has ever come to revolt or *coup d'état*" and the fears it raised among political leaders lingered long after the event (Kohn, 1975, p. 17).

In June 1783, a revolt by a segment of the Pennsylvania Line insured that America's heritage of distrusting standing armies would emerge from the war as strong as ever. Two months earlier, Washington had recommended that Congress grant three months' full pay to enlisted men who were no longer obeying their officers. But a financially bankrupt Congress refused to heed Washington's advice. Instead, in June Congress furloughed the soldiers to their homes, pending a discharge once the definitive treaty of peace had been signed, without any provision for settling their accounts or a word of appreciation. Outraged, 80 new recruits of the Pennsylvania Line marched from Lancaster to Philadelphia, joined several hundred other angry soldiers quartered in the city, and barricaded several members of Congress and the Executive Council of Pennsylvania in the State House demanding their pay before they went home. The revolt quickly petered out, however, when several congressmen walked out of the State House unharmed amid insults shouted by drunken soldiers. Alarmed, Congress moved from Philadelphia to Princeton, and revolutionaries everywhere noted the army's threat to civil authority.

Meanwhile, the rest of the Continental Army troops decided not to wait for their pay and complied with the congressional furlough. By mid-June most of the disgruntled enlisted men had started for home, while 700 soldiers were retained for garrison duty. The Continental Army disbanded unhappily, amid threats of mutinies and coups.

3 Washington's "Sentiments on a Peace Establishment"

In the midst of the Continental Army's unruly demobilization, Congress was forced to consider what kind of permanent military organization to create, because the New York and Pennsylvania authorities requested military aid for negotiating Amerindian treaties and garrisoning British-occupied forts. In April 1783, in response to a congressional committee, Washington sent Congress his "Sentiments on a Peace Establishment," outlining his understanding of the nation's future military needs and American republicanism. Washington advocated a small permanent army of 2,631 men designed to protect the frontier and to serve as a nucleus for security in a general war. He also recommended that a national militia be established, consisting of a reserve force of all male citizens aged between 18 and 55 and a select group of young men aged 18 to 25 specially trained for military emergencies. Washington's "Sentiments," a product of wartime experience, represented the nationalists' new understanding of republicanism, which now emphasized military preparedness, a select militia, and a peacetime standing army to protect republican institutions from foreign invasion and domestic insurrection. The "Sentiments" became the basis for all subsequent discussion about the organization of the armed forces in the early Republic.

In the immediate postwar era, Washington's proposals never stood a chance of enactment because of the nation's financial weakness and Congress's traditional fears of a standing army in peacetime. On June 2, 1784, Congress ordered General Henry Knox, the ranking senior officer, to discharge all but 80 soldiers. Nevertheless, recognizing that Amerindian defense demanded a larger force, Congress the next day erected the first national peacetime military force in American history by recommending that several states furnish 700 men from their militias to serve one year. Although only Pennsylvania met its quota of soldiers, Congress had created the First American Regiment.

4 Shays's Rebellion

Throughout the Confederation era (1781–9), America's military weakness was manifest, especially in coping with Amerindian threats in the Northwest and South and with British refusal to abandon their forts in the Northwest, as the Treaty of Paris stipulated. In addition, Congress looked on helplessly as Spain closed the Mississippi to all United States shipping and stirred up secessionist sentiment in the Southwest (*see* chapter 49, §2). The low point in the Confederation Congress's military experience occurred in September 1786, when a former Revolutionary War officer, Daniel Shays, and 1,100 debt-ridden farmers marched to the Court of Common Pleas in Hampshire County, Massachusetts, to prevent the seizure of their property for the payment of debts and taxes. Eight hundred militiamen, called out by the Confederation Congress to defend the court, refused to act because they sympathized with the rioters. Consequently, in October, Congress called upon the states for $530,000 in order to raise a special force of 1,340 men to crush the rebellion. Only Virginia responded. More than any other single event during the Confederation period, Shays's Rebellion revealed the inadequacy of Congress's military powers under the Articles of Confederation.

Most importantly, Shays's Rebellion galvanized the movement to revise the Articles of Confederation and led directly to the calling of the Constitutional Convention. When the delegates met in Philadelphia in May 1787, opponents of a strong central government, termed Anti-Federalists by their detractors, denounced the Constitution's military provisions using Real Whig arguments against standing armies. Anti-Federalists particularly feared giving the national government the power to tax and control of the military. They worried that the new government would use a professional army to collect unjust taxes and questioned whether the country needed a standing army when at peace. The Massachusetts delegate Elbridge Gerry even suggested that the Constitution should limit the national army to 3,000 men. For the Anti-Federalists, the militia was sufficient for the nation's defense.

5 The Constitution's Military Provisions

The Federalists – nationalist supporters of the Constitution – defended the Constitution's military provisions by turning to the "lessons" of the Revolutionary War. They argued that, had the United States relied on citizen soldiers alone during the war, America would have lost its independence. Although the Federalists credited the Continental Army with America's military victory, they argued that a national military force, encompassing both regular and militia soldiers, was essential to the preservation of America's Independence. Such a force, Federalists explained, would prevent the proliferation of standing armies within each state and thus forestall the Confederation's collapse into warring sections. They also argued that, because of America's geographic isolation, the nation required only a small military establishment to protect the frontier, seaports, and federal arsenals. Thus the Federalists directly confronted Anti-Federalists' fears of centralized military power by arguing that the Constitution's military provisions were necessary for the survival of America's republican institutions.

Compared with the Articles of Confederation, the Constitution's military clauses represented a significant triumph for the nationalists. The proposed Constitution gave Congress the exclusive right to declare war and raise and support both an army and a navy, with the sole proviso that no army appropriation should run longer than two years. The President was made Commander-in-Chief of the armed forces and authorized to appoint military officers with the advice and consent of the Senate. In its militia provisions, the Constitution also signified an advance over the Articles of Confederation. Congress was authorized to call out the state militia in order to enforce federal law, maintain civil order, and repel invasions; and to exert control over the organization, arming, and disciplining of the state units. Both clauses represented radical departures from the tradition of virtual independence which colonial and state militias had enjoyed.

Although the Constitution's military clauses represented a nationalistic triumph, other constitutional provisions undercut federal control of the military by creating a series of barriers against the possibility of military despotism. Control of the military was divided by vesting the executive branch, not Congress, with its command, although the Commander-in-Chief was in turn dependent on the Congress for military appropriations. The Constitution also divided military power between the federal government and the states. The states retained their militias and could be called into federal service only for limited purposes. The Second Amendment to the Constitution further guaranteed the existence of the state militias by mandating that "a well-regulated militia being necessary to the security of a free state, the right of the people to bear arms shall not be infringed." Many Anti-Federalists felt that the state militias would be a counterweight to any possible misuse of a national standing army.

6 The Legion of the United States and the Uniform Militia Act

The ratification of the Constitution had little immediate effect on the nation's military establishment. Rather, it laid the foundations upon which a stronger national power might be built in the future. Congress initially rejected Secretary of War Henry Knox's proposal to increase the regular army from 840 to 2,033 men and to provide for a select militia similar to the one Washington proposed. But because Amerindian relations in the Northwest were fast deteriorating, Congress resolved in 1790 to increase the First American Regiment's strength to 1,216 men. In the wake of the crushing defeats that the Northwest Amerindians administered to the militia-dominated Regiment in 1790 and 1791, however (*see* chapter 51), Congress authorized for three years a reorganized, regular army of more than 5,000 men, dubbed the Legion of the United States. Significantly, after the defeat of the Northwest Amerindians by General Anthony Wayne at the Battle of Fallen Timbers (1794) and the signing of the Treaty of Grenville, Congress did not dismantle the Legion. Instead, in March 1796, Congress accepted the necessity of a small peacetime standing army to garrison frontier posts, coastal forts, and federal arsenals. The continuance of the Legion constituted a watershed in the creation of America's permanent military establishment: it was the beginning of the nation's acceptance in principal of a standing army in peacetime.

Problems with the Northwest Amerindians, as well as persistent anti-standing army ideology, also led Congress in 1792 to enact the Uniform Militia Act which, contrary to Knox's proposal for a select militia under federal control, provided for universal military training and delegated to the states the responsibility for enrolling all male citizens aged 18 to 45 for militia duty. Congress thus provided loopholes in the law to allow the states to evade compliance with federal guidelines. It failed to provide procedures for training the militia, to institute a system of inspection, or to impose penalties on either the states or individuals for non-compliance with its provisions. Historians have failed to agree on the merits of the Uniform Militia Act. Scholars such as John K. Mahon have denounced the Militia Act as a "virtual abdication by the federal government of all authority over the state militias" (Mahon, 1983, p. 56). On the other side, Russell Weigley, while admitting the Act's military deficiencies, praises it for preserving the tradition of a citizen soldiery. Henceforth, America's permanent military establishment would continue to build upon two foundations: the regulars in the United States Army and the Militia Act of 1792.

FURTHER READING

Carp, E. Wayne: "The problem of national defense in the early republic," *The American Revolution: its Character and Limits*, ed. Jack P. Greene (New York: New York University Press, 1987), 14– 50.

Cress, Lawrence Delbert: *Citizens in Arms: the Army and Militia in American Society to the War of 1812* (Chapel Hill: University of North Carolina Press, 1982).

Gross, Robert A., (ed.): *In Debt to Shays: The Bicentennial of an Agrarian Rebellion* (Charlottesville and London: University of Virginia Press, 1993).

Hatch, Louis Clinton: *The Administration of the American Revolution* (New York: Longmans, Green and Co., 1904).

Kohn, Richard H.: *Eagle and Sword: the Beginnings of the Military Establishment in America* (New York: Free Press, 1975).

Mahon, John K.: *History of the Militia and the National Guard* (New York and London: Macmillan, 1983).

Weigley, Russell F.: *History of the United States Army*, enlarged edn. (Bloomington: Indiana University Press, 1984).

CHAPTER FORTY-EIGHT

Currency, taxation, and finance, 1775–1787

ROBERT A. BECKER

THE Revolution created a financial crisis in the rebelling colonies. Colonial taxes had been very light, but the rebels had to raise unprecedented sums to continue the war, creating in the process huge public debts in every state. At the same time, Congress issued a national currency and spent it, creating a national debt, although it had no independent taxing powers whatever. As both state and national governments struggled to raise enough to continue the war, and after it, to pay their war debts, fierce disputes arose about how best to do both. Despite all their difficulties, the new republics and the Continental Congress managed to raise enough through currency emissions, taxes, loans, and occasional confiscations to secure Independence. In the postwar years, several of the states managed, as well, to reduce significantly their own and the nation's remaining debts. Out of their experience with wartime taxes and with the collapse of the Continental currency in the middle of the war, Americans drew conclusions about the nature (and worth) of their first constitution, the Articles of Confederation, and about the viability of the state-centered republican government it established, some concluding that it was best to locate fiscal and monetary authority in the states, which could respond quickly to local crises and needs, while others concluded that economic stability (and thus effective government) could be achieved only if those powers were located in a national government, far from the influence of popular majorities in the several states. Their experiences directly affected the movement for a new national government that ended in the Philadelphia Convention of 1787, and shaped the content of the Constitution it produced.

1 The Beginnings of National Finance

When the Second Continental Congress convened at Philadelphia in May 1775 the colonies were already at war, and by the end of June Congress began taking on the responsibilities of a government. It raised an army and declared the colonies collectively responsible for what was spent defending their common cause. How that money should be raised, however, posed a dilemma. Barring the question of what authority Congress had to tax anyone, there was the problem of whether a people brought to war in protest over British taxes could safely be asked to pay unprecedented American ones. Prudently choosing not to press the matter, Congress instead resorted to the colonial governments' customary way of raising money during crises, issuing paper currency – a practice "so ingrained in the colonists that nothing else was seriously considered" (Ferguson, 1961, p. 26).

The colonies had normally issued currency in two ways. Some had printed bills of credit and loaned them out, at interest, to individuals who put up land as security. This not only put the money into circulation quickly, it provided a reliable public income (the interest payments) that kept taxes low. New York, for example, had £40,000 out on loan and made £1,350 a year from it until the Currency Act of 1764 ended the practice. Pennsylvania took in about £2,000 a year in interest from its loan office until 1768. Delaware normally paid all of its regular government expenses from interest on its bills of credit. But loan office revenues were slow to come in because the interest payments began only a year after the money was loaned out. More commonly, and especially during wars, the colonies had simply printed money and spent it while promising to collect future taxes to redeem it. Bills so issued were, in effect, tax anticipation notes.

In the critical months after Lexington and Concord, Congress busily printed money (creating a national currency) and spent it (creating a national debt). It expected each rebelling colony, ultimately, to sink (i.e., to tax in and remove from circulation) a sum in proportion to its population. It could have left it up to each colony to emit its proportion of the money, but an irrefutably *national* currency had important advantages. Congress could create and spend it as rapidly as necessary without having to ask anyone's approval or to wait for the various provincial congresses to act. And such a currency would serve, in Gouverneur Morris's words, as a "bond of union to the Associated colonies" (Burnett, 1941, p. 81). In June 1775, Congress issued $2,000,000 in currency. In July it printed $1,000,000 more and then $3,000,000 more before the year's end. It prudently chose to delay redemption (i.e., the date on which it would ask the states to start taxing the money in) until 1779, thus also postponing the sensitive matter of deciding exactly how large a share of this new national debt each rebelling colony should shoulder.

That these measures were woefully inadequate soon became clear. As rebellion turned to revolution and the price of independence rose beyond what even the gloomiest reluctant rebel had imagined possible, Congress discovered that it had no choice but to "stuff…the maw of the Revolution with paper money" (Ferguson, 1961, p. 29). By the end of 1776 there was $25,000,000 in Continental currency in circulation and more obviously on the way. With expenses running at about $1,000,000 a week in paper by mid-1778, Congress began printing currency in lots of five or ten

million every few weeks. It had printed more than $241,000,000 by 1780 when it finally abandoned new emissions.

Inevitably, the currency depreciated (see table 1). By July 1777 Continental currency had lost two-thirds of its face value (that is, it took 3 Continental to purchase $1 specie). By January 1779 it took $8 Continental to buy $1 specie. By October it took $30. One year later it took $77. By April 1781 Continentals circulated at more than 167 to 1 against specie. To stem the decline (and the resulting upward spiral of prices), Congress called upon the states to fix prices, confiscate loyalist property, and begin taxing in specie and the Continental paper already issued. In November it asked the states for $5,000,000 to be sent to the common treasury in 1778. By the fall of 1779 it had requested $95,000,000, and it expected $135,000,000 in 1780. That did not include the $6,000,000 a year in Continental currency it had asked the states to retire from circulation (by taxes) every year beginning in 1779 (Ferguson, 1961, pp. 33–4). Some states began confiscating loyalist property, but the effect on the worth of Continental currency or on the cost of the war was negligible. (Jackson Turner Main estimates that confiscated loyalist property amounted to less than 4 percent of the worth of all property, real and personal, in the colonies [Main, 1973, p. 330].) Only taxation held real promise as a way of propping up the currency and managing the debt. But Congress had no power, in law or in fact, to tax or to compel the states to tax. Under the Articles of Confederation, "all charges of war and all other expenses that shall be incurred for the common defense or general welfare" were to be "defrayed out of a common treasury, which shall be supplied by the several states, in proportion to the value of all land within each state…" The resulting taxes could only be "laid and levied by the authority and direction of the legislatures of the several states…" (Tansill, 1927, pp. 30–1). Congress, then, merely had the right to ask the states to tax on its behalf. In fact, its requisitions produced relatively little real income. E. J. Ferguson estimates, for example, that the $12,897,575 Congress had received by requisition by

Table 1   Depreciation of Continental currency (currency required to purchase $1.00 specie)

	1777	1778	1779	1780	1781
January	1.25	4.00	8.00	42.50	100.00
April	2.00	6.00	16.00	60.00	167.50
July	3.00	4.00	19.00	62.50	
October	3.00	5.00	30.00	77.50	

Source: Ferguson, 1961, p. 32.

1780 was worth only $776,000 in specie (Ferguson, 1961, p. 35).

Next to simply printing money and receiving state contributions, Congress's only significant source of revenue was loans. Benjamin Franklin and Silas Deane arranged a £1,000,000 loan from the French Farmers General in March 1777, secured by promised delivery of American tobacco to France. American envoys won a direct subsidy from France of 2,000,000 livres in 1777 and had secured 4,000,000 in loans and another 5,000,000 in supplies by 1779. Smaller Dutch and Spanish subsidies brought direct foreign aid for the Revolution by early 1781 to $2,213,000 in specie (Ferguson, 1961, pp. 34–42). Virtually all of it was spent in Europe on war supplies and its impact on the worth of the national currency was negligible.

Congress borrowed from Americans too. It opened a Continental Loan Office to sell bonds paying 4 percent interest to the public. Congress was, in effect, asking buyers to bet on rebel victory in the war. Relatively few bonds sold. The interest was too low to be attractive (private loans paid from 8 to 18 percent interest). And of course, if the war was lost, the bonds would be worthless, whereas private debts might still be collected through the postwar English courts. Congress raised the interest to 6 percent in February 1777, and in September it offered to pay the interest in bills of exchange (in effect, in specie, or nearly so) drawn against French subsidies supplied to the Revolution's agents in France. Even so, only $3,330,000 worth sold by the time Congress withdrew the offer in March 1778. Thereafter, Continental bonds paid interest only in paper money, which depreciated at

an appalling rate. Nevertheless, the bonds depreciated less and more slowly than Continental currency did. All told, the Loan Office disposed of about $60,000,000 in Loan Office Certificates (as they were known) before Congress closed it in 1781 (Ferguson, 1961, pp. 37–9).

Congress was also obligated for millions worth of military supply certificates, which were written by army quartermasters and other Continental supply officers to pay for goods seized and services coerced by the army, or voluntarily provided by patriots, and which did not, as a rule, pay interest. These were, in effect, merely congressional IOUs (as were the certificates issued to soldiers in lieu of pay) and the total was enormous. E. James Ferguson estimates $95,000,000 worth had been issued by late 1781 in only ten states (Ferguson, 1961, p. 63). As the Continental currency depreciated, the worth of the certificates depreciated too. By 1780, or even earlier, few accepted them unless coerced, and those who saw their property seized and paid for with quartermasters' certificates believed, with some justice, that their goods had simply been confiscated.

By late 1779 Continental currency depreciation was so out of hand, and Congress's efforts to support the national currency had had so little effect, that it stopped printing money and devised a plan to replace the existing Continental paper with a new, more valuable and less volatile currency. In March 1780 Congress revalued the outstanding Continental currency at 40 to 1 (i.e., it declared each $40 in currency to be worth $1 in specie, which substantially overvalued the currency) and called on the states to tax in all of the old money over the next year.

For every $40 in old money a state collected and destroyed, it would receive $2 in new Continental money, 60 percent of which it could keep for its own purposes and 40 percent of which Congress would spend. The new money's success depended on the taxing ability of states which were themselves facing financial crises similar to the one Congress faced, and had been since the opening days of the war.

2 Financing Revolution in the States

As British authority collapsed in the early spring of 1775, the provisional revolutionary governments and colonial assemblies (where they continued to sit) began to raise money to fight a war they hoped would last only months. By mid-summer, however, these nascent rebel governments understood that they faced prolonged war. To pay for it, they turned to the same sources Congress relied on, borrowing money and emitting currency backed by promises of taxes at some conveniently distant date.

This was unavoidable, for the imposition of high taxes (and sometimes any taxes) threatened to undermine support for the Revolution. The New York Provincial Congress warned in the spring and summer of 1775 that any attempt to tax would provoke "popular disgust ... or opposition." Under the circumstances, it told Congress in May, collecting taxes was "clearly impossible" (NY Provincial Congress, 1842, vol. 1, pp. 14, 92; vol. 2, pp. 17–18). Delaware's cautious assembly, fearing wholesale desertions to the King's colors, flatly refused to tax. The provisional revolutionary governments of Virginia, North Carolina, and Georgia all issued paper and postponed taxing. The South Carolina Provincial Congress printed £1,870,000 in paper between June 1775 and March 1776 without collecting new taxes. Those few rebelling colonies which tried to tax early in the war ran into stiff public resistance. New Jersey, for example, had to resort to force and confiscations to collect even part of the £10,000 tax it levied in June 1775.

Another problem the new governments faced was the uncertainty of their own legitimacy. By what authority did they claim the right to tax anyone? Backcountry settlers in New Hampshire, for example, insisted that the Revolution had placed them in a state of nature and thus they owed unquestioned obedience (and taxes) to no government, royal or rebel, until a new constitution was drafted and properly ratified. Others felt the same.

Issuing paper money while avoiding taxes also let the rebelling states put off deciding how much people should pay. Once taxing began, the new states could not avoid the question of what constituted *just* taxation. Were the old colonial tax systems, thought by many to be discriminatory and oppressive, simply to be reenacted by the new republics? Or would new, more equitable systems have to be devised? Resolving such questions would create divisions within the rebel legislatures that they could ill afford. Not taxing allowed these troublesome matters to be shunted aside and the various state governments to appear more united than in fact they were. Under the circumstances, fighting first and paying later made political sense.

Massachusetts's Provincial Congress issued £26,000 in paper in May 1775, £100,000 in August, and £75,000 more in December, with taxes to redeem some of it put off until the 1780s. New Hampshire issued £40,000 in 1776, with some of the sinking fund taxes delayed to the 1790s. Rhode Island issued money in September without bothering to name any sinking taxes at all. By the summer of 1776 New York had emitted £300,000 with virtually no funding in place. By the end of 1775 the several states had borrowed more than £1,000,000 from their own citizens and issued more than £3,000,000 in paper. By January 1778 the states had probably put in circulation £7,000,000 in paper of one sort or another (Main, 1973, pp. 224–5).

Most of this paper was made legal tender in hopes of forcing its acceptance by merchants and farmers. With money from various sources flooding the new states, with taxes to support it not yet levied or not effectively collected, with continental and state supply officers bidding against each other for military supplies, and with bad news from the battlefields undermining confidence in the rebel cause, what resulted was unavoidable: prices soared and the state currencies depreciated. In trying to stem the collapse of their currencies, however, the states had an advantage the Congress lacked: they could tax, presuming they could muster the will to do so. Beginning in 1777, most of them did.

In that year, all the states save Delaware, New York, and Georgia began levying high taxes to reduce the amount of circulating paper, to raise money to supply the Continental Army and the state militias, and to meet, whenever possible, Congress's requisitions. To make these levies more palatable, many of the states substantially reformed their tax laws. Virginia, for example, eventually replaced a land tax that fell equally on every acre with an *ad valorem* land tax. Maryland enshrined the ability-to-pay principle in its new state constitution, which denounced poll taxes as "grievous and oppressive." Paupers aside, it insisted, "every ... person in the state ought to contribute his proportion of public taxes for the support of the government according to his actual worth in real or personal property ..." (Shipton, 1955, No. 14836).

The amounts levied were huge compared with the taxes colonists had been accustomed to paying. Rhode Island, for example, which normally operated its colonial government on £4,000 a year, levied taxes of £96,000 in 1777 and £94,000 in 1778, and had levied a total of nearly half a million in taxes by the end of 1779. Even allowing for inflation, these were wholly unprecedented levies. In a two-year period (1778 and 1779), Pennsylvania levied £5,000,000. In no year between 1763 and 1775 had colonial Pennsylvania raised more than £34,000 in taxes.

Complaints, evasion, and occasional rioting followed. And finally, state taxes failed either to shore up the Continental currency or to raise enough to keep paying and adequately supplying the Continental Army and state militias. New York, for example, managed to collect only about a third of all the taxes it levied from 1777 to 1781. By the summer of 1782 even so ardent a Continental nationalist as Alexander Hamilton had to concede that his fellow New Yorkers could not (rather than would not) pay all that Congress asked of them. By 1782 uncollected taxes in Pennsylvania alone totaled £3,300,000 in Continental currency, £84,700 in state currency, and £19,500 in specie. Loyalists often had to be forced to pay, which was difficult and at times impossible in states with large Tory populations. Even enthusiastic rebels often refused to pay specie taxes and insisted that they be permitted to pay any tax in Continental currency or any other government (state or national) note they had been forced to take in payment for confiscated goods or coerced service. They were reluctant to pay even Continental paper on time for, the longer they delayed, the more it depreciated and the cheaper the tax became. Most of what did come in, however, was Continental paper (now much devalued), much of which was burned, and therefore could not be used to pay for men and supplies. War crises forced some states to begin printing still more money even as Congress begged the states to stop and to bend all their efforts towards supporting the national currency. The same military crises forced commissary and quartermaster officers to continue issuing certificates in huge quantities. And rampaging inflation meant that, even when large sums were taxed in, they bought fewer and fewer supplies. By December 1780, therefore, it was clear that Congress's refunding plan had failed. By April 1781 it cost $150 Continental to buy $1 specie, and soon after it passed at $500 to $1 or more. By mid-1781 the national currency had collapsed and been abandoned by Congress and the public.

The Continental currency had, despite its chaotic end, served its purpose. It financed the first years of the Revolution when no other funds were readily available. From France, Benjamin Franklin delivered its eulogy:

The general effect of the depreciation among the inhabitants of the states has been this, that it has operated as a *gradual tax* upon them, their business has been done and paid for by the paper money, and every man has paid his share of the tax according to the time he retained any of the money in his hands, and to the depreciation within that time. Thus it has proved a tax on money, a kind of property very difficult to be taxed in any other mode; and it has fallen more equally than many other taxes, as those people paid most, who being richest had most money passing through their hands (Franklin, 1819, p. 477).

Thus some $226,000,000 worth of what E. James Ferguson calls the "common debt" of the Revolution simply disappeared (Ferguson, 1961, p. 67). The debt represented by the Loan Office Certificates, however (i.e., Continental bonds), Congress refused to abandon, establishing instead a scale of depreciation to reduce it to its specie value at the time it was contracted. Congress insisted that it alone remained obligated for both principal and interest. For those who hoped to increase the power of Congress in general and its fiscal authority in particular, the existence of an exclusively *national* debt was critical.

3 The Attempt to Reinvigorate Congress

By 1781 Congress had already relinquished some of the powers of a sovereign national government to the states. It no longer issued a national currency and had stopped paying the army (an unquestionably national responsibility that several states began to assume instead; Congress would not resume responsibility for the army's pay until 1783). Some members of Congress who saw in the erosion of Congress's financial autonomy a threat to the union thought it essential to win for Congress financial independence and so to re-establish its sovereign authority as a national government.

Led by these Continental nationalists, in the first months of 1781 Congress asked the states for the power to collect a 5 percent impost on all foreign goods imported into the United States. Under the Articles of Confederation, however, it could not be done without the unanimous consent of the states. Congress could only make its request and then wait for the states to act. It did act to reorganize the executive departments of the Confederation, replacing the often factious committees that oversaw finance, military, and diplomatic affairs with departments headed by single executive officers.

To run the new Department of Finance, Congress chose Robert Morris, a prominent Philadelphia merchant and committed nationalist who sat in Congress from 1775 to 1778.

Morris took office in June 1780, shortly before Washington began his campaign against Cornwallis. He spent his first months juggling foreign loans, importuning merchants, harassing states to send the supplies they had promised, and pledging his own credit to arrange the supplies and transport needed to shift Washington's army from New York to Virginia.

Foreign loans and subsidies, particularly from France (nearly 4,000,000 in specie during his first year in office alone, more money than France had supplied in all the earlier years of the war combined [Ferguson, 1961, p. 126]) made Morris's early success possible. When news of Cornwallis's surrender reached Europe, Dutch investors (who had sniffed skeptically at American loans earlier) became willing to lend large sums. Yorktown bought for the Continental nationalists the time they wanted to reorganize the national finances and to re-establish national credit so that the new nation might enter the postwar years (now evidently approaching) with an efficient national government that could establish a national currency, fund the national debt, and guarantee fiscal stability. Morris began by consolidating the national debt as a prelude to funding it. This involved two things: first, calling in all the still outstanding individual claims upon the Congress, reducing them to specie value in accord with a scale of depreciation, and exchanging them for new interest-bearing Continental notes (which debt Morris estimated would amount to $30,000,000); and second, once the war ended, settling accounts between the national government and the states by deciding how much each had spent in the common cause. During the war, Congress had issued currency, borrowed money at home and in Europe, and issued, through its agents, an untold number of notes and certificates of public debt (i.e., the commissary and quartermasters' certificates, and others issued to soldiers in lieu of pay). So had the states. Congress needed to know the dollar

Table 2 The total paid to and received from each state by Congress during the Revolutionary War (in $)

State	Paid to state	Received from state
New Hampshire	440,974	466,544
Massachusetts	1,245,737	3,167,020
Rhode Island	1,028,511	310,395
Connecticut	1,016,273	1,607,295
New York	822,803	1,545,889
New Jersey	366,729	512,916
Pennsylvania	2,087,276	2,629,410
Delaware	63,817	208,878
Maryland	609,617	945,537
Virginia	482,881	1,963,811
North Carolina	788,031	219,835
South Carolina	1,014,808	499,325
Georgia	679,412	122,744

Source: Nevins, 1924, p. 478.

value of each state's contributions (so it could credit them), and the amount it had sent to each state to conduct the war (so it could bill them). That herculean task was not completed until 1790, when Alexander Hamilton reported the totals to the new United States Congress (see table 2). Morris would have preferred that Congress simply take over and agree to pay all the states' Revolutionary War debts, but that implied an accretion of national authority that the states were, as yet, unwilling to brook.

Starting in 1782, Continental commissioners in each state began receiving claims against the government, verifying them, reducing them to what they had been worth in specie at the time they were incurred, and exchanging them for new interest bearing Continental bonds. This consolidated national debt (which included the old Loan Office debt, plus the new consolidated quartermasters' certificates and soldiers' claims) totaled about $27,000,000 in specie. Morris proposed that Congress pay only the interest on the new, consolidated debt and "leave posterity to pay the principle" (Nettels, 1962, p. 33). He recommended national land, poll, and excise taxes and a national tariff on imported goods and urged the states to meet Congress's requisitions as rapidly as possible. To tide Congress over until the Articles were properly

amended, Morris helped organize the Bank of North America, which made short-term loans to the government, and he issued notes, backed by his personal credit, to pay government bills. Finally, however, his plans to restore the nation's credit and Congress's authority depended on matters beyond his control – on the states' willingness to deliver to Congress substantial tax revenues (and especially specie) and to surrender the very autonomy over taxes they had contested with England in the Revolution. What they might have been willing to do during the crisis of war, facing defeat as an alternative, they were not willing to do once the war had evidently been won. By the end of 1782 the great financial problem facing the states was no longer how to finance a war of national survival, but how they might best retire the state and national Revolutionary War debts.

Morris had hoped that national creditors would pressure their state governments to grant Congress the power to tax, and, to that end, he suspended interest payments on the national debt in 1782. Instead, many began urging the states to take over payment of the national debt themselves, to assume responsibility for paying both the principal and interest owed to their own citizens. Some states had been paying at least part of the national debt since 1780, when

Congress stopped paying the army. In 1782 Maryland offered to exchange state bonds paying 6 percent interest for Continental notes held by its citizens. Other states did likewise. By the mid-1780s three states (Pennsylvania, Maryland, and New York) had thus converted more than $9,000,000 of Continental debt into state debt. To slow down the states' assumption of the national debt, Congress began in 1784 to pay the interest it owed not in specie (which it did not have), but in new certificates (called "indents" after the way they were oddly bordered on one side to discourage counterfeiting). They were simply another form of Congressional IOU, and, even though the states could tax them in and pay a portion of their requisitions to Congress with the indents, they were not popular with creditors and soon began to depreciate.

By 1786 it was also clear that all 13 states were unlikely ever to approve the still unratified impost plan, much less any wider taxing powers for Congress. In addition, the states were forwarding so little money to Congress that, while it could meet its day-to-day expenses, it had to default on payment of some of its European loans. By August 1786 the Board of Treasury (a committee which assumed control of the nation's finances when Morris resigned in 1785) had abandoned hope of enhancing Congress's powers and recommended that Congress simply distribute what remained of the federal debt among the states and allow each to retire its share as it saw fit. Congressional nationalists opposed the idea, for in their view formally abandoning the national debt to the states meant abandoning sovereignty to the states, which they were not yet prepared to do. Still, by 1786 Congress appeared increasingly moribund, the national debt was being converted piecemeal, by state action, into state debt, and the Continental nationalists' plans seemed to have collapsed along with the autonomy of the Congress on which they had pinned their hopes.

4 Funding the Debt: the States

The states ended the war, as did Congress, with massive debts to pay. Virginia's public debt stood at £4,250,000 in 1784; Massachusetts's at about £1,500,000 in 1785. The state debts included money owed for supplies, their old depreciated war currencies, some of which still circulated, and debts owed to soldiers for back pay. The post-revolutionary states regularly allocated 50 to 90 percent of their revenues to pay the interest they owed on their revolutionary debts. To raise it, and some principal, the states levied heavy new general taxes, and tried where possible to collect indirect taxes, such as imposts – the very revenues Congress wanted to appropriate for the national debt. The politics of postwar finance and taxation in every state was, then, a matter of vigorous and occasionally violent dispute.

The states handled their debt in various ways. Virginia, for example, reduced the outstanding debt to its depreciated value, (i.e., its postwar value in specie), calling in its still circulating war currency, and exchanging it (some at 1,000 to 1) for new interest-bearing state bonds. Similarly, it sank much of what it owed its soldiers by either accepting soldiers' certificates (issued in lieu of pay) for western lands, or by passing taxes payable in such certificates. On the other hand, Massachusetts consolidated its debt not at its current postwar value, but at its value in specie at the time the debts were incurred. This left the state with a staggering specie debt (£1,600,000) which required high specie taxes to pay it. The legislature's refusal to relent on its deflationary debt policy in the midst of the postwar depression was in part responsible for the outbreak of rioting in western Massachusetts known as Shays's Rebellion (*see* chapter 47, §4). Throughout the new republic, as taxes rose to sink the states' debts in the midst of deflation and depression, angry taxpayers began demanding relief – tax abatements and postponements, the right to pay in virtually any sort of outstanding state or federal notes or certificates, or to pay in commodities and produce. Most states (Massachusetts excepted) adopted extensive tax relief programs in the mid-1780s. Among the most popular demands of the protesters, and politically the most volatile, was the renewed emission of state legal-tender paper money which, harassed taxpayers believed, would make both taxes and private debts easier to pay.

In 1785 Pennsylvania's legislature responded with £150,000 in bills of credit. It reserved two-thirds of that to pay interest owed to Pennsylvanians on the state and national debt, and made the rest available as loans, backed by land as security. South Carolina emitted £100,000 to be lent out to landowners. North Carolina issued £100,000 in legal-tender paper. In 1786 New York printed £200,000, New Jersey emitted £100,000, Georgia £30,000, and Rhode Island £100,000. The states' experience with the new paper varied. Some issues were managed wisely, held their value, and provided relief to taxpayers and income to the state. Other issues, however, were so bitterly fought by creditors (who were often required by law to take them at face value, but who just as often flatly refused to accept the money except at a discount, if they would accept it at all) and so badly managed that they depreciated rapidly. Rhode Island's attempts to force its money into circulation became notorious and reinforced the continental nationalists' belief that the state legislatures were too prone to truckle to the mob, especially on money matters, and too likely to consult the public will rather than the public good. Under the Rhode Island currency law, debtors had to accept the paper at full face value for their debts (i.e., they could not demand a discount for taking it, even though it had lost 75 percent of its specie value within a year of being issued). If a creditor refused to accept it, the debtor could deposit paper sufficient to clear his debt with a court and have it declared paid. The money was then forfeit to the state if the creditor still refused to take it. This not only helped wipe out much private debt in Rhode Island, it also helped sink the state's Revolutionary War debts, since those who refused to accept state paper in payment at its full face value saw the debts they held declared forfeit. In 1788, then, when it took $8 in Rhode Island currency to buy $1 in specie, public creditors were forced either to accept the paper (and thus accept only one-eighth of the specie value of what they were owed in full payment), or to refuse it and receive nothing. (Supporters of the plan countered that much of the debt had been bought up by speculators at ten cents on the dollar, so, even at eight to one, they were in effect getting a premium, not taking a loss.) By such methods, Rhode Island had substantially reduced its Revolutionary War debt by the 1790s.

All told, the states were remarkably successful in the postwar years in managing their war debts, servicing the national debt, and financing their operations, while providing practical relief to pressed debtors, public and private, who were cash poor in the depressed postwar economy. The "liquidated" domestic debt of Congress (i.e., the war debt owed to Americans that had been verified, reduced to its specie value at the time it was incurred, and converted to interest-bearing bonds) stood in 1787 at only £28,000,000. The republic's foreign war debt in 1788 was only £10,275,000 more (Jensen, 1950, p. 383).

The methods by which all this had been accomplished, however – devaluation of the debt, currency inflation, tax suspensions and abatements, and the impoverishment of Congress – served only to convince Morris, Hamilton, Madison, and other continental nationalists that the Articles of Confederation were fatally flawed, and that the Republic's prosperity (and its survival) depended upon a new constitutional order that would place national fiscal and monetary policy beyond the reach of popular whim and state legislators. In the aftermath of Shays's Rebellion, their hopes for change rode exclusively on the Federal Convention called to meet in Philadelphia the following summer. Their unhappiness with the Republic's experience in currency, finance, and taxation helped shape both the fiscal powers the new Constitution located firmly in federal hands and the clear limits it established on the monetary powers of the states.

FURTHER READING

Anderson, W. G.: *The Price of Liberty: the Public Dept of the Revolution* (Charlottesville: University Press of Virginia, 1983).

Becker, R. A.: *Revolution, Reform and the Politics of American Taxation* (Baton Rouge: Louisiana State University Press, 1980).

Burnett, E. C.: *The Continental Congress* (New York: Macmillan, 1941).

Ferguson, E. J.: *The Power of the Purse: a History of American Public Finance, 1776–1790* (Chapel Hill: University of North Carolina Press, 1961).

——: "The nationalists of 1781–1783 and the economic interpretation of the constitution," *Journal of American History*, 56 (1969), 241–61.

Franklin, B.: "Of the paper money of the United States of America," *The Posthumous and Other Writings of Benjamin Franklin*, ed. W. T. Franklin, 2 vols. (London: Henry Colburn, 1819), 473–9.

Jensen, M.: *The New Nation: a History of the United States During the Confederation, 1781–1789* (New York: Knopf, 1950).

Kaminski, J. P.: "Democracy run rampant," *The Human Dimensions of Nation Making: Essays on Colonial and Revolutionary America*, ed. J. K. Martin (Madison: State Historical Society of Wisconsin, 1976), 243–69.

Main, J. T.: *The Sovereign States* (New York: Watts, Franklin, 1973).

Nettels, C. P.: *The Emergence of a National Economy, 1775–1815* (New York: Holt, Reinhart and Winston, 1962).

Nevins, A.: *The American States During and After the Revolution, 1775–1789* (New York: Macmillan, 1924).

[New York Provincial Congress], *Journals of the Provincial Congress, Provincial Convention, Committee of Safety of the State of New York, 1775–1777*, 2 vols. (Albany: 1842).

Shipton, C. K. (ed.): *Early American Imprints, 1639–1800: a Microprint Compilation by the American Antiquarian Society* (Worcester, Mass.: American Antiquarian Society, 1955–).

Tansill, C. C. (ed.): *Documents Illustrating the Formation of the Union of the American States* (Washington, DC: US Government Printing Office, 1927).

Ver Steeg, C. L.: *Robert Morris, Revolutionary Financier* (Philadelphia: University of Pennsylvania Press, 1954).

CHAPTER FORTY-NINE

Foreign relations, after 1783

JONATHAN R. DULL

THE 1783 Peace of Paris brought the United States recognition of her Independence, the territorial boundaries she had claimed, and even continuation of American sharing of Britain's fishing grounds (*see* chapter 44, §6). To the shock and disappointment of Americans, however, subsequent events demonstrated that the power of the United States was largely illusory. Great Britain excluded Americans from most trade with the British West Indies and refused to evacuate nine military posts within the borders of the United States. Spain closed the Mississippi River to American shipping and France largely disappointed the expectations of Americans who hoped she would break Britain's near monopoly of American markets. Even the Barbary States of northern Africa treated the United States with contempt. Congress found itself unable to compel the compliance of the individual American states that was necessary for a coherent national foreign policy; starved of revenue, unable to raise an army or navy, lacking even the means of commercial retaliation, Congress, indeed, was almost helpless in international affairs. This situation helped prompt the adoption of the Constitution, which was intended among other purposes to permit the United States to act more effectively in its relations with other nations. While the Constitution alleviated some problems, there were others which it could not solve. The United States was still economically backward and lacked the means to build a modern army and navy to rival those of the great powers of Europe. Protected by geography, America preserved her Independence, but not until well after her industrial

revolution did she become an international great power.

1 America's Gains from the Treaty of Paris

The disappointments of the post-Revolutionary War years were all the more acute because of the exorbitant expectations raised by the 1783 peace treaty. Except for Florida (which she had not sought) all the territory between the Appalachians, the Great Lakes, and the Mississippi was accorded to her. Although establishing exact borders with Spanish Florida and British Canada would present unexpected difficulties, the United States had won a great diplomatic victory. The extent of this territory, however, was not a reflection of a dominant American military or legal claim to the area. Except for a few Spanish, British, and American military posts (and some scattered settlements in Kentucky and Tennessee), the area beyond the Appalachians was populated only by Amerindian tribes, whose rights were not considered during the peace negotiations. The fact that the entire area was accorded to the United States rather than to Spain or Britain should be attributed to the dynamics of the peace negotiations themselves rather than to a pre-existing superiority of American claims. The prime minister of Britain, William Petty, Earl of Shelburne, abandoned Britain's claims to the area as a negotiating tactic to split the United States from Britain's other enemies, France, Spain, and the Netherlands. This sacrifice, necessary if Shelburne were to achieve peace and the opportunity to implement domestic reforms, seems not to have been too painful for him. Shelburne apparently believed that Britain, which maintained control of the St. Lawrence, would still dominate the region economically by buying its produce and selling it British manufactures. Spain was a more serious rival; the peace commissioner John Jay feared that France would dictate a partition of the area between Spain and the United States. France, however, had no designs on Canada and hence little interest in the region. The French foreign minister, Charles Gravier, Comte de Vergennes, feared a deterioration of France's military situation and wished above all for a speedy peace; Spain had more pressing desires elsewhere, such as Gibraltar, Minorca, and Florida, and had little to offer in exchange for them. Thus, only the United States seriously pressed a claim to the area and, thanks to Shelburne's needs and the astuteness of the American peace commissioners, chiefly Franklin, was able to obtain it in the provisional agreement of November 29, 1782 and the final treaty of September 3, 1783.

Unfortunately for the United States, effective control of the West depended on military posts such as Niagara, Detroit, and Michilmackinac. The United States won these posts in the peace treaty but she could not force the British to evacuate them. Britain thus was able to hold them hostage to force American compliance with other articles in the peace treaty. The American peace commissioners (Franklin, Jay, John Adams, and Henry Laurens) had been forced to make last-minute concessions on two issues: payment of debts to British merchants and compensation to loyalists for confiscated property. On the former issue the commissioners made commitments which the individual American states failed to honor, giving the British a justifiable excuse not to evacuate the nine forts they still held. On the latter issue the commissioners promised to recommend to the individual states that they offer redress to the loyalists; when their promise proved meaningless, British public opinion was further alienated.

The peace treaty was also flawed by various imprecisions. One, already mentioned, was the lack of clarity in delineating borders. Due largely to deficiencies in mapping, the border between the northeastern United States and Canada was drawn in a contradictory manner, engendering disputes that were not resolved until 1842. (A less significant error was also made about the northwestern corner of the United States.) Britain was also partially responsible for the ambiguity concerning the northern portion of her former colony of West Florida (which extended to the Mississippi River). The provisional treaty with the United States detached this area from Florida and awarded it to the United States, but a month later the British assigned all of Florida to Spain. The final treaties failed to resolve the issue, which became an object of negotiation between the United States and Spain. Article 3 of the treaty, which assigned the Americans limited rights to catch and dry fish from the Newfoundland and St. Lawrence fishing banks, also was ambiguous; disputes over fishing rights, although partially resolved in 1818, bedeviled relations between the United States and Great Britain for more than a century.

2 Postwar Relations with Britain, Spain, and France

The key issue regarding the treaty, however, was not the precision of its language, but rather the spirit in which it was interpreted. Ironically the United States paid a price for its very success in the peace negotiations. Shelburne, who seems to have genuinely wished for good relations with the United States, undermined his parliamentary majority by the generous terms of peace with the United States and Britain's other opponents. Parliament stopped short of rejecting the peace agreement, but it drove Shelburne from office and refused his legislation permitting Americans to share in British trade. The coalition government of Lord North and Charles James Fox which succeeded Shelburne was far less friendly to America. The change in British attitudes was dramatically demonstrated by the July 2, 1783 Order in Council by which the Americans were largely denied commercial access to the British West Indies. Subsequent orders in council placed restrictions on American

trade with Canada, Britain, and Ireland. By
1787–9, American trade with the West Indies
was barely half what it had been in 1770–2
(although precision is impossible because
of extensive smuggling). John Adams, the
American minister to the British court, tried
unsuccessfully for three years to obtain redress.
While British trade prospered, severe hardships were suffered by American shipbuilders,
merchants, farmers, and fishermen.

The United States was subjected by Spain
to further economic dislocations. The conditional peace agreement between Britain and
the United States promised the Americans
continued navigation of the Mississippi, but
the subsequent Anglo-Spanish agreement on
Florida left both banks of the lower river in
Spanish possession. In 1784 Spain closed
the lower river to American shipping. She
then sent a diplomatic representative, Diego
de Gardoqui, to negotiate the navigation
and border issues with John Jay, the new
American Secretary of State. Jay, despairing
of reopening the river, suggested to Congress it forbear navigation of the river for
25 or 30 years in exchange for Spain's opening her European ports to American ships
and goods; because of opposition from
southern states he failed to obtain the necessary congressional authorization and the
disputes were not resolved until the 1795
Pinckney Treaty.

The difficulties with Britain and Spain
were made more difficult by the effective
dissolution of America's alliance with France.
The French monarchy, facing the threat of
bankruptcy and attempting to preserve the
diplomatic status quo in Europe, had little
attention to spare for America. France did
open certain West Indian ports to some
American goods in 1784, but in general
she greatly disappointed those such as the
American Minister to France, Thomas
Jefferson, who hoped French trade would
help break America's dependence on Britain.
French merchants lacked knowledge of
American markets and did not have the
credit resources to match those of British
merchants. The United States signed commercial treaties with the Netherlands (1782),
Sweden (1783), and Prussia (1785), but
these too did little to break the British stranglehold; Great Britain continued to take

nearly half of America's exports and to provide almost all her imports.

Perhaps the most embarrassing failure
of American foreign policy resulted from the
withdrawal of British naval protection for
American merchant shipping in the Mediterranean. The sale of the few surviving American
warships from the Revolutionary War left
this shipping totally exposed to the privateers of the North African Barbary States.
Agreement was reached with Morocco, but
Algiers, Tripoli, and Tunis continued with
impunity to capture American ships.

Congress had neither the military nor the
commercial means to retaliate against any
foreign opponent. It could not even control
the 13 states of the American union. As
already mentioned, the individual states
embroiled Congress with Britain by block-
ing payment of debts to British merchants
and compensation to former loyalists.
Indeed, America virtually had 13 separate
foreign policies, as particular states ratified
the peace treaty individually, established
their own trade policies, sought foreign
loans, and negotiated independently with
both Amerindian tribes and foreign states.
The opposition of a single state was sufficient to block congressional attempts to
raise a federal revenue; only the Dutch loans
contracted in 1782 and 1784 kept the
government from bankruptcy, and by 1787
hopes for further loans seemed dim.
Without revenue Congress could not hope
to raise a real army or to rebuild the navy;
the latter disappeared totally and the former
was too weak to prevent settlers from
encroaching on Amerindian lands or to
protect them from Amerindian retaliation.
Disillusioned by Congress's inability to force
the British to evacuate their posts, to open
the Mississippi for their produce, or to
defend them from Amerindian attack, frontiersmen in Kentucky and Tennessee began
contacts with British and Spanish officials.
Separatist movements arose in Vermont and
even on the small island of Nantucket.

3   The Effect of the Constitution on American Foreign Relations

Economic hardship, threats to American
unity, and a sense of national humiliation

were factors in the summoning of the Constitutional convention. They also influenced debate within the Convention and provided reasons to support ratification of the Constitution. The new frame of government promised to alleviate some of the foreign policy difficulties of postwar America. It strengthened the executive, empowering the president to appoint the secretary of state, to draft treaties and, with congressional concurrence, to declare war. With its new ability to establish taxes, raise an army and navy, and regulate trade, the federal government acquired the means in theory to make itself respected abroad. Nevertheless, the Constitution could not rectify all the underlying weaknesses which relegated the United States to the ranks of the lesser international powers.

The central source of weakness was the American economy. The United States of the late eighteenth century was still an underdeveloped country by the standards of Western Europe. The American population, while growing rapidly, was still well below that of the European major powers (except for Prussia). America lacked the industrial development to compete with Britain even for American markets (with the exception of the largely self-sufficient and economically primitive frontier). Moreover, the United States was woefully short of banking and credit facilities. Like other economically subservient states, America served chiefly as a provider of raw materials (such as foodstuffs, tobacco, indigo and, increasingly, cotton) to more developed economies such as Britain's. Lacking a sufficient economic base, the United States could not create the huge and complex armies and navies by which the great powers of Europe enforced their will. The obstacles to such creations were administrative as well as material. During the Revolution the United States had found several generals of great ability – Washington, Knox, Greene – but it could not count on such continued good fortune. As the War of 1812 would demonstrate, it was not easy to find officers to raise, train, provision, and coordinate large bodies of troops (and fleets of ships). The United

States was also handicapped by pervasive rivalries among the states and between sections of the country, East versus West as well as North versus South. This made it difficult to implement effective commercial, diplomatic, or military policies. Fortunately for America these weaknesses were counterbalanced by the security accorded by geography. Protected by the width of the Atlantic and the vastness of her size, America's survival was not really menaced, at least by outside forces. Other nations might harm the United States, but only her own disunity could destroy her. The greatest challenge to her unity lay 75 years in the future; once that was mastered the United States could resume her other great revolution, the Industrial Revolution, which would raise her first to the ranks of the great powers and then to their leadership.

FURTHER READING

Bemis, Samuel Flagg: *Pinckney's Treaty: America's Advantage from Europe's Distress*, rev. edn. (New Haven, Conn.: Yale University Press, 1960).

Giunta, Mary A.: *The Emerging Nation: A Documentary History of the Foreign Relations of the United States under the Articles of Confederation, 1780–1789*, 3 vols. (Washington, DC: National Historical Publications and Records Commission, 1996).

Kaplan, Lawrence S.: *Entangling Alliances with None: American Foreign Policy in the Age of Jefferson* (Kent, Ohio, and London: Kent State University Press, 1987).

Marks, Frederick W., III: *Independence on Trial: Foreign Affairs and the Making of the Constitution* (Baton Rouge: Louisiana State University Press, 1973).

Ritcheson, Charles R.: *Aftermath of Revolution: British Policy Towards the United States, 1783–1795* (Dallas: Southern Methodist University Press, 1969).

Whitaker, Arthur Preston: *The Spanish-American Frontier, 1783–1795: the Westward Movement and the Spanish Retreat in the Mississippi Valley* (Boston and New York: Houghton Mifflin, 1927).

Wright, J. Leitch: *British and the American Frontier, 1783–1815* (Athens: University of Georgia Press, 1975).

CHAPTER FIFTY

Slavery and anti-slavery

SYLVIA R. FREY

NEW World slavery had its origin in the vast area located between the lapping waters of the Atlantic Ocean on the south and the looming Kong Mountains on the north, the Volta River on the west, and the Niger River in the Gulf of Benin on the east. For nearly four centuries the three powerful and highly complex African civilizations of Benin, Dahomey, and Yoruba supplied slave labor to the West Indies and the Americas. Slavery had, in one form or another, existed from antiquity: in Plato's Athens, in Caesar's Rome, and in Christian Europe. Although slavery had long since died out in most of Western Europe, it remained at least a marginal institution in Spain and Portugal, and it existed in Africa itself, albeit in a relatively mild form. Despite differences from area to area, and even from tribe to tribe, the African system of slavery was deeply rooted in the general social and political structure. The majority of domestic slaves were debtors, whose enslavement was often payment for a bad debt; prisoners taken in war or kidnapped from other tribes; or criminals enslaved for antisocial crimes, such as adultery or theft. Most African slaves were regarded as valuable and useful people. More often than not, they were recognized as members of their owners' households. They enjoyed certain social rights, including marriage and rights of inheritance for their children, as well as protection against want or ill-use.

1 The Beginnings of the Modern Slave Trade

The year 1441 is generally accepted as the official beginning, so to speak, of the modern international slave trade, upon which New World slavery was based. In the first recorded skirmish between Europeans and Africans south of the Sahara, a young Portuguese explorer named Antam Goncalvez took 12 Africans captive and carried them to Lisbon as a gift for Prince Henry. In 1443–4 a second cargo followed. Thereafter a steady stream of Portuguese caravels descended on the surf-beaten African coast. The exploring navigators were soon followed by sea-traders, whose trading posts, called factories, spread with daunting speed southwards from the estuary of Senegal to Sierra Leone on the Guinea Coast. Within ten years after the trade was initiated Portugal was importing 1,000 Africans a year. The discovery of America by Columbus in 1492, Pedro Alvares Cabral's landing in Brazil eight years later, followed by Balboa's sighting of the Pacific Ocean altered drastically the nature of the slave trade.

Although European merchant adventurers had been making regular sea voyages round the western bulge of Africa and their fortified factories dotted the Guinea coast, the slave trade played only a small role in Europe's economic life. The planting of the first New World colony by Spain and the establishment in 1503 of the encomienda system led to a brief and tragic experiment with Amerindian slave labor. Ravaging disease decimated the Amerindian population and led to an acute labor shortage. The labor shortage, in turn, was exacerbated by the first Spanish shipment in 1515 of slave-produced sugar grown in the West Indies, which marked the beginning of Europe's transition to capitalism. To relieve the problem of labor supply, Charles V approved the importation of slaves directly from Africa. Three years later the first cargo arrived. Within 50 years of the discovery of America, the annual rate of direct shipment from Africa to Spanish colonial America was running at several thousand. The profits from the slave trade soon attracted competition from France and England. The spread of European settlement across the Atlantic created a new demand for slaves and brought the Dutch, the Danes, and the Swedes into the rapidly developing trade. The introduction of sugar into the French West Indies in 1640 precipitated an enormous expansion of the trade in the seventeenth century.

The establishment of the European slave trade provided the framework for the rise of organized slave raiding and warfare in the forest belt of sub-Saharan Africa, which in turn became the chief instruments to build up African trading empires. With muskets and gunpowder obtained through the European trade, chiefdoms (such as the once petty Akan state) began organized slave raiding and warfare on lesser states in the interior. Their success at controlling the trade and establishing markets promoted the rise in the eighteenth century of the Ashanti Union in what is now northern Ghana; of Oyo, the great center of the Yoruba people; of the Kingdom of Benin in the forests west of the Niger; and of the remarkable Fon Kingdom of Dahomey, whose port Ouidah controlled the trade with the Europeans. The long-range impact of the slave trade on West Africa over four centuries has not been calculated. The transformation of formerly peaceful, peasant communities into militarized slave raiding states destroyed human and material resources which might have been diverted to more creative enterprises. The demographic consequences alone were staggering. Global estimates on the number of people exported from Africa across the Atlantic have been calculated at 11,698,000.

2 The Early Slave Trade in America

For the Europeans and the Americans, however, the slave trade provided the basis for the development of capitalism. Slave labor on plantations and mines in the New World made possible the development of tropical and semi-tropical America and allowed the accumulation of capital necessary to exploit the mineral and agricultural resources of the New World colonies. The creation of the various slave regimes of the New World was immediately influenced by local economic forces. In the mainland colonies of British North America, the character of slavery was determined by the rise of staple crop agriculture and the plantation system. It was first introduced into the British mainland colonies in 1619, when a Dutch man-of-war deposited 20 Africans captured from a Spanish vessel bound for the West Indies on the sandy coast of Virginia. Claiming a need for food, the captain of the vessel offered to trade his human cargo for "victualle." His offer was accepted, thus inaugurating the nefarious traffic in human flesh. For many years afterwards, slavery existed without sanction of law, but perforce of custom. In 1661, however, the Virginia Assembly, the oldest representative body in British America, approved a declaration that children should follow the condition of their mothers. By it, Virginia made slavery statutory and hereditary – an attitude which set it apart from all other slave systems in history. In 1670 the assembly approved another act declaring that "all servants not christians," who entered the colony "by shipping," should be "slaves for their lives," thus establishing perpetual chattel slavery.

The legal institutionalization of slavery in Virginia, followed a quarter century later by the development of comprehensive slave codes, ran parallel to several other developments, the most significant being the growth in the size of the black population and the rise of staple agriculture. For most of the seventeenth century, however, Blacks constituted only about 3 percent of the Chesapeake population. The majority were imported from the West Indies. Most lived on small plantations of fewer than 11 slaves and were engaged in the small-scale production of tobacco. Between 1727 and 1769, however, 39,679 slaves were imported into Virginia, four-fifths of them from Africa. By 1770 slaves represented 40 percent of the population of Virginia and 30 percent of the population of Maryland.

A number of factors were responsible for the growth of slavery in the Chesapeake. First was the rapid rise of tobacco, the earliest experiments on which were carried out by John Rolfe in 1612. The royal prohibition on the production of tobacco in England and the higher cost of Spanish leaf created an expanding market for Chesapeake tobacco in England. The reorganization of the tobacco trade early in the eighteenth century by Scottish merchants, who landed huge contracts from the French tobacco monopoly, contributed to the explosive growth of the industry. The expanding market in turn produced a large demand for labor, which was temporarily satisfied by a flood of white emigrants from England. High mortality rates in the Chesapeake and rising real wages in England cut short that source of supply and contributed significantly to the demand for slave labor. Despite recurring depressions in the industry, expansion continued to the Revolution, and Chesapeake planters with access to capital were able to build up immense estates, their home plantations averaging 3,000 acres and 80 slaves.

In the meantime, a different type of plantation economy was developing along the low coastal plains of South Carolina, southern North Carolina, and Georgia. Black slavery in Carolina originated with the founding of the colony in 1670. The Fundamental Constitutions promised land grants to persons who brought slaves to the colony. Barbadians constituted one-third of the early settlers and many of them brought their slaves with them. The introduction of rice seed from Madagascar, and its successful cultivation on the low-lying islands and marshes and along the riverbanks, led to the development of a staple economy centered on the production of rice, the large-scale production of which coincided with the emergence in 1720 of a clearcut black majority in the colony. In the 1740s a second staple crop, indigo, was introduced by Eliza Lucas on her father's plantation in Wapoo Creek. Although slavery was banned in Georgia until 1751, Carolina migrants quickly forged a plantation economy which

closely resembled that of South Carolina. Situated between Virginia and South Carolina, the colony of North Carolina shared characteristics of each of her more prosperous neighbors. In the northern part, adjacent to Virginia, tobacco was grown; in a small area of the Cape Fear valley rice was cultivated. The mainstay of the colonial economy was, however, naval stores, most of which were produced in the southern part.

Plantation societies

Differences in the various plantation societies were the result of a combination of factors peculiar to each system. Chief among these were the different geographic and environmental conditions, the economics of production, the culture of the master class, and the provenance of the slave population. The older, more stable plantation society of the Chesapeake was characterized by a type of paternalism that expressed itself in distinctive patterns of management and labor organization. The strict regimentation required in tobacco cultivation led to a reliance on gang labor and on maximum surveillance and control. On small farm units of fewer than 20 slaves, where a majority of Chesapeake slaves resided, every step of the production cycle was supervised by the master. Slave drivers and foremen carried out some of these functions on larger units, but masters, eager to maximize production, tended to maintain centralized control. In some cases, though not in all, the paternalistic system resulted in improved material circumstances but relatively less individual freedom for the slave population.

An entirely different plantation ethos characterized the lowcountry plantation system. Whereas the majority of Chesapeake slaves lived with resident owners, lowcountry slaves often did not. Masters eager to escape the disease-ridden environment of the rice fields spent part of each year in Beaufort or Charles Town, leaving the supervision of daily plantation activities in the hands of overseers and black drivers. The grueling and unhealthy nature of the work involved in rice cultivation made the task system a more practical form of labor organization in the lower South. The relative lack of supervision and the slaves' freedom to engage in production for private use, once the individual work assignment was complete, resulted in greater autonomy for the lowcountry slave population and in a more exploitative mentality among the planter class.

The differences between one plantation society and another were also owing to the disparate origins, different patterns and rates of growth, and relative size of the slave populations of the various regions. By the eve of the American Revolution, more than 270,000 slaves lived in the colonies of Virginia and Maryland, approximately 66 percent of them in the tidewater, the remainder in the developing piedmont. The early slave trade to the Chesapeake dealt mainly in slaves from the West Indies. Beginning in the 1680s slaves were imported directly from Africa, an estimated 90 percent of them in English shipping. After 1769, however, the importation of African slaves declined dramatically owing to a combination of factors. The major factor was the changing demographic configuration. By and large, Virginians preferred Africans from the Niger Delta, perhaps because tobacco culture required less physical strength, and an estimated 37.7 percent of all eighteenth-century imports were from the Bight of Biafra. Virginians cared less for slaves from Kongo-Angola, probably because the long voyage left the Africans weak, and only 15.7 percent were from Angola. Until roughly 1740 the Chesapeake slave population was culturally diverse, disproportionately male, and widely dispersed throughout the region on small plantations. A more generally balanced sex ratio after 1740, together with improved nutrition and epidemiological conditions and greater family stability, made natural reproduction possible. The shift from tobacco to the less labor-intensive cultivation of wheat, beginning in the 1760s, produced a slave surplus, leading in 1778 to Virginia's prohibition of the slave trade, to the passage in 1782 of a law permitting manumission, and to a similar ban on importations adopted by Maryland in 1783. The slave surplus in Virginia also contributed to the practice of hiring slaves out and, in the post-revolutionary era, to the growth of the domestic slave trade between Virginia and the lower South. Both Maryland and Virginia supported the federal prohibition of 1807 on the external trade.

3 The Growth of the Slave Population

Although the lowcountry slave population had begun to grow naturally, its increase in the eighteenth century still depended on continual immigration. Shipping records indicate that between 1672 and 1775 nearly 90,000 black slaves entered the port of Charles Town, the largest and most dynamic of the five colonial ports engaged in the slave trade from Africa. Approximately half of the slaves transhipped from Charles Town were sent to Savannah or Sunbury in Georgia. North Carolina received the second largest number, and the remainder were sent to the other English colonies along the Atlantic coast, to European colonies in Florida, Mobile, and New Orleans, or to the West Indies and the Caribbean. South Carolina planters, who demonstrated an acute awareness of ethnicity, preferred slaves from the Guinea coast, Gambia, Sierra Leone, and Angola, because they were presumed to have characteristics suited to certain kinds of work. During the colonial period nearly 8,000 Africans from Gambia were sold into slavery in South Carolina. The second largest number of Africans brought to colonial South Carolina was from Angola. Between 1735 and 1740 Kongo-Angolans constituted 70 percent of South Carolina's slave population, and they remained the dominant group throughout the century. Slaves from Sierra Leone constituted the third largest group in terms of total numbers. Up to 7,000 slaves per year were exported from Bance Island, a slave trading station at the mouth of the Sierra Leone River, which was operated by Richard Oswald of London. On the eve of the Revolution, South Carolina's slave population numbered 100,000, compared with 70,000 Whites. Predominantly young, male, and African, it was heavily concentrated in the lowcountry, some 55,058 in the Charles Town district alone. Although

South Carolina's southern neighbor Georgia was late in inaugurating slavery, its slave population had grown to 15,000, two-thirds of whom lived in the lowcountry.

Influences of slavery on the plantation system

Although other variables enter into it, it is now increasingly recognized that the distinctive features of the lowcountry plantation system owe a great deal to the origins of the slave population. It is, for example, probable that the highly profitable rice plantation system of South Carolina and Georgia relied heavily on the technical knowledge of slaves from the "Rice Coast" of West Africa, where local farmers had been cultivating wet rice on the flood plains and dry rice on the hillsides for centuries before the Portuguese introduced different varieties of paddy rice from Asia in the sixteenth century. By the eighteenth century, West African farmers were using elaborate irrigation systems in the cultivation of wet rice. In addition to the technical expertise and labor patterns that they brought, it is also possible that "Rice Coast" slaves contributed to the technology of rice cultivation. Wooden mortars and pestles, used to process rice, and "fanners," the large winnowing baskets used to separate the grain and chaff, which are still in use in Sierra Leone today, were perhaps introduced by West Africans, who may also have contributed to the system of sluices, banks, and ditches used in the cultivation of wet rice.

The lowcountry slave population also had a significant linguistic and cultural impact, particularly in the Sea Island Region, whose semi-tropical climate and disease environment led to the geographical and social isolation of the black population and permitted the development of an independent slave culture strongly influenced by African patterns. The preponderance of peoples from the Kongo-Angola area and from Gambia and Sierra Leone made possible the development of a distinctive language, which retained many elements of African languages. Known as Gullah, it contained thousands of African words and place names, which suggests the influence of several language patterns, including the Tshi (Gold

Coast), KiKongo (Kongo-Angola), and Mande (Upper Guinea). Drawing upon African cultural patterns, lowcountry slaves re-created a world of aesthetic autonomy in music and dance, in stoneware and basketry, in wood sculpture and architecture, in style of worship, and in burial customs, much of which survives today.

Slavery in the North

Although slavery is traditionally associated with the southern colonies, it was an established institution in all of the 13 British mainland colonies, and several of the northern colonies were actively engaged in the slave trade. Important socio-economic differences distinguished the New England and middle colonies from the southern colonies, however, and guaranteed that slavery would remain a marginal institution. By contrast to the southern colonies, which made a rapid transition from subsistence to commercial agriculture, the New England economic system was, under the constraining influence of geography and religion, gradually transformed from household production to a commercialized economy. Although slavery existed, in Massachusetts as early as 1633, the slave population of New England never exceeded 16,000. The middle colonies developed a more varied economic life and relied upon a mix of white wage labor and slave labor. In parts of New York, where slavery was introduced as early as 1628, and in East Jersey, Blacks constituted up to 14 percent of the population. Elsewhere they represented only a fractional minority of the total. Native-born, English speaking, the relatively small black populations of New England and the middle colonies enjoyed the benefits of education and church membership, thus making their integration into the community possible.

4   The Anti-Slavery Movement

Although it was a vital part of the labor system only in the South, slavery enjoyed almost universal acceptance. No systematic body of thought against it existed, while philosophical justifications for it were as old as the institution itself. From the classical and hellenistic period, Greek and Roman writers had constructed philosophical defenses for the overriding importance of property rights. Because slaves constituted a special form of property in classical antiquity, it was necessary to devise a rationalizing ideology for the specific problem of slavery. Greek and Roman writers constructed two main types of philosophical justification: the first, the theory of "natural slavery" suggested by Plato and fully developed by Aristotle, argued that certain people are slaves by nature and actually benefit by slavery; the second type represented slavery as the result of accident rather than nature, and denied that a "good" person could ever "really" be a slave at all. Orthodox Christian writers generally accepted the latter view. Early church fathers, such as St. Augustine, viewed slavery as evil in principle but accepted it as divinely ordained. New Testament writers advanced the idea of the equality of souls before God, but made no effort to prescribe a general code of morality with respect to economic or political behavior, under which rubric slavery fell. The result was that Christianity offered no unqualified denunciation of private property ownership or of slavery or kindred forms of unfree labor.

Religious

Paradoxically the roots of anti-slavery sentiment were religious in origin. The first explicit religious condemnation of slavery in America was the 1688 Germantown petition of the Mennonites, a sect similar to the Quakers. The mildly worded Germantown Protest, which argued from the golden rule, went unheeded. It was soon followed, however, by more elaborate, distinctly religious anti-slavery literature, most of it written by Quakers such as George Keith, John Hepburn, Ralph Sandiford, and Benjamin Lay. At least one New England Puritan, Judge Samuel Sewell, was among the anti-slavery pioneers. Sewell's tract *The Selling of Joseph* (1701) attacked the Biblical arguments traditionally used to justify slavery and advanced the opinion that, as children of God, Blacks had "equal Right unto Liberty," an original right which could not

be forfeited either by consent or by captivity in war.

No practical results came of any of these early efforts until the evangelical upsurge known as the Great Awakening swept through New England and the middle colonies, beginning in the 1740s. The frenzy of religious revivalism associated with it reinvigorated the Quaker anti-slavery tradition and produced a flood of anti-slavery tracts, the most influential of which were written by Anthony Benezet and John Woolman. Benezet, a Quaker schoolmaster in the Friends' English School in Philadelphia, wrote nine tracts between the late 1750s and his death in 1784. The three which are considered most important are *A Short Account of That Part of Africa, Inhabited by the Negroes* (1762), *A Caution and Warning to Great Britain and her Colonies* (1766), and *Some Historical Account of Guinea* (1771). The practical issue of Benezet's tracts, which were directed at the suppression of the slave trade, were apparent on both sides of the Atlantic. His *Short Account* apparently influenced the great English barrister Granville Sharp, who in 1772 led the successful court battle to free James Somerset, a slave in England. His *Historical Account* attracted the attention of Thomas Clarkson, who directed the successful fight to abolish the British slave trade in 1807. At Benezet's urging the prominent Philadelphia physician Benjamin Rush published his influential *An Address to the Inhabitants of the British Settlements in America, Upon Slave-Keeping* (1773). Although Benjamin Franklin's *Observations Concerning the Increase of Mankind* (1751) represented the first American attack on slavery from an economic and demographic perspective, Franklin too was influenced by the moral arguments of Benezet.

Woolman's efforts were directed at the Quaker community. For a quarter of a century Woolman traveled from Quaker meeting to meeting, trying to persuade his fellow Quakers to free their slaves. His extended tours of Maryland, Virginia, and North Carolina in 1746 and again in 1757 gave him first-hand experience with slavery and powerfully influenced his essay *Some Considerations on the Keeping of Negroes*, the first part of which appeared in 1754, the second in 1762. In it Woolman laid down the basic tenets of religious anti-slavery thought: the brotherhood of all God's children as partakers of the Inner Light; liberty as the gift of God to all his children; the entitlement of all God's children to "treatment according to the Golden Rule." Woolman's work had a notable impact among Quakers. In 1754 the Philadelphia Yearly approved a resolution written by him advising members of constituent meetings against purchasing slaves. In 1755 the Yearly advised monthly meetings to admonish any friend who persisted in the practice of buying slaves. In 1758 the Woolmanites scored a major victory with the adoption by the Yearly of the 1758 minute enjoining Friends to free their slaves or face discipline from the monthly meetings. The Philadelphia example spread through New England and New York, whose yearly meetings also approved minutes outlawing slavery. In New England, where the slave population was small and assimilable, and in Pennsylvania and New York, where Quaker influence was strong, slavery was practically abandoned by the Quakers before the Revolutionary War. Outside the Society of Friends, the religious movement did not produce important results until the revolutionary era, when the religious and moral movement began to converge with new political and economic ideas to produce a searing intellectual indictment of slavery.

Secular

The tradition of religious anti-slavery in New England and the middle colonies intersected with two independent but parallel systems of thought and culminated eventually in a powerful secular anti-slavery movement. The first developed out of the writings of John Locke, the seventeenth-century English philosopher whose ideas were formulated in opposition politics under Charles II. In their struggle with Britain over imperial policies, revolutionary leaders relied upon a popularized version of Lockean philosophy, which affirmed the existence of immutable laws of nature and

the doctrine of natural rights, whose guiding values of liberty and equality found resonance in the religious principles of the spiritual equality of all God's children and liberty as His special gift to each of them equally. Although Locke himself had justified slavery, the French philosopher Montesquieu, in his *Spirit of the Laws* (1748), was the first to expound the theory that slavery was forbidden by natural law, an argument later vaguely made by Woolman and by Benezet, whose *A Caution and Warning ...* quoted from the writings of Montesquieu. The rising tide of anti-slavery thought was supported by the publication in 1776 of Adam Smith's *Wealth of Nations*, whose utilitarian arguments that slavery was the "dearest of any" form of labor seemed to fit the economic realities of the late eighteenth century.

The three convergent, often interlocking, movements produced a fundamental intellectual reorientation, whose leading religious or moral, political and economic motifs raised questions about the obvious contradictions between society's professed values, religious and secular, and the existence of chattel slavery. Although most Americans drew back from the logic of their own arguments when it came to Blacks, the Boston Revolutionary James Otis did not. In *The Rights of the British Colonies Asserted and Proved* (1764), essentially an argument against the British writs of assistance, Otis bluntly asserted that "The Colonists are by the law of nature free born, as indeed all men are, white or black." During the controversy over the Stamp Act, anti-slavery literature began to proliferate. Produced by a diverse group of ministers, lawyers, merchants, and schoolteachers, it appealed to both religious sanctions and natural law. Among the anti-slavery advocates were Blacks themselves, including the poet Phillis Wheatley, whose work gained international recognition, and the one-time slave Caesar Sarter, whose essay on slavery appeared in the *Essex Journal*. "Freedom suits" brought by slaves against their masters in New England courts gave practical application to the ideas of anti-slavery writers, as did the wartime flight of thousands of slaves to the British Army.

5   Emancipation in the North

The practical issue of the intellectual anti-slavery movement was a trend in the northern states towards gradual emancipation, the preliminary to which was the passage of slave-trade legislation. In 1766, the year of the repeal of the Stamp Act, Boston instructed its representatives to "move for a law, to prohibit the importation and purchasing of slaves for the future." A number of New England towns approved similar instructions, and in 1767 the General Court debated but declined to take action on several bills prohibiting or restricting the slave trade. In 1771 a prohibitory bill passed the House and Council, but Governor Thomas Hutchinson refused to sign it. Although Massachusetts did not succeed in prohibiting the slave trade until 1788, Pennsylvania (1773), Rhode Island (1774), and Connecticut (1774) all passed prohibitory acts, and the general Articles of Association adopted by the first Continental Congress in 1774 contained a slave-trade clause which pledged the Association "neither [to] import nor purchase any slave imported after the first day of December next," after which time it agreed "wholly [to] discontinue the slave trade" and "neither [to] be concerned in it ourselves" nor to "hire our vessels, nor sell our commodities or manufacturers to those who are concerned in it."

Efforts to remove restraints on manumission, which existed in many states, were the next steps on the road to emancipation. Encouraged by petitions from Quakers and local abolitionist societies, several northern states adopted measures to facilitate voluntary manumission. Delaware approved a measure permitting manumission by will or other instrument (1787), and similar acts were passed in New Jersey (1786, 1798), New York (1785, 1788), Kentucky (1798, 1800), and Tennessee (1801). Concern that the freedmen might become a public charge led most states to establish age limitations and impose restrictions, including the requirement that the manumittor provide some form of maintenance for freedmen. During the Revolutionary War years, all of the northern states except New York and New Jersey took steps to abolish slavery.

Actual emancipation in the northern states was achieved by a variety of means: direct legislative action, direct constitutional provision, and the judicial process as supplementary to the Constitution. Early attempts at legislative emancipation in New England and New Jersey failed, but in 1780 the Pennsylvania Assembly enacted the first gradual emancipation law in American history. In New York and New Jersey, where slavery was more deeply entrenched, gradual emancipation legislation was not adopted until 1799 and 1804 respectively, New Jersey being the last state to do so before the Civil War. Both states made emancipation contingent upon the inclusion of abandonment clauses, which permitted owners of Negro children freed by the act to abandon them a year after birth, after which time they were considered paupers and therefore subject to be bound out to service by the overseers of the poor. Since the law did not prohibit overseers from binding out children to the very masters who had abandoned them, masters were entitled to receive reimbursement from the towns for the support of the children they had abandoned.

Although the doctrine of natural rights was the foundation upon which all states constructed their new state constitutions, only that of Vermont provided for the total prohibition of slavery. It, however, established the precedent for similar action in the new states formed from the Northwest Territory. In Massachusetts and New Hampshire emancipation was accomplished by constitutional provision supplemented by judicial action. After petition campaigns waged by slaves in both states failed to achieve legislative emancipation, slaves, aided by anti-slavery lawyers, began suing for freedom in the courts. In the 1781 case of *Brom and Bett v. John Ashley*, heard in the Inferior Court of Common Pleas, Great Barrington, Massachusetts, Elizabeth Freeman, or "Bett," argued that the phrase in the new Massachusetts Constitution of 1780 declaring all individuals were "born free and equal" applied to black as well as white Americans. Bett's claim to a share in the heritage of the Revolution established the precedent for a series of court decisions which effectively destroyed slavery in Massachusetts.

6 Entrenchment and Expansion in the South

Although the northern record of emancipation was sullied by the general refusal to offer to freed Blacks full membership in the political community or to alter in any way their degraded social status, by a slow, often tortuous process, slavery was gradually abolished in all of the northern states. In the southern states it emerged from the Revolution as a firmly entrenched sectional institution, thus foreshadowing conflict at some remoter date. There are several reasons for these divergent developments, including the lack of economic dependence on slavery in the northern states, and the fact that the major intellectual tradition of religious radicalism reinforced by revolutionary ideology, which gave impetus to the anti-slavery movement in New England and the middle colonies, was largely absent in the South. The period of intense religious revivalism known as the First Great Awakening was also experienced in the South, but its geographic strength was limited to a few counties in Virginia's piedmont and the upper tidewater. Before the tradition of religious anti-slavery could become very deeply rooted, popular attention was preoccupied with the events of the imperial conflict.

White southerners also had a different conception of revolutionary ideology. Although they embraced the ideology of republicanism, which espoused the notions of liberty and equality, they had built a social order upon the contrary ideal of inequality. The ideal of equality, which captivated so many of their northern countrymen, held no allure for a people committed to slavery, for it was identified by them with racial anarchy and barbarism. From the white southern perspective, an ordered inequality was the best safeguard of harmony and peace. Unable to identify fully with the values of equality and liberty that were projected by the language of republicanism, white southerners fastened upon the rights of property as the focal point of their attachment to republican thought.

The experience of the Revolutionary War reinforced these ideas. Years of military occupation, continuous naval assaults, and bitter internecine warfare produced massive damage and overwhelming chaos in the South. British efforts to use slavery as a matter of tactics threatened to shatter social cohesion and to destroy the existing social order. The flight of thousands of slaves to the British Army or to sanctuaries in the developing Southwest and in Florida contributed to the devastation of southern plantation economies and to the severe depletion of the slave labor force. Faced with the disintegration of their society and the forfeiture of their material power, southerners emerged from the war, not persuaded to end slavery, but convinced that its restoration was the indispensable condition for the economic rehabilitation of the entire region.

The result was the further entrenchment of slavery everywhere in the South except Maryland, and its expansion westwards: into the southside and transmontane areas of Virginia and the backcountry of Georgia and South Carolina; across the Allegheny Mountains into Kentucky and Tennessee; and southwest to frontier plantations in Mississippi and Alabama. During and after the Revolution, Maryland's slave population grew slowly. A small state with no hinterland for expansion, in 1783 Maryland removed restraints on manumission, and by 1810 more than 20 percent of the state's black population was free. By contrast, neighboring Virginia's slave population nearly doubled between 1755 and 1782, most of the growth owing to natural increase. Left by the transition from tobacco to wheat with a superfluity of slaves, tidewater planters resorted to the manumission, transfer, and sale of the surplus. In 1782 Virginia revised the slave code to permit individual manumission, and some 10,000 slaves were subsequently freed. During the 1790s and 1800s many times that number were taken into Kentucky and Tennessee by the hundreds of small, middling, and larger planters fleeing the depression-ridden tidewater, or were marketed in slave-hungry Georgia and South Carolina. When that source of supply proved inadequate to meet the insatiable demand, planters from the lower South began importing slaves from Africa. Between 1783 and 1807 an estimated 100,000 Africans were imported into Savannah and Charleston to meet frontier demands in the back country. By 1790 Georgia's slave population was almost 30,000, nearly double the prewar figure. South Carolina, which lost an estimated one-quarter of its slave force during the war, imported almost 20,000 Africans before 1800, and between 1800 and 1807, when the slave trade was closed by federal law, another 39,075. The closing of the international trade accelerated the domestic trade, and between 1810 and 1820 approximately 137,000 slaves from the Chesapeake were marketed in Mississippi, Alabama, and the developing area west of the Mississippi River.

Unsuccessful anti-slavery movements

By the time the postwar anti-slavery movement was launched in the South, slavery was the pivotal institution of southern society. The catalyst for the short-lived crusade was the Second Great Awakening, which broke out on the banks of the James River in 1785 and erupted intermittently thereafter until 1820. Unorganized and generally confined to a handful of European evangelical leaders and northern itinerant preachers, the movement was inaugurated by Methodist conferences in 1780, 1783, and 1784, the last the Baltimore "Christmas" Conference, which directed members of the Society to manumit their slaves or face excommunication. When the English churchmen Thomas Coke, the first superintendent of the church in America, and Francis Asbury, ordained a superintendent by Coke, attempted to enforce the injunction among Virginia Methodists, they met with bitter hostility and open threats of violence. As a consequence, the so-called Slave Rule was suspended in 1785, barely six months after it was adopted. Coke and Asbury then launched a petition campaign for the general emancipation of Virginia slaves. Although a number of the great Virginians

of the revolutionary generation, including Washington, Jefferson, Madison, and Mason, were philosophically opposed to slavery, none was willing publicly to support the anti-slavery movement. The petition campaign was rejected by the Virginia Assembly and stirred a pro-slavery attack. Methodist efforts to achieve gradual emancipation continued intermittently until 1808, when the denominational effort was abandoned in favor of spiritual salvation of the slave population of the South.

The congregational organization of the Baptist polity militated against an organizational anti-slavery effort. In Virginia, the center of southern Baptist strength, the Baptist General Committee of the state adopted a resolution drafted by John Leland, a Massachusetts native, condemning slavery, but it failed to win support in the associations. Advised by the Roanoke and Strawberry associations against further interference with the institution of slavery, the General Committee decided in 1793 to drop the divisive issue on the grounds that it was a matter more appropriately decided by the state. David Barrow, a native of Virginia, led a short-lived but significant anti-slavery movement in Kentucky. Finding no anti-slavery sentiment in the regular Baptist associations, Barrow formed the Licking-Locust Association, Friends of Humanity, and through it preached emancipationism. After Barrow's death in 1819 the movement rapidly disintegrated, however. Although Baptist churches in the lower South contained thousands of black members, there was no Baptist anti-slavery sentiment outside Virginia and Kentucky.

The American Revolution produced an ambiguous legacy. It created the illusion of a young nation united on the principles of liberty and equality, when in fact from the very inception there were invidious divisions along geographical, demographic, and ideological lines. Building upon the revolutionary ideal of political freedom, the "commerical" states of the North moved towards the gradual extinction of slavery. Driven by a different set of imperatives, the "plantation" states of the South entrenched and extended slavery, the very antithesis of freedom. The federal Constitution, which banned the slave trade after 1808 but implicitly recognized the existence of slavery, preserved the moral contradictions present in the situation and passed on to another generation the problem of creating the "more perfect union."

FURTHER READING

Berlin, Ira, and Hoffman, Ronald: *Slavery and Freedom in the Age of the American Revolution* (Charlottesville: Published for the United States Capitol Historical Society by the University Press of Virginia, 1983).

Bruns, Roger (ed.): *Am I Not a Man and a Brother: the Antislavery Crusade of Revolutionary America, 1688–1788* (New York: Chelsea House Publishers, 1977).

Curtin, Phillip D.: *The Atlantic Slave Trade: a Census* (Madison, Milwaukee and London: University of Wisconsin Press, 1969).

Essig, James D.: *The Bonds of Wickedness: American Evangelicals Against Slavery, 1770–1808* (Philadelphia: Temple University Press, c. 1982).

Kulikoff, Allan: "A 'prolifick' people: black population growth in the Chesapeake colonies, 1700–1790," *Southern Studies*, 16 (1977).

Littlefield, Daniel C.: *Rice and Slaves: Ethnicity and the Slave Trade in Colonial South Carolina* (Baton Rouge: Louisiana State University Press, 1981).

Locke, Mary Stoughton: *Anti-Slavery in America from the Introduction of African Slaves to the Prohibition of the Slave-Trade (1619–1808)* (Boston: Ginn, 1901).

McLeod, Duncan J.: *Slavery, Race and the American Revolution* (Cambridge.: Cambridge University Press, 1974).

Morgan, Edmund: *American Slavery, American Freedom: the Ordeal of Colonial Virginia* (New York.: W. W. Norton, 1975).

Pole, J. R.: "Slavery and Revolution: the conscience of the rich," *Paths to the American Past* (New York: Oxford University Press, 1979).

Wood, Peter H.: *Black Majority: Negroes in Colonial South Carolina, from 1670 through the Stono Rebellion* (New York: Alfred A. Knopf, 1974).

Zilversmit, Arthur: *The First Emancipation: the Abolition of Slavery in the North* (Chicago and London: University of Chicago Press, 1967).

CHAPTER FIFTY-ONE

Amerindians and the new republic

JAMES H. MERRELL

IT did not bode well for relations between the new republic and its native neighbors that the only reference to Amerindians in the Declaration of Independence was to "merciless Indian savages." Nor did it help that during the Revolutionary War most tribes sided with Great Britain. After the war ended in 1783 the new nation sought to punish the Amerindians for their loyalty to the King. The peace treaty with Britain gave the United States claim to all of the lands east of the Mississippi River, and the victorious Americans began trying to convince the Amerindians of the claim's validity. But native resistance soon compelled the federal government to adopt a more pacific approach. Beginning in the late 1780s the new nation was negotiating for Amerindian lands and promising money, supplies, and civilization in exchange. This policy, which lasted into the 1820s, was only slightly more successful. Opposition from frontier settlers, from the states, and from the Amerindians themselves combined with a lack of commitment to native rights at the national level to hamper the policy's effectiveness, helping to pave the way for the Amerindians' removal from the East after Andrew Jackson's election to the presidency in 1828.

1 The Indians and the Revolutionary War

At the outbreak of the American Revolution there were perhaps 200,000 Amerindians living east of the Mississippi River, made up of 85 different nations. The vast majority of these nations planned to stay out of the conflict between England and her rebellious colonies. "We are unwilling to join on either side ..., for we love you both – old England and new," the Oneidas explained to the governor of Connecticut in March 1775, a month before the fighting began at Lexington and Concord (Graymont, 1972, p. 58). Initially both Britain and America, aware that Amerindian allies could be expensive and unpredictable, were inclined to respect the natives' wishes. But the temptation to recruit Amerindian warriors – and the fear that the other side would recruit them first – proved too great to resist. By the time Americans officially declared their Independence in July 1776, both sides were seeking Amerindian allies.

Most Amerindians, forced to make a choice in order to continue receiving essential trade goods, ended up supporting the King. While abandoning neutrality was often a difficult and painful decision, choosing between Britain and America was not. The British had a history of trying to protect Amerindian land from encroachments; the Americans had a history of making those encroachments. The British had long supplied Amerindians with gifts, and continued to do so after 1776; the hard-pressed Americans were unable to match the Crown's largesse. In addition, the British Americans most influential among the natives, such as John Stuart in the South and Guy Johnson among the Iroquois, remained loyal to the King; the Americans had no one with their prestige. In the end, most of the Amerindians who did join the patriot cause were from small enclaves located amid the colonial settlements – such as the Marshpees on Cape Cod and the Catawbas in the Carolina piedmont – or, like the Oneidas, were heavily influenced by a prorebel missionary. Together all of these pro-American Amerindian allies were few compared to the estimated 13,000 native men who fought for the British.

North and South, during the war Americans felt the effects of Britain's successful recruiting among the Amerindians. In 1776, for example, Cherokee war parties struck all along the southern frontier, while in 1778 the Iroquois launched attacks on New York and Pennsylvania. In the Ohio River valley an alliance of Amerindian nations – including Delawares, Shawnees, Wyandots, and Miamis – used British supplies and sometimes British troops to maintain their control of the region. Many Amerindians who remained loyal to the Crown paid dearly, however. American forces struck back, invading the Cherokees' mountain homes in 1776 and 1780, in 1779 marching into the heart of Iroquoia under Major General John Sullivan, and in 1780 and 1782 attacking the Shawnees in the Ohio country.

2 The Treaty of Paris and the Theory of Conquest

The Amerindians' suffering during the Revolutionary War continued in another form once peace was made in 1783, for in the Treaty of Paris that ended the conflict Britain ceded to the United States all of the lands east of the Mississippi River. Since none of the Amerindian nations living on those lands had surrendered to the Americans and no native diplomats were at the treaty negotiations, the news that the King had granted away all of their territory came as quite a shock to the natives. It was especially surprising because the Amerindians had scored some of their greatest victories of the war in 1782: the Iroquois were still attacking settlements in the Mohawk Valley, and farther west Amerindian loyalists defeated the Americans on the banks of Lake Erie and at Blue Licks in Kentucky. To Britain's native allies, it looked like the war was all but won; now the English had made a shameful peace, and the Amerindians were furious. At the British

post at Niagara the Iroquois bluntly told the commander "that if it was really true that the English had basely betrayed them by pretending to give up their Country to the Americans without their Consent, or Consulting them, it was an Act of Cruelty and injustice that Christians only were capable of doing" (Calloway, 1987, pp. 10–11).

Nonetheless the deed was done, and the victorious Americans soon began trying to put the treaty's terms into effect. In the autumn of 1783 Congress sent commissioners into Amerindian country armed with a theory of conquest derived from the Treaty of Paris. By defeating Great Britain, the argument went, the United States had also defeated Britain's Amerindian allies, and was therefore entitled to all of the Amerindians' lands. Thus the American commissioners came not to buy Amerindian territory but to demonstrate the new nation's generosity by returning to the Amerindians some of what once had been theirs. "We claim the country by conquest," federal agents informed Delawares and Wyandots in 1785, "and are to give not to receive" (Downes, 1940, p. 294). When, in the following year, a Shawnee protested that "God gave us this country, ... it is all ours," he was advised to "stop persisting in your folly" (Horsman, 1967, p. 22).

Behind the commissioners' strong words lay the new nation's urgent need for more land. To federal officials the Amerindian territory promised rescue from bankruptcy: those acres would either be granted to veterans to fulfill the government's promises of land bounties to soldiers or sold outright to settlers and speculators to raise money. On paper the plan appeared to be working. Between October 1784 and January 1786 the United States all but dictated treaties to the Six Nations and the Shawnees, to a confederacy of western Amerindians including Wyandots, Delawares, Chippewas, and Ottawas, and in the South to the Cherokees, Choctaws, and Chickasaws. But appearances were deceiving. The Amerindians later repudiated these agreements, stating that those who had assented to the terms were under duress or else had no authority to sign. Reiterating their arguments against the conquest theory, native leaders swore to defend

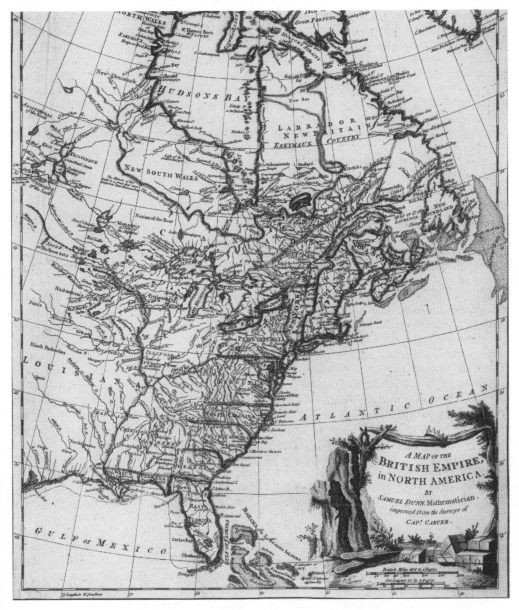

Map 8 The location of many Amerindian nations, on a British map of 1776.
Reproduced by permission of the Bodleian Library, Oxford, U.K.
Copyright©Bodleian Library.

the boundaries they had established in treaties with Britain before the Revolution.

The Amerindians had the resources to back up their threats. The Spanish remained in Florida, the British (defying the Treaty of Paris) in the Old Northwest; both encouraged native resistance and sent supplies to further that resistance. Among the Amerindians were men such as the Mohawk Joseph Brant and the Creek Alexander McGillivray, men with the vision and the political skills in both native and European cultures needed for leadership. McGillivray, with Spanish support, unified the Creeks and turned the nation against the United States so effectively that federal representatives "could not get enough of them to come to a meeting to justify a peace treaty on any terms" (Jones, 1982, p. 154). Brant used his influence among both the British and the Amerindians to help forge a confederacy of northern nations that rejected any treaty made without the unanimous approval of every member of the confederacy.

Citizens of the new nation were undeterred by the work of the British and Spanish, Brant and McGillivray. Those near the frontier saw a vast expanse of territory that, to their minds, was not put to proper use, and during the 1780s settlers poured across Amerindian boundaries to occupy the north side of the Ohio River as well as new territory in Georgia and Tennessee. The Amerindians made good on their promise to defend their homelands. In the latter half of the 1780s native war parties drove out many of the invaders in the South while their counterparts along the Ohio River picked off boats loaded with new settlers bound for Amerindian country. Efforts by the United States to punish the natives for these attacks were disastrous failures. In October 1790 Amerindian defenders badly mauled General Josiah Harmar's army when it invaded western Ohio. A year later, not far away, they all but destroyed General Arthur St. Clair's forces near what is now Fort Wayne, Indiana. In a few hours half of the 1,400 militia and American regulars were killed or wounded and the survivors were fleeing in panic back to the Ohio.

These defeats only proved what some of the new nation's leaders had suspected all along. However attractive the conquest theory might be, it was only a theory, and the United States lacked the means to make it reality. A national army with fewer than 700 men in 1789 (when the Creeks alone had between 3,500 and 6,000 warriors) was not going to subdue the Amerindians, even with the help of militia. Nor was it likely to force Spain to stop supplying the Creeks or compel Britain to abide by the Treaty of Paris and abandon the forts it still held in the Old Northwest.

3 The Policy of Negotiation

Clearly if the young nation was to expand it was going to have to find a better way to come to terms with its Amerindian neighbors. Beginning in the mid-1780s some federal officials began to lobby for a different approach. Most outspoken among them was Henry Knox. Knox had been a general in the War for Independence; after 1785 he was Secretary of War under the Articles of Confederation and in George Washington's administration. As a military man, Knox knew that crushing Amerindian resistance was impossible. As a government official, he recognized that military operations were an expense the republic could ill afford. As a patriot, he was concerned that land grabs and skirmishes with the natives would be an everlasting stain on the republic's record. Finally, as a product of the Enlightenment, he believed that environment shaped a people's culture, and that a change in environment could help raise the Amerindian from "savagery" to "civilization." Drawing upon all of these sources, Knox argued that there was a better way to pacify the Amerindians and acquire their territory at the same time. Recognize the Amerindians' right to the soil, he urged. Negotiate for that land in good faith, and pay for any cessions made. Finally, repay the Amerindians not only with cash but also with teachers, preachers, plows, and other tools of civilization. Such a policy, he argued, would save money, bring honor to the republic, and still allow for the nation's expansion.

Others, including Washington and many members of Congress, shared Knox's views, and in the late 1780s the talk of conquest faded. In August 1787 Congress advocated dropping "a language of superiority and command" in favor of dealing "with the Indians more on a footing of equality, ... and instead of attempting to give lands to the Indians to proceed on the principle of fairly purchasing of them" (Horsman, 1967, pp. 41–2). This less belligerent policy – which in fact was a return to British practice before 1776 – continued after a new federal government was established under the Constitution. The nation's new framework of government scarcely mentioned Amerindians – saying only that Congress had the power "to regulate commerce with foreign nations, and among the several States, and with the Indian tribes." Nonetheless, this provision, and the Constitution's treaty-making clause, empowered the federal government to pass a series of laws in the early 1790s establishing a national policy that respected Amerindian land rights, acquired those lands through treaties confirmed by the Senate, and promoted civilization among the natives.

The Amerindian policy formulated during the late 1780s and early 1790s was to remain in place for the next four decades, even though the Amerindians' military power steadily declined. For all of those 40 years, the policy met with stiff and sometimes violent opposition. Much of that resistance came from the frontier, where settlers did not share their national leaders' views on Amerindians. In 1800, for example, Arthur St. Clair, then governor of the Northwest Territory, reported that Amerindians regularly faced "injustice and wrongs of the most provoking character, for which I have never heard that any person was ever brought to justice" (Edmunds, 1983, p. 22). Despite federal treaties making peace, setting boundaries, and promising punishment of trespassers, the frontier folk would not be stopped. "We think that the United States do not want our lands," Cherokee leaders told federal officials; "but we know as well who do want them – the frontier people want them" (Horsman, 1967, p. 118).

The states contributed in their own way to resistance to federal policy. Before the Revolution each colony had enjoyed wide latitude in dealing with Amerindians, and after 1776 the states were reluctant to give up their traditional powers. The first federal constitution, the Articles of Confederation, had done little to encourage them. Article 9 gave Congress "the sole and exclusive right and power of ... regulating trade and managing all affairs, with the Indians, not members of any of the states, provided that the legislative right of any state within its own limits not be infringed or violated." Obviously this was open to interpretation, and the states took it to mean that they could deal with the Amerindians much as they always had. During the 1780s various states, on their own initiative, fought or negotiated with various native nations. In the fall of 1784, for example, the Iroquois met representatives from New York, the United States, and Pennsylvania in turn. Indeed, of the 21 treaties Amerindians made between May 1783 and November 1786, only six were with the United States; seven were with individual states, two more were with the putative state of Franklin, the rest were either with Spain or with individuals. The Constitution, and the federal laws that followed, took power away from the states; nonetheless, some still made trouble. Besides complaining that Amerindian land cessions were not going fast enough, states such as Georgia encouraged settlers to violate treaties and cross boundary lines in an attempt to increase the pressure on the federal government to step up the pace of negotiations.

As if opposition from settlers and their state governments were not enough, the nation's efforts to implement its Amerindian policy also had to contend with Amerindian reluctance. While the United States plan of recognizing Amerindian rights to the soil was an improvement over the conquest theory, that new policy was accompanied by relentless pressure to sell land. Amerindians resented this pressure and, often, the civilization program that went with it. Native resentment took several forms after 1800. Among Senecas, Shawnees, and Creeks, nativistic prophets won large followings by urging a return to traditional values. In some nations – the Shawnees and Creeks especially – this nativism spilled over into open warfare during the War of 1812. The government's civilization program enjoyed more success elsewhere. Many Cherokees learned English, converted to Christianity, established cotton plantations, and obeyed a law code modeled on those of their white neighbors. The problem was that even the Cherokees most willing to accommodate America's civilization plans were not willing to sell their nation's lands, at least not at the rate the United States demanded. In fact, these acculturated natives were economically, socially, politically, and educationally better equipped to resist the American advance. Thus whatever the response – violent resistance by nativists, a religious movement such as those headed by the Shawnee Prophet and the Seneca Handsome Lake, or accommodation – Amerindian opposition was as difficult to overcome as that of the settlers and the states.

Added to all of these opponents was one final problem: the doubts at the federal level, where the policy was formulated and implemented. The policy's sponsors faced two dilemmas. First, the government placed greater emphasis on western expansion than on fair treatment of the natives. If the two policies clashed, if tribes refused to retreat before the white advance, they were manipulated, even coerced, into signing treaties. The second problem was that policy makers were increasingly pessimistic about the Amerindians' prospects for civilization. Even Knox had known that the task of transforming Amerindians into white people would be difficult; as resistance continued and even mounted, Knox's successors in the federal government became convinced that it was not only difficult, it was

impossible. With the election of the frontiersman and Amerindian fighter Andrew Jackson in 1828, the republic's treatment of Amerindians would change dramatically from the course charted after the Revolution.

FURTHER READING

Calloway, Colin G.: *The American Revolution in Indian Country: Crisis and Diversity in Native American Communities* (New York: Cambridge University Press, 1995).

Dowd, Gregory Evans: *A Spirited Resistance: The North American Indian Struggle for Unity, 1745–1815* (Baltimore, Md.: Johns Hopkins University Press, 1992).

Horsman, Reginald: *Expansion and American Indian Policy, 1783–1812* (East Lansing: Michigan State University Press, 1967).

Jones, Dorothy V.: *License for Empire: Colonialism by Treaty in Early America* (Chicago: University of Chicago Press, 1982).

Martin, Joel W.: *Sacred Revolt: The Muskogees' Struggle for a New World* (Boston: Beacon Press, 1991).

McLoughlin, William G.: *Cherokee Renascence in the New Republic* (Princeton: Princeton University Press, 1986).

Merrell, James H.: "Declarations of independence: Indian–white relations in the new nation," *The American Revolution: its Character and Limits*, ed. Jack P. Greene (New York and London: New York University Press, 1987), 197–223.

Prucha, Francis Paul: *American Indian Policy in the Formative Years: the Trade and Intercourse Acts, 1790–1834* (Cambridge, Mass., 1962), repr. (Lincoln: University of Nebraska Press, 1970).

Sheehan, Bernard W.: *Seeds of Extinction: Jeffersonian Philanthropy and the American Indian* (Chapel Hill: University of North Carolina Press, 1973).

CHAPTER FIFTY-TWO

The impact of the Revolution on the role, status, and experience of women

BETTY WOOD

WOMEN from all walks of life played a visible and significant part in the struggle for American Independence. However, the female experience during the revolutionary era was diverse. Women's perceptions of, and reactions to, the revolutionary movement were shaped by their class and race, as well as by their gender. Although the Revolution prompted a reappraisal of women and their role in the new republic, the lives of most women did not change dramatically during the first decade or so of American Independence. In the short term the Revolution neither ended nor inaugurated a "Golden Age" for American women.

Contrary to the impression conveyed by successive generations of male historians, and that which still pervades the popular view of the American Revolution on both sides of the Atlantic, the female experience during the revolutionary era amounted to rather more than Betsy Ross stitching her flag, Phillis Wheatley writing her poetry, and Abigail Adams urging her husband John and his fellow delegates meeting in Philadelphia in 1776 to "Remember the Ladies." Research dating from the 1970s, mainly undertaken by female scholars, has largely succeeded in exploding the traditional assumptions, myths, and stereotypes that have permeated the historiography of the American Revolution ever since the late eighteenth century. They have been replaced by far more subtle, comprehensive and realistic assessments of the often very different perceptions and activities of American women during the momentous and turbulent years of the 1760s, 1770s, and 1780s.

Although, everywhere on the mainland, they were denied the franchise, and therefore effectively excluded from any formal participation in political life, women from all social classes contributed in various, and often quite tangible, ways to the shaping and timing of the decision for American Independence. Moreover, by their efforts on the home front, but not necessarily only in the home, they also played a significant part in ensuring the eventual achievement of that Independence.

1 The Role of Women in Pre-Revolutionary America

The longer-term forces at work in the societies and economies of British America that both encouraged and enabled women to participate in the revolutionary movement were of critical and continuing importance in shaping their status, their daily lives, and the esteem in which they were held both within their families and their communities. The complex demographic, social, economic, and cultural processes that ever since the late seventeenth century had interacted to cause the ever-increasing modernization of American but especially of northern society were, and would remain, profoundly important in defining both the experiences and the perceptions of women. Also, they would help to shape the ways in which women were perceived and perceived each other. The twin processes of urbanization and industrialization, the inexorable growth of market economies and consumerism, exerted an enduring, and arguably in the longer term a rather more tangible, influence on the lives of American women than either republican ideology or the transient events of the War for Independence.

In the South, which was not entirely immune from the process of modernization, the growth and institutionalization of black slavery after the late seventeenth century played a decisive and invidious part in shaping both the status and the daily lives of women. Race was of fundamental significance in delineating the range of interactions deemed possible and desirable between white and black women. White and black women alike, and indeed black men also, even if in rather different ways, were to be the victims of the often-ambiguous sexual attitudes and behavior of white men. By the mid-eighteenth century race was, and despite the challenge posed to the institution of slavery during the revolutionary era, would remain by far the most potent and divisive force in defining the experiences and attitudes of all southern women.

Predictably, the revolutionary era was not marked by a uniform or unifying cluster of distinctively female ideas, perceptions, or patterns of behavior. Class, race, and place of residence, as well as gender, all contributed to the shaping of what were often dramatically different female experiences, to the definition of female ambitions and aspirations, and to the opening and closing of windows of opportunity for women. The lives of some women, black and white, would be completely and permanently transformed because of the American Revolution. However, as far as most were concerned, the end of the war and the political settlements of the 1780s meant simply a return to their "normal" roles and responsibilities.

For hundreds of white women, of all ages and social ranks, the decision for American Independence meant only the shattering of the world they had known, an abrupt and often traumatic break with the past, and an uncertain future. These women and girls may or may not have completely endorsed the loyalist sympathies of their husbands and fathers, but for them the American Revolution was to mean an often involuntary and permanent exile in England, Canada, or the Caribbean. For many black women too, the loyalist sympathies of their

masters and mistresses could also mean their enforced removal from the mainland, often to the harsher slave regimes of Britain's sugar islands.

Women's exclusion from political life

To all intents and purposes, women were excluded from any formal participation in the political life of the mainland colonies. Politics and government, both at the local and increasingly at the intercolonial level, were very much a male preserve. In all its aspects, men dominated the formal political movement from resistance to revolution. The decision for American Independence was taken in and by exclusively male political forums. However, this male dominance of the halls of government, which would not change with the securing of Independence, should not be allowed to obscure the fervor with which many American women embraced the patriot cause or the significance of their albeit, and necessarily, informal political contribution to that cause.

Women's work outside the household

Some scholars have regarded the colonial period, but more especially perhaps the seventeenth century, as being something of a "Golden Age" for American women. In some senses, this was indeed the case. During the initial stages of settlement, in the labor-hungry communities of both North and South, the willingness of women to work at quite often arduous physical tasks outside the household, traditionally the preserve of men, often earned them the high esteem of their menfolk. Much the same held true in other "frontier" societies as settlement expanded through the colonial period. In these communities, because of their scarcity and the value of their labor, women enjoyed something approximating a social and economic equality with men, if only an equality of physical hardship and deprivation. Probably it was a situation which not all women relished. However, it was a temporary and expedient equality, born of necessity rather than indicative of a fundamental reassessment of the status and role of women which would persist as these often-precarious frontier communities were transformed into more settled and stable societies.

2 Old World Perceptions of Women

The evolving societies of early America relied heavily on Old World perceptions and definitions of the role and status of women. The colonists had no intention of jettisoning the social thought, roles, and relationships which underpinned English society. What they sought to create in the New World were their own versions, sometimes highly idealized or anachronistic versions, of that society. Certain of the perceptions and definitions which informed the shaping of the colonial societies established in the seventeenth century, not least those concerning the appropriate legal status of women, would be modified in and by the requirements imposed by the American environment. Yet both in theory and in practice, the status and role of women everywhere in British America bore more than a passing resemblance to the English model. Crossing the Atlantic did not produce a dramatic or permanent change in the status of women or, it might be added, in the attitude of most women towards their designated role in society. In some respects, and despite the consequences for women of the increasing modernization of colonial society, which arguably did more than anything else to confirm and reinforce gender distinctions, very little changed during the colonial period, at least in the working lives of women and men.

The ideal colonial woman

The ideal and idealized colonial woman, the woman who would have been lauded by both John Winthrop and Thomas Jefferson, was one who fulfilled the role of obedient wife, fruitful mother, efficient homemaker, and dutiful daughter. As in England, the woman's place was most definitely in the home, in the domestic as opposed to the public sphere. The patriarchal family, which everywhere on the mainland was regarded as the essential cornerstone of an ordered and orderly society, was expected to be the center of the woman's world, the reason for her existence. A woman's importance lay in what she contributed as a wife and mother to the formation and continuing cohesion of the family unit. Her broader civic duty lay in the influence she might bring to bear on shaping, and perhaps moderating, the opinions and attitudes of her husband and sons. However, her husband was the undisputed head of the family. He was the ultimate decision-maker whose word was, if necessary, law.

Education

The often limited formal and informal education of girls and young women was designed to fit them for their roles as wives, mothers, and homemakers. Higher education was effectively closed to them: men deemed it both unnecessary and beyond their intellectual capacity. Entry into most professions, except school teaching, was an avenue closed to women. The expectation was that any work they undertook would be within a family oriented domestic context.

Religion

In many respects it was religion which provided those women who wanted it with a legitimate entrée into the wider world. Of course, it was unthinkable to male divines, priests, and clergy that women should be accorded any formal ministerial recognition or responsibilities. Only in the Quaker communities, founded in the late seventeenth century, did women enjoy anything like complete equality of religious participation and involvement. So far as most other Protestant sects and denominations were concerned, religious activities provided an appropriate sphere in which women might cultivate and apply what were widely regarded as the quintessential female virtues of piety, humility, and charity.

Single women

Marriage and motherhood were regarded as a woman's main role and objective in life. The high incidence of marriage and remarriage, as well as the high rate of natural increase, in the mainland colonies suggests that most women conformed to these expectations of them, if only because to remain single was to invite sarcasm and ridicule. How many colonial marriages were happy must remain a matter for conjecture. Legal separations were possible and, if she were the injured party, the wife could expect continuing material support from her husband. Divorce was a virtually impossible option for either partner.

The only sure ways for a woman to gain a significant measure of, if not complete, control over her own destiny were to remain single, be legally separated or divorced from her husband, or to be widowed. True, such women had to make their way and support themselves in what was very much a man's world, and their social class as well as their gender determined just how hard a struggle that might be. Yet in terms of their legal status and standing, and particularly in respect of their property rights, these women enjoyed various benefits which, in theory at any rate, were largely denied to married women.

In practice, however, both within and outside the domestic sphere, the status, esteem accorded to, and the daily lives of women in mid-eighteenth century America did not always correspond precisely with the image and expectations of the "ideal woman." Within the home, the wife's input into decision-making reflected the nature of her marriage, her husband's character, and his assessment of what she brought or contributed to the family. Not all colonial husbands and fathers were petty tyrants who ruled their households with a rod of iron. Many regarded their wives as partners rather than as subordinates, or as ornaments, and acknowledged the contribution they had made to the family estate, as well as their competence to manage the same, by naming them as their executrices. Indeed, during their lifetimes many husbands willingly left their wives in charge of their affairs while they were away at war or on political or other business.

Working women

Colonial women in the middling and lower ranks of society retained an importance as economic producers. Many continued to work alongside their menfolk in the agricultural economies of the mainland and in the towns they filled various skilled and semi-skilled occupations. The skills acquired by women stood them in good stead if they remained single or if they were widowed. The competence of colonial women was not in doubt, and they both took pride in and drew inspiration from the recognition of that fact.

3   The Revolutionary Era

Women's awareness of political life

Never, since the days of Anne Hutchinson in Massachusetts and Margaret Brent in Maryland, had colonial women been uninterested, passive, and mute observers of the world around them. However, few women stepped so completely outside their assigned gender roles as did Hutchinson and Brent to voice opinions and engage in public activities that explicitly challenged the exclusive authority claimed by men. Those who did were depicted as posing an unacceptable threat to the maintenance of an ordered and orderly patriarchal society and their deviant behavior was often ascribed to witchcraft or other sinister motives.

Most colonial women did not behave in such an assertive and, from the male standpoint, such a deeply threatening manner as had Hutchinson and Brent during the 1630s. This did not mean that, by the mid-eighteenth century, all women had unthinkingly and uncritically internalized the role of wife and mother. They did not totally lack the inclination, intellectual ability, and confidence to take cognizance of, and seek an active part in defining, the rapidly changing world around them and their designated place in that world.

Women in all social classes, and of all ethnicities and nationalities, were not insulated from, or totally uninvolved in, the political, religious, and social discourses taking place in the communities in which they lived. To a great extent, however, their awareness of and participation in these discourses depended upon images and information presented to them by men. Most of the literature available for their consumption, be it in the form of newspapers, pamphlets, or books had been produced by men for other men. This did not necessarily mean that all women could, or wished to, read such materials; that those who did so were incapable of assessing the merit of their contents; or that women simply mimicked the attitudes of male authors as well as those of their husbands and fathers. What it did often mean, though, was that women were obliged to operate within an intellectual frame of reference largely designed by men.

Although denied a formal role in the political lives of their communities, many colonial women took both a keen and an active interest in politics. Their political involvement, the options open to them, and their modes of behavior reflected both their stations in life and, to a considerable degree, the stratagems devised and deemed appropriate for them by men. In the increasingly tumultuous political life of the major port towns of the northern colonies women, probably drawn mainly from the lower ranks of society, were visible and accepted members of the "urban crowd." In a manner which both reflected and reinforced their familial responsibilities, women were highly visible in the urban food riots of the years immediately preceding the War for Independence. Moreover, it was by no means unknown for women to campaign quite openly for candidates in local elections. Thus white Georgians, male and female, do not appear to have been unduly surprised, let alone scandalized, by the fact that in 1768 Mrs. Heriot Crook and Mrs. James Mossman, the wives of two prominent planters, rode around the countryside campaigning on behalf of Sir Patrick Houstoun's candidacy for a seat in the Lower House of Assembly.

As of the early 1760s, women in all walks of life were *au fait* with the institutions and imperatives of the political worlds in which they lived. They could and did assess for themselves the merits of the competing claims of British and American ideologues and politicians. Individually and collectively, women's voices were heard during the 1760s and 1770s – not for the first time, but on a scale hitherto unknown. Significantly, men were not always concerned to silence them. On the contrary, colonial politicians saw women as invaluable, indeed as absolutely necessary, allies in the struggle they were waging against the British, and quite explicitly solicited their support.

Patriot women

There are innumerable examples of women's commitment to, and support for, the patriot cause both before and during the War for Independence. Among the best known is the resolution drafted in October 1774 by 51 women from Edenton, North Carolina. These women declared their unwavering allegiance to their patriot cause and their intent to do all in their power to further it. Equally well known are the 36 women in Philadelphia who in 1780 spearheaded an immensely successful campaign to raise money to help equip American troops. Within a matter of weeks they had collected around $300,000.

Not only in North Carolina and Pennsylvania, but in every colony, women were seizing the initiative. Yet they were participating in a campaign devised and largely orchestrated by men. Those men had fairly explicit ideas about the most appropriate ways in which women could most appropriately assist them. During the 1760s and early 1770s male patriots freely acknowledged that the success of the most potent weapon in their political armoury, the boycotting of British goods, depended upon the cooperation of women, upon their willingness to change their patterns of consumption. Many women, in all ranks of society, and regardless of the cost to themselves, were ready to do precisely that. Male patriots also suggested that women could express their support for the American cause not only by wearing homespun clothes but also by making them. It was in their homes, sitting at their spinning wheels and looms, that women could make an invaluable political contribution. And this is exactly what many women, rich and poor did, often with enormous gusto and enthusiasm. Patriot men were concerned to ensure that the political horizons of women did not extend too far outside the domestic sphere.

Working women

In some ways, the War for Independence had essentially similar consequences for women as had all previous colonial wars. Out of necessity they were required to fill various economic roles often closed to them in peacetime. As the men in their families went off to fight, for whichever side, so women found themselves being left to run the family farm or business. For some this might have been an unwelcome, but not necessarily a daunting, prospect. Most assumed that when their menfolk returned from the war they would resume their usual familial roles and, more often than not, this is exactly what happened. Of course, many men did not return from the war. For their wives this meant not only the trauma of bereavement but also the psychological, and sometimes the material, consequences of adjusting to widowhood.

Black women

Whether they lived in the North or in the South, bondwomen and men must have hoped that the political rhetoric of the patriots, their demands for liberty and freedom from tyrannical British policies that threatened to "enslave" them, might ultimately be translated into a successful campaign to bring about the ending of the institution of slavery as a matter of public policy. By late 1775 a pragmatic British policy of recruiting male slaves into their armies, and offering freedom to those who survived the war, also offered the prospect of liberty, at least for some enslaved people. Everywhere in the mainland, enslaved women as well as enslaved men took advantage of the dislocations of war to abscond in search of their freedom from bondage. For most, however, that freedom would prove both precarious and temporary.

In some respects it was patriot ideology rather than the War for Independence *per se* which seemed to hold out the best prospect of freedom, if not complete equality, for black women and men, both in the northern and southern states. To some degree, that prospect began to be realized during the 1770s and 1780s, albeit often gradually and grudgingly in the North and, through the device of private manumission, on a much more limited scale in the South. Yet nowhere in the early republic did freedom imply any form of equality. In the southern states most enslaved people ended the revolutionary era as they had begun it: as chattel slaves. The end of the Revolutionary War, and the expansion of cotton cultivation into the southern backcountry, brought even greater hardship to bondwomen and men. During the 1780s and 1790s slave-owning rapidly became a stronger institution, and on a far larger scale, than had been the case before the war. The political accommodations and compromises made in Philadelphia in 1787 effectively ruled out the possibility that this situation would change in the foreseeable future.

Many people, on both sides of the Atlantic, had pointed to the apparent inconsistency, if not the hypocrisy, of a patriot ideology which demanded freedom, liberty, and equality for white Americans but which denied those selfsame things to African Americans. But, with the notable exception of Thomas Paine, no patriot pamphleteer or politician suggested or even hinted that women too might legitimately claim full and equal participation in the political society which men were so busy defining and bringing into existence. Neither did American women make the same claim on their own behalf or, during the 1790s, enthusiastically applaud Mary Wollstonecraft when she did.

4 The New Republican Woman

Yet the social and political discourses of the revolutionary era could not, and did not, totally avoid the questions of women's rights and their role in the new republic. In fact, it was the greater visibility of women during the imperial crisis of the 1760s and 1770s, together with their contribution to the patriot war effort, that prompted an intense examination of assumptions and attitudes that previously had been largely taken for granted by both sexes. During the 1780s, with the achievement of American Independence, the debate focused on the attributes that made for the "ideal" republican woman; the role of women in the new republic; and how women might best be prepared for their designated role. The outcome of that debate, in which women participated, was to return women to the private, domestic sphere from which it seemed by their actions, if not by their words, they might be trying to escape.

The woman's view

The political upheavals and disruptions of the revolutionary era did not dramatically change the self-perception of American women, or at least of those middle- and upper-class women who committed their thoughts to paper. Both before, during, and after the War for Independence, these women did not argue for a complete redefinition of their role and status, which, amongst other things, would have accorded them complete political equality with men. As Abigail Adams put it – and she was by no means atypical of women in her social class – "if man is Lord, women is Lordess – that is what I contend for." When she urged the delegates meeting in Philadelphia to "Remember the Ladies," she was not, and probably would not have dreamed of, suggesting that Jefferson amend the Declaration of Independence to read "All men and women are created equal." What Abigail Adams was demanding was an equality of status and esteem for the private sphere in which women operated.

Marriage

Abigail Adams and other women of her social class were essentially conservative and they would not have dissented from the almost universally held view of the social and moral role, function, and significance of marriage and the family. From their perspective, the family was an essential cornerstone of an ordered and orderly society. They were appalled by Paine and Wollstonecrafts's critiques of marriage and horrified by the way in which the latter practiced what she preached. The path suggested by Paine and Wollstonecraft pointed, or seemed to them to be pointing, to a complete breakdown of society – to social chaos, disorder, and anarchy. For women to step from the private to the public sphere, assuming that they had the time to combine the roles of wife, mother, and homemaker with the demands of a public career, would be one step along that dangerous path. The vehement denunciation by elite women of state constitutions and election laws which, with the notable exception of those of New Jersey, explicitly denied women the possibility of formal participation in political life, would have been more surprising than their apparently placid acceptance of this state of affairs. The dearth of first hand written evidence makes it difficult to ascertain the perceptions of women further down the social scale.

Attributes of the republican woman

A principal concern of some upper- and middle-class women during the 1780s and 1790s, and one which they shared with some men – most notably perhaps with Benjamin Rush – was that of defining the attributes of the "ideal" republican woman and determining how girls and young women might best be prepared to fulfill their designated role in the new republic.

In some ways, and drawing heavily from the classical tradition, the "ideal" republican woman shared many of the same qualities, and was required to display many of the same virtues, as the "ideal" Roman matron. Her civic duty lay in the benign, almost civilizing, influence which she exerted over her husband and sons in ensuring that they became wise, virtuous, just, and compassionate members of the body politic and, if called upon, good rulers.

Education

The "ideal" republican women was not a frivolous, empty-headed ornament. On the contrary, she was expected to be a competent partner who could engage in serious discourse on a wide range of matters with her husband and sons. The problem was, as Benjamin Rush, Judith Sargent Murray, and others realized, that the traditional modes and methods of educating girls, when they were educated at all, scarcely fitted them for such an awesome responsibility. Girls had to be educated, and suitably educated, if they were ever to live up to the high expectations of the republican woman. The "ideal" republican had to know how to manage an efficient household, but she also had to know something about those subjects which would be of interest and concern to her husband. In what was to be one of the more tangible benefits accruing to women as a direct result of the American Revolution, much greater attention than ever before came to be paid to the formal education of girls. Everywhere in the mainland, the 1780s, and 1790s saw the founding of schools and academies which accepted female pupils.

Comparatively few female lives, black or white, in North or South, town or countryside, remained completely untouched or unaffected by the ideas and events of the American Revolution. Women's commitment and contribution to the revolutionary cause earned them the respect of men. But although white women came to be regarded in a more positive light during the 1770s, 1780s, and 1790s, these decades did not witness any "revolutionary" change in the status, roles, and daily lives of American women.

FURTHER READING

Berkin, Carol R.: *First Generations. Women in Colonial America* (New York: Hill and Wang, 1996).

Gunderson Joan R.: *To Be Useful to the World: Women in Revolutionary America, 1740–1790* (New York: Twayne Publishers, 1996).

Hoffman, Ronald, and Albert, Peter J. (eds.): *Women in the Age of the American Revolution* (Charlottesville: University Press of Virginia for the United States Capitol History Society, 1989).

Kerber, Linda K.: *Women of the Republic: Intellect and Ideology in Revolutionary America* (Chapel Hill: University of North Carolina Press for the Institute of Early American History and Culture, 1980).

——.: "'I Have Done Much to Carry on the War': Women and the Shaping of Ideology after the American Revolution," *Women and Politics in the Age of the Democratic Revolution*, eds. H. B. Applewhite and D. G. Levy (Ann Arbor: The University of Michigan Press, 1990).

Norton, Mary Beth: *Liberty's Daughters: The Revolutionary Experiences of American Women, 1750–1800* (Boston: Little, Brown, 1980).

Young, Alfred: "The Women of Boston: 'Persons of Consequence' in the Making of the American Revolution, 1765–1776," *Women and Politics in the Age of the Democratic Revolution*, eds. H. B. Applewhite and D. G. Levy (Ann Arbor: The University of Michigan Press, 1990).

CHAPTER FIFTY-THREE

The impact of the Revolution on education

MELVIN YAZAWA

1 Revolutionary Republicanism

THE American Revolution was never simply a movement for colonial independence. Partly of necessity, but primarily by choice, independent Americans were to be citizens of a republic. And because Americans seemed to be so advantageously positioned to attempt an experiment in republicanism, having been conditioned by colonial practices and being able to draw upon an accumulation of past wisdom, the fate of the new nation was supposed to determine once and for all whether men were capable of governing themselves without the benefit of kings or lords. The revolutionary generation, as Robert Livingston declared in 1787, was thus never destined for a "humble peace and ignominious obscurity." If they succeeded in proving a republican system to be workable and durable, their success would be emulated elsewhere in the world and the realm of liberty would be extended; if they failed, their failure would establish the limits of human aspirations.

Revolutionary republicans confronted two major obstacles to success. First, in a republic, ordinary men must behave in an extraordinary fashion. For self-government to work, citizens must be willing to sacrifice their selfish interests for the good of the whole; otherwise, chaos reigns and the orderly rule of a monarch becomes a welcomed alternative. It was precisely this quality of "civic virtue" that was missing from past republican experiments and, consequently, led to their demise. Were Americans sufficiently virtuous? From the outset of the imperial crisis to 1776, the revolutionaries were convinced of their moral superiority. Indeed, independence was necessary in large part because the revolutionaries had come to consider Britain and the British people to be lost in corruption. Unless a speedy separation was effected, Americans could expect to be tainted with British vices. This heady notion was quickly dispelled once the fighting began in earnest.

Wartime experiences – flagging enthusiasm after 1776, declining enlistments, battlefield reverses, looting and the destruction of private property by revolutionary forces, and disciplinary problems among soldiers and civilians alike – understandably undermined all initial assumptions of moral superiority. Although some may have hoped that the end of the war and the enduring commitment to republicanism might effect a moral regeneration among Americans, they were soon disappointed. David Ramsay, the South Carolina physician and revolutionary historian, echoed a common complaint in 1785 when he lamented over the "declension of our public virtue." Liberty and independence, rather than encouraging sentiments of gratitude and sacrifice, had given rise to "Pride, Luxury, dissipation & a long train of unsuitable vices."

The second obstacle to the success of the revolutionary experiment in republicanism was rooted in the circumstance and composition of the American population. The conventional wisdom of the eighteenth century recommended republican systems rather reluctantly, and then only for small states encompassing a homogeneous population.

Was the new American nation too large? Were its people too diverse for republican self-rule? James Madison, of course, provided a measure of reassurance by reversing the logic of the conventional argument for small republics. Contrary to common belief, Madison said in *The Federalist* no. 10, stability was more likely to be achieved in a large republic than in a small one. In an extended republic comprising a vast array of competing interests the formation of an unjust combination constituting a majority of the whole was highly improbable. Separate factions would lack either a common motive or a convenient opportunity to form a self-interested majority capable of subverting minority rights. Civic action, under these circumstances, "could seldom take place on any other principles than those of justice and the general good." Underlying Madison's logic, however, was the assumption that the competing interests would, in the end, recognize the general good and make the private concessions necessary to secure it. Ultimately, then, as Madison acknowledged, disparate interests must be contained within a "practicable sphere."

The very nature of the obstacles suggested a solution. Education, properly conceived and executed, might remedy any defects in the American character. "Education," Thomas Jefferson explained, "engrafts a new man on the native stock, and improves what in nature was vicious and perverse into qualities of virtue and social worth." For the newly independent and infinitely diverse American people the establishment of a national system of education promised to be especially beneficial. In addition to engrafting qualities of virtue essential in a republic, a common education might forge an otherwise discordant conglomeration of factions into a harmonious whole. As Benjamin Rush, the prominent Philadelphia physician and signer of the Declaration of Independence, noted, education "will render the mass of the people more homogeneous and thereby fit them more easily for uniform and peaceable government."

2 Republican Education

The American revolutionaries said and wrote much about education in the new republic. Common themes, however, quickly emerged. First, they conceived of education broadly. Few writers were willing to confine their thoughts to the mechanics of reading, writing, and arithmetic. The vast majority instead viewed education as nothing less than the process by which the uninitiated were transformed into full participating members of society. Robert Coram, editor of the *Delaware Gazette*, offered a succinct definition of education in his 1791 plan for a national system of schools. Education, Coram said, entails the "instruction of youth in certain rules of conduct by which they will be enabled to support themselves when they come to age and to know the obligations they are under to that society of which they constitute a part."

Since 1776, "that society" was of course republican, and the "obligations" youths were expected eventually to assume were the obligations of self-governing citizenship. Accordingly, the second common theme of the revolutionary educational theorists emphasized the necessity of a system of education that would disseminate knowledge widely. If the dissemination of knowledge failed to keep up with the extension of political rights, then the bulk of the people would take on civic responsibilities for which they were poorly prepared and the American republic would likely experience a speedy decline. Educated citizens, on the other hand, might advance the common good and prolong the life of the republic. They would, in the first place, choose their rulers wisely and thereby reduce the chances of ambitious or venal men ever being entrusted with power. But even if magistrates, once elected, attempted to abuse their power, an informed and vigilant populace would quickly check such transgressions. Despots survived only by maintaining "a dark cloud of ignorance" over their subjects, declared Simeon Doggett, a New England Unitarian minister and former tutor at the College of Rhode Island (Brown). Therefore, "let general information and a just knowledge of the rights of man be diffused through the great bulk of the people in any nation, and it will not be in the power of all the combined despots on earth to enslave them."

Two additional considerations strengthened the case for an extensive system of education in the new republic. First, revolutionary writers tended to couple knowledge with virtue and liberty; ignorance with vice and tyranny. In the *Spirit of the Laws* (1748), Montesquieu made famous the idea that systems of government and education ultimately must coincide. Despotic states might ignore the principles of education (indeed they were well advised to do so), but democratic republics were dependent on the powers of education. Only through education might ordinary men be inspired to place public over private interest, a choice that was "ever arduous and painful" to make. Education thus exercised and extended the "crude wisdom which nature bestows," Samuel Harrison Smith observed. Smith, the Philadelphia journalist who later founded the Jeffersonian newspaper the *National Intelligencer*, argued that the "diffusion of knowledge actually produces some virtues, which without it would have no existence." Most important to the life of the republic, knowledge tended to inspire a "spirit of universal philanthropy" and to lift the "mind to an elevation infinitely superior to the sensation of individual regard." In short, education grafted a spirit of selflessness onto originally selfish stock.

A second consideration usually associated with the notion of the importance of disseminating knowledge widely focused on the nature and necessity of female education. The life of the republic was dependent on the moral character of its citizenry, and women as mothers were the chief guarantors of civic virtue within the family. It was commonly known, as Benjamin Rush remarked in 1786, that "*first* impressions upon the mind are the most durable." And because the first impressions of children were ordinarily derived from their mothers, it was essential that women be qualified for this responsibility. In addition to the "usual branches" of domestic education, then, women needed to be "instructed in the principles of liberty and government." No plan of republican education would be complete if it ignored the women of the republic.

Republican systems of education, then, had to be inclusive. However, a system that embraced every part of the community would still be inadequate if it did not provide for the filtration of talent. Most revolutionary leaders assumed that the majority of men were unfit to manage the abstruse affairs of state. Natural aristocrats, an elite group defined by superior talents rather than inherited family position, were best able to protect the welfare of the whole. A third common theme in the literature on education thus described a graduated arrangement of increasingly restrictive institutions designed to single out the naturally superior. Jefferson offered the best summary discussion of this theme. In his *Notes on the State of Virginia*, he described an arrangement of local district schools, county grammar schools, and the College of William and Mary. At each level, the "best geniuses will be raked from the rubbish," Jefferson said. Other writers also commented on the utility of selective promotions. A graduated system of education supposedly reflected the natural order of the world. God, it was commonly assumed, had distributed natural abilities in unequal portions; a republican system of education should complement this natural order. Samuel Knox, a Presbyterian minister and educator whose ideas were probably influenced by the writings of Jefferson, believed that a hierarchical arrangement geared for the advancement of "such as discovered the brightest genius" was in the best interest of America. Each level of institution might then be structured to accommodate a particular group of citizens whose natural abilities could carry them no further. In the end, every citizen would theoretically be prepared to assume his particular station in the republic.

Finally, because of the heightened political significance of education in the new nation, the revolutionaries insisted that it must become a public responsibility. "Wisdom and knowledge, as well as virtue, diffused generally among the body of the people, being necessary for the preservation of their rights and liberties," declared the Massachusetts Constitution of 1780, it is the "duty of legislatures and magistrates" to extend the "opportunities and advantages of education in the various parts of the country." The dissemination of knowledge was "so momentously important," said Samuel Harrison Smith, that it "must not be left to the negligence of individuals." In America, circumstances not only justified, they dictated the "establishment of a system which shall place under a control, independent of and superior to parental authority, the education of children." Robert Coram fully endorsed these sentiments. "Education should not be left to the caprice or negligence of parents, to chance," he cautioned. Independence and the commitment to republican government thus accelerated the trend, well underway by the middle of the eighteenth century, towards the enlargement of the civic responsibilities of the state (in caring for orphans and the poor, for example) and the diminution of the social space occupied by the family.

An obvious corollary of this final theme of public supervision over education was the insistence on the part of the revolutionary writers that the youth of America be educated within the borders of the new nation. To do otherwise would be shameful. The practice of sending students abroad was, as the Georgia legislature announced in 1785, "too humiliating an acknowledgement of the ignorance or inferiority of our own" institutions. Before the Revolution, such a practice was perhaps "an appropriate reflection of our servile station in the British Empire," Noah Webster said. But whatever propriety there existed "ceased with our political relation to Great Britain." To continue sending American youths abroad for an education was inconsistent with true independence. Furthermore, the benefits of education, especially in an extended republic as diverse as the American polity, were unavoidably tied to geography. The smooth functioning of countervailing factions within Madison's "practicable sphere" was dependent on the power of education to encourage self-interested men willingly to make the compromises necessary to secure the common good. In other words, each faction ultimately must be inspired by a love for the republic; otherwise, the array of competing interests would be productive only of anarchy and confusion. This love for the republic, or patriotism, was an affection that had to be consciously inculcated in the minds of youngsters. Webster prescribed a program of instruction that began with a kind of political catechism: "As soon as ... [the American child] opens his lips, he should rehearse the history of his own country; he should lisp the praise of liberty and of those illustrious heroes and statesmen who have wrought a revolution in her favor." The alternative to this sort of patriotic education on American soil was a foreign education that regrettably would give rise to an attachment to foreign governments or to principles foreign to America.

3 Republican Schooling

The revolutionaries' insistence on the establishment of an American system of publicly supervised institutions of education that would promote the welfare and ensure the permanence of the republic manifested itself in a variety of ways. Indeed, given the importance of the subject, the novelty of the situation, and the tradition of localism that was rooted in the American colonial past, institutional multiplicity was perhaps all but inevitable.

The pace of activity in the realm of public education varied from state to state and between localities. The New England states, building on precedents and priorities set during the colonial period, led the way in the creation of institutions at the lower levels. Massachusetts, in particular, was inclined to codify its intention to educate its citizens. In addition to its 1780 constitution, which charged magistrates and legislators to promote institutions of learning, Massachusetts enacted a public schooling law in 1789. According to its provisions, towns comprising at least 50 families had to furnish six months of schooling during the year; towns of 200 families were required also to support a grammar school. There was little resistance to the 1789 law because, as Lawrence A. Cremin has observed (1980), it merely "codified the commonplace." Massachusetts towns and their inhabitants had, in the course of the last decades of the eighteenth century, grown accustomed to the idea of schooling and schoolgoing.

Although Massachusetts was an early champion of public education, it made almost no attempts to subsume its various institutions under one administrative organization. Thus in 1837, when Horace Mann became secretary of the newly created Massachusetts board of education, he complained about the absence of a "common, superintending power" over the 3,000 public schools in the Commonwealth. Each school was "governed by its own habits, traditions, and local customs"; consequently, the various schools remained "strangers and aliens to each other."

Unlike Massachusetts, New York attempted early to effect a grand design for a system of integrated institutions. Beginning in 1784, New York officials sought to implement an administrative structure that would promote learning throughout the state and serve as a supervisory body for all of the state's various academic institutions. The initial legislation in 1784 established the University of the State of New York and lodged broad administrative powers in its board of regents. Unfortunately, the first board was dominated by King's College men and remained preoccupied with the affairs of that institution (renamed Columbia by the 1784 law). A revised law in 1787 restructured the university as a more representative and comprehensive organization for regulating the state's colleges and schools. Again, however, the university failed to operate as an administrative unit for the state. Not until 1812 did the legislature, acting on a report commissioned by Governor Daniel D. Tompkins, pass a law erecting an alternative to the system first described in 1784. The 1812 law appointed a superintendent of schools whose responsibilities included the management of a three-tiered organization comprising local districts, towns, and the state. As a result of the 1812 legislation, institutions chartered by the legislature existed alongside academies chartered by the regents of the university. Also, local districts set up high schools under their own auspices. In the early years of the republic, therefore, New York succeeded in developing institutions that disseminated knowledge more widely, but it failed to realize fully its design to bring all of these institutions under one uniform administration.

In the South, educational systems, especially at the lower levels, developed more slowly than they did elsewhere. Virginia often led the way, although not without setbacks of its own. The 1779 Bill for the More General Diffusion of Knowledge, drafted by Jefferson, called for a division of each county into units called "hundreds" and the creation of publicly supported elementary schools in each hundred as well as grammar schools in each county. The bill, Jefferson said, would prepare the people to "understand their rights, to maintain them, and to exercise with intelligence their parts in self-government." The measure came before the legislature in 1780, 1785, and 1786, but failed to pass. In 1796 the Virginia legislature did enact that portion of the bill that provided for the creation of elementary schools. However, the 1796 law let each local county court decide whether to institute the program. None did.

From the late eighteenth century through the 1840s, Virginians tried repeatedly to develop a comprehensive school system. In 1810 the legislature established an endowment for the "sole benefit of a school or schools, to be kept in each and every county." Although a modest endowment initially, the fund grew in 1816 when it became the repository of money owed to Virginia by the federal government. Unfortunately, competing factions, each with its own plan for the income generated by the fund, effectively stalled the implementation of any program of comprehensive schooling. Jefferson himself, in 1816–17, helped to defeat a measure sponsored by Charles Fenton Mercer that would have created an integrated system of primary schools, academies, colleges, and a state university located in the Shenandoah Valley. Jefferson opposed the Mercer plan in part for partisan reasons – Mercer was a Federalist spokesman for western interests in the Virginia House of Delegates – and in part because he had advanced a plan of his own which called for the location of the state's university in his home county of Albemarle. Neither Mercer nor Jefferson was able to gain the votes necessary for implementing his program. The result was a substitute measure that allowed only the accommodation of the children of the poor in already existing elementary schools. A subsequent piece of legislation in 1829 made publicly supported schooling for the poor mandatory. Virginia, thus, had made advances in public schooling in the early years of the republic; however, only in the education of paupers did it achieve a degree of uniformity.

4 Assessment

What, ultimately, did the founding fathers achieve in the realm of education? There are at least two ways of addressing this question: first by examining the institutional changes that came in the wake of Independence and second by assessing the long-range impact of altered expectations among the bulk of the citizenry.

Some present-day critics of the revolutionary generation's commitment to education have noted that no statewide systems of public schooling were completed in the immediate postwar years. In short, the charge is that the deeds of the founding fathers failed to keep up with their words. Such criticism, however, ignores the flurry of activity in institution-building in the last quarter of the eighteenth century. Between 1775 and 1800, for example, academies flourished. At a time when the boundary between public and private schooling was still in the process of being defined, academies were not only the principal institutions of secondary education but were often supported through a combination of public taxes and private subscriptions. A quick count shows that Virginia chartered 20 academies during these years; Massachusetts, 17; New York, 19; Pennsylvania, 11; and Maryland, 7. Many more academies went unchartered; thus we know that in these states alone there were probably between 100 and 200 new institutions of secondary education after the Revolution.

At the level of higher education, the revolutionaries' achievement was perhaps even more impressive. The life of the republic was dependent on the preparation of ordinary men and women for extraordinary responsibilities, but it was also dependent on the selection of men of superior virtue and talent for public offices. As Jefferson remarked, "that form of government is the best which provides the most effectually for a pure selection of ... natural aristoi into the offices of government." Colleges were, therefore, essential to the success of the republic because, by singling out the naturally gifted for special training, they facilitated the process of pure selection. Between 1783 and 1800, 16 new colleges opened that still exist today. At least five other colleges gained state charters but failed to survive the nineteenth century. In the immediate postwar years, then, the number of colleges operating in the new nation more than tripled.

As impressive as the numbers of new colleges founded was the trend towards publicly supported institutions. In the 1780s and 1790s, the state universities of Georgia, North Carolina, and Vermont received their charters. In addition, St. John's College (Maryland), Transylvania University (Kentucky), the College of Charleston, Williams College (Massachusetts), and Bowdoin College (Maine) either originated under state auspices or maintained a quasi-public character in spite of denominational affiliations. Indeed, it was this connection to the public realm that often determined the nature and pace of internal developments in the various institutions. For example, curricular changes – especially an increased emphasis on politics and modern history, English grammar, mathematics, moral philosophy, and natural sciences – reflected the perceived need for both "practical" and patriotic education in the new republic. Furthermore, the intrusion of outside concerns into college hallways altered the expectations of students and faculty alike. This publicly inspired alteration leads us to the second way of assessing the educational achievements of the founding fathers.

American colleges, understandably, had become increasingly politicized in the course of the Independence movement, and politicization did not end with the end of the war. On the contrary, colleges remained arenas of public controversy and were embroiled in the ongoing political struggles of the 1780s and 1790s. The debate over the federal Constitution, Hamiltonian finances, the French Revolution, the Jay Treaty, and other issues forced the various campuses to choose sides. By the end of the 1790s, New England colleges were recognizably Federalist while the College of William and Mary was decidedly Republican. In the long run, this sort of political identification impeded the development of unified state-wide systems of public education. Thus Jefferson, it will be recalled, prevented the implementation of the Federalist Charles Fenton Mercer's comprehensive plan of 1816–17. Ironically, what present-day critics are wont to identify as evidence of disinterest on the part of the revolutionaries is evidence of precisely the opposite. Because education was so important to them and because the stakes were so high – involving, they believed, the fate of the republic itself – competing factions among the founding fathers found it difficult in the extreme to establish comprehensive systems of education.

The founding fathers' emphasis on the importance of an educated citizenry also led to a fundamental change in the student population. Jefferson and others envisioned a change at the elementary and secondary levels of schooling; however, the transformation of the collegiate population was perhaps the most revealing demographic change in the early republic. Between the 1790s and the 1820s, collegiate populations became more heterogeneous in terms of social background, geographical origins, and age composition. In New England colleges, where the evidence is most complete, larger numbers of needy students began arriving on the various campuses. Yale, as one student observed in 1822, became a "strange medly" of the sons of "wealthy merchants and poor farmers ... of aristocratic planters and poor backwoodsmen." The change in the student population was even more dramatic at the newer colleges. Institutions founded in the last half of the eighteenth century and the early decades of the nineteenth century recruited the rural poor. By 1830 nearly 200 students, approximately 13 percent of the total New England college population, were indigents. Older students entering the various colleges added to the heterogeneity of the student population. Again, changes were most immediately apparent on the newer campuses. Students entering college after the age of

21 constituted one-third of the combined populations of such colleges as Brown, Dartmouth, Williams, Bowdoin, Colby, Amherst, and the University of Vermont.

The medley of students entering American colleges during the early republic put an end to the colonial ideal of *in loco parentis*, the notion that colleges were carefully controlled communal environments in which college authorities acted as parental figures. Poorer students often lived with families in nearby towns or farms rather than in college residential halls. Furthermore, some colleges were forced to alter school routines to accommodate their students' seasonal patterns of work. Finally, mature men in their twenties when they entered college were unlikely to put up with campus rituals that made them errand boys of adolescent sophomores.

The Revolution thus had both an immediate and a long-range impact on American education. The revolutionaries equated education with the dissemination of virtue and knowledge and, consequently, viewed its success as intricately intertwined with the success of the republic itself. Subsequent generations of Americans would modify the content as well as the rationale for comprehensive systems of education; however, the priorities set by the revolutionaries remained influential. The idea that education was too important to be left entirely to private and parental influences, that institutions of learning be inclusive and patriotic, and that the bulk of the people be rendered safe for self-government through instruction continued to resonate in the thoughts of Americans in the nineteenth and twentieth centuries.

FURTHER READING

Allmendinger, David F., Jr.: *Paupers and Scholars: the Transformation of Student Life in Nineteenth-Century New England* (New York: St. Martin's Press, 1975).

Bushman, Richard L.: *The Refinement of America: Persons, Houses, Cities* (New York: Alfred A. Knopf, 1992).

Cremin, Lawrence A.: *American Education: the Colonial Experience, 1607–1783* (New York: Harper & Row, 1970).

——: *American Education: the National Experience, 1783–1876* (New York: Harper & Row, 1980).

Hellenbrand, Harold: *The Unfinished Revolution: Education and Politics in the Thought of Thomas Jefferson* (Newark, Del.: University of Delaware Press, 1990).

Herbst, Jurgen: *From Crisis to Crisis: American College Government, 1636–1819* (Cambridge, Mass.: Harvard University Press, 1982).

Middlekauff, Robert: *Ancients and Axioms: Secondary Education in Eighteenth-century New England* (New Haven, Conn.: Yale University Press, 1963).

Miller, Howard: *The Revolutionary College: American Presbyterian Higher Education, 1707–1837* (New York: New York University Press, 1976).

Novak, Steven J.: *The Rights of Youth: American Colleges and Student Revolt, 1798–1815* (Cambridge, Mass.: Harvard University Press, 1977).

Robson, David W.: *Educating Republicans: the College in the Era of the American Revolution, 1750–1800* (Westport, Conn.: Greenwood Press, 1985).

Wallach, Glenn: *Obedient Sons: the Discourse of Youth and Generations in American Culture, 1630–1860* (Amherst, Mass.: University of Massachusetts Press, 1997).

Wood, Gordon S.: *The Radicalism of the American Revolution* (New York: Alfred A. Knopf, 1992).

Yazawa, Melvin: *From Colonies to Commonwealth: Familial Ideology and the Beginnings of the American Republic* (Baltimore: Johns Hopkins University Press, 1985).

CHAPTER FIFTY-FOUR

The impact of the Revolution on social problems: poverty, insanity, and crime

MELVIN YAZAWA

HOW revolutionary was the American Revolution? In the realm of politics and ideology, the impact of the Revolution was conspicuous. The switch from being loyal subjects of a king to being independent citizens of a republic entailed, we know, much more than simply a modification in the forms of rulership. But how much change did the Revolution produce in American society? Social evolution is an ongoing phenomenon; it becomes difficult to determine, therefore, which changes in society were due to the Revolution itself and which were due to evolutionary impulses that owed little if any of their impetus to the imperial crisis. In assessing the impact of the Revolution on social problems, we must begin with an understanding of long-range trends that preceded the mid-century crisis. Ultimately, as we shall see, changes in social and political perceptions were intimately intertwined.

1 Poverty

The problems associated with poverty and providing for the poor did not sprout suddenly as a result of the Revolution. To be sure, the War of Independence exacerbated the conditions of the poor and may temporarily have added to the total number of needy in America. Wartime dislocations were unavoidable: seaport economies were disrupted, towns and communities occupied, the laboring poor burdened with military service, and destitute war widows left to care for dependent children. But the problem of poverty was more deeply rooted in the

American past. Gradually, over the course of the eighteenth century, a growing class of poor inhabitants appeared in every colony.

Historians have identified at least two factors that contributed to the swelling of the ranks of the poor. First, the pressure of an ever-increasing population on a limited supply of land may have resulted in a declining standard of living for many third- and fourth-generation sons. After the first decades of the eighteenth century, especially in the older agricultural communities of New England, opportunities dwindled as successive generations typically held fewer and fewer acres of land per capita and brought even marginal lands into cultivation. The fact that there were growing concentrations of wealth at the top of the social pyramid and an emergence of larger numbers of paupers in these communities led the historian Kenneth A. Lockridge (1970) to suggest that American society was becoming "Europeanized." Second, between the Glorious Revolution and the 1760s, the colonists participated in a series of imperial wars that made military contractors and a few merchants wealthy but hurt those at the edges of poverty in America's urban centers. A recurrent cycle of heavy taxes to finance the wars, inflation, wartime boom and post-war depression characterized the experiences of the inhabitants of Boston, New York, and Philadelphia from King William's War (1689–99) to the Seven Years' War (1756–63). Increased numbers of fatherless and husbandless families, along with impoverished war veterans, added to the woes of these cities. By the 1760s a class of genuinely poor people made up between 10 and 20 percent of the populations of these seaboard centers.

If the problems of poverty were not new by the time of the Revolution, neither were the solutions. In the seventeenth and first half of the eighteenth century, colonial authorities relied primarily on informal means of rendering assistance. For the most part, this meant that relatives of the needy took them into their homes. Private keepers shored up the system by boarding some of the poor and charging towns for their services. By the latter half of the eighteenth century, however, the trend towards institutionalization was apparent. In the principal urban centers first, publicly supported almshouses replaced the system of lodging the poor with kin or neighbors. Boston, where the problem of poverty appeared early, built its almshouse in 1685; Philadelphia and New York built theirs in 1732 and 1736 respectively. Rural communities followed suit in the late colonial and revolutionary years.

The timing of the switch from boarding out the poor to placing them in institutions varied, but the trend was unmistakable. There were two reasons for this transformation in the colonial poor-relief system. First, communal authorities found it increasingly difficult financially to cope with the growing numbers of impoverished inhabitants. Even with the proliferation of mutual-aid societies and the charitable contributions of such groups as the Society for the Propagation of the Gospel in New York and the Quakers in Pennsylvania, the cost of poor relief rose rapidly after mid-century. The boarding-out system was expensive and subject to overcharging by unscrupulous private keepers. Replacing it with publicly administered poorhouses, at the very least, might reduce the incidence of corruption by reducing the number of keepers who needed to be policed.

In addition to keeping costs down, institutionalization served a second purpose: it conveniently subjected the poor to efforts at rehabilitation. The colonial poor had always been easy targets of suspicion. Several colonies, beginning with Massachusetts in 1699, passed workhouse legislation aimed initially at dissuading "Rogues, Vagabonds, [and] Common Beggars" from entering their jurisdictions. As the number of needy rose and the cost of maintaining them increased, the distinction between the unfortunate poor and idle vagabonds became blurred. In Pennsylvania, for example, where the number of needy requiring assistance in the early 1760s so increased that the almshouse filled to overflowing with five or six beds stuffed into rooms ten or eleven feet square, the overseers of the poor petitioned the legislature to authorize the construction of a new almshouse and workhouse. The legislature responded in 1766 with the creation of a corporation of Contributors to the Relief and Employment of the Poor. The Contributors, most of whom were Quaker merchants, were to pay for the construction of a new "bettering house," but could count on funds from the provincial poor tax to help with operating expenses. The financial difficulties of the contributorship, which was forced to borrow over one-half of the £11,750 required to complete the building, coupled with stresses created in trying to accommodate approximately 360 persons admitted annually between 1768 and 1775, must have soured the dispositions of the new managers of the bettering house. It is also true, however, that they were philosophically inclined to view their charges as being sorely in need of personal reformation. Relief efforts outside the almshouse must be phased out, the managers argued, because they were utterly "inconsistent with and subversive of the Nature and Design" of the new institution. Relief must be offered in conjunction with rehabilitation. House rules, therefore, strictly supervised the hours of sleeping and waking, eating and working. In this way, the managers of the bettering house hoped, habits of industry might be inculcated among the internees to save them from perpetual poverty.

How did the American Revolution affect the poor and patterns of poor relief established in the colonial period? Although the Revolution did not significantly alter the social structure of America, some scholars have argued that the perceptions of the poor changed dramatically in this era. The historian Gary B. Nash (1979), in particular, contends that the urban poor of the 1760s and 1770s responded not only to the constitutional principles enunciated in revolutionary pamphlets, but also to the conditions of their lives. They adhered to a "popular ideology" that ultimately led them to consider the proper distribution of wealth in America. As a New Yorker asked in 1765, was it equitable "that 99, rather 999, should suffer for the Extravagance or Grandeur of one? Especially when it is considered that Men frequently owe their Wealth to the impoverishment of their Neighbours?" Nash's argument is suggestive and intriguing. Whether changing social and economic circumstances contributed to the politicization of the urban poor and provided the impetus for their participation in the Independence movement, however, remains a matter of considerable debate among historians. There is some evidence to suggest that the imperial crisis and the natural rights proclamations of the revolutionary leaders accentuated the resentments of the laboring poor and other "outsiders" and contributed to the decline of deference in the new nation. If the perceptions of the poor probably underwent some changes as a result of the Revolution, perceptions about the poor were also affected.

The movement towards institutionalizing the poor was not stalled by the Revolution. On the contrary, the republican doctrine of the revolutionaries encompassed certain ideas about the poor that amplified the need for almshouses. For a republic to survive, all agreed, its citizens had to be virtuous. The classical definition of civic virtue stressed self-sacrifice for the good of the whole. The founding fathers, however, discovered that this definition was too constraining and too often contradicted by the reality of their own behavior. Consequently, in the 1780s and 1790s, their understanding of virtue placed a premium not on self-abnegation, but on industriousness. The good citizen was an active and diligent worker. "Idleness," which bred depravity and poverty, replaced "luxury" as the greatest threat to the welfare of the republic. The idea expressed earlier by the managers of the Pennsylvania "bettering house," that the poor required rehabilitation, was supported by ideological

imperatives after the Revolution. The poor appeared blameworthy for their own impoverishment, especially in America where, it was commonly asserted, the natural abundance of the land returned a comfortable sufficiency with little exertion.

By the 1820s, when state legislatures began sponsoring systematic examinations of the dimensions of poverty within their borders, distrust of the poor seemed customary. The prevalence of pauperism amidst the scarcity of the Old World was unavoidable and tragic, but its presence in America was mortifying. "In this country," investigators in New York reported, "the labour of three days will readily supply the wants of seven." Thus only the indolence and dissipation of the poor could account for their misery; in a country where "all the necessaries of life are so abundant and cheap ... there can be no danger of a meritorious individual being allowed to suffer." If the character of the poor accounted for the persistence of poverty, its reformation held the key to eliminating poverty in the republic. Almshouses, similar to those established in the late colonial period, flourished between the 1810s and 1830s. And, much like the managers of the Pennsylvania "bettering house," the new almshouse planners aimed at inculcating habits of diligence and industry among the internees by strictly regulating their behavior. Order, regularity, discipline, constancy, obedience, and respect for authority were lessons to be learned through exacting routines. Well-regulated poorhouses, reformers believed, would finally put an end to the embarrassing anomaly of poverty in America.

2 Insanity

In the half century before the Revolution, the American colonists' understanding of the nature and treatment of insanity underwent a fundamental transformation. First, providential or supernatural explanations gave way to natural ones. Rather than tracing the causes of insanity to sources outside human control, experts increasingly focused on human factors. And, in part because of the rise of an increasingly professional medical establishment, physicians came to replace ministers as the chief authorities on insanity. Eighteenth-century physicians were not always clear about what they meant by insanity, let alone what the symptoms of the various forms of derangement were, but they were quite definite about its causes. As a rule, they identified two sets of natural causes: predisposing and precipitating. Predisposing causes included such factors as heredity, climate, and systems of government. Precipitating causes were events or activities that immediately preceded and seemed to incite bouts of derangement; these included excessive love, grief, anger, fear, envy, and pride. Because madness was a disease with natural origins, there was room for optimism about its treatment. The worst effects of all predisposing and precipitating causes of insanity might be ameliorated by the application of medical remedies.

Having affixed a medical face to madness, most commentators suggested cures for the disease. To begin with, it seemed wise to remove the afflicted from the general population and to place them in secured settings. Confinement of the insane promised to accomplish two things at once: prevent the insane from injuring anyone and thus promote the peace and safety of the general public, and subject the insane to the sort of custodial care most conducive to affecting a cure and thus promote their own welfare. Unfortunately, good intentions were rarely enough. Confinement was ordinarily onerous and often cruel. It could hardly have been otherwise. Before 1752, when the Pennsylvania Hospital admitted its first patients, the mentally ill were incarcerated in jails and almshouses. Without the benefit of trials and without formal commitment proceedings, the insane became inmates. Confinement was an end in itself.

Finally, treatment of the mentally ill increasingly became the responsibility of medical institutions. The history of the Pennsylvania Hospital illuminates the nature of the changes taking place in America. In the 1730s, Philadelphians began using their almshouse as a place of confinement for many of the city's most unruly cases of insanity. By mid-century, the almshouse was overcrowded and the Pennsylvania Assembly was forced to grant a charter to a group of prominent philanthropists to establish a hospital whose mission would include the care and treatment of the insane. The founders of the Pennsylvania Hospital, Benjamin Franklin among them, hoped that the afflicted would benefit from the medical remedies afforded them: the insane might be cured of their malady if they were "subjected to proper management for their recovery." For the first time in American history, a public institution agreed to receive the mentally ill for curative treatment.

The early history of the Pennsylvania Hospital failed to support its founders' initial optimism. Insane patients lived in prisonlike basement cells and found their movements further restricted by leg chains, manacles, and "Mad shirts." Attending physicians usually focused their attention on the most recently admitted patients. Such neglect, however, may have been a blessing in disguise for the remaining inmates. Medical treatment tended to stress physical therapeutics. Preternatural excitement in the blood vessels of the brain needed to be relieved; consequently, bleeding, purges, emetics, and blistering were often prescribed for all forms of derangement.

In the late eighteenth century, psychologically oriented treatments came to complement, if not replace, these grimly heroic measures. By the time the new wing of the Pennsylvania Hospital – a west wing intended solely for the care of the insane – was completed in 1796, gentler prescriptions were in order. However, the "moral treatment" movement, which emphasized a humanitarian approach to patients' physical and emotional needs, was not a direct product of the American Revolution. Its inspiration, instead, came from across the Atlantic via the experiments of Philippe Pinel in France and William Tuke in England. Tuke, the founder of the asylum at York whose therapy included a mild regimen of entertainment, exercise, good food, and comfortable lodgings, was especially influential among American reformers.

How did the Revolution affect the perception and treatment of insanity in America? The Revolution reinforced and accelerated the movement towards asylum-building. The commitment to republicanism placed a premium on the civic competence of the individual citizen. Independent participation in the affairs of the republic required self-discipline and a rational understanding of self-interest. The insane, by any of the definitions offed by eighteenth-century physicians and informed laymen, were incapable of precisely this sort of rational calculation. Passions, which normally were under the control of the faculty of reason and therefore restrained in their operations, were excessive in the insane. The Revolution, unfortunately, seemed to have predisposed some people to bouts of passionate excess. At the very moment when self-control became essential to their political survival, Americans were in danger of losing it. The connection between political and biological health thus may have given a special poignancy to the challenge of insanity in America.

The revolutionary generation also subscribed eagerly to Enlightenment ideas of progress and the perfectibility of human nature. "This empire is commencing at a period when every species of knowledge, natural and moral, is arrived at a state of perfection, which the world never before saw," Timothy Dwight, patriot preacher and later Hartford Wit, boasted in 1776. Not surprisingly, eighteenth-century notions of curing the insane through the application of a therapeutic regimen struck a responsive chord among American reformers. Indeed, believing themselves to be blessed with superior knowledge and unburdened by the habits of the Old World, Americans expected to improve on all facets of the treatment of the insane.

The urgency of the situation, coupled with enlightened optimism, conspired to advance asylum-building in the early republic. In 1776 only the Pennsylvania Hospital and the Eastern Lunatic Hospital at Williamsburg – the first public hospital built exclusively for the treatment of the insane – combined confinement with curative treatment. Between the end of the War of Independence and 1825, however, seven other states established provisions for hospitalizing the insane: New York, Maryland, Massachusetts, Kentucky, South Carolina, Ohio, and Connecticut. And in 1825, with the founding of the Western Lunatic Asylum at Staunton, Virginia became the first state with two public hospitals for the mentally ill.

All of these public and semi-public institutions followed similar internal routines. They adopted a variation of the "moral treatment" system Tuke implemented at the York Retreat in England. The Friends' Asylum (1817) in Pennsylvania, the Bloomingdale Asylum (1821) in New York, and the Hartford Retreat (1821) in Connecticut, in particular, attempted to employ Tuke's methods. The process of effecting a cure began with the removal of the afflicted from his familiar surroundings. As the indefatigable Philadelphia physician Benjamin Rush advised, the "first thing to be done … is to remove the patient from his family and from the society of persons" to whom he had been accustomed. The patient would benefit from the immediate suspension of the precipitating causes of his distraction. Furthermore, once institutionalized, the patient came under the "complete government" of the attending physicians and received "remedies with ease, certainty and success." Moral treatment entailed exposure of the patients to a world of precise schedules, regular work routines, systematic procedures, and disciplined habits. In the end, it was hoped, such treatment would reduce psychological stress and promote mental health.

American asylums, however, even more than their European counterparts, continued to rely on medical therapeutics. American physicians held on longer to the theory that insanity was a somatic disease, that it was due to abnormalities or lesions in the brain. Reformers insisted that moral treatment be used in conjunction with physical prescriptions. Rush's influential *Medical Inquiries and Observations upon the Diseases of the Mind* (1812), the first serious American contribution to the study of mental illness, recapitulated many of the postulates of moral treatment. But Rush also prescribed copious bleeding ("from 20 to 40 ounces of blood may be taken at once") along with daily purges ("so as to excite an artificial diarrhea"), emetics (to "assist purges in exciting the alimentary canal"), and blistering (so that diseases "intrenched … in the brain" may be "dislodged"). Rush's "tranquilizer," consisting of a sturdy chair with straps that kept a patient seated upright and immobile, was ideal for treatment involving the "application of cold water and ice to the head, and warm water to the feet." Tuke's vision of institutions where "everything is done to make the patients as comfortable as they can be" existed in an uneasy alliance with more heroic remedies in the asylums of the early republic. Nevertheless, the idea that insanity was a disease best treated in an expertly managed environment was part of the conventional wisdom of reform by the early decades of the nineteenth century.

3 Crime

Crime, like poverty and insanity, was part of the fabric of colonial society. How did the Revolution affect this social problem? In order to answer this question we must differentiate between the incidence of crime itself and society's perceptions of criminal activity. The former deals with changes in crime rates over an extended period; the latter focuses on the impact of Independence on Americans' understanding of the obligations they were under in dealing with crime.

The calculation of crime rates is fraught with problems. Historians are limited by the sources at hand, and, where criminality is concerned, the sources are primarily in the form of court records. These are often incomplete, as in the case of Virginia, where trial court records for the years 1777–88 were lost during the Civil War. Even if complete runs of court proceedings were available, however, the historian would still have to move cautiously, because such records include only the accused who had successfully been apprehended and bound over for trial. Whether officially recorded crime accurately reflects actual levels of criminality is a puzzle that cannot be fully resolved. Furthermore, differences in societal and prosecutorial priorities almost surely account for differences in the rates of certain recorded crimes. For example, studies done of Massachusetts and Richmond, Virginia, in the early national period, conclude that rape "as a significant legal phenomenon simply did not exist" before 1800. It is

unlikely that rape did not occur in these years; it is far more likely that victims did not seek redress through the court system. What happened in courts may thus have little to do with what happened in the larger society.

With these caveats in mind, historians have nevertheless traced long-range patterns in identifiable criminal behavior. Their findings suggest that, for most of the eighteenth century, crime rates remained quite stable. Because of regional variations and differences in judicial procedures, intercolonial or interstate comparisons are not very meaningful; however, within specific locales, changes over time are accounted for largely in terms of population growth. Crime rates increased as the population increased, and only occasionally, as in New York in the 1730s and 1760s, did crime rise faster than population.

Although official crime rates did not change dramatically over the course of the century, the kinds of crimes being prosecuted in some states did. In revolutionary Massachusetts, where the change is best documented, theft-related crimes replaced violations of the moral or religious order as the offenses most frequently prosecuted. Whereas, in the two decades before Independence, only about 13 percent of all prosecutions involved crimes against property, by the early decades of the nineteenth century that figure had risen to over 40 percent. Meanwhile, prosecutions for crimes of morality dropped from over 50 percent to about 7 percent. The legal historian William E. Nelson contends that this change reflects the transforming power of the American Revolution. Concern over property rights, which after all had been instrumental in the colonists' protests against the actions of King and Parliament, superseded ethical and moral concerns. Even after Independence, the revolutionary generation continued to equate protection of property with the preservation of liberty.

For Nelson, the Revolution marked a turning point, if not in overall crime rates then in the definition of crime in America. Other historians, however, have questioned the relationship between the Revolution and the transformation of criminality in

Massachusetts. First, the shift from ethical considerations to the protection of property was well underway by the mid-eighteenth century. Prosecution of sexual misconduct peaked in the early 1730s and declined thereafter. Furthermore, authorities tended increasingly to focus on cases of illegitimacy in order to settle questions of child support rather than to express moral disapproval. The trend away from a definition of crime as sin thus preceded the imperial crisis. Second, increases in crimes against property possibly reflected changes in actual behavior resulting from long-term social and economic developments. An expanding commerical economy could conceivably have fostered an increase in burglary and larceny by separating places of employment from private residences and by making transactions more impersonal and stolen property more difficult to identify. Also, migration into and out of many Massachusetts towns experiencing commercial growth undermined the old order of the community and thereby weakened the efficacy of communal oversight. Finally, by the early nineteenth century, social stratification had contributed to a heightened sense of cohesiveness among the various economic and occupational classes. One result of this development may have been the use of judicial proceedings by the propertied to bolster their control over the poor and propertyless; at any rate, the latter groups were more often charged with and convicted for crimes against property.

If the impact of the Revolution on the prosecution of theft was somewhat oblique, its effect on the punishment of crime was direct. Influenced by the writings of Cesare Beccaria and Montesquieu, the revolutionaries came to believe that they were obligated to apply the principles of the Enlightenment to criminal law in the new republic. From Montesquieu's *Spirit of the Laws*, published in 1748, they learned that "severity of punishments is fitter for despotic governments, whose principle is terror, than for … a republic, whose spring is … virtue." Indeed, because the "imagination grows accustomed" to habitual severity, harsh punishments eventually lose their ability to deter "great crime" and thus corrupt the very spirit of the republic. If severe punishments would not discourage crime, what would? Beccaria's *Essay on Crimes and Punishments* (1764) provided the answer. Certainty of punishment, not extreme harshness, was an effective deterrent. In an enlightened system of correction, every penalty must be proportioned to the offense committed and must be administered without exception.

In revolutionary America the application of these lessons is seen most clearly in the campaign to limit the use of capital punishment. William Bradford, the attorney-general of Pennsylvania, was a leader in the movement. In 1792 Bradford was distressed because he thought independent Americans were still operating under criminal codes imposed upon them by a "corrupted monarchy." The death penalty, in particular, was "an exotic plant and not the native growth of Pennsylvania," said Bradford. His fellow Pennsylvanian Benjamin Rush added that republics founded on "peaceful and benevolent" principles ought not to adhere to a system of punishment that was the "natural offspring of monarchical governments." In addition to such concerns over the propriety of the death penalty, republican reformers voiced a practical objection. Capital punishment was so contrary to humanity that juries might choose to acquit a criminal rather than to execute him. As a result, the system of punishment became unpredictable and the efficacy of all laws was undermined. Relying on variations of these arguments, late eighteenth- and early nineteenth-century reformers in Pennsylvania, New York, and Virginia successfully curtailed the number of offenses punishable by death in their respective states. And increasingly, it appears, executions elsewhere were confined to murder convictions. Nineteenth-century Massachusetts laws, for example, allowed the death penalty for six crimes, including burglary and robbery. In the 1780s, 29 felons were executed; of these, 23 were guilty of burglary or robbery while four were convicted murderers. Over the next 30 years, a total of 17 persons were executed – 11 for murder, but only one for burglary. Laws may have remained the same, but the application of the laws reflected attitudinal changes initiated by the Revolution.

In place of capital punishment, American reformers suggested incarceration. If, as William Bradford said, the death penalty was an abomination in the "bosom of a youthful republic," imprisonment was an ideal alternative. First, it could be tailored to reflect the seriousness of each offense, thus ensuring that the principles of proportionality and certainty of punishment were honored. Second, and more immediately relevant, the inmates themselves would benefit from the experience. Prisons, like poorhouses and asylums, promised reformation. Criminals, perhaps even more than the insane, stood a good chance of being cured of their disorder while incarcerated.

The revolutionaries' optimism concerning the rehabilitative powers of prisons was founded on their belief that the human mind was the seat not only of such intellectual faculties as memory and understanding, but of a "moral faculty." Relying heavily on the ideas championed by the philosophers of the Scottish Enlightenment, American reformers argued that the moral faculty regulated one's ethical posture. It followed that the moral faculties of criminals were deranged or diseased. The key to the reform impulse lay in the realization that a person's moral faculty was as responsive to physical causes as his physical being. In a properly structured institutional environment, every moral precept would be accompanied by a physical regimen. As the moral faculty healed, disorder would give way to order and vice would succumb to virtue.

Given the leadership roles assumed by Pennsylvanians such as Rush and Bradford, it is hardly surprising that the first penitentiary in the new republic was located in their state. The Walnut Street Jail, erected in 1773 and designated as a penitentiary-house by the Pennsylvania Assembly in 1789, successfully incorporated the basic principles of the reformers. In its heyday from 1790 to 1799, the Walnut Street Jail became the model for penal reform in the United States and Europe. Caleb Lownes, a Quaker merchant and an Inspector of the Jail in the 1790s, captured the spirit of its advocates when he chided those who thought prisoners

deserved only to be "perpetually tormented and punished." The prisoner, Lownes said, "is a rational being of like feelings" with ourselves. "Mild regulations, strictly enjoined," and not severity, would advance the cause of rehabilitation. The "rules of the house" thus covered a wide spectrum of daily and weekly routines. From employment to leisure-time activities, from daily diet to divine worship, the inmates of the Walnut Street Jail found their lives closely monitored. Even personal hygiene was a matter of public supervision: prisoners "shall be shaved twice a week, their hair cut once a month, change their linen once a week, and regularly wash their face and hands every morning." Prisoners who distinguished themselves by strict attention to the rules could expect "rewards"; conversely, offenders would suffer "close, solitary confinement." Within the walls of the penitentiary, isolated from outside contact and subjected to "mild, yet firm measures," the criminal would be reclaimed by civil society.

After 1799 the Walnut Street Jail fell into disrepair. Persistent problems of overcrowding quickly rendered the "rules of the house" all but meaningless. By 1835, when the institution was finally abandoned, it was no longer in the forefront of penal reform. That honor belonged to New York's Auburn state prison, established in 1819, and to Philadelphia's Eastern State Penitentiary, which opened in 1829. Still, it is important to note that the precedent and practices set by the Walnut Street Jail were reflected in the designs and operations of these latter-day institutions.

The period from the 1820s to the 1840s was, we know, characterized by a ferment for reform. Among other things, Americans began wholeheartedly to embrace the almshouse, asylum, and penitentiary as solutions to the problems afflicting the poor, the insane, and the criminally inclined in society. Although the number of such institutions constructed in these years outpaced all earlier efforts, the enthusiasm for institutional solutions was not new. Nineteenth-century reformers drew their inspiration from an earlier generation of optimistic social planners. The impact of the Revolution on the social perceptions of Americans thus had a lasting influence on the policies of the republic.

FURTHER READING

Alexander, John K.: *Render Them Submissive: Responses to Poverty in Philadelphia, 1760–1800* (Amherst, Mass.: University of Massachusetts Press, 1980).

Beattie, J. M.: *Crime and the Courts in England, 1660–1800* (Princeton, NJ: Princeton University Press, 1986).

Cray, Robert E., Jr.: *Paupers and Poor Relief in New York City and its Rural Environs, 1700–1830* (Philadelphia: Temple University Press, 1988).

Dain, Norman: *Concepts of Insanity in the United States, 1789–1865* (New Brunswick, NJ: Rutgers University Press, 1964).

Deutsch, Albert: *The Mentally Ill in America: a History of their Care and Treatment from Colonial Times* (Garden City, NY: Doubleday, Duran and Co., 1938).

Ekirch, Roger A.: *Bound for America: the Transportation of British Convicts to the Colonies, 1718–1775* (Oxford: Oxford University Press, 1987).

Greenberg, Douglas: *Crime and Law Enforcement in the Colony of New York, 1681–1776* (Ithaca, NY: Cornell University Press, 1974).

Hindus, Michael Stephen: *Prison and Plantation: Crime, Justice, and Authority in Massachusetts and South Carolina, 1767–1878* (Chapel Hill: University of North Carolina Press, 1980).

Jimenez, Mary Ann: *Changing Faces of Madness: Early American Attitudes and Treatment of the Insane* (Hanover, NH: University Press of New England, 1987).

Nash, Gary B.: *The Urban Crucible: Social Change, Political Consciousness, and the Origins of the American Revolution* (Cambridge, Mass.: Harvard University Press, 1979).

Nelson, William E.: *Americanization of the Common Law: the Impact of Legal Change on Massachusetts Society, 1760–1830* (Cambridge, Mass.: Harvard University Press, 1975).

Rothman, David J.: *The Discovery of the Asylum: Social Order and Disorder in the New Republic* (Boston: Little, Brown and Co., 1971).

Smith, Billy G.: *The "Lower Sort": Philadelphia's Laboring People, 1750–1800* (Ithaca, NY: Cornell University Press, 1990).

CHAPTER FIFTY-FIVE

The impact of the Revolution on church and state

ROBERT M. CALHOON

CHURCH–STATE relations in the American Revolution differed from state to state and region to region; at the same time, unifying forces within American religious life and more divisive tendencies implicit in American religious individualism cut across state and regional lines – paradoxically unifying the polity and attenuating the links between churches and politics. The ambiguous language of the First Amendment to the Constitution, conjoining a ban on established churches with the protection of the free exercise of religion, reflected that complex heritage. In the five southern colonies and in several New York counties, patriot regimes disestablished the Anglican Church; in Connecticut and Massachusetts they allowed the Congregational Church to retain its legal establishment; in the rest of the revolutionary states they protected freedom of conscience while largely restricting office-holding to Protestants.

1 Virginia

Although the Virginia Declaration of Rights guaranteed freedom of conscience and the legislature substantially disestablished the Anglican Church in 1776, the "Bill for Exempting Dissenters from Contributing to the Support of the Church" left open the possibility of a general assessment of taxpayers for the support of Christian instruction. Assessment bills in 1779 and 1784 would have allowed individuals to designate their own churches as the recipients of their payments and would have placed all undesignated assessments in a pool for

distribution to all Christian churches. An especially revealing document, the 1779 bill contained a cumbersome definition of a "Christian" church and stipulated that "no Person whatsoever shall speak any thing in their Religious Assemblies disrespectfully or Seditiously of the Government of this State."

Religious assessment became the central issue in the decade-long struggle over religious policy in Virginia. Led by staunch Anglicans in the aristocracy, by tidewater Presbyterians, and – for complex, murky reasons – by Patrick Henry, the pro-assessment forces believed that "a general diffusion of Christian knowledge hath a natural tendency to correct the morals of men, restrain their vices, and preserve the peace of society" (Buckley, 1977, p. 186). In opposition, Jefferson, Madison, Shenandoah Valley Presbyterians, and the state's Baptist and Methodist evangelicals contended that religious practice was private and voluntary and that any government sponsorship of religious teaching, no matter how benign or even-handed, was fraught with potential mischief.

Although enactment of religious assessment seemed assured in 1785, Madison skillfully mobilized a coalition of evangelical and rationalist opponents of state-promulgated religious teaching. His "Memorial and Remonstrance against Religious Assessments" blended religious fears of assessment with philosophical beliefs in private judgment. Sensing that public sentiment was running in his favor, Madison sought a dramatic victory by proposing defeat of assessment through the vehicle of adopting Thomas Jefferson's Statute for Religious

Freedom, drafted in 1779. When Jefferson's bill passed in December 1785 by a vote of 74 to 20, freedom of conscience and its inviolability from government influence became fundamental law in Virginia. Jefferson's statute reaffirmed the will of the people as the arbiter of issues of liberty and the extent of governmental power.

Madison saw religion and piety as useful means in the building of a functioning republican order. In the "Memorial and Remonstrance," therefore, he made philosophical arguments uphold the positive value of freedom of conscience, while pious sentiments evoked revulsion at the harm done by the public enforcement of religion. The first of 15 numbered paragraphs in the document linked the whole issue of freedom and religion to Enlightenment experience. It quoted Article XVI of the Virginia Declaration of Rights (1776) that "the duty we owe to our Creator can be directed only by reason and conviction," and then paraphrased the language of Jefferson's proposed Statute on religious Liberty by asserting that "the opinions of men, depending [as they must] only on the evidence contemplated by their own minds, cannot follow the dictates of other men" (Jefferson's bill declared that "God hath created the mind free" and "altogether insusceptible of restraint"). From these presuppositions, and probably from Locke's *Letter on Toleration*, Madison drew two conclusions: first, that "homage" to the "Creator" preceded "both in order of time and in degree of obligation ... the claims of civil society" and, second, that "religion is wholly exempt from" the "cognizance" of "civil society." A person entering into a political compact "must always do it with a reservation of his duty to the ... universal sovereign."

Madison devoted the remainder of the "Memorial and Remonstrance" to a blending of the secular and spiritual concerns. While his arguments were eclectic, the rhetoric subtly mixed evangelical fears of secular impurity with rationalist aversion to encroachments on private judgment. He argued that the power to establish Christianity as the favored recipient of public financial support – adroitly equating assessment with establishment – enabled government to establish particular sects of Christians over others and to enforce conformity, praised the "primitive" Christianity that existed before the rise of ecclesiastical establishment, and, in the same breath, incorporated Jefferson's charge that established churches "beget habits of hypocrisy and meanness." He reminded his readers that the avowed purpose of assessment was the instilling of a particular kind of self-control – "correct the morals of men, restrain their vices, and preserve the peace of society" – by denouncing the use of "religion as an engine of civil policy." In a still more pointed reference to the religious implications of assessment, he questioned whether a public official could be a "competent judge of religious truth"; no evangelical reader of the awkward, and narrowly Anglican, five-part definition of a Christian Church in the 1779 assessment bill could fail to find that formulation theologically offensive.

Equally distasteful to Baptists and Methodists was a well-meaning provision in the 1784 bill allowing sects without ministers – Mennonites and Quakers – to receive funds designated for them directly rather than through clergymen. Madison seized on this notion to illustrate the dangers of allowing legislators to make religious designations. "Are the Quakers and the Mennonists the only sects who think a compulsive support of their religions unnecessary and unwarrantable?" Madison demanded; "can their piety alone be entrusted with the care of public worship? Ought their religions to be endowed above all others with extraordinary privileges by which proselytes may be induced from all others?" Nothing of the kind was intended by the provisions of the 1784 bill, nor did Mennonite and Quaker practice involve the stealing of proselytes. Madison did not let these facts stand in the way of scoring the telling point that legislation hinging on matters of internal church polity inevitably would arouse destructive jealousies. Religion lay beyond the authority of the state, he declared, moving boldly in the direction of secular libertarianism, in the same way as did "all our fundamental rights" (Hutchinson, vol. 8, 1973, pp. 299–304).

2 The Other Southern States

In the other southern states, the disestab-
lishment of the Church of England and the
creation of some degree of public sanction
for Protestant Christianity proceeded with
less controversy than in Virginia. In South
Carolina the 1776 Provincial Congress left
Anglicanism established, and the following
year dissenters led by the Congregationalist
minister William Tennent asked for "equal
and free religious privileges" for "all
Protestants" (Curry, 1986, p. 148).

The 1778 constitution restricted office-
holding to Protestants and allowed all
churches which endorsed the existence and
public worship of one God, rewards and
punishment in an afterlife, the truth of
Christianity and the Bible, and the obligation of all citizens to bear witness to the
truth when asked by government to do so.
These provisions satisfied Tennent. South
Carolina in effect established Protestantism
but provided no public support for the
churches.

The 1776 North Carolina Constitution
restricted office-holding to those who did
not deny the "truth of the Protestant religion" nor hold "religious principles incompatible with the freedom and safety of the
state" (Calhoon, 1976, p. 69). This provision did not prevent the distinguished jurist
William Gaston, a Roman Catholic, from
accepting appointment to the state Supreme
Court in 1833 on the grounds that he did
affirm the truths of Protestant Christianity
as well as others peculiar to Catholicism,
nor did it deter the legislature from seating
Jacob Henry, a Jew, in 1809 as the representative from Carteret County.

The Georgia Constitution likewise limited office-holding to Protestants. It also
adopted language on the financial support
of religion which left open the possibility of
use of public funds, by counties, for the
support of Christian ministers, but the practice never went into effect, and the 1798
state constitution abolished it.

The Maryland Constitution of 1776
promised religious liberty to all Christians,
while declaring the worship of God, in
the manner each individual "thinks most
acceptable," a public duty. Adopting a law

authorizing religious assessment in 1784,
the legislature affirmed its power to "interpose in matters of religion as far as concerns
the general peace and welfare of the community." The following year, newly elected
anti-assessment legislators managed to
defeat a bill putting religious assessment
into effect; Marylanders, one lawmaker
observed, had begun "to taste the sweets of
religious liberty" (Curry, 1986, pp. 154–7).

3 New England

Congregationalists in Massachusetts and
Connecticut, on the other hand, had tasted
the sweets of organic community life in
which a publicly supported church in each
town upheld moral values on which the
community rested. Where Virginia leaders
of the Revolution divided into those supporting public maintenance of religion and
those opposed to it, the leadership of the
Revolution in these two states preserved an
established Congregationalist Church. The
Separate Baptists led by Isaac Backus, a
sect which had arisen during the Great
Awakening of the 1740s as a powerful evangelical rival of both New Light revivalist
Congregationalists and Old Light tradition-
alists, represented the only opposition to
the maintenance of the establishment in the
Bay Colony. The audacious demands of
some Baptists for abolition of church taxes
during the revolutionary crisis of 1774 and
the apolitical indifference of others to the
patriot cause thereafter had tainted them
with an undeserved reputation for Toryism,
weakening their public voice in the debate
over church and state in 1780.

The 1780 Massachusetts Constitution
contained two provisions on religion.
Section Two stated paradoxically that it is
the "duty" of each citizen to worship "the
SUPREME BEING," while also being free
to do so according to "the dictates of his
own conscience." Section Three reasoned
that the dependence of order and government upon the "piety, religion, and morality" of the people justified and necessitated
public support of ministers and teachers of
religion and authorized the towns to provide
such payments. Each citizen could specify

which church his own taxes should support; so long as churches conducted themselves "peaceably," no one sect could be legally subordinated to another. John Adams had misgivings about Section Three, but he reluctantly supported it as an integral part of the new constitution, with which he was generally pleased. The only notable figure to oppose Section Three, Joseph Hawley of Northampton, privately regretted the "looseness and uncertainty of language" in the document and questioned whether the unalienable freedom of man, upheld in the constitution, did not take precedence over the strategy of preserving order through moral and religious suasion. But Hawley's objections were restricted to private correspondence and anonymous newspaper essays. In 1810, Theophilus Parsons, a member of the committee which drafted Section Three, offered in a state Supreme Court decision this convoluted but intriguing explanation of the intent of the framers: "the convention acted on the ground that the moral duties are essential to the welfare of a free state"; religious liberty might conflict with the right of the state to spend public funds for socially necessary purposes, such as the support of religious education, Parsons conceded, but the "protection of persons and property," engendered by religion, helped resolve the contradiction between freedom of conscience and the maintenance of public morality (McLoughlin, 1971, pp. 603–4, 611).

Section Three not only sought to reconcile freedom of conscience with the inculcation of respect for property; it also sought to harmonize public maintenance of Congregationalist churches with sectarian equality. The final clause forbad "subordination of any one sect or denomination to another ... by law" (Curry, 1986, p. 174). Towns were free to apply public funds to the support of whichever ministry they chose; in Massachusetts the dominance of the Congregationalists invariably qualified the church for public support. Led by Isaac Backus, Massachusetts Baptists contended that religion was a matter between God and each individual and that the state had no business paying support to any ministers. Backus, it should be noted, based this claim

on grounds very different from those taken by dissenters in Virginia. He conflated religious liberty and Christian liberty; the former was freedom from human interference in belief or worship, while the latter derived from the irresistible working of the Spirit in the lives of believers. Christian liberty, as Backus understood it, required that believers obey God exclusively and that the community become open to the conversion of all. The result of this uninhibited spirituality, Backus confidently predicted, would be the creation of the Christian republic. He therefore supported Sabbath observance laws, military chaplains, and exclusion of non-Protestants from office as desirable public policies.

Connecticut, the other state with a modified establishment of Congregationalists, avoided much of this controversy by simply adopting its colonial charter to serve as a state constitution by removing references to the King. As the Reverend Judah Champion explained in 1776,

our civil liberties ... are nearly connected with ... our religious [liberties] .... Our religious privileges are not inferior to our civil [duties] ... None may impose for doctrine the commandments of men or force others to believe with them ... But if any, under the pretense of conscience, sap the foundations of civil society, ... they are to be restrained by the civil arm. (Curry, 1986, pp. 178–9).

As in Massachusetts, Baptists in Connecticut opposed only the public payment of ministers and the humiliating requirement that members of other churches secure certificates of their financial support of their own church bodies. In several Connecticut towns the Congregationalists were a minority or were too poor to support an established church if Baptist, Quaker, or episcopal neighbors, or disaffected Congregationalists secured exemption from church taxes. In these cases the legislature repeatedly fashioned compromises, giving Congregationalists the power to tax all inhabitants who did not present exemption certificates and then in 1791 allowing dissenters to produce their own certificates rather than those issued by a dissenting minister or church official.

Colonial New Hampshire had a system of church–state relations modeled on that of Massachusetts. In towns with Presbyterian majorities, however, special laws created two tax-supported parishes in which Presbyterians alone gave certificates of tax exemption to town officials, thus signalling their status as dissenters. After Independence, the state tried to compel Baptists to support Congregationalist ministers and, when controversy erupted, granted them specific exemptions. In some cases Baptists became the majority within a town, whereupon they simply exempted themselves. In New London a Baptist minister accepted the position as the town's paid clergyman, but under pressure from Isaac Backus relinquished it on the ground that it was "bondage to be supported by tax and compulsion" (Curry, 1986, p. 187).

Vermont's 1777 constitution required office-holders to be Protestants who believed in God and in the divine inspiration of the Old and New Testaments, and it allowed towns to support "ministers of the gospel" on petition of seven inhabitants and poll of two-thirds of the voters. The legislators assumed that most such publicly supported clergy would be Congregationalists, but significantly did not preclude other denominations. In 1785 Vermont required "every sect or denomination … to keep up some form of religious worship," implicitly omitting any compulsory payment of support from the populace (Curry, 1986, pp. 188–9).

In both New Hampshire and Vermont, the Congregationalist establishment quietly atrophied after 1790. Baptists in Connecticut suffered under the hegemony of the Congregationalist-dominated Federalist Party throughout the early national period, but when the party began to disintegrate after 1816 the Baptists became valuable members of the Republican coalition which came to power in 1817 and the following year revised the state's 1776 constitution (which was essentially the 1661 colonial charter with references to the King expunged). "The course which the Baptists and Methodists are pursuing" in the campaign for a new constitution, one Federalist observed, "is indeed extraordinary. The ground taken by these sectaries [i.e., adamant

demands for complete separation of church and state] seems to preclude every argument that might be adduced in support of the principle on which our laws are founded" (McLoughlin, 1971, p. 1050). "The Federalists never did understand the practice of pressure politics by interest groups," Williams G. McLoughlin succinctly observed.

In Massachusetts as well, declining Federalist and ascendant Republican Party strength prepared the way for the overthrow of Congregationalist privileges, but here partisan conflict became intertwined with the split among Congregationalists over the doctrine of the Trinity and the validity of Unitarian rationalism. In town after town Unitarian majorities took over Congregationalist churches and with them public tax support. In the Dedham Case (1812–21), the courts upheld the power of a majority of church members over that of the ruling deacons to control church property and appoint ministers. During the 1820s, Massachusetts evangelicals stood aloof from the Republicans, but the latter shrewdly played on evangelical fears that "religion enforced by law leads to craft, fraud, deceit, treachery, hypocrisy, and every other evil thing" (McLoughlin, 1971, p. 1204) to gain control of the legislature in 1823. In 1824 the Republicans enacted a law simplifying the creation of self-incorporated religious bodies and easing requirement for dissenters seeking exemption from church taxes. When this law did nothing to help Trinitarian Congregationalists regain control of established churches under Unitarian control, the Trinitarian Congregationalists became disenchanted with the whole idea of public support for religion – paving the way for abolition of such support altogether in 1833.

4 New York, Pennsylvania, and Rhode Island

New York, Pennsylvania, and Rhode Island were far more pluralistic than the Anglican-dissenter South or the Congregationalist-Baptist New England. Following Roger William's insistence on the inviolability of conscience, Rhode Island proscribed any public subsidy for churches, though the colony kept such a low profile in matters of church and state that few people in colonial America knew of this practice, and Williams himself slipped into obscurity after his death until rediscovered by Isaac Backus in the 1740s. Colonial Rhode Island did bar Jews from office-holding and during the Seven Years' War required Roman Catholics to take an oath of allegiance. After Independence Rhode Island was the only state other than Virginia to abolish all religious discrimination. During the colonial period, New York established tax support for Protestant churches in four southern counties without specifying the Anglican Church as the intended recipient of public support. In practice and public perception, this arrangement did establish the Church of England, a privilege fortified when in 1753 King's College – over bitter Presbyterian opposition – was created under modified Anglican control. In 1777 the legislature, without admitting that an establishment of religion had ever existed in New York, abolished any presumed claim to public support of episcopal churches, though it did impose a test oath on Catholics.

Pennsylvania developed the most complex and modern form of church–state relations. Quakers and German Pietists shared a total aversion to state interference in religion, and the unique positions of these two persuasions effectively separated church and state. However, German Reformed and Lutheran disputes over church property originally serving both German-speaking groups involved civil courts in colonial Pennsylvania in religious disputes:

Religious liberty divorced theological conflicts from the state. The colony allowed trustees of religious groups to hold property; if there were schisms or dissension within a church, the courts decided the matter based upon property law, not ecclesiastical precedent. The state would not try to determine whether either of two feuding religious groups was legitimately entitled to claim the property as being truly Presbyterian, Baptist, Lutheran, or Reformed. (Frost, 1988, p. 330)

When the Ephrata Community (a Dunker enclave) practiced celibacy, some husbands of women who deserted their families to join the community sued for alienation of affections; Pennsylvania colonial courts refused to accept jurisdiction in the matter. The Moravian community at Bethlehem became a self-governing entity in which communal property-owning stood outside of provincial law – a situation the Moravians and the colonial government secured by allowing Moravians to hold the key offices of justice of the peace and representative to the Assembly. After the War for Independence the Pennsylvania Quakers reconsidered their relationship to the political and social order, they abandoned their old stance as the one true church, and accepted the status of a Protestant denomination. The 1776 Pennsylvania Constitution required legislators to affirm their belief in God and in the truth of the Old and New Testaments. Early legislation in the Commonwealth of Pennsylvania made blasphemy, profanity, drunkenness, and theater-going illegal. At the request of Jews, legislators' adherence to the New Testament was dropped. The 1790 constitution – which scrapped the radical democratic features of the 1776 document – followed on professedly moral grounds the earlier instrument on blasphemy and drunkenness and allowed non-discriminatory public support of religion.

5 The First Amendment to the Constitution

The intention of the religious freedom provisions of the First Amendment must be determined from the terms of the amendment itself, the brief and somewhat cryptic debate in the First Congress, the context of church–state relations during the 1780s, and cross-currents of Federalist and Anti-Federalist thought which led to the adoption of a Bill of Rights. Stung by Anti-Federalist attacks over the absence of libertarian guarantees in the Constitution, Madison duly asked the House of Representatives to consider a bill of rights. In May 1789 he proposed that "the civil rights of none shall be abridged on account of religious belief or worship, nor shall any national religion be established, nor shall the full and equal rights of conscience be in any manner, or on any pretext, infringed" (Curry, 1986,

p. 199). In August the House considered the issue. Elbridge Gerry wanted to proscribe imposition of "religious doctrines" rather than beliefs or worship – a reflection of historic Puritan aversion to Anglicanism. Roger Sherman thought the amendment unnecessary because Congress had no jurisdiction over religion. Daniel Carroll of Maryland preferred a simple ban on imposed articles of faith lest a more extensive guarantee arouse religious divisions within American society, to which Madison replied that the "necessary and proper" clause might well be interpreted as giving Congress a pretext to legislate on matters of religion. Both Peter Sylvester of New York and Benjamin Huntington of Connecticut feared the amendment would endanger religion itself, Sylvester referring darkly to the possible abolishing of religion and Huntington pointing more to the licentiousness he perceived existing in Rhode Island, where no public support of churches existed. Samuel Livermore of New Hampshire preferred a simple ban on laws "touching on religion or infringing the right of conscience" (Curry, 1986, p. 201). Ranging from religious support for civic virtue to rationalist libertarianism, these comments were representative of views on church and state in the period.

After two days of Select Committee discussion of the amendment, a new proposal emerged, reflecting Madison's views: "no state shall infringe the equal rights of conscience." Thomas Tucker of South Carolina objected prophetically that the probable target of the amendment would be states hauled into court by aggrieved sects, and Madison assured him that he did not want to disrupt the existing balance between state autonomy and the federal judiciary. Ironically, Tucker did not pursue the matter. On August 21 Fisher Ames of Massachusetts suggested that "Congress shall make no law establishing religion, or to prevent the free exercise thereof, or to infringe the rights of conscience." The Senate version changed this language to a prohibition on laws "establishing articles of faith or a mode of worship, or prohibiting the free exercise of religion." On September 25 the House proposed and the Senate accepted what became the terms of the First Amendment: "Congress shall make no law respecting the establishment of religion or prohibiting the free exercise thereof" (Curry, 1986, pp. 206–7).

The legislative record of these debates and votes is very sparse, but one crucial piece of evidence exists in the Senate journal. During a closed debate in that body, a proposal to allow non-discriminatory public support for religion was initially approved and then withdrawn, probably in anticipation of Madison's objections in the House. Here was a distinct echo of the assessment controversy in Virginia; the Senate retreat on this key point strongly supports the position taken by the Supreme Court in *Everson vs. New Jersey* (1947), which maintained in matters of public education a formal barrier between church and state.

FURTHER READING

Buckley, Thomas E.: *Church and State in Revolutionary Virginia, 1776–1787* (Charlottesville: University of Virginia Press, 1977).

Calhoon, Robert M.: *Religion and the American Revolution in North Carolina* (Raleigh: North Carolina Division of Archives and History, 1976).

Clinton, Robert Lowry: *God and Man in the Law: The Foundations of Anglo-American Constitutionalism* (Lawrence: University Press of Kansas, 1997).

Curry, Thomas J.: *The First Freedoms: Church and State in America to the Passage of the First Amendment* (New York: Oxford University Press, 1986).

Dreisbach, Daniel L. ed.: *Religion and Politics in the Early Republic: Jasper Adams and the Church-State Debate* (Lexington: University Press of Kentucky, 1996).

——: "'Sowing Useful Truths and Principles': The Danbury Baptists, Thomas Jefferson, and the 'Wall of Separation,'" *Journal of Church and State*, 39 (1997), 455–501.

Frost, J. William: "Pennsylvania Institutes Religious Liberty, 1682–1860," *Pennsylvania Magazine of History and Biography*, 110 (1988), 327–47.

Hutchinson, William T. et al. (eds.): *The Papers of James Madison* (Chicago: University of Chicago Press, 1962–).

McClellan, James: *Joseph Story and the American Constitution: A Study in Political and Legal Thought* (Norman: University of Oklahoma Press, 1971).

McLoughlin, William G.: *New England Dissent, 1630–1833: the Baptists and the Separation of Church and State* (Cambridge, Mass.: Harvard University Press, 1971).

Pole, J. R.: *The Pursuit of Equality in American History* (Berkeley: University of California Press, 1978).

West, John G. Jr.: *The Politics of Revelation and Reason: Religion and Civic Life in the New Nation* (Lawrence: University Press of Kansas, 1996).

Wilson, John F. (ed.): *Church and State in America: a Bibliographical Guide: the Colonial and Early National Periods* (Westport, Conn.: Greenwood Press, 1986).

Zuckert, Catherine: "Not by Preaching: Tocqueville on the Role of Religion in American Democracy," *Review of Politics*, 43 (1981), 259–80.

CHAPTER FIFTY-SIX

Law: continuity and reform

J. R. POLE

WHEN the Continental Congress severed the American connection with Great Britain, the individual states, claiming to have succeeded to British sovereignty, assumed the full power to make domestic laws for America. This meant that there were now fourteen law-making authorities (including the Congress, when it adopted general interstate measures); but the laws passed by the former colonial assemblies differed significantly among themselves. Since English common law had been adopted by all the colonies, the new state legislatures had to decide not only what new laws to make, but what to retain of the common law heritage. Parliament also had enacted statutes affecting the colonies (some of these had precipitated the colonial revolt); and assembly laws had always been subject to disallowance by the British privy council in the name of the crown if they infringed the royal prerogative or were held to be contrary to British imperial policy. In fact the crown recognized most colonial legislation as meeting local interests; but these factors reminded the colonists that they had never been their own legal masters. Now that the old colonies were new states, it would have been both impractical and unnecessary to abolish all existing laws that were stamped with British authority; such a policy would have caused both moral and legal chaos; it would also have been pointless, since the colonies along with their British contemporaries revered the common law as the chief safeguard of their liberties and property.

Any attempt to assess the consequences of the American Revolution on the internal development of American law must therefore begin with the existing state of the law, including both English law in the colonies and domestic colonial legislation. And this assessment must include the extent to which the colonies had absorbed or adapted the common law as expounded in English reports. Here we encounter an important difference between mother county and colonies, or center and periphery. For many centuries, much English law had been made not by Parliament but by the courts. Decisions had hardened into rules, which had gradually hardened into a concept of *precedent*. When the central English courts of Westminster encountered difficulties for which the law recorded in their books did not provide, they interpreted the law by inventing doctrines or maxims which accorded with common law principles. These came to be known as legal fictions, which exactly described them. Colonial courts (whose records were not printed) lacked either the machinery or the authority to be so high-handed, had an inadequate body of case law to build on, had little locally established concept of precedent, and often cited English decisions as authority for their own. Most positive colonial law-making, on the other hand, was done by the assemblies. Since local conditions varied greatly there could be no uniform policy or pattern.

One of the internal differences with the most lasting social consequences was in the laws governing inheritance. New England favoured partible inheritance – sharing landed property equally among sons; colonies dominated by great estates such as

New York, Virginia, and South Carolina tended to consolidate these holdings by the rule of primogeniture, everything (if, as often happened, the owner left no will) going to the eldest son. Moreover, estates were often entailed, an ancient legal device by which they could not be broken up by any one owner, but were handed down from generation to generation; although Virginia planters and New York manorial lords sometimes promoted private bills to dock entails on their estates, the long-term effect, especially in Virginia, consolidated vast properties in the hands of a few families. Entail offended the new republican spirit – and was often a nuisance to landowners. In 1776, Jefferson introduced legislation in Virginia to abolish entails. But despite revolutionary rhetoric, it took longer to abolish primogeniture, which, over prolonged opposition, was accomplished in 1785. In other states where these relics of English and feudal law survived, they crumbled more easily. But there were other political and social differences that resulted from long-standing differences among the colonial regions.

The most momentous of these differences, both from Britain and among the colonies, was legislation to establish racial slavery. Vestiges of slavery survived in Britain, possibly increasing in the eighteenth century with the growth of slave labour on the plantations in the Caribbean islands and continental colonies. But an important English ruling in 1706 (*Smith v. Gould*) declared that being an African could not be proof of being a slave, because the common law had no knowledge of (and so could not enforce distinctions based on) differences among men (the word *race* had not acquired its present sense). As a general principle, ever since the Middle Ages, the common law had preferred freedom to slavery or villeinage, and had tended to mitigate the latter condition. In the colonies, where African slaves were being imported in ever increasing numbers, legal principles were re-made to conform to the needs of a society where race virtually determined slave status. Before the end of the seventeenth century, Virginia and Maryland had legislated to establish slavery as an attribute of

race, determined by the status of the mother, as well as outlawing interracial sexual relations. Indentured servitude by contrast was always for a fixed term, not above seven years. In 1705, the Virginia assembly legislated to treat slaves as real property like land; in 1727, enlarging on this, to make it possible to entail slave property. The legal status of entailed slaves was, however, highly problematic, and in 1768, after going up to the privy council without being finally resolved, the issue came before the general (or appeal) court of the province. There the statute was strictly construed to confine the "real estate" character of slaves to descent and dower. The court (led by Chancellor George Wythe, the young Jefferson's law teacher) was not willing to enlarge legal fictions in the interests of slavery. The whole complicated story illustrated the problems that inevitably followed from the "Americanization" of the common law to accommodate slavery. Meanwhile in Britain a small but valuable quantity of slave property was employed in domestic service in aristocratic households, and there was a slave market in Liverpool; but British law was moving slowly in the opposite direction. When challenged before Lord Chief Justice Mansfield in the famous case of *Somerset v. Stuart* (1772) slavery could not be sustained in the absence of positive law; this and subsequent cases eroded its legal foundations, and slavery died out – as a result of judicial law-making. The immense business interests involved in the African slave trade fought off abolition until Parliament acted in 1807; in the United States following a provision of the Constitution, Congress abolished the importation of slaves in 1808. This can be considered a long-term outcome of the Revolution. But not a necessary outcome. The Revolution was waged to protect the right of free men to control their property, and slaves were property. But the states lying above the Mason-Dixon line were less dependent on slave labour than those to the south; they were more willing to be moved by the idea that the right to liberty, another tenet of the Revolution, was universal – as the Declaration of Independence claimed. Pennsylvania – powerfully influenced by the

Quakers, and citing the universalist philosophy of the Revolution – led the way
by enacting legislation for gradual – very
gradual – emancipation in 1780; in
Massachusetts the courts, in a series of cases
beginning in 1781, held slavery to be
incompatible with the meaning of the
Declaration of Rights in the state constitution of 1780. By 1804 all the northern
states had introduced measures of gradual
emancipation; slavery was excluded from
the coming settlements in the vast Ohio
Valley under provisions of the congressionally enacted Northwest Ordinance of 1787.

Thus, although the Revolution joined the
moral impulse for enacting the principles
of liberty with the political opportunity,
with the result that the northern territories grew as both free from slavery and – an
important corollary – were generally settled
by a white population, these developments
also revealed the ominous signs of a deepening rift between north and south. The
emancipations – many of them voluntary –
of the revolutionary era also brought into
existence a virtual under-class of free
Americans of African descent – in common
usage, free Negroes. After about 1790, free
Negroes were subjected, by law, to economic and residential restraints; in racial
matters, American law continued its unchallenged adaptation to American conditions.

One of the points made by John
Dickinson in his widely read *Letters from a
Farmer in Pennsylvania* (1767–8) – and he
was really much more a lawyer than a
farmer – was the need for clarification of the
extent of the common law's validity in
the colonies. But independence confronted
the law-makers with new and complex
problems; the common law was English
law, but it had entered into the fabric of
their institutions, it was also *their* law, and it
protected the rights they were defending.

The Continental Congress in September,
1774, proclaimed the colonies' equal right
to the common law. British measures such
as the creation of an admiralty court to sit –
without juries – in Halifax, Nova Scotia,
and the purported intention to convey
colonists accused of treason for trial in
England, struck at common law rights.
Americans, however, continued to cling to

the protection of the common law; as late as
1788, anti-federalists such as Patrick Henry
attacked the proposed Constitution on the
ground that it would supersede the common law while offering American citizens
no equivalent safeguard. Moreover, a high
proportion of the leading colonial spokesmen were lawyers themselves; they had
a kind of double standard as representative leaders of public opinion, who also
claimed the qualification of their own elite
professional status; this status depended
on highly specialized training in the massive and often obscure tomes of ancient
English authors – Fortescue, Littleton,
Coke, Bacon, Hale, and many others –
culminating in William Blackstone's recent
four-volume *Commentaries on the Laws of
England* (1765–69). Blackstone was the
first Vinerian Professor of English Law at
the University of Oxford. To these were
added the handbooks for the use of justices
of the peace, notably Michael Dalton's seventeenth century *Country Justice* and in
1736 a Virginia product, George Webb's
Justice of the Peace, which told county courts
about forms of writs, conditions of contracts, and legal procedures; meanwhile the
English reports were a continuing source of
legal education.

The policy adopted by state legislatures
was to allow British statutes applying to the
colonies to remain in force until repealed
by the state, and to terminate English judicial authority at 1776. In fact, however,
American lawyers and judges continued
to read the English reports, and the sense
of ultimate authority emanating from
Westminster proved hard to shake off; by
the early nineteenth century, this elite status
and the common law tradition created acute
tensions within American society.

The legal status of women in the colonies
was governed by common law rules which
subordinated them to men. A single woman
controlled her own property; but on marriage, her personality was considered to be
merged with her husband's, and her property was merged into his. On her husband's
death, a woman was normally entitled to
dower rights of one third of her husband's
estate. The appearance of Blackstone's *Commentaries* had, for a legal text, dramatic

impact and lasting influence. One of its effects was to reinforce the subordination of the *feme couverte* – an expression for a married woman left over from the French which had once been the official language of English law. Blackstone confirmed that the law considered husband and wife to be one person, "and that one is the husband." He also considered that this gave wives special protection and claimed that women were the "favourites" of the law. In one sense this was true: the doctrine made husbands accountable for their wives' debts. Colonial newspapers frequently carried announcements by deserted husbands disclaiming all responsibility for debts contracted by runaway wives. (Whether these disclaimers were ever tested in court is not known.) In England, women – many of them married but often separated – were involved in numerous business activities, and Lord Mansfield, who presided over the King's Bench from 1756 to 1788, did much to adapt the common law to their needs – also protecting their husbands. Similar reforms did not follow in the wake of revolution in America, but had to await the next century. Women took many active roles in the military, economic and social upheaval of the Revolution. But the political independence of the states left women's legal status largely unchanged either for better or worse; in fact, political independence now had the effect of *shielding* the American variants of common law from the influence of English developments.

Equality before the law was a cardinal republican (and Enlightenment) principle, but in certain respects the law maintained gradations of social status. Relations between masters and servants – a term that took in all employees – took their origin in the English Statute of Artificers of 1563; when American artisans were able to improve their economic standing it was a result of leverage through labour shortages rather than law reform. As late as the Jackson period, a mechanics' lien law, to give artisans a claim for compensation for work partly completed, was a major demand of workingmen's parties. Master-and-servant principles made it a more serious crime for a worker to strike his master

than for the master to strike his servant. They also made a master responsible for damages through his servant's negligence. These principles did not change with the Revolution. But an employer who struck an American servant would be likely to lose his service. American "servants" soon renounced that designation, to be called "help."

Although American society was heavily agricultural, its development and increasing wealth were spurred by an ever-increasing external and internal trade. From the legal point of view, this made it necessary to be able to recover debts and enforce contracts. English contract law had matured before the foundation of the colonies. American courts took over the rule that "parol," i.e. verbal contracts were valid in law, which covered the great majority of agreements struck between farmers and merchants. Colonial courts also appear to have accepted the "will" theory of contract, which meant that the court would try to ascertain and enforce the mutual intention of the parties, even though they might not have been recorded according to strict legal rules. Colonial courts no less than English ones had to assure themselves that the bargain was fair – that there was no deceit, intimidation, or concealment of relevant information; on the other hand, neither common law no chancery courts would go out of their way to bend legal precepts in the interests of parties who had been foolishly negligent. They had no doctrine of *caveat emptor* ("let the buyer beware") but they did expect persons with adult wills to look after their own interests. None of this was changed by the Revolution because none of it needed to be changed. The spread of long-distance transactions, which required an increasing use of formal instruments and observance of rules, introduced no new legal principles. But the violent fluctuations in currency values following Independence often seemed to creditors and holders of one or another form of government certificates to be a violation of faith. The new Constitution contained a clause prohibiting the states from infringing the obligations of contract, which was defended by James Madison, writing as Publius in *The Federalist* (no. 44) with a specific allusion to these currency debasements. The framers of the Constitution deliberately entrenched contract and the rights of property as *constitutional* principles – from which Congress, however, was exempt. If this development was only a remote result of independence from Britain, it was a result – perhaps the culmination – of the Revolution itself.

The protection of property rights did not extend to the estates of loyalists, which were seized on a large scale as a forfeit for treason. But these measures did not introduce any modification of the overriding principle of the sanctity of private property. The Bill of Rights duly affirmed in the Fifth Amendment that "takings," or appropriations required by government in the public interest (which was a borrowing from royal prerogative) were to be permitted only with fair compensation. And in one respect property rights were reinforced by the provision in the Constitution itself (Article 3, section 3) that conviction for treason was not to cause forfeiture of the rights of heirs. Punishment fell on the individual, not the "blood" – i.e. the family; this was certainly symbolic of the transition from feudal to republican ideas of justice.

Certain principles which had entered into common law were enshrined in the Bill of Rights. These included protection against unreasonable searches and seizures, the right against self-incrimination and the prohibition of "cruel and unusual" punishment – language taken from the English Bill of Rights of 1689. The First Amendment right to freedom of speech and press and of public assembly and the right of petition were lessons of history reinforced by the Revolution; they were culminating results of the Revolution itself.

Americans contributed to the Enlightenment as well as receiving from it. In criminal law this followed in part from the theories of the Italian philosopher Cesare Beccaria, whose proto-utilitarian treatise *Of Crimes and Punishments* (1763) had great influence in Europe. Beccaria taught that punishments should be appropriate to the crime, making certainty rather than severity the principle of deterrence. Americans led by example, and Virginia, under Jefferson's influence, led America. Sanguinary physical punishments such as flogging were everywhere – though not all at once – commuted to fines and imprisonment; capital punishment (at least for the free) was retained only for murder and treason. (Jefferson was afterward ashamed that they had retained the *lex talionis*, or castration for rape.) Enacted in Virginia, these reforms were everywhere – though not all at once – copied in other states. These steps necessitated the development of the prison – or "penitentiary," an American word – as an institution, and gave rise to much new thought about the aims and practice of punishment.

In law as in other respects, the American Revolution can be characterized as a revolution in opportunity. Early jurists of the Republic such as Zephaniah Swift in Connecticut and St. George Tucker in Virginia extolled the republican character of American law, Swift claiming that in Connecticut, local customs, enforced through legislation, had liberalized common law rules (particularly in favor of women) long before the Revolution. But not all opportunities led in the same direction, and "republican" principles were sometimes indistinguishable from the imperatives of economic development.

One of the most important fields, however, in which law acted as the lever of reform was that of religion, also pioneered in Virginia. The principle of freedom of religious conscience (already historic in Rhode Island) was planted anew in Virginia's revolutionary constitution, though without being clearly defined. By 1786 Madison had succeeded by adroit diplomacy and a superbly drafted pamphlet in steering Jefferson's Statute for Religious Freedom through the legislature. This statute, which prohibited any official connection with any religion, formed a prototype for the First Amendment, which forbade Congress to impose any form of religious establishment – while leaving individual states free to do so. This was the basis of Jefferson's famous, if hyperbolic, "wall of separation" between church and state.

Other essays in this volume deal with the concepts of the rule of law and sovereignty. Here it will suffice to say that the severance from Britain and from monarchy was undertaken in the name of the sovereignty of the people. This was an extremely vague notion, capable of all sorts of interpretation, manipulation and abuse; but joined with the principle of government by consent and through representation, it did amount to a definitive repudiation of the idea that the right to rule and the obligation to obey were inherited respectively by rulers and ruled.

FURTHER READING

Baker, J. H.: *An Introduction to English Legal History* (London: Butterworth, 1994).

Cooke, Jacob E. ed.: *The Federalist* (Middletown, Conn.: Wesleyan University Press, 1961).

Hoffer, Peter Charles: *Law and People in Colonial America*, 2nd edn. (Baltimore: Johns Hopkins University Press, 1997).

Horwitz, Morton J.: *The Transformation of American Law, 1780–1860* (Cambridge, Mass.: Harvard University Press, 1977).

Kent, James: *Commentaries on American Law*, 4 vols. (New York: O. Halstead, 1826–30).

Kerber, Linda K.: *Women of the Republic: Intellect and Ideology in Revolutionary America* (Chapel Hill: University of North Carolina Press, 1980).

Lieberman, David: *The Province of Legislation Determined: Legal Thought in Eighteenth Century Britain* (Cambridge: Cambridge University Press, 1989).

Mann, Bruce H.: *Neighbors and Strangers: Law and Community in Early Connecticut* (Chapel Hill: University of North Carolina Press, 1987).

Nedelsky, Jennifer: *Private Property and the Limits of American Constitutionalism: the Madisonian Framework and its Legacy* (Chicago: University of Chicago Press, 1991).

Nelson, William E.: *Americanization of the Common Law: the Impact of Legal Change on Massachusetts Society, 1760–1830* (Cambridge, Mass.: Harvard University Press, 1975).

Reid, John Philip: *Constitutional History of the American Revolution* (Madison, Wis., and London: University of Wisconsin Press, 1993).

Roeber, A. G.: *Faithful Magistrates and Republican Lawyers: Creators of Virginia Legal Culture, 1680–1810* (Chapel Hill, University of North Carolina Press, 1981).

Salmon, Marylynn: *Women and the Law of Property in Early America* (Chapel Hill, University of North Carolina Press, 1982).

Steinfeld, Robert J.: *The Invention of Free Labor: the Employment Relation in English and American Legal Culture, 1350–1870* (Chapel Hill: University of North Carolina Press, 1991).

Stimson, Sharon: *The American Revolution in the Law* (Basingstoke: Macmillan, 1990).

Teeven, Kevin M.: *The History of the Anglo-American Law of Contract* (New York, Westport, Con., and London: Greenwood Press, 1990).

Tomlins, Christopher: *Law, Labor and Ideology in the Early American Republic* (Cambridge: Cambridge University Press, 1993).

CHAPTER FIFTY-SEVEN

Confederation: movement for a stronger union

MARK D. KAPLANOFF

IN order to endure, any constitution – even a written one – must allow orderly development in political practice and constitutional interpretation. Initially, it appeared that the Articles of Confederation provided a framework within which a successful process of evolution might have taken place. Together, though, the end of the Revolutionary War and the boldness of some attempts at altering the Articles ended the possibility of continued development; ultimately, in order to secure the "perpetual union" which the Articles promised, it was necessary to bypass them altogether.

1 Frustration and the New Nationalism

Even before the Articles of Confederation were finally ratified, problems were apparent and various expedients necessary. (The Articles were proposed by Congress to the states on November 15, 1777 and formally ratified on March 1, 1781; *see* chapter 35). The nation had a war to fight, and Congress was increasingly hard pressed; in some areas it made significant innovations, but generally it simply muddled through. Congress gradually pushed ahead in creating a new administrative structure for the national government. In October 1777 Congress decided to create Boards of War, Treasury, and Admiralty, each with a professional administrative staff. Beginning in 1777 it established various bodies which heard admiralty appeals from state courts (which decided admiralty cases in the first instance); these were the first federal courts, and they exercised

the first federal appellate jurisdiction. Besides structural innovations, there were also developments in constitutional theory. In September 1779 the President of Congress (John Jay) argued that a complete and lasting union had been formed in 1775–6 and that the nation already had enduring powers and responsibilities. By defining treason, requiring oaths of allegiance, and issuing passports and, implicitly, by the provisions in the Articles requiring interstate comity, a doctrine of national citizenship began to emerge. Finally, as Congress struggled to secure cooperation from recalcitrant states, some congressmen (notably James Madison) began to argue that Congress under the Articles had all implied powers necessary to fulfil its obligations, including the power to coerce uncooperative states.

Yet scattered achievements should not mask the fact that Congress was unable to meet many of its responsibilities and was increasingly forced to rely on the states. Internal factionalism hindered the formulation of foreign policy. Proposals to reform national finances were stalled by political bickering, then ineffective when belatedly put into effect. Problems of supplying the army mounted. As early as the autumn of 1779, Congress began to transfer responsibility for provisioning the army to the states, but they were often unwilling or unable to respond. The result was bitter political acrimony and real hardship for the army; however, men were kept in the field, diplomacy continued, and independence remained in prospect. In the circumstances an independent United States would not have had a powerful, elaborately structured national government, but it is likely that the union would have endured and a workable system of federalism might have evolved.

But circumstances did not permit the experiment; a fiscal crisis intervened. Starting in 1776, Congress had issued paper currency and other paper obligations which circulated as money (eventually amounting to more than $200,000,000), and the value of the paper soon began to plummet (*see* chapter 48, §2). By 1778 inflation at Philadelphia reached levels in excess of 20 percent a month, and nothing – not state taxation, local price-fixing movements, or national fiscal reform – was able to stabilize the value of the paper. With a limited stock of specie and a worthless currency, the army could not purchase supplies, commerce dried up, farmers refused to market their crops, and the cities were short of food. Something had to be done.

A small group of men perceived the crisis as an opportunity and began to formulate a comprehensive program for reform and national development – Philip Schuyler, James Duane, Gouverneur Morris, and Alexander Hamilton among the most active. All were friends and professional colleagues, all sat in Congress for New York at some time, all had ties with the army's general staff, all had family links to New York's landed and mercantile elite. The two youngest, Morris and Hamilton, had the boldest vision; impatient with America's present difficulties, they looked forward to a time when the United States would become a great empire. (The word itself, used by both Morris and Hamilton, distinguished their rhetoric from the austere republicanism of most of their contemporaries.) The genesis of their proposals could be found in private memoranda and correspondence as early as 1778. By 1780 their ideas were well developed, and Hamilton presented their vision in its fullest form in his "Continentalist" letters published (somewhat after their composition) in 1781–2.

These impatient nationalists drew many problems together – currency collapse, a powerless national government, congressional indecision – and proposed a wide-ranging scheme of reform. They called for a convention of the states empowered to create a new framework of government. National government should have full sovereignty except for states' "internal police," it should have an explicit power to coerce states which did not comply with congressional requisitions, and it should also have independent sources of revenue – an impost (customs duties), a land tax, and an excise. They particularly wanted to create strong executive offices. These bold political proposals were, moreover, matched by a bold vision of political economy. First, they proposed to fund the national debt by converting all Continental paper money and paper obligations into long-term interest-bearing bonds with interest guaranteed by new national revenues. This would relieve Congress of the short-term need to repay its debts, secure the government's ability to borrow, cause public creditors to support the national government, and create a body of capital for productive investment. Additionally, a national bank (with part of its capital based on the new bonds) would facilitate treasury and commercial transactions, further increase the supply of capital, and allocate credit to the most productive sectors of the economy.

These men had a bold vision of "development economics" with the United States as an underdeveloped nation. Since the beginning of the century Britain had experimented with fiscal and economic reforms which ultimately created the machinery of a modern nation state and which promoted new capital markets, industrial development, and rapid economic growth. But it had been precisely this nexus of administrative and fiscal reform – when applied to the colonies – which had sparked the American Revolution. Most revolutionaries had contrasted American simplicity with the degeneration and corruption which they saw developing in Britain; they sought to preserve a simpler, freer way of life, freed from the encroachments of a developing nation state or advanced fiscal and credit systems. Men like Hamilton disagreed; theirs was a nationalism of a new sort. Where others saw threat, they saw potential; for them, Britain was the model and Independence merely the prelude to a great experiment in nation-building.

This "new nationalism" was too bold for its time, but it had a lasting importance. Morris and Duane hesitated about making their full program public. General Schuyler worked throughout 1780 for a convention of the states to refashion national government. In the autumn his proposals were supported by the New York legislature and a convention of delegates from New York and the New England states. But the boldness of the movement alienated even those congressmen committed to strengthening national government and, once submitted to Congress, the proposals were quietly forgotten. By early 1781 the convention movement had been superseded by Congress's own, more modest reform efforts. Yet an important beginning had been made. Over the following years suggestions of a national convention were often repeated; more importantly, visions of a great new nation became increasingly attractive amidst the commercial and political frustrations of the next few years. At America's two greatest urban and commercial centers the "new nationalists" themselves remained politically active and professionally successful, a small and committed group of men ready for other opportunities to initiate the great task of nation-building.

2   Morris, Madison, Congress, and Newburgh

During the fall and winter of 1780–1, Congress presented a threefold plan of reform. In September, it requested states with extensive unsettled territories in the West to cede part of their lands to the nation. On February 3, 1781 it proposed an amendment to the Articles empowering the national government to levy an impost of 5 percent on imported goods. Four days later it created three executive departments, Finance, War, and Marine (a Department of Foreign Affairs had been established a month earlier), each under the control of a single officer. Together, these developments were limited efforts to address the familiar problems of finance and administration, not a fundamental attempt to reshape national government. Indeed Congress shied away from more sweeping reforms, particularly on the crucial question of nation–state

relations. Several congressional committees addressed broad questions of amending the Articles of Confederation. The most detailed report (August 22, 1781) proposed seven additional articles changing regulations about congressional quorums and voting and granting Congress powers to admit new states, to levy taxes, and to coerce states which did not comply with congressional requisitions. The report was forgotten after cursory discussion. The proposal most often mooted – some sort of coercive power over uncooperative states – was never formally voted upon. Even those members committed to strengthening national government realized that Congress's standing was not sufficient to win approval for such a fundamental addition to congressional authority.

Within the national government the initiative passed to the newly appointed Superintendent of Finance, Robert Morris. Not until Franklin Roosevelt would an American chief executive assume office at a time of such financial crisis and public paralysis, and, as with Roosevelt, Morris's personality and personal proposals defined the terms of national political debate once he was in office. But in two important ways Morris's situation differed from that of Roosevelt. Firstly, Roosevelt devoted his career to politics; Morris was a merchant (in twentieth-century terms, a broker, investor, and arbitrageur), and he had a merchant's disdain for politics and politicians. Secondly, Morris did not command an organized political party, nor did he have the means to shape mass public opinion.

Morris's program provoked immediate and enduring controversy. Did he intend to go as far as the younger "new nationalists" (two of whom, Gouverneur Morris and Alexander Hamilton, were among his closest associates)? Morris himself never set out his ideals of constitutional development at any length. Contemporary critics accused him of seeking to establish an aristocratic regime based on favoritism and corruption. Historians have charged that he sought to create a strong nation state, dominated by conservative capitalists, and supportive of their interests. More recently, though, others have argued that Morris was hesitant about constitutional change and merely seeking a few limited new powers for national government. (For this point of view, with citations to earlier work on the other side, see Rakove, 1979, 298–307.) Whatever the constitutional implications, the specific economic proposals of the Morris program were enough to elicit deep opposition. He sought to balance national government's current income and expenditure, to secure new revenues for Congress, to consolidate all Congress's past financial obligations into a funded national debt, and to establish a national bank. It was a program designed not merely to win the war but to establish the basis of long-term economic development; however, only a handful of Americans at the time saw anything but threat in the adoption of such a British-style system of political economy.

Even Congress, where the defects of national government were most keenly felt, refused to accept much of Morris's program; Congress readily approved administrative reform, cost-cutting, and foreign subsidies but shied away from new and long-lasting commitments. In August 1781 Morris proposed new federal taxes – a land tax, a poll tax, and an excise; Congress never acted on the proposals. In February 1782 Morris made his first formal proposal to fund the Continental debt, a proposal repeated and developed in his detailed report on public credit on July 27, 1782. Even though French subsidies were reduced after the victory at Yorktown (October 19, 1781) and the states showed decreasing inclination to comply with congressional demands, Congress disregarded Morris's proposals and continued to pass requisitions vainly hoping to meet current obligations while waiting for approval of the impost of 1781.

Ever impatient of politics and politicians, Morris began to recruit support from pressure groups outside Congress. The first to which he turned was the Philadelphia financial community. Arguing that it would be invidious to pay some creditors and not others, Morris proposed in June 1782 that interest payments be suspended on most of the publicly held Continental debt. Meanwhile, he cooperated with a Philadelphia committee of public creditors which lobbied for new national revenues in order to fund

the Continental debt. Congress continued to wait. In November, however, the Rhode Island legislature refused to ratify the impost proposal on the grounds that it threatened the principles of the Articles of Confederation. A congressional delegation set out in December to urge the state to change its mind but turned back when news arrived that Virginia had rescinded its earlier ratification. Meanwhile, the states continued to evade congressional requisitions, interest payments were suspended, and the Philadelphia creditors now sought aid from their state. Despite congressional protests that the state was impinging upon national authority, Pennsylvania in December decided to service that part of the national debt owed to its citizens. Morris's own program had been rejected, his efforts had provoked a backlash which killed the earlier impost proposal, and his erstwhile allies now proposed the transfer of a national responsibility to the states.

Thereupon Morris turned to a second, more threatening interest group – the army. A peace treaty had not yet been concluded, the British still occupied several Atlantic ports (including New York City), and a large Continental force remained encamped at Newburgh, New York. Since 1781, moreover, Morris had suspended army pay (while continuing to pay administration officials), blaming the states' failure to meet congressional requisitions. In December 1782 a small group of officers petitioned Congress for immediate relief, stating that Congress could expect "at least a mutiny" if no action was taken.

Throughout the winter, the atmosphere of crisis increased. Congress consulted Morris, who replied that the army's demands could not be met without granting the government his recommended new powers of taxation. He also offered his resignation and began correspondence with dissatisfied officers at Newburgh. There were further protests at the camp and public threats of recourse to force. Fortunately, by mid-March two Virginians intervened. At a dramatic meeting at Newburgh on March 15, 1783 George Washington, the army's Commander-in-Chief, outfaced the hotheads who were threatening mutiny. Meanwhile, in Congress, James Madison had begun to fashion acceptable compromise proposals for national finance.

Was there a real threat of a coup? Certainly many had reason to play up the threat of mutiny. Afterwards there was persistent suspicion against some of the young officers and some of Morris's younger associates (particularly Gouverneur Morris), although Robert Morris himself generally escaped blame. It will probably never be possible to tell how far things might have gone; it is not the custom for people who dabble in treason to keep detailed records. Military unrest does have a way of getting out of hand, and democratic traditions – indeed any traditions – had not become well established in national politics. Fortunately, as things turned out, Newburgh helped to shape tradition, by defining lasting limits on military involvement in American politics.

Appropriately the architect of Congress's final response to the crisis of 1783 was James Madison – the nationalist in Congress with the greatest concern for constitutional propriety. Madison was a nationalist in the sense that he wanted to strengthen the national government and its authority, but he had different experiences, temperament, and ideals from the Morrisite nationalists. From his arrival in Congress in 1780, Madison worried that national government did not have sufficient powers, but he also fretted about the precise definition of the powers it had. During 1780 and 1781 he advocated an amendment to the Articles to give Congress coercive powers over states which failed to meet congressional directives, and he argued that Congress had implied powers under the Articles in order to fulfil the broad purposes of the Confederation. Later, he served on important committees which considered fiscal affairs and generally advocated measures proposed by Robert Morris, but there were always differences between Madison and the Morris group. Madison always saw the profits from the disposal of western lands as a potentially important financial asset for Congress. (Morris doubted that much money could readily be secured this way.) Madison questioned both the wisdom and constitutional propriety of chartering a bank and disliked plans for a long-term funded public debt. The Morrisites hoped

to use fiscal policy to promote new forms of economic growth and the development of a powerful nation. Madison sought to confine national government to its appropriate limits, to limit advanced economic development, and to preserve an egalitarian, agrarian society.

In late February 1783 Madison began to work out a compromise. He proposed a three-part program: there was to be a revised and limited impost (lasting only 25 years, with the states responsible for collection). New taxes were to be enacted by the states dedicated to servicing the national debt. Finally, the method of allocating national expenses between the states was to be changed from the existing, unworkable scheme based on land values to a system based simply on population (with five slaves being counted as equivalent to three free men). After much debate and minor amendment the proposals were approved by Congress on April 18, 1783 and sent to the states. Significantly, Morris's strongest supporter in Congress, Alexander Hamilton, opposed the package on grounds that it did not go far enough.

The congressional program of April 1783 was the last attempt at comprehensive reform of government under the Articles of Confederation. After three years' debate it looked as if a workable compromise had been reached, yet the proposals themselves indicated how the ambit of possible reform had narrowed. Although the problems of national government had intensified, the final proposals were much less than Morris had advocated, less even than those considered by Congress before Morris had taken office. Since then a well-articulated opposition had arisen to increased central power, and Congress rightly realized that any proposal to strengthen national government would be met with suspicion. The heritage of Robert Morris's administration was an ambivalent one. He had succeeded in financing America's final military effort, and in the long run his efforts foreshadowed the Hamiltonian program of the 1790s, so important in setting up the new government under a new constitution. In its immediate aftermath, however, Morris's administration acted as an inoculation; it inspired a vigorous and successful opposition to Congress's efforts to reform government under the Articles of Confederation.

3   Congress in Peace and Difficulty

After 1783 the momentum of nationalism dissipated; Congress's problems did not. Morris finally left office in November 1784, and the most active nationalists had retired from Congress before that. The states responded slowly to the amendments to the Articles proposed in 1783, but by 1786 it became clear that the amendments had failed. Meanwhile, Congress had to grapple with familiar financial difficulties and also to confront new problems about the West and peacetime diplomacy. Only in the West was significant progress made, but even there policy was not properly implemented because of lack of resources. The men who took over the leadership of Congress after the spring of 1783 had an ideological commitment to maintaining the strict limits on government established under the Articles of Confederation. Successive difficulties persuaded even them that national government needed strengthening; by 1787 they spoke of the need for greater power in almost Morrisite terms, but they proposed nothing concrete. The standing of Congress had fallen so low that it could not even propose reforms necessary for its own preservation.

The West, the area of Congress's greatest conceptual achievement in these years, was also the source of immense practical frustration. As early as 1780 negotiations had begun between Congress and Virginia (the state with the largest claims to unoccupied lands in the West) about ceding an area in the West to Congress. Squabbling over terms delayed the final cession until March 1, 1784, after which Congress for the first time exercised authority over a national domain (*see* chapter 46, §3). Under the Articles, Congress had no authority for domestic governance, but the area was now outside state jurisdiction, and Congress was able to act without challenge. In a series of measures beginning in 1784 and culminating with the Northwest Ordinance of 1787,

Congress planned the orderly development of the national domain. Lands were to be surveyed systematically and sold to settlers on reasonable terms, but funds were lacking to implement the plan, and little money was ever raised from land sales.

Peacetime diplomacy also turned out to be fraught with difficulties (*see* chapter 49). Americans had been able to secure a highly satisfactory treaty of peace with Britain in 1783. Afterwards, recalcitrant states did not abide by the terms of the peace treaty concerning restitution for confiscated loyalist property and the payment of debts owed to British nationals. In retaliation, Britain refused to vacate certain forts in the American West. An economic downturn and hostile British commercial policy caused Americans to seek new trading partners, and Congress's representatives sought to negotiate treaties of amity and commerce with most of the powers of Europe; with little to bargain with, they were generally unsuccessful. Spain, which controlled Louisiana, declared in 1784 that the free navigation of the Mississippi would no longer be allowed. In subsequent negotiations, the American representative sought to alter his instructions in order to concede western navigation in return for privileges in Atlantic commerce with Spain; the request provoked such bitterness that contemporaries spoke seriously of possible division of the union along sectional lines.

National finances also degenerated after 1783. Congress had to depend on the increasingly unworkable system of requisitions. By cutting expenses to the bone, Congress was able to maintain a balance between current receipts and expenditure for a couple of years, but beginning in 1786 the Continental treasury ran an ever-increasing deficit. Moreover, cost-cutting was achieved by measures which diminished national authority. During these years individual states began to service the Continental debt owed to their residents. Left with the foreign debt to deal with, Congress coped by suspending payments to France and Spain and trying to maintain its credit in Amsterdam, but by 1786 it appeared that it would be necessary to default on the Dutch loans as well. Congress was failing to meet its international obligations, even when reduced to a minimum, and on the point of losing its sole remaining dependable source of funds.

Although the fundamental problem in national government remained that of federalism – the proper relation of the nation and the states – the implications had become much more serious. The question was no longer of the role of the states within the union but the nature of the union itself. During the war Congress had coped, albeit sometimes by desperate expedients, with the "external" business of diplomacy, defense, and international borrowing; now this business simply could not be managed. Internally, the Articles envisaged an American "common market" in which the free inhabitants of any state could do business in every state on an equal footing, yet the various state fiscal systems often discriminated against non-residents. The "perpetual union" of the Articles was clearly not developing as planned.

In the circumstances it was surprising how little Congress proposed by way of reform; indeed, as problems mounted, Congress grew perceptibly more hesitant. In July 1783 the British Government ordered the closure of West Indian ports to American ships, and there were widespread demands for retaliation. On April 30, 1784 Congress proposed an amendment granting powers during 15 years to ban foreign ships from American ports and to restrict the trade of foreign merchants. The states were slow to reply, the commercial situation deteriorated, and merchants petitioned for more forceful measures. A year later a congressional committee proposed an amendment granting permanent power to regulate foreign and interstate commerce and to impose import and export duties. (This was distinguished from the still-pending impost proposal of 1783 by handing over both the revenue from the duties and the responsibility for collecting them to the individual states.) Throughout the summer Congress intermittently debated the report, but it fell foul of North–South sectionalism and familiar fears about over-mighty central government, and no proposal was sent to the states.

By the spring of 1786 it was clear that all amendments already proposed were unlikely to succeed. Some congressmen sought to seize the initiative and make one last effort at comprehensive reform. In May, Charles Pinckney proposed that Congress appoint a grand committee to review national affairs and then issue a call for a national convention to consider the report; in August the committee recommended seven additional Articles. Six dealt with familiar problems of regulating trade, raising revenue, and securing observance of treaties and national laws; the seventh addressed the increasing difficulty of maintaining a quorum in Congress. The proposals considered in 1785 about trade regulation were reiterated. Financial penalties could be imposed on states late in meeting requisitions, and Congress was to be given the ultimate right to raise taxes in any persistently uncooperative state. Future revenue amendments would require the assent of only 11 states, and, in the most striking innovation, a federal court would be established with appellate jurisdiction over decisions of state courts on international law, foreign affairs, national revenue, and congressional trade regulation. These proposals did not fundamentally depart from the Articles as traditionally understood. Only one new federal power was proposed – the long-advocated one to regulate commerce. The states retained their role in implementing congressional policy, and non-compliance was to be dealt with not by coercion but by financial sanctions and judicial review. Although Congress took the unusual step of publicizing the committee proposals, debate was desultory, and they were never formally acted upon. A failure of nerve was apparent by late 1786. Efforts ceased even to secure the approval of earlier proposals. (All amendments formally proposed by Congress had achieved ratification by at least 11 states, and the 1784 request for power to pass navigation acts had been ratified by every state, although the varied forms of ratification needed reconciliation.) By default, the initiative in reforming national government passed outside Congress.

Why was it so difficult for Congress to secure amendments? The fate of the 1783 impost proposal illustrated the problems. Prominent congressmen privately hoped it would fail, warning that independent revenue for Congress would strengthen "aristocratical influence" and "establish" an "arbitrary Government." Within the states amendment was hotly contested. Approval in the critical states of Massachusetts (1783) and Virginia (1784) was secured only by the influence of John Adams and George Washington respectively. In Connecticut feelings were particularly high against the commutation of army officers' pensions, and the impost was twice rejected before eventual approval in 1784. Rhode Island held out until 1785. Georgia, which generally showed little interest in national affairs, delayed ratification until 1786. When the impost was finally killed by squabbling between Congress and New York about the measure's implementation (the state insisted upon appointing local collectors of the impost), the outcome seemed almost the result of exhaustion.

Three lessons could be drawn from this unedifying story, and they applied to all congressional business after 1783. One set of difficulties was structural and procedural – the requirements of unanimity for amendment and high majorities for congressional decisions and quorums. A broader question was that of Congress's standing. Effective government was carried out by the states; little attention was paid to Congress by ordinary people or even by state legislatures. Finally, there was the problem of ideological resistance to central power. Constantly reiterated, Whiggish fears of taxes, aristocracy, and tyranny took on a reality of their own. By 1786 the minimum proposals necessary to make national government workable under the Articles were subject to fierce and principled resistance. The earlier opposition to Robert Morris had borne its poisoned fruit.

4 The Road to Philadelphia

Although national government by the mid-1780s was no longer able to respond positively to its difficulties, there remained two areas of creative tension in national affairs. One was in the relationship between the states and the nation. Although the constitutional system of federalism under the Articles had proved unworkable, at another, deeper level the authority of the states and the nation had developed in a reciprocal fashion, and the creative interplay continued, albeit in different ways. On the eve of the Revolution, provincial assemblies had called the Continental Congress into being, and Congress, in turn, had given vital sanction to organization of the new state governments. Ten years later, as Congress foundered, it was constitutional development within the states which provided the model and state legislatures which provided the sanction for a successful movement to remake national government. Moreover, a perceived political crisis within the stages did much to strengthen the cause of national reform. The second area of tension was in the relationship between America and Britain. Americans could not easily shed their British heritage; inherited attitudes and ideas continued to shape their understanding of politics and of nationhood. It was, however, a more mundane connection with Britain which provided the specific opportunity to initiate reform. Britain remained America's most important trading partner, and (in terms of the long-term norms of American development) international trade had a particularly important role in the American economy. After the peace Americans experienced an extraordinarily sharp and painful trade cycle. The resulting crisis sparked new popular support for strengthening national authority, exacerbated political problems within the states, and provided the catalyst for a successful movement to reconstruct national government.

Only twice have major wars been fought on American soil, and in both cases they precipitated enormous constitutional creativity and unprecedented political bitterness. Up to 1786 the creativity and the conflict were most apparent within the individual states. The most important legacy of this period was the development of a new American conception of constitutionalism. It was out of the varied experience of the 13 states during this decade that Americans came to understand how legitimate government should be instituted (a constitutional convention, popular ratification, and a constitution unalterable by the ordinary process of legislation) and how government should be structured (a bicameral legislature, a separate executive, and an independent judiciary). Likewise, this was a time of unprecedented rise in the level of governmental activity in the states, whether measured by the volume of legislation, levels of taxation and expenditure, or the number of cases before the courts. Finally, there was a marked broadening of participation in politics, both in theory and in practice. More men voted, representation was extended to areas previously denied, and formerly excluded interest groups demanded that their interests be attended to; although there were still limits on democracy, practice was gradually broadening expectations. Varied demands, of course, could not all be met, and the level of political contentiousness rose along with the increases in participation and governmental activity.

Political controversy was also shaped and exacerbated by the economic relationship with Britain. America was dependent on Britain for both markets and credit, and complex links of loans and transactions tied even the most isolated farming community to transatlantic markets. General participation in an economy based on agricultural exports and extensive credit did not mean, however, that all Americans shared, or thought that they shared, a common interest. In the seaports and the nearby developed hinterland the level of economic activity visibly depended upon international trade. In isolated farming areas the connection with international trade was less apparent, much less of what was produced was sent to market, and cash was scarce, but ultimately the backwoods economy was also tied into transatlantic exchange, even though in different ways than those from more developed areas. Moreover, the division between isolated rural areas and the more advanced ones was the fundamental division which shaped the politics within the states. Although there were not organized political parties in the modern sense, historians have identified a consistent pattern of cleavage in state politics between backwoods "localists" and "cosmopolitans"

from the more developed areas. (The terms are defined and explored more fully in Main, 1973.) This political conflict was well established by mid-decade, but it was exacerbated by the postwar economic cycle. At the end of the war there was enormous pent-up demand for imports from Britain. There was no corresponding rise in demand for American exports; instead British policy actively sought to restrict American exports in order to encourage Canadian development. The result was a trade imbalance. By the end of 1784 a severe economic contraction was underway, and the impact on politics soon followed.

In 1785 and 1786 the dominant political questions within each state revolved around debt, and local controversy began to inspire a new conservative nationalism. The states had heavy public debts from the Revolution. Taxpayers were increasingly in arrears. Individuals were hard pressed to pay their private debts. Many demanded government action, but there was marked disagreement about what to do. Generally "cosmopolitans" favored enforcing existing contracts, levying taxes to pay public obligations in full, and embarking on government-sponsored schemes to promote commercial recovery. "Localists," on the other hand, advocated debtor relief, reduced taxes, and cutbacks in government activity. Whatever the results in individual states (and they varied widely), conservative "cosmopolitans" had reason for anxiety. If "localists" dominated the politics of a given state, conservatives were obviously dissatisfied; on the other hand, if "cosmopolitans" enacted a conservative fiscal program, it was likely to meet violent resistance. (Shays's Rebellion in Massachusetts during the winter of 1786–7 was merely the most widely publicized of many violent episodes.) By 1786 a number of influential men had begun to speculate that a strengthened national government with a broader sphere of authority might be an attractive alternative to state politics with its rancor and excess.

More immediately, retaliation was demanded against Britain's trade policy. During 1785 the press and public meetings discussed possible measures, including congressional regulation of commerce, state tariffs, and private boycotts of British goods. Soon it became clear that local action by itself would be unsatisfactory, as competing ports might take advantage of local tariffs or non-importation to win business away from rivals. For any policy of commercial retaliation to work, it had to work nationwide, and the campaign increasingly focused on the effort to secure ratification of the 1785 proposal to give Congress power over trade. For the first time there was a broad-based popular movement advocating stronger national authority.

Ironically, the events which finally gave coherence and effectiveness to the impulses for reshaping national government began not in one of the great northern port cities but in Virginia. The unexpected location had profound importance, for it meant that the movement did not begin in the rarified world of the northern urban elite, nor was it initially shaped by contention and partisanship. Instead it began with the largest state in the union and the most respected man in America sensibly transacting a bit of down-to-earth business. Both Virginia and Maryland claimed authority over the navigation of the Potomac, and importers took advantage of the confusion to evade customs. In March 1784 James Madison suggested that the issues be resolved by commissioners appointed by the two states; this was accepted, and after some mishaps and delay the commissioners met at George Washington's home at Mount Vernon on March 25, 1785. The commissioners agreed on a wide variety of issues; they settled questions about navigation and naval jurisdiction and recommended that the two states coordinate their currencies, their customs duties, and their methods of dealing with protested bills of exchange. The commissioners carefully stipulated that navigation should be open to people of all states and wrote to the government of Pennsylvania (into whose territory it was hoped to extend the navigation of the Potomac) suggesting that Pennsylvania should cooperate with their recommendations. The Mount Vernon Conference had raised questions of national importance about commerce, currency, navigation, and debt, and, more significantly, it

provided an example of effective interstate cooperation.

The lesson was not lost on the most thoughtful nationalist in Virginia. Since leaving Congress, Madison had served in the Virginia legislature, where he was accepted as an authority on national affairs and where he sought to secure state ratification of the various amendments proposed to strengthen the Articles. When the commissioners' proposals were considered, Madison argued that they should be submitted to Congress under Article VI of the Confederation (which required congressional consent for any "treaty, confederation, or alliance" between states), but the legislature chose to ratify on its own. Madison then quietly pushed a proposal that Virginia invite all states to appoint commissioners to meet to discuss "such commercial regulations [as] may be necessary to their common interest and their permanent harmony." Considered on the final day of the legislative session, the motion passed with little fanfare, and other states were duly invited to send representatives to a meeting at Annapolis in September 1786.

Rather few states chose to do so. By any reasonable standard the Annapolis Convention was not a success, but it did provide a framework within which to work and a new definition of the scope of reform. Eight states responded favorably to Virginia's invitation, but for various reasons commissioners appeared from only five. The Convention met on only three days and chose not to make concrete recommendations. Instead, the commissioners invited the states to select representatives for a further convention to assemble in Philadelphia in May 1787. But significant things were achieved. Firstly, urban and commercial nationalists from the Mid-Atlantic states enlisted in the Virginia-based movement for reform. Secondly, they broadened the definition of possible objects. Those proposed by the Virginia legislature had been limited, and Madison in particular aspired to nothing more than congressional power to regulate trade. The New Jersey delegation, on the other hand, had broad authority to consider any matters necessary to the "common interest," and a delegate from Philadelphia recommended a general enquiry into the commercial laws of individual states. The major contribution, however, was made by Alexander Hamilton, a representative from New York. Hamilton had never abandoned his early advocacy of a national convention with plenipotentiary powers to change the Articles. Now he was able to graft his proposal onto the more modest Virginia scheme. As the draftsman of the Convention's address to the states (for which he has always been given credit), Hamilton proposed a wide brief for delegates to the Philadelphia Convention – "to devise such further provisions as shall appear to them necessary to render the constitution of the Federal Government adequate to the exigencies of the Union." The Convention's resolutions were then sent to the Congress and the states.

During the next months things went the reformers' way. Congress was understandably cool and did not act until February 21, 1787, when it declared that it would be "expedient" to hold a convention "for the sole and express purpose of revising the Articles of Confederation." Already five states had acted on their own to name delegates, and in the end eight of the 12 states which sent delegates gave them authority to work under the sort of broad remit proposed at Annapolis rather than the narrower one recommended by Congress. Around the union distinguished men who had previously stood aloof from efforts at reforming national government were now willing to serve as delegates. Public opinion was also shifting. There was a sense of crisis as stalemate and sectional rancor continued in Congress and open rebellion broke out in Massachusetts. Among those in national politics, including even those who would later oppose the new Constitution, there was by 1787 a broad consensus for fundamental reform.

Meanwhile, Madison systematically studied history and political theory and considered the problems of state and national politics in order to determine the principles upon which American government should be based. His conclusions were enormously creative. In his most fundamental innovation he proposed that national government

ought to operate directly upon the people (rather than acting through the intermediate agency of the states) and that it ought to receive its authority from the people (rather than from the states). This insight, first of all, allowed a new understanding of federalism. If the sovereign people delegated authority both to the national government and the states, the national government could be given power to act independently in its own sphere and also to impose certain restrictions on state activity. Although the specific mechanism which Madison envisaged – a federal negative on state laws – was rejected, limits on state authority imposed under the terms of the Federal Constitution have become a fundamental feature of American federalism. Secondly, the idea of deriving national authority from the people allowed Madison to abandon old notions of a confederation of states and to draw on the new American experience of constitutionalism in order to propose ways to create and structure national government. Its Constitution should be drawn up by a convention and ratified by the people. Drawing upon traditional theories of mixed government as well as the practical experience of the states, Madison proposed a complex structure for national government with an independent executive and judiciary enforcing the enactments of a bicameral legislature. The precise details which he proposed in the Virginia Plan (present at the beginning of the Philadelphia Convention) were not accepted, and other nationalists disagreed not only about details but some of the principles behind them. Nonetheless Madison provided the agenda, and, once it was accepted, delegates at Philadelphia could discuss national government in familiar terms they had learned from constitution-making in the states.

When the Federal Convention assembled at Philadelphia in May 1787 the movement for a stronger national government was returning to its birthplace, but success was only ensured because the route had included a detour through Virginia. The high-toned nationalism of the "new nationalists" in 1779–81 and the Morrisites in 1781–3 had been both premature and ultimately unrealizable. Nationalism needed a broader constituency than a small arrogant urban elite. Time was needed not only to realize the full problems of the nation but also to draw upon the lessons of the states. This is what the Virginians contributed on the way to Philadelphia.

5 A More Perfect Union

From beginning to end, government under the Articles of Confederation was a creature of the Revolutionary War. The exigencies of wartime diplomacy prompted Congress to propose the Articles to the states, and military responsibility forced Congress to exercise broad authority. It was a time of constant crisis, myriad expedients, and ultimate victory. Victory, however, diminished Congress's responsibilities and made the need to strengthen national government less compelling. The threat of military intervention, whether real or fanciful, fueled a suspicion of central power which frustrated any attempts to reform the Articles. The business of the Revolution, however, was not finished, and Congress was unable to deal with pressing problems of finance and diplomacy within an unworkable constitutional system and after a precipitous loss of its own public standing.

Yet it was also the heritage of the war which made possible the resurrection and transfiguration of national government. It was the war which gave birth to American nationalism; for the first time, people of all states cooperated in a common cause, came to expect mutual rights and privileges, and began to share a sense of national identity. The problem, of course, was that Americans also paid allegiance to their individual states and that the states successfully carried out most of the necessary business of governing. Both in theory and practice it was difficult to work out how the states and the national government could coexist effectively. The very notion of federalism (formally defined as a political system in which two governments exercise jurisdiction over the same territory and neither has the power to destroy the other) was – and is – difficult to conceive. The practical problems of defining the sphere of national government and working out the boundaries of national and state power proved impossible to solve under the Articles of Confederation, yet the years of frustration highlighted the problems and forced some men to begin searching for new solutions. With a bold disregard of grammar and an even bolder optimism, the new Constitution of 1787 promised Americans "a more perfect Union"; it was only after the experience of the Articles that the promise could be made and later realized.

FURTHER READING

Burnett, E. C.: *The Continental Congress* (New York: Macmillan, 1941).

Ferguson, E. J.: *The Power of the Purse: a History of American Public Finance, 1776–1790* (Chapel Hill: University of North Carolina Press, 1961).

Jensen, M.: *The Articles of Confederation: an Interpretation of the Social-Constitutional History of the American Revolution, 1774–1781* (Madison: University of Wisconsin Press, 1940).

——: *The New Nation: a History of the United States during the Confederation, 1781–1789* (New York: Alfred A. Knopf, 1950).

Main, J. T.: *Political Parties Before the Constitution* (Chapel Hill: University of North Carolina Press, 1973).

Morris, R. B.: *The Forging of the Union, 1781–1789* (New York: Harper & Row, 1987).

Rakove, J. N.: *The Beginnings of National Politics: an Interpretive History of the Continental Congress* (New York: Alfred A. Knopf, 1979).

Wood, G. S.: *The Creation of the American Republic, 1776–1787* (Chapel Hill: University of North Carolina Press, 1969).

CHAPTER FIFTY-EIGHT

The Federal Convention and the Constitution

MARK D. KAPLANOFF

THE Federal Convention met at Philadelphia from May 25 to September 17, 1787; during that time 55 delegates from 12 states took part in drafting the Constitution, which remains (with amendments) the fundamental law of the United States. (Of the 13 original states Rhode Island did not participate.) The most basic question that historians have asked about the Constitution has been whether it should be seen as a counter-revolutionary effort to limit the internal effects of the American Revolution or a pragmatic attempt to secure its success after difficult times during the early and mid-1780s. In one particular version of this discussion scholars (drawing especially on the work of Charles A. Beard) have debated whether delegates sought to defend the interests of commercial and financial property-holders. Others, looking in detail at the dynamics of decision-making within the Convention, have emphasized the conflicts during the drafting process and the difficulties resolving them; writing in this vein, one early historian summed up the Constitution as "a bundle of compromises" (Farrand, 1904, p. 484). Three compromises in particular have been identified as the most important. In the Connecticut Compromise of early July small states secured equal representation for all states in the US Senate. The slave trade compromise of late August forbade federal interference with the foreign slave trade before 1808 and granted certain other guarantees to southern planters. The compromise about the presidency in early September established the intricate method of electing the US President. Other historians, however, have correctly emphasized the shared experience and common goals which allowed the delegates to reach agreement on a radically new plan for national government.

1 Background

Delegates, for the most part, had personal experience of national affairs and agreed that the powers of the national government needed substantially to be increased. Of the 55 delegates who attended, 42 had served in Continental Congresses or in Congress under the Articles of Confederation. Others had served in the Continental Army, several on its general staff. Delegates tended to be well-to-do lawyers, planters, and merchants. They were well educated (26 had graduated from college, nine from Princeton) and well prepared. James Madison of Virginia, who has deservedly been called the "Father of the Constitution," had served in Congress for many years and had long advocated strengthening the federal government; during the winter of 1786–7 he had made an intensive study of political theory in preparation for framing a new constitution. As early as 1781 Alexander Hamilton of New York had proposed a convention to draft a new framework for national government. Among other active nationalist delegates at the Convention were Gouverneur Morris and James Wilson of Pennsylvania, Rufus King of Massachusetts, and Charles Pinckney of South Carolina; all were young, college-educated lawyers with experience in Congress. Although less active, Benjamin

Franklin of Pennsylvania and George Washington of Virginia (who presided over the Convention) were the best-known Americans of their day, and their presence and quiet approval ultimately did much to strengthen the nationalists' cause. Among other prominent and active delegates were John Dickinson of Delaware, Roger Sherman and Oliver Ellsworth of Connecticut, Elbridge Gerry of Massachusetts, and George Mason and Edmund Randolph of Virginia. Of these the first three were delegates from smaller states, initially critical but committed nationalists after the Connecticut Compromise; the second three were at first active supporters of a stronger national government but later refused to sign the Constitution. The one consistently active and articulate opponent of the nationalist view at the Convention was Luther Martin of Maryland, a lawyer and public official whose career and vision had remained firmly state-centered. Generally, though, few politicians with a localist orientation attended the Convention, and those there who held such views said little or chose to leave.

Circumstances outside the Convention also worked in favor of strengthening the national government. Under the Articles of Confederation, the federal government was unable to raise sufficient funds to pay its debts and expenses. It could not secure compliance by the states with international treaties, and sectional division within Congress thwarted diplomatic negotiations. Over the years various proposals had been made to grant the federal government an independent revenue, power over international and interstate commerce, and even coercive powers over the states, yet all the proposals had failed. The severe contraction in international trade and credit in 1784–5 had led to widespread distress and had embittered the already strife-ridden politics within the individual states. Debtors struggled for relief, and in several states violence broke out, most frighteningly in Shays's Rebellion in Massachusetts. Many prominent men worried that the idealism of the Revolution was degenerating into selfish, unjust politics and internecine strife, and some began to see that strengthening the national government might work to curb the excesses of the states. General apprehension of crisis and the failure of earlier attempts at amending the Articles of Confederation allowed nationalists at Philadelphia to argue that the Convention provided the last chance for fundamental and necessary reform.

Arrangements within the Convention also favored the nationalists. They set the agenda at the beginning, and more cautious delegates never successfully forced the debate onto other ground. The secrecy in which the delegates debated allowed them to explore wide-ranging proposals. Yet the more avid nationalists did not railroad their proposals through; the rules and practices of the Convention facilitated consensus-building. After giving brief notice any delegate was allowed to reopen discussion on any point, and debates and votes were often repeated. Discussion was exhaustive, and delegates spoke freely. Although the rules allowed a decision by a simple majority (voting was by state, and each state had one vote), delegates were reluctant to conclude controversial business if voting remained closely divided.

Voting patterns reveal some of the results of these arrangements. More than 560 roll-call votes were recorded during the course of the Convention and statistical analysis shows that voting alignments can be divided into four chronological periods. Within each period there were two opposing blocs of states, and the times when voting alignments shifted coincided closely with the three major compromises. It was also significant that no state was always on the losing side; each state was part of a majority coalition during at least one period.

2 The Virginia and New Jersey Plans

The Convention began its substantive business on May 29 when Edmund Randolph introduced the so-called Virginia Plan, a set of 15 brief resolutions sketching an entirely new model for a national government. Authorship has been universally ascribed to James Madison (probably with some collaboration by other Virginia delegates). Summarizing the audacious nature of the plan, one historian concluded that it "proposed, in effect, a sovereign parliament for America" (Murrin, 1987, p. 598). The new national government represented individual citizens (to a degree) and could act directly upon them. The national legislature would have power to pass laws "in all cases to which the separate states are incompetent, or in which the harmony of the United States may be interrupted by the exercise of individual legislation," to "negative" state laws "contravening … the articles of union," and to use force against recalcitrant states (Farrand, 1937, vol. 1, p. 21). The legislature was to have two houses, the lower house elected by the people, the upper elected by the lower. Each state was to be represented in each house in proportion either to taxes ("contributions") or to free population. There was to be a national judiciary and an executive elected by the legislature for an unspecified term and ineligible for re-election. A Council of Revision drawn from the executive and the judiciary was to exercise a veto on legislation. Generally, though, details of the structure and powers of the executive and judiciary were vague. Provision was also made for the admission of new states, for amendment, and for ratification by a popular convention or conventions.

For the next two weeks the Virginia Plan was virtually unchallenged. Although some delegates complained that the proposals exceeded their authority, on May 30 the Convention agreed to support a government *"national & supreme"* and proceeded to debate the individual resolutions of the plan. In the most important decision of these days it was voted on June 6 that state representation in the national legislature and the apportionment of internal taxes would be proportional to the total free population plus three-fifths of the slave population, the so-called three-fifths clause. (This formula had first been proposed by Congress in 1783 as the basis for apportioning taxes among the states.) Other decisions fixed seven-year terms for the upper house of the legislature, three-year for the lower, with the upper house elected by state legislatures. Delegates decided that there should be a single executive serving a seven-year term. The Council of Revision was rejected and

the executive given a veto subject to being overturned by a vote of two-thirds in each house of the legislature. The provision for coercing states was dropped. It was decided to create a national judiciary (which had not existed under the Articles of Confederation). Although the Convention was moving remarkably quickly, a note of caution was sounded as delegates from smaller states warned that they would never accept representation in both houses of the legislature proportional to state population.

The apparently easy momentum of the nationalists was halted on June 14 when William Paterson of New Jersey introduced an alternative "purely federal" plan. Jointly prepared by members of the New Jersey, Connecticut, New York, Maryland, and possibly Delaware delegations, the so-called New Jersey Plan proposed keeping a unicameral national legislature in which each state had one vote, but even this plan went significantly beyond the Articles of Confederation. The national government was to have new powers – power to raise money through customs duties and a stamp tax, power to regulate commerce, and power to compel delinquent states to honor financial requisitions. There was to be a plural executive (elected by Congress) and a national judiciary. Finally, in the most innovative provision, acts of Congress and treaties were to be "the supreme law of the respective states" and binding on state courts.

Debate over the New Jersey Plan was brief, and it was rejected decisively. Paterson and Luther Martin made theoretical arguments in its favor based on state sovereignty and also argued that public opinion was unprepared for more radical changes. Opponents replied that the Convention was free to propose anything and criticized the injustice of the plan and likely impotence of the government it proposed. On June 19 the Convention voted by seven states to three (with one divided) to abandon the proposals. Connecticut and Maryland, whose delegates had been involved in drafting the plan, were among the states who failed to support it. The plan and its fate vividly illustrated the dilemma of delegates from the smaller states. Many of them wished to make substantial enlargements in the powers and structure of the national government but only if they were guaranteed that their states would not be overwhelmed within it.

3 The Connecticut Compromise and Federalism

For the next two weeks the Convention made little progress. Debate ranged over many issues, but the question of representation in the national legislature had to be resolved before others could be addressed. Representation proportional to population in both houses was supported by six well-populated or growing states (Massachusetts, Pennsylvania, Virginia, North Carolina, South Carolina, and Georgia) but opposed by five other states (Connecticut, New York, New Jersey, Delaware, and Maryland). Debate became increasingly acrimonious, supporters of proportional representation charged their opponents with narrow self-interest, delegates on the other side refused to yield, and some even threatened to withdraw.

The impasse was broken in early July. On July 2 there was a tie vote on representation. (The vote of Georgia was divided.) Immediately Roger Sherman of Connecticut proposed that the matter be referred to a committee, which was then chosen with one member from each state. None of the strongest advocates of representation proportional to population was included; large-state members were generally moderates while those from the other states were insistent on some equality of state representation. Three days later the chairman, Elbridge Gerry, reported its proposal: states should have equal votes in the upper house while money bills should originate in the lower house and not be subject to amendment in the upper. (This has come to be called the Connecticut (or Great) Compromise; equal representation for states in the upper house had been first suggested by delegates from Connecticut and by John Dickinson of Delaware in early June and formally proposed by the Connecticut delegation after the defeat of the New Jersey Plan.) For two weeks the decision was delayed. (During this time the Convention approved the system of reapportioning congressional seats according to periodic censuses.) On July 16 the compromise was finally accepted with five states voting in favor, four against, and one divided. (Georgia now voted against compromise, but North Carolina voted in favor. Massachusetts's vote was divided. No delegates from New York or New Hampshire were present.)

The outcome was really a concession not a compromise. Georgia and North Carolina, which defected from the "large-state" bloc on crucial votes, were relatively unpopulated and undeveloped states, large states only in terms of anticipated growth. Elbridge Gerry, who chaired the committee and helped divide the vote of Massachusetts, was an older, conservative delegate never committed to the expansive nationalism of some of his younger colleagues. Generally, though, what lay behind the compromise was a sense of crisis and impasse; delegates from the smaller states would not cooperate without some concession. Many "large-state" delegates were unhappy (notably James Madison), and some went so far as to hold a meeting the next morning to try to concert a strategy to overturn the compromise, but they were unable to agree even among themselves, and the decision was not reconsidered in the Convention itself once the final vote was taken.

Afterwards, from July 17 to 26, the Convention dealt with miscellaneous points before adjourning while a committee produced a draft constitution. The jurisdiction of the federal courts was extended and the negative on state laws rejected. This was a significant retreat from the grant of broad and coercive powers to the national government over the states in the Virginia Plan. Along with the Connecticut Compromise these decisions initiated the development of America's distinctive federalism – a system in which both the states and federal government maintain large areas of their own competence and federal courts act as arbiters of the limits of state and federal power.

4 Nationalism and Sectionalism

The drafting committee (Committee of Detail) met on July 26 and reported on

August 6. Under the chairmanship of John Rutledge of South Carolina, it consisted of five members, among whom James Wilson was probably the most active. Beginning with the amended Virginia Plan and drawing upon the constitutions of the states (particularly Massachusetts and New York) and the Articles of Confederation, the committee produced a document closely resembling the final Constitution. Much was set out in detail which had only been sketched previously, including provisions for the internal organization of Congress, a definition of the jurisdiction of the courts, and a grant of powers to the President.

In two important ways the committee went beyond what the Convention had already decided; the draft set out a list of specific powers granted to the national government (along with a complementary list of powers denied to state governments), and it made the first detailed provisions for the executive and judiciary. The powers granted included – among others – powers to tax and to borrow money, to regulate foreign and interstate commerce, to make war, and to establish inferior courts and criminal law in certain areas, along with the right to enact all laws "necessary and proper" to execute these or other powers vested in the federal government by the Constitution. Although the grant was broad-ranging, it was also significant that powers were specifically enumerated and limited. State governments were forbidden to engage in diplomatic relations (including relations with each other) or to wage wars of their own, and were also prohibited from coining money, issuing paper money "without the consent" of Congress, or laying duties on imports. For the first time the President was given independent powers in foreign and military affairs and also the right to recommend legislation. In the section on the judiciary, the draft provided for inferior federal courts (in addition to and subordinate to the Supreme Court) and gave a broad definition of the jurisdiction of federal courts. The conception of a sovereign legislature was giving way to a new vision of a separate legislature, executive, and judiciary, each with independent powers. The draft did not, however, set out the relationship

between the three branches in the form finally approved; the President was still to be elected by Congress, the Senate had powers to make treaties, to make judicial and diplomatic appointments, and to act independently in settling disputes between states, and the Supreme Court was to try impeachments. The draft also contained other miscellaneous provisions that were later rejected – a fixed ratio of representation to population in apportioning the House of Representatives, a requirement for a three-quarters majority in Congress to override a veto and two-thirds to admit a new state, and a proposal for property qualifications for federal officers.

The draft also made three concessions to southern interests. This was most immediately a response to the demand by Charles Cotesworth Pinckney of South Carolina on July 23 for "some security to the Southern States agst. an emancipation of slaves, and taxes on exports." But an accommodation of southern interests was also fostered by the widespread recognition of the fundamental nature of the North–South division. The draft made three explicit concessions to the South: no tax or duty was to be laid upon exports, the slave trade ("the migration or importation of such persons as the several states shall think proper to admit") was neither to be taxed nor prohibited, and no navigation act was to be passed without a two-thirds majority in each house of Congress. (Southerners feared that measures to promote northern shipping might increase freight costs on their exports.)

During the next three weeks questions about slavery provoked bitter controversy. On August 8 northern delegates attacked slavery on both pragmatic and moral grounds and proposed taking no account of slaves in allocating congressional representation, but the three-fifths clause was reaffirmed by a vote of ten states to one (New Jersey). On August 21–2 critics of slavery were joined by the largest slaveholder in the Convention, George Mason, who bemoaned slavery and attacked the slave trade in particular. South Carolinians replied by impugning the motives of Virginians (who, they claimed, would profit if the closure of the foreign slave trade increased the value of their existing holdings) and defending slavery on grounds of economics and morality. They were joined by northerners (notably Roger Sherman and Oliver Ellsworth from Connecticut) who did not wish to upset a delicate sectional balance. The matter was referred to a committee which reported its proposals on August 24. Congress could not stop the slave trade until 1800 (but could impose a limited tax upon it), the prohibition on export duties was reiterated, but the requirement of a two-thirds majority for navigation acts was abandoned. There was desultory debate up until August 29, and delegates from South Carolina were able to secure an additional eight years for the slave trade (until 1808) and a new clause (copied from the Northwest Ordinance) requiring states to return fugitive slaves apprehended within their borders. On the only significant roll-call vote (to extend the time during which the slave trade was protected), the three states of the Deep South (Georgia, South Carolina, and North Carolina) were joined by the New England states (New Hampshire, Massachusetts, and Connecticut) and Maryland.

Of the three major "compromises" in the Convention, the slave trade compromise provides the clearest example of give-and-take between readily identifiable interest groups. The multiplicity of issues raised and the inter-regional nature of the alliances made it possible to do business. So too did the desire – expressed even by the most violent speakers for and against slavery – to strike a bargain. Although it took time to work out the details, the broad outlines of a possible compromise had been apparent from the start, and the final terms were accepted with little difficulty.

Certainly questions relating to slavery were among the most vexatious at the Convention, but the overall importance of slavery in the formation of the Constitution should not be overestimated. Representatives of no other sectional interest (and there were several which had previously provoked bitter quarrels in national politics) made such strident and persistent demands, but business was done when it had to be, and the issue did not dominate the proceedings of the Convention nor intrude much into the text of the Constitution. As one historian has pointed out, "It would have been impossible to establish a national government in the eighteenth century without recognizing slavery in some way" (Ohline, 1971, p. 582). The provisions in the Constitution which dealt directly with slavery were the three-fifths clause (with consequences for congressional apportionment, for taxation and, in the final draft, for the election of the President), the protection of the slave trade, and the fugitive slave clause. (Some historians have also seen concern to protect slavery in provisions about citizenship and domestic violence and a few other miscellaneous clauses, but it is unlikely that slavery was a primary consideration in drafting these other articles.) More significantly the word "slave" was deliberately not used in the text, it being thought wrong, in Madison's words of August 25, "to admit in the Constitution the idea that there could be property in men." The omission was revealing both of the moral issue and the difficulty that participants had in confronting it. The Constitution neither strengthened nor undermined slavery; faced with a fundamental moral problem, the delegates chose ultimately to avert their gaze.

5 The Presidency

By the end of August the most important unresolved issues related to the presidency. From the beginning it had been clear that the executive would pose particular difficulties for the Convention. Americans of the revolutionary generation were deeply suspicious of executive power and had no obvious models for a national executive. Prior Congresses had tried various ways of delegating executive power, but none had been notably successful and almost no reference was made to them at the Convention. Constitutions of the individual states contained a bewildering variety of provisions about state executives. Finally, as the rest of the draft Constitution evolved, interest groups emerged with stakes in specific proposals about the executive.

Nevertheless, there was always a small group committed to a strong and energetic presidency, most notably James Wilson,

Gouverneur Morris, and Alexander Hamilton. All had been associated with Robert Morris during the difficult years when he managed national finances (*see* chapter 48, §3), and they had concluded that the United States needed a much more effective administration. They also had theories about the necessity of energetic government and strong leadership in nation-building. (Even though they often cooperated with men like Madison, there was an important distinction between their "executive" nationalism and the more "parliamentary" vision of the Virginia Plan.) Throughout the Convention these men fought to have the President elected independently of the legislature, to give him a veto, and to grant him considerable powers of his own. These delegates were always a minority, but they achieved a surprising amount, and their achievements can be attributed to tenacity and exceptional skill in parliamentary maneuver.

It was determining the method of electing the President (along with the closely related issue of length of term and the possibility of re-eligibility) that caused particular difficulty throughout the Convention. The initial decision of May 29 that the executive be chosen by the legislature for a seven-year term with no possibility of re-election was opposed by a small group who advocated popular election (principally James Wilson and other "executive" nationalists) and by others who wished to give state governments a role in the election. Questions were raised whether election by the legislature would undermine the executive's independence, whether a long term would make him too powerful, and whether ineligibility for re-election would destroy an incentive for good behavior. Later on, practical questions of interest intruded as well; small states opposed allocating votes on population alone, the South insisted upon taking some account of slaves (hence opposing popular election), peripheral states worried about a body of electors assembling at a central place.

The result was continuing dissatisfaction. Time and again the delegates returned to the problems of election, term, and re-eligibility in a situation that one historian has

compared to "three-dimensional chess" (Roche, 1961, p. 810). Various proposals suggested that the President be elected by electors chosen by state legislatures; by state governors or electors chosen by them; by the national legislature choosing among nominees made by the people; by the national legislature in the first instance with re-election by electors chosen by state legislatures; even by a group of national legislators chosen by lot. None of these suggestions found much support. Terms were proposed ranging from two years to life ("during good behavior"), and ineligibility and re-eligibility were canvassed again and again. In mid-July a proposal by Oliver Ellsworth for an electoral college briefly commanded majority support but foundered on fears by larger states about the allocation of electors. Although unable to settle on an alternative, delegates were increasingly worried by objections to legislative election, and their anxieties and divisions were skillfully exploited by James Wilson and Gouverneur Morris. The final break came late in August. Playing on small-state apprehensions that the votes of the Senate would be swamped in legislative election by joint ballot of both houses, Gouverneur Morris moved election by electors once again, and several consequent motions resulted in tie votes. The deadlock was apparent, and on August 31 the Convention referred the question of presidential election to the "Committee on Postponed Matters" appointed that day.

This committee (chaired by David Brearly and including both Madison and Gouverneur Morris) proposed an acceptable, if inelegant, solution on September 4. The President was to serve for a four-year term with no limit on re-eligibility. He was to be elected by electors voting in their respective states (which reassured states at the periphery). Each state could choose its electors as its legislature directed (leaving open the possibility of popular participation), and each state was entitled to a number of electors equal to the state's combined representation in both houses of Congress. (This took account of free population and of the slaves of the South but gave less populous states a small bonus from their representation in the Senate.) If no candidate received a majority, election would be made by the Senate (a further sop to the small states). This last point alone proved unacceptable. Delegates feared concentrating too much power in the Senate, and on September 6 the proposal was amended so that inconclusive contests would be settled by the House of Representatives, "the members from each State having one vote." At last the system of presidential election was complete.

The question of the President's powers was neither addressed at such length nor settled so clearly. The Virginia Plan contained the potentially broad grant of "the executive rights vested in Congress by the Confederation," but after objections in early June executive authority was reduced to powers to execute the laws and to appoint to some offices. (The Senate, it was proposed, would appoint most high officers.) This was the situation until the Committee of Detail reported in early August. In a passage almost certainly drafted by James Wilson and closely modeled on the New York state constitution (which established the strongest executive in the 13 states), the report gave substantial independent powers to the President. He was to be Commander-in-Chief of the armed forces. He was authorized to carry on diplomacy (although the Senate was still empowered to make treaties). He had a role to play in legislation with power to recommend measures to Congress and to exercise a veto, although it could be overturned by a vote of two-thirds in each house of Congress.

The proposed powers provoked surprisingly little discussion or opposition; as business continued, the Convention even increased presidential powers. Instead of creating a council of state which might have circumscribed the President's freedom to act in administrative affairs, the brief provisions about the heads of executive departments seem to envision them in a subordinate role. The President was authorized to make treaties and to appoint judges and ambassadors with the "advice and consent" of the Senate. (The meaning of the phrase was unclear at the time, but in practice the initiative passed to the President (*see* Rakove, 1984).) Moreover, in the final text there was a contrast between the grant of legislative powers "herein specified" to Congress and the grant of executive powers without qualification to the President. It was later argued (by some former delegates among others) that the Constitution grants the President executive powers broadly understood of which the specific ones mentioned are merely examples.

In the presidency the Convention created an office with considerable independence and potential. The President had independent powers and a source of election independent of Congress. Drafting left room for the expansion of presidential authority by usage and interpretation. Yet the executive's role was not completely separated from that of the legislature or judiciary. As they fitted the executive into the new structure of government, delegates were beginning to work according to the evolving theory of "checks and balances." The older doctrine of "separation of powers" sought to isolate completely independent roles for legislature, executive, and judiciary (*see* chapter 88, §4). The framers of the Constitution did seek to give each of the three branches of government a role of its own but also to commingle their activities to a degree, in order that the business of government would be carried on with deliberation and restraint and also so that any branch that tried to exceed its legitimate powers could be curbed by the others.

6 Other Business; Other Views

The judiciary was the branch of government to which the Convention paid least attention. In the initial discussion of the Virginia Plan the proposal for a national judiciary was easily accepted, but it was decided not to have federal courts inferior to the Supreme Court. In practice this would have left most of the adjudication of federal law to state courts, and this was explicitly proposed in the New Jersey Plan. Indeed this would have been the effect of the first version of the eventual "supremacy clause," which was proposed on July 17 by the most ardent supporter of states' rights at the Convention, Luther Martin, as an alternative to a federal negative on state laws. His proposal that federal laws and treaties should be "the supreme law of the individual states" and the courts of the states "bound thereby in their decisions, any thing in the respective laws of the individual states to the contrary notwithstanding" was accepted unanimously. As things then stood, this meant that state courts would have decided questions of federal law bound by state rules of procedure and state constitutions; subsequent development altered things completely. On July 18 the Convention decided to provide for inferior federal courts. Later on, Martin's proposal itself was amended to make state constitutions (as well as laws) subordinate to the federal Constitution (as well as to federal laws and treaties). Still, details about the judiciary were so sketchy in the Constitution that the work was only truly completed by the Judiciary Act of 1789 (principally written by the former delegate Oliver Ellsworth). This Act not only defined the structure of federal courts and their particular jurisdiction but established an appellate jurisdiction whereby federal courts could review state court decisions that assertedly conflicted with the federal Constitution or laws. In this final refinement of American federalism, federal courts adjudicated federal laws, state courts adjudicated state laws, but federal courts had the final say in resolving conflicts between state and national authority.

The courts were not, however, given a final say in determining the limits of federal authority; the Constitution is notably silent on judicial review – the principle that the courts are the final interpreters of the Constitution with the power to void unconstitutional acts by other branches of government – although it has become a fundamental feature of American constitutional law. Some delegates did make incidental remarks assuming that the courts would exercise some sort of review, but others rejected it unequivocally, and it is probable that a majority of delegates who thought about the question would have maintained that each branch of government had the authority to interpret the Constitution for itself but not to bind other branches. On the other hand, the supremacy clause did make the most forceful statement of judicial authority in any American constitution to date, the doctrine of judicial review was already developing in American courts, and it was later possible to argue that it was implied in the Constitution. Certainly historians continue to disagree about the delegates' intentions and about the general understanding of judicial review at the time. (For good statements of conflicting points of view, see Rossum, 1987, pp. 232–9 and McCaughey, 1989, pp. 491–7.)

Likewise significant in the development of constitutional law were the prohibitions on state governments. The Committee of Detail in early August proposed the first specific restraints, which were designed to keep states from meddling in military affairs, diplomacy, or international trade. Also included was a prohibition on states (without the consent of Congress) emitting bills of credit or making anything but specie legal tender in payment of debts. These restrictions on economic regulation were debated and extended in late August (although the debates were brief and rather confused) and strengthened further by the final drafting committee. The final text of the Constitution also prohibited states passing any "ex post facto Law, or Law impairing the Obligation of Contracts" – the so-called contract clause. These limits on the powers of state governments to regulate domestic economic affairs have attracted much attention from historians who have argued that the Constitution was designed to protect property rights, but the principal concern of the delegates was probably to secure an orderly and uniform system of interstate commerce, an American "common market." It is also true that people in 1787–8 (including delegates to the Convention) were uncertain about the precise significance of these provisions, and for many years afterwards the restrictions seem to have had little practical effect (see Boyd, 1987). They were important not because they immediately increased the exercise of federal power but because they opened the way for increases in the future.

Meanwhile, during August, the Convention had gone through the draft Constitution making several important changes and additions which were later incorporated in the final document. Rejecting a fixed ratio of representatives to population, delegates established a small House of Representatives that need not grow too large in the future. The Convention declined to fix property qualifications for federal office-holding or suffrage in federal elections; voting in federal elections was to be open to all who voted for state legislatures, which left precise suffrage requirements up to the individual states. Delegates decided that the Constitution should go into effect when ratified by popular conventions in nine states. (This echoed the condition in the Articles of Confederation requiring consent of nine states on important questions but avoided the requirement under the Articles for unanimous consent of the states for amendment.) When the question of western lands arose, delegates chose not to sanction extending federal control over any territory already under the jurisdiction of one of the existing states, but they did give the federal government authority over territory outside state boundaries and also provided for the easy admission of new states into the Union.

As the debate went on, a few delegates were becoming increasingly alienated, including three – Mason, Gerry, and Randolph – who had played prominent and constructive roles earlier in the Convention. Unlike other unsatisfied delegates, who simply departed, these three continued active until the end. Harking back to older, revolutionary suspicions of power and corruption, they expressed worries that the central government would be too strong, that the liberties of the people were threatened, and, to a lesser extent, that the independence of the states was at risk. They also felt that the interests of their own regions were not properly protected. Throughout August they lodged continuous objections to the powers of the President and the Senate and the possibility of collusion between them. They proposed detailed restrictions on federal military power and expressed strong anxieties about the small number of people necessary to make treaties and to regulate trade. Although some of Mason, Gerry, and Randolph's specific proposals were accepted, by the end of the month each had made it clear that he might not accept the Convention's final proposals, and Mason had called for a second convention. Early in September Mason proposed the creation of a small council of state drawn from different regions of the country in order to check the President's power and to safeguard regional interests. On September 12 Gerry and Mason proposed adding a bill of rights to the Constitution.

This proposal illustrated the often positive nature of Mason, Gerry, and Randolph's opposition. Their political instincts were sound and their suggestion constructive. The decision not to include a bill of rights (taken with little discussion and by a unanimous vote) was undoubtedly a liability during the ratification debate. The first ten amendments to the Constitution (drafted by James Madison) promptly added one (see chapter 33, §3), and it did not weaken the new government; instead it helped to secure the long-term acceptance of the Constitution and played a fundamental role in the later development of American constitutionalism. Even if they were critical of many details, Mason, Gerry, and Randolph did want a stronger national government substantially like the one proposed; ultimately their opposition led not to the rejection of the Constitution but to its modification and completion.

Meanwhile, in the first weeks of September, the Convention moved to put the finishing touches on the proposed constitution. The Committee on Postponed Matters proposed an acceptable method of impeachment in which the House of Representatives would vote an indictment (impeachment) and the Senate would act as a court to try the officer impeached. James Madison proposed a workable process of amendment whereby amendments could be proposed by either two-thirds of Congress or two-thirds of the state legislatures and then be accepted when ratified by three-quarters of the states. On September 8 the Convention appointed a five-member Committee of Style to draft the final text of the Constitution; it included Madison and Hamilton, but it is generally conceded that Gouverneur Morris was the principal draftsman. The committee's report was debated from September 12 to 15 and accepted with only minor changes. On September 16, after the three remaining opponents restated their objections, the amended document was accepted by a unanimous vote of the states present. The next day, with Washington presiding and Benjamin Franklin delivering a brief valedictory, the engrossed Constitution was read and signed, and the Convention adjourned to await the decisions of the state ratifying conventions.

7 Conclusion: The Constitution

Writing shortly after the Convention (in *The Federalist*, no. 45), James Madison gave his judgment of what the Constitution had achieved: "The changes which it proposes, consist much less in an addition of NEW POWERS to the Union, than in the invigoration of its ORIGINAL POWERS," an invigoration accomplished by constructing "a more effectual mode of administering them." This comment by "the Father of the Constitution" suggests how best to judge the document. The change in the demarcation of power was not great; the federal government was given limited new powers (principally long-advocated ones over trade and revenue), and limited restrictions were imposed on state governments. On the other hand, there was a marked change in the structure of government (and thereby in the potential to exercise federal power more effectively). The article on the legislature created a government which represented the people and made laws which acted directly upon them. The next article instituted a federal executive endowed with broad competence. The provisions on the judiciary and the law not only made the Constitution supreme law but ensured that it could be pleaded as ordinary law in every court in the land. The states had a role to play in federal government and broad areas of their own authority, but they also had to obey the law.

Even if the results were a departure from recent practice, this did not mean that they departed from revolutionary principles or recent experience. The American Revolution had sought to preserve liberty and the rule of law. In the heady days of 1775–6 the struggle had been carried on by mass action and the assertion of local rights. During the long years of war and troubled peace, action by crowds and committees proved cumbersome and often intrusive on private rights; in a series of practical experiments in constitutionalism, more structured governments had been established in the states with greater legitimacy but more carefully limited powers. Nationalism too was a product of Revolution, and the army and Congress were America's first national institutions. In 1775 boycotting British trade had seemed not only a good political tactic but an assertion of America's sturdy self-reliance; economic setbacks over the next decade demonstrated Americans' dependence on world trade and the need for effective commercial policy. This was the background against which the delegates acted and against which their achievement can be judged. The Constitution created an American common market, an effective national government, a workable scheme of federalism, an embryonic system of constitutionalism limiting both state and national authority, and a scheme of representation open-ended enough to evolve towards representative democracy.

This did not mean that the framers thought that they had settled all possible specific questions about the nature and limits of governmental authority in the United States. Later, in *The Federalist*, no. 48, Madison himself sadly acknowledged that "mere parchment barriers" could never be relied on completely to prevent abuses of power. What the framers sought to create was quite literally a framework, a set of rules within which a continuing process of evolution and definition could take place. Their greatest achievement at the time was to find workable solutions to problems which had arisen during the Revolution and its aftermath; their greatest legacy was to create a system sufficiently open-ended to allow their successors to solve other problems as they arose in the future.

FURTHER READING

Beard, C. A.: *An Economic Interpretation of the Constitution of the United States* (New York: 1913); repr. (New York: Free Press, 1986).

Boyd, S. R.: "The contract clause and the evolution of American federalism, 1789–1815," *William and Mary Quarterly*, 44 (1987), 529–48.

Farrand, M.: "Compromises of the Constitution," *American Historical Review*, 9 (1904), 479–89.

——: *The Framing of the Constitution of the United States* (New Haven, Conn., and London: 1913); repr. (New Haven and London: Yale University Press, 1962).

Farrand, M. (ed.): *The Records of the Federal Convention of 1787*, rev. edn., 4 vols. (New Haven, Conn.: Yale University Press, 1937; London: Oxford University Press, 1937); repr., 5 vols. (New Haven and London: Yale University Press, 1987). Vol. 5, *Supplement to Max Farrand's The Records of the Federal Convention of 1787*, ed. J. H. Hutson.

Finkelman, P.: "Slavery and the constitutional convention: making a covenant with death," *Beyond Confederation: Origins of the Constitution and American National Identity*, ed. R. Beeman, S. Botein and E. C. Carter (Chapel Hill and London: University of North Carolina Press, 1987).

Jillson, C. C.: "Constitution-making: alignment and realignment in the federal convention of 1787," *American Political Science Review*, 75 (1981), 598–612.

Levy, L. W. and Mahoney, D. J. (eds.): *The Framing and Ratification of the Constitution* (New York: Macmillan, 1987; London: Collier Macmillan, 1987).

McCaughey, E.: "*Marbury v. Madison*: have we missed the real meaning?," *Presidential Studies Quarterly*, 19 (1989), 491–528.

Murrin, J. M.: "Gordon S. Wood and the search for liberal America," *William and Mary Quarterly*, 44 (1987), 597–601.

Ohline, H. A.: "Republicanism and slavery: origins of the three-fifths clause in the United States Constitution," *William and Mary Quarterly*, 28 (1971), 563–84.

Rakove, J. N.: "Solving a constitutional puzzle: the treatymaking clause as a case study," *Perspectives in American History*, 1 (1984), 233–81.

Riker, W. H.: "The heresthetics of constitution-making: the presidency in 1787, with comments on determinism and rational choice," *American Political Science Review*, 78 (1984), 1–16.

Roche, J. P.: "The founding fathers: a reform caucus in action," *American Political Science Review*, 55 (1961), 799–816.

Rossiter, C.: *1787: the Grand Convention* (New York: Macmillan, 1966; London: Collier Macmillan, 1966).

Rossum, R. A.: "The courts and the judicial power," *The Framing and Ratification of the Constitution* (New York: Macmillan, 1987; London: Collier Macmillan, 1987), 222–41.

CHAPTER FIFTY-NINE

The debate over ratification of the Constitution

MURRAY DRY

WHEN the Federal Convention adjourned on September 17, 1787, it sent the completed Constitution to Congress with a resolution that "the preceding Constitution be laid before the United States in Congress assembled, and...afterwards be submitted to a Convention of Delegates, chosen in each State by the People thereof, under the Recommendation of its Legislature, for their Assent and Ratification" (Farrand, 1937, vol. 1, p. 665). Thus began a remarkably full, candid, and thoughtful popular deliberation on the future of republican government in America. It took place in the newspapers, with the most important essays receiving wide circulation in different states, in pamphlets, and, ultimately, in the several state ratification conventions, whose members were either chosen by the state legislatures or elected directly by the people. The Constitution's acceptance was assured on July 26, 1788, when New York became the eleventh state to ratify, and by the time Rhode Island ratified the Constitution, on May 29, 1790, more than 1,900 convention votes had been cast: 1,157 for the Constitution, 761 against (see table 1).

Table 1 Ratification of the Constitution: dates and votes by state convention

State	Date	Vote
Delaware	December 7, 1787	30–0
Pennsylvania	December 12, 1787	46–23
New Jersey	December 18, 1787	38–0
Georgia	January 2, 1788	26–0
Connecticut	January 9, 1788	128–40
Massachusetts	February 6, 1788	187–168
Maryland	April 21, 1788	63–11
South Carolina	May 23, 1788	149–73
New Hampshire	June 21, 1788	57–47[a]
Virginia	June 26, 1788	89–79
New York	July 26, 1788	30–27
North Carolina	August 1, 1788	84–184
	November 21, 1789	194–77[b]
Rhode Island	May 29, 1790	34–32[c]
Total		1,157–761

Sources: Elliot, 1891, except for [a]: Walker, 1888, pp. 42–3, 45; [b]: Trenholme, 1932, p. 238; and [c]: Kaminski, 1989, pp. 385, 390, note 55.

Notwithstanding each state's distinctive interests and personalities, one can with justification speak about the ratification debate in general terms. Both Federalist supporters of the Constitution and Anti-Federalist critics appealed to the principles of the American Revolution, swore their dedication to the Union, and claimed to be acting on true federal and republican principles. The purpose of this essay is to explain the ratification debate in light of these grounds of agreement. Part 1 reviews the major decisions of the Federal Convention, introduces the major protagonists, and describes each party's approach to the debate and manner of framing the issue; part 2 examines the deepest ground of disagreement between the Federalists and Anti-Federalists, the nature of republican government; part 3 discusses the most important constitutional applications of that disagreement over republican government, those involving federalism and the separation of powers; part 4 considers the argument over the absence of a bill of rights; and the conclusion considers the significance of the ratification debate for the principles of the American Revolution as well as subsequent constitutional development in America.

1 Points of Departure

The work of the Federal Convention and the "non-signers"

The framers of the Constitution decided to establish a genuine government for the Union, rather than to attempt to strengthen a mere Congress whose powers depended on the good will of the states. They also compromised on legislative apportionment, with equality in the Senate, to satisfy the small states, and on slavery and commercial regulation of navigation, to satisfy sectional concerns of North and South. The first decision accounts for the departures and opposition of the framers John Lansing and Robert Yates of New York and Luther Martin and John Francis Mercer of Maryland, and the sectional compromises account, in large part, for the non-signing of George Mason and Edmund Randolph of Virginia and Elbridge Gerry of Massachusetts. (Mason and Randolph also opposed the unitary executive, all three feared the power of the Senate, and Mason called for a bill of rights.) Randolph wrote a public letter explaining his refusal to sign and urging a second convention. Then, under James Madison's influence, he supported the Constitution in the Virginia convention, explaining his shift in terms of the needs of union, the fact that nine states had already ratified, and Massachusetts's proposal for recommendatory amendments (Elliot, 1891, vol. 3, pp. 25–6).

Identifying the protagonists and their writings

The major ratification debates took place in Pennsylvania (November–December 1787), Massachusetts (January–February 1788), Virginia (June 1788), and New York (June–July 1788). In Pennsylvania, James Wilson was the major spokesman for the Constitution, and he was assisted by Benjamin Rush and Thomas McKean. William Findley, John Smilie, and Robert Whitehall opposed ratification. In Massachusetts, no prominent Anti-Federalists were among the convention delegates, although Gerry was present to answer questions in writing. The major Federalists were Rufus King, Nathaniel Gorham, and Fisher Ames. In addition, John Hancock and Samuel Adams played a major role in the recommendatory amendments proposal (Gillespie, 1989, pp. 141–61). In Virginia, the debate was largely between the Anti-Federalist Patrick Henry and James Madison, the "Father of the Constitution." Henry was assisted by Mason, William Grayson, and James Monroe. Madison was assisted by Randolph, Edmund Pendleton, Arthur Lee, George and Wilson Nicholas, and John Marshall. In New York, the debate was largely between Alexander Hamilton, in support of the Constitution, and Melancton Smith, who recommended significant amendments but then voted to ratify. Hamilton was assisted by Robert Livingston and John Jay, Smith by Lansing.

When we turn to the major writings of the Federalists and Anti-Federalists, we encounter numerous pseudonyms. That is because the eighteenth-century practice was to emphasize the argument rather than the authority of the individual. The Federalists had the advantage, however: everyone knew that George Washington and Benjamin Franklin supported the Constitution, and the authors of the famous *Federalist Papers*, Alexander Hamilton, James Madison, and John Jay, who wrote under the pseudonym "Publius," were identified soon after publication. Likewise, Oliver Ellsworth was soon identified as the author of the "Landholder" essays, John Jay was known as the author of a pamphlet by "A Citizen of New York" in support of the Constitution, and two of James Wilson's most important speeches were published in pamphlet form (Ford, 1982, p. 137; Ford, 1888, pp. 67, 155; McMaster and Stone, 1888, pp. 217–31). The case is different with the Anti-Federalists. "Centinel," the major Pennsylvania Anti-Federal writer, was probably George Bryan, but his son, Samuel, also claimed authorship. "Agrippa," the major Massachusetts Anti-Federalist, appears to have been James Winthrop. It is unclear, however, whether New York's "Cato" was Governor George Clinton, and the evidence is only circumstantial for identifying the Maryland "Farmer" as John Francis Mercer. Not even the authors of the two best and most important Anti-Federal writings, the *Letters from the Federal Farmer* and the *Essays of Brutus*, long thought to be Richard Henry Lee and Robert Yates respectively, can be identified with certainty (Storing, 1981, intros. to 2.7, 4.6, 2.6, 5.1, 2.8, 2.9; Wood, 1974).

Two approaches to the ratification debate

Both parties to the debate expressed support for a candid examination of the Constitution and both identified good government with individual liberty (Storing, 1981, 2.9.2, 2.9.24, and Cooke, 1961, 1, 10, and 51). There was only partial agreement on the urgency of the situation, however. According to Publius, which name Hamilton chose after Publius Valerius, surnamed Publicola, a Roman consul in the first year of the Republic, "the crisis, at which we are arrived," may well determine "whether societies of men are really capable or not, of establishing good government from reflection and choice, or whether they

are forever destined to depend, for their political constitutions, on accident and force" (Cooke, 1961, 1, p. 3). While both the Federal Farmer and Brutus referred to the country's critical situation (Storing, 1981, 2.8.1, 2.8.3, and 2.9.2), they thought there was plenty of time and the people should not be rushed. "Remember," Brutus wrote, "when the people once part with power, they can seldom or never resume it again but by force" (Storing, 1981, 2.9.3). But Patrick Henry refused to accept the critical period argument: "Sir, it is the fortune of a free people not to be intimated by imaginary dangers. Fear is the passion of slaves. Our political and natural hemisphere[s] are now equally tranquil" (Elliot, 1891, vol. 3, p. 140).

Likewise, each side connected the debate over the Constitution to the principles of the Revolution differently. An Anti-Federalist from Massachusetts, writing as "A Republican Federalist," saw little difference between Great Britain and Congress.

The Revolution which separated the United States from Great-Britain was not more important to the liberties of America, than that which will result from the adoption of the new system. The *former* freed us from a *foreign subjugation*, and there is too much reason to apprehend, that the *latter* will reduce us to a *federal domination*. (Storing, 1981, 4.13.13)

In the New York Convention, Thomas Treadwell decried the absence of a bill of rights as "depart[ing] widely from the principles and political faith of '76, when the spirit of liberty ran high, and danger put a curb on ambition" (Elliot, 1891, vol. 2, p. 401).

On the other side, Hamilton, also in the New York Convention, suggested that, while an "extreme spirit of jealousy" was "natural" "[i]n the commencement of a revolution which received its birth from the usurpations of tyranny," it had become "predominant and excessive" (Elliot, 1891, vol. 2, p. 301; *see also* Cooke, 1961, 1, p. 5). And John Marshall, in a speech supporting the Constitution in the Virginia Convention, emphasized the difference between Congress and Parliament (Elliot, 1891, vol. 3, pp. 225–6).

2 Two Views of Republican Government

The above remarks suggest that the Federalists and Anti-Federalists understood the requirements of republican government differently. The Anti-Federal position is presented first, because it was the deepest ground of the critics' opposition to the Constitution and the Federalists were forced to respond to it.

The Anti-Federalist conception emphasized persuasion over coercion and drew on two sources, Montesquieu's discussion of republics and the constitutional controversy which led to the American Revolution. From Montesquieu, they argued that only a small territory and homogeneous population could support republican government; otherwise "the public good is sacrificed to a thousand views…and depends on accidents" (Storing, 1981, 2.9.11). From the Revolution, they argued that two essential ingredients of republican government, a substantial representation and jury trial, were not secure. A full and equal representation "is that which possesses the same interests, feelings, opinions, and views the people themselves would were they all assembled," it required regulation so that "every order of men in the community, according to the common course of elections, can have a share in [government]," including "professional men, merchants, traders, farmers, mechanics etc" (Storing, 1981, 2.8.15). The jury trial concern was twofold; article three provided for appellate review, by the Supreme Court, of all cases "in law and fact." That Congress could make exceptions to this was no guarantee that it would. And no jury trial was provided for in civil cases.

The Anti-Federalist "small republic" position differs from each of its sources. Montesquieu's argument about the public good went together with more restrictions on individual freedom than the Anti-Federalists, in general, supported. George Mason's proposal for a sumptuary law, to discourage consumption, is an illustrative exception to the rule (Farrand, 1937, vol. 2, pp. 344, 606). Likewise, the emphasis on representation moved away from Montesquieu's republic, where no such substitute for civic participation is mentioned. Except for "A Maryland Farmer," who proposed the direct government of the citizens with the Swiss cantons as his model, the Anti-Federalists took representation for granted. As for the revolutionary argument concerning "no taxation without representation," the application was imperfect, since in that case, unlike the one presented by the Constitution, no American had a vote for any representative in Parliament. The Anti-Federalists meant that the proposed federal representation was inadequate.

To explain what he meant by a substantial representation, the Federal Farmer argued that, while there was no constitutional aristocracy in America, there was a natural aristocracy, in contrast to a natural democracy; the former class consisted of governors, members of Congress, state senators, the principal officers of Congress, the superior judges, the "most eminent professional men," and the wealthy; the latter included "in general the yeomanry, the subordinate officers, civil and military, the fishermen, mechanics and traders, many of the merchants and professional men" (Storing, 1981, 2.8.97). The elective principle produces a substantial representation of the natural democracy, or the middling class, in the state governments; but in the federal government under the Constitution, election is bound to produce a largely if not exclusively aristocratic body.

The Federalist conception of republican government emphasized election as the means to an effective administration of government. The most extensive formulations came from a speech by James Wilson, on November 24, 1787 in the Pennsylvania Convention, which was subsequently published in pamphlet form, and from the *Federalist Papers*.

Wilson argued that representation was the key to America's superiority over both ancient governments and the British Constitution:

the world has left to America the glory and happiness of forming a government where representation shall at once supply the basis and the cement of the superstructure. For representation,

Sir, is the true chain between the people and those to whom they entrust the administration of the government; and though it may consist of many links, its strength and brightness never should be impaired. (McMaster and Stone, 1888, pp. 222, 223)

Wilson concluded by suggesting that the different "links" between the people and their representatives provided for the best possible government. "In its principles, Sir, it is purely democratical; varying indeed, in its form, in order to admit all the advantages, and to exclude all the disadvantages which are incidental to the known and established constitutions of government" (McMaster and Stone, 1888, pp. 230–1).

While Madison employed the term "republic" to distinguish direct from representative democracy, he also emphasized election as the essential and defining character of such a government (Cooke, 1961, 39, p. 251). Moreover, Madison's argument in *The Federalist*, no. 10, reveals how election over the extended sphere improves republican government by refining it. The founder's task is to control the effects of faction, of interested and/or passionate action which violates the rights of citizens and/or the permanent and aggregate interests of the community. Since the majority principle was strong in America, it would control a minority faction; the real problem consisted in the majority faction, which threatened majority tyranny. Assuming that people will tend to give their suffrage to those who are able, election, in contrast to lottery, will result in the selection of the more able, and to a greater extent in a large, diverse constituency, where the competition will be keener for the relatively fewer seats. This could be called the "refinement" view of representation, in contrast to the Anti-Federal emphasis on "reflection." In addition, if the larger constituencies are also made up of more diverse economic interests, and Madison assumed they would be in America, then the candidates will have to moderate their views to gain a majority, just as the elected representatives will have to do the same thing in order to form legislative majorities.

Hamilton provided a more direct reply to the Anti-Federal argument concerning the class character of representation in *The Federalist* and in the New York convention. First, he claimed that "the idea of an actual representation of all classes of the people by persons of each class is altogether visionary," since as long as people are free to choose, those in certain professions will defer to those in others. Hamilton argued that there were three key classes, or interests, in American society – the commercial, the landed, and the learned professions. As the merchant is the natural representative of the mechanics and manufacturers, so the large landholder is, especially on matters involving taxes, the natural representative of the small landholder; and the men of the learned professions, lawyers especially, will have the confidence of all parts of society (Cooke 1961, 35, pp. 219–20).

The Anti-Federalists challenged the alleged harmony of interests between large and small landholders, and they did not all share Hamilton's confidence in men of the learned professions. In the Massachusetts convention, Amos Singletary said:

These lawyers, and men of learning, and moneyed men, that talk so finely, and gloss over matters so smoothly, to make us poor illiterate people swallow down the pill, expect to get into Congress themselves; they expect to be the managers of this Constitution, and get all the power and all the money into their own hands, and then they will swallow up all us little folks, like the great Leviathan. (Elliott, 1891, vol. 2, p. 102)

Such distrust was the basis of the Anti-Federal concern that a government too far removed from the people could not keep their confidence.

The fullest exchange on the character of representation in the new government took place between Smith and Hamilton in the New York convention. After defining natural aristocracy in terms of birth, education, talents, and wealth, as the Federal Farmer did, Smith made two claims on behalf of the middling class, or yeomanry. First, they were by habit and necessity "more temperate, of better morals, and of less ambition, than the great." Second, they were "the best possible security to liberty," "because the interests of both the rich and the poor are involved in that of the middling class.

No burden can be laid on the poor but what will sensibly affect the middling class" (Elliot, 1891, pp. 246–8).

Smith's argument was fully consistent with free choice, as long as the number of representatives was substantial enough for the yeomanry (or middling class) to get elected, and it was sound should that class embody the entire community. It also combined the Anti-Federal focus on civic virtue with the need to rely on representation.

In reply, Hamilton advanced two unusual and provocative arguments. First, "as riches increase and accumulate in few hands…, virtue will be… considered as only a graceful appendage of wealth, and the tendency of things will be to depart from the republican standard" (Elliot, 1891, vol. 2, p. 256). This hinted at a new republican form, where inequality of condition would flourish; perhaps that is why Hamilton sometimes used the term representative government (Elliot, 1891, vol. 2, p. 353). Then, he went after Smith's celebration of the middling class.

It is a harsh doctrine that men grow wicked in proportion as they improve and enlighten their minds. Experience has by no means justified us in the supposition that there is more virtue in one class of men than in another. Look through the rich and the poor of the community, the learned and the ignorant. Where does virtue predominate? The difference indeed consists, not in the quantity, but kind, of vices which are incident to various classes; and here the advantage of character belongs to the wealthy. Their vices are probably more favorable to the prosperity of the state than those of the indigent, and partake less of moral depravity. (Elliot, vol. 2, p. 257)

What Hamilton saw as a division between the few and the many, Smith saw as a tripartite division, with an agricultural middle class holding the balance of power. Hamilton said inequality was inevitable if individual liberty was secured (Madison says the same in *The Federalist*, no. 10) and, if forced to choose, he opted for the public benefits of the vices of the few wealthy. Smith did not regard substantial inequality as inevitable and found the frugal yeoman as the representative of the public good.

Another element of Anti-Federal republicanism concerned the importance of religion as a source of character formation and a common set of beliefs. For example, in the Massachusetts convention, Charles Turner argued that "without the prevalence of *Christian piety, and morals*, the best republican Constitution can never save us from slavery and ruin." If the Constitution was to be ratified, he hoped the legislature would recommend to the several states that laws be passed providing for religious education.

May *religion*, with sanctity of morals[,] prevail and *increase*, that the patriotic civilian and ruler may have the *sublime, parental* satisfaction of *eagerly* embracing every opportunity of mitigating the rigours of government, in proportion to that increase of morality which may render the people more capable of being *a law unto themselves*. (Storing, 1981, 4.18.2)

Others, including the Federal Farmer, criticized the Constitution's lack of any qualifications for office, aside from age, citizenship, and residency: "It can be no objection to the elected, that they are Christians, Pagans, Mohametans [*sic*], or Jews; that they are of any colour, rich or poor, convict or not. Hence, many men may be elected who cannot be electors" (Storing, 1981, 2.8.150). Herbert Storing has pointed out that the "Anti-Federalist position was not so much that government ought to foster religion as that the consolidating Constitution threatened the healthy religious situation as it then existed in the states" (Storing, 1981, vol. 1, p. 23).

The Federalists, who emphasized the checking of ambition by ambition, assumed the requisite amount of civic virtue (Cooke, 51, 55, pp. 349, 378).

This disagreement over the nature of republican government has been described in two different ways: as a social conflict between the many and the few, in which the Anti-Federalists spoke for the "radical Whig tradition of mistrust of governmental authority," while the Federalists "meant to restore and to prolong the traditional kind of elitist influence in politics that social developments, especially since the Revolution, were undermining" (Wood, 1969, pp. 520, 513); and as a political disagreement over whether republican government based on the principles of individual liberty and consent could succeed over an extended territory and population (Storing, 1981, vol. 1, pp. 5–6, 71–5). One difficulty with the former interpretation, however, is that the Constitution the Federalists were defending contained no property qualification for any offices, and it was generally known that the suffrage requirements, which were left to the states, would become more popular (Farrand, 1937, vol. 1, p. 49).

3 The Constitutional Structure and Powers: Federalism and the Separation of Powers

We turn now to an examination of the most important constitutional issues: federalism and separation of powers.

Federalism

The federalism topics involve disputes over terminology (who were the true federalists?), over the preamble and the legality of the proposed Constitution, and over several provisions of Article 1.

The Anti-Federalists charged that the supporters' appropriation of the name Federalists was an act of larceny, since they were the true federalists (Storing, 1981, vol. 1, pp. 8, 80). This issue was complicated by the ambiguity of usage during the Confederation period and the subsequent change in meanings as a result of the Constitution and the ratification debate. During the Confederation period, "federal" referred to measures designed to support and strengthen Congress. At the same time, the federal principle meant that the states were primary, not the Union, and hence it was appropriate for the state legislatures to control the unicameral Congress, through election, recall, and federation reliance on state requisitions of men and money. As supporters of a measure to strengthen the authority of the Union, the Constitution, the Federalists had a claim on their name; on the other hand, the opponents argued that the measures proposed were so strong as to go beyond the federal principle.

Both sides revised their views in light of the Constitution. The Federalists used the compromise over legislative apportionment and other provisions recognizing the states

to argue that the Constitution was "partly federal, partly national." Most of the Anti-Federalists, on the other hand, moved away from the standard view of federalism, since they agreed that the Articles of Confederation were inadequate, precisely because requisitions, previously understood as the essence of a federal system, did not work, and they preferred to revise the proposed Constitution (Dry, 1989, pp. 65–9).

The debate over the preamble and the proposed mode of ratification of the Constitution shows how the terminological dispute was connected to a substantive issue. For example, when the preamble came under discussion in the Virginia Convention, Patrick Henry dramatically objected:

My political curiosity, exclusive of my anxious solicitude for the public welfare, leads me to ask who authorized them to speak the language of *We the People*, instead of *We the States*. States are the characteristic, and the soul of a confederation. If the states be not the agents of this compact, it must be one great, consolidated, national government, of the people of all the states. (Elliot, 1891, vol. 3, p. 22)

With Congress's limited instructions to the Federal Convention, to meet "for the sole and express purpose of revising the Articles of Confederation" in mind, Henry and other Anti-Federalists questioned the legality of the Federal Convention's work (Storing, 1981, vol. pp. 12–14). The standard answer to this objection was that the Constitution was but a proposal until ratified by the people through specifically chosen conventions (*see* Wilson in McMaster and Stone, 1888, 219–20). But this reply was not sufficient to legitimate the ratification provision, which violated the Articles of Confederation in two ways: the ratification of nine states, rather than all 13, was sufficient to bring the Constitution into being, and the state legislatures were bypassed for the conventions. Luther Martin pressed this objection in the Federal Convention and again in his *Genuine Information* (Storing, 1981, 2.14.114). The fullest defense, alluded to in the Federal Convention by Hamilton and spelled out by Madison in *The Federalist*, no. 40, was that the mode of ratification was an exercise of the people's right to form and re-form governments, i.e., to revolution (Farrand, 1937, vol. 1, p. 283; Cooke, 1961, p. 265). Beyond the legal point, the Federalists, especially Madison, argued that a popular form of ratification, that is, through state conventions rather than state legislatures, was necessary to assure the supremacy of the new federal government (Farrand, 1937, vol. 1, pp. 122–3).

Due to the importance of federalism for the ratification debate, the major state ratification conventions focused their attention on provisions in Article 1, to which we now turn. Topics of discussion included representation, the two- and six-year terms of office for the House and Senate, the "time, place, and manner" clause, and the extent of the legislative powers.

The concern about the possible misuse of the "time, place, and manner" clause reflects the extent of distrust more than any solid argument; Congress had to be able to provide for its own elections if a recalcitrant state (i.e., Rhode Island) refused to do so. The rotation and recall argument, which was not made in connection with the popularly elected House of Representatives, reflects the traditional notion of federalism. If, as the Federalists claimed, the Senate was the branch of government representing the states, the state governments should be able to control their senators. But many were satisfied with the key elements of the compromise, according to which the states did elect their senators and were guaranteed their equal representation (Constitution, Article V). The argument for an increase in representation, which Smith and many other Anti-Federalists made, ultimately gets directed at a reduction in federal legislative powers. That is because no reasonable increase in federal representation could match the extent of representation in the states.

Hence the major Anti-Federal argument for constitutional change was for a redistribution of the powers of government, as between the nation and the states, to reflect the distribution of representation. Their most important proposals concerned restrictions on the federal powers to tax and to raise armies; the former should be limited to the power to tax foreign imports, and the latter should not extend to a general power to raise armies in time of peace, unless two-thirds of both houses support it (Storing, 2.9.126). Thus they attempted to reply to Hamilton's great challenge, expressed in *The Federalist*, no. 23, that one not embrace the contradiction of, on the one hand, supporting union and entrusting certain national objectives to the federal government, and, on the other hand, refusing to grant ample powers for the attainment of those objectives (Cooke, 1961, p. 151). To the question of how one could foresee the extent of the powers necessary for raising and supporting armies, Brutus assumed that the power would be granted when truly needed, and he also argued that the object of government in the United States was not only to "preserve the general government, and provide for the common defence and general welfare of the union," but also to support the state governments (Storing, 1981, 2.9.80). Seven state conventions proposed limits on the federal tax power, to the import tax, with requisitions as the backup provision; five state conventions proposed restrictions on standing armies; and four state conventions proposed a limitation on the powers to those "expressly" delegated (see table 2, p. 486).

The separation of powers

The separation of powers objections involved the powers of the Senate, the re-eligibility of the executive and the absence of a council of appointment, and the judiciary.

The Anti-Federalists' position on the separation of powers reflected their judgment that the threat to republican government came from a concentration of power in the hands of the few. Patrick Henry, Centinel, and A Maryland Farmer argued that the proposed Constitution was an unsuccessful hybrid of the pure separation of powers, which to them meant legislative supremacy, and mixed government, which required a hereditary monarch and nobility. Since the materials for a mixed government were not present in America, the only sound choice was to construct a government with a simple structure, where the middling class would

Table 2 Major amendments proposed by the Anti-Federalists, state by state

	Pa	Ma	Md	SC	NH	Va	NY	NC	RI
Jury trial in civil cases	×̲	×	×		×	×	×	×	×
Jury trial in criminal cases with no appeal on matters of fact			×						
No interference in state election laws unless the state fails to provide for elections	×̲	×	×̲	×	×	×	×	×	×
State control of its militia	×̲		×̲			×	×	×	×
Strict separation of powers	×̲					×		×	×
Non-supremacy of treaties	×̲							×	
Restriction of jurisdiction of federal courts	×̲	×	×		×	×	×	×	×
Limitation of powers to those "expressly" or "clearly" delegated		×	×	×	×		×		
No direct taxation unless the import tax is insufficient and/or requisitions fail		×	×̲	×	×	×	×	×	×
No congressionally authorized monopolies		×			×		×		×
Special two-thirds congressional majority required for navigation acts						×		×	
Restrictions on a standing army			×̲		×	×	×	×	×
Limitation on presidential re-eligibility						×	×	×	
Limitation on Senate re-eligibility							×		
State recall of senators							×		×
Oath not to violate state constitutions							×		
Provision for freedom of speech and/or press	×̲	×				×	×		
Provision for freedom of religion and/or rights of conscience			×̲		×		×		×

Sources: Schwartz, 1980, pp. 658–60, 712–13, 732–5, 756–7, 760–1, 840–5, 911–18; and Elliot, 1981, vol. 1, pp. 334–7, vol. 4, p. 249.
Note: ×̲ indicates that the proposed amendment was defeated; all others were passed.

predominate in the legislature and the legislature would be the supreme branch of government (Storing, 1981, vol. 1, pp. 53–63).

The most common Anti-Federalist criticism of the Senate, in addition to the absence of rotation and recall, discussed above, concerned that body's participation in the appointment and treaty-making powers. The Anti-Federalists preferred a council of appointment, elected by the legislature, as many of the state constitutions provided, and many preferred that treaties be approved by both houses.

The Anti-Federalist assessment of the executive was surprisingly moderate, in light of their apprehension about consolidated government. While Mason and Randolph opposed unity in the Federal Convention, neither made this point in expressing his objections after the Federal Convention adjourned, and there was general acceptance of a unitary executive, except, of course, for the council of appointment. The Anti-Federalists did oppose re-eligibility, however, which Hamilton and other Federalists regarded as an essential inducement to channeling ambition into constitutionally constructive action, good behavior. Most Anti-Federalists accepted the qualified veto also (Dry, 1987, pp. 285–7).

As for the judiciary, Brutus's prescient account anticipated the full development of both judicial review and federal judicial power (Storing, 1981, 2.9.130–196). By extending the judicial power to all cases in law and equity arising under the Constitution, Article 111 permitted the courts "to give the Constitution a legal construction." That plus the equity jurisdiction gave the courts the power "to explain the Constitution according to the reasoning spirit of it, without being confined to the words or letter." Hence, "the real effect of this system of government will … be brought home to the feelings of the people through the medium of the judicial power" (Storing, 1981, 2.9.30).

Brutus argued that the courts should not be permitted to interpret the Constitution against acts of Congress, or, alternatively, if they were to have that power, they should be responsible to the electorate. He also that lower federal courts were unnecessary, as the states could provide the courts of first resort (Storing, 1981, 2.9.169, 183).

The fullest Federalist account of the separation of powers in the Constitution came from the *Federalist Papers*. To defend the Constitution's assignment of powers to the different branches of government, Madison argued that, rightly understood, which meant on the basis of Montesquieu's example of England and the state constitutions, the doctrine of the separation of powers was fully compatible with some sharing or overlapping of powers among the different branches, that it did not require a pure separation of kinds of power into distinct branches. It is an impressive argument.

To appreciate how the Anti-Federalists could object, it is necessary to recall that the most famous authors of the doctrine, Locke and Montesquieu, supported constitutional monarchy. Might not the republican form of government affect which branch receives

the appointment power, the treaty-making power, and the direction of foreign affairs generally? And what about the number of individuals assigned to each branch? James Wilson, for example, shared the Anti-Federal concern that the Senate might have too much power (McMaster and Stone, 1888, pp. 326–7).

Hamilton's account of the judiciary in the *Federalist Papers* was in direct response to Brutus's essays. A comparison of *The Federalist*, no. 51, where the separation of powers doctrine was presented in terms of ambition checking ambition, with *The Federalist*, no. 78, where the judiciary was first discussed and its good behavior tenure was defended, yields the following tension. In the former Madison asserted that "the interest of the man must be connected with the constitutional rights of the place," and in the latter Hamilton maintained that a written constitution required, for its protection, a learned judiciary, insulated from popular control, whose "proper and peculiar province" was "the interpretation of the laws." The judiciary provided a distinctive function, and judges were expected to interpret the laws with learning and disinterestedness (Stoner, 1987, pp. 208–16).

Brutus agreed about the distinctiveness of the courts, but he thought the judiciary should not have the power to construe the Constitution. For Hamilton, the judges acted as the people's representatives in government by upholding the Constitution, which the people, through their popular ratification conventions, have laid down as their frame of government and fundamental law. The written Constitution plus an independent judiciary produces what is known as judicial review, the doctrine that a law contrary to the "manifest tenor" of the Constitution is void, or the Constitution has no legal standing (Cooke, 1961, 78, pp. 524–5).

The question whether or not to have lower federal courts with full jurisdiction over all cases in law and equity arising under the Constitution concerned federalism again. Brutus's proposal to rely on state courts to adjudicate federal questions was inconsistent with the new form of federalism, but it must be acknowledged that he predicted what came to be called "loose construction."

4 The Bill of Rights: An Anti-Federalist Victory, of Sorts

The most common Anti-Federal argument against the Constitution concerned the absence of a bill of rights, and, in a certain sense, it was their only successful position. The Constitution would not have been ratified without the promise, first made in the Massachusetts Convention and subsequently accepted, that recommendatory amendments accompanying a vote for unconditional ratification would be considered by Congress (Rutland, 1983, pp. 143–9). An examination of the arguments for and against the need for a bill of rights show the Anti-Federalists to have had the stronger argument.

The main Federalist arguments in defense of the Constitution without a bill of rights were: first, the entire Constitution, as it provides for a well-framed government with power checking power and offices filled by election, is a bill of rights; second, there is an internal bill of rights, especially in Article 1, sections 9 and 10; and third, unlike the state governments, the federal government is one of enumerated powers, and hence what is not enumerated is not given, and the state bills of rights remain in force (McMaster and Stone, 1888, pp. 143–4, 252–4; Cooke, 1961, 84). The Anti-Federal responses, in reverse order, were: first, the clear supremacy of the federal Constitution and the extensiveness of the powers granted call into question any reliance on the state bills of rights on the one hand, or the implied restrictions on powers on the other; second, to the extent that one might rely on the principle of implied restrictions on powers, the very fact that certain restrictions are noted suggests, if anything, that what is not expressly reserved is granted; and third, the general argument about a well-constructed government points back to the discussions of federalism and republican government (Storing, 1981, 2.9.22–33; vol. 1, pp. 64–70).

An examination of the major Anti-Federal proposals for amendments reveals the significance of the federalism issue as well as the differences between most of their proposals and what eventually resulted in the first ten amendments (table 2).

In one sense, however, the Anti-Federalist demand for a bill of rights derived from their understanding of republican government. That goes back to the importance of mild government and the educational value of proclaiming the rights and keeping the people aware of them. As the Federal Farmer put it, "If a nation means its systems, religious or political, shall have duration, it ought to recognize the leading principles of them in the front page of every family book" (Storing, 1981, 2.8.196). The affirmation of rights against the government does reflect Anti-Federal constitutionalism. Unlike several state bills of rights, however, the rights enumerated in the Bill of Rights are largely individual rather than collective. Consequently, the civic education that the Bill of Rights has provided has been primarily to support individual rights rather than obligations to the community.

5 Conclusion

The ratification of the Constitution established the American frame of government and thereby completed the American Revolution, since the principles of the Revolution looked up to collective self-government in the service of individual liberty, the natural rights of life, liberty, and the pursuit of happiness. Consideration of the arguments on the merits, as presented in the ratification conventions and in the fullest and most thoughtful writings on the Constitution, yields the conclusion that the Federalists won because they had the better argument (Storing, 1981, vol. 1, p. 71). The Anti-Federal critics were in part the victims of their own candid patriotism; they wanted to secure the blessings of liberty, and they acknowledged that this required a genuine government, rather than modified Articles of Confederation. Hence, they never could answer Hamilton's charge that they were attempting to reconcile contradictions by agreeing to the proper objects of a national government but refusing to grant the necessary powers, i.e., the powers to tax and raise armies without limit (Cooke, 1961, 23, p. 151). To assume that there were limits to the resources that might be necessary to wage war or enforce treaties, or to assume that the states could be relied on to supply what was needed in an emergency, was to overlook the lessons of the Confederation period.

The Anti-Federalists nonetheless deserve to be considered junior partners to the Federalists in the crowning achievement of the American founding. First, they were thoughtful critics of a new form of republican government, one that emphasized effective administration and relied primarily on self-interest rather than love of country. Future generations of Americans have found it useful to be reminded of the limits of this largely successful "low but solid" approach to free government. Second, the Anti-Federalists' call for a bill of rights did succeed, even if it was not all that they had in mind. Third, on important constitutional issues, federalism and the separation of powers, Anti-Federalist arguments survived ratification, albeit with modification. This is especially true with federalism, where advocates of both the strict construction of federal legislative powers and the states'-rights view of the union attempted to achieve the Anti-Federal objective of a balance between the nation and the states. Examples of the strict construction view include the opposition of Madison and Jefferson to the establishment of a national bank, in 1790, under the implied powers doctrine; examples of the states'-rights view include Madison's and Jefferson's opposition to the Alien and Sedition Acts of 1798, John Calhoun's nullification argument in the 1850s, and the secessionist argument at the outset of the Civil War. As for the separation of powers, two disputes can be connected to the ratification debate: the ongoing debate, since Washington's Neutrality Declaration in 1793, over the scope of executive power in war and foreign affairs, and the more recent division between supporters of the Bill of Rights, which includes the judicial power of enforcing rights against the government, and supporters of the Constitution, meaning primarily the separation of powers and checks and balances among the political branches of government. This division departs somewhat from the ratification debate, as each side favors strong national government; the partisans of the Bill of Rights resemble the Anti-Federalists in their distrust of government, but not in their reliance on a strong federal judiciary to protect individual rights.

Finally, the contemporary disagreement about liberalism and republicanism, or individual rights versus communal, or communitarian, concerns (Sandel, 1984, pp. 1–11), can be related to the ratification debate over republican government. The contemporary communitarian position is not necessarily against big government, however, and the Anti-Federalist "small republic" position acknowledged the primacy of individual liberty.

FURTHER READING

Berman, Richard, Botein, Stephen and Carter, Edward C. II (eds.): *Beyond Confederation: Origins of the Constitution and American National Identity* (Chapel Hill: University of North Carolina Press, 1987).

Cooke, Jacob (ed.): *The Federalist* (Cleveland and New York: World Publishing Co., 1961) [Internal citations refer to an essay number and, where appropriate, a page number as well; since the essay numbers are standard in all full editions, and the differences in the text are insignificant, any full edition of *The Federalist* may be consulted]

Dry, Murray: "The Anti-Federalists and the Constitution," *Principles of the Constitutional Order*, ed. Robert L. Utley Jr. (Lanham, Md.: University Press of America, 1989), 63–88.

——: "The case against ratification: Anti-Federal constitutional thought," *The Framing and Ratification of the Constitution*, ed. Leonard W. Levy and Dennis J. Mahoney (New York: Macmillan, 1987), 271–91.

Elliot, Jonathan: *The Debates of the State Conventions on the Adoption of the Federal Constitution, as Recommended by the General Convention at Philadelphia in 1787*, 3rd edn. (Philadelphia: Lippincott, 1891).

Farrand, Max (ed.): *The Records of the Federal Convention*, rev. edn. in 4 vols. (New Haven, Conn.: Yale University Press, 1937).

Ford, Paul Leicester (ed.): *Essays on the Constitution of the United States* (Brooklyn, NY: 1892); repr. (New York: Burt Franklin, 1970).

——: *Pamphlets on the Constitution of the United States, Published During its Discussion by the People, 1787–1788* (Brooklyn, NY: 1888); repr. (New York: Burt Franklin, 1971).

Gillespie, Michael: "Massachusetts," *Ratifying the Constitution*, ed. Michael Gillespie and Michael Liensch (Lawrence: University of Kansas Press, 1989), 138–67.

Gillespie, Michael, and Liensch, Michael (eds.): *Ratifying the Constitution* (Lawrence: University of Kansas Press, 1989).

Jensen, Merrill, Kaminski, John P., and Saladino, Gaspare J., et al. (eds.): *The Documentary History of the Ratification of the Constitution*, 12 vols. to date (Madison: State Historical Society of Wisconsin, 1976–).

Kaminski, John P.: "Rhode Island," *Ratifying the Constitution*, ed. Michael Gillespie and Michael Liensch (Lawrence: University of Kansas Press, 1989), 368–90.

Kesler, Charles (ed.): *Saving the Revolution: the Federalist Papers and the American Founding* (New York: Free Press, 1987).

Levy, Leonard W., and Mahoney, Dennis J. (eds.): *The Framing and Ratification of the Constitution* (New York: Macmillan, 1987).

McMaster, John Bach, and Stone, Frederick D.: *Pennsylvania and the Federal Constitution* (Philadelphia: Pennsylvania Historical Society, 1888).

Main, Jackson Turner: *The Antifederalists: Critics of the Constitution* (Chapel Hill: University of North Carolina Press, 1960).

Rutland, Robert Allen: *The Ordeal of the Constitution: the Anti-Federalists and the Ratification Struggle of 1787–1788* (Norman: University of Oklahoma Press, 1966).

——: *The Birth of the Bill of Rights: 1776–1791*, rev. edn. (Boston: Northeastern University Press, 1983).

Sandel, Michael (ed.): *Liberalism and its Critics* (New York: New York University Press, 1984).

Schwartz, Bernard: *The Roots of the Bill of Rights*, 5 vols. (New York: Chelsea House Publishers, 1980).

Stoner, James: "Constitutionalism and judging in the *Federalist*," *Saving the Revolution: the Federalist Papers and the American Founding*, ed. Charles Kesler (New York: Free Press, 1987), 203–18.

Storing, Herbert J.: "The 'other' Federalist papers: a preliminary sketch," *Political Science Reviewer*, 6 (1976), 215–47.

——: *The Complete Anti-Federalist*, 7 vols. (Chicago: University of Chicago Press, 1981); first vol. separately pubd as *What the Anti-Federalists Were For!* [Internal references refer to the volume, entry number, and paragraph]. An abridged one-volume version of *The Complete Anti-Federalist* was published under the title, *The Anti-Federalist: Writings of the Opponents of the Constitution* (Chicago: University of Chicago Press, 1985).

Trenholme, Louise Irby: *The Ratification of the Federal Costitution in North Carolina* (New York: Columbia University Press, 1932).

Walker, Joseph B.: *A History of the New Hampshire Convention* (Boston: Supples and Hurd, 1888).

Wood, Gordon S.: *Creation of the American Republic, 1776–1787* (Chapel Hill: University of North Carolina Press, 1969).

——: "The Authorship of *The Letters from the Federal Farmer*," *William and Mary Quarterly*, 31 (1974), 299–308.

PART IV

External Effects of the Revolution

CHAPTER SIXTY

Great Britain in the aftermath of the American Revolution

IAN R. CHRISTIE

THE series of setbacks and defeats encountered by the British in the American War of Independence – the surrender of Burgoyne's army at Saratoga, the subsequent intervention of France and Spain, the capture of Cornwallis's army at Yorktown – followed by the acknowledgment of the secession of the 13 North American colonies, created serious political tensions within Great Britain, and generated a sense of despondency about the country's future. Among the members of the political class, from the King downwards, the fear spread that its position as a leading great power had been destroyed, and that French world ascendancy was unavoidable. Very few far-sighted people – though there were a few – foresaw that the political independence of America would strike no serious blow at the natural economic interdependence of the two English-speaking communities. Even fewer foresaw the remarkable recovery of British power within a few years of the signing of a humiliating peace. In the immediate period of wartime and postwar crisis recriminations over the responsibility for disaster created bitter tensions among the politicians, and the repercussions spread widely among an informed public in the middling ranks of society. From the beginning of 1780 till the summer of 1784 the domestic political atmosphere was one of constant strain, until at last, with the war over and the process of repair and reconstruction begun, the natural conservative stability of the nation reasserted itself.

1 Britain and Europe

French statesmen believed in 1783 that they had successfully cut Great Britain down to size, and for the time being at least the country's pretensions to rank as a great power had been seriously checked. With the winning of Independence by the Americans the Crown had lost a quarter of its subjects and a good deal more than a quarter of the economic resources, including shipping and seamen, which contributed to the sinews of war. In strategic terms the balance had been tilted adversely both in the New and in the Old World. American mainland bases which had provided a back-up for the defense of the West Indian portion of the British Empire had gone, and the return of East and West Florida to Spain enhanced that nation's military and naval position in the Caribbean. The situation of the British in the West Indies was also weakened by the cession of Tobago and St. Lucia, while in the Mediterranean the return of Minorca to Spain deprived the nation of an important naval base, the loss of which was to be signally felt at the beginning of the next round of wars against the Bourbon powers. Although in North America the British still retained possession of Newfoundland, Canada, and the maritime provinces of Nova Scotia and New Brunswick, these represented little in the way of strength, and it was by no means clear whether Canada, in particular, might be a liability rather than an asset, a pawn in American hands readily open to invasion if ever the Americans saw fit to join any combination of Britain's enemies.

From the diplomatic viewpoint the war appeared to have clinched, to the advantage of France, the growing alienation of the British from one of their traditional allies – the United Provinces – which had already begun to show itself during the Seven Years' War. And by a cautious avoidance of any aggressive move against Hanover the French had managed to humiliate Britain without creating east of the Rhine any apprehensions about the balance of power which might have attracted European states towards the British camp. The general attitude in Europe immediately after the war was that Britain had become a negligible quantity in the scales of power, no longer alliance-worthy – a country which might be ignored in the considerations of European power politics.

Nevertheless, as events were soon to show, the situation was far from irretrievable. The British Isles still remained a formidable base for naval power, as its rulers well understood, and the impetus of the wartime naval construction program was determinedly prolonged into the years of peace. Whatever the losses in the West, the British position in the East had not been adversely affected. French pressures and pretensions had been beaten off, and, if anything, the British hold on India had been consolidated, carrying with it both present and future commercial advantage. The Dutch rivals in this area had been worsted and humiliated, being obliged by the peace terms to abandon their Indian trading base at Negapatam and to concede British demands for freedom of navigation in the Spice Islands. The great ships of the British East India Company still brought in their lucrative cargoes from Canton. Britain's freedom in the sea lanes was still secure in the East and in the West, and, within three or four years after being written off as of no account, British governments were once again exerting their weight in Europe, combatting French pretensions, and entering into the diplomatic combinations with Holland and Prussia which made up the Triple Alliance system of 1788. Behind this modest recovery on the international stage lay a saga of internal political recovery,

administrative and financial modernization, and economic advance.

2 Domestic Political Difficulties

Defeat in America temporarily disrupted the normal pattern of British domestic politics. Up till 1779 the ministry headed by Lord North appeared stable internally and assured of general support within Parliament and out-of-doors. The Declaration of Independence had appeared to vindicate the Cassandra-like prophecies of ministers, that from the start the colonial protests about Parliament's powers had been leading up to a repudiation of imperial control; and many of the men who had previously sympathized with the colonists and had signed petitions in their favor were alienated from them by the Declaration. The government at first received wide support for its policy of preserving imperial unity by force of arms, and it was not until defeat at Saratoga had shown up the limitations of British military power, and till France and Spain had become involved in support of the Americans, that disillusionment began to spread.

At one level this was manifested by dissensions within the ministry ostensibly over Ireland (*see* chapter 62). During much of 1779 the administration seemed in a parlous state. The Earl of Suffolk, Secretary of State for the Northern Department, was incapacitated and died in office. Through much of the year Lord North appeared to be on the verge of a nervous breakdown and unable to take steps either to secure the appointment of a successor or to deal with the pressures upon him from the Southern Secretary and the President of the Council to take decisive measures to resolve Irish grievances. Eventually these two ministers resigned, and the administration was reconstituted with two new secretaries of state. Thereafter it was to soldier on with a narrower political base until the virtual withdrawal of parliamentary confidence in March 1782 in the wake of the second major British military defeat at the hands of the colonists at Yorktown.

At another level discontent found a focus in the county association movement launched by Christopher Wyvill at York in December 1779. This public agitation, organized initially by the local gentry, and keyed to securing support from the upper and middling classes of society, began as a campaign to reduce taxation by curbing what was believed to be governmental corruption and extravagance, regarded as the mainstay of a misguided and inefficient administration in Parliament. As a protest by hard-pressed tax-payers it initially attracted wide support, and the leaders of opposition in Parliament soon sought to exploit it and fill their sails with the fair wind of public opinion. In response to widespread petitioning by the associators the opposition brought forth its program of legislation against placemen, contractors, and electors who held posts in the revenue services. The government managed to beat off this attack in Parliament; and in the face of temporary military success in South Carolina and a conservative reaction against the attempt by Wyvill to bring forward a measure securing more frequent general elections, the popular movement had lost steam by the summer. It proved impossible to resuscitate it to any extent the following year and, in the event, it played no part in the bringing down of the government in the early months of 1782.

3 The Resignation of Lord North

The resignation of Lord North and his colleagues in March 1782 was due entirely to a withdrawal of parliamentary confidence. There is little doubt that North himself welcomed it as a release from an intolerable situation. For although he and most of the ministers were now convinced that the country would have to cut its losses in America, the King, whose chosen servants they were, remained obstinately determined beyond the eleventh hour to try to salvage something out of the wreck by military means. So long as George III remained adamantly opposed to any peace recognizing American Independence, North could not make the about-turn on policy which would have enabled him to retain support in Parliament: although the existing majority remained on the whole well-disposed towards him, its members could see no

alternative to deserting the ministry in divisions in the House of Commons if the war was to be brought to an end. Finally, in mid-March 1782, it was the privately expressed intention of some independent country gentlemen, whose defection would be decisive, to do just that, which enabled North to wring out of the King a reluctant permission to announce his resignation.

This move destroyed altogether for the time being the normal pattern of eighteenth-century politics, whereby a group of ministers of the monarch's choice stood secure in the support of safe majorities in the two Houses of Parliament, while opposition politicians unavailingly sought to undermine their reputations with the public and make their situations untenable, but could rarely achieve more than the occasional rejection of an unpopular government measure. Now George III found himself obliged to recruit a new administration from politicians nearly all of whom for one reason or another had incurred his disapproval or dislike – in most instances because of incompatibility of views on the American question. Not only this, but he was obliged to acquiesce in a ministerial commitment to make peace on the basis of American Independence, which he thought ruinous to the kingdom for whose fate and prosperity he as monarch bore responsibility. Also he was constrained to accept a program of administrative reform which involved ministerial and, in some degree, parliamentary interference with the running of executive government which he felt to be his particular constitutional responsibility. To his mind the pretensions of the main opposition party, led by the Marquis of Rockingham, to a lion's share of leading positions in the new administration reflected the behavior of "faction," which on principle he disapproved.

Such was the turmoil into which defeat in America had thrown the state of politics that the King's early attempts to restore what might be considered from his point of view a state of normality proved distinctly unhappy in their results. During the three months' duration of the administration nominally headed at the Treasury by Rockingham (not a single speech by whom in the House of Lords is reported for that period) George III systematically tried to shore up the situation as co-premier of the Home Secretary, the Earl of Shelburne. Not only did he find Shelburne more congenial to work with, but he was aware that Shelburne, like his former political mentor, William Pitt, Earl of Chatham, was averse from seeing parliamentary encroachments upon the royal prerogative, symbolized both by the Rockinghamites' claim to hold office whether the King liked it or no and by their program of "economical reform." The royal stance led naturally in July 1782 to the appointment of Shelburne as First Lord of the Treasury on the death of Rockingham, a move which exacerbated interparty jealousies and resulted in the withdrawal from office of Charles James Fox and other leaders of the Rockingham connection.

4 The Fox–North Coalition and the East India Legislation

This political maneuvering on the King's part was doomed to failure since the balance of forces in the Commons made it unviable. In the Parliament which had been elected in 1780 Shelburne and his friends commanded only exiguous personal support, insufficient in combination with the court and administration party to ensure safe majorities in parliamentary divisions. The Rockinghamite party remained a formidable force; but so also did North and his considerable following, and Shelburne was in no situation to pay the sort of political price for support that North might have found acceptable. The decision of North and Fox to join forces in February 1783 meant irretrievable disaster for Shelburne in the House of Commons. Shelburne was particularly vulnerable because on him fell the primary responsibility for negotiating a peace which many politicians believed gave too much away unnecessarily in America to the United States and in particular failed to secure any guarantee for loyalists of reinstatement in their lands or of compensation in respect of property confiscated or destroyed. In February 1783 votes of censure on the peace terms in the Commons spelled the necessity for resignation to Shelburne just

as, a year before, the imminent threat of the passage of a vote of no-confidence had spelled the end for Lord North.

After stubbornly resisting the inevitable through an inter-ministerium of some six weeks, George III had no alternative but to bow to the situation and admit the leaders of the Fox–North coalition to office. Even more than the events of March 1782 he felt this to be an inadmissible invasion of his prerogative of selecting ministers. Oppressed with the feeling that, with the royal functions reduced to a nullity, he could no longer effectively serve the country in his royal role, for a brief space he seriously contemplated abdication. At this point, perhaps, came the peak in the graph of the distortions introduced into British politics by the American winning of independence. In the end wiser counsels prevailed. From politicians who had no sympathy with either North or Fox came hints that perhaps in due course a situation which the King – and not the King alone – regarded as a gross violation of the Constitution might be set to rights.

Ultimately, the return to a traditional pattern of politics, and the vindication of the royal prerogative, followed with surprising speed, within less than a year. This process of readjustment was greatly facilitated involuntarily by the leaders of the Fox–North coalition themselves. A thorough overhaul of the relationships between the royal administration and the role of the East India Company as the governing authority in large parts of the Indian sub-continent was long overdue. The coalition ministry was bound to tackle this problem. But it did so in such a way as to make itself both unpopular and highly vulnerable. The measures foreshadowed in its proposed East India legislation of December 1783 entailed invasions of chartered rights which had not been fully negotiated and agreed (and probably would not have been agreed) by all concerned. In particular, the intended conferment of powers to make appointments in India upon a body of parliamentary commissioners nominated by the coalition appeared to place in the hands of the coalition parties a vast reservoir of patronage carrying political influence far greater than the royal patronage recently curbed by the Rockingham administration's economical reform legislation of 1782. Some zealous constitutional reformers, Wyvill among them, felt that all power in the state would be transferred from the royal administration to Charles Fox as the dominant personality in the coalition, and ludicrous charges were made against him of aspiring to usurp control of the state like another Cromwell.

5 The Establishment in Office of Pitt

The affairs of the nascent British Empire in the East thus contributed to bring an end to the distortions in British politics set up by the American achievement of independence. In December 1783 the way was clear for the King to turn the tables on the coalition, for royal influence to sway the votes of the House of Lords against Fox's East India Bill, and for the coalition ministers to be dismissed and a new administration recruited from non-coalition politicians headed by the youthful William Pitt.

In the early weeks of 1784, although the small Fox–North majority in the Commons created difficulties for Pitt, a massive display of public opinion in the form of addresses and petitions revealed widespread support for the King's action. This show of public opinion was confirmed by the general election of April 1784. Not only were some of North's closest supporters displaced in a number of nomination boroughs where he had arranged seats for them in 1780, but many Foxites lost their elections in open constituencies after acrimonious public political debates in which a general distrust of the coalition was clearly evident. In the new Parliament Pitt had an assured majority. Thus, within two years of the end of the American war politics had returned to their accustomed channel. So, in the longer term the consequences of the American Revolution for British politics were minimal. Tensions which might have been if not dangerous at least debilitating had been eliminated. King and ministers were again at one. The government was once again clearly the King's government, conducted by ministers of the King's choice, as it had been in the 1770s. Parliamentary support for the ministry was assured. Opposition was once

again reduced to a powerless rump in Parliament, capable of creating occasional embarrassment for ministers – as it was to do in respect of Pitt's proposed Irish legislation in 1785 – but not of effectively challenging their tenure of office and power. One innovation indeed there was. To hold a general election only three and a half years after the previous one was unprecedented in the Hanoverian period, and the part played by the elections of 1784 in the resolution of the political crisis of the previous 12 months gave an enhanced importance to the role of public opinion in political affairs. This apart, the political machine during the administration of the younger Pitt continued to function much as it had done under the 12-year leadership of Lord North.

6 Industrialization and Financial Reform

The restoration of political stability was undoubtedly one important factor in British recovery after the loss of the American colonies. Two other factors in particular deserve mention. One – industrialization – owed little or nothing to the influence of the American Revolution, save insofar as war stimulated demand for military and naval clothing and weaponry. But the expansion in metallurgy and the truly dramatic increase in textile production, with consequent stimulus to export and import trade, soon made up any deficiencies in the nation's economy that might have been expected to arise from the loss of the American war. The lift-off of the cotton industry in the years after the war was phenomenal and is easily discernible from the customs figures for imports of cotton wool: in 1870 rather under 7 million lbs., in 1785 more than 15 million, and in 1790 doubling to more than 30 million. There is ample evidence over this period for a wide diffusion of modest prosperity in the form of higher earnings among large sections of the working people as well as among small businessmen. Canal-building, road construction, the beginnings of the erection of factories, and the growth of industrial villages were all facets of the development of an indispensable infrastructure for industrialization, forming a basis for national power and prosperity hardly conceivable in the war-disaster years of 1781–2.

The other factor of recovery – administrative and financial reform – was much more directly a product of the American crisis, for in part it was engendered by the pressures created by the war. One of North's most successful counter-strokes to the parliamentary opposition's campaign against alleged extravagance and corruption at the beginning of 1780 was to secure parliamentary approval for the establishment of a statutory commission of inquiry into the public accounts, rather than an opposition-sponsored parliamentary committee of inquiry which would have devoted its energies to political point-scoring. The commission voted into being in 1780 carried out over several years a thorough examination of the procedures of the revenue and spending departments, and laid an indispensable foundation for reforms undertaken after 1784 by the younger Pitt in the administration of the revenue and the control of expenditure.

North himself, before his resignation, had begun to experiment with a broadening of the basis of taxation, introducing an inhabited-house duty and a tax on male servants in 1778. After 1784 Pitt's attempts to extend the catchment area of taxation still further were not always successful, but he achieved considerable success in combatting loss of revenue through smuggling by the reduction of the various customs duties, particularly on tea and wines. More effective in achieving efficiency in the collection of revenues was his reapportionment of responsibility for this among the various existing agencies. Regularity in administration was imposed by a new treasury commission of audit. Simplicity in government accounting was achieved by the creation of the consolidated fund, and the public credit was enormously strengthened by Pitt's reorganization of the sinking fund. Much of all this financial reform was based on the reports of North's commission, which continued its work up to 1787, and can therefore be seen as a direct effect of the American crisis. It was of particular significance that under the impact and strain of unsuccessful war the political and administrative machinery of

Great Britain should so effectively stand up to the task of self-examination and reform, effectively contributing to the achievement of national recovery. In this, above all, the contrast between Britain and France was particularly marked. Indeed, it is not too much to say that the work of the commission on the public accounts marked the divide between the *ancien régime* system of financial administration the country had inherited from the Middle Ages and a modern, efficient administrative machine based on some degree of cost efficiency and eliminating, at least to some extent, surviving inefficient and sinecure offices. Although many reforms remained to be achieved, Britain emerged from the American crisis with a financial system much superior to that with which it had entered it.

In sum, restored political stability, a relatively effective financial system, and a thriving industrializing economy all combined within a very few years of the American Revolution to re-establish national self-confidence and the sinews of power in Great Britain.

FURTHER READING

Binney, J. E. D.: *British Public Finance and Administration, 1774–1792* (Oxford: Clarendon Press, 1958).

Butterfield, Sir Herbert: *George III, Lord North, and the People, 1779–1780* (London: Bell and Sons, 1949).

Cannon, John: *The Fox–North Coalition: Crisis of the Constitution, 1782–4* (Cambridge: Cambridge University Press, 1969).

Christie, Ian R.: *The End of North's Ministry, 1780–1782* (London: Macmillan, 1958).

——: *Wars and Revolutions: Britain, 1760–1815* (London: Edward Arnold; Cambridge, Mass.: Harvard University Press, 1982), chapters 6–8 and chapter bibliographies.

——: *Stress and Stability in Late Eighteenth-Century Britain: Reflections on the British Avoidance of Revolution* (Oxford and New York: Oxford University Press, 1984), chapters 3 and 5.

Ehrman, John: *The Younger Pitt: the Years of Acclaim* (London: Constable, 1969).

Watson, J. Steven: *The Reign of George III, 1760–1815* (Oxford: Clarendon Press, 1960), chapters 9–11.

CHAPTER SIXTY-ONE

The American Revolution in Canada

ELIZABETH MANCKE

THE American Revolution prefigures the imminent independence of most of the Americas from European colonization. In Saint Domingue free blacks and slaves wrested their independence not just from their domestic masters but from France as well. Wars of independence from Mexico to Argentina made Spain, like France, empire-poor. By 1825 only Britain retained continental colonies in North America, and indeed had consolidated its control over them. This retention of a transcontinental empire (what would become the future state of Canada) and not just a few islands, the fate of Spain's and France's American empires, has puzzled scholars and occasionally irritated an expansionist United States, a reminder that its conquest of the British Empire in the Americas had been only partial.

Britain's persistence as the only European colonial power on continental North America raises major questions about the nature of the American Revolution and the British Empire. Why did British subjects in Nova Scotia, Quebec, the Island of St. John, and Newfoundland not embrace the armed rebellion that led fellow subjects to independence? What was the impact of war and its immediate aftermath in these remaining parts of British North America? And to what extent did these loyal polities accept the social and humanitarian ethos of the revolutionary era having rejected its militancy and immediate political agenda?

1 The Years of Resistance

When armed conflict began in 1775, there were approximately 125,000 European inhabitants in what is now Canada: 90,000 in Quebec; 20,000 in Nova Scotia (which in 1775 also included present-day New Brunswick); 1,000 on the Island of St. John (later to be called Prince Edward Island); 12,000 permanent residents of Newfoundland; and a few hundred in fur trade posts scattered throughout the west.

For these British subjects, the fundamental constitutional issue of the patriot cause – whether Parliament should legislate for the colonies – was moot. Parliament had legislated for Newfoundland since the mid-seventeenth century. Lacking an island-based, year-round government, Newfoundland was politically an extension of metropolitan Britain. Nova Scotia, conquered in 1710 and ceded by the French in the Treaty of Utrecht in 1713, had always had a government under the Crown-in-Parliament. Without an assembly until 1758 to raise taxes, it was governed parsimoniously until 1749 when Parliament began voting monies to build Halifax as the northern American naval port. Parliamentary funds subsequently paid for the settlement of foreign Protestants in Halifax and Lunenburg, and subsidized the settlement of 7,000 New Englanders in the 1760s.

In 1763, the French territories of the Island of St. John and Cape Breton were ceded to Britain and attached to the government of Nova Scotia. Settlement of Cape Breton was minimal. The Island of St. John was divided by Britain into 20,000-acre townships and granted to British proprietors, most of whom were prominent elites associated with the Earl of Egmont. In 1768 they requested and received the right to separate from Nova Scotia and establish a new colonial government, provided it could be funded from quitrents. These British-based proprietors had no interest in breaking the imperial tie. Their tenants, most of whom were Highland Scots, supported Britain in the war, as did large numbers of fellow Highlanders throughout North America.

Quebec, conquered from and ceded by the French in the Seven Years' War, was constitutionally subordinate to the Crown-in-Parliament and acceded to parliamentary legislation, most notably with the 1774 Quebec Act. In the West, the Proclamation of 1763, however haphazardly applied, served the interests of Amerindians, while the Quebec Act extended French civil law into the *pays de haut* where the largest European-descended population was French-speaking and Catholic. British fur trading merchants, connected through Montreal to European markets, supported the British government which tried to curb, or at least slow, the expansion of agricultural settlement into the transappalachian West (*see* chapter 19).

2 The Years of War

While British subjects in Nova Scotia, Newfoundland, the Island of St. John, and Quebec largely remained observers of the resistance, the outbreak of fighting in April 1775 would make colonists from Newfoundland to the Caribbean participants in a civil war. Troop movements, disruptions in shipping, rerouting of the provisioning trades, and privateering caused upheaval, privation, and loss of life and property in settlements all along the Atlantic littoral. In Nova Scotia and Quebec, patriots battled briefly and unsuccessfully for the support of these colonies in the war, and on the western and southern frontiers of Quebec, fighting among Amerindians, Americans, and British troops continued until 1782.

Quebec

A former colony of France and hence a former enemy, the colony of Quebec was an enigma for British Americans. After its cession to Britain in 1763, it became a symbol

of the autocratic government that many colonists believed Britain wanted to inflict on all the colonies. In their estimation, the Quebec Act was one of the Coercive Acts designed to legislate colonists into submission and bridle their customary institutions of self-government (*see* chapter 24). Some patriots believed that given proper encouragement Quebec would join the United Colonies, and George Washington feared that the British possession of Quebec, bordering New England and New York, made them vulnerable to attack. With these considerations in mind, the Continental Army undertook an offensive invasion of the colony in the fall of 1775, one of its few in a largely defensive war.

The two-pronged attack began in September with Richard Montgomery, a former British army officer, leading one column of 2,000 men up Lake Champlain and the Richelieu River, and Benedict Arnold leading another 1,000 men up the Kennebec River in Maine. Montgomery's troops, arriving in early November, found a sparsely defended colony. The year before Governor Guy Carleton had returned from Britain with the Quebec Act in hand. Confident that he would be governing a contented and loyal populace, he had acceded to General Thomas Gage's request for troops and had sent to Boston all but a few hundred men, which he stationed in Montreal under his command. Upon an American invasion, Carleton discovered to his chagrin and dismay that the Quebec Act had not rendered French Canadians pliant subjects. They would not heed militia musters to defend the colony against the invading armies, nor did Britain's Amerindian allies wish to defend the colony in what they considered to be an unnatural war between brothers.

While Montgomery captured Fort St. Jean on the Richelieu River and turned his army towards Montreal, Carleton fled for Quebec City anxious to defend the seat of government. The major defense of the colony came from approximately 600 British regulars and the Royal Highland Emigrants, a new regiment organized by Allan Maclean. He had received permission to form two battalions, one recruited among Highlanders in Quebec and New York, the other in Nova Scotia and the Island of St. John. The Royal Highland Emigrants became renowned as among the most loyal of the British troops raised in North America.

In early December Montgomery and Arnold met with their armies outside Quebec City. Without sufficient supplies for a prolonged siege of the city, they attacked on December 31. The British won the battle, Montgomery was killed, and a wounded Arnold assumed command of both patriot armies. Although losing the battle for Quebec City, the Americans were not yet a defeated army and settled in for the winter. While French Canadians had proved willing provisioners of the invading armies so long as they carried hard money to pay for food and lodging, by winter the Americans had little but the unacceptable Continental currency. Nor were Canadians interested in joining the war against Britain or sympathetic to pillaging troops. By late winter, many patriot soldiers had deserted for home, smallpox had claimed its due, and hunger, threadbare clothes, and a dwindling supply of arms and ammunition made the Continental Army a tiresome guest in the Canadian countryside. Benjamin Franklin led a delegation from the Continental Congress to negotiate with the Canadians about joining the revolt, but discovered that without more to offer than paper money and an unwelcome army, the Canadians declined to join the war against Britain.

The spring thaw of the St. Lawrence brought British reinforcements, and patriot troops headed home, moving just far enough in advance of the British that they took or destroyed bateaux, barges, and other vessels necessary for the movement of troops and material down the Richelieu River and Lake Champlain. Forced to build new watercraft, the British army delayed an attack on New England and New York until the summer of 1777. The American occupation of Quebec tarnished Carleton's military reputation and he was relieved of his command of the Canadian-based troops, though continued his duties as the civilian governor. His military replacement John Burgoyne had an even more ignominious Canadian tour, leading troops into the Battle of Saratoga, one of the major British defeats of the war. In June 1778, Frederick Haldimand replaced both Carleton and Burgoyne.

While fighting had expended itself in the settlements between Quebec City and Montreal before the Declaration of Independence, the larger context of the war kept the colony unsettled. With France's entry into the war in 1778, rumors of a French invasion began circulating. The positive response of many French Canadians disturbed the British, who did not want a war in Quebec, and the Americans, who did not want France re-established in North America. As a consequence, the Americans decided in the fall of 1780 to postpone indefinitely a joint French-American attack on Quebec. Meanwhile, French naval action disrupted transatlantic shipping that had repercussions on Quebec's western and southern frontiers where relations with Amerindian allies were kept precariously balanced through the generous distribution of gifts.

Not only was Haldimand responsible for keeping the St. Lawrence settlements out of the war, his jurisdiction included the western posts of Kaskaskia, Vincennes, Detroit, Michilimackinac, and Niagara. The month after his arrival in Quebec, George Rogers Clark and a band of Americans captured Kaskaskia before moving on to take Vincennes. Haldimand promptly issued orders to the lieutenant governors of Detroit and Michilimackinac to distribute whatever gifts were necessary to maintain Amerindian alliances. At Fort Niagara, loyalist refugees took shelter and organized a regiment that engaged in vengeful raids in the Mohawk Valley. Maintaining a flow of provisions and gifts for thousands of Amerindian allies, loyalist refugees, and troops at Niagara, Detroit, and Michilimackinac was an enormous logistical task. Haldimand detailed troops to build the first canals to avoid some of the cumbersome portages on the water route between the St. Lawrence and the Great Lakes. Back in Montreal he negotiated with touchy British merchants, who still resented the Quebec Act, and wrote justifications to London to explain escalating expenses.

Meanwhile in London and Paris, British treaty negotiators, wanting to keep the

French marginalized, had countered Franklin's demand for all of Quebec with an offer of the lands between the Great Lakes and the Ohio River. Back in the colony, colonial officials, British merchants, Canadians, fur traders in the west, and Amerindian allies felt betrayed by the territorial concession. The Montreal fur merchants intensified their penetration of the northwestern fur country, where in 1778, Peter Pond had crossed into the arctic drainage basin and in 1798 Alexander Mackenzie would reach the Pacific. Loyalists, many of the early ones Mohawks and Highland Scots, resettled in Quebec. And despite cession of the lands south of the Great Lakes, the British retained control of western forts in the territory until after Jay's Treaty in 1794.

The Atlantic region

While Guy Carleton had been overly confident of the loyalty of Canadians, Governor Francis Legge was highly suspicious of Nova Scotians, approximately 50 percent of whom hailed from New England. Scholars have also been suspicious of why Nova Scotians did not revolt, often assuming that they should have and therefore tried to answer a counterfactual question about what they did not do.

Legge's exaggerated distrust of the Yankees was not entirely groundless. During the tenure of Governor Charles Lawrence, they had agitated for an assembly, which the Board of Trade finally ordered him to call in 1758. In the early 1760s, New England settlers had protested the absence of town government, though on that issue the Board of Trade advised the King to disallow legislation to create some self-government in the settlements. A few Nova Scotians in Halifax and Liverpool had protested the Stamp Act. For Legge, the capstone came in the late fall of 1775 when he ordered the militia to Halifax to protect the city. Some units rejoined that they desired "to be neuter" and objected to leaving their families and property unprotected from privateers (quoted in Brebner, 1937, p. 310). None heeded Legge's orders.

For Legge, the militia's refusal to defend Halifax was obstinate disloyalty. For historians, the Nova Scotian response has been literally interpreted as neutrality or as confusion. All have probably made too much of a few scraps of evidence and not enough of the larger context. Legge was an inept, if not incompetent, governor and discrediting one's colonial critics with aspersions on their loyalty was common political fare. Legge's panic in the fall of 1775 was not entirely groundless. Patriots had seized a British naval vessel in Machias and the British had retaliated by burning Falmouth (now Portland), Maine. Benedict Arnold was marching his army up the Kennebec River towards Quebec. And patriot-licensed privateers preyed on British shipping and Nova Scotia settlements. But given these circumstances, settlers along the South Shore and Bay of Fundy knew that it was wisest for their militias, even if wretchedly armed, to stay at home. So in time-honored, British-American fashion, they asserted local control of their militias. Similar wartime disputes over the control of militias set governors against colonists in the West Indies (*see* chapter 63).

What Legge and many historians have not mentioned is that in 1775 the Nova Scotia Assembly did pass a militia bill and wrote a memorial to London recommending changes in the governance of the empire in the interest of alleviating the problems that were contributing to armed conflict. Merchants in the farming settlements of the Minas Basin loaded vessels with food and wood to provision troops in Boston. And most active supporters of the rebellion had already left the province for New England, thus dissipating what revolutionary potential might have existed.

Unlike Quebec, the Continental Congress expressed little interest in Nova Scotia and rebuffed the invasion proposal submitted by John Allan and Jonathan Eddy, two Nova Scotians from the Isthmus of Chignecto. Allan and Eddy, overestimating the political alienation of their fellow settlers, recruited 80 men from Machias, Maine, and Maugerville, Nova Scotia, the latter a struggling, isolated community on the St. John

River. Joined by approximately 100 men when they reached the Chignecto settlements at the head of the Bay of Fundy, they attacked Fort Cumberland in August 1776. The British quickly responded with reinforcements and Allan's and Eddy's modest army withdrew and retreated to the United States. Such was the extent of the contest for the hearts and minds of Nova Scotians. Faced with a choice between joining patriot interests and remaining loyal, the majority chose loyalty.

For the next seven years of war, residents of the Atlantic region remained on constant alert for privateers and no one escaped their impact. They captured large numbers of trading vessels. Simeon Perkins and his associates in Liverpool, Nova Scotia had lost four vessels by the end of 1776. Finally in 1778 they applied to the Nova Scotia government for licences to arm their own vessels as privateers. Most towns and villages in Nova Scotia, the Island of St. John, and Newfoundland had been threatened, if not invaded, by privateers who burned houses, barns, and fishing shacks, killed livestock, and plundered moveable property.

In Newfoundland, long dependent on provisions from New England and the Mid-Atlantic, as well as Ireland, privateering produced famine-level food shortages. Privateers preying on the banks fleet made off-shore fishing so prohibitively costly and dangerous that it collapsed during the war, thereby furthering Newfoundland's immiseration. Throughout the region, the presence of large numbers of British soldiers and sailors pushed up prices for already scarce foodstuffs. Conditions became so desperate in Newfoundland that after the war the British government inquired into the trading practices for provisioning the island, and reopened trade with the United States rather than leave residents overly dependent on West Country and Irish merchants. But it would take the French Revolutionary and Napoleonic Wars before Britain finally conceded that Newfoundland needed proper government and appointed the first year-round governor in 1824.

The end of the war transformed Nova Scotia and the Island of St. John. More loyalists relocated to Nova Scotia than to any other part of British North America, nearly tripling the colony's population until Britain created New Brunswick and Cape Breton as separate colonies. The high demand for peacetime services and British subsidies to pay for refugee relocation buoyed the economy. Nova Scotia's trade rebounded as merchants gained new markets in the Caribbean, now closed to American shipping. The governments of both Nova Scotia and the Island of St. John began escheat and distraint proceedings to void the pre-revolutionary grants of absentee landowners who had either not fulfilled the terms of their grants or had defaulted on their quitrents. In Nova Scotia the land recovery and redistribution proceeded with few challenges, but on the Island of St. John the colonial government's questionable practices met with vociferous protests, and political battles over land ownership and use would persist into the mid-nineteenth century.

3 The Age of Revolution

The age of revolution in the Americas is so associated with independence from European colonial powers that the persistence of colonialism in what became Canada is often defined as counter-revolutionary. This descriptor would have shocked many colonial officials who found these remaining British colonial subjects dangerously republican in their sentiments. In turn, many colonists found official policies such as toleration of Catholicism and measures against slavery excessively liberal. The commitment to an imperial tie did not mean that British North Americans and British officials rejected a range of values associated with the revolutionary era, including greater participation in government, religious toleration and freedom, and the end of slavery. Indeed, by European standards, whether British or continental, and in some instances by American standards, British North America was progressive. But colonialism persisted and many reforms came through state mandate or elite decisions rather than through populist activism.

Political change

Thousands of loyalists upon arriving in Nova Scotia and Quebec agitated vociferously for their political rights, forcing Britain to redefine colonial jurisdictions and governors to relinquish powers. Approximately 35,000 loyalists emigrated to Nova Scotia in 1782 and 1783 as the British evacuated New York, Charleston, Savannah, and St. Augustine. Nearly half settled on the St. John River and down the west side of the Bay of Fundy and promptly requested that they be separated from Nova Scotia and given a new colonial government. In response, Britain created the colonies of New Brunswick and Cape Breton (reunited with Nova Scotia in 1820). In Nova Scotia proper, loyalist members of the assembly allied with outport MLAs to break the power of Halifax interests and to press for assembly control of revenues. While they failed to achieve the latter goal, they did gain control over the dispersement of road monies, one of the largest expenditures in the colony's budget.

In Quebec, the absence of an assembly and English civil law gave 10,000 loyalists ready-made grievances. After strenuous protestations from alliances of newly arrived loyalists and prewar English and French Canadians, Parliament responded in 1791 with the passage of the Constitutional Act which divided Quebec at the Ottawa River into the two colonies of Lower and Upper Canada. Each colony received an assembly. In Upper Canada, English civil law was restored. In Lower Canada, French civil law continued, as did the rights of Catholics and the Catholic Church.

In all these colonies, loyalists allied with existing colonists, whether French or British, to provide the critical mass to challenge and check the power of the governors and councils, who had greater powers than had executives in the former 13 colonies. As a consequence, political battles involved expanding the powers of the assemblies at the expense of executives, essentially the opposite of political battles in the former 13 colonies at the time of the Revolution. Not until the 1840s, after serious political unrest the previous decade, would British

North American executive councils be chosen from the assembly and be "responsible" to the electorate.

Religion

For British colonial officials anxious for the speedy establishment of stable and economical governments, which generally meant limited coercion and maximum allegiance, the extension of religious toleration became an effective means to avoid social tensions. In 1759, Governor Lawrence of Nova Scotia promised prospective New England settlers that there would be religious toleration for all Protestant dissenters, including no direct taxes to the established Anglican Church. The executive proclamation gave Nova Scotians a more liberal religious policy than those in many of the older colonies, such as Connecticut or Massachusetts.

After the conquest of Canada in 1760, the British governors began easing the strictures of the Test Act to allow Catholics to serve on juries. The need to stabilize the government of Quebec and allow French Canadians to hold public office contributed to the 1774 Quebec Act which gave Catholics in Quebec greater political rights than elsewhere in Britain or British America. In Britain's reassessment of Newfoundland after the war, the government decided to permit Catholic priests to minister to the island's large population of Irish Catholic residents.

In Nova Scotia and subsequently in other heavily Protestant areas of British North America, the toleration of Protestant diversity and the absence of local governments that regulated religious observance created an institutional environment that was highly conducive to experimental religious movements. Some movements achieved denominational definition, while others were flashes in the fires of religious enthusiasm that spread across British North America from the 1770s to the 1820s. The phenomenon began in 1775 when a 27-year-old Nova Scotian of Rhode Island birth had a profound religious conversion. In sorting through the experience, he came to believe that God was loving not wrathful, in contrast to New England teaching. Feeling himself called to preach this message, though only a humble farmer, he found himself challenging New England strictures about the need for an educated clergy. Rejecting the New England theology and standards of his youth, but operating within New England beliefs about individual conversion experiences, he struck out in 1776 as an itinerant minister, preaching in meeting-houses throughout western Nova Scotia.

Alline's conversion in 1775 was surely influenced by the political uncertainty throughout British America. The large numbers of ministerless churches in the colony contributed to warm receptions by people weary of the vigilance and deprivation of wartime. While he organized just a few churches in Nova Scotia, his writings became central to Free Will Baptist theology as it developed in New England after the Revolution and spread back into the Maritime colonies.

Alline's ministry came at the front edge of a wave of itinerancy in new areas of settlement. By the end of the war, Methodist and Baptist itinerants criss-crossed British North America and the United States preaching, inspiring revivals, and establishing churches, often in settlements without a settled minister. Charles Inglis, the first Anglican bishop in North America, found the religious ferment repugnant and unsettling. He, along with most colonial governors, believed that religious unrest would lead to political unrest. They schemed unsuccessfully, and it proved unnecessarily, for ways to curb the religious diversity that their predecessors' reforms had made possible. By the early nineteenth century, the rising tide of British emigration and a strengthened attachment to the empire helped to moderate expressions of religious enthusiasm.

Free Blacks, slaves, and abolition

Among the flood of war refugees leaving the new United States in 1782 and 1783 were thousands of Blacks, both slave and free. The numbers leaving for Nova Scotia and Quebec are inconclusive, but we know that approximately 3,000 free Blacks, alone, embarked in New York for Nova Scotia in 1783. Free Blacks probably accounted for 10 percent of the loyalists in British North America, with hundreds more Blacks arriving as the slaves of the refugees. This large postwar influx of Blacks (which would be reinforced by maroon refugees during the Napoleonic Wars) swelled their numbers in colonies where Blacks and the institution of slavery had been marginal, and precipitated social scrutiny of their condition and place in British North America.

Free Blacks who became loyalists had gone behind British lines in response to promises of freedom, as former slaves on sequestered plantations, or as already free Blacks. Identifying themselves as loyal supporters of the British Empire, they expected some parity of treatment with white loyalists, though they received far less. Segregated from Whites in their own communities, officials put them at the end of the queue for provisions, clothing and temporary housing, as well as for the distribution of land. Blacks who finally received land grants, and it was far from all those who were eligible, were given approximately 50 acres in comparison to the 200 acres granted to most white loyalists. Obliged to accept lower wages than white laborers, free Blacks also found themselves segregated in churches and schools.

Disillusioned with their second-class status after the revolutionary promise of freedom, land, and homes of their own, Blacks in Nova Scotia and New Brunswick were highly receptive to the plans of the Sierra Leone Company to establish a new British colony in West Africa. By January 1792, nearly 1,200 of them accepted the company's offer of free passage, land, and racial equality, and embarked in Halifax for Sierra Leone, the first former slaves to resettle in Africa.

The attack on slavery in British North America came from abolition-minded elites who used their public offices to constrain and then eliminate the institution. Upper Canada's first governor, James Graves Simcoe, arrived from Britain already opposed to slavery on constitutional and religious grounds. In 1793, the third year of his tenure, he instructed the attorney general, John White, to introduce legislation to abolish slavery. A mere two weeks later the assembly, with over a third of its members slaveholders, unanimously passed compromise legislation prohibiting the further importation of slaves and providing for gradual abolition. Activist opponents of slavery in Lower Canada and Nova Scotia were justices who used their power to interpret the law to end slavery. In a notorious 1800 case in New Brunswick, the four-member bench gave a split decision on whether slavery was legal in the colony. At the end of the case, one of the two slave-holding judges freed his slaves. While not ending slavery in the colony, slaveowners were put on warning that many of their fellow elites had little tolerance for the institution. By the 1820s, slavery had been largely eliminated. When the British Parliament passed legislation in 1833 to abolish slavery in the empire, it enumerated colonies where slaveowners would be eligible for compensation. The absence of all the British North American colonies from mention in the legislation is testimony to the fact that case by case, slavery had been made an untenable institution.

In matters of politics, religion, and social policy, these loyal colonies of British North America remained committed to reform. But in reaction to their republican neighbors to the south and the legacy of the War for Independence, they believed reform should happen without armed conflict, reinforcing, and indeed providing substance to, the characterization that they were conservative and deferential.

FURTHER READING

Brebner, J. B.: *The Neutral Yankees of Nova Scotia: A Marginal Colony During the American Revolution* (New York: Columbia University Press, 1937).

Bumsted, J. M.: "1763–1783: Resettlement and Rebellion," in *The Atlantic Region to Confederation: A History*, eds. P. A. Buckner and J. G. Reid (Toronto: University of Toronto Press, 1994), 156–83.

Clarke, E.: *The Siege of Fort Cumberland, 1776: An Episode in the American Revolution* (Montreal and Kingston: McGill-Queen's University Press, 1995).

Condon, A. G.: "1783–1800: Loyalist Arrival, Acadian Return, Imperial Reform," in *The Atlantic Region to Confederation: A History*, eds. P. A. Buckner and J. G. Reid (Toronto: University of Toronto Press, 1994), 183–209.

Errington, J.: *The Lion, The Eagle, and Upper Canada: A Developing Colonial Ideology* (Kingston and Montreal: McGill-Queen's University Press, 1987).

MacKinnon, N.: *This Unfriendly Soil: The Loyalist Experience in Nova Scotia, 1783–1791* (Kingston and Montreal: McGill-Queen's University Press, 1986).

Mancke, E.: "Another British America: A Canadian Model for the Early Modern British Empire." *Journal of Imperial and Commonwealth History* 25 (1997), 1–36.

Neatby, H.: *Quebec, 1760–1791* (Toronto: McClelland & Stewart, 1966).

Stewart, G. and Rawlyk, G. A.: *A People Highly Favoured of God: The Nova Scotia Yankees and the American Revolution* (Toronto: Macmillan, 1972).

Walker, J. W. St. G.: *The Black Loyalists: The Search for a Promised Land in Nova Scotia and Sierra Leone 1783–1870* (New York: Africana Publishing Company, 1976).

Winks, R. W.: *The Blacks in Canada: A History*, 2nd edn. (Montreal and Kingston: McGill-Queen's University Press, 1997).

CHAPTER SIXTY-TWO

The American Revolution and Ireland

MAURICE J. BRIC

BEFORE 1776, a shared constitutional status and political discourse bound Ireland and the sibling colonies of British North America. Discursive themes were essentially shaped by reference to the imperial matrix in London. Accordingly, Irish patriots believed that American writers such as John Dickinson and James Wilson were developing themes first set forth by William Molyneux (1656–98) and Jonathan Swift (1667–1745). By the 1770s, the cause of America was the cause of Ireland.

Both Molyneux (in the 1690s) and Swift (in the 1720s) had established the outlines of a patriotic agenda that incorporated each side of the British Atlantic world: the independence of local legislatures, freedom of trade, and political reform. As the preeminent vehicle for this agenda, the American Revolution could hardly be denounced by the members of the Irish Parliament without their admitting that the British Parliament had the right to tax the Irish. Accordingly, while commemorative dinners, addresses and parades celebrated the assertion of the "liberties of America," patriotic leaders and clubs in Ireland kept in close contact with their American colleagues in order to ensure that, as the (Dublin) *Freeman's Journal* put it on February 18, 1766, British policy in America was not "part of a plan of Humiliation nearer home."

Irish newspapers also published a stream of reports on the background to and the movement towards American Independence. These reports were drawn from a variety of sources, including the legislative assemblies, contemporary American publications and newspapers, and the debates and resolutions of various revolutionary groups.

Relatively few pamphlets on the American Revolution were published in Ireland. Although these, together with newspaper essays, affected the Lord Lieutenant in 1779 "with more terror than 10,000 soldiers," the fact is that they largely ignored the ideological themes of the Revolution for the narrower political capital of condemning what Benjamin Franklin termed "the heavy yoke of tyranny" in Ireland itself. Therefore the celebrated *Letter to the Town of Boston*, penned by the Irish patriot leader Charles Lucas (1713–71) in 1770, ignored the great constitutional concerns of the day and largely confined itself to berating the "base, perfidious, vindictive, rapacious Ministers" of the British Government. Similarly, proposals made in America by Franklin for a "consolidating union" between Ireland, Britain, and the colonies, and in England by William Pulteney to set up a "general Parliament, to take care of the general interests of the whole" were misunderstood or ignored by Irish patriots.

1 The Immediate Reaction in Ireland to the Revolution

For all the rhetorical protestations of fellowship, patriotic Irish reaction to the American Revolution was less pro-American than anti-government and this may account for the Revolution's minimal impact on contemporary Ireland. At parliamentary level, the Irish were more interested in the internal and organizational character of their own

Parliament than in its ideological basis, and the American Revolution did not alter this.

To a large extent also, the influence of the American Revolution on Ireland was determined, and ultimately limited, by that sense of domestic insecurity that had long molded the development of eighteenth-century Irish politics. This was highlighted by the announced participation of France (June 1778) and (a year later) Spain in the Anglo-American conflict. These declarations constituted the ultimate threat to the interlocking system of established networks, ties, and traditions that bound Ireland and Britain.

Accordingly, while the Irish Parliament expressed its "abhorrence" of the developing Revolutionary War, Henry Grattan (1746–1820) and his patriot colleagues drew a fine line between their view of the Anglo-American war and a potential threat from Catholic France. Their loyalty to the British Crown in the face of a foreign enemy was always unconditional.

Outside Parliament, the loyalty of even the island's most vocal pro-American group, the Irish Presbyterians, was also never in doubt. Should "necessity" call them forth to oppose "the jealous enemies" of their ancient liberties and religion, wrote one of their ministers, William Steele Dickson, "we are ready to approve ourselves the steady friends of the constitution." Well might the Lord Lieutenant conclude that the notion of a French war had "not only altered the language but the disposition" of the revolutionaries' strongest supporters in Ireland.

2   The Political Situation in Late Eighteenth-Century Ireland

These reactions to the development of the American Revolution reflected not only traditional fears but also the shifting alignments of late eighteenth-century Irish politics. These had been complicated by the residency of the Lord Lieutenant (from 1767) and by the presumed threat to a Protestant ascendancy based on land from a rising Catholic and Protestant bourgeoisie based on commerce and the professions.

Both the socio-economic and the political status of the Catholic leadership was greatly undermined by the Penal Laws. These laws, the majority of which were passed between 1695 and 1704, effectively placed everybody outside the Established (Anglican) Church in a legal limbo. However, because the laws contained loopholes on the acquisition of commercial wealth, a new Catholic middle class emerged. Not only did this emerging group challenge what was left of the traditionally landed leadership but it actively sought some sort of accommodation with the Hanoverian Succession. Through the Test Act of 1774, the abjuration of both the temporal and the deposing powers of the papacy, the renunciation of loyalty to the exiled Stuart dynasty, and the proclamation of loyalty to George III set the scene for the repeal of many of the Penal Laws.

The quest not only to change old attitudes to the Stuarts but to prove Catholic loyalty to George III shaped the reactions of Ireland's Catholics to the American Revolution. In February 1779, Dr. John Troy, bishop of Ossory (1776–86), condemned the Americans as "rebels" and called on all Catholics to "be loyal." A year earlier, on the French declaration of war, six Catholic peers and 300 other lay leaders expressed both their "abhorrence at the unnatural rebellion" in America and their loyalty to George III. However, as with the political emphasis of the patriots, this was less a protest against the American Revolution *per se* than one to the administration that Catholic Ireland could be "trusted" with liberation from the Penal Laws.

As an aspect of negotiations on repeal of the Penal Laws, most Catholic leaders agreed with this emphasis and shared in the contemporary reassessment of their traditional affinity towards France. However, although it was a strategy that was politically pragmatic, it also smothered differences between the older Catholic peerage and the newer bourgeois "intruders" as to who would lead Irish Catholicism into the nineteenth century. By and large, the aristocratic Catholic leaders of the 1770s had had relatively little emotional or personal attachment to America. For many Catholic merchants, however, Europe had been replaced by America in their affections as a result of their involvement in transatlantic commerce. Especially in the southern ports of Ireland, these merchants were affected by the embargo of February 1776 which forbade the export of provisions (except corn) to all countries other than Great Britain and the loyal colonies.

3 The American Example Inspires Moves Towards Irish Liberty

The embargo inspired a number of resolutions and petitions. In June 1776, for example, a petition to George III from the merchants of Cork linked the "ruination" of their American trade to a call for the dismissal of Lord North, while several other cities and counties resolved not to import British goods. Such protests inevitably invited comparisons with revolutionary America. British Whigs warned North that Ireland might "go the way of" America, as rumors circulated that Franklin, then American minister to France, had been empowered "to treat with Ireland on commerce and matters of mutual interest and support."

In April 1778 a British parliamentary committee sought to prevent what it saw as the further dismemberment of the British Empire and recommended the suspension of Ireland's trade restrictions. But protectionist resentment in Britain undermined these parliamentary moves, and consequently the non-importation movement blossomed during late 1778 and 1779. The "armed associations" of Irish patriotism, the Volunteers, grew to an estimated 40,000 by the end of 1779, while within the blossoming non-importation movement, both inside and outside the Irish Parliament, the slogans of revolutionary America found a rhetorical home in Volunteer resolutions and reviews.

In November 1779 Dublin mobs protested against government policy and decorated the cannons outside the Irish Parliament with the legend "a free trade or else." Although the effects of the embargo on Irish commerce are unclear, opposition to it enlivened the patriot movement and, in

Edmund Burke's words, changed "a mere question of commerce into a question of state." Indeed, with rumors that the French were mounting an invasion of Ireland, some saw the free trade movement as an aspect of the second front that the French had opened in mid-1778.

In the face of the protests in Ireland, North was obliged to introduce "free trade" measures in December 1779 and February 1780. While these concessions were welcomed in Ireland, they "ought not," as John Adams reported to Congress, " to be considered as anything more than a great beginning" of a patriotic campaign to redress constitutional disabilities as well.

These disabilities were enshrined, first, in Poynings's Law (1495), which stipulated that bills had to be initiated in the English Privy Council and that, consequently, the Irish Parliament could only consent to (or reject) bills and, second, in the so-called Declaratory Act, which proclaimed the right of the British Parliament to legislate for Ireland. In April 1780 Grattan observed that "a country enlightened as Ireland, chartered as Ireland, armed as Ireland, and injured as Ireland, will be satisfied with nothing less than liberty." For the next two years the Lord Lieutenant, the Earl of Carlisle (1780–4), and his chief secretary William Eden, who had earlier sought to negotiate with the American rebels, now sought to conciliate the Irish patriots.

Such experience of the realities of American patriotism as well as the quickening pace of Volunteer activity in Ireland convinced the administration of Ireland that it had no alternative but to advise the repeal of the Declaratory Act and the alteration of Poynings's Law. Although the concessions of 1782 were limited, they were sufficient to ensure that the revolutionary American path would not be taken by Irish patriots. The British Government felt assured of their ultimate loyalty, and, although its responses to both "free trade" and legislative independence were influenced by events in America, Carlisle accurately concluded that Irish and American patriotism were following divergent courses.

Carlisle believed that Irish patriots less understood the American Revolution than related it to their own domestic situation. Thus, although Irish responses to the Revolution revealed the effects of a wide range of ideological, personal, religious, and regional factors, in the last analysis they were pragmatic. The American Revolution revealed and, to some extent, inspired changes in the Irish polity in a crucial period of its development.

FURTHER READING

Bric, Maurice J.: "Ireland and the Broadening of the Late Eighteenth-Century Philadelphia Polity" (Ph.D. dissertation, Johns Hopkins University, 1990).

——: "The Irish and the 'New Politics' in America," *The Irish in America: Emigration, Assimilation, and Impact*, ed. P. J. Drudy (Cambridge: Cambridge University Press, 1985).

Doyle, David Noel: *Ireland, Irishmen and Revolutionary America* (Cork: Mercier Press, 1981).

Edwards, Owen Dudley: "The American Image of Ireland: a Study of its Early Phases," *Perspectives in American History*, 4 (1970), 199–284.

Johnston, Edith Mary: *Ireland in the Eighteenth Century* (Dublin: Gill & Macmillan, 1974).

Kraus, Michael: "America and the Irish Revolutionary Movement in the Eighteenth Century," *The Era of the American Revolution*, ed. Richard B. Morris (New York: Harper & Row, 1939).

McDowell, R. B.: *Irish Public Opinion, 1760–1800* (London: Faber & Faber, 1943).

——: *Ireland in the Age of Imperialism and Revolution, 1760–1801* (Oxford: Oxford University Press, 1979).

O'Connell, Maurice: *Irish Politics and Social Conflict in the Age of the American Revolution* (Philadelphia: University of Pennsylvania Press, 1965).

CHAPTER SIXTY-THREE

The American Revolution and the sugar colonies, 1775–1783

SELWYN H. H. CARRINGTON

1 Pre-war Relations – Interdependence

IT is generally held that, without unrestricted access to American markets, the plantation system of the British West Indies would not have developed so fully and the importance of the sugar colonies to British economic growth during the eighteenth century would have been far less significant. In fact, the insecurity of their artificial economy was not apparent to the majority of planters and merchants because their unrestricted commercial system functioned smoothly until the dispute between Britain and America erupted. Yet there were signs that any attempt at interference with this commercial relationship was fraught with disastrous implications for the survival of the plantation system.

In the commerce that developed, not only did the Americans supply the planters with a variety of foodstuffs and lumber and consume large portions of their rum and minor products, but they were also the mainstay of the carrying trade between the continent and the West Indies (Edwards, 1794, p. 399). These vessels were mainly brigs, schooners, and snows, ranging from 30 to 90 tons, and were well-suited to the transportation of bulky commodities (Bell, 1917, p. 278) "over shallows and Bars," often offloading their goods in creeks and small bays which were unsuited to large merchantmen.[1]

American monopoly of intercolonial shipping had posed serious threats to British shipping interests. The economist Josiah Tucker wrote that the Americans were poised to engross not only that branch of the trade but also the carrying trade between Britain and the West Indies. John Adams was equally aware of British opposition, and is credited with the epigram "The Americans were spreading too much canvass on the seas and their wings needed clipping."[2] It was, however, Lord Sheffield who cited American competition as justification for excluding the United States from the West Indian carrying trade in the post-1783 period. He wrote:

The American shipping, by various means, were monopolizing this business; they used to give their lumber at half price to those who would load their vessels with sugar. They were encouraged, and sent away loaded in a few weeks, while our ships were often obliged to come away half loaded. One consequence was that British sugar ships were gradually lessening in number, every man concerned in … withdrawing himself as fast as he could. (Sheffield, 1784, p. 163)

Taken together, America and the West Indies comprised the major trading block in an area encompassing Canada, the Spanish mainland, and the Caribbean. Furthermore, Britain could not compete with the Americans, whose products were cheaper and much more geared to a slave economy. Any interference with American–West Indian commercial relations threatened the pre-eminent position of the West Indies as the center of the British imperial economic system. The Earl of Dartmouth expressed most clearly the hopes and fears of many: "The State of Affairs in North America and particularly in the New England Colonies is become very serious. It is to be hoped however that nothing will happen to obstruct the Commerce that for mutual interest ought to be cherished on both sides."[3]

2 The War and West Indian Trade

The outbreak of fighting between Britain and the American colonies had deep and lasting consequences for the sugar colonies. Previous eighteenth-century wars had been mere annoyances and had posed no serious threat to the plantation system. Colonial shipping was protected by a strong Royal Navy; freight and insurance rates remained low; the slave trade, although affected, met the needs of the planters and merchant classes; and of course food and lumber reached the islands in large enough quantities. In fact, historians have observed that on these occasions colonial commerce "prospered more than in times of peace" (Pares, 1963, p. 471; Sheridan, 1973, p. 266). During the American war, however, West Indian trade with the United States was first affected by two Restraining Acts passed early in 1775, and was later terminated by the Prohibitory Act of 1776. Thereafter emerged a number of crises which contributed to the retardation and subsequent decline of the sugar economy.

The Prohibitory Act terminated all commercial intercourse between the West Indies and the rebellious colonies. Canada, Nova Scotia, and Newfoundland were expected to fill the vacuum. However, certain provisos exempted categories of American vessels from capture, and also allowed British merchants to trade with loyal colonies of those areas under the control of British forces. These loopholes worked to the benefit of American merchants and their West Indian sympathizers,[4] and led to an extensive illegal trade in arms, ammunition, and some plantation supplies with the rebels (Ford, 1904: 11, pp. 257–9; Setser, 1937, p. 11).

After 1776 the planters faced severe shortages of all categories of foodstuffs, lumber, and other plantation supplies. As a corollary, prices increased significantly, and the general conditions of the sugar plantations were aptly described by John Pinney, an attorney and planter of Nevis, "You have

no idea of the distressed and unhappy state of this country."[5]

In order to prevent devastation to life and property, many planters tinkered with the plantation system by attempting self-sufficiency through the production of local food. Overall, the gains were minimal, while the losses in sugar production from labor shortages were quite marked. The very nature of the monocultural sugar plantation system made even this temporary alternative unworkable, and for survival the planters embarked on a frantic search for external sources of food and lumber. Jamaica introduced a bounty system which facilitated the importation of American supplies through the foreign free ports; the Antiguan Assembly passed a bill for this purpose but the latter was rejected by the Council. Barbados did nothing in this area, believing that market conditions would have a greater impact. Some governors, however, such as William Mathew Burt of the Leeward Islands, supported the importation of foreign goods, but this was rejected by the Colonial Office as an infringement of British commercial policy (Carrington, 1987, pp. 828–9).

The cessation of American–West Indian commerce initiated a "redirection of trade" which saw the expansion of business between the sugar colonies and the United Kingdom. Agents from Scottish and other merchant-houses were sent out to secure new business and to direct the trade on a commission basis. However, there were several disadvantages to the planters: insurance costs spiralled as there was need for special clauses to allow vessels to ply among the islands; American privateers had a devastating effect on the trade and inter-island shipping; the quantity of supplies was inadequate, and spoilage further reduced it. Furthermore, related factors such as increased demand for Scottish and Irish herrings, high freight insurance, lighterage, commission, and other charges pushed the costs of food for the slaves beyond the ability of planters to pay and maintain profits. In order to lessen the hardships to West Indian planters, Parliament allowed the export of food to the islands and removed all restrictions on Irish–West Indian trade between 1778 and 1780. Larger quantities of beef, pork, and herrings reached the islands, but it is doubtful that this quality of food was given to the slaves.[6]

Commercial gains to the West Indies were negligible. Ireland imported minimal tropical products and the value of her imports declined substantially between 1778 and 1783, while Irish exports to the West Indies increased. The imports of West Indian products into Scotland increased initially to fill the vacuum created by the loss of the tobacco trade (Sheridan, 1976, p. 618). But this development was short-lived, and, as the Scottish economy went into recession and large quantities of West Indian products rotted in warehouses, Houston and Company's letters to its agents reflect the general situation: "We have resolved to restrict trade to the West Indies."[7] It then stopped the practice of taking sugar estates for mortgages, and it resolved that nothing could induce the company "to go deeper into the West Indian trade."[8]

Throughout most of the war, the main source of food for West Indian slaves was the neighboring foreign islands, which continued to receive unlimited quantities of American products. Hence the British sugar colonies were hit by continuing food shortages with tragic results. Deaths from malnutrition among the slaves reached several thousands in the Leeward Islands and Jamaica. An estimated 5,000 slaves perished in Barbados between 1780 and 1781; the slave population declined from 78,874 in 1774 to 63,248 in 1781, and in 1784 it was given as 61,808. Faced with heavy losses, some planters re-emigrated to England, as exemplified by Pinney's letter to his uncle. "I want to contract my concerns here and fix a fund in England – not solely to depend upon estates subject to every calamity" (Pares, 1950, pp. 93–4).[9]

Thus the loss of the American source of foodstuffs and plantation supplies led to two major problems. First, the decrease in the labor force through heavy losses among the slave population, especially since the slave trade had declined markedly as a result of the war; and then, as a corollary, there was a decline in the quantity of West Indian products exported to Britain. Despite this, there was an inadequate number of ships to transport Caribbean products to Britain for several reasons. The most significant were: a large number of merchantmen was requisitioned for war services; prohibition of American–West Indian commerce removed an extremely large portion of British shipping; a large portion of merchant vessels captured by American privateers was not replaced because of high labor costs and the shortage and high costs of material.

In addition to the economic woes which resulted from the American war, there was a significant psychological blow. The Revolution had virtually broken the spirit of numerous planters, who lost the resilience so characteristic of this group in the eighteenth century. Furthermore, the loss of direct trade with America had another ominous consequence. If forced the merchants and planters to depend on the foreign islands for their American supplies, thus creating an extensive illegal trade between United States and West Indian merchants in foreign colonial ports – a situation which continued in the post-1783 period, despite the tightening of British mercantilist policies. The West Indian sugar economy also went into a decline from which it never truly recovered.

3 American Privateering: Its Consequences

Privateering was a traditional wartime activity of the colonists. Yet, although previously it had only minimal effect on colonial trade, efforts were made by Britain to regulate the activity of enemy privateers (Bemis, 1935, p. 55). In all previous wars the Admiralty contended mainly with French privateers and was able to estimate their number and to restrict their movements by employing an effective convoy system.[10] On the contrary, during the American war, the Admiralty was unable to estimate the numbers and strength of rebel privateers which infested the secluded creeks and small bays around the Caribbean islands. The latter thus successfully blockaded colonial ports, captured merchant vessels, and seriously threatened British colonial commerce as well as the security of the islands (Davis,

1962, p. 332). American privateers fulfilled two extremely important functions: they became a weapon in America's fight for independence, and they were an important means of transporting arms and munitions of war and tropical products to the continent.

In order to fulfil the first function, the privateers attacked West Indian shipping as the vessels made their way unprotected from Barbados through the network of foreign and British islands to Jamaica. Cruisers were normally employed to protect the trade but, in order to do so, the strength of the naval force along the American coast would have had to be weakened.

Many of the American privateers found protection in the ports of the foreign governments, where there were hundreds of United States supporters as well as agents of Congress and some states. Some of the most famous were William Bingham and Richard Harrison, representatives for Virginia and Maryland, at Martinique (Brown, 1937, pp. 54–9); Stephen Ceronio at Cape François in St. Domingue; and Abraham van Bibber and Samuel Curson at St. Eustatius. Many pursued their private enterprises with the help of resident Americans or British merchants. They secured British registers for American privateers and other vessels to be used if stopped by ships of the Royal Navy. For example, John Spear of Antigua received cargoes of provisions and lumber from his father, William Spear of Baltimore, through the services of Abraham van Bibber, without paying commission. John agreed to provide Abraham with British manufactures, gunpowder, arms, and registers for rebel vessels.

The Edenton merchant William Savage, in transacting a business deal with John Crohon and Company of St. Eustatius, advised the firm to secure the support of the British West Indians, without which it would fail. Likewise, Isaac Gouverneur, the agent for Braxton, Willing and Morris of Philadelphia, also received invaluable support from William Mactier (McTair) of St. Kitts. In Jamaica, Joseph and Eliphalet Fitch, formerly of Boston, provided American rebel vessels with invaluable information about the movement of British warships. These activities enabled the privateers to evade capture and to distress British shipping.

From July 1776, all vessels belonging to British subjects, except those owned by the Bermudians and Bahamians, were subject to capture (Maclay, 1924, p. 69). Congress as well as many states joined private individuals in sending small navies of warships and privateers on expeditions in the Caribbean (Paullin, 1906, pp. 441–9; 452–3). During these voyages they captured hundreds of West Indian ships laden with rum, molasses, sugar, indigo, and other tropical products. On occasions, Continental warships fought battles with ships of the Royal Navy. The success of the *Alfred* (Captain Elisha Hinman) is a classic example; on a trip to the Caribbean in 1777 it captured the *Druid* (Captain Cateret Bourchier). This incident sparked complaints about Lord Howe's handling of the fleet in America, and the lack of protection for the West Indian trade.

The privateers and Continental warships also made physical attacks on the islands. A few cases would illustrate their successes. In May 1777 part of the crew of the *Oliver Cromwell* landed at Sandy Point, Tobago (a plaque marks this incursion). Several months later a party of American rebels landed at Bloody Bay in the same island and carried off the gunpowder. Early in 1779 another village, Charlotteville, was successfully attacked.[11] Dominica was also besieged by privateers, and in the case of Barbados, the *Johnson* of a mere eight guns terrorized coastal estates and the colony's trade (Schomburgk, 1848, pp. 335–6). The village of Moryeau in Grenada was burnt and American vessels carried off the gunpowder.

The successful harassment of the islands and their trade served the American war effort well. The British Government had to withdraw parts of the navy blockading the coast to protect the islands, thus enabling American privateers to sail unmolested to the United States with the necessities of war. These attacks by rebel privateers added immensely to the planters' struggle for survival, and at times may even have influenced their opposition to British imperial rule (Carrington, 1988, pp. 84–101).

4 American War: Its Political and Constitutional Impact

One of the more interesting but relatively unexplored areas is the impact of the American Revolution on political and constitutional development in the West Indies. Like many in the United States, several colonists in the islands believed in the emerging ideology of the "Rights of Man," and for most of the second half of the eighteenth century West Indians, too, struggled to control such areas as taxation, the appropriation and expenditure of public money, the upholding of the rights and privileges of their Assembly, the control of all local appointments which they previously held, the usurpation of greater portions of the executive power, the prevention of the unwarranted removal of judges and other local officers, and the forcing of Parliament to abolish those parts of its commercial laws antithetical to colonial trade. In fact, the American concept of "no taxation without representation" originated in Barbados in 1651, when the Assembly denied the British Parliament the right to legislate for the island, since "legislation without representation was a violation of the rights of Englishmen." In Jamaica in 1680, the Assembly successfully established its right to legislate in all domestic matters (Schuyler, 1929, pp. 103–16; Williams, 1970, pp. 179–80; cf. Boyd, 1974, p. 548; Goveia, 1956, pp. 56–7), and finally it was a Grenadian planter who filed a suit in England that led to Lord Mansfield's famous ruling in 1774 in *Campbell vs. Hall.*

In his litigation against William Hall, a Collector of the Customs, Alexander Campbell argued that the Crown had surrendered its right to tax the colonies when local legislatures were established. In this historical and celebrated decision, Lord Mansfield upheld the contention that "Royal Orders" could not supersede the laws and were unenforceable in the colonies without authorization of the local legislatures. This ruling came at the height of the dispute between Britain and her colonies in America, and the colonists welcomed it as supporting their struggle against subjugation by the British Parliament.

Hence many of the constitutional claims of the period did not originate with the American War, although influenced by it, but were well known and discussed throughout the islands. The 1774 "Petition and Memorial" to King George III in support of the Americans in their dispute with Parliament was a restatement of the Jamaican Assembly's constitutional position in an earlier petition in 1766, when it was involved in the protracted Oliphant Case controversy. Other pro-American addresses came from Tobago, from the Assembly of Grenada and the Grenadines, and from the Council of St. Vincent. The Assembly of Barbados, while not overtly pro-American, established a fund for the people of Boston and despatched a petition to the King critical of British policy.

Not only did the assemblies forward petitions and other documents establishing the principles on which the Americans were fighting for their freedom; many West Indians openly spoke in favor of rebellion and even drank to the American struggle as the "Immortal Honour of Incountering death in every form rather than submit to slavery," which they equated with a submission to British authority. In Jamaica, support for the Americans abated after an abortive slave rebellion in 1776 among the house slaves who were imbued with the "spirit of Dear Liberty,"[12] who were emulating the planters' avowed stance, and who themselves wished to gain their freedom. The political and constitutional crises which occurred in Jamaica, Barbados, Grenada, St. Vincent, and the Leeward Islands from 1774 to 1783 were primarily influenced by the pro-republican ideology of a large number of the inhabitants, as well as an accelerated effort on the part of many assemblies to gain power over the executive branch, since they viewed Britain's attempt to subdue the colonists by force as a threat to their own political existence.

There thus developed a struggle for power centered around four traditional areas – the control of internal taxation and the disbursement of the public revenue; the composition and proceedings of the assemblies which embodied their right to appoint their own officers and to have a greater say in the executive decision-making process; the control of the local militia and the islands' defenses; and, in general, a stricter observance of basic parliamentary privileges.

One of the first areas of the prerogative to be attacked was defense, including the governors' total control of the forts, fortifications, public works, martial law, and the control of the militia during this period. In Jamaica in 1778 the Assembly took control of the area by naming all its members and the entire Council to join the Governor as Commissioners for Forts, Fortifications and Public Buildings. His function was now one of making recommendations only. In Barbados, St. Vincent, Antigua, St. Kitts, and Grenada, the assemblies assumed control of public works, including forts and fortifications, by their insistence on examining public accounts before payments were authorized; all works to be paid out of the public purse had to be vetted by the assemblies before the governors could undertake them.

Another area of grave concern in the islands was the declaration of martial law, the calling out and drilling of the militia. There were always complaints of governors' misuse of this prerogative; but there is little doubt that the war in America motivated the West Indian assemblies to seek greater control over martial law and the militia. After a protracted dispute, in 1779 the legislature of Jamaica passed an Act establishing the Assembly, the Council and the Governor of the Council of War. This thus gave the Assembly control of the militia and martial law. While the Barbados Assembly did not take the same path, it refused to pass a militia bill over the consequences of which it would have no control. It thus told both governors Edward Hay and James Cuninghame that it was "most unwilling ... in times too ... propitious to the claims of civil liberty in the Colonies than ever, to renounce a principle of attachment so Honorable to Society, and enforce Obedience to a power congenial with the Habits of despotic sway."[13] Repeated calls for a militia act met with no success in St. Vincent. In those islands where the assemblies passed legislation to regulate the militia they were useless. Most contained no articles of war,

penalties for desertion were unenforceable, and a majority of the inhabitants refused to cooperate.

The Americans had included the unwarranted removal of judges as one of its main complaints against the King in their "Declaration of the Rights of Man." Since 1751 the Jamaica Assembly had sought to give security of tenure of office to judges in the island by legislation which was allowed "to lie on the table" in England. The dismissal of four judges in 1778 led to a prolonged constitutional crisis until January 1781, when the Judges Act was passed giving tenure *quamdiu se bene gesserint* (also expressed as *ad vitam aut culpam* – privilege to be held during good behavior). After 1783 the Act was incorporated into the Governor's Instructions. In Barbados the question was also debated and was cited as a grievance by the Assembly. Although it did not pass legislation as in the case of Jamaica, its opposition to unjustified removals was recognized. There is therefore little doubt that the upheaval caused by the American war had enabled the judges in most islands to hold their places *quamdiu se bene gesserint*, and not *durante bene placito* (during the pleasure of the grantor) as before the war (Carrington, 1988, pp. 128–61).

5   Conclusion: A Summary

The impact of the American War of Independence on the economy of the West Indies is fairly well known. The war had caused severe hardships, and the islands went into a state of economic decline from which only minimal recovery was made as late as the 1790s. The political and constitutional impact is less well known. It is quite clear that the American Revolution had found support among a large sector of the inhabitants who shared the political and constitutional ideology of the Americans, as demonstrated in the writings of Edward Long and Bryan Edwards, as well as in the celebrated victory for the Grenada planters in Lord Mansfield's ruling in *Campbell vs. Hall* in 1774 and in the continuous persecution of some governors, as in the case of Valentine Morris of St. Vincent from 1775 to the island's capture in 1779.

It was during this period of crisis in the British Empire that the assemblies vociferously made their claims of co-equality with the British House of Commons. In addition, they refused to raise taxes; they restricted the governors' powers in every facet of political life; they usurped executive power and they persecuted all colonial officials opposed to their tactics and/or ideology. This opposition formed part of a wider movement which was manifested in the American War of Independence. All the governors who served in the West Indies during this period complained of the rise of a "republican spirit," which to the planters meant the retention of power in their hands. Valentine Morris of St. Vincent, John Dalling of Jamaica, Edward Hay and James Cuninghame of Barbados, and Lord George Macartney of Grenada shared William Mathew Burt's observation of the state of politics in the Leeward Islands: "Others in this part of the world have caught the infection from America and deeply tinged with the principles of Republicanism, attempt bringing all to a level."[14]

Horatio Nelson reached a similar conclusion (Nicolas, 1845, 1: p. 114), as did Sir Guy Carleton, former Governor of Canada and Commander-in-Chief of British forces in America during the war, who strongly opposed free trade between the West Indies and the United States. He wrote: "It is not in the Revolted provinces alone that a Republican spirit is to be found, but the tint has … spread to other parts of America and to the West Indies."[15] During the American war, therefore, the colonial system was indeed severely tested and, although the islands remained "loyal" to Britain, the planters in their political and constitutional disputes, arising at times out of their declining economic conditions, sought to establish the common ideology of the "Rights of Man," and they severely tested the imperial ties.

REFERENCES

1 Minutes of the Committee of the Privy Council (1784). B.T. 5/1 fo. 27d. Edward Long: "History of Jamaica," Vol. 1. British Museum: Add. MS 12,404, 402d. See also Carrington, Selwyn H.H.: *The British West Indies During the American Revolution*, and Hewitts, M. J.: "The West Indies in the American Revolution," D.Phil. thesis, Oxford University, 1936.

2 Josiah Tucker: "The State of the Nation in 1777, compared with the State of the Nation in the famous year of conquest and Glory of 1759" (1777). Bristol Public Library: Jefferies Collection of MSS. Vol. VII, fo. 87. I wish to thank the late Professor Julian P. Boyd for supplying the anecdote.

3 The Earl of Dartmouth to Edward Payne, October 5, 1774. C.O. 152/54.

4 Merchants of Grenada to Lord Macartney, June 3, 1977. Adm. 1/310, fo. 123; James Young to Philip Stephens, June 12, 1777. *Ibid.*, fos. 114–114d; Clark Gayton to John Dalling in Journal of the Assembly of Jamaica, October 31, 1777. C.O. 140/59; Macartney to Sir William Howe, November 16, 1778. C.O. 101/21, fo. 198.

5 John Pinney to William Croker, June 1778. Letter Book 4, p. 220.

6 Houston and Company to James Smith, October 1, 1776. Houston Papers: H.L.S. MS. 8,793, p. 55, Houston and Company to John Constable, February 7, 1777. *Ibid.*, p. 170; Houston and Company to Lewis Chavel & Co., October 13, 1777. *Ibid.*, p. 39. "Invoice of Fifty Barrels Herrings … on Account and Risque of William Bryan Ese. of Jamaica," September 17, 1777. Chisholme Papers: N.L.S. MS. 188:75, fo. 34.

7 Houston & Company to Turner & Paul, May 27, 1777. N.L.S. MS. 8,793, p. 325.

8 Houston & Co. to Samuel Cary, April 9, 1778. N.L.S. MS. 8,793, p. 428.

9 Cf. Pinney to Simon Pretor, June 12, 1777. Pinney Papers. Letter Book 2, p. 114.

10 R. P. Crowhurst: "British Oceanic Convoys in the Seven Years War, 1756–1763," Ph.D. thesis, University of London, 1970.

11 Peter Campbell to Lord Macartney, July 6, 1777. C.O. 101/20, fo. 211d; "Memorial of the Proprietors … in Tobago" to Lord George Germain (1777). *Ibid.*, fo. 242; cf. May 28, 1778. C.O. 101/21, fo. 150; Extract of a letter from Lieutenant Oswald Clark, January 18, 1779. C.O. 101/23, fos. 78–78d; cf. Macartney to Germain, January 28, 1779. *Ibid.*, fos. 76–76d.

12 R. Lindsay to Dr. Robert Robertson, August 6, 1776. Robertson–MacDonald Papers. N.L.S. MS. 3,942, fos. 260d-261.

13 Journal of the Assembly of Barbados, October 1, 1776. C.O. 31/39.

14 William Mathew Burt to Germain, October 25, 1780. C.O. 152/60, fo. 258.
15 "Minutes of the Committee of the Privy Council for Trade," March 16, 1784. B.T. 5/1, fo. 14d.

FURTHER READING

Bell, Herbert C.: "The West Indian trade before the American Revolution," *American Historical Review*, 22 (1917).

Bemis, Samuel Flagg: *The Diplomacy of the American Revolution* (New York: American Historical Association, 1935).

Boyd, Julian P.: "Jefferson's expression of the American mind," *Virginia Quarterly Review*, 50, 4 (1974).

Brown, Margaret L.: "William Bingham: agent of the Continental Congress in Martinique," *Pennsylvania Magazine of History and Biography*, 61 (1937).

Carrington, Selwyn H. H.: "The American Revolution and the British West Indies' Economy," *Journal of Interdisciplinary History*, 17, 4 (1987), 823–50.

——: *The British West Indies During the American Revolution* (Holland: Royal Institute of Linguistics and Anthropology/Foris Publications, 1988).

——: "The American Revolution, British Policy and the West Indian Economy, 1775–1808". *Review Interamericana*, Vol. XXII: nos. 1–2 (Summer, 1992), 72–108.

——: "The British West Indies Economy and the Industrial Capitalist Revolution, 1775–1846," in Alan Cobley ed., *Crossroads of Empire: the Caribbean Connection, 1492–1992* (Cave Hill, Barbados: Department of History, 1994).

——: "The United States and the British West Indian Trade, 1783–1807" in Roderick A. McDonald, ed., *West Indies Accounts: Essays on the history of the British Caribbean and the Atlantic Economy in honor of Richard Sheridan* (The Press: University of the West Indies, Mona, Jamaica, 1996), 149–68.

Davis, Ralph: *The Rise of the English Shipping Industry in the Seventeenth and Eighteenth Centuries* (London: Macmillan, 1962).

Edwards, Bryan: *The History, Civil and Commercial, of the British Colonies in the West Indies*, 2 vols. (London: Stockdale, 1794).

Ford, Worthington Chauncery (ed.): *Journals of the Continental Congress, 1774–1789* (Washington: 1904).

Goveia, Elsa V.: *A Study of the Historiography of the British West Indies to the End of the Nineteenth Century* (Mexico: 1956).

Maclay, Edgar Stanton: *A History of American Privateers* (London: Appleton, 1924).

Nicolas, Sir Charles Harris (ed.) *The Despatches and Letters of Admiral Lord Viscount Nelson*, 7 vols. (London: 1845–6).

Pares, Richard: *A West India Fortune* (London: Longmans and Green, 1950).

——: *War and Trade in the West Indies, 1739–1763* (London: Cass, 1963).

Paullin, Charles Oscar: *The Navy of the American Revolution: its Administration, its policy and its Achievements* (Cleveland: Burrows, 1906).

Schomburgk, R. H.: *The History of Barbados* (London: 1848).

Schuyler, Robert L.: *Parliament and the British Empire: Some Constitutional Controversies Concerning Imperial Legislative Jurisdiction* (New York: Columbia University Press, 1929).

Setser, Vernon G.: *The Commercial Reciprocity Policy of the United States, 1774–1829* (Philadelphia: University of Pennsylvania Press, 1937).

Sheffield, John: *Observations on the Commerce of the American States* (Dublin: 1784).

Sheridan, Richard: *Sugar and Slavery: an Economic History of the British West Indies, 1623–1775* (Baltimore: Johns Hopkins University Press, 1973).

——: "The crisis of slave subsistence in the British West Indies during and after the American Revolution," *William and Mary Quarterly*, 33 (1976).

Williams, Eric Eustace: *From Columbus to Castro: the History of the Caribbean, 1492–1969* (London: Deutsch, 1970).

CHAPTER SIXTY-FOUR

The effects of the American Revolution on France and its empire

DAVID P. GEGGUS

THE American Revolution gave *ancien régime* France its last foreign policy success, a very popular war that brought revenge for the humiliations of 1756–63, but at a cost many historians have considered disastrous. Within five years of the war's end the French Government was bankrupted and forced to embark on revolutionary reorganization that within another five years brought the abolition of the aristocracy, the overthrow of the monarchy, and the start of another, far more costly, war against almost the whole of Europe. Both the financial and ideological impact on France of its participation in the War of Independence are controversial. The American and French revolutions were similarly engendered by wider movements in the Western world, which led governments to extend their fiscal demands at the same time that libertarian and egalitarian ideas gained currency. Moreover, the French Revolution was an event of much greater magnitude and expressed deep-rooted domestic tensions. Even so, the American Revolution probably hastened the outbreak of the great upheaval in France and helped shape its early years.

1 The French Government

From the very end of the Seven Years' War in 1763, the French Government began preparing for a new conflict with Britain that would avenge its disastrous losses. As early as 1775, the foreign minister, Charles Gravier, Comte de Vergennes, recognized that the crisis in North America might bring such an opportunity. Despite opposition from the finance minister Turgot and the reluctance of the young Louis XVI to support a revolt against a legitimate sovereign, Vergennes obtained permission in May 1776 secretly to assist the rebel colonists. Pierre-Augustin Caron de Beaumarchais was engaged as an intermediary, and the departure of volunteers for America was tacitly countenanced. Although Vergennes feared the impact of "so terrible an eruption" (Manceron, 1978, p. 153) on France's own colonies, his ministry instructed the pro-government press to publicize the patriot cause, and even founded a newspaper, *Les Affaires de l'Angleterre et de l'Amérique*, for this purpose.

France declared war in June 1778, four months after concluding treaties of alliance and trade with the confederated colonies. The decision actively to intervene resulted not from Franklin's persuasive diplomacy, but from the assurance brought by the victory at Saratoga that the rebellion would not collapse. The government's aims were limited. England was to be weakened by the loss of the 13 colonies, and France, it was hoped, would benefit commercially. To La Fayette's dismay, Versailles displayed no desire to reconquer French Canada. A continued British presence in North America was considered necessary to limit the power of the emergent new state, whose future alliance was not seriously valued. American brusqueness during the peace negotiations, and the failure of French merchants after 1783 to make inroads into the North American market, helped maintain the

French Government in its aristocratic cool-
ness towards the United States (*see* chapters
44 and 49).

2 Public Opinion

In their struggle against bigotry and injustice at home, social commentators such
as Voltaire had since the 1730s depicted
British North America as a land of prosperity and religious toleration, popularizing the
image of "the virtuous Quaker" free of Old
World corruption. However, before the
Stamp Act crisis, Frenchmen knew and
cared little about the 13 colonies. Benjamin
Franklin's defense of the colonies before
Parliament, and his subsequent visit to Paris
in 1767 at the invitation of the French
Government, set in motion a current of
pro-Americanism that would not diminish
for 25 years.

French interest in North America was
therefore already growing when the events
of 1776 sent a wave of emotional enthusiasm through France, expressed in poetry,
plays, and novels, banquets, new fashions,
new books about America, and translations
of old ones. Aristocratic young men, eager
to fight the traditional foe, took ship for the
New World to offer their military services.
In salons, colleges, and academies, reading
clubs and masonic lodges, the meaning of
the Revolution was avidly discussed. The
periodical press, expanding fast in these
years, carried not only frequent war reports,
but also the writings of colonial patriots and
the acts and resolutions of their legislatures.
The state constitutions and bills of rights
were published in French at least five times
between 1777 and 1786, and, like the
Declaration of Independence, were deliberately ignored by the government censor.

Interest in the Revolution was also promoted by the increase of personal contacts, hitherto rare, between Americans and
Frenchmen. When most well-to-do French
persons still wore powdered wigs, plain-
dressed American sea-captains, merchants,
and diplomats created a vivid impression.
Benjamin Franklin, who was regarded as the
personification of New World virtue and
simplicity, became a household name after
his return in 1776, and his picture appeared
on all manner of everyday items. Both
Franklin and John Paul Jones were received
at court, sculpted by Houdon, and admitted into the new masonic lodge of the
Nine Sisters. Other members included
the future revolutionaries Brissot, Sieyès,
Danton, Pétion, Condorcet, and Camille
Desmoulins. Franklin played a major role in
the propagation of occult masonry, and his
and George Washington's membership facilitated French identification with the patriot
cause. A different type of contact came
through the 8,000 French soldiers who
served in the United States and returned
home to recount their experiences. Peace
brought the establishment of a regular
packet service between the two countries,
and the flood of publications continued
through the 1780s.

Two levels of public opinion may be distinguished. The most popular form, a vague
pro-Americanism, was rooted in a jingoistic
Anglophobia that generated enthusiasm for
the insurgents because they were enemies
of the British. Among the politically conscious, those who were pro-reform and anti-
autocratic saw the American Revolution as
a vindication of their own ideas and an
inspiration for their own struggle against
royal absolutism and social injustice. In
the 1780 edition of the Abbé Raynal's
very influential *History of the two Indies*,
Diderot inserted two chapters on North
America, which, while justifying the
colonists' rebellion, covertly attacked the
foundations of *ancien régime* France and
caused the book to be banned.

There is no form of government with the prerogative of being immutable; no political authority
which, created yesterday or a thousand years ago,
cannot be abrogated in ten years or tomorrow;
no power, however respectable or sacred, that is
authorized to regard the state as its property.
(Raynal, [1780] 1981, p. 325)

Both these trends in opinion were reinforced by the fashionable literary image of
the noble savage and his colonial counterpart, the noble frontiersman. The resulting
vision of America was frequently an idealized distortion that depicted an undiffer-
entiated nation of hard-working, godly
farmers who lived in harmony, free of

jealousy, greed, and intolerance. This "American mirage" reflected French pre-occupations with social privilege, corruption, and despotism as much as transatlantic realities. This is well illustrated by the French edition of St. Jean de Crèvecoeur's *Letters of an American Farmer*, which became more sentimental and propagandist in its revised translation. Americans in France, such as Franklin, Jefferson, and Philip Mazzei, attempted to promote a more realistic image. However, first-hand experience was no guarantee of accuracy; the radical journalist Jacques-Pierre Brissot, founder of the "Société Gallo-Américaine," visited the United States in 1788, but proved one of the fiercest defenders of the American myth. Myth or not, he declared, it served a purpose.

Rather than introducing new ideas, the American Revolution catalyzed trends already present in *ancien régime* France. As early as the 1750s, Frenchmen began to claim they were living in a dynamic new era of change, and the liberal, egalitarian, assumptions of the Enlightenment had become commonplace long before the War of Independence. By the 1760s even aristocratic opponents of the Crown were using words such as "nation," "constitution," and "citizen." By 1776 the phrase "imprescriptible and inalienable rights" was already in use. The very fact that the ideology of the American Revolution was not novel, and spoke to existing aspirations, helps explain the enthusiasm that greeted it. It also renders it extremely difficult to assess America's impact on the development of French opinion.

For the youthful La Fayette, one can say his conversion to the cause of moderate constitutionalism was directly owing to his pursuit of military honors. And his fellow officer the Comte de Ségur later reminisced, "I was far from being the only one whose heart palpitated at the sound of the growing awakening of liberty, seeking to shake off the yoke of arbitrary power" (Cobban, 1963, p. 122). On the other hand, Condorcet and Brissot, two of the most influential "Americanists," had both read Rousseau before reading the Declaration of Independence. Beaumarchais had written the anti-aristocratic *Marriage of Figaro* before being won over to the cause of the insurgents, though he could not get it published until the 1780s. The Marquis de Chastellux, who published in 1786 a popular account of his wartime experience in Rochambeau's army, had already praised American society in his *De la félicité publique* in 1772. This serves as a reminder that much of what the French found admirable in North America, such as religious toleration, the absence of institutionalized privilege, and freedom of speech, was not a product of the Revolution at all.

What was stunningly unique about the events in America was that they put into action what hitherto Frenchmen had merely discussed as abstract propositions. Contemporaries familiar with the concept of a social contract felt they were witnessing, as if in the primeval past, the birth of a new society. For a nation completely lacking a political life, America provided a practical demonstration of successful and sweeping political reform. That this was achieved without considerable bloodshed or persecution brought a new respectability to the idea of revolutionary change, and inspired belief in a new era of progress. Governments truly could be made accountable to their subjects.

The spectacle of European ideas being applied across the ocean also reinforced their claim to be considered as universal truths. The physiocrat and former minister Turgot opposed on financial grounds France's assisting the rebel colonists, but in 1778 he wrote to Joseph Price that they were the hope of the human race and perhaps would provide a model for it. Even the royal censor, the Abbé Genty, declared in a prize essay: "The independence of the Anglo-Americans is the event most likely to accelerate the revolution which must bring happiness on earth. In the bosom of this new republic are true treasures that will enrich the world" (Mornet, 1933, pp. 396–7).

Although difficult to prove, contemplation of the American dream must have increased the dissatisfaction of at least those already dissatisfied with the *ancien régime* in France. One may surmise from the events of the 1780s that the focusing of national attention on the American

Revolution made French opinion more impatient of despotic authority and social inegality, and more ready to consider radical reform and republicanism as workable options for some societies. The theory of enlightened despotism no longer found champions among intellectuals. And the role in limiting royal power claimed for the aristocracy, in theory by Montesquieu and in practice by the *parlements* (the chief law courts), was less readily accepted.

Here several qualifications need to be introduced. There is no evidence that any French soldier returned from America a convinced revolutionary. Indeed the word would not be coined, by Mirabeau, until 1789, and some claim that the modern concept of revolution came not from the Atlantic world or the Enlightenment but from German Illuminism. Similarly, contemporary interest in republican democracy was also fueled in the 1780s by a growing fascination with Ancient Greek and Roman culture. This helped increase the popularity of Rousseau as a political thinker and diminish that of Montesquieu. It also reduced the reputation of the British Constitution. *Anglomanes* thus gave ground to more democratic *Américanistes* in the postwar years for reasons besides the triumph of the United States. Nevertheless, despite having participated through their wartime alliance in the overthrow of a legitimate sovereign, the French gave no sign of seeking a republic themselves when their own revolution began. One might add that the exhilarating sense of living in a new age of progress also owed as much to the Enlightenment as to the American Revolution, which it pre-dated. It was as the Enlightenment in action that the Revolution was hailed in Condorcet's *De l'influence de la Révolution d'Amérique sur l'Europe* (1786), which was the period's most powerful statement of the idea of progress. In his later history of the world, Condorcet depicted the Revolution as a great event, a harbinger of the French Revolution, but even so, only one link in the chain stretching from Descartes to the foundation of the French republic, which constituted the ninth age of history.

Another problem in assessing America's impact on France is that it did not provide a clear-cut example. While most states had two-chamber assemblies, and few yet had elected governors, it was the constitution of Pennsylvania that gained greatest praise from commentators such as Turgot, Condorcet, and Brissot. Although favoring a very restricted franchise, they saw little good in the separation of powers, and thought the Federal Constitution made the presidency too powerful. Not only John Adams but also Thomas Jefferson seemed somewhat conservative in the company of such men, whom they met as ambassadors in Europe. Ironically, one way the Revolution undermined the position of the French aristocracy was by the creation of the hereditary order for veteran officers, the Order of Cincinnatus. Perceived as an incipient nobility, this created uproar among admirers of America, led by the Comte de Mirabeau, and engendered a heated debate on the evils of aristocracy. It should be said, however, that the controversy was secretly initiated by Franklin.

In addition to such critical analysis by the friends of America, there were some overtly hostile currents in French thought. The theory of American degeneracy, derived from Buffon and applied to the New World's Caucasian inhabitants by De Pauw, was also a product of these years, though it could make little headway given the physical presence in Paris of Franklin and Jefferson. Many aristocrats who crossed the Atlantic did not like what they found there, and came back critics of American society. And royalists and conservatives naturally were happy to predict disaster for the new republic. French attitudes towards the 13 former colonies nonetheless remained overwhelmingly favorable down through the early years of the French Revolution.

3   French Finances

The chaotic system of French Government accounting made it very difficult even for the King's ministers to know the government's true financial position. For this reason the financial impact on France of intervention in North America is a rather murky subject. Historians have often claimed that the price of American Independence was the French Revolution, since it began with the financial crisis of 1786. Jacques Necker, the finance minister from 1777 to 1781, is generally blamed for funding the war solely with loans at very high interest, and for covering up their impact in his published accounts. Recent research shows that Necker's loans were not as expensive as once thought. Moreover, although the war cost France more than 1,000 million livres, and Necker's loans totalled more than 500 million, his peacetime successors also borrowed very heavily. The apparent miracle of financing a war without recourse to taxation certainly impeded the postwar implementation of much-needed tax reform. However, the war was far from solely responsible for the bankruptcy of 1788.

4   The French Revolution

When assessing the American impact on the French Revolution, the same problems arise as with the development of French opinion in the preceding decade. Driven forward by internal forces, the French Revolution could probably have unfolded in much the same way had the United States never existed. However, in the influence of certain individuals, perhaps in some constitutional forms and reforms, one may see the imprint of American example. The onset of the Revolution and the hostility of foreign powers undoubtedly made Frenchmen feel closer to the United States, and the active involvement of Americans such as John Paul Jones, Joel Barlow, and Thomas Paine helped intensify pro-American sentiment during the early years of the Revolution. The death of Franklin, for example, made a profound impact on all levels of Parisian society.

The concepts of a constitutional convention, a written constitution, and a declaration of rights, in the forms they were best known in France, can be called American concepts. The Estates-General were called in France shortly after the United States had ratified its own Federal Constitution. State constitutions and bills of rights had been meticulously analyzed in France for more than a decade. Although the Estates-General was a medieval body, it was commonly

expected that it would provide France with a constitution. This it began to do, on transforming itself into a National Constituent Assembly in June 1789. Its Declaration of the Rights of Man bore close resemblance to the Virginia Declaration of Rights, though it was more self-consciously universalist. La Fayette, advised by Jefferson, and Mounier, another admirer of the United States, had a major share in writing the document.

Potentially the most direct link between the American and French revolutions is provided by the peasant soldiers who served in Rochambeau's army. On campaign in North America, they witnessed first-hand the life of prosperous small farmers, who knew nothing of the seigneurial exactions and high taxes that burdened rural France. The regions in which the soldiers were most heavily recruited were also those that experienced the worst rioting in 1789 against the relics of the feudal regime in the countryside. It is tempting to imagine that these veterans returned to their villages with broadened horizons, and encouraged their neighbors to be less accepting of existing inequalities. However, it is not known how many troops had returned by 1789 to the districts they had originally left. It is possible simply that the poorest rural areas produced most popular discontent and most recruits for the army.

In the debates of September 1789 on the form of the new constitution the opposing parties both appealed to American example. The supporters of bicameralism and a strong executive were resoundingly defeated. Although their plan conformed most closely to American precedent, and had the backing of Jefferson, they were known as *Anglomanes* or *Monarchiens*. Those favoring a single-chamber legislature and a temporary royal veto included the leading *Américanistes*, Brissot and Condorcet, though their chief spokesman, the Abbé Sieyès displayed little interest in American affairs. American influence on the question is thus difficult to assign. John Adams, curiously, approved of the outcome. He recognized that, under a balanced government, the progress of reform would have been jeopardized owing to the existence of an hereditary monarch and aristocracy in France.

Of the French officers who participated in the War of Independence, only a handful were prominent in the French Revolution. The Marquis de La Fayette, seconded by Charles de Lameth, played a major role in breaking down barriers between the aristocracy and Third Estate in the period 1787–9. As head of the Paris National Guard, however, he became more notable for attempting to restrain rather than further the course of the Revolution. The Comte de Custine became a general in the army of the Republic, but was executed for treason. Mention could also be made of Du Châtelet, a journalistic collaborator of Condorcet.

Condorcet and Brissot proved to be very influential figures during the years of 1789–92, both as journalists and politicians. Their ideas prevailed in many key controversies, such as over the Declaration of the Rights of Man, the form of the constitution, the abolition of privilege, and the declaration of war in 1792. However, although they had been enthusiastic interpreters of America, their ideas notably evolved in response to domestic pressures during the course of the French Revolution. This is particularly true of their republicanism. Condorcet had as early as 1774 denounced kings as the dupes of priests, and in 1786 had declared a republic to be the best form of government. However, not till the King fled Paris in June 1791, proving himself an enemy of the Revolution, did Condorcet call for a French republic. Brissot also proved a reluctant republican. Nevertheless, he did make frequent references to American precedent when rousing public opinion to support a war against the hostile monarchies of Europe. "With few soldiers [the Americans] won numerous battles against the superior forces of the English, and it was because their cause was just" (Gidney, 1930, p. 123).

With the triumph of moderate constitutionalism in 1789 the symbolic importance to France of the United States declined. It was among the supporters of constitutional monarchy that the American myth had most appeal, and as the Revolution moved to the left the United States found fewer admirers. Brissot attempted to reverse this trend, when he published in April 1791 his *Nouveau voyage dans les Etats-Unis de l'Amérique septentrionale*. He acknowledged that, having won their own liberty, the French did not need any lessons from the Americans in that area. However, for the secret of preserving that liberty the United States remained an important object of study. By forcing France into war in 1792, Brissot was paradoxically to be largely responsible that this lesson was never learned.

5   The French Colonies

The impact of the American Revolution on France's colonial empire was felt most perceptibly in the Caribbean colony of Saint Domingue (modern Haiti), which was the world's major producer of sugar and coffee. With a population in 1789 of 60,000 Whites and free coloreds and a half million slaves, its 8,000 plantations made it one of the wealthiest European colonies. It accounted for some two-fifths of French overseas trade and had been the engine of France's great commercial expansion during the eighteenth century. Saint Domingue experienced its own complex and extremely destructive revolution simultaneous with the revolution in France. Beginning in 1788 as a movement of wealthy planters for greater colonial autonomy, it resulted in the expulsion of all Whites and the creation of the independent state of Haiti in 1804. Although the American Revolution was not of critical importance in the causation of this upheaval, it does seem to have played a multi-faceted role in raising tensions within the colony on the eve of the revolution that would destroy it.

Unlike their British counterparts and neighbors, French colonists lacked any system of representative government. They also suffered more severely from metropolitan laws of trade. These forced them to pay high prices for imports and denied them access to the foreign markets where most of their produce was eventually sold to the sole profit of French merchants. France's Caribbean colonies, therefore, had more substantive reasons for rebellion than any British possessions, and indeed since 1770 Raynal and other French writers had predicted eventual colonial secession. However, vulnerability to slave revolts, to naval blockade, and to foreign invasion made West Indian islands (whose wealthiest proprietors resided in France) particularly dependent on their mother countries for protection. This considerably reduced the relevance to them of the example of the American Revolution. Dissident planters in Saint Domingue tended to be Anglophiles who looked to a British takeover rather than independence. Perhaps for this reason the struggle of the 13 colonies excited among them no obvious sympathy for the insurgents.

Nevertheless, the desire for self-government had a long history in Saint Domingue and it was notably strengthened by the War of Independence. Aside from its (apparently slight) ideological impact, the American Revolution gave Saint Domingue a tempting taste of free trade. When France intervened in the conflict, colonial administrators (liberally interpreting the Franco-American trade treaty) opened the colony's ports to Yankee traders, who supplied its needs more cheaply than could French merchants. These commercial contacts were continued in restricted form after the war through a new system of free ports, which were visited in the late 1780s by more than 600 American vessels per year, chiefly from Massachusetts and Philadelphia. Numerous American merchants established themselves at Cap Français and Port au Prince, and by 1790 Saint Domingue was absorbing 10 percent of United States exports. The free-port trade, however, was heavily taxed and subjected to frustrating prohibitions. It also provoked a retaliatory increase in freight charges by resentful French merchants. In addition, smuggling was curtailed by new measures reminiscent of British action in North America 20 years before.

Such conflicts of interest encouraged planters to think of themselves as "Americans" rather than Frenchmen. When prominent colonists established a scientific society at Cap Français in 1784 they called it "Le Cercle des Philadelphes." Among the many adepts of occult freemasonry who were members was Bacon de la Chevalerie, who had links with the Nine Sisters' Lodge in

Paris and who five years later became the first revolutionary leader in Saint Domingue. Ironically, friction between colony and metropolis reached its height at a time when both the Minister of Marine (La Luzerne) and the Colonial Intendant (Barbé de Marbois) were former diplomats who had served in Philadelphia during the war.

The abolition of slavery in northern states such as Massachusetts, where freed Blacks migrated to the seaports, must have been discussed in Saint Domingue by visiting American seamen, but it is not known how this affected the slaves. The American Revolution certainly had more direct impact on the colony's free colored community, which formed a sort of middle class of mixed racial descent and was victimized by an entrenched system of discrimination. In 1779 a special regiment of free coloreds was raised and, along with a battalion of Whites, sent to Georgia to fight alongside the rebel colonists at Savannah. The regiment's muster roll reads like a list of future revolutionaries. Besides the future King Henry Christophe, it included many of the leaders who, in the 1790s, would direct the struggle for civil rights and then free colored domination in Saint Domingue. Such men returned from Georgia with military experience and a new sense of their own importance. For the first time they cautiously began to pressure an intransigent government to dismantle the system of racial inequality.

Autonomist and secessionist attitudes among Saint Domingue Whites, and aspirations for freedom and equality among its non-Whites, also developed in response to the appearance in Paris in 1788 of an anti-slavery society called the "Amis des Noirs." Founded by Brissot, its members included Condorcet, Mirabeau, and La Fayette. The question here is to what extent the movement was inspired by the American Revolution. Anti-slavery thought in France certainly long pre-dated the revolt of the 13 colonies, and Condorcet was an abolitionist by 1776. In La Fayette's case, it was apparently his experiences in North America that converted him, for on his return he immediately began an experiment with freed slaves in France's Guiana colony. Other veterans, however, reported that North American slaves were relatively well treated. Neither Washington nor Jefferson chose to encourage the movement. The key figure was Brissot. His interest in anti-slavery and the initial proposal for an abolition society, which was founded before his trip to the United States, came from his Quaker friends in London. Even so, he subsequently made ample use of American evidence to buttress his arguments about the safety of abolishing the slave trade, the superiority of free labor, and the ability of Blacks. With the outbreak of the French Revolution, the "Amis des Noirs" became active supporters of the free coloreds and the principal bugaboo of the white colonists.

In these ways the American Revolution helped prepare the ground for the Haitian Revolution. Whether the Whites' desires for autonomy, the free coloreds' for equality, or the slaves' for freedom would of themselves have led to rebellion is a matter of speculation. However, it was clearly the French Revolution that precipitated Saint Domingue's destruction. Weakening the traditional sources of authority in the colonies, it not only inflamed social and political aspirations but also undermined the institutions that had held them in check. Initiating a decade of turmoil in Saint Domingue, it thus brought into existence the New World's second independent state.

FURTHER READING

Bodinier, G.: *Les officiers de l'armée royale, combattants de la guerre d'Indépendance des Etats-Unis: de Yorktown à l'an II* (Officers of the Royal Army: Veterans of the American War of Independence from Yorktown to the Year II) (Vincennes: Service Historique de l'Armée de Terre, 1983).

Cobban, A.: *A History of Modern France*, 3 vols. vol. 1, *Old Regime and Revolution, 1715–1799* (Baltimore: Penguin, 1963).

Debbasch, Y.: *Couleur et liberté* (Color and liberty) (Paris: 1967).

Echeverria, D.: *Mirage in the West: A History of the French Image of American Society to 1815* (New York: Octagon Books, 1966).

Frostin, C.: *Les révoltes blanches à Saint-Domingue aux xviie et xviiie siècles* (White revolts in Saint Domingue during the seventeenth and eighteenth centuries) (Paris: L'Ecole, 1975).

Gidney, L.: *L'influence des Etats-Unis d'Amérique sur Brissot, Condorcet et Mme Roland* (The influence of the United States on Brissot, Condorcet, and Mme Roland) (Paris: Rieder, 1930).

Harris, R. D.: *Necker, Reform Statesman of the Ancien Regime* (Berkeley: University of California Press, 1979).

Manceron, C.: *The Wind from America, 1778–1781* (New York: Alfred Knopf, 1978).

McDonald, F.: "The Relation of French Peasant Veterans of the American Revolution to the Fall of Feudalism in France." *Agricultural History* 25 (1951), 151–61.

Mornet, D.: *Les origines intellectuelles de la Révolution Française (1715–1787)* (Intellectual origins of the French Revolution) (Paris: Armand Colin, 1933).

Palmer, R. R.: *The Age of the Democratic Revolution: A Political History of Europe and America, 1760–1800*, 2 vols. vol. 1, *The Challenge* (Princeton: Princeton University Press, 1959).

Perrault, G.: *Le secret du roi*, 3 vols. vol. 3, *La revanche américaine* (The King's Secret: The American Revenge) (Paris: Fayard, 1996).

Raynal, G. T.: *Histoire philosophique et politique des deux Indes* (Philosophical and Historical History of the Two Indies) (Paris: 1780); repr., ed. Y. Bénot (Paris: Maspéro, 1981).

CHAPTER SIXTY-FIVE

The impact of the American Revolution on Spain and Portugal and their empires

KENNETH MAXWELL

1 Introduction

HISTORY writing since the Second World War has tended to de-emphasize the role of individuals, institutions and events and, instead, has sought to plot the longer-term trends in economic development, to delineate social and economic structures and to track shifts in mentalities. Topics such as the impact of the American Revolution on the territories of the other European colonial powers to its south have been, as a consequence, much neglected. Although much has been achieved by this emphasis, and conjunctural economic analysis and an understanding of the social complexity of the Americas is essential to any understanding of the reception of the North American Revolution in Latin America, it has also led to the almost total exclusion of detailed examinations of elites or institutions, and above all of intellectual life and politics, all areas in which the impact of the North American model was, of course, most influential among Latin Americans of the late colonial period. Hence today we tend to know more about slaves than their masters; more about the forced Amerindian labor drafts of upper Peru (contemporary Bolivia) than the attitudes of Peruvian merchants and bureaucrats in Lima; more about Mexican silver production than the political role of mining entrepreneurs. As to intellectual history, the most recent work on the Enlightenment in Latin America – a decisive framework for explaining what was and what was not taken from the North American example by the Latin American

elites of the period – is 20 years old, and the best account remains the collection of essays edited by Arthur Whitaker in the early 1940s (twice reissued in the early 1960s, but long since out of print). A third problem is related to context. That is, we have a division of historical output concerning Latin America into two broad categories, one which might be called the vertical dimension, the other the horizontal. The vertical dimension is a form of history writing confined by the geographical limits of what became after Independence national entities. National histories inevitably stress originality and uniqueness rather than any common colonial background, and are sometimes hostile to a point of view that would place the new nations that emerged in Latin America within an international or a comparative framework, or even within a colonial or neo-colonial context. The horizontal dimension is of course the comparative one – but this is also something we lack for Latin America. The *Cambridge History of Latin America* (Cambridge, 1984–), for example, is almost totally devoid of comparative analysis, especially in its colonial and early national volumes, a factor emphasized by the ease with which the original volumes are now being subdivided and reissued as what are essentially national histories. And a final caveat: according to the latest textbook in the field, *Early Latin America* by Stuart B. Schwartz and James Lockhart (Cambridge, 1983), this topic is not very important at all. To them the Latin American revolutions (and, by implication, the American Revolution, which they mention twice in a text of 480 pages) were no revolutions at all, and national independence a shadow thing at best. As they put it, "It has been said often and truly that the division between colonial and national periods is an artificial one especially in the social, economic, and cultural domains where so much current scholarly interest lies."

This is not the view of radical comparativists such as Susan Deans and Edward Countryman ("Independence and Revolution in the Americas," *Radical History*, 27 (May 1983), 144–72). For them independence, that is, political emancipation from Europe, was a critical transition which at the very least requires an inquiry into the place of Latin America within the process of industrial, political and social transformation that flowed from the circum-Atlantic upheavals of the late eighteenth century, of which the American Revolution was, of course, the most dramatic colonial manifestation. The question they raise is one raised some time ago by Stanley and Barbara Stein (1970); which is: why at Independence did the histories of South and North America diverge so dramatically, or, to put the question in Immanuel Wallerstein's terms, how was it that North America moved from the periphery to the core of the world system, while Latin America remained peripheral? Brazilian historians such as Fernando Novais and Emilia Viotti da Costa have also been concerned to place the late eighteenth- and early nineteenth-century experience of Brazil within the context of a crisis of the old regime and the old colonial system in the face of the Atlantic and industrial revolutions. Less work of this nature has been undertaken on Spanish America, although Tulio Halperin has long focused on the economic and political complexities of the independence period, both in the La Plata region and more broadly in Spanish America (*Reforma y disolución de los impérios Ibéricos, 1750–1850* [Madrid: Alianza, 1985]). Nancy Farriss in her book on the Maya sees the impact of the reformist proto-liberal policies of the Spanish Bourbons as marking the critical divide in the history of Meso-America. Much of the new economic history of late colonial Mexico is seeking some

explanation for the paradox of coexisting boom and rising social tensions within the most important of Spain's colonial holdings in the Western Hemisphere. But the important point about these disagreements is to emphasize that the issue of the significance of the impact of the American Revolution on developments in Latin America is not one which should be assumed, but which requires justification.

Above all, we are here talking about process, or rather about three discrete processes. One involves ideas in their social context. For Latin America and the Iberian powers Spain under Carlos III (1759–88) and for Portugal during the long predominance of the Marques de Pombal (1750–77), led to major reform in the management of colonial affairs that in some instances served to preempt and in others to mitigate the impact of the American Revolution. Secondly, there is the issue of revolution as example and as potentiality, involving the creative articulation of new institutional mechanisms of government. In both Brazil during the late 1780s and Spanish America in the aftermath of the Wars of Independence, the North American constitutional as well as the federal model proved attractive. Thirdly, we are dealing with colonial opposition to metropolitan powers; that is, the preeminent lesson of the North American example was the successful waging of War of Independence. It is in this aspect, of course, that the ambiguity of the Iberian and Ibero-American role is most apparent, since Spain in particular was an important component of the European alliance that helped the North Americans escape from British rule. And many would-be Latin American nationalists saw Britain as a potential ally against Spain. Process, therefore, is an element in the period because we are dealing with a complex interaction involving the impact of the Enlightenment as well as the coincidental experimentation with new state institutional forms (confederation, federalism, constitution-making, bills of rights, etc.), as well as a process of decolonization. All imply a delinking and a reformulation of previously set patterns; an upsetting, changing and resetting of the context within which collectivities define themselves.

There are two major paradigms for examining the impact of the North Atlantic democratic revolutions in Latin America. First, there is the Robert Palmer–Jacques Godechot vision of an Atlantic-based transformation, an essentially political and institutional view which sees mutual influence in political theory, constitutional experimentation and the politics of democratic incorporation. In this view the Enlightenment is a positive, benign and causative influence, essentially a progressive force.

A second view is a more economistic one – partly Marxian but also capable of incorporating much of classical liberalism – that is, it is a view that sees a general crisis of the old colonial system which affects the British Empire in the 1770s and the Spanish and Portuguese in the early nineteenth century, all of which flows from the shift from commercial to industrial capitalism. In this view the intellectual contribution is minimal. The revolutions in America, both North and South, represent a shift from formal to informal domination, with the newly industrializing states of Europe – especially Britain – replacing the decaying bureaucratic and mercantilist empires of Spain and Portugal.

2 Brazil

How do Brazil and Spanish America fit into this picture? The case of Brazil is especially interesting since, given the Atlantic focus of its trade, its large slave population and its close links via Lisbon to the British-dominated commercial system of the North Atlantic, its local elites were closely attuned to the events surrounding the struggle between Britain and its North American colonies.

The economic characteristics of the eighteenth-century Portuguese-Atlantic system were first, the preeminence of colonial, mainly Brazilian, staples. Second, the growth, decline and revival of manufacturing industry in Portugal was inversely proportional to the rise and fall of gold production in the Brazilian interior. That is to say, Portuguese domestic manufacturing thrived before 1700, and again after 1777, but languished during the golden age. This had major implications for Portuguese foreign and colonial policy. Portugal also remained

throughout the eighteenth century a chronic grain importer – from Northern Europe at the beginning of the century and from North America, especially Virginia and the Carolinas, towards the end. This fact during the 1780s and 1790s had a major impact on the attitudes of the new North American republic, marked especially in the person of Thomas Jefferson, towards protonationalist republican movements in Brazil. These attitudes were ambivalent at best when Virginia's trade with Portugal was placed in the balance against support for nationalist movements of uncertain origin in Portugal's vast South American territories.

Finally, the eighteenth-century Luso-Atlantic world was characterized by the struggle between France and England, a struggle which increasingly compromised Portugal. Lisbon tried to accommodate both, but by its very Atlantic nature, and because of the central economic role of Brazil within the Luso-Atlantic commercial system, Portugal was tied inextricably to Britain and, though it always sought to remain neutral and retain thereby the prosperous entrepôt function of Lisbon for the export of colonial products, it was very rarely able to maintain neutrality long. It was this need for the external political and military support in Europe which was of course at the core of the commercial concessions Portugal had made to England in the 1640s, and which Brazil for similar reasons would be obliged to concede again in Britain in 1810. It was the French seizure of Lisbon in 1807 which forced the effective political and economic emancipation of Brazil in 1808 by neutralizing the power of those in Portugal opposed to recognition of Brazil's central political role, collapsing thereby the structure of the Luso-Atlantic system as it had existed since the 1660s and replacing Lisbon as the required intermediary by direct access between the rest of Europe and the Brazilian ports.

The role of Brazil in Portuguese calculations and diplomacy, economic and institutional, thus held much higher priority than did the colonial weight of North America in British calculations. Preoccupation with the development of the Portuguese Atlantic empire on the one hand, and with

Portugal's diminished stature and apparent backwardness on the other, permeated the Portuguese intellectual milieu of the age.

Portuguese policy under the Marquês de Pombal

The most dramatic reformulation of Portugal's policy towards Brazil occurred during the long period of rule by the Marquês de Pombal. Pombal himself took much from classic mercantilist theory and practice in his policy-making, both from its British and its French or Colbertian origins, but the use of the term mercantilism to describe Pombal's policy is not entirely appropriate. Mercantilism, when defined narrowly, describes a policy whereby trade is regulated, taxed and subsidized by the state to promote an influx of gold and silver. The objective of such state intervention is aimed more broadly at achieving a favorable balance of trade.

Pombal's policy was at once more limited and more focused than this. Its objective was to use mercantilist techniques – monopoly companies, regulation, taxation and subsidies – to facilitate capital accumulation by individual national merchants. This aid to individual Portuguese capitalists had wider objectives and consequences because it was part and parcel of a scheme to fortify the nation's bargaining power within the international commercial system.

The problem for an enlightened Iberian economic nationalist, which is perhaps a more accurate way to describe Pombal, was not so much to encourage the influx of precious metals; this was rarely a problem for Iberian economic policy-makers given the fact that Spain and Portugal and their empires were the principal source of the world's bullion supply in this period – gold from Brazil and silver from Peru and Mexico. The dilemma was precisely the opposite, that is, policy-making needed to devise measures to retain capital within their own economic system and at the same time to multiply the positive and diminish the negative economic impact of being producers of precious metals. The theory and practice of mercantilism was, after all, the creation of bullion-poor northwestern Europe. The application of the theory and practice of mercantilism in the bullion-rich Iberian peninsula was bound to be partial because the end of the policy was fundamentally different from that sought by mercantilism's progenitors. The Iberians aimed to retain bullion, the northwest Europeans aimed to attract it.

Pombal's methods reflected, in fact, the peculiarities of Portugal's position within the Luso-American system, and the particular impact on Portuguese entrepreneurship of the Brazilian gold boom between 1700 and 1760. Essentially, the all-powerful minister placed the power of the state decisively on one side of the conflict that had developed between Portuguese entrepreneurs as a consequence of the gold boom. He chose the large established merchants over their smaller competitiors because he saw the small merchants as mere creatures or commission agents of the foreigners. With support from the state he hoped the large Portuguese merchants in time would be able to challenge the foreigners at their own game. His economic policy was a logical one in view of Portugal's position within the eighteenth-century international trading system. It protected mutually beneficial trade (such as the Portuguese wine trade) but it also sought to develop a powerful national class of businessmen with the capital resources and the business skills to compete in the international as well as in the Portuguese domestic market with their foreign, especially British, competitors. It was not an easy policy to pursue, at least overtly, because it was essential to achieve this outcome without bringing into question the political and military support the treaties with Britain guaranteed and which was essential if Spanish ambitions were to be kept at bay.

At the same time in Brazil, in striking contrast to the Bourbon reformers in Spanish America, Pombal sought to incorporate and coopt the Brazilian oligarchy. Portugal was after all a small country with a large empire. It did not possess the resources of a Britain or a France. It did not have the military capabilities or the economic resources to force Brazil into a subservient role. Indeed, as Pombal had watched the British attempt to repress the rebellious colonists in

English-speaking North America during the 1770s, he was fortified in his belief that conciliation was a more effective weapon against colonial uprisings than military force.

Portugal's colonial policy under Pombal in effect served to diffuse tensions within the colonial nexus by preventing any polarization along colonial versus metropolitan lines. The intervention of the Pombaline state had almost always been sectoral; that is, it had swung state support behind one side in a series of pre-existing conflicts which themselves bridged the metropolitan– colonial divide. Hence Pombal supported the large entrepreneurs against their smaller competitors; he had aided the Church and educational reformers such as the Oratorians while destroying the Jesuits and their colleges; he had crushed powerful elements among the old aristocracy while encouraging the access of businessmen to noble status. The benefits as well as the displeasure of the Pombaline state, in other words, helped and hindered both Brazilian and Portuguese, forging in fact a series of alliances across the Atlantic as well as counter-alliances which linked Portuguese and Brazilian interests at a variety of levels. Some of these results of policy were unintentional; but the conciliatory aspect of Pombal's policy towards powerful Brazilian interests was entirely explicit.

The fundamental problem for Portugal, however, arose from the logic of the Brazil-based Atlantic system within which Pombal had operated. In the final analysis, Brazil would inevitably become the dominant partner within the Portuguese-speaking empire. If the political constraints, which had governed the whole period from the 1660s to the end of the eighteenth century, also changed, that is, if for example Great Britain no longer saw it as in her own interest to protect Portugal from her continental neighbors, then the British might opt for a direct relationship with the colony rather than with the mother country. Since the whole basis of Portugal's prosperity had been built on the manipulation of colonial monopolies, cash-crop exports, colonial markets and colonial gold, such a rupture would bring fundamental change, and would close an epoch.

The Minas Conspiracy of 1789

Nevertheless, despite, and in many respects as a result of, these structural conditions of Portugal's relationship with Brazil, the American Revolution had an immediate and very explicit impact in the most important province of late colonial Brazil, Minas Gerais. The starting-point here is an economic one. As the gold bloom faded in the late eighteenth century, the diverse pressures arising from the growth of import-substituting industries in both the metropolis and Brazil after Pombal's fall from office in 1777 challenged the conciliatory basis of his system. With the rise of manufacturing came the rise in influence of powerful new lobbies on both sides of the Atlantic. By the 1780s, the Portuguese Government was faced with a choice, Either the maxims of the classic mercantilist tradition had to be abandoned, or they had to be more strictly observed. In other words, Brazil had to return to a more classically colonial status or the issue had to be confronted as to how and when Brazil's central status in the economic system was to be consolidated by a recognition of its potential political role.

The problem with the traditional view of metropolitan–colonial relationships espoused by Melo e Castro, Pombal's successor in colonial policy-making, and the manufacturing interests which stood behind him, was that broader changes within the international economic and political system were making the whole rationale of their fiercely neo-mercantilist position increasingly anachronistic. In England the Industrial Revolution was underway, which was to transform over the next 30 years the competitive position of the British textile industry in international markets. In addition, the lessons the British were to learn from the loss of their North American colonies led to a policy which would seek direct access to South American markets, even at the expense of the old privileged trading relationships in Europe. Moreover, the tensions within the Luso-Brazilian system itself threatened to become serious. The interests of the local oligarchies in Brazil had been woven so closely into the structure of administration that, in some regions, especially those less linked to the cash-crop export sector, such as the interior captaincy of the Minas Gerais, and where changing economic conditions were leading to a strong desire for economic autonomy, many now saw their self-interests at variance with those of the imperial policy-makers in Lisbon.

The intellectual climate in Brazil had changed too. Especially important was the fact that the international context had been transformed by the successful revolt of the British colonies in North America, an event which had profound impact on many educated Brazilians. The hardening of colonial policy particularly with respect to the collection of tax arrears and the suppression of colonial enterprises – especially manufacturing – led in 1789 to the Minas Conspiracy, where important members of the oligarchy in Minas Gerais prepared to move in armed rebellion against the Portuguese Crown and establish an independent and republican government. Their plot was betrayed and failed, but it shocked the system profoundly.

The Minas Conspiracy was a complex, tragic affair; yet because of its timing, 1789, it provides a unique perspective on the intellectual climate in one part of Latin America in the period between the American and French revolutions. Its failure, in fact, is the reason we know so much about the conspirators – their lives, their ideas, their assets. Once the conspiracy was denounced and its instigators imprisoned, they were interrogated, their properties were confiscated and their words were remembered, recorded and used against them by the agents of the Portuguese Crown. For the historian this provides a treasure trove because it is one of those rare occasions where ideas, reading patterns and concrete proposals can be seen quite explicitly in the context of a proposed rebellion. The task of the leading intellectuals of the region, men such as Gonzaga, a magistrate, Claudio Manuel da Costa, a lawyer, and Luis Vieira, a priest, had been to formulate the laws and constitution of the new state and provide the ideological justification for the break with Portugal. All three men were well informed of events in Europe, two of them educated there. They all possessed good libraries; that of Vieira contained more than 600 volumes. Books

and information often reached them more rapidly than official dispatches passed through the cumbersome bureaucracy from Lisbon to the captaincy's governor. Vieira's cosmopolitan collection of books contained Robertson's *Histoire de l'Amérique*, the *Encyclopédie*, as well as the works of Bielfeld, Voltaire and Condillac. Claudio Manuel da Costa was reputed to have translated Adam Smith's *Wealth of Nations*. And circulating among the conspirators was a copy of the *Loix constitutives des Etats-Unis de l'Amérique* (1778), which contained the Articles of Confederation and the constitutions of Pennsylvania, New Jersey, Delaware, Maryland, Virginia, the Carolinas and Massachusetts. They possessed constitutional commentaries by Raynal and Mably, and Raynal's lengthy discussion of the history of Brazil in his *Histoire philosophique et politique* was much debated. Gonzaga had long been interested in jurisprudence. His famous *Cartas chilenas*, a satirical poem set ostensibly in Chile, was in fact an attack aimed very directly at the governor of Minas and his cronies. Luis Vieira had often argued against Portugal's right to dominion in America, and was a warm admirer of the North Americans' struggle for independence. The conspirators had in fact in 1787 established a secret contact with the United States via Thomas Jefferson while he was ambassador to France, a meeting about which Jefferson had informed the Committee of Secret Correspondence of the Continental Congress. Jefferson himself was ambivalent – Virginia grain was exported to Portugal.

Although the program of the conspiracy reflected the specific and immediate compulsions which had thoroughly alienated the leading citizens of Minas Gerais from the Portuguese Crown and forced along the path of revolution, and tax arrears and threatened tax levies were important stimulants to rebellion in Minas as in North America, it also reflected the presence among their ranks of those able and distinguished magistrates, lawyers and clerics who had been forced into a reassessment of the colonial relationship by other motives, and who drew their inspiration from the example of North America, the constitutions of the

American states and the works of the Abbé Raynal.

From the fragments of information that exist, an outline of their proposals can be rediscovered. The system of the government was to be republican. Restrictions and monopolies were to be abolished. Manufactories were to be established and the exploitation of iron ore deposits encouraged. A gunpowder factory would be set up. Freedom was to be granted to native-born slaves and mulattos. A university would be founded in Vila Rica. All women who produced a certain number of children were to receive a prize at the expense of the state. There was to be no standing army. All citizens were instead to bear arms and when necessary to serve in a national militia. Parliaments were to be established in each town, subordinate to a supreme parliament in the capital. For the first three years Gonzaga would rule – after which time there would be annual elections. No distinctions or restrictions of dress would be tolerated, and the elite would be obliged to wear locally manufactured products. All debtors to the royal treasury would be pardoned.

Strong tones of economic nationalism were present in the discourse of the plotters. The sentiment was most explicit in the statements of Tiradentes, a junior military officer of the Minas Dragoons and the only victim of the plot, whose hanging and quartering by the Portuguese later made him one of republican Brazil's national heroes. He praised the beauty and natural resources of Minas as being the best in the world in words reminiscent of the Abbé Raynal's. Free, and a republic like British America, Brazil could be even greater, he claimed, because it was better endowed by nature. With the establishment of manufactories, Tiradentes said, there would be no need to import commodities from abroad. Brazil was a land which had within itself all that was needed; no other country was required for its sustenance. The reason for the country's poverty despite all these riches, he said, was "because Europe, like a sponge, was sucking all the substance, sending out every three years governors, bringing with them a gang that they called servants, who after devouring the honor, finances, and offices

that should have belonged to the natives returned happily to Portugal bloated with riches." Colonel Gomes, another conspirator, claimed that the merchants of Rio de Janeiro were behind the uprising to make an English America. "The Abby Raynal had been a writer of great vision," one of the conspirators observed, "for he had prognosticated the uprising of North America, and the captaincy of Minas Gerais was now in the same circumstances."

The conspiracy in Minas Gerais moreover had occurred at a special moment in time. The plot was concerted before the French Revolution. But the arrest, the trial and the sentencing of those involved coincided with growing revolutionary turmoil in Europe. The chronological relationship of the Minas Conspiracy to the French Revolution is of critical importance. The Minas oligarchs had believed they could control and manipulate the popular will. Remarkably they had spoken of freeing Brazilian-born slaves. They had taken as their example the American Revolution, where political readjustments in their view had taken place without social upheaval. But the example of the American patriots had not prepared them for the spectacular repercussions of the French Revolution in the Americas. The revolt of the slaves on the French sugar island of Saint Domingue (Haiti) during 1792 brought an awful awakening to those slaveowners who had talked naively of republics and revolt and ignored the social and racial consequences of their words.

The Bahian plot of 1798

In the climate of opinion that followed the Saint Domingue revolt, the discovery of plans for an armed uprising by the mulatto artisans of Bahia during 1798 had a very special impact; the plans demonstrated what thinking Whites had already begun to realize: that ideas of social equality propagated within a society where a mere third of the population was white risked being interpreted in racial terms. The Bahian affair revealed the politicization of levels of society barely concerned in the Minas Conspiracy. The middle-aged lawyers, magistrates and clerics in Minas Gerais (most of them opulent, members of racially exclusive brotherhoods and slave owners) contrasted markedly with the young mulatto artisans, soldiers, sharecroppers and salaried schoolteachers implicated in the Bahian plot. Embittered and anticlerical, the Bahian mulattos were as opposed to rich Brazilians as to Portuguese dominion. They welcomed social turmoil, proposed an overthrow of existing structures, and sought an egalitarian and democratic society where differences of race would be no impediment to employment and social mobility. The pardo [mulatto] tailor João de Deos, one of the leaders who at the time of his arrest possessed eight children and no more than 80 reis, proclaimed that "All [Brazilians] would become Frenchmen, in order to live in equality and abundance … . They would destroy the public officials, attack the monasteries, open the port … and reduce all to an entire revolution, so that all might be rich and taken out of poverty, and that the differences between white and brown would be extinguished, and that all without discrimination would be admitted to positions and occupations."

It was obviously not the North American patriots that provided the example for João de Deos and his colleagues. They also sought to raise up public opinion. Handwritten manifestos appeared throughout Bahia on August 12, 1798. Addressed to the "Republican Bahian People" in the name of the "supreme tribunal of Bahian democracy," the manifestos called for the extermination of the "detestable metropolitan yoke of Portugal." Clergy who preached against popular liberty were threatened. "All citizens, especially mulattoes and blacks," were told that "all are equal, there will be no differences, there will be freedom, equality and fraternity." There was no equivocation over slavery: "all black and brown slaves are to be free so that there will be no slavery whatsoever." The government would be "democratic, free and independent." "The happy time of out liberty is about to arrive, the time when all will be brothers, the time when all will be equal."

As in the case of Minas nine years previously, the Bahian artisans were caught redhanded. The appearance of the manifestos

in Bahia, the demand for liberty, equality and fraternity, and the racial composition of the conspiratorial conclave, however, provoked a reaction out of all proportion to the incidents themselves. The arrested conspirators were all hanged and quartered or transported to be abandoned on the coast of Africa. Since 1792, slaveowners throughout the Americas had barely hidden their concern that the revolution in the Caribbean might prove contagious. For slaveowners in Brazil, at least, the words of the Bahian mulattos made the contagion of Saint Domingue a concrete reality.

Portuguese steps to accommodate tensions in Brazil

With republicanism discredited by the abortive uprising in Minas Gerais and later association with social and racial turmoil, there was room for metropolitan initiatives. And, for the white minority in Portuguese America, the failure of the elitist movement in Minas Gerais during 1789 and the threat from below revealed by the Bahian artisans in 1798 provided two powerful incentives for compromise with the metropolis. Psychologically, the situation was propitious for accommodation.

The recognition of this fact by influential members of the Portuguese Government during the 1790s had profound impact on the future development of Brazil. It was at this point that a group of skillful and enlightened ministers took over the reins of government in Lisbon. One Luis Pinto de Sousa Coutinho became Portugal's foreign minister. He was a man with firsthand knowledge of Brazilian conditions, having distinguished himself as governor of Mato Grosso (1769–72) before being appointed as ambassador to the Court of St. James. In Britain he had provided William Robertson with information on South America for Robertson's famous history, a service he had also provided for the Abbé Raynal some years earlier. Once back in Lisbon, Luis Pinto made contact with Brazilian intellectuals. On May 31, 1790 he sent two of the more promising young Brazilians to Paris to take courses in physics and mineralogy. Afterwards the scholars were to visit the mines of Saxony, Bohemia and Hungary, and to return to Portugal by way of Scandinavia and Great Britain.

The leader of the expedition, Manuel Ferreira da Camara, had close links with those caught up in the events of Minas Gerais. His elder brother was implicated on several occasions during the judicial inquiry into the conspiracy, and had fled from Minas by way of the backlands to Bahia. Luis Pinto's extension of the powerful protection of his office to these young Brazilian scholars during the critical year of 1790, and his remarkable act of faith in sponsoring the visit to the center of European social and political upheaval, can be considered quite remarkable.

The reasoning behind these actions was explained by another leader of this group of enlightened ministers, D. Rodrigo de Sousa Coutinho. In 1779 Rodrigo had visited Paris, where he met the Abbé Raynal. He told Raynal that the population and resources of France would have made her insupportable to the rest of Europe were it not for the disorder of her financial administration. Raynal replied that "Providence had given France the forces but refused her good sense. France would indeed be terrible if her natural power was matched by a just and wise administration." Writing to his sister, Rodrigo later wondered: "What would be better for Europe, to be a factory of the English or a slave of France? The only thing that can console us is the almost total impossibility of France reforming her system of government." Reform of course came through revolution, and France's power was projected over Europe by the regime of Napoleon Bonaparte, and it was just as formidable as Rodrigo has suspected it could be.

Rodrigo attributed the collapse of the French monarchy to its fiscal situation. His opposition to monopolies and the contracting of revenues and his fervent support of an efficient and solvent financial administration grew from his belief that intelligent reform was essential if Portugal were to avoid a similar collapse. The revolution in France, he believed, should accelerate reform in Portugal, not delay it. To achieve sound fiscal policies, Rodrigo recommended "wise and enlightened reforms, executed by intelligent men, capable of forming well organized systems, the utility of which would be recognized by all." His optimism epitomized that of the Enlightenment itself. In 1801 Rodrigo went so far as to propose the establishment of the monarchy in Brazil, a compromise that promised political change without social disintegration. The task of formulating these plans was largely turned over to the young Brazilians whose European educational expedition the government had sponsored.

The recognition of the central place of Brazil in the Luso-Brazilian commercial system, and the open espousal in 1801 of the need to move the court to Brazil, was of course strenuously opposed by powerful vested interests in Portugal. Portuguese neutrality during the revolutionary wars in Europe brought great prosperity. The opulent Portuguese merchant industrialists were well aware that this wealth arose from the control of the re-export of colonial staples such as cotton, sugar, tobacco and hides, not to mention the retention of captive markets in Brazil for their manufactured goods. The ideas of making Brazil the center of the Portuguese Empire had also become a position acceptable to the British. In 1803 the British envoy in Lisbon, Robert Fitzgerald, was already advising London that "the British property within [Portugal itself] forms no object of great national importance - especially when in the opposite balance are viewed the innumerable advantages to be derived from an open and unrestricted trade with the Brazils." The project became a reality nonetheless when in 1807 Napoleonic troops crossed the frontier from Spain and moved rapidly on Lisbon. It is vital to emphasize, however, that the decision of the Portuguese court to move to Brazil was not a panic measure. Napoleon's invasion of 1807 in fact served to neutralize opposition to the move. The Portuguese fleet was ready – treasure, archives and the apparatus of a bureaucracy loaded for the retreat across the Atlantic. And, as we have seen, the process of the last two decades of the eighteenth century in Brazil had made many previously skeptical Brazilians receptive to the idea of a New World monarchy. D. João, the Prince Regent, arrived in

Rio de Janeiro in 1808 after a brief stay in Bahia, not as an exile but as the head of a functioning national state. 1808 may therefore be viewed as a real watershed in both Brazilian and Portuguese history.

3 Spain

The example of the American Revolution was particularly important in Brazil for reasons that lay in the coincidence of its anti-colonial message with severe tension between Lisbon and a major segment of the local elite in the one area in the Portuguese territories in the Americas with the capacity to articulate as well as make effective an independent state, possessing as it did in the 1780s adequate revenues, military forces, administrative experience and a close attention to international developments. That it failed despite all these elements is an indication of how difficult the achievement of colonial independence would be in Ibero-America.

The circumstances in the core regions of Spanish America were even less propitious. The impact of the American Revolution would here be confined to the peripheries. Very little impact can be discerned in the two great core regions of Spanish dominion, Peru and Mexico. In many respects, the North Americans, in terms of trade, influence and contacts, followed the sea-lanes, and their role was most significant within the Caribbean and along the coastlines, where they had long been involved in the transatlantic complex as purveyors of codfish, sugar, slaves, grain, tobacco and, most recently, cotton. But here it was the North American commercial role within the Atlantic commercial systems as a whole that was decisive. The grain trade, in particular, found ready customers in the Iberian peninsula among the colonial overlords of South and Central America. And trade more than republican ideology would be the watchword in the United States' dealings with both Spain and Portugal. These powers, Spain in particular, had aided in very substantial ways the attainment of American Independence: it was a connection which made for some caution when it came to aiding and abetting revolutionaries to the south, at least until the Napoleonic period, when for all effective purposes the United States gained direct access to Spanish American ports (smuggling had already long existed) and Spain to all intents and purposes lost direct administrative control of its empire in America owing to British control of the sea-lanes.

But, for other reasons, the ground in Spanish America was not fertile for the American model. The eighteenth century had seen three major processes at work. First, the old monopolistic trading connection of Atlantic convoys of protected ships sailing on a regular pattern between the Caribbean and monopoly port of Seville (later Cadiz) had been superseded by a *de facto* diversification of trade. Some of this diversification was illegal – but like the trade through Jamaica, where the North Americans were actively involved, this had become a substantial contribution to overall Atlantic commerce. Spain had also eventually permitted other Spanish ports into Atlantic commerce, gradually ending the Cadiz monopoly between 1765 and 1789, as well as given formal administrative recognition to the peripheral coastal regions away from the old Highland Amerindian populated core areas (where Spain's major bases in the Western hemisphere had been since the time of the Conquest). Thus, while Lima and Mexico City remained important, new regions, such as the Rio de la Plata, Caracas and Cuba, also developed. These previous backwaters – good for provisions but producing very little else – all became major exporters in the late eighteenth century – Buenos Aires, an exporter of salt beef, silver, hides and grains; Caracas for cacao and hides; Cuba, especially after the revolt in Haiti, a major center for sugar and slaves. Second, from mid-century on, Spain had attempted to implement a series of major administrative, mercantile and fiscal reforms aimed at the enhancement of the power of the metropolis through the more efficient exploitation of its colonies. As in Portugal, there had been growing awareness in Spain that its role as a great power was severely undermined by the failure to adapt to modern conditions; which in eighteenth-century terms meant using the power of the state to increase revenues and impose a more centralized administrative system. This preoccupation with national regeneration was in the forefront of the minds of several high government officials. Jose de Carvajal, for example, foreign minister from 1746 to 1759, saw Spanish America as the means for Spain to recuperate its position in Europe if the recourses could be more effectively utilized. The 1743 proposal of José de Campillo, minister of finance, in which he called for a "New System for the American Economy" (Nuevo Sistema de Gobierno Económico para la América), encapsulated the intention to turn to the empire as a market for Spanish manufactures and as a source of raw materials. Campillo wished to see a system of general inspectors (visitas generales), the creation of intendancies, and the introduction of "free trade" into colonial administration. The intendant system had been previously adopted in Spain itself and established a system of provincial governors with a mixture of military, financial and judicial authority directly responsible to Madrid. It was, however, the Bourbon monarch Carlos III (1759–88) whose reign became associated with the implementation of a series of far-reaching new governmental measures for the administration of the vast Spanish territories in the New World. The urgency of these reforms became more than ever evident after the seizure of Havana by the British in 1762 during the Seven Years' War.

The administration of colonial territories under Carlos III

The Spanish Bourbon reforms took place against the background of demographic and economic recovery in much of Spanish America, and much controversy exists among historians as to the cause and effect of reform and prosperity. It is generally agreed, however, that the impact of the new governmental measures varied considerably from region to region. One immediate consequence was that tensions were aggravated between European Spaniards and the old Latin American white creole oligarchies which had for several centuries, it should be remembered, found a political niche within local administrations throughout the Americas. The Bourbon reforms, especially the intendant system, were therefore first introduced in the regions where the old creole oligarchies were less formidable; Cuba after 1764 and the Rio de la Plata after 1776. Only in 1784 was the system initiated in Peru and in 1786 in Mexico. Spain's involvement in the war of North American independence also had the effect of bringing major new fiscal demands. The articulation of the new systems owed much to the reforming visitor general of New Spain (Mexico), José de Galvez (1765–71), who later became long-term secretary for the Indies (1776–87). His objective in Mexico had encompassed the establishment of a tobacco monopoly (to raise revenue), the reorganization and raising of the sales tax (the Alcabala), the stimulation of silver production (by lowering the price of mercury) and the expulsion of the Jesuit order.

Thirdly, this ferment of innovation and the reaction to it revealed just how complex Spanish American colonial society had become by the late eighteenth century and how difficult it would be in Spanish America either for a clear regional focus for proto-nationalistic sentiment to emerge, or for the creation of a cohesive social base to support any rebellion against Spain. Internal social, racial and caste divisions permeated colonial society, and it was very difficult anywhere in Spanish America for European Spaniards living in the colonies, creole magistrates, soldiers and local businessmen to come together in even the embryonic nationalist movement which had made the idea of an independent Minas Gerais on the North American model so pertinent in Brazil in 1788–9.

Social unrest and incipient nationalism

Movements of social protest did, of course, emerge in Spanish America and with much more violence, bloodshed and disruption than ever occurred in Brazil. But those movements were limited in their ideological content. They did not make the leap from protest against bad government to an attack on the rule of Spain in America. The most significant of these movements of protest and rebellion, the Comunero rebellion in New Granada (present-day Colombia and Venezuela) in 1781 and the Tupac Amaru rebellion in upper Peru (present-day Bolivia) in 1780–1, never projected themselves into an anti-colonial struggle, and both, especially the latter, served to terrify the creole elites and make them acutely aware of the risk of race and ethnic violence implicit in the complexity of Spanish America's social makeup.

Given the heterogeneity of Spanish America in the late eighteenth century, the uneven impact of imperial reform, the diversification of the economic system and its reorientation towards the Atlantic trading system in the new peripheral growth areas such as Venezuela and the Rio de la Plata, as well as the limited anti-colonial sentiment apparent in the rebellions of the 1780s, incipient nationalism was, when it emerged, more a characteristic of disgruntled elites than of the masses. The latter were on the whole more preoccupied with immediate inequalities and exploitation than with intra-imperial injustices, and felt more actually the oppression of the local oligarchies than of the Crown in Madrid. The rebels in both upper Peru and Venezuela in fact had looked to the Crown for redress of grievances. The notion of independence from Spain, of a colonial emancipation from Europe, was hence confined to a very small number of the white creole elite and developed after the putative popular revolts of the early 1780s had been repressed. These aspirations also were of a reformist rather than a revolutionary nature, and, while the institutional model of the new North American nation was often an inspiration, in terms of overseas contacts and hope of assistance it was England to which they looked rather than to the United States.

A Spanish version of the proclamations of the Continental Congress was in the hands of the Venezuelan conspirators of 1797 (the conspiracy of Manuel Guel and José Maria España) who hoped to establish an independent republic on the North American model. And by the turn of the century works by John Adams, Washington and Jefferson were circulating in both Mexico and South America. Key leaders of the independence movement, most notably Francisco de Miranda, visited the United States, as did Simon Bolivar, who admired Washington, though he was not uncritical of the North American system. Miranda in particular summed up the complex reaction to the events of 1776 in North America and 1789 in France. "We have before our eyes two great examples," he wrote in 1799, "the American and the French Revolutions: let us prudently imitate the first and carefully shun the second." After the revolt in French Saint Domingue, as in Brazil, property owners throughout Spanish America became even more cautious, especially if that property included African slaves. "I confess that as much as I desire the liberty and independence of the New World," Miranda observed, "I fear anarchy and revolution even more." This attitude was to be the legacy of the revolutionary period, and it meant that the United States model after the turn of the century would be viewed as one which matched social conservatism with political independence from Spain.

4 Conclusions

In summary, then, in the case of Portugal and Brazil, the basic argument has been that during the period between 1750 and 1808 it had become very evident that the impact of the American Revolution in Brazil, which was a powerful influence before 1789, was nonetheless diluted and eventually rejected by the mid-1790s. This rejection was partly owing to the failure of the attempt in Brazil during early 1789 to set up an independent state modeled on the United States, but it was due also to the counter-influences of the French Revolution and most particularly the manifestation of the French Revolution in the Americas, the great slave revolt in the French Antilles.

The white Brazilian elite, slaveowners and those opposed to slavery alike, found by the 1790s that republicanism and democracy were concepts too dangerous for experimentation within a society half-slave, and where Blacks outnumbered Whites two to one. The consequence was that those who avidly and approvingly followed the events in North America before 1790 turned away from the North American model, and, encouraged by the Portuguese metropolitan government, which had learned its own lessons from the revolt of the 13 colonies, embraced monarchy in the interests of preserving the status quo against racial and social upheaval. A similar interaction between the chronology of revolutions and elite attitudes took place in all the American states and ex-colonies where slavery was entrenched.

The Haitian revolt also had a critical impact on the attitudes of the governments of Spain, France and Britain towards America, in the latter case being a principal cause of the profound shift in policy with respect to colonial rebellions in the Western Hemisphere, making them all much more cautious.

In mainland Spanish America, independence followed from external more than internal events: the collapse of the Bourbon monarchy in Spain itself in the face of the Napoleonic onslaught in 1808. Unlike in Portugal, where the French invasion brought about a denouement to the dilemmas of the metropolitan–colonial relationship with the removal of the Portuguese court to Brazil and the *de facto* (later *de jure*) establishment of Rio de Janeiro as the seat of a New World monarchy, in Spain the invasion in effect cut Spanish America loose of the old metropolis for a critical six years between 1808 and 1814, with major consequences for Spanish American unity and stability. The successor Spanish American republics often took shape within the new boundaries imposed by the eighteenth-century reformers, but they all faced massive problems of internal social cohesion and economic and administrative dislocations. The conflicting pressure arising from unequal economic growth within the Spanish Empire in America, the ambiguities of an administrative reform which was in part an attempt to respond to those changes, as well as the several social, ethnic and racial tensions which permeated the social makeup of Spanish America had all served to limit the development of a broad-based anti-colonial sentiment before 1808, and fragmented the social bases of support for a nationalistic project on the North American model, limiting thereby the potential impact of the North American example. Again, as in the lowland tropical areas of the Western Hemisphere, the example

of Haiti reinforced the fears arising from the bloody uprisings in upper Peru in the early 1780s. Those who saw the American model as relevant tended after 1800 to see it as the conservative option. Latin Americans were interested in the United States as a model for nation-building; federalism, for example, proved attractive to many. But, for an effective partnership, they more often looked to Great Britain and to trade: espousing "liberalism" in the sense of access to world commerce rather than liberalism in the sense of democracy.

For Latin America, especially for the areas where plantation economies and African slavery predominated, it is essential, therefore, to look at the relationship between the three revolutions of the late eighteenth century, the American, the French, and the Haitian, and for Spanish America to look to the vicissitudes of the eighteenth-century experience with reform and rebellion. From the perspective of the Americas at the time, the great slave revolt of 1792 in French Saint Domingue was a second "American" revolution that seemed no less important than the first. It brought to the forefront of elite consciousness fears and tensions inherent in plantation systems throughout the New World. Within the empires of Spain and Portugal the Haitian revolt served to stimulate both a reapproximation between local oligarchs and the more progressive elements within the metropolitan governments as in the Portuguese-speaking empire, and as in Spanish America made it inevitable that the independence movements when eventually they came would always find questions of race, class and social stability close to the surface. Whereas in the 1780s would-be Latin American revolutionaries had found inspiration in George Washington, by the 1790s they recoiled in fear before the example of Toussaint L'Ouverture.

FURTHER READING

Adrien, Kenneth J., and Johnson, Lyman L.: *The Political Economy of Spanish America in the Age of Revolution 1750–1850* (Albuquerque, 1994).

Alden, Dauril: "The Marques of Pombal and the American Revolution," *The Americas*, 17, 4 (1961), 369–82.

Aldridge, O. A. (ed.): *The Ibero-American Enlightenment* (Urbana, Il, 1971).

Barbier, Jacques A.: *Reform and Politics in Bourbon Chile, 1755–1790* (Ottawa, 1980).

Barbier, Jacques, and Kuethe, Allan (eds.): *The North American Role in the Spanish Imperial Economy 1760–1819* (Manchester, 1984).

Brading, D.: *The First America: The Spanish Monarchy, Creole Patriots and the Liberal State, 1492–1866* (Cambridge, 1991).

——: *Miners and Merchants in Bourbon Mexico* (Cambridge: Cambridge University Press, 1973).

Dominguez, Jorge: *Insurrection or Loyalty: The Breakdown of the Spanish Empire* (Cambridge Mass, 1980).

Fisher, H. E. S.: *The Portugal Trade: a Study of Anglo-Portuguese Commerce, 1700–1770* (London, 1971).

Fisher, J. R.: *Government and Society in Colonial Peru* (London: Athlone, 1970).

Fisher, John, Kuethe, Allan J., and McFarland, Anthony (eds): *Reform and Insurrection in Bourbon New Granada and Peru* (Baton Rouge La., 1990).

Geggus, David: *Slavery, War and Revolution: The British Occupation of Saint Domingue, 1793–1798* (Oxford, 1982).

Godinho, Vitorino Magalhães: *Prix et monnaies au Portugal, 1750–1850* (Paris, 1955).

Gonzalez, António, Garcia-Baquero: *Cadiz y el Atlántico (1717–1778)*, 2 vols. (Seville, 1976).

Guerra, Francois-Xavier: *Modernidad e Independencias. Ensayos sobre las revoluciones hispánicas* (Madrid, 1992).

Halparin, Tulio: *Politics, Economics and Society in Argentina in the Revolutionary Period* (Cambridge, 1975).

Hamnet, Brian R.: "Process and Pattern: A Reexamination of the Ibero-American Independence Movements 1808–1826" *Journal of Latin American Studies*, vol. 29, p. 2, (May 1997), 279–328.

Herr, Richard, *The Eighteenth Century Revolution in Spain* (Princeton, NJ: Princeton University Press, 1988).

Jacobson, Nils, and Puhle, Hans-Jürgen (eds.): *The Economics of Mexico and Peru During the Late Colonial Period, 1700–1810* (Berlin: Colloquium Verlag, 1986).

Langley, Lester D.: *The Americas in the Age of Revolution 1750–1850* (Newhaven: Yale University Press, 1996).

Liss, Peggy K.: *Atlantic Empires: the Networks of Trade and Revolution, 1713–1826* (Baltimore: Johns Hopkins University Press, 1983).

Lynch, John: *Spanish Colonial Administration, 1782–1810* (London, 1958).

——: *The Spanish American Revolutions, 1808–1826* (London, 1975).

Mattoso, Kátia M. de Queirós: *Presença francesa no movimento democrático Biano de 1798* (Baia, 1969).

——: "Conjoncture et société au Brasil à la fin du XVIII siècle, prix et salaires et à la vielle de la revolution des alfaiates, Bahia, 1798," *Cahiers des Ameriques Latins*, 5 (1970), 33–53.

Maxwell, Kenneth R.: *Conflicts and Conspiracies: Brazil and Portugal, 1750–1808* (New York: Cambridge University Press, 1973).

——: *Pombal, Paradox of the Enlightenment* (Cambridge: Cambridge University Press, 1995).

Mota, Carlos Guilherme: *Atitudes de inovação no Brasil, 1789–1801* (Lisbon: 1972).

Novais, Fernando: *Portugal e Brasil na crise do antigo sistema colonial (1777–1808)* (São Paulo, 1978).

Pagden, Anthony: *Spanish Imperalism and the Political Imagination: Studies in European and Spanish American Social and Political Theory, 1513–1830* (New Haven, 1990).

Palmer, R. R.: *The Age of Democratic Revolution*, 2 vols. (Princeton, NJ: Princeton University Press, 1959, 1964).

Pedreira, Jorge Miguel Viana: *Estructura Industrial e Mercado Colonial: Portugal e Brasil 1780–1830* (Lisbon, 1994).

Phelan, John Leddy: *The People and the King: the Communero Revolution in Colombia, 1781* (Madison, 1978).

Rodriguez O, Jaime E.: *Mexico and the Age of Democratic Revolution 1750–1850* (Boulder, 1994).

Ruy, Afonso: *A Primeira revolução social brasileira (1798)* (São Paulo, 1942).

Stein, Stanley J., and Stein, Barbara H.: *The Colonial Heritage of Latin America* (New York: Oxford University Press, 1970).

Tavares, Luis Henrique Dias: *História de sedição intentada na Bahia em 1798* (São Paulo, 1975).

Valentim, Alexandre: *Os Sentidos do Império: Questão Nacional e questão colonial na Crise do antigo Regime Português* (Oporto, 1993).

Whitaker, A. P. (ed.): *Latin America and the Enlightenment* (Ithaca, NY: Cornell University Press, 1961).

——: *The United States and the Independence of Latin America* (Baltimore: Johns Hopkins University Press, 1941).

CHAPTER SIXTY-SIX

The influence of the American Revolution in the Netherlands

JAN WILLEM SCHULTE NORDHOLT AND WIM KLOOSTER

THE Dutch Republic, officially called the Republic of the Seven United Netherlands, was an oligarchy, where the power was in the hands of a small elite of regents and a Stadtholder, who were, however, divided among themselves. The great majority of the Dutch people had no influence at all in government. Not surprisingly, therefore, the rebellion of the Americans against their British King George III was received with mixed feelings. The conservative circles around the Stadtholder, Prince William V, who was himself a cousin of George III, were strongly opposed to the Americans, but they found a great deal of sympathy among the burghers who were hankering after a voice in the government. The example of the American Revolution led to an intensification of the party strife between, on the one hand, the court, most of the regents, and the clergy of the Established (Dutch Reformed) Church, supported by the lower classes, and, on the other, the anti-Orangist regents, the *petit bourgeoisie*, and the dissenters, who formed a coalition, which was soon to assume the noble name of Patriots.

1 Dutch Relations with the British and the Americans

From the very beginning there were difficulties. Since the early seventeenth century there had been a Scottish brigade stationed in the Netherlands, and in times of war England could request the use of these troops. This is what George III immediately did in 1775, but in the Republic this sending of the soldiers to support the King against his own subjects met with strong opposition. It was argued that after all England was not at war, but was being confronted with an internal uprising. In essence this resistance was the first protest of the patriots against the pro-British policy of the Stadtholder. It was headed by a nobleman, a deputy of the States of the Province of Overijssel, Johan Derk van der Capellen tot de Poll, who soon developed into the great leader of the pro-American party. The Dutch Government preferred to remain neutral in the conflict between England and its colonies. One of the reasons was that there was a great deal of money to be earned under the circumstances. Via the island of St. Eustatius in the Caribbean an enormous contraband trade of weapons and munition for the American rebels got under way.

The Americans, on their part, were looking to the Netherlands for financial and diplomatic support. At the suggestion of Benjamin Franklin, Congress had in 1776 appointed an agent in The Hague, the first offical representative of America in a foreign country. This was a Swiss intellectual, Charles Guillaume Frédéric Dumas. Dumas was the rare example of a pure enthusiast, who fervently believed in the American cause. He was all ardor and hence not very suited for a diplomatic role; his influence was limited and he was not able to accomplish much of significance. Curiously enough, the first secret Dutch–American treaty, between the city of Amsterdam and the

American agent William Lee, which was concluded at Aix-la-Chapelle in 1778, was negotiated without his knowledge. But Dumas did play an important role when in 1779 John Paul Jones sailed his fleet into the roads of Texel. It was he who organized the support for Jones. And it was he who with his propaganda paved the way for John Adams. Some years earlier he had invited Benjamin Franklin to come to Holland and he had promised that he would be his John the Baptist. Now he could accomplish that role for John Adams.

With the arrival of John Adams in the Republic in the summer of 1780, Dutch–American relations entered a new phase. Adams came to Holland with the goal of obtaining loans from the Amsterdam bankers, but he soon realized that an official recognition of the American Republic by the Dutch Government was an important condition for the achievement of his goal. He first settled in Amsterdam, where he tried to gain the support of the Patriot leaders. He also made attempts to influence the press, and for that purpose he made friends with important Dutch journalists such as Johan Luzac, editor of the *Gazette de Leyde*, a French-language paper which was being read all over Europe. In Amsterdam he supported a French writer, Antoine Marie Cérisier, and induced him to start the publishing of another paper, *Le Politique Hollandais*, again in French. Impatient as he was, Adams could not wait for the moment when it would please the Dutch Government to receive him. Against the advice of Franklin he decided on his own impetuous so-called militia diplomacy. He drew up a "Memorial to their High Mightinesses the States General of the United Netherlands," which he not only presented at The Hague but also had translated and printed in Dutch, English, and French. The document, which was written in fervid language, apppealed to the supposed exact similarity between the two countries, which had both fought a revolution against a foreign king, had the same Protestant religion, the same love of freedom, and the same spirit of commerce and free enterprise. He therefore pleaded for speedy recognition.

2 War between Britain and the Netherlands

In the meantime Adams's efforts had been made considerably easier by the fact that in December 1780 war had broken out between Great Britain and the Netherlands. In September 1780 the British had arrested the new American envoy to the Netherlands, Henry Laurens, on the open sea when he was on his way to Holland, and among his papers they had found the text of the secret treaty of Aix-la-Chapelle. This gave them the long-wanted excuse to declare war on the Dutch Republic and make an end to the smuggling of arms to the American rebels. Their first act of war was the conquest of the island of St. Eustatius and the complete destruction of all the Dutch warehouses there. The Dutch suffered heavy losses during the war: many of their ships were captured and their entire trade was paralyzed. In spite of the fact that a naval battle at the Dogger Bank in the summer of 1781 remained undecided, Britain still maintained her position as the ruler of the seas.

The war caused a good deal of commotion in the Republic and the protest against weak government policy was increasing rapidly. The Stadtholder was singled out for blame for the unhappy state of affairs. In September 1781 an anonymous pamphlet entitled *To the People of the Netherlands*, which was strongly anti-Orangist and which demanded greater popular influence, proved to be enormously successful. It was written, as it turned out much later, by Johan Derk van der Capellen. But van der Capellen worked not only in secret. He openly called on the people to arm themselves as the Americans had done. At the same time he appealed to the burghers to exert their influence by presenting petitions to the government. This very moderate form of democracy was practiced for the first time in the winter of 1781–2, when in many cities petitions, called requests, were drafted demanding the recognition of the American Republic. Expectations were running high indeed, especially after the capitulation of Yorktown. America was regarded as an inexhaustible new market.

3 The Influence of John Adams and the American Constitution on Dutch Political Thought

The American cause became very popular. In February 1782 the States of Friesland were the first to acknowledge the United States. The other provinces soon followed suit and on April 19, 1782 recognition was extended by the States General, the highest sovereign of the Republic. So John Adams became the first American envoy in the Netherlands. Through the mediation of Dumas, who served as his *chargé d'affaires*, he had by then already bought a house in The Hague, which thus became the first American embassy building on foreign soil. Moreover, in October 1782 a Treaty of Amity and Commerce between the Dutch and American Republics was signed. This was soon to be followed by the coveted loans from the Amsterdam bankers, which in the course of the next few years were to reach the amount of 30 million guilders. These loans formed the financial foundation of the United States.

After the peace treaty of Paris, Adams was appointed as ambassador to the court of St. James (1785), but he also continued in his post in The Hague. In 1788, in the company of Thomas Jefferson, who was then American ambassador in Paris, he paid his last visit to the Amsterdam bankers and departed for America. He had been completely successful in achieving his objectives in the Netherlands.

But John Adams did not only change the political relations between Holland and the United States. He was also very much concerned with ideas. His ideological influence on the political thinking of the Patriots was considerable. It was owing to his efforts that a collection of all the constitutions of the 13 American states and of the Articles of Confederation was published in Dutch translation. Dutch reformers who had for a long time been struggling with the problems of a federal state were very interested in the American solutions to that problem. In 1784 the young Rutger Jan Schimmelpenninck, who was later to become one of the most important leaders of the Batavian Republic, wrote a dissertation on *A Well Organized Popular Government*, in which he closely followed the model of the Constitution of Massachusetts, written by John Adams.

But in constitutional matters things never got beyond the planning stage. Nothing ever came of all the beautiful porposals for constitutional reform which were drafted by the Patriots during the years 1782 to 1787. In the latter year all their hopes were completely frustrated: through the intervention of England and Prussia the semi-civil war which had been raging between the Orangists and the patriots suddenly came to an end. With this counter-revolution the authority of the Stadtholder was reinstated and the Patriots were forced to flee to France. America had also lost its popularity; in The Hague there was even an anti-American riot in front of the embassy, where Dumas was living at the time. It was, in all probability, another "first" – the first "Yankee-go-home" manifestation in the world.

It is perhaps pure coincidence, unless we accept that all these events were part of the same struggle towards a democratic revolution, that in that same year the new Constitution was drafted in Philadelphia. However, in spite of the internal turmoil, the American Constitution attracted considerable attention and admiration among the intellectuals in the Netherlands. Johan Luzac published it first in his *Gazette de Leyde* and soon the Dutch papers followed suit and gave at least abstracts from it. A scholar, Gerhard Dumbar, wrote a three-part volume explaining the new Constitution to the Dutch people (*The Old and New Constitutions of the United States, explained in their Foundations from the best Sources*, Amsterdam, 1793–6). But it was not only the Patriots who expressed their admiration. The Constitution also appealed to conservatives. The brilliant young statesman Gijsbert Karel van Hogendorp, who had visited the new nation in 1783–4 and been very disappointed by the (in his opinion) far too loose structure of the American republic, was now of the opinion that with the Constitution, by introducing a safeguard against too much popular influence, America had found the ideal balance between order and freedom.

But the American example could nevertheless not serve as a model for the Dutch. First the counter-revolution of 1787 restored the *ancien régime* of the Stadtholder and made all reforms impossible. Then, in 1795, the old government was indeed dismantled, but now the French model became the dominant one. In 1795 the revolutionary armies of the French Republic occupied the Netherlands and put an end to the old Dutch Republic. The Stadtholder escaped to England, and the Patriots, who had fled eight years earlier, returned in triumph and founded the Batavian Republic. Now the achievements of the French Revolution, such as equality before the law, the abolition of the Established Church, and other similar reforms were carried through. An elected General Assembly set to work to draft a constitution. During the endless debates that followed, America was not forgotten, but by now it was the conservatives who put their trust in the American example. The radical reformers referred to the French model. They wanted to abolish federalism entirely and therefore called themselves Unitarists. The more conservative members, on the other hand, pleaded for the preservation of the old provinces and consequently called themselves Federalists, with a clear reference to America. It is true that there was a certain irony in this use of the same word. In America federalism stood for unity, in the Netherlands for variety. Yet American and Dutch Federalists had much in common: they were both rather conservative and afraid of too much democracy, and hence supporters of a mixed form of government and a separation of powers.

But no discussion could disguise the indisputable fact that the French model was compellingly close, the American far away. The Batavian Republic was increasingly becoming a satellite of France and was experiencing various *coups d'état*, where the French examples, more or less radical according to the situation in France itself, served as a model. America was disappearing behind the horizon.

After the so-called French era (1795–1813), independence was restored in the Netherlands. The son of the last Stadtholder returned as King William I. A constitution was drafted by Van Hogendorp. In this document the American influence is of little significance. It is true that, to a certain extent, Van Hogendorp sought to retain the provincial differences, but he did so without following the American model. Dutch provinces do not have anything like the same power as American states. National unity was the dominating force in the new Kingdom of the Netherlands. America remained an example from afar, which does not mean that John Adams was not right in proclaiming that there were (and are) many common values between the two countries.

FURTHER READING

Edler, Friedrich: *The Dutch Republic and the American Revolution* (Baltimore: Johns Hopkins Press, 1911).

Foley, Mary Briant: *The Triumph of Militia Diplomacy: John Adams in the Netherlands, 1780–82* (Ph.D. dissertation, Loyola University, Chicago, 1968).

Hutson, James H.: *John Adams and the Diplomacy of the American Revolution* (Lexington, KY: University Press of Kentucky, 1980).

Klein, S. R. E.: *Patriots Republikanisme. Politieke cultuur in Nederland (1766–1787)* (Political Culture in the Netherlands (1766–1787)) (Amsterdam: Amsterdam University Press, 1995).

Mecking, G. J.: "Mr. Gerhard Dumbar, een verlicht historicus?" *Overijsselse Historische Bijdragen*, 100 (1985), 167–93.

Morison, Samuel E.: *John Paul Jones: a Sailor's Biography* (Boston: Little, Brown, 1959).

Poelgeest, Bart van: "The influence of the American Constitution on Dutch lawyers, judged by the Dutch debate on judicial review," in *The US Constitution: after 200 years*, ed. Rob Kroes and Eduard van de Bilt (Amsterdam: Free University Press, 1988), 137–59.

Riker, William H.: "Dutch and American federalism," *Journal of the History of Ideas*, 18 (1957), 495–521.

Schulte Nordholt, J. W.: "The example of the Dutch Republic for American federalism," in *Federalism: history and current significance of a form of government*, ed. J. C. Boogman and

G. N. van der Plaat (The Hague: M. Nijhoff, 1980), 65–77.

Schulte Nordholt, J. W.: *Voorbeeld in de verte: de invloed van de Amerikaanse revolutie in Nederland* (Baarn: 1979), trans. Herbert H. Rowen, *The Dutch Republic and American Independence* (Chapel Hill: University of North Carolina Press, 1982).

Welling, G. M.: *The Prize of Neutrality. Trade relations between Amsterdam and North America 1771–1817. A study in computational history* (Ph.D. dissertation, Rijksuniversiteit Groningen, 1998).

Wijk, F. W. van: *De Republiek en Amerika, 1776–1782* (Leiden: E.J. Brill, 1921).

Winter, P. J. van: *Het aandeel van den Amsterdamschen handel aan den opbouw van het Amerikaansche Gemeenebest*, 2 · vols. (The Hague: Martinus Nijhoff, 1927–33).

CHAPTER SIXTY-SEVEN

The influence of the American Revolution in Germany

HORST DIPPEL

THE American Revolution came upon a divided Germany, divided into a multitude of independent or semi-independent states with different political allegiances and military engagements or responsibilities, divided into heterogeneous economic interests, religious affiliations, and traditional political orientations, divided into different classes of people with unequal means of access to information and sources of knowledge and with different, even opposing social and political interests. Besides these major divisions, there existed some important commonalities, such as a general lack of received political ideas and movements in terms of modern party politics, of a powerful bourgeoisie as an accepted political force pressing for reforms, of profound knowledge of what the American Revolution was all about, and – and this is no contradiction – of a general interest in American affairs and a widespread enthusiasm for the American Revolution.

1 German Politics and the American Revolution

The French and Indian War in its European theater had engaged the two major German powers, Prussia and Austria, the first as British, the second as French ally. Though Frederick II of Prussia mistrusted British politics since the accession of George III, he was well aware in subsequent years that for economic, political, and military reasons he could not come out openly with an anti-British policy. He was ready in the 1770s to tolerate American emissaries in Prussia buying war supplies, made vague hints of a recognition of American Independence if France preceded, and did not object to former Prussian officers entering into American services, such as Baron Friedrich Wilhelm August von Steuben as the most famous of them. Once, he even prevented German troops hired by the British for fighting in America from crossing his territory. But any further provocation might have hurt Prussia's export trade and its political interests seriously. American Independence was not formally recognized until 1783; a treaty of amity and commerce, however, already concluded in 1785 and due to the negotiations of John Quincy Adams in Berlin, was renewed in 1799.

The Prussian king and his government had hardly more sympathy with the rebellious Americans than the emperor in Vienna whose political and economic interests appeared to be far less involved than those of Prussia. The American Revolution hardly touched official policy and, therefore, even allowed for experiments with American constitutional ideas in Tuscany during the 1780s, instigated by Grand Duke Peter Leopold, the emperor's brother and successor in 1790. As emperor, however, he was strictly opposed to any form of modern constitution, anywhere.

Of the other German princes, nobody ruled a territory large enough to allow for a foreign policy that went beyond France or Great Britain in the West. Nevertheless, some ten of them tried to profit from American affairs and according to a long-standing tradition offered Britain troops for the war in its rebellious colonies in order to improve their budget. Some 30,000 of these were finally hired by Britain and came to be styled indiscriminately in America as "Hessians." To be precise, slightly more than half of them came from Hesse-Kassel, whereas the rest were roughly evenly divided among Ansbach-Bayreuth, Brunswick, Waldeck, Anhalt-Zerbst, and Hesse-Hanau, while two or three other German princes were less successful in selling troops to Britain. Americans as well as British fought alongside German troops. Some 1,000–2,000 had either individually offered their service to America, or as most of them did, joined with the French troops as German regiments constantly in French service. The result was that at Yorktown German troops fought on both sides.

2 Loyalties and Interests

As it happened, all the princes selling troops to Britain came from Protestant Germany. Of course, they did not sell their standing armies but only regiments especially raised for the purpose of service in America, and they recruited them not only in their own territories but also legally or illegally all over Protestant Germany as well as in Prussia and Hanover, the German possession of King George III. For almost 100 years England had been the bulwark of Protestant Europe against Catholic France and its political aspirations. Some of these traditional loyalties, in many parts of northern Germany combined with definite economic interests, were still alive. Additionally, not only those in Protestant Germany but almost all who had read Voltaire, Montesquieu, Delorme and others admired the British political system and tended to consider Britain the land of liberty.

Though the Enlightenment had made progress, traditional values and loyalties still had their meaning well beyond Protestant Germany. But the overtly political connotations of Enlightenment philosophy so obvious in France were hardly to be grasped in Germany. Here, no ground was prepared for the ideas of the American Revolution by imminent political demands or protests or by a national bourgeoisie that intellectually set the tone from the nation's capital. Nothing approaching "public opinion" existed yet in a rural Germany divided into states containing small towns, where even Vienna, Berlin, Hamburg, or Cologne, failed to achieve national importance in political or intellectual terms. Localism and isolation characterized German life, with an aristocracy thoroughly influenced by French culture and the lower classes mostly illiterate.

3 The impact of the Ideas of the American Revolution

In 1776, the American Revolution with its ideas and ideals broke into this divided and traditionally orientated German world and electrified the imagination. Words such as liberty, equality, property, rights, and others ringing over the ocean had a familiar sound and seemed easily accessible. For the educated classes the Enlightenment had given meaning to these words, though only indirectly in a political sense, while the rest of the population had no difficulty in making sense of such concepts. Thus almost overnight, the American Revolution became extremely popular in Germany.

The popularity of this event, the details of which were basically completely unknown, was strange. German enthusiasm was not preceded by years of debate about British policy and American arguments. But in 1776 with war and independence across the ocean, with recruiting officers sweeping large parts of Germany, and with soldiers on their march to America, the American Revolution gained momentum in German towns and villages. A public political debate about America arose all of a sudden, the extent of which Germany had hardly ever seen before. Newspapers and journals were full of American news, hundreds of books were published, either by German authors or translated from French, English, or other languages. To tens of thousands even private information by way of letters from America was now and then available.

All kinds of information about America poured into Germany. Especially in the newspapers most of it centered on the war in America with its daily news and never-ending rumors about American success or failure. In comparison with the War of Independence, however, the American Revolution hardly showed up in them. In the journals and books it fared only slightly better. Not more than a handful of publications between October 1776 and the end of the century contained a complete German translation of the Declaration of Independence. The Federal Constitution of 1787 saw even less publicity, and the first and only German edition of American state constitutions appeared in 1785, seven years after the first French edition, and years after similar publications in London and the Netherlands. Some may have seen *The Federalist* in the French translation of 1792, but the first German translation was only published in 1950.

Why were key documents of the American Revolution not readily available in Germany? Germans were enthusiastic about the American Revolution and – with some dissent in English Hanover – generally agreed that America had succeeded England as the land of liberty. Why did they not bother to found their judgment more solidly? The answer plainly reveals the German situation in contrast to that in France. German enthusiasm, sincere as it was, was motivated by the persuasion that the Americans had succeeded in transforming Enlightenment ideals from the realm of theory to down-to-earth practice. They had demonstrated that these ideals would work, i.e. that the Enlightenment ideals were justified and true. According to them, Americans had proved nothing less than the victory of the Enlightenment. Every enlightened contemporary could rejoice over their victory.

The equation of the American Revolution with the Enlightenment had two consequences. On the one hand, there was no need to go into details and to bother about specific documents to prove the case. On the other hand, German *Aufklärer* could leave the situation at this point. Basically, the American Revolution was a philosophical event. It had proved that this philosophy was true, for it demonstrated that the step from theory to practice was possible. Germany was not the place to imitate the

Americans because the situation there did not allow for anything comparable. There was no way to perform an equivalent step, and any detailed study of further documents would make no change with regard to this assessment.

4 The French Revolution and the New Interpretation of the American Revolution

Change came again abruptly. With the outbreak of the French Revolution the German philosophical interpretation of the American Revolution collapsed. Now, the American Revolution seemed to repeat itself in the first country of Europe, and no further doubt was allowed about its imminent practical political meaning. Obviously, its principles could bring about change in the political reality of Europe. Liberty and equality could change people's lives. Under this impression, quite a few Germans became revolutionaries, a rather new phenomenon in Germany. During the American Revolution just one really radical treatise was published, and on its publication the author, Johann Christian Schmohl, decided to emigrate to America, which he never lived to see, for he drowned near the Bermudas.

Even those who did not become revolutionaries had become politically more alert. Hardly any of them lost their admiration for America, and even those more skeptical in the past now tended to appreciate the American Revolution, as it had been so much more orderly and bloodless than the French Revolution with its horrific terror. It was this evaluation that necessitated a more detailed look back at the American Revolution beyond philosophical reflections or the uncritical admiration of its heroes, especially Benjamin Franklin and George Washington. Now its principles and proceedings had to be analyzed more carefully to prove, as ever more Germans came to believe during the 1790s, that the American Revolution was a "good" revolution, while the French Revolution was a "bad" revolution. The United States and France had little in common; distant America might remain a self-sufficient ideal, while France was expanding dangerously, and required individual attention, meaning either revolution or reaction.

The American Revolution survived the challenge of the French Revolution. Even though it was studied in Germany in more detail, it remained, after all, an ideal. This was not the continued philosophical interpretation of the 1780s, for the reality of the American Revolution was understood as the result of a specific American environment inherently different from the European situation. Thus, while the admiration continued, the American Revolution had again lost its real meaning for Germany. Though it had helped to articulate political attitudes even before the advent of the French Revolution, it failed to make its supporters identify with it. Instead of delivering a catalog of demands for political reform, it continued to be a point of reference, however, to an ideal world, insurmountably different from the European world.

FURTHER READING

Atwood, Rodney: *Hessians, Mercenaries from Hessen-Kassel in the American Revolution* (Cambridge: Cambridge University Press, 1980).

Dippel, Horst: *Americana Germanica, 1770–1800. Bibliographie deutscher Amerikaliteratur* (Bibliography of German literature on [North] America) (Stuttgart: J. B. Metzlersche Verlagsbuchhandlung, 1976).

——: *Germany and the American Revolution, 1770–1800. A Sociohistorical Investigation of Late Eighteenth-Century Political Thinking*, Forward by R. R. Palmer (Chapel Hill, NC: University of North Carolina Press, 1977).

Kroeger, Alfred: *Geburt der USA. German Newspaper Accounts of the American Revolution* (Madison: State Historical Society of Wisconsin, 1962).

Palmer, Robert R.: *The Age of the Democratic Revolution: A Political History of Europe and America, 1760–1800*, 2 vols. (Princeton, NJ: Princeton University Press, 1959–64).

Wilke, Juergen: "Agenda-setting in an historical perspective: The coverage of the American Revolution in the German press (1773–83)," *European Journal of Communication* 10 (1995), 63–86.

CHAPTER SIXTY-EIGHT

The influence of the American Revolution in Russia

HANS ROGGER

SOVIET historians describe the American "bourgeois" revolution as above all a war for national independence. That view prevailed also in the government of Catherine II (1762–96) and among those of her subjects who could follow public affairs. This is one reason for the tolerant, even benign, official and non-official reactions to American events. Others were their remoteness from Russia and the opportunities they presented to her diplomacy and trade.

1 Official Relations

Although relations between Russia and Britain were friendly, the request George III made in 1775 for 20,000 Russian troops to be sent to America was refused by Catherine and her advisers. They had just put down the Pugachev rebellion and ended a long war with Turkey, and were not averse to seeing Britain embroiled in a distant conflict which the Empress might arbitrate with benefit to her prestige and influence. It was a conflict, moreover, for which the intransigence of the English was blamed and which they were not believed certain to win. "Patient neutrality" was the course adopted while awaiting the outcome of the war and profiting from the increase in trade it brought.

In 1780, patient neutrality turned into "armed neutrality." Supported by other states whose vessels the British had seized, Russia declared that neutral ships might freely sail to belligerents' ports; that enemy goods in neutral ships, except war contraband, were not subject to seizure; and that a blockade had to be enforced rather than merely proclaimed. Russia's defense of neutral shipping was a boon to the fledgling republic and greeted as such by its leaders, who in the same year appointed the first American diplomat to St. Petersburg. Francis Dana was to "engage Her Imperial Majesty to favour and support the sovereignty and independence of these United States" (Bashkina, 1980, p. 98).

During his stay (1781–3), Dana was neither received nor recognized in his official capacity. To avoid antagonizing England and to keep open the possibility of her mediation, Catherine observed "strict impartiality." When Britain recognized the Independence of the United States, Russian representatives abroad were allowed to deal with them as with other republics. Although full and formal relations did not begin until 1809, quasi-official, commercial, and private contacts increased in the 1780s and became cordial during the next two decades.

2 Popular Opinion

Despite the Empress's distaste for their act of rebellion, the colonists enjoyed the sympathy of many, perhaps most, educated Russians. Catherine's son, the Grand Duke Paul, in 1781 praised the Americans for their "internal force and virtue" (Griffiths, 1969, p. 22), reflecting the general view that they were moderate and reasonable men whom English ineptness and arrogance had goaded into disaffection. Russians' opinions of the new nation's struggle, laws, and institutions were shaped by foreign writers and journals, by one Russian book and several translated volumes, and increasingly by their own press, which was for the most part favorable to the Americans.

This was especially true of one of the country's two newspapers, the *Moscow Gazette*. For Nikolai Novikov, its publisher and a leading figure of the Russian Enlightenment, the foundation of the American republic was as much a moral as a political act, and Franklin was a kindred spirit in the fight against the vices of courts and aristocrats. Posterity, the newspaper predicted, would revere him as a divinity; as electricity had transformed physics, events in the colonies would transform all of politics. Washington was declared to be greater than other patriots and liberators, for he had founded a nation that would "become a refuge for the liberty which luxury and depravity had driven from Europe" (Bolkhovitinov, 1976, p. 159). John Adams was praised for his republican simplicity of dress and bearing, the fervor of his republican convictions, and the eloquence with which these were expressed.

In his *Journey from Petersburg to Moscow* (1790), Aleksandr Radishchev, Russia's first radical, voiced boldly the revolutionary implications of the war. More than a national conflict, it was a popular rising against the abuses of arbitrary government, part of the fight for the freedom and dignity of all men which the Americans had waged willingly and won by their own efforts. Theirs was not an army of ignorant conscripts or mercenaries, but a host of free men who were inspired, like their leader, by the love of liberty. They had preserved that precious gift, proclaiming freedom of the press and civil liberty. Not even slavery, which Novikov too condemned, extinguished for Radishchev America's achievement; few Russians after him spoke of it with such passion.

Frightened by the French Revolution, Catherine suppressed the *Journey* and exiled its author. Yet, in a time of reaction, America appeared as the one nation where liberty and law survived. Demanding these for Russia, the officers who staged the ill-fated rebellion of December 1825 looked to a revolution that had avoided terror and despotism to erect a constitutional federation in which the rights of citizens were secure and the powers of government restrained. America showed that a state need not be cruel to be strong or rulers tyrannical to be obeyed. The Decembrists' failure and growing awareness

of America's defects – crass commercialism, corrupt politicians, fickle electorates – dimmed the bright image of the young republic. But its chief features endured: the public and private virtues of its founders, the laws and institutions created by them.

America's youth would always be the period of greatest attractiveness to Russians; radical or conservative antipathy never displaced totally their original, largely liberal, image of the United States. But, like liberalism itself, it made no permanent conquest of the Russian mind, although democrats and socialists did on occasion invoke the principles and achievements of the Revolution as models or a source of hope.

FURTHER READING

Allen, Robert V.: *Russia Looks at America: The View to 1917* (Washington: Library of Congress, 1988).

Bashkina, N. N. et al. (eds.): *The United States and Russia: the Beginning of Relations, 1765–1815* (Washington: Government Printing Office, 1980).

Blakely, Allison: "American Influences on Russian Reformist Thought in the Era of the French Revolution," *Russian Review*, vol. 52, no. 4 (October 1993), 451–71.

Bolkhovitinov, N. N.: *Stanovlenie russko-amerikanskikh otnoshenii 1775–1815* (Moscow: Nauka, 1966); trans. Elena Levin, *The Beginnings of Russian-American Relations, 1775–1815* (Cambridge, Mass., and London: Harvard University Press, 1975).

——: *Rossiia i voina SShA za nezavisimost' 1775–1783* (Moscow: Mysl', 1976); trans. C. Jay Smith, *Russia and the American Revolution* (Tallahassee, Fla: Diplomatic Press, 1976).

Griffiths, D. M.: "Nikita Panin, Russian diplomacy, and the American Revolution," *Slavic Review*, 28 (1969), 1–24.

Hecht, David: *Russian Radicals Look to America* (Cambridge, Mass.: Harvard University Press, 1947).

Laserson, M. M.: *The American Impact on Russia, 1784–1917* (New York: Macmillan, 1950).

Nikoliukin, Aleksandr N.: *A Russian Discovery of America* (Moscow: Progress, 1987).

Rogger, Hans: "How the Soviets see us," *Shared Destiny: Fifty Years of Soviet-American Relations*, ed. Mark Garrison and Abbott Gleason (Boston: Beacon Press, 1985), 107–45.

Saul, Norman E.: *Distant Friends: The United States and Russia, 1763–1867* (Lawrence: University Press of Kansas, 1991).

PART V

Internal Developments after the Revolution

CHAPTER SIXTY-NINE

The economic and demographic consequences of the American Revolution

MARY M. SCHWEITZER

THE long-run economic and demographic consequences of the American Revolution are inseparable, because economic well-being is measured in the lives of individuals. In the eighteenth century, economic prosperity translated into longevity, good health, having children and grandchildren, and ensuring they were settled as adults in their own *independent* households. By this yardstick, the political economy of revolutionary America was both a stunning success, and a dismal failure. For the majority of British America, the period saw prosperity unknown elsewhere. The century between 1740 and 1840 also saw the emergence of the modern phenomenon of economic growth whereby each generation has available not only as much as the previous one, but more – the kernel of truth behind the myth of the "American dream." The population of the United States doubled between 1776 and 1800, the space of one generation, despite the interference of a very serious, long, and hard-fought war.

At the same time, however, one out of five Americans lived a cruel mockery of this household-centered economy – possessing no rights to even form a household, let alone have any say in its disposition. The end of the Revolution also signaled the beginning of the Hundred Years' War of conquest, death, and banishment of Amerindian nationals. The same political economy that enabled a spectacularly successful agrarian economy to thrive, permitting generations of independent farm households to flourish, also enabled the choice to be made to keep one-fifth of Americans in slavery, and to conduct a prolonged war against another large segment of the population. We can never fully understand ourselves as a nation, or the economic policies implicitly buried within the nation's institutional framework, until we have confronted this Janus-faced past.

At the end of this essay we shall return to the long-run economic and demographic implications of the institutional choices made during the period of revolutionary change in early modern America. First, however, we must focus more closely on the short-run causes and effects of the events that shaped the creation of a new nation, from Lexington and Concord to the ratification of the Bill of Rights.

1 The Immediate Costs of the Revolution

The Revolution was costly to America, both in lives and possessions. At the beginning of the war, a little more than 2 million people inhabited the British American mainland colonies south of Canada; by the end, the number had reached 3 million. Roughly half of this population was under the age of 16; another half was female. Estimates of the number of soldiers who fought at some time during the war vary from 100–200,000; perhaps half of all men of "fighting age" served in the military during the war. The fighting itself thus had an impact on every American household and every American community.

The most serious cost of the war was death or disfigurement – at least one in five soldiers were casualties of the war effort. Next came the losses suffered in households where a healthy adult male was imperative to the economic structure. War-widows could survive as shopkeepers in the city, but it was very difficult for a woman to run a farm without the help of a male partner (as was the reverse, but it was men who left). Most communities and families suffered economic losses while their men were away at war; for some the losses would be permanent.

The war also brought with it destruction of physical property – the capital stock of the nation. Southeast Pennsylvania, New Jersey, and Delaware suffered greatly from raids by both armies for food. The American army left behind Continental notes that proved nearly worthless; the British simply took what they wanted. In addition, the British burned houses, barns, fences, and outbuildings, and dismantled mills, smashing or carting away the expensive French millstones that gave Pennsylvania super fine flour such a high price abroad. Both armies took livestock and horses, although the Americans might leave a cow and a horse; the British even took the seed corn.

Areas close to water were vulnerable to raids by the British navy – farms in the Chesapeake region of Delaware and Maryland and towns along the Connecticut seacoast were destroyed, sometimes in repeat raids to torch what had just been rebuilt. In addition to the loss of farms and villages, both areas were centers of shipbuilding, and the British destroyed both the ships and drydocks. Early in the war, Norfolk, Virginia, a rising seaport that looked as if it would become a serious competitor to Baltimore in the West Indies trade, was so completely destroyed it would take nearly two centuries to recover its position as the largest city in Virginia. Both Charleston and Savannah spent years under siege, eventually to be sacked when the defense collapsed. Cornwallis's march through the Carolinas and Virginia wrought deliberate

destruction in a manner not unlike that of General Sherman in a later war.

There are no precise estimates of the damage caused by the American Revolution as there are for the Civil War. The literary evidence, however, indicates destruction on a very high level for this supposedly capital-poor nation. In that context, it is intriguing that only Norfolk failed to recover. Both Connecticut and Pennsylvania were already entering the stage of modern economic growth when the war decades hit; costly war damage caused a significant retreat in the last decades of the 1700s, but they would both be back on track within a decade of the ratification of the Constitution.

Given that those who suffered the most losses of the war were either soldiers and their families, or those in the pathway of suppliers for either army, the failure of Congress to find a way to legitimately reimburse soldiers and small suppliers for their goods and services contributed even more to the unequal distribution of the costs of war. Some states tried to make up for the failures of Congress by supplementing Continental payments to their own citizens with state notes, but by and large most of the losses due to the collapse of the "national" currency, the "Continental," or the failure of Congress to reimburse those who held Continental notes, were never recouped.

The problem stemmed from Congress having behaved as a national government when true sovereignty always rested with the nation-states created in 1776. The treaty of 1783 created not a single independent nation, but "13 free and independent states," listed by name. During the period between effective peace (1781) and the ratification of the US Constitution (1788), the state legislatures came to the reluctant decision that the very powers for which they had fought so hard – to control domestic economic policy – were going to have to be shared with a new federal government.

2 Economic Sovereignty in Revolutionary America

The Revolution was a war of preservation, not upheaval. During the first half of the 1700s, each colony wrested effective control over the policies essential to economic independence: taxation, money creation, and internal development. At the war's end, in 1782, these powers remained in the hands of the several state legislatures with one important exception: Virginia, succumbing to Maryland's power play with Cornwallis barreling toward the Chesapeake, gave up all claims to the regions west of Pennsylvania and north of the Ohio River in exchange for Maryland's signing the Articles of Confederation. Had this not occurred, control of the lands that became Ohio, Indiana, Illinois, Michigan, Wisconsin, and perhaps even southwest Pennsylvania, would have legally remained in the hands of the Virginia legislature – and Virginia land speculators (often a redundancy). Instead, a new entity was created, the "Northwest Territory," created not as a colony of a state, nor a colony of all the states, but a special type of government intended to evolve into equality with its neighbors – a truly revolutionary conception. Virginia, however, had already set in motion the means by which its land west of the Appalachians and south of the Ohio would become a state – Kentucky.

It is difficult to recapture the degree to which so much of later American history was impacted by this happenstance. No one paid much attention at the time, because the lands were still very much in the hands of Amerindian nationals. Because Congress – and not Virginia (or the Ohio Company) – had control over the construction of the territory's first government, Thomas Jefferson was able to engineer a remarkable coup: the new Northwest Territory would become the first fully slave-free region in the new United States.

Plans were underway to create new colonies west of the Appalachians before the ink was dry on the Treaty of Ghent. Vandalia, Franklinia, and Transylvania were very much alive in the minds of western settlers when Congress redrew the boundaries using rivers as borders instead of the original plans, which would have used them as centers. Franklinia would have included much of the area that today follows the Pittsburgh Steelers – portions of Pennsylvania, Ohio, and West Virginia. Transylvania would have combined the mountainous regions of the

South into one giant state. Vandalia was to be formed around the intersection of the Illinois, Ohio, and Mississippi Rivers – a region already cleared out and occupied by a once-strong Amerindian trading nation (the heirs of Cahokia) as well as the site of a French colonial village.

Vandalia and Franklinia made geographic sense: certainly a state combining southeastern Ohio, southwestern Pennsylvania (including Pittsburgh), and northern West Virginia would have had a cohesion that cartographically defined Pennsylvania definitely lacks. Similarly, the Ohio River valley had a natural unity that did not match well with the geography, or future economic development, of the Great Lakes region. All three states: Ohio, Indiana, and Illinois, retain a deep sense of separation between their own north and south.

However, Vandalia and Franklinia would have been slave states. Congress drew the borders of the Northwest Territories along north–south lines (rather than the east–west boundary of Kentucky and Tennessee), then settled the long-standing dispute between Virginia and Pennsylvania over ownership of the Pittsburgh region by ordering a formal extension of the Mason-Dixon line almost to the Ohio. The result would be a slave-free North extending much further south than would have probably emerged had the region been left to develop naturally. The decision to ban slavery north of the Ohio, and extend Pennsylvania's government (which had just voted in the first – albeit weak – emancipation law) due west 50 miles south of Pittsburgh, was most likely the most important action taken by the short-lived Confederation government. Certainly the history of America in the nineteenth century would have been very different had that boundary not been drawn where it was.

After the passage of the Northwest Territory and the determination of boundaries between Virginia and Pennsylvania, no actions taken by the Confederation government had any impact on the economy of the states. To the contrary, the state legislatures made it very clear who was in charge of economic policy. Yet by 1788, the states were willing to give up powers over economic policy dating back to the previous century, to a new national government. Why?

The end of the Revolution created 13 free and independent states – and a fourteenth maverick. (Vermont, which had declared independence, ratified a constitution, was governed by a legislature and sent troops to fight in the war, was technically still a part of New York State, and Congress had no power to require New York to give it up.) Each legislature assumed that it would be back to business as usual, without the annoying interference from London that had increased every year since 1750. To find the source of essential sovereignty during the Revolution and the Confederation period, one need look no further than the right to tax, because scholars of the day (and many now) pointed to the right of taxation as the essential characteristic of economic and political power.

The Confederation had no powers to tax.

This was no accident. By refusing to give up any parcel of their right to tax, the state legislatures sent the clear message that *they*, not Continental Congress, would possess ultimate sovereignty in the postwar era. It is possible that, had the war lasted sufficiently long, the states would have given in on the tax issue, as Virginia eventually gave in on the western lands. But the war ended, and with it all pressure to give up that most critical of state powers: taxation.

With no power to raise taxes, Congress issued paper currency, a standard method in the colonies/states for financing wars. But each of the 14 states (the 13 plus Vermont) issued its own paper currency, and each of the currencies not only added to the total money supply (and hence inflation), but also directly competed with the new "Continentals." Monetary theorists suggest that fiat money (money that has value because the government declares it to be valuable, not because it can be exchanged for some real good) will hold its value if (and only if) it is accepted by the government as payment for … taxes. *The Confederation had no powers to tax*. If the Confederation's fiat money ("Continentals") were to have any hopes of stability, it would have to be accepted at par in payment for state taxes. Once again, the states refused to cooperate. With nothing to support their value but good will, it should be no surprise that the Continentals quickly plummeted in value to near zero.

The result was a sharp rise in prices between 1777 and 1781, followed by an equally rapid fall. By 1785, prices had stabilized, and the states had returned to the monetary policies they had practiced before the war. States such as Pennsylvania, with a history of successful issues of paper currency, continued that practice with no mishaps. States such as Virginia, where the tidewater economy had little need of paper currency because tobacco inspection notes served effectively as a form of money, the legislature continually battled over whether or not to issue paper. Rhode Island reverted to its pre-1750 practice of finance-by-arbitrage, a practice with major ramifications later. The ease with which the states returned to business as usual with regard to monetary policy belies the usual historical accounts that paper money was such a huge disaster. The *Continentals* were a disaster – mostly for the soldiers and provisioners who had to accept them in payment. But the householders of eighteenth-century America possessed a sophisticated understanding of money as a commodity and had had decades of experience using different types of money as competing commodities. State currencies circulated along with Chesapeake tobacco inspection notes, certificates for British sterling, the occasional British coin, and more commonly Dutch and Spanish coins from the West Indies trade. The Spanish *dolare* was such a common unit of exchange that was adopted for the new national curency, which would be called "dollars." Continentals were simply one form of currency among many; one that failed. The problem was not the concept of fiat money – the problem was the gross inequity with which the Continentals were distributed under the full knowledge that they stood little chance of holding their value. Some states tried to make it up to their own citizens with supplementary payments, but others were left with nothing.

Wars are expensive. Troops must be provisioned, material produced only to be destroyed. Unless there is enormous productive slack in the economy (as was true in the United States in 1940), the only way to finance a war is to divert current production away from consumers and investors toward the war effort. Direct taxation seems an obvious possibility, but it also tends to substantially reduce civilian support for the war. In this case, it was impossible because ... *Congress had no powers to tax*. The states did have the power to tax, and they did tax their citizens – but they proved stubbornly reluctant to turn much of that over to the Confederation government.

When Congress emitted Continentals, they knew it would cause inflation; they hoped it would not be too bad; they later would claim they had no idea that it would prove as disastrous as it did. The Confederation was neither the first nor the last American government to finance a war using inflation. Inflation forced people to make do with less. As a result, current production was diverted from consumption and investment to the war effort – the identical effect that would have been caused by direct taxation. Unlike a tax, however, where the distributional effects are visible, the uneven burden of inflation makes it difficult to tell who's paying for the war.

Historians could not have been further from the mark when they forced the Populist/Progressive view of farmers and banking upon the revolutionary era. True enough, all other things being equal, holders of real wealth (such as farmland) will benefit from inflation; creditors will benefit from deflation. But the farmers, artisans, storekeepers, and merchants of early America never lobbied for artificial movements of prices or the value of money – when one group or another went to the legislature or courts it almost always stemmed from a *loss* of monetary stability, not a desire to create more.

The pace of financial transactions in the late eighteenth century was glacial. Merchants, shopkeepers, and farmers seldom balanced their books. Individual accounts were cleared out at irregular intervals; the cautious creditor converted a book debt into a note after about two years, but it might not be paid for another five. There was no debtor or creditor class; had there been, a large number of people would have had no idea which group they fell into. Only when a person died were all the debts paid, credits called in, or the paper transferred to others – and then the books were literally and finally closed. Often no one really knew how large or small the estate was – or if it was consumed by debt, until this "final reckoning." Contrary to the stereotype, merchants often died deep in debt, while farmers' estates might contain a long list of people to who they had extended credit.

Rapid inflation followed by rapid deflation favored no one. There were windfall gains, and windfall losses, but it all happened too quickly for anybody to plan them. The complex network of debt and credit that extended throughout the colonies was thrown into total disarray when prices more than doubled in the space of four years, then halved again a couple of years later. And then, just as suddenly, it all balanced out. By 1785 prices were again stable, and would remain so in most places. The states that as colonies had a history of fiscal responsibility with fiat money – such as Pennsylvania with its land bank – returned to their old, successful practices. Those whose citizens had long quarreled about whether or not to issue paper currency – such as Virginia – returned to quarreling (and relying on Pennsylvania's currency as the means of exchange in the backcountry). Rhode Island's creatively irresponsible legislators returned to their old practices of finance through arbitrage – printing massive issues of paper currency, benefiting from the lag in the price correction mechanisms in their neighboring states, and enjoying the benefits of extra cash, for Rhode Islanders alone, while inflation spread over New England.

At the end of years of price disruption caused by the war, legislative dockets were clogged with requests for private laws that would straighten out the mess by revaluing personal debts as close to real terms as possible. British observers (and later historians) would think such machinations reckless, but indexing was probably the most sensible economic solution to the one-time mess that had been created. The legislatures consciously strove, where possible, to prevent both windfall gains and windfall losses due to six brief years of unusually massive price movements.

As private debtors and creditors turned to the legislatures to clarify the true meaning of their contracts, so too the farming population turned to the courts to clarify their own debts and credits – and in states with land taxes, to revalue the assessments that determined the amount of tax owed. Historians have often read into the capture of rural courts in western Massachusetts (Shays's Rebellion) the beginnings of a class revolution – for better or worse. At the time, however, it was a fairly common occurrence, a type of injunction to stop courts from acting to foreclose on farms until an unsettled situation could be clarified. Many of the states had legislation directed towards precisely this type of situation. In Pennsylvania, farmers were generally given a period of seven years to restructure their debt and pay it off a little at a time, while continuing to operate their farms. This practice was explicitly drawn from the rules of the Friends' Meetings (Quakers). Friends were required by their faith to keep "friendly disputes" out of the court system. Instead, they were handled by local men's monthly meetings. The Philadelphia Annual Meeting of 1705 instructed the men's monthly meetings to choose two respected men to assist their "friend" in restructuring the debt, negotiating a system of payments so creditors would be satisfied, and help devise a more efficient budget for running the farm so the farmer would not again succumb to serious indebtedness. In short, the Pennsylvania Society of Friends had created an effective type of bankruptcy proceeding 100 years before economists and legal historians believe the concept of bankruptcy first appeared. Neighbors outside the Friends' community would often request the services of the Meeting to arbitrate contract disputes or set up a bankruptcy; by mid-century the Pennsylvania legislature had formalized many of the bankruptcy provisions into law.

The movement to persuade courts to stop foreclosing on farms based upon erroneous valuations of the farms' worth – just like the movement to create indexing for the period of rapid price movements – rested on a common understanding that nominal values can differ wildly from real values. Throughout the colonial period, local courts and legislatures had consistently indicated that economic rules should be based upon real values rather than nominal ones. Ironically, it was not from a lack of familiarity with cash or prices – but rather a thorough understanding of the limits of prices as a mechanism for valuation.

Most states handled the problem effectively. When Virginia farmers took over the courts, the legislature responded by indexing the real value of debts for the years of rapid price changes. There was barely a ripple of commentary. Pennsylvania had plenty of revenue from its land bank, liquor taxes, and a high tariff on goods passing through the port of Philadelphia. There was also a long tradition of refusing to pay colony-wide taxes. From 1717 through 1755, the local poor taxes were regularly met, but no government could collect a penny in colony-wide revenues (and the Proprietor saw very little in the way of the "quitrents" that were technically owed to him by all landowners). During the Revolution and the 1780s, Pennsylvania farmers, low on cash, did not bother the courts. They simply refused to pay. Year after year tax collectors from western counties would return to Philadelphia and apologize for having failed to collect taxes. Year after year, the legislature would scold the tax collectors and instruct them to try to do better next year. Nothing else ever happened.

In this context, Shays's Rebellion was a standard response to an unusual economic occurence. The dramatic break with the past was not the "rebellion," but the reaction in Boston. Perhaps the legislature was edgy about paper currency because of Rhode Island's misbehavior – but Massachusetts had already enacted a law declaring Rhode Island currency useful for payment of debts to their citizens (as had New Hamsphire and Connecticut). Perhaps the refusal of New York to recognize Vermont, and Vermont's idle threat to join Canada, made them particularly nervous about the Connecticut River Valley. Or perhaps they were just too sure of themselves, too contemptuous of western country bumpkins.

Whatever the cause, the decision to send the Massachusetts militia out to quell the "insurrection" was an enormous political error – the hardliners were voted out of office in the next election, and the legislature taken over by Shays's sympathizers.

In a similar vein, Washington's march on western Pennsylvania during the Whiskey Rebellion of 1794 established federal dominance – Pennsylvania would have negotiated with the rebels, but was overruled by the federal government. Washington also succeeded in sending a message of strength to foreign governments. But Washington's march on western Pennsylvania eventually spelled the beginning of the end for the Federalists. The Whiskey Tax *was* unfair – whiskey was a chief export only in the backcountry regions; no other region was so singled out. If the purpose was to tax a price-inelastic export, why was tobacco not added to the bill? Clearly the worst fears of western Anti-Federalists had been realized: whereas they had reasonable representation in the state government, they were too much of a minority in the federal government to be able to defend themselves politically against such an imposition. Many of the out-of-state soldiers in Washington's army (particular those from Massachusetts) understood this all too well. A number remained in Pennsylvania, and Pennsylvania would become a center of Democrat Republican activity leading up to Jefferson's election in 1800.

The mechanics of restructuring the value of contracts in the face of massive price movements had little to do with coherent "creditor" or "debtor" interests. Wartime inflation wreaked havoc for a very brief period within the financial structure of the nation, and then the situation corrected itself – in some cases with help from the state legislatures. The one segment of the population unusually hard hit by the inflation were the actual recipients of the Continentals; soldiers, small provisioners, and their families – already contributing greatly to the war effort – were forced to contribute even more by being paid in worthless paper. The assault of the Masachusetts legislature on its western farming region was particularly insensitive given that western farmers

(such as Daniel Shays), who had lost significant agricultural income during the war while in the army, were only to be paid in Continentals. What was the legislature thinking when it began foreclosing on the farms of these families for "nonpayment of taxes?" Perhaps the holders of the federal debt would have to wait a bit longer for specie payments to recover *their* losses, but to do so by adding to the burdens already carried by their citizen farmers was a bit much.

In the meantime, Rhode Island had resurrected its fiscal policies from the prewar era. The little state had discovered that if it printed a large issue of paper currency, both the state and its local citizens could use it to pay debts – particularly to creditors outside the state – before the legal balancing mechanisms caught up. The rest of New England, forced to pay with inflation for Rhode Island's monetary largesse, had acquiesced in 1750 to an agreement with the Board of Trade that prohibited all issues of paper currency in New England – essentially giving up their own powers to print paper money in exchange for putting a stop to Rhode Island's. This provision was never applied outside of New England, with the issue quickly becoming moot at the start of the Seven Years' War (which ended up being financed by paper money issues). However, newly freed from the Board of Trade, Rhode Island found itself able once again to participate in this unusual practice of finance-by-arbitrage: financing activities in Rhode Island by benefiting from a gap in the legal and actual exchange rate between two money supplies.

Both situations came to a peak in the last months of 1786 and carried into 1787. Newspapers throughout the colonies carried stories of Rhode Island merchants fleeing their customers who were trying to pay them in rapidly depreciating Rhode Island currency. It did not bode well for future interstate economic cooperation when Massachusetts, New Hampshire, and Connecticut passed laws exempting their own citizens from having to accept Rhode Island currency as payment from Rhode Island debtors. Next came the stories about Shays's Rebellion. First, the newspapers wrote of the harsh decision by the Massachusetts legislature to insist on tax payments in specie (coin), which was itself a dear commodity in the backcountry. Massachusetts' decision to send in troops was far more alarming for many outside of New England, because *their* governments *would not have done that*. Such reckless behavior could have triggered an uprising in a region already angry over New York's continued blackballing of Vermont in Continental Congress, a single vote that, because of the rules of the Articles of Confederation, continued to keep the fourteenth original state in limbo.

The end result of the fiasco of the "Continentals" was a stengthening of the movement toward a stronger federal government – not because one class of "creditors" wished to regain power that had fallen into the hands of a class of "debtors" but because it had become clear that the state money supplies were interdependent. The actions of one state could dramatically impact on the fortunes of another, and there was no mechanism by which to regain balance.

The state legislatures had thought that freedom was a return to "normalcy" – but it was not. The prewar distribution of power had included one element that would prove to be necessary in the new environment: the Board of Trade. The new states needed some entity with enough power to prevent a rogue state from damaging the economies of its neighbors. The "negative" tone of the Constitution – prohibiting behaviors rather than promoting them – borrowed heavily on the experience of living with the Board of Trade, which seldom acted, but always remained a presence in decision-making because of the limits that were set on any individual colony's ability to improvise.

War finance had other implications for the life of the Confederation government. Unable to tax, unable to distribute a form of currency that would hold its value, the Confederation turned to creditors at home and abroad. Domestic lenders contributed ten times the financing of foreign governments, but the debts owed the latter would present far more of a political problem.

Wars both ruin and create fortunes, and it can be sheer luck on which side of the line a person finally lands. The Revolution created a cocky *nouveau riche* class that had learned to use government to get its way. On paper, and from the distance of a century, it might look as if those who had purchased congressional debt instruments were being cheated out of their due compensation by the refusal of most states to prioritize that debt over others, but this view ignores the reality that there were many ways in which to obtain extended credit for the war effort, and the purchase of paper bills of credit was only one. By turning first to straightening out the internal tangle of private loans and public taxes, translating nominal values into real, the states wisely chose to return their own economies to a semblance of order *first*. Most states were intensely conscious of the burdens their soldiers had suffered and had no intention of compounding those burdens just so that one segment of the population could escape their share of the economic losses of the war. As nationalist activist James Wilson pointed out, many of those who held the congressional debts by the mid-1780s had purchased them during the years of wild price movements; they did so fully aware of the risks, and they were just going to have to wait until the postwar turmoil settled down. In short, it was the Massachusetts legislature and Boston creditors who fomented rebellion – not Shays and his neighbors. But the aggressive war creditors did foreshadow the way financial disputes would be handled in the future. The agricultural nation-states of eighteenth-century America were long used to operating with real values, not nominal values, as their guide – much to the dismay of their British overseers. A new generation of lawyers and financial speculators had arisen, who would insist upon the claims of paper documents as having primacy over other forms of evidence in the completion of economic transactions. The spirit of a contract would get lost in the lawyers' determination to enforce the language. In part this shift was inevitable: colonists had become used to the flexibility of the local courts, run by local men or rising professional politicians with no desire to anger their constituents. Powerless to act formally to prevent both Parliament, and British investors in the American colonial system from selling promises to the ambitious, Americans had often turned to their local courts for redress where, using "custom" as the yardstick rather than the language of a contract signed 2,000 miles overseas, a local judge could prevent the unfair confiscation of a farm with two generations of improvements by negotiating a satisfactory solution for the English speculator. Similarly, local judges had protected the interests of American merchants who trafficked in illegal West Indies trade with foreign islands by refusing to enforce the penalties for smuggling – after the merchants had negotiated a "fair" deal with the customs collectors for a lower sum.

The newly independent nation-states were going to have to come to terms with the reality that *they* were now the rule-makers, and that mischievous behavior used to evade British laws could now be turned on them. Conversely, the citizenry had to learn that they no longer needed to revert to traditional means of getting the government's attention – such as taking over the courts. In a republic, such unpopular policies passed by one's government could be changed simply by changing the representatives in the government. In the mid-1780s, the countryside reverted to traditional methods and stopped court proceedings until the legislatures listened to their needs. Shays's farmers lost in the first round, when the Massachusetts army freed the courts and returned them to business as usual. However, they won the second by voting out the legislature that had made that choice. In 1794, Washington's prominent military occupation of western Pennsylvania shocked those who believed the rebels to be well within their political rights; but the lesson learned once again was that it was not necessary to capture the courts when you could change the government itself by voting. Washington's actions settled the issue of state vs. federal jurisdiction, overruling Pennsylvania's request for mediation by sending in troops, but it also set the stage for the end of the Federalist phase of national government and Jefferson's "revolution" of 1800.

All governments make choices regarding the difference between *real* economic transactions, and their paper representations. Unpredictable external shifts in the value of money or short-term natural disasters that left some debtors temporarily unable to honor their contracts had been viewed by colonial legislatures and courts, in general, as outside the realm of normal economic activities. Nonpayment of debts because of an unusual situation was different from nonpayment of debts because the debtor had proved incompetent in his affairs. The colonials understood that contracts contained underlying assumptions about the future, and were loath to assign windfall gains or windfall losses to either party when those assumptions had been dramatically altered through no one's fault.

Ironically, the federal courts would adamantly refuse such leeway for individuals, yet they saw nothing wrong with structuring a legal mechanism by which groups of investors could enjoy that very privilege. The institution of the corporation reinstated the practical views of colonial judges and legislators by permitting individuals limited liability when a corporation went bankrupt – that is, mechanisms were instituted to try to prevent risk-taking investment from ruining entrepreneurs entirely. How was this different when the entrepreneur was a farmer and the risk-taking involved improvements to the land? Theoretically, not at all. The Pennsylvania Society of Friends' effective bankruptcy procedures for farmers were identical in purpose and theory to the incorporation and bankruptcy laws of the early national period. Contemporary historians are so used to the legal fiction of the corporation as individual and the legal construction of "limited liability" that they have forgotten both are as artificial an imposition upon the "free market" as the older tradition of restructuring nominal debts after a period of rapid price changes, or protecting the farmers' investment in improvements upon the land by holding off foreclosures after unforeseen disasters. Why would one be considered morally correct and the other not? Because historians have forgotten that both involved deliberate choices as to the parameters within which the so-called "free market" would operate.

In the long run, federal emphasis on nominal contracts over real economic evidence stemmed not from the policies of

Alexander Hamilton or Robert Morris, but from the needs of southern slaveowners to draw very rigid lines in the law with regard to the type of "property" they referred to as "slaves." Southern totalitarianism required the most strict enforcement of anything having to do with the rights of slaves – or those who might be slaves (Americans of African descent). The fierce nature of the fight over the *Amistad* affair (Africans bound for New World slavery took over the slave ship, only to find themselves in a New England jail indicted for piracy on the high seas – the Africans won at the local level, but the Federal Government took the case all the way to the Supreme Court where, astonishingly, they won again) demonstrates the degree to which southern leadership felt there could be no grey areas with regard to the laws that kept one-tenth of the national population in permanent bondage. This rigid enforcement of contract over common sense became embedded in American economic jurisprudence, to the benefit of those who later formed corporations. The Supreme Court decisions creating the corporate structure and defense of the contract so praised for encouraging American risk-taking and, hence, economic growth was made by southern-dominated courts. Later, a southern-dominated court would choose to apply the Fourteenth Amendment (protecting the rights of citizens) in defense of corporations' rights to engage child labor, striking down child labor laws – yet refuse to apply it in defense of the rights of southerners of African descent to put forward candidates for office and vote. The political economy of southern slaveholding was very different from that of the small family farm economy that dominated revolutionary America – when searching for the changes in the political and economic parameters that ensued in the next century, historians have erred in omitting the role of southern slaveholding totalitarianism.

There is no way of telling whether the states would have continued to choose differently from the Federal Government. The same decision-makers controlled state legislatures who would control federal courts. Over the nineteenth century the value of the paper contract would become increasingly important to those who lived in slaveholding regions. Large slaveholders were far more powerful in the Federal Government than non-farming capitalist entrepreneurs, even when outnumbered by northerners, because they voted in blocks. Their descendants would continue to shape national economic policy disproportionately through southern control of Congress for decades after the war ended. This approach to republican government, where the opposition is not debated but demonized, is once again exerting enormous influence over federal policies.

One more issue involving debtors and courts during the revolutionary era needs to be clarified. In Virginia, there were three types of debts that were being debated in the state legislature over this period. First, there was Virginia's share of the war effort, debts the state owed to Congress and Congress owed to creditors. Second, there were the same valuation problems experienced throughout the colonies, brought about by the rapid rise and fall of prices during the war. A third problem pertained to tobacco producers who had been able to avoid paying off their debts to British creditors through the war, and now wanted to forget them altogether. England made repayment of these *private* debts to English citizens a condition of the peace, but only Virginia could enforce it. Somehow these three very different problems have been conflated into one by generations of historians. The perceived moral issues – and contractual obligations – in the three situations were *very* different. Hence, Shenandoah voters could favor the restructuring of personal debts, oppose the plan to obliterate all private debts to British citizens, and be completely indifferent to the problem of Virginia's share of the Continental debts. Once again, it is easy to see why most active politicians of the day believed the holders of the federal debt were just going to have to wait a while – it did not come from any theoretical animosity towards creditors, or a desire to welsh on payments now that the hard times were over. Rather, there were many difficult problems on the agenda of each state legislature, and those of the federal creditors clearly fell pretty low on the scale of immediate priorities. The cavalier treatment by Congress of their citizen-soldiers' needs for provisioning and payment due for services had not encouraged state legislators to push Congress's needs any further up the queue.

In general, the state governments handled the financial disruption caused by the war competently, restoring their economies to normalcy within a surprisingly short period of time. There were three financial issues, however, that the states did not – and could not – deal with, and these proved increasingly troubling as the states tried to return to the old *status quo*.

The international debt posed a far more serious potential danger than that of the internal creditors. The most important source of overseas financial capital during the war had been England's enemies, France and the Netherlands. For both nations and their nationals, the Confederation took on a significance far exceeding its reality – a misconception that congressional diplomats Ben Franklin, Thomas Jefferson, and John Adams did little to discourage. The reality of a set of fairly independent nation-states, rather than a unified nation with a number of subsidiary governments, would not have looked promising to Europeans. Far better to stress the paper identity of the Confederation than admit to the absence of any real powers in Congress. Conversely, European financing was late to arrive, and nowhere near sufficient to pay the direct costs of the war. As a consequence, many state politicians never fully understood the significance or size of the foreign debt.

European nationals read the impotence of Congress in this matter as a sign of disrespect and immaturity at first, a sign of dangerous impotence as time went on. No matter how responsible individual states were in their fiscal practices, the chances of receiving financing from abroad were distinctly lessened by the inability of Congress to at least make a dent in the monies owed abroad. Far worse, if the European nations began to sense that Congress could not control the eastern seaboard of the United States (let alone the large western territories still in possession of Amerindian nations), they might act to protect – or further – their

own interests in the area. Spain posed a real danger in the South with its possessions in Florida, along the Gulf Coast, and across the Mississippi. Spanish troops began to venture out from the Gulf Coast into Creek and Choctaw lands for the first time in two centuries (having been convinced very early on that the interior had nothing to offer them that warranted facing the fierce resistance of these two well-entrenched nations). Rumors reached Congress that Spanish soldiers were occupying Mussel Shoals in the northwest hinterland of South Carolina. The new settlers of the Pittsburgh and Kentucky regions were themselves alarmed by Spain's threats to shut down their access to the port of New Orleans, the most cost-efficient path for trading goods between the Ohio Valley and the Atlantic Coast. For some state legislators, the foreign threat was becoming very real – but for others, it remained distant and inconsequential compared to local problems. As Congress increasingly failed to reach a quorum, those with interests to the west increasingly fretted over the dangers.

At the same time, Great Britain had put into effect the obvious: if the American states were no longer part of the British Empire, then they would no longer have trading privileges with the British West Indies. Many Americans had convinced themselves that West Indian merchants would never permit this in Parliament – but the West Indies were losing favor in London. The prohibition hurt some merchants worse than others; Americans were too experienced at smuggling to be completely denied access anywhere so far from London. However, the appropriate response in the international game of trade regulation would be for the Americans to place a tax on imports of British manufactured goods – giving West Indian representatives an ally in their fight for open trade. The newspapers were full of complaints about British factors (representatives of merchant houses) "dumping" manufactured goods onto the market by simply unloading their ships and holding an auction, bypassing the shopkeepers entirely. The reader should keep in mind that this "dumping" was unfortunate from the point of view of a shopkeeper specializing in British manufactures, but a wonderful boon for consumers who purchased British goods. Shopkeepers and merchants joined together to pass a strong tariff on British imports. The dangers of leaving the main powers of economic policy in the hands of the states became apparent once more. Three times Congress tried to enact a law taxing British imports. But, *Congress did not have the power to tax*. Each state had to pass identically worded legislation for the tariff to take effect, and every attempt Congress made was stymied by one state – ironically, a different state each of the three times (Rhode Island, New York, and Pennsylvania).

Those states dependent upon international ports outside their borders were also becoming increasingly frustrated by having to pay taxes on imports through their natural trading ports that would benefit only the neighboring state government. New Hampshire and parts of Connecticut were dependent upon Boston; western Connecticut and northern New Jersey dependent upon New York City; southern New Jersey and Delaware (as well as the great backcountry through Virginia into the Carolinas) dependent upon Philadelphia, and, with the wartime destruction of Norfolk, the Virginia tidewater found itself dependent upon Baltimore. New Jersey, Delaware, and Connecticut advertised tax-free ports. Wilmington succeeded in capturing Philadelphia's flour export trade (and hence the milling industry that accompanied it), but imports continued to go through Philadelphia. New Jersey and Connecticut drew up flyers to distribute overseas, advertising Perth Amboy, Burlington, and New Haven, respectively, as free ports, but the stranglehold of Philadelphia and New York City on their international trade could not be broken. From their perspective, not only was Congress impotent to pass a tariff that seemed an obvious diplomatic necessity, but Congress also could not step in to require the fortunate states with international ports to share some of that revenue with their less fortunate neighbors.

Virginia tried several approaches to the disadvantage of having no international port. Advertising Alexandria as a free port would not have been particularly helpful,

since Baltimore was already thriving with this method. Instead, Virginia enacted a law to tax foreign products brought across state lines into Virginia – a tax that collectors found exceedingly difficult to enforce, and when enforced, never really distinguished between imported manufactures and goods manufactured in other states, specifically Pennsylvania. At the same time, Virginia enacted a law taxing goods brought into Virginia ports on "foreign bottoms" (ships), the definition of "foreign" being any ship not manufactured in Virginia. Whereas the taxation of Pennsylvania products could be portrayed as inadvertent, this law clearly violated the proscription in the Articles that states would not tax each other's products. Congress issued a formal complaint; Virginia apologized and promised to do better – but as the state legislature had once played games with such restraints set on their powers by London, they now did the same with Congress. They did nothing; the laws remained on the books. Fortunately, the laws proved inconsequential because overland taxation was very difficult to enforce, and the tax on foreign shipping ended up encouraging trade through Georgetown, Maryland, on the opposite shore, instead of helping Virginia's shipbuilding industry. The point had been made, and so noted, however: despite the clear language of the Articles of Confederation, Congress had no powers with which to prevent a state enacting protective tariffs against other states. Over the next half century, the states would enter into intense competition among themselves in the race to capture the western trade. Because the Constitution created a more powerful government than that of Congress, their only tools were internal improvements and minor local boosterism. The nineteenth century would have proceeded very differently had the states retained powers to compete by enacting trade barriers, instead of investing in infrastructure.

When George Washington was a young surveyor for the Ohio Company two decades earlier, he had seen the future: trade with the Ohio Valley. Now that the war had ended, he set about to secure for Arlington (conveniently located next to his home at Mt. Vernon) the role of the "next"

Philadelphia by diverting the western trade down the Potomac instead of across the mountains to Philadelphia, or by the Mississippi–Gulf of Mexico route to existing Atlantic ports. Hence his great project of the period: the Chesapeake and Delaware Canal. This project would, however, require the cooperation of the neighboring state of Maryland, and here arose the third problem with Congress's inability to act.

Washington called for a bilateral commission between Maryland and Virginia to regulate trade. Representatives of both states met at Mt. Vernon in 1785 to iron out a set of agreements on legislation to enact in each state during the next session. Washington's pet project of creating a route west required as a first step that the Potomac River be dredged and locks installed at the lower falls. Second, basic rules for fishing rights in the Chesapeake Bay had to be agreed upon. Both groups agreed on a set of identical tariffs on imported goods. Finally, the representatives agreed to set Virginia and Maryland paper currency at par – in effect to join their currencies into one.

Only the dredging of the Potomac met with any serious opposition. The Baltimore papers complained loudly that Maryland should not be in the business of diverting trade from Baltimore to a city in a "foreign state," as one letter-writer referred to Virginia. Maryland itself was in the midst of negotiations with Pennsylvania to have the Susquehanna River dredged – the issue was finally resolved by a tradeoff whereby Pennsylvania agreed to dredge the Susquehanna if Maryland would permit Pennsylvania to construct a canal across the upper end of the Delmarva Peninsula, connecting the two great bays, the Chesapeake and the Delaware. Washington offered to set up a trilateral conference with Pennsylvania and Maryland, which soon mushroomed into a proposal for a multistate conference on trade to be held in Annapolis the following year.

At this point many who were knowledgeable about political economic theory became alarmed. If the states signed separate treaties regarding trade and money *outside* of Congress, the Confederation Government would die. The Annapolis convention itself

was a failure – Maryland refused to send representatives because the Maryland legislature did not want to do anything to scuttle the Articles. The New England delegation was late to arrive, and Alexander Hamilton took that opportunity to call for another convention, to be held in the summer of 1787 in Philadelphia, to amend the Articles of Confederation to include powers of taxation, specifically tariffs, and perhaps other powers to determine economic policy.

Once again, those knowledgeable in political economy voiced the fear that such an amendment would vest too much power in Congress. With Rhode Island's printing presses churning out paper money, Massachusetts' army marching on western farmers, Spain rattling sabers in the southwest, Britain refusing to evacuate Great Lakes forts, Virginia proving that Congress could not stop a state from enacting and enforcing protective tariffs, and the impost having failed once again to pass Congress, political leaders began seriously to consider the probability that the states had no choice: they would have to give up a portion of their precious rights to control economic policy to a larger central government.

As the Maryland legislature had commented in refusing to attend the Annapolis conference, granting the right to tax, to control trade, and to manage the money supply would confer upon Congress a level of sovereignty the Confederation had never possessed. Once delegates became convinced that this would have to be done, they also realized that the structure of the Articles of Confederation was inadequate to handle the powers that would soon be conferred. Hence, a meeting that was first called to amend the Articles had already become a convention to create a whole new Federal Government, with a new Constitution modeled on those in force in the 14 states, before the delegates even arrived in Philadelphia. A weak protest by New Jersey was quickly outvoted, and the delegates set down to the real task of creating a new nation – and ending the period of the individual nation-state.

The Constitution was first and foremost a political document. When historians reach back and try to read a significant shift in economic theory, power, or practice into the document, they ignore the history of the colonial/state legislatures through generations of local rule, and a little more than a decade of independent nation-state status. There was no need to "protect private property" – Anglo-American jurisprudence leaned heavily on contract law, and private property had been "protected" from the first day of settlement. Differences could arise over the definitions of property and ownership – whether the spirit or the letter of a contract should be enforced – but no one in the colonies seriously contested the validity of contract law.

The economics of the Constitution consisted in the shift from total control over economic policy within the states, to control over significant segments of economic policy by the new Federal Government. Since these policies carried with them enormous powers, the Federal Government had to be structured in a manner comparable to the states, with particular attention made to the checks and balances that prevented one faction from dominating the government. These men were well seasoned in discussing these issues. Individual states had chosen different mechanisms; individuals differed on how much power to leave in the hands of state and local governments – but the basic issue was not in dispute. *If* Congress was to be handed the powers of taxation, international trade regulation, full powers to enforce interstate trade disputes, and control over the money supply (imperative to New Englanders), *then* a new government structure equal to the task of using those powers had to be created.

The finished product was *almost* satisfactory, but not quite. The Constitution would not have been ratified had there not been an agreement to add a set of amendments ensuring the rights of individuals – particularly with regard to the courts – and the continued rights of states to practice those powers that had not been ceded to the new government. The first Congress fulfilled its obligation and passed what is known today as the Bill of Rights, the first ten amendments. The significance of the Bill of Rights is one reason that Madison's "Federalist X" is wholly inadequate as an intepretation of

the Constitution: at the time, Madison staunchly opposed the idea. Only later, when he understood the amendments were inevitable, did he step forward to write them (to retain control over their content). The Constitution was born out of disputes over the proper relationships among society, economics, and government – in the end, with the Bill of Rights attached, it succeeded because it embodied compromise between contending theories, rather than the full conquest by holders of one view over those of another. To portray the Constitution as if it had been handed down from a mountain carved on stone tablets, or to use Madison as the embodiment of the sentiments of a mythical set of politicians called the "Founding Fathers," is to completely ignore the actual debates in favor of a carefully created myth. By ignoring the degree to which the construction of the new nation came about because of the willingness of Federalists to agree to attach a Bill of Rights, we fail to see the degree to which disagreement was both institutionalized and given a peaceful outlet. Furthermore, the reliance today by jurists on *Federalist X* dooms us to an interpretation formed at the beginning of this century by scholars steeped in British contract law, nineteenth-century British theories of the fixed stages of economic history and the progressive march to "rational" government, *and* a period of history where southern political economy still had enormous influence on the national landscape through the Supreme Court and the domination of Congress through committee chairmanships. It is difficult to see the original meanings of the Constitution through all the veils of interpretation that later generations have placed upon it.

3 The Political Economy of Revolutionary America

The historiography of the revolutionary economy is way overdue for revisions. A longstanding historical focus on the well-being of merchants, or international trade, is misleading because neither was representative of the period, nor a harbinger of the future. True enough, British economic growth coincided with the introduction of textile mills and the rise in factory production – but the same was not true of America. There is no single model of economic modernization; different countries have taken different paths, at different times. In the American case, there were few gains to be made from cramming large numbers of women and children into a four-storey building for 70-hour weeks. Most Americans well understood that the nation's trading advantage came from its agricultural sector, which had the added bonus of providing a healthy way for children to grow up.

The underlying basis of American economic growth to 1880 was rapid innovation in farm family production, based on changes both in agriculture and in household work. Manufactured products from new types of plows, to combines, to the vacuum-sealed glass bottle contributed to this massive increase in productivity. However, innovation in finance, reductions in transportation costs, and the rapid distribution of information within the farming sector (made possible by very high literacy rates) were equally important. Labor productivity in agriculture increased *fourfold* to 1880. The foundations of economic modernization in America occurred not in factories but on farms.

The participation of the revolutionary period in the commencement of American economic growth can best be explained by examining three important innovations of the late eighteenth century. In 1790, Oliver Evans built a fully automated flour mill on the banks of the Red Clay Creek near Wilmington, Delaware: a single worker poured the grain into the top of the mill, and the finished product, finely milled flour, emerged at the bottom already bagged. A second important innovation was the application of the steam engine to river travel on the Delaware River and the Hudson. The third was the creation of a more efficient butter churn, essential to the growing dairy industry in southeast Pennsylvania – an industry run by women. In all three cases, the goal was to save *time* and *distance*. Time was a precious commodity to farming families, who often juggled several different

sources of income to make more efficient use of family skills. Transportation costs were the greatest impediment to the formation of internal markets; the soldiers at Valley Forge went hungry while large supplies of foodstuffs piled up in Winchester, Virginia, because they could not get the product to the source of the demand. Finally, Pennsylvania flour may have been destined for southern Europe or the West Indies – increasingly, however, it ended up in New England, where the Hessian fly had destroyed the area's wheat products and they now had to import grain. A thriving trade in dairy products to support the city of Philadelphia replaced the earlier wheat-growing economy of the near counties in southeast Pennsylvania; as early as the 1740s women in Chester County marketed large amounts of butter and cheese to the iron-milling town of Coventry Forge. Steamboats were used for internal trade, not overseas shipping. In short, the economy of America was turning inward.

Both economic and demographic statistics support the contention that by 1750, domestic trade was increasing at a far more rapid pace than international. The Great Valley of the Appalachians, America's first "Midwest," was settled between the 1730s and 1750s; by the second generation the arduous work of farm investment was mostly complete. The first building constructed was usually a Presbyterian church (that doubled in the afternoon as Lutheran); next came the tavern. By the 1750s, the region was dotted with water-driven mills for making flour and fulling wool. The inland city of Lancaster (one of the ten largest cities in the new United States) had once traded German-manufactured linens east to Coventry Forge in exchange for iron products west; by the Revolution the city was known for its innovative "rifle," a long-barreled gun with a "rifled" spiraling groove inside the barrel, the first truly accurate shooting weapon. Later known as the Kentucky rifle, Lancaster's rifles supplied the backcountry sharpshooters of the Revolution who so terrorized the British Army on the march from Charleston to Yorktown. Carlisle and Reading, Pennsylvania, were known for hat production; other inland towns would produce boots on a mass scale for the war effort. The Great Valley of the Appalachians, which spread from Albany southwest to Winston-Salem, North Carolina, could hardly be called a "frontier" in 1776, let alone 1790.

With the war's end, agriculture settlement rapidly expanded west. The spark that started the Seven Years' War (French and Indian War) came from young George Washington's attempts to survey southwest Pennsylvania for the Virginia partners in the "Ohio Company." By the 1780s, the Pittsburgh region was contested territory claimed by both Pennsylvania and Virginia; Congress ruled that the Mason-Dixon line be extended; whatever was to the north would belong to Pennsylvania. By then, however, settlers were already pushing along down the Ohio River into central Kentucky, joining other settlers who had come overland. Kentucky was so densely populated that Congress declared it a state in 1792; Tennessee became a state in 1796, and only seven years later Ohio was added. Although sometimes the settlement process was eased by the takeover of a village site abandoned by a defeated Amerindian nation, such rapid development entailed a very high rate of capital formation – cleared land, barns, houses, outbuildings, fences, roads, and public buildings; the growth of crossroads villages such as Gettysburg, Winchester, Staunton, and Salem; the beginning of urban development at Pittsburgh, Cincinnati, Lexington.

The coastal cities expanded as well: New York City, Philadelphia, Baltimore, Boston, Charleston, Newport, and many others grew rapidly in population despite the movement of many urban dwellers to the west. Philadephia's newspapers in the 1780s described fights between crews of ships trying to dock in the same space at the crowded port. In this context, the petty ups and downs of a few coastal merchants hardly seem representative of the larger picture of economic growth. If trans-Atlantic trade stagnated or even declined, it was more than balanced by the enormous expansion westward. What did it matter if New England merchants had not yet reached the point where they were building profitable

textile mills? Real investment was taking place all over the new nation. The economy of postwar America was clearly thriving.

The rural world of small, family-run farms, crossroads villages, taverns, mills, and churches extended from Maine west to the Connecticut and Hudson River Valleys; south through the Mid-Atlantic into the Eastern Shore of the Chesapeake in one direction, Charlottesville in the other; and from Albany southwest down the Great Valley of the Appalachians – the Lehigh, Lebanon, and Cumberland Valleys of Pennsylvania, the Shenandoah and the Great Valley of Virginia, finally spilling out into the Carolina interior. It extended through mountain passes into the new West. There was not yet a delineated North and South (contemporaries spoke of "the East," or New England, the middle colonies, the south, and the backcountry). Slave-owning families traveled west, but slaves were not profitable on wheat- or corn-growing farms and it was amazing how quickly one's conscience could speak up against an institution when it was no longer of use. The two major centers of slaveholding remained in the Chesapeake and low-land South Carolina. At the time of the writing of the US Constitution, Virginia had the largest number of free Blacks in the nation. Free Blacks farmsteaded in New Jersey, Pennsylvania, and Massachusetts; Philadelphia's free black population was itself the size of a small city, and had just created the first free congregation run by Blacks for Blacks, the first African Methodist Episcopal Church. Free Americans of African heritage formed a large percentage of the mariner population; others practiced artisan trades and a few became merchants.

Was there a moment when slavery could have been ended by government fiat, rather than bloody war? If so, this was that moment: in Philadelphia, in 1787, when the motion was put before the convention to include an emancipation clause in the new Constitution. But the moment passed. Some form of an anti-slavery clause (perhaps modeled after the ones being passed in the North at the time, freeing all slaves born after a certain year at the age of 21 and thus slowly abolishing the institution) probably could have won enough votes to be included. But only a small minority of delegates felt passionately that slavery should be banned, and South Carolina threatened to walk if the subject was even discussed. South Carolina's delegates hinted at a possible alliance with Spain to the south and west if the Constitution prohibited slavery. Should someone have called South Carolina's bluff? Two hundred years later, it is easy to fervently wish they had. But they did not.

When questioned later, some delegates claimed that they did not act because they believed slavery to be on its way out as an institution. It certainly appeared that way in Virginia, where the major slave stronghold, the Chesapeake, was suffering greatly from economic decline. No one ever got the chance to find out, because within a decade the parameters had shifted once more. Eli Whitney's invention of the cotton gin gave new life to the institution, rendering slaveholding intensely profitable on plantations far west of the Atlantic Coast. In an unseemly disregard for their fathers' dying wishes, young heirs dragged wills into court that had freed the family slaves at the patriarch's death, and had them broken on technicalities. In the grab for more slaves, woe unto the free Black who fell into debt, for he could be sold back into slavery. Who knows how many Blacks lost their freedom surreptitiously in the rapid grab for slaves that followed the news that cotton could be profitably produced in the US? Who knows how many freed Blacks snatched back into slavery were directly related to those who stole their lives away once more? Virginia had very few free Blacks when the next census was taken. Those who remained free left.

By 1800, the North and the South were formed and fixed, one free, one slave, guaranteeing that one day war would erupt over the continued incarceration of one group of Americans by another. This was no hazy medievalist throwback, pre-capitalist traditional society, slow and foolish in its insistence on the maintenance of a dying way of life. Slaveowning was reborn in the 1790s because it was *profitable*. Until the first years

of the Civil War, investment in slavery outperformed any type of investment in manufacturing or transportation. And this does not even take into account the bonus of the cheap labor. Many economists have tried to estimate whether slaves earned as much as free labor. The question is absurd. If slaves had received compensation equal to that of free Blacks, *they would not have had to be enslaved*. But they could not be treated as if they were free, because the most essential goals of all American householders were violated by the very institution. Slaveowners would not give up control over the destiny of slave families, or children born into slavery. In a society that valued the economic independence of the household above all, slavery required the cruelest of sacrifices. And everyone (except, of course, slaves and free Blacks), pretended not to notice.

When historians use the concept of "precapitalism," or "pre-market mentalities," or any other narrowly defined economic category to gerrymander slavery outside the economic history of America, they are only following the lead of generations of South Carolina intellectuals who also went to a great deal of effort to present themselves as "different." Since *we* no longer permit slavery, that rather lets us all off the hook. It was a "peculiar" institution without consequence or guilt. These were not the *ad hoc* reasonings of armchair pamphleteers: many of the theories southerners would use to defend slavery (and later segregation) were constructed by an economics professor at the University of South Carolina in the 1830s, and were on the cutting edge of the romantic nationalist school of economics at the time. How ironic that he would eventually leave South Carolina for Germany, where these theories flourished and eventually gave rise to the concept of national socialism – or Nazism. Stripped bare of the fiction of medieval remnants or non-market behavior, the institution of slavery (and segregation) can only be described as the explicit creation of a terroristic, totalitarian state, for the sole purpose of financial profits for those in power.

In 1787, there was a moment when slavery could have been ended by the stroke of a pen. South Carolina and Georgia might have been lost to the United States – and with them, Alabama and Mississippi (still territories of those two states). Conversely, slavery might have been too expensive for this small segment of the continent to hold on to by themselves. The success of the Northwest Ordnance in keeping slavery out of all territories north of the Ohio suggests that anti-slavery laws could have been obeyed. The mad grab for slaves at the end of the 1790s in Virginia suggests the opposite. One thing is clear: had the Revolution never occurred, the crisis over slavery would have arisen earlier rather than later, when Britain outlawed the institution in all British colonies. Barely a generation after the invention of the cotton gin, the law would have faced a South where slavery was now fully entrenched. Surely the result would then have been revolution, but of a very different nature than the one that occurred in 1776, and most likely with different boundaries. No, the moment when slavery had the least toehold on American society was 1787, and that moment was lost.

Whether or not a constitutional prohibition could have stopped the spread of slavery after the 1790s, the fact remains that no such effort was made. Can an omission be called an "effect"? Probably not, although eventually the full weight of the Constitution would be brought to bear on the last southern efforts to support slavery: in the Dred Scott decision, it was southern slave interests which claimed that "property rights" and "interstate commerce" overruled individual freedoms guaranteed by another state's constitution; likewise, it was Wisconsin which invoked states' rights to avoid having to enforce the Fugitive Slave Act, and a Southern Supreme Court which ruled that federal law prevailed. By not ending slavery, the Constitution carried with it tacit approval.

For the next several decades, the North would go its way, and the South another. For years southerners – and historians – agreed that the North's economic growth in the antebellum period was itself due to the institution of slavery, pointing to textile mills, financial advisers, and provisioners of plantation supplies. On closer analysis, however, it has become clear that the South

as a region was far more self-sufficient than everyone had assumed – indeed, the antebellum South was more diversified than it would be 50 years later. Southern markets were not essential to the maintenance of northern economic growth. One Constitution governed two very different political economies. What remnants of the needs of slaveowners remain embedded in our national institutions, in the ways we approach economic policy? Perhaps two: the conviction that some people do not "deserve" the same rights in America as others; and the loss of the original focus on the well-being of the individual household.

Honest appraisal of the economic and demographic consequences of the American Revolution requires the ability to admit complexity and paradox – and face the possibility that there could have been other outcomes by which all Americans shared in the prosperity that was restricted only to some. The historians who see only "economic growth," or "tradition and market," or "pre-capitalist and capitalist," only serve to support the intellectual mechanism that rendered this part of the American Revolution invisible, or at best, interesting but tangential to the "real story."

Neither the American Revolution nor the Constitution were based on a goal of freedom for the individual to earn what he/she wants, to spend what he/she wants, to ignore what he/she wants. "Independence" meant that households were *not dependent upon* others for their livelihood. "Freedom of choice" for one's children required a basic level of income so no one went without proper clothing, shelter, or food. Independence meant that the next generation would not be hampered by the untimely loss of a parent, or the inconvenience of five daughters instead of four sons. *Household independence* could only come from *household well-being*, and the promise of economic growth to provide an income base for future household independence in the face of tremendous population growth. Unmarried males, without a household to support, were taxed at enormously high rates to help those households with the wrong demographic mix to completely care for themselves.

The right to "life, liberty, and the pursuit of happiness" was the right to shelter, food, and clothing; and it was *inalienable* – could not be sold or bargained away, and most certainly did not have to be "earned."

In addition to a convenient lapse of memory that has forgotten that one-fifth of all Americans lived in slavery during the revolutionary period, our national histories also too easily assume that "westward expansion" was inevitable, that the nations between the 13 states and the Pacific Ocean were not "real" nations, and by extension, their peoples not "real" either.

The consequences of the war proved an unmitigated disaster for the millions of people living within nations geographically situated between the new United States and the Pacific Ocean. The so-called "western campaign" of the American Revolution, wherein Iroquois territory was invaded, conquered, and its inhabitants reduced to refugees on their own land, marked the beginning of 100 years of invasion, conquest, and banishment. The British would not have – could not have – stood in the way of their colonies' march to the Mississippi. However, they would have protected the boundary rights of Iroquoia and the Cherokee lands, forcing migration in other directions. Whatever the sins of the British Empire in India and Africa – and they were many – Indians and Africans lived on to reclaim their nations in modern times. A similar consequence within the boundaries of the United States today is unimaginable. Only the Navajo and Pueblo nations of the American southwest retain any significant portion of their native land, in part because of early Spanish occupation, and in part because no Europeans wanted the land. All hopes of a future America where present and past nations could have coexisted in peace ended in 1783, when European nations ceded all rights to remaining British lands to the new United States.

The long-run economic and demographic consequences of the American Revolution thus present us with an unavoidable paradox. The documents and institutions that provided the opportunity for household independence and economic growth for Americans of European descent, doomed those of African descent, and Amerindian nationals, to socio-economic totalitarianism and destruction. There are thus three very different stories that we could tell about the impact of the Revolution. Somehow we will have to learn to acknowledge these three stories without requiring that one be dependent upon the other, because that is an assumption, not a scholarly conclusion based upon consideration of the evidence. As historians once had to forget about the Revolution to understand the revolutionary era, we must now forget what we think was necessary or inevitable in the evolution of the three economic histories of America. Only when we have understood them as experienced at the time can we return to examining the interrelationships, multiple causalities, and perhaps find the turning points where a different choice could have been made. Only when we understand the *full* political economy of early America as it existed then, without deciding in advance which categories of person or economic activity are important, and which are irrelevant, will we be able to understand the long-run impact of that political economy on the documents that have shaped the history of this nation.

The goal of the American Revolution was to maintain the economic independence of households. This was not a privilege to be "earned," but an *inalienable* right – a right that could not be sold, bargained, or rationalized away. If we learn how to extend that goal to *all* members of *all* households, perhaps we can regain the best of the revolutionary political economy and finally let go of the worst.

FURTHER READING

Appleby, Joyce: *Capitalism and a New Social Order: The Republican Vision of the 1790s* (New York University Press, 1984).

Bailyn, Bernard and Philip D. Morgan: *Strangers Within the Realm: Cultural Margins of the First British Empire* (Chapel Hill: University of North Carolina Press, 1991).

Berlin, Ira and Ronald Hoffman, eds.: *Slavery and Freedom in the Age of the American Revolution* (Charlottesville: University of Virginia Press, 1983).

Carp, E. Wayne: *To Starve the Army at Pleasure: Continental Army Administration and American Political Culture, 1775–1783* (Chapel Hill: University of North Carolina Press, 1984).

Countryman, Edward: *The American Revolution* (New York: Hill and Wang, 1985).

Dowd, Gregory Evans: *A Spirited Resistance: The North American Indian Struggle for Unity, 1745–1815* (Baltimore: Johns Hopkins University Press, 1992).

Graymont, Barbara: *The Iroquois in the American Revolution* (Syracuse: Syracuse University Press, 1972).

Greene, Jack P. ed.: *The American Revolution: Its Character and Limits* (New York: New York University Press, 1987).

——: *Pursuits of Happiness: The Social Development of Early Modern British Colonies and the Formation of American Culture* (Chapel Hill: University of North Carolina Press, 1988).

Higginbotham, Don: *The War of American Independence: Military Attitudes, Policies, and Practice, 1763–1789* (NY: Macmillan, 1971).

——: *War and Society in Revolutionary America: The Wider Dimensions of Conflict* (Columbia: University of South Carolina Press, 1988).

Hoffman, Ronald, Thad W. Tate, and Peter Albert, eds.: *An Uncivil War: The Southern Backcountry During the American Revolution* (Charlottesville: University of Virginia Press, 1985).

Kerber, Linda: *Women of the Republic: Intellect and Ideology in Revolutionary America* (Chapel Hill: University of North Carolina Press, 1980).

McCoy, Drew R.: *The Elusive Republic: Political Economy in Jeffersonian America* (Chapel Hill: University of North Carolina Press, 1980).

McLeod, Duncan: *Slavery, Race and the American Revolution* (Cambridge: Cambridge University Press, 1974).

Middlekauff, Robert: *The Glorious Cause: The American Revolution, 1763–1789* (Oxford: Oxford University Press, 1982).

Nash, Gary B. and Jean R. Soderlund: *Freedom by Degrees: Emancipation in Pennsylvania and its Aftermath* (Oxford: Oxford University Press, 1991).

Nettels, Curtis P.: *The Emergence of a National Economy, 1775–1815* (New York: Holt, Reinhart and Winston, 1862).

Norton, Mary Beth: *Liberty's Daughters: The Revolutionary Experience of American Women, 1750–1800* (Boston: Little, Brown and Co., 1980).

Onuf, Peter S.: *Statehood and Union: A History of the Northwest Ordinance* (Bloomington: Indiana University Press, 1987).

Perkins, Edwin J.: *The Economy of Colonial America*, 2nd edn. (New York: Columbia University Press, 1988).

——: *American Public Finance and Financial Services, 1700–1815* (Columbus: Ohio State University Press, 1994).

Pole, J. R.: "Slavery and Revolution: the Conscience of the Rich," *Paths to the American Past* (Oxford: Oxford University Press, 1979).

Quarles, Benjamin: *The Negro in the American Revolution* (Chapel Hill, University of North Carolina Press, 1961).

Richter, Dan and James H. Merrill, eds.: *Beyond the Covenant Chain: The Iroquois and Their Neighbors in Indian North America, 1600–1800* (Syracuse: Syracuse University Press, 1987).

Schweitzer, Mary: *Custom and Contract: Household, Government and the Economy in Colonial Pennsylvania* (New York: Columbia University Press, 1987).

Shy, John: *A People Numerous and Armed: Reflections on the Military Struggle for American Independence* (New York: Oxford University Press, 1976).

Smith, Billy G.: *The 'Lower Sort': Philadelphia's Laboring People, 1750–1800* (Ithaca, NY: Cornell University Press, 1990).

White, Richard: *The Middle Ground: Indians, Empires, and Republics in the Great Lakes Region, 1750–1815* (Cambridge: Cambridge University Press, 1991).

Wood, Gordon S.: *The Creation of the American Republic, 1776–1787* (Chapel Hill: University of North Carolina Press, 1969).

CHAPTER SEVENTY

The religious consequences of the Revolution

ROBERT M. CALHOON

THE most immediate effect of religion on the newly independent American republic was ideological. Moderate Calvinism helped knit together into a coherent civic creed the two main divergent strands of revolutionary thought. The older of these was *contractualism*, derived from the Puritans and from John Locke. It justified revolution as the righteous response to the British tyranny which had violated the compact between the sovereign and the people. The newer one – also popularized and emphasized by Calvinist clergymen – was *republicanism*, originating in Cicero's Rome, resurrected by Renaissance civic humanists, adopted by English opposition theorists in the 1720s and 1730s and by Scottish moral philosophers two decades later, and thence transmitted to America in books and pamphlets as well as through the minds of publicists who crossed the Atlantic. Republicanism intermingled readily with Old Testament notions of a sinful people who had a Lockean covenant with a stern but loving Creator. Republicanism was communal and pessimistic; secularized Lockean Calvinism was optimistic and individualistic. Preachers, infusing both traditions with Biblical images, were particularly adept at combining and harmonizing these dark and light elements in patriot political consciousness.

1 Lockean Calvinism and Republicanism

New England Congregationalists

New England Congregationist sermons of the pre-revolutionary period enunciated the classic American reformulation of Locke. "Once it was acknowledged," in these pulpits, "that rulers were more likely to violate the common interest than were subjects," it was "reasonable to endow the people with a right to frame a constitution 'as the standing measure of the proceedings of government' for their own protection and to solicit their ruler's consent to it" (Buel, 1964, pp. 170–1). This discovery of divinely sanctioned fundamental law was profoundly conservative in the sense that it obligated subjects to be dutiful, watchful, and conscientious about public affairs, but also radical in its assumption that sinfulness concentrated within the bowels of government was far more immoral, destructive, and obnoxious to the Lord of the universe than the isolated misdeeds of individuals. The contract meant that, to counter the misdeeds of a ruler, the people had to act in concert with dignity, eloquent rhetoric, and personal self-sacrifice in order to vindicate the cause of liberty and the legitimate interests of the community.

As the struggle for liberty shifted from resistance to revolution a mutually constraining compact came under severe stress; accordingly New England clergymen took the lead in using millennial rhetoric and radical English opposition thought to express a darker and more desperate vision: images such as "the great whore of Babylon" from Revelation, as well as older notions of New England as the chronically sinning children of Israel who continually tested the patience of a loving but stern father, introduced just the note of terror into revolutionary politics that republicans such as Cicero or Machiavelli considered necessary to summon men to the common defense of liberty. Linking Lockean contractualism and the republican apprehension together most securely was the old idea of a Puritan ethic – a calling from God to every believer to consider salvation, talent, ambition, productivity, and family responsibilities as gifts of God to be employed with discipline and thrift. Revolutionary clergymen readily applied the Puritan ethic to politics, considering liberty itself a gift held in trust. Sacrifice in the public cause then became a purging, purifying experience which expelled dangerous poisons of selfishness, complacency, and political myopia from the human spirit and replaced them with life-giving qualities of zeal, energy, and sagacity. "We boast of liberty, and value ourselves much on being free, when at the same time we have been taken captive by Satan at his pleasure," explained one Massachusetts preacher in 1774: "This is a much more shocking absurdity than it would be for a man confined in a dungeon to boast that he is a liberty because he is not called on, in providence, to go into the field and labour," to which another added, "it is an indispensable duty, my brethren, which we owe to God and our country, to rouse up and bestir ourselves, being animated with a noble zeal for the sacred cause of liberty" (Stout, 1986, pp. 297–8).

North Carolina Presbyterians

Combining Lockean obligation and republican zeal, David Caldwell, a Presbyterian minister in piedmont North Carolina, blamed tyranny on human slothfulness – political inactivity, unreflectiveness, apathy and stupid concern with personal comfort – and he assigned to the spirit of God the task of redeeming the slothful and filling the human frame with activity, poise, and libertarian consciousness. The political and social implications of these tendencies in human nature, for Caldwell, were ominous. Throughout history "sloth" as a state of mind and body and as a moral condition had tempted rulers to exercise tyrannical power. The slothful were people who seemed, to arrogant and unreflective rulers,

to be fit objects of unbridled governmental coercion. The "ignorance, disregard of moral obligation, and supreme love of ease" of the groveling sluggard corresponded exactly with a tyrant's appetite and cynicism. Not only did the slothful encourage and facilitate oppression, their own "shame" and "sinking spirits," their own pitiful compliance and submission became self-made chains of slavery. The miraculous way in which God might intervene to preserve colonial liberty, Caldwell declared, would occur only as the Holy Spirit penetrated the encrustations of habit and lethargy and converted the soul, the conscience, the moral sense within the human frame into something graceful and swift and responsive (Calhoon, 1988, pp. 94–5).

The stresses of war strained this compound of Lockean and republican religious thought about politics. The savage irregular warfare in North Carolina during 1781 prompted Samuel McCorkle, a Presbyterian minister from Rowan County, North Carolina, to warn that "a plundering Whig is worse than a non-plundering Tory." "It is in your interest to join with the [latter], if disposed to join you, [and] to support and execute the laws upon the [former], if indisposed to repent or restore," he instructed North Carolina leaders in a sermon on "The Crime and Curse of Plundering." McCorkle equated plundering of helpless Tories with the looting of "silver and … gold and vessels of brass and iron" by an Israelite soldier named Achan in the Book of Joshua, which "kindled … the anger of the Lord against the children of Israel." McCorkle's argument, in fine republican pessimism, held that individual enterprise and enrichment did energize society but also had a corrosive influence. No one had a right to injure the public good in the pursuit of private gain, and in war the line between rational self-interest and besotted greed and vengeance became perilously thin (Calhoon, 1988, p. 80).

Chaplains in the Continental Army

Another vivid measure of the stress between Lockean duty and republican heroism appeared in the service of chaplains to the Continental Army. Abiel Leonard, minister of the Congregationalist church in Woodstock, Connecticut, joined Washington's army in early 1776. "He engaged early in the army and has been indefatigable in the duties of his station," observed General Nathanael Greene; "in a word he has done every thing in his power both in and out of the line of duty to promote the good of the service." A year later Leonard was sick and worried about the health and well-being of his family. On the way back from furlough, Washington reprimanded him for overstaying his leave. That night, while staying in a tavern and deeply depressed, he slit his throat with a razor. "The cut is so near his chin that the tongue is wounded and he cannot speak, but writes … [and has] expressed a great desire to get well." Leonard died 18 days later. Those who knew Leonard and his ability to inspire the troops attributed his wound to a "fit of lunacy, … how soon may reason be unsealed." Religious zeal functioned imperfectly as a remedy to the psychological toll taken by life in the army (Royster, 1979, pp. 173–4).

2 Nationalism: John Witherspoon and James Madison

With the successful winning of independence, Lockean and republican influences continued to inform American religious experience in two major ways. Nationalists such as John Witherspoon of the College of New Jersey at Princeton, and his student, James Madison, drew on both Lockean and republican traditions for guidance in political realism and a vision of the future of the republic based on both Enlightenment and Calvinist concepts of human nature. Localists and democrats, on the other hand, suspicious of concentrations of power and of hierarchies in society, used the same ideas to promote egalitarianism and anti-institutionalism.

Witherspoon's republicanism was a mixture of Calvinist doctrines of depravity and civic humanist notions about virtue. To enable them to understand evil, Witherspoon told his students that God had "implanted" in human beings "conscience, enlightened by reason, [by] experience, and [by] every way … we … learn the will of our Maker." This formulation was the very conception of

human nature that Witherspoon had condemned time and again in Scotland as leader of the orthodox wing of the Presbyterian Church of Scotland opposing the influence of Scottish moral philosophers, especially Francis Hutcheson. In 1758 he scornfully dismissed Enlightenment Christianity in Scotland as "a pliant and fashionable scheme of religion, a fine theory of virtue and morality" (Calhoon, 1988, p. 81).

Witherspoon's theological reorientation, following his installation as President of Princeton in 1768, has perplexed historians more than it did his contemporaries. American Presbyterians knew little of the ecclesiastical wars in Scotland, and the Trustees of the College of New Jersey were attracted to Witherspoon more for his reputed erudition and eloquence than for his orthodoxy. Once in America he sought to revitalize the finances and academic stature of the college by nurturing a new consensus among American Presbyterians based on Scottish moral philosophy as well as self-conscious piety.

Madison's analysis of constitutionalism easily adopted the framework Witherspoon had taught him at Princeton 17 years earlier. Witherspoon's didactic "virtue/vice" and "ethics/politics" polarities were, to start with, spacious and subtle enough to provide Madison a framework for an elegant, persuasive political theory. The creative tension in Witherspoon's concept of virtue and vice was his paradoxical treatment of human action as an expression of virtue and yet the dependence of such action on divine grace. Whether or not he resolved his paradox by assigning the moral sense a critical role in the work of redemption, or merely trusted that, in America, Providence would enhance the potency of virtue among sinful men, Witherspoon certainly did envision a symbiotic tie between vice and virtue which would fashion a secularized Calvinism that filled a real need in early national political culture.

Madison made the most of this discovery. "As long as the connection subsists between his reason and his self-love," he predicted, "[man's] opinions and his passions will have a reciprocal influence on each other," with passions "attach[ing] themselves" in dangerous ways to rational thought. "The first object of government" was to protect society from destructive jealousies over material inequality especially fomented by organized groups of factions united by a common sense of deprivation. "The latent causes of faction," Madison concluded, "are sown in the nature of man." Thence arose disputes over religion and politics, rivalries between the followers of different leaders, the influence of demagogues, and the persistence of "frivolous and fanciful" dissatisfactions. "But the most common and durable source of faction has been the various and unequal distribution of property" – debtors and creditors, "landed," "manufacturing," "mercantile," and "monied" interests. These political actors, left to their own devices, would "clog the administration" of government and "convulse the society."

Madison saw the solution in the ideological materials with which Americans were already familiar – and in human nature and social reality itself. He sought to remove the most prominent of the conditions: provinciality, isolation, and localized conflict, which encouraged "men of factious tempers, of local prejudices, or of sinister designs" to "obtain the suffrages and betray the interests of the people." "An extensive republic" would enlarge the pool of talented, public-spirited candidates for office and focus public attention on issues of the common weal. Admittedly, Madison adroitly conceded, the creation of a spacious republic carried with it the risk of "render[ing] the representative too little acquainted with all" the "local circumstances and lesser interests" of his constituents. But, turning this difficulty to his own advantage, Madison reminded his readers that these were the very circumstances that encouraged narrowly self-interested behaviour and made legislators "too little fit to comprehend and pursue great and national objects." Intrinsic to human society, according to Madison's formulation, was a kind of latent, moral inertia that could be overcome only by a quickened pace of moral stimulation and intellectual challenge (Calhoon, 1988, pp. 85–6). Jefferson's Virginia Statute for Religious Liberty was adopted by the legislature fortuitously in 1786 when support flagged for a clumsy but superficially popular plan for public subsidization of ministerial salaries. Madison seized this opportunity to discredit as well as defeat this "religious assessment" plan by arguing brilliantly that even non-sectarian governmental inculcation of religion would debase the human spirit and subvert the public good.

3 Religious Educational Philosophy: Benjamin Rush and Henry Allason

While eschewing direct public entanglement in religion, republicans employed religious teachings as well as Enlightenment philosophical arguments to construct an educational philosophy appropriate to the needs of the new nation. It taught, according to Benjamin Rush, that each "pupil … does not belong to himself but … is public property" (Yazawa, 1985, p. 143).

Rush believed that evangelical Christianity was a natural re-enforcement of republicanism and the only means of containing "the irregular and compulsive impulses of the human heart" which weaned individuals away from devotion to the common weal. The cause of liberty could have lasting meaning, he warned, only if it was a prelude to *"the salvation of all mankind"*:

Republican forms of government are the best repositories of the Gospel: I therefore suppose they are intended as preludes to a glorious manifestation of its power and influence upon the hearts of men. The language of these free and equal governments seems to be like that of John the Baptist of old, "Prepare ye the way of the Lord – make his paths strait."

If Christian discipleship was an antidote to the individualism of egocentric desires flying off in all directions, then, in Rush's thinking, infusing civic virtue with the "power" of "the gospel" would create a disciplined, sustainable experiment in republican government. Personal service to the community – especially moral leadership inspired by worship – would fill individuals with premonitions of immortality and assure them of fame beyond the grave. "How delightful to a good man should be the thoughts of surviving himself," he told Elhanan Winchester, who had just published a funeral sermon about John Wesley and a volume on prophesy:

your works however much neglected or opposed now will be precious to those generations which are to follow us ... The persons who are to exist a hundred years hence are as much our fellow creatures as ... are our contemporaries. It only requires more grace to love them than the persons whom we see ... every day; but in proportion as we attain to this supreme act of love, we approach nearer the source of all love.

That kind of ardent service of fellow souls yet unborn was, for Rush, the essence of republican self-denial.

Christianity in a republic appealed to Rush, not only as a way of fixing ambition on the spiritual well-being of others but also as the only reliable way of deepening personal consciousness and effecting a reformation of the deepest roots of behavior. By fusing republican notions about equality and virtue to Christian habits of introspection and humility, Rush developed a theory about education and discipline. "Solitude," he insisted, was the only appropriate form of discipline in a republic:

Too much cannot be said in favor of SOLITUDE as a means of reformation, which should be the *only* end of *all* punishment. Men are wicked only from not *thinking*. O! that they would *consider*, is the language of inspiration. A wheelbarrow, a whipping post, nay even a gibbet, are all light punishments compared with letting a man's conscience loose upon him in solitude. Company, conversation, and even business are the opiates of the Spirit of God in the human heart. For this reason, a bad man should be left for some time without anything to employ his hands in his confinement. Every *thought* should recoil wholly upon *himself*.

The process by which solitude turned an individual "wholly upon himself" was for Rush the essence of pious individualism (Rush, 1951, pp. 511–12, 611–12).

One evangelical schoolmaster found the process of inculcating virtue to be an especially compelling calling. "In order to be virtuous," Henry Allason, a self-educated Methodist teacher in Maryland, reminded himself in 1807, "a man must resist his propensities, inclinations, and tastes, and maintain an incessant conflict with himself" that is between the guidance of the "heart"

and the demands of "ambition" and public expectation. Learning to work through such experiences, Allason believed, required teachers who could "preside" over a schoolroom: "men well recommended, not given to intrigue and hence to loss of virtue. We should not ask if he is a wit, a bright man, a philosopher, but is he fond of children, does he frequent the unfortunate rather than the great?" Such a teacher would remember that the only punishment appropriate in a republican culture was exclusion of an offender from the company of other students, an "exile" proportionate to the seriousness of the offense and administered in a manner respectful of the student's personal dignity.

Tying these standards and assumptions together was Allason's belief that

nothing is durable, virtue alone excepted. Personal beauty passes quickly away, fortune inspires extravagant inclinations, grandeur fatigues, reputation is uncertain, talents, nay genius itself are liable to be impaired. But virtue is ever beautiful, ever diversified, ever equal, and ever vigorous because it is resigned to all events, to privations as well as to enjoyments, to death as to life, happy ... [am I] if I have been able to contribute ... toward redressing some of the evils which oppress my country and to open some new prospect of felicity.

Education for a republican like Allason was decidedly more public and shared than personal and private; happiness and virtue could only be known in civic activity. Allason felt this ideal constantly slipping away, retrievable only by recurrence to first principles of self-discipline and comradeship with others. To be a republican was to seize the day and live out a credo of public service and unselfishness before evanescent favorable circumstances evaporated (Calhoon, 1988, pp. 124–5).

4 New Evangelical Sects

In contrast with Enlightenment evangelicals such as Witherspoon and Madison, who conceived of constitutions and political discourse as instruments of "conflict resolution," the many Anti-Federalist Baptists and Methodists, and some Presbyterians, opposed ratification of the Constitution.

They valued instead "conflict management" as an ongoing function of churches and communities in which elites did not achieve predominance and irrepressible democratic impulses did not dissipate in the quest for national stability. Lemuel Burkitt, a Separate-Baptist minister in Hertford County, addressed large, spirited crowds during the ratification struggle in North Carolina. His "peroration did not address religious liberty, the constitutional issue historians have characteristically associated with religious dissenters in the South… Instead he raised an issue associated with the Harringtonian [republican] tradition of Anglo-American political thought, namely the dangers of a standing army and centralization of power" (Marini, 1990). This kind of localized, community rooted, communal evangelicalism swept away Congregationalism in northern New England during the revolutionary era, as Freewill Baptists, Shakers, and Universalists created hundreds of new churches. Influenced in part by the revivals in Nova Scotia led by Henry Alline, these radical sects on the outer edges of revolutionary New England developed in their worship and especially in their hymnody a "language of the soul" which was sensuous, personal, otherworldly, and didactic (Marini, 1982, pp. 156–71).

A less visible and more precarious variety of marginal evangelical churches were black churches in Wilmington, Charleston, Savannah, and elsewhere in the South. William Meredith, a Methodist missionary from the West Indies, settled in Wilmington in 1795, preached to Blacks, and organized an all-black congregation which built its own meeting-house. There Blacks conducted their own services for nearly 15 years until the arrival of the white Methodist minister William Capers, whose parishioners appropriated the "negro meeting-house" (Hinks, 1989, p. 34). Andrew Bryan, a slave owned by Whitefield's convert Jonathan Bryan, began preaching to Savannah Blacks in 1782. Fearful of slaves being taken away by the departing British, patriot officials in Savannah ordered him whipped, but he *"would freely suffer death for the cause of Jesus Christ"* (Raboteau, 1978, p. 141), a willingness to endure punishment like that of the

apostles in the book of Acts which shamed officials into releasing him.

The spread of evangelical Christianity among slaves and free Blacks in Virginia, the Carolinas, and Georgia after the Revolution sent unmistakable tremors throughout the region. A slave scare – fear of imminent servile uprising – in eastern North Carolina in 1802 took place in the very localities where biracial conversions and baptisms in 1822, led by Denmark Vesey, drew their ideology and inspiration from Christian millennialism. Probably influenced by Vesey, the first full-scale indictment of slavery written by an American Black, David Walker's *Appeal to the Coloured Citizens of the World* (1829), proceeded from the assumption that "the day of our redemption from abject wretchedness draweth near when we shall be enabled… to stretch forth our hand to the LORD our GOD, but there must be a willingness on our part for GOD to do these things for us!" (Hinks, 1989, p. 1).

Ultimately the most far-reaching religious consequences of the Revolution came between the 1820s and the 1850s, when evangelical zeal, a millennial sense of being a chosen people, and the new cultural milieu of romanticism combined to undergird a wide-ranging set of movements known as romantic reform. Some of the artistic and intellectual leaders for abolitionism, women's rights, public education, temperance, and the rights of Amerindians became Unitarians – those former Congregationalists who rejected orthodox theology – and their off-shoot the Transcendentalists, who sought to infuse rational religion with spiritual joy. But the rank and file of romantic reform movements came from evangelical churches and channeled the optimistic, Arminian, and millennial expectancy of religious revivalism in the early nineteenth century into a crusade to purify American society. James G. Birney, a Princeton graduate practicing law in Alabama in 1817, experienced conversion at a revival meeting. His first response to that religious experience was to become a lawyer for Amerindians being forced from their ancestral lands, and in 1832 he became an agent of the American Colonization Society. Disappointed in the response of other slaveowners to colonization, he moved to Kentucky and then to Ohio, where he edited abolitionist newspapers. In 1837 he became Secretary of the American Anti-Slavery Society and in 1840 and 1844 an anti-slavery candidate for President. New England missionaries to the Cherokees waged a long and losing struggle in the courts to protect that tribe from removal from Georgia to reservations west of the Mississippi. The more pervasive impact of Christianity on Amerindians, however, was the Jeffersonian conviction, rooted in a deistic view of creation and ethics, that Amerindians could be civilized and thereby converted into yeoman farmers – a vision which ironically paved the way for the destruction of Amerindian civilization by the relentless expansion to the west of yeoman farmers of European descent.

FURTHER READING

Buel, Richard: "Democracy and the American Revolution: a frame of reference," *William and Mary Quarterly*, 21 (1964), 165–90.

Calhoon, Robert M.: *Evangelicals and Conservatives in the Early South, 1740–1861* (Columbia: University of South Carolina Press, 1988).

Hatch, Nathan O.: *The Sacred Cause of Liberty: Republican Thought and the Millennium in Revolutionary New England* (New Haven: Yale University Press, 1977).

Heyrman, Christine Leigh: *Southern Cross: the Beginnings of the Bible Belt* (New York: Knopf, 1997).

Hinks, Peter P.: *To Awaken My Afflicted Brethren: David Walker and the Problem of Antebellum Slave Resistance* (University Park: Pennsylvania State University Press, 1997).

Isaac, Rhys: *The Transformation of Virginia, 1740–1790* (Chapel Hill: University of North Carolina Press, 1982).

Marini, Stephen A.: *Radical Sects of Revolutionary New England* (Cambridge, Mass.: Harvard University Press, 1982).

——: "Religion, Politics, and Ratification," *Religion in a Revolutionary Age*, ed. Ronald Hoffman and Peter J. Alberts (Charlottesville: University of Virginia Press, forthcoming).

Noll, Mark A.: *Princeton and the Republic, 1768–1822: The Search for a Christian Enlightenment in the Era of Samuel Stanhope Smith* (Princeton: Princeton University Press, 1989).

Raboteau, Albert J.: *Slave Religion: the "Invisible Institution" in the Antebellum South* (New York: Oxford University Press, 1978).

Royster, Charles: *A Revolutionary People at War: the Continental Army and American Character, 1775–1783* (Chapel Hill: University of North Carolina Press, 1979).

Rush, Benjamin: *Letters of Benjamin Rush*, ed. Lyman H. Butterfield (Princeton, NJ: Princeton University Press, 1951).

Stout, Harry S.: *The New England Soul: Preaching and Religious Culture in Colonial New England* (New York: Oxford University Press, 1986).

Yazawa, Melvin: *From Colonies to Commonwealth: Familial Ideology and the Beginnings of the American Republic* (Baltimore: Johns Hopkins University Press, 1985).

CHAPTER SEVENTY-ONE

The cultural effects of the Revolution

NORMAN S. GRABO

THE strongest cultural impact of the American Revolution was on the verbal arts – poetry, fiction, theater, and the popular press. But even there the result was not a drastic change from how things had been before the Revolution. Rather the war and the resulting shifts in social governance seem to have accelerated a general movement towards a distinct cultural identity that had been underway at least since the 1750s. The war released great pent-up energies that were determinedly self-reflective and patriotic and at the same time fiercely determined to meet the marks set by English and European civilization. The sciences – particularly medicine – struggled to find a professional identity and quality without achieving any spectacular advances. At the same time American painting soared in sophistication and accomplishment, but it would be hard to say that either sluggishness in the sciences or the brilliance of painting owed much directly to the Revolution. What the culture of letters showed, however, was that the Revolution confirmed already dawning hopes and inspired great visions of a practical glory in the future. It forced a potent ethnic mix to embark on a long and ongoing voyage of self-definition.

1 Cultural Diversity

When Rip Van Winkle woke up – having slept right through the Revolution – nothing had changed, except the color of George's coat on the tavern sign, from red to blue. Looking back in his *Travels* from about the same vantage point as Washington Irving (1817), Timothy Dwight, the president of Yale, generally agreed: the basic revolution in American culture had occurred in the late 1750s when Americans played their little part in the worldwide conflict known as the Seven Years' War. Massive influxes of both British and French soldiery brought with them new tastes, habits, and manners. They brought as well new literary works and criticism, new standards in painting, new music, theater, and most important, new ideas.

Boys born in the early 1750s were in college when revolutionary anxiety was growing intense – at Harvard, Yale, Princeton, Pennsylvania, Columbia, and Rhode Island. All Christian and ministerial to begin with, these cultural instruments provided in the 1770s increasing numbers of boys with a systematic exposure to Enlightenment attitudes developing both in France and Britain. America's future ministers, lawyers and judges, statesmen and politicians, teachers, scientists, and tradesmen were being groomed for a world that had not been visible to their fathers.

More important as instruments of cultural expression were the many newspapers (since 1690) and magazines (since 1740) that sprang up and died as rapidly as weeds. Couriers, post-boys, and gazettes flourished and failed quickly. But they could be found in any port city, and, although they were pitched at relatively local subscribers, their uniform pretentions to intellectual authority and disinterested rationality generated a sense of standardized, somewhat abstracted, provincial manners, customs, diversions, and concerns that may be somewhat misleading. This phenomenon of the absorption of local and individual voices into a more depersonalized and general intellectual discourse has come to be known recently as the "public sphere," heavily dependent upon the duplication and distribution of the printed word. Published weekly, twice weekly, and monthly, these popular press forms were generally divided into departments or sections, like modern periodicals – with a period intelligencer (covering international events from Europe to China), an encyclopedia essay, the serialization of a history or travel account, an Addisonian essay, and sometimes a poetical miscellany, but almost always some kind of serious "entertainment," usually on the first page. Newspapers also printed port news – dates of arrival and departure, occasionally notice of goods – and noticed merchandise for sale – fabrics or ribbons, anvils, slaves, land, and livestock. In exceptionally diverse and sophisticated Charles Town the *South Carolina Gazette* outdid most in its announcements of concerts, theatrical performances, dance and music lessons, even the manufacture and repair of musical instruments.

When the British occupied Charles Town under General Henry Clinton, it seemed through all the colonies as if their most elegant and charming cultural center had been violated. Finally persuaded to an alliance with the revolutionaries, France's first effort was to harry the occupiers of Charles Town, which was in many respects a French spa, even to its use of the French language. The complete dominance of English in the popular press masks what must have been a powerful multiplicity of tongues and accents. The sounds of Africa, Europe, the Mediterranean, and the West Indies enriched the coastal air as much as did the spices and aromas of various ethnic cuisines. Provost William Smith of the College of Pennsylvania discussed contemporary educational theory in elegant English, with a strong overlay of Aberdeen Scots, and the enormously successful publisher Mathew Carey kept the lilt of his native Irish alive, no doubt tinged by his years as an apprentice printer in Paris, long after his postwar emigration to Philadelphia. We tend to forget that passionate conversations about religion and politics, as well as family matters,

were as likely to be thought through and spoken in vigorous German, French, Dutch, Yoruba, Gullah, Spanish, Swedish, or Farsi before they assumed the public voice of printed English, a form of apparently benign oppression that went unchallenged by the Revolution.

In the wake of warfare, as young American idealists welcomed peace, some saw this linguistic diversity as the inheritance of Babel. They yearned for, even prophesied, a world where nationalism would be transcended by an international language identical with reason and based on the morality of nature. They never specified what language that would be.

The college generation of the early 1770s was only eight to 12 years old when the British Admiralty tightened trade restrictions. A young boy such as Philip Freneau, whose father sailed trading vessels between New York, Philadelphia, Haiti, Jamaica, and Charles Town, would surely not have known or cared about British restrictions on colonial trade and manufacture. But he would have heard his father's complaints about the difficulty of making a living at sea – the high costs of insurance and the heavy risk capital, to say nothing of the dangers, and then the additional taxes! He would have heard them in salty French. There must have been a deep anger and sullenness – one rarely articulated or preserved, and therefore difficult to document – in those boys. Whether they came from the sea or from ministerial households, villages or farms, they seem to have come of age with a great sense of material deprivation, and a sullen hostility to arbitrary authority. Even their best suits were made abroad – not because foreign clothing was better (although it was), but because remote administrators in England would not permit the manufacture of finished goods in America. Timber, fish, bread and grain, mineral ores, indigo, and other raw materials found a long and expensive way around to American use.

2 Poetry and Theory of the Arts

By 1770 the boys were voicing their unrest in a curiously formal way. Commencement

Day became an occasion for producing cele-
bratory orations and poems, addressed to
parents, trustees, and invited dignitaries,
prominent citizens, and public officials.
Poems on the "Rising glory of America"
began to spring up on these occasions,
visionary poems not content with self-
congratulation, but full of a future that did
not include colonial limitations. Typically
these poems – such as the best known by
Philip Freneau (1752–1832) and his friend
Hugh Henry Brackenridge (1748–1816) at
Princeton – progressed through a series of
set themes: firstly the discovery of the
Americas, secondly the present accomplishments of Americans in science and the useful arts, thirdly future expansion westward
across the continent, fourthly commerce as
the chief instrument of civilization, and
lastly the future preeminence of America in
the fine arts. These subtle manifestations of
American "Manifest Destiny" built on the
economic imperialism of an unrestricted
commerce had so little basis in experience
they must be seen as expressing the fantasies
of an oppressed mentality.

Such poems were often courteously
printed, either in newspapers or separately,
setting the manner for later Federalist-
inspired Forefathers' Day and Fourth of July
occasions well into the nineteenth century.
Especially at Yale the genre took on considerable force. John Trumbull (1750–1831),
who apparently began the mode, gave it up
after some satirical turns. But his friend
Timothy Dwight (1752–1817), who would
later become an eminent president of Yale
(1795–1817), emphasized the new opportunity opened by the Revolution in his alle-
gory of Joshua's epic revolt in *The Conquest
of Canaan* (published in 1785 and dedicated
to Washington as the new Joshua, but actually written during the war). Joshua shows
an America at the last stage before the apoc-
alyptic destruction of the world and a new
millennial order.

Dwight's student Joel Barlow (1754–
1812) found the allegorical equivalent of
George Washington not in Joshua or elsewhere in the Bible, but in Christopher
Columbus and the original lawgiver of
Peru, the Incan Manco Capac, who had to
fight and destroy in order to bring about a

social order designed for the benefit of
mankind. Barlow's *The Vision of Columbus*
was published in 1787 – the year of the
Constitutional Convention in Philadelphia –
though much of it had been written during
the war. It shows again that in periods of
crisis, when American writers tried to define
exactly who they were, they looked back to
Hispanic discoveries and to the civilizations
of Aztec Mexico and Incan Peru, acknowledging in a rudimentary way a revolutionary consciousness of the importance of
Hispanic elements in the American experience, even while political relationships with
Spain remained strained.

Young collegians were as likely to think
themselves "Sons of Columbus" as "Sons of
Liberty," plowing what Walt Whitman
would call 100 years later a water "Passage
to India." Such grandiose ideas flourished
especially at Yale, which throughout the
1770s turned to the serious study of Lord
Kames's eye-opening *Elements of Criticism*
(1762). Kames taught Americans that the
fine arts were more than entertainment or
recreative diversions, that they were significant expressions of human nature, especially
of human passions. Since the will is itself
but a mode of passion, to control the
images by which it operates can deeply
affect personal choices in areas of ethics and
morality. Of course (as Jonathan Edwards
had been urging since the 1740s), this argument was also valid in terms of social and
political behavior. No prince, said Kames,
can wisely ignore the role of the fine arts in
furthering political order, and a generation
of Americans came out of the Revolution
believing that no republic could ignore that
role either.

Kames almost completely secularized
American thinking about the arts. For him
the Bible was essentially a collection of literary images from whose congruity and propriety one's sentiments might usefully be
refined. Art – whether architecture, garden-
ing, or literature (and especially theater) –
depended upon the suitability of images to
their referents in nature. Thus a Kamesian
analysis of the political situation in America
might argue that King George (to whom
the *Elements* was dedicated) had failed to
produce an image of proper government in

the colonies. The incongruities between right principles and actual policy were so great as to be ludicrous. Merely to describe them would be to write satire, which punishes by ridicule and laughter. On the other hand, Kames's notions of suitability and propriety were so fussy as to encourage in young and only moderately talented poets the most grand and pompous trash. The sublime visionary poems, for example, all derive from Virgil's *Aeneid*, somewhat pneumatically pumped up by Miltonic overtones of *Paradise Lost*. How could American resistance not be compared to the glory and grandeur of Ancient Greece and Rome? Here were the new Columbuses, like Adam on the verge of a great new beginning.

At a more general level something of the same lesson was being acquired through popular fiction. English novels, especially by Defoe and Richardson, circulated widely in America after 1744, subtly insinuating sentimental notions of family duties. Like *Robinson Crusoe*, whose hero's anxious years of isolation are framed by the parable of the prodigal son, novels reinforced a sense of mutual pious duties between parents and children. Children owed proper respect and obedience to their parents. But parents also had special obligations towards the welfare of their children which, if not observed, justified breaking the family ties. In short, reading Americans had had a long indoctrination into the grounds of justifiable revolt. How deep that psychological preparation was may be questionable, but there was certainly, on one hand, an audience alert to British appeals to its wayward and ungrateful colonial children, and, on the other, to the revolutionary accusations against British cruel and irresponsible parenthood in such documents as Thomas Jefferson's Declaration of Independence and Thomas Paine's *Common Sense* and *The Crisis*.

Kames argued that the end of study of the fine arts was the formation of taste, that somewhat mysterious capacity to distinguish the good from the bad. At some level taste became indistinguishable from a Moral Sense, which, presumed to be universal, lay beyond the reach of nationalist politics. This leads to the irony, then, of cultural elitists joining the cause of nationalist reformation on the grounds of a theory quite inimical to their actions. This irony was compounded by the fact that once the Continental Army had taken the field it became the chief institution to patronize promising men of "genius," as they were then called. Men of literary talents especially found appointments as brigade chaplains. Timothy Dwight, Joel Barlow, Hugh Brackenridge, and the future dramatist Royall Tyler were among the most prominent of the young literary men who found time and support for writing in the army.

While some writers shared Freneau's bitterness at the war's disruption of artistic ambitions – "An age employed in edging steel / Can no poetic raptures feel" – others, such as Dwight and Barlow, saw warfare itself as ennobling. For both men war is the mother of fame, honor, glory, and bravery. They perceive events through highly posed martial gestures. These are presumed to realize the noblest potentialities of human nature. Dwight, for example, sought to represent manners that "might belong to the amiable and virtuous, of every age: such as elevated without design, refined without ceremony, elegant without fashion, and agreeable, because they are ornamented with sincerity, dignity, and religion, not because they are polished by art and education." In a poem conspicuously dedicated to General Washington, this description was quickly applied to the revolutionary hero, and is a fair representation of most portraits, painted as well as verbal, of revolutionary leaders both during and after the war.

More than Dwight, Barlow was a painterly poet, casting subjects into scenic tableaux, making word paintings of one patriotic hero after another, or of whole gatherings of heroes arranged as in a pageant (for example, his description of the Philadelphia debate leading to the Declaration of Independence). The poem attempts to stop the action of the present, to freeze it at those points where every gesture, every bit of color and costume, is laden with significance.

But whereas a superior poet like Freneau found himself overwhelmed by the torrent of immediate details, actors, and events, Dwight and Barlow controlled the Revolution by containing it within an overarching design. For Dwight that design was the millennium that would follow the apocalypse of Revelation. For Barlow, too, the Revolution was an intermediary step towards a millennium, but one achieved by natural causes. It would take the shape of one world of free international commerce, a congress of united nations, adoption of a single language, and a patriotism defined by universal principles of morality rather than national boundaries. In both views the Revolution was celebrated for its necessary but temporary character, and the fledgling United States was seen rather as a means to some providential design than as an end in itself. This could yet be a spur to very practical social activity: Barlow envisioned a system of canals tied to natural watercourses that would penetrate inland America and finally enable commerce to move easily and cheaply from coast to coast. His young friend the inventor Robert Fulton enthusiastically joined in that vision.

3 Science and Medicine

Perhaps the end of Barlow's vision of combined poetry and engineering helped spur the scientific expedition of Meriwether Lewis and William Clark, not merely into the interior, but all the way to the Pacific (1804–6). The primitive character of that adventure tells much about the state of post-revolutionary science in America. Following the Newtonian view of a mechanistic universe susceptible to rational principles, Americans tended to study the factual edges – Cotton Mather, hybridization of corn; John Winthrop IV, earthquakes; Franklin, electricity – using the Royal Society of London as the most eminent medium for sharing information and speculations. But the war ravaged most scientific activity, closing institutions, destroying books, and scattering the curious.

Indeed, science still seemed to be a branch of polite literature before the turn of the century, something one talked about with other intellectually disposed young men at one's boarding house or convivial club, where attorneys, clergymen, physicians, and merchants mingled. Physics, agronomy,

chemistry, botany, zoology, geography, and geology all stood in need of data, of agreed-upon morphologies, and of basic theory. Medicine represents the disarray of science at that time, the disastrous yellow fever plague that struck Philadelphia in the summer of 1793 providing a test case. No one had the slightest knowledge of the nature or causes of diseases such as smallpox, diphtheria, or yellow fever. Hospitals were quickly overcrowded and badly managed. Those who could, fled, including inadequately educated medical practitioners. Hospitalization was a death sentence for thousands.

The mayhem was no less than it had been during the war, where disease destroyed more human life, on both sides, than did fighting. Dr. Benjamin Rush, a signer of the Declaration of Independence, surgeon general to the Continental Army, the most distinguished leader in medical education at the time, and a worldwide model for compassionate treatment of the mentally disturbed, was helpless before the onslaught of the annual plague. Like other natural philosophers, Rush had no pathology, no genetics, no germ theory, no simple tools like thermometers, no statistics or applicable mathematics, and no workable chemistry with which even to understand let alone battle this and other diseases.

Deluged equally with an overload of data and speculation, Americans joined in efforts – usually local in character – to form professional societies and journals to share and preserve their interests. These led inevitably to hospital administrative reforms, better sanitation, emphasis on preventive medicine, and higher standards for research, education, and certification. New Jersey had a medical society by 1766; during and after the war similar associations arose in Massachusetts (1781), New Hampshire (1791), Connecticut (1792), and Delaware (1789). With Mitchill and Smith's *American Medical Repository* (started in 1797), at least the groundwork was laid for professionalizing that branch of science. Other disciplines were undergoing the same kind of development: agriculture with the New Jersey Society for the Promotion of Agriculture, Commerce, and Art (1781); astronomy – perhaps the leading American science of the period under David Rittenhouse – in the rejuvenated American Philosophical Society (originally begun in 1743–4); law in several state bar organizations; and sociology under the Virginia Constitutional Society (1784) and other societies designed to apply scientific principles and procedures to questions of social and political behavior. Attributing any of these developments directly to the Revolution seems problematic at best. More obvious were the technological inventions brought on by the war itself – Eli Whitney's assembly-line production of rifles with interchangeable parts, Fulton's improvements on torpedoes and submarines, the military use of hot-air balloons, and the idea of armored warships. These would have far-reaching practical implications, some of which were not realized for another 50 years.

The spirit of science even found a significant place in religion, where skepticism first floated a deistic religion of nature or rational religion, in works such as Thomas Paine's *The Age of Reason* (1794–6) and Ethan Allen's *Reason the Only Oracle of Man* (1784). Condemned by some such as Dwight as simple atheism and "infidelity," this use of science led eventually – through the influence of young intellectuals such as those gathered in Boston as the Anthology Society, with its institutional embodiment in the Boston Athenaeum – to the scientific examination of the Bible and the development of Germanic principles of criticism as expressed in their *Monthly Anthology* (1803–11).

4 Manners and the Stage

The Revolution also reinforced the long-lived American advocacy of plainness in speech, dress, buildings, and manners – obviously making a virtue of necessity. But it was more than that, for it was a studied plainness, as it had been for Puritan preachers in the early seventeenth century. The most dramatic examples are probably the radical appeals of Thomas Paine in *The Crisis* (1776) and *Common Sense* (1776–83), and *The Federalist Papers* (1787–8) by John Jay, James Madison, and Alexander Hamilton. All were calls to a dangerous

commitment in desperate circumstances; all equally show the possibility of passionate resolve tied to rational constraint, clear thinking, and arresting simplicity. Radical reformers took pains not to appear lunatic.

Benjamin Franklin especially epitomized affected Yankee simplicity during his many years as an American agent in France, where courtiers and philosophers found him more charming and agreeable than did many of his American associates. With comic exaggeration, this characterization found its way onto the stage in plays such as the appropriately titled *The Contrast* (1787) by Royall Tyler (1757–1826), in the guise of simple but honest Jonathan, the absolute foil to Chesterfieldian British manners.

What we might call amateur theater dates in America from 1598 in El Paso, Texas, with the Oñate expedition, and presumably was not unusual in taverns in earliest Virginia. The more sophisticated French in Nova Scotia wrote original masques as early as Marc Lescarbot's *Neptune's Triumph* in 1607. But as a professional art form it did not exist until Lewis Hallam's American Company appeared to tour the coastal cities in 1752. Military regiments enacted Addison's *Cato* (1713) – a tragedy of patriotic self-sacrifice set in colonial Africa which was trotted out through the century whenever lessons in patriotism required reinvigorating. During the war *Cato* emerged, and on both sides. Although theater was outlawed by the Continental Congress, it persisted, sometimes attended by General Washington himself, with Philip Freneau, the future ardent Anti-Federalist, willingly writing a prologue for one performance honoring the present general.

From *The Group* (1775) by Mercy Warren (1728–1814), the "old lady" who wrung praise even from strong Federalist / Tory critics, to *André* (1797) by William Dunlap (1766–1839), the Revolution provided subjects for stirring and vivacious images that did not fail to move deep political passions. Honoring the much admired Major André was perfectly acceptable, but when in the play his rebellious American friend Captain Bland passionately denounced the declared execution of the hero/spy by pulling the regimental cockade from his hat and throwing it to the floor, the audience rose up in angry repudiation, and the scene had to be rewritten before the play could find approval. We might surmise then that the chief impact of the Revolution was to provide images of acceptable political and social behavior, and thereby to break down local resistances to theater, although it would take another century before a respectable drama would take its place in American cultural life.

5 Music and Painting

When the exalted images and sentences of the serious poets were put upon the stage in costume and gesture they tended towards bombast, melodrama, or operatic hyperbole. There was a good deal of music in the plays of the time, beginning with a ballad opera called *The Disappointment* (1767), featuring a black dandy named Raccoon, the invention of either Colonel Thomas Forrest or Andrew Barton. This was a great age of English vocal music, when British quarterlies regularly reviewed currently published music for home performance. Tunes were often traditional, with new words set to fit a current occasion – such as the politics of revolution – or dramatic situation. And although Francis Hopkinson (1731–91), who first came to public attention as a college student in Pennsylvania in the 1750s, was both composer and lyricist, his words (preserved in anthologies) have outlasted his melodies. We have thus tended to lose the robust reality of rousing music sung in camps, in taverns, in social clubs and singing schools, and in political meetings, as well as on the stage.

Instrumental music, essentially non-referential, seems to have been unaffected by the Revolution in any direct way. The outstanding Andrew Law (1749–1821) stood out among choral tunesmiths of the time such as Oliver Holden (1765–1844), William Selby (?1738–98), Benjamin Carr (1768–1831), Rayner Taylor (1747–1825), and dozens of others who set music to psalms, hymns, anthems, and show songs, all within an English or European tradition, regardless of the politics or theology of the words they set. The eccentric, self-taught Boston tanner

and composer William Billings (1746–1800), himself an ardent revolutionary whose "Chester" was a patriotic fifist's delight during the war, had declared his own independence from Anglo-European musical decorums as early as 1770, however. But his quirky – some say grotesque or primitive – effects strike one as only accidentally connected with the politics of the time. Military bands doubtless introduced symphonic music for the first time to many Americans.

Somewhat more surprising, perhaps, is the absence of revolutionary influence in American painting. Unlike music, the field of painting seemed suddenly overwhelmed with world-class talent. This was due in no small part to the influence of the Scotsman John Smibert (1688–1751), who was a decent portrait artist and not a bad landscape painter, but whose main importance may have resided in his making available his wide collection of copies and "antiquities" for aspiring young painters to study in Boston. Benjamin West (1738–1820), who did not need Smibert's material and who went on to become King George III's Court Painter, John Singleton Copley (1738–1815), Gilbert Stuart (1755–1828), Charles Willson Peale (1741–1827), whose Baltimore Museum (1814) became the first public museum in the country, and a score of other talented and ambitious painters found their way in the 1760s and 1770s to England, especially to study at West's atelier in London after 1764. They exhibited portraits and historical paintings in Europe as well, to considerable and well-deserved acclaim. On both sides of the ocean there were prominent and wealthy clients to capture on canvas and, as the Revolution threw up new heroes, soldiers, statesmen, and ambassadors, plenty of subjects. But again, except for changes in costume, whatever advances came along in this art were owed to influences other than the Revolution.

The most distinctively American style during that time was the primitivism or naive style of Paul Revere (1735–1818) or Winthrop Chandler (1747–90), with its roots clearly in the tradition of Puritan limners of the preceding century. During the American Revolution, English and European artists were more likely to be fascinated by Winckelmann's post-1755 excavations of Pompeii, with their new revelations of ancient dress, furniture, buildings, and other designs, study of which would technically affect historical paintings. Some of this was carried by Americans into paintings recording stirring moments in the conflict – as Trumbull's *The Battle of Bunker's Hill* – but even the patriotic subject often seems an occasion for the display of technical virtuosity rather than a deeply felt display of change in the social and political world. In any event, American painters equalled British painters in the age of Reynolds and Gainsborough too quickly and too easily, and gained almost too ready acceptance for there to be a visual correspondence to the political and ideological turmoil.

6 History and the Novel

Even in the verbal arts, where the Revolution was articulated most consciously – in law and rhetoric and public policy, the theater, the press, and poetry and fiction, one must conclude that the primary impact of the Revolution on cultural activity was its energizing divisiveness. It drove a deep wedge, first between revolutionaries and loyalists, and later between democrats and Federalists. These divisions required on each side clarity of self-definition and fierce assertions of equality of accomplishment. If anywhere, here is where Jürgen Habermas's concept of a public sphere with a deep dependence upon the culture of print should come into play, but it seems to be most evident and useful with respect to political pamphleteering, exactly where one would expect it. Given the strange malleability of theatrical speech and the powerful though never literally transcribed, let alone printed, oratory from Patrick Henry to Fisher Ames, one should probably employ such tempting theories with a considerable degree of caution.

Hostilities between America and England released great cultural energies, and with them great fears. Hector St. John Crèvecoeur's *Letters from an American Farmer* (1782) depict with great vivacity the nightmare terror of revolution, its apparent

enforcement of barbaric and savage inclinations in all peoples. In contrast, Thomas Jefferson's *Notes on Virginia* (1785) displayed elegantly that in climate and natural phenomena America equalled any place in creation. The Connecticut Wits elaborately exhibited a self-destructive America plummeting headlong towards anarchy in their *American Antiquities* (1787–8), while at the same time the *Federalist Papers* demonstrated an American capacity for political philosophy unmatched in the modern world. Snarling Freneau, the "smutty linkboy to the muses," hammered away insistently at the aristocratic pretensions of the Federalists, while the Federalist Joseph Dennie (1768–1812) argued annoyingly and alliteratively against Jeffersonian democrats in his great periodical *The Port Folio* (1801–27).

That this vituperative and often quite unfocused spirit of debate was actually moving in positive and definitive directions may be seen in the establishment of several new colleges; the beginnings of local historical societies, with the radical printer Isaiah Thomas's American Antiquarian Society at Worcester (1812); and with self-reflective publications such as Jeremy Belknap's *History of New Hampshire* (1784, 1791, 1792), Jedediah Morse's *American Geography* (1789); and Noah Webster's *An American Dictionary of the English Language* (1828, on work begun in the 1780s). Such reactions to the Revolution would carry their cultural consequences through the 1790s and into the nineteenth century.

By 1789, when *The Power of Sympathy* by William Hill Brown (?1765–93) initiated the American novel, Americans, especially young women, were already addicted to reading fiction – all imported. They thrilled to threats of seduction, rape, abandonment, yielding to the blandishments of irresponsible rakes (often British officers), and hoping for rescue by an honorable American – the pattern brilliantly caught in the immensely popular *Charlotte Temple* (1794), by Susanna Rowson (1762–1824), song and dancing actress, teacher, and historian. Snappish editorials and thundering sermons could not stem the habit. Brown even incorporates anti-novel warnings within his novel – a

feature that constituted a common amuse-
ment in the form. Tabitha Tenney (1762–
1837) made that joke the central feature of
her satirical misadventures of Dorcasina
Sheldon in *Female Quixotism* (1801).

Most such work, like the scandalous *The
Coquette* (1797), by Hannah Foster (1759–
1840) were strongly didactic and sentimental, and pretended to be true historical tales.
Even in their frequently epistolary form they
trumpet their British origins, and revolutionary reflections tend to be quite incidental.
The case is different, however, with Hugh
Henry Brackenridge, whose career took him
first into teaching, then law, and then frontier politics in Pittsburgh. His massive
Modern Chivalry (1792, 1793, 1797, 1815)
like Tenney's *Quixotism*, turns to Cervantes
as a model, but then accretes into what
seems to be a purposeful formlessness, variously described as an anthology, miscellany,
hodge-podge, rhapsody, farrago, medley,
salmagundi, and Lucianic or Menippean
satire – which I would call the essential
American literary form. In Brackenridge's
case the genre covers everything – the impos-
sibilities of the Articles of Confederation,
hopeless tax collecting, pretentious universities and learned societies, elections run on
rum, slavery and race relationships, greed
and power hunger, property qualifications
for the franchise, dancing, and presidential
levees. These are strung in a series of alter-
nating essays, sketches, anecdotes, jokes, and
adventures involving the learned rationalist
Captain Farrago and his disaster-prone companion, the bog-trotter Teague O'Regan.

More complex are the gothic romances of
Charles Brockden Brown (1770–1810),
especially *Wieland* (1798), *Arthur Mervyn*
(1799, 1800), *Ormond* (1799), and *Edgar
Huntly* (1799). Rife with images of irrational terror, benighted fanaticism, misled
revolutionary idealism, psychic disorders
and downright insanity, Brown's novels
imply a post-revolutionary America deeply
anxious about its existence in the political
wilderness of modern democracy. Still reel-
ing from the terrible aftermath of the
French Revolution, these intense tales may

easily be seen as allegorical cautions against
too facile a trust in human reason, order,
high hopes, and Columbian symbolism.

Brown and Brackenridge are – each in his
way – penetrating critics of the Revolution,
without succumbing to the fierce factionalism that captured other powerful voices
such as Joseph Dennie and Philip Freneau.
They announce the possibility that will
be realized in the impresario character of
others – the great Philadelphia publisher
Mathew Carey and the poet-playwright-
theatrical manager-biographer-historian-and-
painter William Dunlap (also of Philadelphia
and New York). Figures of no mean cultural
influence themselves, they energized and
enabled others to give voice, music, color,
myths, memories, and form to the violence
of independence.

FURTHER READING

Buell, Lawrence: *New England Literary Culture:
From Revolution through Renaissance*
(Cambridge: Cambridge University Press,
1986).

Davis, R. B.: *Intellectual Life in the Colonial
South, 1585–1763*. 3 vols. (Knoxville:
University of Knoxville Press, 1978).

Fliegelman, Jay: *Prodigals & Pilgrims: The
American Revolution against Patriarchal
Authority, 1750–1800* (Cambridge: Cambridge
University Press, 1982).

Greene, Jack P.: *Pursuits of Happiness: The Social
Development of Early Modern British Colonies
and the Formation of American Culture* (Chapel
Hill: University of North Carolina Press,
1988).

Nye, Russel B.: *The Cultural Life of the New
Nation, 1776–1830* (New York: Harper &
Row, 1960).

Silverman, Kenneth: *A Cultural History of the
American Revolution: Painting, Music,
Literature, and the Theatre in the Colonies and
the United States from the Treaty of Paris to the
Inauguration of George Washington, 1763–1789*
(New York: Thomas Y. Crowell Company,
1976).

Warner, Michael: *The Letters of the Republic:
Publication and the Public Sphere in Eighteenth-
Century America* (Cambridge, MA: Harvard
University Press, 1990).

CHAPTER SEVENTY-TWO

The effects of the Revolution on language

JOHN ALGEO

THE Revolution created a new national variety of English as well as a new nation. Although American English became a distinct entity almost as soon as the first settlers from Britain arrived in the New World, its status as an institutionalized or standard variety of the language had to await the Revolution and subsequent efforts to create a culturally, as well as politically, independent society. Today, American is spoken by more persons than any other variety of the language; consequently British and other varieties of English around the globe are massively influenced by it and thus by the linguistic consequences of the Revolution.

Those consequences appear in both the system of the language and attitudes towards it. A language system consists of words, spoken or written, related to each other by grammar and used by its speakers to interact. But a language also involves the attitudes of its speakers towards the world and the language itself. The effects of the Revolution can be seen in all these aspects: the system of words, pronunciations, spellings, grammar, and meanings, but also strikingly in the attitudes of speakers of American English.

1 Settlement

The American colonies were settled from many regions of the motherland. The diverse cultural traditions of seventeenth- and eighteenth-century Britain were exported with concentrations in various colonies: the Puritans from the eastern counties to New England, the Cavaliers and their indentured servants from southern England to Virginia, the Quakers from northern England to the Delaware valley, and the Scots and Scots-Irish to the Appalachian range and elsewhere in South Carolina and Georgia. Those groups brought with them their ways of speaking English along with other cultural features that have survived as identifiable strains even in present-day national life (Fischer, 1989). Alongside the four major strains, other regional cultures were Dutch in the Hudson valley; African and West Indian in coastal South Carolina and Georgia; Highland Scots in the Carolinas; Swedish, German, French, and others elsewhere.

If we knew a great deal more than we do about language varieties in the British Isles from the end of the sixteenth century, when the first colonists learned their English, through the time of the Revolution, we could trace the roots of American English with more confidence than in fact is possible. Unfortunately, the English of England during American colonial days is the least well described of all its historical periods. The detailed study of English in America during the same period is even less satisfactory. Consequently much of what can be said about the earliest linguistic relationships between Britain and America must remain a matter of likely generalities rather than documented fact.

The lack of certainty about origins extends also to subvarieties of American English, such as the speechways of the early Africans in the American colonies and hence of their present-day descendants. Concerning the genesis of Black English, as these speech-ways have been called, there are two major theories, neither of which has enough factual support to silence the other, but each of which enjoys outspoken support from its adherents.

One theory is that the African slaves, originating from many different tribes, came to America without a significant common language. On the plantations, they learned English from the overseers, and thus Black English is a variety of provincial British English with an admixture of African elements and other modifications springing from the manner and circumstances in which it was acquired.

The other theory is that many African slaves came to America already knowing a pidgin with English elements in it – a pidgin being a simplified speechway combining features from two or more languages and used for communication among people who normally speak different languages. On the plantations, the pidgin was the only way many of the slaves could communicate among themselves, and it had the added advantage of shutting out the slave master. So it was used as the primary language of the slaves; that is, it became a creole. As time passed, this creole accepted increasingly many features from standard English, thus becoming more like it.

According to the first of these theories, Black English began as a subdialect of southern American English, to which African elements were added. In the second, it began as a creole, a non-English language, which has assimilated to English. The historical facts are not adequate for choosing confidently between the two theories, so present-day views of Black English and its history are governed largely by political or other affective responses. The genesis of Black English lies in pre-revolutionary days, but the nature of that genesis is obscure. What is clear is that Black English is one of the strains from which American English has drawn.

Like the African forced immigrants and their speech, the social groups from Old England who settled in various colonies, bringing with them the speechways of the homeland, had an influence that has survived in present-day American dialects. The New England colonies extended their influence westwards, as the present-day Northern dialect region. The Delaware valley colonies likewise extended westwards as the North Midland dialect region. The colonies from Virginia southwards became the Southern or Coastal Southern dialect region along the Atlantic and Gulf coasts. And the southern Appalachian settlements expanded westwards to the Ozarks and beyond as the South Midland or Mountain Southern dialect region. The persistence of colonial settlement patterns in twentieth-century dialect regions is notable.

2 Colonial Homogenization and Differentiation

In addition to the cultural differences of colonial America and their persistence, however, a complementary tendency to homogenization is equally notable. The language of the colonies and the early nation seemed to contemporary observers to be remarkably uniform, foreshadowing the rise of American English as an identifiable, relatively homogeneous variety. As John Witherspoon, a Scots Presbyterian minister who became President of Princeton University, put it in 1781:

The vulgar in America speak much better than the vulgar in Great-Britain, for a very obvious reason, viz. that being much more unsettled, and moving frequently from place to place, they are not so liable to local peculiarities either in accent or phraseology. There is a greater difference in dialect between one county and another in Britain, than there is between one state and another in America. (Mathews, 1931, p. 16)

The pressure towards a colonial speech more uniform than that of the mother country can be seen also in Australia, New Zealand, South Africa, and of course Canada. This colonial homogenization is a consequence of the fact that colonists who speak different motherland dialects adapt to one another, with a resulting partial loss of differentiating features and the appearance of a more uniform variety of the language. It is often claimed that colonial varieties of speech are more conservative than the language of the mother country; it is, however, difficult to measure degrees of innovation versus conservatism in pronunciation, vocabulary, and grammar, so the reality of "colonial lag" (as it is called) is disputed. The existence of colonial homogenization, on the other hand, is easier to document and to explain.

Although the colonists brought their English speechways with them, certain forces operated from the beginning to make English in America different from that in Britain: language drift, the new physical and social environment, and contacts with other languages.

There is an inevitable drift in the history of languages by which small changes are continually introduced. Within a relatively homogeneous speech community whose members are in frequent contact with each other, innovations will either be spread quickly to most members of the community or be suppressed. Thus, although the language of the community changes, it does so uniformly, thus maintaining its identity.

When one speech community is divided from another, however, so that their members interact less frequently or in restricted ways, each community will drift in its own direction. If two communities are divided for an extended period, the result will be distinct dialects of the common language, or eventually even separate languages.

The Atlantic Ocean was an effective barrier to easy communication, guaranteeing that over time the language of the colonies and that of the motherland would drift apart. And so they did, eventually creating distinct British and American varieties of English. Since the colonists, however distant they might be from each other, were more likely to interact directly with each other than with persons still in the British Isles, they tended to grow linguistically more alike and less like those in Britain. Hence the phenomenon of colonial homogenization.

The natural tendency of a language to change is reinforced when its speakers encounter new circumstances of life. In that case, the vocabulary especially is rapidly modified, by using old words in new ways (as *creek* for a stream rather than an estuary),

by making new words from old words or word-parts (as *scrub oak* for a type of tree), or by borrowing words from other languages (as *squash* from Algonquian or *cookie* from Dutch). Exposure to new experiences is a powerful motive for language innovation. The colonists met new topography, climate, flora, fauna, and humanity. They found themselves in new social groupings. The result was an adaptation of their language to the new circumstances in which they used it.

The English colonists were not alone in the New World; the Amerindians who held the land before them were still there. So were colonists and entrepreneurs from other European nations: Dutch, Swedes, French, Germans, and, to the south, Spaniards. Shortly they were joined by Africans, many brought immediately from the Caribbean. As English-speaking colonists interacted with those peoples, they were influenced by them.

3 Attitudes to American English

As a result of the factors of drift, environmental pressure, and foreign contacts, the English of the American colonies began to differentiate at once from that of the homeland and to acquire a character and system of its own. Changes in the English of America were noticed early. In 1735 One traveler in Georgia, Francis Moore, observing the location of the town of Savannah, complained, "... the bank of the river (which they in barbarous English call a bluff) is steep..." (Mathews, 1931, p. 13).

Most of the early comments were complaints. Any change in language has always tended to be seen as degeneration by those who have not yet participated in the change. That tendency was especially strong in the eighteenth century, when "ascertaining, correcting, and polishing" the language, before "fixing" it to prevent further change, were taken as self-evidently desirable aims. Thus American and British English began the process of mutual differentiation with the first permanent English settlement in 1607. But Americans and Britons alike tended to regard the features differentiating the two varieties as flaws in American.

Despite Witherspoon's complimentary view that the vulgar in America speak much better than their counterparts in the old country, his examples of Americanisms consisted of American provincialisms, vulgarisms, common or personal blunders, cant phrases, and other departures from the standard of England. The Revolution contributed to the actual differentiation of the two varieties, as any major political and social event will, for example, by ending old political institutions and creating new ones to which the vocabulary had to adjust. However, the major linguistic effect of the Revolution was not on the language system, but rather on linguistic attitudes. And that change in attitude came about only gradually.

Long after the Revolution, many Americans continued to look to London for their linguistic model. John Pickering, in his *Vocabulary or Collection of Words and Phrases Which Have Been Supposed to Be Peculiar to the United States of America* (1816), confessed that

none of our countrymen, not even those, who are the most zealous in supporting what they imagine to be the honour of the *American* character, will contend, that we have not in some instances departed from the standard of the language. (Mathews, 1931, p. 67)

The standard, for Pickering and many others, was still that "spoken and written in England at the present day." But the intoxicating sense of new nationhood brought others to the conclusion that political independence was imperfect without cultural independence as well. That conclusion revalued the differences distinguishing American from British and reformed attitudes towards the language.

The quest for cultural independence led to a promotion of American letters and of the American version of the English language. The political patriotism that underlay the Revolution was matched by linguistic patriotism on the part of an anonymous American writing in 1774:

The English language has been greatly improved in Britain within a century, but its highest perfection, with every other branch of human knowledge, is perhaps reserved for this Land of light and freedom. As the people through this extensive country will speak English, their advantages

for polishing their language will be great, and vastly superior to what the people in England ever enjoyed. (Mathews, 1931, p. 40)

Among the founding fathers, John Adams held similar views, based upon his assumption that, since a republic requires eloquence for advancement to its public offices, its language will be of "the greatest purity, copiousness, and perfection." Although Adams's crystal ball may have been clouded with respect to the linguistic effects of political rhetoric, it was clear enough about the future of the English language when in 1780 he wrote to the President of Congress:

English is destined to be in the next and succeeding centuries more generally the language of the world than Latin was in the last or French is in the present age. The reason of this is obvious, because the increasing population in America, and their universal connection and correspondence with all nations will, aided by the influence of England in the world, whether great or small, force their language into general use, in spite of all the obstacles that may be thrown in their way, if any such there should be. (Mathews, 1931, p. 42)

The most notable figure in promoting American English was Noah Webster, who may be accounted a Founding Father of American English, if not of the republic. Today Webster is remembered chiefly as the embodiment of American lexicography, the creator of "Webster's Dictionary," which in the popular mind is less a particular book than an archetypal one. He is also associated with the "Blue-backed speller" and spelling reform. Both those activities were related to Webster's advocacy of "Federal English" as the language of the new nation (Baron, 1982).

Ironically, Webster's dictionary was not particularly American in content and his influence on American spelling was not innovative, but regulatory. As Thomas Pyles has remarked, Webster's

use of American writings [as illustrations in his *American Dictionary*] is actually the principal justification for the use of *American* in the title, for despite all his high-sounding talk about an American language, Webster really had little conception of the differences between American and British English in his day. (Pyles, 1952, p. 120)

Similarly, it is often assumed that characteristically American spellings were invented by Noah Webster. He was very influential in popularizing certain spellings in America, but he did not originate them. Rather, from the competing variety of a less orthographically rigid age, he chose already existing options such as *center*, *color*, and *check* on such grounds as simplicity, analogy, or etymology. British practice settled on different options: *centre*, *colour*, *cheque*.

As important as Webster's role in American lexicography and orthography was, perhaps his greatest contribution was promoting a sense of pride in distinctively American language variants. As Pyles put it,

Webster was certainly one of the most influential commentators upon language who ever lived. More than any other single person, he shaped the course of American English, for he supplied us with the schoolmaster's authority which we needed for self-confidence. (Pyles, 1952, p. 123)

That is, Webster's contribution was less to the ways Americans use English than to the attitudes they have towards their own usage.

4 Later Developments

Webster did not, however, settle the question of the identity of American English as a distinct standard. Overt arguments and covert preferences contended through the nineteenth century and into the early decades of the twentieth. Second only to Webster as an influence on attitudes towards American English was H. L. Mencken, the Baltimore journalist and social critic whose anti-British and pro-German sentiments made it expedient for him to turn to a subject less explosive than international politics during World War I. Consequently in 1919 he published his polemical work *The American Language*, which went through four editions and two supplements before it was abridged and updated by Raven I. McDavid, Jr., in 1963.

In the first edition of his book, Mencken's thesis was that British and American English were two streams whose divergence since the Revolution was becoming so great that they were well on their way to being separate languages, hence his title. Mencken supported this thesis partly through an elaborate joke by which he compared a formal, prim British style with a highly colloquial, slangy, or folksy American one.

Mencken's thesis was attacked by George Philip Krapp in his more sober but also less entertaining response, *The English Language in America* (1925), the title of which also announces its thesis. But Mencken himself recognized that his thesis had been wrong and therefore modified it to argue that in fact the two streams were converging. However, since the American stream was many times larger than the British and, in Mencken's view, a great deal more vital, he predicted the increasing Americanization of British English, foreseeing much the same future as had John Adams a century and a half earlier.

Language development is a slow process. The structural differences between present day American and British English are minor (Algeo, 1988); vocabulary differences are greater. Both are the consequence of impulses set in motion by the colonization of America. The attitudes that recognize American as the major national variety of the English language alongside British spring from and still echo the Revolution.

FURTHER READING

Algeo, John: "British and American Grammatical Differences," *International Journal of Lexicography*, 1 (1988), 1–31.

Baron, Dennis E.: *Grammar and Good Taste: Reforming the American Language* (New Haven, Conn.: Yale University Press, 1982).

Fischer, D. H.: *Albion's Seed: Four British Folkways in America* (New York: Oxford University Press, 1989).

Krapp, George Philip: *The English Language in America*, 2 vols. (1925), repr. (New York: Ungar, 1960).

Mathews, M. M.: *The Beginnings of American English* (1931), repr. (Chicago: University of Chicago Press, 1963).

Mathews, M. M. (ed.): *A Dictionary of Americanisms on Historical Principles* (Chicago: University of Chicago Press, 1951).

Mencken, H. L.: *The American Language* (1919, 1921, 1923, 1936, 1945, 1951), abridged and augmented by Raven I. McDavid, Jr. (New York: Knopf, 1963).

Pyles, Thomas: *Words and Ways of American English* (New York: Random House, 1952).

CHAPTER SEVENTY-THREE

Medicine before and after the Revolution

MARY E. FISSELL

FOR much of the eighteenth century, medicine in America strongly resembled its counterpart in Britain. While regional differences in health and medical provision were marked, most inhabitants of the 13 colonies experienced health care organized on British models. During the Revolution, military medicine was severely hampered by lack of organization and sufficient funds. The Revolution intensified and accelerated some changes in the professional structures of medicine, but little substantial innovation can be traced to the war. Nor did medicine notably alter patterns of mortality in this period.

1 Healers and Healing

As in the mother country, health care was provided by a wide range of practitioners. For most Americans, self-medication or domestic medicine was a first line of defense. Books such as William Buchan's *Domestic Medicine* (1769) or S. A. Tissot's *Advice to the People* (first English edition 1765) were imported from England and reprinted in the colonies. In the late eighteenth century medicine chests for the home were commercially produced and sold widely. These often contained fairly orthodox remedies, and may have helped to make domestic practice more equivalent to health care provided by full-time practitioners. Many patent remedies were bought and sold over the counter; these were often old British standbys such as Bateman's Drops or Dover's Powders, fundamentals of domestic and professional practice alike. What little is known about popular healing suggests that,

like its British equivalent, it depended upon a congeries of beliefs deriving from Galenic theory and magical ideas.

The line between home healing and that provided by a "professional" was vague; many practiced medicine with little training and on a part-time basis. Even for trained practitioners, medicine was often a part-time, even casual, occupation. For example, Joseph Pynchon, a leading mid-century Boston practitioner, had started his career in his spare time while serving in the General Court. On the elite level, men of learning might be very knowledgeable about medicine. For example, Benjamin Franklin was sometimes referred to as a medical man because of his invention of bifocals and research on electricity, although he did not train as a physician. So, too, those few who received a college education often acquired some medical knowledge; the University of Virginia provided medical education to all its undergraduates until 1830.

The distinctions between physicians, surgeons, and apothecaries typical of London medicine rarely applied in the colonies. In part this was due to the lack of physicians – few MDs emigrated and few colonists could afford a European training. But even the few physicians in large cities often compounded and sold drugs, a practice which their English brethren could not have countenanced. By the late eighteenth century a few American cities were beginning to afford opportunities for genteel medical practice. But, as in the mother country, the typical practitioner was a surgeon-apothecary, the ancestor of the general practitioner.

These medical men were either trained through apprenticeship or were self-taught. Apprenticeship, although sometimes denigrated by later graduates of medical schools, provided a fairly cheap and often effective means of one-to-one instruction. In rural areas where practitioners traveled many miles on horseback to see patients (almost all medical care took place within the patient's home) the apprentice provided valuable assistance.

Midwifery was very much a female pursuit – again, often a part-time one. Childbirth was an occasion for women to join together in support, and most births were attended and managed by a group of the mother's friends and relatives in addition to the midwife. By 1800 this pattern had altered for urban wealthy women, who began to rely upon male midwives, usually surgeons. These men, such as Dr. William Shippen of Philadelphia, took a more interventionist approach to labor and delivery, using opium, bloodletting, and forceps.

For much of the century, American therapeutics were transplanted British ones, with the addition of a few Amerindian remedies like sassafras. Many therapeutic agents were intended to rid the body of noxious humors, so patients expected and experienced bleeding, purging, blistering, and vomiting. Historians have characterized American medical practice as pragmatic, free from the overly theoretical debates and speculative systems which afflicted learned European medicine of the period.

But in the last decades of the century, patients began to undergo what is referred to as "heroic" medicine, so-called because of its dramatic and severely debilitating effects, caused by intensive bleeding and purging. Some of the responsibility for this therapeutic style must be given to Benjamin Rush the Philadelphia physician and educator whose name became a byword for bloodletting. Rush advocated a medical system which was the direct descendant of those described by his Edinburgh teachers William Cullen and John Brown. Where Cullen and Brown emphasized that the body in illness was either under- or over-stimulated, Rush thought he had found a unitary cause of disease in morbid excitement. William Cobbett remarked that Rush's medicine was one of those great discoveries made from time to time for the depopulation of the earth, but Cobbett's sarcasm did not dent Rush's reputation as an outstanding medical man or diminish the popularity of heroic medicine.

2 Medicine in the Revolution

Unlike many other wars, the American Revolutionary War did not promote medical innovations or lead to the restructuring of the profession. Throughout the war, medical provision for the military was hampered by two serious problems: the lack of trained and equipped surgeons, and organizational difficulties which were worsened by political squabbles among the top ranks. Both contributed to the large numbers of deaths from disease; typical estimates suggest that, for each soldier killed by the enemy, nine died from disease.

Most of the ailments which struck the American forces were those familiar to any eighteenth-century military operation: dysentery, smallpox, venereal disease, and camp fevers (probably typhus and typhoid). Malaria also plagued the troops, especially as campaigns moved south. Smallpox was especially severe in the early years of the war, and in New England, where inoculation had sometimes been banned. After the first two years of war smallpox became less significant, since by then many troops had either succumbed or been inoculated. Similarly, as discipline became better in the forces, the standards of camp hygiene improved, and dysentery and diarrhea declined. However, the Americans always suffered more from enteric diseases than did the British, who were better-disciplined and equipped with surgeons who could draw upon considerable experience in military hygiene and medicine.

The problems of medical organization were basically those of integrating various provincial units, creating a functioning hierarchy, and ensuring adequate funding – none of which was fully resolved. In February 1775 the Provincial Congress of Massachusetts appointed Drs. Benjamin Church and Joseph Warren to oversee the medical needs of the local militia. A few months later the Massachusetts Committee on Public Safety found that regimental surgeons were not always adequately trained.

Such conflicts between regimental surgeons (usually political appointments) and centralized authority were often repeated throughout the war. In May 1775 the Continental Congress created an Army Medical Department and named Benjamin Church its first Director-General. The department's difficulties in integrating regimental surgeons were exacerbated by lack of funds; the Continental Congress and Washington himself failed to appreciate the costs of medical care. Regimental surgeons, for example, initially did not receive medical supplies from the department and were chronically lacking in essentials such as bandages and blankets. It was not until January 1779 that the Continental Congress finally allocated monies for medical supplies for the regimental surgeons.

Church's career was terminated when a treasonable letter from him to a British officer was intercepted. In October 1775 Dr. John Morgan, a Philadelphia physician and founder of the first American medical school, was appointed in Church's stead. Unfortunately, the choice of Morgan seems to have led to a series of notable conflicts between leading Philadelphia medical men serving in various military capacities. Morgan attempted to institute a system of examinations for hospital mates and regimental surgeons and mates, and to standardize medical military discipline. But he continued to face substantial organizational difficulties and limited funds, problems exacerbated by his inability to avoid political wrangling. Morgan's old rival Dr. William Shippen, Jr., was put in charge of the Flying Camp in New Jersey and then, in October 1776, appointed to oversee army medicine west of the Hudson. Morgan and Shippen feuded over supplies and authority, with Shippen complaining directly to the Congress about outbreaks of illness in the winter campaigns of 1776–7. Then Morgan attempted to court-martial Dr. Samuel Stringer, who oversaw army medicine in northern New York State, for misconduct. But in January 1777 the Congress fired both Morgan and Stringer.

To Morgan's chagrin, Shippen was appointed Director-General in his stead.

Under Shippen's guidance, Congress adopted a plan in April 1777 to increase the pay of medical personnel and to organize the department into four regions. Drs. Jonathan Potts, Isaac Foster, and Benjamin Rush headed the northern, eastern, and middle divisions, while Dr. William Rickman enjoyed greater autonomy as director of the southern region. As a result, a direct chain of command was set up from regimental surgeon to director and regional hospitals were inaugurated, although organizational difficulties did not disappear as a result.

The dispute between Morgan and Shippen took on a new dimension when Benjamin Rush accused Shippen of war profiteering. Congress relieved the Director-General of the responsibility of supplying hospitals in February 1778, but the problems with Shippen's administration were not resolved and Rush kept up his attacks. In June 1779 Morgan made a formal accusation of misconduct to Congress. Shippen stood trial in early 1780, faced with charges of peculation, neglect of patients, and financial mismanagement. In July he was discharged from arrest, having been acquitted on four of the five counts. But neither his name nor reputation was cleared, and in January 1781 Shippen resigned. His replacement, Dr. John Cochran, completed the reorganization of the medical department by subsuming all four regions under his direct control. But he continued to have problems ensuring that the medical department had sufficient funds – in the spring of 1781 he noted that one hospital had been forced to permit ambulatory patients to beg for food. By avoiding the political in-fighting which characterized the administrations of his predecessors, Cochran continued in office until the signing of the peace treaty.

3 Professional Structures

Although most medical practitioners continued to be self-taught or apprenticeship-trained, the medical professions in large cities became stratified in the last three decades of the century. New institutions, such as hospitals and medical schools, reflected and accelerated this trend. But local medical cultures remained strong; for instance, the patterns of development in Boston and Philadelphia were markedly different.

The first hospital in the 13 colonies was founded in Philadelphia in 1751, and the consequences of its foundation shaped Philadelphia medicine into the next century. As in some provincial British cities, the hospital assumed an educational function; apprentices walked the wards and were given lectures by the hospital staff. The new institution was a voluntary one, run by a lay board, and staffed by medical men who were not paid for their attendance. Philadelphia already had an almshouse where inhabitants received medical care from a paid staff, and this quickly became a stepping-stone for younger medical men ultimately hoping to attain a prestigious hospital post.

In 1765 John Morgan took Philadelphia medical education a step further with the foundation of a medical school. During the Revolution the school closed (many of its staff were directly involved in the war), but despite political wrangling medical lectures were resumed after the war. In 1786 a dispensary was added to the roster of the city's medical charities. The College of Physicians, founded in the following year, was an elite and prestigious group of medical men elected to their posts.

Boston's medical societies, on the other hand, were similar to the first state medical society in America, that of New Jersey (founded 1766). Such societies were intended to regulate practice, not honor leading medical men. The Boston Medical Society (founded 1781) examined and licensed practitioners. The society also established an influential fee-bill which dictated fees for various medical services, in effect creating a medical cartel of fixed prices.

Post-revolutionary Boston's medical life was characterized by the founding of learned institutions, often of an elitist nature, such as the Medical Society, the Boston Athenaeum, and the Historical Society. Medical lectures had been given by John Warren to army surgeons during the war, and in 1782 the Harvard corporation appointed three professors of medicine. Some have seen these foundations as a wave of American institution-building, intended to replace or repudiate British models. Others have argued that Boston was just catching up with Philadelphia.

Both cities continued to develop distinctive medical cultures. For example, Philadelphia medicine was strongly influenced by the Edinburgh medical school; many more Philadelphians than Bostonians trained in Edinburgh. Philadelphians were used to walking the wards, receiving extensive clinical instruction, and being offered the opportunity for anatomy and dissection. But Bostonians lacked hospital training until the medical school moved to Boston in 1810, and, when they did go abroad, they tended to choose London. Reciprocally, Edinburgh offered Philadelphians theoretical models of medicine as well as many personal connections. No doubt students' choices were also shaped by their parents' purses; Bostonians often had commercial links with London rather than Edinburgh, making the metropolis a practical option.

Despite the establishment of additional medical schools, including Kings in New York City (1768) and Dartmouth in New Hampshire (1800), medical training continued on traditional lines in many parts of the country. One of the Pennsylvania medical school's first graduates, for example, trained more than 50 apprentices during his career. So, too, domestic medicine and patent remedies continued to flourish; professional structures did not immediately alter patterns of health care.

4 Health

Nor can it be said that medical initiatives dramatically altered patterns of mortality in the new nation. At the time of the Revolution, at least three different patterns of mortality characterized the colonies.

New arrivals to the Chesapeake and southern colonies could expect about a year of "seasoning," in which they were vulnerable to very high mortality from such unfamiliar diseases as *falciparum* malaria (British colonists knew only the milder *vivax* form) and yellow fever, as well as familiar ailments like dysentery and typhoid. But even those who weathered this severe initial period still experienced much higher mortality than in the Mid-Atlantic and New England colonies, although those who lived inland, away from salt water, fared somewhat better. Black slaves who survived their passage were somewhat better equipped than white settlers to withstand malaria and yellow fever, but were particularly prey to respiratory ailments, worms, and dietary deficiencies.

In contrast, contemporaries noted the healthiness of rural New England, which did not experience the southern pattern of sharp annual peaks in mortality. However, towns and villages did undergo severe mortality crises caused by epidemics of diphtheria, smallpox, dysentery, and fevers. Ironically, the very healthiness of rural New England – its lack of endemic disease, its salubrious environment, and its relatively small numbers of new immigrants – made for occasional severe epidemics.

Towns and cities in the Mid-Atlantic and New England colonies fell somewhere between the two extremes of rural New England and the South. Ports were host to endemic disease as well as epidemics. Smallpox remained one of the most dreaded epidemic diseases, recurring every few decades despite the availability of inoculation. At the end of the century smallpox was rivaled by yellow fever, which killed 10 percent of Philadelphia's population in the epidemic of 1793. In major cities endemic diseases of poverty had also become significant killers – consumption, for example, was often the leading cause of death in large cities by the turn of the century.

The one notable contribution post-revolutionary medicine made to eradicating disease was the introduction of vaccination for smallpox. This was safer than inoculation, since it involved infection with cowpox, a milder ailment than the smallpox it protected against. In 1799 Dr. Benjamin Waterhouse, the professor of the theory and practice of medicine at Harvard, received a copy of Edward Jenner's pamphlet which described vaccination. Waterhouse published an account of vaccination in a Boston newspaper, and over the next three years obtained vaccine material from England and carried out tests to show that vaccination protected against smallpox.

FURTHER READING

Bell, W.: *John Morgan, Continental Doctor* (Philadelphia: University of Pennsylvania Press, 1965).

Cash, P., Christianson, E. H., and Estes, J. W. (eds.): *Medicine in Colonial Massachusetts* (Boston: Colonial Society of Massachusetts, 1980).

Dobson, M.: "Mortality gradients and disease exchanges: comparisons from old England and colonial America," *Social History of Medicine*, 2 (1989), 259–97.

Shryock, R.: *Medicine and Society in America, 1660–1860* (Ithaca: Cornell University Press, 1962).

CHAPTER SEVENTY-FOUR

The construction of gender in a republican world

RUTH H. BLOCH

REFERENCES to gender continuously intruded into American revolutionary discourse, for notions of civic morality were repeatedly encoded in language describing ideal masculine and feminine traits. Between the 1760s and 1790s, moreover, dominant ideals of masculinity and femininity were subtly transformed. What had earlier been an essentially male standard of public virtue gradually gave way to a conception of social morality as largely depending on female influence. Ideas about the proper arena in which to perform civic obligations concurrently shifted away from the military and government towards the private institutions of the church and the family. A new view of appropriate relationships within the family served to elevate the status of wives and mothers, whose very femininity was now often perceived as indispensable to the maintenance of republican virtue.

How much these underlying changes in conceptions of gender were specifically due to the events of the Revolution is a debatable question. A similar upgrading of the roles of wife and mother occurred, for example, among the English bourgeoisie during the same general period. In its broadest sense, this reconstruction of gender relations can be associated with the long-term development of the commercial economy and the ascendancy of a pre-Romantic culture of sentimentalism as much as with the American Revolution itself. Across the Atlantic world the ascendant commercial middle classes increasingly celebrated the value of private domestic life, and the

emotionalism previously held against women came to be viewed in a positive light.

In America, however, the Revolution did cast these general, transatlantic changes in a specifically republican and national framework. Both the history of female participation in the patriot cause and the growth of female education in the early republic pushed towards a more generous assessment of women's capabilities (*see* chapter 52, §§3 and 4). Since gender symbolism permeated revolutionary debate, moreover, critical changes in republican ideology hinged in part on the revision of gender definitions. The shift from a masculine to a feminine conception of virtue simultaneously reflected a new understanding of gender relations and a new understanding of republicanism itself.

Unlike other concepts associated with American revolutionary ideology – such as liberty, equality, property, happiness – gender was not, however, considered by eighteenth-century Americans themselves to be a revolutionary issue. Republican ideology contained no explicit call for the reconstruction of popular understandings of masculinity and femininity. Whatever tensions and changes occurred in gender relations during the American Revolution were barely noticed by contemporaries. For the most part even those who commented explicitly on such matters as marriage and female education assumed the continuance of a legal and political system that institutionalized female subordination and relegated men and women to fundamentally different social roles.

1 The Masculine Concept of Power

The main intellectual sources of early revolutionary ideology, Lockean liberalism and classical republicanism, both assumed the dependency and invisibility of women. According to each of these traditions, citizenship was based on a combination of property-holding and military service. For both, the fundamental contest for power within states was a male drama including in its cast of characters free propertyholders, noblemen, and kings. Opposition to absolute despotism was justified in the interest of preserving the liberty and independence of a citizenry that was composed of self-reliant, rights-holding, and arms-bearing men (*see* chapter 87, §2).

Frequently such a conflict between tyrant and subject was described in familial terms. Royalists had long employed the metaphor of paternal authority to legitimate monarchical rule. A king, argued James I, can be compared with "Fathers of families; for a King is trewly *Parens patriae*, the politique father of his people" (McIlwain, 1918, p. 307). In his anti-patriarchal argument against Filmer, Locke had redefined citizenship as a contractual agreement analogous to marriage. Yet both marriage and the subordination of women still remained, in his view, outside politics. The invention of the state was an exclusively masculine act.

In the early revolutionary movement, American patriot ideology drew heavily from both liberal and classical republican thought in its formulations of the imperial conflict. The metaphor of England as the "mother country" had in traditional royalist fashion long pointed to the familial obligations and loyalties inherent in the imperial system. Initially American patriots expressed themselves in these conventional terms in the hope of achieving peaceful reconciliation. As James Otis phrased his appeal in response to the Revenue Act of 1764, "few if any instances can be given where colonies have been disposed to forsake or disobey a tender mother" (Otis, [1764] 1965, p. 448). As the struggle with Britain intensified, however, the image of the imperial mother quickly turned from tender to cruel. In 1765 John Adams likened mother Britain to the monstrous Lady Macbeth, who would have "plucked her nipple from the [infant's] boneless gums,/And dashed the brains out" (Adams, 1850–6, 3: p. 464). The tyrannical lust for power represented a violation of the feminine maternal principle earlier associated with benign imperial rule. Power itself was typically symbolized as aggressively masculine, embodied above all in the supposedly ruthless and self-interested machinations of the King's notorious ministers.

The King himself was usually spared such negative characterizations until the mid-1770s. Until then, protestations of loyalty still typically sought to distance expressions of filial love for the father from the outrage expressed towards his ministers. Yet after the battles of Concord and Lexington, the image of George III as a heartless father emerged with a vengeance. "We swore allegiance to him as a *King*, not as a *Tyrant*," a patriot newspaper angrily declared in 1775, "as a *Father*, not as a *Murderer*" (*Boston Gazette*, July 17, 1775). Crystallizing this growing anti-patriarchal sentiment, Thomas Paine's *Common Sense* characterized George III as "the royal Brute of Britain." As Paine elaborated the familiar familial analogy, America was best understood not as a dependent child but as an adolescent son coming of age. King George figured in his pamphlet as a "wretch, that with the pretended title FATHER OF HIS PEOPLE can unfeelingly hear of their slaughter, and composedly sleep with their blood upon his soul" (Paine, [1776] 1976, p. 92).

2 The Feminine Concept of Liberty

If the image of tyrannical power was aggressively male, the image of its symbolic opposite, liberty, was passively female. Particularly in the early years of the revolutionary movement, liberty was commonly depicted as delicate and vulnerable, susceptible to brutal acts of violence suggestive of rape. Cartoons and other graphic portrayals of the imperial struggle often presented America as a chaste virgin. The portrait of America as an Amerindian princess uncorrupted by European civilization was a common variation on this theme. Another popular feminine image of America was drawn from the Book of Revelation – that of the unprotected woman in the wilderness encountering the wrath of the anti-Christian dragon. Taken together, these various patriotic representations of women highlighted the fragility of American liberty in the face of British power.

3 The Militant Ideal of Masculine Virtue

The symbolic dualism of active male power and passive female virtue was particularly pronounced during the period of resistance in the 1760s and early 1770s. As the patriot movement progressed from resistance to rebellion, however, an alternative masculine ideal of virtue rose to the fore. Paine's influential view of America as an adolescent boy chafing against unjust parental restrictions merged in the mid-1770s with a patriotic ideal of youthful male heroism. In accord with fundamental assumptions of classical republicanism, the language of republicanism in the opening years of the war glorified the physical courage and valiant self-sacrifice of male citizen-soldiers. Military service offered young men the promise of public glory and fame. At the height of the military vogue, a toast on the first anniversary of American Independence made the underlying exclusion of women from this militant conception of citizenship particularly clear, declaring, "May only those Americans enjoy freedom who are ready to die for its defence" (Royster, 1979, p. 32).

Ironically, women were in fact present in the American Army as camp followers. Far from being valorized for their participation, however, they only embarrassed the military leadership. A suggestive woodcut of a woman posed with a gun occasionally appeared in publications of the 1770s, but this image of female militancy predated the conflict with Britain and the stories it was chosen to illustrate had no connection to the American Revolutionary War. Only later would the disguised woman soldier Deborah Sampson Gannett become the popular heroine of American folklore. The term "manly" became itself nearly synonymous with public virtue in revolutionary discourse. "Effeminacy," on the contrary, signified laziness, cowardliness, and corruption.

"Idleness is the mother or nurse of almost every vice," explained the college president John Witherspoon in a patriotic sermon predicting the victory of American troops over "those effeminate and delicate soldiers, who are nursed in the lap of self-indulgence" (Witherspoon, 1776, pp. 56–7).

This ideological association of femininity with laziness and luxury left little room for a republican ideal of woman analogous to that of the militant republican man. Women received recognition as patriots only rarely in the 1760s and 1770s, and then primarily for acts of stoic self-denial in support of the cause. They were praised for abstaining from extravagant imported goods and for laboring to produce homespun yarn, both as individuals and occasionally as "Daughters of Liberty." Women who worked hard and spurned luxury could thus be perceived as renouncing "effeminacy" and as conforming in a limited way to the essentially masculine ideal of republican virtue. A patriotic speech delivered by a young college graduate in 1780 praised the "ladies" for "their admiration of military virtue" and "their generous contributions to relieve the wants of the defenders of their country" (Kerber, 1980, p. 106). Women were similarly valorized in revolutionary propaganda for eagerly sending their men into battle. Young single women ostensibly favored the amorous attentions of courageous soldiers, for, in the words of a patriotic poem of 1778, *"Love hates a coward's impotent embrace"* (Royster, 1979, p. 30). One Philadelphia newspaper publicized the fighting words of a New Jersey matron to her soldier grandsons, "Let me beg of you … that if you fall, it may be like men" (Kerber, 1989, p. 21). At the height of the military fervor, the feminine conception of liberty as passive and in need of protection thus merged with the otherwise highly masculine version of heroic republican virtue.

4 A Less Combative Ideal: Family Life

The symbolic elevation of the male soldier proved, however, short-lived. In the face of growing anxieties about corruption and social disorder both during and after the war, American revolutionaries needed to establish a less combative ideal of republican citizenship consistent with peace and stability.

Widespread political disillusionment in the 1780s undercut earlier millennial expectations of social perfection. Americans lost their earlier confidence that liberty would be preserved if it depended for its survival on the self-sacrificial virtue of the people.

The ideological transformation that underlay the United States Constitution redefined the relationship of men to the state. No longer urged into direct public service, ordinary citizens could, argued the authors of the *Federalist Papers*, indirectly contribute to the greater public good by exercising their freedom to pursue separate and competing interests. The state would protect itself against the destructive forces of selfish factionalism through an election system designed to filter out the most local and particular interests and a structure of government based on the institutional mechanisms of checks and balances. The active display of public virtue, still expected among civic leaders, was no longer required of the majority of republican men.

Not that the revolutionary generation altogether abandoned its hopes for a virtuous society. The virtue that had earlier been associated with the collective, public life gradually became redefined as a private, individual characteristic. Instead of being demonstrated in political activism and public service, it became chiefly manifest in the personal relationships of friendship and family.

This shift away from the earlier valorization of public virtue corresponded to a change in the representation of gender within republican ideology. The increased emphasis on the virtues of private life focused greater amounts of attention on emotional relationships between women and men. Just as the patriarchal family had long stood for royalists as a natural justification of monarchical government, so American revolutionaries devised their own republican understandings of courtship and marriage. Novels and magazines of the 1780s and 1790s excoriated parents for arranging mercenary marriages detrimental to their children's happiness. Couples were to marry out of neither self-interest nor lust but affectionate friendship. The marital relationship was idealized as voluntary and equal,

a metaphor for the relationship between citizens in a republic. And the future of the nation depended on the capacity for mutual love that was best learned in marriage. "That MAN who resolves to live without WOMAN, or that WOMAN who resolves to live without MAN, are ENEMIES TO THE COMMUNITY in which they dwell," pronounced a piece on the "Genius of Liberty" printed in 1798 (Lewis, 1987, p. 709).

5   The New Civic Role of Women

Yet the egalitarian values expressed in this republican conception of marriage reflected no commitment to the political or social equality of women and men. Unlike French revolutionary women, who insisted on bearing arms and forming their own republican societies, American women never claimed universal rights for themselves. Instead of appealing to the ideal of universal equality, the primary justification for female self-assertion was made on the grounds of gender difference. The feminine qualities of sympathy, delicacy, and piety would, according to this view, soften the sensibilities of otherwise overly aggressive and self-interested men. One anonymous tract of 1787 entitled *Women Invited to War* called American women to a collective religious crusade against postwar corruption and greed. Women were increasingly accorded recognition for a new civic role, that of requiring proper republican behavior of male suitors, husbands, and sons. As a Columbia College orator expounded upon the public importance of this private influence, "Yes, ye fair, the reformation of the world is in your power" (*New York Magazine*, May 1795, p. 298).

These new ideals of femininity found repeated expression in the growing body of literature in the early republic devoted to female education. Male leaders such as Benjamin Rush began to insist that American women needed greater knowledge in order to inculcate proper republican manners and morals in their husbands and children. Not only men but educated and articulate women, ranging from the sentimental novelist Hannah Foster to the political polemicist and historian Mercy Otis Warren, contributed to the delineation of the roles of republican wife and mother. Even Judith Sargent Murray, who came the closest to anticipating Mary Wollstonecraft in her insistence upon women's innate rational capacities, never rejected the centrality of marriage and motherhood.

While differing from the modern idea of social and political equality, a feminine principle thus entered into conceptions of the relationship between civil society and the republican polity. This was a new development in the history of American political thought, one anticipated by neither classical republican nor classical liberal theory. Women were now increasingly represented as a crucial part of the republican moral order even as they remained outside the institutions of government. The expanded definition of female civil obligations also enhanced women's domestic status, challenging, if by no means eliminating, older hierarchies within the family. In the new symbolic order, the republican wife and mother can be seen as the counterpart to the image of the benevolently paternal Founding Fathers. Moral guides rather than imperious rulers, these new models of political authority replaced the earlier patriarchal ideal of monarchy while retaining the analogy between the family and state. In the course of reformulating this analogy, gender relations had been significantly redefined.

These ideological changes never overcame strict limitations in the appropriate roles for republican women, however. The more elevated notion of the civic value of personal domestic relationships gave rise to a still more deeply gendered definition of public and private spheres. The Revolution provided no impetus to re-evaluate the context of male economic and political power that rendered women ultimately dependent for all their newfound authority within the home. The idealization of domestic relationships encouraged the privatization of morality, a process which indirectly sanctioned men's pursuit of self-interest in the public domain. The republican construction of gender – built on the premise that female virtue could counteract male selfishness – at once increased the public value attributed to women and widened the symbolic polarity between feminine dependency and masculine autonomy within subsequent American culture.

FURTHER READING

Adams, John: *The Works of John Adams*, ed. C. F. Adams (Boston, 1850–6).

Bloch, Ruth H.: "The gendered meanings of virtue in revolutionary America," *Signs: Journal of Women in Culture and Society*, 13 (1987), 37–58.

Kerber, Linda K., *Women of the Republic: Intellect and Ideology in Revolutionary America* (Chapel Hill: University of North Carolina Press, 1980).

——: "'History can do it no justice': women and the reinterpretation of the American Revolution," *Women in the Age of the American Revolution*, ed. Ronald Hoffman and Peter J. Albert (Charlottesville: University Press of Virginia, 1989).

Kerber, Linda K., et al.: "Beyond roles, beyond spheres: thinking about gender in the early republic," *William and Mary Quarterly*, 46 (1989), 565–85.

Lewis, Jan: "The republican wife: virtue and seduction in the early republic," *William and Mary Quarterly*, 44 (1987), 690–721.

McIlwain, Charles: *The Political Works of James I* (Cambridge: Cambridge University Press, 1918).

Paine, Thomas: *Common Sense* (Philadelphia, 1776); repr., ed. Isaac Kramnick (New York: Penguin, 1976).

Otis, James: *The Rights of the British Colonies Asserted and Proved* (1764), in *Pamphlets of the American Revolution*, ed. Bernard Bailyn (Cambridge, Mass.: Harvard University Press, 1965).

Royster, Charles: *A Revolutionary People at War* (Chapel Hill: University of North Carolina Press, 1979).

Smith-Rosenberg, Carroll: "Domesticating 'virtue': coquettes and revolutionaries in young America," *Literature and the Body: Essays on Populations and Persons*, ed. Elaine Scarry (Baltimore: John Hopkins University Press, 1988), 160–84.

Witherspoon, John: *The Dominion of Providence* (Philadelphia, 1776).

CHAPTER SEVENTY-FIVE

The construction of race in republican America

JAMES SIDBURY

DISCUSSIONS of race in early republican America must be couched in carefully qualified language, because the modern Western concept of "race" was emerging during precisely this time. Over the course of the nineteenth century, social and natural scientists in Europe and the Americas built on Enlightenment proto-racial theories to argue that human kind could be divided into various numbers of racial sub-categories. Members of each racial group were believed to differ from members of other racial groups in consistent ways that were stable and inherited across generations. While the particular indices of difference – skull size or shape, sexual "ardency," intelligence-test score, or athletic ability – have varied over time and space, the belief in stable inherited difference has remained a staple of racial thought. Although the overwhelming majority of late twentieth-century scholars have come to reject such racial thought, the sense of difference that these nineteenth-century theories described remains the object of inquiry for most historians tracing "race" in history.

In the wake of the civil rights movement, historians have paid increasing attention to the place of racial difference in the American Revolution. The reasons for this growing interest are rooted in both the salience of racial issues in late twentieth-century America and the apparent contradictions inherent in a revolution officially devoted to the claim that "all men are created equal" but led by slaveholders. While much of the historiography has focused on the moral and political failings of the Founding Fathers, especially Thomas Jefferson, many historians in recent years have turned away from a simple focus on what the Founding Fathers did or did not do. Such scholars have chosen instead to explore the broader meanings of racial difference and of the status of non-white peoples during the era of the American Revolution. Simultaneously, more attention has been paid to what people of color themselves did during and immediately after the American Revolution, and how their actions affected the course of the Revolution and early republic. This new scholarship has uncovered an irony that is consonant with, but in some ways deeper than, that of the existence of slavery in a republic founded on liberty. It is becoming increasingly clear that the era of the American Revolution was both a formative era in the development of racial thought among white Americans – the time during which a sense of whiteness was first articulated – and the period in which Amerindians and African Americans responded by enunciating clear senses of racial difference and unity in their own struggles for equality in the new nation. The Revolution, with its ringing endorsements of man's natural equality before God, also helped spawn the racial ideologies that have alternately divided and inspired Americans ever since.

1 The Emergence of White Identity

Current scholarship sheds the clearest light on the conceptions of racial difference that prevailed among Whites in early republican America. European settlers in North America had, of course, been living in close proximity to indigenous Americans and to Africans and people of African descent for close to two centuries by the time of the American Revolution. Europeans responded to these peoples in complicated ways during the colonial period, but that complexity cannot alter the obvious ways in which white settlers believed themselves different from Blacks and Amerindians. Nonetheless, in a monarchical system in which hierarchy was considered natural, British Americans had little incentive to question or explain those differences with intellectual rigor. By replacing the Crown's authority with an appeal to natural rights and popular sovereignty, however, the American Revolution necessitated a more formal conception of the place of black and red peoples in the new republic. Regardless of the specific intent of the signers of the Declaration of Independence, a nation formally devoted to the "self evident" claim that "all men are created equal" and endowed by "their Creator with certain inalienable rights" had to grapple with the persistence of slavery and the unequal status of Amerindians. Some white Americans responded by fighting against slavery and some sought to protect Amerindians' claims to their land. Others sought to explain away the seeming contradictions, and in doing so they forged definitions of citizenship that helped produce white racial identity.

The libertarian ideology of the American Revolution inevitably highlighted the existence of chattel slavery in the new republic. Indeed, many white Americans grew disenchanted with slavery, and in the three decades following the end of the Revolutionary War anti-slavery activists put slavery on the road to abolition in seven states: Vermont, Pennsylvania, Massachusetts, Connecticut, Rhode Island, New York, and New Jersey. The national government also took a stand against the extension of slavery into the Old Northwest and came close to adopting a similar position regarding slavery in the Old Southwest (present day Alabama and Mississippi). And in 1807 Congress passed a law closing the Atlantic slave trade to the United States. In each case anti-slavery sentiment combined with other forces to produce change, and together these actions reflect the distaste for slavery that emerged in the era of the American Revolution, a distaste that could prove decisive where slavery's roots were shallow.

In the other states of the new union, however, slavery played a more central role in regional economics and societies. From the Chesapeake south to Georgia, colonial elites' wealth had grown out of the labor of enslaved people. The 1790s invention of the cotton gin further entrenched slavery in the southern states by simplifying the processing of short-staple cotton and thus opening up the Old Southwest to large-scale plantation agriculture. Though the Revolution could and did inspire anti-slavery thought and action within the slave societies of the southern states – manumission laws were liberalized and many white southerners supported the closing of the Atlantic slave trade – outright attacks on the institution were less effective. There are, of course, simple economic reasons for this, but they are inseparable from ideological complexities: because slaves were both people and property, revolutionary ideology offered equal sanction to masters' claims to the inviolability of their property rights and slaves' claims to their human rights. Formal conceptions of white people as inherently – "racially" – different from black people arose out of this tension. During the decades following the Revolution these conceptions were expressed by white Americans of different classes in northern and southern states.

Early explanations for this difference oscillated between two poles rooted in Enlightenment thought: the belief that slavery made blacks different from whites was rooted in environmentalist theories of human development, while the claim that blacks were inherently inferior rested upon the urge toward scientific classification. Explanations were not, of course, always given. When, in his *Letters from an American Farmer* (1782), J. Hector St. John de Crèvecoeur described the "new race of men" called Americans, he mentioned descendants of the English, French, and Dutch while silently excluding Blacks and

Amerindians. Those who did seek to explain the exclusion ranged from some scientists who claimed that Blacks would become white after generations in America's "moderate" climate, to Benjamin Rush, the Philadelphia anti-slavery activist, who speculated that black skin resulted from generations of African leprosy that modern science might "cure," to Thomas Jefferson, who maintained in *Notes on the State of Virginia* (1782) that "physical distinctions" proved a "difference of race" between black and white people, and concluded that it was not Blacks' "condition [as slaves] then, but nature, which has produced the distinction." The connection between racial categorization and the problem of slavery in republican America is underscored by the fact that Jefferson's invocation of nature's role in producing races came during an extended explanation of the barriers to ending slavery in Virginia. Given their belief in the inherent differences between the races, Jefferson and others implied that the new republic could only prosper under the secure control of the superior race – whites. Stronger supporters of slavery went further to argue that race-based bondage helped ensure the survival of republican government by guaranteeing a level of equality among all white citizens.

While clear intellectual explanations of this belief were, by their nature, only offered by elites, ample evidence indicates widespread consensus. From legislative petitions in Virginia in the 1780s, to state constitutional debates in South Carolina during the 1790s, to racially exclusive ceremonies celebrating the new nation in northern towns and cities during the decades following Independence, people of European descent in various localities throughout the United States made clear that their vision of the nation did not include black citizens. In 1790, the first federal naturalization act passed after the adoption of the Constitution ratified that vision by offering the possibility of citizenship to any "free white" immigrant who lived in the United States for two years. Even as northern and southern states began down the roads that would lead one section to slavery and the other toward freedom, many white

Americans throughout the union expressed a growing sense that the new nation was and should remain a white nation.

2   The Emergence of Amerindian Identity

Amerindians were not as central as Blacks to white Americans' developing sense of racial identity, but they were profoundly affected by the American Revolution and the new nation that it created. By the era of the Revolution, Amerindians, like Blacks, had long been suffering oppression at the hands of white Americans. The Americans' victory in the Revolution unleashed western settlement, greatly accelerating the rate at which Amerindians in the Ohio country and the Old Southwest were dispossessed of their land, so the Revolution was generally a disaster for native peoples. That onslaught of invaders helped stimulate native spiritual and political leaders from several different peoples – most prominently the Delaware and the Shawnee – to seek a new level of unity among all tribal groups, a unity explicitly based on the notion that Amerindians were different from white people. This conviction of Amerindian racial unity emerged at roughly the same time as European settlers in the east articulated a sense of white identity.

For much of the colonial period, different native peoples had fought, traded, and negotiated with one another as well as with various European powers. Myriad diplomatic and military possibilities had constantly been created by shifting lines of friendship and competition among different native peoples as well as among British, French, and Spanish settlers. Between 1763 and 1815, however, the possibilities for Amerindians to find a middle ground among different European powers diminished as the French were expelled from North America and the British presence grew fainter. Amerindians living south of Canada and east of the Mississippi River faced the growing threat of white American settlers with fewer realistic hopes for useful diplomatic or military alliances with France, England, or Spain. Leaders of the new American republic argued that

Amerindians were primitive and needed to adapt to the arrival of "civilized" whites by adopting their ways, accepting Christianity, and settling down into European-style agricultural communities. American settlers and politicians pressured Amerindians to sign treaties granting settlers' rights to most native land. In return Amerindians would receive help with the "civilizing" process. White leaders maintained that over time, as Amerindians became civilized, they would be absorbed into the new nation, and, in keeping with that claim, some treaties between Amerindians and the Federal Government specified ways in which individuals could achieve citizenship by separating themselves from their tribe.

These conditions helped give greater currency to several Amerindian religious leaders' visions of native unity. These leaders called on Amerindians throughout the Ohio and Mississippi River valleys to recognize that they were racially different from white and black people, to reject those aspects of white culture – especially alcohol – that rendered Amerindians dependent on trade with the settlers who were taking up the land, and to unify as a single people to defend their land and way of life. This critique of Amerindian assimilation did not originate in the post-revolutionary era. As early as the 1760s the Delaware prophet Neolin helped inspire Pontiac's war against the British, a war that entailed both military strikes against British forts and a spiritual strike against many European ways within Amerindian country.

Pontiac was defeated, but Neolin's campaign to unify and purify Amerindian peoples proved more enduring. The Revolutionary War temporarily revived opportunities for different Amerindian villages and tribal groups to play white powers against one another and to enhance their own power through access to European goods. However, the defeat of the British and Britain's slow but persistent withdrawal from the western regions of the new United States left western Amerindians from the Ohio country to New Orleans without reliable European allies. Amerindian villages were increasingly divided about how to respond to these new conditions. Some

Amerindian leaders argued that their people had little choice but to cooperate with representatives of the new American republic and to seek to win the best terms possible. Others continued in the tradition of Neolin and Pontiac to push for Amerindian unity and resistance to white encroachment on their land. The late 1780s and early 1790s witnessed a major alliance that included members of Amerindian nations extending from the Shawnee and Delaware in the Ohio country down to the Creek and Cherokee in the South. American troops under General Anthony Wayne broke this confederacy at the Battle of Fallen Timbers in 1794, but the spirit of resistance did not die. It re-emerged under the leadership of Tecumseh and the spiritual leader Tenskwatawa ("The Prophet") to fuel a final attempt to forge unity among the eastern woodlands Amerindians during the first decade of the nineteenth century. It, too, was crushed militarily, this time by troops under William Henry Harrison at the Battle of Tippecanoe in 1811.

The military defeats suffered by these prophets of Amerindian unity cannot, however, obscure their role in forging a sense of racial identity among Amerindians from the Ohio country in the North to present-day Louisiana in the South. Famous prophets like Neolin and Tenskwatawa shared a belief in Amerindian unity with many less well-documented Amerindian spiritual figures. Some of these figures argued that Amerindian peoples had been created by an Amerindian deity while white and black people had been created by another god. All maintained that native peoples' only hope to regain mastery over their own fate lay in turning away from the village, ethnic, and regional rivalries that hindered unified resistance to white settlers. Amerindians had, in short, to accept a common identity as Amerindians and to fight together against the white settlers who sought to take their land. This battle would, of necessity, be cultural as well as military.

It would be misleading to suggest that all, or even most, eastern Amerindians came to accept this "racialized" vision of the world during the decades following the American Revolution. Some native peoples – most famously the Cherokee – concluded that continued military resistance would prove suicidal and attempted to conform to white demands that they "civilize." Many Amerindians living farther to the east along the seaboard remained beyond the sphere of the prophets, and they increasingly blended into African American communities. Even those peoples from whom prophetic nativists arose included many Amerindians who chose to pursue the most cooperative relationships they could with white settlers and governments. Nonetheless, an explicitly articulated proto-racial sense of Amerindian unity emerged among important eastern groups during the American Revolution and the era of the early republic, and that racial identity has remained an important force in the history of Amerindians in the United States.

3   The Emergence of African Identity

The Revolution produced more ambiguous effects for black Americans than for Amerindians. Many enslaved blacks joined the British army during the Revolutionary War, seeking and sometimes winning freedom by fighting against the patriot forces with their racially defined conception of human liberty. A smaller number fought for the American side and won their freedom from grateful state governments after the war. Many more black Americans achieved freedom as a result of the emancipation movements that triumphed in northern states after the war or the liberalized manumission laws that helped produce rapidly growing free black populations throughout the upper southern states during the final decades of the eighteenth century. And with the closing of the Atlantic slave trade in 1808, the African-born among North American slaves – already a minority in most communities – became a smaller and smaller minority in comparison to American-born (or "creole") slaves. All of this occurred while, as noted earlier, white Americans articulated increasingly racist conceptions of black Americans, and as southern states became increasingly committed to protecting slavery within the new union. In this complicated and difficult

environment black Americans began to offer a vision of "African" identity that stood as an alternative to the derogatory one coming to dominate white America.

Enslaved Africans and people of African descent had begun to develop shared identities in Britain's North American colonies prior to the American Revolution. Creoles became predominant among the enslaved in the Chesapeake region by the middle of the eighteenth century, and western expansion extended black kinship networks throughout the state. High mortality among those consigned to the rice swamps of South Carolina and Georgia resulted in larger and steadier importations of African people and probably more persistence of ethnic tension among Blacks in the lowcountry, but creole languages – Gullah in South Carolina and Geechie in Georgia – developed during the eighteenth century, and they served to tie together enslaved people on the rice coast. Smaller black populations lived north of the Chesapeake, and they too left sporadic evidence of their emerging sense of identity in the form of public ceremonies in which they came together to elect "negro governors" of their regions. Each of these cases suggests an emerging local sense of racial identity among people from various African societies and their descendants.

During and after the American Revolution these local senses of unity began to be transformed into a broader diasporic or racial identity. The creation of a national union putatively devoted to equality and the discussions of racial equality and inequality that the union stimulated played a role in this development, but they alone cannot explain the flowering of diasporic institutions that occurred in the wake of the Revolution. Beginning with the founding of the Prince Hall African Masonic Lodge in Boston during the Revolutionary War and continuing through the first two decades of the nineteenth century, black people up and down the Atlantic seaboard founded institutions that incorporated "African" in their names. The most famous of these was the African Methodist Episcopal Church, founded in 1816, but it was far from unusual. Black people from Savannah, Georgia to Boston, Massachusetts founded other "African" churches of various denominations, and free black people in northern cities also built "African" schools, fraternal groups, and self-help organizations. Members of these organizations – at least those in the North where such activity was possible – expressed their identification with their fellow "African" in America by parading and petitioning in favor of the abolition of slavery and the slave trade throughout the new nation. They also celebrated victories against slavery and helped shelter runaway slaves who escaped from the South. In speeches and pamphlets that they produced in support of such activity, they also developed visions of racial identity rooted in newly articulated understandings of "African" history. Some appeals to shared history focused on the recent past, tracing the oppression shared by black victims of slavery and highlighting the Haitian Revolution's destruction of a slave regime; others claimed shared glory by turning to classical history and the contributions of ancient Egypt to Greek and thus Western civilization; still others maintained that sub-Saharan African peoples and their descendants could all trace their genealogies to a common Old Testament past. Whatever combination of these arguments different authors or speakers used, many asserted a shared history for black people in Africa and the Americas, and they emphasized the victories that slaves had won against their masters, from Moses and the biblical exodus to Toussaint L'Ouverture and the creation of the first black republic in the Americas. In the process they rejected the negative connotations that whites placed on "African" identity, while asserting a positive racial identity rooted in a shared past. Many believed that black people in Haiti, on the west coast of Africa, and in North America shared a future just as their forebears had shared a past. Both past and future were rooted in a common racial identity.

4 Conclusion

The period stretching from the American Revolution through the first decades of the nineteenth century – the era of the early American republic – witnessed fundamental developments in the history of race in the United States. Much that was new in that period can be traced to the tension rooted in the persistence of slavery in a republic formally devoted to the doctrine of natural equality. Americans of European descent responded to the paradox of slavery in a "free" republic by arguing that slavery could persist in the United States precisely because those enslaved were inherently incapable – racially incapable – of achieving the self-reliance and virtue required of republican citizens. Some proponents of this argument sought to portray the reliance on black slavery as a pillar in the system of republican society.

Amerindians and black Americans responded to emerging visions of the United States as a white republic by forging oppositional senses of racial identity. Ironically it was Amerindian prophets with their claims for racial polygenesis who most clearly anticipated some of the content of classic nineteenth-century racist thought. They argued that Amerindian people, regardless of their tribal affiliations, were fundamentally different from white and black people, and thus that Amerindians had to reject the invaders from Europe and Africa in order to recover the form of life intended for them by their creator. Formative figures in early black racial thought rooted "African" identity in historical argument rather than in claims to essential difference. But because so much of the discourse of early black racial identity responded to white racial thought – especially to Jefferson's assertions of black inferiority in the *Notes on the State of Virginia* – by proclaiming an unappreciated history of black achievement stretching from the present back into the classical past, black authors often imported implications of essential difference from the texts they sought to refute.

Few would question the damage that has been done by the sense of white identity that began to come into its own during the early republican period in the United States. Amerindian and black senses of racial identity have not had equally negative effects, in part because they arose in opposition to the dominant group's claim to racial superiority and in part because throughout the history of the United States they have helped to fuel fights for greater equality. Nonetheless, there is an irony in the degree to which the era of the American Revolution, with its lofty invocations of the natural equality of all people, spawned inherently exclusive racial identities among black, red, and white Americans. In 1782 the Continental Congress chose "E Pluribus Unum" (From many, one) as the motto of the new nation. While the motto was originally intended to refer to the forging of a single nation out of the 13 colonies, it quickly became a richer metaphor for the process through which American nationality encompassed people from many different nations and made of them one. Recent scholarship on race in the early republic suggests that the process was richer still. The forging of a nation out of 13 British colonies involved the forging of American nationalism out of English and other European peoples. The exclusion of Amerindians and Blacks from that process stimulated each to make of their many ethnic or tribal groupings one racial identity. Each group sought a unity based implicitly or explicitly on the exclusion of the others, and together they helped create the basis for the multi-racial society that emerged in the United States.

FURTHER READING

Bethel, Elizabeth Rauh: *The Roots of African-American Identity: Memory and History in Antebellum Free Communities* (New York: St. Martin's Press, 1997).

Dowd, Gregory Evans: *A Spirited Resistance: The North American Indian Struggle for Unity, 1745–1815* (Baltimore and London: Johns Hopkins University Press, 1992).

Jordan, Winthrop D.: *White Over Black: American Attitudes Toward the Negro, 1550–1812* (Chapel Hill, NC: The Institute of Early American History and Culture by the University of North Carolina Press, 1968).

MacLeod, Duncan J.: "Toward Caste," in *Slavery and Freedom in the Age of the American Revolution*, eds. Ira Berlin and Ronald Hoffman (Charlottesville, Va.: United States Capitol Historical Society by the University Press of Virginia, 1983), 217–36.

Morgan, Edmund S.: *American Slavery, American Freedom: The Ordeal of Colonial Virginia* (New York, W. W. Norton and Sons, 1975).

Sidbury, James: *Ploughshares into Swords: Race, Rebellion, and Identity in Gabriel's Virginia, 1730–1810* (Cambridge: Cambridge University Press, 1997).

White, Shane: "'It Was a Proud Day': African Americans, festivals, and parades in the North, 1741–1834," *Journal of American History* 81 (1994) 13–50.

CHAPTER SEVENTY-SIX

The construction of social status in revolutionary America

CHRISTINE DANIELS

REVOLUTIONARY Americans constructed social status in much the same
way as did contemporary Britons. They
lacked the well-developed conception of
social class that would emerge in the nineteenth century. Rather, they saw society as
organized vertically around communities,
families, occupations, and skills. They put
central emphasis upon wealth and the
degree of independence from external control that it conferred. They also considered one's legal condition, distinguishing
between free masters (including unmarried
or widowed women) and various legal dependents, especially servants and slaves under their
command. They distinguished between husbands and wives, parents and children, and
children with and without parents. They also
took the measure of people by the degree of
their education, learning, and professional
skills, and made a sharp distinction between
those people who worked with their hands
and the much smaller population of gentle
folk – planters, wealthy farmers, merchants,
lawyers, doctors, and clergymen, who did
not. Finally, by the early years of the new
republic, they were able to represent such
distinctions with some precision through
new varieties of consumer goods, many
of them imported from Great Britain or
Europe.

An individual's freedom from dependence
resonated with the economic reality of the
early colonies. Anglo-America was, from
its inception, land- and resource-rich and
labor-poor. The colonies south of New
England, moreover, depended upon staple

crops for their existence. Tobacco in the
Chesapeake, rice in the lower South and
sugar in the West Indies all demanded intense
labor, while free laborers were only to be had
at great expense. As a result, seventeenth-
century landholders in the Anglo-American
colonies relied upon an assortment of bound
laborers, most notably indentured servants
and slaves.

Early colonial masters needed to command
sufficient labor to build farms and plantations. As a result, such embryonic elites as
the seventeenth-century colonies possessed
were recognized by their mastery of laborers, rather than their ownership of vast
quantities of unimproved land. As late as
the final quarter of the eighteenth century,
revolutionary America's single most important social divide lay, not between economic
elites and other classes, but between people
who were independents and their dependents. While this distinction was most pronounced during the seventeenth century, it
continued through the eighteenth; by 1775,
no more than 15 percent of the population
of revolutionary America could be termed
independents, although this was an impres-
sively large proportion by contemporary
standards. An independent was a person (an
adult male or *feme sole*) who possessed sufficient property to leave him or her theoretically free from the control of other persons;
dependents (married women, children, servants, slaves or others) were subject to the
will of the independent upon whom they
relied for their support. The legal control of
dependents by independents – which was

elaborated socially into the concept of patriarchy – permeated all aspects of revolutionary America. When the rule of the state was weak (as it was in early America until the Civil War), patriarchy assumed a great deal of governance.

Independents exercised legal and economic command over dependents. Patriarchs, who interacted with the political and legal systems, were to keep order in their households, and to insure that household members did not disturb the civil peace. They were empowered to employ moderate physical chastisement, if necessary, to do so. Dependents had no political voice, and their access to the law was restricted. Nor did dependents possess economic freedom; married women's property, for example, passed to their husbands upon marriage, unless both parties had agreed otherwise while the woman was still *sole*. Servants and slaves were also (theoretically, at least) forbidden to trade with anyone other than their master.

Colonial communities used this familial model to provide for all social deviants – criminals, orphans, the insane, the blind, and the aged. Revolutionary America possessed neither social welfare systems, police forces, nor penitentiaries; in the absence of such institutions, patriarchs performed the roles of all three. County governments, knowing their constituents, refused to raise sufficient taxes to provide social services, such as prisons, orphanages, or hospitals. Instead, independent householders provided space in their homes for all people who were not to be trusted at liberty, or who could not help themselves. This practice provided patriarchal control of and support for irregular people who might otherwise disrupt communities. The householders who kept them, married men or widows, expected compensation for their efforts and received it as a credit on their county taxes.

A man's standing within political structures and his recognition as a person worthy of independence, however, were based not only on how well he controlled his dependents, but on how generously and honestly he supported them. Independents were expected to sustain dependents adequately and treat them fairly, even affectionately. They were responsible for the civil education

of the persons who relied upon them. If a patriarch failed to treat his dependents responsibly, he violated the implicit social terms on which his control was based. With the important single exception of slaves, however, independents did not own their dependents. Dependents were neither discrete political nor economic persons, but they were discrete legal persons, not things.

Commanding labor was a mark of an independent man's standing during the seventeenth century. As the eighteenth century wore on, however, and the older-settled regions of the colonies became increasingly populous, good land in such areas became scarce, while slave work forces increased. By the time of the American Revolution, few freed servants or younger sons of middling farmers or planters could acquire improved land in long-established communities. As the long-settled regions of the colonies became increasingly populous, however, the command of real property became a more important mark of a person's status. This trend was especially marked in the urban areas of the colonies and the new nation.

Land had little value until it was improved – occupied, cleared, drained, planted, and fenced, with houses and outbuildings erected. Unimproved lands were worth only a few pennies an acre. In contrast, by 1774, improved lands in populous Suffolk or Essex County, Massachusetts were often valued at £10 per acre or more. As population and capital improvements increased, wealth in long-settled regions, both real and personal, became increasingly concentrated in the hands of elites. Farm-building created opportunities for accumulation which permitted some men to outstrip their neighbors. In the colonies south of New England, slavery furthered the progress of inequality by enabling some men to command far larger work forces than others. Finally, while the diversification of the mainland colonial economies (underway by the early eighteenth century) created new economic opportunities, many small and middling planters and farmers did not have the resources to invest in necessary capital equipment to exploit these opportunities. As a result, real wealth became disproportionately concentrated in the hands of elites – the 5–10 percent of colonial adult males which included leading merchants, farmers and planters, and professionals in the older areas of the colonies.

On the other hand, opportunities to acquire land grew rapidly in areas beyond the first and second tiers of settlement after 1780. While many elite people and some middling and laboring people elected to remain in long-settled areas, others left for the frontiers. By the beginning of the Revolution, for example, slightly more than half of Virginia's population lived either in the Piedmont or the Shenandoah Valley, while the rest remained in the tidewater. Material success or the lack thereof in one's home community was always one of the most important factors in a man's decision to stay put or move on, although family ties became increasingly important after the first generation or two of settlement in a given area in keeping some free residents in place.

The increasing concentration of wealth in the hands of elites was not necessarily a simple upward trend in pre-revolutionary America. In some rural areas, for example, this bias peaked during the first decade of the eighteenth century. In Philadelphia and other urban areas, it peaked immediately after the Seven Years' War. The general progress of inequality, however, continually drifted upward. In the rural Chesapeake by the 1770s, 20 percent of the property holders owned nearly 70 percent of the wealth; in rural New England, almost 65 percent; in the rural Middle Colonies, nearly 55 percent; and in Philadelphia, 85 percent. This concentration of inequality continued – in fact, escalated – after the end of the American Revolution.

Tenancy also rose gradually throughout the eighteenth century in long-established rural areas. In one old Maryland county by the 1750s, for example, more than 56 percent of households were established on rented lands, up from 35 percent during the 1730s. Before the middle of the eighteenth century, moreover, many young people rented land while saving money to purchase their own farms, and many long-term leases offered opportunities to acquire some "sweat equity" in capital improvements made to leased lands. The terms of these leases,

however, often became less advantageous to lessees as the century progressed, while more people became tenants for life.

But grinding poverty was unusual in the rural colonies, even in long-settled regions. Throughout the eighteenth century, most rural working people and their families, even those who owned no land, were able to cobble together a livelihood through a mix of wage labor, work in various commercial endeavors (such as crafts or fishing ventures), and tenancy. Such families, of course, virtually always relied, at least in part, on the wage labor of both parents, and often of the older children as well, to survive.

Colonial farmers, planters, and merchants hired rural wage laborers for virtually all occasional tasks. Rural working men drained new land, set weirs and seines for spring fishing, felled and mauled trees into lumber, plowed, planted, harvested, and threshed wheat. They mowed marsh hay, husked corn, and swingled flax, and sometimes worked at crafts, especially weaving and tanning. Rural working women made butter, cheese, cider, honey, soap, and candles, and raised poultry, for sale to local stores. They often spun yarn and sometimes wove cloth for the same markets. By the mid-eighteenth century, free women in the Mid-Atlantic at least occasionally reaped wheat. Most would not have had enough upper body strength to use a scythe, and used smaller and less efficient sickles. Women received less than half of a man's wage for reaping, but every hand counted during the harvest. Not all hired laborers were white; African Americans also worked as free laborers in rural areas, particularly in the Mid-Atlantic region from North Carolina to Pennsylvania.

Even widows and orphans could support themselves, albeit meagerly, in rural areas. Widow Mary Betson, for example, occupied a small, raw tenancy in Maryland during the mid-1740s. Her lease included the right to take a certain amount of firewood each year, and her household included her teenage daughter and a young hired boy. With her boy's help, she grew corn and a ran a few hogs in the woods for meat. She and her daughter sold chickens and turkeys, and made shirts, breeches, stockings, and gloves for sale. County governments, too, sometimes hired widows to care for the very old, the crippled and the insane, although in rural areas of the colonies and of the new nation few people who were not sick or disabled received long-term poor relief. Rural poverty, despite its bleakness and monotony, did not often involve starving or freezing to death.

Although they lived adequately, however, all working people, rural and urban, who did not own real property in a world that lacked insurance and social services lived close to disaster. Landless workers had little protection from ill fortune. If either spouse in a working family was seriously injured or died while his or her children were still very young or the workers themselves were elderly, their families were often sent into a downward spiral of debt.

Widow Margaret Kibby of Cecil County, Maryland, for example, had "procur[ed] by her Labour a comfortable & necessary subsistance," before a run of bad luck and ill-health. "Thro ye bad Conduct of a Midwife," Kibby "was greatly hurt," and after her husband died, the complications of that traumatic childbirth rendered her unable any longer "to Work for a Living." Another woman, Susannah Temple, "with the assistance of her late husband" supported "herself with some little Credit & without running into Debt." After "a violent illness," however, "she lost the use of her limbs," and was incapable of "Spinning or doing other work to gain a Support her hands being quite useless." In 1786, her husband died. "[L]osing this rod" reduced Temple to "the humanity of her neighbors & the sale of what few things" she had. (Manuscript 231, Cecil County Petitions to the Court, Maryland Historical Society, Baltimore, Maryland.)

But if, in general, the rich were becoming richer in eighteenth-century America, so were the middling and the poor. While economic opportunities became more restricted in developed areas, the constant improvement of western lands and the progressive diversification of the colonies' economy insured that the early American pie grew ever larger. Between 1750 and 1776, the colonial economy experienced its longest and most pronounced period of growth ever. On the eve of the American Revolution, per capita domestic product was higher than it had ever been, higher than that of any other nation in the world, and considerably higher than it would be again in the United States for some time, possibly as late as 1840.

By the final quarter of the eighteenth century, an increasingly diverse economy created a growing array of occupational niches, particularly in urban areas. As commercial entrepôts, cities particularly hosted an increasing variety of vocations by the 1770s, particularly for the artisan and laboring classes. During the second half of the eighteenth century, for example, sailors comprised one-fifth of the working men in Philadelphia, while artisans and laborers who supplied goods and services to the commercial sector (draymen, shallopmen, coopers, farriers, wheelwrights, sailmakers, and the like) constituted another 15 percent. Most of the remainder produced goods or performed services for Philadelphia's local retail market, which was in turn fueled by the growth of the city's overseas trade. Urban laborers loaded ballast into or unloaded cargoes from waiting ships, collected crops from the surrounding countryside, and delivered wheat and oats to the mercantile mills they themselves had helped to build.

By the third quarter of the eighteenth century as well, urban working-class people had begun to comport and present themselves differently from middle-class people. Their clothes (designed for ease of movement while working) fit them loosely, and were made of plain durable stuff; working men's trousers and aprons were often leather. In fact, simply wearing trousers, rather than breeches, proclaimed a working man in the late eighteenth century. More outré male laborers, including sailors and some apprentices, sported earrings and tattoos as well. Such tattoos proclaimed their attachments to specific crafts (seagoing or artisan), family members or nations. While elite men wore powdered wigs, and middling men wore natural ones, working men wore their own hair. Some workers, such as sailors, in fact proclaimed their trades with their extremely long pigtails. Working-class women often labored only in their shifts, jackets and short petticoats, wearing neither stays nor stockings. Elites, in contrast, wore clothes cut to fit their bodies more closely, and studied their movements to emphasize grace. Elite men abandoned breeches for trousers after the Revolution, but their elegant cut and expensive materials still proclaimed class differences.

Education, too, from the mastery of reading in the Bible to complex accounting and the learned professions, marked elaborate social distinctions in revolutionary America. Differing educational accomplishments had long distinguished between people of differing social classes and genders. During the seventeenth and most of the eighteenth centuries, reading and writing were taught as separate skills, both in Britain and in British America. Reading instruction was conducted orally, and required no writing practice. Many people, including working-class men and virtually all women, learned to read without ever learning to write. Even many women who conducted "dame schools," where young children learned reading, could not themselves write. Writing, on the other hand, was considered a skill restricted to middle- and upper-class men; writing masters often served an apprenticeship to learn their craft as other artisans did. While reading was considered an important means of imbibing religious, political, and other forms of information, writing was considered a job-related skill of most use to men such as merchants, skilled craftsmen, great planters, ministers, and lawyers who kept financial records, wrote sermons and the like.

By the very late eighteenth century, increasing numbers of women and some working-class men were learning to write, and to master some arithmetic as well. Working-class women did not generally partake of the same benefits until the 1820s, when more public schools became available, at least in urban areas. This post-revolutionary trend toward increasing education was notable throughout the former colonies, but most especially in cities such as Boston and Philadelphia. A rapid increase in urban commerce in part spurred this growth. City life demanded the ability to buy and sell goods or to settle accounts with shopkeepers

without being cheated. Working people in rural areas, however, did not benefit from increasing standards of education before the 1840s, if then. And few working people at any time, even the functionally literate, achieved the levels of learning that elite people did.

From 1776 to 1793, however, both elite and laboring people shared in the devastating financial effects of their separation from Great Britain. This decline was due, in part, to the physical destruction of the Revolutionary War, in part to internal disruptions and dislocations in markets, and in part to the closure of British ports, including those in the West Indies, to mainland shipping.

The colonies south of Maryland had borne the brunt of the depredations of the British Army during the last years of the Revolution. After 1779, the British Army had abandoned its efforts to reconcile the colonial population, and had, as a result, destroyed many generations of capital and labor invested in farm building in Virginia, the Carolinas, and Georgia. Francis Richardson, returning to his South Carolina plantation through lands previously occupied by British troops noted the "general doom and destruction which fell on every part of the State," and described the formerly large rice plantations as being shrunk "into small truck patches; stock of every description had been taken for the use of the British army; fences gone ..., and rank thistle nodded in the wind" (Frey, 1991, p. 207). Thomas Jefferson similarly described the ruin of Monticello after the British had occupied Virginia. He stated that General Cornwallis had "destroyed all my growing crops of corn and tobacco, he burned all my barns" after "having first taken ... all my stocks of cattle, sheep and hogs for the sustenance of his army." Cornwallis also carried off all of Jefferson's horses "capable of service: of those too young for service he cut the throats, and he burned all the fences on the plantations, so as to leave it an absolute waste" (Frey, 1991, p. 167).

Nor did the southern colonies recover quickly from these depredations. By the 1790s, the British Empire had resumed trade with the former colonies, albeit with mercantile restrictions. While the New

England and middle colonies had once again attained their prewar per capita output, Maryland and Virginia's per capita output had fallen to 61 percent of its prewar total, while that of the Carolinas and Georgia had fallen to 50 percent.

The destruction wrought by the British Army also contributed to the decline of many formerly populous market towns in the southernmost mainland colonies. Norfolk and Williamsburg, Virginia, each lost more than half of its population during the British occupation. Jamestown was left "merely the rubbish of a town," while Suffolk, North Carolina, which before the war had "a good trade in pitch, tar, timber and other products" was burned to the ground (Frey, 1991, p. 216).

After the Revolution, moreover, the new states were denied access to all British markets, those in the British West Indies and Newfoundland. The latter two markets had consumed provisions, such as wheat and other grains, flour and preserved meats from the Mid-Atlantic and lower Southern colonies for years; the West Indies had purchased timber and lumber as well.

The new national economy only began to recover in earnest after the ratification of Jay's Treaty in 1794, which regulated commerce between Great Britain and the United States. Among other provisions, it reopened British ports to certain American vessels. Under its terms, the value of US exports rose from $33 million to $94 million by 1800.

Wealthy families, especially mercantile families in urban areas, benefitted most from the recovery of the 1790s, and accelerated the trend toward wealth concentration present in cities before the Revolution. By the 1770s, for example, the top 10 percent of Philadelphia's wealth holders possessed about 80 percent of the city's wealth; by 1798, that figure had risen to 98 percent. Mercantile fortunes of more than £20,000 (stated in constant value) were rare in revolutionary Philadelphia, but commonplace by the 1790s. Moreover, the proportion of that city's taxpayers designated as "gentleman" or "esquire," increased five times from the 1770s to the 1790s.

The increasing concentration of wealth in a few elite hands after the Revolution was accompanied by accentuated conspicuous consumption. This increase was particularly marked in the building and woodworking trades, as homes and furniture became an important means of distinguishing between elites from other groups; such possessions both reflected and reinforced their owners' status and standing within society.

Consumerism was not a new concept during the post-revolutionary era; by the 1720s, the ownership of specific possessions set off colonial elites from the middling and lower sorts. Many such possessions, however, had already trickled down to the middling and working classes by the beginning of the Revolution. Tea drinking was one ritual shared by all classes, for example, and its practice relied on the possession of certain goods. Tea itself was an exotic new beverage by the early eighteenth century, while preparing it, serving it, and drinking it required new utensils – tea caddies, strainers, teapots, and slops bowls – and the knowledge of using them properly. By the 1760s, even working-class people drank tea and were familiar with the proper forms for dispensing and consuming it.

It was more difficult, of course, for other groups to imitate elites in their use of items more expensive and durable than a tea set. After the Revolution, furniture, coaches, and houses became the most important consumer emblems for wealthy people, particularly in American cities. In fact, in an ironic twist, such goods became considerably more British than they had been during the colonial period, when architectural styles had been shaped both by local, vernacular traditions and by a pursuit of English gentility. By the 1790s and 1800s, American building styles followed British fashion more closely than they had during the colonial period. While some critics complained that this fashion offended against republican virtue, architects and cabinetmakers in American cities such as Philadelphia, Boston, and Charleston nonetheless pursued British styles farther than they had previously. Foreign visitors to the United States during the 1790s often commented that wealthy urban residents of the new republic used their houses, furniture, clothing, and coaches to establish more decided class lines than elsewhere. To the English-born architect Benjamin Latrobe, for example, US homes were not "neat and plain" as republicanism demanded, but were instead "structures copied from the palaces of the corrupt age of Diocletian, or the still more absurd and debased taste of Louis the XIV" (Carson et al., eds., 1994, p. 57).

Especially in urban areas, the rich grew richer at the expense of, rather than together with, the poor. Urban gentry often spent their wealth in ways – such as purchasing imported consumer goods – that failed to trickle down to middling and lower sorts in American cities or to have multiplier effects on the local economy. Only a few laborers, including those who served the export trade, recovered part of their pre-revolutionary status. From the 1770s until the 1790s, aggregate real wages for the laborers and journeymen in Philadelphia fluctuated from 20 to 25 percent below their 1760 level. But journeymen shoemakers, for example, who made slave shoes for export to other states and the West Indies, as well as shoes for British soldiers fighting in the Napoleonic Wars, and whose work was protected by increasingly stiff tariffs on imported shoes, recovered more completely than did journeymen tailors, whose clients were more intent than ever on acquiring English goods. The golden portrait of preindustrial craftsmen that many historians of the industrial revolution find so powerful, which depicts early artisans as self-sufficient artists constantly challenged by their work who participated actively in a collective artisan culture, in fact describes a minute number of elite artisans, usually in capital-intensive trades such as coachmaking or goldsmithing.

While the quality of very elite housing improved after the Revolution, that of the lower sort declined, as classes grew increasingly disparate. Members of the lower sort increasingly lived and worked in modest, poorly finished and dimly lighted homes. By the late 1790s, a typical urban working-class tenement might be a single-storey home, 12 feet wide by 18 feet long, which housed a family of seven, and often an unmarried male boarder or two. In contrast, a wealthy merchant might have a three-storey home about as wide but three times

as long, complete with outbuildings such as kitchens and washhouses.

Laboring people were also hard put to furnish their homes adequately, and often lacked the amenities found as a matter of course in wealthier households, including candles, spoons, plates, kitchen utensils, chamber pots, and chairs. Benjamin Rush, a Philadelphia physician who often worked among the poor during the 1790s, noted that on his visits to their homes he often climbed to the upper storey of their "huts" via a ladder, and "many times have been obliged to rest my weary limbs upon the bedside of the sick (for want of chairs)" (Smith, 1990, p. 162).

All but the wealthiest people in eighteenth-century cities, moreover, walked rather than took a carriage to their destinations. As a result, cities such as Philadelphia were becoming segregated by class by the third quarter of the eighteenth century, a trend which escalated considerably after the Revolution. Poor people increasingly moved to the peripheries of cities as wealthier people purchased homes near business centers. Between 1780 and 1800, laborers congregated in the northern, southern, and western areas of Philadelphia, while elites clustered on High Street near the Delaware River. By 1800, Philadelphia, like other American cities, had assumed a classic preindustrial shape, where wealthy people clustered near the center of town and progressively poorer rings of middling classes and laborers radiated out from that center, as poor people were shunted into more and more crowded tenement neighborhoods. While the bottom 40 percent of taxpayers were distributed fairly evenly throughout the city on the eve of the Revolution, virtually all of them had moved to areas of exclusively low-rent housing by 1800.

As a result, poor neighborhoods became progressively more crowded by the end of the eighteenth century. Urban laboring people increasingly dwelt in houses built cheek-by-jowl, with tiny yards which opened onto crowded alleys. The increasing density of people in these neighborhoods created unsanitary conditions and higher death rates. Municipal governments spent relatively little money in working-class neighborhoods;

streets went unpaved, watchmen came only sporadically, and mounds of garbage fed a multitude of rats and other vermin.

The economic adversity that followed the War of Independence, therefore, reversed itself only for some urban working people by the 1790s. More and more poor people in cities began to fill their bellies with grain instead of meat, to triple up in ramshackle, ill-furnished tenements, to take in additional lodgers and to go without firewood or warm clothing during bitter winter weather. Both spouses in working-class families continued to labor while their standard of living, particularly in cities, fell below a bare existence.

FURTHER READING

Carr, Lois Green, and Russell R. Menard: "Wealth and welfare in early Maryland: Evidence from St. Mary's County," *William and Mary Quarterly* 56 (1999), 95–120.

Carson, Cary et al., eds.: *Of Consuming Interests: The Style of Life in the Eighteenth Century* (Charlottesville, VA: University Press of Virginia, 1994).

Frey, Sylvia: *Water From the Rock: Black Resistance in a Revolutionary Age* (Princeton, NJ: Princeton University Press, 1991).

Hoffman, Ronald et al., eds.: *The Economy of Early America: The Revolutionary Period, 1763–1790* (Charlottesville, VA: University Press of Virginia, 1988).

McCusker, John J.: "Measuring colonial gross domestic product: An introduction," *William and Mary Quarterly* 56 (1999), 3–8.

Main, Gloria L., and Jackson T. Main: "The red queen in New England?," *William and Mary Quarterly* 56 (1999), 121–51.

Newman, Simon P.: "Reading the bodies of early American seafarers," *William and Mary Quarterly* 55 (1998), 59–82.

Smith, Billy G.: *The 'Lower Sort': Philadelphia's Laboring People, 1750–1800* (Ithaca, NY: Cornell University Press, 1990).

Walsh, Lorena S.: "Summing the parts: Implications for estimating Chesapeake output and income subregionally," *William and Mary Quarterly* 56 (1999), 53–94.

Part VI

Concepts

CHAPTER SEVENTY-SEVEN

Liberty

ELISE MARIENSTRAS

"THE history of our country is the history of liberty," wrote the poet and diplomat Joel Barlow in 1810. Indeed, liberty was the key word of the Revolution. The figure of liberty was drawn, painted, and embroidered. Trees of liberty were planted. Poems, ballads, and sermons were written in celebration of liberty. Liberty was cited as one of the "unalienable rights" in the Declaration of Independence, and was the main right to be protected by the First Ten Amendments to the Constitution.

However, from the beginning of the conflict with the mother country in the early 1760s, to the Declaration of Independence in 1776, and through the adoption of the Bill of Rights 15 years later, the meaning of liberty changed as it was understood differently. Liberty is one of the concepts whose significance is most flexible, being discussed in different languages at different times according to the political philosophy of the men who speak of it. At the time of the Revolution, three different meanings at least were attached to the word "liberty": the most conservative trend among the revolutionary leaders – the "reluctant revolutionaries" such as John Jay – understood liberty in a rather limited fashion; the moderate or Whig wing – people such as John Adams – insisted on its links with order and property; the radicals – artisans, small farmers, and spokesmen such as Thomas Paine – viewed liberty as a principle and as a natural right which justified an individual's stand if he happened to oppose authority.

Moreover, one must take into account the diverse conceptions of liberty inherent in the traditions in which American views and practices of liberty were grounded. The British colonists had been nurtured on the old English contradiction between the idea of royal prerogative and the freedom of subjects. Two revolutions centering merely around this issue were won in the seventeenth century. The colonists were well aware of that history. They were also heirs to a Western tradition which started, as J. G. A. Pocock terms it, at the "Machiavellian moment" in sixteenth-century Florence, where philosophers enunciated the basic principles of a *res publica* (Pocock, 1975). The paramount principle was the collective or republican notion of liberty, for which the citizens would be ready to sacrifice their lives. According to that conception, individual freedom was to be second to collective liberty. Later, at the time of the Enlightenment, political writers hesitated between these two conceptions. So did the American Founding Fathers and the people: within two decades they shifted from one conception to the other.

1 The First Phase of the Revolution: "Liberty Against Tyranny"

At the beginning of the colonial crisis, in the 1760s and early 1770s, the American revolutionary leaders merely relied on their own experience and rights as Englishmen. They rested these rights on the theories of liberty underlying the British common law and its effects on the juridical system. They opposed the conservative, "court" party conception of the Tories in England and of those colonists such as Jonathan Boucher or Peter Oliver, who were to become "loyalists" and who envisaged liberty as resulting from a "mixed" government in which the different parts of the nation, represented by the King, the Lords, and the Commons, were balanced against one another and where tradition and history were the best safeguards of public freedom. Thomas Hutchinson, Governor of Massachusetts, even denied to the colonies the privilege of enjoying in full the free system of government that was in force in Britain. "Massachusettensis" (Daniel Leonard), the opponent of John Adams, wrote that the Revolution, then within sight, would sacrifice "real liberty to licentiousness" (Massachusettensis [1775] 1972, Letter III). According to the British Tories and the colonial loyalists, liberty was always relative. It was granted by the government within the limits that were necessary to the maintenance of law and order.

In contrast, the "Country" party writers were merely influenced by John Locke's *Second Treatise of Government* or, in the first period of their resistance to the Navigation Acts, by Trenchard's and Gordon's *Cato's Letters* (1721). Like the early eighteenth-century radical writers, they affirmed that liberty was a fragile good, constantly threatened by the tendency of the rulers to abuse their powers and to use their military forces as potential weapons against the freedom of the governed. Like Trenchard and Gordon, they contended that liberty was the concern of the governed only, and that it rested on the will of the people to put checks on the rulers' power.

They also diverged from the conservative writers on the definition of the source of liberty. Whereas the latter limited freedom to what was granted to the governed by the rulers, early Whig leaders insisted on the "natural" origins of freedom, born, as John Locke had explained, out of the state of nature, and further preserved by the people when they entered a compact to form a civil society. Civil liberty is, according to Lockean thought, the continuation of natural liberty, limited only by the interests of the other members of the society. Liberty cannot be granted: it is a common and universal good, to which all men in society are entitled and which they can voluntarily diminish only by a preliminary compact.

Therefore, following James Otis's *Rights of the British Colonies Asserted and Proved* – a pamphlet written to deny the right of Parliament to levy a tax on sugar (1764) – the early revolutionary leaders stressed their rights to British constitutional freedom, and at the same time their right to natural "truth, equity, and justice."

As the conflict with Britain developed with the Stamp Act crisis, the colonists found it more and more necessary to distinguish their own rights from the traditional rights of the British people. Richard Bland, for instance, wrote in 1769:

I have observed before that, when subjects are deprived of their civil rights, or are dissatisfied with the place they hold in the community, they have a natural right to quit the society of which they are members and to retire in another country. Now when men exercise these rights and withdraw themselves from their country, they recover their natural freedom and independence. (Bland, 1769, p. 12)

Eight years later, in a pamphlet originally meant as Virginia's instructions to its delegation to the Continental Congress, Thomas Jefferson argued that emigration from Britain was at the root of the rights of American British colonists. In this tract, Jefferson elaborated on Richard Bland's and James Wilson's theories of the right to freedom of emigration and on emigration as the source of a new liberty. Indeed, the colonists had left England as free British subjects. Their emigration had made them free, even though they still paid allegiance to the King. Denying the right of the King to ultimate proprietorship of their lands in America, Jefferson presented American freedom as a step towards greater liberty. *A Summary View of the Rights of British America* (Williamsburg, [1774]) is a strong plea in favor of liberty as an individual right, and primarily as a right to property of land in freehold. By having come to a new country and entered there into a new compact, the British emigrants had applied their exertion to acquire new lands, to reclaim them, and to plant on them.

Thus, as the Navigation Acts and constitutional conflict went on, the colonists started to give liberty a broader meaning. Besides, while, until the eve of Independence, liberty was seen mainly as a right to be defended *against* encroachments by the British executive and legislative power, it then took a new, more active sense. It became the cornerstone of the republic.

2 The Decisive Step of the Revolution: Republican Liberty

When the Second Continental Congress decided, in July 1776, that separation from the mother country had become inevitable, its members would have been embarrassed to continue defining their right to freedom merely on the basis of the British Constitution and of their rights as Englishmen. The "self-evident" rights enumerated in the Declaration of Independence were basically natural and universal. As independent citizens, the former Sons of Liberty, the minutemen and the continental privates, the pamphleteers and the members of the Continental Congress henceforth considered themselves as the true protectors of liberty. A new nation was born; sovereignty had changed hands from the King in Parliament to the People; it then devolved onto the several states of the Confederation. In the contest between proponents of a strong central government and supporters of the sovereignty of the states, the latter associated liberty with popular local control. But, for all the revolutionaries, liberty was to be the guiding principle for the creation of the republic. The American citizens thus started to see it as formative of the character and culture of the American people. From being British, liberty became American.

A fourfold definition of American liberty was now at hand: it was a liberty inscribed in geography and space; it was a liberty created by the American citizens; it was the cause of all mankind; and it would be the basic principle of the new civil society.

Firstly, the new nation rested its liberty on such principles as Thomas Jefferson, Richard Bland, and Benjamin Franklin had described before Independence: Americans were at a great distance from Europe. An ocean – as Jefferson and Washington would later argue in their "non entangling alliances"

theories – was a natural and providential barrier against oppression from the outside world. And the enormous potential resources of a vast continent were enough to make the young republic independent from another country, and individuals free from economic exploitation. In *Common Sense* (1776), Thomas Paine used the cosmic metaphor of stars and planets to demonstrate that it was contrary to the laws of nature to make a continent the satellite of a small island. On this matter, Paine did not repeat Franklin's and John Adams's prophecies that, one day, "America would become the center of empire" and that "America, an immense territory, favored by nature ... will ... be able to shake off any shackles that may be imposed upon her and perhaps place them upon the imposers" (Van Doren, 1947, p. 256).

Instead, Paine and many others gave liberty a second meaning: American liberty would be the outset of a great human future. From America, it would expand over the whole planet. "Liberty is the spirit and genius, not only of the gospel, but of the whole of that revelation, we have first and last, received from God," wrote John Mellen (Mellen, 1795, p. 9). For the American revolutionaries, liberty played the main part in revolutionary religious and civil millennialism.

Ironically, in the late 1770s, liberty took a third meaning which was more nationalistic than universal. American revolutionaries described liberty as being particular to those emigrants who fled European tyrannical powers, thrived in the New World, and retained their ancient love for liberty. From then on, the American nation would ever be described as the land of liberty; liberalism would be conceived as the main component of the United States system of government as well as its main ideology.

The fourth and principal feature of liberty as it was conceived and glorified in the years following the Revolution was republicanism. Far from being new to the former colonists, the tradition of the "commonwealthman" inherited from the British revolutions was revived and strengthened in the new revolutionary era. Maxims like those written by Benjamin Rush to his wife in 1776 were common: "The new era will be characterized by freedom…without licentiousness, government without tyranny, and religion without superstition…" (Butterfield, 1951, 1: p. 99).

Yet the revolutionaries continued to fear abuse of power from the government. In the new republic, however, the most threatening danger for liberty might be an excess of freedom, a misunderstanding of the true meaning of liberty, and above all the constant possibility of a failing of civic virtue. One of the keywords of this era was "republican virtue," a quality without which civil liberty would be a vain term. Now, the revolutionary leaders were facing a situation where the tyrant could be the people themselves or their representatives. Sermons as well as speeches, patriotic poems, and dramas stressed the importance of preserving republican liberty, even at the expense of individual freedom. "A citizen owes everything to the Commonwealth," wrote Samuel Adams to Caleb Davis in 1781 (Cushing, 1904–8, IV: p. 255). And Benjamin Rush was even more radical when writing "Every man in a republic is public property" (Wood, 1969, p. 61). These assertions did not lead to a negation of the principle of individual liberty. On the contrary, during the decade following the Declaration of Independence, liberty was even more cherished than before. It only changed from a negative, defensive concept to a positive, dynamic one. Liberty was to be the cornerstone of a republic in which the sovereign people would never, as Josiah Quincy put it, be "interested to injure themselves" (ibid) Their liberties depended on the collective freedom of the body politic. The solution rested on the construction of a commonwealth which would provide at once public freedom and citizens' participation in political power.

3   Liberty and Liberties in the Federation

The abstract concept of liberty such as the early revolutionaries had thought of was mostly inspired by the ancient republics, small enough to allow the citizens to put direct checks on the government. The ideal republic was a small one, inhabited by a limited number of citizens. In America, however, the space was almost limitless, and the population was growing fast. Each state was already larger than Athens had been, and in order to survive the states needed to unite into a great republic. How could liberty be protected when the citizens could not govern by themselves, but were to trust representatives? Those who were to be known as Anti-Federalists vested the protection of liberty in the several states. States' rights against a national government's tendency to encroach on civil liberties became, in the 1780s, the principal concern of the American republicans. Only in the states would property, individual safety, and freedom of expression, religion, and self-defense be guaranteed and protected.

Indeed, with the establishment of new governments in the several states, constitutions were adopted which provided for the preservation of freedom through a balance of powers. Everywhere, bills of rights were adopted, more or less copied after the Virginia Bill of Rights of 1776. Besides, liberty gradually ceased to be spelled in the singular and became plural, often replaced by the wording "freedom of" with a limited sense.

Indeed, when the Constitutional Convention met in Philadelphia in March 1787, many of the delegates were more concerned with the menace "anarchy" or "popular licentiousness" presented to property than by an ideal of republican collective liberty. The principle of the safety of individual property seemed threatened by the recent Shays's rebellion or by the abolitionists aggressively opposing slavery. From 1787 on a tension developed between republicanism and liberalism. Both ideologies cared for liberty. Neither required a commitment to egalitarianism. But each conceived of liberty and social order in different terms.

Although the Federalists conceded some provisions which limited the power of the Federal Government and guaranteed habeas corpus, they did not explicitly provide for rights to specific liberties in the Constitution. The checks and balances system of government and the federal organization of the Union were considered by the authors of the *Federalist Papers* as sufficient safeguards against abuse of authority. The spirit of 1776 was over. With institutionalization, republican ideology and its rigid moral demands were henceforth relegated to mere rhetoric. From then on liberty was generally conceived as the sum of individual rights, and the public good was envisioned as the satisfaction of individual self-interest.

Above all, liberty came to be identified with the protection of private property. Although the Bill of Rights also guaranteed freedom of the press, of opinion, of expression, and of religion, property of one's own body and one's goods became the liberties most often fought for. But physical and civil liberty were still not enjoyed by everyone. The Constitution had not banned slavery.

Some of the revolutionaries, politicians or clergymen, continued to envision a republic where liberty could be enjoyed by all men. For those who were not content with mere rhetoric on liberty but who exalted the new nation as destined to embody a secularized New Jerusalem, chattel slavery appeared as a thorn in the body of the republic, and as a sin to be condemned: "The new Jerusalem is free in a more exalted sense than the church on earth," wrote James Dana in a thundering sermon against the slave trade (Dana, 1791).

But although the slave trade was eventually banned by Congress in 1808, the institution of chattel slavery would endure for almost one century after the colonists had fought against what they termed the British policy of "enslaving" them. Until the Civil War slaveholders and abolitionists would debate over the compatibility of slavery and the principles embodied in the Declaration of Independence and the Bill of Rights. New England and the Mid-Atlantic states did not wait long to free their slaves. But for most of the southerners chattel slavery was not incompatible with a republic founded upon individual freedom. Neither did women or Amerindians have access to complete liberty as it was granted to white men. For a long time the concept of liberty was to remain limited.

From the revolutionary period, however, American citizens had gained much in the matter of freedom. Liberty, fragile as it would always be, now rested on a Constitution and a Bill of Rights which could always be referred to when freedom was at risk. The Virginia Statute of Religious Liberty of 1786 became a landmark in the new freedom of religion. The Establishment clause and the Free Exercise clause, included in the First Amendment, provided once and for all for the separation of Church and State and for equal protection of all faiths and opinions. The First Ten Amendments to the Constitution had been conceived as fundamental safeguards for the citizens against any abuse of power. By enumerating the different fields of liberty, they also achieved the transformation of what had been a rather abstract concept into a series of concrete liberties whose embodiment and enlargement were always possible. Later on, disinherited individuals or groups would struggle in order to carry out into the social, economical, and political spheres the promises which had been inscribed in the fundamental documents.

FURTHER READING

Bailyn, Bernard: *The Ideological Origins of the American Revolution* (Cambridge, Mass.: Harvard University Press, 1967).

Bland, Richard: *An Enquiry into the Rights of the British Colonies* (Williamsburg, 1769); repr. in *A Collection of Tracts*, 4 vols. (London, 1773).

Butterfield, L. H. (ed.): *Letters of Benjamin Rush*, 2 vols. (Princeton, NJ: Princeton University Press, 1951).

Cushing, Henry A. (ed.): *The Writings of Samuel Adams*, 4 vols. (New York: G.P. Putnam's Sons, 1904–8).

Dana, James: *The African Slave Trade: a Discourse Delivered Before the Connecticut Society for the Promotion of Freedom by the Pastor of the First Congregational Church in Said City* (New Haven, 1791).

Kammen, Michael: *Spheres of Liberty; Changing Perceptions of Liberty in the American Culture* (Madison: University of Wisconsin Press, 1986).

Massachusettensis [Leonard, Daniel]: *To the Inhabitants of the Province of Massachusetts Bay* (Boston, 1775); repr. in *The American Colonial Crisis*, ed. James Mason (New York: Harper and Row, 1972).

Mellen, John: *The Great and Happy Doctrine of Liberty* (Boston, 1795).

Otis, James: *Rights of the British Colonies Asserted and Proved* (Boston, 1764).

Pocock, J. G. A.: *The Machiavellian Moment: Florentine Political Thought and the Atlantic Political Tradition* (Princeton, NJ: Princeton University Press, 1975).

Reid, Phillip: *The Concept of Liberty in the Age of the American Revolution* (Chicago: University of Chicago Press, 1988).

Trenchard, John, and Gordon, Thomas: *Cato's Letters* (London, 1721).

Van Doren, Carl (ed.): *Letters and Papers of Benjamin Franklin and Richard Jackson* (Philadelphia: American Philosophical Society, 1947).

Wood, Gordon: *The Creation of the American Republic, 1776–1787* (Chapel Hill: University of North Carolina Press, 1969).

CHAPTER SEVENTY-EIGHT

Equality

J. R. POLE

THE United States was almost certainly the first country to base its existence on an abstract principle of social relations. The Continental Congress adopted the statement that "all men are created equal" as the fundamental moral precept of the Declaration of Independence. Americans also believed in other principles, notably liberty. But equality is prior to and more fundamental than liberty in the canon of American principles: for if all men, or all persons, are equal *in rights*, then all must be equal in their right to liberty; no single American can have a greater right, or a right to more liberty, than any other.

But equality is also a relative value. Colonial society was in many respects more wide open than was generally the case in Europe. But it was also a slave society, and in other areas property-owners depended considerably on indentured service. There was a more conscious claim to equality of status than in European nations, but there were also enormous disparities: disparities of wealth, and disparities of associated social status and political power.

Personal ambition played a forceful part in the hopes and expectations of innumerable colonials, and ambition is not an inherently egalitarian type of motivation. The abstract principle of equality would have seemed an unlikely candidate for the central role it was soon to attain in formal American ideology.

1 Equality of Status

Yet, in spite of these discouragements, many reports from the 1760s and 1770s indicating a restless drive for economic opportunity and social recognition among the more subordinate classes of the population carried messages reflecting a demand for equality. After the repeal of the Stamp Act, Anne Grant, the daughter of a great proprietor in Albany County, New York, recorded a little sardonically that her father's visitors "from Hampshire or Connecticut," recent settlers in the neighborhood, "came in without knocking; sat down without invitation; and lighted their pipe without ceremony; then talked of buying land; and finally, began a discourse of politics, which would have done honor to Praise-God Barebones, or any of the members of his Parliament." In Massachusetts, a few months after the Stamp Act riots, Thomas Cushing wrote anxiously to Thoms Hutchinson, Lieutenant-Governor and Chief Justice of the province, "A Spirit of Levillism Seems to go Through the Country, and very little distinction between the highest and lowest in Office." In Philadelphia, a Church of England cleric observed soon afterwards that "the poorest labourer on the shore of the Delaware thinks himself entitled to deliver his opinions in matters of religion and politics with as much freedom as the gentleman and the scholar." Even in Virginia the newly rising religious sect of Separate Baptists was carrying a message of brotherhood and sisterhood that challenged the supremacy of the Established Church – and this was perceived as a threat to supremacy in society as well as religion.

2 Collective and Individual Equality

Thus, although colonial America produced very little egalitarian political theory, there was an undertow of sometimes violent social demand. Americans were increasingly sensitive to questions of equality in two broadly defined areas. The first was the collective level: as British subjects, Americans were fully entitled to all the privileges and protections that Britons enjoyed at home under the common law. But there was conspicuous contrast of treatment. In Massachusetts in 1761 the Superior Court authorized customs officers to use writs of assistance, which permitted them to enter private premises; but only two years later the Court of Common Pleas in London declared that general warrants – whose effects were closely similar – were illegal. When Charles Townshend as Chancellor of the Exchequer introduced his Tariff Act in 1767 he specifically included a power to use writs of assistance in the colonies. The English cases had been widely reported in the colonial newspapers, which brought home the difference of treatment under the common law. This issue was an important theme in John Dickinson's *Letters from a Farmer in Pennsylvania*, published in late 1767 and 1768.

Parliamentary taxation without representation was a still more glaring demonstration of the same point: it was an offense against their lawful rights as British subjects; but at the emotional level it was no less serious as an offense against their dignity and self-respect. In other more personal ways British superiority wounded colonial sentiments. Probably none of these was more significant for the future than the painful susceptibility of the young Virginia militia colonel George Washington, who badly wanted a commission from the King. Washington failed in this aspiration and deeply resented being out-ranked by commissioned officers junior to him.

This collective theme culminated in the Declaration of Independence, with the assertion that the time had come for "one people" to assume its equal station among the nations. But Thomas Jefferson, in his *Summary View of the Rights of British America*, had already written two years earlier that *every individual* American was the equal of *every individual* in Britain, thus bringing together the collective and the individual themes of equality. And in many sectors of colonial society the individual theme was more prominent and immediate than the still latent issue of national status.

3   The Equalizing Process of Revolution

It is doubtful, however, whether this theme would have been able to gain effective political leverage if the quarrel with Britain had not taken place when it did. After momentary upsurges of protest, ordinary colonists tended generally to accept the posture of deference to their superiors just as their counterparts did in Britain; men of old family, of large estates or property, of law and learning seldom had much difficulty in reasserting their traditional sway over the minds of the less educated – and less organized – men in humbler walks of life. The revolutionary upheaval unsettled these habits of mind, however. The suffrage was already widespread, extending to nearly all small freeholders and many urban artisans, and the sheer necessities of revolutionary organization called for the creation of numerous local committees, which brought thousands of local people into active, if limited, political power. The leaders of society could not ignore these men, who played a crucial role in enforcing such measures as the non-importation agreements. The Revolution, among many other things, was a process of widespread popular political mobilization. It was an equalizing process.

4   The Various Categories of Equality

But even equality could not mean the same thing for everybody. Considered at the individual level, equality broke down into a variety of segments, which are susceptible to separate analysis.

Equality before the law

The cardinal Enlightenment principle was that of equality before the law, which was a matter of very general agreement in America. (Such anomalies as benefit of clergy, which actually saved many individuals from execution, were gradually abolished.)

The exceptions to this generalization fell along lines not of social or economic class, but of gender and race. Women occupied a separate sector of society, in which their role was not less important than men's but was theoretically sheltered behind the legal privileges of the male sex. Not all women felt that this theory worked to their advantage or protection, and many women took part in local economic life and had access to the courts when their interests were affected. But they had no direct access to the political process. Married women were held to be inferior to their husbands in law, and lost control of their property on marriage. (A wife who murdered her husband was guilty of petit treason, and liable to be burned to death, not hanged.) Slaves had no legal rights and no normal access to the legal system, although there were some striking exceptions. For some years after the Revolution, the courts of Virginia and Maryland were surprisingly sympathetic to claims to freedom based on oral evidence and memory given by other slaves.

Political equality

At the level of political rights, equality was becoming an active principle of participation both in elections and in committees. But political rights were generally held to be associated with property, both in the right of suffrage and in the equally important matter of the distribution of representatives. The idea that individuals might have an equal right to vote simply *as individuals* was not sufficiently established to form a political program. Individual political equality did make an advance in the revolutionary process, but it did so in alliance with the interests of high concentrations of property. Thus in Boston, which had been badly under-represented before the Revolution, the men of property wanted more representation, and they acquired it on the basis of Boston's population being much larger than that of other towns. Boston's representation in the Assembly at once went up from four to 12. This principle was very gradually generalized. By the time of the Federal Constitution, one man,

one vote in equal electoral districts was an accepted principle.

Religious equality

The demand for religious equality was sectarian before it was individual. The challenge of the Separate Baptists in several colonies and the claims of other minority sects put intense pressure on the prevailing religious establishments. Jefferson's famous Statute for Religious Freedom eventually prevailed in Virginia in 1786, and laid the groundwork for the First Amendment to the United States Constitution – also, like the Virginia Statute, introduced by Madison. This established the formal neutrality of the Federal Government in all matters of religion, leaving the states to follow their own preferences.

Equality of opportunity

Glimmerings of the idea of equality of opportunity were perceived in demands for access to economic privileges before the Revolution; they grew in number and confidence after the war. Hamilton, writing *Federalist*, no. 36, expressed the conviction that America could, and under the Constitution would, give opportunities to all who deserved them: "There are strong minds in every walk of life that will rise superior to the disadvantages of situation, and will command the tribute due to their merit, not only from the classes to which they particularly belong, but from society in general. The door ought to be equally open to all ..."

Equality of esteem

Pervading all these can be discerned a passionate demand for equality of esteem. The Revolution spurred people in many downtrodden walks of life, including white women, free Blacks, and slaves, to become conscious of their moral worth. Political and legal institutions did not fully respond to these demands; America remained in many respects an unequal society, but even so it was a society that had to respond to demands based on these concepts.

5 The Language of Equality

The principles of equality which did so much to inspire the American Revolution, and to express its motivation, were no sudden outcropping, but had ancestors in politics, ideas, law, and religion reaching far back into English history. When the revolutionary legislatures (in Massachusetts, a state convention) came to draw up republican constitutions for their newly independent states, they adopted a principle, derived from John Locke, which had certain egalitarian implications. They explained the existence of society and government as resulting from contracts, or agreements among individuals who were thought to have been roaming around, in a state of nature, at liberty but badly in need of order, protection, and rules by which to live. This picture was not intended as a metaphor; it represented a literal belief, which had been imported into colonial thinking by generations of English political thinkers and publicists who were widely read in the colonies; the idea had already been demolished by the philosopher David Hume, but had been even more recently reinforced by a brief remark in Blackstone's influential *Commentaries on the Laws of England*. This work was very widely accepted as gospel in colonial legal circles. At least in the more Calvinistic colonies, the American statemakers may also have been influenced by the tradition of covenant theology, which saw the church as formed by voluntary, individual acts; and it matters here that both the common law of contract and Puritan theology regarded the original acts of covenanting or contracting as done by individuals who, in that capacity, were *equals*. Although there were many and deep class-bound inequalities in Britain, and many subtle social inflections in colonial life, the common law would not enforce a contract if either party had been subjected to coercive pressure or deceit; in both common law and equity (administered by chancery courts) a valid contract was based on an assumed agreement between equal wills.

None of this mandated any particular *form* of government, and the constitutions of the new states varied considerably; in fact most of them included additional protections for the higher ranks of property – though these qualifications soon failed to function. But the appeal of equality had the advantage of political popularity, and in the long run also enjoyed the more effective moral leverage.

The framers of the Federal Constitution, which was an indirect but overwhelmingly important result of the Revolution, created a government which (setting aside the powers reserved to the states,) bore directly on the citizens as individuals. And although electoral arrangements were placed in state hands, the provisions for representation reflected the principle that electoral districts should be as nearly as possible equal in population – not in wealth, taxable property or any other resources, but people. There is no specific sanction in the Constitution for the representation of interests, ethnic minorities, or other groups – only of aggregations of individuals. This individualist principle was often perverted in subsequent generations – by political parties, economic and demographic groups, and racial separationists. But it was this individualist principle which provided the underpinning for the reapportionment judgments of the Supreme Court under Chief Justice Earl Warren in the 1960s. Essentially, shorn of extrinsic detail, the tenor of those judgments was to return to the original constitutional principle of one person, one vote in equal electoral districts. The equality principle had proved to have more staying power than its enemies had given it credit for.

Although the Constitution was not heralded into the world by any great declaration of principles, some of its provisions carried an ideological charge, and much of that charge reflected a concern for legal and political equality. The Constitution forbade titles of nobility; as far as law and government were concerned, all citizens were of one rank; it also abolished the medieval law of attainder, under which conviction for treason not only condemned the guilty party, but deprived his heirs of their inheritance. The Bill of Rights in its turn was entirely based on the assumption that all rights under the Constitution were equal rights. In the great struggle against slavery the nation's commitment to equality also exerted moral leverage. As early as 1781 the Massachusetts Superior Court declared that the language of the recently adopted state Constitution was incompatible with the existence of slavery in the state; as late as 1860, when the Republican Party convention was wavering in face of southern secession, the veteran abolitionist Joshua Giddings in a speech of thunder virtually compelled the delegates formally to adopt the Declaration of Independence.

The Revolution did not enact equality – indeed, it couldn't even find a consistent definition. But it put a potent weapon in the hands of the oppressed. If it was not a set of laws, it was a language. Under British rule, the language of political and social relations was paternalistic; it assumed the subordination of the peers to the monarch, of the common people to the peerage, of the colonies to the parent country, of servants to masters, of wives and children to the father, of the people to their rulers, and, of course, to the monarch. The language of the Republic no longer had to accommodate either monarchy, hereditary privilege or a prescriptive right to rule; it assumed that equality was the norm in most of these relations, and weakened the grip if it did not abolish the power of many traditional superiors. There were to be many and bitter struggles for equality, complicated by various and sometimes conflicting ideals. Some of these conflicts, social, educational, economic, geographical, even linguistic, have not been fully resolved. But in a republican society, when equality was denied, there was always a case to answer. If the struggles have had to be constantly renewed, the argument has been and continues to be fought out in the egalitarian language of the Republic.

FURTHER READING

Baer, Judith A.: *Equality Under the Constitution: Reclaiming the Fourteenth Amendment*, (Ithaca and London: Cornell University Press, 1983).

Becker, Carl L.: *The Declaration of Independence* (New York: Vintage Books, 1959).

Davis, David Brion: *The Problem of Slavery in Western Culture* (Ithaca, NY: Cornell University Press, 1966).

Dworkin, Ronald: *Taking Rights Seriously* (Cambridge, Mass: Harvard University Press, 1977).

Epstein, David E.: *The Political Theory of The Federalist* (Chicago: University of Chicago Press, 1984).

Lakoff, Sanford A.: *Equality in Political Philosophy* (Cambridge, Mass: Harvard University Press, 1964).

Pole, J. R.: *The Pursuit of Equality in American History* rev. 2nd edn. (Berkeley, CA: University of California Press, 1993).

Rae, Douglas et al.: *Equalities* (Cambridge, Mass: Harvard University Press, 1981).

Verba, Sidney and Gary R. Orren: *Equality in America: the View from the Top* (Cambridge, Mass., and London: Harvard University Press, 1985).

White, Morton: *The Political Philosophy of the American Revolution* (New York: Oxford University Press, 1978).

Wood, Gordon S.: *The Creation of the American Republic* (Chapel Hill: University of North Carolina Press for the Institute of Early American History and Culture, 1969).

CHAPTER SEVENTY-NINE

Property

ALAN FREEMAN AND ELIZABETH MENSCH

> This land is my land,
> this land ain't your land.
> I gotta shotgun
> and you ain't got one.
> If you don't get off,
> I'll blow your head off.
> This land is
> PRIVATE PROPERTY.
> > Anon

THE concept of property serves to define one's simultaneous relationship to others and to resources. Historically, the key American resource has been land. The bit of schoolyard doggerel quoted above captures, in an appropriately aggressive way, the concept of property that has been dominant in American culture since the early nineteenth century: exclusive, possessive, and individualistic, a personal right of territorial sovereignty.

With their characteristic tendency to universalize themselves, Americans take for granted that "property" has always meant a liberal, privatized, protected right. Yet the message of history is contingency. A quick visit to America's past reveals that the modern concept of property did not triumph until after the Constitution of 1787. During the long colonial period property acquired a variety of meanings utterly at odds with the modern, liberal definition. The Revolution then triggered a period of rhetorical excess and lively enthusiasm that threatened to subject property to the leveling passions of a free and democratic people. Against that background, the architects of the Constitution built an institutional and conceptual web to secure property from the whims of the masses.

1 The Colonial Period

Widely read in the colonies were the Whig articles of Gordon and Trenchard, first published in England in the 1720s. They proclaimed:

And as Happiness is the Effect of Independency, and Independency is the Effect of Property: so certain Property is the Effect of Liberty alone, and can only be secured by the Laws of Liberty. (Mensch, 1982, p. 641)

Similarly Sir William Blackstone, whose famous *Commentaries on the Laws of England* appeared in the colonies in 1771–2, proclaimed that "There is nothing which so generally strikes the imagination, and engages the affections of mankind, as the right of property" (Blackstone, 1766, p. 2). Americans on the eve of their Revolution could readily agree on their shared affection for property, so long as the rhetoric was sufficiently vague to obscure significant differences.

Those differences had emerged with the earliest settlements, and often reflected particular regional needs or prior English experience. Land might serve as a basis for community organization, a source of subsistence, a resource for the production of revenue, a commodity exchangeable for speculation, or a power base for a carefully structured social/political hierarchy. These functions often overlapped and collided with one another. Although the cumbersome and intricate English common law of property was available to every colony, regional selectivity led to lack of uniformity in application.

In New England, property, while privately owned, was subordinate to community organization. Under the "township" model developed in Massachusetts, the founding fathers of each new township held both political authority and title to the land, and land was distributed in proportion to the wealth or status of the original heads of household. The founders also controlled undistributed land, subjecting newcomers to strict social authority – not usually resented by a people communally committed to their "Bible commonwealth." That commitment led New Englanders to reject feudal incidents, such as quitrents. Their "General Lauues and Libertyes" of 1648 (Massachusetts) provided that

all our Lands and Heritages shall be free from all Fines and Licenses upon alienations, and from all Hariots, Wardships, Liveries, Primerseizens, year, day and wast, Escheats and forfeitures, upon the death of Parents or Ancesters, be they natural, unnatural, casual or judicial and that for ever.

Notably, they also rejected primogeniture.

In the South property ownership contemplated more individual initiative and resourcefulness. In Virginia, by the 1620s the leaders were "tough, unsentimental, quick-tempered, crudely ambitious men concerned with profits and increased landholding, not the grace of life" (Bailyn, 1977, p. 44). The result was a system of large tobacco plantations dependent for labor first on English indentured servants and later on black slaves. With expansion, vast tracts of undeveloped land were acquired through paper transactions without any care in survey or description. Meanwhile, actual settlers gradually began to occupy those same tracts of land. Inevitable was the resulting conflict between property as subsistence and livelihood, and property as asset exchangeable for speculation. On the eve of the Revolution it was apparent that the fiction of pure "title by occupancy," so fondly embraced by English common law, could not survive the strain, but neither could the elaborate claims of paper title wholly unrelated to possession and use.

Close to the feudal tradition of property as carefully structured hierarchy were the huge land grants that established Pennsylvania, the Carolinas, Maryland, and much of provincial New York. For example, from the time of its founding by the Dutch, New York had been characterized by land grants of hundreds of thousands of acres. Conferred on a few political favorites, those vast grants were conceived by royal governors as a way of maintaining a hierarchically structured, Crown-centered political and religious authority, especially as against rampant sectarian diversity. Many grant proprietors were given the authority to conduct manor courts and name ministers, as well as to collect rents. While often not exercised, such authority was understood as a natural extension of the Crown's own unitary prerogative authority over provincial law, religion, and land. Provincial grantees also soon recognized their grants' potential as a source of capital accumulation. Thus Robert Livingston argued that proprietors of large grants could, by extracting rents from tenants, "oblige their Tenants to ... raise more than they consume" (McAnnear, 1940, p. 88). This would provide proprietors with the capital required for investment in mills, where wheat could be efficiently processed and also concentrated in the hands of a few landlord merchants for investment on the world market.

In marked contrast, many New York communities, especially separatist townships on Long Island, developed a roughly egalitarian model. Land was often distributed in lots based on family size, and grants were subject to condition of settlement: absentee landowning led to forfeiture, and contracts to sell unimproved land could be voided. The goal was that none should use land for purely speculative profit or to gain power over others. This model was closely associated with the most direct forms of participatory democracy, along with sectarian religious enthusiasm: the ultimate goal of property arrangements was the "enlargement of the Kingdom of Christ in the Congregational way and all other means of comfort in subordination thereunto" (Mensch, 1982, p. 650).

Implicit in this New York contrast was a conflict over theories of both property and political participation. Building on both the civic humanist tradition and the "yeoman farmer" imagery of England, most eighteenth-century political theorists assumed that only a freeholder could exercise sufficient independence to support responsible and autonomous political judgment. In the colonies, as in England, the propertyless were regarded as too dependent and morally unfit for political participation. In seventeenth-century Virginia, for example, all freemen had been permitted to vote until declining mortality rates gave rise to a sizeable class of servants and ex-servants, a "giddy multitude," a propertyless "rabble" (Fredrickson, 1981, p. 62). In 1670 Virginians adopted a property qualification for suffrage, as had every colony but one by the time of the Revolution.

Conversely, at the other extreme were the assertions of radical democracy unleashed during the English Civil War, captured by the pervasive claim "the voice of the People is the voice of God." That position could lead to redistribution of property to achieve equality and an independent electorate. The influential English republican theorist James Harrington taught that a stable commonwealth depended upon the people's owning at least three-quarters of the land, or the "over-balance." Ownership of the over-balance by the few rather than the many necessitated an "agrarian" law to correct the balance through redistribution. Such a scheme was consistent with the experience of colonists from areas like Long Island, where an egalitarian distribution of property was specifically intended to ensure democracy.

One solution to the assumed link between property and politics was simply to rely on the vast land resources in the New World to enable settlers to become landholders

through industry and effort, and thereby to join the political community. This approach led to conflict when actual settlers struggled to preserve their claims against huge landowners, whose paper titles derived from mysterious "sovereigns" and their grantees. To recognize titles based on occupancy and use collided with property as exchangeable commodity, necessary to the development of commerce and trade. Furthermore, to reject the Crown as legitimate source of title placed a dangerous power in the people themselves. John Locke's natural law theories were an effort to challenge Crown prerogative without yielding to the most radical claims of the people, providing an important model for post-revolutionary notions of property. Notably, however, Locke's own views were not unambiguously liberal and modern. Much in the natural law tradition he invoked supported communitarian visions of property, being premised on the assumption that God originally gave land to all men in common and that only sin led to private entitlement. Locke was concerned with theology and virtue, not just property rights, and even retained doubts about the legitimacy of excessive accumulation. Nor was he prepared to repudiate aristocracy altogether in the quest for possessive individualism. Indeed, Locke himself joined a failed North Carolina settlement scheme which linked land-ownership to political status in an elaborate balance between aristocracy and democracy (*see also* chapter 11, §1).

2   The Revolution and its Aftermath

In the immediate post-revolutionary period Americans sought to build a true republic. That meant not merely eliminating English domination, but reordering politics and social relations towards the realization of virtue. Many post-revolutionary theorists, influenced by Harrington, assumed that property was therefore properly subject to political control. At the end of the war an anonymous pamphleteer in South Carolina quoted *Cato's Letters* approvingly: "Men in moderate circumstances, are most virtuous. An equality of estate, will give an equality of power; and equality of power is a natural commonwealth" (McDonald, 1985, p. 89). Some gentlemen of large "estate" were surprisingly willing to put theory into practice. Thomas Jefferson, for example, proposed that Virginia distribute 50 acres of land to all citizens (a category limited, of course, to white males) willing to farm, for the sake of ensuring an independent electorate; and he proposed a Harringtonian agrarian law to limit holdings.

More alarming to the elite intelligentsia was the eager embrace of republican theory by those whom genteel society could never consider gentlemen. "When the pot boils the scum will rise," James Otis had warned, and his prediction came true with a vengeance (Wood, 1969, p. 476). Those elected to state legislatures were often of low social standing; nor did they seem the "natural aristocrats" who could be expected to lead a virtuous republic. As one complaint stated, men fit only to "patch a shoe" suddenly felt qualified to "patch the state" (Wood, 1969, p. 477).

State legislators were bent on instituting property reform: the only question was whether that reform would result in a broad program of mandatory republican equality. In the years just before the war lawyers had given renewed emphasis to feudal forms – engaging, for example, in solemn discussion of feudal incidents of tenure such as knight service. Post-revolutionary state legislators, however, quickly abolished all forms perceived locally as feudal. Their clear preference for allodial, rather than tenurial, landholding represented rejection of feudal hierarchy and Crown privilege. Similarly, the fee tail was almost universally scorned. An Act of 1776 in Virginia abolished entail because it did "injury to the morals of youth" (McDonald, 1985, p. 12) and discouraged trade and improvement of land.

Elites feared that this zeal to reform would not be confined to archaic relics of a feudal past, but would threaten all legally acquired inequality. Most at risk were the large estates based on "paper title" and the speculative investment they made possible. Montesquieu had written of the importance of regulating contracting in a republic, to preserve equality and the virtues of "frugality" and "simplicity." Sparta, often touted as a model of civic virtue, had forbidden trade and mandated equality of landholding. In that spirit of "simplicity" most states passed laws to control spending, especially for luxuries, and many state constitutions required such laws. The Massachusetts Bill of Rights, for instance, announced that principles of "piety, justice, moderation, temperance, industry and frugality" were necessary to preserve "liberty," so that the people had a "right" to require observation of those principles in legislation (McDonald, 1985, p. 90).

Even more extreme was the wholesale expropriation of loyalist estates which quickly followed the war. Estimates indicate that the value of property confiscated by state bills of attainder amounted to more than $20 million, almost a tenth of the value of all improved real estate. This breaking up of "dangerous monopolies of land" was often accompanied by demagoguery, and led to speculative gain for insiders. Still, most states mandated resale into small parcels to promote republican independence. Given that legislative zeal, many feared a general levelling of property. While wholesale redistribution of all large holdings never became the norm, and the fever for confiscation had abated by 1787, other legislation further underscored the leveling potential of democracy. Debt relief was common; so was the printing of paper money. Regulation of prices and wages was routine, and many people advocated abolition of monopolies and corporations as vestiges of Crown privilege. Such pervasive legislative control over wealth suggested that the nightmare version of republicanism could easily become reality: to subordinate property to the requirements of democracy meant not the triumph of reason and virtue, but mob rule.

The challenge of the 1780s was to develop a notion of property that would stem majoritarian excesses, without appealing to now-despised aristocratic institutions. Throughout the colonies the notion of ownership "right" had been rooted in a conception of title as derived from the Crown. The post-revolutionary survival of that right required conceptual transformation. While the vagaries of natural law theory and the technicalities of the common law tradition provided useful reference points, their quite various interpretations in the colonies left no uniform law or practice, and no coherent theory of property right.

That such a right was developed is a tribute to the sophistication of the framers and to the Supreme Court justices who later enunciated Federalist theory. Even before the Constitutional Convention, future Federalists, especially in New York, had become adept at protecting large property holdings from democratic excess. Alexander Hamilton, invoking both natural and common law, had successfully argued in court against enforcement of an anti-Tory Trespass Act. In an atmosphere of frenzied confiscation, Hamilton's victory was a firm stroke against Tory-baiting. It also provided an important (albeit ambiguous) precedent for judicial review by interposing "law" between property and democratic legislation, without appeal to Crown grant rights.

Similarly, in a striking symbolic success, New York's political elite protected a huge land grant to a despised institution, Trinity Church in Manhattan. Trinity, whose advisers included Hamilton and John Jay, had a long, inglorious history: her holdings were based on a flimsy Crown grant from a corrupt royal governor who had established her in order to impose Anglicanism on a resentful, dissenting populace. During the war most of her officers remained staunchly and arrogantly loyalist. Calls for confiscation of her land arose immediately after patriot victory, and early state proceedings were directed towards that end. Yet the politically adroit elite in New York severed Trinity's link to Anglicanism's Crown-based ecclesiastical structure and then quelled the call for confiscation by petitioning for a fresh title premised on the church's newly assumed identity as private rightholder, as both religious body and owner of property.

Such victories against the confiscatory spirit were not simply crass protection of established interests; nor were they mere retreat to feudalism. Instead, they represented a modern, Humean conception of republicanism. Hume, whose work influenced both Hamilton and Madison, explicitly rejected republicanism as realization of

Spartan simplicity and equality (*see* chapter 11, §6). A polity like Sparta, Hume argued, was "violent and contrary to the more natural and usual course of things... [for it] aggrandizes the public by the poverty of individuals" (Stourzh, 1970, pp. 71–2). The less circumspect Hobbes declared outright, "the *wealth* and *riches* of all the particular members, are the *strength* of the commonwealth" (Stourzh, 1970, p. 73).

Hamilton became the frankest spokesman for the "modern policy," as it came to be called. The goal was to encourage the "natural" appetite for personal gain by protecting private wealth, for private wealth would ultimately lead to national prosperity. Inevitably, as Hamilton honestly acknowledged, the classical goal of republican virtue would have to surrender to the modern, enlightened goal of commercial development. Hamilton thus reminded the delegates to the Federal Convention, "the difference of property is already great amongst us. Commerce and industry will still increase the disparity. Your government must meet this state of things..." As he stated at the New York Ratifying Convention, "as riches increase and accumulate in a few hands; as luxury prevails in society; virtue will be in a greater degree considered as only a graceful appendage of wealth, and the tendency of things will be to depart from the republican standard" (Stourzh, 1970, pp. 70–1).

Thus Federalists were delicately poised on the threshhold of modernity. They had rejected not only feudalism, but also the classic conception of republican virtue which depended upon "frugality" and equality. The dilemma was to formulate a conceptual scheme for protecting property which was not outrageously antithetical to republican principles, yet would effectively interpose a wedge between democratic people (public) and economic advantage (private). Their stroke of genius was to propose that the people themselves were the architects of that wedge.

The new conception of property as private right reached its fruition through the Constitution of 1787, which supplied the one ingredient previously missing – an authoritative source. Emerging property theory in the 1780s had still been uncomfortably dependent upon natural law to insulate property from legislative interference. The new Constitution provided a crucial text in the form of the "contract clause" ("No State shall…pass any…Law impairing the Obligation of Contracts…"). That text, combined with the theory of judicial review articulated by Hamilton in *The Federalist*, no. 78, provided the basis for an inviolable right of property, derived from the republican people themselves, but protected from their majoritarian excess by their own constitutionally structured judiciary.

The famous case of *Fletcher v. Peck* (1810) offered a dramatic opportunity for the realization of this new theory of property rights. In January 1795 the Georgia legislature, through outright bribery led by one of its United States senators, had corruptly deeded more than 35 million acres of its western lands (including all of the present state of Mississippi) to speculators. A year later a new legislature, elected to end corruption, voted to repeal the grant. The case would not be decided by the Supreme Court until 1810. Yet in 1796, within a month of the repeal legislation, Hamilton wrote a legal opinion arguing that Georgia had no power to repeal the corrupt grant. Hamilton contended that "every grant from one to another, whether the grantor be a state or an individual, is virtually a contract that the grantee shall hold and enjoy the thing granted against the grantor, and his representatives." He therefore concluded, "taking the terms of the Constitution in their large sense," that the revocation by Georgia was in violation of the contract clause of the Constitution (Magrath, 1966, p. 150).

Chief Justice Marshall's famous opinion in *Fletcher v. Peck* followed Hamilton's reasoning and reached the same conclusion. Marshall offered a deft blend of natural law and English common law (the *bona fide* purchaser doctrine), yet relied ultimately, as did Hamilton, on the *constitutional text*. That the source of title was the sovereign state (and corruptly so) made no difference, as Trinity's tainted source of title had also made no difference. In the new world of private right-holders all are equally secure against the interference of the state.

The genius of the solution is its relationship to Hamilton's theory of judicial review. The ultimate source of sovereignty is the people. In theory, the people acted directly as a body when ratifying the Constitution ('We the people…'). Yet the Constitution, as a legal text, can be authoritatively interpreted only by those trained in the "artificial reason" of the law. Thus the people, by adopting the Constitution, effected a Hobbesian covenant, even a political transubstantiation: they relocated their sovereignty in an intricate web of institutional arrangements whose meaning now belonged to a judicial priesthood. In so doing they surrendered forever their active democratic control over property rights.

That the Constitution's solemn role was the careful protection of property was not lost on influential members of the emerging American judiciary. John Marshall made that clear during his more than 30 years as Chief Justice. As the almost equally famous Justice Joseph Story put it in 1829, upon his inauguration as Dane Professor of Law at Harvard: "[T]he lawyer's most glorious and not infrequently perilous" duty was to guard the "sacred rights of property" from the "rapacity" of the majority. Only the "solitary citadel" of justice stood between property and mob rule. It was the lawyer's noble task to man that citadel, whatever the cost. "What sacrifice could be more pure than in such a cause? What martyrdom more worthy to be canonized in our hearts?" (Story, 1829).

FURTHER READING

Alexander, Gregory S.: *Commodity and Property: Competing Visions of Property in American Legal Thought 1776–1970* (Chicago and London: University of Chicago Press, 1997).

Appleby, J.: "Republicanism in old and new contexts," *William and Mary Quarterly*, 43 (1986), 20–34.

Bailyn, B.: "Shaping the republic," in Bailyn, B., Davis, D. B., Donald, D. H., Thomas, J. L., Wiebe, R. H., and Wood, G. S.: *The Great Republic: a History of the American People* (Lexington, Mass.: D. C. Heath, 1977), 1–227.

Banning, L.: "Jeffersonian ideology revisited: liberal and classical ideas in the new American republic," *William and Mary Quarterly*, 43 (1986), 3–19.

Blackstone, W.: *Commentaries on the Laws of England*, 4 vols. vol. 2, *Book the Second* (Oxford: 1766), repr. (London: Dawsons, 1966).

Cunliffe, M.: "Property," *Encyclopedia of American Political History*, ed. J. Greene (New York: Charles Scribner's Sons, 1984), vol. 2, pp. 1018–30.

Dunn, J.: "From applied theology to social analysis: the break between John Locke and the Scottish Enlightenment," *Wealth and Virtue: the Shaping of Political Economy in the Scottish Enlightenment*, ed. I. Hont and M. Ignatieff (Cambridge: Cambridge University Press, 1983).

Fredrickson, G.: *White Supremacy: a Comparative Study in American and South African History* (New York and London: Oxford University Press, 1981).

Katz, Stanley N.: "Republicanism and the Law of Inheritance in the American Revolutionary Era," *Michigan Law Review*, 76 (1977), 1.

Kloppenberg, J. T.: "The virtues of liberalism: Christianity, republicanism, and ethics in early American political discourse," *Journal of American History*, 74 (1987), 9–33.

McAnnear: "Mr. Robert R. Livingston's reasons against a land tax," *Journal of Political Economy*, 48 (1940), 63.

McDonald, F.: *Novus Ordo Seclorum: the Intellectual Origins of the Constitution* (Lawrence: University Press of Kansas, 1985).

Magrath, C. P.: *Yazoo: Law and Politics in the New Republic: the Case of Fletcher v. Peck* (Providence, RI: Brown University Press, 1966).

Mensch, E.: "The colonial origins of liberal property rights," *Buffalo Law Review*, 31 (1982), 635–735.

Minogue, K. R.: "The concept of property and its contemporary significance," *Nomos*, 22 (*Property*) (1980), 3–27.

Morgan, E.: *Inventing the People: the Rise of Popular Sovereignty in England and America* (New York and London: W. W. Norton, 1988).

Pocock, J. G. A. (ed.): *The Political Works of James Harrington* (Cambridge: Cambridge University Press, 1977).

——: *Virtue, Commerce, and History* (Cambridge: Cambridge University Press, 1985).

Story, J.: *Discourse upon the Inauguration of the Author as Dane Professor of Law*, 1829; unpubd, Cornell Law School Collection.

Stourzh, G.: *Alexander Hamilton and the Idea of Republican Government* (Stanford, Calif.: Stanford University Press, 1970).

Wood, G. S.: *The Creation of the American Republic, 1776–1787* (Chapel Hill: University of North Carolina Press, 1969).

CHAPTER EIGHTY

The rule of law

JOHN P. REID

THE concept of the rule of law during the second half of the eighteenth century is not easily defined as it meant one thing in North America and had for some decades been taking on a quite different definition in Great Britain. In Great Britain its scope and theory was narrowing from what it had been – or what its exponents had tried to make it mean – in Stuart times. Put in historical perspective, the definition of the rule of law in Great Britain had been changing from what it still means in the twentieth-century United States to what it would mean in nineteenth- and twentieth-century Great Britain. Put in terms of eighteenth-century common-law jurisprudence, the concept of the rule of law in Great Britain was coming to mean adherence to the command of the legislature and ceasing to mean adherence to "right" over "power".[1]

1 Contrasting Concepts of the Rule of Law

As an ideal, the concept of the rule of law in eighteenth-century Great Britain was a support for liberty as liberty was then defined – as a restraint on governmental power, especially arbitrary power, and less, as we would think of it, as liberating the individual. One fundamental element of liberty was the certainty of law, and the certainty of law was established, in part, by the rule of law. "Free Government is the protecting the People in their Liberties by stated Rules," Thomas Gordon had pointed out earlier in the century. "Only the Checks put upon Magistrates make Nations free,"

his colleague John Trenchard agreed, "and only the want of such Checks makes them Slaves."[2] In the American colonies the concept was summed up by the Connecticut clergymen Jared Eliot. "Blessed be God… We live under a Legal Government," he said, explaining that by "Legal" he meant "Limited." "It is a Corner-Stone in our Political Building, *That no mans* Life, *Limb, Name or Estate, shall be taken away but by his Peers and by the known Laws of the Land.*"[3] What distinguished "Law and Freedom from Violence and Slavery," Edmund Burke added, "is, that the property vested in the Subject by a known Law – and forfeited by no delinquency defined by a known [law] could [not] be taken away from him by any power or authority whatsoever."[4]

At its strongest, the rule of law was a general principle that government and governed alike are subject to due process. In popular expression, the concept of the rule of law defined government as "The empire of laws, and not of men,"[5] or the circumscribing of power by "some settled Rule or Order of Operation."[6] In the seventeenth century the ideal of the rule of law had obtained constitutional primacy because the power it circumscribed was monarchy. "[I]t is one of the Fundamentals of Law," the prosecutor of Charles I had asserted, "that the King is not above the Law, but the Law [is] above the King."[7] Charles could be criminally charged because a prince disobeying the law was a "rebel."[8] "King Charles," an eighteenth-century writer explained, "either could not, or would not distinguish, between the executive power, which our Constitution has lodged in the Crown, and the supreme power, which our Constitution hath lodged in the law of the land, and no where else."[9] When these words were written in 1771, "law of the land" may have meant something quite different in Great Britain than in the colonies. It is most unlikely that a majority of Britons at that time thought of "law of the land" or "rule of law" as expressing fundamental or immutable law, rather than merely positive law. The Crown might still be subject to the rule of law, but in Great Britain "law" in this sense was coming to mean what Parliament declared. It was that change in the concept of "law" – whether we call it fundamental, immutable, or constitutional – that American Whigs resisted.

2   British Law Defined as Statute

Although theory was changing and it is difficult to tell just when certain principles became dominant, it seems safe to assert that, by the age of the American Revolution in Great Britain, the rule of law no longer included the notion of the sovereignty of law over the ruler. It may even be that the rule of law had become procedural only, not substantive, holding that government actions must conform to legislative command while that command could change at legislative will. In other words, the rule of law now restrained power from violating liberty largely by limiting the definition of liberty to the legislatively permitted "An *English* individual," a writer who thought American resistance in 1775 was legal explained, "cannot, by the supreme authority, be deprived of liberty, unless by virtue of some law, which his representative has had a part in framing."[10] The word "law" in this context had shrunk from meaning "right" to meaning "statute." It was enough that laws be promulgated and certain for the rule of law to serve the liberty of the individual. "To assert an absolute exemption from imprisonment in all cases," Blackstone protested, "is inconsistent with every idea of law …: but the glory of the English law consists in clearly defining the times, the causes, and the extent, when, wherefore, and to what degree, the imprisonment of the subject may be lawful."[11]

As understood in Great Britain, therefore, the principle of the rule of law may not have restrained parliamentary power so much as guided it. Certainty of procedure was perhaps its most basic and most universally recognized element, and meant, in John Locke's words, "to govern by *promulgated establish'd Laws*, not to be varied in particular Cases."[12] Almost as well known, although in eighteenth-century Great Britain as likely to be breached as to be honored, were the elements that punishment should not be *ex post facto* and property should not be taken without compensation. Another aspect of the rule of law was protection of legal rights. "[T]he very Essence of Government," as an anonymous commentator on revolutionary principles pointed out, "consists in making and executing Stated Rules, for the determining of all Civil Differences, and in doing all other Acts that tend to secure the Subjects against all Enemies Foreign and Domestick, in the quiet Possession of their legal Rights."[13] The most salient expression of the rule of law in eighteenth-century Great Britain, however, the one that American Whigs most likely thought of first when asked if Great Britain was ruled by the rule of law, was the principle of equal application. "Laws, in a Free State," it was said, should be equally applied. "[T]he Peer should possess no privilege destructive to the Commoner; the Layman obtain no Favour which is denied the Priest; nor the Necessitious excluded from the Justice which is granted to the Wealthy," or, in the words of Locke, there was but "one Rule for Rich and Poor, for the Favourite at Court, and the Country Man at Plough."[14]

3   Americans and Arbitrary Power

In the American colonies the concept of the rule of law was more English than contemporary British, that is, it was closer to the constitutional values of seventeenth-century England than to the newer constitutional understanding of eighteenth-century Great Britain. For Americans, the rule of law primarily meant to be free of arbitrary power. To understand what colonial Whigs meant by the rule of law, therefore, it is necessary to define what they (and eighteenth-century

Britons) meant by arbitrary power, and to do that we must rid ourselves of twentieth-century thoughts about arbitrariness having something to do with despotism, tyranny, or cruel government. It may today, but that was not the legal definition in the eighteenth century. Then it was not the harshness, the brutality, or the certainty of the exercise of power that made government arbitrary. It was, rather, the possession of power unchecked. Tyrannical power was abuse of power, arbitrary power was power without restraint.

In eighteenth-century parlance on both sides of the Atlantic, arbitrary was the difference between liberty and slavery, right and power, constitutional and unconstitutional. To the eighteenth-century American legal mind, knowing what was arbitrary delineated the concept of the rule of law. "For it is certain," Jared Eliot reminded Connecticut's law-makers in 1738, "*That to the Constitution of every Government, Absolute Sovereignty must lodge somewhere*. So that according to this Maxim, Every Government must be Arbitrary and Despotick. The difference seems to be here; Arbitrary Despotick Government, is, When this Sovereign Power is directed by the Passions, Ignorance & Lust of them that Rule. And a Legal Government, is, When this Arbitrary & Sovereign Power puts it self under Restraints, and lays it self under Limitations."[15] It was, Viscount Bolingbroke had said, a matter of power and not of the type and structure of government. Whether power was vested in a single monarch, in "the *principal Persons of the Community*, or in the *whole Body of the People*," was immaterial. What matters is whether power is without control. "Such Governments are Governments of *arbitrary Will*," he concluded.[16]

Just as the eighteenth-century concept of arbitrariness should not be confused with cruelness or terror, for it could be benevolent, mild, and materially beneficial, so it should not be confounded with absoluteness. "[E]ven *absolute Power*," John Locke pointed out, "where it is necessary, is *not Arbitrary* by being absolute, but is still limited by that reason, and confined to those ends, which required it in some Cases to be absolute," such as martial discipline which vests an army officer with power to order a trooper to die but cannot "command that Soldier to give him one penny of his Money."[17] Law was the distinction. If the officer acted within the parameters of the law, his absolute orders were not arbitrary. That element – law or the rule of law – was all important to eighteenth-century constitutional thought. For "court whigs", Reed Browning has pointed out – and also, it should be added, for most educated Britons and Americans – there were "but two types of government: arbitrary and lawful,"[18] or, as John Arbuthnott explained in 1733, "what is not legal is arbitrary."[19]

4 The British and Parliament

For the British of the age of the American Revolution this meaning of "legal" had changed as the constitutional principle emerged that Parliament could not be arbitrary in law. English constitutional history, especially the history of the Glorious Revolution, taught Britons that Parliament was the institutionalization of liberty, and, as a consequence, law that was the command of Parliament was the law of liberty. The Glorious Revolution had established the principle of parliamentary supremacy over the Crown. Once Parliament attempted to extend that supremacy by claiming parliamentary sovereignty over the law and the Constitution, the American theory of the rule of law could not survive in the British constitutional world. The fact that the concept of the rule of law, for so long understood to be a barrier constraining the power of the Crown on behalf of liberty, would not be extended to restrain parliamentary power, sums up much of the American Revolution's constitutional controversy. Legal theory in Britain was drawing apart from legal theory in the colonies primarily on the issue of constitutional restraint on legislative authority. The difference was summarized by a pamphlet published in Philadelphia the year of the Declaration of Independence. "No country can be called *free* which is governed by an absolute power," the pamphleteer contended; "and it matters not whether it be an absolute royal power or an absolute legislative power, as the consequence will be the same to the people."[20] British lawyers may have been reluctant to do so, but soon they would acknowledge an absolute power in Parliament.

Americans may not have appreciated how deep the gulf had become. The realization that some Britons now equated law, liberty, and constitutionalism with parliamentary legislation could have staggered American constitutionalists had the fact sunk into their legal consciousness. They would never break free of the fundamentals of anti-Stuart constitutionalism in which power unrestrained was not legal. They could not see what difference it made for arbitrary decision to be legislative rather than monarchical. "There cannot be a more dangerous doctrine in a state, than to admit that the legislative power has a right to alter the constitution," another Philadelphian wrote, also in 1776. "For as the Constitution limits the authority of the legislature; if the legislature can alter the constitution, they can give themselves what bounds they please."[21] It is not an exaggeration to suggest that the legal aspects of the American Revolution could be told under the title *In Defense of the Rule of Law*.

REFERENCES

1 For the eighteenth-century dichotomy between "right" and "power" in jurisprudential theory, *see* John Phillip Reid: "In the taught tradition: the meaning of law in Massachusetts-Bay two hundred years ago," *Suffolk University Law Review*, 15 (summer 1980), 947–61.

2 Gordon: Letter of 20 January 1721, *Cato's Letters: or, Essays on Liberty, Civil and Religious, And other Important Subjects. In Four Volumes*, 6th edn. (London, 1755), 2: 249; Trenchard: Letter of February 9, 1722, *ibid.*, 4: 81.

3 Jared Eliot: *Give Cesar his Due. Or, the Obligation that Subjects are under to their Civil Rulers, as was shewed in a Sermon Preach'd before the General Assembly of the Colony of Connecticut at Hartford, May the 11th, 1738. The Day for the Election of the Honourable the Governour, the Deputy-Governour, and the Worshipful Assistants* (New London, Connecticut, 1738), 36.

4 Speech of Edmund Burke, Commons Debates, 26 May 1767, *The Writings and Speeches of Edmund Burke*, ed. Paul Langford (Oxford: Clarendon Press, 1981), 2: 65.

5 [Charles Inglis:] *The True Interest of America Impartially Stated, in Certain Strictures on a Pamphlet Intitled Common Sense*, 2nd edn. (Philadelphia, 1776), 12.

6 Anon.: *The Fatal Consequences of the Want of System in the Conduct of Public Affairs* (London, 1757), 2. 1722, *ibid.*, 4: 81.

7 John Cook: *King Charl[e]s his Case, an Appeal to all Rational Men, Concerning his Tryal at the High Court of Justice. Being for the most part that which was intended to have been delivered at the Bar, if the King had Pleaded to the Charge, and put himself upon a fair Tryal* (London, 1649), 6.

8 *Boston Evening-Post* (March 25, 1771), p. 2, col. 1. *See also New York Evening-Post* (December 7, 1747), repr. *Boston Evening-Post* (December 28, 1747), p. 1, col. 2.

9 Anon.: *An Historical Essay on the English Constitution: Or, an impartial Inquiry into the Elective Power of the People, from the first Establishment of the Saxons in the Kingdom. Wherein the Right of Parliament, to Tax our distant Provinces, is explained, and justified, upon such constitutional Principles as will afford an equal Security to the Colonists, as to their Brethren at Home* (London, 1771), 80.

10 Anon.: *Resistance no Rebellion: In Answer to Doctor Johnson's Taxation no Tyranny* (London, 1775), 14.

11 William Blackstone: *Commentaries on the Laws of England* (Oxford, 1765–9), 3: 133.

12 John Locke: *Two Treatises of Government: a Critical Edition with an Introduction and Apparatus Criticus*, ed. Peter Laslett, 2nd edn. (Cambridge: 1967), Book 2, Sec. 142.

13 Anon.: *The Revolution and Anti-Revolution Principles Stated and Compar'd, the Constitution Explain'd and Vindicated, and the Justice and Necessity of Excluding the Pretender, Maintain'd against the Book Entituled Hereditary Right of the Crown of England Asserted* (London, 1714), 15.

14 [John Shebbeare:] *A Second Letter to the People of England on Foreign Subsidies, Subsidary Armies, and their Consequences to this Nation*, 4th edn. (London, 1756), 17; John Locke, *supra* note 12, Book 2, Sec. 142.

15 Jared Eliot: *supra* note 3, 36 footnote.

16 [Henry Saint John, Viscount Bolingbroke:] *A Dissertation upon Parties; In Several Letters to Caleb D'Anvers, Esq.*, 2nd edn. (London, 1735), 159.

17 John Locke: *supra* note 12, Book 2, Sec. 139.

18 Reed Browning: *Political and Constitutional Ideas of the Court Whigs* (Baton Rouge: Louisiana State University Press, 1982), 196.

19 *The Freeholder's Political Catechism. Written by Dr. [John] Arbuthnot* ([London], 1769), 9.

20 Anon.: *Four Letters on Interesting Subjects* (Philadelphia, 1776), 19.

21 Demophilus: *The Genuine Principles of the Ancient Saxon, or English Constitution Carefully collected from the best Authorities: With some Observations, on their peculiar fitness, for the United Colonies in general, and Pennsylvania in particular* (Philadelphia, 1776), 35.

FURTHER READING

Reid, John Phillip: "In legitimate strips: the concept of 'arbitrary,' the supremacy of Parliament, and the coming of the American Revolution," *Hofstra Law Review*, 5 (spring 1977), 459–99.

——: *The Concept of Liberty in the Age of the American Revolution* (Chicago: University of Chicago Press, 1988).

Thompson, E. P.: *Whigs and Hunters: the Origin of the Black Act* (1975).

CHAPTER EIGHTY-ONE

Consent

DONALD S. LUTZ

AMERICANS justified their break with Britain on the grounds that they should be subject only to laws to which they had consented. The Declaration of Independence is deservedly famous for stating a robust doctrine of consent, and for reflecting the importance of the concept for American political thought. The American notion of consent was partly derived from English common law, but between 1620 and 1776 the colonists developed a perspective that varied considerably from the one held in Britain. The process was not one of consciously modifying an existing theory. Rather, the colonists first developed institutions that met their needs and strongly held values, and then they appropriated from European thinkers theories that supported what they were already doing. By 1776 Americans had a fully articulated theory of consent undergirding a set of well-established consent-based institutions. An important feature of American consent theory by this time was the assumption of popular sovereignty, an idea that had never taken hold in Britain. Between 1776 and 1787 theory and institutions evolved in the direction of a more active, direct, and continuous notion of consent. The United States Constitution successfully combined effective government with institutions of consent at the national level, although an ambiguity in consent theory remained for Americans to resolve.

1 The Magna Carta and Colonial Charters

Consent as a political concept in England is usually traced back to the Magna Carta

signed in AD 1215. King John had been forced by his barons to agree to a number of articles limiting the power of the monarch, including one that held the king could not tax the barons without their consent. Over time the meetings for obtaining consent evolved into Parliament, a body of representatives elected by men of property. Although Magna Carta was an agreement between the aristocracy and the king, the wording of the tax provision was very general and supported the conclusion that no man should be taxed without his consent. As a result of Magna Carta, therefore, the English linked consent with taxation, considered an elected legislature the primary consent-giving institution, and in the long-run viewed consent as being relevant to any property owner whether a member of the aristocracy or not.

The link between Magna Carta and the American Revolution was the colonial charter. All charters, beginning with Queen Elizabeth's Letters Patent to Sir Humphrey Gilbert (1578), contained two critical provisions. First, English colonists brought with them the rights of Englishmen, which meant the common law. Magna Carta had for several hundred years been printed as the first common law statute, and thus Englishmen brought with them the right not to be taxed without their consent, and the implied right to representation in an elected legislature as the means for giving consent. The second key provision in colonial charters was to make explicit the implied right to an elected legislature. Colonists were allowed to erect their own local governments, as long as the laws they passed were not contrary to the laws of England.

However, important differences in their circumstances led the colonists to develop a markedly different set of institutions from those found in Britain. The right to vote in England had been defined by statute since 1430 to require the ownership of enough property to earn 40 shillings in rent per year, which usually amounted to about 50 acres. The distribution of land by the late eighteenth century produced a regularly voting electorate of about 5 or 6 percent of adult males. In America, where land was cheap and plentiful, and with no prior claims of ownership by the aristocracy and gentry to contest, a similar 50-acre requirement enfranchised most white adult males. Thus, even though American statutes generally required about the same amount of property in order to vote, the electorate in America was about ten times the percentage of the male population as it was in England.

Forced to rely upon themselves for survival, the colonists produced a considerable number of foundation documents designed to elicit cooperation from everyone. The Mayflower Compact (1620), the Pilgrim Code of Law (1636), the Fundamental Orders of Connecticut (1639), and the Rhode Island Acts and Orders (1647) are some early examples. The last three effectively functioned as what we now call constitutions.

These documents had several important characteristics in common, one of which was that they were signed by all adult males. The signatures showed that consent for the political institutions created by each document was being given by the people as a whole. The American view thus required popular consent, and implied popular sovereignty, before there was a political theory justifying either. In New England Thomas Hooker and Roger Williams wrote tracts during the 1630s and 1640s which argued for popular consent based on religious principles derived from a dissenting Protestant reading of the Bible. Religious reasoning was important for explaining the emergence of documents founded upon popular consent in New England before

anywhere else, but similar documents were eventually written throughout the colonies.

Colonial documents of political foundation thus rested upon *de facto* popular consent. These documents made an elective legislature the central consent-giving body, as was the case in Britain, but then tied the legislature to popular consent through annual elections by a broadly defined electorate. All of this happened before James Harrington, Thomas Hobbes, Algernon Sidney, John Locke, or Charles-Louis de Secondat, Baron de Montesquieu, wrote their influential tracts on consent. Eventually, the theories of these Europeans were appropriated to justify and underwrite what had already been developed institutionally in the colonies.

2 Competing Theories of Consent

When the British Parliament levied a series of taxes in the Stamp Act (1765) and the Townshend Acts (1767) to defray expenses from the recent war with France, the colonists objected. Benjamin Franklin testified before Parliament that the colonists did not object to paying their fair share for a war that was fought, in part, to protect them, but they were only willing to pay taxes levied by legislatures elected through their own consent. Since the colonists were not represented in Parliament, any tax levied by it upon the colonies was taxation without their consent. The colonists also argued that they were operating under charters from the king, and these charters granted them the right to create their own legislatures and elect their own representatives.

The argument made little sense to most Britons, since the vast majority of British subjects could not vote yet were considered represented in Parliament. It was a matter of more than numbers. The British by this date saw Parliament as sovereign, whereas the Americans saw the people as sovereign. The argument was rooted at least as much in divergent interests – British mercantilism versus colonial aspirations for economic development, for instance – as it was about constitutional principles. But their differing views on consent inclined the Americans to make a case they found to be reasonable and compelling given their experiences, while at the same time inclining the British to defend a position reasonable and compelling from their experiences. Efforts at conciliation often foundered upon conflicting habits of thought, and the mental blinders they produced, as much as on an inability or unwillingness to compromise on concrete political or economic issues. The American Revolution thus resulted, at least in part, from competing theories of consent.

3   "Passive" and "Active" Consent: Locke and Sidney

John Locke's *Two Treatises of Civil Government* (1690) had an ironic place in the dispute. By British standards Locke was too insistent upon Parliament's dependence on the consent of the majority, and therefore he was largely ignored by British commentators in the late eighteenth century. By American standards Locke did not impute enough of a role to majority consent, but he was widely cited by Americans in a manner that attributed to him a more radical theory than he actually defended. In fact, the position argued by the Americans was more congruent with Algernon Sidney's theory in *Discourses Concerning Government* (1698), although largely by accident rather than through conscious borrowing.

Both Sidney and Locke saw civil society as resting upon a compact in which each individual consents to be bound by the will of the majority. Whatever form of government the majority establishes is thereby presumed to rest upon the consent of all. In other words, the original compact has two parts or two aspects. The first part is a unanimous agreement to be bound by the majority, and the second is the agreement by the majority to a particular form of government. This much Sidney, Locke, and the Americans had in common.

However, Locke's theory of consent is weaker than that advocated by Sidney and the Americans for two reasons. First of all, Locke argues that, when a person comes of age, that person gives his tacit consent to the compact by not leaving the country or resisting the government, and by taking advantage of the laws, especially those protecting property. In such a fashion, says Locke, most of us pass without noticing into civil society. Second, Locke has little to say about consent beyond its role in the original compact. He does not argue for the necessity of elections or any other instrument of continuing consent. This is not enough for Sidney. He denies that tacit consent is meaningful. Every person must willingly and consciously give his consent. Furthermore, government must rest on continuously recurring consent, otherwise the notion of consent is vitiated.

The differences in these two theories of consent can be put another way. For Sidney, the unanimous consent upon which the civil society rests in the first place should be an actual event which all newcomers must re-enact. Americans had already developed the concept of a written Constitution signed by all relevant people, or by representatives elected for that express purpose. Newcomers could be added to the civil society by taking an oath to uphold it. This is how Algernon Sidney would have it done, and it might be termed an "active" theory of consent.

Locke, on the other hand, had a "passive" version. As long as one did not specifically object, or act in a manner so as to indicate rejection, consent was assumed. Political theorists frequently refer to Locke's approach as the "acquiescence model." In effect, Locke's theory was that a government had the consent of the people to exist and to act until those people said "no." Sidney's theory was that the government did not have the consent of the people either to exist or to act until the people explicitly said "yes."

We can state the two theories of consent in a more formal manner. Sidney's active, direct, and continuous consent refers to a situation where the right of one man to act in a certain way is conditional upon another man's having expressed the wish that he act that way. Locke's passive, indirect, discontinuous consent involves always acting in a manner that the doer knows, or is assumed to know, will not prevent another from acting. Not only is Locke's notion of consent passive, note that two men need not even meet in order for one to consent to the other's acting – hence such consent is indirect. In Sidney's version there must be some form of direct interaction, and the interaction must take place either continuously or with some frequency.

4 Parliamentary and Popular Sovereignty

One can see, then, that the institution of annual elections reflects Sidney's theory, while Locke would not require such frequency – he never argued for it. Further, Sidney would expect the legislature to mirror the people at large, and he would also expect the people to send demands or instructions to their representatives, instructions which would be heeded. Locke, on the other hand, would expect representatives to deliberate for the common good more or less free from popular instructions, but subject to removal if a majority protested. American consent theory strained toward Sidney's active, direct, continuous approach, although there were a number of Americans who professed Locke's acquiescence version as well. Regardless of the differences, Americans had a strong tendency to believe that government must originate in the consent of the people; whether in Locke's sense or Sidney's sense did not matter. The British, on the other hand, did not think in terms of popular sovereignty. After the Glorious Revolution of 1688, Parliament was held to have ultimate power, and the British developed the legal fiction of the "king in Parliament" to define British sovereignty. Americans had by 1776 come to view parliamentary sovereignty as incompatible with popular sovereignty.

Americans were concerned not only with how to structure the act of consent upon which government rested, but also with who should give consent, on what range of issues, and through what processes or procedures. The broadest-known existing electorate became even broader. Efforts were made to tie legislatures more closely to the consent of the majority. Annual elections were already in use in every state, but some went further. For example, Pennsylvania required that before a bill become a law it had to be passed a second time by next year's legislature, with the people being able to question members of the legislature during the intervening election. Most interesting is what happened to the framing and ratification process for constitutions themselves.

Britain had no written constitution, yet it was assumed by Americans that government had to rest upon such consent-giving instruments. However, it had been a century or more since those now known as Americans had engaged in constitution writing, and at first the method for consenting to a new constitution did not completely match the theory. The first six state constitutions were written and adopted by state legislatures, although in each case the legislature met in special session as a convention. Even with the legislatures tied to a broadly defined electorate through annual elections this did not seem congruent with popular consent in a direct sense. In August 1776, three months after the Declaration of Independence, Delaware became the first state to elect a special body to write a state constitution, followed in 1777 by New York, whose legislature felt that "the right of framing, creating or new modeling civil government is, and ought to be in the people." Such practice became standard after this, although not until the Massachusetts document in 1780 and the second New Hampshire constitution in 1784 was the document also submitted to the people for approval in a popular referendum. These two changes made the practice of consent theory completely congruent with popular sovereignty. The American commitment to popular consent along the lines described by Algernon Sidney thus moved them to invent new constitutional methods for coherently and consistently expressing this conviction.

5 The Declaration of Independence

Consent tended to become so active, direct, and continuous after 1776 that some, such as James Madison, feared American institutions would be undermined by the very consent theory upon which they were built. Madison and other Federalists were able to design a national Constitution which combined effective government with consent-giving institutions at the national level.

The Declaration of Independence is the document in which the American people consent to the creation of a civil society known as the United States of America. It proclaims itself to be a unanimous declaration in the title, and the list of signatures at the end is the familiar American method going back to the Mayflower Compact (1620) of consenting to the creation of a civil society through one's own signature or the signature of an elected representative. The United States Constitution is the agreement creating a form of government. We have here, then, the documentary expression of the double compact advocated by both Locke and Sidney, but implemented in the active sense preferred by Sidney. Both agreements, however, reflect an ambiguity in the American notion of consent.

The Declaration does not address a situation where individual Americans are in a state of nature. Each lives under an already operating government based upon his consent at the colony level. Rather, it is a situation where "it becomes necessary for one people to dissolve the Political Bands which have connected them with another." The people are acting, not a collection of individuals. Most of the document is a list of abuses which Americans had suffered as a people at the hands of the English. Communitarianism, not individualism, permeates the list of abuses. The phrase "all men are created equal" thus has a double meaning with respect to consent. Liberty and equality pertain to individuals in the state of nature, but are focused upon the community in civil society. The American people are equal to the English people precisely because both peoples are composed of individuals who would be equal in the state of nature with the same ability to give or withhold consent. Put most directly, the Declaration enunciates the basic American view that consent is given individually because consent rests on all individuals, but the agreement collects the individual acts of consent to create the consent of the people, an entity in itself.

The important question then becomes, does the Declaration of Independence rest upon the consent of all Americans directly, or upon their consent collected as members of a state? In the second instance consent would be direct from individual to state, but indirect from individual to nation, so that the agreement is really between the states as collective entities. The evidence in both the Declaration and the Constitution is contradictory. The central position of federalism in the Constitution, whereby a person is simultaneously a citizen of a state and the United States, clearly implies that we should read the two founding documents as being based upon the simultaneous consent of both individual Americans and collections of individuals in the states. This paradox, or ambiguity, in American consent theory guaranteed that the concept of consent would continue to play a central role in future American politics.

FURTHER READING

Franklin, Julian S.: *John Locke and the Theory of Sovereignty* (Cambridge: Cambridge University Press, 1978).

Lutz, Donald S.: *Popular Consent and Popular Control: Whig Political Theory in the Early State Constitutions* (Baton Rouge: Louisiana State University Press, 1980).

Morgan, Edmund S.: *Inventing the People: the Rise of Popular Sovereignty in England and America* (New York: W. W. Norton, 1988).

Parsons, Theophilus: *The Essex Result* (Newburyport, Mass.: 1778); repr. in *The Popular Sources of Authority*, ed. Oscar Handlin and Mary Handlin (Cambridge, Mass.: Harvard University Press, 1966), 324–65.

Partridge, P. H.: *Consent and Consensus* (New York: Praeger Publishers, 1971).

Plamenatz, J. P.: *Consent, Freedom, and Political Obligation*, 2nd edn. (Oxford: Oxford University Press, 1968).

Pole, J. R.: *Political Representation in England and the Origins of the American Republic* (Berkeley: University of California Press, 1971).

CHAPTER EIGHTY-TWO

Happiness

JAN LEWIS

THE term "happiness" is a key word in the revolutionary vocabulary because American patriots often asserted its assurance as the object of government and its pursuit as one of mankind's inalienable rights. Both of these usages of the concept have been immortalized in the second paragraph of the Declaration of Independence, although the precise meaning attached to the word as well as the possible sources for Thomas Jefferson's phrasing have long been contested by scholars. It is worth quoting this section of the Declaration in its entirety, for it establishes the context for understanding the meaning of happiness not only to the revolutionary generation, but also to all those who have debated it since then:

We hold these truths to be self-evident, that all men are created equal, that they are endowed by their Creator with certain unalienable Rights, that among these are Life, Liberty and the pursuit of Happiness. – That to secure these rights, Governments are instituted among Men, deriving their just powers from the consent of the governed, – That whenever any Form of Government, becomes destructive of these ends, it is the Right of the People to alter or to abolish it, and to institute new Government, laying its foundation on such principles and organizing powers in such form, as to them shall seem most likely to effect their Safety and Happiness. (Becker, 1969, p. 186).

Jefferson had used the term happiness a third time in his rough draft of the Declaration, in the penultimate paragraph, when, after rehearsing the revolutionaries' grievances against their "British brethren," he observed that "the road to happiness and to glory is open to us too; we will climb apart from them" (Becker, 1969, p. 169). Although this section was dropped from the version adopted and signed in Philadelphia, there is no record that either of the other uses of "happiness" was questioned or debated. Therefore we may conclude that the meaning of the concept was either so clear and commonly understood that no comment was required, or that its connotation was so vague and ambiguous that each could attach to it his own definition.

Not until almost half a century had passed would the sources – and hence the intent – of the happiness passages be questioned. Then, John Adams pointed to James Otis's pamphlet *The Rights of the British Colonies Asserted and Proved* (Boston, 1764) as the model, and Richard Henry Lee to John Locke's *Two Treatises of Government* (1690). Both Adams and Lee were correct, at least to the extent that both the philosophy and phrasing of the Declaration, including the happiness passages, were strikingly similar to those of works known to have circulated in the colonies in the years before 1776. Jefferson himself disclaimed originality, saying in a letter to Lee (May 8, 1825) that the Declaration was "intended to be an expression of the American mind ... all its authority rests on the harmonizing sentiments of the day" (Koch and Peden, 1944, p. 719) – not only Locke, but Aristotle, Cicero, Sidney, and others (*see* chapter 33). Most of those who have interpreted the meaning of happiness in the Declaration since have followed Lee's lead and found in Locke the most important key to Jefferson's intent. Recently, scholars who believe that revolutionary theorists drew as much, if not more, from Scottish Enlightenment thinkers have argued that happiness was a social more than an individualist concept (*see* chapter 11, §§1 and 6).

1 The Influence of Locke: Property as a Condition of Happiness

The case for Locke's influence – stated perhaps most forcefully by Carl Becker, who wrote in *The Declaration of Independence* (1922) that "Jefferson copied Locke" – rests upon the similarity of reasoning and rhetoric both. The entire document, and especially the first paragraph of the Declaration, may be read as a restatement of Locke's doctrines of natural rights, the compact theory of government, and the right to resist tyranny. It has been argued that Jefferson merely substituted the rhetorically more felicitous "pursuit of happiness" for Locke's characteristic invocation of "property," and that consequently "the pursuit of happiness" should be translated as "property." Locke, incidentally, never used the precise phrase "life, liberty, and property," but instead spoke of "life, liberty, and estate" and "lives, liberties, and fortunes" (Locke, 1690, pp. 387, 420), and intended the term "property" to embrace all three elements of that which he believed a man possessed by natural right (p. 414). Nonetheless, the term "life, liberty, and property" had been used in important revolutionary documents, so there is good authority for interpreting "happiness" as "property." The Declaration of Colonial Rights and Grievances, adopted by the First Continental Congress on October 1, 1774, asserted that the colonists were "entitled to life, liberty and property" (Morris, 1970, p. 132), and James Otis in *The Rights of the British Colonies Asserted and Proved* (1764) said that government was designed "above all things to provide for the security, the quiet, and happy enjoyment of life, liberty, and property" (Otis, in Schlesinger, 1964, p. 326). The Virginia Declaration of Rights (June 1776), written by George Mason, noted that

all men are created equally free and independent, and have certain inherent natural rights, of which they cannot, by any compact, deprive or divest

their posterity; among which are the enjoyment of life and liberty, with the means of acquiring and possessing property, and pursuing and obtaining happiness and safety. (Mason, in Jones, 1953, p. 12).

Jefferson's debt to Mason and, if not as directly, Locke is clear. That "happiness" might mean "property" was one of "the harmonizing sentiments of the day."

To say that the philosophy of the Declaration was Lockean and that happiness ought to be translated as property is to underscore the individualistic and contractarian aspects of revolutionary thought. Such an interpretation suggests that the purpose of government is to protect the individual and to secure his rights and possessions. Indeed, Locke wrote that "the great and chief end of men's uniting into commonwealths, and putting themselves under government, is the preservation of their property" (Locke, 1690, p. 412). The common good entailed the protection of the individual and his property. The Lockean reading of the meaning of happiness likewise implies that human happiness proceeds from the individual's enjoyment, improvement, and use of his possessions. It is well known that Jefferson and other revolutionaries believed that property was prerequisite to individual independence, and hence citizenship, so that a Lockean interpretation of happiness need not be read as narrowly economic or necessarily protocapitalist. At the time of the Revolution, most American political writers believed that their society was uniquely egalitarian, that property was held or was available to virtually all white men, and that, as James Madison later recalled, "a provision for the rights of persons was supposed to include of itself those of property" (Madison, in Wood, 1969, p. 412). Protecting property and preserving liberty were virtually identical, or, as Locke had seen it, the one included the other.

2 The Eighteenth-Century Use of the Term

Interpreting "happiness" as "property" is therefore consistent with the tenets of republicanism. Nonetheless, some of the scholars who have illuminated the republican dimension to revolutionary thought have found the Lockean reading of the meaning of happiness deficient. They note that Jefferson had abundant opportunity to use the word "property" in the Declaration, but clearly chose not to. Moreover, Jefferson recommended that the Marquis de La Fayette excise the inalienable right of property (*propriété*) from the draft of the Declaration of Human Rights that he wrote for France in 1788 (Willis, 1978, p. 230). Perhaps Jefferson had reasons other than felicity of style for naming the pursuit of happiness, but not property, as an inalienable right.

Those who have questioned the Lockean, individualist interpretation of "happiness" have observed that the term was in wide use among eighteenth-century political and moral theorists, so that, when Jefferson chose it, he intended it to evoke the meanings associated with happiness rather than those attached to property. When theorists used the term, they usually differentiated between a social and an individual happiness. The distinction is most clear in John Adams's *Thoughts on Government* (1776), where it is noted that "upon this point all speculative politicians will agree, that the happiness of society is the end of government, as all divines and moral philosophers will agree that the happiness of the individual is the end of man" (Adams, 1851). Like Adams, most political writers concerned themselves primarily with the social construction of happiness. Josiah Quincy, Jr., in his *Observations on the Act of Parliament Commonly Called the Boston Port-Bill* (1774), claimed that the object of government was "the greatest happiness of the greatest number" (Quincy, in Schlesinger, 1964, p. 326), while Richard Henry Lee hoped, a month after the signing of the Declaration, that "by a wise and just confederation, the happiness of America will be secured" (Lee, 1911). Three years later, in his *Bill for the More General Diffusion of Knowledge*, Jefferson himself suggested that a system of public education would be "expedient for promoting public happiness" (Jefferson, 1779). It was this public or social happiness that Jefferson seemed to have in mind when he

wrote, in the Declaration, that it is the right of the people to create, alter, or abolish government in order "to effect their safety and happiness."

3 Wilson, Burlamaqui, and Hutcheson: Public Happiness

When revolutionary theorists spoke of the happiness of society, they seemed to intend more than the sum total of individual happinesses. Even if it is granted that the phrase "the pursuit of happiness" derives from Locke and means the right of the individual to be secure in his property, there is considerable evidence that revolutionary thinkers understood something different by public happiness. The meaning of this term is suggested by one of the other works commonly supposed to be a source for the Declaration. Jefferson copied portions of James Wilson's *Considerations on the Nature and Extent of the Legislative Authority of the British Parliament* (1774) into his *Commonplace Book* although, curiously, not this passage, which bears a striking resemblance to the second paragraph of the Declaration:

All men are, by nature, equal and free: no one has a right to any authority over another without his consent: all lawful government is founded in the consent of those who are subject to it: such consent was given with a view to ensure and to increase the happiness of the governed, above what they would enjoy in an independent and unconnected state of nature. The consequence is that the happiness of the society is the first law of every government. (Wilson, in Becker, 1969, p. 108)

As Jefferson would later do, Wilson invoked both the Lockean social compact theory of government and the public conceptualization of happiness.

Wilson cited as his source the Swiss jurist Jean Jacques Burlamaqui, who held that God, "by creating us, proposed our preservation, perfection, and happiness" (Burlamaqui, 1807). Burlamaqui believed, consequently, that individuals had an obligation to pursue their happiness, and that this duty preceded any actions by men themselves. The pursuit of happiness, then, was a "primitive" right, whereas property – and the consequent right to protect it – was "adventitious," proceeding from men's efforts to satisfy their wants. Jefferson's enumeration of the pursuit of happiness as one of mankind's inalienable rights, then, is consistent with the views expressed in Burlamaqui's *Principles of Natural and Politic Law*, a French edition of which he purchased in 1769 (White, 1978, p. 37).

Another of Burlamaqui's modifications of Locke is relevant to an understanding of the meaning of "happiness." Like Locke, Burlamaqui rejected the notion of innate ideas, but, while Locke believed that moral truths could be discerned by reason, Burlamaqui attempted to reconcile Locke's rationalism with the doctrines of the Scottish Enlightenment philosopher Francis Hutcheson, who held that men were born with an innate moral sense. According to Morton White, Burlamaqui believed that both reason and the moral sense were inherent, that both lead to the truth, and that "reason verifies what the moral sense first brings to our attention" (White, 1978, p. 111). At the time he wrote the Declaration, Jefferson seems to have followed Burlamaqui in subscribing to both a Lockean rationalism and a Scottish Enlightenment sensationalism, and, like Burlamaqui, he generally gave priority to reason, which verified, clarified, and developed the impressions conveyed by the moral sense.

This understanding of Jefferson's epistemology may clarify his use of the term "happiness," for Garry Wills has recently argued that Jefferson's intellectual debt was primarily to the Scottish Enlightenment philosophers, particularly Hutcheson, and that, consequently, we should look to Hutcheson for an understanding of "happiness." Hutcheson believed that it is benevolence that is the source of happiness, for we become happy "when we reflect upon our having done virtuous actions." Because "the surest way to promote ... private happiness [is] to do publicly useful actions," happiness might be attained only in society. And it followed that "the action is best which procures the greatest happiness of the greatest numbers" and that "the general happiness is the supreme end of all political union" (Hutcheson, 1755, 1726). American revolutionary theorists who echoed Hutcheson

were not utilitarians, for they grounded happiness in a "self-evident" truth, perceived by an intuitive reason or an innate moral sense, rather than in social usefulness. Nor were they individualists, for they held that happiness derived not from the gratification of self-interest, but from doing good for others.

4　From Communalism to Individualism

At the time the Declaration was written, both the Lockean and Hutchesonian definitions of "happiness" were in use among American revolutionary theorists. Whether by accident or intent, when Jefferson harmonized the "sentiments of the day," he invoked both the individualist and the social meanings of the term. Yet at the time he wrote, there was no apparent inconsistency, for few saw any necessary conflict between the rights of the individual and the welfare of the entire society. Just as Jefferson believed he could harmonize the sentiments of the day, so most revolutionary thinkers believed that a properly working government could harmonize the interests of its citizens, securing simultaneously and reciprocally the happiness of the individual and the society.

Over the course of the Revolution, this inherently unstable consensus on the meaning of happiness would fracture. The factious and self-interested actions of the American people themselves convinced Madison, among others, that the individual pursuing his own happiness might undermine that of the society at large; it appeared evident that the interests of the individual and the society were not identical. Indeed, it is not clear that the American people, as distinguished from revolutionary ideologues, conceptualized happiness in public terms. Jack P. Greene has suggested that the conditions of settlement of the colonies so enhanced individual autonomy that, by the time of the Revolution, at least, the pursuit of happiness meant, essentially, personal independence – the ability to provide for oneself and one's family and be free from the intrusions of government or society (Greene, 1988). Such a notion of independence was, of course, profoundly individualistic and essentially Lockean in its conceptualization. To be sure, historians have debated precisely when the balance in America was tipped from communalism to individualism, but it is generally agreed that the spread of an individualist practice of happiness was one of the underlying social causes of the Revolution, and that the Revolution itself only exacerbated that trend (*see* chapter 7, §§2, 3, and 4). Whatever its intent, the Declaration's phrase "pursuit of happiness" seemed to legitimate the individualistic strivings of the American people.

In the decades after the Revolution, American men and women would come to define happiness almost exclusively in private, personal terms. If happiness retained its Lockean association with property and, consequently, material well-being, it also acquired an emotional connotation, as men and women came to expect that they should find happiness at home, in the intimate relationships of the family. In this sense, the history of the concept "happiness" is similar to that of "virtue," a related term, and one equally significant in the revolutionary vocabulary. As Ruth H. Bloch has demonstrated, the term "virtue" had two meanings; public virtue referred to the willingness of the individual to sacrifice his self-interest for the public good, while private virtue suggested a number of personal qualities, such as piety and frugality (Bloch, 1987). In the decades after the Revolution, "virtue" was stripped of its public meaning, so that it eventually came to be associated almost entirely with admirable personal characteristics, especially those of women (*see* chapter 77, §§4 and 5). Although the meaning of happiness was never feminized in the same way, it also lost its public connotations, so that, ultimately, most Americans would define and pursue it in private and personal ways. It was left for later generations to rediscover the more complex understanding of happiness that was embraced by Jefferson and his colleagues in the revolutionary endeavor.

FURTHER READING

Adams, John: "Thoughts on Government," *Works of John Adams*, ed. C. F. Adams (Boston, 1851), IV, 193; repr. in White, 1978, 233.

Becker, Carl L.: *The Declaration of Independence: A Study in the History of Political Ideas* (1922); 3rd edn. (New York: Alfred A. Knopf, 1969).

Bloch, Ruth H.: "The gendered meanings of virtue in revolutionary America," *Signs: Journal of Women in Culture and Society*, 13 (1987), 37–58.

Burlamaqui, Jean Jacques: *Principles of Natural and Political Law*, trans. Thomas Nugent (Cambridge, Mass.: 1807), Part II, Chapter IV, Section VI; repr. in White (1978), 162.

Ganter, Herbert Lawrence: "Jefferson's 'pursuit of happiness' and some forgotten men," *William and Mary Quarterly*, 16 (1936), 422–34, 558–85.

Greene, Jack P.: *Pursuits of Happiness: the Social Development of Early Modern British Colonies and the Formation of American Culture* (Chapel Hill: University of North Carolina Press, 1988).

Hamowy, Ronald: "Jefferson and the Scottish Enlightenment: a critique of Garry Wills's *Inventing America: Jefferson's Declaration of Independence*," *William and Mary Quarterly*, 36 (1979), 503–23.

Hutcheson, Francis: *An Inquiry into the Original of our Ideas of Beauty and Virtue*, 2nd edn. (1726), 177; repr. in Margaret Canovan: "The un-Benthamite utilitarianism of Joseph Priestly," *Journal of the History of Ideas*, 45 (1984), 436.

——: *A System of Moral Philosophy*, vol. II (1755); repr. in Wills, 1978, 252.

Jefferson, Thomas: *Bill for the More General Diffusion of Knowledge* (1779), in *The Papers of Thomas Jefferson*, ed. Julian Boyd (Princeton, 1950), II, 526–33; repr. in David M. Post: "Jeffersonian revisions of Locke: education, property-rights, and liberty," *Journal of the History of Ideas*, 47 (1986), 153.

Koch, Adrienne, and Peden, William: *The Life and Selected Writings of Thomas Jefferson* (New York: Modern Library, 1944).

Lee, Richard Henry: *The Letters of Richard Henry Lee*, ed. James C. Ballagh (New York: Macmillan, 1911), I, 211; repr. in Ganter (1936), 585.

Locke, John: *Works*, 10 vols. vol. 5, *Two Treatises of Government* (1690) (London: Thomas Tegg, 1823), repr. (Germany: Scientia Verlag Allen, 1963).

Madison, James: "Observations on Jefferson's Draft of a Constitution for Virginia" (1788), *The Papers of Thomas Jefferson*, ed. Julian Boyd (Princeton, 1950), VI, 310; also repr. in Gordon S. Wood: *The Creation of the American Republic, 1776–1787* (Chapel Hill: University of North Carolina Press, 1969), 410.

Mason, George: *Virginia Declaration of Rights* (1776), in Kate Mason Rowland, *The Life of George Mason* (New York and London: 1892), Appendix X, I, 434; also in Howard Mumford Jones: *The Pursuit of Happiness* (Ithaca: Cornell University Press, 1953; repr. 1966), 12.

Morris, Richard B. (ed.): *The American Revolution, 1763–1783* (New York: Harper and Row, 1970).

Otis, James: *The Rights of the British Colonies Asserted and Proved* (Boston: 1764), in *Some Political Writings*, ed. Charles F. Mullett (University of Missouri Studies, 4, 1929), 309; also repr. in Arthur M. Schlesinger: "The lost meaning of 'the pursuit of happiness'," *William and Mary Quarterly*, 21 (1964), 326.

Quincy, Josiah: "Observations on the Act of Parliament commonly called the Boston Port-Bill," *Memoir of the Life of Josiah Quincy, Junior, of Massachusetts, 1774–1775*, 2nd edn. (Boston: 1874). 323; also repr. in Arthur M. Schlesinger: "The lost meaning of 'the pursuit of happiness,'" *William and Mary Quarterly*, 21 (1964), 326.

White, Morton: *The Philosophy of the American Revolution* (New York: Oxford University Press, 1978).

Wills, Garry: *Inventing America: Jefferson's Declaration of Independence* (New York: Doubleday, 1978).

Wilson, James, *Considerations on the Nature and Extent of the Legislative Authority of the British Parliament* (1774), repr. in Becker, 1969, 108.

CHAPTER EIGHTY-THREE

Suffrage and representation

ROSEMARIE ZAGARRI

BEGINNING in 1962, the United States Supreme Court embarked on a series of decisions which mandated that all state legislatures be apportioned according to the principle of "one person, one vote." This principle actually embodies two distinct concepts: the idea that each person is entitled to the vote and the notion that each person's vote should be worth the same as every other person's. The former is achieved through universal adult suffrage; the latter through numerical apportionment, which makes representation in the legislature proportionate to population. The idea of "one person, one vote" first appeared during the American Revolution. In the years thereafter it gained a permanent place in both the state and the federal governments. However, it took almost two centuries for these principles to be fully realized in practice.

1 Concepts of Representation in the Revolutionary Era

Representation was at the center of the American controversy with Great Britain. As the colonies developed, each one established a system of representative government, modeled on Parliament, in which the lower house of the assembly was popularly elected. The colonists believed that only their colonial assemblies – their elected representatives – had the right to tax them. Before the Sugar and Stamp Acts of 1764 and 1765, Parliament had never attempted to tax the colonists. Previous Acts had been designed to regulate trade or to provide for the defense of the colonies. In the wake of the budget crisis following the Seven Years' War, however, Parliament tried for the first time to pass laws for the explicit purpose of generating revenue – in other words, to tax the colonists without their consent.

In the debate over the Stamp Act, it became clear that concepts of representation in England and the colonies had diverged. Defenders of the Stamp Act in Britain promoted an idea known as "virtual" representation. Parliament, they said, legislated for the good of the entire realm. Although Americans did not send representatives to the House of Commons, their interests were known and taken into account there. The colonists, they argued, were as well represented as any non-elector in England. The Americans, however, insisted that only their elected representatives could tax them. They rejected virtual representation and the comparison with non-electors in England. Because of the large distance separating England and America, Members of Parliament could not have a direct knowledge of the colonists' situation or interests. They claimed that even those who could not vote in England could personally convey their needs or express their displeasure to Members of Parliament. Even more important, in England representatives were subject to the same laws as the people. This was not the case with America. Representatives in the House of Commons could impose harsh taxes on the colonies without ever feeling the effects themselves or seeing the consequences before their eyes. To tolerate the Stamp Act, it was said, would mean to permit the possibility of an unending string of ever more burdensome taxes.

The Stamp Act crisis forced Americans to define their understanding of representation, an understanding which they expanded upon in the subsequent debates leading up to the Revolution. Close ties should exist between the constituents and their legislators. The people should know and be known by their representatives – personally, if possible. The legislature should reflect precisely the interests and wishes of those that elected them. The representatives should legislate as the people would, were they all able to be present. Unless the people's desires conflicted with the common good, they should promote the interests of their local constituency above all others. This notion of representation, though adequate for governing the colonies, effectively limited the compass of republican government to a small area.

2   Representation in the States

As Americans focused their attention on representation issues, they began to realize that the structure of representation in their own governments was inadequate and, in many cases, unjust. In all the colonies before the Revolution, the corporate method of apportioning representatives prevailed. Under this system the legislature determined how many representatives communities, such as counties, towns, or parishes, would be allowed to send. In some colonies each community sent the same number of representatives to the legislature. In Virginia, for example, each county was entitled to send two delegates to the House of Burgesses, while in Connecticut each town received two representatives in the lower house. In other colonies the apportionment was more arbitrary and left to the whim of the legislators. In South Carolina the assembly seemed to have no method at all for determining the number of representatives assigned to each parish. They wanted to preserve the power of the older, more established regions by giving them the preponderance of representatives. No colony conducted regular censuses before the Revolution, and no colony sytematically based its representation on population.

Inequalities under the corporate system of apportionment had grown increasingly apparent by the eve of the American Revolution. Since the legislators controlled the distribution of representatives, they wanted to prevent the diminution of their own power. They had a stake in preserving the status quo. As a result, they often refused to grant representation to new communities or failed to give extra representatives to more populous areas. Because the regions closest to the coast were the most long-settled, the legislatures tended to be dominated by easterners. By 1775, for example, Pennsylvania's three eastern counties had 26 delegates, while eight western counties, containing more than half the population, had only 15. As larger numbers of settlers moved into the interior, more people either had no representatives or so few that they had no real power in the assembly. Even before the Revolution, some colonists began to protest against inequities in their own legislatures.

The revolutionaries' emphasis on equality and natural rights reinforced the importance of making every elector's vote equal to every other elector's. Under the corporate system of representation this was not the case. When a county of 2,000 inhabitants received the same number of representatives as a county with 10,000, the vote of a person in the county with 2,000 was worth more and had more influence on the outcome of the election. Moreover, under the corporate system the majority of people might not have the majority of votes in the assembly. If communities rather than individuals were the basic unit of representation, then a majority of communities containing less than half the population might have more representatives than communities that had more people, as demonstrated in the example of Pennsylvania given above.

During the Revolution most of the states wrote new constitutions which altered the structures of their governments. Some states took this opportunity to correct problems in their method of apportioning representatives. First of all, many states took apportionment out of the hands of the legislators and made it a part of their constitutions. By describing the method of distributing representatives in the document which formed the fundamental law of the state, apportionment would be less likely to be manipulated to the advantage of certain legislators and regions at the expense of others.

Then the states faced even more difficult problems: overcoming the resistance of an entrenched elite in the legislature and finding a new system of apportionment to replace corporate representation. In Massachusetts, for example, large numbers of people in the seaboard towns cooperated with the great commercial and shipping interests there to overcome the opposition of legislators to a new system based on numbers of people, or on property owned, or on some combination of these factors. In other states increasingly numerous westerners also placed pressure on the assemblies. In any case, the method Americans most often turned to was proportional, or numerical, representation. Under this system the number of representatives was made proportionate to the population. In other words, a ratio was established between the people and their representatives – for example, one legislator for every 30,000 inhabitants. This method assumed that the individual rather than the community formed the basic unit of representation. Communities – counties, towns, parishes, or specially created legislative districts – received representation in proportion to their strength in numbers. Political units with more people received more representatives; those with fewer people received fewer representatives. Numerical representation would insure that the majority would rule.

In their first state constitutions, Pennsylvania, New York, Massachusetts, and New Hampshire quickly implemented some form of numerical representation in the lower houses of their state legislatures. In 1789 Georgia followed suit. Both South Carolina and New Jersey acknowledged the principle of numerical representation in their early constitutions, but South Carolina did not actually institute the system until 1808 and New Jersey not until 1844. The Northwest Ordinance of 1787 prescribed the method for the new states carved out of the Ohio Territory. All but two of the 20 states entering the Union between 1789 and 1860 provided for numerical representation in at least one house of their legislatures.

In the wake of the Revolution, then, most states did accept the notion of numerical representation in some form. Some states only used the method in one house. Some states used a combination of property and

population in determining representation. Most states defined the represented population as something less than the total number of inhabitants. The Massachusetts and Pennsylvania constitutions, for example, counted only taxable inhabitants: the Georgia constitution, like the United States Constitution, included all Whites but only three-fifths of all Blacks. Nevertheless, the principle and practice of numerical apportionment was well established. In the last decades of the nineteenth century, however, an intense rivalry developed between rural areas and the increasingly populous cities. State legislatures, dominated by rural interests, began to deviate substantially from the norm of numerical representation. Inequities had become so common and so severe that the Supreme Court, beginning in 1962 with *Baker v. Carr*, issued a series of decisions designed to compel states to maintain proportional representation in both houses of their legislatures as well as in their congressional districts. The Court imposed from above a standard that had emerged from below in the revolutionary era.

3 Representation for the Nation

At the federal level, the most important decision concerning representation occurred at the Constitutional Convention in Philadelphia during the summer of 1787. Delegates from the larger states – states which either had large populations or expected to have large populations in the near future – argued for numerical representation in both houses of the national legislature. Representatives from the smaller states insisted that the states deserved to be represented as states – in other words, as corporate entities – in at least one house. This split represented the most serious threat to the success of the Philadelphia convention. Neither side wanted to back down; both sides claimed that they were correct. In fact, the smaller states did have the long colonial tradition of corporate representation on their side. The large states, however, had the greater fairness of the numerical system to support their position. After debating the issue for over one and a half months, a compromise was reached. The Great Compromise (sometimes called the Connecticut Compromise) included, among other things, provisions which made representation proportionate to population in the lower house of the national legislature and equal for each state in the upper house. It also included a clause requiring a decennial census for the purpose of keeping representation in the lower house commensurate with population. The convention's resolution of this vexing question, then, produced a system that combined both new and old concepts of representation.

Concepts of representation were also central in the debate over the ratification of the United States Constitution. The opponents of the Constitution, the Anti-Federalists, maintained that it was impossible to establish a republic in an area as large as the United States. Following Montesquieu, they claimed that republics could exist only in small territories having homogeneous populations. A large republic was bound, they said, to degenerate into despotism or split into many warring factions. They criticized the proposed system of representation because it lacked the personal intimacy of representation at the state level. The Congress, they said, had too few members to represent such a numerous, diverse population. Only wealthy, prominent – and unrepresentative – individuals would be elected to federal office. As a result, the federal representation would be detached and unresponsive to the needs and wishes of the constituents.

The Federalist supporters of the Constitution responded by proposing a new concept of representation. In *The Federalist* no. 10 James Madison gave the classical formulation of this theory. Madison argued that representative government was not only possible, but preferable, in a large territory. Factious majorities, seeking to promote their own selfish interests, represented the gravest threat to the stability of the country; these could not be stopped by normal democratic processes. In the United States, however, the population was so diverse and so spread out over a vast area that it would be impossible for factious majorities to form.

Even more important, however, was Madison's distinction between a democracy and a republic. A democracy, he said, was a form of government in which all the electors must meet personally to vote on every issue. A republic, on the other hand, was a form in which the people elect representatives to conduct the public business for them. The process of election would help filter out corrupt and untrustworthy candidates and raise to office those who were worthy of the public trust. The wisest and the most virtuous would prevail. Federal representation was of a different stripe from that in the states. Congressmen need not have personal knowledge of nor personal contact with their constituents. They would govern in the national interest, removed from the particularistic concerns of the states. The Federalists, then, formulated a new concept of representation better suited to American circumstances. Ironically, the Federalists' theory bore more than a passing resemblance to the discredited concept of virtual representation that many Americans had so vigorously opposed.

4 Suffrage

The Revolution also catalyzed sentiment in favor of expanding the franchise by reducing or abolishing property qualifications for voting. The colonies had followed the practice in England of requiring electors to own a certain amount of wealth or property before being allowed to cast a ballot. In England, the standard was possession of a 40-shilling freehold; that is, to own land worth 40 shillings per year in rental value or income. Because of the scarcity of land in England, this represented a substantial sum and prevented the majority of Englishmen from voting. In seventeenth-century elections in England, no more than one-fifth of the adult male population could vote. Although some colonies, such as Rhode Island and eighteenth-century Massachusetts, adopted the 40-shilling rule, many set their own requirements in terms of acreage. North Carolina and Georgia, for example, insisted that the voter own 50 acres of land; Virginia required the voter to own 100 acres of vacant land or 25 acres of improved land. Other colonies had variations on these basic requirements, which changed somewhat over time.

An elaborate rationale existed to justify the need for property qualifications for voting. It was believed that only property owners had a real stake in society, a permanent interest in the government's future. They were the ones on whom taxes fell most heavily. Only they had the independence to vote for the best candidate; poorer individuals might sell their votes or be susceptible to bribery.

Yet the property qualification for voting had a far different effect in the colonies than in England. Because land was cheap and abundant in America, most men owned property. As a result, the vast majority of white males were eligible to vote; whether they exercised this privilege was another matter. Although the numbers varied over time and from colony to colony, it is believed that from 50 to 80 percent of the white male population could vote in colony-wide elections before the Revolution. Furthermore, colonists with little or no property were often allowed to vote for the town or county officials even when they could not vote for delegates to the legislative assembly. Unlike in England, then, the property qualifications for voting did not prove to be a highly restrictive barrier to political participation in the colonies.

Nevertheless, property qualifications for voting came under attack during the revolutionary era. There had been some pressure in the late colonial period to reduce or abolish property qualifications. News that radicals in Britain such as Joseph Priestly and James Burgh were demanding liberalization of the franchise strengthened American commitment to the cause. After 1767, however, Britain refused to allow any colony to alter the structure of its government and so no changes were made. The revolutionary crisis intensified demands. Once the fighting began, some soldiers realized that, although they were expected to die for their country, they could not vote for their elected officials. The protests against taxation without representation led naturally to objections to representation without suffrage.

As was the case with apportionment, the writing of the new state constitutions provided the opportunity for states to reform injustices in their electoral system. Pennsylvania, North Carolina, New Hampshire, New Jersey, Maryland, and New York all reduced the property qualifications for voting during the Revolution. Some states, such as New York and North Carolina, instituted lower property qualifications for those voting for members of the lower house and higher qualifications for those voting for the upper house. Pennsylvania established the most generous rule, extending the franchise to all adult white male taxpayers. (Vermont, which was at this time not a part of the Union, was even more liberal. In 1777 it gave the franchise to all adult males who would take the Freeman's Oath, thus becoming the first place to establish universal manhood suffrage.) Over the next several decades, more and more states followed Pennsylvania's lead. By 1824 the right to vote had become independent of property ownership and taxpaying. Nearly all adult white males were allowed to vote, except in Rhode Island, Virginia, and Louisiana, which still retained more restrictive requirements.

5   The Exclusion of Women, Slaves, and Free Blacks

As ratified in 1789, the US Constitution did not prescribe national qualifications for the franchise; individual states set these standards. In the years following the American Revolution, state constitutions differed significantly in their suffrage requirements. For the most part, the liberalization in the franchise did not extend to women and non-Whites. As political dependents, women and black people were thought to have no need to vote; their husbands or masters took their interests into account when they voted. As economic dependents, women and Blacks might be susceptible to bribery or corruption, selling their vote to the highest bidder. Yet while white women could claim certain civil rights, such as the right to freedom of speech, trial by jury, and the right to petition, all slaves, men and women alike, were regarded as political nonentities, lacking even basic civil rights.

Yet the egalitarian principles of the American Revolution did inspire a few states to extend the franchise beyond its traditional limits. In their first state constitutions, New York, New Jersey, Pennsylvania, and North Carolina allowed free Blacks to vote on the same terms as Whites. This experiment in racial equality, however, was short-lived. By the 1820s increasing racism led to the disenfranchisment of free Blacks. In some states, free Blacks were even expelled, prohibited from living within state boundaries.

No state specifically granted women the right to vote. The New Jersey Constitution of 1776, however, employed gender-neutral language in allowing "inhabitants" who met the £50 property requirement to exercise the franchise. Whatever the origins of this provision, in 1790 state legislators affirmed the principle of female suffrage by passing an electoral statute that used the term "he" and "she" in discussing voters. Few women, besides wealthy widows, could meet the property requirement. Nonetheless, beginning in 1797, small numbers of women (probably no more than a few hundred in any given election) did vote in both state and federal elections. In 1807 election fraud and a lingering suspicion of the female franchise led legislators from both political parties to pass a law prohibiting women from voting. Free Blacks were disenfranchised at the same time. Interestingly enough, women apparently neither protested against nor objected to their loss. After that time, most new state constitutions explicitly limited suffrage to white males.

While suffrage requirements within the states tended to be exclusive, the basis of representation in the US Constitution was more broadly inclusive. According to the Constitution, representatives for the lower house of Congress should be apportioned according to the total number of "inhabitants," regardless of age, sex, or condition. Total population was chosen in preference to more restrictive categories such as the number of property holders, electors, or taxpayers. In other words, population, rather than wealth or territory, was to be the basis of representation in Congress. Whereas older theories of representation had insisted that power should follow property, the emerging American notion suggested that all people deserved to have their interests represented in the legislature. By implication, then, women were virtually represented in Congress.

The same was not true for black people. At the Constitutional Convention, northerners, who wanted the South to pay taxes on slaves but not to gain more representatives

in the House of Representatives, clashed with southerners, who wished to maximize their representation and minimize their taxes. Delegates compromised on a 3:5 ratio in order to prevent southerners from abandoning the Convention. Under this plan, only a portion of the slave population would be taxed and represented in Congress. It was a compromise that satisfied no one completely, and which embedded racial distinctions into the nation's founding document. (Significantly, the text of the Constitution does not include the word "slave," though the allusion is clear.) In addition, the 3:5 ratio implied that slaves occupied an anomalous status, existing as both persons and property. The contradictions in this policy quickly became apparent in subsequent legal decisions and ultimately had to be resolved through force of arms.

Over time, the ideal of equal representation became more fully realized. The Fourteenth Amendment, passed in 1868, granted equal protection by the law to all persons, and extended citizenship to all males, regardless of race. The same amendment explicitly excluded women from the privileges of citizenship. The Fifteenth Amendment prohibited people from being denied the right to vote for reasons of race, color, or previous condition of servitude. Not until 1920 did women receive their full share of representation, when the Nineteenth Amendment guaranteed women the right to vote. While many changes have been made, and more groups enfranchised, even today Americans struggle to put into practice the principle first articulated during the American Revolution: equal representation for all.

FURTHER READING

Dinkin, Robert J.: *Voting in Revolutionary America: A Study of Elections in the Original Thirteen States, 1776–1789* (Westport: Greenwood Press, 1982).

Klinghoffer, Judith Apter and Lois Elkis: "'The Petticoat Electors': Women's Suffrage in New Jersey, 1776–1807," *Journal of the Early Republic*, vol. 12 (Summer 1992), 159–93.

Lewis, Jan: "'Of Every Age Sex & Condition': The Representation of Women in the Constitution," *Journal of the Early Republic*, vol. 15 (Fall 1995), 359–87.

Pole, J. R.: *Political Representation in England and the Origins of the American Republic* (1966), paperback edn. (Berkeley, University of California Press, 1971).

Rakove, Jack N.: *Original Meanings: Politics and Ideas in the Making of the Constitution* (New York: Alfred A. Knopf, 1996).

Williamson, Chilton.: *American Suffrage: From Property to Democracy, 1760–1860* (Princeton: Princeton University Press, 1960).

Zagarri, Rosemarie.: *The Politics of Size: Representation in the United States, 1776–1850* (Ithaca: Cornell University Press, 1987).

CHAPTER EIGHTY-FOUR

Republicanism

ROBERT E. SHALHOPE

IMMEDIATELY upon declaring their Independence from the British monarchy in 1776, Americans committed themselves to establishing republican forms of government. They set about drafting constitutions within their newly formed states that would confirm the legitimate authority of the people. Intent upon creating a republican political system within their new nation, Americans actually created much more – a republican society. Even before the end of the Revolution, republicanism had become a cultural system that permeated every facet of American life – a pervasive ideology that would affect the behavior and thought of Americans for years to come.

1 John Locke and the Eighteenth-Century "Commonwealthmen"

In their effort to present a cogent intellectual defense against the actions of Parliament following the end of the Seven Years' War (1763), Americans drew upon a wide variety of sources – classical antiquity, the English common law, and Enlightenment rationalism. While most of these served an illustrative rather than a determinative role in their thought, the work of John Locke (1632–1704) stood out as a major exception. Indeed, by the 1760s, his belief that the people retained the right to rebel against unlawful or oppressive authorities had become entrenched in the consciousness of articulate and inarticulate colonists alike. Locke's principles and his ideas regarding the social contract could be employed to highlight the resistant rather than the submissive side of the traditional protection–allegiance

covenant between king and people. For many colonists, then, Locke helped smooth the way towards resistance without a radical departure from a familiar, traditional ideology. His ideas became the essential and familiar conduit for changed colonial beliefs.

While Lockean principles underlay the colonial perception of the relationship between rulers and the ruled, a group of English writers – eighteenth-century transmitters of the radical social and political thought of the Civil War and Commonwealth era – provided the colonists with a theory of politics that simultaneously explained why the British behaved as they did in the post-1763 years and provided the ideological basis for an American response. From the 1720s onwards, men such as John Trenchard, Thomas Gordon, Robert Viscount Molesworth, Richard Price, and James Burgh offered Americans a cohesive set of ideas that fused classical thought, common law theories, and Enlightenment principles into a coherent whole and which provided both clarity and direction to the colonial opposition. Under the intense pressure of events after 1763, the ideas of these men became integrated into a comprehensive and forceful image of politics and society that penetrated widely and deeply throughout colonial culture to form the essential substructure of American republicanism.

The writings of these eighteenth-century "commonwealthmen" emerged from a bitter hostility towards social, economic, and political forces transforming English society after the Glorious Revolution of 1688. These men perceived their society as degenerate and diseased, corrupted by vice and luxury and materialistic, commercial values. Behind this perception lay a political critique: excessive governmental power was spawning the decadence and decay eating away at the very foundations of English society and was rapidly carrying the nation towards the fate of ancient Rome.

While such ideas gained little popularity within English society, they became increasingly popular and influential in the American colonies. This body of opposition thought literally permeated colonial culture throughout the 1760s and 1770s. There the imposition of new colonial legislation after 1763 raised troubling questions, questions for which English radical and opposition writers seemed to provide particularly reasonable and uniquely relevant answers. Within this context, a comprehensive theory of politics emerged throughout the American colonies that made sense of the bewildering changes of the mid-eighteenth century for a great many diverse sorts of Americans.

2 Power and Liberty

This theory of politics focused on the role of power – defined as the control or domination of some men over others within American lives. For Americans, the disposition of power lurked behind every political event; it was the ultimate explanation for whatever political behavior they observed. Power became omnipresent in public affairs and always aggressively expanded beyond its just and safe limits. It was this aggressiveness that so troubled provincial writers because, in their minds, justice, equity, and liberty always fell victim to the inordinate demands of power. As a consequence, they saw the public world separated into two innately antagonistic spheres: power and liberty. The first, constantly and brutally assertive, must always be opposed, while the second, delicately innocent and passive, required a ceaseless and vigilant defense. From this basic insight colonial authors drew a central, all-important conclusion: the preservation of liberty relied entirely upon the moral strength and vigilance of the people. Only they could maintain effective restraints on those who wielded power.

Such a perspective led many colonists to see a pattern to the new British actions, a pattern whose meaning became unmistakably clear in light of Americans' understanding of opposition literature. Britain was succumbing to the all-too-familiar tendencies seen throughout history for nations to degenerate with age, to fall prey to the madness and corruption of power. Viewed in this manner, the actions taken by the British represented not merely mistaken or ill-advised behavior, but a deliberate attack upon liberty in Britain that was spreading its poison to the American colonies through unconstitutional taxes, an invasion of placemen, a purposeful weakening of the colonial judiciary, plural office-holding, an undermining of the prerogatives of the provincial assemblies, and the presence of a standing army. If unchecked, such a plot could destroy the sacred British Constitution and with it all the protection for individual liberties.

The belief that they faced a ministerial conspiracy against liberty transformed the meaning of resistance, in the minds of many colonists, from a Constitutional quarrel over the power of Parliament to govern them to a world-regenerative creed. In their minds, the lamp of liberty burned brightly only in the American provinces. Not to resist the British would be treasonable to themselves and to posterity. Out of these beliefs emerged the American perception of republicanism as the great moral force within their culture and throughout the Western world.

A belief in the regenerative quality of their resistance meant, for many Americans, that the Revolution was more than just a political revolt; it represented the creation of a fresh world, a republican world. Consequently, republicanism stood for more than simply the substitution of an elective system for a monarchy. It infused the political break from Britain with a moral fervor and an idealism linked inextricably with the very character of American society. The sacrifice of individual interests to a greater common good comprised both the essence of republicanism and the idealistic goal of the Revolution. Thus, the Revolution represented more than a rejection of British corruption. It required a reformation within provincial societies as well, a reformation defined in republican terms. For most Americans, republicanism expressed a longing for a communal attempt to control the bewildering and selfish impulses generated by the emergence of a capitalistic market economy in their midst. Emphasizing a morality of social cohesion, these people hoped to create an organic state joining individual citizens together into an indissoluble union of harmony and benevolence: a true republic. Theirs was a noble, though fragile, ideal because republics, by definition, depend entirely upon the character and spirit of their citizens. Unique among all polities, republics necessitate an absence of selfishness and luxury; their very existence rests upon virtue – the willingness of citizens to place the common good above their private desires. The presence or absence of virtue, therefore, determines whether or not a society remains republican. For Americans, the moral character of their society formed the prime measure of the success or failure of their revolution: republicanism blended indistinguishably with political revolution and moral regeneration.

On the eve of the Revolution, then, Americans embraced a distinctive set of political, social, and ethical attitudes that united them against the British. Assuming that history revealed a continual struggle between the spheres of liberty and power, American revolutionaries quickly formed a consensus in which the concept of republicanism epitomized the new social and political world they believed they were creating. Preserving a republican polity meant protecting liberty from ceaseless aggressions of power. In addition, since Americans believed that what made republics great or what ultimately destroyed them was not force of arms but the character and spirit of the people, public virtue became the essential prerequisite for good government. A people practicing frugality, industry, temperance, and simplicity constituted sound republican stock, while those who wallowed in luxury were corrupt and would corrupt others. Since furthering the public good – the exclusive purpose of republican government – required the constant sacrifice of individual interests to the greater needs of the whole, the people, conceived of as a homogeneous body (especially

when set against their rulers) became the great determinant of whether a republic lived or died. Thus, republicanism meant maintaining public and private virtue, internal unity, social solidarity, and vigilance against the corruptions of power. United in this frame of mind, Americans set out to gain their independence and to establish a new republic.

3 Republicanism and Liberalism

While the bulk of Americans espoused republican ideas in their struggle against the British, these ideas did not bear the same meaning for everyone involved. Indeed, it soon became apparent that republicanism represented a general consensus solely because it rested on such vague premises. Few things were certain: Americans believed that republicanism meant the elimination of an aristocracy and a monarchy as well as the absence of inherited authority and unearned privilege. Beyond this, agreement vanished – what form a republican government should assume and, more importantly, what constituted a republican society remained unclear. With the passage of time, it became apparent that republicanism and revolution carried different meanings in various regions of the country and even different meanings for distinct groups within the same locale. Some people enthusiastically accepted the New World market relations, while others remained deeply anti-capitalistic. Some wanted to retain a communal society based on social hierarchy, others desired an open, competitive society without regard for rank or status, while still others preferred a simple, homogeneous society of relative equality held together by deep corporate bonds. These disparate desires emerged as discrete fragments of two cultural impulses – republicanism and liberalism – coursing through the lives of late eighteenth-century Americans. At times, the two appeared to run parallel to one another, at others they seemed in direct conflict, and quite often they melded into a nearly indistinguishable whole. In many ways, republicanism – a familiar ideology permeating all walks of life – shaped Americans' minds; it offered them a self-image that provided meaning and identity to their lives.

Liberalism – as yet an unarticulated behavioral pattern more than a sharply delineated mode of thought – unconsciously shaped their day-to-day activity.

Most Americans clung to a harmonious, corporate view of themselves and their society even while behaving in a materialistic, utilitarian manner in their daily lives. Thus, while rapidly transforming their society in an open, competitive, modern direction, Americans idealized communal harmony and a virtuous social order. Republicanism condemned the values of a burgeoning capitalistic economy and placed a premium upon an ordered, disciplined personal liberty restricted by the civic obligations dictated by public virtue. In this sense, republicanism formalized or ritualized a mode of thought that ran counter to the flow of history; it idealized the traditional values of a world rapidly fading rather than the market conditions and liberal capitalistic mentality swiftly emerging in the late eighteenth century. And yet the confrontation with the British in the 1760s and the 1770s instilled new vigor into traditional republican values by stigmatizing the institutions, values, and attitudes of a mother country poised on the verge of the Industrial Revolution. Consequently, the Revolution sanctified virtue (defined as the subordination of self to the greater good of the community), corporate harmony, unity, and equality at the very moment when those values had already become anachronistic.

This resulted in ambivalence, inconsistencies, and ironic incongruities. Americans wrestled with changes that transformed their society while continuing to idealize an essentially premodern set of values. Economic, social, and political changes began to alter institutions and modes of behavior in fundamental and dramatic ways. More and more isolated agrarian villages began to be tied into larger commercial networks; opportunities abounded that revealed the unlimited potential for human freedom; and the bonds holding together families, churches, and communities eroded and in many cases simply fell away. Americans found themselves caught up in confusing ambiguities arising from a tension between old values and new modes of behavior. And yet the conflict between traditional republican values and newly emerging liberal behavior patterns never became so clearcut as to set one specific set of ideas in direct opposition to another. Indeed, this tension seethed as fiercely within single individuals and groups as it did between competing elements within American society. As a result, Americans could, and did, believe simultaneously in corporate needs and individual rights. They never had a sense of having to choose between two starkly contrasting traditions – republicanism and liberalism. Instead, they domesticated classical republicanism to fit their contemporary needs; they unselfconsciously amalgamated inherited assumptions with their liberal actions.

4 Republican Interpretation of the War

The tension between republican ideology and liberal behavior patterns carried throughout the Revolution. And yet the war itself, or rather its victory, prompted most Americans to view their efforts in republican terms and to enshrine these values in the meaning of the war. Most Americans entered the Revolution with the millennial expectation of creating a new republican society comprised of virtuous citizens free of Old World corruption. The Revolution carried the promise of regeneration with a desperate insistency born of the doubts and uncertainties arising from transformations already affecting the colonial societies. During the course of the war, however, American behavior had manifested disturbing and disappointing signs of European vice: sectional, factional, and personal rivalries emerged; public officials and governmental contractors indulged in widespread graft and corruption; farmers demanded usurious prices for their crops, while merchants displayed similar greed in selling their trade goods; many individuals engaged in a lucrative trade with the enemy; and others strove desperately to avoid military service. The techniques employed to win the war also raised grave questions about the republican character of Americans: the Continental Government found itself forced to conscript citizens, to confiscate property, and to engage the mysterious and very likely corrupt financial and administrative talents of shrewd and ambitious individuals. Worst of all, the militia – the backbone of a republican society – proved ineffective; only the creation of a regular army with rigorously disciplined soldiers and self-seeking ambitious officers saved the cause.

Despite these experiences, Americans chose to believe that their victory represented a confirmation of their moral strengths, a testament to their republican ideals. in 1783 they celebrated public virtue, not its failure. To preserve their millennial vision of the future, Americans could not recognize the reality of the many questionable expedients employed to win the war. Concerned about their failures and anxious about their bequest to posterity, the revolutionary generation redefined its experiences and made them as virtuous and as heroic as they ought to have been. Thus, victory – gained by the fallible, partial, and selfish efforts of many Americans – allowed an entire generation to ignore these unpleasant realities and to claim that it had remained true to the republican standards of 1775. They offered those standards and the image of a unified, virtuous republican citizenry to future generations. To celebrate the victory was to celebrate the regenerative character of the revolutionary movement. The young nation's triumph validated a unique national character based upon the predominance of republican virtue. The language of the revolutionary victors belied their experiences during the war just as republican language had belied the experiences of Americans for several decades before the outbreak of the Revolution. Republican ideals expressed a reaction against tendencies actually dominant in colonial society, not their political fulfillment. Classical republicanism expressed seemingly anachronistic ideas at the very moment when the circumstances of the American Revolution transformed them into a national ideology.

5 Post-Revolutionary Republicanism

By the end of the eighteenth century, the American commitment to republicanism had grown even stronger than it had been in 1776. Republicanism existed as a social fact, a cultural system whose tenets permeated American society. Throughout the decades following the outbreak of the Revolution America had indeed become republican, but hardly in the manner intended by its early leaders. During this time economic and demographic changes taking place at an unparalleled rate began to work fundamental transformations within the new nation. Geographic expansion spawned incredible mobility, and great numbers of Americans became involved in the market economy and strived to gain all the advantages they could from their new-found social and economic autonomy.

Revolutionary republicanism, rather than constraining these activities, seemed to encourage them and to afford them legitimacy. The emphasis placed upon equality in revolutionary rhetoric stimulated great numbers of previously deferential men to question all forms of authority and to challenge distinctions of every sort. Rather than generating an increased commitment to order, harmony, and virtue, republicanism appeared to be fostering an acquisitive individualism heedless of the common good or the benevolent leadership of a natural elite. Post-revolutionary America, instead of becoming the New World embodiment of transcendent classical values, appeared increasingly materialistic, utilitarian, and licentious: austerity gave way to prosperity; virtue appeared more and more to connote the individual pursuit of wealth through hard work rather than an unselfish devotion to the collective good. No longer a simple, ordered community under the benign leadership of a natural elite, America seemed instead to be moving towards a materialistic and utilitarian nation increasingly responsive to the desires of ordinary, obscure individuals.

The rapid democratization and vulgarization that took place in American society throughout the last decades of the eighteenth century helped create a far more open and liberal society than had been anticipated by most revolutionary leaders. Indeed, the transformations taking place within American society throughout these years were so complex and indeliberate, so much a mixture of day-to-day responses to a rapidly changing socio-economic environment, that most

Americans were unaware of the direction such changes were taking them and their society. Their commitment to republicanism allowed them to continue to imagine themselves as members of a virtuous, harmonious organic society long after the social foundations of such a society had eroded. The fact that republican language became increasingly disembodied from the changing cultural context made self-awareness all that much more difficult. The presence of an ideology as powerful as republicanism fostered an unconscious tendency among the dominant majority of Americans to make reality amenable to ideas, and ideas to reality, so as to create an integral world view credible enough to foster a collective as well as an individual sense of identity and security. Adherence to republican ideals helped to ease the strains present within late eighteenth-century American society. It allowed groups and individuals to dissociate themselves, their institutions, and their society from harmful and evil actions. It allowed – even impelled – men to view themselves as committed to the harmony, order, and communal well-being of a republican society while actively creating an aggressive, individualistic, liberal, and materialistic one. Ironically, then, republicanism provided the fertile seedbed within which the individualistic liberalism of the nineteenth century took root.

FURTHER READING

Appleby, Joyce: *Liberalism and Republicanism in the Historical Imagination* (Cambridge, Mass.: Harvard University Press, 1992).

Bailyn, Bernard: *The Ideological Origins of the American Revolution* (Cambridge, Mass.: Harvard University Press, 1967).

Kloppenberg, James T.: "The virtues of liberalism: Christianity, republicanism and ethics in early American political discourse," *Journal of American History*, 74 (1987), 9–33.

Kramnick, Isaac: *Republicanism and Bourgeois Radicalism: Political Ideology in Late Eighteenth-Century England and America* (Ithaca and London: Cornell University Press, 1990).

Rahe, Paul A.: *Republics Ancient and Modern: Classical Republicanism and the American Revolution* (Chapel Hill: University of North Carolina Press, 1992).

Shalhope, Robert E.: *The Roots of Democracy: American Thought and Culture, 1760–1800* (Boston: Twayne, 1990).

——: *Bennington and the Green Mountain Boys: The Emergence of Liberal Democracy in Vermont, 1760–1850* (Baltimore: Johns Hopkins University Press, 1996).

Watts, Steven: *The Republic Reborn: War and the Making of Liberal America, 1790–1820* (Baltimore: Johns Hopkins University Press, 1987).

Wood, Gordon: *The Creation of the American Republic, 1776–1787* (Chapel Hill: University of North Carolina Press, 1969).

——: *The Radicalism of the American Revolution* (New York: Alfred A. Knopf, 1992).

CHAPTER EIGHTY-FIVE

Sovereignty

PETER S. ONUF

DEFINING and locating sovereignty, the ultimate authority in a political community, represented a major conceptual and practical challenge to the American revolutionaries. The idea that there had to be a single, absolute power to decide and command contradicted the colonists' experience in the empire; furthermore, the distribution of power between states and central governments guaranteed that any effort to locate such a power would fail. In the decade preceding Independence, American patriots organized resistance to parliamentary claims to sovereignty over the colonies, thus reinforcing the colonists' traditional hostility to centralized authority. But Independence did not resolve the problem of sovereignty: the revolutionaries now had to construct a political order that would gain recognition from foreign powers and command the allegiance of American citizens. The success of the Revolution did not depend on the establishment of a supreme, sovereign lawmaking authority, but the new regime did have to achieve legitimacy, both at home and abroad.

As the institutional embodiment of the "common cause," the Continental Congress succeeded to many functions of the British Crown, particularly in managing foreign-policy and in promoting the states' collective interests. As a result, Congress naturally laid claim to the aura of legitimacy traditionally surrounding royal government. The transfer of authority from Crown to Congress did not, however, resolve the sovereignty question, but instead brought to the fore fundamental tensions and contradictions in British constitutionalism. First, the revolutionaries deconstructed the orthodox British notion of sovereignty, denying that the authority of the Crown merged with that of the other branches in Parliament. Americans proclaimed their loyalty to a king whose personal "sovereignty" or prerogative – considered apart from his role in Parliament – was constitutionally limited. Congress, by succeeding to this authority, might thus be considered "sovereign," but only in a sense that contemporaneous British commentators would have considered anachronistic.

The American situation was further complicated by the revolutionaries' determination to preserve the political integrity of colony-states with legislative and taxing authority within their respective jurisdictions. The revolutionaries thus faced the daunting tasks of locating effective authority *among* as well as *within* their newly constituted governments. They had to establish procedures for adjudicating the kinds of jurisdictional conflicts which the successful assertion of parliamentary sovereignty would, by definition, have eliminated.

1 Parliamentary Sovereignty

The revolutionaries' protracted efforts to establish an effective and legitimate new political order represented an answer to the British idea of parliamentary sovereignty set forth by William Blackstone in his influential *Commentaries on the Laws of England* (1765–9). Parliament "hath sovereign and uncontrollable authority in making, confirming, enlarging, restraining, abrogating, repealing, reviving and expounding of laws," he wrote, "this being the place where that absolute despotic power, which must in all governments reside somewhere, is entrusted by the constitution of these kingdoms" (Greene, 1967, p. 87). Blackstone thus formulated the modern conception of sovereignty, against which American constitutional claims now appear reactionary and anachronistic. But the colonists could plausibly argue that the sovereignty asserted by Parliament represented a dangerous innovation in British constitutionalism, particularly when extended to the empire as a whole. Defenders of parliamentary supremacy saw that body as the palladium of British liberty, and so could not imagine that its "absolute despotic power" jeopardized the integrity of the British Constitution or the sanctity of British rights. In the constitutional struggles of the previous century Parliament had successfully curbed royal prerogative, the greatest threat to the Constitution. But British constitutionalists remained "fearful of resurgent monarchy," wrote the legal historian John Phillip Reid, and therefore "insisted that parliamentary sovereignty must not be diluted by the slightest iota" (Reid, 1987, p. 262). As a result, even Britons who sympathized with the American cause were appalled by the colonists' apparent willingness to jeopardize their rights by renouncing parliamentary protection and inviting the Crown to play a larger role in imperial governance.

Because of the enormous discrepancy between parliamentary claims to sovereignty and actual conditions in the empire, the Americans were well situated to see potentially dangerous contradictions in the new constitutional orthodoxy. Parliamentary sovereignty over the colonies might have seemed a logical and necessary extension of its sovereignty in Britain, but colonists could assert that Parliament had, in fact, never played a significant role in governing the empire. By contrast, the King's presence was pervasive and his authority was generally revered; Crown appointees constituted the "government" in each colony as well as the governing apparatus of the imperial state.

Colonial protests against innovations in British policy centered on the issue of representation. Americans questioned the central premise of the new orthodoxy, that the King-in-Parliament "represented" – was in some sense identical with – the British state and, by extension, the imperial state. Reasonably enough, colonial polemicists such as Daniel Dulany denied that any colonist "is or can be *actually* or *virtually* represented by the British *House of Commons*" (Bailyn, 1965, pp. 618–19). The administration's argument for "virtual" representation, based on the analogy between the colonies and various unrepresented municipalities in Britain, illuminated the defective premises of parliamentary pretensions. "To what purpose," wondered James Otis, "is it to ring everlasting changes ... on the cases of Manchester, Birmingham, and Sheffield, who return no members? If those by now so considerable places are not represented, they ought to be" (quoted in Bailyn, 1967, p. 169). The plausibility of the claim that Parliament legitimately exercised "despotic" authority depended on a willingness to embrace the fiction that that body was truly representative. Therefore, the logic of the idea of sovereignty itself – not an anachronistic attachment to "pre-modern" constitutional forms – drove Americans to resist parliamentary pretensions.

The radical idea that the British Government was an artificial, despotic, unrepresentative encumbrance on the British people as well as on the American colonists was most fully developed by Thomas Paine in *Common Sense*. The British Constitution, wrote Paine, consisted of the "base remains of two ancient tyrannies" – "the remains of monarchical tyranny in the person of the king" and "the remains of aristocratical tyranny in the persons of the peers" – "compounded with some new republican materials" in the House of Commons (Greene, 1967, p. 272). Paine thus questioned the legitimacy of the respective branches: William the Conqueror, for instance, was a "French bastard" and "a very paltry rascally original" for the modern monarchy (Greene, 1967, p. 275). But more significant than these sensational thrusts was the assumption Paine shared with many of his American readers that the "compounding" of the branches in the orthodox conception of King-in-Parliament was fundamentally illegitimate. Neo-Harringtonian critics of the Whig ascendancy had long since warned that the constitutional independence of the

Commons was jeopardized by the King's influence and patronage. "These means of subversion are known collectively as corruption," wrote J. G. A. Pocock, "and if ever Parliament or those who elect them – for corruption may occur at this point too – should be wholly corrupt, then there will be an end of independence and liberty" (Pocock, 1973, p. 125). Even before the onset of the imperial crisis, colonists tended to view the British Constitution from this dissenting perspective. After 1763, repeated encroachments on American rights appeared to justify the pessimistic conclusion that the historic balance of powers in the British Government no longer operated effectively to protect constitutional liberties. The result was a growing disparity between British and American perspectives on the character of the imperial state and the scope of parliamentary authority. For orthodox Whigs, cooperation among the branches and the assertion of parliamentary sovereignty signified the final perfection of British constitutionalism; for Americans, the despotic power of a corrupt Parliament was neither sovereign nor constitutional.

2 Popular Sovereignty

The colonists based their claims to English rights on an idealized conception of the "ancient constitution." But the debate over representation also forced Americans to grapple with the distinctively modern dilemma of political legitimacy. As the revolutionaries rejected imperial rule, they recognized the importance of connecting the emerging governmental infrastructure with the larger political community. The fiction of parliamentary sovereignty may have been exploded, but patriot leaders had to construct a more plausible fiction of their own. The ultimate solution was to invoke the idea of "popular sovereignty," a notion deeply imbedded in British constitutionalism and most succinctly expressed by the great contract theorists. But who were the "sovereign" people in 1776? Divided by political, ethnic, and religious differences, Americans did not speak with a single voice or express a single, sovereign will. The belated, controversial decision for independence clearly revealed America's disunited state. Ironically, it was only *after* Independence had been achieved and the new states had consolidated their authority that the notion of a sovereign American people began to make sense. Before the revolutionaries could invoke the sovereignty of the people they had to construct a regime in which the people could believe. Not surprisingly, they borrowed heavily from the old imperial order.

In the final, crucial phase of the imperial crisis, when the Americans explicitly rejected Parliament's jurisdiction, they insisted that their allegiance to the King provided the only constitutional foundation for imperial rule. "Our allegiance to his majesty," John Adams wrote in his *Novanglus* letters (1775), "is not due by virtue of any act of a British parliament, but by our own charter and province laws." George III, it followed, was "king of the Massachusetts, king of Rhode Island, king of Connecticut, &c." (Mason, 1972, p. 208). Of course, the sovereignty of such a king bore little resemblance to the sovereignty claimed by Parliament; royal prerogative was constitutionally limited and did not include "despotic" law-making powers. From the colonial perspective, the apotheosis of royal authority did not represent a reversion to divine right absolutism, but rather a final, desperate effort to guarantee colonial rights within the imperial framework.

3 Congress

The American conception of the imperial constitution flowed logically from the colonial assemblies' aggressive claims to local legislative supremacy and control over taxation. But American legislators did not seek to exercise the full range of sovereign powers and their protestations of loyalty to the Crown were genuine. The assemblies played an increasingly equivocal and tentative role as the final break approached, precisely because of a pervasive sense of the insufficiency of their legitimate powers. During this period, according to Jerrilyn Marston, Americans were "loathe to destroy the precious constitutional balance by removing the symbol of political authority, the king" (Marston, 1987, p. 33). Meanwhile, Congress took the lead in organizing the intercolonial resistance movement and began to exercise a broad range of sovereign powers; perhaps most crucially, colonists agreed that Congress should speak for all the colonies in representing American grievances to the King and in seeking some sort of constitutional accommodation. George III's unwillingness to deal with Congress, a body with no constitutional standing, and his determination to uphold parliamentary authority precluded any settlement, hastened the movement for independence, and facilitated the transfer of legitimate authority to Congress.

Because Congress thus stood in the place of the King, the colonies were able to make the transition to independent statehood with relative ease. After sanctioning various *ad hoc* arrangements in specific colonies, in May 1776 Congress urged revolutionaries to form new governments "where no government sufficient to the exigencies of their affairs" had yet been established (Greene, 1967, p. 283). The question of which came first – the new states or the new national government – is a perennial favorite among constitutional historians, but can never be resolved. Clearly, the different levels of government drew legitimacy from each other and the interdependence of local and central authorities was well established before Independence. As a result, the revolutionary leadership institutionalized a broad distribution of powers in the new regime that was fundamentally incompatible with a Blackstonian definition of sovereignty. On one hand, the state governments extended their jurisdictions and gained legitimacy through the process of constitution-writing. At the same time, however, the exigencies of warfare and diplomacy reinforced the importance of Congress's role as successor to the Crown's executive powers while illuminating its defects as a national legislature.

The great paradox of early American constitutional development was that Congress should exercise so many attributes of sovereignty without any constitutional sanction. The Articles of Confederation were sent out to the states in 1777 but did not gain unanimous approval and go into effect until 1781. The contrast between Congress and the state governments is striking: at first, the states hesitated to act without congressional authorization; thereafter, constitutional revision in the states increasingly depended on explicit popular approval. But the idea that the legitimacy of congressional authority should be grounded directly in the sovereign people did not take hold until reformers pushed for a new Federal Constitution in 1787. Nor did the state legislatures play a crucial part in legitimizing Congress; if anything, the declining prestige and growing ineffectiveness of Congress during the period when the Articles were in effect (1781–9) suggests the opposite conclusion.

Both the original impulse towards confederation and the ratification of the Articles reflected strategic and diplomatic imperatives. Congressmen needed to convince skeptical foreign powers that they were empowered to enter into engagements on behalf of the American people. Many congressmen were also persuaded of the necessity for resolving outstanding differences among the states and providing for the authoritative determination of future conflicts. In neither case, however, did congressmen assume that their authority rested solely or primarily on the states' ratification of a continental constitution. More plausibly, confederation would be a means of binding the states not to interfere with Congress as it exercised sovereign powers it already legitimately enjoyed. But, once the confederation was finally completed, the results were disappointing to nationalist-minded politicians. With victory soon in hand, the need for a national sovereignty no longer seemed compelling. The focus of confederation politics thus shifted towards the kind of inter-state and inter-sectional conflicts that the need for wartime cooperation had held in check. As a result, the Articles functioned less as a national charter than as a treaty of alliance among semi-sovereign states.

4 Federal Union

Dissatisfaction with the Articles reflected growing ambiguity about the functions of Congress and the legitimacy of its authority. Critics complained that the central government was constitutionally incapable of fulfilling its mandate and that the state governments were all too eager to fill the resulting power vacuum. During the "critical" period before the meeting of the Constitutional Convention in the summer of 1787, frustrated nationalists began to argue that only a king could effectively exercise national sovereignty. But the founders contrived a radically different solution to the crisis of legitimate authority. Concluding that the monarchical model was inadequate to the exigencies of national government, the founders sought to construct a true national legislature as well as an efficient and powerful executive. Because the reconstituted union would itself be a kind of state – and not simply a league of states – the founders recognized the need to ground its authority in popular consent. The federal union was like a "pyramid," proclaimed the Pennsylvanian James Wilson, and therefore must rest on as "broad a basis as possible" (Onuf, 1983, pp. 202–3).

The idea of popular sovereignty had a long history in Anglo-American thought and practice. But the legitimacy of the central government had never before depended on the consent of the people. The genius of the founders was not only to borrow constitutional forms from the states, but to establish their authority on the same foundation. Thus, implementation of the new system depended on its ratification by specially elected state conventions, not by the state governments; members of the lower house of the new congress were to be popularly elected. It would be a mistake, however, to exaggerate either the extent of popular power or the importance of popular consent in the new federal union. The states continued to play a crucial role in the national government through representation in the Senate, and the popular will was only indirectly expressed in choosing the new national executive. As a result, Anti-Federalists had little difficulty in showing that the proposed system was not truly popular or representative by state constitutional standards. But such criticism was beside the point. The Federalists simply had to establish that the state governments did not "represent" the American people exclusively. If the states were not sovereign in this sense, the principle of popular sovereignty did not therefore necessarily preclude the expansion of national power.

By directly appealing to the sovereign people, the Federalists hoped to discredit the states' pretensions to sovereignty. "The people of America have mistaken the meaning of the word *sovereignty*," Benjamin Rush wrote in 1786: "hence each state pretends to be sovereign. In Europe it is applied only to those states which possess the power of making war and peace" (Onuf, 1983, pp. 7–8). The Federalists pursued this line of argument in the ratification debates, suggesting that Congress's "imbecility" under the Articles and the tendency for the states to fill the resulting power vacuum would destroy the union. The danger was that the states would then assume all the attributes of sovereignty, thus jeopardizing their republican constitutions. Implicit in these dire predictions was a conception of national sovereignty derived from the imperial executive and subsequently exercised more or less effectively by Congress – despite inter-state and inter-sectional jealousies and notwithstanding constitutional obstacles incorporated in the Articles of Confederation.

Yet, just as the Federalists' appropriation of the idea of popular sovereignty helped neutralize the resistance of sovereign states, the establishment of a national constitutional order helped mitigate fears that perfecting the union meant a return to despotic, monarchical rule. The crisis of legitimate authority during America's "critical period" reflected pervasive confusion about the source and scope of authority at all levels of American government. If the states were not truly "sovereign" – and could not be so without destroying the union – the putatively sovereign Congress was not the government of a true state, and therefore could not command the loyalty and resources of the American people. But the federal Constitution enabled Americans to transcend the antagonism among the states and between the states and Congress that had been institutionalized in the Articles of Confederation.

The Federalists persuasively argued that Americans did not have to choose between state governments resting on popular consent and a strong national government wielding a sovereign, superintending authority somehow derived from the old imperial regime. But neither the states nor Congress should be considered "sovereign," insisted supporters of the new regime. The recent history of state constitutional development emphasized the distinction between the sovereign people – the constituent power – and their governments. Federalists exploited this crucial distinction as they sought to legitimize the radical expansion of federal power. According to their conception of popular sovereignty, Americans should be able to distinguish between the source of legitimate authority and the various governments charged with its exercise.

The paradoxical result of dissociating legitimate authority from its institutional forms was that all American governments gained in legitimacy. As Nathaniel Chipman of Vermont wrote, shortly after the new government was established: "solely an impression of the efficiency of the federal government, favored perhaps, by its national magnitude and importance, added, at the instant of organization, a degree of energy to the state governments, and put an end to those factions and turbulent commotions, which made some of them tremble for their political existence" (Onuf, 1983, p. 273). Simply, the Americans had achieved – or were under the "impression" that they had achieved – the integration between governmental authority and political community on which modern conceptions of sovereignty are premised.

FURTHER READING

Bailyn, B.: *Pamphlets of the American Revolution, 1750–1765* (Cambridge, Mass.: Harvard University Press, 1965).

——: *The Ideological Origins of the American Revolution* (Cambridge, Mass.: Harvard University Press, 1967).

Greene, J. P. (ed.): *Colonies to Nation, 1763–1789: a Documentary History of the American Revolution* (New York: McGraw-Hill, 1967).

Marston, J.: *King and Congress: the Transfer of Political Legitimacy, 1774–1776* (Princeton, NJ: Princeton University Press, 1987).

Mason, B. (ed.): *The American Colonial Crisis: the Daniel Leonard–John Adams Letters to the Press, 1774–1775* (New York: Harper & Row, 1972).

Morgan. E. S.: *Inventing the People: the Rise of Popular Sovereignty in England and America* (New York: W. W. Norton, 1988).

Onuf, P. S.: *The Origins of the Federal Republic: Jurisdictional Controversies in the United States, 1775–1787* (Philadelphia: University of Pennsylvania Press, 1983).

——: "State sovereignty and the making of the constitution," *Conceptual Change and the Constitution,* eds. T. Ball and J. G. A. Pocock (Lawrence: University Press of Kansas, 1988), 78–98.

——: *Jefferson's Empire: The Language of American Nationhood* (Charlottesville: University Press of Virginia, 1999).

Pocock, J. G. A.: "Machiavelli, Harrington, and English political ideologies in the eighteenth century," *Politics, Language and Time: Essays on Political Thought and History* (New York: Atheneum, 1973), 104–47.

Pole, J. R.: *The Gift of Government: Political Responsibility from the English Restoration to American Independence* (Athens: University of Georgia Press, 1983).

Reid, J. P.: *Constitutional History of American Revolution: the Authority to Tax* (Madison: University of Wisconsin Press, 1987).

Wood, G. S.: *The Creation of the American Republic, 1776–1787* (Chapel Hill: University of North Carolina Press, 1969).

CHAPTER EIGHTY-SIX

Nationality and citizenship

ELISE MARIENSTRAS

AT the end of the eighteenth century it was generally agreed that the newborn United States did not resemble any other known nation. There was no uniform language. No common history was shared by the inhabitants. Few people yet had family graves with ancestors buried in what would become the national territory. The new state did not aim to restore the legitimacy of an earlier nation state. Until the very moment of the Declaration of Independence the colonists had been the subjects of the British Crown, which means that they had been members of the British nation (Pole, 1973, p. 3). When they severed their allegiance to the King, the revolutionaries broke at the same moment their ties to British nationality and their identity as British subjects. They were suddenly compelled to define themselves anew.

Significantly, at the time of the Revolution and for a few decades longer, the former colonists debated over the name of the new nation. Some, including the poet Joel Barlow, preferred "Columbia," in which he found a resonance of his own nationalist epic "The Dream of Columbia" (Barlow, 1807). "America" seemed improper to many, since it referred to a continent rather than to a nation within its borders. Eventually the new nation was named "United States," a political term and not, like Spain, England, or France, a word derived from the name of a people. Moreover, some of the political and intellectual leaders regretted, as did Jedidiah Morse in 1792, that, although she had become formally independent, America was still dependent on Great Britain for her manners, her laws, and her education

(Morse, 1792, p. 212). Morse argued for keeping the young men at home instead of sending them to study in England. Noah Webster, the "Schoolmaster to America," as his biographer called him (Warfel, 1936), contemplated a reformation of the English language which would at once "naturalize" the English tongue into American (Webster, 1783). These are some of the indications of the difficulty of defining the United States as a nation. Historians have tried to handle this issue by assigning to the American nation a special character derived from the circumstances of its birth, or its environment, or a particular turn of the American mind. They have echoed the perplexities assailing the American revolutionaries who had to invent a new kind of citizenship as well as a new nationality.

Many questions arose as soon as the Americans ceased to consider themselves British and settled down to the task of building a nation. Since the 1750s the colonists had assumed three kinds of identity, calling themselves indifferently British-Americans, British subjects, or by the adjective derived from the name of their province. After Independence they were left with two identities, not being sure which, the national or the provincial, should prevail. When they became 13 "independent states" the colonies had yet to find what would be the cement of a united body, and how to transform former subjects into citizens of a nation-state as well as of a particular provincial state. The problems that arose were of a cultural, an institutional, and a political nature.

1 A Problematic Nation

The Declaration of Independence, by which the revolutionary leaders officially proclaimed that the colonists no longer belonged to the British Empire, did not hint at the issue of nationality. The colonists' right to secede from Great Britain was said to be based upon universal natural rights rather than upon particular national rights. And the last paragraph of the Declaration referred only to the political and international powers of the new independent states without mentioning that they now constituted a nation.

Indeed, in the late 1770s and afterwards, the Founding Fathers were so doubtful about the existence of the nation that they, as it were, suppressed the word from the official language and replaced it by the word "Union," which is still more often used than "nation." For instance, in 1787–8 the promoters of the Constitutional Convention changed the name by which they were known from "Nationalists" to "Federalists." The terms "nation" and "nationalist" held negative implications for people who feared the tyranny of a strong, centralized government. In order to win the ratification elections over the Anti-Federalists, James Madison and Alexander Hamilton wrote, in *The Federalist Papers*, that the new government would be partly national, partly federal.

This does not mean that only the Federalists desired to establish a nation. The Anti-Federalists merely objected to a national government which would invade individual liberties. The Federalists believed in the necessity of a strong federal state, fit to protect property and national prosperity. But Federalists and Republicans shared a fundamental creed: the necessity to preserve the Union, that is, the nation.

The question which then arose was: to what extent did ordinary people share this sense of unity, of national identity? Did the colonists, as some historians argue (Merritt, 1966), begin to be conscious of being different from their English "brothers" in 1763, after the Seven Years' War? Or had they, on the contrary, become more and more Anglicized in the second half of the eighteenth century, importing more and more European goods, copying more frequently English manners and culture, and even reviving such old English traditions as feudal tenancy, which had then almost disappeared from England (Murrin, 1987)?

Indeed, during the colonial era the 13 coastal colonies, although they enjoyed a large degree of autonomy, were offshoots of the British nation. The empire was conceived as nothing other than a geographical extension of the kingdom. *Jus sanguinis* applied to all inhabitants on condition that they were freemen and Christians. No matter where they resided, or whence they came, all members of the empire were supposed to be inheritors of the same past, of the same traditions, of the same destiny. As they maintained when they rebelled, the colonists were entitled to the rights and liberties of every British subject. On the eve of the American Revolution they were thus previleged British subjects, and they were proud of their nationality.

One must, however, take into account the particularities of the British Americans, and firstly, that they or their ancestors had emigrated from Europe, were confronting a new environment, and were meeting men whose races and cultures were different from those of any European people. Moreover, coming from different parts of Europe, Euro-Americans did not share a common past. They did not eat the same foods, speak the same languages, or belong to the same churches (Morse, 1792). By dealing with the Amerindians who stood in the path they were ready to conquer or with the imported Africans, whom they deemed inferior to themselves, the colonists had innovated – they had lived through experiences unknown in Europe. They had been "creolized" (Breen, 1984, pp. 195–232).

Did they cease for this reason to be British? Until 1776 the colonists continued to pay their allegiance to the King. They claimed to be loyal British subjects and, moreover, affectionate and obedient "children" of the mother country – a patriarchal metaphor which Thomas Paine vigorously repudiated in *Common Sense*, but which nevertheless was frequently used in the post-revolutionary United States as a way of depicting the ties between the citizens and the nation or the nation's "father," George Washington.

Changing allegiance from England to the United States took, in the words of the leaders, but a short time. John Adams later wrote that the Revolution was in the hearts of the people long before it came to their minds (Adams, 1818). Yet, the transformation which changed the British colonists into American citizens was a slow process. Before Independence, members of the elite tried to resist it. They kept close relations with the mother country. Although they had a very different way of life from that of their counterparts living in England, they thought of themselves as sharing in the English culture. During the Revolution some of them chose to stay loyal to the King, and left America when the war broke. The case of the loyalists, who continued their allegiance to the Crown and returned to the mother country or fled to Canada while keeping a strong affection for the country where they were born or where they had lived, is a good, though paradoxical, indicator of the complex meaning of the American sense of national identity.

2 American Nationality as a Collective and Individual Sense of Belonging

The American nation was so new in kind that the revolutionary leaders had to "invent" a new way of attaching the people's sense of identity to it. Members of the American elite, who had initiated the rebellion against the Crown, had no difficulty in shifting their allegiance from Great Britain to the new nation. But the plain people, who were devoid of political power, were not used to mixing their private and public identities. The idea of a national community was foreign to most of them. They had been used to separating in their minds the concept of a state which had been embodied by a distant king and the only real community they knew, which was the local one.

Although they had a strong symbolic sense of British nationality, they were much more involved in their local affiliations. They had a physical knowledge of the limits of their county and province; they had walked through their fields to the next town and church, and participated in local institutions and politics. Now they had to lodge their collective and their personal identity in the same place, a place, however, which was to be apprehended differently at both levels. The problem faced by the early national-era leaders was to help fuse the former colonists' personal sense of belonging into a collective, national attachment to the new nation. This was a process which was to take many years and which would never be completely achieved. Mental dimensions of space, of time, of kinship were to be enlarged. The diversity of the peoples and of the different states had to be overcome and a sense of national unity built through the creation of institutions, the invention of rituals, and the working together of all the parts of the nation in order to achieve a common goal.

The new nation had to be created in the minds of the people as well as in the juridical realm and on the battlefield. The former colonists were induced to think of the United States not only as a federation of 13 governments, but as a newborn being, made of several million people, promised to a brilliant future, and endowed with the mission to protect and spread liberty all over the world a – mission, according to John Adams, inherited from the early Puritans or, as argued by others such as Thomas Jefferson, from the Saxon ancestors. With the help of what historians have come to name "civil religion," with which the clergy, the political leaders, and the intellectuals concurred, the new nation was to be an "imagined community" (Anderson, 1983, Bellah, 1967).

Civil religion provided at once an ideological content to citizenship and a fervent spirit of patriotism. As soon as Independence was proclaimed, patriotism relied on ideology more than upon traditional national feelings. By shifting the nature of the cause they were struggling for, from a customary conflict between national foes to the modern ideological antagonism of liberty against tyranny, the patriot leaders laid the first basis for a national identity and character. Civil religion thus became the means by which every member of the nation was to be united in a common creed. With the help of new symbols and rituals, the farmer and the mechanic, from their limited view of a close community, were brought to envision the national destiny. The national flag, iconograpic representations of Liberty, Fourth of July processions, festivals and celebrations such as George Washington's birthday, days of fasting ordered by Congress – all involved the citizens in new, "invented" traditions which would become part of a common national culture.

3 Forging an American Citizen

There was still another condition to the durability of the nation. The American citizen himself had to forget his ancient being and be transformed into a "new man." "The principle of patriotism," wrote Benjamin Rush, "stands in need of the reinforcement of prejudices in favor of our country, and it is well known that our strongest prejudices are formed in the first one and twenty years of our lives" (Rush, 1786). This is the reason why some of the most eminent of the early national leaders devoted so much attention to education. The republican citizen's virtue was to be inculcated from early childhood. Early national-era textbooks, initiated by Noah Webster's *Spelling Book*, were meant as instruments of civic education. Indeed, the schoolteacher was to be the first, if modest, builder of American citizenship.

However, the legal status and definition of citizenship remained ambiguous for a long time. It was not until after the Civil War that a general and national definition of the American citizen appeared in the Fourteenth Amendment to the Constitution.

Indeed, the question of citizenship arose as soon as the colonists denounced their allegiance to the King, even before Independence was proclaimed: in January 1776 New Hampshire adopted a new constitution, and was soon followed by South Carolina, which, in March 1776, required all its officers to swear an oath "to support, maintain, and defend" the provisional constitution (Kettner, 1978, p. 175). All at once, the traditional oath of allegiance to the King was dropped from the rebellious documents, as if allegiance had simply shifted from the monarch to the new independent and sovereign states.

In so doing, local assemblies, conventions, or committees acted as representatives of all the inhabitants, or at least of the majority of them. The loyalists, or the people who disagreed with the majority decisions, were at first considered as a minority who had to comply with the general will. But war, cases of plotting, espionage, and counterfeiting forced the states and the Continental Congress to separate more clearly the people who agreed with the new policies from those who stayed loyal to the King. Thus, in a pragmatic manner, the states and the Continental Congress took the first steps towards defining the status of the inhabitants. On June 24, 1776 Congress resolved that

all persons residing within any of the United Colonies, and deriving their protection from the laws of the same, owe allegiance to the said laws, and are members of such colony; ... [and] that all persons, members of, or owing allegiance to any of the United Colonies ... who shall levy war against any of the said colonies ..., or be adherents to the king of Great Britain ... are guilty of treason against such colony. (*Journals of the Continental Congress*, V, pp. 475–6)

A few days later, the Declaration of Independence repeated in other words the assertion that, in the same manner as allegiance to the King had been tied to his duty of protection, so was citizenship in the new states dependent upon a contract which provided for state protection to the citizens in return for their allegiance to the republican government.

Thus citizenship was defined through allegiance, as it used to be in the British Empire. But now that the people had become sovereign, citizenship came to be considered as contractual and volitionary. A further step was taken when, after the treaty of peace in 1783, questions of debts, confiscation, or inheritance required that a distinction be made between what the British tradition called "the natural" subjects of the King, who were named "real subjects" in the diplomatic documents, and the citizens of the United States. Originally, most Americans had been "natural" subjects. Again, the notion of volitionary personal allegiance was used to distinguish citizens from aliens. However, the status of the *"ante-nati"* was not definitely solved, and it was debated with reference to

Calvin's case, which Sir Edward Coke had reported in 1607, when, the kingdoms of Scotland and England being united under the same king, the nationality of Scottish subjects became an issue. Two centuries later the arguments of Sir Edward Coke were recalled, proving that the question of nationality and citizenship, as new as it presented itself in the United States, also carried on the old British tradition.

More easy to solve than such legal cases, the process of naturalization provided citizenship to those aliens who were ready to swear their loyalty to the revolutionary United States. After some confusion about which, of the separate states or the Union, would be entitled to determine the rules of naturalization, the Federal Constitution of 1787 determined a national standard of naturalization through laws voted by Congress. Several Acts were adopted, in 1795, in 1798, and in 1802, the last one becoming the main legal document on citizenship up to the Civil War. Significantly, these naturalization laws differed mainly about the time of residence which was required from the applicant to be granted American nationality. From two years to 14, it was eventually settled at five years, considered enough for those imbued with "foreign principles" to assimilate the habits, values, and mode of thought necessary for responsible participation in a self-governing republican community (Kettner, 1978, p. 219). For, although citizenship was primarily considered a matter of personal election, the political community did not open its doors to everyone without qualification. The Federal Constitution, as well as the states, reserved citizenship to white freemen, implicitly excluding Blacks, even though they were free, and Amerindians who belonged to tribes, then considered as foreign nations. Citizenship was not extended to Blacks before 1868 or to Amerindians before 1924. White women also, while they could be treated as citizens in economic matters, were not entitled to all the privileges of citizenship before 1919.

For those who were admitted as citizens, citizenship, however, was an ambivalent concept and reality. The Constitution did not solve the indetermination of citizenship which had come out of the Revolution. The Articles of Confederation had paved the way for a dual citizenship. Article IV of this first American Constitution had stated that "the free inhabitants of each of [the] states ... shall be entitled to all privileges and immunities of free citizens in the several states." There was some debate about the meaning of the phrase "free inhabitants," but it is clear from further documents that, implicitly, the American people were considered at once citizens of their own state and citizens of the United States. A dual citizenship was created, which resembled only in shape the former dual subjectship of the colonists.

The Constitution of 1787, while presenting the concept of citizenship indirectly through naturalization, also made clear that the American inhabitants were citizens both of their state of residence and of the United States as a whole. However, the discussions that arose between Federalists and Republicans about the "implied powers" of Congress involved the idea that a common citizenship in a national political community conflicted with the sovereignty of the states. Political implications of citizenship were referred to only in the articles dealing with eligibility to the highest federal positions. But qualifications for the main political right of the citizen, that of suffrage, were left to each state to decide upon.

Gradually, a vertical integration from the several states to the Union was attempted. The Federalists, particularly, insisted on the necessity of homogenizing the citizens in order for the Union to endure (Washington, vol. 27, p. 50). Once again, it would be left to the Union victory in the Civil War, and its aftermath in reconstruction, to ensure the prevalence of national citizenship over that of the states, and once and for all to confront directly the question of individual citizenship with all the duties and rights attached to it.

FURTHER READING

Adams, John: "To Hezekiah Niles," February 13, 1888, *The Works of John Adams*, 10 vols., ed. C. F. Adams (Boston: Little, Brown & Co., 1856), vol. 10, p. 285.

Anderson, Benedict: *Imagined Communities: Reflections on the Origin and Spread of Nationalism* (London: Verso, New Left Books, 1983).

Barlow, Joel: *The Columbiad: a Poem* (Philadelphia, 1807).

Bellah, Robert N.: "Civil Religion in America," *Daedalus*, 96 (1967), 1–21.

Breen, Timothy: "Creative adaptations: peoples and cultures," *Colonial British America*, ed. J. P. Greene and J. R. Pole (Baltimore and London: Johns Hopkins University Press, 1984).

Kettner, James H.: *The Development of American Citizenship, 1608–1870* (Chapel Hill: University of North Carolina Press, 1978).

Marienstras, Elise: *Nous le peuple: les origines du nationalisme americain* (Paris: Editions Gallimard, 1988).

Merritt, Richard: *Symbols of American Community, 1735–1775* (New Haven, CT: Yale University Press, 1966).

Morse, Jedidiah: *The American Geography* (Philadelphia, 1792).

Murrin, John M.: "'A roof without walls': the dilemma of American national identity," *Beyond Confederation: Origins of the Constitution and American National Identity* (Chapel Hill: University of North Carolina Press, 1987), 333–48.

Pole, Jack R.: *Foundations of American Independence, 1763–1815* (London, 1972); repr. (London and Glasgow; Fontana, 1973).

Rush, Benjamin: *Thoughts upon the Mode of Education Proper in a Republic* (Philadelphia, 1786).

Savelle, Max: "Nationalism and other loyalties in the American revolution," *American Historical Review*, 67 (1962), 901–23.

Warfel, Henry R.: *Noah Webster, Schoolmaster to America* (New York, 1936: repr. 1966).

Washington, George: *The Writings of George Washington*, ed. J. C. Fitzpatrick (Washington, DC: Government Printing Office, 1931–44).

Webster, Noah: *The American Spelling Book* (Boston, 1783).

CHAPTER EIGHTY-SEVEN

The separation of powers

MAURICE J. C. VILE

OF all the decisions taken at the Constitutional Convention in Philadelphia, the decision to build the new system of government on the basis of the doctrine of the separation of powers had the most far-reaching effect. It not only distinguished the American system sharply from the British system, against which the Founding Fathers were reacting, but it also meant that the future development of the American polity was to be very different from that of nearly every other democracy that was to evolve during the nineteenth and twentieth centuries, for the latter were to choose parliamentary government as the pattern for their constitutional arrangements.

1 The Concept of the Separation of Powers and the English Civil War

The concept of separating the exercise of the legislative and executive functions, and entrusting them to different branches of government, had its roots in Greek political thought, was echoed by Cicero, and was developed by Marsilius of Padua in the fourteenth century and embodied in the institutions of the Venetian Republic. The transformation of these ancient and medieval concepts into a modern form which could reasonably be labeled the doctrine of the separation of powers, took place, however, during the English Civil War, and attained its most clear and precise expression during the Protectorate. The battle between King and Parliament served to sharpen the distinctions made between the functions of government which had previously characterized the accepted constitutional theory,

the mixture of monarchy, aristocracy, and democracy – King, Lords, and Commons. At the extreme, the opponents of the royal power argued with Milton that the King should have no function in the making of the law, but should be concerned solely with its execution. With the execution of the King and the abolition of the House of Lords, the need was clear for a new constitution of government, and in 1653 the *Instrument of Government*, although never implemented, provided the first written constitution of modern times. The *Instrument* entrusted the legislative power to Parliament, giving the Protector only a suspensive veto of 20 days, and in Article II confided the "exercise of the chief magistracy and the administration of the government" to the Lord Protector. The defense of the *Instrument, A True State of the Case of the Commonwealth*, published in 1654 and probably written by Marchamont Nedham, set out the necessity for the separation of the executive and legislative powers if corruption and tyranny were to be avoided. Nedham's second work, *The Excellencie of a Free State* (1656), reiterated that "A fifth Errour in Policy hath been this, viz. a permitting of the Legislative and Executive Powers of a State, to vest in one and the same hands and persons." According to John Adams, Nedham's work was well known in colonial America. Indeed, the momentous events taking place in England had their impact in the colonies, and in Massachusetts in 1679 the Elders of the Church asserted that the Charter of the Company of Massachusetts Bay had set up a "distribution of differing interest of power and privilege between the magistrates and freemen, and the distinct exercise of legislative and executive power."

2 Eighteenth-Century Constitutional Theorists

The ideas which were evolved in England in the mid-seventeenth century were further developed by Locke, Montesquieu, and Blackstone, in a much less extreme form, one which was adapted to the restored monarchy and the mixed and balanced constitution of post-revolutionary England, and which fitted well with the forms of government then established in the American colonies themselves. The separation of powers remained an essential element in the constitution of a free state, but the branches of government must have the ability to prevent the abuse of power by the others. Montesquieu summed up his view thus: "Here, then, is the fundamental constitution of the government we are treating of. The legislative body being composed of two parts, they check one another by the mutual privilege of rejecting. They are both restrained by the executive power, as the executive is by the legislative." The eighteenth-century constitutional theorists also abandoned the twofold division of the functions of government into legislation and execution which had largely characterized the preceding century, and asserted the importance of a separate judicial function of government, and, following the Bill of Rights, the independence of the judges. However, with the increasing tension between the American colonies and the mother country in the 1770s, Americans increasingly used the separation of powers to attack the structure and operation of British government, and as a consequence to criticize also the structure of colonial governments. The role of the Governor's Council, which had a finger in every pie, was attacked as an affront to the separation of powers. James Otis, in 1764, mounted a passionate attack upon the appointment of Lieutenant-Governor Hutchinson as Chief Justice of Massachusetts, and demands were made for the exclusion of members of the judiciary from the colonial legislature. Above all, the exercise by the colonial governors of the royal prerogative was under attack, in particular

the exercise of the veto power, which was actively used to disallow bills passed by colonial legislatures, long after the sovereign had, in Jefferson's words, "modestly declined the exercise of this power in that part of his empire called Great Britain." "Demophilus," and other pamphleteers in revolutionary Pennsylvania, demanded that the role of the Governor must be "solely executive," the same demand that the radicals had made during the English revolution.

As in mid-seventeenth century England, the more radical the attack upon the established institutions, the more extreme the demands for the implementation of a thoroughgoing separation of powers. The authority of Montesquieu was invoked on all sides, but the great philosopher's emphasis upon the importance of checks and balances was appealed to only by Tories and by the more conservative elements, whose voices were not very audible amidst the revolutionary fervor of 1775. The radicals in Pennsylvania and in the New Hampshire Grants, later to become the state of Vermont, would have nothing of mixed and balanced government. In the words of the historian Samuel Williams of Vermont, in the "American system of government … the security of the people is derived not from the nice ideal application of checks, ballances, and mechanical powers, among the different parts of the government, but from the responsibility, and dependence of each part of the government, upon the people." In other words the branches of government should be separate from each other, and each answerable directly to the people, not to the other branches. The direct and only check upon each branch of government is, therefore, the electorate, leading to demands for the election not only of legislators and of the head of the executive, but of judges also. Thus began a major strand of American constitutional thought which is still important today, particularly in the sphere of state government.

3 The Drafting of State Constitutions

In the revolutionary atmosphere of 1776, the separation of powers was the only respectable ideological basis for the drafting of constitutions for the newly declared states in order to replace their redundant colonial charters. A clear statement of the doctrine came in the preamble to the Constitution of Virginia of June 1776:

The legislative, executive and judiciary departments shall be separate and distinct, so that neither exercise the powers properly belonging to the other: nor shall any person exercise the powers of more than one of them at the same time, except that the justices of the county courts shall be eligible to either House of Assembly.

All the elements of the doctrine are here – separate branches of government exercising different functions, and a prohibition upon membership of more than one branch at any one time. The last of these characteristics of the doctrine has had the greatest influence on shaping the distinctively American political scene, making "cabinet government" impossible, breaking the link between executive and legislature, and making it possible for legislators to maintain their independence of action without destroying the stability of the executive.

The constitutions of Pennsylvania, Virginia, and of four other states written in 1776 and early 1777 reflected the revolutionary doctrine that power was delegated by the people to the several branches of government. In these constitutions the effort was made to remove all vestiges of prerogative powers; the only exception that was made was to give to some governors the power of pardon or reprieve. No veto power was wielded by the governors of these states. The Constitution of Virginia provided that the governor "shall not, under any pretence, exercise any power or prerogative, by virtue of any law, statute or custom of England." Jefferson later wrote that the Constitution of Virginia was designed to remove all discretionary power from the executive, indeed that no power could be exercised which was not clearly embodied in legislation. The only concession to the theory of checks and balances, associated as it was with notions of monarchy and aristocracy, was the adoption of bicameral legislatures in all but two of these states. Pennsylvania, engaged in an internal upheaval as well as in revolution against Britain, enacted the most radical

constitution, providing for a unicameral assembly, a directly-elected plural executive, the Supreme Executive Council, and a Council of Censors with the duty of enquiring every seven years "whether the legislative and executive branches of government have performed their duty as guardians of the people, or assumed to themselves, or exercised other or greater powers than they are intitled to by the constitution."

The constitution for the new state of Vermont, written in 1777, adopted the same radical pattern as that of Pennsylvania, but the other early state constitutions, such as those of Virginia, Georgia, and Maryland, retained some semblances of the theory of the balanced constitution, in particular bicameralism. However, a reaction very soon set in against what was seen as the effects of extreme democracy, and against the extreme form of the doctrine of the separation of powers, a reaction which was to gain momentum, and to become a vital factor in shaping the Constitution of the United States. The idea that the separation of powers, standing alone as the theoretical basis of a constitutional structure, was an adequate protection against the abuse of power by governments very quickly came under attack. State legislatures began to meddle in all the aspects of government, including the exercise of the judicial power. As Jefferson wrote in his *Notes on the State of Virginia*, published in 1781, the constitution of that state had separated the powers of government, but because "no barrier was provided between the separate powers" the legislature, merely by casting its decisions in the form of legislation, could interfere in those aspects of government which were properly the preserve of the executive and judicial branches. Thus, Jefferson asserted, "all the powers of government, legislative, executive and judiciary, result to the legislative body." Americans learned, as their English forebears had learned during the rule of the Long Parliament, that legislatures can be as tyrannical as kings or governors.

Even in 1777 the Constitution of New York recognized the need for a system of government with greater checks to the exercise of legislative power, but it was in the debates leading to the adoption of the Constitution of Massachusetts in 1780 that the problem of reconciling the separation of powers with the need to provide effective checks to the abuse of power by any of the branches of government was squarely faced. The *Essex Result*, the views of the people of Essex County on the shape of the proposed state constitution, drafted by Theophilus Parsons, clearly set out what was to be the American solution to the problem of ensuring freedom from the exercise of excessive power by government. The *Result* did not in any way recede from a belief in the importance of the separation of powers, but it emphasized that this in itself was not enough. "Each branch is to be independent, and further, to be so balanced, and be able to exert such checks upon the others, as will preserve it from a dependence on, or a union with them." This was exactly the position taken by Madison in the Constitutional Convention in Philadelphia:

If a constitutional discrimination of the departments on paper were a sufficient security to each against encroachments of the others, all further provisions would indeed be superfluous. But experience had taught us a distrust of that security; and that it is necessary to introduce such a balance of powers and interests, as will guarantee the provisions on paper.

4 The Federal Constitution

Although the Federal Constitution represented a movement back towards the principles of the balanced constitution of mid-eighteenth-century Britain, the final result was very different from that model. The Convention specifically rejected the British system of parliamentary government and the role of the Cabinet in that system. James Iredell noted that in England "everybody knows that the whole movement of their government ... [is] directed by their *Cabinet Council*, composed entirely of the principal officers of the great departments," which was, in the view of George Mason, "the worst and most dangerous of all ingredients for such a council in a free country." Resisting the proposal that the President be elected by the legislature, Gouverneur Morris said that in England "the *real* King ... is the Minister ... Our President will be the British Minister, yet we are about to make him appointable

by the Legislature." Along with the rejection of the idea of government by a cabinet went the complete exclusion of office-holders from membership of the legislature, a motion which was accepted by the Convention without opposition. Thus the personnel of the legislative and executive branches were to be completely separate, with the exception of the role of the Vice-President as presiding officer of the Senate. The former prerogatives of the Crown were dealt with by dividing them and distributing them between the President and the Congress – a qualified veto power for the President which can be overturned by the Congress, the presidential appointing power subject to Senate confirmation, and the negotiation of treaties by the President subject to ratification by the Senate. Only the power of pardon remained unscathed from the former powers of the King.

The role of the Supreme Court and the judiciary in this combination of the separation of powers and checks and balances was less clear. A major difference between the *Instrument of Government* of 1653 and the Federal Constitution over a century later was the firm establishment in the latter of a separate and powerful judicial branch; but neither the extent of the power of the judiciary to check the other branches, nor a clear prohibition on dual membership, was provided by the Constitution. There is evidence in the revolutionary period of the development of the idea of judicial review of legislation, of the power of the courts to declare legislature decisions unconstitutional and therefore void. James Wilson argued that case before the Pennsylvania ratifying convention, and Alexander Hamilton in *The Federalist*, no. 78, justified the exercise of judicial power over Acts of Congress. However, it is not until the Supreme Court itself asserted this power that it could clearly be seen to be a consequence of the doctrine of checks and balances which Madison enunciated so clearly in *The Federalist*, no. 47: "Unless these departments be so far connected and blended, as to give to each a constitutional control over the others, the degree of separation which the maxim requires, as essential to a free government, can never in practice be duly maintained."

The acceptance by the Convention of the separation of powers modified by the old theory of checks and balances was not, however, the end of the debate. John Adams, in his *Defence of the Constitutions of the United States* (1787–8), had urged upon the American people the desirability of a return to the old form of mixed government, and, although the Convention did not by any means accept the ideas there set out, Adams's work became the stalking-horse of those who opposed what they saw as monarchical and aristocratic elements in the new constitution. The doctrine of the separation of powers became the most coherent theoretical basis of the Anti-Federalists' attack upon what they saw as, in the words of Nathaniel Chipman in *Sketches of the Principles of Government* (1793), "a confusion of powers," a perpetual war of one part against the others, a situation incompatible with republican government. Jefferson himself, in his later years, returned to the idea that each of the three branches of government should be directly accountable to the people and not to each other, and the great exponent of Jeffersonian Republicanism, John Taylor of Caroline, in his major work, *An Inquiry into the Principles and Policy of the Government of the United States* (1814), presented a coherent and thoroughgoing analysis based upon the separation of powers, rejecting totally the remnants of mixed government to be found in the Federal Constitution. John Taylor drew upon the tradition of radical thought stretching back to the work of Marchamont Nedham during the Protectorate in order to put forward an extreme version of the separation of powers as the basis for a free system of government, but, at the level of the Federal Government at any rate, the triumph of the Federalists was complete, and the American version of a separation of the legislative, executive, and judicial branches of government, in which each could check the others and yet retain its own independence, became the foundation of a uniquely democratic system.

FURTHER READING

Gwyn, W. B.: *The Meaning of the Separation of Powers* (New Orleans: Tulane University Press, 1965).

Levy, L. W.: *Original Intent and the Framers' Constitution* (New York: Macmillan,1988).

Vile, M. J. C.: *Constitution and the Separation of Powers* (Oxford: Clarendon Press, 1967).

CHAPTER EIGHTY-EIGHT

Rights

MICHAEL ZUCKERT

THE American Revolution was mainly about rights: The document announcing the break with Britain justified the colonists' deed in terms of the King's failure to secure their rights. The Americans regularly and eloquently spoke the language of rights both before the Declaration of Independence, in colonial protests against British actions, and after it in American attempts to construct new governments.

1 A Paradox of Rights

Yet controversy pervades the discussion of the role and nature of rights in the Revolution. The Declaration of Independence in its most memorable passages spoke the language of "unalienable rights" and invoked "the laws of nature and of nature's God." Other colonial and then state documents of the era were rife with references to natural rights.

Nonetheless, many students of the Revolution deny the importance of natural rights. A well-known legal historian proclaimed the irrelevance of the Declaration as a document of natural rights and natural law. "The British Constitution, not [the natural rights philosophy] supplied American Whigs with their theoretical motivation... Every right for which the Americans contended was located in British constitutional theory." Another historian has argued that the American position rested not on natural rights but on traditional notions of the rights of Englishmen, the royal charters of the separate colonies and especially on "long standing constitutional custom."

The controversy concerns not whether rights were significant, but which rights were important, natural or constitutional, the "rights of Man" or the "rights of Englishmen." In order to understand what this conflict is about it will be an immense aid to lay out the two different conceptions of rights, the one as articulated in the American Declaration of Independence, the other in the British Declaration of Rights, a document issued at the time of the Glorious Revolution, roughly a century before the American Revolution. A series of "rights variables" together make up what we might call a "regime of rights," and when compared along these dimensions we will see that the English (constitutional) and American (natural) theories of rights differ greatly.

Source of rights

According to the Americans the source of rights is "the creator," who appears to be the God of nature, for the document speaks of "the laws of nature and of nature's God." In principle the God of nature is knowable by all human beings according to public standards of truth; the God of nature is emphatically not the God known only to one or another specific religious tradition.

In the English Declaration, on the other hand, "the rights and liberties asserted and claimed... are the true, ancient and indubitable rights of the people of this kingdom." These are "ancient rights and liberties." The rights do not find their source in nature or nature's God, but in their antiquity: not nature or a divinity but history and prescription.

Possessors of rights

The 1776 Declaration asserts these rights to be the endowment of "all men." They are not limited to members of any sect, or nation. The rights belong to men of other races as well, at least according to those who drafted the American document; they included the accusation that the King had "waged cruel war against human nature itself, violating its most sacred rights of life and liberty in the person of a distant people … [by] carrying them into slavery."

Tracing the source of rights to antiquity and prescription, the English document declares rights that belong only to "the people of this kingdom." Most of the rights proclaimed are not individual rights at all. For instance, the first "right of the people" announced is "that the pretended power of suspending laws, or the execution of laws, by regal authority, without consent of parliament, is illegal." This and most of the other rights are not possessions of the individual English persons, but are powers of parliament, or non-powers of the monarch. This is clearly a very different matter from the kind of individual rights asserted in the natural rights philosophy. It is the "right of the [English] people" that political bodies exercise their own powers, an important feature of constitutional government. This commitment to constitutionalism means, in the first place, a commitment to non-absolutism: the King does not possess powers to make laws (or ignore laws), to tax, to jail people, or to deploy the armed forces of the community alone. The core is the sharing of power. The sharing of power between these political bodies bespeaks a deeper kind of sharing – the joint possession of authority by the different estates or classes of the realm. The English Declaration is promulgated in the names of "lords spiritual and temporal, and commons." The two first comprise the House of Lords, the last is represented in the House of Commons. The Declaration's constitutionalism is this sharing or participation in rule among these elements of the community and the monarch, a sharing meant to procure rule of law, rather than the mere rule of the monarch.

According to the Declaration of Independence, however, all human beings possess their rights as individuals, whatever their place in society. As an endowment from the "creator," the rights are not the gift of history or society, however understood. They are also primitive and original; the rights are possessed prior to the formation of government (conceptually and perhaps historically), for it is for the sake of these rights that "governments are instituted among men."

Duty bearers

Every right in the full sense implies a corresponding duty in someone. In the case of the American Declaration the rights belong to "all men" in a condition prior to and independent of political life. The corresponding duty-bearers would thus seem to be "all comers" – all other human beings and collectivities (e.g. government) when such are in place. The duties in the first instance appear to be merely of forbearance – Peter's right to life implies only Paul's duty not to interfere with Peter's life. Since government is "established" to secure rights according to a kind of contract, government becomes the duty-bearer corresponding not only to the primary natural rights but to a secondary right to security in one's rights. This is more than a duty to forbear; it is the duty to supply the protection of rights. If government fails to live up to its obligation then the people have the right to "alter or abolish" malevolent or incompetent government. This is the so-called right of revolution, which the Declaration of Independence is especially keen to announce.

The duty-bearers corresponding to the rights in the English Declaration are not so easy to identify, because the rights listed are so various. Since they are mostly limitations on the power of the King, or, conversely, affirmations of parliamentary powers, the duty-bearer appears to be the king.

Substance of rights

The American Declaration lists a series of "unalienable rights" as "among" those with which "all men" are "endowed." There is nonetheless a kind of coherence to the list supplied, as there is to the more common list of "life, liberty, and property." Although the Declaration substitutes "pursuit of happiness" for "property," other documents of the revolutionary era make clear that this substitution does not necessarily signify a rejection of the latter right, for many of the state constitutions contained both: obviously the one does not in any sense cancel the other.

The rights listed have a systematic coherence. The right to life is a right to what is most one's own, one's life. Given the nature of a human life, it is difficult to see how it could be anything other than one's own, how it could in any sense belong to others. Given the dependence (or base) of life in or on the body, the right to life must contain a right to bodily immunity, the right not to have one's body seized, invaded, controlled by others.

The right to liberty extends the right to life: not only does one possess a rightful immunity against the depredations of others on one's body, but one has a right to the use of one's body. We can take control of our bodies and invest our bodies' movements with our intentions and purposes. The natural right to liberty proclaims the prima facie rightfulness of active, intentional use of the body. The right to property involves an extension of rights from the spheres of one's own life, body, and actions to the external world. It proclaims the rightful power of human beings to make the external their own in the same way they can make their bodies their own.

The three basic rights together amount to the affirmation of a kind of personal sovereignty, a rightful control over one's person, actions, and possessions in the service of one's intents and purposes. When seen as an integrated system of immunities and controls the specific rights amount to a comprehensive right to pursue a shape and way of life self-chosen.

Their systematic quality differentiates the rights in the American Declaration from those in the English Declaration. The latter lists 13 rights, ranging from the rights that the King should not suspend or dispense with laws, not levy taxes, not keep a standing army without the consent of Parliament, to the rights of subjects "to petition the king," and not to be subjected to excessive bail. Although obviously important, the rights in the Declaration of Rights do not reach the level of fundamentality or coherence

visible in the Declaration of Independence's rights.

Function of rights

According to the American Declaration the securing of natural rights is the only end or purpose of legitimate government. The existence of legitimate government and laws proves that the various rights cannot be "absolutes." The law can legitimately limit rights, and can intrude into the basic sphere of immunities of the individual not only on behalf of the specific rights of others, but in pursuit of "the public good." Rights-securing requires a community and an effective government, and these in turn have many requisites not translatable directly into rights of specific individuals. Equally important, if less obvious, is what we might call a society's "rights infrastructure" – the social institutions and traits of character that make rights-securing possible. Concern for the rights infrastructure may also require that governments provide services beyond direct protection to rights; for example, Thomas Jefferson was of the view that public education was a requisite to the rights infrastructure. The natural rights theory is quite certain in affirming the ends of political life ("to secure these rights"), but there is nonetheless a great range of possibilities as to what this involves in practice. Securing rights serves also as a standard for the invocation of one of the important rights, the right to alter or abolish governments which are "destructive" of the primary rights.

By contrast the English Declaration of Rights is silent on the ends of government. The rights do not function as a justification or triggering condition for the invocation of the right of revolution; the document nowhere invokes or affirms such a right, or describes the action being taken in 1688 as a revolution. The king is said to have "abdicated," not been deposed or overthrown. The rights announced, having far more the character of constitutional powers and arrangements than of rights in the ordinary sense, seem to be means rather than ends. The Declaration of Rights sets out intently silent about the ends these means serve.

2 The American Amalgam

This brief survey of the two rights regimes clarifies how different the two kinds of rights are: one wonders how competent observers can disagree over which of them was the driving presence in the American Revolution. The simple answer to this conundrum lies in the observation that the Revolution was, importantly, about both kinds of rights. The Americans, especially at first, merely agitated for the "rights of Englishmen," rights they claimed under their colonial charters or under the general principles of the Constitution. By 1776 the Americans were also appealing to natural rights. The co-presence of appeals to both constitutional rights and natural rights is best understood in terms of a nearly unique amalgam, comprised of both natural and constitutional rights, that the Americans forged.

The controversy between America and Britain was indeed legal and constitutional. The single most striking fact about that constitutional battle, however, is that both parties appealed to the same constitutional principles, but derived their own version of the normative imperial constitution from that appeal. The British expressed their notion of the constitution most revealingly in the Declaratory Act of 1766, passed at the same time that Parliament repealed the stamp tax. The law put the Americans on notice that Parliament was not conceding an inch on the constitutional principle at stake: "be it declared ... that the said colonies ... in America ... are, and of right ought to be subordinate unto and dependent upon the imperial crown and parliament of Great Britain, [which], had, hath, and of right ought to have full power and authority to make laws and statutes to bind the colonies and people of America ... in all cases whatsoever." Strong stuff, but it was a most plausible interpretation of the British Constitution as revealed in the Declaration of Rights. The mandate there was rule by joint authority of King and Parliament. The Declaratory Act says no less: the colonies are presumed bound and subject to all relevant acts of King and Parliament. Conceding that the Americans possessed "the rights of Englishmen," their right was fulfilled when the King acted in and through Parliament.

The Americans protested that this was not the interpretation they were used to, for King and Parliament had mostly refrained from legislating and taxing the colonies and instead had left such matters to the colonial assemblies. More importantly, the colonists, reading the Constitution through the lens of the natural rights theory of legitimate government, rejected the British interpretation. The British version could not be correct, they thought, once one interpreted the Constitution in terms of the true rationale for constitutional practices. Why, for example did the Constitution require the consent of Parliament to tax measures? Without the consent of Parliament, i.e., of the tax payers or their representatives, the right to property was not recognized; if property could be taken at the will of the King alone, then it was not really property, goods to which the owners had an exclusive right. Under such a regime the subjects would not be recognized as free rights bearers. In the language of the day, they would be "slaves," neither self-owning nor genuinely owners of pieces of the external world.

Parliament could vote taxes for Englishmen without denying their rights because Parliament represented and thus could give consent for the right-bearers. But the colonists did not accept the English view that they were "virtually" represented in Parliament. Parliamentary action *vis-à-vis* them derogated from their status as free and rights-bearing persons, as they understood the situation, just as much as if the King acted alone. The resulting amalgam of constitutional and natural right gave the colonists a perspective on the meaning of the Constitution that was by no means necessary or evident from every point of view. The amalgam in effect replaced the older notion of shared power, which is found in the Declaration of Rights, with the quite different natural rights commitments.

The natural rights philosophy thus gave the Americans a way to interpret the Constitution that was at work even when they were apparently talking only about the Constitution and appealing to constitutional rather than natural rights. It was thus not a major shift for the Americans to give more weight to the purely natural rights aspects of their position when the British authorities resisted the American theory of the Constitution; it was also not inconsistent with this shift for the Americans to continue to insist on their rights as Englishmen.

FURTHER READING

Bailyn, Bernard: *The Ideological Origins of the American Revolution* (Cambridge, Mass.: Belknap Press of Harvard University Press, 1967).

Becker, Carl: *The Declaration of Independence* (New York: Vintage, 1958).

Greene, Jack: *Peripheries and Center: Constitutional Development in the Extended Politics of the British Empire and the United States* (Athens, GA: University of Georgia Press, 1986).

Reid, John Phillip: *Constitutional History of the American Revolution: The Authority of Rights* (Madison: University of Wisconsin Press, 1986).

Rossiter, Clinton: *Seedtime of the Republic: The Origin of the American Tradition of Political Liberty* (New York: Harcourt, Brace, 1953).

Strauss, Leo: *Natural Right and History* (Chicago: University of Chicago Press, 1954).

Tierney, Brian: *The Idea of Natural Rights: Studies on Natural Rights, Natural Law and Church Law 1150–1625* (Atlanta: Scholars Press, 1997).

Tuck, Richard: *Natural Rights Theories: Their Origin and Development* (Cambridge: Cambridge University Press, 1979).

Zuckert, Michael P.: *Natural Rights and the New Republicanism* (Princeton: Princeton University Press, 1994).

Zuckert, Michael P.: *The Natural Rights Republic* (Notre Dame: University of Notre Dame Press, 1996).

CHAPTER EIGHTY-NINE

Virtue

JAMES T. KLOPPENBERG

VIRTUE was ubiquitous in eighteenth-century American discourse. An all-purpose term of approbation, virtue had different, and occasionally incompatible, meanings in different contexts. When Montesquieu distinguished between three sorts of virtue – Christian, political, and moral – in *The Spirit of the Laws*, he was only confirming what contemporaries already knew. While the categories of religion, politics, and ethics may have been separable in principle, however, in linguistic practice they were usually blurred. Understanding the range of meanings associated with virtue in revolutionary America requires distinguishing among these different vocabularies and understanding how they changed from 1763 to 1800.

1 Christian Ideas of Virtue

Virtue lay at the heart of Christian doctrine. While Aquinas followed Aristotle in conceiving of the intellectual and moral virtues as a mean between defects and excesses, he placed primary emphasis on the infused theological virtues of faith, hope, and especially charity, which had no counterpart in ancient philosophy. The Christian ideal of universal benevolence translated into a wide variety of philosophical and political outlooks in America, ranging from the rationalism of Charles Chauncy and Jonathan Mayhew to the Augustinian rigor of Jonathan Edwards, and from the covenant tradition of Puritan New England, which became especially raucous during the Great Awakening, to the far less participatory mainstream Anglicanism of the South. But religion in America remained vibrant throughout the eighteenth century, and representatives of various traditions proclaimed resistance to all forms of oppression, real or imaginary (*see* chapter 8). In his sermon *A Discourse Concerning Unlimited Submission*, delivered in Boston in January 1750, Mayhew warned that "a spirit of domination is always to be guarded against, both in church and state." Virtue required vigilance against "the slavish doctrine of passive obedience and nonresistance" (Bonomi, 1986, p. 196). In a variety of ways, the Protestant inclination to interpret experience in terms of a providential plan shaped Americans' attitudes towards their privileged but fragile status as God's chosen people.

Christian ideas of virtue were sufficiently ambiguous to suggest contradictory implications for public life. The awakening might involve challenging all forms of authority or merely reconstituting it on a purified foundation. The recurring emphasis on man's depravity might signal the distance America had fallen from its lofty aspirations, or it might reflect the chosen community's dogged faithfulness to its original ideals. The commitment to God might require selfless obedience to duty, or it might require the individual's liberation from all merely earthly forms of authority. Different religious communities interpreted virtue in different ways, and their recognition of those disagreements only made their competing claims more strident.

2 Republican Ideas of Virtue

The classical republican tradition likewise contained various conceptions of virtue.

The political ideas of Cicero and Seneca were no more identical than were those of Plato and Aristotle, and the political writings of seventeenth-century English republicans such as John Milton and Algernon Sidney further complicated the notion of civic virtue. Although any generalization about republicanism is perilous, given the breadth of the tradition, American republicans tended to rely on independent citizens to protect fragile civic virtue against the threat of corruption represented by the extension of executive power. The republican ideal of community, in which individuals defined their interests according to their perception of the common good, figured prominently in the political literature produced in America, particularly between the end of the Seven Years' War and the ratification of the Constitution.

Yet just as the Christian ideal of virtue was both central and ambiguous, so the republican ideal of the virtuous citizen was fuzzy. Greek and Roman republicans feared rather than welcomed change. They preferred cities to the countryside, hierarchy to equality, Spartan simplicity to economic prosperity, and military conquest to domestic tranquility. Machiavelli, a more proximate source of republican ideas, elevated the will to combat fortune above the individual's responsibility to adhere to the moral law. The quest for glory was essential to the Renaissance conception of *virtù*. Force and fraud were but part of the standard repertoire of statesmanship, and aspirations to greatness outweighed calculations of justice. As a weapon wielded against perceived corruption, the republican tradition exerted a powerful appeal in America, but Americans who cherished progress, democracy, commerce, and peace felt compelled to reject as much of the republican tradition as they endorsed.

3 Eighteenth-Century Moral Philosophy

Moral philosophy provided a third tradition of discourse on virtue. Understanding these ideas is complicated by the controversies swirling around the ethics of John Locke and Scottish common sense realists such as Francis Hutcheson, Adam Ferguson, Thomas

Reid, and Dugald Stewart. Locke's writings were perhaps more widely cited in America than those of any other thinker. Recent interpretations of his work emphasize the importance of seeing Locke on his own terms rather than as the progenitor of a tradition of "possessive individualism." His concept of individual liberty dissolves if it is removed from the context of divinely established natural law, which encumbers the freedom of individuals at every turn with the powerful commands of duty. Locke's belief in a natural law discernible by reason led him to condemn the unregulated pursuit of self-interest that Thomas Hobbes considered natural and that later writers who celebrated a market economy sanctioned. As Locke wrote to Edward Clarke in April 1687, "He that has not a mastery over his inclinations, he that knows not how to resist the importunity of present pleasure, or pain, for the sake of what, reason tells him, is fit to be done, wants the true principle of Virtue, and industry, and is in danger never to be good for anything" (Dunn, 1985, p. 194). For Locke, as for his American readers, freedom could be exercised virtuously only within the boundaries of natural law discerned by reason.

Scottish moral philosophy appealed to Americans because it offered an ostensibly empirical ethics that did not require invocations of authority yet conformed to conventional Christian conceptions of virtue. The idea of a moral sense that was just as much a part of man as his physical senses proved irresistible in the age of Locke's psychology and Newton's physics. For a culture still strongly committed to traditional religious values, yet searching for alternative ways of justifying these commitments, Scottish common sense realists offered both novelty and reassurance. Different Scots appealed to different Americans, since the Scots' explanations ranged from those grounding the moral sense on feelings, with Hutcheson, to those who grounded it on rational intuition, with Reid. All of these Scottish moralists, however, shared a commitment to the accountability of the individual to the community, and that commitment appealed to Americans as much as did their comforting theories of knowledge.

4 American Virtue in Practice, 1763–90

Although religious, republican, and ethical conceptions of virtue were hardly identical, and in some of their forms quite clearly incompatible, Americans after 1763 imaginatively braided them together. As Gordon Wood has explained, "The traditional covenant theology of Puritanism combined with the political science of the eighteenth century into an imperatively persuasive argument for revolution. Liberal rationalist sensibility blended with Calvinist Christian love to create an essentially common emphasis on the usefulness and goodness of devotion to the general welfare of the community. Religion and republicanism would work hand in hand to create frugality, honesty, self-denial, and benevolence among the people." To use the revealing phrase of Samuel Adams, through revolution America would become "the *Christian* Sparta" (Wood, 1969, p. 118), an amalgamation of Christian benevolence, classical republicanism, and selfless devotion to moral duty.

During the War for Independence, these feelings intensified. When militia men and Continental regulars held their ground against British soldiers, they fortified their courage by pledging to uphold their virtue rather than break and run. Facing a particularly stark conflict between self-interest and duty, they expressed their commitment in the vocabularies of virtue (Middlekauff, 1984, p. 330–1). Women who sustained the revolutionary struggle in a variety of ways likewise learned to think of themselves as virtuous citizens, and some challenged men to extend to them the privileges they had earned as a result of their devotion to the cause of liberty (*see* chapter 52, §4).

Virtue, at least until the achievement of independence, functioned as a fighting word, a challenge boldly hurled against corruption. During the period from 1783 to 1787, virtue no longer meant simply resistance to government and authority. As the bracing experience of war gave way to confederation and disarray, some Americans began to doubt their ability to preserve their new nation. The Reverend Asa Briggs of Vermont warned in his election sermon

of 1786, "Political virtue may serve as a support for a while, but it is not a lasting principle." Virtue, Briggs and others insisted, can only rest on piety (Bloch, 1990, p. 55). Such sentiments found expression in the authorization for public support of religious education and worship in the Massachusetts Constitution of 1780. The Virginia Statute for Religious Freedom of 1786, which challenged the public's authority to dictate belief, was something of an anomaly.

It is possible to interpret the Constitutional Convention as an attempt to create institutions embodying the virtue of a republican citizenry, or as an admission that, since civic virtue is impossible, the aim of politics is merely to harness the effects of vice. Alternatively, the debates on the ratification of the Constitution can be understood to illustrate the persistence of the competing clusters of religious, republican, and ethical ideas about virtue circulating before the revolution. Neither Federalists nor Anti-Federalists fit neatly into the categories of liberalism or republicanism. Spokesmen for both groups expressed ideas drawn from the vocabularies of Christianity, classical republicanism, and Lockean or Scottish common sense philosophy, and both veiled considerations of self-interest with proclamations of their own virtue and their opponents' corruption. In a characteristic formulation, the Yale President Timothy Dwight insisted that a virtuous republic must rest on the pillars of "Piety to God, Good-will to mankind, and the effectual Government of ourselves" (Hatch, 1977, p. 109).

Adams, Madison, and Jefferson

Neither John Adams, James Madison, nor Thomas Jefferson, arguably the most important theorists of the revolutionary generation, fit comfortably within any of these categories. While his early enthusiasm for more popular government gave way to distrust in the wake of Shays's Rebellion and the French Revolution, Adams continued throughout his career to invoke both the Puritan convenantal and classical republican traditions in his writings. Reflecting on his plan for the Massachusetts Constitution, he described it as "Locke, Sidney, and

Rousseau and de Mably reduced to practice" (Adams, 1850–6, IV, p. 216), an apt characterization of the mixture of ideas that seemed so natural to the founders and so unsettles twentieth-century critics.

Likewise Madison, who so soberly described the pervasiveness of self-interest in *The Federalist*, no. 10, slipped easily into the languages of republicanism and Scottish moral philosophy in no. 55:

As there is a degree of depravity in mankind which requires a certain degree of circumspection and distrust: So there are other qualities in human nature, which justify a certain portion of esteem and confidence. Republican government presupposes the existence of these qualities in a higher degree than any other form. Were the pictures which have been drawn by the political jealousy of some among us, faithful likenesses of the human character, the inference would be that there is not sufficient virtue among men for self government; and that nothing less than the chains of despotism can restrain them from destroying and devouring one another. (Madison, Hamilton. and Jay, 1961, p. 378)

Madison was a realist but not a cynic, and he realized that the separation of powers was a necessary but not sufficient condition to insure what he sometimes termed "the common good of the society."

Jefferson too was guardedly optimistic about the harmonious interaction of self-interested individuals only because he believed their inner moral gyroscopes would prevent them from oppressing one another. Jefferson defined self-interest as Locke's virtue rather than Hobbes's possessive individualism. In a letter to Benjamin Rush written in 1803, Jefferson criticized as "defective" ancient republican philosophers' overly narrow conception of those who fall "within the circle of benevolence." The advance of Christian over classical conceptions of virtue, according to Jefferson, lay precisely in the universality of Christian charity, which extends "not only to kindred and friends, to neighbors and countrymen," as does republican duty, "but to all mankind, gathering all into one family, under the bonds of love, charity, peace, common wants and common aims." Finally, in his meditation on the "foundation of morality in man," Jefferson distinguished benevolence from egotism. "Self-love, therefore, is

no part of morality," he wrote to Thomas Law. "It is the sole antagonist of virtue, leading us constantly by our propensities to self-gratification in violation of our moral duties to others … nature hath implanted in our breasts a love of others, a sense of duty to them, a moral instinct, in short, which prompts us irresistibly to feel and to succor their distresses." Jefferson acknowledged the importance of civic virtue, and he insisted on the importance of individual rights, but he never surrendered his devotion to the Christian ideal of universal benevolence as "the most perfect and sublime" conception of ethics (Jefferson, 1984, pp. 1124–5, 1136–7).

5   The Decline of Virtue

References to virtue continued to be widespread in American political discourse through the 1790s, but the accelerating development of the contradictory religious, political, and economic tendencies that began to appear in those years of rapid change gradually destroyed the bonds that might have linked an optimistic and egalitarian republicanism to an ethically attuned and democratically alert liberalism. The latent inconsistencies within these traditions became manifest when the crises that temporarily fused them together were resolved and social and economic change upset their equilibrium. Benjamin Franklin wrote that "only a virtuous people are capable of freedom" (Franklin, 1905–7, IX, p. 80). The American record after the 1790s suggests that a free people may be incapable of virtue. During the early nineteenth century the meaning of virtue lost its earlier religious, civic, and ethical significance and became a label for bourgeois propriety or feminine purity. When independence lost its identification with benevolence, when self-interest was no longer conceived in relation to the egalitarian standard Jefferson upheld – in his theory if not in his practice – then freedom itself, especially the freedom to compete in the race for riches without the restraint of natural law, ironically became an obstacle in the way of justice, a poor substitute for the earlier Christian, republican, and moral conceptions of virtue.

FURTHER READING

Adams, John: *The Works of John Adams*, 10 vols., ed. Charles Francis Adams (Boston, 1850–6).

Bloch, Ruth: "Religion and ideological change in the American Revolution," in *Religion and American Politics*, ed. Mark A. Noll (New York: Oxford University Press, 1990), 44–61.

Bonomi, Patricia: *Under the Cope of Heaven: Religion, Society and Politics in Colonial America* (New York: Oxford University Press, 1986).

Dunn, John: *Rethinking Modern Political Theory* (Cambridge: Cambridge University Press, 1985).

Franklin, Benjamin: *The Writings of Benjamin Franklin*, 10 vols., ed. Albert H. Smyth (New York, 1905–7).

Hatch, Nathan: *The Sacred Cause of Liberty: Republican Thought and the Millennium in Revolutionary New England* (New Haven, Conn.: Yale University Press, 1977).

Jefferson, Thomas: *Writings*, ed. Merrill D. Peterson (New York: Library of America, 1984).

Madison, James, Hamilton, Alexander and Jay, John: *The Federalist*, ed. Jacob E. Cooke (Middletown, Conn.: Wesleyan University Press, 1961).

Midlekauff, Robert: "Why men fought in the American Revolution," in *Saints and Revolutionaries: Essays on Early American History*, ed. David D. Hall et al. (New York: W. W. Norton, 1984), 318–31.

Wood, Gordon: *The Creation of the American Republic, 1776–1787* (Chapel Hill: University of North Carolina Press, 1969).

CHAPTER NINETY

Interests

CATHY MATSON

FOR generations before the American Revolution jurists, policy-makers, and political commentators in the British Empire attached meanings of "interest" primarily to land ownership and the personal character they believed to derive from it. Their views owed much to classical teachings about the political rights and personal virtue that flowed from land ownership, teachings which enjoined early modern British people to restrain group and private interests – especially when they had been detached from the enduring, timeless benefits of landedness – and to identify with a *res publica*. Although many British writers identified the stability of such a public interest with a monarch's political authority over an extensive dominion, by the seventeenth century they more often associated the "interest of the nation" with a mixed government dominated by a gentry "landed interest."

British citizens clung tenaciously to these traditional meanings of interest, but the rapidly changing economic, political, and social conditions of their empire after the mid-1600s prompted new meanings as well. One shift in the definitions of interest derived from new thinking about land. John Locke's writings reflected, among other things, an intellectual shift just underway which questioned the link between land and static inherited social authority and monarchical political structures. As land itself increasingly became a marketable asset, a commodity that individuals and governments bought and sold, Locke and others proposed that it be seen as a means for social advancement, private business transactions, and shifting political authority. Interests

thus became plural, mobile, and affiliated with many kinds of property. Locke offered that the most pernicious effects of competing interests could be nullified by the voluntary compact of free individuals in the commonwealth, attached in their mutual pursuit of prosperity. The political authority of such a compact would flow not from brute force but from the collective of self-regarding individuals who controlled and coordinated interests. Locke's reasoning was especially influential during the years surrounding the Glorious Revolution of 1688.

Although much of Locke's writing reflected new thinking about a landed interest, other observers at about the same time underscored a "financial interest," and a "commercial interest." The former arose from numerous banking and administrative changes arising from the government's imperial expansion and wars. The latter, although it had existed during centuries of international trade, became a far more important topic of commentary among moralists and popular writers when colonial settlement, new consumer goods, and changing urban life evoked notice. A growing commercial elite rivalled the landed gentry for the benefits of government policies, and took on clearer distinctive characteristics. Commerce, remarked its admirers after the 1620s, embodied mobile rather than static property, risk rather than tradition, commodities and financial instruments rather than real estate, expansion and foreign connections rather than the solidification of political authority at home.

A core group of policy-makers in England by the late 1600s merged the perceived benefits of commercial and financial interests into a mercantilist "national interest." Mercantilists argued for regulatory policies to expand foreign trade and hopefully return profits consistently in favor of merchants, small producers, and the Crown. Because nations competed for limited global wealth, the rise of any nation relied upon a higher value of exports than imports; such a favorable balance of trade would make the nation wealthy, and because the rising wealth of Britain implied the impoverishment of foreign nations, a balance of power accrued to Britain as well. By exploiting the great appetites of foreign consumers for British finished goods, traders and policy-makers together could meld commercial interests to the nation's.

By the early 1800s, optimists heralded the benefits not only of group interests, but of private interests as well. They celebrated the material prosperity and institutional maturation of the empire, especially the "sweet" effects of commerce, and the commercial wealth accumulating in the hands of international traders. Expansive, multivariant, and inclusive interests, talents, and tastes all combined creatively, especially in the encounters among buyers and sellers everywhere. Self-interests, properly directed, argued Bernard Mandeville, enhanced the public good. By the 1750s David Hume and Adam Smith, among others, investigated the soothing effects of every individual's "moral sense" and "benevolence" on collections of interests.

Alongside this optimism about the benefits of self-interest, notes of caution rang clearly. Critics of self-interest drew sustenance from the republican or commonwealth tradition that had endured – but also changed – since classical associations of interest with prescriptive rights. By the eighteenth century, republicans wrote that interest was potentially dangerous when it led to excessive pecuniary gain in loaning money, or when private interests vied for political preferment or power and became dangerous to the health of the state itself. Interests were claims, declarations of rights, and bonds that compromised personal independence from obligation to others. By nature, interests represented restless ambitions, disregard for stability, and suggested

loyalties distinct from, or opposed to, those of the entire community, such as when credit and debt networks broke down into contentious interests and jeopardized social order. Although not inherently evil, interests easily became corrupted, fraudulent, irrational, and dangerous to the stability of the polity.

Not only individual self-interests, but the rise of interest groups, drew republican ire. Financial and administrative changes following the Glorious Revolution had, according to republican critics such as John Trenchard and Thomas Gordon, ramified into selfish market relationships and corrupted political preferments. New landed interests did not honor age-old prescriptive rights, but treated property as mobile. New monied interests stretched debt obligations to breaking point, and speculated wildly in banks, annuities, war loans, stocks, bonds, and other "flimsy paper." In commerce, they had flooded polite and civilized society with overextended credit and foreign luxuries. In politics, Court Whigs supposedly fomented and financed endless wars for imperial dominion, and joined forces with factional political interests around Robert Walpole. Together, they built an alarming coalition of merchants and placemen who reoriented policies toward unstable international trading risks, some of them in foreign waters where the danger of provoking further wars with competing empires loomed large. Republican critics doubted that these new interests could advance the empire's wealth and power before they annihilated each other in the scramble for special privileges. The South Sea Bubble of the 1720s made manifest their worst fears when a widespread network of financial speculation collapsed from overextension, nearly ruining thousands of investors ranging from Isaac Newton to groups of English sailors.

American revolutionaries nurtured their independence movement with both republican teachings about the dangers of new interests, and emerging celebrations of public and private interests. By the 1720s, especially in the northern American colonies, legislative assemblies gained significant ascendancy over governors' powers. Men serving in the assemblies at first believed that the slow accretion of authority in these provincial bodies simply expressed varied local interests struggling to be heard; in time, great numbers of Americans believed that the rise of the assemblies' power reflected the collective efforts of numerous economic, social, and intellectual interests to take a place in the very structure of government. Merchants and farmers, eastern and western counties, new townships, contending elite families deliberated in mixed assemblies of interests with direct political influence.

This process of politicizing interests preceded its theoretical articulation. But by the onset of the imperial crisis in America, Edmund Burke and other British parliamentary leaders had begun to portray the House of Commons as an interest-based body. Commerce, banking, military, and professional interests, argued Burke, deserved a legitimate separate representation in Parliament. David Hume, too, insisted that in politics, as in commerce, interests would have a natural tendency to balance each other over time; critics need not fear the corrupting influence of openly stated interests in legislative deliberations.

Yet few Britons expressed clearly who should represent these newly recognized political interests in colonial American assemblies and in Parliament's House of Commons. Tradition held that only the well-born gentry was fit to do so; other citizens would not find enough time from pursuing their economic interests to rule others, or they would fail to rise above their private interests to serve the general welfare. Only members of the gentry shared sufficient "disinterest" to rule. But this traditional view could not take root firmly throughout the colonies because elites comprising "the better sort" remained relatively unstable coalitions of interests, and because gains of political authority among "the lesser sort" formally and informally challenged elite rule after about the 1720s. But no serious alteration in the structure of political representation occurred over these years.

The imperial crisis after 1763 heightened these ambiguities. Already, the colonies had experienced the contradictions of imperial policies which, on the one hand, promised to protect equally all interests within the empire, but, on the other hand, emphasized

that the balance of power among imperial interests should tip toward London at all times. By the early 1760s, colonists began to doubt whether certain important interests were in fact equal within the empire; British policy-makers tightened controls over colonial production, attempted to restrain colonial frontier expansion, and denied colonists political representation at the level of the empire. After 1763 parliamentary debate resulted in what imperial officials called a "new System of Interests" that ratified colonists' subordinate status, and by 1773 the Tea Act gave the East India Company a "monopolied interest" over colonists that disrupted the harmony of the empire.

By 1776, the exigencies of the Revolutionary War focussed meanings of interests in additional ways. As they created new states, many leaders called upon citizens to sacrifice private interests and devote themselves to the common good, an appeal they believed to be grounded on classical republican and corporatist notions of politics and the economy. The army, the state governments, and local committees persistently reminded fellow Americans that privatistic, self-aggrandizing impulses jeopardized the public good. Interests, they warned, easily turned into dangerous factions that threatened to annihilate both the individual rights of particular citizens and the political liberty of all citizens.

But such selflessness proved impossible to sustain, for too many citizens refused to sacrifice their private interests. Farmers in the Mid-Atlantic region and merchants in coastal cities, for example, demanded that the Revolution release private interests from public restraints, that the old regulatory order of mercantilism be dismantled and individual economic freedom finally prevail. Otherwise, some commercial leaders in America insisted, they would starve "on the slender Meals of Patriotism." Newspaper editorials intoned that Americans had the virtue and the will to create a system of orchestrated interests, thereby avoiding the grasping system of special interests represented by Parliament and King.

The war created a frenzy of buying and selling among citizens and soldiers, often in the form of speculative ventures, which in turn gave average farmers, country craftsmen, small privateers, and urban shopkeepers a taste for expansive enterprise. Wartime emissions of paper money, and a boom in credit and debt relations, fueled prospects for bounteous American internal development. A growing – though not completely new – sense of rising "middling interests" in North America permeated revolutionary discussions about the roles of producers, consumers, and wartime suppliers. These interests in turn vied for special favors from policy-makers and strained traditional social relations by emulating the refinement of their betters. Commercial farmers, urban artisans, and small planters strove to prosper from wartime need during the 1770s; many translated their economic interests into serving political positions for the first time. These new voices in politics anticipated that the sovereign states of the Confederation would continue to provide forums for rapid recovery and the expansive energies unleashed in America's vast expanses of unexplored land.

It is one of the great ironies of the American Revolution that this vision of unfettered interests, set free from the bondage of factional self-interests in Parliament and Crown circles, gave way almost immediately to a plethora of regulations, enforcement committees, taxes and requisitions, a contract-bidding system to supply the army, price controls, embargoes, and many other constraints on individual or local actions. There would be no congeries of interested individuals competing freely in markets.

Yet America's experienced revolutionary leaders feared that these new interests arising in the states comprised the most serious threat to the stability of the republic. As republican intellectual traditions had taught, the acquisitive and commercial forces unleashed by the Revolution were always potentially dangerous to political stability, and during the 1780s they seemed to be spinning out of control. Military and congressional leaders lamented that inexperienced, local-minded men with pecuniary ambitions overran the new state legislatures, passing all manner of dangerous paper money and debtor relief laws, as well as market regulations that interfered with individual property rights and harmed creditors. "Little men" who had

parochial views about development and the defense of the republic dominated some state legislatures, reducing their constituents' interests to endless quarrels over temporary, pocketbook responses to local concerns. This fracturing and belittling of interests left the states ill-prepared to consider their relationship to each other and to foreign nations.

As the 1780s progressed, Federalists warned against the kind of interested behavior that used lesser political offices to secure private gain. The social origins of these private interests lay in the rising commercial character of the new republic, the increasing importance of free labor, the accelerating pace of internal and international exchange, and Americans' widespread dedication to getting ahead. James Madison sharply criticized the "immediate augmentation of property and wealth" that infused much of the popular attitude about society and government. Such private interests were dangerous enough when men of commerce and manufacturing introduced great quantities of luxuries to unwary consumers, but dangers grew exponentially when inexperienced democratic interests arose in the state legislatures. By the time Madison wrote *The Federalist* no. 10, it was no longer startling to note that shaping interests in public arguments and seeking to fulfill them in state legislation dominated American political life. Madison, and most Federalists, believed that while the "clashing interests" of groups and private individuals who entered markets in land and goods were not necessarily pernicious, the use of government to serve the goals of myriad shifting interests would, perforce, undermine the integrity of republican state governments. Government should be above interestedness, and its offices should be filled with worthy and virtuous representatives who had significant learning and leisure, and who rose above immediate material pursuits to become "servants of the public good." Only men who were free of interested ties to others could rule according to principle and for "the people" as a whole. Confederation-era states had not measured up to this responsibility. Instead, Federalists argued that the new national government would be a "dispassionate umpire in disputes between different passions and interests," and run by men "whose enlightened views and virtuous sentiments render them superior to local prejudices, and to schemes of injustice." Many leading Federalists also shed their fears about the negative consequences of pursuing interests, and instead adopted optimistic views about the potential for development in America. Interests, when conceived as productive activities, as opposed to contentious self-interests, could be assimilated with hard work and other traditional virtues. Optimistic Federalists raised the prospect of government under the Constitution protecting and furthering "infant interests" in manufacturing and commerce; by avoiding the political corruption of the British state, America's constitutional solution would keep maturing enterprises from threatening the civil polity and the economic virtue of Americans.

New conceptualizations of interests also emerged in the Federalists' solution to the divisive policies and contentious interests in state government during the 1780s. As Madison and others had made abundantly clear, 13 separately sovereign republics under the Confederation plan had proved not to be the glue of the republic, but rather its undoing. Fragmented, distinct interests somehow needed to be refashioned into a more transcendent interest. The federal republic proposed by the Constitution offered such a plan – though many Americans still doubted in 1787 that it offered a truly workable solution – by projecting that similarly situated groups across the nation shared common interests that could be protected and furthered only by the federal political authority outlined in the Constitution. Further, the presence of a vast western hinterland made it imperative to reach beyond the existing jurisdictions of state interests to create a more encompassing national interest that could progressively incorporate territory into the republic. Nationalist merchants and land speculators who favored a strengthened union under the new Constitution insisted that the "natural interests" of development and expansion across new regions provided a valuable counterpoint to the "artificial interests" of states struggling with each other for relative advantage.

By embracing and reshaping perceptions of "interest," many revolutionary leaders took steps that led beyond the constraints of republican warnings. It was hard to find disinterested gentlemen anymore who did not blend their participation in markets with factional politics. By 1788 many Anti-Federalists suspected that the Constitution was little more than a plan to empower a small elite that was deeply "interested" in creating large institutions under their control. Land companies formed by the great post-revolutionary securities holders, and banks whose directors and primary stockholders came from elite kinship networks, were but two of the interests identified with the Federalist agenda. Creditors, brokers, bankers, wholesalers, and great planters variously suffered the same withering Anti-Federalist critique. These Federalists, charged their critics, were not selfless publicly minded leaders, but instead pursued their private interests to a much greater degree than the "little men" in America.

Anti-Federalists certainly accepted the pervasive influence of "interests." But in contrast to Federalists' emphasis on national or transcendent ones, Anti-Federalists insisted that there were "many different classes or orders of people," all shifting in their interests, all requiring distinctive representatives of those interests at different governmental levels. No one of these groups, no particular set of men, could claim a lack of interests – all were equally self-interested – so that governments ought to provide for the representation of each "in just proportion of their best informed men." This perspective had barely emerged during the revolutionary era, but gained prominence during the next years of the republic's ascendancy. Indeed, optimism about bolstering either a Federalist national interest or the plethora of Anti-Federalist local interests would meet continuous strenuous challenges after 1800 when regional and sectional interests vied for their own place in policy ideology.

FURTHER READING

Bacon, Francis: *The Advancement of Learning* (London: 1605), repr., ed. W. A. Wright (Oxford: Oxford University Press, 1963).

Cooke, Jacob, ed.: *The Federalist Papers* (New York, 1787–1788), repr. (Middletown, Conn.: Wesleyan University Press, 1961), esp. no. 10.

Dickson, P. G. M.: *The Financial Revolution in England: A Study in the Development of Public Credit, 1688–1756* (London: Macmillan, 1967).

Hirschman, Albert O.: *The Passions and the Interests: Political Arguments for Capitalism before Its Triumph* (Princeton: Princeton University Press, 1977).

Hobbes, Thomas.: *Leviathan*, (London: 1651), repr. (Harmondworth, Middlesex: Penguin, 1968), ch. 13.

Hume, David.: *Essays, Moral, Political, and Literary*, 2 vols. (London, 1741–2), repr. ed. T. H. Green and T. H. Grose (London: Longmans, Green, & Co., 1875), 1: 76.

——: *David Hume: Writings on Economics*, ed. Eugene Rotwein (Madison: University of Wisconsin Press, 1955), "Of Interest," 47–59.

Hyneman, Charles S., and Donald S. Lutz, eds.: *American Political Writing during the Founding Era, 1760–1805*, 2 vols. (Indianapolis, University of Indiana Press, 1983).

Smith, Adam: *The Wealth of Nations* (London, 1776), repr., ed. Edwin Canaan, 2 vols. in 1 (Chicago: University of Chicago Press, 1976), esp. 1: 477.

Steuart, Sir James: *Inquiry into the Principles of Political Economy*. 2 vols. (London, 1767), repr. ed. A. S. Skinner (Chicago: University of Chicago Press, 1966).

Storing, Herbert J.: *The Complete Anti-Federalist*, 7 vols. (Chicago: University of Chicago Press, 1981).

Chronology

Compiled by STEVEN J. SARSON

POLITICAL AND LEGAL EVENTS	MILITARY CAMPAIGNS, CIVIL ORDER, AND WESTERN SETTLEMENT	SOCIAL, CULTURAL, ECONOMIC, SCIENTIFIC, AND RELIGIOUS DEVELOPMENTS
1688–99	1688–99	1688–99
1688, Dec. 11. Glorious Revolution in England culminates when James II flees; Parliament declares him in abdication, and enthrones William and Mary.		**1688.** Germantown Petition by Pennsylvania Mennonites represents early condemnation of slavery.
1689, Feb. 13. Convention adopts Declaration of Rights, later legislated as Bill of Rights.　**April 18.** Glorious Revolution in America begins with overthrow of Dominion of New England by "Declaration of Gentlemen, Merchants and Inhabitants of Boston." Other New England colonies follow. Leisler's Rebellion topples Andros in New York. John Coode's Protestant Association overthrows Lord Baltimore and converts Maryland to a royal colony for 25 years. Other colonies declare William and Mary King and Queen more peacefully. Many colonies receive new charters.　**Oct.** First appearance of John Locke's (anonymous) *Two Treatises of Civil Government*, which later influenced American revolutionary thought. Also influential was Algernon Sidney's *Discourses Concerning Government* (1699).	**1689, May 12.** William III enters England into Grand Alliance and War of the League of Augsburg (King William's War) against Louis XIV of France. French and Amerindians fight British in America, especially New England, New York, and the West Indies, making this the first of four major wars for empire.	**1689.** Founding of America's first public school, the William Penn Charter School, which charges tuition only to those able to pay.

		1690, Feb. 3. To pay soldiers serving in Quebec, Massachusetts becomes first colony to issue paper money.
		1691. New Massachusetts Charter grants "liberty of conscience" to all Protestant Christians. Severe laws enacted against blasphemy and atheism (Oct. 1697). Maryland establishes the Church of England (1692), rescinding Toleration Act of 1649. Catholics and Quakers object. Board of Trade rejects in 1696 but accedes in 1702.
		1692, March. Children in Salem, Massachusetts, claim to have been bewitched, auguring famous Witch Hunt and trials. **April.** Thomas Neale receives patent for post office in America.
		1693, Feb. 8. Charter granted to College of William and Mary. Building begins in 1695, and is completed in 1702.
1694, Dec. 19. Triennial Act ensures elections in England every three years. **Dec. 28.** Death of Mary. William III remains King.		**1694.** Building of Annapolis, planned town and new capital of Maryland. Virginia follows with Williamsburg in 1699.
1695, April 12. Expiration of Licensing Act ends state censorship in England.		
1696, May 15. Navigation Acts create Board of Trade and Admiralty Courts with jurisdiction over all colonial affairs, including appointment of officials and review of legislation. Board power decreases owing to takeover of colonial gubernatorial appointment by Secretary of State, Southern Department (1703).		**1696, May 15.** Act of Trade (Navigation Acts) excludes foreign shipping from colonies and enumerates goods required to be re-exported through England rather than exported directly to foreign countries. Adds rice, molasses, naval stores (1705–6), copper, beaver and other furs (1721).
	1697, Sept. 30. Treaty of Ryswick ends King William's War with status quo ante bellum in Europe and America.	
	1698, March 20. Pierre Le Moyne d'Iberville enters mouth of Mississippi and begins French settlement of Louisiana territory	

	(purchased by Jefferson 106 years later). New Orleans founded in 1718.	
		1699, March 8. Rev. Thomas Bray founds Society for Promoting Christian Knowledge in London to spread Christianity in "superstitious lands." Bray travels to America on missionary work (Dec. 16).
		June 29. Massachusetts passes America's first workhouse legislation. **Dec. 1.** Woolens Act forbids export of wool manufactures across colonial borders.
1700–9	1700–9	1700–9
		1700–1. Imports from all colonies equal 20% of all imports to Britain. 10% of British manufactures are exported to colonies. Colonial population approximately 275,000.
		1700, June 16. Bray founds Society for the Propagation of the Gospel (SPG), and helps establish America's first publicly funded library in Charles Town, South Carolina. Massachusetts expels Catholics (June 17). North Carolina Vestry Act establishes Church of England (Dec. 15, 1701), disallowed by proprietors but re-enacted in 1705 and 1715. **June 24.** Publication of Samuel Sewell's early anti-slavery tract, *The Selling of Joseph*. Other writings of the decade include Cotton Mather's *Magnalia Christi Americana* (1702); Robert Beverley's *The History and Present State of Virginia* (1705); and Ebenezer Cook's *The Sot-Weed Factor* (1708).

1701, Nov. 8. William Penn grants Charter of Privileges to Pennsylvania.
  March 8. Death of William III. Accession of Queen Anne.
  April 26. New Jersey proprietors surrender authority to Crown.
		1701, Oct. 16. Dissatisfied with liberalism at Harvard, Congregationalists establish a "Collegiate School" at Killingsworth, Connecticut. Later moved to New Haven and renamed Yale (1745).

	1702, May 4. Grand Alliance declares War of Spanish Succession (Queen Anne's War) on France. Early British gains include capture of St. Christopher and Carolinian razing of St. Augustine, Spanish Florida. **July 24.** Antoine de la Mothe Cadillac establishes French settlement at Detroit.	
	1704, Feb. 29. French and Amerindians massacre 50 settlers at Deerfield, western Massachusetts. Haverhill suffers same fate (30 Aug. 1708).	**1704, April 24.** Founding of first successful colonial newspaper, the *Boston News-Letter*.
1706, March. Board of Trade increases power by introducing suspending clause requiring Crown approval before implementation of certain types of colonial legislation.		
1707, March 6. Anne signs Act of Union joining England and Scotland.		
		1709, Sept. 3. Carolina proprietors grant 13,500 acres to sponsors of German and Swiss emigrants.
1710–19	1710–19	1710–19
	1710, Oct. British capture Port Royal and Acadia from France, but fail to capture Quebec.	
	1711, Sept. 22. Tuscarora War begins between Amerindians and encroaching North Carolina settlers. War ends with Whites capturing Ft. Nohuck (March 23, 1713). Tuscaroras migrate north and join Iroquois Nations.	
1712, May 9. Division of Carolinas into separate colonies.		**1712, Aug. 1.** Pennsylvania Assembly levies £20 duty on every imported slave. Board of Trade vetoes this attempt to stem slave trade and vetoes others in 1715 and 1719.
	1713, April 11. Treaty of Utrecht precludes Bourbon succession in Spain. Britain gains Newfoundland, Nova Scotia, Hudson Bay, Nevis, and St. Kitts.	**1713, April 11.** After Treaty of Utrecht, British Government begins encouraging foreign emigration to colonies.

1714, Aug. 1. Death of Anne. Accession of George I and the Hanoverian line. **Aug.** Revival of Privy Council Committee on Colonial Affairs increases imperial bureaucracy and decreases Board of Trade power.		
	1715, April 15. Yamasee War begins between Amerindians and encroaching South Carolina settlers. Peace of January 1716 largely ends Amerindian threat to South Carolinians. Proprietors' disinterest in war leaves settlers bitter.	
1716, May. Septennial Act, promoted by Whigs worried about Jacobites, party struggle, and securing control over Hanoverians, increases life of Parliament to seven years. **1717, July 13.** Appointment of Martin Bladen to Board of Trade, a key figure for 30 years.		
		1718, Feb. American ships allowed into West Indies. Encourages vigorous sugar trade and rum manufacture, especially in New England.
1719, May 11. Earl of Westmoreland appointed President of Board of Trade. **Nov.** Commons House seizes power from proprietors and converts South Carolina into a royal colony.		**1719, Dec. 14.** Founding of the *Boston Gazette*.
1720–9	1720–9	1720–9
1720. In the opinion of the Counsel to the Board of Trade, common law extends to the colonies. **Nov.** Trenchard and Gordon begin publishing *Cato's Letters* in response to South Sea Bubble crisis. Used by Americans to criticize Navigation Laws. **1721, April 1.** Walpole's administration begins years of metropolitan "salutary neglect" of colonial affairs.		**1721, April.** Smallpox epidemic breaks out in Boston. 6,045 out of a population of 10,597 contract the disease before epidemic ends (spring 1722). Dr. Zabdiel Boylston begins

		inoculation treatment (June 26, 1721) and calculates that of 286 persons inoculated only 6 (2.1%) die, while of those 5,759 not inoculated 844 (12.8%) die. Despite the approval of the clergy, popular objections to inoculation remain vehement. Cotton Mather's son and two slaves stoned by mob.
		1723, April. William Price, influenced by Wren's Georgian style, begins building Boston's famous "Old North Church" C of E. It was from this steeple that a lantern was hung in 1775 to signal Paul Revere of British tactics. **Oct.** German Baptists in Germantown, Pennsylvania, found first Dunker Church in America.
1724, April 6. Duke of Newcastle begins benign 24-year tenure as Secretary of State, Southern Department.	**1724, Aug. 14.** Dummer's/ Lovewell's War begins between New Englanders and French-backed Abenaki Amerindians. Settlers win decisive Battle of Fryeburg, Maine (May 9, 1725), but sporadic fighting continues until Abenaki recognize British authority in 1729.	
1727, June 21. Death of George I. Accession of George II.	**1727, Feb.** Beginning of indecisive 13-month Anglo-Spanish War.	**1727, Oct.** Benjamin Franklin begins great public career with establishment of the Junto, an Enlightenment benevolent society. In October 1728 he publishes "Articles of Belief and Acts of Religion," espousing reason as basis of faith, and next year purchases the *Pennsylvania Gazette* as an oracle for his secular and religious beliefs.
		1728. New York City Jews build America's first synagogue.
1730–9	1730–9	1730–9
		1730, May. Virginia passes Tobacco Inspection Act favoring larger producers of better quality leaves. Maryland later follows, with resulting tobacco cutting riots in both colonies.
		1731, May 7. Parliament allows direct export of some colonial products to Ireland.

1732, June 20. Charter and parliamentary subsidies granted to Edward Oglethorpe and trustees for establishment of the colony of Georgia.

1733, March. Walpole faces political difficulties over excise crisis.

1734, Oct. John Peter Zenger, publisher of *New York Weekly Journal*, acquitted of libel charge; landmark case in the history of freedom of speech.

1737, May 25. Thomas Hutchinson begins political career with election to Massachusetts House of Representatives.
    June 27. Lord Monson begins benign term as President of Board of Trade.

1732, June 20. Colony of Georgia established with slavery prohibition and parliamentary subsidies to encourage white settlement, partly in hope of securing South Carolina from dangers of slave revolt and attack from Spanish Florida.

1739, Sept. 9. First of three slave revolts in South Carolina in ne year. 21 Whites and 44 Blacks perish.
    Oct. 23. War of Jenkins's Ear inspired by Captain Robert Jenkins's report to Parliament that Spanish customs officers had cut off his ear for suspected smuggling.

1732. Franklin founds Library Company of Philadelphia, the world's first circulating library. In December 1733 he begins publishing *Poor Richard's Almanack*.

1733, March. Walpole's attempt to increase government finance by replacing tobacco and wine duties with inland duties results in excise crisis.
    May 17. Parliament passes Molasses Act establishing 6d per gallon duty on American imports of the product from the West Indies. Largely avoided by bribes to customs officers.

1734, Dec. Series of emotional conversions brought about by evangelist Jonathan Edwards marks beginning of Great Awakening. Edwards publishes theory and method of converting in his *Personal Narrative* (1739). English Methodist John Wesley begins tour (Feb. 1736), and George Whitefield follows (Aug. 1739).

1735, Feb. First Moravian community established at Savannah, Georgia.

1736, Aug. 6. William Parks begins publishing the *Virginia Gazette*.

1737, March 17. Boston sees first celebration of St. Patrick's Day not held solely in church.

1740–9	1740–9	1740–9
1740, Nov. 10. Publication of Proprietor William Stephens's roseate *A State of the Province of Georgia*. Patrick Tailfer et al. make vitriolic response in *A True and Historical Narrative of the Colony of Georgia* (1741).	**1740, Jan.** James Oglethorpe invades Spanish Florida but fails to capture St. Augustine. **Dec.** War of Jenkins's Ear subsumed by War of Austrian Succession (King George's War) against France and Spain.	**1740.** Eliza Lucas Pinckney experiments with crops, primarily indigo, to supplement South Carolina's rice staple. British Government establishes 6d per pound bounty on indigo in 1748. **Feb. 15.** Naturalization Act empowers colonies to naturalize foreign Protestants resident for seven or more years. **March 25.** Wesley and Whitefield promote building of Bethesda Orphanage in Savannah. Whitefield embarks on tour of New England (1740); Edwards publishes *Some Thoughts Concerning the Present Revival of Religion in New England* and is criticized in Charles Chauncey's *Enthusiasms Described and Cautioned Against* (1742). **Sept. 8.** Nine directors sign articles forming a Land Bank in Massachusetts (credits secured by land) in response to lack of adequate medium of exchange. Legalized by JPs (Dec. 4) amid intense controversy.
	1741, Dec. "Negro Conspiracy" panic in New York City. Savage punishments.	**1741, March.** Parliament extends Bubble Act to colonies, prohibiting formation of corporations without parliamentary consent. Many colonists, including Samuel Adams's father, lose property in resulting Massachusetts Land Bank dissolution.
1742, Feb. 2. Walpole driven from office, the first Prime Minister to resign over defeats in the House of Commons.	**1742, July 7.** Spanish attack on Georgia repelled at Bloody Swamp.	**1742, Sept. 24.** Boston's Faneuil Hall opens to public. Work begins on another famous building, Carpenters Hall in Philadelphia, where the Continental Congress will sit. **1743, May.** Franklin founds the American Philosophical Society. Also co-founds the Academy of Philadelphia (Nov. 1749), later renamed University of Pennsylvania. College of New Jersey, later renamed Princeton University, founded by Presbyterians (Oct. 1746).

1744, Nov. 23. Pelhamites petition George II to force Cartaret to resign, but William Pitt's exclusion from new ministry forces Henry Pelham to resign (Jan. 1746). 1747 elections return Pelhamites to large Commons majority and restore stability to British politics.

1744, March 15. France officially declares war on England.

1745, June 16. New Englanders capture French Ft. Louisburg, Cape Breton Island.
July. Charles Edward Stuart lands in Scotland. Jacobite Uprising peaks with invasion of England (Nov.–Dec.). Last casualties recorded at Clifton (Dec. 18) after which Jacobites disperse and Stuart flees.
Sept. 19. Trespass arrest of Samuel Baldwin of Newark precipitates ten years of sporadic land riots in New Jersey.
Nov. 29. French and Amerindians burn Saratoga, New York.

1745, Jan. 17. Jonas Green founds the *Maryland Gazette*.

1746, May 28. Thomas Hutchinson begins two years as Speaker of Massachusetts House. Becomes Member of Council in May 1749.

1746, March. John Woolman begins tour of Upper South colonies persuading fellow Quakers to free slaves.

1747, May. George II grants 500,000 acres to Ohio Company of Virginia. Virginia Council grants 800,000 acres to Loyal Company (July 12, 1748). Both companies send agents to survey in the early 1750s. French dispatch Jean Baptiste le Moyne de Bienville to make claims and establish forts in the Ohio Valley.

1747, Dec. First appearance of Jared Eliot's, scientific agriculture theories in *An Essay on Field Husbandry*.

1748, Oct. Publication of Montesquieu's *Spirit of the Laws*, which influenced later American constitutional thought.
Nov. 5. Earl of Halifax appointed President of Board of Trade, and Duke of Bedford Secretary of State, Southern Department. Appointment of these activists reflects increased metropolitan concern over growing importance of provinces and with political and social disorders therein. Halifax secures increased Board of Trade power

1748, Oct. 18. Treaty of Aix-la-Chapelle ends French claim to Austria. American gains returned to France. In 1749 Britain establishes Nova Scotia with parliamentary subsidies as full colony and buffer zone.

through greater scrutiny over colonial legislation, power of gubernatorial appointment and oversight, and the establishment of a packet-boat system for greater communication within the empire (1755). Activism temporarily halts, however, with war (1754–63).		**1749, Jan. 10.** Georgia trustees relinquish ban on slavery. **March.** Parliament rejects Board of Trade bill to ban colonial paper money which enabled colonists to pay creditors (often British) in depreciated currency.
1750–9	1750–9	1750–9
1750, Jan. Jonathan Mayhew delivers famous sermon in Boston, *A Discourse Concerning Unlimited Submission*, advocating virtue as a defense against tyranny. **1751, May 9.** Benjamin Franklin elected to Pennsylvania House of Assembly.		**1750, June 24.** Iron Act forbids inter-colonial iron trade but allows duty-free imports to Britain. Currency Act bans issuing of paper money in New England as of September 25, 1751. **1751.** Bishop Thomas Sherlock pushes Parliament for suffragan bishops in America. **May 9.** Franklin publishes "Rattlesnakes for Felons," satirically offering rattlesnakes in exchange for convicts transported to America. Wins Copley Medal of the Royal Society of London for his electrical studies (Nov. 23, 1753). Another scientific achievement was the first clock made entirely in America (1754), built by Benjamin Bannecker, a Maryland free Black. Great writings of the decade include Franklin's *Observations Concerning the Increase of Mankind* (1751); Samuel Johnson's *Elementa Philosophica* (1752); Edwards's *Freedom of Will* (1754); William Smith Jr.'s *The History of the Province of New York* (1757).
1752, April 22. Lt.-Governor Dinwiddie of Virginia attempts to levy fee on land grants. Resulting Pistole Fee Controversy reveals disagreement over nature of property rights between Crown and colonists.	**1752, June.** French attack Pickawillany trading post (at present-day Erie, Pennsylvania) and erect Ft. Presque Isle.	**1752, Aug.** Liberty Bell, a gift from England celebrating Pennsylvania's 50 years under Charter of Privileges, arrives in Philadelphia. Found to be cracked, it is twice recast before being hung in the State House (now Independence Hall). Tolled

June 25. Georgia trustees surrender authority to Crown.

1754, March 6. Death of Pelham inspires George II to complain, "I shall now have no more peace." Duke of Newcastle becomes Prime Minister.

1756, June 29. Newcastle appoints Pitt Secretary of State, forming a coalition government

---

1753, March–April. French erect Fts. Le Boeuf and Verango.

Oct. 31. Governor Dinwiddie of Virginia dispatches George Washington to demand French withdrawal from Ohio territory. Refusal reported in January 1754.

1754, Feb. Dinwiddie orders construction of fort at forks of Ohio River but French seize the site and erect Ft. Duquesne. Washington skirmishes with French at Great Meadows and erects Ft. Necessity (May 28).

June 19. Representatives of Iroquois Nations, New York, Pennsylvania, Maryland, and New England colonies meet for Albany Congress to discuss defense against French. Endorses Franklin's Plan of Union but it is rejected by colonies.

July 3. Washington forced to withdraw from Ft. Necessity, leaving French in control of the Ohio Valley. Marks beginning of series of British defeats.

1755, July 9. William Braddock defeated at Battle of the Wilderness and killed in retreat at Monongahela.

Sept. 8. William Johnson defeats French in Battle of Lake George.

Sept.–Oct. British expel Acadians from Nova Scotia.

1756, Jan. 16. Britain enters alliance with Prussia. France allies with Austria (May 1).

---

in celebration of Stamp Act repeal and Independence, its career as a symbol of liberty continued with the anti-slavery movement. It was cracked on June 8, 1835 while being rung to commemorate the death of Chief Justice Marshall and has remained in this condition ever since.

Sept 5. Lewis Hallam's American Company opens tour with performance of *The Merchant of Venice* in Williamsburg: start of professional theater in America.

1754, Aug. Encouraged by Woolman's *Some Considerations on the Keeping of Negroes* (1754), the Philadelphia Yearly resolves against Quakers buying slaves. Yearly of September 1755 advises monthly meetings to admonish Friends who continue to buy slaves. New York and New England Quakers follow. Woolman again tours the Upper South speaking to Quakers against slavery (1757).

Oct. 31. Founding of Kings College of New York, later renamed Columbia University.

Nov. Scottish philosopher David Hume begins publishing three-volume *The History of England*. Completed in 1762.

with Pitt controlling foreign affairs.
    Sept. Thomas Pownall replaces William Shirley as Governor of Massachusetts, Hutchinson appointed Lt.-Governor.
	Feb. 17. William Johnson appointed to new post of Indian Superintendent for the Northern District, Edmond Atkin for the Southern District.
	    May 15. Declarations mark the official beginning of the Seven Years' War (French and Indian War) after three years of fighting.
	    June 28. French capture Minorca.	

1757, Feb. 3. Pennsylvania elects Franklin agent to England. Franklin also appointed to represent New Jersey, Maryland, and Georgia.	**1757, Aug. 9.** French capture Ft. William Henry.	
1758, Sept. 14. Virginia Assembly passes Two Penny Act, permitting payment of obligations to clergy in tobacco at 2d per pound. Clergy seeks royal disallowance, and metropolitan authorities object to lack of suspending clause. Law finally disallowed by Privy Council.	**1758, July 8.** French capture Ticonderoga, but Pitt's new war policy meets success with capture of Louisburg (July 26), Ft. Frontenac (Aug. 27), Ft. Duquesne (renamed Pittsburg) and Ticonderoga (Nov. 25). **1759.** British capture Ft. Niagara (July 25), Lake Champlain (July 26), and Quebec (except Montreal, Sept. 18).	
1760	1760	1760
June 3. Thomas Pownall becomes Governor of South Carolina. Replaced in Massachusetts by Francis Bernard. Bernard appoints Hutchinson Chief Justice (Nov. 10). **Aug.** New York Governor Cadwallader Colden causes controversy by not granting "good behavior" tenure to new Chief Justice, Benjamin Pratt. Board of Trade reiterates this policy, evoking similar controversies in New Jersey and both Carolinas in the early 1760s. Colden provokes further judicial controversy by overriding jury decision (Oct. 1764). **Oct. 25.** Death of George II. Accession of George III.	**Aug. 8–9.** Cherokees capture Ft. Loudon, Tennessee, and massacre British retreating to Ft. Prince George. **Sept. 8.** French surrender Montreal. Thomas Gage becomes Military Governor of Quebec. British capture Detroit (Nov. 29). **Dec.** Frontier governors instructed to deny land grants in Amerindian territories.	
1761	1761	1761
Feb. Massachusetts Writs of Assistance case; court rules	**Oct. 8.** Death of Indian Superintendent (Southern	

in favor of allowing customs officials to search private homes. Controversy results in James Otis's resignation from admiralty court and publication of his *Vindication of the Conduct of the House of Representatives*. The *Boston Gazette* also establishes itself as a major patriot advocate. **March 21.** Lord Sandys appointed President of Board of Trade. **May 25.** Lord Bute appointed Secretary of State, Northern Department. **Oct. 5.** Pitt resigns over conduct of war. Replaced by Halifax as Secretary of State. Halifax also receives Northern Department post in 1762.	District) Edmond Atkin. Replaced by John Stuart.	
1762	1762	1762
May 26. Resignation of Newcastle. Beginning of Bute ministry. **May.** Bernard and Council spend £72 of Massachusetts public funds fighting French privateers. Legislators object to this violation of their right to oversee appropriations. **Sept.** South Carolina Governor Thomas Boone sparks election controversy and political deadlock by refusing to seat Christopher Gadsden in the Commons House of Assembly.	**Jan.** Britain declares war on Spain. **Feb.** British begin attacking French West Indies. **Nov. 13.** France cedes Louisiana to Spain in secret Treaty of Fontainebleau.	St. Cecilia Society, America's first music society and a gathering place for the elite, established in Charles Town.
1763	1763	1763
March 1. Charles Townshend appointed President of Board of Trade. Replaced by Lords Shelburne (April) and then Hillsborough (May). **April 8.** Resignation of Bute. Beginning of Grenville ministry. **April 23.** John Wilkes attacks the government in issue no. 45 of *The North Briton*. Grenville has Wilkes and 49 associates arrested under general warrant. Obtaining habeas corpus, Wilkes is acquitted through MPs' freedom from conviction for libel. Colonial newspapers sympathize with Wilkes and begin criticizing prospective sugar tax.	**Feb. 10.** Peace of Paris. Britain gains Quebec, Florida, and all North America east of the Mississippi. Military presence of 15 regiments remain under Gage, based in New York. Cost of maintenance estimated at £225,000. Lord Bute suggests colonists should pay. **May 7–Nov. 28.** Pontiac's Uprising. Johnson and Stuart estimate Amerindian population at 10,000. Congress of Augusta (Nov. 5–10) is first of eight pre-Revolution southern Amerindian treaties. **June.** Establishment of Mississippi Company, which	**April.** Customs Board investigation of colonial tax evasion reveals annual revenue from American customs at £1,800. Suggests revitalization of Molasses Act (1733). Parliament passes "An Act for the further Improvement of His Majesties Revenue of Customs" (April 19) for inspection of ships below 50 tons, encouraging seizures, and preventing smuggling. Publication of first volume of Catherine Sawbridge Macaulay's *History of England*. Publication of Rev. East Apthorp's *Considerations of the SPG*. Answered by Jonathan

	begins petitioning for western lands. **Oct. 7.** Royal Proclamation Line forbids settlement west of line marked by Alleghenies. **Dec. 13–27.** Paxton Boys massacre peaceful Conestoga Amerindians and march on Philadelphia.	Mayhew's *Observations on the Charter*, opening controversy on the establishment of an American episcopacy.
1764	**1764**	**1764**
April 5. American Duties Act creates new Vice Admiralty Court in Halifax, Nova Scotia. Publications against the Act include Otis's *Rights of the British Colonists Asserted and Proved*. Thomas Pownall recommends more effective policy from metropolitan viewpoint in *The Administration of the Colonies*. **June 13.** To combat British policy the Massachusetts House establishes the first Committee of Correspondence. **Dec.** John Olyphant of Jamaica refuses to pay libel damages awarded against him, invoking "parliamentary privilege" principle. Governor Lyttelton has Olyphant arrested. House of Assembly frees him and arrests plaintiffs for seizing his property. Controversy paralyzes Jamaican politics for three years.	**Feb. 13.** Disgruntled westerners deliver *A Remonstrance from the Pennsylvania Frontier* to their governor and assembly. **July 10.** Board of Trade issues "Plan of '64" for cooperation with Amerindians. Johnson secures first of 11 pre-Revolution northern Amerindian treaties.	**April 5.** American Duties/Sugar Act replaces Molasses Act with 3d per gallon duty, extends number of goods enumerated under Navigation Acts (all goods enumerated by 1767), and makes duties and fines payable in sterling. Currency Act (April 19) extends prohibition of paper money to colonies south of New York; all paper money in circulation withdrawn. **Aug.** Boston merchants agree on non-importation to counter Sugar Act. Mechanics join agreement (Sept.) and other colonies follow. Publication of Richard Peters's *Thoughts on the Present State of the Church of England in America*, arguing for institution of four suffragan bishops in America. Provokes Archbishops Secker and Drummond to petition for colonial episcopacy.
1765	**1765**	**1765**
March 22. Parliamentary opposition to Stamp Act is led by William Pitt in the Commons and Earl Camden in the Lords. **April.** Samuel Adams resigns as Boston tax collector in response to Stamp Act and is subsequently elected to House of Representatives. Publications against the Act include Otis's *Vindication of the British Colonies*; John Adams's *Dissertation on Canon and Feudal Law*. The Virginian Patrick Henry makes famous "Treason Speech" and Burgesses pass the Virginia Resolutions (May 29). Sons of Liberty organize various colonies. **June 8.** Massachusetts General Court sends Circular to other	**March 24.** Mutiny/Quartering Act obliges colonists to provide barracks and supplies for British soldiers. **Aug. 14.** Bostonians hang Stamp Collector Andrew Oliver in effigy from Liberty Tree and burn his house. Oliver resigns (Aug. 15). Hutchinson's house also burned (Aug. 26). Such acts, though condemned by Sons of Liberty, render Stamp Act unenforceable in most colonies.	**March 22.** Parliament passes Stamp Act to be effective November 1. Attempts compromise by exempting ships under 20 tons from detailed documentation and allows direct importation of colonial iron and lumber to Ireland. **Oct. 28.** New York agreement on non-importation. Other colonists follow. Colonists continue to conduct business without stamps after November 1.

colonies promoting Stamp Act Congress. **July 10.** Resignation of Grenville. Beginning of Rockingham ministry. **Oct. 7–25.** Stamp Act Congress, attended by eight colonies, meets in New York. Ratifies John Dickinson's "Declaration of Rights and Grievances" (Oct. 19).		
1766	1766	1766
March 18. Repeal of Stamp Act. Indemnity Act prevents prosecution of non-compliants. But Declaratory Act asserts Parliament's right to legislate for colonies "in all cases whatso-ever." Sons of Liberty disband. **May.** Death of John Robinson reveals corruption in Virginia gentry, provoking reforms which include separation of offices of Speaker and Treasurer. Tension highest with Robinson's father-in-law, John Chiswell, illegally bailed on a murder charge (June). **July.** Resignation of Rockingham. Beginning of Pitt ministry. Shelburne appointed Secretary of State. Mental health of Pitt (now Earl of Chatham) deteriorates, Charles Townshend becomes *de facto* Prime Minister by September. Lord North becomes Chancellor of the Exchequer. **Dec. 18.** Robert Nugent appointed President of Board of Trade.	**Jan.** Second Quartering Act billets troops on unoccupied dwellings and taverns. New York refuses to comply. Soldiers and citizens brawl in New York streets (Aug. 10–11). **May.** New York City crowd destroys opulent new Chapel St. Theater. Discontented tenants revolt in Hudson Valley. Settlers occupy Monongahela Valley of Pennsylvania without Amerindian consent or purchase. Ohio Company speculates in region of Pittsburgh. Illinois Company petitions for 1.2 million acres in Mississippi Valley.	**Jan. 17.** Petitions of British merchants affected by boycotts reach Parliament. Franklin testifies to Parliament that the Stamp Act is an "internal tax" and that Parliament is restricted to levying "external taxes" (Feb. 13). Parliament repeals (March 18). **Sept.** Charles Townshend begins devising external taxes for America. **Oct.** Anglican convocation in New Jersey petitions Archbishop of Canterbury and Bishops of London and Oxford for American bishoprics. **Nov. 1.** American Trade Act reduces duty on molasses to 1d per gallon and creates two freeports in the Caribbean.
1767	1767	1767
June 29. Townshend Acts create duty collection and enforcement agency, Board of Customs Commissioners, based in Boston. Sons of Liberty reorganize in various colonies. **Sept. 4.** Death of Townshend. Prime Ministerial duties fall to Duke of Grafton. **Nov. 5.** Customs officials arrive in Boston. John Dickinson begins publishing *Letters from a Farmer in Pennsylvania* (dated Nov. 5; published Nov. 30).	**May.** Disorders against Townshend Acts include attack on British sea captain by gentry-led Charles Town mob. Another such attack (Sept.) is led by Mayor of Norfolk, Virginia. **June 6.** New York Assembly finally appropriates money for quartering, but petitions Parliament to repeal. **June 29.** Parliament passes New York Restraining Act nullifying a provisioning act of 1766. Not enforced, however, because of June 6 compliance.	**Feb. 27.** Parliament, despite Townshend's opposition, forces reduction of British land tax. **March 16.** Massachusetts House votes to prohibit slave trade. After four years in committee stage, however, Hutchinson vetoes. **April 23.** Staging of Thomas Godfrey's *The Prince of Parthia* is first performance of a play written by an American. Other achievements include publication of *To the University of Cambridge*, a poem by African-born slave Phillis Wheatley, and

Dec. 30. Massachusetts General Court adopts Samuel Adams's Circular Letter condemning Townshend Acts.		construction of America's first planetarium by David Rittenhouse. **June 29.** Parliament passes Townshend Duties, tariffs on goods imported to America, believing colonists would accept "external" taxes. **Oct.** Second Anglican Convocation in New Jersey. Pamphlet war begins between Thomas Chandler and Charles Chauncey. **Dec. 31.** Non-importation agreements within and among various colonies commence.
1768	1768	1768
Jan. 20. Hillsborough appointed Secretary of new Colonial Department. **Feb. 11.** Adams's Circular Letter appears. **March.** Creation of new Vice Admiralty Courts in Boston, Philadelphia, and Charles Town. **April 21.** Hillsborough instructs Bernard to order Massachusetts General Court to rescind Circular Letter and other Governors to dissolve assemblies before countenancing it. **July 12.** Soame Jenyns appointed President of Board of Trade. **July 18.** *Boston Gazette* publishes "The Liberty Song." **Sept. 22.** Massachusetts Convention meets to discuss Townshend Acts. **Oct.** Chatham, now recovered and horrified at government policy in his absence, resigns. Makes Grafton Prime Minister in name as well as practice.	**March 7.** Board of Trade *Report on the Western Problem* rejects idea of inland colonies, yet Grand Ohio Company petitions for 2.4 million acres for a western proprietary colony (1769). **June 10.** Seizure of John Hancock's sloop causes "Liberty Riot." Bostonians attack Customs Commissioners who withdraw to Castle William (June 11) and request military aid (June 15). **Oct. 1.** Gage's troops arrive in Boston to restore order.	**March.** *New York Gazette* publishes "The American Whig," a Presbyterian attack on episcopalianism. Samuel Seabury and others respond with "A Whip for the American Whig."
1769	1769	1769
Feb. 9. Parliament revives Statute of Henry VIII for juryless trials of provincials in London. **May 16.** George Washington presents George Mason's Virginia Resolves to the Burgesses, who pass them. Massachusetts voters oust rescinders and return supporters of the Circular Letter, including John Hancock.	**Oct. 9.** Regulators petition North Carolina Assembly against eastern economic and political domination.	**Jan. 26.** MP Isaac Barré predicts revolt of colonists if Parliament persists in taxation policy. **May 17.** Prorogued Burgesses meet in Williamsburg tavern and adopt the Virginia Association, a non-importation organization. **June 3.** In Norriton, Philadelphia, William Smith, John Lukens, David Rittenhouse, and John Sellers of the American Philosophical Society participate

Aug. 1. On departure of Bernard, Hutchinson becomes Governor of Massachusetts. **Dec.** South Carolina Commons votes £1,500 to pay debts of John Wilkes, arrested and expelled from Parliament after his election and re-election to the seat for Middlesex.		in international scientific observation of the Transit of Venus over the sun's disk. **Dec.** Cabinet decides to repeal all Townshend Duties except that on tea.
1770	1770	1770
Jan. 31. Resignation of Grafton. Beginning of North ministry. **March.** On Hillsborough's instruction Hutchinson moves Massachusetts General Court to Cambridge. Inspires controversy over metropolitan alteration of colonial custom. Irish patriot Charles Lucas pens *Letter to the Town of Boston* opposing such attacks by the British ministry. Samuel Adams mounts campaign of opposition to British military presence. **April 12.** Repeal of Townshend Acts does not include the principle of making governors and magistrates independent of assemblies and answerable to Crown. **April 14.** British officials threaten Treasurer of South Carolina with severe penalties if any public funds are appropriated without executive approval. Wilkes Fund Controversy paralyzes South Carolina politics until Independence. **Nov.** Maryland Governor Robert Eden's Proclamation setting scale of government officers' fees inspires three-year controversy. Charles Carroll of Carrollton ("First Citizen") establishes himself as patriot leader by opposing Eden.	**Jan. 19.** Confrontations between soldiers and New York citizens culminate in Battle of Golden Hill. **March 5.** Similar confrontations result in King Street Riot (Boston Massacre) in which five die. **Dec. 4.** Verdict in Boston Massacre case acquits six soldiers and finds two guilty of manslaughter. Offenders branded on the thumb.	**March 5.** Parliament debates repeal of Duties. Townshend Acts, except tea duty and Board of Customs Commissioners, repealed on April 12. **Nov. 26.** Thomas Jefferson takes residence in small brick house at Monticello. Building of the mansion began the previous fall. Other achievements include Wheatley's verse commemorating the death of George Whitefield; Bannecker's clock that chimed all hours, the first of its kind in America; and Benjamin Rush's publication of the first American chemistry textbook, *A Syllabus of a Course of Lectures on Chemistry*, and his appointment as America's first Professor of Chemistry at the College of Philadelphia.
1771	1771	1771
Sept. Samuel Adams, concerned about quiescence, proposes network of corresponding societies to instruct and arouse the public. Boston Town Meeting forms Committee of Correspondence. Other towns follow.	**Jan. 15.** Johnson ("Bloody") Act makes Regulator movement treasonable in North Carolina. Governor Tryon crushes Regulators at Alamance Creek, near Hillsborough (May 16).	**Jan.** Non-importation ends and trade returns to normal. **May.** "The Rising Glory of America" is read at Princeton commencement, attended by its co-author, Philip Freneau. **June 4.** Beginning of nine-month convention of clergy in Virginia to discuss the episcopal question.

1772	1772	1772
May. Elbridge Gerry elected to Massachusetts House and Boston Committee of Correspondence. **June 13.** Hutchinson announces he would now receive salary from Crown. General Court expresses resentment at gubernatorial escape from accountability to legislature. **Aug.** Hillsborough resigns as Colonial Secretary in opposition to projected colony of Vandalia in Ohio region. Replaced by Earl of Dartmouth. **Nov.** Boston Committee of Correspondence endorses Samuel Adams's *A State of the Rights of the Colonists* and other writings.	**June 10.** *Gaspée* incident. Rhode Islanders burn Royal Navy schooner. Judge Stephen Hopkins prevents arrest of offenders.	Imports from colonies equal 36% of all imports to Britain. 37% of all British manufactures are exported to the colonies. Colonial population reaches almost 2.5 million.
1773	**1773**	**1773**
Sept. North Carolina Assembly devises new superior court law ignoring royal prohibition of laws for confiscating non-residents' property in debt suits. Controversy paralyzes North Carolina legislature and court system until Independence. **Oct. 16.** Mass meeting in Philadelphia condemns Tea Act. Virginians and Bostonians call on colonists to form inter-colonial correspondence committees. **Dec.** Samuel Adams secures publication of letters by Bernard and Hutchinson advocating reduction of colonial liberties.	**Dec. 16.** Boston Tea Party. Sons of Liberty, disguised as Amerindians, board the *Dartmouth, Eleanor,* and *Beaver* and dump 90,000 lb of East India tea into the harbor. Similar incidents occur in other colonies.	**Jan. 12.** Establishment in Charles Town of America's first museum. Walnut St. Jail in Philadelphia opens, the first American penitentiary. **Feb.** Pennsylvania legislature finally suceeds in killing the slave trade with £20 duty per head. Wheatley publishes *Poems on various subjects, Religious and Moral*. Rush cites Wheatley as evidence that Africans are not inferior to Europeans in *An Address to the Inhabitants of the British Settlements in America, Upon Slave-Keeping*. Mercy Otis Warren writes *The Adulateur*, portraying Hutchinson as "Rapatio." **May 10.** Tea Act gives monopoly to East India Company by grant-ing tax concessions so it could sell at low prices to Americans. **June 15.** Parliament modifies Currency Act to allow issue of paper money through loan offices to pay public debts. **July 14.** First Annual Conference of American Methodists held in Philadelphia.
1774	**1774**	**1774**
Jan. 29. Solicitor General Alexander Wedderburn	**July 12.** Death of Indian Superintendent (Northern	**March.** Barré reminds Parliament of vast importance

humiliates Franklin before Privy Council over release of Hutchinson–Bernard letters and Boston Tea Party. Parliament passes Coercive or Intolerable Acts comprising Boston Port Act (March 31) closing the port; Massachusetts Government Act (May 20) providing that the King appoint Council members and town meetings occur only annually and discuss only local matters; Administration of Justice Act (May 20) providing for trials of provincials in other colonies or in England away from sympathetic juries; Quartering Act (June 2) billeting troops on unoccupied buildings. In addition, the Quebec Act (June 22) transfers jurisdiction of western lands to the Canadian Catholic colony governed by French civil law with no jury trials or elected assembly.

May 13. Gage arrives in Boston to replace Hutchinson as Military Governor.

May 17. Rhode Island issues the first call for a "Grand Congress."

June 17. Massachusetts calls for Continental Congress. All colonies except Georgia begin electing delegates. Gage dissolves Massachusetts General Court. Representatives meet illegally in Concord and invite the Pre-Government Act Council to resume business as if still under the 1691 Charter. Other colonial legislatures similarly ignore prorogations and dissolutions. Joseph Warren presents "Suffolk Resolves" (Sept. 9) calling for non-importation, though most colonies prefer to await actions by Continental Congress. Opposition publications include Thomas Jefferson's *Summary View of the Rights of British America*. Jamaica sends "Petition and Memorial" to George III supporting Massachusetts. Other island governors report a "republican spirit." In Parliament itself Chatham, Wilkes, Edmund Burke, and Isaac Barré maintain vocal dissent.

District) William Johnson. Replaced by his nephew Guy Johnson.

May–Aug. Crowds close Massachusetts court houses in response to Coercive Acts and force judges to resign in public ceremonies.

Sept. 1. Boston-based British troops seize cannon and powder from stores in Cambridge and Charles Town.

Oct. 7. Massachusetts Congress names John Hancock to head Committee of Safety authorized to call out militia. Calls on localities to drill militia (Feb. 1775).

Dec. 14. Warned by Paul Revere of plan to garrison Portsmouth, New Hampshire, a band led by John Sullivan peacefully over-awes guards at Ft. William and Mary and carries off arms and powder.

of American commerce to Britain.

March 8. Massachusetts Assembly attempts to prohibit slave trade but is prorogued next day.

June 5. Solemn League and Covenant, drawn up by Boston Committee of Correspondence, binds subscribers to end trade in and consumption of British imports as of October 1.

Oct. 20. Congress recommends that colonies discourage horse racing, cock fighting, gambling, theater, and other "expensive diversions and entertainments." Evidence shows that such activities continued.

Oct. 24. Congress forms the Continental Association, a non-importation organization, taking effect on December 1. Enforced locally by Committees of Inspection.

Sept. 5. First Continental Congress meets in Philadelphia. Warns Massachusetts to avoid aggression but promises aid if attacked. Rejects Joseph Galloway's "Plan of Union" for an American Congress sharing power with Parliament (Sept. 28). Adopts "Declaration and Resolves" against Intolerable Acts and taxation without representation (Oct. 14). Adopts Continental Association for non-importation and authorizes local Committees of Inspection to enforce embargo if demands not met within one year (Oct. 18). Adjourns (Oct. 26), resolving to reconvene next May. **Oct. 7.** Massachusetts House, meeting in Salem, declares itself a Provincial Congress. **Dec.** Pamphlet controversy between John Adams, writing as "Novanglus" and the Tory Daniel Leonard, as "Massachusettensis," who argues for Crown sovereignty whereby liberty is granted at pleasure. Adams replies that sovereignty is grounded in consent and Parliament's power is limited to regulating external trade.		
1775	1775	1775
Jan. 20. House of Lords rejects Chatham's conciliatory Provisional Bill whereby Parliament would remain sovereign in America but renounce taxation power. Parliament declares Massachusetts in a state of rebellion (Feb. 9) but endorses North's conciliation plan whereby Parliament would forsake all but external taxes on colonies that taxed themselves (Feb. 27). Rejects Burke's conciliation bill entailing acceptance of Continental Congress demands (March 22). **March 21.** Franklin departs England for America. Arrives in Philadelphia May 5. **March 23.** Patrick Henry predicts fighting in	**April 14.** Gage receives letter from Dartmouth commanding forceful implementation of Coercive Acts but refusing request for 20,000 troops to restore order. Dartmouth still believes trouble caused by a few rabble rousers. **April 18–19.** "Midnight Ride" of Paul Revere warns rural patriots that "the British are coming" to seize defense supplies. **April 19.** Battles of Lexington and Concord. Patriots harass redcoat retreat to Boston. Massachusetts Congress mobilizes 13,600 soldiers. Neighboring colonies form militia groups to march on Boston. **May 10.** Ethan Allen and Benedict Arnold capture Ft. Ticonderoga and Crown Point.	**Feb.** Massachusetts Congress appoints Drs. Benjamin Church and Joseph Warren to oversee medical needs of local militia. Committee of Safety later finds surgeons inadequately trained. Congress further shows increased professionalization of medicine through creation of Army Medical Department (May), although it suffered from inadequate funds and feuding administrators. Benjamin Church appointed first Surgeon General of Continental Army (July 25). **Feb. 22.** "American Manufactory of Woolens, Linens and Cottons" established as America's first joint stock company. Shares sold on subscription at £10 each. **March 30.** Parliament passes "New England Trade and

New England in famous "Liberty or Death" speech.

May 10. Second Continental Congress meets in Philadelphia. Resolves to put colonies in a state of defense (May 15).

May 16. Provincial Congress of Massachusetts, after its prospective constitution is rejected by voters in America's first referendum, suggests that Congress write a model constitution.

May 31. Mecklenburg County (North Carolina) Resolutions void all laws and commissions emanating from London.

June 9. Congress recommends Provincial Congress of Massachusetts elect its own executive Council in place of Crown appointees imposed by the Government Act. Massachusetts elects a 28-member alternative council and declares the 1691 Charter a temporary constitution (June 29).

July 6. Congress establishes Post Office with Franklin as Post Master General. Adopts "Olive Branch Petition" to George III explaining necessity of defensive measures, blaming corrupt ministers, and requesting the King to end armed conflict (July 8). Postpones decision on Franklin's Plan for Union and proposals for opening commerce and seeking political alliance with foreign nations (July 21). Rejects North's conciliation plan (July 31). Adjourns (Aug. 2).

Aug. 23. George III rejects the "Olive Branch."

Sept. 12. Congress reconvenes, now with representatives from Georgia, the last mainland colony to send delegates. Recommends that colonies write new constitutions.

Nov. Dartmouth resigns as Colonial Secretary. Replaced by Lord George Germain, Viscount Sackville.

Nov. 4. New Jersey Assembly declares reports of colonists' seeking independence groundless.

Nov. 16. Burke makes famous conciliation speech proposing

May 25. Generals Sir William Howe, Sir Henry Clinton, and John Burgoyne arrive to assist Gage.

May 26. Congress resolves on state of defense, petitions Canadians to join resistance (May 29), forms Continental Army (June 15) of which George Washington takes command (July 3), decides to invade Canada and issues £2,000 in paper money for expenses (June 22), and issues John Dickinson's "Declaration of the Causes and Necessity of Taking up Arms" (July 6).

June 12. Gage imposes martial law, declares Americans in treason, and offers pardon to all those who surrender (except John Hancock and John Adams).

June 17. British capture Bunker Hill but take heavy losses in frontal assault.

Aug. 23. George III proclaims the colonies in "open and avowed rebellion," declaring. "The die is now cast. The colonies must either submit or triumph." North issues "A Proclamation for Suppressing Armed Rebellion."

Sept. 25. Americans invade Canada, reaching Montreal (Dec. 13), where Ethan Allen is captured and held for war's duration. Forced to retreat (Dec. 31).

Oct. 10. Howe succeeds Gage as British Commander-in-Chief.

Nov. 7. Governor Dunmore declares martial law in Virginia, offers freedom to slaves who fight patriot masters (Nov. 17), and wins Battle of Great Bridge (Dec. 11).

Nov. 10. Congress raises two marine battalions, forms navy (Nov. 28), of which Esek Hopkins takes command (Dec. 22).

Nov. 29. Congress forms secret committee to communicate with America's friends. Meets Bonvouloir, who assures French goodwill, use of ports, and neutrality in Canada.

Fisheries Act" banning trade with West Indies but restoring it with Britain. Extended to Pennsylvania, New Jersey, Maryland, Virginia, and South Carolina (April 13).

April 15. Franklin and Rush establish *The Society for the Relief of Free Negroes Unlawfully Held in Bondage*.

May. Massachusetts illegally prints £26,000 paper money. South Carolina prints £1,870,000 (June). Fearing taxes, both emissions funded by borrowing to be redeemed through taxes in the indefinite future. Congress issues £2,000,000 (June 22) and another £4,000,000 by year's end, delaying redemption until 1779.

Oct. 51 women in Edenton, North Carolina, sign pledge to support patriot cause, illustrating the importance of women in the Revolution. Thomas Paine writes article in *Pennsylvania Magazine* espousing women's rights. Other important writings are Warren's *The Group*, again featuring Hutchinson as "Rapatio"; John Trumbull's satire on American Tories, *M'Fingal*; and Samuel Seabury's loyalist *Letters of a Westchester Farmer*.

"Motion for a Bill to Compose American Troubles," advancing a parliamentary supremacy controlled by self-denying ordinance. No such bill is passed. **Dec. 6.** Congress disavows allegiance to Parliament but admits sovereignty of Crown. **Dec. 21.** New Hampshire Provincial Congress meets to draft new constitution. **Dec. 22.** Parliament passes Prohibitory Act on trade with colonies and declares them beyond Crown protection.	Sends Silas Deane to purchase war supplies (March 3, 1776).	
1776	1776	1776

Jan. 5. New Hampshire becomes first colony to write new constitution.
Jan. 10. Publication of Thomas Paine's republican *Common Sense*; John Adams's "Thoughts on Government"; and (anon) *The People the Best Governors*. In England Richard Price publishes *Observations on the Nature of Civil Liberty and Additional Observations* (1777), advocating free states bound to the empire by affection and interest.
Jan. 11. Maryland instructs delegates to Congress not to consent to independence. Massachusetts, however, replaces delegate Thomas Cushing with Elbridge Gerry, making for a small majority in favor of independence by February. South Carolina adopts new constitution erecting the first independently operating government in America (March 26). North Carolina becomes first colony to instruct delegates in Congress to vote for independence, if in concert with others (April 12). Georgia adopts interim constitution (April 15). Pennsylvania election gives victory to opponents of independence (May 1). Rhode Island adopts interim constitution and repudiates allegiance to Crown (May 4).
May 10. Congress adopts John Adams's motion calling on colonies to form their own
	Jan. 1. British warship bombards Norfolk, Virginia.
	Jan. Britain secures treaties with several German states to provide 20,000 mercenary troops for American War.
	Feb. 28. Backcountry Scots Highlander loyalists routed at Moore's Creek Bridge, North Carolina.
	March 5. Americans capture Dorchester Heights and besiege Boston, forcing British evacuation (March 17).
	May 2. Louis XVI permits French foreign minister Comte Vergennes to lend Americans £40,000 through an arms trading company.
	June 7. Americans retreating from Canada defeated at Three Rivers.
	June 27. Thomas Hickey hanged for conspiring to deliver Washington to the British, the first American soldier executed by military court.
	June 28. British fail to take Charles Town and abandon the South for two years. Cherokees attack Carolina rebels but no other southern tribe joins. Johnson fails to secure military support of Iroquois for British.
	July 2. Howe lands on Staten Island with 10,000 troops.
	July 12. Admiral Richard Howe arrives off New York coast with British Navy. Esek Hopkins defeated at Nassau (March),
		March 9. Publication of Adam Smith's *The Wealth of Nations*.
		April 6. Congress resolves to open American ports to all nations except Britain and its dominions and temporarily closes slave trade.
		July 3. Publication of John Leacock's satire of pre-revolutionary politics, *The Fall of British Tyranny*. In addition to *Book of the American Chronicles of the Times* (1774–5), this makes Leacock a leading satirist of his day.
		    Charles Willson Peale, after studying in London under American painter Benjamin West, returns to Philadelphia and begins a brilliant career in portraiture. Before the Revolution many American artists moved to the metropolis; Peale begins a partial migration back.
		    Legend has it that at this time Washington requested Philadelphia seamstress Betsy Ross to produce an American flag. Ross was commissioned by Congress to make various flags but it is not certain she designed or manufactured the stars and stripes.
		Oct. Jefferson's law against entails passes the Virginia legislature. Other colonies follow suit. These acts often merely ban a practice long in decline. Virginia also considers "Bill for Exempting Dissenters from

governments and adds preamble (May 15) that all executive departments of government under Crown authority be suppressed.

May 11. North Carolina adopts provisional constitution. Virginia instructs delegates to vote for independence (May 15).

May 27. Virginia and North Carolina motions for independence laid before Congress. Richard Henry Lee proposes independence (June 7). Some delegations threaten to walk out, Congress postpones voting until July 1 but authorizes a committee headed by Thomas Jefferson to draft Declaration of Independence (June 10) and appoints 13-member committee (one from each delegation) headed by John Dickinson to draft Articles of Confederation (June 12).

June 12. Virginia Convention passes 16 resolutions comprising Declaration of Rights. Adopts new constitution (June 29).

June 19. Government of Pennsylvania overthrown by Committee of Safety. New Pennsylvania Conference discards allegiance to Crown (June 24) and authorizes convention to meet on July 8 and draft constitution. New Jersey adopts new constitution. Grants women's suffrage until revised in 1807 (July 2).

June 24. Congress declares loyalist property open to seizure and recommends confiscation acts (Nov. 27, 1777).

July 2. Congress votes in favor of Lee's resolution. Unanimous except for New York delegates' abstention (not yet authorized to vote for independence). With a few alterations Congress accepts Jefferson's Declaration of Independence (July 4). Read publicly in Philadelphia (July 8) and to Washington's troops in New York (July 9). New York authorizes independence (July 9) and Congress adds the word "unanimous" to the Declaration's preamble (July 15). Engrossed

trapped in Narragansett Bay (Aug.), dismissed by Congress (Jan. 2, 1777).

Aug. 27. Washington, defeated at Long Island, retreats to Manhattan. Captured patriot Nathan Hale achieves martyrdom by proclaiming "I only regret that I have but one life to lose for my country" at his execution. Sullivan captured and sent to Congress as peace envoy.

Sept 11. Staten Island Peace Conference breaks down over American refusal to rescind Declaration of Independence. Congress sends Franklin and Arthur Lee to assist Deane as diplomatic commissioners to France (Sept. 26).

Sept. 15. William Howe captures New York City and invades New Jersey.

Oct. 11. Sir Guy Carleton defeats Benedict Arnold at Valcor Island. American lake fleet destroyed at Split Rock (Oct. 13).

Oct. 28. Howe defeats Washington at White Plains.

Nov. 16–18. Lord Cornwallis captures Fts. Washington and Lee, taking 2,000 prisoners.

Dec. 11. Pursued by Howe, Washington crosses the Delaware. His third in command, Charles Lee, is captured (Dec. 13) and held for 16 months.

Dec. 26. Washington defeats Howe at Trenton and captures 1,000 Hessian troops.

Contributing to the Support of the Church." Begins ten-year struggle over the question of religious liberty.

Nov. Henry Alline begins itinerant preaching in Nova Scotia. That colony, confused over the revolutionary crisis, undergoes a social-religious great awakening.

Dec. 5. Phi Beta Kappa founded at College of William and Mary as a social fraternity.

Dec. $25,000,000 Continental paper money is in circulation.

copy of Declaration signed (Aug. 2). Congress replaces title "United Colonies" with "United States" (Sept. 9). **July 12.** Committee presents draft Articles of Confederation to Congress. Issues of state representation, expense apportionment, and western lands prevent agreement. **Sept. 20.** Delaware writes new constitution. Pennsylvania ratifies its Declaration of Rights and new constitution, the most radical to date (Sept. 28). Maryland adopts Declaration of Rights (Nov. 3) and new constitution (Nov. 8). **Nov.** Rockinghamites formally secede from Parliament in protest against colonial policy. **Dec. 19.** *Philadelphia Journal* publishes first of Paine's Revolutionary War pamphlets, *The American Crisis*, written while serving with Nathanael Greene.		
1777	1777	1777
Jan. 16. Vermont secedes from New York. Its July constitution goes further than that of Pennsylvania by establishing universal manhood suffrage and abolishing slavery. Georgia adopts new constitution (Feb. 4). New York follows (April 20). **April 21.** Congress returns to Articles of Confederation and immediately passes Thomas Burke's (North Carolina) amendment guaranteeing sovereignty of individual states. **Sept. 11.** Delaware adopts Declaration of Rights. **Oct. 7.** Congress endorses one state, one vote principle of Articles. Agrees that expenses of national government be settled according to the amount of surveyed land in each state. Creates Boards of War, Admiralty, and Treasury (Oct. 14). Approves the 13 Articles of Confederation, having somewhat diluted Dickinson's	**Jan. 3.** Washington defeats Howe at Princeton. Howe retreats to New York. **July.** British capture Mt. Defiance (July 2) and Ticonderoga (July 6). Barry St. Leger marches south to join Burgoyne at Albany. His combined British–Amerindian forces attack Oneida Amerindians and destroy Iroquois unity. **July 23.** Howe advances on Pennsylvania with force of 15,000. Defeats Washington at Brandywine (Sept. 11), captures Philadelphia (Sept. 26) and Germantown (Oct. 4). Congress flees Philadelphia for Lancaster, then York, Pennsylvania (Sept. 19–30). **Aug. 4.** Congress replaces Philip John Schuyler with Horatio Gates as Commander of Northern Army. **Sept. 19.** Burgoyne defeats Daniel Morgan at first Battle of	**June 14.** Congress resolves on stars and stripes flag design. **July.** Vermont establishes the first constitution forbidding slavery. Congress finds that Continental currency has lost two-thirds of face value. Loan office sells certificates of various kinds, raising $60,000,000 before its closure in 1781. Delaware, New York, and New Jersey raise taxes to decrease the amount of circulating paper. **Nov.** Congress asks states to raise $5,000,000 for the common treasury.

original nationalist outlook, and issues them to the states for approval (Nov. 15). **Dec. 14.** North Carolina adopts new constitution and Declaration of Rights (Dec. 17).	Bemis Heights, New York, but is defeated by Arnold at the second (Oct. 7) and retreats to Saratoga. **Sept. 25.** Thomas Conway writes letters to Congress and to Gates criticizing certain commanders, including Washington. Washington rebukes Conway, forcing Gates to disavow connection with "Conway Cabal." **Oct. 17.** Gates attacks Burgoyne and secures important victory at Saratoga. Convention of Saratoga transports Burgoyne and 5,700 troops back to England. **Dec. 18.** Washington settles army at Valley Forge for the winter.	
1778	1778	1778
March 19. South Carolina adopts new constitution. Massachusetts voters reject proposed constitution in second referendum. **May 11.** Death of Chatham. **June.** Ten states had either ratified the Articles of Confederation or were preparing to do so. Expecting Delaware, New Jersey, and Maryland to follow, Congress proceeds with French negotiations as if under the Articles.	**Feb. 6.** By Treaty of Amity and Commerce, France promises no peace until Britain recognizes American Independence. France announces treaty terms, confers full diplomatic status on American commissioners, and appoints Conrad Alexandre Gerard Ambassador to the US (March 13). Britain recalls its ambassador to France. Congress replaces Deane, too generous with commissions and suspected of private arms dealings, with John Adams and appoints Franklin Minister to France and John Jay Minister to Spain (March 31). Ratifies treaty (May 4). **Feb. 17.** Parliament appoints Earl of Carlisle to Peace Commission in America. Congress rejects negotiations with Carlisle and declares no terms short of British withdrawal and recognition of independence acceptable (April 22). **April 13.** Admiral d'Estaing and French fleet leave Toulon, arriving off New York on July 11. John Paul Jones illustrates revival of American sea forces by attacking English port of Whitehaven and defeating the *Drake* in the Irish Sea (April 23).	**Jan.** By this time state currency emissions exceed £7,000,000. By mid-year Congress is printing $5–10,000,000 every few weeks. **March 6.** New South Carolina constitution is first of many to restrict office-holding to Protestant Christians. **Dec.** Jefferson's "Bill for the More General Diffusion of Knowledge" passes House but fails in Virginia Senate. A bill of 1796 establishes public elementary schools in each hundred, as Jefferson hoped, but fails to establish grammar schools in each county.

	May 8. Clinton replaces Howe as British Commander-in-Chief. **June 18.** Clinton evacuates Philadelphia to protect New York. **June 28.** Charles Lee engages Clinton at Monmouth. Washington saves Lee from total defeat and retreats to take position at White Plains above New York City. Lee court-martialed and dismissed for ineptitude. **July 3.** Loyalist and Amerindian forces massacre settlers in Wyoming Valley, Pennsylvania. George Rogers Clark captures Kaskasia (July 4) and battles to maintain American dominance in the West. **Aug. 29.** D'Estaing and Sullivan fail in joint offensive on Newport, Rhode Island. **Oct. 3.** Carlisle's *Manifesto and Proclamation* threatens destruction if Americans do not submit to peace. Returns to England (Nov. 27). **Nov. 11.** British and Amerindians inflict Cherry Valley (New York) Massacre. **Dec. 29.** Lord Germain's new southern strategy bears fruit with British capture of Savannah.	
1779	1779	1779
April. People of Massachusetts vote for the first popularly elected Constitutional Convention in American history. Meets on September 1. **June 1.** Thomas Jefferson elected Governor of Virginia. **Sept. 13.** John Jay, President of Congress, issues circular letter to states praising a lasting union and the idea of American nationhood. Reflects a "new nationalism" promoted by Jay and others, notably James Madison. **Oct. 22.** New York, having already seized much loyalist property, institutionalizes the practice with a Confiscation Act. All states follow suit within three years.	**Jan. 29.** Georgia campaign continues with British capture of Augusta. Andrew Pickens defeats loyalists at Kettle Creek (Feb. 14) but loses heavily at Brier Creek (March 3). D'Estaing begins siege of Savannah (April 23). Benjamin Lincoln defeated at Stono Ferry (June 19). **Feb. 3.** William Moultrie repels British at Port Royal, South Carolina. **Feb. 25.** George Rogers Clark captures Vincennes. **March 29.** Congress approves Baron von Steuben's "Blue Book" army regulations. **April 12.** Franco-Spanish Treaty of Aranjuez recruits Spanish aid in American War in exchange for French aid in regaining Gibraltar	**Jan. 14.** Continental currency deemed worth only one-eighth of face value. **Nov. 17.** Currency depreciated to almost one-fortieth of face value. Congress requests $95,000,000 from the states rising to $180,000,000 next year. Asks states to retire $6,000,000 per annum of Continental currency and discontinues printing paper money with more than $241,000,000 already in circulation.

Nov. 15. Earl of Carlisle appointed President of Board of Trade. **Dec.** Christopher Wyvill of Yorkshire launches County Association movement against high taxes, corruption, and for a new triennial act. This, in addition to Wilkes and parliamentary opposition, reflects growing political disaffection in Britain in mid-war years.	and Minorca. Spain declares war on Britain (June 21). **May 10.** British capture and burn Portsmouth and Norfolk, Virginia. **July 15.** Americans capture Stony Point, New York, and Paulus Hook, New Jersey (Aug. 19). **Sept. 23.** John Paul Jones's *Bonhomme Richard* defeats *Serapis* and *Countess of Scarborough* off the east coast of England. **Oct. 11.** Clinton evacuates Rhode Island to concentrate on New York and the South. **Oct. 28.** Suffering heavy losses, d'Estaing withdraws from Savannah.	
1780	1780	1780
March 20. New referendum approves Massachusetts Constitution. Takes effect October 25. **Oct.** Hartford Convention (New England States and New York) agrees on need for stronger central government. Alexander Hamilton and Gouverneur Morris write "Continentalist Letters" to that effect. **Dec. 12.** Lord Grantham appointed President of Board of Trade.	**Feb. 28.** Catherine II of Russia abandons "patient neutrality" policy and forms League of Armed Neutrality with Denmark, Sweden, Prussia, Austria, and Sicily. Congress sends Francis Dana to St. Petersburg (Dec. 19) but he is ignored. **May 2.** Comte de Rochambeau's army leaves Brest, arriving off Rhode Island on July 11. Postponement of Franco-American invasion of Canada alienates *Conadiens.* **May 12.** Clinton captures Charles Town and 5,500 patriots. Provokes bitterness by offering freedom in exchange for oaths of allegiance. Dispatches Cornwallis to complete pacification of South Carolina and Georgia and to invade the Upper South. **May 25.** Two Connecticut regiments mutiny over rations and pay. Curbed by Pennsylvanians. **June 13.** Congress commissions Gates to command new Southern Army. Defeated by Cornwallis at Camden, South Carolina (Aug. 16). Tory Banastre Tarleton defeats Thomas Sumter at Fishing Creek (Aug. 18). Cornwallis invades North Carolina (Sept. 8).	**March 1.** Pennsylvania Act for Emancipation, drawn up by Thomas Paine, is the first Act for gradual abolition of slavery in America. Slaves' children born after the Act were to serve to age 28. Other northern states follow through the end of the century, usually emancipating slaves born after a certain date at age 25 or 28. **May 4.** American Academy of Arts and Sciences chartered at Boston. **May 20.** J. Hector St. John de Crèvecoeur sells manuscript of *Letters from an American Farmer* to Davies and Davis of London. Published early in 1782. **Oct.** Continental currency depreciated to one-seventy-seventh of face value. 36 Philadelphia women launch campaign to equip American troops, collecting around $300,000 in Continental dollars in two weeks.

	Sept. 6. Congress calls on landed states to cede western lands. Promises national domain would be used to benefit all states and that new states would be formed out of ceded lands (Oct. 10). **Sept. 25.** Revealed as a traitor, Benedict Arnold flees to the British, who reward him with money and military command. **Oct. 7.** Nathanael Greene defeats Patrick Ferguson's Tennessee Loyalists, shielding Cornwallis's flank, at Kings Mountain, North Carolina. Cornwallis retreats to Winnsboro, South Carolina. Greene, appointed to command Southern Army (Oct. 14), begins using tactics of guerrilla warfare. Sumter avenges Tarleton at Blackstocks (Nov. 20). **Dec. 20.** British capture Henry Laurens *en route* to Netherlands, discover secret Treaty of Aix-la-Chapelle, and, to prevent Dutch joining League of Armed Neutrality, declare war. British defeat Dutch warships supplying American arms from St. Eustatius.	
1781	1781	1781
Feb. 3. Congress unsuccessfully asks states to amend Articles of Confederation so it can raise 5% impost on foreign goods imported to America. Creates three new executive departments: Finance, War, and Marine (Feb. 7). **Feb. 27.** Maryland ratifies Articles of Confederation, the last state to do so. Articles take full effect (March 1). **Aug. 22.** Congressional Committee report proposes seven amendments to Articles to increase central government power, though never voted on or presented to the states. Elizabeth Freeman ("Bett") wins freedom in case of *Brom and Bett v. Ashley.* Establishing that the 1780 Massachusetts constitutional principle declaring all	**Jan. 1.** 2,400 unpaid Pennsylvania soldiers march on Philadelphia protesting against new recruits receiving $25 commissions. Washington dispatches Robert Howe to quell mutiny. **Jan. 2.** Landless state majority in Congress rejects Virginia's conditional cession of western lands, demanding the whole Kentucky territory and validation of land titles not validated by Virginia. **Jan. 17.** Daniel Morgan defeats Tarleton heavily at Cowpens, North Carolina. Other American successes are Henry Lee's harassment of Carolina loyalists and James Craig's occupation of Wilmington. David Fanning's loyalists begin guerrilla retaliation. Greene marches into	**Feb. 3.** Having revalued currency at 100 to 1, Congress asks states to grant it power to collect duty on imports to America. States refuse, fearing excessive central power. By April currency is worth 167 to 1. It collapses in the summer, giving rise to the phrase "not worth a continental." **May 14.** Robert Morris appointed Superintendent of Finance. Proposes federal land, poll, and excise taxes, and a national bank (May 21). Congress approves national bank to make short-term loans to Congress and pay interest on national debt (May 26). Charters Bank of North America based in Philadelphia with capitalization of $400,000 (Dec. 31).

individuals "born free and equal" applied to Blacks as well as Whites, the case provides for the judicial dismantling of slavery in the state. It also illustrates the considerable power of courts (judicial review had first been established in New Jersey in 1780). Similar cases won in other northern states in the 1780s.

South Carolina and suffers series of defeats but captures some small British posts (April–July). **March 15.** Cornwallis loses one-fourth of his forces at Guilford, North Carolina. Marches on Virginia, almost capturing Governor Jefferson and his assembly at Charlottesville (June 4). Occupies Yorktown (Aug. 1).
April 2. John Barry defeats British ships *Mars* and *Minerva*. French Admiral de Grasse captures Tobago and St. Christopher, and embarks for Chesapeake on April 14. Receives correspondence of May 21 from Washington and Rochambeau to attack the British in Virginia.
June 11. Congress names John Adams, Franklin, Jay, Jefferson, and Laurens to peace commission to England.
Sept. 8. Arnold burns New London, Connecticut, and captures Ft. Griswold. Greene defeated at Eutaw Springs, South Carolina (Sept. 9).
Sept. 10. De Grasse drives British off the Virginia Capes, leaving Cornwallis without naval support. Washington and Rochambeau combine forces of 16,800 at Williamsburg (Sept. 28) and besiege Yorktown (Oct. 9), forcing Cornwallis's decisive surrender (Oct. 18).

1782	1782	1782
March 20. North resigns to avoid further votes of no confidence. Beginning of Rockingham/Shelburne ministry. **July 11.** Parliament abolishes Board of Trade. **July 31.** Death of Rockingham. Shelburne continues as Prime Minister with support of George III but without safe parliamentary majority.	**Feb. 27.** Hearing of Yorktown surrender, Parliament votes to discontinue offensive operations in America. New Shelburne administration (March 20) opens informal peace talks in Paris (April 12.) Formal negotiations begin September 27. **April 4.** Carleton succeeds Clinton as British Commander-in-Chief and begins organizing withdrawal. Evacuates Charleston and Savannah (May 9). **April 12.** British capture de Grasse at Battle of the Saintes, near Jamaica.	**May.** Virginia manumission law results in eventual emancipation of 10,000 slaves. **June 11.** John Adams secures loan of $2,000,000 from the Netherlands. Dutch aid confirmed and extended by Treaty of Amity and Commerce (Oct. 8). **June 20.** Congress adopts Great Seal of the United States. **July 27.** Robert Morris presents Report on Public Credit recommending suspension of interest payments on national debt and Congress taking responsibility for

	April 19. Netherlands becomes first nation formally to recognize the American republic. **Oct. 19.** Congress accepts New York's cession of western lands (also claimed by Virginia). **Nov. 29.** Richard Oswald signs provisional agreement with Franklin, Jay, and Laurens. Recognizes American Independence, cedes all lands between Great Lakes and Mississippi River, and permits continued American participation in British fisheries. Agreement conditional on treaty with France. Vergennes, surprised at British generosity, criticizes US commissioners for not consulting him (Dec. 15). Franklin's tactful reply (Dec. 17) prevents discord.	state debts which it could redeem through taxation. Rejected for fear of excessive central power. National debt assessed at $27,000,000 specie. **Nov. 22.** Harvard appoints three professors of medicine to new medical school. Promoted by Nathan Smith, who went on to found medical schools at Dartmouth (1797), Yale (1810), Bowdoin (1820), and Vermont (1822).
1783	1783	1783
Feb. 24. Concerned over Shelburne's generosity to Americans, Fox and North join forces to provoke his resignation. Fox and North become Secretaries of State in a coalition government with Duke of Portland as figurehead Prime Minister. **April 26.** 7,000 loyalists leave New York, the last of the 100,000 to flee to Canada or Europe from test acts, loyalty oaths, disfranchisement, discriminatory taxes, confiscation, and expulsion. **Oct. 31.** New Hampshire Convention adopts new constitution. Takes effect June 1784. **Nov. 17.** Fox's East India Bill, attempting to usurp power in eastern empire from Crown to Parliament, is defeated amid controversy. Fox resigns and is replaced by King's favorite, William Pitt the younger. Fox–North retain Commons majority and defeat Pitt ministry 16 times in six months.	**Jan. 20.** Armistice in Europe established at near status quo ante bellum, pending formal Anglo-French treaty. **March 10.** Army discontent over pay reaches climax with John Armstrong's "Newburgh Addresses," calling fellow officers to action, and "lash remonstrances" speech criticizing Congress. Washington calms the situation by personally calling for patience and obedience to civil authority (March 15). In Philadelphia Mutiny (June 17), soldiers surround the Pennsylvania State House where Congress is sitting. Peacefully dispersed on June 24. Congress moves to Princeton, then Annapolis. **April 11.** Congress proclaims cessation of war. Ratifies provisional treaty (April 15), begins furloughing army (May 26). **May 2.** Washington submits "Sentiments on a Peace Establishment": a blueprint for a republican militia and civil control thereof. **Sept. 23.** Treaty of Paris confirms provisional treaty and armistice.	**April 3.** Treaty of Amity and Commerce with Sweden. Lord Sheffield's "Observations on the Commerce of the American States" advocates diverting Anglo-American commerce to British vessels and excluding American ships from West Indies. Influences defeat of Pitt's call to allow continued American trade in the islands. **April 18.** Congress proposes two amendments to Articles: one giving it power to raise import duties, the other replacing the system of expense apportionment among the states based on land values with one based on population (including three-fifths of all slaves). Both are rejected. **May 13.** Formation of the Society of Cincinnati with membership restricted to Revolutionary War veterans and their first-born sons. Washington is first president, Hamilton second. Criticized for being aristocratic. Less aristocratic and more ethnic is the Society for the Friendly Sons of St. Patrick of Irish veterans in New York City. **May 30.** Benjamin Towne estab-lishes the first daily newspaper in

	Nov. 25. British troops evacuate New York. **Dec. 23.** Washington resigns commission.	the US, the *Pennsylvania Evening Post*. Noah Webster publishes *A Grammatical Institute of the English Language*, and begins work on his *American Dictionary* (1828).
1784	1784	1784
March 8. Pitt institutes Committee of Council on Trade and Plantations to replace defunct Board of Trade. **March 25.** Dissolution of Parliament. The subsequent elections give large parliamentary majority to Pitt, who forms a ministry of King's favorites. Relative calm returns to British politics which, combined with financial reforms, an industrializing economy, and continued primacy in trade with America, restores confidence and power of British nation within a short time.	**Jan. 14.** Congress ratifies Treaty of Paris. **April 23.** Having finally received unconditional cession of Virginia western lands, Congress considers the first territorial ordinance. Though rejected over size of parcels to be distributed and apportionment of costs among the states (April 30), it provides precedents for methods of state admittance and the grid system. Other states follow Virginia in ceding land. **June 2.** Congress orders Henry Knox to discharge all but 80 soldiers of Continental Army. Rejects Washington's proposal for a small peace-time army but establishes the First American Regiment, 700 men from state militias, to defend the frontier. **Oct.** US begins dictating treaties to Amerindians, often quickly repudiated because made under duress or because of white settler encroachment.	**May 28.** Robert Morris resigns. Replaced by Treasury Board of Samuel Osgood, Walter Livingston, and Arthur Lee. **July 2.** British Order in Council denies American access to West Indies and later Canada, Ireland, and Britain. **July 6.** Richard Price publishes *Observations on the American Revolution*, dedicated to "the Free and United States of America." American achievements include Jeremy Belknap's *History of New Hampshire*; Jedediah Morse's *Geography Made Easy*; Rush's *Enquiry into the Effects of Spirituous Liquors*: and Judith Sargent Murray's "Desultory Thoughts upon the Utility of Encouraging a Degree of Self Complacency, Especially in Female Bosoms." **Aug. 30.** John Greene lands the *Empress of China* at Canton, opening lucrative American China trade. **Nov. 14.** Samuel Seabury consecrated as America's first Episcopal Bishop. **Dec.** Baltimore "Christmas Conference" organizes American Methodist Church. Francis Asbury is co-superintendent and first Bishop. Church instructs members to manumit slaves. Next year, however, Virginia Methodists suspend the "Slave Rule," beginning schism between northern and southern churches.
1785	1785	1785
Jan. 24. Congress appoints James Monroe to lead a committee to draft an appeal to the states to give Congress power to secure treaties with for-eign nations. No action taken.	**Feb. 24.** Congress replaces Franklin with Jefferson as Minister to France and appoints John Adams Minister to Britain. Adams formally demands British withdrawal from US soil in	**March.** Establishment of The Philadelphia Society for Promoting Agriculture, America's first purely agricultural society. Innovations in transportation include institution of the first

July 11. Massachusetts Assembly passes resolution favoring nationalistic revision of Articles of Confederation. Delegates to Congress fail to present it.
Nov. Alexander Hamilton in New York, Benjamin Rush in Pennsylvania, and Aedanus Burke in North Carolina begin campaigns to restore rights and property to loyalists.

accordance with Treaty of Paris (Nov. 30). British reply (Feb. 28, 1786) holds that presence in northern forts will be maintained until Americans fulfill obligations to British creditors and loyalists.
March 8. Congress appoints Knox Secretary of War. Begins more pacific Amerindian policy, creating the first reservations next year.

regular stage routes between Philadelphia, New York City, Albany, and Boston. John Fitch begins pioneering work on steamboats.
March 25. Mt. Vernon Conference promotes free navigation of rivers by states and coordination between states on matters of currency, duties, and debt funding. Most states ban export of goods on British ships. Pennsylvania deals with debt problem by issuing $150,000 in bills of credit. Other states follow. Even where debts are effectively managed, tension between debtors and creditors exists over currency depreciation and taxes. Jefferson proposes national coinage system (July 6), put into effect on August 8, 1786. Many begin to favor greater central government power over the economy.
May 10. Publication of Jefferson's *Notes on Virginia.* Other publications include David Ramsay's *History of the Revolution in South Corolina*; Timothy Dwight's *The Conquest of Canaan,* lionizing Washington; and Macpherson's *Philadelphia Directory*, the first of its kind in America.
May 20. Congress sets aside section 16 of each western reserve township for public schools.
Sept. 10. Treaty of Amity and Commerce with Prussia.

1786	1786	1786

June 26. Congress discusses Charles Pinckney's motion for reorganizing government.
Aug. 7. Congress proposes several amendments pertaining to power over commerce with foreign nations and between states, and power to requisition money from the states. Superseded by Constitutional Convention.
Sept. 11. Annapolis Convention meets. Delegates agree to a more ambitious convention meeting in

Aug. Depression and high taxes provoke indebted farmers in western Massachusetts to revolt. Only Virginia responds to Congress's call for money and men to end Shays's Rebellion. In other states debtor-farmers demand state laws for protection, close courts to prevent debt and tax collection, and attack tax collectors and even legislators. These economic difficulties and problems of internal security highlight inadequacy of

Jan. 16. Passage of Jefferson's Virginia Statute for Religious Freedom.
Jan. 21. At Madison's instigation, Virginia.legislators invite all states to discuss economic and commercial problems at a conference in Annapolis. Depression reaches lowest point in summer, and when US defaults on interest payments to Spain, France, and the Netherlands (Aug.) more become persuaded of need for governmental reform.

Philadelphia in May 1787 to consider provisions "to render the constitution of the Federal Government adequate to the exigencies of the Union" (Hamilton).	government under the Articles of Confederation and increase demands for stronger national government.	**June 28.** In exchange for gifts worth $10,000 the Emperor of Morocco agrees to end privateering on American ships by Mediterranean Barbary pirates.
1787	1787	1787
Feb. 21. Congress approves Convention to revise Articles. **May 25.** 55 delegates to Constitutional Convention (from all states except Rhode Island) meet in Philadelphia. Edmund Randolph introduces the Virginia Plan, probably written by James Madison (May 29). Small state delegates disapprove of representation in federal government according to population. William Patterson introduces "purely federal" New Jersey Plan (June 14) proposing increases in federal power, especially to tax foreign and interstate commerce, *within* the framework of the Articles. To ensure fair representation of small states it proposes one vote per state in federal legislature. Rejected in favor of entirely new national government (June 19). "Connecticut Compromise" (July 16) proposes bicameral legislature with equal state representation in the upper house and representation according to population in the lower, with money bills decided in lower house. Three-fifths of slaves would be counted in representative apportionment in the lower house. **July 19–26.** Convention draws up 23 "fundamental resolutions." forming a rough draft of a Constitution, and appoints Committee of Detail to draft final document. Begins debating draft (Aug. 6). Attack on slavery and three-fifths clause roundly defeated (Aug. 8). Two-year term for congressmen agreed (Aug. 8). Six-year term for senators agreed (Aug. 9). Power of Congress to regulate foreign, interstate, and Amerindian commerce agreed (Aug. 16).	**July 13.** Congress adopts Northwest Ordinance dictating that until a population of 5,000 was reached each area would be ruled by a federal governor. Thereafter a territory could elect an assembly, and when population reached 60,000 free inhabitants it could apply for statehood. Jefferson inserts clause banning slavery in these territories.	**Jan. 1.** Publication of Joel Barlow's *Vision of Columbus*, comparing Washington to the discoverer of America. Also published that year were Rush's *Thoughts upon Female Education* and (anon) *Women Invited to War*, espousing a civic republican role for women in fighting government corruption. Established that year were the Pennsylvania Society for the Encouragement of Manufactures and Useful Arts and the first American cotton mill, at Beverly, Massachusetts, by John Cabot and Joshua Fisher. **May.** Founding of the British Anti-slavery Society.

Congress forbidden from banning African slave trade until 1808 and clause requiring states to return fugitive slaves passed (Aug. 29). **Aug. 31.** Committee of Postponed Matters appointed to consider the presidency. Convention agrees on four-year term for president, electoral college representation for states equal to total representation in Congress, and House of Representatives to vote in the event of a tie (Sept. 6). Many aspects of judicial power and balance of power between governmental branches and state and federal government remain ambiguous. Five-member Committee of Style appointed to make final draft (Sept. 8). **Sept. 12.** Worried about excessive federal and executive power, Elbridge Gerry and George Mason propose a "Bill of Rights." Madison promises one at the first opportunity. **Sept 12–15.** Debate over final draft. Unanimously accepted, with a few minor changes, by delegates of 12 states in attendance (Sept. 16). To become operative when approved by nine states. **Sept. 17.** Convention adjourns. Franklin's closing speech becomes the most reprinted propaganda in favor of adoption. Other Federalist writings include *The Federalist Papers* by Hamilton, Madison, and Jay. Anti-Federalist literature includes Richard Henry Lee's *Letters from the Federal Farmer*, and "Cato's Letters," probably by George Clinton, in the *New York Journal*. **Dec. 7.** Delaware becomes the first state to ratify the Federal Constitution. Followed by Pennsylvania (Dec. 12) and New Jersey (Dec. 18).		
1788	1788	1788
Jan. 2. Georgia ratifies. Followed by Connecticut (Jan. 9) and Massachusetts	**April.** John Adams resigns as Minister to Britain, still unable to secure withdrawal of soldiers	**Feb. 19.** Founding in Paris of French abolition society *Les Amis des Noirs*. Bankruptcy of French

(Feb. 6) proposing nine amendments. In a referendum in which Federalists refuse to participate, Rhode Island rejects the Constitution (March 24). Maryland (April 28) and South Carolina (May 23) ratify.
June 21. New Hampshire, proposing 12 amendments, becomes the ninth state to ratify, meaning the Constitution can go into effect. Virginia ratifies, proposing 20 amendments (June 25). North Carolina decides to withhold ratification until a bill of rights is incorporated (July 21). New York ratifies (July 26).
Sept. 13. Congress names New York as site of new government. Fixes date of elections and meeting of First Congress. Last major act of Confederation Government is acceptance of cession by Maryland of ten square miles for future Federal District of Columbia (Dec. 23).

from northwestern US territories. Other disappointing elements of Treaty of Paris were exclusion of Americans from northern fisheries and West Indian trade by Britain and preclusion from Mississippi trade by Spain. Britain disappointed by inability to secure payment of creditors and compensation to loyalists; France at being unable to break British monopoly of American trade; and Amerindians at British surrender of western lands to the US.

Government occurs, contributed to by the 1 billion livres spent on the American War between 1777 and 1783. Contributes to French Revolution of 1789.

1789	1789	1789

Jan. 7. Presidential electors named by state legislatures. Congressional elections held and Electoral College casts ballots (Feb. 4). First Congress convenes (4 March), though quorum not achieved until April 1 in the House and April 5 in the Senate. Senate declares Washington elected President with 69 votes and John Adams Vice President with 34 (April 6). Washington begins tour from Mt. Vernon to New York (April 16), inaugurated (April 30).
May. Georgia becomes first of many states to rewrite constitutions in early national period.
Aug. 7. Knox appointed first War Secretary, Hamilton first Treasury Secretary (Sept. 2), Samuel Osgood first Post Master General (Sept. 22), Jefferson first Secretary of State (Sept. 26), in Washington's first cabinet.

April 11. John Fenno founds Federalist *Gazette of the United States*. Important publications include William Gordon and David Ramsay's histories of the Revolution, both later revealed to have been plagiarized from wartime reports of the *Annual Register*; Webster's *Dissertation on the English Language*; and the first American novel, William Hill Brown's *The Power of Sympathy*.

Sept. 24. Judiciary Act establishes federal court system. John Jay appointed first Chief Justice. **Sept. 25.** Congress proposes 12 amendments, a "Bill of Rights," to encourage remaining states to adopt the Constitution. **Nov. 21.** North Carolina ratifies.		
1790	1790	1790
May 29. Rhode Island, last of the original 13 states, ratifies.		**March 23.** Franklin's last public writing satirizes slavery and asks Congress to abolish it. Franklin dies on April 17.
1791		
Dec. 15. Adopted by three quarters of the states, the First Ten Amendments to the Constitution, known as the Bill of Rights, go into effect.		

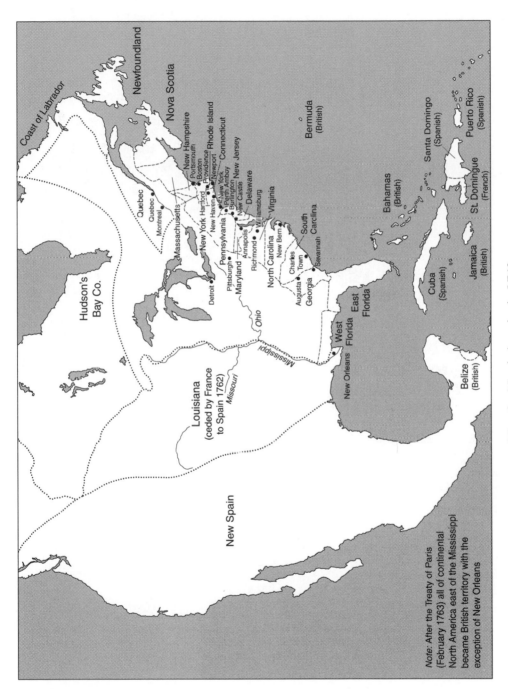

Map 9 North America in 1763.

Note: After the Treaty of Paris (February 1763) all of continental North America east of the Mississippi became British territory with the exception of New Orleans

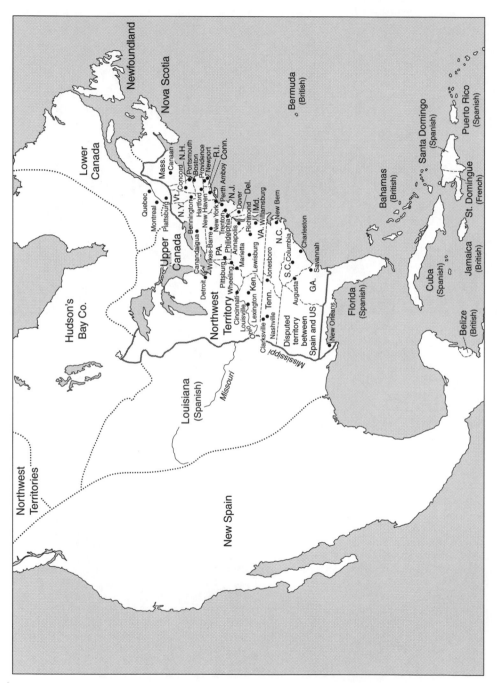

Map 10 North America c. 1796.

Index